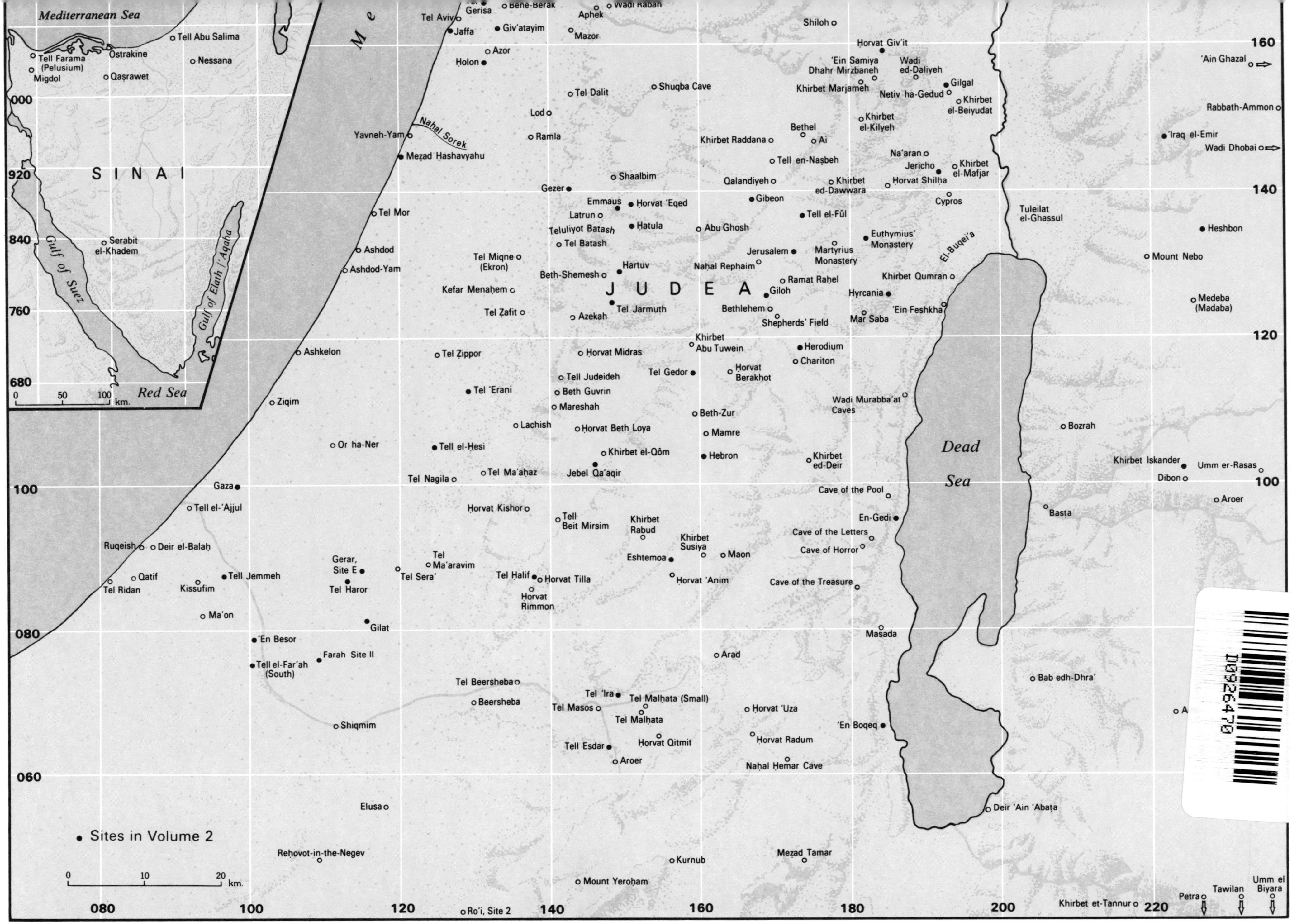
Mediterranean Sea
Tell Farama (Pelusium)
Migdol
Ostrakine
Qaṣrawet
Tell Abu Salima
Nessana
SINAI
Serabit el-Khadem
Gulf of Suez
Gulf of Elath / 'Aqaba
Red Sea
0 50 100 km.
000
920
840
760
680
Me
Tel Aviv
Jaffa
Gerisa
Bene-Berak
Giv'atayim
Azor
Holon
Aphek
Mazor
Wadi Rabah
Yavneh-Yam
Nahal Sorek
Mezad Hashavyahu
Tel Mor
Ashdod
Ashdod-Yam
Ashkelon
Ziqim
Or ha-Ner
Gaza
Tell el-'Ajjul
Ruqeish
Deir el-Balah
Qatif
Tel Ridan
Kissufim
Tell Jemmeh
Ma'on
'En Besor
Tell el-Far'ah (South)
Farah Site II
Gerar, Site E
Tel Haror
Gilat
Tel Ma'aravim
Tel Sera'
Tel Nagila
Tell el-Hesi
Tel 'Erani
Tel Zippor
Kefar Menahem
Tel Miqne (Ekron)
Tel Zafit
Lod
Ramla
Tel Dalit
Gezer
Shaalbim
Shuqba Cave
Emmaus
Horvat 'Eqed
Latrun
Teluliyot Batash
Tel Batash
Hatula
Beth-Shemesh
Hartuv
Azekah
Tel Jarmuth
JUDEA
Horvat Midras
Tell Judeideh
Beth Guvrin
Mareshah
Lachish
Horvat Beth Loya
Khirbet el-Qôm
Jebel Qa'aqir
Tel Ma'ahaz
Horvat Kishor
Tell Beit Mirsim
Tel Halif
Horvat Tilla
Horvat Rimmon
Khirbet Rabud
Eshtemoa
Khirbet Susiya
Horvat 'Anim
Maon
Tel Beersheba
Beersheba
Shiqmim
Tel 'Ira
Tel Masos
Tel Malhata (Small)
Tel Malhata
Tell Esdar
Horvat Qitmit
Aroer
Arad
Elusa
Rehovot-in-the-Negev
Ro'i, Site 2
Mount Yeroham
Kurnub
Mezad Tamar
Horvat 'Uza
Horvat Radum
Nahal Hemar Cave
'En Boqeq
Masada
Cave of the Treasure
Cave of Horror
Cave of the Letters
En-Gedi
Cave of the Pool
Khirbet ed-Deir
Hebron
Mamre
Beth-Zur
Horvat Berakhot
Tel Gedor
Khirbet Abu Tuwein
Herodium
Chariton
Wadi Murabba'at Caves
Bethlehem
Shepherds' Field
Giloh
Ramat Rahel
Mar Saba
Hyrcania
'Ein Feshkha
Khirbet Qumran
El-Buqei'a
Jerusalem
Nahal Rephaim
Martyrius Monastery
Euthymius' Monastery
Abu Ghosh
Gibeon
Tell el-Fûl
Qalandiyeh
Khirbet ed-Dawwara
Tell en-Nasbeh
Khirbet Raddana
Bethel
Ai
Shiloh
Horvat Giv'it
'Ein Samiya
Dhahr Mirzbaneh
Wadi ed-Daliyeh
Khirbet Marjameh
Netiv ha-Gedud
Gilgal
Khirbet el-Beiyudat
Khirbet el-Kilyeh
Na'aran
Jericho
Khirbet el-Mafjar
Horvat Shilha
Cypros
Tuleilat el-Ghassul
Dead Sea
Deir 'Ain 'Abata
Bab edh-Dhra'
Basta
Bozrah
Khirbet Iskander
Dibon
Umm er-Rasas
Aroer
Mount Nebo
Medeba (Madaba)
Heshbon
'Iraq el-Emir
Wadi Dhobai
Rabbath-Ammon
'Ain Ghazal
Khirbet et-Tannur
Petra
Tawilan
Umm el Biyara
Sites in Volume 2
0 10 20 km.
080
100
120
140
160
180
200
220
060

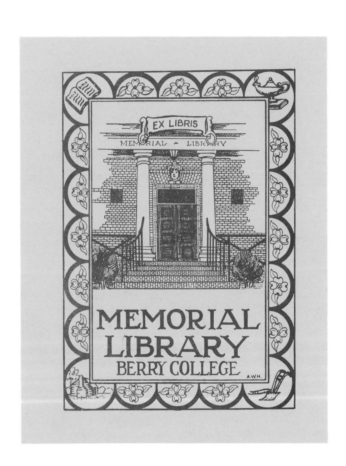

THE NEW ENCYCLOPEDIA OF ARCHAEOLOGICAL EXCAVATIONS IN THE HOLY LAND

EPHRAIM STERN, Editor
Hebrew University of Jerusalem

AYELET LEWINSON-GILBOA, Assistant Editor
Hebrew University of Jerusalem

JOSEPH AVIRAM, Editorial Director
Israel Exploration Society

Volume 2

THE ISRAEL EXPLORATION SOCIETY & CARTA, JERUSALEM

SIMON & SCHUSTER
A Paramount Communications Company

New York London Toronto Sydney Tokyo Singapore

Printing Number 6 5 4 3 2 1

Printed in Israel

Library of Congress Cataloging-in-Publication Data

The New encyclopedia of archaeological excavations in the Holy Land /
editor, Ephraim Stern.
p. cm.
Includes bibliographical references.
ISBN 0-13-276288-9 (set)
ISBN 0-13-276304-4 (v.2)
1. Palestine–Antiquities–Encyclopedias. 2. Bible–Antiquities–
Encyclopedias. 3. Excavations (Archaeology)–Palestine–
Encyclopedias. I. Stern, Ephraim, 1934-
DS111.A2N488 1992
933'.003–dc20

92-17712
CIP

ABBREVIATIONS

a. acre
AH *anno Hegirae*, in the year of the Hegira
Am. Amos
'Arakh. *'Arakhin*
Avot *Pirkei Avot*
A.Z. *'Avodah Zarah*
b. born
B.B. *Bava Batra*
BCE before the common era
Beits. *Beitsah*
Bekh. *Bekhorot*
Ber. *Berakhot*
Bik. *Bikkurim*
B.M. *Bava Metsi'a*
BP before the present
B.Q. *Bava Qamma*
B.T. Babylonian Talmud
c. *circa*, about, approximately
cat. catalogue
CE of the common era
cent. century
cf. *confer*, compare
1 Chr. 1 Chronicles
2 Chr. 2 Chronicles
cm centimeter
Col. Colossians
comp. compiler (pl., comps.)
1 Cor. 1 Corinthians
2 Cor. 2 Corinthians
cu cubic
d. died
Dan. Daniel
Dem. *Dem'ai*
diss. dissertation
div. division
dm decimeter
Dt. Deuteronomy
EB Early Bronze
Eccles. Ecclesiastes
ed. editor (pl., eds.); edition; edited by
'Eduy. *'Eduyyot*
e.g. *exempli gratia*, for example
Eph. Ephesians
'Eruv. *'Eruvin*
ESR Electro Spin Resonance
et al. *et alii*, and others
etc. *et cetera*, and so forth
Ex. Exodus
Ezek. Ezekiel
f. and following (pl., ff.)
fig. figure (pl., figs.)
g gram
Gal. Galatians
Gen. Genesis
Git. *Gittin*
Hab. Habakkuk
Ḥag. *Ḥagigah*
Ḥal. *Ḥallah*
Heb. Hebrews
Hg. Haggai
Hor. *Horayot*
Hos. Hosea
Ḥul. *Ḥullin*
ibid. *ibidem*, in the same place
id. *idem*, the same
in. inch
in prep. in preparation
Iron Iron Age
Is. Isaiah
Jas. James
Jer. Jeremiah
Jg. Judges
Jn. John
Jon. Jonah
Jos. Joshua
J.T. Jerusalem Talmud
Kel. *Kelim*
Ker. *Keritot*
Ket. *Ketubbot*
kg kilogram
1 Kg. 1 Kings
2 Kg. 2 Kings
Kil. *Kil'ayim*
km kilometer
l. locus
Lam. Lamentations
LB Late Bronze
lb. pound
Lev. Leviticus
Lk. Luke
loc. cit. the place cited
m meter
Mal. Malachi
1 Macc. 1 Maccabees
2 Macc. 2 Maccabees
Mak. *Makkot*
Makh. *Makhshirin*
MB Middle Bronze
Meg. *Megillah*
Me'il. *Me'ilah*
Men. *Menaḥot*
mi. mile
Mi. Micah
Mid. *Middot*
mill. millennium
Miq. *Miqva'ot*
Mk. Mark
ml milliliter
mm millimeter
Mo'ed Q. *Mo'ed Qatan*
Mt. Matthew
MT Masoretic text
n. note
Nah. Nahum
Naz. *Nazir*
n.d. no date
Ned. *Nedarim*
Neg. *Nega'im*
Neh. Nehemiah
Nid. *Niddah*
no. number (pl., nos.)
n.p. no place
n.s. new series
Num. Numbers
Ob. Obadiah
Ohal. *Ohalot*
op. cit. *opere citato*, in the work cited
Par. *Parah*
PEF Palestine Exploration Fund
Pes. *Pesaḥim*
Ph.D. Doctor of Philosophy
Phil. Philippians
Philem. Philemon
pl. plate (pl., pls.)
PPN Pre-Pottery Neolithic
PPNA Pre-Pottery Neolithic A
PPNB Pre-Pottery Neolithic B
PPNC Pre-Pottery Neolithic C
Proc. Proceedings
Prov. Proverbs
Ps. Psalms
P.T. Palestinian Talmud
pt. part
1 Pt. 1 Peter
2 Pt. 2 Peter
Qid. *Qiddushin*
Qin. *Qinnim*
q.v. *quod vide*, which see
r. reigned; ruled
Rab. *Rabbah*
rev. revised
Rev. Revelation
Rom. Romans
1 Sam. 1 Samuel
2 Sam. 2 Samuel
San. *Sanhedrin*
sect. section
Shab. *Shabbat*
Shev. *Shevu'ot*
Sheq. *Sheqalim*
Song Song of Solomon
Sot. *Sotah*
sq square
St. Saint (pl., SS.)
Suk. *Sukkah*
Ta'an. *Ta'anit*
Tam. *Tamid*
Tem. *Temurah*
Ter. *Terumot*
1 Thes. 1 Thessalonians
2 Thes. 2 Thessalonians
1 Tim. 1 Timothy
2 Tim. 2 Timothy
TL Thermoluminescence
Toh. *Tohorot*
tr. translator; translated by
Trans. Transactions
Univ. University
UTM Universal Transverse Mercator
Zech. Zechariah
Zeph. Zephaniah

BOOKS/WORKS

Abel, *GP* F. M. Abel, *Géographie de la Palestine* 1–2, Paris 1933–1938
AE *L'Année Épigraphique* (quoted by year and inscription no.)
Aharoni, *LB* Y. Aharoni, *The Land of the Bible: A Historical Geography*, London 1966, 1967 (2d ed.)
Akkadica Supplementum 7–8 (1989) *Archaeology of Jordan* 2/1–12, Field Reports, Surveys and Sites (Akkadica Supplementum 7–8, eds. D. Homes-Fredericq and J. B. Hennessy), Leuven 1989
Alt, *GIPT* A. Alt, *Die Griechischen Inschriften der Palästina Tertia Westlich der Araba*, Berlin and Leipzig 1921 (quoted by inscription no.)
Alt, *KSch.* A. Alt, *Kleine Schriften zur Geschichte des Volkes Israel* 1–3, Munich 1953–1959
American Archaeology in the Mideast *American Archaeology in the Mideast: A History of the ASOR* (ed. P. T. King), Philadelphia 1983
ANET *Ancient Near Eastern Texts Relating to the Old Testament* (ed. J. B. Pritchard), Princeton 1950
ASOR Symposia *Symposia Celebrating the Seventy-fifth Anniversary of the Founding of the American Schools of Oriental Research (1900–1975)* (ed. F. M. Cross, Jr.), Cambridge, Mass. 1979
ASR *Ancient Synagogues Revealed* (ed. L. I. Levine), Jerusalem 1981
Avi-Yonah, *HL* M. Avi-Yonah, *The Holy Land*, Grand Rapids 1966
Baldi D. Baldi, *Enchiridion Locorum Sanctorum*, Jerusalem 1935 (quoted by text no.)
BAR/IS *British Archaeological Reports*, International Series, Oxford
Benoit et al., *Discoveries* 2 P. Benoit, J. T. Milik, and R. de Vaux, *Discoveries in the Judaean Desert* 2 (*Les Grottes de Murabba'at*), Oxford 1961
Bliss–Macalister, *Excavations* F. J. Bliss and R. A. S. Macalister, *Excavations in Palestine during the Years 1898–1900*, London 1902
Brünnow–Domaszewski, *Die Provincia Arabia* R. E. Brünnow and A. V. Domaszewski, *Die Provincia Arabia* 1–3, Strassbourg 1904–1909
CCSL *Corpus Christianorum, Series Latina*, Turnhout
Chron. J. Malalas, *Chronicon* (ed. L. Dindorf)
CIG *Corpus Inscriptionum Graecarum* (ed. A. Boeck), Berlin 1828–1877
CIJ *Corpus Inscriptionum Judaicarum* 1–2 (ed. J.-B. Frey), Rome 1936–1952 (see also Frey, *Corpus* 2)
Clermont-Ganneau, *ARP* C. Clermont-Ganneau, *Archaeological Researches in Palestine* 1–2, London 1896–1899
Clermont-Ganneau, *RAO* C. Clermont-Ganneau, *Recueil d'Archéologie Orientale* 1–8, Paris 1888 ss.
Conder, *SEP* C. R. Conder, *The Survey of Eastern Palestine*, Memoirs 1, London 1889.
Conder–Kitchener, *SWP* C. R. Conder and H. H. Kitchener, *Survey of Western Palestine*, Memoirs 1–3, London 1881–1883
Crowfoot, *Early Churches* J. W. Crowfoot, *Early Churches in Palestine*, London 1941
DACL *Dictionnaire d'Archéologie Chrétienne et de Liturgie*, Paris
Epiph., *Haer.* Epiphanius Constantiniensis Episcopus, *Panarion seu Adversus LXXX Haereses* (ed. K. Holl), Leipzig 1915–1931 (*GCS* 25, 31, 37; also in *PG* 41–42)
Eus., *Onom.* Eusebius, *Das Onomastikon der biblischen Ortsnamen* (ed. E. Klostermann), Leipzig 1904
Fest. Festschrift (in honor of . . .)
Frey, *Corpus* 2 J.-B. Frey, *Corpus Inscriptionum Judaicarum*, Rome 1952
GCS *Die Griechischen Christlichen Schriftsteller der Ersten Jahrhunderte*, Leipzig
Goodenough, *Jewish Symbols* E. R. Goodenough, *Jewish Symbols in the Greco-Roman Period* 1–12, New York 1953–1968
Guérin, *Galilée* V. Guérin, *Description Géographique, Historique et Archéologique de la Palestine, Galilée* 1–2, Paris 1868–1880
Guérin, *Judée* V. Guérin, *Description Géographique, Historique et Archéologique de la Palestine, Judée* 1–3, Paris 1868–1869
Guérin, *Samarie* V. Guérin, *Description Géographique, Historique et Archéologique de la Palestine, Samarie* 1–2, Paris 1874
Harbour Archaeology, 1985 *Harbour Archaeology—Proceedings, 1st International Workshop on Ancient Mediterranean Harbours, Caesarea Maritima 24–28.6.83* (*BAR*/IS 257, ed. A. Raban), Oxford 1985
HE (various authors) *Historia Ecclesiastica*
Hill, *BMC* G. F. Hill, *Catalogue of the Greek Coins in the British Museum, Palestine*, London 1914
Hüttenmeister–Reeg, *Antiken Synagogen* F. Hüttenmeister and G. Reeg, *Die antiken Synagogen* 1–2, Wiesbaden 1977

IGLS *Inscriptiones Grècques et Latines de la Syries* (eds. L. Jalabert and R. Mouder), Paris 1927–

IG Rom. *Inscriptiones Graecae ad res Romanas pertinentes* 1–4 (ed. R. Cagnat), Paris 1911–1927

Itin. Burdig. *Itinerarium Burdigalense*

Josephus, *Antiq.* Josephus Flavius, *Antiquities*

Josephus, *War* Josephus Flavius, *The Jewish War*

Khouri, *Antiquities* R. C. Khouri, *The Antiquities of the Jordan Rift Valley*, 'Amman 1988

Klein, *Corpus* S. Klein, *Jüdisch-palästinisches Corpus Inscriptionum*, Vienna 1920

Kohl–Watzinger, *Synagogen* H. Kohl and C. Watzinger, *Antike Synagogen in Galilaea*, Leipzig 1916

Lidzbarski, *Ephemeris* M. Lidzbarski, *Ephemeris für Semitische Epigraphik* 1–3, Giessen 1902–1915

Musil, *Arabia Petraea* A. Musil, *Arabia Petraea* 1–3, Vienna 1907–1908

Naveh J. Naveh, *On Stone and Mosaic: The Aramaic and Hebrew Inscriptions from Ancient Synagogues*, Tel Aviv 1978 (Hebrew; quoted by inscription no.)

NEAT *Near Eastern Archaeology in the Twentieth Century: Essays in Honor of Nelson Glueck* (ed. J. A. Sanders), Garden City, N.Y. 1970

P Edgar, P Cairo, P Nessana, P Zen. Various collections of papyri

Perrot–Ladiray, *Tombes et Ossuaires* J. Perrot and D. Ladiray, *Tombes et Ossuaires de la région côtière Palestinienne au IVème millénaire avant l'ère Chrétienne* (Mémoires et Travaux du Centre de Recherches Préhistoriques Française de Jérusalem, 1), Paris 1980

PG *Patrologia Graeca* (ed. Migne), Paris

PL *Patrologia Latina* (ed. Migne), Paris

Pliny, *NH* Pliny, *Naturalis Historia*

PPTS The Library of the Palestine Pilgrims' Text Society, London 1897 (quoted by text no.)

Ptol., *Geog.* *Claudii Ptolomei Geographia* (ed. C. S. A. Nobbe), Hildesheim 1966

Recherches Archéologiques en Israël *Recherches Archéologiques en Israël. Publications jubilaire des Amis Belges de l'Université Hébraïque de Jérusalem à l'Occasion de vingt-cinquième ans de l'Institut d'Archéologie. Reine Élisabeth de Belgique*, Leuven 1984

Reeg, *Ortsnamen* G. Reeg, *Die Ortsnamen Israels nach der Rabbinischen Literatur*, Wiesbaden 1989

Robinson, *Biblical Researches* E. Robinson, *Biblical Researches in Palestine* 1–3, London 1841

Saller–Bagatti, *Town of Nebo* S. J. Saller and B. Bagatti, *The Town of Nebo*, Jerusalem 1949

Schürer, *GJV* 2 E. Schürer, *Geschichte des jüdischen Volkes im Zeitalter Jesu Christi* 2, Leipzig 1907

Schürer, *HJP* E. Schürer, *A History of the Jewish People in the Age of Jesus Christ* 1–3 (new rev. ed.), Edinburgh 1973–1986

SEG *Supplementum Epigraphicum Graecum* (quoted by volume and inscription no.)

Society and Economy *Society and Economy in the Eastern Mediterranean, c. 1500–1000 B.C.* (eds. M. Heltzer and E. Lipinski) (Orientalia Lovaniensia Analecta 23), Leuven 1988

Stern, *GLA* M. Stern, *Greek and Latin Authors on Jews and Judaism* 1–3, Jerusalem 1974–1984 (quoted by text no.)

Stern, *Material Culture* E. Stern, *Material Culture of the Land of the Bible in the Persian Period 538–332 B.C.*, Warminster 1982

Strabo *The Geography of Strabo* (ed. H. L. Jones), London 1949–1969

Sukenik, *Ancient Synagogues* E. L. Sukenik, *Ancient Synagogues in Palestine and Greece*, London 1934

Vincent–Abel, *Jérusalem Nouvelle* L. H. Vincent and F. M. Abel, *Jérusalem Nouvelle* 1–4, Paris 1912–1926

Vincent–Stève, *Jérusalem* L. H. Vincent and A. M. Stève, *Jérusalem de l'Ancien Testament* 1–4, Paris 1954–1956

Waddington W. H. Waddington and P. Le Bas, *Voyage Archéologiques en Grèce et Asie Mineure: Inscriptions et Applications*, 3, Paris 1870

Warren–Conder, *SWP—Jerusalem* C. Warren and C. R. Conder, *The Survey of Western Palestine—Jerusalem*, London 1884

Watzinger, *DP* K. Watzinger, *Denkmäler Palästinas* 1–2, Leipzig 1933–1935

Weippert 1988 H. Weippert, *Palästina in Vorhellenistischer Zeit* (Handbuch der Archäologie-Vorderasien 2/1), Munich 1988. Includes Ortsregister

Woolley–Lawrence, *PEFA* 3 C. L. Woolley and T. E. Lawrence, *The Wilderness of Zin* (PEFA 3), London 1915

JOURNALS

AAA Annals of Archaeology and Anthropology
AASOR Annual of the American Schools of Oriental Research
ADAJ Annual of the Department of Antiquities of Jordan
AJA American Journal of Archaeology
AJSLL American Journal of Semitic Languages and Literature
'Alon Bulletin of the Israel Department of Antiquities (Hebrew)
APEF (see *PEFA*)
'Atiqot Journal of the Israel Antiquities Authority
AUSS Andrews University Seminary Studies
AWA Advances in World Archaeology
BA Biblical Archaeologist
BAIAS Bulletin of the Anglo-Israel Archaeology Society
BAR Biblical Archaeology Review
BASOR Bulletin of the American Schools of Oriental Research
BBSAJ Bulletin of the British School of Archaeology in Jerusalem
BIAL Bulletin of the Institute of Archaeology, London
BIES Bulletin of the Israel Exploration Society (Hebrew)
BJPES Bulletin of the Jewish Palestine Exploration Society
BMB Bulletin du Musée de Beyrouth
BS Bibliotheca Sacra
BTS Bible et Terre Sainte
BZ Biblische Zeitschrift
CNI Christian News from Israel
CRAIBL Comptes-rendus, Académie des Inscriptions et Belles-Lettres
EI Eretz-Israel
ESI Excavations and Surveys in Israel
HUCA Hebrew Union College Annual
HUCMS Haifa University Center for Maritime Studies
IEJ Israel Exploration Journal
IJNA The International Journal of Nautical Archaeology and Underwater Exploration
ILN The Illustrated London News
JAOS Journal of the American Oriental Society
JBL Journal of Biblical Literature
JCS Journal of Cuneiform Studies
JEA Journal of Egyptian Archaeology
JFA Journal of Field Archaeology
JNES Journal of Near Eastern Studies
JPOS Journal of the Palestine Oriental Society
JRAI Journal of the Royal Anthropological Institute
JRAS Journal of the Royal Asiatic Society
JRS Journal of Roman Studies
LA Studii Biblici Franciscani Liber Annuus
MdB Le Monde de la Bible
MDOG Mitteilungen der Deutschen Orientalischen Gesellschaft
MUSJ Mélanges de l'Université Saint Joseph de Beyrouth
OLZ Orientalische Literaturzeitung
PEFA Annual of the Palestine Exploration Fund
PEQ Palestine Exploration Quarterly
PJB Palästina Jahrbuch
PMB Palestine Museum Bulletin
QDAP Quarterly of the Department of Antiquities in Palestine
RAr Revue Archéologique
RB Revue Biblique
RHR Revue de l'Histoire des Religions
SHAJ Studies in the History and Archaeology of Jordan
TA Tel Aviv
TLZ Theologische Literaturzeitung
VT Vetus Testamentum
ZAW Zeitschrift für die Alttestamentliche Wissenschaft
ZDPV Zeitschrift des Deutschen Palästina-Vereins

TRANSLITERATION OF HEBREW

Letter	*Name*	*Transliteration*
א	aleph	'
ב	bheth	v
בּ	beth	b
ג	gimel	g
ד	daleth	d
ה	he	h
ו	vav	v, w
ז	zayin	z
ח	cheth	ḥ
ט	tet	ṭ
י	yod	y
כ, ך	khaph	kh
כּ, ךּ	kaph	k
ל	lamed	l
מ, ם	mem	m
נ, ן	nun	n
ס	samekh	s
ע	'ayin	'
פ, ף	phe	f
פּ	pe	p
צ, ץ	tzadhe, ṣadhe	ẓ, ṣ
ק	koph	q
ר	resh	r
שׁ	shin	sh, š
שׂ	sin	s
ת	tav	t

TRANSLITERATION OF GREEK

Letter	*Name*	*Transliteration*
Α α	alpha	a
Β β	beta	b
Γ γ	gamma	g
Δ δ	delta	d
Ε ε	epsilon	e
Ζ ζ	zeta	z
Η η	eta	ē
Θ θ	theta	th
Ι ι	iota	i
Κ κ	kappa	k
Λ λ	lambda	l
Μ μ	mu	m
Ν ν	nu	n
Ξ ξ	xi	z
Ο ο	omicron	o
Π π	pi	p
Ρ ρ	rho	r
Σ σ, ς	sigma	s
Τ τ	tau	t
Υ υ	upsilon	y, u
Φ φ	phi	ph
Χ χ	chi	kh
Ψ ψ	psi	ps
Ω ω	omega	ō

THE NEW ENCYCLOPEDIA OF ARCHAEOLOGICAL EXCAVATIONS IN THE HOLY LAND

E

(CONTINUED)

EMMAUS

IDENTIFICATION

Emmaus is situated at the eastern end of the Ayalon Valley. The name of the city has persisted in the name of the modern Arab village 'Imwas (map reference 149.138), near Latrun, on the old Jerusalem–Tel Aviv road. Emmaus (Ἐμμαοῦς, Ἀμμαοῦς) occupied an important strategic position on the road that ascends from the Coastal Plain to Jerusalem.

HISTORY

Emmaus is first mentioned in 1 Maccabees (3:40, 3:57, 4:3) as the place where the armies of the Seleucid kingdom encamped in their third campaign against Judas Maccabaeus, and where they were defeated and their camp captured. In the middle of the first century BCE, Emmaus was the capital of one of the toparchies of Judea. The Roman commander Cassius sold its inhabitants into slavery and in 4 BCE, following the death of King Herod, it became the center of an insurrection led by the shepherd Athronges. In retaliation, Varus, the proconsul of Syria, set fire to the city. Several tombstones found here, bearing the names of Roman soldiers, indicate that the Fifth Legion was encamped in the city during the First Jewish Revolt. Emmaus was still in existence in the days of Rabbi Akiba and later. During the Bar-Kokhba Revolt, the troops from Petra were stationed here. In the Talmud, the town is referred to as a major site in the Shephelah (J.T., *Shevi'it* 8, 9, 38d) and as a seat of the Samaritans (J.T., *A.Z.* 85, 44d). In the third century CE, Emmaus was granted the status of a city by the emperor Elagabalus (218–222 CE) and named Nicopolis. In the Byzantine period, its vicinity was made unsafe by the brigand Cyriacus, the head of a Jewish and Samaritan band. Samaritan inscriptions were discovered on the site, among them a bilingual inscription in Greek and Samaritan. Following the Arab conquest in 639 CE, Emmaus was struck by a plague that claimed thousands of lives. During the Crusades, a garrison of Knights Templar was stationed there.

Although it is certain that the city of Emmaus-Nicopolis was situated close to 'Imwas, near Latrun, scholars differ over whether it is the Emmaus mentioned in the New Testament (Lk. 24:13), which was 60 (according to some versions 160) stadia from Jerusalem. According to the Gospels, Jesus appeared to two of his disciples there, after his resurrection. Some scholars take this latter Emmaus to be Abu Ghosh, situated between Jerusalem and Emmaus, or el-Qubeibeh, northwest of it.

THE CHURCH

Remains of the church found at the site, called el-Kenisah, attracted the attention of explorers as early as 1875, when J. B. Guillemot excavated there. The main work, however, was carried out in 1924, 1925, and 1927 by the Dominican fathers L. H. Vincent and F. M. Abel, on behalf of the École Biblique et Archéologique Française in Jerusalem. The excavators distinguished the remains of five structures:

Emmaus: general view of the Crusader church, looking east.

Emmaus: plan of the church and baptistery, as proposed by the excavators.

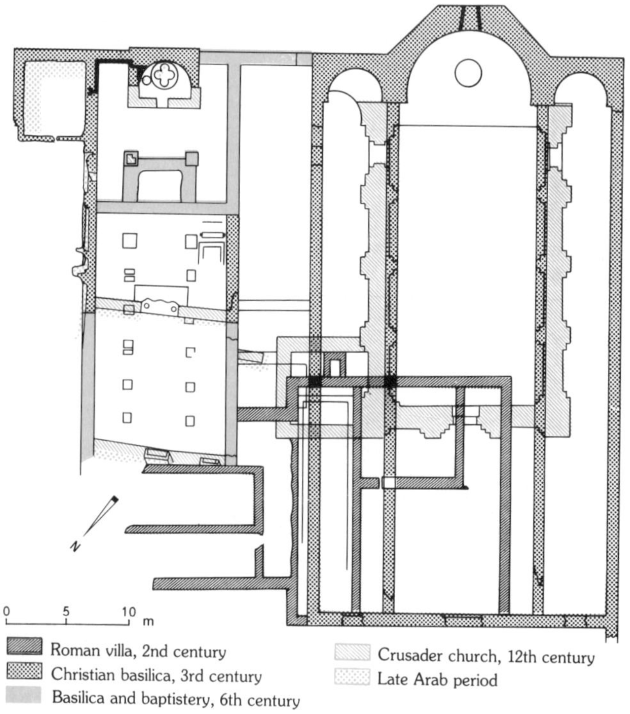

1. Recesses hewn out of the rock and foundations of walls (c. 0.8 m thick) they assigned to the second and first centuries BCE.

2. The remains of a Roman villa dated to the second century CE (building 2), a square structure (18 by 17 m) comprising a long room and a square room (or courtyard) at its northeast extremity. A long courtyard surrounded by porticos runs along the northern side of the building, to which the excavators also assigned a mosaic pavement with floral and guilloche borders. The field of the mosaic was composed of a pattern of circles and octagons combining into squares and lozenges filled with various kinds of guilloche motifs. The extant octagons contain depictions of a lion devouring a bull, a panther savaging a gazelle, and birds perched on lotus flowers. One of the circles contains an inscription that mentions "the other brothers Pelagius and Thomas."

3. A Christian basilica (46.4 by 24.4 m), dated by the excavators to the third century (building 3), was divided into a nave and two aisles by two rows of thirteen columns each. On the east, the basilica ended in three apses. There is no trace of a narthex. The remains of two layers of mosaic pavements are preserved in the west.

4. A two-part parallel structure (building 4) beyond an intermediate hall (5.8 m wide): a basilica (18 by 10 m) with two rows of six columns each, and behind it a baptistery supported by four columns. In the baptistery, a trefoil-shaped stone baptismal font was uncovered, with a smaller baptismal font for children next to it. Near the baptistery is a deep well. The excavators dated the basilica and baptistery to the sixth century. In the baptistery were the remains of mosaics with geometric motifs and a fragment decorated with floral borders with intertwining tendrils. Part of an inscription was also found that mentions an *episcopus* and the laying of the mosaic. Another inscription, in which a certain Johanan and the laying of a mosaic are mentioned, was found near the east end of the basilica's southern aisle.

5. A twelfth-century Crusader church built in the prevailing Romanesque style. These are the best-preserved remains. The Byzantine's church's central apse was reused by the Crusaders as the apse of their own church, to which they added a vaulted hall (23 by 10.25 m). The main entrance to the hall was in the west; two side entrances were made in the vault in front of the apse. As was usual in that period, the roof of the hall rested on four pointed arches with voussoirs supported by pillars attached to the wall of the hall (1.5 m thick). On the western facade of the Crusader church, two freestanding pillars supported a porch in front of the hall's main entrance. Among the smaller finds were fragmentary inscriptions, one of which was bilingual: in Greek, "God is One," and in Samaritan, "Blessed be His name forever." Also found were fragments of the sculpture of an eagle, estimated to have been about 1 m high; the remains of a Byzantine oil press; and numerous architectural fragments. Except for several Arab and Hellenistic-Herodian potsherds, the excavators did not record any ceramic finds from the various periods of construction.

SUMMARY. J. W. Crowfoot observed that the dates suggested by the excavators were unacceptable, at least those assigned to the mosaic pavements and the large basilica. The large church cannot be dated to the third century, a period when Christianity was a prohibited and persecuted religion and its adherents were compelled to worship in private houses (as we know was the case at Dura Europos). The church plan with a triple apse appears for the first time in this country in the days of Theodosius II. It became prevalent in the first half of the fifth century (at Gethsemane and in St. Stephen's), especially in the Negev (at St. Theodore at Eboda [Oboda] and at St. George at Subeita [Sobota], for example). The main church cannot be separated from the

Capital from the Crusader church with a Samaritan inscription: "Blessed be His name forever."

Detail of a mosaic from the Roman villa.

Plan and section of the southern baths, on their reduced scale.

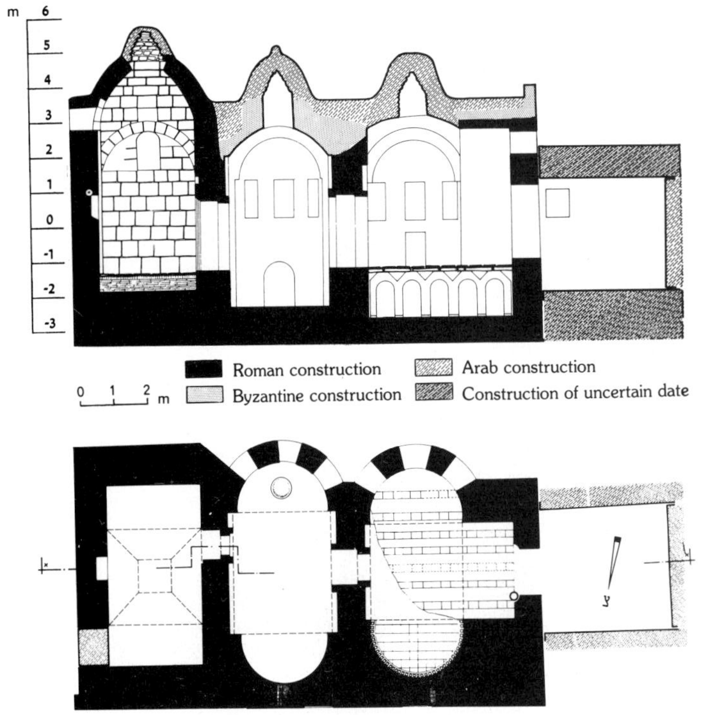

Dome of the frigidarium (room 4), viewed from below.

baptistery. Auxiliary structures such as these are found at many sites, as, for example, at Subeita and Mount Nebo. The mosaics ascribed to the second century are similar in many details to those in the fifth-century church at Heptapegon (q.v.) and even more so to those at Makhatet el-'Urj near Beth Guvrin (see Mareshah and Beth Guvrin), which are presumably from the sixth century. In any case, they have nothing in common with the Roman mosaics. It is difficult to establish dates in the absence of strata, pottery, or coins and in the presence of the many disturbances caused by subsequent building activities. It seems, nevertheless, that a church was erected in the fifth century (building 3) on the foundations of the Constantinian villa (building 2). The additions to the church and the pavements date to the sixth century (building 4).

MICHAEL AVI-YONAH

THE SOUTHERN BATHS

It is accepted at present that the source of the name Emmaus is Ḥamat or possibly Ḥamatah or Ḥamata. In Jewish sources, Emmaus is mentioned as a place of "fine water and a fine dwelling" (*Eccles. Rab.* 7:15)—that is, a place of rest and of baths. This is also alluded to by the name Dimosith by which it is called (*Shab.* 147b, etc.), a name derived from the Greek *dimosion* (δημόσιον λουτρόν), "public bathhouse." The healing properties of the waters of Emmaus are also mentioned by Byzantine writers, who connect those properties with the visit of Jesus to the place (Sozomenus, *HE, PG* 67, 1280). Emmaus' renown was not, however, due solely to its thermal springs, for it also contained rich sources of ordinary water.

Emmaus drew a portion of its water from the spring of 'Eqed at the foot of Giv'at 'Eqed (q.v. Ḥorvat 'Eqed) through a system of three parallel aqueducts. It is possible that not all three of these aqueducts existed at the same time; one of them was restored in the Middle Ages. The system was partially uncovered in 1976 by Y. Hirschfeld, on behalf of the Institute of Archaeology at the Hebrew University of Jerusalem, and in 1984 by E. Shenhav, on behalf of the Jewish National Fund.

It can be reasonably assumed that the southern baths formed only one part of the bath installations at the site, and that the others have not yet been uncovered. The southern baths were preserved due to an unusual series of events. In 636 CE, Abu 'Ubeideh, the commander of the Muslim army, died here of plague, and Emmaus was abandoned in the wake of the epidemic. It was resettled by the Crusaders, who found the baths in ruins and apparently used them as warehouses. The Mamelukes, who sought to reinforce every site's link to Islam, turned the baths at Emmaus into a holy place. The current Arab name of the place, Maqam esh-Sheikh 'Ubeid, may be derived from the name Abu 'Ubeideh. A landslide during the Ottoman period covered the building on three sides, protecting it. Believers ceased to visit and to pray here at around the turn of the twentieth century.

EXCAVATION RESULTS. The site of the southern baths was first surveyed by a team from Tel Aviv University in 1968. In 1977–1978 and 1981–1982, systematic excavations were carried out here under the direction of M. Gichon, with the participation of scholars from the University of Florence.

The southern baths consist of a series of adjoining rooms arranged in a row; the visitor progressed through the rooms, each of which had a special function in the process of cleansing and caring for the body. At the conclusion of his stay in the complex, the bather would retrace his steps and leave through the entrance. At present, the bathhouse contains four rooms preserved to ceiling height; originally, however, the structure contained additional rooms on the north side, and perhaps in the south, as well. These rooms were damaged in one of the many earthquakes that struck the region, perhaps in one of those recorded in 498, 502, and 507 CE. Because the Muslim cemetery surrounding the bathhouse structure could not be excavated, the nature of the additional rooms could not be determined.

The baths were not established before the Severan period, but perhaps after Emmaus-Nicopolis was granted city status (polis) by Elagabalus in 221 CE—at any rate, no later than the early fourth century CE. This date is supported by the discovery of a few third-century sherds and a gem, from the second to third centuries CE, found behind secondary retaining walls in room 3 (see below).

After the damage it had suffered in one of the above-mentioned earthquakes, the complex was restored on a more limited scale (14 by 7.5 m). Two apses in the south project about 2 m; two niches (0.47 m deep and 2 m high) were built in the north wall. Two additional niches were in this wall's original facade. From the lower pavement of the hypocaust to the top of the flat roof, the building is 6 m high. The dome above room 4 (see below) rises to a height

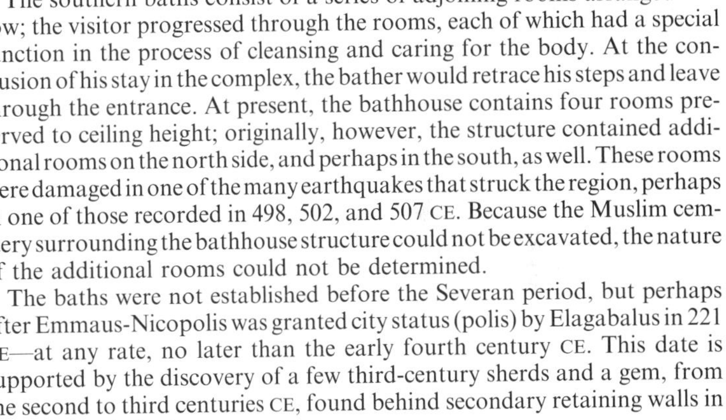

Southwestern niche in the tepidarium (room 3); the windows were blocked in the Middle Ages.

The caldarium (room 2) and the arches of the suspensurae.

of an additional 1.5 m. The walls (1 to 1.5 m thick) were built of well-dressed ashlars in the opus quadratum method (full ashlar construction, with the stone blocks fitted together precisely).

The restored, smaller bathhouse (2.75 by 5.15 m) was entered through a doorway in the northeast corner of room 4. This room had a domed ceiling, composed of four vaulted sections that do not meet at their points, which leaves an opening for ventilation. According to Vitruvius' description of Roman baths (*De Architectura* V, 10, 5), a mechanism for regulating the air in the baths was installed in this opening. Two of the sections of the dome are a continuation of the southern and eastern walls, while the other two are supported by arches. These arches formed deep recesses that may have contained a basin or a bathtub. The room was paved with marble slabs in geometric patterns, which had already been looted in the Middle Ages. The colored wall plaster, which was applied over a base of sherds, has also disappeared almost completely.

Room 4 is the frigidarium in the existing form of the bathhouse, whereas in the original plan it was the tepidarium. This is indicated by the existence under its floor of a duct for hot air, built of fired bricks. The air, which passed through the duct from the hypocaust in room 3 (see below), warmed room 4 to some extent and turned it into a tepidarium.

Room 3, in its original form, was the caldarium; the superheated air reached it through a subterranean passage from the central furnace room (*praefurnium*) adjoining it on the south. The room's barrel-vaulted ashlar ceiling collapsed in the earthquake that destroyed the building and apparently broke the hypocaust system. When the room was restored, the upper pavement and its supports were removed and the pipes (*tubuli*) in its walls, through which the hot air had ascended, were dismantled. Then room 3 became a tepidarium heated by a portable brazier or some other heating arrangement.

Room 2 is similar in shape to room 3, but with the addition of a large square niche on the west side, above the passage to the second furnace room. The tubs for the hottest baths were installed in this niche. The earthquakes did not spare room 2 either, but because it was impossible to remove from it the system of supports for the upper pavement (*suspensurae*) during the restoration, the arches of the system of supports were repaired from time to time.

Because it was not possible to excavate outside the building, the date of construction and the original plan of room 1 could not be determined. This room over the southern praefurnium is built of especially well-smoothed ashlars rising into a barrel vault. Its present dimensions (3.75 by 3.1 m) are probably smaller than the original ones. In any event the room existed, at the latest, in the Byzantine period, after the landslide had covered the south wall of the building to window height. The three windows cut into the eastern niches of rooms 2 and 3 were intended to provide plentiful light, in contrast with the accepted practice in the Byzantine period.

A structure resembling a shed was built on top of the overflowing debris next to the south wall, over a large water container. Pipes ran on the windowsill at the debris level into a niche lined with fired bricks in room 1. Apparently, there was a water tank in this niche as well. According to Vitruvius' description of Roman baths (*De Architectura* V, 10, 1), this room should also have had a third water tank, positioned above the heating duct. Therefore, as far as can be determined, there were three regular tanks in the Emmaus bathhouse: for cold water (outside the structure), for lukewarm water (somewhat closer to the source of heat), and for hot water (above the praefurnium). Room 1, which is located above the praefurnium, may have been the sudatorium.

A portion of the pipe system attached to the walls in room 2 is preserved. This system prevented the air from becoming steam and the walls from becoming wet by only generating heat under the floor. Openings on the sides of the clay pipes enabled the lateral flow of air as well, and chimneys, whose remains are visible in rooms 2 and 3, ensured proper air flow by expelling the cold air and drawing in new hot air from the furnace in the praefurnium.

The upper pavement in room 2 was laid according to the Vitruvian method: a base of pottery tiles on arches and a 35-cm layer of cast and especially hard cement, covered by a pavement of two-shaded marble slabs set into a layer of paving plaster. The method of supporting the upper pavement by a series of parallel brick arches (1.6 m high) and not by piers or colonnettes is uncommon. It can be explained by the wish to add strength and flexibility to the *suspensurae* in baths located in an earthquake-prone area.

In the Crusader period, room 4 was divided into a lower and an upper room by a wooden ceiling installed 2.2 m above the pavement. This ceiling was carried by horizontal beams set in sockets in the walls. It became the pavement of the upper room. The ceiling was dismantled after the Crusaders were driven out, and the building was turned into a Muslim holy place. The believers turned the wall sockets into niches for oil lamps. Fragments of these lamps were found in abundance in the upper strata.

A series of channels belonging to the water-supply and drainage systems was uncovered along the outer walls. The channels were partly built of cement on small stones and of U-shaped stone blocks, covered by flat slabs. Regulation of the water intake was ensured by means of a meticulously constructed, ashlar-built castellum (reservoir), 1.5 m in diameter, connected to the building's northwestern corner. A fine mosaic floor abutting the northern wall and well-carved architectural fragments point to the existence of a palaestra on this side.

MORDECHAI GICHON

General: M. Shiffers, *RB* 2 (1893), 26–40; E. Michon, ibid. 7 (1898), 269–271; I. Benzinger, *ZDPV* 25 (1902), 195–203; M. Riemer, *PJB* 14 (1918), 32–43; G. Beyer, *ZDPV* 56 (1933), 218–246; *The Rosenberger Israel Collection* 3 (City Coins of Palestine), Jerusalem 1977; P. Figueras, *CNI* 26 (1978), 132–134; Y. Hirschfeld, *IEJ* 28 (1978), 86–92; J. Schwartz, ibid. 40 (1990), 45–57.
The church: C. Schick, *ZDPV* 7 (1884), 15–16; *RB* 35 (1926), 117–121; L. H. Vincent and F. M. Abel, *Emmaüs: Sa Basilique et son histoire*, Paris 1932; id., ibid. (Review), *PEQ* 67 (1935), 40–47; L. H. Vincent, *RB* 45 (1936), 403–415; 55 (1948), 348–375; R. de Vaux, ibid. 47 (1938), 244–245; Crowfoot, *Early Churches*, 71, 125, 145; B. Bagatti, *I Monumenti di Emmaus et Qubeibeh e dei Dintorni* 1–2, Jerusalem 1947; id., *Rivista di Archeologia Christiana* 35 (1959), 71–80; M. Avi-Yonah, *The Madaba Mosaic Map*, Jerusalem 1954, 64; D. Buzy, *BTS* 36 (1961), 4–13; J. Finegan, *The Archaeology of the New Testament*, Princeton, N.J. 1969, 177–180; Y. Blomme, *RB* 87 (1980), 404–407; D. Chen, *ZDPV* 97 (1981), 171–177; S. de Sandoli, *Emmaus–el Qubeibeh* (Studium Biblicum Franciscanum Guide-Books), Jerusalem 1959: id., *Emmaus–el Qubeibe: The Sanctuary and Nearby Biblical Sites* 2 (The Holy Places of Palestine), Jerusalem 1980.
The baths: M. Gichon, *IEJ* 29 (1979), 101–110; (with R. Linden) 34 (1984), 156–169; id., *RB* 86; G. Kühnel, *Wall Painting in the Latin Kingdom of Jerusalem* (Frankfurter Forschungen zur Kunst 14), Berlin 1988, 149–180. (1979), 125–126; id., *Archiv für Orientforschung* 27 (1980), 228–233; id., *BAIAS* 6 (1986–1987), 54–57.

'ENAN

IDENTIFICATION

The Natufian site of 'Enan (Mallaḥa) is in the northern Jordan Valley, on the western bank of what was Lake Ḥula, which has been drained. It lies about 100 m west of the Rosh Pinna–Metulla road, on the embankment above the spring of 'Ein Mallaḥa, at 72 m above sea level (map reference 204.277).

EXPLORATION

The site was discovered in 1954, when authorities were laying a water pipe. It was surveyed in 1955 and 1956 by J. Perrot and E. Yeivin, on behalf of the Israel Department of Antiquities and Museums, and was systematically excavated by the Centre de Recherche Français de Jérusalem in two campaigns, from 1959 to 1961 and 1971 to 1975. Perrot was assisted from 1972 to 1975 by M. Lechevallier and then by F. R. Valla. The research was supported by the American Philosophical Society, the Wenner Gren Foundation, the Centre National Français de la Recherche Scientifique (with the participation of several specialists), and the Commission des Fouilles Archéologiques of the French Foreign Ministry. Assistance in Israel came from the Department of Antiquities; the Ḥula Prehistory Museum and A. Assaf; and the Moshe Stekelis Museum of Prehistory in Haifa and M. Davies. Assaf and Davies participated in the research. The excavated area covers over 300 sq m; the total area of the site is estimated at 2,000 sq m.

EXCAVATION RESULTS

STRATIGRAPHY. The main archaeological remains were found above reddish clays containing Mousterian flint tools, at the foot of the limestone foothills in the Galilee mountains. The clays form the bulk of the slope. The remains are from the Epipaleolithic era and, together with the Natufian material, date to between 10,500 and 8300 BCE. The Natufian deposits are up to 2.5 m thick. They contain a dozen layers and occupation floors, grouped into four levels that correspond to four archaeological periods: early (levels IV–III), middle (level II), late (level Ic), and final (level Ia). The early and middle periods, according to Valla, correspond to the Early Natufian, the late period to the Late Natufian, and the final period to the Final Natufian. Samples submitted to carbon-14 analysis have produced the following dates: for level IV—11,590 ± 540 BP (LY 1160: [9640]); level III—11,740 ± 570 BP (LY 1661: [9790]) and 11,310 ± 880 BP (LY 1662: [9360]). Traces of pits with pottery similar to that at Sha'ar ha-Golan were found on the surface.

ECOLOGY AND ENVIRONMENT. 'Enan is situated at the junction of complementary ecological zones: Lake Ḥula and the belt of marshy vegetation that surrounded it, and the highlands of the Golan, Mount Hermon, and the Galilee. Judging from pollen analyses and paleoclimatic data, a higher level of humidity than at present encouraged the development of vegetation

'Enan: general view of the site, looking southeast.

'Enan: plan of the site.

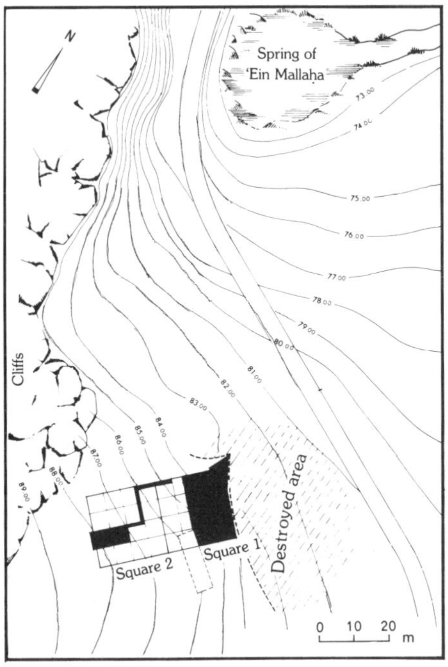

General view of level II.

in the Epipaleolithic era and, consequently, a wide variety and abundance of animal species. The upper Jordan Valley lies in the natural distribution zone of wild cereals; wild wheat was first recognized in Palestine by A. Aaronson at Rosh Pinna. Conditions were optimal for a group that had lived by fishing, hunting, and gathering to settle down and lead a quasi-sedentary life near a perennial and plentiful water source. The sedentary nature of the occupation here is shown by the thickness of the deposits, the importance of the stone structures and heavy equipment, the existence of a cemetery and by the faunal evidence, which proves that animals were hunted year round.

SUBSISTENCE. Analysis of the finds at 'Enan has thrown light on its inhabitants' way of life. Their subsistence was based on fishing and hunting. Medium-sized cyprinoid fish were plentiful (500–1,500 g). Notched pebbles found at the site may have been used as net weights; the fish were decapitated and probably gutted on the spot and then brought back to the village and grilled. Mollusks, crabs, tortoises, lizards, and snakes were also collected. The migratory birds were even more varied and numerous than today; the presence of some species confirms that the climate was cooler and more humid then.

The main sources of meat were gazelle (54 percent of the faunal remains) and other large mammals (roe deer, fallow deer and red deer); wild pig also played an important role. Remains of bovids, wild sheep and wild dog have also been found. Among the carnivores, wolf, fox, wildcats, badger, and marten could have been hunted for their fur; there is clear evidence of the preparation of skins at the site. The use of cereals has often been deduced from the presence of mortars, pestles, and sickles, but these tools could have had other uses. Several grinding stones retain traces of red ocher, and the sickle gloss could have come from cutting bulrushes, whose stems contain silicone. Remains of pistachios and almonds were found.

Plan of part of the Natufian village and burials.

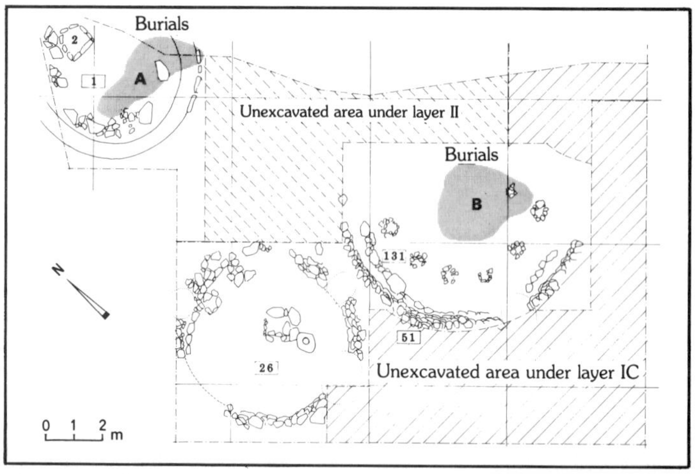

Round stone structure (no. 131) from the Early Natufian period, with a row of depressions for the bases of the columns that supported the roof.

Remains of round stone dwellings with hearths, basins, and other installations.

Building 131: pebbles and bone implements on floors A and B, Early Natufian period.

DWELLINGS. The inhabitants of 'Enan dug circular shelters, 9 m in diameter, into the slope. The surrounding earth was retained by a thick wall built of large field stones. The shelters had earthen roofs supported by posts surrounding the wall. The floors were sometimes paved with large slabs. There is evidence of the use of lime that, mixed with clay, forms an extremely hard mortar when it dries. It was used to coat the walls of small pits dug in the ground. Each shelter had various secondary structures, such as a hearth edged with stones and often a large mortar made of local or basalt stone. The rocks near the site bear many cupmarks. The diameter of the shelters became smaller in the upper level (3 to 4 m). In level Ic, a large area between the dwellings (about a dozen shelters, scattered over 300 sq m) contains several large, bell-shaped "silos," with walls coated with a thick layer of clay and shallow pits coated with lime plaster. These silos are the earliest known in the region; they were in use for a short time during the final period at the site.

TECHNOLOGY. Evidence for the preparation and sewing of skins is provided by the *lissoirs* and double-ended points. Some *aiguilles à passer* could mean that basketwork was done or fishing nets made. Spatula spoons and various composite tools were also found, as were retouchers for pressure-working flint. The bone tools themselves were made using a new and original technique that involved rubbing the bone on a grindstone.

The flint industry was essentially the same as that in the Upper Paleolithic and represents the same range of activities. It includes notched pieces (12 percent), burins (10 percent), retouched flakes and blades (5.5 percent), borers, scrapers, microliths, and some microburins. The new element in the industry is the higher proportion of microliths (45 percent), 10 percent

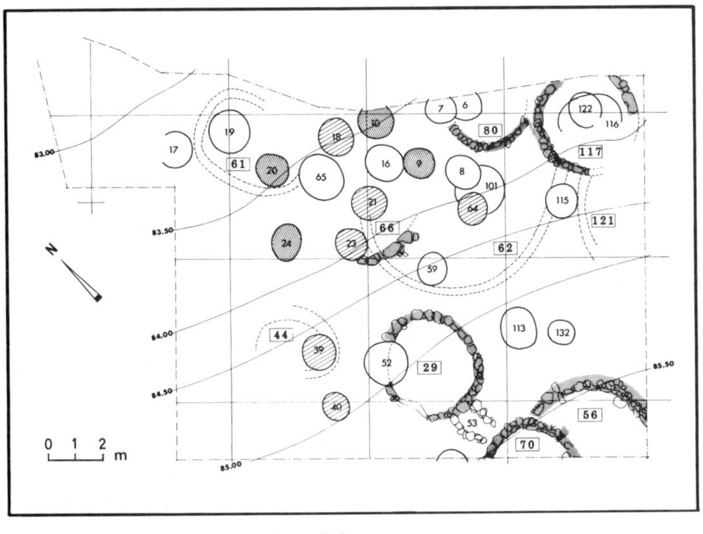

Plan of the cemetery.

Burial under a dwelling.

Burial 3, covered with stone slabs laid in a circle.

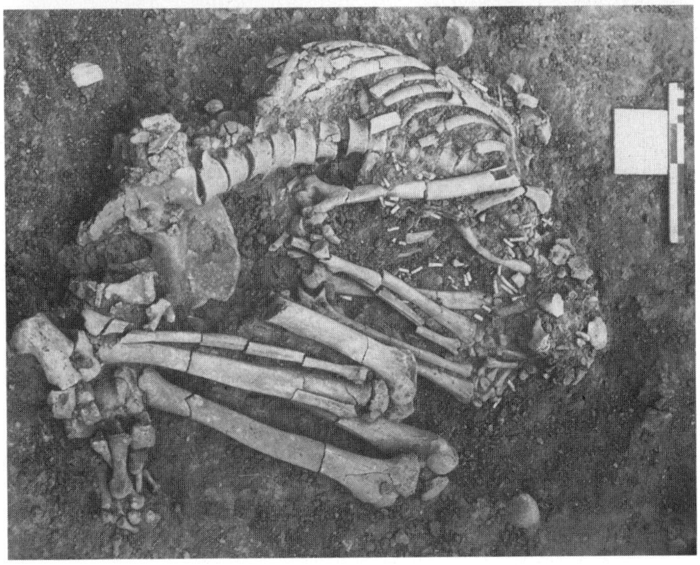

Early Natufian burial of a skeleton with a necklace.

of which are geometric (triangles, rectangles, trapezes, lunates). Half of the lunates (5 percent of the total) have bifacially retouched backs. Toward the end of the period the lunates became smaller, and bifacial retouch became less common. Because of the site's proximity to the great basalt outcrops in the Golan, considerable use was made at 'Enan of basalt to manufacture vases, mortars, pestles, grinding stones, small mortars, and polishing stones. Limestone was rarely used.

BURIALS. About one hundred tombs were discovered within the excavated area. The oldest are primary burials, groups of individuals (10 to 12 skeletons) that seem to represent two or three generations. Each such "cemetery" could have belonged to one family and have been used for the duration of their occupation at the site. The skeletons were not oriented in any particular direction; they were flexed or semiflexed, lying on the side or, more rarely, on the back. Tightly flexed examples are rare, and there are no completely extended burials, as in the el-Wad and Hayonim caves. The arrangement of the skeletons shows the respect paid to the dead: the deceased were buried with their personal ornaments (necklaces and bracelets, see below). There are no funerary offerings. Of particular interest is the burial of an adult with a young canine (a dog or wolf) in level IV; this constitutes the earliest evidence of the link that had begun to form between humans and certain animals. In the late period (level Ic, upper part) some burials were grouped in the area between the dwellings that had been occupied earlier by shallow pits and silos (lower part). Some of the shallow pits were reused for funerary purposes. Two types of burial can be distinguished: (1) successive primary burials in the same pit, whose fill includes large stones; (2) simultaneous burials of several individuals, with their skulls, limbs (often still articulated), and a few other bones. Tomb 9 contains six skulls and remains of eight individuals: three adults, an adolescent, and four children. The impression given by these collective burials is that they could represent a partial transfer from the older type of family cemetery. They are not the genuine secondary burials of the nomadic pastoralists of the fourth millennium BCE. The bones are often covered with red ocher. In one case (tomb 10), gazelle-horn cores were laid near the skulls. Most of the burials in this upper level are marked with large, flat stones that seem to have been standing; these stones can be compared with the disused limestone mortars that accompany the burials on the terraces at el-Wad and Naḥal Oren. In this way, the previously unmarked tomb became visible; the remembrance of the deceased passed from individual to group memory. This idea may have crystallized at the same time as the concept of a community of the dead. The presence of the cemetery reinforced the group's sense of identity and ownership of territory; from then on, it played an important role in the group's organization of space.

THE INHABITANTS. The Natufians of 'Enan were tall (men, 1.74 m; women, 1.62 m). Their skeletons are strikingly sturdy, especially the men's. The skulls are elongated, ovoid, and rather low; seen from behind, they are "house shaped." The face is characterized by heavy supraorbital ridges and large, low eye sockets. The mandible has a very high horizontal branch. The 'Enan skeletons constitute a homogeneous group in the line of development of Upper Paleolithic and Neolithic populations in the Near and Middle East.

Large basalt mortar.

Pebble incised with a human face.

ART. The works of art found at 'Enan are more modest than those found in the caves in the Carmel Range or the Judean Desert, where sedentarization seems to have been less advanced. Two anthropomorphic pebbles were found, as well as a small limestone human figurine with traces of red paint and a stone zoomorphic figurine that may represent a tortoise. Some vases and mortars bear geometric motifs, which do not seem to be functional, in low or high relief. The headbands, belts, and bone and shell necklaces and bracelets found with the burials from the first period may have had a prophylactic function or been purely ornamental. In any case, the symbolism used is not clear.

SOCIAL LIFE. Analysis of the archaeological remains does not reveal any

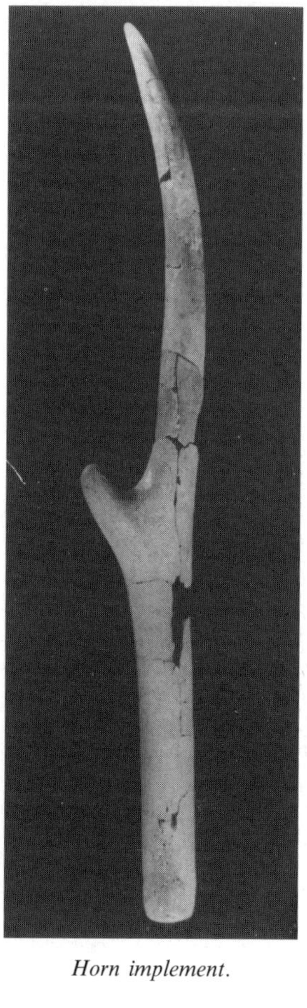

Horn implement.

Burial found between levels I and II.

differences in wealth or status among the site's inhabitants. The society seems to have been egalitarian, with no social stratification or hierarchy.

SUMMARY

The excavated area (300 sq m) at 'Enan reveals a sequence of periods of varying duration, beginning with the Natufian culture (10,500–8500 BCE), that is characterized by sedentary occupation. 'Enan provides the earliest known example of sedentary life in this country, and perhaps in the entire Near East. Since 1960, the research at 'Enan has encouraged the hypothesis that, contrary to accepted opinion, the beginning of sedentary life was not necessarily the result of production subsistence (through domestication of cereals and animals). It seems, rather, that in a favorable environment, an economy based on fishing, hunting, and gathering could lead to the development of sedentarization. In 'Enan's case, it seems to have been the rich fishing available in Lake Ḥula that was the origin of a sedentary life-style; hunting, although important, was not the determining factor. The use of cereals has not been directly proved.

The sedentary life-style involved an immediate change in technology: the construction of shelters and storage facilities, the use of lime plaster, and the refinement of the techniques of food acquisition (net weights for fishing and sickle hafts) and preparation (heavy mortars, pestles, and grindstones). The conceptual and quantitative jump here is most impressive. In the long term, sedentarization brings population growth and regroupings that entail social change; Beisamun, a few hundred meters from 'Enan, extended over 24 a. in the eighth millennium BCE, like Jericho. The sedentary way of life probably played a positive role in the development of the domestication of cereals and certain animals, such as the dog.

The Natufian tradition at 'Enan continued in the country in the Pre-Pottery Neolithic A, which represents the final phase of the Epipaleolithic, at the very end of the Pleistocene. The following period, the Pre-Pottery Neolithic B, bears witness to new influences here, probably from the north. This period saw the first manipulations of cereals and animals, leading to their domestication (thus justifying the designation Neolithic). The economy of the Pre-Pottery Neolithic B was still dominated by a subsistence system based on wild food sources, however, that was essentially the same as that practiced earlier at 'Enan.

Main publications: F. R. Valla, *Les Industries de silex de Mallaha (Eynan) et du Natoufien dans le Levant* (Mémoires et Travaux du Centre de Recherche Français de Jérusalem 3), Paris 1984; J. Bouchud, *La Faune du gisement Natoufien de Mallaha (Eynan), Israel* (Mémoires et Travaux du Centre de Recherche Français de Jérusalem 4), Paris 1987; D. Stordeur, *Outils et armes en os du gisement Natoufien de Mallaha (Eynan), Israel* (Mémoires et Travaux de Centre de Recherches Français de Jérusalem 6), Paris 1988; J. Perrot et al., *Les Hommes de Mallaha (Eynan), Israel* 1–2 (Mémoires et Travaux du Centre de Recherche Français de Jerusalem 7), Paris 1988; G. Dollfus, *Outils, vases et instruments en pierre du gisement Natoufien de Mallaha (Enan)*, Paris (in prep.).

Other studies: J. Perrot, *Antiquity and Survival* 2 (1957), 91–110; id., *IEJ* 7 (1957), 125–127; 10 (1960), 14–22, 257–258; 26 (1976), 47–48; id., *RB* 67 (1960), 257–260; id., *Year Book of the American Philosophical Society* 1960, 543–546; 1962, 604–607; id., *L'Anthropologie* 70 (1966), 437–483; id., *Paléorient* 2 (1974), 485–486; id., *Courrier du CNRS* 22 (1976), 13–18; id. (et al), *Les Hommes de Mallaha* (Review), *Mitekufat Ha'even* 22 (1989), 132*–138*; id., *Investigations in South-Levantine Prehistory: Prehistoire du Sud-Levant* (*BAR*/IS 497, eds. O. Bar-Yosef and B. Vandermeersch), Oxford 1989, 287–296; D. Ferembach, *Comptes-rendus du 6e Congrès Internationale des Sociétés Anthropologiques et Ethnologiques Musée de l'Homme*, Paris 1960, 587–591; id., *L'Anthropologie* 65 (1961), 46–66; A. Biran, *CNI* 12 (1961), 17; 13 (1962), 17; M. C. Cauvin, *L'Anthropologie* 70 (1966), 484–494; M. Lechevallier and J. Perrot, *IEJ* 23 (1973), 107, 239; 25 (1975), 16; id., *RB* 80 (1973), 399–400; 82 (1975), 70–71, 558–559; 84 (1977), 254–255; F. R. Valla, *IEJ* 25 (1975), 1–7, 161; 26 (1976), 47–48; 27 (1977), 42; id., *Paléorient* 3 (1975–1977), 287–292; 14/2 (1988), 283–296; id., *La Recherche* 19/199 (1988), 576–584; id. *Mémoires du Musée de Préhistoire d'Ile de France* 2 (1989), 293–302; id., *The Natufian Culture in the Levant* (International Monographs in Prehistory, Archaeology Series 1, eds. O. Bar-Yosef and F. R. Valla), Ann Arbor 1991, 111–122; O. Soliveres, *Bulletins et Mémoires de la Société Anthropologique de Paris,* Série 13, 3 (1976) 261–279; K. Yassine, *ADAJ* 22 (1977–1978), 14–19; H. Büller, *Traces d'utilisation sur les outils néolithiques du Proche Orient* (Travaux de la Maison de l'Orient 5, ed. M. Cauvin), Lyon 1983, 107–126; E. Eisenberg, *ESI* 2 (1983), 28; id., *'Atiqot* 17 (1985), 59–74; A. Leroi-Gourhan, *Paléorient* 10 (1984), 103–105; *Préhistoire en Israël* (Dossiers d'Archéologie 100), Paris 1985, passim; T. Stech et al., *'Atiqot* 17 (1985), 75–82; A. E. Shimron, ibid., 83–89; Weippert 1988, 87, 91f., 94f.; P. C. Edwards, *Journal of Mediterranean Archaeology* 2 (1989), 5–48; J. Pichon, *Investigations in South-Levantine Prehistory* (op. cit.). 61–74; C. Maréchal, *The Natufian Culture in the Levant* (op. cit.), 589–612.

JEAN PERROT

'EN BESOR

IDENTIFICATION

Tel 'En Besor is situated on a small loess hill in the northwestern Negev desert within the boundaries of the modern Eshkol Park, about 30 km northwest of modern Beersheba (map reference 1013.0795). The hill is approximately 0.4 a. in area. The site is located about 350 m south of the 'En Besor springs ('Ein Shellala in Arabic) and about 500 m southwest of the Early Bronze Age IA "site H," excavated in 1929–1930 by E. MacDonald, a member of the W. M. F. Petrie expedition to Tell el-Far'ah (South) (Tel Sharuhen). The eastern edge of Tel 'En Besor was destroyed during World War I, when the British built a branch line for a railway. The western part of the site is completely eroded, and the archaeological remains at the top of the mound were severely damaged when the site was used as a burial ground by a local Bedouin tribe.

EXCAVATIONS

From 1970 to 1983, salvage excavations were carried out at 'En Besor, under the auspices of the Israel Department of Antiquities and Museums and the Institute of Archaeology at Tel Aviv University, headed by R. Gophna and D. Gazit. In the southern part of the mound (c. 400 sq m) four occupation strata were uncovered: three from the Early Bronze Age and one from the Hellenistic period.

STRATUM IV: EARLY BRONZE AGE IB. The remains of a poor settlement were uncovered along the hill's remaining eastern slope. It was established after the large Early Bronze Age IA village (site H) on the adjacent hill had already been abandoned (see above). Noteworthy among the remains of stratum IV was a round silo base built from stream pebbles and parts of floor segments of structures whose walls were not preserved. Pottery from the Early Bronze Age IB, flint implements, goat and sheep bones, and the carbonized remains of wheat, barley, peas, and grapes were also found.

STRATUM III: EARLY BRONZE AGE IB. Following the abandonment of the first settlement, a brick structure without stone foundations (building A) was constructed on top of the hill and over part of the stratum IV remains. The area of this building is estimated at about 85 sq m. The building was only partially excavated, as its southern and eastern edges had been eroded or

'En Besor: general view.

destroyed as a result of construction in later periods. Various elements discovered in the building indicate that it was constructed by the Egyptians when they controlled 'En Besor, from the end of Dynasty "0" to the beginning of the First Dynasty. These elements include the size of the mud bricks (8 by 12 cm) and the manner in which they were laid and bonded in the walls, the inside partition of the building, and the finds discovered in and around it (in refuse pits).

The western wing of building A was a residence, to the east of which was an open courtyard. Analysis of the building's remains and its contents suggests that the number of its inhabitants did not exceed twelve people. In the house's southern wing, pottery vessels and several installations were revealed, suggesting that a bakery and a brewery were located here. The residence's main entrance was discovered in the north, near remains of the food storeroom. Most of the cylinder seal impressions were found here (see below).

Marble pendant in the shape of a bull's head.

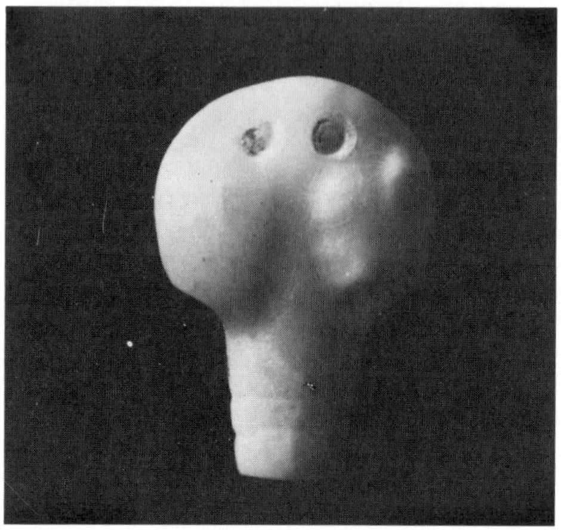

Serekh *inscription of a king from the First Egyptian Dynasty.*

Apart from sherds of several hole-mouth jars, widespread in Canaan in the Early Bronze Age, the rest of the finds uncovered in building A and the refuse pits around it were Egyptian in nature. These include pottery vessels, flint tools (knives and sickle blades), two copper implements (a pin and a harpoon), a marble pendant in the shape of a bull's head, and the lower portion of a faience statuette of a baboon. Also found was the inscribed *serekh* of an Egyptian king, a cylinder seal and dozens of unfired clay pieces bearing Egyptian cylinder seal impressions. Outstanding in the assemblage of Egyptian pottery found in stratum III is the great number of coarse bowl sherds. Bowls of this type were used in Egypt during the first two dynasties for baking a special kind of bread. The incised lines on the inside of several of the bowls at 'En Besor may be the "bakers' marks." Petrographical and chemical analyses of pottery sherds from stratum III revealed that only a small percentage of these were imported from Egypt, while most of them belong to vessels produced locally.

The type of cylinder seals whose impressions were discovered on the unfired clay pieces at 'En Besor were the type used in Egypt to seal containers (leather and other bags, and sacks) primarily designed for dry food products. Fragments of over sixty unfired pieces with decipherable impressions were found. According to A. R. Schulman, who deciphered them, they belonged to sealed containers that arrived at 'En Besor from the royal storehouses in Egypt. In his opinion, on some of the impressions it is possible to read the names of three of the kings of the First Egyptian Dynasty (Djer, Den, and 'Adjib) and the names of several officials. In light of these interpretations, Schulman suggests dating the use of building A to the latter part of the First Dynasty in Egypt—that is, the Early Bronze Age II. S. Mittmann, A. Kaiser, and L. E. Stager differ, suggesting a date at the beginning of the First Dynasty or even earlier, at the end of Dynasty "0." In their view, the building should be dated to the end of the Early Bronze Age IB. This date has been corroborated by the comparative analysis of the Egyptian pottery from stratum III at 'En Besor. Also, petrographic analysis of the mud sealings demonstrated that the clay is local, so it appears that the above-mentioned receptacles were sealed in Canaan.

The building from stratum III is the only Egyptian structure of its kind from the Dynasty "0" period uncovered in Israel or anywhere else outside Egypt. It was probably erected by a royal Egyptian expedition as a way station near 'En Besor on the route from the northern Sinai Desert to Canaan. By means of this way station, the Egyptians were able to oversee the largest and most permanent water source on the border of the settled land, located between the wells of northern Sinai and the springs of the Yarkon River in the central Coastal Plain. It appears that the need to establish a way station near 'En Besor was the result of the close relations that existed between Egypt and southern Canaan at this time.

STRATUM II: EARLY BRONZE AGE II–III. Most of the remains from stratum II were discovered on the mound's southeastern slope, where part of a broadhouse with stone foundations was uncovered (building B). Part of

Egyptian cylinder seal impressions.

Two Egyptian jugs.

the foundation was built on top of pits from stratum III. The pottery from this level is local ware, consisting of fragments of storage jars, jugs, and ledge handles. This pottery dates stratum II to the end of the Early Bronze Age II or the beginning of the Early Bronze Age III.

STRATUM I: THE HELLENISTIC PERIOD. The remains from the Hellenistic level were almost entirely destroyed by modern Bedouin when they dug graves at the top of the site. With the exception of parts of a wall and floor, all that remains from this period are potsherds and a bronze coin found on the surface. The finds date stratum I to the mid-third century BCE.

R. Gophna, *IEJ* 20 (1970), 225; 26 (1976), 199; 40 (1990), 1–11; id., *'Atiqot* 11 (1976), 1–9; 14 (1980), 9–16; id., *TA* 3 (1976), 31–37; 17 (1990), 144–162; id., *Expedition* 20/4 (1978), 5–7; id., *ESI* 1 (1982), 76; 2 (1983), 30; id. (and D. Gazit), *TA* 12 (1985), 9–16; id., *Egypt, Israel, Sinai* (ed. A. F. Rainey), Tel Aviv 1987, 13–21; A. Ben-Tor, *'Atiqot* 11 (1976), 13–15; id., *BASOR* 281 (1991), 3–10; E. Yeivin, ibid., 10–12; id., *Dedicated to the Memory of E. T. Yeivin* (ed. S. Yeivin), Tel Aviv 1980, 5–7; A. R. Schulman, *'Atiqot* 11 (1976), 16–26; 14 (1980), 17–33; id., *Journal of the Society for the Study of Egyptian Antiquities* 13 (1983), 249–251; id., *The Nile Delta in Transition, 4th–3rd Millennium B.C.—Abstracts* (ed. M. Azmi), Cairo 1990; S. Mittmann, *EI* 15 (1981), 1*–9*; T. E. Levy, *BAIAS* 1983–1984, 36–41; N. Porat, *Bulletin of the Egyptological Seminar* 8 (1986–1987), 102–129; id. "Composition of Pottery—Application to the Study of the Interrelations between Canaan and Egypt during the 3rd Millennium B.C." (Ph.D. diss., Hebrew Univ. of Jerusalem 1989); id., *The Nile Delta in Transition* (loc cit.); Weippert 1988 (Ortsregister); I. Gilead (and D. Alon), *Mitekufat Ha'even* 21 (1988), 109*–130*; id. (and Y. Goren), *BASOR* 275 (1989), 5–14; id., *Levant* 22 (1990), 47–63; J. F. Quack, *ZDPV* 105 (1989), 18–26; E. Friedman and R. Gophna, *TA* 17 (1990), 87–90, 144–162.

RAM GOPHNA

'EN BOQEQ

IDENTIFICATION

The oasis of 'En Boqeq (Umm Bagheq) is situated on the shore of the Dead Sea, about 13 km (8 mi.) south of Masada and close to the Dead Sea ford leading to Kir Moab (map reference 185.067). Although smaller, it is similar to the En-Gedi oasis in terms of natural and economic resources. From earliest times, the springs 'En Boqeq and 'En No'it irrigated the fields and orchards in the delta of Năal Boqeq, as well as the terraces on the lower mountain slopes facing the Dead Sea. Archaeological evidence shows that palm trees, as well as medicinal and aromatic plants, were grown on the site. The site may possibly be identified with Tetrapyrgia (Τετραπύργια), mentioned by the Byzantine monk Anastasius in the first half of the seventh century CE (Anastasius, *Questiones, PG* 89, col. 745).

HISTORY

The oasis was probably initially settled in the Hasmonean period, when the first irrigation systems were established. A watchtower from this period, which was later incorporated in the Herodian installation, has been preserved. In the Herodian period, 'En Boqeq was a center for the manufacture of pharmaceuticals and cosmetics. The oasis was destroyed during the First Jewish Revolt (66–73 CE), perhaps in the course of one of the raids carried out by the defenders of Masada against the villages on the shore of the Dead Sea (Josephus, *War* IV, 399–405). During the Bar-Kokhba Revolt, work was resumed in the manufacturing plant as part of the effort to create an economic basis for the struggling state.

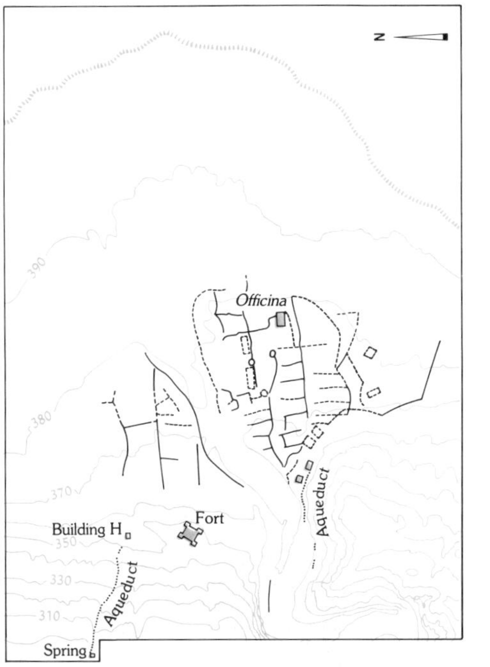

'En Boqeq: map of the oasis.

'En Boqeq oasis with the fortress and ancient orchards at its foot.

*Plan of the Herodian workshop (*officina*).*

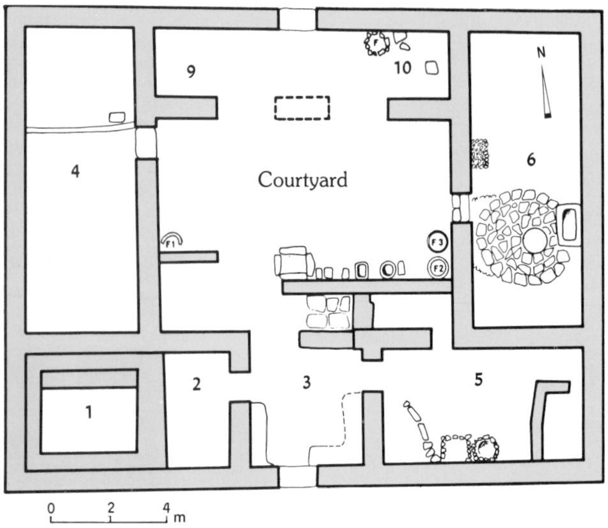

Denarii of Hadrian found in a grave in the officina *courtyard.*

A permanent settlement at the site was renewed only in the first half of the fourth century CE, when a small Roman fort was erected here as part of the eastern frontier fortifications of the Limes Palaestinae. According to a register of Roman armed forces from the late fourth or early fifth century, the soldiers stationed here were probably the Cohors I Flavia, whose headquarters were at Malḥata, or of the Cohors I Palaestinorum, whose headquarters were at Tamara (*Notitia Dignitatum* XXXIV, 40, 45). Evidence of destruction, either by violence, or by one of the earthquakes in the years 363, 419 or 447, and in the early sixth century CE, is clear. The fort was destroyed during the Persian conquest in 614 and hastily repaired in expectation of the Arab invasion. It was inhabited for several decades following the Arab conquest of circa 635, possibly as an industrial site processing products from the Dead Sea. If the identification of the site with Tetrapyrgia is valid (see above), the workers in the oasis at that time were Cypriot prisoners of war.

EXPLORATION

The 'En Boqeq oasis is first mentioned by F. de Saulcy, who visited the site in 1853. A general survey was made in 1931 by F. Frank, followed by one in 1958 by M. Gichon. In 1966, S. Applebaum surveyed the agricultural remains. Excavations were begun by M. Gichon, assisted by B. Sapir (first season) and I. Roll, for the Unit of Frontier Studies of the Classics Department at Tel Aviv University and were continued intermittently until 1975. The last season of excavations, which concentrated on the water-supply installations, was directed by M. Fischer.

EXCAVATION RESULTS

THE HERODIAN WORKSHOP. The workshop, *officina*, is a square structure measuring 20 by 20 m. Its walls are built of two faces of roughly dressed stones with a fill of rubble between them. They are preserved to a height of 1.5 m above the foundations. The upper courses may have been constructed of ashlars similar to those used in the Hasmonean watchtower incorporated in the southwest corner of the fort. These white ashlars were found in various places among the debris.

Four phases of occupation connected with certain changes in the production process (see below) have been distinguished. Phase 1 was Herodian, possibly destroyed during the uprisings following Herod's death (Josephus, *Antiq.* XVII, 269–285). Phase 2 can be assigned to the first procurators, when the area became an imperial estate. Phase 3 belongs to the reign of Agrippa I and the period of the later procurators; and phase 4 belongs to the Bar-Kokhba revolt. It should be noted that, as mentioned above, a Hasmonean tower was found incorporated in the phase 1 structure.

The dating of the phases is based on ceramic and numismatic material. The sherds found at the site are similar to those found at contemporaneous sites in Judea, including some in the immediate vicinity—En-Gedi, Masada, and Qumran. The earliest coins found are of Alexander Jannaeus, while the latest are Hadrianic silver denarii, buried as an offering in a grave dug in the deserted courtyard of the *officina* after the Bar-Kokhba Revolt.

Nabatean pottery, most of it painted, forms part of the material from phases 2 and 3. Nabatean coins, which constitute a third of the numismatic assemblage, attest to the trade relations between Judea and Nabatea, particularly in this frontier region. Moreover, raw materials from South Arabia and the Far East required for the *officina* were probably supplied by Nabatean trade caravans.

The internal plan of the *officina* remained basically unchanged in all its phases. All the rooms abutted the exterior walls and opened onto a central courtyard that was subdivided by partitions to create separate working compounds. The main entrance from the south led into a vestibule with plastered benches. From there a door opened westward into a storeroom. Fragments of the lower part of a large pithos were found in a hollow in the middle of its floor. There was a workroom in the east, in which intricate installations, as in the other working compounds, may be an indication of the raw materials used—buds, blossoms, and leaves of aromatic plants, seeds, fruit, resins, twigs, and bark—for perfumes, pharmaceuticals, and cosmetics. Various operations, including drying, pressing, and boiling, were carried out here.

A narrow (easily guarded) passage led from the vestibule into the courtyard past a staircase ascending to the building's flat roof. Partitions extending into the courtyard from the east and west created five processing and storage units, which may have been roofed by reed mats. The southeast compound may have been the main production plant. Its installations in-

Left: *one of the ovens in the* officina*;*
(right) *bench in the vestibule of the* officina.

The fort, looking northeast.

cluded a stone receptacle for raw materials, a stove for heating and boiling, a grinding platter, a stone basin (or mortar), and a pair of clay ovens faced with stone (F1 and F2). At the top of the ovens was an opening on which (according to al-Kindi, a chemist in the ninth century CE) a basin of water was placed and heated; another vessel, containing substances requiring controlled heating, was set into this basin (the double-boiler method). One of the ovens, F1 (60 cm in diameter), was preserved to a height of 65 cm. Not all of these installations were in use at the same time. This description fits phase 2, in which there is no evidence for the existence of the stove and oven F2.

Two rooms (10 by 3.7 m) were uncovered east and west of the courtyard. The walls and floor of the west room (4) were thickly plastered. Its floor slopes slightly from its northern edge, 3.5 m down toward a 15-cm-high barrier. This was probably the crushing or treading floor. The prepared liquefied or pulverized (by means of a roller?) substance was collected in a sunken, plastered pit (50 by 35 by 55 cm) at the northeastern end of the barrier. Piles of date pits found in the southern part of this room indicate that the date was one of the substances processed here. The substances processed in room 4 may have been transferred for reducing to oven F3 (similar in shape to ovens F1 and F2) in the southeastern part of the courtyard. In the east room (6), which is connected directly to the main plant, the processing work was performed on a round, thickly plastered stone table (diameter, 90 cm) set on a flagstone floor. It may have served as a stand for horizontally operated millstones.

The most elaborate equipment in the workshop belongs to phase 2. Phase 4 was the poorest. At this stage the table in room 6 was covered by destruction debris and was replaced by a small pressing basin.

The watchtower at the southwest corner guarded the plant. Its walls were thicker (1.2 m) than the other walls of the *officina* (0.8 m). As an additional security measure, there was no entrance to the tower from the ground floor.

THE FORT. A square building (20 by 20 m) with four towers (6 by 6 m) projecting from its corners protected the oasis. Its walls, 1.8–2 m wide, still stand to a height of 6 m. They were built of two faces with a rubble fill. The facing stones were not always carefully fitted; in most places small stones were inserted into the joints to produce level horizontal courses. The stone dressing is of uneven quality, probably because the walls were repaired several times in the three hundred years of their existence. A clayey mortar bound the courses, and the doorways and corners were built of ashlars, some of them in secondary use. The building's single gate was closed by a two-leaved wooden door that was studded with iron nails with large heads. It was secured by a horizontal beam and a heavy lock deep in the wall. The gate was 1.8 m wide and as deep as the walls.

Two rows of rooms abutted the walls, one in the north and the other in the east. These rooms opened onto the central open courtyard. In phases 2(?) and 3, wooden sheds were built next to the west wall, and on the eve of the Arab conquest, flimsy structures were added, also on the south side. Thus, the 'En Boqeq fort (*castellum*) was, indeed, as its name implies (if the identification with Tetrapyrgia is to be accepted), a *tetrapyrgos* (four-towered structure). Five phases of occupation were distinguished: phase 1, the reign of the Constantine dynasty; phase 2, from the reign of Valentinian to the second half of the fifth century CE; phase 3, from the second half of the fifth century to the Persian invasion in 614 CE; phase 4, from the reconquest of the country by Heraclius to the Arab conquest in 632–635 CE; and phase 5, the Early Arab period.

The barracks rooms were all preserved to a height of 1.7 m above the floor. The additional height of the external walls (about 2.6 m) and the numerous fallen stones suggest that each row of rooms may have had two stories. The living space in the barracks and the towers, together with the forces necessary for the defense of the perimeter both in an emergency and during the daily routine, suggests that the garrison stationed here numbered forty-five to sixty-five soldiers.

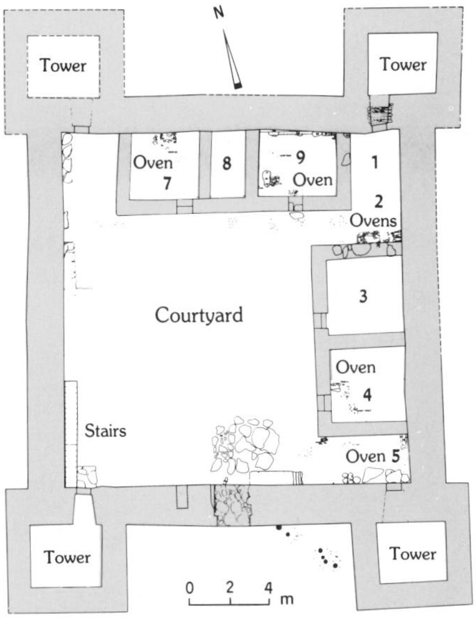

*Plan of the fort (*castellum*).*

Southern facade of the fort, with an entrance gate and two corner towers.

Interior of the fort and the barracks against the eastern wall.

Ashlars in the corner of the fort's southeastern tower.

In phases 1 and 2, regular troops were probably stationed in the fort. The stoves set up in each of the rooms in phase 2 were standard equipment for the *contubernium*—a group of soldiers fighting together, living together, and cooking together. In phase 3, the forces stationed at the fort were made up of *limitanei*, an agricultural militia residing outside the *castellum* walls. The fort now served as an administrative center, in addition to its defensive function as part of the Limes. There is some evidence that in this period medicinal and aromatic herbs were still being cultivated here, and chemicals continued to be extracted from the Dead Sea. The numerous fragments of glass vessels found in some of the phase 3 rooms may represent the remains of containers for these products, which were either marketed in a raw state or processed at the oasis.

Wooden beams in situ in the ceiling of the fort's northeastern tower.

The ceilings in the fort were supported by wooden beams. The towers, too, were divided by wooden ceilings into two stories. These towers probably had flat roofs, which served as the main fighting platforms. Because there is no stone staircase up to the ceiling height of the ground floor, it can be assumed that access to the towers was by wooden ladders, which could be removed if necessary. Thus, the soldiers on the roof could deny their enemies access, even once they had succeeded in penetrating the courtyard. The towers were further protected because their entrances were not higher than 1.6 m and consisted of narrow corridors widening inward, so that a single defender could repel invaders. All the entrances to the towers have relieving arches above the lintel, one of the earliest examples of the use of this stone construction technique.

The builders of the fort wanted it to be both stable and flexible, despite the fact that it was built on a rubble hill in a region prone to earthquakes and landslides. For this reason, the foundations in the east were 2 m deep and the space was filled with tightly packed gravel between stabilizing layers of stamped earth up to ground level. An internal stabilization for the structure was achieved, which contributed to its present good state of preservation.

THE WATER SUPPLY. The waters of 'En Boqeq were carried in an aqueduct 1 km (0.6 mi.) from where the spring issues in Naḥal Boqeq to a series of cisterns at the oasis. Along most of the way, the aqueduct ran on a wall at least 3 m high on the north side of the riverbed. For lack of maintenance, the flow of water in the riverbed has washed away large sections of the aqueduct's

Papyrus fragment with a list of debtors and creditors, from the fort's archives, 6th–7th centuries CE.

'En Boqeq: silver plaque from the fort.

foundations. However, a 2-m-long surviving stretch of the aqueduct attests to the sound construction of the bridge that carried one of the branches(?) of the water supply system to the southern bank of Naḥal Boqeq. It consisted of hollow stone links clinging to the steep slope and continuing farther on as a channel between two low walls; both the walls and the floor were thickly plastered.

Two of the cisterns have been preserved; they measure 3.45 by 11.65 by 12 m and 3.2 by 10.3 by 16.6 m. They were built of large blocks, covered with three layers of plaster laid on potsherds; cohesion was achieved by herringbone incisions. Steps led to the bottom of the aqueduct and a single outlet regulated the amount of water allocated for irrigation.

The waters of 'En No'it were collected nearby in a small nymphaeum (3 by 3 m), erected on a natural terrace above the fort. Installations associated with the spring and its mineral waters were vandalized in the 1960s. Only one aqueduct has survived, which descended at an angle of 35 degrees and carried water over a distance of 200 m to a solid structure (10.25 by 10.25 m). This structure served as a regulating water reservoir that directed the waters of 'En No'it southward to the fort and eastward to the fields at its foot. The aqueduct's U-shaped stone links (width 30 cm, height 17–20 cm) were covered by local limonite.

In the last repair, a stretch of fallen links was replaced by a channel lined with stone and well plastered. Because of their therapeutic properties, the 'En No'it waters probably served for bathing and drinking. The bathing facilities may have been destroyed by modern development activities since 1965. The mineral content of these waters made them more suited for watering palm trees than other plants. The inhabitants of the fort seem to have preferred drinking the waters of 'En Boqeq, and a channel cut in the fort's west wall probably carried that water into the fort either by a branch of the aqueduct, now completely vanished, or, preferably, by trains of beasts of burden.

AGRICULTURAL REMAINS. Terraces, field partition walls, and ancient enclosures were preserved until the 1960 and 1970s. All were built of local fieldstones, in dry courses. To prevent grazing animals from entering the fields, walls up to 2 m high were erected and access to the fields was possible only by steps jutting from both of the wall's faces.

THE EARLY ARAB PERIOD. After the Arab conquest, the site was reoccupied and the buildings were roughly repaired. The debris from this period contains large deposits of Dead Sea chemicals. At that time, a salt or phosphate industry may have existed at the site, or it may have served as a depot for shipping such raw materials westward(?).

F. de Saulcy, *Narrative of a Journey Around the Dead Sea*, London 1857, 252–262; F. Frank, *ZDPV* 57 (1934), 191–194; M. Gichon, *RB* 77 (1970), 579–580; id., *Bonner Jahrbuch* 171 (1971), 386–406; id., *'En Boqeq: Preliminary Report on the 1st Campaign* (Proc., 8th Congress of Roman Frontier Studies), Cardiff 1974, 256–262; id., *PEQ* 106 (1974), 119–139; id., *Akten des 14. Internazionales Limeskongresses 1986 in Carnuntum* (eds. H. Vetters and M. Kandler), Vienna 1990, 193–194; id., *En Boqeq* 1, *Die Ausgrabung einer Oase am Toten Meer*, Mainz (in prep.).

MORDECHAI GICHON

EN-GEDI

IDENTIFICATION AND HISTORY

En-Gedi, an oasis on the western shore of the Dead Sea (map reference 187.098), is one of the most important archaeological sites in the Judean Desert. En-Gedi (Engaddi in Greek and Roman sources and 'Ein Jidi in Arabic) is the name of the perennial spring that flows from a height of 200 m above the Dead Sea. In the cycle of stories about David's flight from Saul, the desert area in the vicinity of the spring is called the "wilderness of En-Gedi" (1 Sam. 24:1). The walled camps at the top of the mountains appear as the "strongholds of En-Gedi" (1 Sam. 23:29). En-Gedi is mentioned in the list of the cities of Judah among those in the wilderness (Jos. 15:62). In a late biblical source, it was somewhat arbitrarily identified with Hazazon-Tamar (2 Chr. 20:2). The site is also mentioned in the Song of Songs (1:14), in connection with its vineyards, and in a prophecy of Ezekiel (47:10).

Various references to En-Gedi are found in sources from the Second Temple and the Roman and Byzantine periods. Josephus lists it among the headquarters of the toparchies of Judea (*War* III, 55) and relates that the Sicarii raided it during the First Revolt against Rome (*War* IV, 402). Pliny (*NH* V, 73) refers to its destruction during the same war. From documents discovered in the Cave of the Letters in Naḥal Ḥever in the Judean Desert, it can be deduced that, during the period preceding the Bar-Kokhba Revolt, En-Gedi was a Jewish village that had become the property of the emperor, and a Roman garrison was stationed there. En-Gedi became one of Bar-Kokhba's administrative and military centers. The church fathers attest in their writings to the existence of a settlement at En-Gedi in the Roman-Byzantine period. Eusebius (*Onom.* 86:18) describes it as a very large Jewish village. According to the sources, En-Gedi was renowned for its excellent dates and crops of balsam-producing plants.

En-Gedi: general view of Tel Goren, looking southeast.

EXCAVATIONS

In 1949, a small expedition headed by B. Mazar on behalf of the Hebrew

General view of Tel Goren, looking east.

University of Jerusalem (with the participation of A. Reifenberg and T. Dothan) began a series of surveys and excavations in the oasis of En-Gedi. Trial soundings at Tel Goren (Tell el-Jurn), a narrow hillock southwest of the plain near Naḥal 'Arugot (map reference 1870.0965), established that from the end of the Iron Age onward this was one of the main centers of settlement in the oasis. On the mound's western slope, the remains of a solid tower, built of rough stones, were ascribed by the excavators to the Hellenistic period. The investigation of the building remains, the terraces on the slopes of the hill, and the aqueducts leading from the spring to reservoirs in the plain has shown that from the Hellenistic to the Byzantine periods an efficient system of agriculture and advanced techniques for collecting water for irrigation were developed. The combination of a tropical climate and an abundant water supply enabled the inhabitants of En-Gedi to develop such systems, to cultivate, in particular, the balsam plants for which En-Gedi became famous. The settlement must have been administered by a central authority that dealt with the construction of terraces, aqueducts, and the network of strongholds and watchtowers.

A second survey was carried out under the direction of Y. Aharoni, and a third under J. Naveh, in 1956 and 1957, respectively. Much was learned in these surveys about the defensive network of the oasis, water-supply systems, and the remains of Chalcolithic construction in the hill terrace above the spring. Archaeological excavations were later carried out at En-Gedi on behalf of the Hebrew University and the Israel Exploration Society. In the first two seasons (1961–1962), the excavations were directed by B. Mazar, I. Dunayevsky, and T. Dothan, and in the following three seasons (1964–1965) by Mazar, assisted by Dunayevsky and E. Stern. From 1970 to 1972, excavations were conducted in the synagogue at En-Gedi on behalf of the Hebrew University, the Israel Department of Antiquities and Museums, and the Israel Exploration Society, under the direction of D. Barag and Y. Porath.

TEL GOREN. During the five seasons, the excavations were concentrated mainly on Tel Goren, the most prominent site in the oasis. The first settlers did not limit themselves to the small summit of this narrow and elongated hill but terraced its steep slopes and built on them. In later periods, the settlement expanded over extensive areas in the plain between Naḥal David and Naḥal 'Arugot. Five occupation levels can be distinguished at Tel Goren. The following strata were found:

Stratum	*Period*
V	End of the Iron Age (c. 630–582 BCE)
IV	Persian period (5th–4th cent. BCE)
III	Hellenistic period (mainly the Hasmonean period, from Alexander Jannaeus to Herod, 103–37 BCE)
II	Early Roman period (mainly the time of the Herodian dynasty, 4 BCE–68 CE)
I	Late Roman and Byzantine periods (2nd–6th cent. CE)

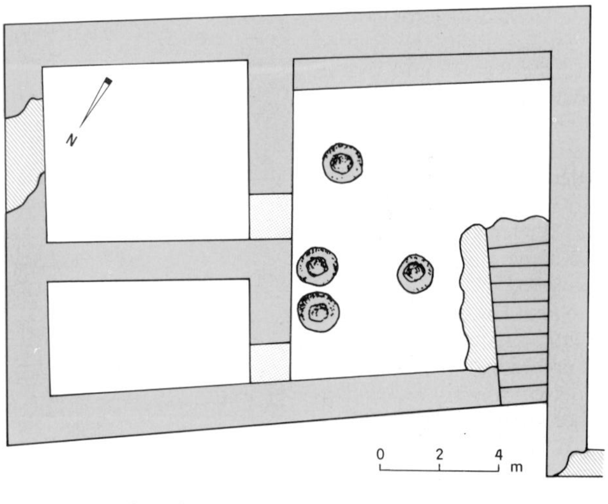

Plan of an Iron Age house from stratum V.

Destruction layer of stratum V.

Stratum V. The earliest settlement at Tel Goren was built on the top of the hill and on the terraces. On the southern slope, the remains cleared consisted mostly of courtyards with adjoining buildings. The numerous finds made here under brick debris and a layer of ash included large pottery vessels (pithoi) shaped like barrels, or vats, with their bases sunk into the ground. In one of the courtyards a row of seven such pithoi was uncovered set close together. They were surrounded by an abundance of pottery vessels—jars, bowls, cooking pots, jugs, juglets, decanters, and lamps—as well as a basalt mortar, perforated clay balls, and lumps of bitumen. Most of the vessels are characteristic of the second half of the seventh and the beginning of the sixth centuries BCE. The buildings on a wide terrace in the middle of the mound's northern slope also belong to this period. The structures had a uniform plan: a courtyard with two interconnected small rooms along one side and stairs leading from the street on the lower terrace giving access to them.

Along this street a group of installations was discovered, including ovens. Pithoi similar to those found on the southern slope, pottery, and metal and bone objects were found in one of the courtyards. The excavators assumed that these structures were used for some special industry, probably for the production of perfume. En-Gedi was known as a center for the cultivation of perfume-producing plants, especially balsam (*opobalsamum*). It can be assumed that the workshops processing such costly products were concentrated at Tel Goren and that the local growers and perfume workers were employed in the royal service. A gloss of Rabbi Joseph on Jeremiah 52:16, "But Nebuzar-adan . . . left certain of the poor of the land to be vinedressers and husbandmen" states that these were the "balsam gatherers from En-Gedi to Ramtha" (B.T: *Shab.* 26a).

Individual finds included a seal impression on a jar handle, showing a double-winged symbol and an inscription in ancient Hebrew that can be read: לנרא (*lnr'*), לנרת (*lnrt*), למרת (*lmrt*), or למרא (*lmr'*). The last reading (belonging to *mr'*) could refer to the Aramaic royal title מרא (lord, sovereign), or be an allusion to Nebuchadnezzar, king of Babylonia. Another find was a small square seal with the Hebrew inscription לאריהו עזריהו (belonging to Uriyahu [son of] ʿAzaryahu). A large limestone stamp bears the name טבשלן (Tobshalon). Near the name is a design resembling the plan of the building in which the seal was found. Another find was a fragment of a store jar inscribed לפטיהו (belonging to Puṭiyahu). Numerous jar handles with

Corner of a room with pottery barrels, from stratum V, on the northern slope.

***Right:** Hebrew seal and impression* לאריהו עזריהו *(l'ryhw 'zryhw), Iron Age.*

***Left:** Hebrew seal* טבשלן *(tbšln), Iron Age; **(right)** Hebrew seal impression* לנרא *(lnr'), Iron Age.*

Fragment of a pottery vessel decorated with reliefs, Iron Age.

rosette stamps were also discovered. One jar handle bearing a *lamelekh* impression with the double-winged symbol was found. The inscription also mentions the town of זיף ("Ziph"). Beside the seal are incised concentric circles, made with a compass. A jar handle stamped with the figure of a horse was also found.

Other finds include stone weights, each marked with the sign representing the shekel standard. In a building on the northern slope (where the Tob-shalon stamp was found) was a pot covered with a lamp. It held a hoard of silver ingots in various shapes that must have been used as currency. In various buildings, silver jewelry—rings, beads, and earrings—was discovered. Although these finds can be dated with certainty to the end of the kingdom of Judah, doubt remains regarding the dating of a potsherd which has no parallel in Palestinian ceramics. The sherd is from a vessel on which pieces of clay were applied in a horizontal row and then stamped with a variety of impressions. Three are identifiable: a bearded man sitting on a chair in a hut(?), his right hand resting on his knee and the left holding some object near his face; a ram with projecting horns; and what appears to be the remains of a mask (or a lion's head?). The stratum V settlement was completely destroyed by a conflagration, perhaps in the year 23 of Nebuchadnezzar's reign (582–581 BCE). (See also Jer. 52:30; Josephus, *Antiq.* X, 181.)

Stratum IV. During the Persian period, the settlement covered the top of the hill and its slopes. Toward the north, it extended considerably beyond the area of the earlier stratum. The structures in stratum IV are impressive in size and strength. Of special interest is the large building situated on the northern slope. It was unearthed under a thick layer of accumulated silt and building debris. Many pottery fragments were found here, the sherds having rolled down from the terraces on the slope. Most of the pottery is characteristic of the Persian period. It includes a jar handle with a seal impression of a roaring lion, handles with יהוד (*Yhwd*), יהד (*Yhd*), and יה (*Yh*) seal impressions, Attic ware, and sherds decorated with triangular, wedge-shaped and reed impressions. A small portion of the pottery finds belongs to types typical of stratum V.

The plan of the large building and the finds discovered there indicate that it was a dwelling, in parts two-storied. The walls, floors, and probably also the ceilings were covered with a thick coat of plaster. Trunks of palm trees were

Jar handle with seal impression, Iron Age.

Yhd *seal impression on a jar handle, Persian period.*

Babylonian seal from the Persian period.

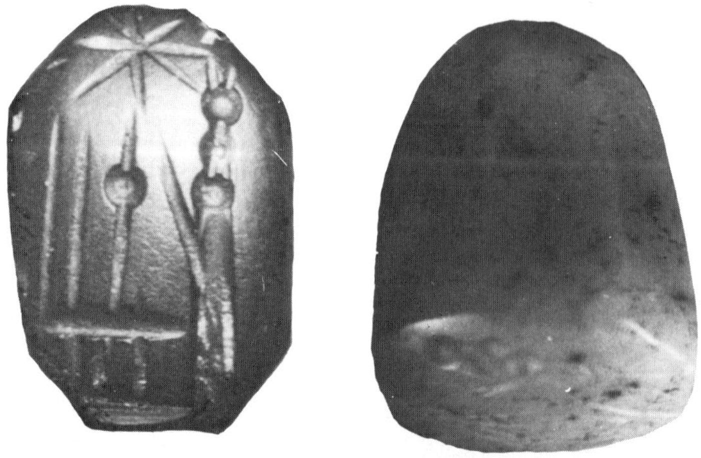

Colored glass pendants, Persian period.

Tel Goren, northern slope: (foreground) building from the Herodian period; (background) building from the Persian period.

used to construct the roof. The building covers an area of about 550 sq m and contains twenty-three rooms, enclosed courtyards, and storerooms of various sizes. The details of the plan raise various problems, especially regarding the connection between the different parts of the building and the entrances to the rooms. A study of the building and the finds (which include Attic pottery) suggests that it was erected in its entirety in the first half of the fifth century BCE and was destroyed in about 400 BCE, or at the beginning of the fourth century BCE. The western wing of the building was restored subsequently for dwelling purposes, perhaps by the inhabitants who remained in En-Gedi after its destruction. The building was used for about fifty years more.

Among the finds in this building was a conical chalcedony seal of the type common in Babylonia from the seventh to fifth centuries BCE. Another seal of the same type was discovered on the mound's southern slope. In addition, two opaque colored-glass pendants—one of the head of a woman wearing earrings and the other the head of a bearded man— and fragments of a rhyton (drinking horn) decorated with a relief of a crouching lioness were found. The pottery on the floors and in the rubble was common the Persian period and includes abundant Attic ware. Of special interest is the rich collection of potsherds from the Persian period, found under a layer of ash in a room in the northern part of the building near the main entrance. The epigraphic finds included two Aramaic ostraca and jar handles with יהד and יה seal impressions that probably originated in the building on the top of the slope.

Other structures were uncovered west and east of the large building and south of it on the rising slope. These were dwelling houses that were separated by narrow lanes. On the southern slope of Tel Goren, part of another large building was cleared, and a few building remains were excavated on the western slope.

Stratum III. A few coins from the time of the Ptolemies and the Seleucids and Early Hellenistic potsherds are evidence of settlement in the oasis in the period of the Diadochi. The palm plantations of En-Gedi are also referred to in Ecclesiasticus 24:14: "I was exalted, like a palm tree in En-Gedi." In the Hasmonean period the place flourished again, especially in the time of Alexander Jannaeus and his successors. This is indicated by numerous coins of Jannaeus collected throughout the oasis, by the finds from the tombs in Naḥal David, and especially by the citadel on the summit of Tel Goren.

The remains of the defense system of the stratum III citadel were uncovered on the top of the mound, along its southern, northern, and western slopes. The citadel consisted of two parts. The western, smaller section was built on a trapezoidal plan. Its walls are 1.2 to 1.4 m wide, and there is a rectangular tower at its western extremity. The eastern section is a large rectangle (width of the walls, 1.7 to 2 m), with a rectangular tower in the southern part. The whole area of the citadel probably covered about 3,500 sq m. The finds that can be attributed to stratum III are not numerous: most can

Tel Goren: tower wall from the Hasmonean period.

be ascribed to the Late Hasmonean period, especially to the time of Jannaeus and his successors. It can be assumed that the citadel was destroyed during the Parthian invasion and in the war of the last Hasmoneans against Herod.

Stratum II. A strong citadel was uncovered in stratum II. Its remains, including walls built of large, rough stones about 2 m thick, were cleared on the top of the mound, along the southern, western, and northern slopes of Tel Goren. Of special interest is the tower at the western extremity, which is separated from the citadel's west wall by a narrow passage. The tower is a solid rectangular structure (14 by 7 m) enclosing two rooms and two narrow cells. The building technique is similar to that of the citadel wall. The details of the tower's plan were elucidated in the first two seasons of excavations. The later excavations at En-Gedi established the dating of the citadel and of the tower. However a reassessment of the finds from the tower and a comparison of the ceramics from Qumran and Masada resulted in a revision of the date of stratum II at Tel Goren to the time of Herod's successors—although the beginning of the stratum may be earlier. The two buildings were destroyed by fire, probably during the First Jewish Revolt against Rome.

A large building discovered on the northern slope of Tel Goren, north of the large Persian building (described above), belongs to the same period. The building consists of a spacious courtyard enclosed by a stone wall. It contained several rooms on its north and west sides. Especially interesting are several ovens set in a row along the southern wall of the courtyard. Near one oven was a large Herodian lamp, sealed with a plug and containing a hoard of 139 coins struck in the sixth year of Agrippa I (42–43 CE), in the fourteenth year of Claudius (54 CE), and in the fifth year of Nero (58–59 CE). Two phases of construction can be distinguished in the rooms. This building may originally have been a public one and only later converted into a private dwelling. The beginning of the later phase is dated by coins of Agrippa I; its destruction is dated by coins from the second year of the revolt found in the ash layer (67–68 CE). A few remains found in the same area date from a period immediately following the destruction of the building.

Stratum I. The remains in stratum I at Tel Goren from the Roman-Byzantine period indicate that there was no permanent settlement then. The structures were temporary and the terraces were used for agriculture. It appears that in this period, as in the preceding ones—at least from the Herodian period onward—the center of the settlement at En-Gedi had moved to the plain east and northeast of Tel Goren, between Naḥal David and Naḥal 'Arugot where remains of structures were found.

THE BATHHOUSE. In its last three seasons, the expedition cleared a bathhouse from the Roman period, situated in the center of the plateau between Naḥal David and Naḥal 'Arugot, about 200 m west of the shore of the Dead Sea. The building is long and narrow (40 by 50 m). Its chambers form one

Roman bathhouse: floor built of Doric capitals taken from the Herodian building.

continuous row, aligned north to south—a rather unusual arrangement that suggests it was part of a larger complex. Visitors entered a vestibule at the bath's northern extremity. After dipping their feet in a small basin, they proceeded to the two dressing rooms. South of these was the bath, which consisited of three units: frigidarium (cold room), tepidarium (warm room), and caldarium (hot room). South of the caldarium was the heating room with the furnace. There is another room whose use is not clear. The frigidarium was paved with carved building stones taken from an earlier building, including eleven Doric capitals. West of the frigidarium was a square, plastered pool, reached through a large opening and by descending two steps. The floors of the tepidarium and caldarium have been destroyed, but the underground rooms and their heating channels are preserved, as is a clay channel covered with ceramic tiles. Through it, the heated air passed from the furnace to the caldarium and from there to the heating channels.

The bath dates from the period between the destruction of the Second Temple in 70 CE and the Bar-Kokhba Revolt in 132. The dating was established by the pottery, the fragments of glass vessels, and the coins, especially a group of six bronze coins that had been hidden in a hollow in a door frame. The oldest of the coins dates to the time of Titus, and the latest were minted in the first year of Hadrian (117 CE). For the construction of the bath, numerous architectural elements were reused: Doric capitals, ashlars, and door and

Roman bathhouse, looking south.

Decorated stones reused in the bathhouse.

Chalcolithic temple, looking west.

window frames. Some of these were decorated in relief. The stones presumably were taken from an important Herodian structure that had stood nearby and had been destroyed during the First Revolt. After the bath was destroyed, part of it may have been converted into temporary dwellings (in the time of Bar-Kokhba?). Only a few building remains from the Roman-Byzantine period are extant here. In a sounding made in the northwestern corner of the bath, a structure was uncovered containing two adjoining pools. The southern and larger of them was reached by descending a flight of stairs. This building was perhaps a mikveh (ritual bath). On the basis of the pottery and the coins, which are dated to the period between the reign of Agrippa I and the second year of the First Revolt, it is possible to ascribe this lower structure to the time before the destruction of the Second Temple.

THE BUILDINGS NEAR THE SPRING. In the second season of excavations, the solid, deep stone foundations of the square tower east of the spring at En-Gedi were unearthed. It had already been explored in previous surveys. It could be established with certainty that the foundations were contemporary with stratum V at Tel Goren and should be dated to the second half of the seventh and the beginning of the sixth centuries BCE. The so-called circular structure was also cleared about 40 m northeast of the spring. This structure was found to be a limekiln of the Roman-Byzantine period. To the same period belongs an ashlar construction discovered on the slope of the ridge near the road leading from the spring to Tel Goren.

THE CHALCOLITHIC ENCLOSURE. During the surveys conducted by Aharoni and Naveh at En-Gedi in 1956–1957, a building complex was discovered on a hill terrace above the En-Gedi spring, some 150 m north of it (map reference 1870.0974). A trial excavation carried out by Naveh showed that this was a public building from the Chalcolithic period. During the second season, systematic excavations on the spot uncovered a sacred enclosure, whose various structures have outstanding plans and architecture. The stone walls are remarkably preserved to a considerable height. The building complex comprised a main building in the north and a smaller building in the east. In the enclosure wall north of the smaller building a gate leads to Naḥal David, and to the south another gateway led to a descent to the spring of En-Gedi. A stone enclosure wall, built in sections, linked the buildings into one unit. In the center of the enclosed courtyard, surrounded by the buildings and the enclosure wall, is a circular structure (diameter, c. 3 m), built of small stones, that probably served a cultic purpose.

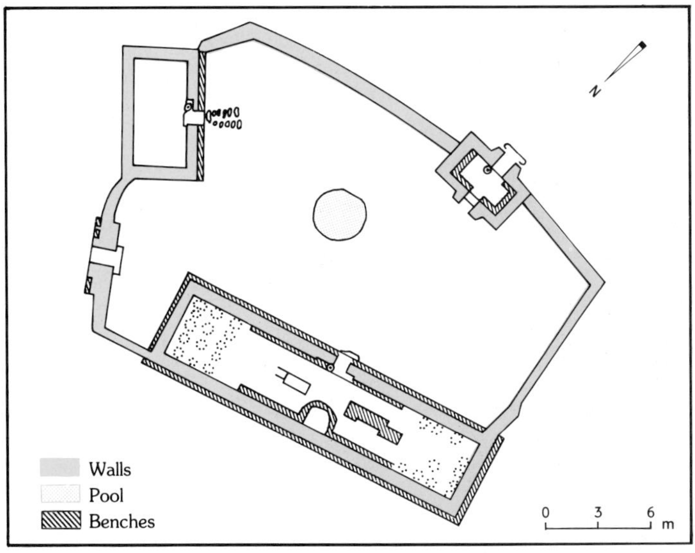

Plan of the Chalcolithic temple.

The main building in the northern part of the enclosure (about 20 m long) is a broadhouse with its entrance in the middle of the long wall on the south side. The door in this structure, as well as the doors in the smaller building and the gateway, opened inward. This is clear from their stone sills, all of which have hinge holes to the left of the entrance. Along the wall opposite the entrance of the main structure was a hoof-shaped niche surrounded by a stone fence. Judging from the remains—animal bones, fragments of pottery, and an accumulation of ashes—it was probably used as an altar. A clay statuette of a bull laden with a pair of churns was also found there. There are stone benches on both sides of the entrance and of the horseshoe-shaped niche. Of special interest are the groups of small pits sunk into the floor near both of the building's short walls. Remains of burned bones, horns, pottery, and a great quantity of ashes were found inside them. The smaller building is also a broadhouse. Its floor is coated with light-colored plaster. A stone-paved path in the center of its long wall led to the courtyard. The gateway consists of a square room with benches built along its walls. The room has two entrances, one in the outer wall and one in the inner wall, opening onto the courtyard.

There is no evidence either of stages of construction or repairs for this building complex: it is to be dated in its entirety to the same limited period. All the pottery finds belong to types characteristic of the late stage of the Ghassulian phase of the Chalcolithic period: small bowls, chalices, and cups. However, they have parallels in the late pottery of the Beersheba culture and of various Chalcolithic sites in the Judean Desert. No domestic ware or remains of dwellings from the Chalcolithic period were found in the enclosure. It seems, therefore, that it was solely a cult place, perhaps even the central sanctuary for the region's inhabitants. In character and plan, it resembles the Chalcolithic sanctuary in stratum XIX at Megiddo. The enclosure at En-Gedi was not destroyed but was abandoned, and when the last worshipers left, they apparently took the cult furniture with them.

BENJAMIN MAZAR

THE SYNAGOGUE. During earthworks carried out in En-Gedi in 1965, the remains of a mosaic floor were discovered about 300 m northeast of the summit of Tel Goren. In 1970–1972, three seasons of excavations were conducted at the site and several synagogues were revealed. The earliest synagogue (stratum IIIB) was trapezoidal: 13.5 m long on its east side, 15.5 m long on the west, and from 9 to 10.5 m wide. There are two entrances in the northern wall, which is oriented toward Jerusalem—one in the center and the other close to the northeast corner. The building's mosaic pavement is made of coarse white stones (25 tesserae per sq dm). In its center is a rectangle (8 by 3 m) of smaller white and black stones (60 tesserae per

*Synagogue: **(below)** plan; **(right)** aerial view.*

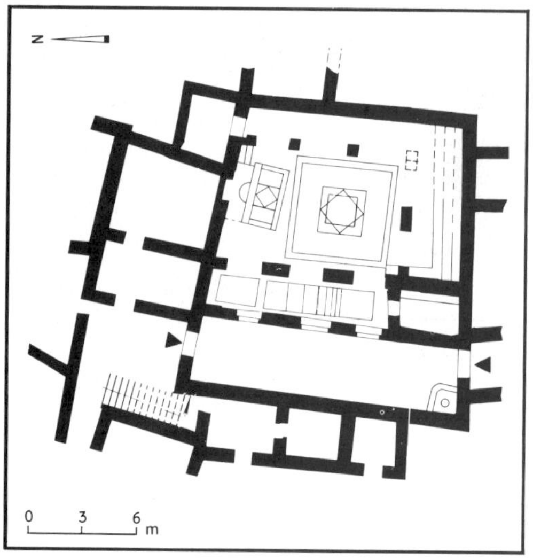

sq dm). The rectangle is surrounded by a frame of black tesserae and inside it are three squares. The southern square is decorated with a swastika made of black tesserae. The middle square was decorated with colorful patterns of which only traces remain. Only fragments of the frame of the northern square are preserved (it was damaged during the construction of the bema of the synagogue in stratum II). It is not yet clear whether the difference between the mosaic rectangle made of small tesserae and the coarser surrounding mosaics is merely a matter of technique or whether the rectangle was laid later within the original pavement. Judging from the lamps and coins preserved in the synagogue's *favissa* in stratum II (see below), this building was constructed in the time of the Severan dynasty, at the end of the second or the beginning of the third century CE. This synagogue was a rather modest prayer hall, very different from the magnificent contemporary synagogues in the Galilee. Swastikas also appear in the carved decorations and mosaic pavements of other synagogues from the Roman-Byzantine period, but not so prominently as at En-Gedi. The symbol was chosen purely for decorative purposes or as a symbol of luck. Under the building remains were found from the end of the Second Temple period, or possibly even from the time of Bar-Kokhba.

General view of the synagogue, looking north.

*Synagogue: **(right)** basin for the ritual washing of the hands, looking south; **(below)** pottery bowl from the end of the Byzantine period, found next to the Torah ark niche.*

Some time later, the building underwent extensive changes (stratum IIIA). The central entrance in the northern wall was blocked by a brick wall and turned into a niche 1.1 m wide and about 0.35 m deep. A broad green band was painted on the plaster on each side of the niche. The Torah ark, which was built of wood and partially protruded into the hall, seems to have stood in this niche. Between the entrance next to the northeast corner and the Torah ark was a stepped seat ("Seat of Moses"), and three stepped benches were constructed along the building's southern wall. The interior, which had previously been one large hall, was divided by pillars into a nave and two aisles (one in the east and one in the south). Three entrances were opened on the west side of the building, and a porch with three columns was built in front of them. The mosaic pavement from stratum IIIB was still in use in stratum IIIA, with only a few changes; in one instance, the pavement was repaired after a fire.

The finds from the excavations are not sufficient to determine the exact date the Torah ark and the "Seat of Moses" were installed, or when changes were made that significantly altered the building's character. It is assumed that these changes took place between the mid-third century and the start of the fourth century CE. It was then that the practice of placing the Torah ark in the wall facing Jerusalem began in synagogues in Palestine and the Diaspora. In the first half of the fourth century CE, En-Gedi was mentioned by Eusebius in the *Onomasticon* as "a very large Jewish village."

The stratum IIIA synagogue was used until the middle or the second half of the fifth century CE, when the synagogue of stratum II was built. In stratum II, a rectangular wooden structure was built in place of the niche that contained the Torah ark. It was 3.25 m wide and extended about 1.5 m into the nave. In the center of the structure was an apse oriented toward Jerusalem; its stone base apparently supported the Torah ark. The interior of the structure (the area

*Synagogue: **(above)** mosaic inscriptions in the western aisle, at the time of discovery; **(left)** central mosaic.*

Bronze menorah during its excavation.

Coin hoard and the goblet in the Torah ark niche.

between the wooden wall and the synagogue's north wall) was used for storage. In front of the wooden structure was a rectangular bema (3.4 by 2 m) surrounded by screens. The area of the porch, to the west of the nave, became the western aisle; to its west a long corridor (narthex) about 3 m wide was built, with entrances in its southern and northern sides. The synagogue was trapezoidal, about 13.5 m long on the east side, about 16 m long on the west side, and about 12.5 m wide. A small room was added to it that was entered through the northeastern wall of the stratum III synagogue. A similar room was built at the southern end of the western aisle. Next to the southern entrance of the corridor-narthex was the basin (*kiyor*) for washing the feet of worshipers, with a clay jar used to store the water found nearby, in situ. A stone basin, also found nearby, may have been used for washing hands. Outside the synagogue, near its northwest corner, were remains of stone stairs leading to the second-story galleries.

A new, colorful mosaic pavement (in white, black, reddish pink, red, brown, yellow, and bluish gray) was laid in the synagogue of stratum II. Near the end of the bema, the mosaic depicts three menorahs, two close to the corners of the bema and one in the center. The mosaic in the nave is decorated with leaves formed by intersecting reddish-pink circles. In the center of the nave's mosaic pavement is a circular medallion inside a lozenge and a square. Four birds are depicted in the medallion, and in each corner of the square a pair of peacocks hold a bunch of grapes. A similar motif, with one bird in the center, decorates the bema's mosaic, and birds within a circle decorate the area near the benches in the southern part of the nave.

The mosaic floor of the western aisle contains five inscriptions in Hebrew and Aramaic. The first quotes 1 Chronicles 1:1–4 ("Adam, Seth, Enosh, Kenan, Mehalalel, Jared, Enoch, Methuselah, Lamech, Noah, Shem, Ham, and Japheth"). The second inscription lists the names of the twelve signs of the zodiac, from Aries (Nissan) to Pisces (Adar), the twelve months of the year starting with Nissan. It then mentions the three patriarchs (Abraham, Isaac, and Jacob), the blessing שלום (Peace), the three companions of Daniel (Hananiah, Mishael, and Azariah), and ends with שלום על ישראל (Peace upon Israel). The third inscription, in Aramaic, opens with a blessing on Yose ʿAzrun (or Irun?) and Hezekiyo (recently J. Naveh suggested the readings ʿAzaryan and Ḥezekian) sons of Ḥalfi; it then continues with warnings to those who commit certain sins—causing dissension in the community, passing on to the Gentiles malicious information, or revealing the secrets of the town. It reads: "The one whose eyes roam over the entire earth and see what is concealed will uproot this person and his seed from under the sun and all the people will say Amen, Amen, Selah."

The fourth inscription, a blessing in Aramaic written in poorly executed script, mentions Rabbi Yose son of Ḥalfi and Hezekiyo (Naveh: Ḥezekian) son of Ḥalfi who have done very much לשמה דרחמנה, שלום (for the Name of the Merciful, Peace). A fifth inscription in Aramaic (which has not been completely published) is a blessing on all the people of the town who renovated the synagogue and also mentions Yonatan the *ḥazan* (a synagogue official). Four of the inscriptions were published in 1971. Since then various interpretations have been proposed and published. Various questions—foremost of which is the identification of the "secrets of the town" that may not be revealed to the Gentiles, still remain unanswered. It is possible that the first two inscriptions were influenced by the *piyutim* (religious hymns) current during the Byzantine period.

The En-Gedi community refrained from decorating its synagogue's mosaic pavement with the signs of the zodiac, as was done in the synagogues at Hammath-Tiberias, Beth Alpha, Ḥusifah, and Naʿaran, even though it did mention the names of the signs in an inscription. This indicates a very conservative attitude toward figural representations at a time when they were being commonly used in synagogues elsewhere in the country. The synagogue's walls and columns were coated with white plaster and decorated with drawings and patterns in red. On one of the pillars a painting of two ships with sails was found, and on a section of plaster the Aramaic word גביה is preserved, apparently part of a blessing.

The stratum II synagogue was built in the middle or late fifth century CE, during the period in which the Jewish community in the oasis flourished. The Jewish town of En-Gedi and its synagogue were destroyed in a violent conflagration.

A hoard of bronze coins in a cloth bundle was found in the courtyard of a house near the synagogue. It included coins from the reigns of Anastasius I (491–518) and Justin I (518–527) to the beginning of the reign of Justinian I (527–565). At the beginning of Justinian I's reign, the Jews suffered persecution—for example, in 531 a church was built over the synagogue at Gerasa. The coins in this hoard suggest that the synagogue, along with all of Jewish En-Gedi, may have been destroyed in that wave of persecution. Interesting finds were discovered in the ashes and ruins of the synagogue. A seven-branched menorah, cast in bronze, about 22 cm wide and 15 cm high, was found close to the Torah ark. Its base was not found, but with it, the menorah's original height would have been 30 to 35 cm. Because there are no sign that the upper portion was joined to a wooden board or any other device used to hold a lamp, it can be assumed that the menorah was purely decorative.

The niche of the Torah ark in stratum III and in the area between it and the inner side of the wooden structure of stratum II may have been used for storage. They are the locations of most of the finds, which include many bronze coins and a vessel in the form of a goblet with a stem with a revolving lid on a hinge (which was not found); a small seven-branched silver lamp, possibly one of the decorations of the Torah ark curtain or one of the ornaments of the mantle of the Torah scroll; pottery lamps; a decorated pottery bowl; and fragments of glass vessels. The extreme aridity at the site also preserved traces of burnt parchments and a wooden disc set at the base of a rod on which a scroll was rolled.

Isolated finds show that subsequently, at the beginning of the seventh century CE, before the Arab conquest, there was some activity at the site, but its nature has not been determined. In the Middle Ages, after some of its building stones had been looted, the site of the synagogue was covered with a thick layer of earth and sherds, including fragments of handmade pottery vessels painted with simple patterns in red and brown.

DAN BARAG

Main publication: B. Mazar et al., *En-Gedi: The First and Second Seasons of Excavations, 1961–1962* ('Atiqot 5), Jerusalem 1966.

Other studies: B. Mazar et al., *IEJ* 11 (1961), 76–77; 12 (1962), 145–146; 14 (1964), 121–130; 17 (1967), 133–143; id., *Archaeology* 16 (1963), 99–107; id., *Archaeological Discoveries in the Holy Land*, New York 1967, 67–76; id., *Archaeology and Old Testament Study* (ed. D. W. Thomas), Oxford 1967, 222–230; id., *RB* 74 1967), 85–86; id., *Archaeology* (Israel Pocket Library), Jerusalem 1974, 83–87; id., *BTS* 162 (1974), 8–17; Y. Yadin, *Jaarbericht Ex Oriente Lux* 17 (1964), 227–241; D. Ussishkin, *BA* 34 (1971), 23–39; id., *TA* 7 (1980), 1–44; D. Barag et al., *RB* 79 (1972), 581–583; 81 (1974), 96–97; id., *ASR*, 116–119; id., *Recherches archéologiques en Israël*, 232–237; A. Kempinski, *IEJ* 22 (1972), 10–15; Y. Meshorer, *Actes du VIIIe Congrés International de Numismatique Sept. 1973*, Paris 1976, 111–112; L. I. Levine, *ASR*, 140–145; J. Porath, *ESI* 1 (1982), 26; G. Hadas, ibid. 4 (1985), 25–26; 7–8 (1988–1989), 51; A. Ofer and J. Porath, ibid. 5 (1986), 26–29; B.-Z. Binyamin, *Immanuel* 21 (1987), 68–79; M. D. Coogan, *PEQ* 119 (1987), 3–4; Weippert 1988 (Ortsregister); R. Amiran, *L'Urbanisation de la Palestine à l'Age du Bronze Ancien (Actes du Colloque d'Emmaüs, 1986*; *BAR*/IS 527, ed. P. de Miroschedji), Oxford 1989, 53–60.

'EN GEV

PREHISTORIC SITES

EXCAVATIONS

During the survey made by D. Ben-Ami of Kibbutz 'En Gev on the eastern side of the Sea of Galilee, the sites of 'En Gev I and IV were discovered on a hill adjacent to the kibbutz, on a flank of the Golan Plateau, about 0.5 km (0.3 mi.) east of the shore. An expedition under the auspices of the Israel Academy of Science and Humanities, directed by M. Stekelis and O. Bar-Yosef, excavated there in the summers of 1963 and 1964. The main excavation took place at 'En Gev I, where a human skeleton was found. Additional test pits were opened in 1965 and 1967–1968 at 'En Gev II, III, and IV.

'EN GEV I. The excavation uncovered six layers (1–6) whose stratigraphy was based on the succession of floors on which large concentrations of flints and bones were exposed. The configurations of the layers suggest a hut dug into the slope of the hill, so that its eastern side was higher than its western side. The floor was a kind of shallow basin enclosed on the east and probably open to the west—the westward elevation of the site (except for the lowest layers, 4–6) suffered from later erosion. The infilling of the floors of the hut indicates a rapid accumulation of sand from the slope between each period of occupation. In layer 4, a hearth with white ash was uncovered. Near the hearth were a basalt mortar and two pestles, one of which was broken. On a paved area at the southern edge of the pit, several horn cores were found. Some large bones were laid on a paved area inside the dwelling pit.

In the center of the pit, in layer 3, a female skeleton lying on its right side was found buried in a shallow grave. The legs were drawn up, the left hand was resting on the thigh, slightly bent, and touching the left leg. The skull, lying on several stones, was crushed. Large animal bones were found around the skull. Based on the position of the burial, it can be assumed that it took place toward the end of the layer 3 occupation.

The lithic industry defines 'En Gev I's material culture as Kebaran. It is characterized by obliquely truncated, backed bladelets. Other characteristics are the Falita points—which relate this culture to other Kebaran sites in Syria and Lebanon—scrapers, burins, denticulates, and several picks. The bone tools are burnishers made of *Oryx* horn cores. The numerous kitchen remains include bones of gazelle, Nubian ibex, fallow deer, roe deer, bovids, wild cat, wolf, and common red fox, as well as several birds and mollusks from a nearby spring.

'EN GEV II. 'En Gev II was found across the gully, about 30 m south of 'En Gev I, on the same topographic elevation (between 150 and 160 m below sea level). Technologically and typologically, the material culture is the same as at 'En Gev I.

'EN GEV III. 'En Gev III is located 25 m west of site II. A cross section of this site showed the same type of pit-dwelling construction as was seen in 'En Gev I. The flint industry is somewhat different, however, as it also includes a few rectangles. This indicates a trend toward geometrization—that is, the transition from Kebaran to Geometric Kebaran.

'EN GEV IV. 'En Gev IV is located on the northern edge of the same hill as the other sites. Its lithic industry, found within a small sounding (2 by 1 m) made in 1968, was characterized by the use of the microburin technique. The products of this technique amount to 50 or 60 percent of the total assemblage of the five layers uncovered. The tools are mainly end scrapers on blades, with some on flakes, and a few burins. The microliths are generally obliquely truncated or micro-gravette points. The geometric microliths include scalene and isosceles triangles and several lunates, all of which are products of the microburin technique. Also found were many notched tools and denticulates, some of which were made on large blades or thick flakes, and a few burins. This flint industry, on typological grounds, seems to be later than the industries at the other sites.

The fauna include horses, wild boar—which did not appear at the other sites—gazelle, some bovids, roe deer, fallow deer, rabbits, wolf, wild cat, some birds, turtles, and fish (from the Sea of Galilee).

SUMMARY. The descending locations of the sites from I to IV probably indicate the regression of the lake as well as the gradual freshening of its water, as testified by the existence of fish remains at site IV. The Kebaran hunters, living in small and probably familial huts on this hill, were provided with abundant game and wild cereals from their immediate environment: the valley near the lake and on the escarpment of the Golan Heights plateau. The evolution of the tool kit is indicated by the typological modifications of the microliths, from nongeometric to a fully geometric type. Such a development is parallel to other Kebaran and Geometric Kebaran sites in other areas of the country.

OFER BAR-YOSEF

'En Gev I: burial in layer 3; skeleton in situ.

EXCAVATIONS ON THE MOUND

IDENTIFICATION

The site, situated on the narrow plain on the eastern shore of the Sea of Galilee (in Arabic, Khirbet el-'Asheq) is today occupied by Kibbutz 'En Gev. The site (c. 250 m long and 120 m wide) rises only a few meters above the plain and has none of the typical characteristics of an ancient mound. It is evident that its inhabitants were content to forgo the natural protection afforded by a hill and to build their settlement on the shore. The site is adjacent to the road that ran from Beth-Shean to the fords of the Jordan and then followed the eastern shore of the Sea of Galilee as far as the environs of 'En Gev. From there, the road went up the Golan Heights to Hippos and Aphek (Fiq) and

Tel 'En Gev: structures from stratum 3.

Stone incense spoon from stratum 3.

continued north to Damascus. The remains found at the site attest to a continuous occupation from the tenth to the second centuries BCE.

EXPLORATION

In 1961, an expedition on behalf of the Israel Department of Antiquities and Museums and the Hebrew University of Jerusalem spent eleven days making exploratory soundings at the site. The expedition was led by B. Mazar, A. Biran, I. Dunayevsky, and M. Dothan, assisted by volunteers from the Absalom Foundation and from *kibbutzim* in the Jordan Valley. Excavations at 'En Gev were resumed in 1990 (see below).

The plan of the ancient city was found to reflect the topography. It was divided into two sections. The southern section was a residential area surrounded by a wall; the northern section, built on an elevation about 3 m high, was a citadel. The trial sounding in the south (area I) sought to trace the fortifications and determine the settlement's stratigraphy. The sounding in the north (areas II–III) was intended to ascertain the nature of the citadel.

EXCAVATION RESULTS

AREA I. The trial trench dug in area I established clearly that the earliest city (stratum 5) had been built on level ground and that the elevated mound consists only of an accumulation of occupational levels. All the layers throughout the excavated area were horizontal, which made it relatively simple to establish the stratigraphy. The five strata provided numerous indications of the settlement's cultural continuity in the Iron Age, from the tenth to the eighth centuries BCE. No remains of other periods were uncovered in this area.

Strata 5–4. A foundation (1.85 m thick) on which a brick wall once stood is assigned to stratum 5, the earliest settlement on the site. The foundation was built of medium-sized, rough stones. When the wall went out of use, it was replaced by a casemate line (stratum 4), whose two walls were built of large, undressed stones with a fill of smaller stones—the southern, or exterior, wall (1.75 m thick and preserved to a height of 0.9 m) and the northern one (1.15 m thick and preserved to a height of 0.45 m). The space between the two walls (1.4 m) is paved with flagstones. The casemate wall is of the type common in the country during Solomon's reign; it resembles the walls at Megiddo (VA–IVB) and Hazor (X–IX). The need for such a massive wall was dictated by the topography of the area—an almost level plain for which strong defenses were necessary.

Few building remains were uncovered in strata 5 and 4. In stratum 5 the remains of a house were found, separated from the nearby city wall by a street (5.5 m wide). The plan of the house could not be established. No remains of buildings were found in stratum 4 because most of the excavation in the trial trench only reached down to stratum 3. The few potsherds found in the two strata (which included fragments of highly burnished Cypriot-Phoenician vessels) are to be assigned to the tenth century BCE.

Strata 3–2. It is evident that after the destruction of the earlier city, new settlers erected a town (stratum 3) on its ruins whose character was altogether different. In building the walls they used the foundations of the outer casemate wall; the inner wall went out of use. The new wall in stratum 3 was buttressed on the outside, apparently at regular intervals; hence, it consisted of alternately narrow (1.75 m) and broad (3.15 m) sections, on the plan of the

Above: storage jar with the inscription "(belonging) to Šqy'" from stratum 2; **(below)** enlarged detail of inscription.

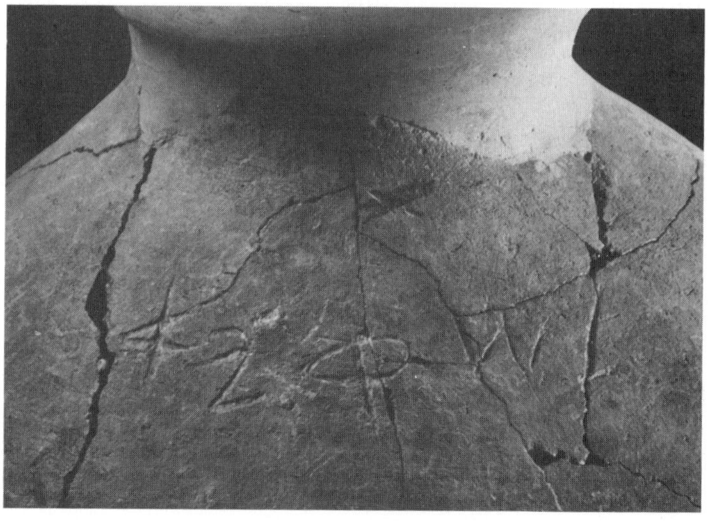

Tel 'En Gev: carved orthostat.

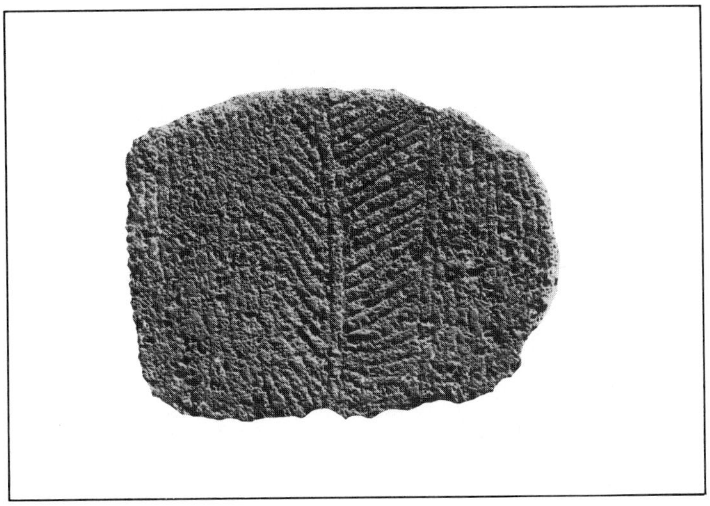

"offsets and insets" common in the ninth century BCE (Megiddo IVA, Hazor VIII). A glacis was added, consisting of a stone revetment supported by the remains of the stratum 5 wall.

Most of the area north of the wall was occupied by a single building separated by only a narrow alley from the wall. The building evidently consisted of a courtyard surrounded by rooms on two or three sides. In one room, which was completely paved with large flagstones, the excavators unearthed a wealth of finds, including ritual libation and incense vessels—a clay incense burner, a stone incense spoon, a small bronze funnel, and decorated pottery vessels. All this may indicate that the room served the cultic needs of a family, similar to the cultic room in house 2081 at Megiddo (strata VA–IVB). North of this room was a courtyard sparsely paved with stones. It had a silo attached to its wall. Within the courtyard several vessels were found, including a storage jar with an Aramaic inscription incised on its shoulder: "belonging to *Shaqiah* [the 'cupbearer']." On paleographical grounds, the inscription can be assigned to no later than the mid-ninth century BCE. *Shaqiah* is evidently the Aramaic equivalent of the Hebrew *mashqeh*, "cupbearer," perhaps the title of a high official in the Aramean kingdom.

Of the many clay vessels found in stratum 3, the majority are typical of pottery from sites in the northern and central part of the country in the ninth century BCE. Some of the pottery was imported, however, especially from the Aramean parts of Syria.

The structures in stratum 2 were built over the ruined stratum 3 buildings after the latter had been burned to the ground. They were constructed according to the same plan, and the wall of stratum 3 continued to be used in stratum 2. It appears that these two strata belong to one historical-cultural period and that after the destruction of city 3, the same inhabitants rebuilt it, albeit with some changes. The thick wall, which in stratum 3 separated the house from the courtyard on the north, was replaced by a wall consisting of a row of pilasters built of flat stones arranged one upon the other with mud-brick fill. The pottery in stratum 2 also did not differ to any marked degree from that in stratum 3.

Stratum 1. The stratum 2 settlement was also destroyed by fire, but this time the destruction was complete. The settlement that followed in stratum 1 was of an altogether different character. On the ruins of stratum 2, the excavators found a public building with generous dimensions. Its stone walls (1.1 m thick) may have served some military purpose; or it may have been a storehouse protected by thick walls. Judging from the pottery, stratum 1 is to be assigned to no later than the eighth century BCE. (The table below gives estimated dates for the strata, from top to bottom.)

AREAS II AND III. At the northeastern tip of the mound, where the citadel stood, two exploratory soundings were made: a small pit in area II and a somewhat larger excavation nearby (area III). These soundings revealed the nature of the citadel and its stratigraphy. It is quite certain that its dimensions were about 60 sq m. Its wall in area II (1.35 m thick and preserved to a height of 4.15 m) was built of large, undressed stones inside and outside, with a fill of smaller stones. Because the wall was built directly on virgin soil, a fill of earth was heaped up on both its sides to a height of 3 m. The citadel's earth floor was laid on this fill. It appears that the builders of the citadel had raised the level of the floor so that the fortress would dominate the entire area.

In area III, four strata were distinguished.

Stratum 4*. Stratum 4* is represented by a layer of earth 1.35 m above virgin soil. In it remains of furnaces, many potsherds, and a considerable amount of charred matter were found. This stratum, which preceded the citadel, was also found in area II, where a pavement of large stones laid on virgin soil was uncovered.

Stratum 3*. Remains of the citadel, which was built on a high fill, are to be assigned to stratum 3*. The thick stone walls that surrounded the fortress were built on virgin soil 1.4 m below the level of the floor. The southern limit of the fill was marked by a heavy brick wall. To the south, the space between the virgin soil and the floor of the citadel was used to build a basement that was divided into rectangular rooms, two of which were uncovered. The rooms were found filled with earth and sherds. In one room, the excavators found large, flat, well-dressed flagstones that evidently had faced the lower part of the citadel's walls and had fallen into the cellar when the ceiling collapsed.

About 10 m south of area III, a section of a stone wall could be seen. Judging from its construction and direction, it was the southern wall of the citadel; it marks the limit of the cellar rooms in the south.

Stratum 2*. Stratum 2* is represented by two stone walls built at right angles to one another. The stratum's earth floor is about 0.5 m higher than the top of the stratum 3* walls.

Stratum 1*. Two stone walls built at right angles to each other and a rough stone pavement about 0.5 m above the level of the floor of stratum 2* were found in stratum 1*. The pottery from this stratum does not differ from that in stratum 2* and belongs to the eighth century BCE.

Date. The dates of the strata range from the beginning of the United Monarchy (the beginning of the tenth century BCE) to the campaign of Tiglath-pileser III (733–732 BCE). The table below presents a tentative synchronization of the strata in area I with those in areas II and III and their approximate dates.

AREA IV. An additional sounding was made near a building used by the fishermen on the kibbutz (area IV). In the early fifties, two basalt orthostats were found there, one of them decorated with a palm tree in relief. The uppermost stratum in this area was assigned to the Hellenistic period; the lower strata paralleled those in areas I, II and III. Persian and Hellenistic vessels and sherds were also found in trenches and ditches dug on the summit of the mound and in the vicinity.

Area I	*Areas II–III*	*Period (BCE)*	*Fortifications*
1	1* 2*	790–733/32: Joash and Jeroboam II, to the campaign of Tiglath-pileser III against Damascus	Unfortified city
2	3*	838–790: Hazael and Ben-hadad III, to the campaigns of Joash against Aram	Citadel and "offset/inset" wall
3		886–838: Ben-hadad I and II (the Omrid dynasty in Israel) to the campaign of Shalmaneser III in northern Transjordan	
4		945–886: the middle of Solomon's reign to the campaign of Ben-hadad I	Citadel and casemate wall
5	4*	990–945: David and the first part of Solomon's reign	Solid wall

BENJAMIN MAZAR

RECENT EXCAVATIONS

Excavations at 'En Gev were resumed in 1990–1991 by a Japanese expedition, under the auspices of the Land of Geshur Project of the Institute of Archaeology at Tel Aviv University, directed by M. Kochavi. The excavations at 'En Gev were directed by H. Kanaseki of Tenri University and H. Ogawa of Keio University.

Because the entire southern (lower) part of the mound was occupied by the houses of Kibbutz 'En Gev, the area selected for excavation was limited to the high part of the mound, in the north—called the citadel by the 1961 expedition. The new excavations took place at the northeastern corner of the citadel, some 70 m east of the previous expedition's areas II and III (referred to in the excavation report as areas B and C). Four strata were distinguished in the new excavation.

Stratum IV. Stratum IV was the earliest stratum identified (the excavators did not reach bedrock). Its main feature was a well-built wall (1.3 m thick) of large stones. This wall runs along the eastern slope of the mound in a north–south direction. On its east was a floor, on which sherds were buried in a layer of black ash some 40 cm thick. The pottery types represented were characteristic of the tenth century BCE. On its west, the wall supported a fill that was intended to raise the ground level of the citadel. The wall was excavated to a depth of 3.5 m without reaching its foundations.

Stratum III. The remains in stratum III included part of a large building, consisting of long halls without pillars—perhaps storerooms. The building's eastern wall ran parallel to the stratum IV fortification wall; the length of the walls running up to it was as much as 18 m.

Stratum II. The area of the stratum III storehouse was occupied in stratum II by a pillared building with three long halls. Its central hall was wider and unpaved, while the two halls flanking it were narrower and paved. Two rows of eleven pillars separated the halls. Each pillar was monolithic, about 1.4 m

General view of 'En Gev.

high and square in cross section. The building was 18 m long (similar in size to the northern pillared buildings at Megiddo). There were no troughs in the building, and there were no holes drilled in the pillars; only a few sherds were found on the floors.

Stratum I. In stratum I a private house, with rooms surrounding a courtyard, was built over the pillared building. Several of the stratum II pillars were used in the floors of the house; a mortar was even cut into one of the pillars. The pottery in this stratum belongs to the Hellenistic period.

SUMMARY

DATING AND STRATIGRAPHY. As the excavations at the site are incomplete, only tentative conclusions are possible. 'En Gev was first occupied in the tenth century BCE; its occupation ended in the Hellenistic period, as the first excavators surmised. The massive stratum IV fortifications (tenth century BCE) unearthed in the new excavations are in accord with the fortifications designated as stratum 3* by the earlier excavators, who, however, dated it to the ninth century BCE. Further excavations may resolve the issue.

IDENTIFICATION. The strong fortifications and public buildings on the site suggest an identification with Aphek, which was an advance Syrian (Aramean) outpost in the ninth and eighth centuries BCE. This identification, originally proposed by M. Dothan, is supported by the results of a survey at Afiq/Fiq, where the name is preserved, but no Iron Age sherds were found. The excavations at Tel Soreg, which is closer to Afiq, revealed evidence of only a small wayside fort in the Iron Age II; this fort was only 20 by 20 m in size and could hardly be identified as the great fortified city from which Ben-hadad went to war and to which he retreated after his defeat by Ahab (1 Kg. 26:30).

MOSHE KOCHAVI

B. Mazar et al., *IEJ* 11 (1961), 192–193; 14 (1964), 1–49; M. Stekelis and O. Bar-Yosef, *L'Anthropologie* 69 (1965), 176–183; B. Arensburg and O. Bar-Yosef, *Paléorient* 1 (1973), 201–206; S. J. M. Davis, "Faunal Remains of Upper Palaeolithic Sites at Ein-Gev (Israel)" (Master's thesis, Hebrew Univ. of Jerusalem 1972); id., *Paléorient* 2 (1974), 453–462; G. Martin, *IEJ* 28 (1978), 262–263; id., *RB* 86 (1979), 109–110; id. (with O. Bar-Yosef), *Paléorient* 3 (1975–1977), 285–286; 5 (1979), 219–220; P. Porat, *Scripta Classica Israelica* 6 (1981–1982), 101; G. W. Ahlström, *TA* 12 (1985), 93–95; D. Kaufman, *Mitekufat Ha'even* 20 (1987), 37*–49*; Weippert 1988 (Ortsregister); P. C. Edwards, *Journal of Mediterranean Archaeology*, 2 (1989), 5–48; M. Kochavi, *IEJ* 39 (1989), 1–17; 41 (1991), 180–184.

'EN NASHUṬ

IDENTIFICATION

A once nameless ruin on the bank of Naḥal Meshushim in the Golan (possibly the site called by G. Schumacher Deir Raḥb), 2.5 km (c. 1.5 mi.), north of Qaṣrin (map reference 2687.2153), is now named after the spring of 'En Nashuṭ on the stream's opposite bank. The ruin is some 6 a. in area; there are a few walls visible above the surface and the remains of two olive presses.

EXPLORATION

The site was discovered in 1969 by Y. Gal, and the location of its synagogue was identified in 1971 by S. Barlev and M. Hartal. They found stones engraved with menorahs and sculpted with a lioness in relief and a Corinthian capital. After it was learned that coins had been plundered from the site, a short trial excavation was conducted in 1971 by M. Ben-Ari. In 1978, a salvage excavation was carried out by Z. Ma'oz, on behalf of the Israel Department of Antiquities and Museums and the Israel Society for the Protection of Nature, Golan Field School. The synagogue is situated at the edge of the site, on its northwestern slope, near a circular structure built over the spring. It is surrounded on three sides by an open area enclosed by retaining walls. The site's remains have not been damaged by later construction.

EXCAVATION RESULTS

STRATUM III (THIRD–FOURTH CENTURIES). Stratum III lies beneath the remains of the synagogue, in the western part of the building and outside it to the southwest. The stratum consists of the remains of walls leveled before the construction of the building in stratum II. Judging from the layout of the walls, there were probably two rooms here. However, the true nature of this stratum, which has been tentatively dated to the fourth century CE, is not sufficiently clear. Sherds and coins dating from the first century CE, as well as some sherds from the Chalcolithic period, were found in various earth fills.

STRATUM IIB (FIFTH CENTURY). Stratum IIB is characterized by the construction of the synagogue. Probes dug in the earth fill of the synagogue's foundations yielded eight coins from the fourth century CE, mainly from the end of the century (383–395 CE). A group of 193 coins (of which 115 have been identified) was found under the paving in front of the main entrance. They were probably buried there during the construction of the synagogue, a tradition found at the synagogues at Qaṣrin, Ḥorvat Kanaf, and Dabiyye. The latest coins dated to the reign of the emperor Honorius (408–423 CE). Another group, stratigraphically associated with the end of stratum III or the beginning of stratum II, was found in a small room to the west of and beneath the synagogue; it included fifty-one coins (of which thirty-four have been identified). The latest have been dated to the reign of the emperor Theodosius II or Valentinian III (425–450 CE). Since both groups are copper coins of the smallest denominations, they were not hoards buried for retrieval, but votive offerings, possibly with some magical significance. Together with other coins found scattered in the foundations, they enable the dating of the stratum II synagogue's construction to the fifth century CE, probably in the middle of that century.

STRATUM IIA (SIXTH CENTURY). Repairs to the synagogue and its final occupation characterize stratum IIA. The base of the Ark of the Law was enlarged, a column was added to the western row of columns, a wall was erected for the narthex in the building's forecourt (to the south), and a new floor was laid for the narthex. These repairs may have been carried out in the wake of an earthquake in the sixth century CE (551 CE?). This stage continued until the synagogue fell into disuse and the village was abandoned. On the basis of a few coins and an intact lamp found on a bench in the synagogue, this abandonment occurred at the end of the sixth or beginning of the seventh century CE.

STRATUM I (MODERN PERIOD). In stratum I, stones were robbed, synagogue remains were destroyed, and many engraved architectural elements were smashed.

'En Nashuṭ: general view of the synagogue, looking west.

THE SYNAGOGUE

The synagogue at 'En Nashuṭ was built on a terrace at the northwestern edge of the village. The eastern wall (0.9 m thick), built of roughly cut stones, served as a retaining wall for the adjacent buildings to the east. The other three walls were 1.1 m thick; their outer faces were built of smooth-basalt ashlars (without mortar), and their inner faces of roughly cut stones. The excavation exposed the prayer hall, an annex in the southeast, the area in front of the entrance in the south, and the base of a staircase built along the northern and eastern walls.

THE PRAYER HALL. The prayer hall is built on a rectangular plan (outer measurements, 12.65 by 11.4 m; inner, 10.45 by 9.35 m). Five square stylobates are preserved in the floor, one still supporting a pedestal, together with the base and part of the column, carved out of a single stone. Judging from the stylobates, the prayer hall was divided into a nave (5.25 m wide) and two aisles by two rows of three columns each. Three basalt benches surround the walls; the upper two were molded with depressions for feet. On the side of the hall facing Jerusalem—the south—an impression of the Ark of the Law was found in the floor plaster, as well as a stone of the lowest step that ascended to the ark. The ark (1.6 by 1.4 m) probably stood to the left of the main entrance; the central opening was destroyed by stone robbing, but fragments of the doorjambs and lintel found nearby, as well as a section of the plaster floor just inside the entrance, indicate its location—off-center in the building's southern (front) wall. The main entrance (estimated width, 1.2 m) was slightly to the west of the central axis in order to accommodate the Ark of the Law in the southern wall. The floor of the hall was made of a fine, white, levigated plaster overlying layers of mortar mixed with small basalt pebbles. Walls, benches and the columns were whitewashed. Patches of plaster survived on the walls, some with incised inscriptions, painted red.

Synagogue: column base decorated with a menorah.

THE ANNEX. The annex is a side room, built alongside the southeastern corner of the prayer hall. Its floor is about 1 m higher than that of the synagogue as a whole. It was reached through a door (1 m wide) in the hall's eastern wall. In stratum IIB, the annex also opened directly into the forecourt to the south, through an ashlar-built entrance. In stratum IIA, this door was sealed and plastered over, replaced by a shelf that functioned as part of a wall cupboard. At the same time, a new plaster floor was added and the walls were replastered, both with grooves in a herringbone pattern.

FORECOURT. A few small Doric capitals, found reused in the paving of stratum IIA, indicate that the synagogue may originally have been fronted by a small covered portico, like the one at the synagogue at Umm el-Qanaṭir. The facade of the 'En Nashuṭ synagogue, built of ashlar blocks, includes the annex as well. Some 1.2 m south of and facing the annex is a solid, square platform, faced with ashlar blocks. It may have been the base of a flight of steps leading from the village to the forecourt. The space between the steps and the door to the annex was paved with fine ashlars. In stratum IIA, a plastered stone bench was built onto the base of the platform. In the same stratum, to the south, a coarsely built wall of roughly cut stones was built, parallel to the synagogue wall. It closed off the court, converting it into a kind of narthex. A new floor was laid in the narthex. It was made of crumbly plaster on top of two layers of paving stones in secondary use—the upper layer of small stones and the lower of larger ones, including ashlars, capitals, and a fragment of an engaged sculpture of a lion. It seems that parts of the original stratum IIA building were damaged, possibly in an earthquake; these were not restored but were incorporated as raw material in the bedding of the floor.

STAIRS TO THE GALLERIES. Attached to the northwestern corner of the prayer hall and outside it, and continuing along the eastern wall, a broad wall (1.2 m wide) was discovered. It may have served as the base of a staircase along the outside wall that climbed to the entrance to the galleries above the annex.

ARCHITECTURE AND DECORATION. The 'En Nashuṭ synagogue is particularly rich in architectural decoration. Two of the pedestals bear reliefs of intricate geometric and floral patterns—rosettes, a double meander, bands of buds—as well as a menorah (on the northeastern pedestal). Two capitals, preserved almost intact and originally part of the columns on the ground floor (as indicated by their diameter), are in the diagonal Ionic

'En Nashuṭ: capital decorated with menorahs from the synagogue.

style. The capital over the northeastern column is particularly notable for its decorations: each of its four faces bears a different design. Among the motifs are a menorah, altar, amphora, flower, a pair of facing birds of prey, and a large nine-branched candelabrum.

The ground-floor columns supported stone architraves and a frieze. The architrave has a bench-shaped cross section, with a diagonal depression between two fasciae. One architrave, which was found broken in two, bore a relief of a Hercules knot whose ends were carved in the shape of snakes' heads, with two rosettes beside them. Incised below the relief was an Aramaic inscription (see below). This architrave, like the capital mentioned above, was found at the foot of the northeastern column. The frieze, found in pieces, has a *cavetto* molding surmounted by baguettes. Column drums whose diameter is smaller than that of the columns on the ground floor, and two Corinthian capitals constitute the remains of the rows of columns on the upper story, which supported the tiled roof. Both aisles probably had galleries. The Corinthian capitals were drilled, in the shallow style characteristic of the fifth century CE. Among the parts of the main entrance found in a heap of material rejected by robbers, south of the building, were the doorjamb stones, carved in Ionic style; a fragment of a lintel with a relief of a wreath around a rosette; and fragments bearing unidentifiable reliefs. On fragments of a flat stone found nearby were low reliefs of two menorahs and between them a lion facing the center. Other parts of the facade included arch stones, a cornice decorated with astragal and egg-and-dart patterns and a vine trellis, a convex frieze adorned with an overlapping leaf pattern and a rosette, and parts of a cyma. Triangular-cut stones indicate that the facade was gabled. The gable may have been topped by the relief of an eagle with outspread wings, like the one at the synagogue at Chorazin; fragments of such a relief were found at the site. Other decorated fragments, whose original location cannot be determined, were found in the heaps of rubble: a large relief of a lioness, a lion's paw, a bird pecking at a bunch of grapes, a sculpted lion's head, a fragment of a capital(?) on which a bird and another animal were carved, and a spirally fluted colonnette. It is noteworthy that carved fragments, apparently plundered from the 'En Nashuṭ synagogue, have been found at neighboring sites, such as Ghadriyye and 'Ein Samsam. At Ghadriyye two pieces from gabled windows with conches inside them were found. At 'Ein Samsam an orthostat was found with a fully sculpted lion's head at its end and, on its side, a relief of a man raising his hands; the man is flanked by a lion and by a lioness suckling a cub, and at both ends of the scene, one of two eagles pecks at bunches of grapes. At the 'En Nashuṭ synagogue, the windows were probably in the front wall; the orthostat may have adorned the base of the Ark of the Law. The scene depicted on it probably represents Daniel in the lions' den, a motif familiar from the synagogues at Susiya and Na'aran.

INSCRIPTIONS. Several inscriptions were found in and around the 'En Nashuṭ synagogue. In the debris, mainly in the northeastern corner of the hall, fragmentary inscriptions, mostly single letters, were found incised and painted in red on chunks of wall plaster. One piece of plaster bore part of a Hebrew inscription in two lines: שה[יתקי]ן... / אמ[ן אמן ס] לה שלום (*šh[ytqy]n. . . / 'm[–'mn s] lh šlwm*). It probably honors donors to the building. An Aramaic inscription that may perpetuate the memory of the principal donor was found on the carved architrave (see above): *'bwn br ywsh* (Abun son of Yose). Two basalt sarcophagus lids were found on the hill to the west of the village. One bore an Aramaic inscription: *šm'wn br 'bwn br šnyn kw* (Shimon son of Abun, twenty-six years old)—perhaps referring to the son of the person honored in the synagogue inscription. The other lid bore a Greek inscription translated "Yose son of Zanos, fifty years old."

COINS AND POTTERY. Some 719 coins were discovered at 'En Nashuṭ, mostly copper *perutot*. Of the 719, 466 were found in the excavation itself. They were identified by D. Ariel. The remainder was collected from the surface and unearthed in the 1971 exploratory excavation. Two of the coins were dated to the period of the procurators in the first century CE and six to the second to third centuries CE. Most (361 coins, or 77 percent of the total) were dated to the fourth century CE, 71 to the fifth, and 26 to the sixth century CE (including three gold tremisses). A relatively small number of sherds was found, mainly in the fills in the synagogue's foundations. Most prominently represented among the sherds were the so-called Galilean bowls and cooking pots; the long time span represented by the pottery—from the end of the second to the mid-fifth centuries CE (and perhaps even later)— does not permit specific conclusions about the occupation of the site during the second to third centuries CE.

SUMMARY

The numismatic and ceramic finds indicate that the site of 'En Nashuṭ was settled in the first century CE and destroyed during the First Jewish Revolt against the Romans. The site probably remained unpopulated (or only sparsely settled) during the second and third centuries. It was resettled toward the end of the third century and at the beginning of the fourth, in the context of the economic revival under Diocletian and Constantine. The synagogue built in the mid-fifth century CE was probably the first at the site. It served the village community until the end of the sixth or the beginning of the seventh centuries CE and was then abandoned. The wealth of architectural and carved elements in this synagogue recalls the synagogues at Chorazin, Shura (on the Rosh Pinna plateau), and ed-Dikkeh, Rafid, and Khaukha in the Golan. This heavily ornamented style is characteristic also of fifth-century churches in Syria but is not known either in Syria or the Golan in the fourth or sixth century CE.

In the synagogue at 'En Nashuṭ, the problem of how the main entrance and the Ark of the Law could both be accommodated in the southern wall of the building was solved: the entrance was made slightly off-center. A similar solution was found in other Golan synagogues (Zumeimira, Umm el-Qanaṭir). A second notable feature in the 'En Nashuṭ synagogue was the spot near the elaborately decorated northeastern column, where the pedestal with meanders and a menorah, as well as the unique carved capital and the architrave with a relief and an inscription honoring the synagogue's donor (see above) were found. This honored position, just opposite the Ark of the Law, was probably the seat of the principal donor, Abun son of Yose, the "village squire," who took pains to decorate it as lavishly as possible. As yet no parallel has been identified for this sociological-architectural phenomenon in other synagogues in the country.

Z. Ma'oz, *ASR*, 105–112; id., *BA* 51 (1988), 116–128; D. T. Ariel, *IEJ* 37 (1987), 147–157.

ZVI URI MA'OZ

'EN SHADUD

IDENTIFICATION

The site of 'En Shadud is situated approximately 200 m east of Tel Shadud (map reference 1724.2294), on the northwest slopes of the Jezreel Valley. Its extent is unknown because most of it was destroyed at the time of its discovery, when an industrial plant was constructed. The site, named after a nearby spring that provides a plentiful water supply, is located on fertile, easily cultivated land. The remains of the ancient settlement were discovered beneath a layer of alluvial soil up to 1 m deep.

EXCAVATIONS

The excavations at the site were carried out on behalf of the Israel Department of Antiquities and Museums under the direction of E. Braun and S. Gibson in two areas, 20 m distant from each other. Two main strata were distinguished in both areas. The earlier settlement was established on virgin soil. The remains of two or three structures were uncovered, but the plan of only one rectangular building could be traced. Access to the building was by means of a step down to a pebble-paved floor, where a stone bench and flat

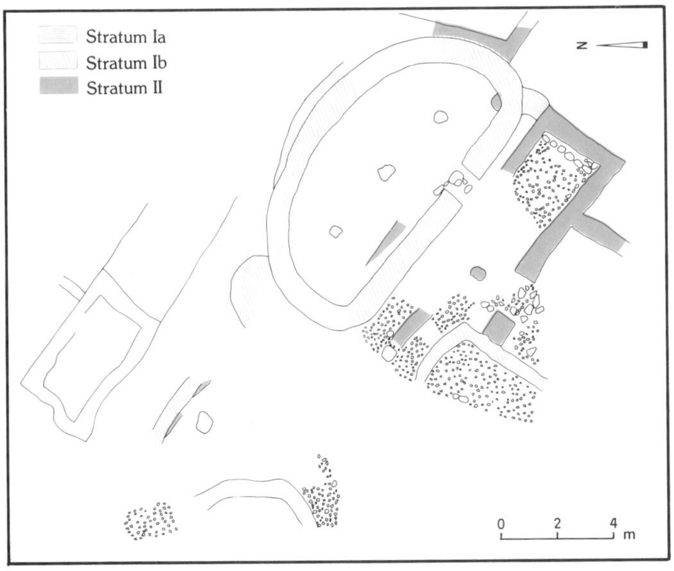

'En Shadud: plan of the site.

stone slabs (column bases) were exposed. A corner of this house, where several querns were found on a flat, basalt-paved surface, was devoted to grinding activities. The later stratum had two phases and was badly disturbed by a phenomenon that can only be described as warping. Horizontal layers were pushed up in places, creating dips and valleys that seriously complicated the stratigraphy. In one instance the top of a single stone wall showed differences of more than 1 m in elevation, even though it had initially been built to the same height along its entire length.

This structure, originally interpreted as a rectangular building with rounded corners, was twisted as a ribbon, due to warping. However, in the light of recent evidence from the contemporary settlements at Qiryat Ata and Kabri, it now seems more advisable to consider the building's plan as sausage shaped, with parallel walls ending in two semicircular apses. This house, with its broadroom affinities and stone pillar bases, combines aspects of the earlier, curvilinear architectural traditions of the Early Bronze Age I found at Yiftaḥel and those of the ubiquitous broadroom, notable in the latter part of this period and in the Early Bronze Age II. A line of several stones near the inner face of the front wall of this building may either represent a bench or an earlier structural phase. During the building's lifetime, rectangular structures existed contemporaneously. In the earlier phase the walls of the various buildings, including the back wall of the curvilinear house, were narrow. In the later phase several earlier walls were reused; new, thicker walls were added; and the rear wall of the curvilinear building was broadened.

In addition to these stratified buildings, several other structures—including a double broadroom paved with stones, a curvilinear wall, and fragments of pebbled surfaces—were uncovered. They could not, however, be assigned with any confidence to a definite stratum.

THE FINDS. The pottery from the two occupational phases is typical of an advanced (post-Yiftaḥel II) stage of the Early Bronze Age I. Most of the vessels are either painted or have a reddish-brown slip, often burnished; some have been decorated in the band-slip technique typical of the northern part of the country. Some gray-burnished ware was also found, mainly small carinated bowls. Hole-mouth jars and pithoi with rail rims and bow rims are also common. Fragments of two basalt bowls with circular wells, a rectangular base, and four strap handles stretching from the rim to the four corners of the base; numerous basalt querns; and several shallow basalt bowls comprise the site's worked stone assemblage. The flint assemblage of 'En Shadud attests to a local, diverse industry of ad hoc tools. Many Canaanite blades, some of them retouched, were recovered, but neither the raw material from which they were made nor their cores was found. The blades may have been brought to the site and finished there. No hunting tools were found, but sickle blades were numerous. The faunal material also supports the assumption that hunting did not play an important role in the village economy, which was based on agriculture and the husbandry of sheep, goat, asses, and pigs. A single rabbit bone suggests that some small game may have been trapped.

The small finds included two cylinder seal impressions on pottery vessels (with parallels in Megiddo stage V), a bead-shaped bone cylinder seal, and a human face modeled on the handle of a small pottery vessel.

DATING. The material culture indicates that both settlement phases at 'En Shadud should be attributed to an advanced phase of the first half of the Early Bronze Age I, similar to that represented at Megiddo (stages V–IV), Beth-Shean XV–XIV, and Qiryat Ata 2. The argument for this dating is the presence of gray-burnished ware and what appears to be the remnant of a tradition of curvilinear architecture that provides a link with the earlier Yiftaḥel II phase of the Early Bronze Age I. However, the absence at 'En Shadud of gray-burnished bowls with a projecting sinuous line of knobs on the angle of carination (vessels commonly found at Yiftaḥel II) and the presence of quantities of red-burnished pottery, the technique of band-slip painting, and the broadroom aspects of the architectural traditions indicate links with the later Early Bronze II period. The virtual identity of the pottery from both phases within the occupation of this site suggests that 'En Shadud was occupied and abandoned within a short span of time during the Early Bronze Age I.

E. Braun, *IEJ* 29 (1979), 234–235; E. Braun and S. Gibson, *BASOR* 253 (1984), 29–40; E. Braun, *'En Shadud: Salvage Excavations at a Farming Community in the Jezreel Valley, Israel* (*BAR*/IS 249), Oxford 1985; ibid. (Review), *PEQ* 122 (1990), 143; ibid. 121 (1989), 1–43; Weippert 1988 (Ortsregister).

ELIOT BRAUN

General view of area A.

'EQED, ḤORVAT

IDENTIFICATION

Ḥorvat 'Eqed is situated on a steep hill 2 km (1 mi.) east of Emmaus about 20 km (12 mi.) west of Jerusalem (map reference 1508.1382). On the east, a saddle connects it to other hills, but on the west, south, and north, it is bordered by steep cliffs. The site was fortified in the late Seleucid or in the Hasmonean period and can perhaps be identified with the fortress built by Bacchides at Emmaus (1 Macc. 9, 50; Josephus, *Antiq.* XIII, 15–16). However, its identification as a royal administrative center set up in this region for the royal Judean estates seems more likely (J.T. *Shevi'it* 9, 2, 38d). The earliest coins at the site are of Demetrius I and Alexander Jannaeus.

Overlying Herodian pottery and coins is a destruction layer from the time of the insurrection against Varus (5–4 BCE), when the area served as a center for Jewish rebels led by Athrongaeus (Josephus, *War* II, 60–63, 71) or from the time of the Jewish revolt against Rome, when Vespasian took Emmaus, in 68 CE (Josephus, *War* IV, 444–445). Secret underground bases were prepared here later, on the eve of the revolt by Bar-Kokhba's fighters, using existing cisterns, burial caves, and other rock-cut underground facilities. They also repaired the fortifications on the hilltop. Coins recovered at the site, which date from the third year of the revolt onward, indicate that the Romans recaptured the place in 134 CE or toward the end of the revolt. In the last stages of the fighting, the defenders probably sought shelter in the caves. The site was not reoccupied after it was destroyed for the second time. Some of the entrances to the underground chambers were sealed by the Romans to prevent them from being used as places of refuge in the future.

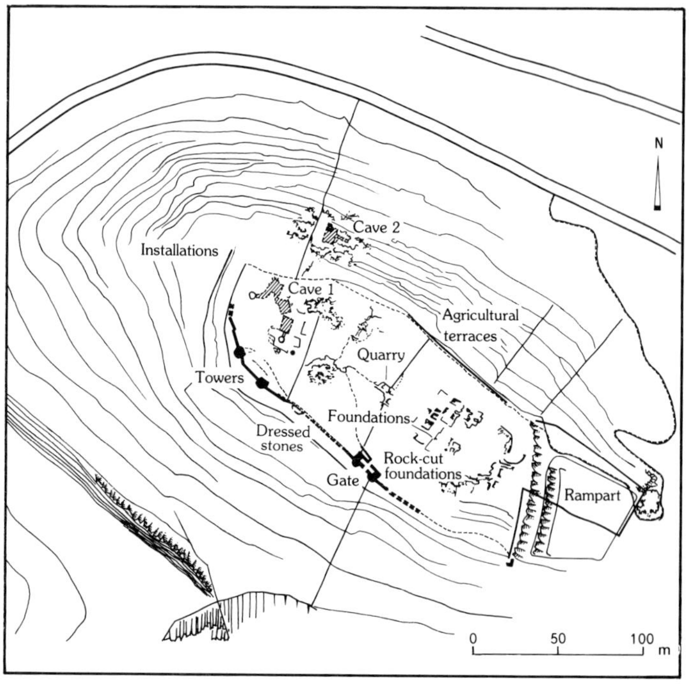

Ḥorvat 'Eqed: plan of the site.

EXCAVATIONS

The first salvage excavation at the entrance to underground complex 1 on the hillside was carried out by E. Damati in 1976 on behalf of the Department of Antiquities and Museums. Excavations on the hilltop, and later in the underground complexes, were conducted by M. Gichon, assisted in 1979 and 1980 by M. Fischer, on behalf of Tel Aviv University, from 1978 to 1980 and in 1983.

THE WALLS ON THE HILLTOP. The hilltop is surrounded by a defensive wall 1,050 m long that enclosed an area of about 400 by 150 m. A gateway and two towers were uncovered in the southern wall. Another tower and a stretch of wall 200 m long were exposed at the western part of the fortification. The wall still stands 7 m above its foundations. The gate was built of finely dressed white ashlars; larger stones were used for the towers. The walls (3.25 m wide) were faced with roughly dressed stones of varying size. At some points the wall is 2 m below ground level so that its foundations could be placed on bedrock, ensuring stability and strength. Furthermore, to protect the foundations against earthquakes and battering rams, retaining walls three courses high were built (at some points) against the outside of the wall. Wherever cracks and crevices were found in the bedrock close to the foundations, they were carefully packed with stones. Two passages (40 by 90 cm)—either for drainage or as emergency exits for sorties—cross the walls, one in the southwest and the other in the west.

The Southwestern Gate. The ashlar-built gate had a single passage (4.5 by 2.37 m) and was roofed by a barrel vault; it is preserved to a height of 1.9 m. Its original height, before the vault collapsed into the passage, was 3.1 m. The door sockets in the threshold attest to a two-leaved door (the iron sheath of one of the hinges is still in the western door socket). The gate passage was paved with stamped earth and had a guard room (3.8 by 0.75 by 1.7 m) on each side that was roofed with heavy stone slabs.

Two massive towers flanked the gate; their rounded fronts (4 m wide at the base) project some 1.25 m from the structure. They were built of large, closely fitted stones to a height of 2 m above ground level. The rooms were probably higher, in order to hinder penetration by the enemy. This device is frequently encountered in Hellenistic fortifications.

The Towers. Two more towers were exposed; both project from the wall inward and outward. The tower (4.68 m long and 5.65 m wide) in the southern part of the western wall was preserved to a height of 2.1 m. It was founded on bedrock and its lower courses were built of large, roughly dressed ashlars. Like the gate towers and the tower in the western part of the southern wall, this tower had no rooms on the ground floor. Like the gate towers, it is rectangular and has a rounded external face.

The Site Within the Walls. No architectural remains were preserved in the area enclosed by the wall, but a few piles of variously dressed ashlars testify that in the fairly recent past large, solid structures were dismantled here. Soundings along the walls did not reveal any remains, and it may well be that this belt along the walls was purposely left empty for security purposes. Only at one point were the foundations for a long structure (3 by 7.5 m) uncovered.

The many rock cuttings within the walls can be interpreted as foundations for buildings, quarries, or as agricultural installations. The latter as well as various agricultural installations around the site reflect the nature of the settlement and its surroundings.

Both the gate towers and the walls show signs of hasty repairs made during the Bar-Kokhba Revolt. Many arrowheads and fragments of other military

View of the southern gate, from the interior.

Southwestern tower, view from inside the fortress.

equipment were found in the debris from this period.

THE UNDERGROUND HIDING COMPLEXES. So far, two underground complexes have been partially investigated. The potsherds recovered date mainly from the time of Bar-Kokhba; a few sherds, including some from the Iron Age II, suggest that, in addition to cisterns, some of the caves are earlier. Complex 1 includes an entrance room, a narrow tunnel, and an inner chamber. The entrance room is an enlarged natural cave measuring 9 by 5 m at its widest point. Niches in the walls extend the cave area. The entrance to the complex, then as today, was hidden by dense vegetation. In the course of time, this entrance, as well as that of complex 2, was damaged. A winding tunnel 12 m long led westward from the entrance room to a bell-shaped cistern that existed before the tunnel. The tunnel is 55 cm wide and between 65 and 80 cm high, so that one person could crawl through the tunnel on hands and knees. Two niches allowed for the passage of another person. The maximum dimensions of the cistern are 2.5 by 7 m. The inner chamber (8 by 8 by 3 m) was hewn by Bar-Kokhba's men. A tunnel similar to the one described above, but shorter, led from it to a larger bell-shaped cistern. Both cisterns provided ventilation and served as emergency exits. Because the secret tunnels entered the cisterns at a height of 2 m above the bottom, the cisterns may have held water up to that height. This arrangement served not only as camouflage, but also provided water for those in hiding.

Complex 2 was entered through a natural crevice in the slope of the hill, which was enlarged to enable a person to crawl through it. This narrow entrance led into a hewn hall (22 by 9 by 4 m). When the hall was discovered, it was free of washed-in soil; its height indicates that it served as a gathering place as well as a storage space. Soot marks on the west wall of the spacious hall indicate that it was lit by torches. Two tunnels issue from this hall, one to the west and the other to the east. Both are full of alluvial soil. The east tunnel (2) was completely excavated. Its dimensions are similar to those of the tunnel in complex 2; it is 4.5 m long and leads into another chamber, basically a natural cave (as yet unexcavated). In both complexes, coins from the Bar-Kokhba Revolt were recovered. A. Kindler deduced from the numerous broken blanks and the like that a Bar-Kokhba mint functioned at the site.

The secret underground complexes here accord with the description by Dio Cassius, the Roman historian of the Severan period, who relates in his *Roman History* (epitome of Book LXIX, 12, 3) that "(the Jews) occupied the advantageous positions in the country and strengthened them with mines and walls in order that they might have places of refuge whenever they should be hard pressed, and might meet together unobserved underground; and they pierced these subterranean passages from above at intervals to let in air and light." The "subterranean passages" may be underground installations such as those at Ḥorvat 'Eqed and the "walls" are regular fortifications like those on the summit. The wish to keep secret the plans for the revolt suggests that the establishment of the underground complexes preceded the construction of the walled fortifications.

The underground complexes at Ḥorvat 'Eqed are part of the phenomenon of contemporary underground installations that have been discovered in different parts of the country. However, Ḥorvat 'Eqed served as a secret base for planning the unexpected attacks on the Romans that ushered in the Bar-Kokhba Revolt. Other sites, at least initially, were places of refuge for the civilian population. In this, Ḥorvat 'Eqed differs from other sites of this type, such as Ḥorvat Moran, Ḥorvat Midras, and Khirbet Daliya.

N. J. Cohen, *Hebrew Studies* (Univ. of Wisconsin) 20–21 (1979–1980), 51–53; M. Gichon, *Archiv für Orientforschung* 28 (1980), 235; id., *JQR* 77 (1986–1987), 23–29; id. (and M. Vitale), *IEJ* 41 (1991), 242–257; E. Damati, *Israel Numismatic Journal* 4 (1980), 27–29; A. Kindler, *Israel Numismatic Journal* 9 (1986–1987), 46–50.

MORDECHAI GICHON

'ERANI, TEL

IDENTIFICATION AND EXPLORATION

Tel 'Erani (Tell esh-Sheikh Aḥmed el-'Areini), one of the most important ancient sites in the eastern part of the Coastal Plain, lies at kilometer 19 on the highway connecting the coastal road (near Ashkelon) with Beth Guvrin, opposite the remains of the abandoned village of 'Iraq el-Manshiyyeh. Naḥal No'am runs south of the site and Naḥal Lachish north of it (map reference 129.113). The total area of the site exceeds 60 a., but its exact limits have not yet been defined (see below). The site consists of three parts:

1. The acropolis (the high mound) has a nearly flat top (c. 4 a.) and rises 32 m above the level of the surrounding plain (152 m above sea level). The slopes of the acropolis hill are quite steep, especially on the east and north. At the highest point of the mound is a small *weli*, the tomb of Sheikh Aḥmed el-'Areini, after whom the local Arabs called the mound. The *weli* is surrounded by modern burials.

2. The high terrace, stretching around the acropolis hill on three sides (west, south, and east) over an area of about 40 a. (including the area under the acropolis). This terrace rises about 15 to 18 m above the surrounding plain, and at its highest point reaches about 138 m above sea level. The acropolis is nearly 17 m higher.

3. The lower terrace around both the acropolis and the higher terrace, gradually sloping down toward and merging into the surrounding plain.

V. Guérin was the first scholar to visit the site, in May 1867. C. Conder, who was here in the 1870s, proposed identifying it with Libnah (Jos. 15:42;

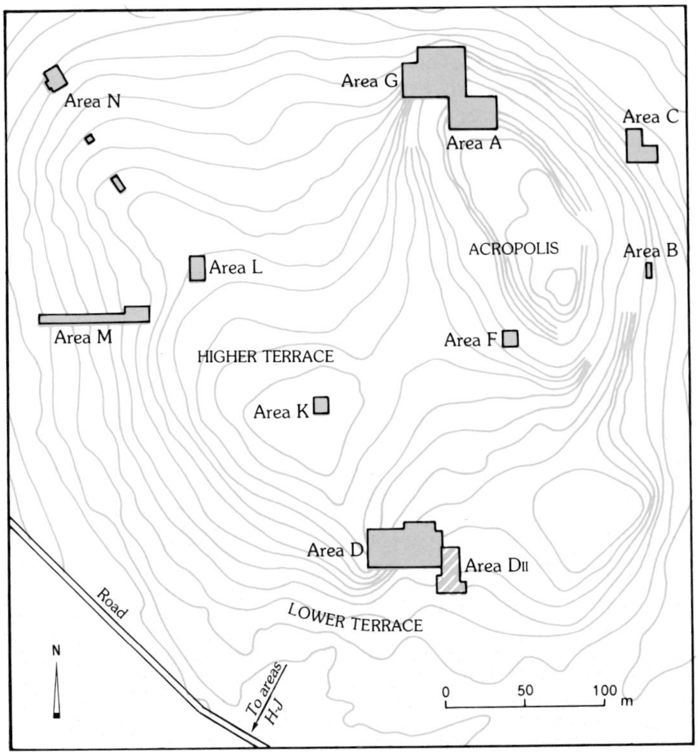

Tel 'Erani: the mound and excavation areas.

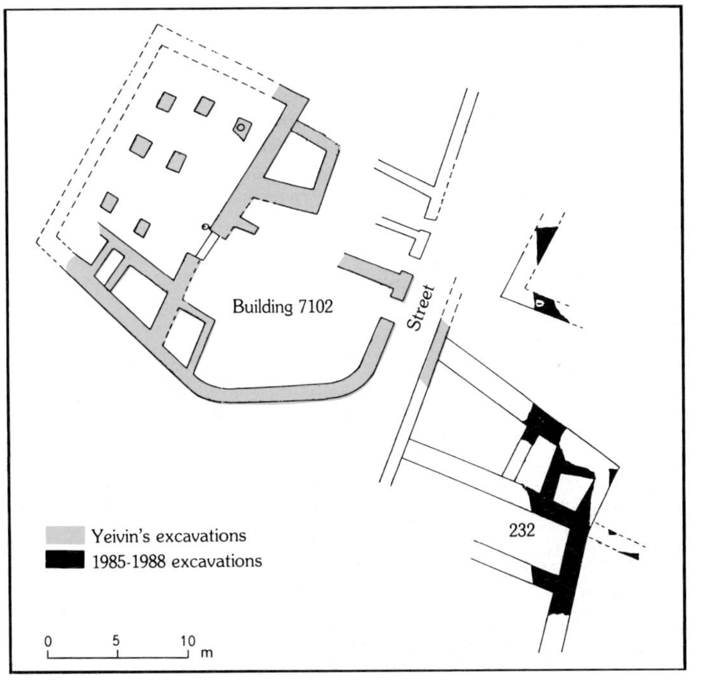

Plan of the EB I buildings in area D.

"the white one"), on the assumption that the settlement had been named after "the hills near it (which) are of very white chalk." H. Guthe was the first to suggest identifying it with Gath of the Philistines. W. F. Albright, who visited the site twice in the early 1920s, independently proposed (in 1923) the same identification, which was accepted by numerous scholars. The Israel Geographic Names Committee named the site Tel Gath. However, later evidence, revealed in the excavation results produced by S. Yeivin, invalidated that identification, and the site was renamed Tel 'Erani. An acceptable identification for Tel 'Erani has yet to be proposed.

HISTORY OF EXCAVATIONS

Six successive seasons of excavations (1956–1961) were carried out at the site on behalf of the Israel Department of Antiquities and Museums. The fourth season was held jointly with the Italian Centro per le Antichita e la Storia dell'Arte del Vicino Oriento of the Istituto per l'Oriente of Rome. S. Yeivin, who directed all the seasons, was assisted by S. Levy until 1960.

In the spring of 1956, a detailed survey of the site was carried out; it revealed ancient remains on the two terraces surrounding the acropolis. In the course of the survey, eight areas were chosen for excavation: three on the acropolis (areas A, E, and G), three along its foot (areas B, C, and F), one on the southern edge of the high terrace (area D), and one in the abandoned village (area H, to examine the possible site of the ancient cemetery). Areas B and E were not excavated. In the course of the work, another area in the abandoned village (area J, a monumental Byzantine structure) and four additional areas on the high terrace (K–N) were excavated. A trial trench was opened down the northwestern slope of the acropolis (almost to the level of the high terrace), south of area G.

In 1985, 1987, and 1988, further excavations were undertaken on the southern high terrace (area D), under the direction of A. Kempinski of Tel Aviv University and I. Gilead of Ben-Gurion University of the Negev. The purpose of these was to extend the area excavated by S. Yeivin to the east and to check the stratigraphic sequence excavated by Yeivin with new dating for the local and Egyptian Early Bronze Age pottery.

EXCAVATION RESULTS

AREAS A AND G. The whole summit of the acropolis was used as a cemetery in post–Byzantine times. In 1956–1957, about two hundred burials, dating from the Early Arab period to the seventeenth century, were uncovered in area A. These interments disturbed the upper strata on the acropolis down to an average depth of 2.5 m below the present surface. Potsherds and small sections of surviving foundations in this disturbed debris indicate that it initially included remains of at least three occupation levels, dating to the Persian and Hellenistic periods. Only at a depth of 2.25 to 2.5 m below the surface of area A did more extensive architectural remains begin to appear. These represented a lower occupation layer (stratum IV), undisturbed by the tombs of later periods. However, the stratum, as well as the one underlying it, was badly disturbed by round silos dug by the inhabitants of the Persian strata (III–II).

The pottery found in stratum IV dates it to the end of the seventh or beginning of the sixth century BCE, but no plausible plan of its architectural remains could be established. Although the underlying layer (stratum V) was also heavily damaged by the Persian silos, certain features could be observed. At different spots, remains of two oblong ovens full of ashes were uncovered. Both were lined with coarse clay, and near each small heaps of slightly flattened spherical pottery "sinkers" (covers) covered with ashes were found. Also in this stratum, outlines of a narrow lane (1.5 m wide) could be observed for the first time. It apparently led from the square in front of the gateway (see below) into the interior of the settlement.

On the slope of the acropolis, about 20 m west of area A, a small area (G) was investigated in the attempt to find the gateway to the acropolis. The remains of four superimposed fortification systems were revealed here. Of the upper three, only the stone foundations of what appeared to be casemate walls have survived. Below the level of these systems, and a short distance west of them, were the remains of a fourth defensive wall, built entirely of baked bricks. In it was a gateway (2.7 m wide). In front of it, outside the walled city, was a pavement of baked bricks, continued southward by a stone-paved approach road, completely destroyed at a short distance to the south. This defense system showed marked signs of a conflagration, which must have destroyed the walled settlement.

Because potsherds were very scarce, it was difficult to assign dates to the different systems of fortifications. To their southwest, the slope of the acropolis was covered by a continuous stretch of a glacis, built up of large, rectangular mud bricks covered by a thin facing of mud plaster. The glacis was laid over a layer of beaten earth that contained some sherds from the Iron Age I.

In the following season (1958), the connection between areas A and G was investigated. At the western edge of area A, ruins of a square structure were uncovered immediately below the surface. They comprised a square room (c. 3.2 by 3.2 m) with remains of a stone pavement in its southwestern part, and a λ-shaped corridor in the southeast and southwest. The structure had been erected over an artificial fill, rising (at the foundations of its walls) to a height of about 1.5 m above the level of the pavement of the square just inside the highest of the four fortification systems in area G. This must have been the town square in front of the gateway to the acropolis (inside the city), similar to squares uncovered in Iron Age strata at other excavated sites.

The lane that led into the city, traces of which had been unearthed in strata V and IV, probably started from the southeastern corner of the town square. It also continued to be observed deeper down, in strata VIII to VI. On the strength of the results obtained from the first five seasons and from the trial trench dug in the sixth season, the stratification in this area is summarized here.

Strata I–III. Stratum I consists of a thick conglomeration of disturbed debris, containing Hellenistic remains (fourth–second centuries BCE). In stratum II, corners of some rooms were uncovered with beaten-earth floors and pottery from the Persian period. Numerous remains of silos from the same period were found both in this level and in the underlying one (stratum III). These two strata belong to the late sixth or early fifth to third centuries BCE. A gap of some seventy to eighty years apparently existed between the occupation of stratum III and the underlying stratum IV.

Stratum IV. Stratum IV (Iron Age III, early sixth century BCE) had been heavily disturbed by silos dug into it from the Persian levels. However, parts of rooms and remains of ovens were distinguished, as well as traces of a lane leading from the gate into the city.

Stratum V. Stratum V dates to the Iron Age III (seventh century BCE). It also had been disturbed by silos. However, the remains of three large buildings as well as wide, pebble-paved courtyards—one with an industrial installation—could be partially traced. The finds include carinated, burnished bowls and fragments of jar handles stamped with *lamelekh* impressions.

Stratum VI. Stratum VI belongs to the Iron Age III (early seventh century BCE). This was the latest layer in which it was possible to trace the complete plans of houses: two adjacent, four-room buildings connected by a communicating doorway, both situated northeast of the previously mentioned lane. The walls were built of mud brick on foundations of one or two courses of pebbles. The outer walls were thicker than the inner ones. The longitudinal, lateral rooms were each separated from the inner courtyard (the room between them) by a row of columns(?) erected on stone bases. Near the eastern building, on the pavement of the lane, fragments of a four-handled jar were found; each handle was stamped with the impression *lamelekh*/*ḥbrn* above and a four-winged scarab. The number of sherds of carinated, burnished bowls diminished considerably in this stratum.

Stratum VII. Stratum VII also belongs to the Iron Age III (late eighth–early seventh centuries BCE). Under the buildings of stratum VI lay remains of two structures with adjacent inner courtyards. Each was surrounded on its other three sides by a row of rooms, one deep on the southwestern side and two deep

General view of area A.

Left: *pottery vessels from the Late Chalcolithic period;* ***(center)*** *pottery vessel engraved with a* serekh *possibly denoting the name of the Egyptian king Narmer;* ***(right)*** *crude cylindrical pottery vessel, Late Chalcolithic period.*

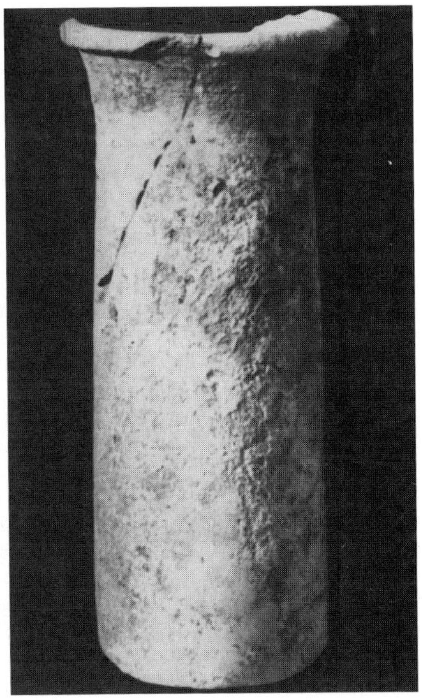

both on the northwestern and northeastern sides. The houses were entered from the lane through doorways in the southern corner of the western building and near the western corner of the eastern building. Each doorway led into a long corridor that communicated with its inner courtyard by means of a second doorway at its opposite end, thus forming an indirect access to the house. In the courtyards there seem to have been sheds with roofs supported on wooden(?) poles that left visible holes in the ground. The lane near the entrances to the buildings was paved with pebbles, and its western part was covered with a thick, hardened lime plaster. A group of pottery vessels found smashed on the floor in one of the rooms of the northwestern building fully established the date of this stratum. Dating was further confirmed by the paleographic evidence of a Hebrew graffito incised on the shoulder of a broken pot, which read *lyḥz'* (belonging to yḥz').

Stratum VIII. Stratum VIII apparently also belongs to the Iron Age III (eighth century BCE). Under the northwestern inner-courtyard building in stratum VIII the remains of a similar structure were uncovered; its courtyard showed signs of two building phases. Remains of another similar building were found under the adjacent house, to the southeast.

Stratum IX. At a depth of some 10 to 15 cm below the foundations of the stratum VIII building, an extensive area of whitewashed mud plaster was uncovered on which no signs of buildings were visible. Near the northern end of the lane, where it opened onto the square in front of the town gate, a rectangular pit was found almost full of slaked lime—undoubtedly the source of the whitewash covering the whole of the area east of the lane. The purpose of this area is not clear, but it seems that it covered a deep earthen fill. This is the only way to account for the sagging of the northwestern corner of the western building in stratum VII, which broke up (diagonally) the paving across a room into two levels and lowered the central part of the western building in stratum VI, tearing its southern wall away from its western one. It seems probable that the uppermost of the casemate systems of fortification in area G (see above) and the paved open square in front of its gateway belong to stratum X—that is, to the stratum beneath the whitewashed mud plaster-covered fill.

Industrial Installations. In the courtyards of all the superimposed buildings in strata VIII to V in area A, remains of industrial installations were found. The stratum V installations were destroyed beyond any possibility of examination. All the installations in strata VII and VI, however, were similar. Each consisted of an oblong structure, plastered and whitewashed on the outside, about 1 m high. The upper surface of each structure showed an oval depression, also plastered and whitewashed. In the center was a slightly raised clay collar surrounding a deeper oval hollow, both mud plastered and whitewashed.

AREAS C AND F. Area C (at the foot of the acropolis, on the north) and area F (on the south) were examined for traces of a possible fosse round the defenses of the acropolis, but none were found. In area F a small area paved with pebbles was uncovered, at some depth, with Iron Age I pottery on it. This may indicate temporary squatting by a seminomadic population.

AREAS H AND J. No traces of ancient burials were found in area H. To the northwest, however, in area J, there were fairly well-preserved remains of a large stone tomb from the Byzantine period that contained numerous disturbed burials (including skulls).

SHMUEL YEIVIN

AREA D. The significance of area D is that it was here that both expeditions—Yeivin's and Kempinski and Gilead's—were able to examine the development of the early settlement which existed here from the end of the fourth to the first third of the third millennia. In addition, two *favissae* from the Persian period and two tombs from the end of the Late Bronze Age (thirteenth century BCE) were uncovered. In the southern part of the area, the edge of a Byzantine cemetery was also found. It was partially excavated by Yeivin and later reexamined by D. Ussishkin. The discovery of the two Late Bronze Age tombs probably indicates that the small contemporary settlement was located on the acropolis.

Yeivin was of the opinion that the early strata at Tel 'Erani contained evidence of cultural continuity from the end of the Chalcolithic period to the earliest phase of the Early Bronze Age I. The results of the latest trial excavations show that there is no cultural continuity here, in the accepted sense of the term, although some pottery has been found that can be regarded as continuations of Chalcolithic prototypes. Yeivin also identified certain ceramic types, of Egyptian origin although made at Tel 'Erani, as vessels made in the Chalcolithic tradition. However, the ceramic assemblage, both local and foreign, and the settlement itself show that a new period had started—the

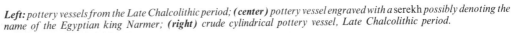

Corner of an EB II structure.

Early Bronze Age I. The few Chalcolithic sherds found in the trial excavations (1985–1988) had been carried to the excavation area by erosional processes and seem to have come from a Chalcolithic site located on the high terrace or perhaps on the acropolis.

Yeivin distinguished twelve strata (XII–I) in his excavations of area D, the earliest of which (XII) he described as a stratum of a "dwelling-pit settlement," founded on virgin soil. In stratum VIII, he found a public building that continued in use up to the end of stratum VI, when it was destroyed in a fierce conflagration. Another public building was erected above it in stratum V, which continued in use, with many modifications, until stratum II, toward the end of the Early Bronze Age II.

In stratum I, from the Early Bronze Age III, the plan and traces of the earlier settlement were still visible to a certain extent. Yeivin found several phases here in the best-preserved area, the upper part of area D. B. Brandl, in his analysis of Yeivin's excavations, has suggested that stratum I contains the remains of rectangular ramps and fills of mud-brick material, like the ramps and stone fill excavated at Tel Jarmuth. He interprets them as the defensive wall of the Early Bronze Age III town. This analysis is currently based only on Yeivin's plans and has not been tested by excavation.

The aim of the more recent excavations (1985–1988) was to examine the stratigraphy and chronology suggested by Yeivin and his team and other scholars who had analyzed the excavation and its results. Of particular interest also was the site's close ties with predynastic Egypt and the issue of the beginning of urbanization in southern Canaan. The new excavations and the reevaluation of Yeivin's stratigraphic sequence were based on a central section, which ran along the western edge of the new excavation area, and on 4-by-4-m squares and dividing balks 1 m wide between the squares. The results show that in many instances the strata defined by Yeivin were actually different stages of the same stratum. Instead of Yeivin's twelve strata in area D, five definite strata (A–E) were distinguished.

The earliest stage was a settlement of small buildings, adjoined by pits dug in virgin soil. The virgin soil stratum was labeled E, while the stratum of pits and buildings was assigned the letter D. This stratum is parallel to Yeivin's stages (strata) XII and XI, and perhaps even X. The pottery from stratum D dates to the Early Bronze Age I; it includes hole-mouth jars, large and small bowls, some of which were made in the "Chalcolithic" tradition—that is, the late variant of V-shaped bowls. The superbly fired storage jars are of the southern type and are slipped with whitewash and painted with red stripes. Egyptian vessels or local imitations of them were found in this stratum. Several lumps of clay were also found, which bore impressions of seals of the type found at Naḥal Besor in the Negev.

Above this settlement was the first occupation at Tel 'Erani with the hallmarks of a city. It covered about 50 a. and was labeled stratum C. It included several stages and is parallel to Yeivin's stages (strata) X to VI. A large building (structure 232) in this stratum is identical in its method of construction, although not in its plan, to the nearby public building (building 7102) uncovered by Yeivin. Building 7102 (c. 20 by 24 m) had a paved courtyard at its southeastern corner; two rows of rooms were built on the north and west. The central room (c. 12 by 14 m) was particularly interesting; it contained seven pillars, whose square bases were found in situ. The new excavations uncovered a house to the east of this structure; the thickness of its walls and its method of construction were identical to those of building 7102. The building's northern row of rooms and central room have been uncovered to date. The mud-brick walls are about 1 m thick and were preserved to a height of about 2.8 m (both in the area excavated by Yeivin and that excavated by Kempinski and Gilead). The size of these buildings, their careful planning, and their centralized groups of rooms rather than isolated single-chambered units (as in other contemporary towns, such as Arad) indicate that the process of urbanization started in stratum C.

A carbon-14 analysis carried out on a sample from stratum C provided a date of about 3352 to 3090 BCE, which closely matches the date obtained from an analysis of the pottery—about 3200 to 3100 BCE. The pottery found in stratum C is very similar to that from stratum D. Here, too, well-fired, "metallic" fired storage jars with red-painted vertical stripes are very common. The Egyptian pottery includes tear-shaped vessels, open bowls, and baking trays. Several of the vessels were made locally, indicating the presence of Egyptians here. This stratum also yielded a lump of clay with remains of a seal impression, like the ones found at Naḥal Besor. The impression is too obscure for the name of the king or official to be read. Stratum C has been dated on the basis of the assemblage of local pottery, which is early in date but still within the Early Bronze Age I; the Egyptian pottery dates to the period before the First Dynasty. The end of the stratum must therefore antedate the rise of that dynasty.

Stratum C was destroyed in a conflagration; the mud-brick debris from its large structures filled in the buildings, creating an extensive, flat area on which the stratum B town was built (Yeivin's strata V–II). The destruction of these buildings undoubtedly reflects the destruction of the entire town. The new settlement was slightly smaller, as is apparent from the large areas not rebuilt, to the southeast of building 7102 and south of structure 232. The builders of stratum B made use of the projecting stumps of the earlier walls where these were preserved above the level of the mud-brick debris, especially in the northern parts of the structure. The plan of this area was now completely different: several fairly small structures were built above building 7102, the most interesting of which was a house with a corner courtyard. The pillars from building 7102 were not reused; another structure

Area A: four-room house, Iron II.

Clay Astarte figurine with a bird-shaped head, Iron Age.

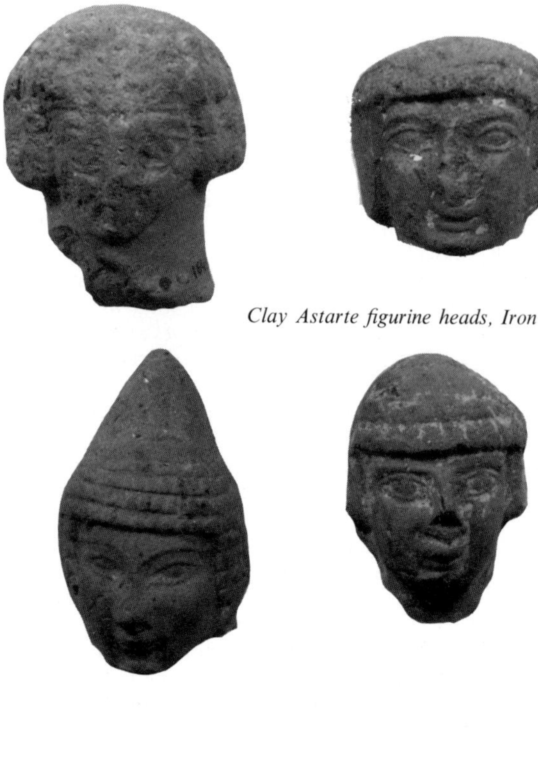

Clay Astarte figurine heads, Iron Age.

was built to its north, so far only partially excavated.

Above the northern part of structure 232, a building was erected whose plan is not yet clear. In the earlier stage of stratum B (Yeivin's stratum V), a sherd from an Egyptian storage jar was found, inscribed with the name of Narmer, the last king of Dynasty "0" of Egypt. Associated finds include many examples of cylindrical, white-slipped and burnished vessels, characteristic of the early First Dynasty period. Several sherds of these vessels were also found in the new excavations, which together with the Narmer inscription invite a date for the beginning of this stratum of about 3000 BCE.

The end of stratum B (Yeivin's stratum II) is still not clear, but judging from the ceramic finds, it may belong to the Early Bronze Age II. Stratum A (Yeivin's stratum I) is composed of several stages. Yeivin himself distinguished three building phases in the area excavated on the north of the lower terrace. The new excavations only revealed accumulations of debris from the Early Bronze Age III.

Two Late Bronze Age II tombs were dug into these accumulations. One is that of an adult and contains pottery and a scarab dated by Brandl to the reign of Ramses II. The second tomb was that of a young man. Some Iron Age II pits, which belong to the settlement on the acropolis, and the two Persian period *favissae* attest to the later occupation of area D: a group of clay figurines and fragments of stone statues from the Persian period were found in an eroded layer of clean sand (in a pit at the northeastern corner of area D); this seems to have been a *favissa* for sacred offerings from a temple whose remains are still concealed in the Persian strata on the acropolis or on the middle terrace. Similar finds were discovered in similar circumstances at Makmish and Tel Ẓippor. The Byzantine cemetery uncovered in the southern part of area D belonged to a relatively large settlement located under the modern industrial area of Qiryat Gat.

Fortifications. Such an important Early Bronze Age city must have been surrounded by a wall. The problem of its location interested Yeivin, and in order to solve it he excavated areas M and N. In area N, part of a wall was found that was attributed, on the basis of the pottery found above it, to stratum VI, equivalent to stratum C in the new excavations. Brandl believes that the wall and the two towers that adjoin it date to the Early Bronze Age III. This hypothesis is supported by the remains of mud-brick debris in area D, which Brandl interprets as a fill that served as the base for the city wall. In this writer's opinion, there is still no proof for this late date for the wall (as long as the strata adjoining the wall on the inside are unexcavated); it should be regarded as the wall of the stratum C city, from the period immediately before the beginning of the First Dynasty in Egypt.

STRATIGRAPHY AT TEL 'ERANI

Yeivin (1956–1961)	*Kempinski and Gilead (1985, 1987–1988)*
Post I, I	Stratum A
II–V	Stratum B
VI–VIII (IX)	Stratum C
(X) XI–XII	Stratum D
Virgin soil	Stratum E

AHARON KEMPINSKI

AREAS K–M. To ascertain the density of occupation on the high terrace, three spot areas were explored on its surface. In area K, at the highest point of the terrace (139 m above sea level), remains of some pavements were uncovered to a depth of about 1 m below the surface soil swept down from the acropolis by winter rains; at 138.4 to 138.5 m above sea level, remains of a potter's kiln, a cooking oven(?), and small sections of beaten-earth floors were uncovered, all of them dating to the Iron Age II. At a depth of some 2.5 m below the surface sections of Early Bronze Age II mud-brick walls appeared.

In area L, on the northwestern part of the high terrace, the surface of which was lower than that of area K, remains of mud-brick walls also were uncovered just below surface level. These also dated to the Early Bronze Age II.

In area M, southwest of area L, on the western edge of the high terrace, similar mud-brick remains belonging to the Early Bronze Age II included a broad stretch of a mud-brick belt. It was later identified (in the light of discoveries made in area N) as the ruins of the thick wall that had encompassed the city (see below).

AREA N. An aerial photograph taken before the start of the excavations showed a sharp and clearly marked boundary line between areas of differing colors along the northern edge of the high terrace. It was therefore decided in 1960 to examine this region. A trench was opened, running a long distance south of the edge of the terrace at this spot, up to the boundary line already mentioned. It was later extended far to the northwest, into the surrounding plain, by means of small, square pits.

At a depth of a few centimeters below the surface of the high terrace, mud-brick structures appeared in the trench (area N) along its entire length. Ceramic evidence pointed to the Early Bronze Age II. In the small pits

Figurine of a horseman, Persian period.

sunk in the lower area outside the border line, scattered sherds from the same period were found, mixed with alluvial soil, to a depth of about 1 m below the surface. The most interesting finds, however, were uncovered on the border seen in the aerial photograph, which coincided with the edge of the high terrace. Immediately below the surface, an extensive belt of mud bricks came to light. It soon became apparent that this represented a massive circumvallation protected on the outside (north) by a thick, mud-plastered glacis. Over the latter, remains of a small, square tower were uncovered (near the edge of the wall). West of it, at a distance of 5 m, were scanty remains of the eastern part of a similar tower.

This trial trench was widened in 1961. It was then ascertained that the thickness of the wall was at least 8 m here. On top of the glacis, a miniature juglet with a rounded base and a disproportionately large loop handle was found; it is characteristic of the ware associated with stratum VI in area D. It seems probable, therefore, that the wall already existed at the time of the stratum VI occupation. Trial sections cut in the inner and outer faces of the wall showed that originally—apparently in the occupational level corresponding to stratum VII in area D—a mud-brick wall some 2 m thick (at the rear of the later massive circumvallation) was erected around the settlement. A thin, vertical line of burned material along its outer face indicates that this original fortification was intentionally set on fire (by a besieging force?). It was rebuilt in its massive form by the settlers of stratum VI.

Although the stratum VI city had been stormed (there were traces of burning at this stage), the same system of fortifications seems also to have protected the stratum V settlement. On the other hand, the remains of stratum IV (in area D) seem to lie over the line of the wall (seen in the aerial photograph), indicating that the settlement was an open one, like that of stratum III.

A new aerial photograph shows that the northern end of the eastern fortification wall crossed Naḥal Shiqma, turned southwestward at a sharp angle, recrossed Naḥal Shiqma, and continued in the same direction toward the line uncovered in area N. Thus, the wall enclosed a built-up area of about 60 a.

Among the finds unearthed in area N, on the burned floor of the lower occupational level inside the wall (stratum VII?), was the almost complete horn of a mouflon, a wild sheep. It was, however, so badly burned it powdered to dust immediately after being photographed in situ. Another find was a group of copper scales attached to each other. Similar scales were later disovered in a treasure trove at Kefar Monash (q.v. Tel Ḥefer). These were found in the upper level of occupation inside the wall (stratum VI). In a burned layer outside the wall a copper ax of the Late Gerzean Egyptian type was found.

SHMUEL YEIVIN

Survey and identification: Conder–Kitchener, *SWP* 3, 259; W. F. Albright, *AASOR* 2–3 (1921–1922), 11; id., *BASOR* 17 (1925), 8; G. Beyer, *ZDPV* 57 (1934), 148f.

Excavation reports: S. Yeivin, *Encyclopaedia Biblica* 7–8 (Language Academy Publications), Jerusalem 1960, 224; id., *IEJ* 10 (1960), 193–203; 11 (1961), 191; id., *RB* 67 (1960), 391–394; 69 (1962), 395–397; id.,

First Preliminary Report on the Excavations at Tel "Gat" (1956–1958), Jerusalem 1961; id., *Oriens Antiquus* 2 (1963), 205–213; id., *4th World Congress of Jewish Studies* 1, Jerusalem 1967, 45–48; id., *JNES* 27 (1968), 37–49; A. Ciasca, *Oriens Antiquus* 1 (1962), 25–29; 2 (1963), 45–63; A. F. Rainey, *The Biblical World* (ed. C. F. Pfeiffer), Grand Rapids 1966, 573–574; id., *CNI* 17/2–3 (1966), 30–38; 17/4, 23–24; id., *EI* 12 (1975), 63*–76*; R. Amiran, *Israel Museum News* 8 (1970), 89–94; A. Slatkine, *Museum Ha'aretz Yearbook* 15–16 (1972–1973), 104–107; R. Gophna, *TA* 3 (1976), 31–37; id., *Egypt, Israel, Sinai* (ed. A. F. Rainey), Tel Aviv 1987, 13–21; J. M. Weinstein, *BASOR* 256 (1984), 61–69; A. Kempinski and I. Gilead, *ESI* 4 (1985), 29–30; 7–8 (1988–1989), 58–59; id., *IEJ* 38 (1988), 88–90; id., *TA* 18 (1991), 164–191; A. Kempinski, *The Nile Delta in Transition, 4th–3rd Millennium B.C.: Abstracts* (ed. M. Azmi), Cairo 1990; S. A. Rosen, *IEJ* 38 (1988), 105–116; M. Wright, *BA* 48 (1985), 240–253; N. Porat, *Bulletin of the Egyptological Seminar* 8 (1986–1987), 109–129; Weippert 1988 (Ortsregister); *L'Urbanisation de la Palestine à l'Age du Bronze Ancien* (*BAR*/IS 527, ed. P. de Miroschedji), Oxford 1989, 163–168 (A. Kempinski); 357–387 (B. Brandl); 423–432 (S. P. Tutundzic); A. Ben-Tor, *BASOR* 281 (1991), 3–10; A. Miller Rosen, *TA* 18 (1991), 192–204.

'ERAV, ḤORVAT

IDENTIFICATION

Ḥorvat 'Erav (Khirbet 'Iribbin) is located in upper Galilee on a hill 490 m above sea level, about 1.5 km (1 mi.) east of Kibbutz Adamit (map reference 1716.2764). The site should probably be identified with either Rosh Maya or Bikhrah, both settlements in the Tyre district mentioned in the Talmud. Ḥorvat 'Erav was surveyed in 1981–1982 by Z. Ilan, who also headed excavations at the site from 1982 to 1984—the first on the Adamit plateau—on behalf of the Israel Department of Antiquities and Museums. The survey recorded numerous houses, caves, cisterns, and pools; decorated architectural elements; a stone (tombstone?) with a Greek inscription; a lintel bearing a *tabula ansata* that contains an incised geometric pattern and a cross; and several pairs of oil-press posts, some of them in situ. The pottery collected on the site dates to the Iron Age II, the Hellenistic, Byzantine, Early Arab, and Medieval periods. During the survey, a Byzantine church at the northeastern end of the settlement was measured, and another church, which was discovered in the southwest of the early settlement, was excavated. The existence of two churches in what had presumably been a Jewish village reflects a situation typical at other early Jewish settlements in the region (such as at Ḥanita and Beẓet), which contained churches but no Jewish remains.

THE CHURCHES

EASTERN CHURCH. The eastern church is a basilical structure (16 by 20 m) that is part of a larger complex with several rooms to the south, one of which may have served as a chapel. The church has a rounded central apse flanked by square apses. The prayer hall is divided by two rows of columns into a nave and aisles. Most of the columns were recovered on the site and two are still standing in situ. A stone with a *tabula ansata* containing an incised figure of a woman—a saint or an empress—was found in the central of the three entrances in the western facade. Close by was the altar of the church, which has a design of triangles incised on its upper part (0.45 by 1 m). A colorful mosaic pavement was uncovered in the northern aisle. In the atrium, a vaulted cistern has survived in its entirety.

WESTERN CHURCH. The western church (14.1 by 17.9 m) is oriented east to west. Only half of it was uncovered in the excavations. It is located in the center of an enclosed area, possibly a monastery, whose southern wall is built close to the cliff of Naḥal Beẓet. Slightly below the cliff's edge are Byzantine hermit cells. The prayer hall was divided by two rows of five columns each into a nave and two aisles. The columns stood on pedestals carved in relief, some with crosses that were defaced at a later period. Four capitals were also found: one is Ionic, another bears a relief of a temple facade, and the others are carved with crosses. A large bema, 0.4 m above the nave floor, was uncovered in the eastern half of the hall. There were three apses in the eastern wall—a large central apse with two plastered benches (synthronon), flanked by smaller apses, with a niche in the upper part. The hall was paved with fine mosaics (132 tesserae per sq dm), in which red and blue predominate, in geometric and floral designs.

Three entrances were uncovered in the church's southern wall, the easternmost of which apparently led to a chapel. To the north of the hall is a cistern, and a second one is in the atrium, west of the narthex. The fill above the pavement contained hundreds of pottery oil lamps from the Arab period, including dozens of whole ones. Five types of lamps could be discerned, the most common being the beehive type; glazed lamps were also found. Remains of buildings from the Mameluke period are visible on top of this fill. The building was probably erected in the Late Byzantine period, in the sixth to seventh centuries, and continued in use during the Early Arab period. In the Crusader period, the place came into use again, apparently as a pilgrimage site, but not necessarily as an active church. The settlement here during this period was integrated into the grouping of rural settlements that existed at that time in the region.

Z. Ilan, *ESI* 1 (1982), 26–27; 6 (1987–1988), 53–54.

ZVI ILAN

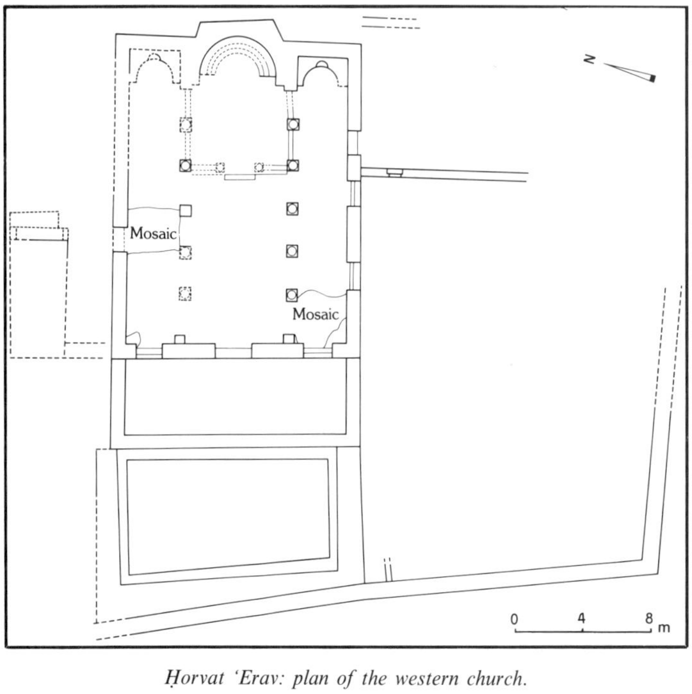

Ḥorvat 'Erav: plan of the western church.

Above: *capital bearing a relief of a temple facade, from the western church.*

Western church: part of the mosaic floor in the southern aisle.

ESDAR, TELL

IDENTIFICATION

Tell Esdar is a loess hill, approximately 5 a. in area, situated on the west bank of the Aroer Valley, midway between Beersheba and Dimona (map reference 1475.0645) in the Negev desert. The remains of several periods of settlement are visible on the surface of the hill. The site attracted settlers because of the underground water in the bed of the nearby valley. Tell Esdar was first discovered by N. Glueck in 1956.

EXCAVATIONS

A salvage excavation was conducted at the site in December 1963 and January 1964 under the direction of M. Kochavi, on behalf of the Israel Department of Antiquities. The remains on the surface were examined, and a trench was dug on the south side of the mound. Five periods of settlement were distinguished: stratum I—Roman-Byzantine period; stratum II—Iron Age IIA; stratum III—Iron Age IB; stratum IVA—Early Bronze Age II; stratum IVB—Chalcolithic period.

In stratum IVB the remains of silos were found, some built and some dug into the ground, as well as ashpits and floors. The stratum belongs to the Beersheba culture of the Chalcolithic period, as was indicated by the painted pottery, fragments of churns, flint axes, and an agate pendant.

Stratum IVA contained a collection of large fan scrapers, about 20 centimeters in diameter, which were decorated with various incised patterns. Scrapers of this type and similar incised decorations are known from other Early Bronze Age sites in the Negev. The ledge handles and rims of hole-mouth jars found are typical of the Early Bronze Age II. Stratum IV was encountered in all excavated areas on the mound, either as a single stratum of remains, or beneath the Iron Age strata.

Stratum III represents the most important stratum on the mound. It was the first excavated village that dates from the period of Israelite settlement in the Negev. The houses were built on the summit of the hill in a circle about 100 m in diameter.

Eight houses were cleared in stratum III, and the remains of another two were distinguished at surface level. The houses were built close together and apparently also served as a defensive wall. All the doorways were on the inside, facing the center of the circle. The remains of these houses had lain exposed since the time of their destruction, and they were severely damaged by erosion and agricultural activities. The plan of only one of the buildings was intact. It consisted of three areas, with a court separated from the living and working rooms by a row of pillars. Smashed domestic vessels lay on the plaster floors of the dwellings—testimony to the settlement's sudden destruction. Among the typical finds of this stratum were thirty-six storage jars, with high necks and pointed bases; chalices, found with lamps, suggesting that the chalices served as stands for the lamps; large jugs with a trefoil mouth, and shallow carinated cooking pots with handles. The pottery showed no sign of slip, burnish, or decoration. This stratum was attributed to the second half of the eleventh century BCE.

Stratum II was found only on the southern slope of the mound, where a three-room house was uncovered with stone floors and silos and two subsidiary buildings. The pottery with slip and burnish and the differences in the form of the bowls, storage jars, cooking pots, jugs, and juglets distinguish this settlement from its predecessor. The settlement was dated to the late tenth century BCE.

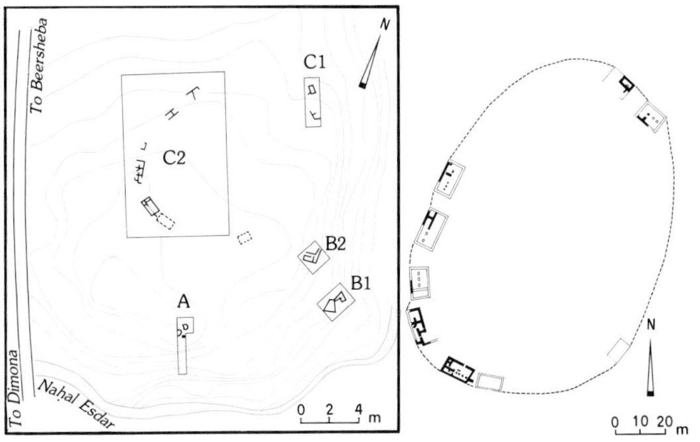

*Tell Esdar: **(left:)** map of the mound, excavation areas, and major remains in strata III and II; **(right)** plan of stratum III, Iron IB.*

To stratum I were ascribed terraces used in agriculture. Roman-Byzantine potsherds were found scattered over the surface of the mound.

SUMMARY

The earliest settlement at Tell Esdar (stratum IVB), is one of the many Chalcolithic sites of the Beersheba culture found in the northern Negev. After a gap in occupation, the site was again inhabited in the Early Bronze Age II (stratum IVA), a period of prosperity in the Beersheba Valley, the Negev, and Sinai. Only in the Iron Age, 1,500 years later, was occupation resumed on the mound. This settlement, stratum III, was apparently founded by the Israelite tribes and is one of the earliest Israelite sites in the Negev. The sudden destruction of the settlement may have been caused by a surprise raid by the Amalekites, with whom Saul fought to protect the Israelite southernmost settlements (1 Sam. 15). In the tenth century BCE, Tell Esdar (stratum II) apparently was a farm, one of the *ḥaẓerim* (unfortified satellite settlements) that took root in the Negev of Judah during such periods of relative calm as the reigns of David and Solomon.

N. Glueck, *BASOR* 145 (1957), 14 (site 308); A. Biran, *CNI* 15 (1964), 21–22; M. Kochavi, *IEJ* 14 (1964), 111–112; id., *Israel Youth Horizon* 7/4 (1965), 15–17; id., *RB* 72 (1965), 560–561; R. Cohen, *IEJ* 28 (1978), 185–189; I. Finkelstein, *JNES* 47 (1988), 244–245; Weippert 1988 (Ortsregister).

MOSHE KOCHAVI

ESHTEMOA

IDENTIFICATION

Eshtemoa has been identified with the Arab village of es-Samu' in the southern Judean Hills, about 14 km (8.5 mi.) south of Hebron (map reference 156.089). Eshtemoa was a town in the territory of Judah (Jos. 15:50) that was granted to the Levites (Jos. 21:14; 1 Chr. 6:42). David sent part of the spoils taken in his campaign against the Amalekites to the elders of the city (1 Sam. 30:28). According to Eusebius, "a very large Jewish village" existed here as late as the fourth century CE (*Onom.* 26, 11; 86, 20).

EXPLORATION

Building blocks decorated with menorahs and other motifs, discovered by various explorers in the second half of the nineteenth and the early twentieth centuries, attested to the existence of a synagogue at the site. In 1934, L. A. Mayer and A. Reifenberg succeeded in locating its ruins, and in the winter of 1935–1936 they undertook an exploratory excavation on behalf of the Hebrew University of Jerusalem; however, due to the political disturbances that broke out that year, work was stopped. At that time, the synagogue building was being used for habitation by the villagers, who built their houses on top, inside, and adjoining it. That made the excavators' work more difficult: the synagogue's plan could only be reconstructed on the basis of the sections that were visible. In 1969–1970, excavations at the site were resumed, under the

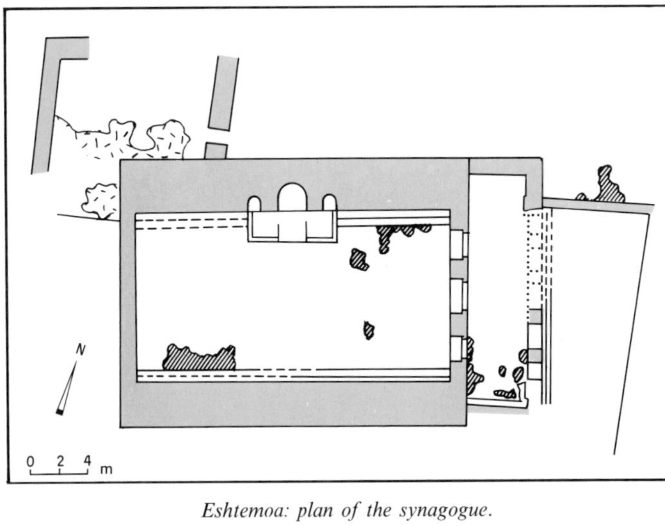

Eshtemoa: plan of the synagogue.

General view of the synagogue, looking west.

Western wall of the synagogue, from the outside.

direction of Z. Yeivin, staff officer for archaeology in Judea and Samaria.
THE SYNAGOGUE. The synagogue is a rectangular structure (inner measurements c. 20 by 10 m), with long north and south walls and short east and west walls. Its three entrances are located in the east wall. In front of the facade is a portico (15 by 5 m) that opens onto a well-preserved street or a piazza paved with large flagstones. The street is bounded on the north by a raised step at a right angle to the steps leading to the portico. To the south was an open piazza, and to the east is the local mosque. The remains of an ancient entrance are visible at the continuation of the mosque wall to the south. It is noteworthy that the alignment of the synagogue steps does not correspond to the alignment of the flagstones in the piazza, indicating that the synagogue was probably built after the pavement. Three steps (partly preserved in the southern section) led up to the portico that consisted of four columns flanked by two pilasters (the south pilaster is well preserved). The cistern next to the north pilaster is still in use. A stone bench is preserved next to the south wall of the portico.

The synagogue had three entrances in the east wall; the central doorway is wider and higher than the two lateral ones. The east wall and the doorways are preserved to a considerable height. The three doorways were set into a frame carved in relief that enclosed their tops. The facade's proposed reconstruction shows that this frame enclosed the doorways on three sides, creating a single decorative unit. The lintel of the central doorway is emphasized by a wider frame. The right doorjamb of the right-hand doorway is preserved to its full height, together with its ornamentation. The lintel set at present above the central doorway does not belong to it, and the east and west doorways are now blocked.

Stone decorated with a menorah.

The preserved height of the west wall is about 7 m; of the east wall (with doorways), about 4 m; of the north wall, 3 m; and of the south wall, 1 m or less. The long north and south walls are 3 to 3.5 m wide, while the west and east walls are 1.2 to 1.5 m wide.

The interior of the synagogue was a hall that was not subdivided by columns. Its principal elements were the Ark of the Law, the bema, and the three niches in the north wall. The records of the first 1936 excavations include a photograph of a niche and next to it an inscription in Hebrew letters, which the excavators did not decipher. In 1968, part of the niche was found destroyed, and nothing remained of the inscription. Steps probably led up to the ark from the center of the bema; they crossed the bema and reached the central niche, which was flanked by the two smaller niches. Presumably the central, larger niche housed the Ark of the Law, while the two lateral niches were intended to contain menorahs. Two stone benches, one above the other, extended between the bema and the east wall; the benches between the bema and the west wall are not preserved. Evidence of some construction in three phases was uncovered in this area, perhaps representing the remains of a high pulpit from which the Torah was read. Two stone benches are preserved along the entire south wall. The benches are cut by a miḥrab, probably built in the tenth century, when the building served as a mosque.

No traces of columns or pillars were found in the synagogue. The building could have been covered by a tiled gabled roof with a broad span supported by a strong wooden structure that rested on the two thick walls in the north and in the south. Close to the outside northwest corner, the remains of a room were uncovered that seem to be contemporaneous with the synagogue. This room was part of the group of structures that surrounded the synagogue building.

The local mosque is east of the synagogue. Remains of an ancient wall with an entrance in it are visible farther along the wall of the mosque on the south. Both the entrance and the wall correspond to the alignment of the pavement of the synagogue piazza. A rock-cut cistern close to the north corner, and next to the west wall, probably formed part of the synagogue's drainage system.

The Mosaic Pavement. The synagogue was paved with mosaics. Their bedding, which consisted of pebbles mixed with plaster, survived in the western section. Only a few scattered fragments of a mosaic with floral and geometric

Mosaic floor of the synagogue with the Aramaic inscription: "L'azar the Priest."

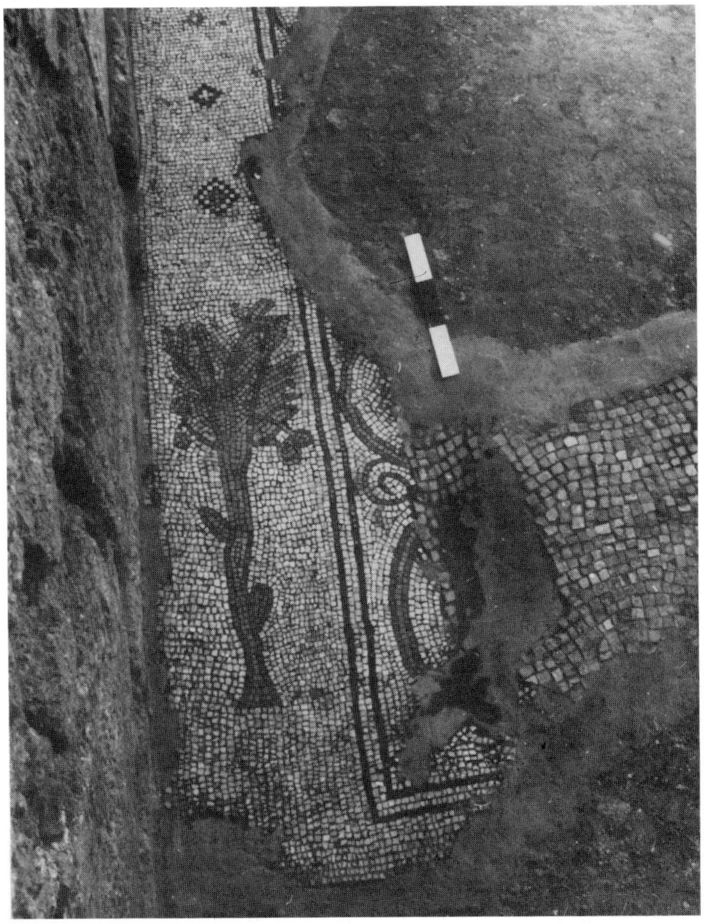

Part of the mosaic in the exedra near the eastern wall.

designs have survived. In a small section of the portico, close to the east wall and next to the doorway in the south, a five-color mosaic depicting a tree was uncovered. Several repairs are visible: the original mosaic was made of small tesserae (1 sq cm each) and was later repaired with larger (1.5–2 sq cm) white tesserae. Next to the miḥrab and under a section of the southern benches, remains were exposed of the later mosaic, done in large white tesserae. These remains attest to the construction or repair of the benches, at least in this place, in a later phase, following the repair of the original mosaic. A similar later mosaic was uncovered next to the east section of the north wall. Of special interest is a fragment of mosaic adjoining the second pilaster south of the portico. This mosaic contains an Aramaic inscription in small black tesserae (similar in size to those in the original mosaic) set into a white background. The width of the inscription was limited, because the mosaic artist matched it to the width of the pilaster it adjoins. The inscription reads: דכיר לטב לעזר כהנ(א) / ובנוי דינב חד טר / (מי)סין מן פעל(ה) (Remembered be for good L'azar the Priest and his sons who gave one tremissis of his property.)

A stretch of wall oriented east to west and built of smoothed stones without mortar was uncovered on bedrock, under the early pavement southeast of the synagogue. Pottery from the ninth and eighth centuries BCE found on bedrock attests to the period the wall was erected. This wall belongs to a large building—part of the Israelite settlement at Eshtemoa, whose remains are located among the houses of the present village and on the nearby mound.

The bema and niches in the synagogue.

Fragment of a marble menorah depicting a lion leaning against a branch.

THE SILVER HOARD. Adjoining the north wall of the synagogue is a room that was used as a dwelling until the 1968 excavations. Five jugs containing a hoard of silver from the Iron Age were found under the floor of this room, on bedrock. Two of the jugs were intact; the others were found broken, with their contents scattered. Three of the jugs are similar in shape and size, and two bear a one-word inscription on the shoulder written in red ink with a broad quill: חמש (a fifth part or five). In one of the inscriptions the letter ש is reversed. The hoard contains about 26 kg of silver, in variously shaped pieces, including a large quantity of shapeless castings, pieces of cut silver, and jewelry rejects (in a wide range of shapes). Some of the castings and pieces remained in the jugs, and some were stuck together in lumps, as a result of oxidization. A portion of the material was cleaned and examined.

The very large quantity of silver in the hoard would have exceeded the needs of a single individual or even a silversmith. Undoubtedly, the items were collected for the value of the silver metal, and not for their esthetic value. The pure silver content in various items reaches 70 to 97 percent. The pieces had been intentionally selected, for nothing but silver was found in the hoard. The silver castings are not uniform in composition, suggesting that they were collected from numerous sources. The items may have been taxes or spoils collected from different sources and their arrangement in five jugs may indicate five separate sources of the silver. The pottery jugs belong to an early phase of the Iron Age, from the late tenth to the ninth centuries BCE, a date that corresponds to the script of the above-mentioned inscriptions.

It is possible that the hoard is connected with the administrative system of the Israelite kingdom, established in Solomon's reign, which continued to exist after his death. The Levite cities, including Eshtemoa, played an important role in the royal administration (Jos. 21:14; 1 Chr. 6:42). Although the date does not correspond, mention should be made of 1 Samuel (30:26–28): "When David came to Ziklag, he sent part of the spoil to his friends, the elders of Judah, saying, 'Here is a present for you from the spoil of the enemies of the Lord'; it was for those in Bethel, in Ramoth of the Negeb, in Jattir, in Aroer, in Siphmoth, in Eshtemoa."

The earliest finds discovered in the synagogue area therefore belong to the Iron Age (tenth to ninth centuries BCE), and the latest finds are from the fourth to fifth centuries CE. Other finds date from the Middle Ages to the present.

L. A. Mayer and A. Reifenberg, *QDAP* 6 (1938), 221–222; id., *JPOS* 19 (1939–1940), 314–326; E. L. Sukenik, *Rabinowitz Bulletin* 1 (1949), 16; Goodenough, *Jewish Symbols* 1, 232–236; Z. Yeivin, *RB* 77 (1970), 401–402; id., *IEJ* 21 (1971), 174–175; id., *ASR*, 120–122; id., *BAR* 13/6 (1987), 38–44; M. S. Balmuth, *Actes du 8e Congres International de Numismatique New York–Washington Sept. 1973*, Paris 1976, 27–30; R. Hachlili, *BASOR* 223 (1976), 43–53.

ZEEV YEIVIN

Eshtemoa: jewelry from the silver hoard, 10th–9th centuries BCE.

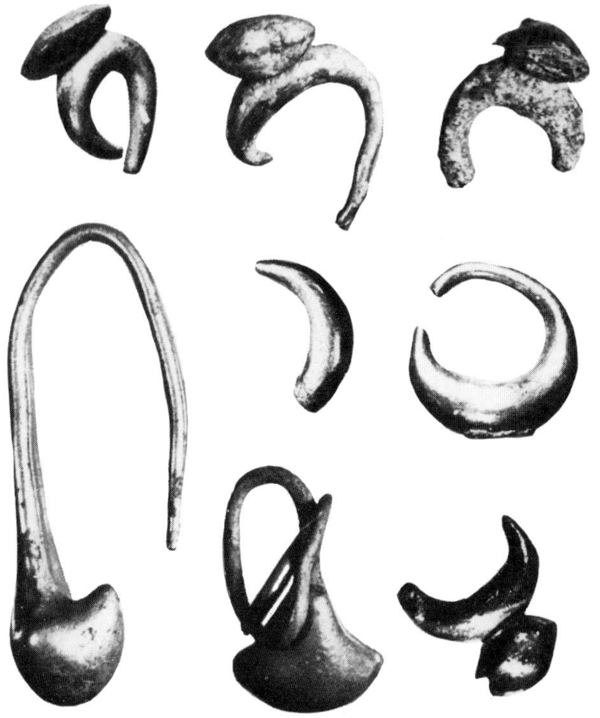

A jug from the silver hoard, 10th–9th centuries BCE.

ESUR, TEL

IDENTIFICATION

Tel Esur (Tell el-Asawir) is situated at the southern entrance to Naḥal 'Iron (Megiddo Pass) near the so-called Via Maris, about 10 km (6 mi.) north of Ḥadera (map reference 152.209). The site, which covers an area of about 7.4 a. and rises 7 to 11 m above the surrounding country, lies in the midst of an area of rich soil and abundant springs. In the course of a survey conducted on the surface and at the foot of the mound, potsherds were found indicating that a settlement existed on the site from the Late Chalcolithic or Early Bronze Age I period until the end of the fifteenth century BCE and again from the ninth century BCE up to and including the Byzantine period.

A. Alt's identification of the mound with Yaḥam, which is mentioned as the starting point of Thutmose III's march against Megiddo, is not shared by most scholars, who are inclined to identify Yaḥam with Khirbet Yamah, 13 km (8 mi.) south of Tel Esur. Alt later identified the site with Arubboth, a

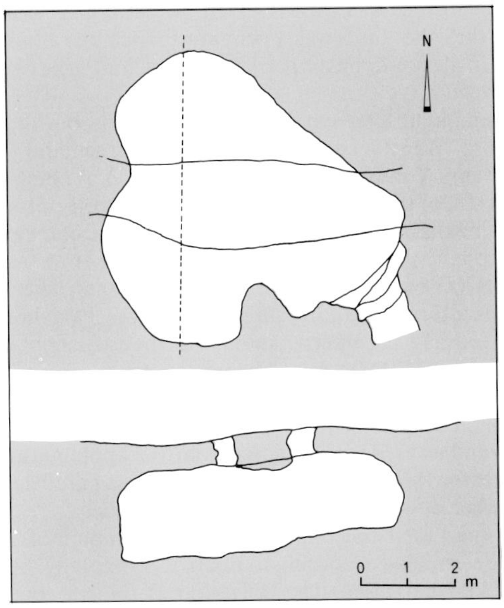

Tel Esur: plan and cross section of the burial cave.

Selection of pottery from the cave: ***(above)*** *red-burnished jugs;* ***(below left and right)*** *gray-burnished bowls.*

place included in Solomon's third district (1 Kg. 4:10), but this identification is unconvincing because no potsherds from the tenth century BCE have been found on the mound.

BURIAL CAVE

Several burial caves were found near the mound, especially to the east of it. One of the caves, found in the bed of Naḥal 'Iron, about 500 m east of the mound, was excavated by M. Dothan in 1953 on behalf of the Israel Department of Antiquities. The mouth of the cave was covered with a layer of debris. Underneath, five steps led to an irregularly shaped room whose maximum length and width were about 6 m and whose height was about 1.8 m.

MIDDLE BRONZE AGE. The upper burials, found at a depth of about 50 cm, contained skeletons and pottery. From the position of the skeletons and the distribution of the vessels, it is evident that the graves had been looted. On the basis of the potsherds, especially those of jugs and bowls, these burials appear to date to the second half of the Middle Bronze Age IIB, approximately the seventeenth century BCE. At a slightly lower level four pottery, Middle Bronze Age IA vessels were found but no remains of a burial. They evidently are the remains of an extensive burial area inside the cave that had been cleared for that purpose in the Middle Bronze Age.

LATE CHALCOLITHIC (EARLY BRONZE I) PERIOD. Two layers of burials were uncovered in the loose, moist soil at the bottom of the cave. It was impossible to distinguish clearly between them because the burials and the funerary offerings in both layers were mixed. Hundreds of vessels, many intact, were found, and in several places the bones of skeletons and a number of skulls were uncovered. The skulls were severed from the bodies and only a few bones were scattered among them. Most of the bones were found inside vessels that covered almost the entire floor of the cave. The condition of the bones indicates that this was a grave in which limbs were reburied (secondary burial). The burial offerings included beads, pendants, flint and stone artifacts, and copper rings. This burial layer, which was rich in finds, dates to the last stage of the Late Chalcolithic period (beginning of the Early Bronze Age I).

THE FINDS. Most of the pottery is similar to that found at other sites from the Late Chalcolithic, or Early Bronze I, period. The vessels were handmade for

Pottery vessels from Tel Esur.

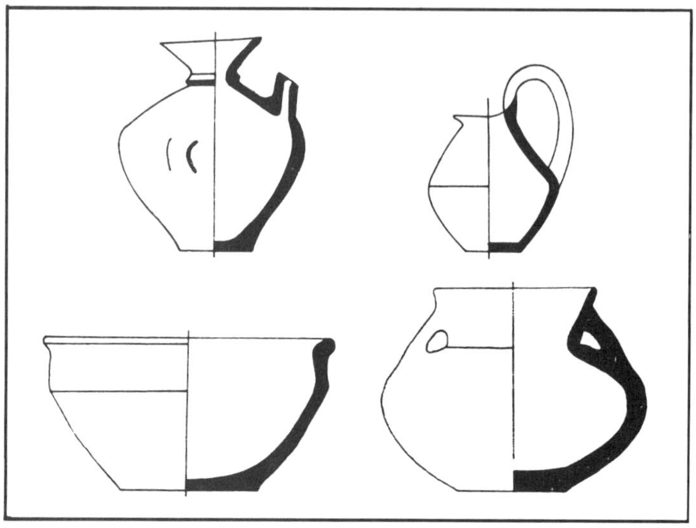

the most part, but some were made on a slow wheel (tournette). A few were burnished. The main forms include a jug with a high loop handle; a red-burnished jug with a spout and a ridged neck; a red-burnished *amphoriskos* in the form of a gourd; and a gray-burnished bowl, which is the distinctive hallmark of the period. Also found were a red-burnished bowl and pots decorated with paint, which are well known from this period, especially in the southern part of the country. Many of the pottery types are derived from the Ghassulian culture, but they were also prevalent in the Late Chalcolithic period and the beginning of the Early Bronze Age. Parallels are also found in the pre-dynastic cultures of Egypt (Gerzeh, Ma'adi) and Mesopotamia (Uruk). Among the other finds was a pendant shaped like a bull's head, which had its origin in the pre-dynastic period in Egypt, and three rings made of almost pure copper.

Human bones were found in at least sixty-five pottery vessels, but there must have been many more. Many vessels were found overturned and the bones scattered beside them. A minimum estimate, based on a count of complete sets of human teeth, of the number of people buried in the pottery vessels would be 38; the maximum estimate is 105. Of the four complete skulls, two are dolichocephalic and two brachycephalic (Alpine).

THE RELATIVE AND ABSOLUTE CHRONOLOGY. The finds in the earliest layer of the grave indicate that the culture of the early stage of the Late Chalcolithic (Early Bronze Age I) period had been perpetuated, but they also contain elements belonging to the Early Bronze Age. The pottery from this phase found at Tel Esur shows characteristics of both the southern and northern parts of the country. Several objects clearly exhibit an Egyptian origin. A communal burial of limbs and severed heads, known from Mesopotamia and Egypt, was uncovered here for the first time in Israel. Its closest parallels in the country are in a number of cemeteries at Jericho and Gezer.

The date of the grave, the Late Chalcolithic period or beginning of the Early Bronze Age I, was determined according to relative chronology, by a comparative study of finds from parallel sites: Tell el-Far'ah (North), Beth-Shean (stratum XVI), Megiddo (part of stratum XIX and stages 6–7), Jericho (part of stratum VII), various graves at site H in Naḥal Besor, and others. On the basis of Egyptian chronology, the absolute date of the grave can be fixed in the thirty-second century BCE, a date that tallies with the results obtained from a carbon-14 examination of grave A-94 at Jericho, where the finds were similar.

M. Dothan, *IEJ* 3 (1953), 263; J. Leibovitch, *CNI* 5 (1954), 25; A. Alt, *Kleine Schriften* 1, Munich 1959, 102; D. Ferembach, *IEJ* 9 (1959), 221–228; R. Amiran, *NEAT*, 89, 99; Weippert 1988 (Ortsregister); *'Atiqot* 21 (in prep.).

MOSHE DOTHAN

EUTHYMIUS' MONASTERY

IDENTIFICATION

Euthymius' Monastery (Khan el-Aḥmar) is located in the industrial zone of Mishor Adummim, about 10 km (6 mi.) east of Jerusalem (map reference 1819.1333). Cyril of Scythopolis (Beth-Shean), the biographer of Euthymius, provides an exact topographical description of the monastery. It was located, according to him, on a small hill surrounded on the east and west by two especially beautiful valleys that meet and converge on the south side.

HISTORY

The monastery of Saint Euthymius was founded in 428 as a laura (q.v. Monasteries). This laura was unique in its status and central location, and the number of its monks quickly rose to fifty. According to Cyril's description, a garden containing a reservoir was planted next to the laura's church and the bakery. In accordance with Saint Euthymius' will, the monastery was reestablished as a coenobium, containing a church and a refectory, as well as

Euthymius' Monastery: aerial view, looking south.

Plan of the monastery complex.

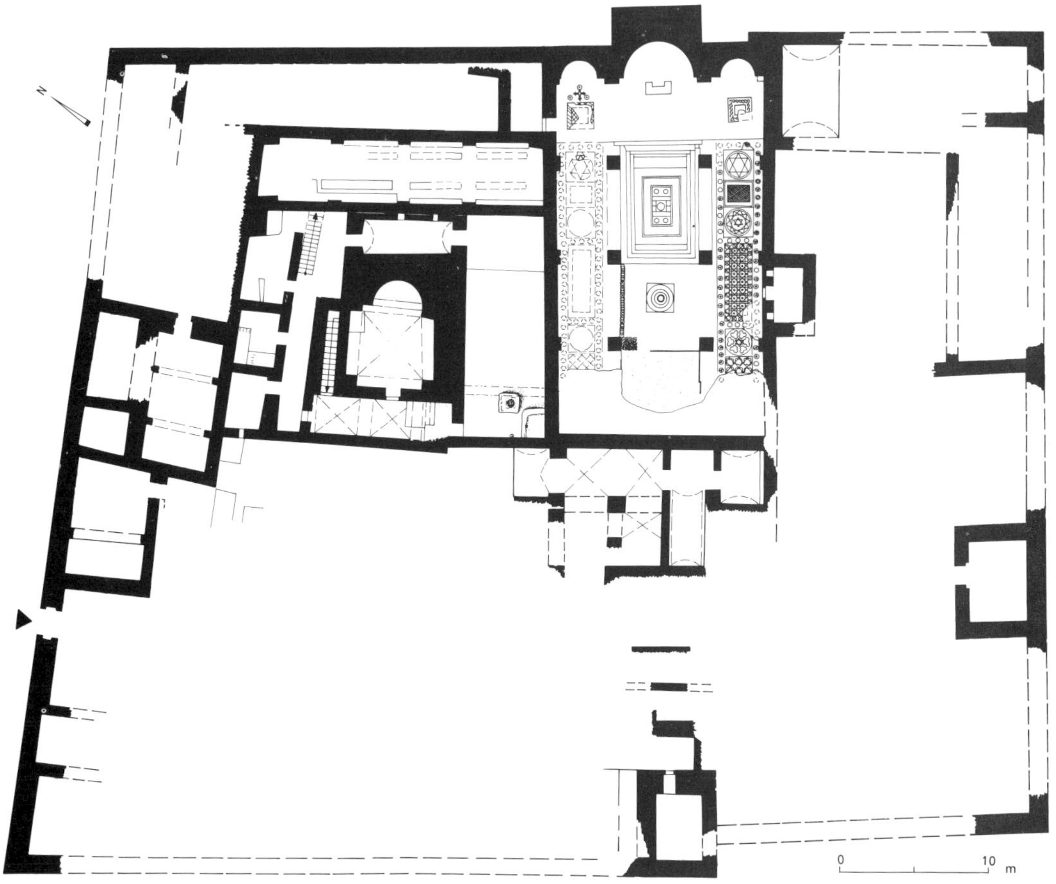

a tower, and surrounded by a wall. The coenobium was dedicated in 482 CE.

Twenty years after the Arab conquest of Palestine, in the summer of 659, the monastery was severely damaged by an earthquake that also destroyed Jericho and the monastery of Saint John the Baptist overlooking the Jordan River. Most of the remains visible at the site today belong to the repairs of the earthquake damages carried out by the monks in the late seventh or early eighth century CE. In the early ninth century, the monastery was attacked by desert nomads, the Saracens, but continued to exist. The tombs of Euthymius and of other holy fathers are mentioned in the work of a Russian pilgrim, Abbot Daniel, in 1107 (PPTS IV, 3, 35–36). In the twelfth century, extensive restoration and construction works were carried out in the monastery, including the repaving of the church, the building of a chapel over the tomb of Euthymius, and he construction of additional rooms and halls. The restored monastery is described in the work of Iohannes Phocas, a pilgrim who visited the monastery in 1185 (PPTS V, 3, 25). The site was abandoned in the late twelfth or early thirteenth century and presumably became a caravanserai serving Muslim pilgrims going up to Jerusalem from the traditional tomb of Moses, Nebi Musa, in the Hyrcania Valley east of the monastery.

EXPLORATION

The monastery of Saint Euthymius was the first monastery in the Judean Desert in which archaeological excavations were conducted. It was excavated from 1927 to 1930 by D. Chitty, on behalf of the British School of Archaeology in Jerusalem. Chitty concentrated on uncovering the church and the structure of the adjoining crypt. In the 1970s, Y. Meimaris excavated here, extending the previously excavated areas. In 1987, excavations were resumed by Y. Hirschfeld and R. Birger-Calderon, on behalf of the Institute of Archaeology at the Hebrew University of Jerusalem. The monastery's successive stages were uncovered and the tower structure in its north wing was partially excavated.

EXCAVATION RESULTS

The monastery complex (65 m long from north to south and 54 m wide from west to east) is surrounded by a wall of ashlar construction. The entrance gate to the complex is in the north wall. It is built of stones with drafted margins and is preserved in its entirety (2.1 m wide and c. 3.2 m high), including the pointed arch at the top. The gate and the walls probably belong to the last building phase of the monastery, in the twelfth century.

THE CHURCH. The church in the east wing is the most impressive and prominent structure in the monastery. It stands on a substructure of three vaults. Soundings showed that both the vaults and the church above them were rebuilt at the beginning of the Early Arab period, apparently in the wake of the earthquake of 659. An extensive and comprehensive restoration of the church structure and its embellishments was carried out in the twelfth century. The church is rectangular (13.8 by 25.4 m) and is divided into a nave and two aisles by two rows of three stone pillars each. A colorful mosaic pavement decorated with geometric designs and animal representations is preserved in the south aisle. The style of the mosaics indicates a date in the Umayyad period. The nave, which is paved with stone tiles in different sizes and colors (opus sectile), is dated to the twelfth century. Chitty's excavations uncovered parts of frescoes on the church walls and fragments of an altar table, chancel screens, windows, and windowpanes.

THE CRYPT. North of the church Chitty completely exposed the crypt of Euthymius. In the Byzantine period, this crypt attracted many thousands of

The crypt, looking northeast.

Euthymius' Monastery: part of mosaic floor in the southern aisle of the church, Umayyad period.

pilgrims. Its location at the center of the monastery and the passages leading to it attest to the important role it played in the life of the community. Thirteen narrow steps led down into the burial chamber. The crypt consists of a central chamber and a smaller adjoining chamber to the west of it. The main hall is rectangular (4.7 by 5.8 m) and its walls and vaulted ceiling are built of fine ashlars. Nine masonry burial troughs (average length 2 m, width 0.5–0.7 m) were uncovered under the paving stones (most of which are missing). A few contained skeletons stacked one on top of the other, as well as funerary offerings, mainly Byzantine pottery lamps. According to Cyril's description, Saint Euthymius was buried in the central tomb. The second burial chamber was uncovered in Meimaris' excavations. A low, narrow passage connects the two chambers. The method and quality of construction of the walls and vaulted ceiling in the smaller burial chamber (2.4 by 8.5 m) are identical to those in the central chamber. Two large burial troughs for group burial, separated by a narrow passage as wide as the entrance, were cut into the floor of the chamber. The troughs are well plastered and contained the skeletal remains of more than one hundred monks, who were presumably of high standing or high monastic rank.

Passageways, a tower, a row of rooms (north of the crypt), the refectory, dating from a later phase, and other structures were excavated in the monastery, in addition to the church and the crypt. Many wings connected with the daily life of the monastery, such as monastic cells, storerooms, stables, and perhaps also a hostel (possibly mentioned in literary sources) are buried under mounds of debris, awaiting excavation.

Main publication: Y. E. Meimaris, *The Monastery of Saint Euthymios the Great at Khan el-Ahmar, in the Wilderness of Judaea: Rescue Excavations and Basic Protection Measures, 1976–1979, Preliminary Report*, Athens 1989.

Other studies: D. J. Chitty and A. H. M. Jones, *PEQ* 61 (1929), 98–102, 175–178; 62 (1930), 43–47, 150–153; 64 (1932), 188–203; Y. Hirschfeld, *ESI* 3 (1984), 80; id., *The Judean Desert Monasteries in the Byzantine Period*, New Haven (in prep.); R. Birger and Y. Hirschfeld, *ESI* 7–8 (1988–1989), 110; Y. E. Meimaris (Review), *LA* 40 (1990), 524–526.

YIZHAR HIRSCHFELD

'EVRON

THE PREHISTORIC SITES

IDENTIFICATION

In the 1940s, several prehistoric artifacts (among them an elephant's tusk and some stone implements) were found in the vicinity of Kibbutz 'Evron (southeast of Nahariya) in the western Galilee. In the excavations and surveys carried out by archaeologists and kibbutz members, four adjacent sites were discovered—all Paleolithic—that were later termed the quarry site, the orange grove site, the Zinat site, and the ha-Shikkun site. All are located in a drainage valley at the edge of the easternmost of the three *kurkar* ridges of the western Galilee coast.

QUARRY SITE. The quarry site is located in a *kurkar* quarry, within a stratigraphic section that is among the most complete known on the eastern Mediterranean Coastal Plain. It comprises the following layers:

1. At the section's top is a layer of dark or black clay, 2 m thick; the Zinat site is located within it, to the west of the quarry site.
2. A layer of gravel, 1 to 2 m thick.
3. A layer of red clay, 1 to 2 m thick; the orange grove site was apparently deposited in it, adjacent to and west of the quarry.
4. A gray-yellow layer, 2 m thick.
5. A reddish *ḥamra* layer, 1.5 m thick; the quarry site is located at its top.
6. A *kurkar* layer, 4 m thick.
7. A Miocene clay layer.

The quarry site was excavated in 1976–1977 on behalf of the Israel Department of Antiquities and Museums and Haifa University, under the direction of M. W. Prausnitz and A. Ronen, and in 1985 by A. Ronen. Three levels were uncovered, each containing concentrations of animal bones and stone tools. These levels may represent a single occupational horizon, from which there has been a vertical dispersal of small bones and artifacts. It seems to have been a butchering site of hunted animals or scavenged carcasses. The faunal remains include bones of elephant (*Mammuthus trogontherii*), hippopotamus (*Hippopotamus cf. amphibius*), boar (*Kolpochaerus evronensis*), deer, and hyena.

The flint tools recovered here include hand axes and flake tools. The hand axes are very large and thick, measuring up to 20 cm in length; they were shaped by the removal of a few flakes, which left deep scars. Some have sharp points and others have chisel-like points. In contrast, the flake tools are very small (most of them c. 3 cm long). They include a large number of notches and chopping tools. The presence of a large number of roundish limestone concentrates ("Elijah's watermelons") is noteworthy. These may have been used both to knap stone tools and to split animal bones in order to extract the marrow. The site's stone industry belongs to the Early Acheulean. Although the stratigraphical-geological data, the faunal remains, and the stone implements testify to the site's antiquity, its precise age cannot be determined. It is estimated that the quarry site is earlier than 500,000 BP. A primary reconstruction of environmental conditions indicates the proximity of a body of water (a wadi or swamp), on whose banks humans hunted or scavenged other predators' prey.

ORANGE GROVE SITE. The orange grove site consists only of surface finds. It is located to the west of the quarry, on dark-red soil that is attributable to stage 3 of the quarry's section. Here, several well-made hand axes were found, with more flakes removed than from the quarry site's artifacts; they exhibit a higher level of symmetry. This small assemblage is attributable to the Middle Acheulean, as its estimated age falls between those of the quarry and Zinat sites.

ZINAT SITE. The Zinat site is in a shallow depression adjacent to the *kurkar* ridge, within dark clay identical to layer 1 of the quarry's section. This is thus the youngest site attributable to the stratigraphical section. In 1949, the site

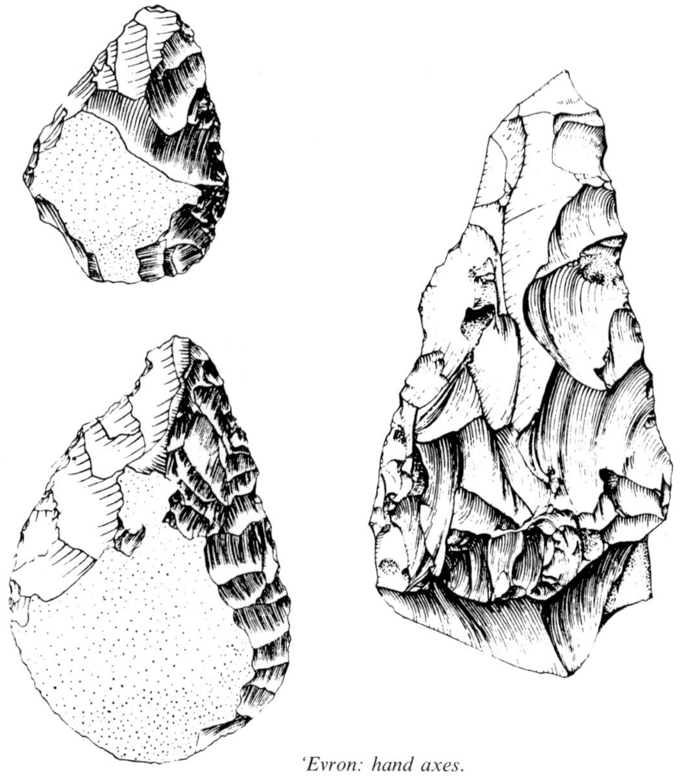

'Evron: hand axes.

was tested by M. Stekelis, and several hundred items were later collected by kibbutz members. The tools include hand axes and flake tools; both groups differ from those recovered from the quarry site. The hand axes, which measure, on average, about 9 cm, are symmetrical and well made. The flake tools, made in the Levallois technique, are mainly side scrapers and points. This assemblage is characteristic of the Late Acheulean. A broken elephant tusk is the only faunal evidence from the site. The shallow depression in which the site is located may once have been a swamp or a small lake, in whose vicinity hunter groups used to lie in wait for their prey.

HA-SHIKKUN SITE. The ha-Shikkun site was discovered in the 1980s by kibbutz members. It is located on a low hill at the foot of the *kurkar* ridge and to its east, a little to the north of the Zinat site. This assemblage, not yet fully studied, includes thin, delicate hand axes and many flake tools, mainly side scrapers, among which the Yabrudian type is prominent. This site may belong to the Acheulo-Yabrudian stage, which followed the final Acheulean. Should this be the case, the ha-Shikkun site would be the latest of the 'Evron sites. Worth noting is the location of the site on a hilltop, as opposed to the location of the other, low-lying 'Evron sites.

The western edges of the western Galilee drainage valley, adjacent to the *kurkar* ridge delimiting it, thus served for a long time as an encampment on the Paleolithic hunters' route. It seems that prehistoric man's preference for this area was related to its seasonal swamps or lakes, which attracted a variety of animals.

(See also Churches)

The prehistoric site: A. Issar and U. Kafri, *Israel Journal of Earth Sciences* 18 (1969), 147; M. W. Prausnitz, *IEJ* 19 (1969), 129–136; M. W. Prausnitz and A. Ronen, ibid. 27 (1977), 162–163; A. Ronen (and A. Amiel), *Paléorient* 2 (1974), 167–173; id., *ESI* 5 (1986), 33; D. Gilead and A. Ronen, *EI* 13 (1977), 56*–86*; Weippert 1988, 74–76, 664; L. Kolska Horwitz and E. Tchernov, *Mitekufat Ha'even* 22 (1989), 7*–14*.

The church: M. Avi-Yonah, *CNI* 5 (1955), 21–22; A. Jacques, *EI* 19 (1987), 54*–56*; V. Tzaferis, ibid., 36*–53*.

The amulet: R. Kotansky, *'Atiqot* 20 (1991), 81–87.

AVRAHAM RONEN

EẒBA' CAVE

IDENTIFICATION

The Eẓba' (Abu Uṣba) Cave is situated high above the riverbed on a bluff on the southern bank of Naḥal Oren, near the point where it emerges from Mount Carmel (map reference 1480.2385). The cave consists of three chambers: the first (10 by 15 m) is accessible through a corridor (c. 6 m long) and is penetrated by daylight. The second is smaller, and the third, the largest, is pitch dark. At the entrance to the cave is a small terrace with a radius of 18 m.

EXCAVATIONS

In 1941, M. Stekelis explored the Eẓba' Cave and discovered that its prehistoric occupants had settled mainly in the first chamber, which receives daylight; the third chamber contained only insignificant remains. A sounding made on the terrace yielded mixed finds: a collection of Roman-Byzantine sherds, Upper Natufian and Mousterian flint implements, and pottery similar to layer B material (see below).

Because the deposits in chamber I were undisturbed, Stekelis was able to establish their stratigraphic sequence:

LAYER A: up to 0.90 m thick, with black earth, contained modern remains.

LAYER B1: 0.90 to 1.15 m thick, with soft reddish-brown cave earth, contained flint implements, potsherds, and fauna.

LAYER B2: 1.15 to 1.65 m thick, with compact reddish-brown cave earth, contained flint implements, potsherds, and fauna.

LAYER C: 1.65 to 2.35 m thick, with stalactite crust and breccia, contained bones and Levalloiso-Mousterian flint implements.

LAYER D: 2.35 m thick, rested on bedrock.

Both phases of layer B yielded a culture that was named Uṣbian because of its unique characteristics. Although this layer was found only in chamber I, the abundance of its material made it the essential part of the excavation.

In layer C, about 350 objects were collected, including about forty tools, retouched points, and side scrapers. This industry resembles the Upper Levalloiso-Mousterian stratum B at Tabun Cave and stratum G at el-Wad Cave.

In layer B, the flint implements could be divided into two groups: one related to the Upper Natufian and the other completely unrelated to the Natufian. To the first group belong microburins, lunates with Helwan-type retouch, blades with inverse retouch, Natufian sickle blades, truncated burins, retouched microliths, scalene triangles, and various scrapers. To this group Stekelis added three adzes, similar to those found at el-Wad Cave in Natufian layer B1. The second group included primitive arrowheads with points but without tangs, as well as denticulated (sawlike) sickle blades made by the pressure-retouch technique.

The pottery found in this layer was of poor quality, handmade, and fired in an open hearth. Some sherds had been petrified by the infiltration of calcium carbonate. The few fragments found were rims, walls, bases, and handles, the latter including lug and knob handles. A few showed traces of red-brown, yellow-brown, and gray-brown paint. Others bore incised decorations.

In Stekelis's opinion, layer B represents a homogeneous culture belonging to a small, poor community that may have occupied the site for only a short time. The inhabitants were primarily hunters and fishermen, but the sickle blades, axes, and pottery indicate incipient agriculture.

The fauna of layer B was studied by G. Haas. Attention was focused on the microfauna, for it represented many biotopes. Because the cave is situated in a mountainous ridge, next to a spring and not far from the coast, the fauna represents a cross section of different regions. The amphibian species point to the existence of a spring near the site and of swamps on the shore. The reptilian remains belong to species living exclusively in Mediterranean evergreen scrubwood. The birds include rockbreeders, forest dwellers, and winter residents. The existence of a forest is proved by the presence of mammals as well as the absence of arid-region rodents. Alongside the forest dwellers, land animals living in open spaces, such as *Gazella, Hyena,* and *Equus*, are also found. Haas does not consider the preponderance of *Gazella* over *Dama* to be proof of climatic variation, for biotopes suitable for both animals existed side by side. Possibly, too, hunters preferred one animal to the other.

The biotope of layer B at the Eẓba' Cave is not different from that found on the site today, except that it had a much denser forest than at present. The faunal study shows the coexistence of forest dwellers with arid-land animals.

After the results of the excavation had been published, W. F. Albright and others contended that layer B was a mixture of Natufian flint implements with Neolithic or Chalcolithic pottery. They did not accept Stekelis's assertion that it was an undisturbed layer with very early pottery that could not be dated by its decoration but could be compared with a coarse, equally undatable pottery found by D. Garrod at the el-Wad Cave. In Albright's view, a Pre-Pottery Neolithic period existed between the Upper Natufian and the Pottery Neolithic as it appeared in J. Garstang's excavation at Jericho. Albright considered stratum B a mixed layer with both Natufian and Pottery Neolithic. The former included mainly the lunates with Helwan-type retouch and the sickle blades, and the latter the denticulated sickle blades, the arrowheads with pressure retouch, the adzes, and the pottery. In Stekelis's opinion, layer B was undisturbed and belongs to the Pottery Neolithic culture in which earlier elements were preserved, particularly tools of Natufian tradition.

W. F. Albright, *BASOR* 86 (1942), 10–14; 89 (1943), 24–25; M. Stekelis, ibid. 86 (1942), 2–10; 89 (1943), 22–24; id., *QDAP* 11 (1944), 115–118; M. Stekelis and G. Haas, *IEJ* 2 (1952), 15–47; M. Almagro, *Ampurias* 14 (1952), 184–186; Y. Olami, *Prehistoric Carmel*, Jerusalem 1984; Weippert 1988, 88.

OFER BAR-YOSEF

F

FAR'AH, SITE II

IDENTIFICATION

Far'ah II is in the northwestern Negev desert, on the bank of Naḥal Besor. It was discovered in 1972 by D. Price-Williams, and was excavated from 1976 to 1978 by the archaeology division at Ben-Gurion University of the Negev, under the direction of I. Gilead.

DESCRIPTION

The site dates to the Middle Paleolithic period. It is embedded in the silt deposits on the bank of Naḥal Besor, about 350 m east-northeast of Tell el-Far'ah (South). The land in the vicinity of the site is 100 m above sea level. Naḥal Besor cuts down into this plain to an elevation of 75 m above sea level. At the base of the sections cut by the wadi (dry stream bed) is a layer of pebbles 5 m thick. These are the remains of the former wadi bed; they contain flint artifacts from the Middle Paleolithic. Above the layer of pebbles, a thick layer of silt (19–20 m) has accumulated. The upper level of this layer is used today as agricultural land; it contains Chalcolithic and Early Bronze Age sites found by E. MacDonald. Far'ah II, rising 83.5 m above sea level, was covered by a very thick layer of silt deposited by Naḥal Besor. At some stage in the past, intensive erosion of these deposits created a badlands formation, particularly in the vicinity of the wadi bank. This process removed large portions of the deposits, under which the sites were buried. Flint implements and a living surface preserved under 3 m of silt deposits were recovered.

THE FINDS

Two layers of finds were revealed, each 5 to 8 cm thick. They were separated by a layer of clay containing very few artifacts. Seventy sq m of the upper layer and 13.5 sq m of the lower layer were excavated. The finds from the upper phase were scattered on top of a compressed layer of clay sloping slightly southwest to northeast. They included a large quantity of flint and limestone tools, animal bones, and charcoal particles. The fact that so many artifacts were deposited in such a thin layer indicates that the site was occupied for a relatively short period. The hunter-gatherers who used this site probably carried out a number of different activities in the various parts of the living surface. The surface was covered soon after the site was abandoned, so there were no major changes in the location of the flint artifacts and bones.

At the southwestern edge—the highest part—of the site, a small area was uncovered with a layer of reddish soil under a layer of ashes. The ashes contained bones and charred flint implements. It seems that this was a hearth used, inter alia, for cooking meat. In the 2 sq m to the east of the hearth, a large number of animal bones was found, in what was probably a refuse dump. Smaller amounts of bones were found elsewhere on the living surface. They indicate that the animals hunted included cattle, wild ass, large antelope, gazelle, and a large camel. Fragments of ostrich eggshells and thinner eggshells, perhaps of bustard, were also found. This is the richest collection of animal remains from this period in the Negev, where the soil does not usually preserve animal bones. The charcoal remains were identified as juniper. From the animal and plant remains, an environment with few trees can be reconstructed that is not very different from the modern landscape.

All over the living surface a large number of flint implements was found. They were knapped using a limestone hammerstone from small flint pebbles, found in abundance in the wadi bed. The pebbles were brought to the site and knapped, and selected flakes were worked to produce tools. This is evident from the fact that about thirty-five flakes, found within a radius of one meter, were collected and reconstructed into an almost complete pebble. From the 3,702 items sampled for preliminary analysis, 206 tools were identified, the most common among them being Levalloiso-Mousterian points and flakes (40 percent), natural backed knives (37 percent), and notches (8 percent). At other contemporary sites in the region, typical Mousterian tools such as scrapers are common, but at Far'ah II these tools are very rare (1.6 percent). While in the rest of the country the Levalloiso-Mousterian technique was widely used to manufacture points, flakes, and blades, the use of this technique was limited at Far'ah II. Of the hundreds of flakes, blades, and tools examined, only 5 percent were made using the Levallois technique. This phenomenon is also known from other open-air sites from the area of Sede Boqer. Dozens of limestone artifacts were also found, some of them charred pebbles and hammerstones. A few were also knapped and used as tools.

SUMMARY

Settlements from the Middle Paleolithic period, usually open-air sites, are scattered throughout the country. Most of them have been almost completely eroded and destroyed; except for a few flint implements, there is not enough evidence to reconstruct their inhabitants' way of life. A small number of open-air sites, particularly in the Negev, have been preserved in situ, and one of the most important is Far'ah II. Unlike other contemporary sites, both open-air and cave dwellings, the living surfaces have been preserved here just as they were left by their inhabitants. These remains reveal that the prehistoric hunters here engaged in tool knapping and food preparation. When the site was deserted, the surface was quickly covered. When the inhabitants returned they found a clean, new surface.

D. Price-Williams, *Nature* 242 (1973), 501–503; id., *Archaeological Theory and Practice* (ed. D. Strong), London 1973, 193–216; id., *BIAL* 12 (1975), 123–143; R. A. M. Gardner, *Journal of Archaeological Science* 4 (1977), 337–386; I. Gilead and O. Bar-Yosef, *IEJ* 27 (1977), 236; I. Gilead, ibid. 30 (1980), 52–62; id. (and C. Grigson), *Proceedings of the Prehistoric Society* 50 (1984), 71–97; id., *L'Anthropologie* 92 (1988), 797–807.

ISAAC GILEAD

Far'ah II and the badlands area near Tell el-Far'ah (South).

FAR'AH, TELL EL- (NORTH)

IDENTIFICATION AND HISTORY

Tell el-Far'ah (in the north, as distinct from the southern site, which is also called Tel Sharuhen) lies 11 km (7 mi.) northeast of Shechem, on the Nablus–Tubas road (map reference 1823.1822). The mound stands near the source of the Far'ah brook, which flows down to the Jordan River. It is situated on a rocky ridge that slopes in a southwest–northeast direction. Two springs, 'Ein Far'ah to the north and 'Ein Daleib to the south, supply the site with ample water. The fertile valley of Wadi Far'ah is the main thoroughfare between the Jordan Valley and the western mountain district.

Various scholars have attempted to identify the site with a biblical town. K. Budde, G. Dalman, and A. Alt considered it to be the Ophrah of Abiezer; F. M. Abel suggested Beth-Barah (Jg. 7:24); and W. F. Albright identified it with Tirzah. The latter view has been borne out by the excavations and is accepted today by most scholars. It is an identification based on the following considerations: Tell el-Far'ah is situated in the territory of Manasseh, which included Tirzah. In the biblical account of the daughters of Zelophehad (Num. 26:33, 36:10–11; Jos. 17:3), Tirzah and Hoglah are mentioned together, and the Samaria ostraca enable locating Hoglah not far from Tell el-Far'ah. Moreover, the archaeological finds at Tell el-Far'ah agree with Tirzah's biblical history. In the beginning, Tirzah was a Canaanite town (like Tell el-Far'ah). The stratum attributed to the Late Bronze Age shows signs of destruction, which can be regarded as the result of the Israelite conquest. Tirzah, as the capital of the kingdom of Israel, corresponds to stratum III at Tell el-Far'ah. This level was devastated during the Omrid capture of the town, subsequent to Zimri's seizure of power (c. 885 BCE). The fortress in the northwestern corner may be the king's castle mentioned in 1 Kings 16:15–18, which Zimri himself set on fire and in which he met his death. Omri was able to rebuild Tirzah and to set up his residence there only at the end of a four-year struggle with his rival, Tibni. The foundations sunk into level III probably belong to his structures. However, after two years, Omri transferred the capital to Samaria (cf. 1 Kg. 16:23–24). This explains why there are buildings in the area that were never completed. The royal household and military and state officials left Tirzah, undoubtedly followed by the artisans and merchants. It is quite possible that the town was completely abandoned for some time. This would explain the paucity of the interim stratum, apparently constructed after a short period of settlement. As the Northern Kingdom flourished under Joash and Jeroboam II, Tirzah, too, enjoyed a measure of prosperity. It is from this town that Menahem launched his attack on Samaria (2 Kg. 15:14). Stratum II represents this era with its magnificent structures and administrative headquarters. As some have suggested, these may have served Menahem, if indeed he held sway at Tirzah. During the Assyrian invasion of the Northern Kingdom (c. 732 BCE), the town was captured. The destruction in stratum II dates from that time.

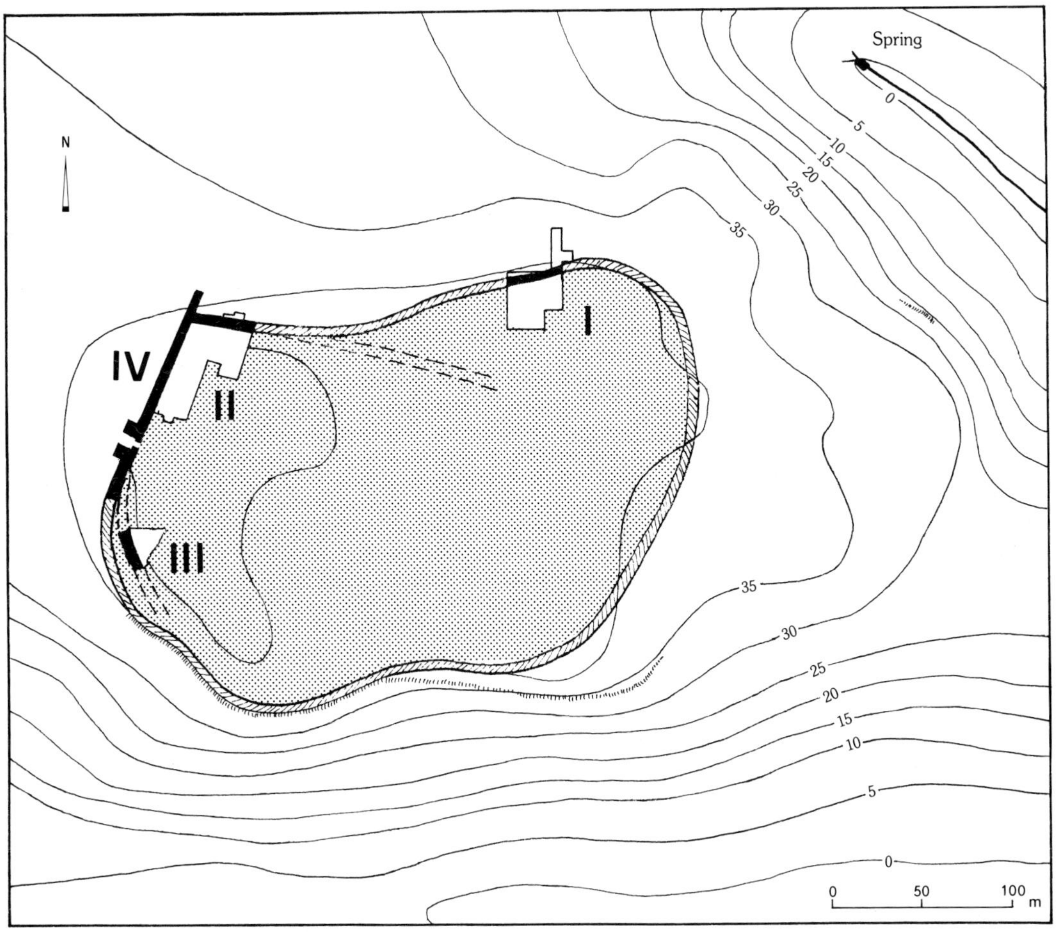

Tell el-Far'ah (North): plan of the mound and excavation areas.

The École Biblique et Archéologique Française in Jerusalem conducted nine seasons of excavations at the site, between 1946 and 1960, under the direction of R. de Vaux.

ROLAND DE VAUX

NEOLITHIC PERIOD TO MIDDLE BRONZE AGE

EXCAVATIONS

The remains of the early periods at Tell el-Far'ah (North) were excavated in four different areas, designated I to IV in the final reports.

Area I. Area I is located in the northern sector of the site, in the direction of the Far'ah spring. It was excavated in 1946–1947; above bedrock, a succession of strata were revealed that were labeled "Enéolithique moyen," "Enéolithique supérieur," "Ancien Bronze I," "Ancien Bronze IIa," "Ancien Bronze IIb," and "Moyen Bronze II." It should be noted that after the Early Bronze Age this area was extramural.

Area II. Area II occupies the northwestern part of the site. The excavations, conducted here from 1950 to 1959 on about 1,100 sq m, isolated a succession of strata initially ascribed to the "Néolithique," "Chalcolithique moyen," "Chalcolithique supérieur," "Ancien Bronze I," "Ancien Bronze II," and "Moyen Bronze II." In the sequence of the "Ancien Bronze I" and "Ancien Bronze II," six strata, or rather six phases of occupation, were recognized and called "période 1" to "période 5" and "période finale"; they have been labeled here strata IV1 to IV6. Similarly, six phases of occupation were identified in the Middle Bronze Age II that were called strata A1 to A2 and B1 to B5 in the final publication.

Area III. Area III, located to the southwest of the site, was excavated in 1960. Above some pockets in the bedrock containing Early Bronze Age I sherds, four phases of the Early Bronze Age II and at least five phases of the Middle Bronze Age II occupation were discovered. This area was also extramural after the Early Bronze Age.

Area IV. Area IV is the extension of area II outside the line of the Early and Middle Bronze Age fortifications. Above the Early Bronze Age fortifications, two phases (A1 and A2) of the Middle Bronze Age II occupation prior to the erection of the Middle Bronze Age rampart were identified.

STRATIGRAPHY

The following chart is intended to eliminate confusion arising from the changes in terminology used in the preliminary reports to designate assemblages that were sometimes mixed. The "Enéolithique moyen" and part of the "Enéolithique supérieur" of the first two seasons in area I encompass two periods that were later distinguished as "Chalcolithique moyen" and "Chalcolithique supérieur" and correspond respectively to the Early and Late Chalcolithic and to the Early Bronze Age I in current terminology. Part of the Enéolithique supérieur and the Ancien Bronze I of the first two seasons in area I were later ascribed to a single period called Ancien Bronze I; this period corresponds to the beginning of the Early Bronze Age II in current terminology. The period called Ancien Bronze II (or Ancien Bronze IIa and IIb) in the preliminary reports corresponds to a later stage of the Early Bronze Age II. In the current reworking of the Tell el-Far'ah stratigraphy, the periods of occupation under consideration have been labeled I to V.

The chart indicates the main phases in the early history of Tell el-Far'ah. The site was first inhabited in the Pre-Pottery Neolithic B and then abandoned until the second half of the fifth millennium. It seems to have been sparsely occupied in the Chalcolithic period, and then more heavily and continuously from about the middle of the Early Bronze Age I until the very end of the Early Bronze Age II. It was then abandoned until the Middle Bronze Age IIA, when reoccupation is indicated by some graves. It seems to have been a small rural settlement in the Middle Bronze Age IIA and IIB, but became a fortified city in the Middle Bronze Age IIC. From then on, occupation was continuous until the Iron Age.

Period	*Area I*	*Area II*	*Area III*	*Area IV*
I PPNB	*Bedrock*	"Néolithique"		
	H i a t u s			
II Chalcolithic Early / Late	"Enéolithique moyen"	"Chalcolithique moyen"	*Bedrock*	
III EB I	"Enéolithique supérieur"	"Chalcolithique supérieur"	"Chalcolithique supérieur"	*Bedrock*
IV EB II	"Ancien Bronze I" "Ancien Bronze IIa" "Ancien Bronze IIb"	1 2 3 "Ancien Bronze I" 4 5 6 "Ancien Bronze II"	a b "Ancien Bronze I" c d "Ancien Bronze II"	EB Fortifications Phases: IA IB IIA IIB IIC
	H i a t u s			
V MB IIA	Burials	Burials	Burials	Burial
MB IIB	Strata and burials	Burials	Burials	Strata A 1–2
MB IIC	Strata and burials	Strata B 1–5 / Underground Temple	Strata	MB II Fortifications

PERIOD I: PRE-POTTERY NEOLITHIC B PERIOD. The first settlers were attracted by the powerful Far'ah spring as early as the seventh millennium. The scattered remains of their settlement, which was apparently small and poor, were revealed in area II only. They consisted of oval depressions (c. 0.5 m deep, up to 4.5 m long, and 3 m wide) established in virgin soil with a lime-plaster floor and one or several hearths. The excavator interpreted these structures as pit dwellings. The associated material comprises basalt implements (cylindrical pestles, shallow vessels, and a disc-shaped grinding stone), bone tools (awls and spatulae), flint tools (mainly axes, picks, chisels, scrapers, and serrated sickle blades), and a quantity of arrowheads of Pre-Pottery Neolithic B types.

PERIOD II: CHALCOLITHIC PERIOD. Settlement. In most places in area II, the Pre-Pottery Neolithic B remains are covered by a thin layer of sterile earth overlaid by layers of stones and earth associated with another series of pit dwellings resembling circular or oval huts, attributable to the Chalcolithic period. These dwellings have been explored by means of several narrow trenches and seem to be sparsely distributed over the excavated area. They are marked by shallow pits less than 0.8 m deep and measuring between 2 and 4.5 m in diameter, with a plastered or beaten-earth floor associated with fireplaces, some stone slabs, and pits. The abundant small stones filling the depressions derive presumably from mud walls built around the rim of the pit to support the superstructure.

The pottery, which appears rather coarse, is usually light buff and occasionally red-slipped. It is characterized by large bowls with straight sides (sometimes with a painted band on the outside of the rim or with a shallow pedestal base), bow-rim jars, and hole-mouth jars with finger-impressed applied bands under the rim. Noteworthy are typological details like mat-impressed bases, thick horizontal ledge handles with large finger impressions, loop handles with an enlarged attachment to the vessel's body, and an occasional incised herringbone-pattern decoration. This assemblage is reminiscent of the later strata of the Jericho Pottery Neolithic B, but may have been partially contemporary with the Ghassulian Chalcolithic, as

EB house.

suggested by the rare occurrence of Late Ghassulian sherds.

The associated flint industry includes finely and deeply serrated sickle blades, picks, axes, and arrowheads in the Late Neolithic tradition. Basalt cylindrical or conical pestles are also numerous.

Cave U. Special mention should be made of a cave discovered on the southern slope of the mound. Designated "Grotte U," it seems to have been used initially as a dwelling in the Early Chalcolithic period. In a late phase of the Ghassulian Chalcolithic, it was reused as a burial cave, as indicated by four burials and by a fragment of a house-shaped ceramic ossuary. The pottery includes a series of cream-ware vessels (of a type well known in a Late Chalcolithic phase at Tuleilat el-Ghassul and in the Beersheba area), small V-shaped bowls, and a fragment of a churn.

THE EARLY BRONZE AGE I: PERIOD III. Settlement. In most places in area II, the Early Bronze Age I is separated from the Chalcolithic by a thin layer of sterile earth. Its stratigraphic appearance, however, is similar: it is also marked by layers of small stones presumably deriving from the mud walls of pit dwellings. These structures are the only dwelling remains observed in this stratum and are identical to those of the preceding Chalcolithic period. This similarity explains de Vaux's inclination to group the two periods under the same "Chalcolithic" label. The Early Bronze Age I occupation was much denser, however.

Cemeteries. Several cemeteries have been identified in the immediate vicinity of the mound. One burial ground is located about 500 m to the south of the mound, toward Wadi ed-Daleib; another is some 1,200 m to the north of the tell, on the slopes of Wadi er-Resif; and a third one may have existed on the eastern side of the mound. Altogether, seventeen tombs have been excavated, but it is known that many more were subjected to illicit excavations in the 1960s and 1970s in a radius of fewer than 5 km (3 mi.) around the tell. These numerous burials suggest that, in the second half of the fourth millennium, an increasingly large number of pastoral nomads had begun to settle in this area, and that the settlement at Tell el-Far'ah became a central place for them.

The tombs, hewn out of the soft chalk with flint tools, were intended for mass burials. The largest (tomb 3) measured 8 by 6.5 m and is almost 2 m high, while the smallest does not exceed 2.5 by 2 by 1.5 m. As most of the tombs had been reused in the Early Bronze Age II and in the Middle and Late Bronze ages, and the majority of the bones had disintegrated, it was not possible to ascertain the position in which the bodies were buried or the number of burials. The large number of individuals buried in the tombs can nevertheless be inferred from the abundance of offerings—up to 204 vessels in the case of tomb 5.

Material Culture. Most typical of the period is its pottery, which is completely new in ware, shape, and decoration. Although the cemeteries have yielded mostly funerary vessels with shapes seldom encountered on the tell and the abundant domestic vessels were not attested in the tombs, the two assemblages can be considered basically contemporary. They date mostly to the Early Bronze Age IB phase, although part of the assemblage and some tombs (especially tomb 3 in the northern cemetery) can be dated to the second half of the Early Bronze Age IA (c. 3300 BCE).

Typological analysis shows that the pottery industry was predominantly local. A few imported vessels, or vessels imitating nonlocal pottery, indicate, however, that a segment of the population kept close ties with adjacent regions (the Jordan Valley, Beth-Shean Valley, Esdraelon Plain, and Sharon Plain). The overwhelming majority of the vessels belong to common or red-burnished wares. The most typical local shapes are ovoid bowls, shallow bowls with a discoid flat base and a protuberance (an omphalos) at the bottom, bag-shaped or pear-shaped juglets with a high loop handle, small

EB II structures.

spouted jars, and pots with two handles and an opening in the shape of the figure 8 when seen from above. Gray-burnished-ware bowls with or without a pedestal base are rare on the tell but well attested in the tombs. They appear in two varieties of ware and shape: one is "northern," and quite rare, being known only in tomb 3 and on the tell; and the other is local and comparatively more frequent, presumably intended only for funerary purposes, as it was not found on the tell. Painted ware is rare. Typical on the mound is an abundance of red coarse ware of the Tell Umm Ḥamad esh-Sharqiyya (Proto-Urban D) type, represented mainly by basins and pithoi with heavy plastic decoration with finger or nail impressions.

The associated flint industry is equally new. It is of the Canaanean type and represented mainly by Canaanean blades and tabular scrapers, with a few borers. This impoverishment of the flint tool kit is indicative of the growing importance of metal tools and weapons, which make their first appearance in period III. They are represented in the tombs by a few chisels, by copper daggers with a central rib and rivets for attachment, and by rings made with a coiled wire. A silver goblet whose shape was inspired by contemporary carinated cups is especially noteworthy. Basalt bowls, a mace head, beads of various types in carnelian and faience, pendants of *Aspatharia* shells from the Nile River, and bracelets manufactured from *Lambis truncata*, a large mollusc from the Red Sea, were also recovered.

EARLY BRONZE AGE II: PERIOD IV. The beginning of the Early Bronze Age II (de Vaux's Ancien Bronze I) marks a radical change in the history of the settlement. In area II, the houses from the first Early Bronze Age II stratum (stratum IV1) were built directly over the ruins of the latest pit houses from the Early Bronze Age I and are stratigraphically related to the base of the first city wall. This simultaneous appearance at Tell el-Far'ah of architecture and fortifications is synchronous with marked changes in the pottery assemblages—hence, de Vaux's justified insistence on the sharp break between the Early Bronze Age I and II periods at Tell el-Far'ah and elsewhere in Canaan.

From then on, the evolution of the Early Bronze Age takes place without major interruption. In the three areas where remains of this period have been excavated, it is marked by successive reconstructions that did not alter the major lines of the urban layout established at the beginning of the period. In area II, these reconstructions correspond to strata IV2 to IV6.

Fortifications. From its inception, the Early Bronze Age II town was pro-

View of the stairs against the inner face of the EB stone rampart; (foreground) note the drainage channel, area II, stratum IV3.

Typical EB I pottery from the necropolis; the two vessels on the left are local gray-burnished ware.

tected by strong fortifications. In use for a period of about four centuries, they underwent several changes and rebuildings. Two major phases were distinguished in this history, corresponding to the erection of two successive ramparts. The first, built at the very beginning of the Early Bronze Age II occupation at the site, is a 3-m-thick brick wall built on solid stone foundations (phase IA = stratum IV1). Attested on the west side of the town (area II), on a straight line for a distance of 125 m, it may have enclosed a settlement of about 12.5 a. It was reinforced with a bastion (or a large buttress) 2.5 m thick and at least 9 m long, and possibly with towers. Later, it seems to have had an outer wall (1.15 m thick) built some 3 m in front of the rampart (phase IB = stratum IV2).

Following a few destructions, a second rampart, this time in stone, was erected (phase IIA = stratum IV4). On the west side, it rests against the outer face of the old brick rampart and brings the total thickness of the fortifications to nearly 6 m. It was preceded by a small wall (0.75 m thick) that created a passage 1.25 m wide along the foot of the new rampart. On the north side, the line of defense was moved back by about 12 m and the new stone rampart, erected over the ruined stratum IV3 houses, abutted the inner face of the old brick rampart on the west. The stone rampart here is between 5.5 and 7 m thick. On its outer face, it has a small "glacis," 1.7 m high, composed of layers of clay inclined at a 30-degree angle. On its inner face, it has a stone staircase, of which the first ten steps are preserved, leading to its top. This stone rampart was also found in area I near the northeastern corner of the city, where it is 8 m thick and has an inner stone buttress 1 m deep and 2.5 m long.

In a later phase (phase IIB = stratum IV5), the slope along the fortifications on the west side was covered by a fill of earth over 7 m long and more than 2 m high; this fill was arranged in terraces with two small retaining walls and thus formed a sort of glacis. Finally (phase IIC), the old brick rampart collapsed inside the town under the combined weight of this pseudo-glacis and the stone rampart. The damages were then hastily repaired and a small outer wall was added on the top of the pseudo-glacis, while new houses were built over the layer of fallen bricks (stratum IV6).

City Gate. Access to this part of the site was through a fortified city gate established at the beginning of the Early Bronze Age II with the construction of the initial brick rampart. It is composed of a 2.5-m-wide opening through the rampart flanked by two square brick towers set on stone foundations and attached to the rampart. Measuring 7.5 by 8 m and 7.25 by 7.75 m, with walls 2 m thick, these towers isolate a passageway 7 m long and 3.5 m wide. Their brick masonry has been preserved to a height of 4 m. The passageway and the towers were covered; door sockets found in situ indicate that the door could be closed by means of two folding panels.

In the Early Bronze Age II, this large structure underwent several changes. Phase II corresponds to a major reshuffling: following a fire whose debris had raised the floor level at the entrance, a ramp ascending from the outside was established in the passageway, comprised of five steps of beaten earth supported by tree trunks; several repairs and consolidations were also made in and around the towers. Phase III, possibly contemporary with phase IIB of the fortifications, is marked by the closing of the gate: a stone wall (4.5 m thick) was constructed at the exit of the passageway, transforming the gate into a kind of bastion. Phase IV saw the reopening of the gate: the blocking wall was buried under a fill accumulated to a height of up to 2 m, and a new passageway was formed over it. By then, the towers were not in use; the northern one had its entrance blocked and the southern one was largely ruined.

EB II street with a central drain, area II, stratum IV2.

Urbanism. These strong fortifications protected a well-urbanized settlement. At least in the excavated areas, the transition from the period III village of huts to the period IV town is quite sudden. Although it is doubtful that the new urban settlement was planned from its inception, the main lines of the urban layout seem to be established in area II at the end of stratum IV1 and were preserved almost to the end of the Early Bronze Age II occupation. They include two streets (2 m wide) that presumably cross each other at the place of the underground Middle Bronze Age temple (see below). Some of these streets had stone-lined drainage channels whose network was modified over time; one of these channels passed under the stone rampart to the north of area II. Together with a passage running along the inner face of the rampart, the streets isolated groups of houses.

DWELLINGS. Ordinary dwellings were composed of one rectangular room and a courtyard; there were seldom more than two communicating rooms. The entrance was either on the long or on the short side, usually close to a corner. Floors and walls were usually plastered. Roofs were supported by a series of wooden posts placed on stone slabs arranged on an axial line. Many of the houses had stone benches along one or two adjacent walls, infrequently on three or four sides. Inside the rooms, domestic installations included

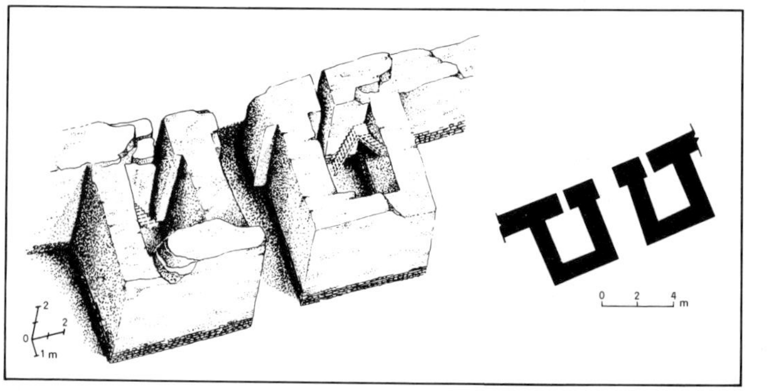

*EB city gate, phase I: **(left)** general view; **(right)** reconstruction and plan.*

stone-lined basins, pithoi sunk in the ground up to the neck, or freestanding pithoi resting on a stone or on a pottery slab; in the courtyards, they included stone-lined underground silos and fireplaces sometimes incorporated in a small rectangular stone structure that may have been a kitchen.

TEMPLE(?). Some buildings may have had a special function. A building ascribed to the first Early Bronze Age II stratum (stratum IV1) was identified by de Vaux as a temple because of its careful construction and peculiar layout—distinct from that of the surrounding domestic houses. It is comprised of an open hall that opens on the east into a small room surrounded by benches. Its plan, however, differs from that of all other contemporary temples in the country.

"INDUSTRIAL" INSTALLATIONS. Some possible "industrial" installations were also recognized. A circular structure (diameter, 3 m) ascribed to stratum IV3a might have been a potter's kiln. There is no doubt about the function of a large, well-constructed structure (diameter, 2.6 m) excavated in stratum IV4: it is certainly a potter's kiln. It is comprised of a firing chamber above a half-buried furnace; the floor of the firing chamber is pierced by nine holes and rests on a central pillar. Such an elaborate installation suggests the existence of a professional potter. It is interesting to witness its appearance at a time when highly fired (metallic ware) vessels become frequent at the site. In addition, two possible potter's workshops marked by concentrations of finely ground calcite, to be used as temper, and various tools were observed.

Burials. The Early Bronze Age II necropolis has not been located. However, several Early Bronze Age I tombs were reused in this period (tombs 2, 3, 5, 13, 14, and 16, among others).

Pottery. Changes in pottery are marked at the beginning of the period: the majority of the Early Bronze Age I pottery types had already disappeared in the first Early Bronze Age II stratum (IV1). They were replaced by new types, some derived from an earlier tradition, but most of them entirely new. Subsequently, the changes were gradual, with the pottery showing a strong typological continuity throughout the various strata of the Early Bronze Age II occupation. However, statistical analysis revealed two phases, IVA and

EB II potter's kiln in area II, stratum IV4.

IVB, corresponding respectively to de Vaux's Ancien Bronze I and Ancien Bronze II; the first corresponds to strata IV1 and IV2 and the second to strata IV4 to IV6, stratum IV3 being transitional. Typical of the earlier strata are small bowls with a sinuous profile; deeply carinated small bowls with straight or concave sides; large bowls with an incurved rim and flattened top; rather deep platters; and pithoi with a vertical or slightly outcurved neck. The carinated bowls in metallic ware and the jugs of the Abydos type appear only from stratum IV3 onward. They are typical of the later strata, together with shallower platters, bottles, and pithoi with an outcurved neck.

Abandonment. In area II, the last stratum of the period (stratum IV6) shows a sparser occupation and a dissolution of the urban layout, as if the city were already in the process of depopulation. This suggests a peaceful termination for the Early Bronze Age occupation. On the basis of the pottery typology, the abandonment took place at the very end of the Early Bronze Age II (c. 2600 BCE). No pottery type dating to the Early Bronze Age III has been identified.

Most of the smaller sites in Wadi Far'ah were abandoned at the same time. The area remained inhabited, however: Mitḥam Wadi Far'ah, a newly founded enclosure site midway between Tell el-Far'ah and the Jordan Valley, and Khirbet el-Makhruq, at the exit of the wadi in the Jordan Valley, were prosperous Early Bronze Age III settlements. There is also evidence of settlements dating to the Intermediate Bronze Age (Middle Bronze Age I) period in Wadi Far'ah. The tell itself, however, remained deserted until the Middle Bronze Age IIA.

THE MIDDLE BRONZE AGE II: PERIOD V. Tell el-Far'ah was resettled at some time in the first half of the Middle Bronze Age IIA, in about 1900 BCE. Two major phases of occupation, VA and VB, were distinguished in areas II and III. The first phase corresponds to an open village dated to the Middle Bronze Age IIA and IIB and the second to an unfortified and then to a fortified town in the Middle Bronze Age IIC.

Phase VA: Village Phase. The new Middle Bronze Age settlement remained rural for a long time. Its nucleus has not been identified; it was probably located near the center of the tell. The excavations have reached only open spaces at the periphery of a small village that had no other protection than the slope of the tell; natural caves in the rock scarp sheltered some troglodytes (Grotte T).

In phase VA, these open spaces surrounding the village were intermittently used for burials and for settlement. The clearest stratigraphy was obtained in area IV, above the Early Bronze Age fortifications, where two phases of burials alternating with two strata of building remains (A1, A2) have been identified. With more or less clarity, this sequence also applies to the other areas of excavation.

SEQUENCE OF OCCUPATION. The oldest remains left by the new settlers is *tombe* B in area I, dated to the first third of the Middle Bronze Age IIA. Later, a late Middle Bronze Age IIA grave of an adult (*tombe* I, before stratum A1) was dug in area IV into the northern tower of the ruined Early Bronze Age gate. A series of child burials was also dug into the Early Bronze Age ruins in area II (*tombes* W–Y and AB) and in area III (*tombes* AN and AD).

In the next phase (Middle Bronze Age IIB), while the vicinity of area I (*tombes* G–H) and of area II (*tombe* AA) remained mainly a burial ground,

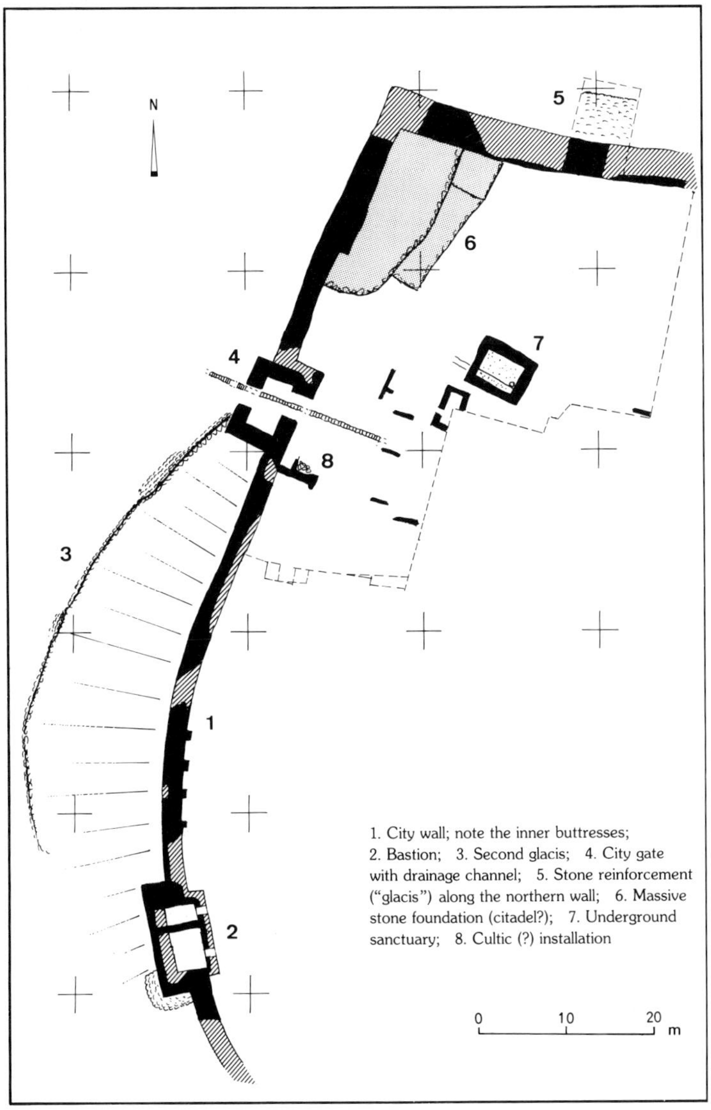

Plan of area II, stratum VB3–5, MB IIC.

the first houses appeared in area IV directly over the remains of the Early Bronze Age fortifications. Stratum A1 has a continuous series of rooms (length, 48 m), interrupted only by a passage(?) at the future location of the city gate. The largest rooms measure up to 7.5 by 3.5 m and are not interconnected; the entrance to each was through a door on its eastern side. Stratum A2 represents a rebuilding with a reuse of earlier walls as foundations for the new houses.

In area III, there are few contemporary remains of the phase VA occupation: traces of walls, drains, an oven, and also three graves of adults and one grave of a child (*tombes* AM, AN, AD, and AJ) dug in the open spaces between houses or during gaps in occupation. The latest of these graves (*tombe* AM) dates to the late Middle Bronze Age IIB or early Middle Bronze Age IIC.

BURIALS. The deceased were buried in the ground, alone, or in groups (one adult and one child). Only the newborns were buried under the floors of houses, usually in a jar. In addition, some tombs in the Early Bronze Age necropolis might have been reused at that time, as suggested by the case of tomb 16, which has yielded early Middle Bronze Age IIA pottery comparable to that in *tombe* B.

Phase VB: Urban Phase. The transition from phase VA to phase VB is marked by the expansion of the original rural settlement, which soon assumed an urban appearance. Area II is the only area where the complete stratigraphy of the urban phase, involving five superimposed strata (B1–B5) could be observed. However, the first two strata, B1 and B2, antedate the building of the fortifications.

PREFORTIFICATION STRATA. Strata B1 and B2 represent the first extension of the settlement beyond the limits of its nucleus. They are marked by fragmentary remains of houses with silos and by burials of newborns dug under the floors of the houses. The associated material dates to the beginning of the Middle Bronze Age IIC.

FORTIFICATIONS. The erection of the fortifications is dated to stratum B3, possibly in about 1600 BCE. The town enclosed by the rampart was smaller than the Early Bronze Age town: the city wall excluded the greater part of the northern sector and part of the southwestern sector of the earlier town. Notwithstanding minor changes and repairs, two major phases were recognized in the history of the fortifications on the western part of the site.

The first phase of fortifications consisted of a freestanding wall associated with a city gate, a bastion, and possibly a citadel. The wall is 2.2 m thick and its solid stone foundations are preserved to a height of 1 to 2.3 m. On the western side, it was constructed on top of the ruins of the Early Bronze Age brick wall. It followed the same line up to the Early Bronze Age city gate, from which it moved eastward. On the northern side, it was built on top of the (second) Early Bronze Age (stone) wall but did not follow the same line. It soon turned in an east–southeast direction, thus leaving the greater part of the northern section of the earlier town outside the wall. For all or part of its length, its inner face presents a series of stone buttresses 0.5 to 0.8 m deep and 1 to 1.4 m wide, placed at intervals of 2 to 2.8 m.

This rampart's major feature is a city gate, located to the north of the Early Bronze Age gate, directly on the Early Bronze Age brick bastion, which provided a solid foundation. Protruding 5 m from the line of the rampart, it is a direct-entrance gateway consisting of a single broadroom (6 by 3.5 m) with an outer doorway 2.5 m wide and an inner one 3 m wide. The walls are 1.5 to 1.8 m thick.

About 50 m south of the gate, the southwestern corner of the city was defended by a bastion 12.7 m long and 3 m deep. It contained two interconnected rooms, one measuring 4.5 by 3.5 m and the other only 1.8 by 3.5 m, each accessible from inside the city. Some 35 m north of the gate, the northwestern corner of the city was occupied by a massive stone platform (19 by 8 m) later widened by stone reinforcements. This large structure was interpreted by the excavator as the foundation of a destroyed "citadel."

Sometime later, in their second phase, the fortifications were strengthened by the addition of an earthen glacis. This was realized in two phases. Established between the bastion and the gate, the first glacis consisted of compact, sterile black earth dumped on the slope; it was separated from the wall by a stone-lined fosse nearly 10 m wide on the south, but gradually narrowing as it approached the gate. Later, a new and larger glacis was established with sterile red earth. Crescent-shaped in plan, with a maximum width of 16 m, it covered the preceding glacis and buried the foot of the wall from the city gate to the edge of the steep slope of Wadi ed-Daleib. Downslope, it rested against a retaining wall built with heavy masonry and preserved up to 2.8 m high.

These earthworks do not exist south of the bastion—where the steep slope of Wadi ed-Daleib was probably considered sufficient natural protection—or along the northern side of the town. Here, the rampart had no earthen glacis but only a small stone "glacis," or rather an accumulation of stones, about 4 m wide and at least 3 m high, laid against the foot of the wall.

URBANISM. With the building of the city wall, the settlement became urban and witnessed a higher density of construction. A well-built stone-lined drainage channel (0.5 m wide and 0.6 m deep), covered by stone slabs, was cleared for a length of 22 m in area II; it ran along a street and went through the gate in a straight line. In the same area, the contemporary houses had been damaged by the construction of the underground temple (see below) and by post–Middle Bronze Age building activities. The excavations revealed only fragmentary remains of rectangular houses lined up parallel to the rampart and containing domestic installations and pits. In area III, however, well-preserved architectural remains were found, consisting of several strata of workshops and storerooms, all attached to the wall.

Drainage channel beneath the city gate, MB IIC.

MIDDLE BRONZE CULTIC INSTALLATIONS. Some construction of a public nature was also identified. The most remarkable was found in area II: it is an underground chamber (4.8 by 3.6 m) excavated in stratum B3 at a depth of more than 2.6 m. The walls are 1 to 1.4 m thick and have only an inner face. They and the floors were plastered and a bench was built along the western wall; a jar was sunk into the floor near the southern corner, later replaced by an 0.8-m-deep stone-lined pit. The problem of access to this room and its eventual relationship to a surface building could not be solved. The structure was probably in use from the time of stratum B3 to that of stratum B5, which marks the end of the Middle Bronze Age IIC at Tell el-Far'ah. Besides pottery, the most remarkable find was that of bones of suckling pigs (*Sus scrofa*). The excavator compared this installation to an underground cella discovered in stratum V at Alalakh in Syria and interpreted it as a sanctuary dedicated to a divinity whose cult was marked by the sacrifice of pigs.

Another possible cultic installation was found near the entrance in the city gate, a few meters from its south side. In the Middle Bronze Age, it appeared as a paved area (1.5 by 1 m) partly enclosed by a wall. It was understood by the excavator to be a cultic installation, a forerunner of those on the same spot in the Late Bronze and Iron ages and presumably devoted to the cult of a divinity associated with the city gate and symbolized by a standing stone (*maṣṣeba*).

BURIALS. The only burials found on the tell from phase VB are of newborns in large jars with two or three small jars as offerings (*tombes* J–L, N–P, R, and S). The older children and the adults may have been buried outside of the tell in shaft tombs, as suggested by the reuse in the Middle Bronze Age IIB–C of several Early Bronze Age I tombs in the southern necropolis (tombs 3, 5, 7, 11, and 12).

PIERRE DE MIROSCHEDJI

LATE BRONZE AGE TO THE ROMAN PERIOD

LATE BRONZE AGE: PERIOD VI. Poorly preserved remains attesting to a Late Bronze Age occupation at Tell el-Far'ah are still under study. They cover a period of about three centuries, perhaps into the sixteenth century BCE. There is no definitive gap between this period and the Middle Bronze Age II. No town plan could be reconstructed, as the traces are too fragmentary and scattered, but there is some indication that the rampart and the western gate existed in the Late Bronze Age.

The earlier building remains include well-built walls with two stone faces. The later house plans are still square, although less well built, with narrower walls. The superimposed floor levels and wall repairs indicate that some of the buildings were in use over a long period.

Contemporary pottery was found both at the site and in the tombs; in addition to the local products, assemblages include imported Mycenean and Cypriot ware.

Few tombs from this period are known; some Middle Bronze Age ones were reused. Infant burials in jars were found under the house floors, while all the adult inhumations were located outside the town, sometimes even in Chalcolithic tombs.

THE IRON AGE: PERIOD VII. Iron Age remains were found in all the excavation areas on the mound, especially on the west, in trenches II and III, where extensive traces of three superimposed towns were found. These were remarkably well preserved and covered five successive periods (VIIa–e), lasting until the site was abandoned at the end of the seventh century BCE.

Period VIIa. The remains from period VIIa, which were excavated only in the northern part of trench II (gate sector), were founded on the Late Bronze Age walls. The houses did not abut the rampart as in the Middle Bronze Age, but were aligned north–south and east–west; this alignment continued throughout the Iron Age. The building the excavators called the Late Bronze Age temple was actually an Iron Age residential building that was rebuilt several times up to the end of period VIId, as is attested by its plan and pottery. It was built directly above the Middle Bronze Age subterranean sanctuary (see above). A silver-plated bronze plaque depicting the goddess Hathor was found in the underlying stratum. The building's plan is clearer in level VIIb. One of its rooms yielded two terra-cotta chalices that led the excavator to interpret the structure as a temple. While its interpretation as a house is certain, it is possible that it also served some cultic function, which suggests a type of worship incorporated in domestic life. Although it is poorly preserved, this level provides evidence of major refurbishment (VIIa$_1$), a sign of continuity between this period and the next.

Period VIIb. The period VIIb level was built on the remains of period VIIa and repeats its plan while developing it. The town underwent a period of renewal; the quasi-systematic use of new plans and urban features bears witness to some authority being responsible for the organization of public life. The Middle Bronze Age fortifications and gate were rebuilt. Stone benches were built against the western block of the gate and an installation consisting of a basin and a hewn stone pillar set on a base was constructed in the road leading from the inner gate to the town, without blocking it. These must have been a libation basin and a *maṣṣeba*, a ritual standing stone, of the sort found at Taanach and Arad. The role played by this monument at the entrance to the town finds an echo in 2 Kings 23:8: "and he broke down the high places of the gates . . . which were on one's left at the gate of the city." This installation was in use throughout the Iron Age, and the basin was enlarged in period VIId. The Middle Bronze Age traditions concerning the location of cultic sites are known to have been preserved in the Israelite period. The gate opened onto a square, and an orthogonal network of roads divided the houses into blocks.

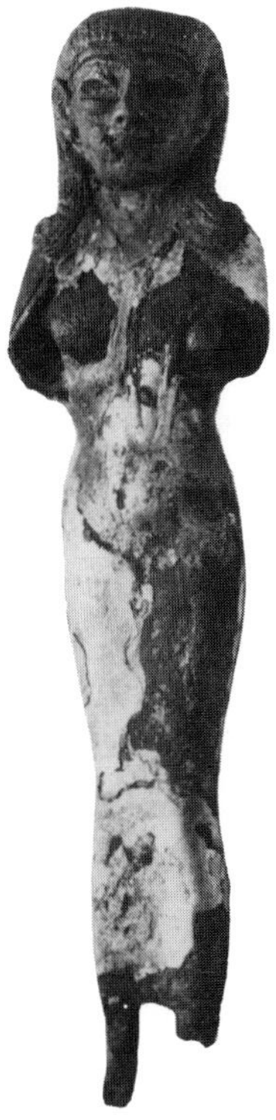

Silver-plated bronze figurine of the goddess Hathor, period VI, LB.

The houses were built without any foundations over the ruins of period VIIa; they occasionally follow the same plan and have stone-faced walls. Almost all the structures have the same plan: they are rectangular and are divided into three parts. An oblong courtyard opens to the street and the rooms; it is flanked on its entrance side by two open rooms, with pillars along their sides, that are often paved and were used as kitchens or workshops. Closed rooms in a horseshoe arrangement surround the courtyard at the rear, with a second story above them. This part of the structure was reserved for storage rooms and residential quarters. At Tell el-Far'ah, this tripartite division, rather than the number of rooms (as in the "four-room house"), is characteristic of the Iron Age. It is a very elaborate concept of an urban residence, neatly incorporating workshop and residential areas. It appears fully developed in the tenth century BCE, without any visible development in earlier periods. This house type, found from this time onward at many sites in the country, is unique to the ancient Near East.

The raising of some streets and the repair and refurbishing of houses without altering their original plan bear witness to the long duration of this period. The abundant pottery is mostly domestic in character, although a clay temple model, with parallels at Megiddo and in Cyprus and Transjordan, was also found. It can be dated to the tenth and early ninth centuries BCE.

Period VIIc. The destruction of level VIIb was followed by the abandonment of the site. The first evidence of the town's reconstruction appears to the north, at the level of the gate (which then lay in ruins), and consists of a large complex of public buildings. Several features suggest that it was never finished (abandoned building materials, partly-dressed stones, the absence of ruins). It was aligned in the same direction as the buildings in level VIIb, and its foundations were based on the earlier level's remains. The main building consisted of a central courtyard surrounded by three large rooms. The walls were faced with stone on both sides and were reinforced on the facade and at the corners by pilasters. The structure was well built, using fine ashlars, some of them bossed; the stones' oblique dressing resembles that of the masonry in the palace at Samaria. The pottery found nearby on a plastered floor is comparable to that found at Megiddo, stratum IV.

The destruction of level VIIb may have taken place at the time of Omri's conquest; if so, then the unfinished building in level VIIc would bear witness to the reconstruction of the capital, interrupted when it was transferred to Samaria. This hypothesis, suggested by the excavator, R. de Vaux, is supported by the analysis of the ceramic material.

Period VIId. The thickness of the destruction layer that seals level VIIb varies; it reveals that the abandonment of the site did not last long and was interrupted by the building attempt visible in level VIIc. The quality and importance of the structures in period VIId are remarkable, as is their almost hierarchical arrangement from north to south (with the gate, the stela monument, the palace, the public buildings, the patrician houses, and the

Terra-cotta model of temple flanked by columns with inverted proto-Aeolic capitals, period VIIb.

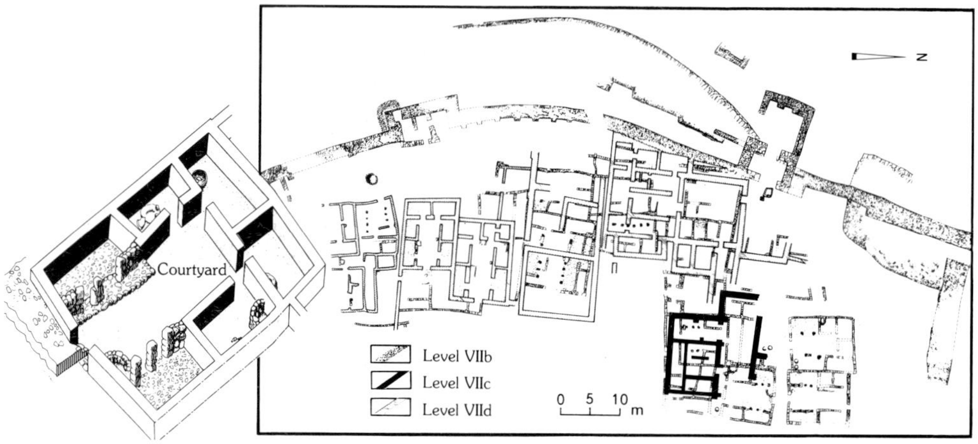

Left: *isometric reconstruction of house 436, period VIIb;* ***(right)*** *plan of area II, stratum VII, Iron II.*

dwellings of the poor). This town was unfortified and had no rampart. The gate was partly rebuilt, and its eastern block disappeared. The level VIIb monument was reconstructed, a larger basin was built over the old one, and the stela was replaced. The major feature of this period was the construction of a palace. It was very large, and it was aligned in the same direction as the unfinished building from level VIIc—although it was larger and was surrounded by annexes. In front of it was a huge square, paved courtyard whose asymmetrically sited entrance faced the gate monument. As in the case of the structures from the preceding period and most of the buildings from period VIId the palace was well built, following a regular plan. Certain of its elements also appear in structures at Megiddo, Hazor, and Tell Beit Mirsim, where the presence of foreign influence has been suggested. A large quantity of pottery was found here, including 150 storage jars from a room at the bottom of the palace and several terra-cotta "bathtubs" and basins in the central room.

To the north, a wall separates the houses of the patrician class, which were carefully built to the same plan as that used in level VIIb, from those of the poor. The latter were built back to back in blocks and resemble the houses of level VIIb. Very large quantities of pottery characteristic of the eighth century BCE, including Samaria ware, were found in this level, which was violently destroyed in the Assyrian conquest. The town seems to have been burned when Samaria was conquered by Sargon II in 721 BCE.

House 328, 8th century BCE.

Corner of unfinished building 411, period VIIc, 9th century BCE.

Periods VIIe and VIIe$_1$. The town was immediately reoccupied (period VIIe), but its remains have only been found in the area of the palace and the gate. The ruined gate was completely blocked, and the rebuilt palace shows no major alterations. In contrast, the basin and *maṣṣeba* were enclosed in a large, square area, crudely paved and communicating with the palace's great courtyard. The permanence of this cultic site, reconstructed after each destruction of the town throughout the Iron Age, indicates that the town must always have been reoccupied by its original inhabitants. However, the discovery of carinated Assyrian bowls indicates that an Assyrian garrison or colonists must also have occupied the site. This type of pottery, identified by W. M. F. Petrie at Tell Jemmeh, reproduces metal prototypes that appear in reliefs from Assyrian palaces and that were found at Nimrud in Sargon II's palace; in Israel it is known from the end of the eighth and the beginning of the seventh centuries BCE, particularly at Samaria and Hazor.

The town gradually declined in importance (period VIIe$_1$). The palace was subdivided by poorly built partitions, the cultic place was abandoned, and the basin was turned into a drinking trough. A small farming community occupied the site, as is indicated by a silo and a large threshing floor. The site was gradually abandoned in the seventh to sixth centuries BCE, although some finds can be attributed to the Hellenistic and Roman periods. A Muslim cemetery from the thirteenth and fourteenth centuries CE badly damaged the earlier remains.

STRATIGRAPHY AT TELL EL-FAR'AH, LATE BRONZE AND IRON AGES

Preliminary reports	*Period*	*Date (BCE)*	*Observations*
Stratum 4	VIIa	12th–11th cent.	Unfortified town, badly damaged
Stratum 3	VIIb	(11th)–10th cent.	Rebuilt rampart; black-on-red pottery
"Unfinished building"	VIIc	Early 9th cent.	Short-lived new town
Stratum 2*	VIId	9th–8th cent.	Fortified town; "Samaria ware"
Stratum 1	VIIe	7th cent.	Garrison; "Assyrian" pottery
	VIIe$_1$	6th–5th cent.	"Squatters"; Iron II and Persian pottery

ALAIN CHAMBON

Early excavation reports: W. F. Albright, *JPOS* 11 (1931), 241–251; R. de Vaux (and A. M. Stève), *RB* 54 (1947), 394–433, 573–589; 55 (1948), 544–580; 56 (1949), 102–138; id., ibid. 58 (1951), 393–430, 566–590; 59 (1952), 551–583; 62 (1955), 541–589; 64 (1957), 552–580; 67 (1970), 245–247; 68 (1961), 557–592; 69 (1962), 212–253; id., *Archaeology and Old Testament Studies* (ed. D. W. Thomas), Oxford 1967, 371–383.
Main publications: J. Mallet, *Tell el-Far'ah (Région de Napluse): L'Installation du Moyen Bronze antérieure au rempart* (Cahiers de la Revue Biblique 14), Paris 1973; id., *Tell el-Far'ah 2: Le Bronze Moyen, Stratigraphie des Vestiges du Bronze Moyen II* (Recherche sur les Civilisations—Mémoires 66), 3 vols., Paris 1987; A. Chambon, *Tell el-Far'ah 1: L'Âge du Fer* (Recherche sur les Civilisations, Mémoires 31), Paris 1984.
Other studies: G. E. Wright, *BA* 12 (1949), 66–68; J. Gray, *PEQ* 84 (1952), 110–113; R. de Vaux, ibid. 88 (1956), 125–140; id., *Von Ugarit nach Qumran* (O. Eissfeldt, Fest; Beihefte *ZAW* 77), Berlin 1958, 250–265; C. Picard, *RAr* (1958) A, 91–93; U. Joachims, *ZDPV* 76 (1960), 73–96; J. L. Huot, *RB* 74 (1967), 517–554; J. Mallet, *Tell el-Far'ah (Région de Napluse)* (Reviews), *PEQ* 106 (1974), 167. — *JBL* 94 (1975), 607–608; id., *RB* 81 (1974), 423–431; 84 (1977), 108–112; P. de Miroschedji, *Contribution à l'étude de l'urbanisation en Palestine à l'Âge du Bronze Ancien* 1–2, (Ph.D. diss., Univ. of Paris, 1976), 13–24, 74–81, 90–95, 97–99, 115–119, 179, 183–184; id., *Tell el-Far'ah 2* (Reviews), *Paléorient* 15/2 (1989), 154–159. — *Syria* 67 (1990), 524–525; E. Otto, *ZDPV* 94 (1978), 108–118; R. Amiran, *R. Hecht Fest.*, Jerusalem 1979, 115–118; *Biblical Archaeology Society Newsletter* 2/2 (1981), 1–2; M. D. Fowler, *PEQ* 113 (1981), 27–31; A. Chambon, *Tell el-Far'ah 1* (Reviews), *Paléorient* 10/2 (1984), 130–131. — *Syria* 61 (1984), 339–340. — *ZDPV* 101 (1985), 178–183. — *BASOR* 267 (1987), 84–86. — *Archiv für Orientforshung* 35 (1988), 236–237; *Buried History* 22/1 (1986), 14–24; Weippert 1988 (Ortsregister); H. Brodsky, *Bible Review* 5/1 (1989), 38–44.

En-Gedi: the mosaic floor and bema in the stratum II synagogue, looking north.

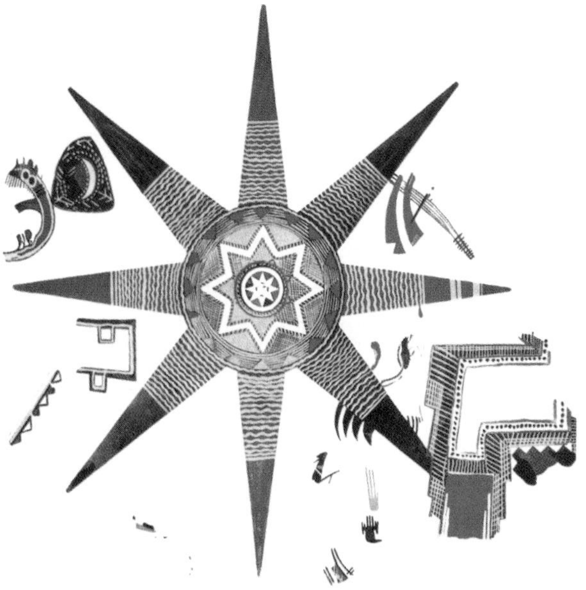

Tuleilat el-Ghassul: Chalcolithic wall paintings.

FAR'AH, TELL EL- (SOUTH)

IDENTIFICATION AND HISTORY

Tel Sharuhen (Tell el-Far'ah, South, not to be confused with Tell el-Far'ah, North, in the northern hill region) was the site of one of the most important cities in the Negev desert in antiquity. It is located approximately 24 km (15 mi.) south of Gaza and 20 km (18.5 mi.) west of Beersheba (map reference 100.076). W. F. Albright's suggestion that the site be identified with the Sharuhen mentioned in descriptions of Egyptian military expeditions and in the Bible is accepted by most scholars (but q.v. Tell el-'Ajjul). It has erroneously been identified by W. M. F. Petrie with biblical Beth-Pelet (Jos. 15:27) on unsound etymological grounds. Sharuhen is mentioned in three Egyptian sources: Ahmose's account of the Hyksos' expulsion relates that the Egyptians laid siege to Sharuhen for three years. Sharuhen appears again in the description of Thutmose III's first campaign, where it is stated: "The garrison which was there was in the town of Sharuhen, while from Iursa to the outer ends of the earth had become rebellious against his majesty." It is last mentioned in the description of Pharaoh Shishak's campaign. All these sources clearly indicate that Sharuhen was situated not far from the Via Maris. In the Bible, Sharuhen is mentioned only in Joshua 19:6. In the parallel verse, Joshua 15:32, the name Shilhim appears instead of Sharuhen. In Shishak's roster the name is also written SRḤM = SLḤYIM (no. 125). The name Sharuhen does not appear in the Septuagint. The town's name is translated as "their fields." The mound lies on a natural hill, about 100 m above sea level, near Naḥal Besor. It is about 16.5 a. in area and contains an accumulation of approximately 14 m of occupational debris.

EXCAVATIONS

W. M. F. Petrie conducted excavations at the site in 1928 and 1929 on behalf of the British School of Archaeology in Egypt. The first volume of his report was published in 1930 and dealt with the excavations conducted at the north end of the mound and in several cemeteries. The second volume (written by E. MacDonald, J. L. Starkey, and G. L. Harding) appeared in 1932 and contained the reports of the excavations of the early sites at the foot of the mound and of additional cemeteries, as well as excavations at the south end of the mound and the extension of the excavation on the north side. The two seasons of excavation at Tell el-Far'ah brought to light a nearly continuous occupation from the Middle Bronze Age IIB to Roman times. The latest remains are trenches from World War I, which crisscross the surface of the site.

MIDDLE BRONZE AGE IIB. The first settlement on the mound was established by the Hyksos. Its characteristic feature is a glacis topped by a wall. The east side of the mound is defended by a steep slope descending to Naḥal Besor; on the north and south sides, the natural slopes run down to its tributaries. The slopes were smoothed to prevent ascent by the enemy. The west side, lacking natural protection, was fortified by a fosse 24 m wide at the top; its outer bank descends 8 m at a 40-degree angle. The glacis sloped 18 m at a 33-degree angle from its top to the upper edge of the fosse. The glacis, made of beaten earth, was leveled off at the top to form a foundation for the wall. At the top of the natural slope at the north end of the mound a rampart 5 m wide stood 6 m above the hill. At three places within the rampart, excavations revealed an earth fill sandwiched between two brick walls (the inner 1.5 m thick and the outer 0.6 m thick).

The Gate. At the top of a ravine at the northwest corner of the mound, Petrie

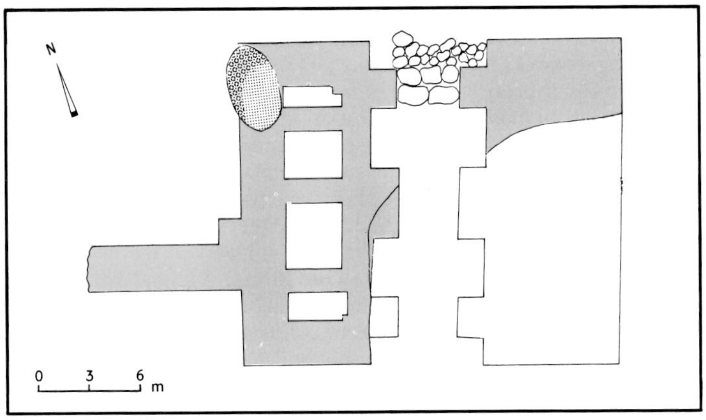

Plan of the southern gate, MB II.

uncovered what he described as a threshold of large stones. Because this was the easiest approach to the mound, he believed that the stones represented the remains of the city gate. However, the remains were too scanty for such a conclusion, especially when at the south end of the mound the well-preserved remains were found of a fine mud-brick gate built on leveled earth with an underbedding of sand (like the rampart in the northeast corner at the top of the slope). The entrance (18 by 3.5 m) in the gate, which was flanked by two towers, contained three pairs of piers (each 2 m wide), which divided it into two broadrooms, entered through three narrow passages. The floor of these rooms stood 2 m above the level of the central entrance. Of the towers flanking the gate, only the northwestern one has survived. It contained four small chambers. A stone-paved threshold and two sandstone steps led from the gate into the city. The construction of the wall on the gate side and its juncture with the gate are not explained in the excavation report, but according to the plan, about a third of the tower projects from the line of the wall. Petrie mentioned another section of wall belonging to this gate, which was uncovered in the trench on the west side of the mound. The ceramic finds indicate that the gate was in use during both the Middle Bronze Age II and the Late Bronze Age, and indeed two separate stages of construction were distinguished: the first of brick and the second of clay piled on top of the earlier foundations. Similar gates, also connected with Hyksos fortifications, are found at sites dating from the same period, such as Beth-Shemesh, Gezer, Hazor, Megiddo, Shechem, and Tell Beit Mirsim. As at Tell el-Far'ah, at most of these sites the gate was also built in the Middle Bronze Age II and continued in use during the Late Bronze Age.

The Hyksos Buildings. The second season's digging at the north end of the mound brought to light architectural remains dating to the Middle Bronze Age II. Here, as in the section of the southern gate, the area was first leveled with a layer of earth on which the building foundations were laid. The remains were not clear, and the plan of the structure was not established. Directly above the Hyksos walls was a building with a paved courtyard and rooms on three sides (the fourth side was not excavated). In two rooms west of the courtyard ovens were found. The building, which was destroyed by fire, most probably dates to the Late Bronze Age II.

LATE BRONZE AGE. The Residency. A large building (25 by 22 m) at the northern section of the mound is by far the finest structure uncovered in the excavations. Its foundations are brick, in places set on a single stone course,

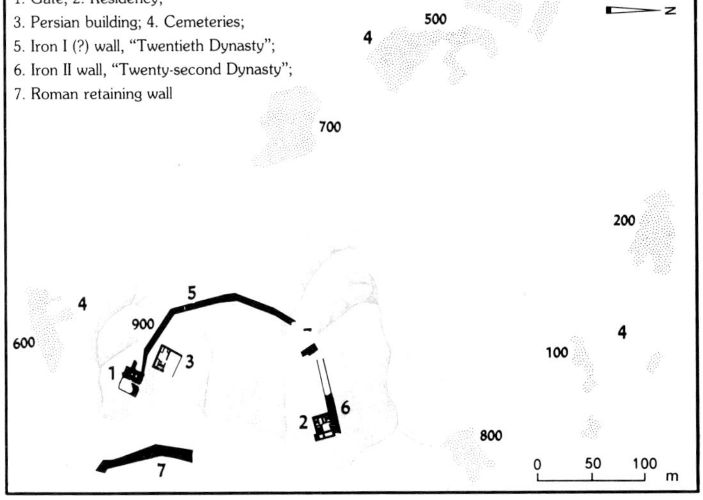

Tell el-Far'ah (South): plan of the mound and cemeteries.

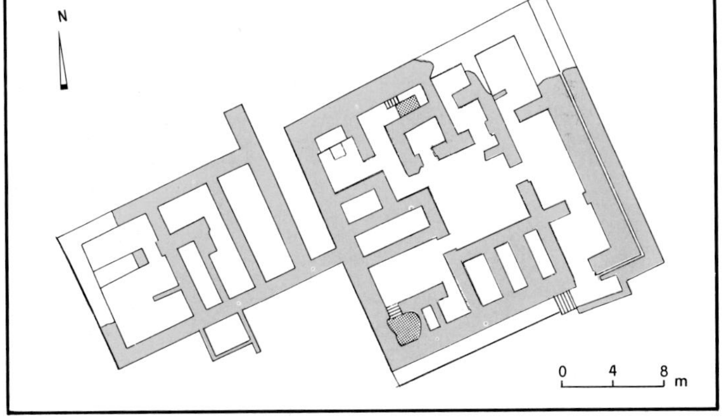

Plan of the residency, LB.

and lie directly on the Hyksos rampart in the north. The structure is made up of rooms on all four sides of a central courtyard. The bedroom has a raised platform set in a recess, which apparently served as a couch or bed. Adjoining the bedroom is a bathroom containing a plastered water tank raised about 1 m above the floor and reached by a flight of plastered steps. In a storeroom in the building remains of forty-five store jars were found, some of which were sealed with conical clay stoppers stamped with the figure of a god riding a lion. Adjoining this building to the west stood a smaller building (19 by 22 m), which probably housed the domestic offices and services. The residency was entered through a large paved courtyard, from which a flight of steps led to the building itself. The pavement of the courtyard shows traces of a path leading to the gate. Remains of steps leading either to the roof or to a second story were found in a small room in the southwest of the building. The residency was built at the end of the Late Bronze Age and apparently remained in existence until the eleventh century BCE, when it was destroyed by fire. It underwent at least two stages of construction on the same foundations, but the dates of these stages cannot be determined. The general plan is surprisingly similar to buildings of the Nineteenth Dynasty in Egypt. Of special interest are two finds, apparently dating to the beginning of the building's existence (the end of the thirteenth century BCE). The first, found in the courtyard, is the fragment of a jar inscribed with a cartouche of Seti II (end of the Nineteenth Dynasty). The other is a small charred wooden box found in one of the rooms. It is decorated with carved ivory inlays of a hunt in the swamps and the figures of a ruler, his servants, and dancing girls. The scenes themselves are clearly Egyptian, but the workmanship is Canaanite. Mycenean motifs also appear.

THE IRON AGE. The excavator suggested that the city wall shown in one of the plans of the excavation reports belongs to the Twentieth Dynasty. If that is so, then Sharuhen is one of only a few cities known to have been fortified during the Iron Age I.

The next level of occupation is found mainly to the south of the residency. Petrie also noted traces of later construction in the residency itself. The inhabitants of level X apparently added walls and floors to the ruins of the residency (which were still standing to a considerable height at that time) and reoccupied it. To the south, however, they erected new buildings.

According to the plan, level X is divided into two phases. Various architectural remains can be discerned, but they are not sufficient to give a clear picture of the buildings in this level. The finds date the level to the Iron Age IIA.

The next level, V-W, consists of a number of different phases. As Petrie himself states, it is quite difficult to arrive at a clear plan of any of the buildings. The only clear section is VK-VE, a paved courtyard (c. 2 m wide) in which the bottom sections of four pillars were found. It is very similar to the courtyard of the typical Israelite house, partially covered by a low roof supported on pillars. The roofed half of the courtyard housed the domestic animals, while the various household tasks were carried out in the other half. No trace has survived of any rooms around the courtyard. Most of the walls in this level were built of bricks on stone foundations. The excavators uncovered several sections of paved floor (probably of courtyards) and a large number of ovens. Level T-U seems to have been a phase of considerably more activity, but it too is quite fragmentary and cannot be fully understood.

Level R-S contains some of the finest architecture at Tell el Far'ah. At the

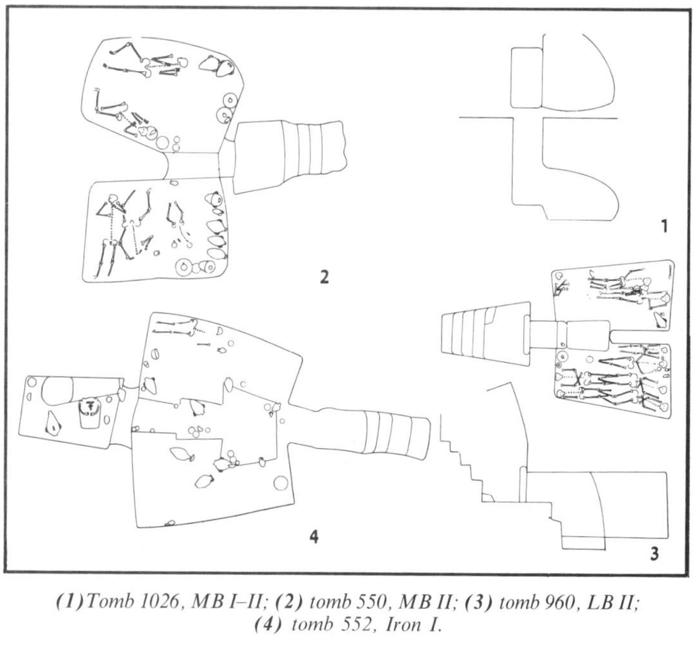

(1) Tomb 1026, MB I–II; (2) tomb 550, MB II; (3) tomb 960, LB II; (4) tomb 552, Iron I.

Anthropoid coffin lid from tomb 552, Iron I.

northern end of this level, the excavators uncovered a massive brick wall (5 m wide) built on a foundation of a single course of stone set deep into a layer of ash. Facing it was a brick retaining wall (2 m thick), whose foundations were somewhat higher than those of the first wall. Nearby stood a building (23 by 10 m) on a brick foundation, set in a layer of sand. The building consisted of a long courtyard enclosed by rooms on the north, south, and west sides. Various other sections of buildings also attest to intensive building activity in this level. It is difficult to determine the dates of the last two levels. The ceramic finds were mixed and also included pottery from the Persian period. Petrie ascribed level R-S to Pharaoh Shishak who, in Petrie's opinion, rebuilt the cities in southern Palestine after having conquered them.

None of the cemeteries at Tell el-Far'ah contained burials from the middle of the ninth to the seventh centuries BCE—a fact that may indicate a gap in settlement on the mound in that period. It is therefore possible that "Shishak's level," the last of the Iron Age settlements, actually dates to the end of Iron Age II (the seventh to the sixth centuries BCE) and was established during one of the periods of southward expansion of the late Judean kingdom.

The architectural remains above the gates in the southern part of the mound are too fragmentary to form a clear picture. In the north, the Persian remains are very meager, and in the south only one structure recognizable as a house was found. It was square, with a large courtyard and rooms along the south side that were probably built around another interior courtyard.

THE ROMAN PERIOD. A clear plan was obtained of the Roman settlement. At the northern end of the mound stood a fortified structure (20 by 15 m) with stone foundations. It consisted of a courtyard with rooms on three sides. To the west of this structure were two thick, well-built, parallel walls (perhaps the remnants of a gate) and a large hall with two columns covered with white stucco. On the floor of the hall three hoards of coins were found dating from the first century CE. At the center of the mound, not far below the surface, the stone foundations of Roman houses were exposed; in the southern part of the mound were remains of long, parallel halls, similar to Roman army barracks or storehouses. On the east, at the foot of the mound, stood a retaining wall (c. 100 m long and 10 m thick) constructed of carefully laid courses of sandstone bound with small stones and mortar. At the time of the excavations, the wall stood 3 m above ground level, but it was not fully excavated. Petrie records the discovery of some sherds of Roman pottery in the wall. No remains later than the first century CE were discovered in the excavations, except for a stamped Byzantine clay stopper that was picked up on the surface of the mound.

THE CEMETERIES. A large part of both seasons of excavations was devoted to the numerous cemeteries around the mound. More than 350 tombs, lying mostly to the north, south, and west, were excavated. Unfortunately, Petrie's descriptions of the tombs are rather brief and sometimes incomplete.

Middle Bronze Age II Burials. Tombs from the Middle Bronze Age II were found in cemeteries 500, 700, and 1000. Cemetery 1000 contained rectangular shaft graves with one or two burial chambers, occasionally separated by a high step. In cemetery 500, two other types of tombs were discovered. One consisted of a long, narrow stepped passageway (dromos) leading from the north toward two oval burial chambers that communicated via a very large opening. The second type also had a stepped passageway, but it led down to two rectangular burial chambers. The threshold at the entrance to the chambers was raised and extended inward to form a high step between them. Between the two burial chambers, a partition wall built as a continuation of the high step supported the ceiling.

Late Bronze Age Burials. Burials from the Late Bronze Age were found in cemeteries 100, 500, 600, and 900. The most interesting of these are the tombs of cemetery 900; they had been dug into the slope of the glacis, which had gone out of use. Tomb construction had improved greatly over the previous period. Now a stepped passageway on the west led to the tomb entrance and to a pit at the center of the tomb. A wide ledge ran along the walls of the tomb. The burial chambers were either square or round, and some tombs contained two chambers. Tomb 960 was the only one that had not been plundered or damaged. In it ten skeletons were laid full length on their backs, with their heads against the chamber walls. In tomb 902, nine skeletons were found; several Mycenean vessels had been placed at the head of one of them. Cemetery 900 was very rich in finds, which included pottery decorated with animal motifs characteristic of Late Bronze Age ceramics. This cemetery dates from the thirteenth to the middle of the twelfth centuries BCE—that is, prior to the beginning of the Philistine settlement here.

Iron Age I Burials. Burials dating to the Iron Age I were found in most of the cemeteries excavated. They confirm the stratigraphic evidence—namely, that a rich and densely populated settlement flourished here in this period. Of special importance are four tombs that, together with a fifth smaller one, Petrie designated as the "graves of the five lords of the Philistines." These tombs consist of a passageway of six or seven steps that lead down into a nearly square chamber. The steps continue in the chamber proper to a rectangular depression cut in the center of the floor. In two of the tombs (542 and 552) this rectangular depression extends beyond the wall opposite the entrance and leads into another small chamber cut along the tomb's central axis. The dead, it seems, were laid both in the central depression and on the ledge around it, but with no particular orientation. These tombs contained very rich finds, including an especially large quantity of Philistine pottery. Worthy of special note are two cigar-shaped anthropoid clay coffins from tombs 552 and 562. The human faces depicted on the lids have a short beard, and the arms emerge from behind the ears and join beneath the beard. Similar coffins are known from Beth-Shean, Lachish, and Deir el-Balaḥ, from Saḥab in Transjordan, and from Egypt. The Philistine tombs date from the twelfth to the eleventh centuries BCE. According to both Petrie and Albright, their chronological sequence was 542, 552, 532, 562. Cemetery 100 also belongs to the Iron Age I (and to the end of the Late Bronze Age). Its tombs are small and carelessly made, and most of them were plundered in antiquity.

Iron Age II Burials. Cemetery 200 belongs to the Iron Age II, with most of its tombs dating to the tenth and beginning of the ninth centuries BCE. The tombs were cut deep into the ground and lined with stone. They were usually covered with large stone slabs on which vessels had been placed after the tomb was sealed—apparently brought as offerings to the dead. Most of these tombs contained rich finds, including a large quantity of jewelry including armlets, rings, and necklaces. Tomb 201 may have been a family burial place; despite its small size (3.8 by 1.2 by 1.7 m), at least 116 adults were buried in it.

Burials in pottery vessels were also discovered in cemetery 200. The jars, similar in shape to Phoenician vessels, lay near the surface. They had been closed with inverted bowls or piles of stones. Inside were charred bones and small offering bowls. The finds in this cemetery included a Hebrew seal on

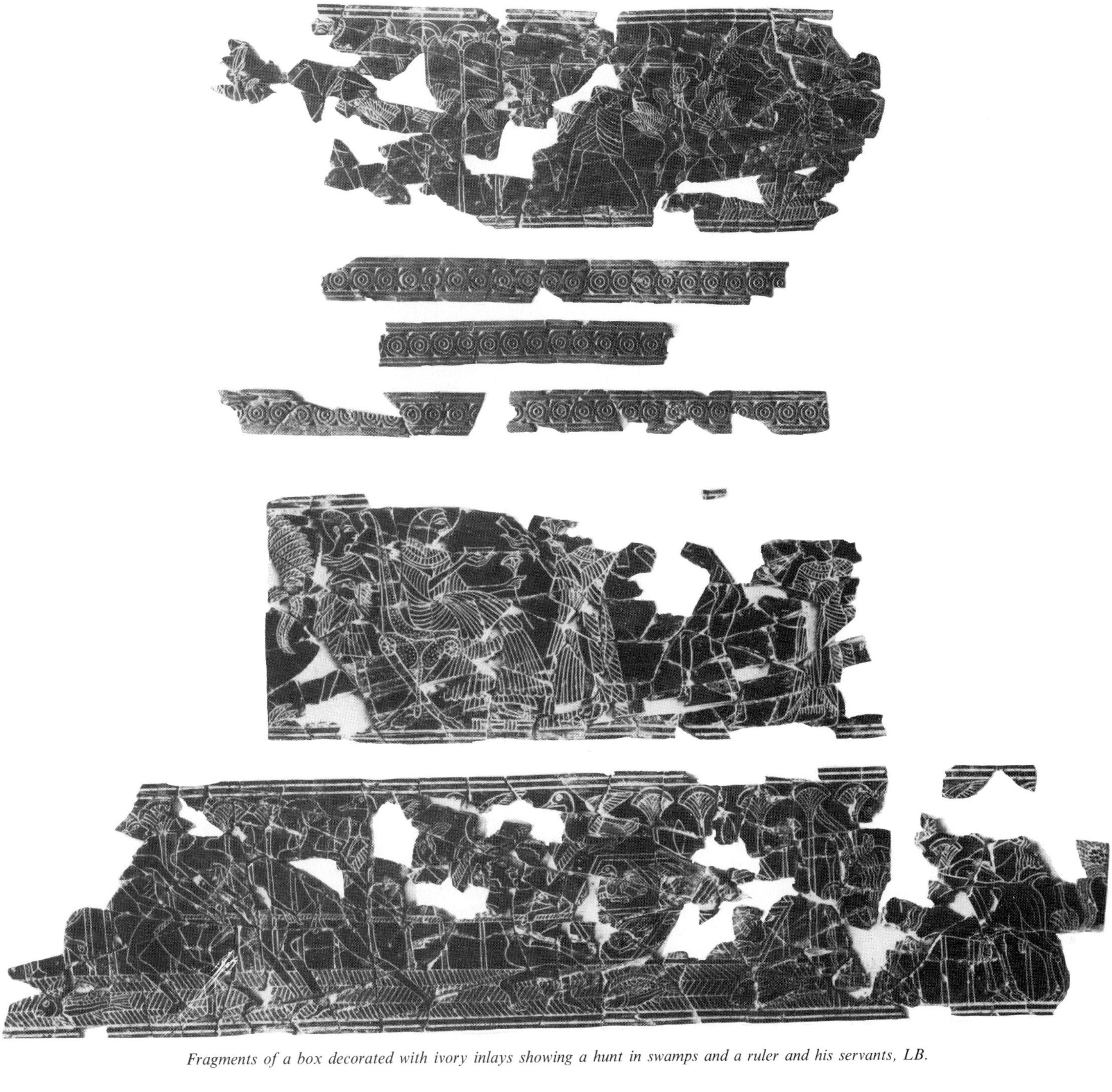

Fragments of a box decorated with ivory inlays showing a hunt in swamps and a ruler and his servants, LB.

Tell el-Far'ah (South): Aramaic ostracon, c. 300 BCE.

which a griffon wearing the double crown of Egypt and the Hebrew inscription *lḥym* were carved (tomb 228). As already mentioned, no burials were found dating from the eighth and seventh centuries BCE. This may indicate a gap in settlement on the site.

Persian Period Burials. Burials from the Persian period were discovered in cemeteries 100, 600, and 800. Tomb 650 consisted of a large burial chamber with a bricked-up entrance and a forecourt. This tomb yielded the metal frame of a couch on which the corners and tie rods were connected to the legs, a silver fluted bowl with an omphalos bottom, kohl vials, and a silver dipper with a handle shaped like a girl swimming. On one of the corners of the metal couch frame were several Phoenician letters. This grave is dated to the fifth or fourth century BCE.

A great quantity of metal objects was uncovered in the cemeteries at Tell el-Far'ah, among them iron weapons, which make their first appearance here in graves from the Iron Age I. Four different types of metal bowls were discovered in the cemeteries. Two are characteristic of the Iron Age and two of the Persian period. Metal strainers were also found, as well as spoons with handles terminating in duck's heads. An ostracon inscribed in Aramaic and dating to approximately 300 BCE was found on the surface of the mound.

YAEL YISRAELI

ḤAẒERIM (FARMS) NEAR TELL EL-FAR'AH

Six Iron Age settlements were examined in the vicinity of South Tell el-Far'ah by R. Gophna, during a survey and soundings conducted from 1960 to 1963 in the region of Naḥal Besor, on behalf of the Israel Department of Antiquities. The settlements contained remains of huts, grain pits, millstones, ovens, and pottery. None of the sites, which ranged in size from 0.5 to 2.5 a., revealed significant occupational debris or archaeological finds. The ceramic assemblages were homogeneous throughout. The evidence indicates that these settlements existed for a very short time only. Five of the six sites can be dated to the Iron Age IIA. The sixth, the largest of the group, was settled during the Iron Age IIC.

It is possible that these sites are the biblical *ḥaẓerim* (farms) that existed at various times during the Iron Age in the vicinity of the large settlement at Tell el-Far'ah. Their connection with Tell el-Far'ah seems obvious because of their proximity (1.5 to 6 km [1 to 4 mi.]) and because the mound was visible from all of them. Moreover, the pottery found in each of them is identical with that discovered by Petrie's expedition in the excavations at Tell el-Far'ah. The pottery from the five *ḥaẓerim* dating to the Iron Age IIA was found in strata X, V, and W of the mound. The ceramic finds at the sixth *ḥaẓer*, dating to the Iron Age IIC, have their counterpart, apparently, in level R-S on the mound.

RAM GOPHNA

Identification: W. F. Albright, *BASOR* 33 (1929), 7; Abel, *GP* 2, 451; A. Kempinski, *IEJ* 24 (1974), 145–152; W. H. Shea, ibid. 29 (1979), 1–5.

Main publications: W. M. F. Petrie, *Beth Pelet* 1, London 1930; E. MacDonald et al., *Beth Pelet* 2, London 1932; D. Price-Williams, *The Tombs of the Middle Bronze Age II Period from the "500" Cemetery at Tell Far'a (South)*, London 1977.

Other studies: J. G. Duncan (with contributions by J. L. Starkey and W. M. F. Petrie), *Corpus of Palestinian Pottery*, London 1930; J. H. Iliffe, *QDAP* 4 (1935), 182–186; J. Waldbaum, *AJA* 70 (1966), 331–340; W. H. Stiebing, Jr., ibid. 74 (1970), 139–143; D. Price-Williams, *An Examination of Middle Bronze Age II Typology and Sequence Dating in Palestine, with Particular Reference to the Tombs of Jericho and Fara (South)* 1–2 (Ph.D. diss., Univ. of London 1975); id., *"500" Cemetery* (Reviews), *ZDPV* 95 (1979), 210–211. — *PEQ* 112 (1980), 66–67; R. Cohen, *IEJ* 27 (1977), 170; K. R. Maxwell-Hyslop, *Archaeology in the Levant* (K. M. Kenyon Fest.), Warminster 1978, 180–182; id. et al., *Levant* 10 (1978), 112–115; T. L. McClellan, *JFA* 6 (1979), 57–73; H. Liebowitz, *IEJ* 30 (1980), 162–169; D. Gazit, *ESI* 4 (1985), 28; J. N. Tubb, *PEQ* 118 (1986), 51–65; L. Khalil, *BIAL* 23 (1986–1987), 171–178; M. O'D. Shea, ibid., 161–169; E. D. Oren, *Journal of the Society for the Study of Egyptian Antiquities* 14 (1984), 47–48; C. Uehlinger, *ZDPV* 104 (1988), 5–25; Weippert 1988 (Ortsregister); J. K. Hoffmeier, *Levant* 23 (1991), 117–124; J. Weinstein, ibid., 105–115; B. G. Wood, *BAR* 17/6 (1991), 50–52.

Tomb 650: silver bowl and ladle, Persian period.

FEJJA

IDENTIFICATION

The ruins of the Arab village of Fejja (map reference 141.165), today within the municipal boundaries of Petaḥ Tiqva, are located about 5 km (3 mi.) from the mound of Aphek. The name Fejja recalls the Greek name of the Hellenistic site, Pegai (πηγαί) (The Springs). Pegai is mentioned for the first time in 259 BCE, in the Zenon papyri (*PSI* 406), as a frontier post, probably between Samaria and the territory of the Greek polis on the Coastal Plain. For topographical reasons, and especially because of the lack of springs at Fejja, this post seems to have been actually located near the source of the Yarkon River at Tel Aphek (map reference 143.168) some distance from Fejja. Mishnaic sources mention Mei-Pigah ("waters of Pigah" in Mishnah *Par.* 8:10) or simply Pigah (Tosefta *Ter.* 1:15). In the Mishnah, Aphek is usually known as Antipatris, a city founded by Herod. Possibly the whole area around Aphek was called The Springs, from the Hellenistic period onward. This would explain the persistence of the name at such a distance from the actual sources.

EXPLORATION

In 1951, J. Kaplan carried out an archaeological survey in Fejja and later excavated here on a small scale (see below). The survey showed that the Arab village was built on formerly uninhabited land. Ancient remains, however, were found some dozen meters north of the village. The remains were found

Fejja: round winery pit (no. 2), area C, Roman period.

scattered through three areas, all in the same vicinity. Area A, the closest to the ruins of the village, was made up of whitish-gray earth that contained a great number of sherds from the Middle Bronze Age II and Persian period. Area B extended over a strip of grayish earth, northwest of area A and parallel to the Lod–Petaḥ Tiqva road. The ground in this area was covered with small field stones and many sherds from the Persian period and Iron Age II. In area C, about 100 m northeast of area A, there were a number of structures, the remnants of a wine industry: winepresses and wine cellars sunk into the ground.

EXCAVATIONS

In 1963, J. Kaplan carried out trial excavations in areas A and B, assisted by R. Cohen. In area A, five short trenches were dug 2 by 3 m each. In trench A1, two levels of settlement were revealed but no building remains. The upper level dated to the Middle Bronze Age IIB–C and the lower one, which was built on virgin soil, to the Middle Bronze Age IIA. Trench A2 yielded similar finds with the addition of a single potsherd (bow rim) belonging to the Wadi Rabah culture and two Ghassulian potsherds. A number of Iron Age II sherds were also found, and on the surface, near trench A1, lay a coin of Alexander Jannaeus.

In trench B, a 60-cm-thick layer dating to the Persian period was followed by two Middle Bronze Age strata, the first belonging to the Middle Bronze Age IIB–C and the second (built on virgin soil) to Middle Bronze Age IIA.

In trench C, immediately below the surface, a Roman level of settlement was uncovered. It contained, inter alia, a Roman coin from the first century CE. Below the Roman stratum was a Middle Bronze Age IIB–C level of settlement, containing two sections of mud-brick walls. On the floor by these walls were sherds of juglets and jars from the Middle Bronze Age IIB–C. Below this stratum was a Middle Bronze Age IIA level founded on virgin soil. In the upper part of this level, the foundations of a stone wall were uncovered.

Trench D was apparently outside the ancient zone of area A. The top layer yielded only a throwout of mixed Persian and Middle Bronze Age pottery fragments. The earth beneath this mixed layer was sandy and in it were discovered, inter alia, fragments of a basalt bowl whose rim was decorated on the interior with incised hatched triangles typical of the Chalcolithic period.

Area C contained remains of winepresses and cellars for the wine industry, all dating to the Roman period. The remnants of three different installations were uncovered. Number 1 was for the most part in ruins, with only a part of the mosaic-paved treading floor remaining. Number 2 was also almost completely damaged, save for part of a round winery pit, with a mosaic floor paved in a pattern of circles. Number 3 was almost completely preserved. A section of the treading floor and the entire square winery pit were cleared. The floor of the pit was paved with mosaics. A lead pipe was found running from the treading floor to the pit.

SUMMARY

The presence on the site of a potsherd from the Wadi Rabah culture, of Ghassulian pottery, and of fragments of a Ghassulian basalt bowl provides evidence that remains of settlements belonging to these periods are buried nearby. Investigations in the trenches showed that the site was established and reached its height of development chiefly during the two phases of the Middle Bronze Age IIA and IIB–C, from which time building remains were also found. The settlement of Fejja at that period was doubtless connected with the mother settlement of Tel Aphek, which was first excavated in the 1930s by J. Ory. The extent of the settlement in the Iron Age II was not examined, but it appears to have been limited. In contrast, the Persian stratum (apparently fifth century BCE) revealed extensive settlement. The lack of Hellenistic remains is not surprising, as has been pointed out above. It was only in the first century CE that settlement was renewed to continue throughout the Roman-Byzantine period.

A. Alt, *ZDPV* 45 (1922), 220–223.

JACOB KAPLAN

FÛL, TELL EL-

IDENTIFICATION

Tell el-Fûl is part of the ridge north of Jerusalem that becomes Mount Scopus and the Mount of Olives to the south, some 5 km (3 mi.) north of the city's Damascus Gate. It stands in some isolation, with no other promontories nearby. It is situated on the crest of a watershed rising 862 m above sea level (map reference 1719.1367). On a clear day, from the top of the mound, the Dead Sea is visible to the southeast; northeast, the view is toward Geba and Michmash; northwest lies Nebi Samwil, and there is a commanding view of Jerusalem sprawled over the hills to the south. The ancient north–south road ran along the foot of Tell el-Fûl to the west, as does the modern one. Its location and panoramic view have made it an important strategic site.

Tel el-Fûl means "Mound of Horse Beans" in Arabic. It rises about 30 m above the surrounding plain, with a relatively level summit (c. 150 m north to south and 90 m east to west). It is not strictly a tell, as the occupational debris was seldom as much as 2 m. Most scholars identify the site with biblical Gibeah (Gibeah of Benjamin, Gibeah of Saul).

C. Warren carried out a two-week excavation at Tell el-Fûl in 1868 and C. R. Conder described the remains in 1874, but the debate over the identification with Gibeah of Saul continued until W. F. Albright's excavation in 1922–1923 (see below).

HISTORY

Gibeah (the Gibeah of Benjamin and the Gibeah of Saul) was the center of the territory of the tribe of Benjamin during the period of the Judges, and it was the royal residence during King Saul's reign. The town has several appellations in the Bible (cf. Jg. 20:4, 20:14, 20:19; 1 Chr. 11:31). In some cases, the names Geba and Gibeah are confused. During its first period of settlement, Gibeah was apparently the capital of the Benjaminites, located on the main road leading from Judah and Jerusalem northward to Mount Ephraim (Jg. 19:11–13). The destruction of the town by burning is the subject of a story in Judges 19–20. Saul lived there before he rose to royal rank (1 Sam. 10:26, 11:4). Although the grave of his father, Kish, was in Zela (2 Sam. 21:14), his family's lands were probably near Gibeah. Saul's genealogy, as preserved in 1 Chronicles 8:29 ff., speaks of Gibeon as the place of origin of his family. However, we know that after the victory of Saul and Jonathan over the Philistines, Gibeah became the king's residence. It was then renamed Gibeah of Saul (1 Sam. 15:34 ff.).

Tell el-Fûl: plan of fortress II; proposed reconstruction after the 1964 season.

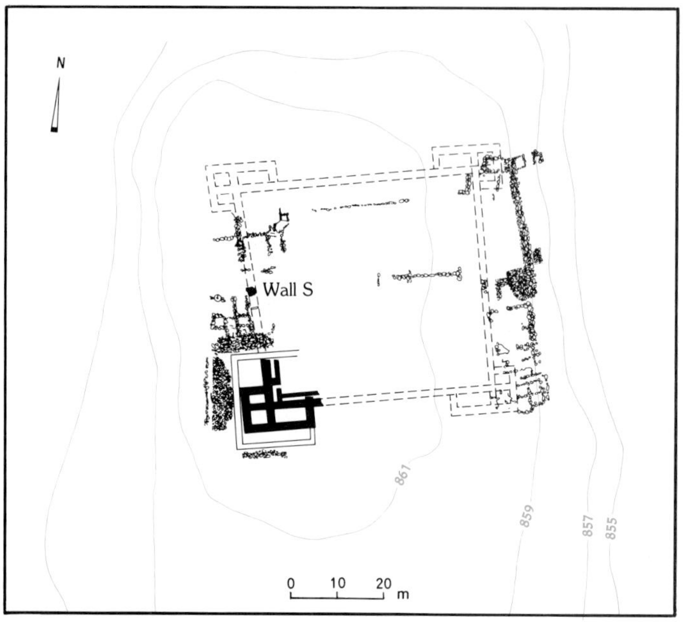

Plan of fortress III and the casemate system.

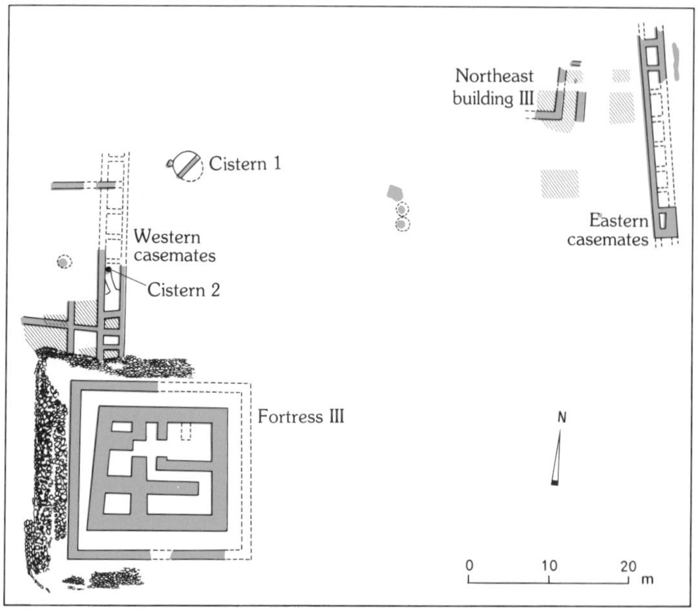

One of David's warriors came from this town: "Ittai the son of Ribai of Gibeah of the Benjaminites" (2 Sam. 23:29; 1 Chr. 11:31). According to 1 Chronicles 12:3, "Ahiezer, then Joash, both sons of Shemaah of Gibeah," were among Saul's kinsmen who came to David at Ziklag. Michaiah, the daughter of Uriel, who was the mother of Abijah, king of Judah, was also from Gibeah (2 Chr. 13:2). The abandonment of Gibeah is mentioned in the description of the putative route of the Assyrian invasion from the north (Is. 10:29). There is little information about Gibeah from later periods. Josephus (*War* V, 51) mentions a village named Gibeah of Saul, about 30 stadia (about 5.5 km) north of Jerusalem, near which Titus camped the night before he attacked Jerusalem.

EXCAVATIONS

W. F. Albright, on behalf of the American Schools of Oriental Research, conducted two campaigns at Tell el-Fûl ten years apart (1922–1923 and 1933). The publication from his second campaign did not appear until 1960 and raised some new problems concerning the possible date of the fortress on the site and of the other periods of occupation. For this reason, in 1964, P. W. Lapp (with Albright's concurrence and assisted by J. L. Kelso) conducted a six-week salvage excavation in 1964 at Tell el-Fûl, before King Hussein's plans to build a West Bank palace on the ancient site were underway. Lapp's work, in the main, confirmed Albright's earlier conclusions—the first campaign somewhat more than the second—and clarified the occupational history of Tell el-Fûl.

Only a handful of scattered pre-Iron I sherds were uncovered in the 1964 campaign and, although some are mentioned in connection with earlier excavations, none are published. There was some evidence of the pre-fortress phase, period I (c. 1200 BCE), beneath the period II wall on bedrock and on a floor on the eastern side of the mound. There was no evidence of destruction, but abandonment is usually associated with the revenge against the Benjaminites as recorded in Judges 19–20.

CHRONOLOGICAL TABLE OF TELL EL-FÛL, ACCORDING TO LAPP (1964)

Period	*Date*
I	1200-1150 BCE (pre-fortress)
II	1025-950 BCE (fortresses I and II)
III	650-587 BCE, phase A (fortress III)
	587-538 BCE, phase B
IV	175-135 BCE, phase A
	135-100 BCE, phase B
	100-63 BCE, phase C
V	c. 70 CE

PERIOD II (FORTRESSES I AND II). The construction of the first fortress on the mound, fortress I, is characterized by large, roughly dressed stones laid in irregular courses. Only the southwest corner tower and parts of the adjacent casemate walls were preserved. Based on Albright's reconstruction, the fortress was a rectangle with casemate walls and reinforcing towers, presumably one in each corner. Some casemates were filled with earth and stones, whereas others were used for storage, having doorways into the fortress. This would make the length of the fortress about 52 m, its width 35 m, and the preserved area of the tower about 13 by 9 m. According to Albright, Saul built fortress I. A. Alt and B. Mazar have suggested that it was one of a series of Philistine fortresses built to control the principal trade routes and was later occupied by Saul, during whose reign fortress II was built. The original conclusion drawn by L. A. Sinclair that fortress I was built by Saul and that David may have repaired it (fortress II) following the original plan must now be reconsidered. Claims have been made that the fortress was actually Hellenistic. In the fortress proper, an iron plow tip came to light. This and a similar plow tip from Beth-Shemesh are among the earliest known iron objects from the Israelite period.

Part of the western casemate wall.

Jar handles stamped Yršlm ***(left)*** *and* Yhd ***(right)***, *Hellenistic period.*

One of the principle objectives of the third campaign was to reassess the date of the fortifications, especially the fortress attributed to Saul. A trench laid out northwest of the tower Albright excavated yielded clear Iron Age IC pottery in undisturbed debris against the tower's north face and in its foundation trench. This pottery, exclusively from the post-Philistine phase of the Iron Age I, definitely dates the tower to the time of Saul, as Albright maintained. In the second campaign, Albright claimed substantial rebuilding following a major destruction; however, the evidence from the third campaign neither confirmed nor denied his conclusions about the two successive fortresses in the Iron Age I. Albright thought the tower he unearthed in the southwest was one of the four corner towers of Saul's fortress, using as his model other fortresses known from that period. Questions had been raised in the scholarly community concerning this reconstruction and his claim for a casemate wall, which would be one of the earliest in the country. In the third campaign, excavations north of the tower revealed a 3-m segment of a wall (wall S) approximately on line with the west wall (the 1.5-m discrepancy could be due to the contours of the hill). Three more stones from the wall were uncovered 2.75 m to the south, and a deposit of period II sherds was found on bedrock at the base of the Iron Age II revetment against the tower. The wall S extension, however, was beyond Albright's reconstruction of the fortress, so the fortification probably fitted the contours of the hill better than he supposed. Lapp found no evidence for a casemate and noted that Albright's inner casemate wall at the southwest corner of the fortress was not bonded to the outer wall but had straight joints. It is doubtful that there was a casemate fortification at this time.

PERIOD III. Refinements in pottery chronology point to the second half of the seventh and the sixth centuries BCE (Late Iron Age II and exilic period) for the principal period III occupation at Tell el-Fûl. It was probably during Josiah's reign (640–609 BCE), when he attempted to extend his kingdom northward, that fortress III was rebuilt over the remains of the Iron Age I tower and a casemate wall was constructed. The destruction of the fortress is attributed to Nebuchadnezzar's campaign in 588–587 BCE. The earlier excavations found widespread destruction in the fortress area, but in 1964 the only evidence was an ashy layer in one building on the northeast. Once the fortress was useless, the Babylonians may have been unconcerned with the remainder of the town's inhabitants and allowed them to live in peace. Occupation did continue, probably throughout the exilic period (period IIIB) and then the site was abandoned; the inhabitants may have joined the returnees to Jerusalem.

Thus, there were two defensive elements in the Late Iron Age II: a revetted tower and its casemate wall system. The tower probably served as a *migdal*, or watchtower; its principal function was as a lookout post for Jerusalem against surprise attacks, and, if necessary, to take the brunt of any surprise itself. Its stronger walls and sloping revetment set it off from the usual Negev forts to which it has been compared. On the other hand, it is its thin and relatively feeble casemate construction that makes it comparable to the Negev fortresses, rather than the stronger Iron Age II casemates at Kadesh-Barnea and Arad, for example. Tell el-Fûl's casemates were keyed

Casemate wall of period III: plastered basins from the Hellenistic period were built inside.

into the Iron Age II revetted tower, extending north. Where the casemates were uncovered on the eastern side of the mound, they may have been related to a revetted tower on the northeast (removed by later Hellenistic construction). The towers and casemate walls gave limited protection against a major attack, but they did provide domestic space and storage for the families and supporters who manned the fort.

The Tell el-Fûl period IIIA pottery is comparable to other Late Iron Age II ceramic groups, such as those at Beth-Zur (stratum III), Lachish (II), the very latest stratum at Tell Beit Mirsim, Ramat Raḥel (VA), and En-Gedi (V). The earliest Tell el-Fûl Iron Age II pottery (limited almost completely to the midfield silos) dates to about 700 BCE, along with Ramat Raḥel (VB) and the Beth-Zur pottery cache, slightly later than the Iron Age II pottery of Lachish III, Tell Beit Mirsim A2, Beth-Shemesh IIC, and Beersheba II. Tell el-Fûl period IIIB pottery dates to the exilic period (c. 587–532 BCE). Comparable pottery groups come from Bethel (locus sub-104), Beth-Shemesh (tomb 14), Gibeon (part of mixed groups), Tell en-Naṣbeh (some cisterns), Lachish (some tombs), and Samaria (some in period VIII). Tell el-Fûl's homogeneous pottery from the exilic period makes an important contribution to the pottery chronology of this period.

PERIOD IV. The principal Hellenistic occupation (period IV) belonged to the second century BCE, mainly toward the end of the century (period IVB). After the Albright campaigns and before pottery chronology of this period was well established, the period IV material was dated as early as the seventh century BCE (after 1922), but mainly to the third century BCE (after 1933). There was a possible light occupation at the end of the third century BCE, some occupation from 175 to 135 BCE (phase IVA), and some from 100 to 63 BCE (IVC), but the site flourished from 135 to 100 BCE (phase IVB). In addition to the pottery, which is now well-known, some coins, an ostracon, and two stamped jar handles provided chronological pegs. All evidence of fortress IV had been removed before the third campaign, but excavation revealed that the casemate rooms were reused and occupation had spread outside the walls to the edges of the mound. An interesting double vat installation was uncovered in the southwest area, above earlier Iron Age II installations. What may have been a tower on the northeast was excavated; a three-room house in two phases was found inside the wall, west of the tower.

PERIOD V. Roman pottery from period V (c. 70 CE) points to a settlement of short duration—several months to a few years. Occupation layers in the northwest indicated more than a Roman campsite, but it did not compare to the flourishing occupation of periods III and IV. A small number of Roman sherds was recovered in all three campaigns, although a clear distinction between the Hellenistic and Roman periods was not made until the third campaign.

THE SILOS. Silos hewn in the bedrock were found throughout the excavations in all the campaigns. Most of them were probably dug early in the occupational history of Tell el-Fûl and were used in succeeding periods. Because the contents had been deposited during the last use of the silo or accidentally during subsequent occupations of the site, they were not useful for dating the silo's original construction. Several were below Hellenistic floors or were covered by Hellenistic or even Iron Age II walls. The silos can be generally divided into two groups: large silos with an average depth of 2.26 m and small ones about 1.6 m deep. Some were capped or had recesses for caps. Silos with similar contents and a similar geological makeup are recorded from Tell en-Naṣbeh, and the "wine cellars" found at Gibeon are comparable to the large Tell el-Fûl silos. It is probable that at all three sites (which have similar occupational histories and are in the same geographic area), the silos housed storage jars filled with grain or liquids. Many of the silos were dug in the Iron Age I, more were cut in the Iron Age II, and some were in use for as long as the site was occupied.

Main publications: W. F. Albright, *Excavations and Results of Tell el-Ful (Gibeah of Saul)* (AASOR 4), New Haven 1924; N. L. Lapp, *The Third Campaign at Tell el-Ful: The Excavations of 1964* (AASOR 45), Cambridge, Mass. 1981.

Other studies: Conder–Kitchener, *SWP* 3, 158–160; V. Guérin, *Description de la Palestine, Samarie* 1, 188ff.; Alt, *KSch.* 2, 31, n. 1; 3, 259; K. Galling, *Biblisches Reallexicon* (Handbuch zum Alten Testament), Tübingen 1937, 193; A. Demsky, *BASOR* 212 (1973), 26–31; J. M. Miller, *ZDPV* 99 (1983), 121–122; E. Puech, *BASOR* 261 (1986), 69–72; Weippert 1988 (Ortsregister); P. M. Arnold, *Gibeah: The Search for a Biblical City* (Journal for the Study of the Old Testament Supplement Series 79), Sheffield 1990.

Albright excavations: W. F. Albright, *BASOR* 52 (1933), 6–12; L. A. Sinclair, *AASOR* 34–35 (1960), 1–52; id., *BA* 27 (1964), 52–64.

Lapp excavations: L. A. Sinclair, *BA* 27 (1964), 52–64; P. W. Lapp, ibid. 28 (1965), 2–10; id., *Archäologie und Altes Testament* (K. Galling Fest.), Tübingen 1970, 179–197; id., *The Tale of the Tell*, Pittsburgh 1975, 83–90; N. L. Lapp, *BASOR* 223 (1976), 25–42; id., *The Third Campaign* (Reviews), *PEQ* 116 (1984), 73. — *ZDPV* 103 (1987), 226–230; E. Puech, *BASOR* 261 (1986), 69–72.

NANCY L. LAPP

G

GALILEE

The mountains of Lower Galilee rise about 600 m above sea level, whereas those of Upper Galilee attain elevations of up to about 1,200 m. The east–west mountain ranges of Lower Galilee are interspersed with fertile valleys, affording easy passage, while Upper Galilee consists of rugged mountain blocks and only a few valleys. The Galilee is composed mostly of chalk, limestone, and dolomite, with extensive basalt-covered areas in its eastern part. Although the soil is largely fertile, much of the region's hilly area is strewn with boulders. Lower Galilee has a warmer climate than Upper Galilee; the former's average annual rainfall is about 600 m, while that of Upper Galilee is about 800 mm. Most of the Galilee's natural vegetation is Mediterranean wood, whose components vary according to climate, amount of rainfall, and the types of soil and rock.

PREHISTORIC PERIODS

Human occupation in the prehistoric periods, known from Upper and Lower Galilee, the Ḥula Basin, and the Coastal Plain of western Galilee, is summarized below.

LOWER PALEOLITHIC PERIOD. One of the country's earliest sites from the Lower Paleolithic period is located near Kibbutz 'Evron in western Galilee. It dates to over half a million years ago. The lithics and faunal remains, including those of an elephant, a rare species of warthog, and other animals (q.v. 'Evron) indicate that the site was used for hunting and butchering prey. Another exceptional site is Gesher Benot Ya'aqov, where the earliest layer (dated c. 500,000 BP) yielded basalt hand axes—unique in Israel (q.v. Gesher Benot Ya'aqov). A few flint tools were found underneath the basalt cover at Ramat Yir'on, in Upper Galilee. These artifacts predate the basalt lava flow, which is dated to 2.4 million years ago.

Sites from the Late Acheulean culture, dating to the terminal Lower Paleolithic, were mostly detected on Eocene plateaus or basalt flows at Ramat Yir'on and Bar'am. Similar remains were found at Ma'ayan Barukh and near Kibbutz 'Evron. Remains of the culture termed Yabrudian, from the terminal Lower Paleolithic (130,000 BP?), were recovered in the Zuttiyeh Cave in Naḥal 'Amud (q.v.). This layer yielded a human cranium, so far the earliest human remains recovered in Israel.

MIDDLE PALEOLITHIC PERIOD. Unlike the Lower Paleolithic remains, which were mainly found at open-air sites, Middle Paleolithic remains were discovered in caves, such as the Zuttiyeh, 'Amud, and Shovakh caves in Naḥal 'Amud (q.v.); the Qafzeh Cave (q.v.) near Nazareth; and Hayonim Cave (q.v.) in western Galilee. The flint tools characteristic of the preceding period—hand axes—are replaced by scrapers, points, and denticulates. A novel feature in this period is the relatively large number of skeletons that were carefully interred, for the first time in human history. A burial in a flexed position was found in the 'Amud Cave and a burial ground containing sixteen skeletons was found in the Qafzeh Cave. The man from Naḥal 'Amud is morphologically similar to the Neanderthal, whereas the Qafzeh population is of a modern human type. Both human types manufactured the same lithic artifacts and existed under the same socioeconomic conditions.

UPPER PALEOLITHIC PERIOD. The Upper Paleolithic remains, characterized by blades, end scrapers, and burins, were, as in the Middle Paleolithic, found only in caves. Upper Paleolithic layers were detected in Hayonim Cave, the Qafzeh Cave, and the Emireh Cave at Naḥal 'Amud. No skeletons dating from this period were found in the Galilee.

EPIPALEOLITHIC OR TERMINAL PALEOLITHIC PERIOD. The Epipaleolithic period is divided into the Kebaran (20,000–12,000 BP) and the Natufian (12,000–10,000 BP) stages. Kebaran remains were detected on the terraces fronting the Hayonim and Emireh caves, and in the bed of Naḥal Dishon, near 'En Miri. The Kebaran stage is characterized by an abundance of microliths and by temporary encampments. The succeeding Natufian stage marks the onset of sedentarism and the appearance of sickle blades and what might be regarded as art objects. The Natufian stage is known from Hayonim Cave and from 'Enan (q.v.) in the Ḥula Basin, at both of which a large number of burials was unearthed (about forty in the former and one hundred in the latter). The village found at 'Enan featured circular structures (diameter, 5–10 m) that were partially dug into the ground and faced with stones. Within and near the structures were plastered silos, apparently used to store cereals. The floors of several structures were plastered and even painted. In one of the graves, a human body was interred with a young dog. This is one of the earliest direct archaeological examples of the man-dog link, long before the domestication of any other animal.

NEOLITHIC PERIOD. In the Neolithic period (10,000–7000 BP), animal husbandry and agriculture were already being practiced. Sites from this period in the Galilee extend from Achzib, on the coast, to the Tanur waterfall, and from the Beth Netofa Valley to Ḥanita. The most intensively explored Neolithic sites are Beisamûn (q.v.) in the Ḥula Basin and Yiftaḥel in the Beth Netofa Valley. At both sites, rectangular structures with plastered floors, hearths, post holes, various installations, and storage pits were found. The tools characteristic of the period are arrowheads, axes (some of them polished), sickle blades, and awls. Human burials with their skulls removed were found under the house floors, and at Beisamun there were two plastered skulls, of the type found along the Jordan Valley, from Jericho through Rabbath-Ammon and up to Tell Ramad in Syria.

M. W. Prausnitz, *IEJ* 9 (1959), 166–174; 19 (1969), 129–136; E. de Vaumas, ibid. 13 (1963), 195–207; M. Lechevallier and G. Dollfus, *EI* 11 (1973), 9*–21*; R. Frankel and R. Gophna, *TA* 7 (1980), 65–69; A. Brosh and M. Ohel, *Paléorient* 7/1 (1981), 23–32; M. T. Ohel, *Proceedings of the Prehistoric Society* 48 (1982); 29–43; 52 (1986), 247–280; id., *Archaeology* 36/4 (1983), 64–65, 77; id., *Bullétin de la Société Préhistorique Francaise* 80 (1983), 179–183; id., *Anthropos* 80 (1985), 199–225; id., *The Acheulean of the Yiron Plateau, Israel* (*BAR*/IS 307), Oxford 1986; ibid. (Review), *AJA* 92 (1988), 443. — *Mitekufat Ha'even* 21 1988), 165*–171*. — *PEQ* 121 (1989), 151; id., *Mitekufat Ha'even* 19 (1986), 12*–30*; id., *Investigations in South Levantine Prehistory: Préhistoire du Sud-Levant* (*BAR*/IS 497, eds. O. Bar-Yosef and B. Vandermeersch), Oxford 1989, 113–123; id., *Lithic Analysis of Acheulean Assemblages from the Avivim Sites, Israel* (*BAR*/IS 562), Oxford 1990; id., *PEQ* 123 (1991), 33–47; G. Bruder, *Mitekufat Ha'even* 18 (1985), 13*–20*; M. Weinstein-Evron, *Pollen et Spores* 28 (1986), 157–165; I. Hershkovitz and A. Gopher, *Paléorient* 14/1 (1988), 119–125; Weippert 1988, 75f.; A. Gopher, *Mitekufat Ha'even* 22 (1989), 82*–92*.

AVRAHAM RONEN

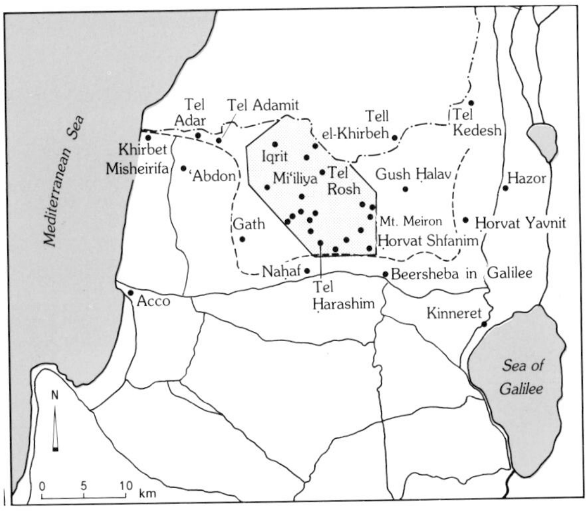

Upper Galilee: map of the main sites.

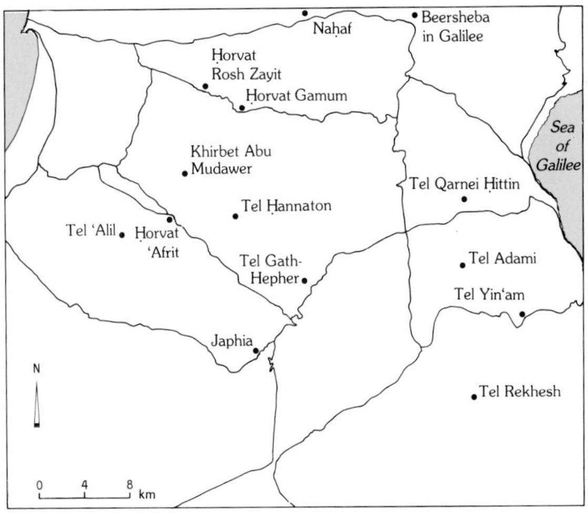

Lower Galilee: map of the main sites.

CHALCOLITHIC TO PERSIAN PERIODS

EXPLORATION

The Galilee has been somewhat neglected in archaeological research. Extensive excavations of major tells have been carried out only at Dan (q.v.) and Hazor (q.v.) and limited work was conducted at Tel Kedesh (q.v.). Initial surveys were conducted in the early 1920s by several scholars, among them W. F. Albright, J. Garstang, and A. Saarisalo. Later, from 1950 to 1953, parts of Upper Galilee were surveyed by R. Amiran and Y. Aharoni, who also excavated limited areas at Tel Kedesh and Tel Ḥarashim (see below). N. Zori surveyed the eastern Lower Galilee from the 1950s through the mid-1960s.

Systematic surveys of the Galilee were only initiated by the Israel Archaeological Survey in the mid-1970s, when Y. Olami, R. Frankel, A. Raban, and Z. Gal worked in western Lower Galilee, western Upper Galilee, the Nazareth Hills, and eastern Lower Galilee, respectively. A survey of selected sites in Upper Galilee was conducted by R. Frankel and M. Aviam in 1989–1990. As of this writing, the surveys are still underway. A periodical review based on data gathered in the various surveys follows.

CHALCOLITHIC PERIOD. One of the earliest sites discovered so far is in Naḥal Ẓippori, at the entrance to Moshav Ẓippori (map reference 1761.2374). Here, the pre-Ghassulian site was cut by the Nazareth–Shefar'am highway. Debris, foundations of walls, and plaster floors were observed in the sections. The pottery recovered here consists mostly of shiny red-slipped ware. The Ghassulian phase is represented by various sites, among them a cluster of sites around the western edge of the Beth Netofa Valley, Mi'ar (map reference 1735.2533), and the Dalton plateau (map reference 193.269). Chalcolithic Golan ware has been found at several Galilean sites, as far west as Naḥal Eblayim (map reference 1747.2488). Cultural connections with sites along the Coastal Plain north of Israel can be observed at several sites in the western Galilee, for example, at Abu Sinan (map reference 1664.2631).

EARLY BRONZE AGE I–III. The Early Bronze Age I occupation is represented by rural sites as well as a few tells. Most of these sites are characterized mainly by grain-washed ware. The Early Bronze Age II–III occupation is represented by some major sites that apparently were fortified cities: Tel 'Alil (Ras 'Alil), Miẓpe Zebulun, Giv'at Rabi, Ḥorvat Bor Nishbar (Bir Maksur), Tel Ḥannaton, Tel Gath-Hepher, Tel Rekhesh, Ḥorvat Shaḥal, Ḥorvat Rigma, Ḥorvat Ẓalmon, Naḥaf, Farod, Tel Rosh, Iqrit, and Jish, as well as Tel Kedesh (q.v. Kedesh in Upper Galilee) and Me'ona (q.v.), which have been partly excavated.

Ḥorvat Shaḥal Taḥtit.

MIDDLE BRONZE AGE I. Several types of caves from the Middle Bronze Age I have been excavated. Most were burial caves (Naḥaf), but there were also dwelling caves, like the one at Tel Ḥarashim (see below), and a unique cult cave near Tel Kedesh (q.v. Kedesh in Upper Galilee). Some other sites have been surveyed, such as the settlement at Murhan on the southern margins of eastern Lower Galilee.

MIDDLE BRONZE AGE II. The settlement pattern in the Middle Bronze Age II consisted of major sites along with rural sites. The main tells are Japhia, Tel Gath-Hepher, Tel Ḥannaton, Tel Rekhesh, Tel Rosh, and Tel

Tel Ḥannaton.

Kedesh, none of which have yet been excavated. Only a few burial caves from this period have been excavated: Tur'an, Safed (Wadi Ḥamrah), and Sasa.

LATE BRONZE AGE. In the Late Bronze Age, the Galilee was poorly settled. Of the large tells, only Tel Ḥannaton, Tel Gath-Hepher, Tel Rekhesh, Tel Qarnei Ḥittin, Tel Yin'am, Tel Kedesh, Ṭayṭabeh, and Tel Rosh were occupied. At Tel Rekhesh a piece broken from a royal Egyptian stela was found on the surface. Tell el-Wawiyat (q.v.) is an excavated rural site. Of the large sites, only Tel Yin'am (q.v.), Tel Kedesh, and Tel Qarnei Ḥittin (see below) have been partially excavated.

IRON AGE I. In the Iron Age, the Galilee was settled by a network of rural sites, many of which have been found in the surveys. Several have been excavated: Sasa, Tel Ḥarashim, Mount Adir (see below), and Ḥorvat 'Avot (q.v.). The material culture shows local as well as Phoenician characteristics.

IRON AGE II. The Iron Age II is characterized by the establishment of many fortified cities and by an elaborate pattern of settlements consisting of cities, villages, farms, and isolated small sites. Some of the major cities existed at Tel Ḥannaton, Tel Gath-Hepher, Tel Rekhesh, Tel Qarnei Ḥittin, Tel Adami, Japhia, Iqrit, Tel Rosh, Tell el-Khirbeh, Tel Kedesh, and Jish. It seems that the entire Galilee was abandoned after the Assyrian campaign of Tiglath-pileser III in 733–732 BCE. For more then a century, the region was almost completely deserted.

PERSIAN PERIOD. It was only in the late sixth and fifth centuries BCE that the region was reoccupied. It was settled by a network of small rural sites that were the hinterland of the large coastal cities. Many of these settlements occupied sites that had never before been settled. A remarkable site is the sacred enclosure at Mount Miẓpe Yammim (q.v.).

EXCAVATIONS

TEL ḤARASHIM. Tel Ḥarashim is situated on a peak that dominates the mountainous area south of Peqi'in in Upper Galilee (map reference 1814.2636). It indicates the existence of a typical Iron Age I settlement in the region. The ruins extend over 1 to 1.5 a. and form several cultivated terraces. Trial excavations were carried out in the northwestern corner of the site by Y. Aharoni, on behalf of the Israel Department of Antiquities and Museums. The following four occupation layers were uncovered in a 7-by-10-m area.

Stratum IV revealed a Middle Bronze Age I dwelling cave, whose ceiling had collapsed. The pottery found in this level included a large pithos, an envelope ledge handle, and numerous sherds with rope and combed decoration.

Stratum III dates to the early phase of the Iron Age. The main structure found is a 6.25-by-5.25-m chamber that served as a bronze foundry. Stone shelves were found near three of the walls and the remains of a large kiln near the fourth wall. The entrance was in the southwestern corner, to the left of which stood a *tabun* (oven) made of the upper part of a large jar turned upside down. On the *tabun* were fragments of a cooking pot. On and near the shelves, various stone bowls, a clay smelting furnace, and two horn-shaped casting ladles were found. The pottery included large collared-rim jars and cooking pots.

Tel Ḥarashim: krater and pithoi, Iron I.

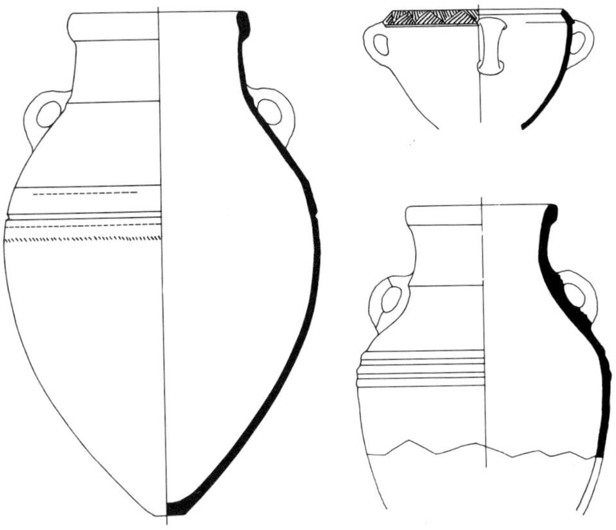

The Stratum II settlement was erected after a certain gap. To this level belong two parallel walls (each 1.25 m wide), with straight partitions between them, probably part of a casemate wall. Two building phases, both from the Iron Age II, were distinguished in this level.

Stratum I, the upper layer, contained Persian and Hellenistic pottery, including Rhodian stamped jar handles, but no building remains.

TEL MADOR (KHIRBET ABU MUDAWER). Tel Mador is located on an isolated summit on the northern side of Naḥal Eblayim (Wadi I'billin), 5 km (3 mi.) east of the Acco Plain, in Lower Galilee (map reference 170.247). Although the mound is badly eroded, there is a clear outline of fortifications around the site, with several areas containing ancient debris. In the excavations in 1980, directed by Z. Gal on behalf of Tel Aviv University, two areas were dug along the wall: area A on the northern side of the mound and area B in the northwest corner, where a small depression resembling a gateway was visible. Two strata were distinguished in each area: stratum I contained two Persian phases and stratum II contained three Iron Age II phases. In addition, some sherds from the Early Bronze Age I and the Byzantine period were found.

Area A. STRATUM II: CITY WALL. Stratum II consisted of the city wall (2.3 m wide and 1 m high), made of undressed stones established on bedrock. Only the wall's inner face was preserved. The earliest phase of occupation (stratum IIC) was characterized by a beaten-earth floor along the wall's inner side.

Tel Mador in Naḥal Eblayim.

Tel Qarnei Ḥittin: general plan.

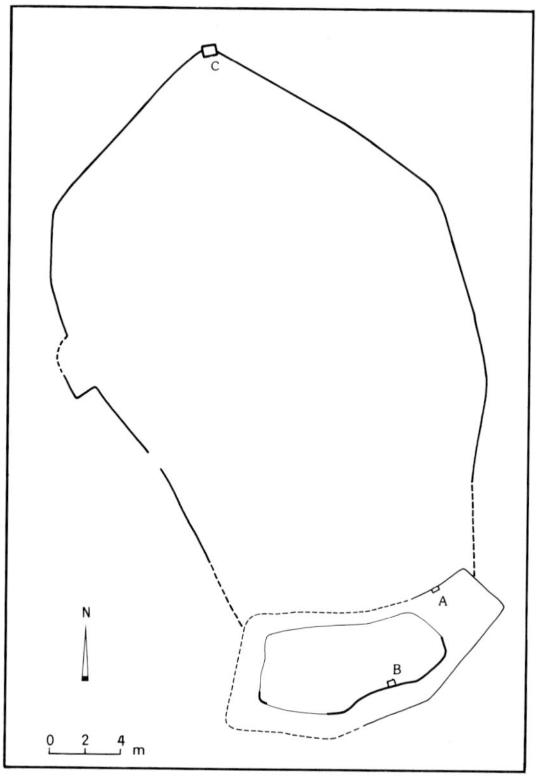

Stratum IIB was represented by part of a small building with a doorway with a stone jamb near the wall. A stone-paved drain led from the building through the wall toward the mound's northern slope. Stratum IIA consisted of a large wall attached to the city wall.

STRATUM I. A fill of soil and pebbles containing large quantities of Persian period pottery was found on top of stratum II, creating a terrace (stratum IB). A building consisting of a wall and a beaten-earth floor, including a small stone installation and pottery, were found. Stratum IA was represented by the wall of a building with stone paving.

Area B. CITY WALL. The fortifications in area B consisted of a corner created by the western and southern walls with a small gate. The 15 m of the west wall that were exposed show two phases. The earlier wall was 3 m wide; it appears that the earlier gate, of which one pilaster has been uncovered, was also built in this phase. The later city wall (2.3 m wide), was visible on the surface between the two areas. The gate is 2 m wide and its outer corners were protected by pebble revetments, which created a gentle, paved slope. A path, beginning on the easternmost moderate slope of the mound and supported by a terrace, leads toward the gate.

STRATUM II. Stratum IIC consisted of the earliest debris founded on bedrock, associated with the earlier city wall. In stratum IIB, a beaten-earth floor adjacent to the city wall, as well as floors associated with one of the gate pilasters, was found. The later city wall and gate were built in stratum IIB. A beaten-earth floor adjacent to the corner of the city wall was revealed.

STRATUM I. Stratum IB was represented by a fill of earth and pebbles that sealed all the earlier debris. This resulted in a mix of pottery from the two strata. The massive fill eventually turned the early city wall into a revetment terrace, on which a beaten-earth-and-pebble floor was built (stratum IA).

Tell Sasa, stratum 3: decorated kernos, 11th century BCE.

TEL QARNEI ḤITTIN. Tel Qarnei Ḥittin is located on an isolated volcanic summit above the valley of Arbel, through which the Via Maris passed to the Lower Galilee plateaus (map reference 1933.2447). The site is identified with biblical Madon/Merom (Jos. 11:1, 11:5). It is composed of two main parts: a volcanic crater encircled by a ruined wall, partially preserved along its edges; and a southern summit containing the remains of two fortification systems, one of which circles the entire summit and the other only the upper terrace. The three fortification systems were investigated in the excavations directed by Z. Gal in 1976, on behalf of the Israel Department of Antiquities and Museums.

Area A. The 2.6-m-wide wall on the northern edge of the southern summit was built of large basalt boulders preserved to a height of 1.6 m. Inside the wall, a floor of basalt pebbles was found with a wall adjacent to it. These were covered by a layer of ash from the conflagration that destroyed the city. The pottery in this destruction level dates to the fourteenth to thirteenth centuries BCE. The basalt-pebble floor had been cut by an Iron Age I pit, in which a few sherds of a collared-rim jar were found.

Area B. A probe was dug along the upper wall on the southern edge of the southern summit, exposing the wall's outer face and a wide foundation. The few sherds found there date from the tenth to eighth centuries BCE.

Area C. In order to date the ruined city wall visible along the edges of the crater, the tower on the northern summit was excavated. The wall's lowest course was uncovered in this probe, where pottery from the tenth to eighth centuries BCE was found. All the pottery gathered in the crater was from the same period.

Summary. A Late Bronze Age fortress existed on the southern summit, followed by a large Iron Age II city that extended over the entire volcanic peak. It seems that the southern summit functioned as an acropolis in the Iron Age II city. The city was probably destroyed during Tiglath-pileser's campaign in 733–732 BCE.

Tell Sasa, stratum 3: inverted jar sunk in a plastered floor, 11th century BCE.

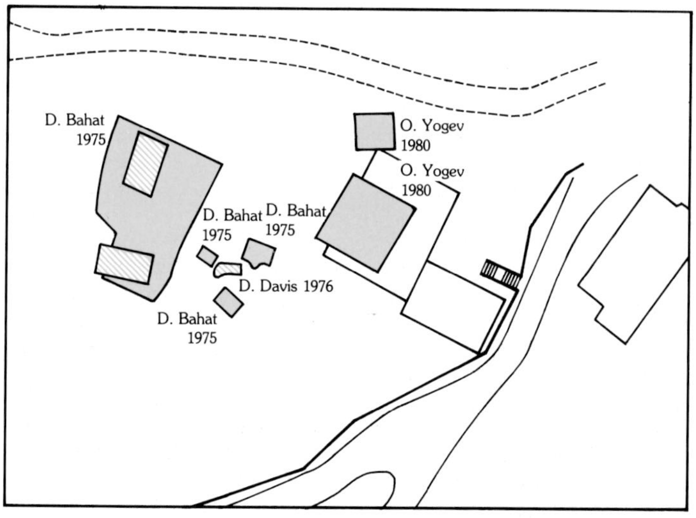

Tell Sasa: general plan.

Mount Adir, stratum III: iron pick, Iron I.

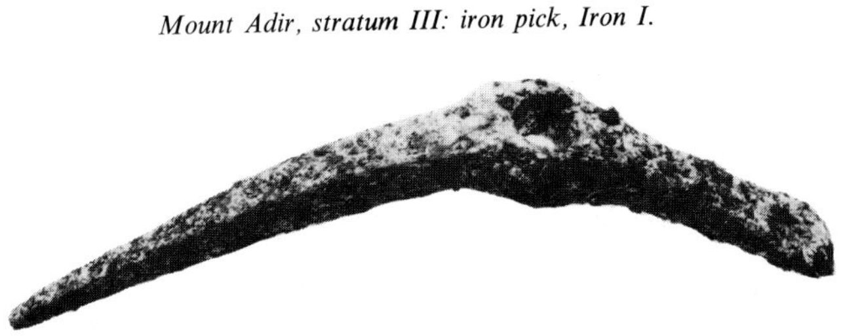

SASA. Sasa is located on a summit at the foothill of Mount Meiron in Upper Galilee (map reference 1873.2704). Several salvage excavations were conducted here by B. Gus-Silberstein, D. Davis, and D. Bahat on behalf of the Israel Department of Antiquitites and Museums in the mid-1970s, and by O. Yogev in 1980. In the course of these excavations it became clear that the site had been occupied in the Middle Bronze Age IIB, the Iron Age I, and the Roman period. Of these periods, the most significant remains revealed so far were those from the Iron Age I. Three strata were excavated. Stratum I was represented by fragments of floors and walls, and stratum II by several stone walls and possibly also a silo. Stratum III was based on bedrock. It consisted of three rooms of a possible single building. The walls were apparently plastered and painted with red dots. All the pottery dates to the eleventh century BCE and consists mostly of collared-rim pithoi and cooking pots. Among the pottery an elaborate kernos was also found.

MOUNT ADIR. Mount Adir (map reference 1851.2708) is one of the highest mountains (1,006 m above sea level) in the central Upper Galilee. The thickly forested summit overlooks the northern Upper Galilee, south Lebanon, the Mediterranean Sea to the west, and Mount Meiron to the east. As a result of construction work, soundings were conducted by F. Vitto in 1975, followed by a salvage excavation conducted by D. Davis in 1976, both on behalf of the Israel Department of Antiquities and Museums. The excavated area was 100 sq m at the northwestern corner of the summit, where the casemate fortifications of a fortress covering an area of about 2.5 a. were revealed. Three building levels, spanning the eleventh to the ninth centuries BCE, were distinguished.

STRATUM III. The outer walls of the casemates are 1.25 m wide and have foundation trenches hewn into the limestone bedrock. These walls were supported by a glacis, which was preserved to an average height of 2 m. The inner casemate walls were one meter wide and formed two casemates. Directly below the floor surface of the northern casemate an iron pick was found. This pick shows advanced typological and technological features and was probably used to excavate the wall's foundation trenches. The southern casemate contained large pithoi sherds and small vessels.

STRATUM II. The outer walls and the glacis continued into the second level, and alterations were made to enlarge the casemates. The new casemates extended eastward and southward from a corner casemate (4 by 4 m) and were interconnected by passages 1.5 m wide. Inward from the casemates a courtyard area was excavated that contained two semicircular hearths and finds indicative of intensive activity. The pottery recovered from the floor of the courtyard included mostly storage vessels.

STRATUM I. In the last level of occupation the fortress's outer walls continued to be used, while the inner walls of the casemates were dismantled and replaced by two new walls. These walls, laid directly over a floor in stratum II, formed a smaller corner casemate (4 by 2.4 m) and an eastern casemate. The walls were preserved to a height of three courses and had no associated floors. The site was apparently then abandoned.

Galilee Hills in the Chalcolithic and Bronze Ages: W. F. Albright, *BASOR* 19 (1925), 10–13; 29 (1928), 1–8; 35 (1929), 8–10; R. de Vaux, *Cambridge Ancient History*, 3rd ed., 1 (1970), 498–538, 657–662; M. Tadmor, *IEJ* 28 (1978), 1–90; A. Ben-Tor, *Cylinder Seals of 3rd Millennium Palestine* (BASOR Supplement Series 22), Cambridge, Mass. 1978; Z. Gal, *TA* 8 (1982), 78–86; 15–16 (1988–1989), 56–64; id., *ESI* 2 (1983), 65; id., *ZDPV* 101 (1985), 114–127; id., *IEJ* 38 (1988), 1–5; id., *BASOR* 272 (1988), 79–84; id., *Map of Gazit (46) 19–22* (Archaeological Survey of Israel), Jerusalem 1991; I. Gilead, *Paléorient* 15/1 (1989), 263–267.
Upper Galilee in the Iron Age I: J. Garstang, *Joshua-Judges*, London 1931, passim; Y. Aharoni, *Antiquity and Survival* 2 (1957), 142–150; id., *LB*, 219–220; id., *NEAT*, 254–267.
Tel Ḥarashim: Y. Aharoni, *Antiquity and Survival* 2 (1957), 131–150; I. Finkelstein, *The Archaeology of the Israelite Settlement*, Jerusalem 1988 (index); Weippert 1988, 379.
Tel Qarnei Ḥittin: *The Horns of Ḥattin* (Proc. of the 2nd Conference of the Society for the Crusaders and the Latin East, Jerusalem and Haifa, 2–6 July 1987, ed. B. Z. Kedar), Jerusalem (in prep.).
Sasa: *BAR* 2/2 (1976), 5, 29; E. Braun, *ESI* 1(1982), 104; L. Kolska Horwitz, *IEJ* 37 (1987), 251–255; Weippert 1988, 75 f.; A. M. Maeir and Y. Garfinkel, *Levant* 24 (in prep.).
Mount Adir: D. Davis et al., *JNES* 44 (1985), 41–51.

ZVI GAL

THE HELLENISTIC TO BYZANTINE PERIODS

More is known, and in greater detail, of Upper Galilee between the Hellenistic and Byzantine periods than of Lower Galilee. A survey of sites from the late periods in Upper Galilee, completed in 1990, indicates a considerable number of Hellenistic sites in various parts of Upper Galilee, contrary to the findings of previous surveys and publications. Moreover, during and after the Hellenistic period, the number of sites in the Galilee continued to rise, until the end of the Byzantine period, despite occasional cases of abandonment and decline.

From the Hellenistic through the Byzantine periods, the western parts of the Galilee remained very much under the sway of the large cities of Tyre and Acco. By the end of the Hellenistic period, probably in the wake of the Hasmonean conquest, the Galilee had become the most important center in Palestine for olive oil production. One result of the surveys was to permit a clear demarcation of the borders between areas of mostly Jewish population and regions inhabited largely by pagans (in the Hellenistic and Roman periods) and Christians (in the Byzantine period).

HELLENISTIC PERIOD. The survey revealed that in Upper Galilee, particularly in its mountainous parts, there was a concentration of small villages, some of them settled since the end of the Persian period. Typical of this period are crudely made storage jars and bowls, mostly handmade, of pinkish clay containing a large quantity of coarse grits. This ware was also found in one-level sites together with imported ware and coins from the Hellenistic period. Excavations by R. Frankel on Mount Miẓpe Yammim showed that this ware originates in the Persian period. Similar sherds were also found at some sites in Lower Galilee, but its main source seems to have been in south Lebanon and Upper Galilee.

Acco (q.v.) was the capital of the Galilee at the beginning of the Hellenistic period. Its reestablishment as a Greek polis by the Ptolemies, as indicated by its Greek name, Ptolemais, enhanced its importance, which was then further reinforced by its large harbor, its control of a major highway (one branch of the Via Maris), its plentiful water sources, including an aqueduct that brought water through a rock-cut tunnel from the Kabri springs, and the large amounts of land available to it. Acco's importance can also be seen in the system of fortresses built to its east to protect its agricultural hinterland and the main roads leading to it: the fortresses at Sha'ar ha-'Amaqim (q.v.), Wadi Rushmiyye on Mount Carmel, Tefen, Mount Sneh, and other sites where evidence was found of a military presence in the Hellenistic period.

Other large settlements in the Galilee in the Hellenistic period were the cities of Cadasa (q.v. Kedesh in Upper Galilee), Philoteria (q.v. Beth Yeraḥ), Beersheba in Galilee (where the survey found remains of a walled city some 15 a. in area; see below), Ḥorvat Devora at the foot of Mount Tabor, and the fortress on the summit of Mount Tabor (Polybius V, 70).

In the reign of Alexander Jannaeus, or perhaps even earlier, under Judah Aristobulus, Jewish settlements began to spring up all over the Galilee. Some of the small (probably pagan) sites from the Hellenistic period had been abandoned at the end of the Seleucid period—the latest coins found there date to the second century BCE—others, in which Hasmonean coins were found, were settled continuously and became Jewish villages. Altogether, ninety-three Hellenistic sites have been discovered in Upper Galilee.

EARLY ROMAN PERIOD. In the Early Roman period, the Galilee was an important Jewish center within the borders of Jewish Palestine established by the Hasmonean kings. In the early part of the period, Sepphoris (q.v.) was the Galilean capital, but later the foundation of Tiberias (q.v.) presented it with a competitor. In western Galilee, on the other hand, the domination of Tyre and Acco was unchallenged. The most dramatic event to occur in the Galilee in this period, clearly reflected by the archaeological finds, took place in 67 CE, the first stage of the Jewish War against Rome, in which battles swept through the Galilee. At that time, Josephus fortified a series of settlements here and prepared for the revolt (*War* II, 572–576; *Life*

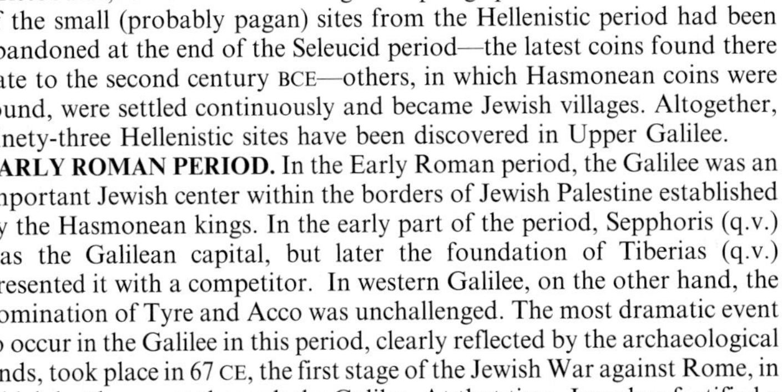

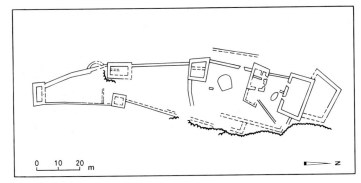

Plan of the Tefen fortress, Hellenistic period.

Ḥorvat Ruma: plan of an underground refuge system, Early Roman period.

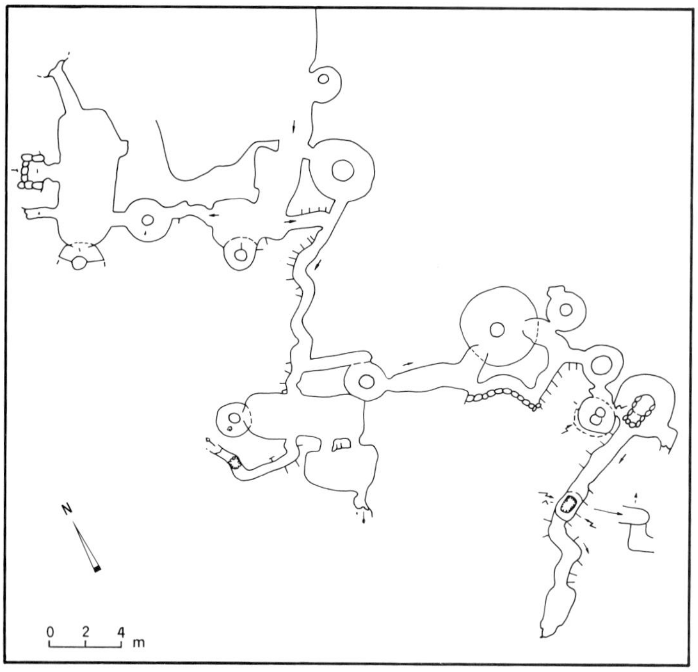

187–188); many of the settlements have been identified, chief among them being Jotapata (Yodfat), the site of one of the fiercest battles of the revolt.

JOTAPATA. A recent survey and trial excavation at Jotapata (map reference 176.248) produced evidence for the truth of Josephus' account: the city was completely surrounded by a wall, most of which survives. Jotapata occupied not only the rocky summit of the hill, but also the eastern slope (as at Gamala, q.v.) and the low ridge running south from the summit. A ballista stone and an iron sword were found at the foot of the northern wall. Numismatic finds also indicate that the city was abandoned in the first century. A complex of oil presses was discovered in a cave on the eastern slope of the hill. An excavation conducted here by M. Aviam revealed parts of an oil press typical of the Early Roman period. Of the many sherds found at the bottom of the weights pit, the earliest were from the first century BCE and the latest were from the second half of the first century CE.

North of the fortified hill are the remains of Khirbet Jifat. Among the sherds found here in the survey, only a few were from the Early Roman period; most were from the Late Roman and Byzantine periods. This provides evidence for the location of "New Jotapata" as opposed to "Old Jotapata" (Mishnah, *'Arakh.* 9:6).

BEERSHEBA IN GALILEE. The Hellenistic fortifications on the hill of Galilean Beersheba (map reference 189:259) continued in use in the Early Roman period, up to the second century. On Mount Nittai, adjacent to Arbel (q.v.), the survey revealed the remains of a wall with towers facing west, protecting the cave complex. This complex was presumably prepared before the Jewish War; Josephus describes it as "the walls on the caverns around the Sea of Gennesareth" (*War* II, 573). A wall found on Mount Tabor has been dated to the Hellenistic period; it is probably the wall Josephus claims to have built in only forty days, using the remains of ancient walls.

MEROTH. At Meroth (map reference 199.270; q.v.) the survey and excavations identified remains of a wall, towers, and perhaps also a fosse. Sherds and coins unearthed at the site indicate that it was settled as early as the first century BCE. These finds support the conjecture that this is indeed the site mentioned by this name in Josephus' works (*War* II, 573; *Life*, 188).

GISCHALA. Limited salvage excavations at Gischala (Gush Ḥalav, map reference 191.270; q.v.) revealed a section of a large earthen rampart around the southwestern corner of the mound. None of the sherds found in the rampart postdate the first century; this may well be the remains of the city fortifications built by John son of Levi (*War* II, 575).

No remains or coins from the time of the Bar-Kokhba Revolt have been found in the Galilee, and the literary evidence is also extremely sparse. Subterranean passages leading to halls and rooms, similar to those common in the Judean foothills, have been discovered at many sites in the Galilee; these are considered proof by some scholars that the Second Revolt also spread to the Galilee, but to date no conclusive evidence has been found. The underground systems are probably associated, both in the Galilee and in Judea, with the First Revolt as well. Systems of this kind have been discovered in the Galilee at Sulem (map reference 181.223), Japhia (q.v.), Nazareth (q.v.), Sepphoris (q.v.), Lubiyya (Lavi; map reference 190.242), Ḥorvat Ivzam (map reference 195.237), Ḥorvat Ruma (map reference 177.243), 'Ilabun (map reference 187.249), Ḥorvat Neṭofa (map reference 186.248), Ḥorvat Mimlaḥ (map reference 191.251), Ḥorvat Ravid (map reference 194.252), Yaquq (Ḥuqqoq; map reference 195.254), Mount Ḥazon (map reference 187.256), 'Iyye Me'arot (map reference 200.266), Ḥorvat Qiyuma (map reference 194.266), Meroth, Kefar Neburaya (see Nabratein), and elsewhere. In 1992, two such systems were excavated at Kafr Kana and at I'billin. In both, pottery and other finds dating to the first and second centuries CE were uncovered.

LATE ROMAN PERIOD. With the first appearance of fine synagogues in the Jewish villages of the Galilee, in the mid-third century, a clear borderline can be observed between the Jewish population and the areas of pagan settlement. As of the time of writing, no remains clearly identifiable as synagogues have been located north of a line drawn through Sasa, Bar'am, and Qaẓyon. Similarly, no synagogues have been identified west of the Peqi'in–Rama line in Upper Galilee, or west of a line through Rama, I'billin (Eblayim), and Tiv'on in Lower Galilee. The southernmost synagogues in the Galilee in the Roman period were found in the Nazareth hills. There may have been Jewish settlements beyond these borders, but if so, their remains have not come to light. At the same time, there were certainly Jewish communities in mixed cities.

North of the synagogue line in Upper Galilee, the remains of two pagan temples and an inscription attesting to the existence of another building were found. The earliest of these is the temple at Jebel Balaṭ. This site was surveyed by V. Guérin and the Palestine Exploration Fund, who pointed out its considerable similarity to the synagogues. The recent survey (1990) examined the date of its construction and its period of use (made possible by modern construction activity in the area). There was probably a holy place here as early as the Hellenistic period, but the building presently visible on the surface, which includes a portico of monolithic columns and architraves, dates to the Early Roman period. The survey revealed that it was not used later than the second century.

The temple excavated at Kedesh (q.v. Kedesh in Upper Galilee) is the most impressive Roman temple surviving in Israel. Its proximity to the Galilean synagogues and the architectural affinity between the two types point to the architectural roots of the synagogue in the Talmudic era. Judging from the

Ḥanita: part of the bema's mosaic and Greek inscription, Byzantine period.

Christian burial cave near Kibbutz Loḥamei ha-Geta'ot, Byzantine period: plan and sections.

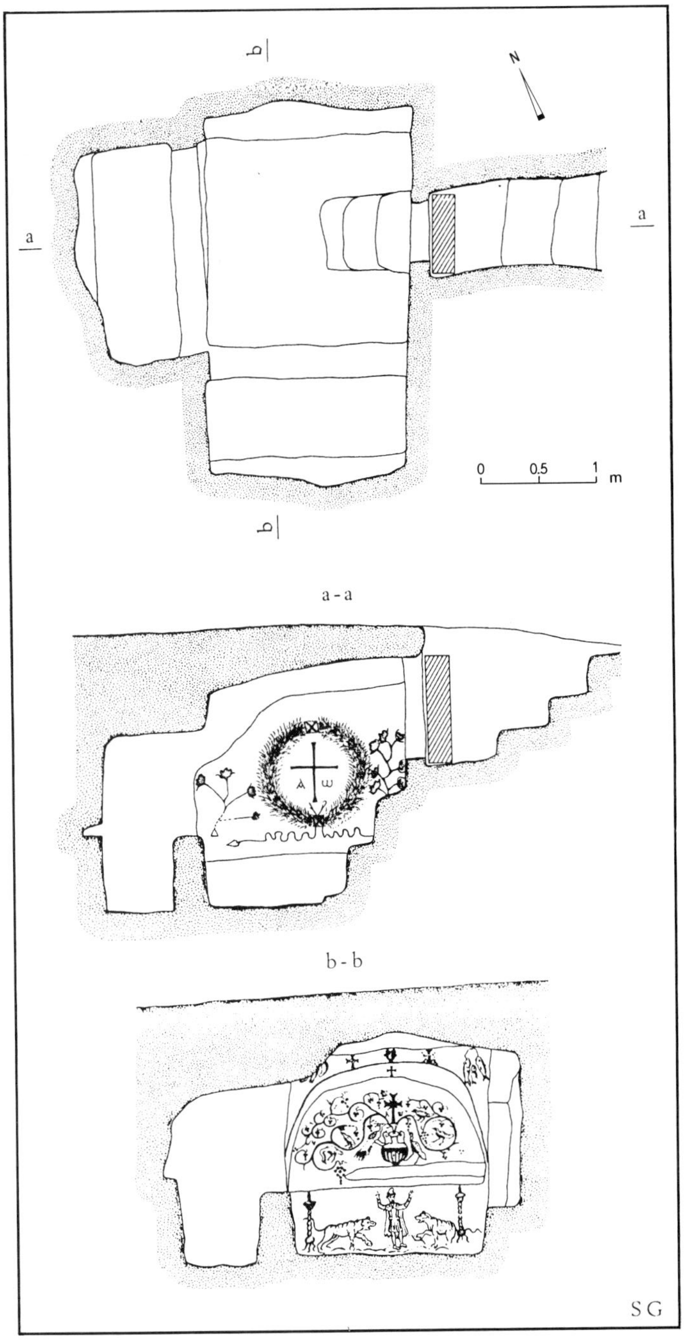

Khirbet el-Waziyya: part of the church's mosaic floor, Byzantine period.

material finds, the building was erected in the second half of the second century, was in use mainly in the third century, and ceased to exist in the fourth. Northwest of Kedesh, at a site now in Lebanese territory, an inscription dedicated to Apollo and Diana was discovered in the nineteenth century. It probably originated in a temple contemporaneous with the temple at Kedesh. Numerous remains of temples have been found in the region, but no synagogues, indicating that the rural population of the area was pagan.

A total of 138 sites dating to the Roman period have been discovered in Upper Galilee.

Roman Roads. The Galilee was a rural region in the Roman period, with only three cities: Acco (the non-Jewish capital of the region) and Sepphoris and Tiberias (the Jewish capitals); hence, there was no continuation of a network of imperial Roman roads in this part of Palestine. Three roads crossed the Galilee from north to south; two were continuations of international continental roads, and the other was a coastal road linking Acco to Antioch. The remains of the latter were unearthed in the excavations at Nahariya (q.v.) and some of its milestones were found along the coast between Shavei Ẓion and Nahariya. A Latin inscription discovered at Nahariya indicates that the road was built in Nero's reign (first century, *AE* 1948, no. 142). Another road linked Tiberias to Banias (Panias). Two rock-cut ascents of this road, surveyed on the eastern outskirts of the Galilee, indicate that a length of it west of the Sea of Galilee turned north and crossed the Jordan River, cutting across the Chorazin plateau. The third road linked Legio (Kefar 'Otnai) and Sepphoris, whose importance increased after the Sixth Legion had been stationed at Legio in the period between the two revolts. The evidence for this road is provided by a few paved sections and milestones, the latter bearing inscriptions dating the building of the road to 130 CE.

Two important roads ran from west to east. The first was the Acco–Tiberias road, whose remains have been identified in some areas, such as along the bed of Naḥal Eblayim, where several concentrations of milestones have been discovered. A long stretch of this road, which was one of the broadest in the Roman period, has been discovered in the Beth Rimmon (Tur'an) Valley, and some additional sections have been surveyed in the vicinity of the Golani road junction. It probably had a branch leading off to Sepphoris, the Jewish capital of the Galilee. Another length of a typical Roman road, with uninscribed milestons, was surveyed to the south; this was apparently the line of the road running from Acco toward Sepphoris, which ultimately linked up with the Legio–Sepphoris road.

The second road connected Banias with Tyre. Stretches of this road are known in the region of the Banias stream, and some of its milestones have been discovered near Kefar Yuval. The exact line of this road was identified in the area of Misgav 'Am near the present Israel–Lebanon border; it described a winding route up from the foothills. Two sections actually overcame a height differential of some 600 m and cut across the ridge of the "Galilee Panhandle" along the saddle of 'Adisa village in Lebanon; from there the road continued through the mountainous country of southern Lebanon toward Tyre.

BYZANTINE PERIOD. The Byzantine period was one of prosperity in the Galilee, during which new settlements were established and large areas of arable land made fit for cultivation. Throughout the period, the Jewish population of eastern Galilee continued to flourish. More synagogues of the "Galilean" type (q.v. Synagogues) sprang up, their walls built of ashlar masonry, and their imposing facades facing south and adorned with rich architectural decorations. It was in this period that Christianity first emerged as a leading force in Palestine in general and in the Galilee in particular, as evidenced by the construction of churches and monasteries, some infringing on traditionally Jewish territory.

The survey of Upper Galilee identified 162 sites from the Byzantine period.

Ḥorvat Ḥesheq: reliquary in the southern apse.

Ḥorvat Ḥesheq: general view.

Some of them were definitely established on virgin soil. One, Ḥorvat Batah, is now in the heart of the modern town of Karmi'el (map reference 178.258). Two churches were excavated here, one of them part of a monastery. In the Byzantine period, this was the site of a large village (more than 6 a.), surrounded by a massive wall that also encircled the monastery at the foot of the hill. The excavations revealed remains of houses, cisterns and reservoirs, industrial installations, and rock-cut tombs in the vicinity. Not far from the village were three other churches. The village was founded in the second half of the fourth century and abandoned in the seventh century.

Jewish settlement in the Galilee continued without interruption throughout the Byzantine period, despite the religious and economic competition of Christianity authorities. This continuity is evident from the erection of both residential buildings (at Sepphoris, Khirbet Shema', Gush Ḥalav, Nabratein, Chorazin, Capernaum, and Kafr Maṣr) and synagogues at these sites, as well as at Meroth (q.v.) and Ḥorvat Shura. Some Jewish settlements remained deserted in this period, such as Beth She'arim, at the border of Lower Galilee and the Jezreel Valley, and Meiron. Some scholars attribute this situation to the aftermath of the revolt against Gallus Caesar in 351 CE, while others associate it with local events.

The increase in the Christian population of the Galilee was concentrated in three areas. One was the environs of the Sea of Galilee, where two of the most hallowed Christian shrines in the north were built: at Ṭabgha (q.v. Heptapegon) and at Capernaum (q.v.). Also known from this period are the great monastery at Kursi (q.v.), the Christian district capital of Sussita (see Hippos) with its five churches, and the churches at Beth Yeraḥ (q.v.). A second focus of settlement was the Nazareth-Mount Tabor region. Three churches were built on the summit of Mount Tabor, one at Kefar Devora, two at Kafr Kama, and a few monasteries in the eastern part of the region. The third region was western Galilee, where Aviam has surveyed a large number of Christian settlements, including more than fifty churches, architectural elements decorated with crosses, and tombs adorned with crosses. In addition, many churches were excavated in this region in the past, such as at Shavei Ẓion (see Churches), Nahariya (q.v.), 'Evron (see Churches), and el-Makr.

Types of Churches in the Galilee. Most of the Galilean churches are triapsidal structures. Their mosaics commonly feature a pattern of budlike scales and the central areas are surrounded by friezes depicting animal and human figures. The mosaics in the smaller churches are composed of geometric patterns. Churches in western Galilee show unmistakable evidence of the existence of galleries (see below) with limestone parapets. In three western Galilean churches—'Evron, Shelomi, and Kabri—inscriptions in Syriac were found, an indication that the indigenous Semitic population had converted to Christianity. Greek inscriptions in other churches also feature names of Semitic origin.

Some sites in the Galilee produced the remains of churches associated with large settlements—towns or villages: Shavei Ẓion, 'Evron, Giv'at Katznelson (in Nahariya), and Kafr Kama (see also Nahariya, Tell Keisan, and Churches). Characteristic of most of these churches are their spaciousness, rich architectural decoration, marble appurtenances, and magnificent mosaic floors. Two other churches were discovered at Khirbet el-Waziyya,

Ḥorvat Ḥesheq: bronze chandelier from the church.

Ḥorvat Ḥesheq: mosaic with the church's date of construction, next to its main entrance.

Mt. Gerizim: overview of building A, Hellenistic period.

Gilat: "Ram Carrying Cornets" statuette, Chalcolithic period.

Ḥammat Gader: decorated marble fountains in the Hall of Fountains.

Gilat: "Woman with Churn" statuette, Chalcolithic period.

Ḥammat Gader: view of Tell Bani.

Ḥorvat Ḥesheq: isometric reconstruction of the church.

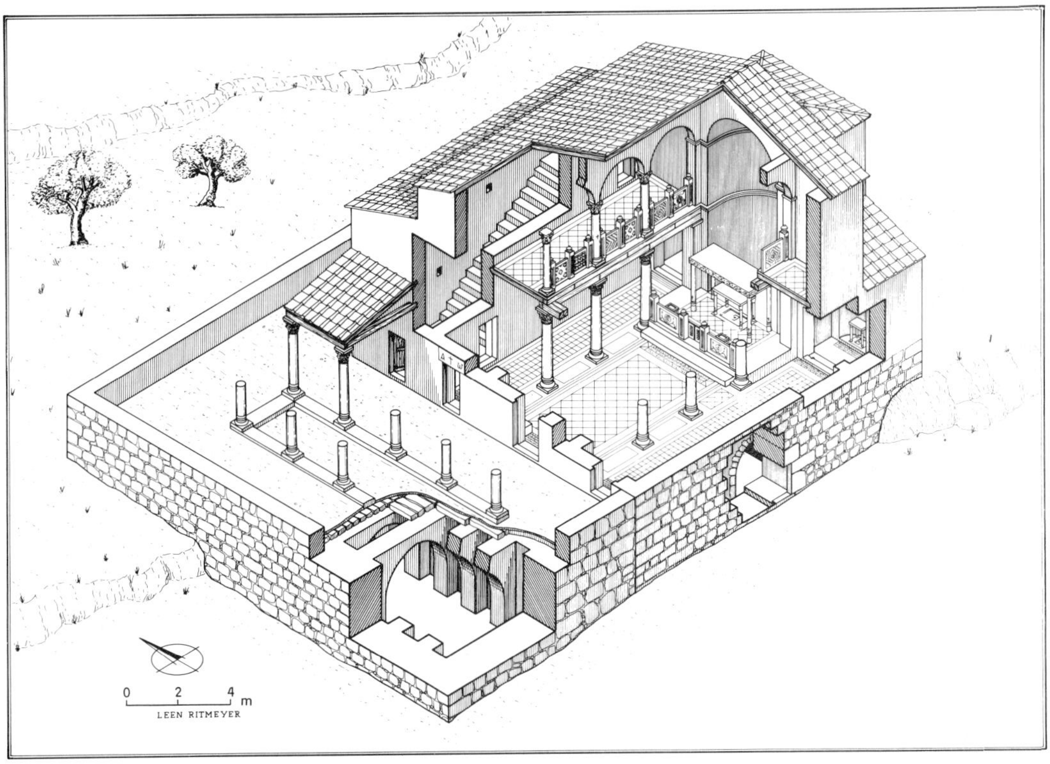

near Julis, a site occupying an area of some 15 a. (map reference 168.259). At the top of the hill were the remains of a church, with a broad flight of stairs (c. 15 m wide) leading up to its doors. At the eastern end of the site, Aviam uncovered the remains of a church (37 by 32 m—one of the largest discovered in the Galilee—paved entirely with mosaics. A frieze of acanthus leaves, forming medallions with depictions of animals runs around the border of the mosaic. The churches at Ḥorvat 'Erav (q.v.), 'Arabbe, Suḥmata, Rama, el-Makr, Mi'iliya, and other sites are smaller structures, serving medium-sized and small villages all over the Galilee.

MONASTERIES AND THEIR CHURCHES. Although historical sources do not have much to say about Christian monastic life in the Galilee, excavations and surveys have unearthed evidence of numerous groups of monks who settled in the region. The Byzantine remains exposed on the summit of Mount Tabor probably belong to a church (perhaps with a monastery attached to it) for which there is also historical evidence. The caves around the summit may have been used by hermits who belonged to the monastery. At Shelomi the rooms of a small building, perhaps a monastery farm, were excavated. The mosaic inscription discovered there mentions the name and title of the father superior.

Surveys in western Galilee have identified several sites probably used as monasteries, some also containing small churches, such as at Khirbet Qaṣr in the Tefen region. There, excavations of an oil press revealed architectural elements belonging to a church (a chancel screen post and two fragments of decorated limestone slabs). In the Byzantine period, hermits frequented the small caves in the clifflike banks of some of the streams, such as Naḥal Aviv,

Ḥorvat Ḥesheq: southern apse and the mosaic floors in front of it.

Naḥal Keziv, Naḥal Beẓet, Naḥal Namer, and the cave at the foot of Mount Qedumim (Jebel el-Qafṣa, Saltus Domini), near the village of Iksal.

CULT OF SAINTS IN FAMILY CHURCHES. The remains of a family church were unearthed in Ḥorvat Ḥesheq in the Tefen region. This area was one of those settled for the first time in the Byzantine period, when four villages and two monasteries were established. The central village was Ḥorvat Maḥoz, where the remains of two churches were found. Around the village were three more small churches, one of which is that at Ḥorvat Ḥesheq, which has been excavated.

ḤORVAT ḤESHEQ. The church at Ḥorvat Ḥesheq (map reference 1754.2419) was built on a platform formed by a small burial chamber with a vaulted ceiling. Close by was a cistern, roofed with stone slabs supported on arches. On this platform, a small church (11 by 8.5 m) was erected with an atrium, narthex, and facade containing three entrances. The central apse was preserved to a height of 4 m. The excavations exposed the nave, the southern aisle, the central apse and the bema in front of it, and the southern apse. The mosaic floor, which is completely preserved, is decorated with geometric patterns and five inscriptions. The mosaic tells the history of the family of Demetrios the deacon and Georgios his son, the builders of the church. The inscription in the main entrance dates the construction of the church to April 518. Besides being a family church (the tomb in the foundations probably had something to do with this), the church was dedicated to at least two saints. A reliquary in the central apse preserved the remains of Saint George, the patron saint of the church; the name of Saint Sergius was inscribed opposite the reliquary in the southern apse. As the church was in an uninhabited area and no paved roads led to it, it was never robbed, so that its architectural elements were found intact. An important feature of this church was its galleries, with their beautifully decorated stone parapets fashioned out of the local stone. In the excavator's opinion, the galleries in synagogues were of a similar design.

The two small churches east of Ḥorvat Ḥesheq were probably also family churches in which the relics of saints were venerated. The same applies to the small churches around Khirbet Waziyya and Ḥorvat Bata.

SUMMARY

The Christian settlement in Upper Galilee did not encroach on the areas of Jewish settlement. Lower Galilee, however, reveals a different picture: churches and monasteries were found close to the remains of Jewish settlements. Many of the most hallowed Christian sites are in Lower Galilee, as were the two Jewish capitals of the Galilee, Sepphoris and Tiberias. Upper Galilee was a rural area, part of a continuous strip of Jewish settlements that flowed into the central Golan.

Christian churches and the religious establishment suffered greatly in the Persian conquest of 613 when large churches were burned. Some of the rural Christian population nevertheless remained in their villages. The Jewish population was not affected, and there is archaeological evidence for the existence of synagogues after the Persian occupation. An additional blow to the Christian population came with the Arab invasion of 638. Once again, however, synagogues and Jewish settlements were not harmed. There is evidence at Kefar Neburaya (Nabratein) and Meroth for continued activity of the local synagogues even under Arab rule, but almost all the churches ceased to operate, with the exception of the upper church at Ḥorvat Bata.

Guérin, *Galilée* 3, Paris 1880; Conder–Kitchener, *SWP* 1, London 1881; B. Bar-Kochva, *IEJ* 24 (1974), 108–116; E. Meyers, *BASOR* 221 (1976), 93–101; id. et al., ibid. 230 (1978), 1–24; D. Groh, *Explore* 3 (1977), 78–93; S. Freyne, *Galilee from Alexander the Great to Hadrian, 323 B.C.E. to 135 C.E.* (University of Notre Dame Center for the Study of Judaism and Christianity in Antiquity 5), Wilmington 1980; D. Barag, *Israel Numismatic Journal* 6–7 (1982–1983), 7–13; F. Diez-Fernándes, *Ceramica Comun Romana de la Galilea (63 A.C.–350 D.C.)*, Madrid 1983; ibid. (Reviews), *Aula Orientalis* 1 (1983), 290–292. — *JAOS* 106 (1986), 369–370; M. Goodman, *State and Society in Roman Galilee, A.D. 132–212* (Oxford Centre for Post-Graduate Hebrew Studies Series), Totowa, N.J. 1983; ibid. (Reviews), *JQR* 75 (1984), 89–90. — *IEJ* 36 (1986), 115–117; D. Adan-Bayewitz, "Manufacture and Local Trade in the Galilee of Roman-Byzantine Palestine: A Case Study" (Ph.D. diss., Hebrew Univ. of Jerusalem 1985); R. Frankel, *ESI* 4 (1985), 110–114; C. Dauphin, *EI* 19 (1987), 2*–9*: A. Jacques, ibid., 54*–56*; V. Tzaferis, ibid., 36*–53*; Z. Ilan, *ESI* 9 (1989–1990), 14–16; M. Aviam, *Christian Archaeology in the Holy Land* (V. C. Corbo Fest., Studium Biblicum Franciscanum Collectio Maior 36), Jerusalem 1990, 351–378; B. Bagatti, *Ancient Christian Villages of Galilee* (Studium Biblicum Franciscanum Collectio Minor 13), Jerusalem 1990; J. Briend, *Transeuphratène* 2 (1990), 109–123; P. W. Walker, *Holy City, Holy Places?: Christian Attitudes to Jerusalem and the Holy Land in the Fourth Century* (Oxford Early Christian Studies), Oxford 1990, 133–170.

MORDECHAI AVIAM

Ḥorvat Ḥesheq: column and stone slabs from the gallery parapet.

GAMALA

IDENTIFICATION

Gamala is located in the southern Golan, on a rocky ridge (map reference 219.256), that is very narrow at the top. The ridge rises about 230 m above the surrounding area, to a maximum of 330 m. The hill is shaped like the hump of a camel (*gamal* in Hebrew, hence its name). In Arabic it is called es-Sunas. The hill separates Naḥal Daliyyot from Naḥal Gamla and is connected by a narrow saddle to a higher plateau. The slope facing south–southeast, upon which the city was built, is broader and more moderate than the northern one. The identification of Gamala with this hill was first proposed by Y. Gal in 1968. It was confirmed by S. Gutman, initially in a survey he conducted in 1970 and later in excavations he carried out from 1976 onward on behalf of the Israel Department of Antiquities and Museums. The earlier identifications of Gamala include the hill of Sussita—Tell el-Ḥuṣn or Qal'at el-Ḥuṣn (L. Oliphant, S. Merrill, J. P. Van Kasteren, B. Z. Luria) and Tell ed-Dara' on the eastern bank of Naḥal Raqqad (K. Furrer, G. Dalman, G. Schumacher).

HISTORY

Gamala is located in the lower Golan (Josephus, *War* IV, 2). It is first mentioned in Josephus' account of Alexander Jannaeus' campaign to conquer Gilead and the Golan, in about 83 to 80 BCE, in which Jannaeus deposed Demetrius, the governor of the district (*War* I, 105; *Antiq.* XIII, 394). During the census of Quirinius in Judea (6 CE), Judas of the Golan, from the city of Gamala, and the Pharisee Zadok, one of the founders of the Zealot sect, headed the civil rebellion (*Antiq.* XVIII, 4). Gamala was included in the kingdom of Agrippa II (*Antiq.* XVIII, 4), and at the beginning of the revolt it kept its allegiance to the Romans (*Life* 11, 61). Gamala then switched its allegiance to the rebels and was put under the command of Josephus, who fortified it by building a wall around it (*Life* 177–185; *War* II, 568–574). Agrippa sent troops to recapture Gamala (*Life* 114), but a seven-month siege in 67 CE failed to take it (*War* IV, 10). The town was finally conquered by the intervention of Vespasian and his legions in the autumn of 67 CE (*War* IV, 3–83). In the Mishnah (*'Arakh.* 9, 6), Gamala is included in the list of walled cities dating from the time of Joshua the son of Nun. Josephus provides a detailed description of the city and the topography of the hill on which it was built, as well as of Vespasian's siege and the struggle waged by the city's defenders (*War* IV, 1–83; cf. Suetonius, *De Vita Caesarum*, Titus 4). The remains found in the city are mainly from the Jewish Revolt; some are from the Hellenistic period. The earliest coin found at the site is of Antiochus I Soter, from 280 BCE. The latest coins are of Antonius Felix, the last of the procurators in Judea to mint coins—they were struck between 41 and 59 CE,

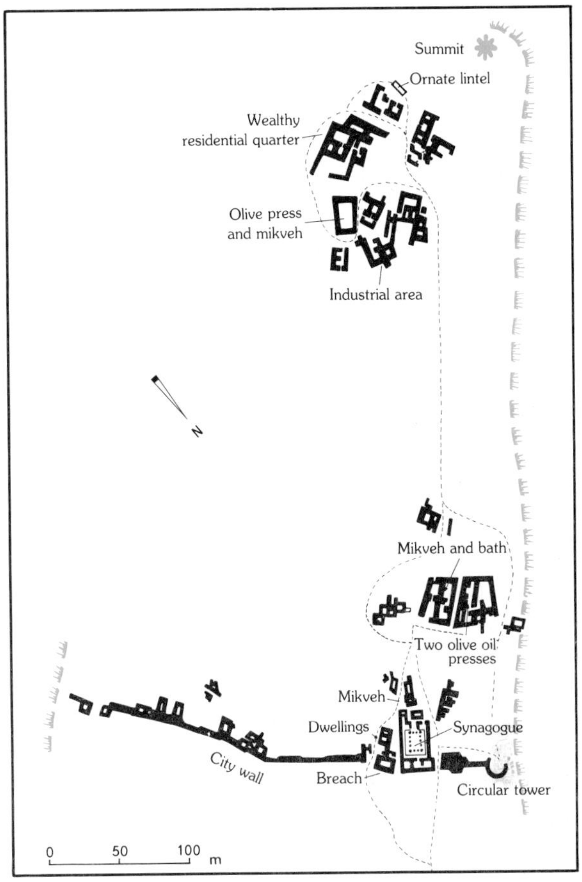

Gamala: general plan of the city.

General view, looking west.

Area G: breach in the city wall.

during the reigns of Claudius and Nero; a coin of Acco from the time of Vespasian; and six coins "for the redemption of h[oly] Jerusalem," of a type found only at Gamala. These coins mark the period of the Jewish Revolt and the fall of Gamala.

EXCAVATION RESULTS

THE WALL. The wall encompassing Gamala extends for about 350 m on the east, separating the settlement from the saddle. On its other sides, the city was protected by steep cliffs. The wall was built section by section and is not homogeneous. Some sections incorporate the walls of the outermost buildings, and in a few places the wall is built over earlier structures. Its thickness was obtained by the partial or complete blocking of rooms, which also provided it with towers. The section adjoining the synagogue (see below) was clearly built of large, massive stones in regular courses. At the top of the ridge the remains of a round tower were uncovered; to its south a rectangular tower adjoined the wall near the presumed entrance to the city, close to the synagogue. A section of the wall (c. 30.5 m long) separating the two towers is built of small stones. Its courses are not regular, and it is not integrated with the towers. It was erected over a building that had stood between the circular tower and the synagogue. At the juncture of this section of the wall with the section adjoining the synagogue, the wall had been breached by the besiegers. The breach was closed and then reopened, but it was never repaired again. Hundreds of slingstones of various sizes and iron arrowheads were found on both sides of this wall. There are also signs of a breach in the wall to the south of the synagogue (area G; see below). Here, in addition to many slingstones and iron arrowheads, nails were found that may have been used to built the siege ladders. Farther south along the wall are the bases of two additional rectangular towers with a passage between them. Part of a silver-coated helmet with cheek pieces and a fragment of body armor were also found.

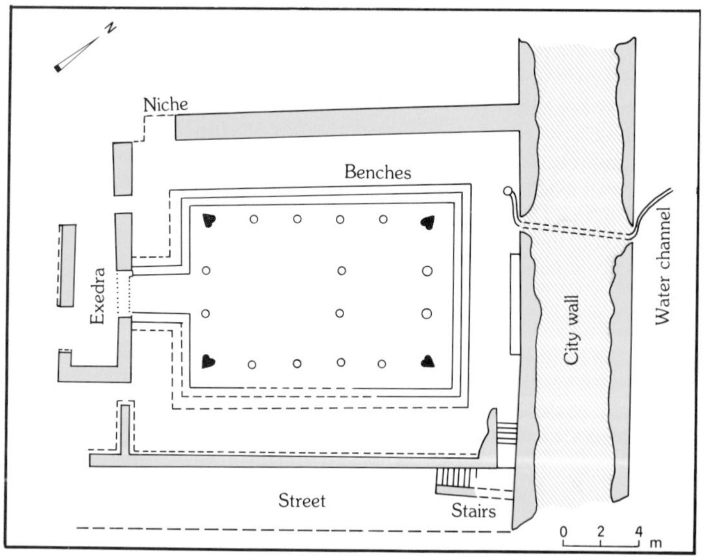

THE SYNAGOGUE. The synagogue was uncovered in the first season of excavations, and several soundings were carried out in it. It was built at the eastern approaches to Gamala, perhaps during the time of Alexander Jannaeus. It was destroyed by the Roman legions commanded by Vespasian and Titus when they took the city in 67 CE. It is a rectangular structure (25.5 by 17 m) built on a northeast–southwest axis (the builders apparently wished to orient it to the south but were prevented by the steepness of the slope). Its unpaved hall (13.4 m long and 9.3 m wide) is lined with benches with stone paving at their feet: four benches on the east, at the head of which is a basalt-paved platform and behind which is a fifth bench, adjoined to the wall; three benches on the northeast; and two benches on the southwest. The benches on the south are not completely preserved.

Four raised platforms surround the hall. On its southwest are two entrances: a narrow one leading to the northern platform and a wide one leading to the center of the hall. In the corners of the hall, heart-

Above right: *plan of the synagogue;* ***(right)*** *overview of the synagogue, looking east.*

Area A: the synagogue complex and the buildings on the mound's slope, looking north.

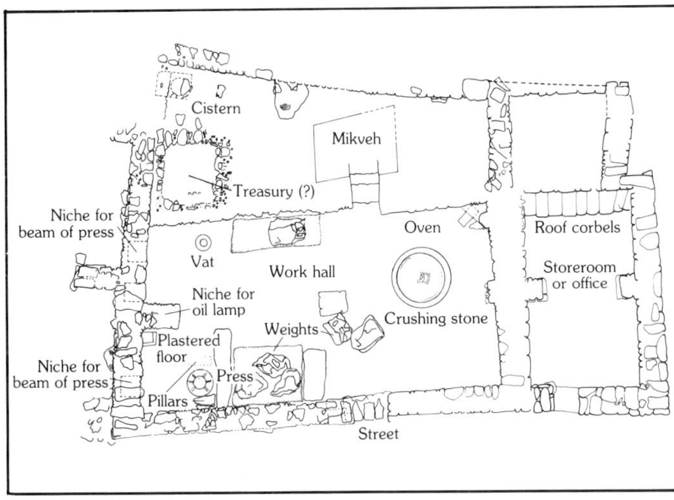

Area R: plan of the olive press.

Coin with inscription: "For the redemption of h[oly] Jerusalem."

shaped columns (diomedian) supported the roof. Between the columns, along the paving at the foot of the benches, slabs used as bases for the columns extend inward: four in the north, four in the south, and two each in the east and west. At the northern part of the basalt-paved platform, above the four benches along the eastern wall, the paving was destroyed and shows signs of burning. A water channel was discovered here, coming from the east and passing through the wall. It ends in a small basin that may have been used for washing hands. To the west of the synagogue is an exedra, in front of which an open court forms the southern part of the synagogue. To the west of this court is the ritual bath.

THE RITUAL BATH. The ritual bath (mikveh) is a rectangular structure. Its north–south walls are 4 m long, and its east–west walls, 4.5 m. All the walls were coated with several layers of waterproof plaster. The bottom of each wall ends—at a depth of 1.55 m—in a 0.4-m-wide shelf; the water in the ritual bath apparently reached this level. The wall rises to a height of an additional 1.55 m above this shelf. The southern wall survived to a height of 3.15 m, and the northern wall to a height of 2.02 m—the height of the entrance to the bath. This entrance is in the bath's southern wall. From it, a series of four steps leads down into the bath. There are traces of more steps (probably two) leading up to the entrance. The width of the two bottom steps ensured a steady stance for those immersing themselves, both short and tall, as required by Jewish law. Water entered the bath through a channel that collected rainwater from the roof of the synagogue. This channel was uncovered where it passes through the exedra and the synagogue's courtyard.

THE STUDY ROOM. Several rooms were found to the east of the synagogue, within the first section of the city wall. A wall was found in the northern part of the southernmost room. It crosses the city wall from east to west and contained an entrance to the north. The room and the entrance were found filled with stones, most of them field stones mixed with brittle material and a few sherds from the Roman period. The room had been deliberately filled in order to thicken the wall. When the excavators cleared it, benches were found around it: two on the east and on the north, one on the west and on the south, and one on either side of the entrance. In the western wall, which abuts the synagogue, there apparently was a window through to the hall of the synagogue. This was probably a study room attached to the synagogue. The synagogue, adjoined by a study room, a ritual bath, and a courtyard, thereby constituted a community center of

Area R: olive press (with restored arches).

sorts for study and prayer, while the Temple in Jerusalem was still in existence.

THE BUILDINGS WITHIN THE WALL. The excavations at Gamala were conducted outside the city wall—along its entire length and inside and adjacent to it. The buildings inside the wall were erected in descending blocks, going down the slope to the south. Between each two blocks a lane led into the city. Not all the buildings along the wall were uncovered in the excavations, but from those excavated on the upper portions of the ridge, in the center, and at the southern end of the settlement, a picture emerges of destruction and devastation by the Roman legions.

Area C. Area C is located to the south of the synagogue. It was an open alley that could be entered from the public area. It led to the synagogue courtyard on the west, which was on a higher level; they were connected by several steps. In the eastern part of the alley many arrowheads and slingstones were found. The entrance to the settlement via the alley was between two blocks: the synagogue on the north and the complex of the area G buildings on the south. This entranceway was blocked as part of the preparations for the revolt and was breached during the fighting. A retaining wall for the path coming from the east is visible outside the city wall. Inside the city wall, in the retaining wall for the synagogue steps, is a *leḥi*, a pole erected to permit carrying on the Sabbath (see Tosefta, *'Eruv.* 8, 5 and 9, 3; J.T., *Pes.* 1, 27b).

Area G. In Area G, which is located at a lower level to the south of the synagogue, two dwellings were uncovered 5.5 m below the alley, one on the east and one on the west. There are six rooms in the eastern dwelling; the two farthest east adjoin the city wall. Within these rooms it is possible to walk along a depression in the city wall. It was through these rooms that the Roman legions broke into the city, through a breach in the wall 5 m wide. Here, traces of burning and many slingstones of various sizes were found, as in the area outside the wall, opposite the breach. In addition, all the rooms in the eastern dwelling contained charred bones, arrowheads from both bows and catapults, many nails, oil lamps of the type used at the time of the revolt, pieces of metal, fragments of glass vessels, and various coins, including some of Claudius (41–54 CE) and of Alexander Jannaeus. In the southwestern corner of one of the rooms was a grinding installation on a raised base (0.87 m above the floor). It consists of a lower basalt millstone and an upper millstone that could be operated by one person. The room's white plaster floor is preserved; sherds and nails were found on it.

Areas S and R. Areas S and R are at the southwestern part of Gamala, far from where the battle for the city was fought and lost. It is from here, however, that, when the battle was decided, the defenders leaped into the the valleys, fleeing from the Roman legionaries. This western area seems to have been a wealthy residential quarter. The buildings were of dressed stones and the quality of construction was high. Areas S and R were combined into a single excavation area, in the southwestern part of the city. Work here began with the last buildings on the southern slope and then moved to the north, to the basalt cliffs at the top of the ridge. This basalt layer had disintegrated, and the huge boulders that had rolled down from it into the residential quarter were integrated into the walls of rooms. Most of the buildings in area S include remains of colored and white plaster of excellent quality, reminiscent of the painted plaster in the palaces on Masada. The buildings here were erected in a beehive plan, in blocks that follow the contour of the hill. In this area, however, a narrow street, ascending south to north, was also uncovered, along with several narrow streets separating one block from another.

THE OLIVE PRESS. An olive press dating to the beginning of the first century CE was uncovered in area R, in a rectangular room (11 m from east–west and

Group of pottery bottles, Early Roman period.

*Area R: **(above)** hoard of silver Tyrian shekels and silver* sela'im *discovered near the entrance to the olive press; **(below)** lead medallions, Early Roman period.*

5.5 m south–north). It was dated by two of the coins found in it. The first is a coin of Vespasian, minted in Acco at the beginning of the First Revolt. On the obverse is the likeness of Nero, and on the reverse the symbols of the Roman legions. The other is a bronze coin unique to Gamala: on one side appears "For the redemption of," and on the other, "Holy Jerusalem." The floor of the room was laid on limestone bedrock. In its center a column supports two arches, one extending to the east and the other west. The room was roofed with basalt slabs, like the ceilings from the Byzantine period in the buildings in the Hauran and the Golan. The existence of such roofing as early as the first century is highly significant. At the juncture of the room's east and north walls is an installation that may be an oven. A basin (external diameter, 1.8 m; internal diameter, 1.2 m) has a crushing stone on an axial post at its center. In the western part of the room two presses, with all their fixed parts, for extracting the oil from the crushed olives were found in situ. In the western part of the south wall there is a niche in the wall for the beam of one press. To the east of this wall is the vat of the olive press—a plastered platform with a basin in its northwestern corner to receive the oil. Between the two posts a storage vat for the oil is cut in the limestone bedrock, with a basalt stone in its upper part. To the east of the storage vat, a trench with five stone weights in it is cut in the limestone bedrock. In the other press two posts, a niche in the wall for the press beam, the vat of the olive press, and a storage vat were also found in situ. In the storage vat of this press, however, the basalt part is missing, and in the trench to its east only one weight was found.

A ritual bath with steps is hewn in the limestone bedrock of the room's north wall and is coated with high-quality plaster. The existence of a ritual bath in a room with an olive press is of considerable significance. It attests to the care taken during the Second Temple period to ensure that oil would be produced by individuals who were in a state of ritual purity. To the east of the olive press and adjacent to it is a small room with a single arch and a stone roof whose nature is still unclear.

THE LARGE HOUSE. Above the oil press, to the north, a courtyard was uncovered, paved with dressed stones. The courtyard was the entrance to a large house containing a small room and a large hall whose walls and floor were coated with fine plaster. Traces of a fierce conflagration were found here. In the northern walls of both rooms are two entrances that led deeper into the house. They have not yet been excavated. To the east of the large house is a paved piazza, and to its north is a well-built staircase 4 m wide. East of the staircase is a series of rooms, possibly shops, and south of them is a narrow east–west street. A cave hewn in the limestone bedrock was found inside one of the rooms/shops. Next to it was a grinding installation with two conical lower millstones and a single upper millstone.

Ballista stones.

Area B. Area B was excavated in the eastern part of the city. It extends from the top of the ridge toward the contour line above the synagogue. Two blocks of buildings, consisting of tightly packed rooms and dwellings, were uncovered here. Between them a narrow street runs east to west. Various objects and installations were found in the two blocks, with two occupation strata visible: on the top of the ridge and on its slope an occupation stratum from the Early Bronze Age lies beneath a settlement from the Hellenistic period, which reused part of the walls from the earlier settlement. In the upper block, buildings were constructed on the remains of two earlier olive presses. These two stages of building date to the first century BCE. In one of the rooms, the skeleton of a horse and part of its bit were found. In rooms in the southern block, ovens and pottery vessels were uncovered in situ. A complex of washing and purification installations was also found: a ritual bath with steps and a floor of undressed stones in front of it, and to the east of it a low pool with a bathtub next to it. In this block of buildings, the excavations reached the Early Bronze Age stratum, which contained pottery vessels; there were no signs of construction or finds from the period of the First Revolt here. Although the excavator has not yet succeeded in interpreting the two building phases or the destruction from the Hellenistic period, the finds can be dated up to the time of King Herod (37–4 BCE).

B. Bar-Kochva, *ZDPV* 92 (1976), 54–71; S. Gutman, *Archéologia* 110 (1977), 66–69; id., *BAR* 5/1 (1979), 12–19; id., *ASR*, 30–34; id., *Ariel* 52 (1982), 18–25; id., *ESI* 3 (1984), 26–27; (with D. Wagner), 5 (1986), 38–41; (et al.) 9 (1989–1990), 9–13; A. C. Sundberg Jr., *Explore* 3 (1977), 44–56; Z. Ma'oz, *Israel—Land and Nature* 3 (1978), 138–142; id., *ASR*, 35–41; *BAR* 5/1 (1979), 12–27; *Boletin Arqueologico* 5 (1979), 12–19; J. Potin, *MdB* 8 (1979), 53–55; A. Kenan, *Ariel* 52 (1982), 4–17; D. Wagner, *Olive Oil in Antiquity* (Conference, eds. M. Heltzer and D. Eitam), Haifa 1987, 187–191; G. Foerster, *MdB* 57 (1989), 9–14; Y. Olami, *Mitekufat Ha'even* 22 (1989), 115*–128*.

SHMARYAHU GUTMAN

***Left:** bronze arrowheads (Hellenistic period) and iron arrowheads, Early Roman period; **(right)** iron spearhead, Early Roman period.*

GAZA

IDENTIFICATION AND HISTORY

Tell Ḥarube, or Tell 'Azza, is the site of ancient Gaza. It is situated on Israel's southern Coastal Plain, about 5 km (3 mi.) from the Mediterranean Sea, in the northeastern part of the modern city (map reference 100.100). Its location corresponds with the description of Arrian, writing in the second century CE (*Anabasis* II, 26, 1). The Roman city and the medieval city extended to the seashore.

Gaza is first mentioned in literary sources in the fifteenth century BCE, by the name of Gazat, in the list of conquests of Pharaoh Thutmose III, where it is described as "a prize city of the governor." Following its conquest by this Pharaoh more than fifty Egyptian military campaigns were conducted in the area. Maintaining sovereignty over this region was a primary concern of Egyptian rulers. In Egyptian reliefs it is called "the [city] of Canaan." Gaza is also mentioned in the el-Amarna and Taanach tablets as an Egyptian administrative center. In Joshua 15:47 and Judges 1:18, Gaza is allotted to the tribe of Judah, and in Joshua 13:3, 1 Samuel 6:17, and Jeremiah 25:20, it is part of the Philistine Pentapolis. It became the southernmost city of the Philistine Pentapolis at the beginning of the twelfth century BCE. The Philistine temple of Dagon was located here.

In 734 BCE, the Assyrian king Tiglath-pileser III captured Gaza. However, it remained a Philistine city, and the short-lived conquest of King Hezekiah (2 Kg. 18:8) did not alter its status. Pharaoh Necho II occupied Gaza briefly in 609 BCE. Under the Persians, Gaza became an important royal fortress. It is called Kadytis by Herodotus (II, 159). In 332 BCE, it was the only city in the region to oppose Alexander the Great, who besieged it and sold its people into slavery.

In the Hellenistic period, Gaza was the northern outpost of the Ptolemies, until its capture by Antiochus III in 198 BCE. The city was attacked by Jonathan the Hasmonean in 145 BCE (1 Macc. 11:61–62) but was taken only by Alexander Jannaeus in 96 BCE after a long siege. It is the "desert Gaza" (ἔρημος Γάζα) in the New Testament (Acts 8:26), so called because of its destruction by Alexander Jannaeus. The city was restored by Pompey and rebuilt by Gabinius, the procurator of Syria, in 57 BCE. King Herod held it for a short time. After his death, the city was under the Roman proconsul of Syria.

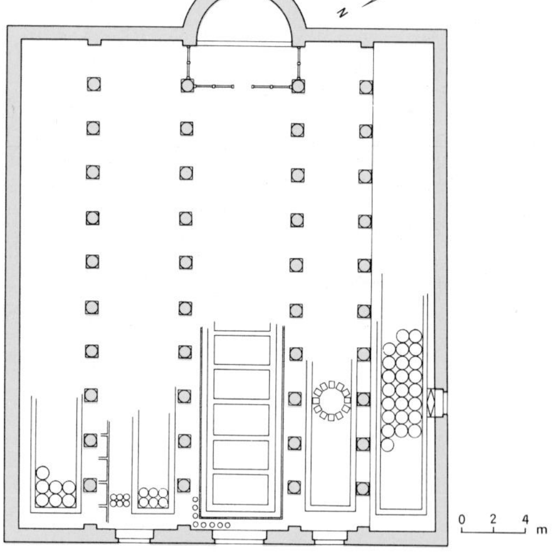

Gaza: plan of the synagogue.

Gaza flourished under Roman rule. A famous school of rhetoric was established here, as well as magnificent temples—of Zeus, Helios, Aphrodite, Apollo, Athene, and the local Tyche (goddess of fortune). The largest of the sanctuaries was that of Marnas (a Cretan deity), the city's main god. Marnas' name also appears on the city's coins. Worship of him continued even after Byzantine-Christian rule was firmly established here. It was only in the fifth century CE, when Christianity became the ruling religion, that the temple of Marnas and those of the other deities were destroyed.

From the fifth century CE onward, Gaza was a prominent city in the Byzantine world. Many famous scholars taught in its school of rhetoric, the most important of whom was Procopius of Gaza (born at the end of the fifth century). On the Medeba map, Gaza is shown as a large city with colonnaded streets crossing it and a large basilica in its center. The New City (Neapolis) developed around the harbor and was known as Maiumas Neapolis (map reference 095.103). It was called Constantia from the fourth century CE onward. Its fair (*panegyris*) was one of the three main fairs in Roman Palestine. Jews settled in Gaza during the Roman and Byzantine periods.

Mosaic of David playing the harp, from the synagogue.

From the synagogue: mosaic pavement in the southern aisle.

From the synagogue: details of the mosaic in the southern aisle; (left to right) lioness, zebra, and tigress.

According to Christian sources, a number of churches were built in Gaza during the Early Byzantine period. A graphic account of the construction of the church of Eudoxia—the Eudoxiana—is presented by the deacon Mark in his *Life of Porphyry*. The Eudoxiana was erected on the site of the large and famous pagan temple, the Marneion. The church was designed and erected by the architect Rufinus, who was brought from Antioch by the bishop Porphyry. Records show that its construction may have taken from five to ten years. It was said to be larger than all other contemporary churches. Indeed, it was criticized as being too large for the local Christian congregation. The church was completed in about 408 CE. No trace of it has been found. The Eudoxiana was a magnificent cruciform church. Its interior was decorated with thirty-two monolithic columns of marble from Carystus in Euboea, which were sent to Gaza on Eudoxia's order.

A second church at Gaza was that of Saint Sergius, but it has not been discovered either. Its mosaics are described at length by Choricius, bishop of Gaza. It was founded in the sixth century by a governor of the city named Stephen. Choricius also describes the mosaics of a third church at Gaza, that of Saint Stephen. They included the figure of the founder holding a model of the church and the figure of Saint John the Baptist. No trace of this church has yet been found.

In a great battle fought near Gaza in 635, the Arabs vanquished the Byzantine army. The city itself fell soon afterward. It became the seat of the governor of the Negev, as is known from the Nessana papyri. The Jewish and Samaritan communities here flourished under Arab rule. In 1149, King Baldwin I of Jerusalem occupied Gaza, and the Crusaders renamed it Gadres. From the time of Baldwin III (1152) it was a Templar stronghold. In 1170, it fell to Saladin. Under Mameluke rule, Gaza was the capital of a district (*mamlaka*) covering the whole Coastal Plain up to 'Atlit. The city continued to flourish under Ottoman rule, when it was the capital of a sanjak, a center of commerce, and a way station for caravans from Egypt to Palestine and Syria.

EXCAVATIONS

THE MOUND. The mound of ancient Gaza was partly excavated by W. J. Phythian-Adams on behalf of the Palestine Exploration Fund in 1922. Three trenches (main cut, cross trench, and ravine cut) were dug without any connection between them. Five brick city walls were discovered and marked brown, red, gray, and green. Also found was a glacis made of field stones, which ran obliquely into the mound and apparently abutted some portion of the main (brown) wall. The associated pottery showed, however, that the glacis belonged to a decadent period in the city's Philistine history, a period that seemed, to the excavator, to have closed with a disaster and perhaps with total abandonment, at least in part of the site.

Archaeological excavation revealed no Hellenistic remains of importance on the mound of Gaza. In the Roman era, the Hellenistic city on the coast apparently disappeared.

In his attempt to assign relative dates to the five brick walls mentioned above, Phythian-Adams arrived at the following conclusions: the massive brown wall is the uppermost and latest in the city; the glacis and the brown wall were built at the time of Alexander the Great (332 BCE); the preceding red wall goes back to the sixth or fifth century BCE, and possibly even earlier, to the days of Pharaoh Necho (609–593 BCE), who apparently inflicted severe damage on the town (Jer. 47:1); and the gray and green walls may date from the middle of the second millennium or to the arrival of the Philistines. According to the excavator's report, no datable pottery relating to these ancient walls was found. The chronology of the walls was estimated by comparison with the depth of the Late Bronze Age remains in the main cut.

In the trenches, Phythian-Adams found various ceramic types, including pottery from the Late Bronze Age (Cypriot base-ring ware, white-slip wish-bone-handle bowls, and part of a pointed juglet), Iron Age I (Philistine), and Iron Age II (burnished ware). The upper debris consisted of a mixture of glazed Early Arab fragments, masses of Roman and Byzantine sherds, some Hellenistic sherds, and numerous fragments of glass from those periods.

THE SYNAGOGUE. In 1965, a mosaic pavement from an ancient synagogue was discovered on the seashore at Gaza, about 300 m south of the present harbor. The Egyptian Department of Antiquities conducted rescue excavations there, and a brief note was published on the results. Systematic excavations were carried out at the site in the summer of 1967, under the direction of A. Ovadiah, on behalf of the Israel Department of Antiquities and Museums, and with the cooperation of the Gaza Military Government. A second season of excavations was conducted at the site, also

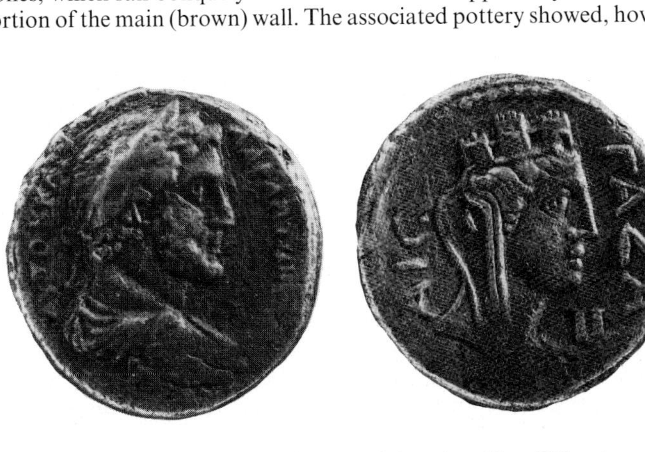

Coin minted in Gaza in the time of Antoninus Pius (151 CE).

From the synagogue: Greek inscription in the southern aisle.

Facade of the Great Mosque (originally the Church of St. John the Baptist, built in the Crusader period).

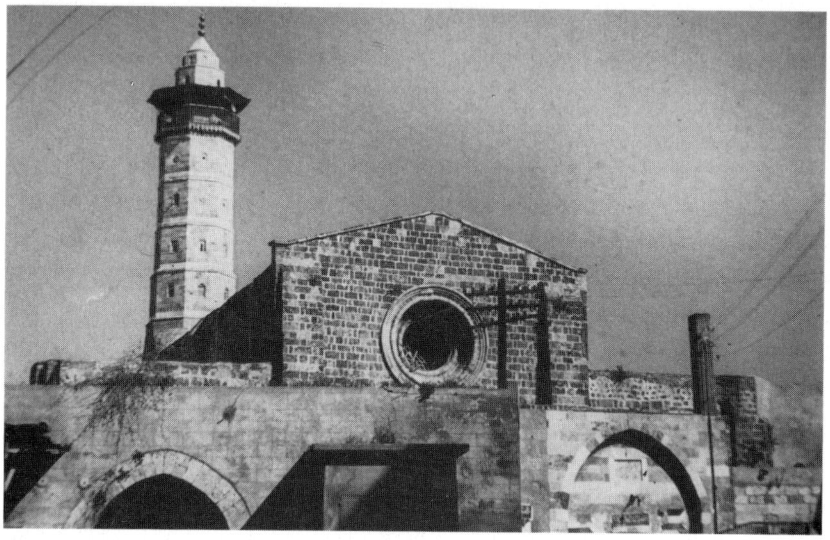

Eastern entrance to the ancient marketplace of Gaza, Mameluke period.

under Ovadiah's direction, late in 1976, on behalf of the archaeology officer of the Gaza region. The excavations were concentrated in several areas: the synagogue, the industrial installations west of it, and the areas east and north of it.

Only the synagogue's mosaic pavement has survived, and even this only partially. The remains, however, point to a large (c. 30 by 26 m) building with an east–west orientation. It consisted of a wide nave flanked by two aisles on each side, making five halls altogether. This differs from other ancient Palestinian synagogues. The halls were apparently separated by rows of columns. There were probably three entrances in the western wall: a central one leading to the nave and two side entrances leading to the inner northern and southern aisles. There apparently was an additional entrance in the southern wall. On the east side of the building was an apse (reconstructed), 3 m deep, that would have held the Ark of the Law.

The nave was originally paved in mosaic, although later it was almost entirely repaved with large marble slabs, only a few of which remain. The surviving section of the mosaic at the westernmost side of the nave depicts King David as Orpheus, dressed in Byzantine royal garments and playing a lyre. Above the instrument is the Hebrew legend דויד (David). Around the king are a lion cub, a giraffe, and a snake, all listening to the music. A border of geometric patterns surrounds the scene.

The mosaic pavement in the southernmost aisle is better preserved: a geometric border surrounds a floral motif (vine trellis) that forms medallions in which various animals are enclosed. This mosaic is very similar to those in the Ma'on (Nirim) synagogue and the Shellal church, which are also from the sixth century CE. Thus, it can be assumed that the pavements at these sites, which are all in the Gaza region, along with those in the Ḥaẓor-Ashdod and Be'er Shema' (northern Negev) churches, were made in the same workshop. In one of the medallions of the Gaza mosaic, a Greek inscription commemorates the names of the donors ("Menaḥem and Yeshua, the sons of the late Isses, timber merchants") and the date (508/509 CE).

Marble screens, marble basins with Greek inscriptions, and other finds support the assumption that this large building, with its colorful mosaic pavements, was indeed a synagogue. Other indications are the typically Jewish names in the Greek inscriptions (Menaḥem, Yeshua, Roubelos [Reuven], Binyamin); the expression "holy place" in the mosaic inscription; the figure of King David with his name written in square Hebrew script; and the building's east–west orientation. The synagogue seems to have belonged to Maritime Gaza—Constantia Maiumas Neapolis. Evidence for the end of the synagogue (it was destroyed in a fire) is provided by clay "slipper" or Sassanian lamps from the end of the Byzantine period (late sixth to early seventh centuries CE). Such types continue just into the Early Arab period. Thus, the synagogue and its environs were probably destroyed in the first half of the seventh century, during the Sassanian-Persian conquest (614–627 CE), or during the Arab conquest (end of the 630s).

INDUSTRIAL COMPLEX UNDER THE SYNAGOGUE. To the west of the synagogue, but on a level about 2.5 m lower, the excavations uncovered a well-preserved industrial complex, probably a dye works. This complex, which covers more than 250 to 300 sq m, is surrounded by a mud wall and is built on a stone foundation. It consists of two rooms: an eastern one with four large reservoirs and two smaller ones, and a western room with two reservoirs. Three limestone basins found here were probably used to grind colors for dyeing. Remains of charred wood and ashes indicate that the building had a wooden roof that collapsed when the structure was destroyed by fire.

East of the dye works is a mud-paved street, 3 m wide, running north to south. On the far side of this street, five rooms of a large building were uncovered (more rooms lie under the floor of the synagogue). The house was carefully built, with mud walls on a *kurkar* foundation. The walls, which are preserved to a height of 1 to 1.5 m, were carefully smoothed and meet at right angles. The rooms are quite large (c. 5 by 7 m). In two of them there is debris from the mud walls, brought down by the fire. It can be assumed that this building and the industrial works were destroyed at the same time. The building's use is uncertain; it may have been a residence or a large storeroom.

Above the floors, within the heaps of sand that accumulated over the course of time, were assorted finds: coins, sherds, complete vessels, tiles, a stone anchor, bronze and iron nails, and needles for repairing nets. These finds, many of which were not in situ, provide evidence that at the end of the fifth and beginning of the sixth centuries the synagogue's builders reused the ruins of this building and filled them with whatever materials were available to a height of about 2 m, to create a platform for the synagogue. They laid a layer of mud about 20 cm thick on this platform, as a base for the mosaic pavement. One of the finds from the debris under the synagogue's pavement is a fragment of a stone grinding bowl, apparently from the fourth century CE. On its rim a two-line Greek inscription is engraved in monumental script: "Whatever is necessary." This was apparently an incantation or invocation, a sign that the bowl would always be brimming over. The finds in the fill—the stone anchor and needles—and the above-mentioned industrial works suggest that there were two residential quarters in this part of the city: one for those involved in the dye industry and another for fishermen.

About 10 m northeast of the synagogue, at a depth of about 2.5 m, is a reservoir (1.1 by 1.45 by 2.6 m) with a ruined eastern wall. At the bottom of its southeastern corner is the lower half of a clay pipe that transferred water to an adjoining reservoir, which is completely destroyed. Ash and charring marks in the two reservoirs show that the complex was destroyed in a fire.

THE FORTIFICATIONS. About 650 m to the north of the synagogue, only a few meters from the sea, is a massive ashlar construction (c. 5 m wide). The stones are laid in alternating courses, one of headers and the next of stretchers, or in courses in which headers and stretchers alternate in the same course. The construction is preserved to a height of about 3 m. Sherds from the Early Byzantine period were found in the debris above this construction, at a height of about 1.5 m. This construction is so massive that it almost certainly belongs to the system of fortifications of Maritime Gaza (Constantia Maiumas Neapolis). This may be the western end of the southern city wall, or a tower at its western end. If this assumption is correct, then the synagogue was built outside the city walls. The survey and soundings carried out south of the synagogue area revealed no built remains or pottery to indicate settlement or fortifications in the area. These fortifications belong to the early stage of settlement in Gaza–Maiumas—to the fourth and fifth centuries CE. They apparently were still in existence in the sixth and first half of the seventh centuries.

THE GREAT MOSQUE (DJAMI EL-KEBIR). The Great Mosque is at the center of the modern city. The building was originally a twelfth-century Crusader cathedral dedicated to Saint John the Baptist. The Crusader church was located on the probable site of the Eudoxiana. The church is completely preserved, although over the course of time a few changes were made. To this day its decorated, magnificent facade, with its arched, characteristic Crusader entrances, is visible. The church was a basilical building with rows of double columns, one above the other, separating the nave from the aisles. When the building was turned into a mosque, its southern and southeastern sides were enlarged and a miḥrab was added. The minaret was built on the eastern side, probably on the site of the Crusader church's belfry tower.

The buildings in the marketplace area and near the Great Mosque are decorated according to the Mameluke (*ablaq*) style prevalent in Palestine, as in Cairo, in the fourteenth to sixteenth centuries. Some granite columns, which probably originated in Roman and Byzantine buildings, are scattered around the Great Mosque.

MISCELLANEOUS FINDS AND REMAINS. Evidence of a Jewish community at Gaza in the Early Byzantine period is also provided by a relief (deliberately destroyed a few years ago) of a seven-branched menorah, a shofar, a lulab, and an ethrog inside a wreath and a bilingual inscription in Hebrew and Greek—"Ḥananiah, son of Jacob"—in a *tabula ansata*, on a column in the Great Mosque. The column very likely came from an ancient synagogue. Also found in Gaza are a Greek inscription engraved on a synagogue screen mentioning Jacob, son of Eleazar, who "renovated the structure of the niche of this holy place together with its screen from the ground up"; a fragment of a marble slab from a synagogue screen on which a menorah was carved with a shofar and lulab; and small fragments of inscriptions.

A colossal seated statue of Zeus, the largest known from the Roman period (second century CE), was found in the vicinity of Gaza at the end of the nineteenth century. It is now exhibited in the Istanbul Archaeological Museum.

Main publications: M. A. Mayer, *A History of the City of Gaza*, New York 1907; G. Downey, *Gaza in the Early Sixth Century* (Centers of Civilization Series 8), Norman, Okl. 1963; C. A. M. Glucker, *The City of Gaza in the Roman and Byzantine Periods* (*BAR*/IS 325), Oxford 1987.

Other studies: W. J. Phythian-Adams, *PEQ* 55 (1923), 11–36; R. W. Hamilton, ibid. 62 (1930), 178–191; G. Downey, *The Dome: A Study in the History of Ideas* (by E. B. Smith; Princeton Monographs in Art and Archaeology 25), Princeton 1950, 155–157; Goodenough, *Jewish Symbols* 1, 223; 3, figs. 583–584; J. Leclant, *Orientalia* 35 (1966), 135, pls. XXXIX–XL; M. Philonenko, *Revue d'Histoire et de Philosophie Religieuses* 47 (1967), 355–357; A. Ovadiah, *IEJ* 19 (1969), 193–198; 27 (1977), 176–178; id., *RB* 82 (1975), 552–557; 84 (1977), 418–422; id., *Atti del IXe Congresso Internazionale di Archeologia Cristiana* (*Roma, 21–27 Sept. 1975*) 2, Rome 1978, 385–391; id., *ASR*, 129–132; L. Y. Rahmani, *IEJ* 20 (1970), 105–108; 31 (1981), 72–80; 33 (1983), 219–230; U. Rappaport, ibid. 20 (1970), 75–80; H. Stern, *CRAIBL* 1970, 63–79; I. Kertesz, *Studia Aegyptiaca* 1 (V. Wessetzky Fest.), Budapest 1974, 231–241; M. Avi-Yonah, *Colloque International pour l'Étude de la Mosaique Antique* 2 (*Vienne 1971*), Paris 1975, 377–382; id., *Art in Ancient Palestine*, Jerusalem 1981, 389–395; F. Vitto, *RB* 82 (1975), 240–245; M. Barasch, *Assaph* 1 (1980), 1–41; A. Kasher, *Jerusalem Cathedra* 2 (1982), 63–78; H. J. Katzenstein, *JAOS* 102 (1982), 111–114; id., *VT* 33 (1983), 249–250; id., *Transeuphratène* 1 (1989), 67–86; D. O. Edzard, *Biblical Archaeology Today*, Jerusalem 1985, 248–259; P. Mayerson, *BASOR* 257 (1985), 75–80; A. Kempinski, *IEJ* 37 (1987), 20–24; J. Naveh, ibid., 26–27; C. Uehlinger, *ZDPV* 104 (1988), 5–25; Weippert 1988 (Ortsregister); S. Wimmer, *Jahrbuch des Deutschen Evangeloschen Instituts für Altertumswissenschaft des Heiligen Landes* 1 (1989), 47–48, 50; L. Mildenberg, *Transeuphratène* 2 (1990), 137–146.

ASHER OVADIAH

Overview of the industrial installation, street, and houses, looking southwest.

Left: *fragment of a marble chancel screen;* ***(right)*** *relief of a menorah and a bilingual inscription in Hebrew and Greek, "Ḥananiah son of Jacob," found on a column in secondary use in the Great Mosque.*

GEDOR, TEL

IDENTIFICATION

Tel Gedor is located in the Hebron Hills, north of the village of Beit Ummar, about 11 km (7 mi.) north of Hebron (map reference 1588.1156). An archaeological survey carried out at the site yielded pottery sherds dating from the Late Bronze Age (on the lower terraces), the Iron Age, and the Persian, Hellenistic, Roman, Byzantine, and Mameluke periods. Gedor is mentioned in the Bible as part of the territory allotted to Judah in the hill country (Jos. 15:58), together with Halhul and Beth-Zur. It is also mentioned in 1 Chronicles 4:4: "and Penuel was the father of Gedor" (these are the sons of Hur, the firstborn of Ephrata, father of Bethlehem). The site should be identified with Beth-Gader, an important settlement center mentioned with Bethlehem in 1 Chronicles 2:51: "Salma, the father of Bethlehem, and Hareph the father of Beth-Gader." Several scholars suggest identifying the site with Geder, mentioned in the list of royal Canaanite cities in Joshua 12:13.

Tel Gedor: assemblage of pottery and alabaster vessels from the burial cave.

EXCAVATIONS

In the summer of 1974, a burial cave from the Late Bronze Age, which contained pottery, metal ware, small objects, and bones, was found by locals. Later it was examined by A. Abu-Argul of the Israel Department of Antiquities and Museums. The pottery included many bowls, both carinated and rounded (some decorated), as well as kraters with vertical lug handles, several of which bore a metope decoration. Several complete chalices were found, along with many chalice fragments, biconical juglets (some decorated), jugs, flasks, *amphoriskoi*, lamps, and storage jar fragments. Among the pottery vessels were Cypriot and Aegean imports. The Cypriot imports included base-ring II vessels, milk bowls of the white-slip II type, and shaved juglets. A vessel from Crete represents the sole Aegean import. Of special interest is a round bowl with a flaring rim and flat base, made of light-colored clay mixed with fine temper and decorated inside and out with a black and red design on an orange background. This bowl belongs to the Midianite ware group.

The metal implements in the burial cave included a trident, sickle blades, swords, spearheads, and arrowheads, as well as a rectangular plaque, jewelry, fibulae, and a gold ring. Other finds include a glass vessel fragment, two alabaster vessels, spindle whorls, and Nile shells.

The cave probably was a family burial place, used over a period of about two hundred years—from the beginning of the fourteenth to the end of the thirteenth centuries BCE. The finds reflect the family's wealth, while the presence of many weapons may indicate that some of its members were warriors.

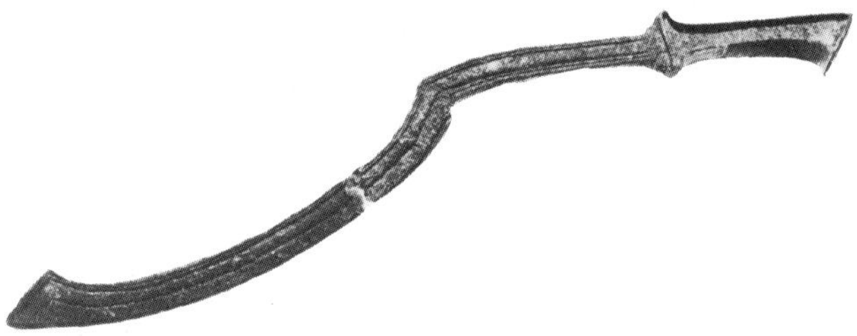

Sickle sword.

V. Hankey, *EI* 15 (1981), 33*–38*.

SARAH BEN-ARIEH

*Decorated Midianite bowl: **(left)** exterior; **(right)** interior.*

GERAR, SITE E

IDENTIFICATION AND EXPLORATION

Many Chalcolithic sites are scattered along the banks of Naḥal Gerar, especially between Tel Sera' and Tel Haror. These sites were first surveyed by D. Alon under the auspices of the Israel Department of Antiquities and Museums. The largest, designated Gerar E, is found close to the intersection between Naḥal Gerar and Naḥal ha-Gedi and east of it, in the clay deposits along the right bank of Naḥal Gerar (map reference 11459.08868). Limited excavations were conducted on the site under the same auspices during the 1970s. Three seasons of more extensive excavations were carried out from 1981 to 1983, directed by I. Gilead and J. Perrot. These excavations were part of the Land of Gerar Project, a joint project of the Ben-Gurion University in Beersheba, the Centre National de la Recherche Scientifique in Jerusalem, and Brandeis University in Waltham, Massachusetts.

EXCAVATIONS

The Chalcolithic site in Naḥal Gerar is situated on the upper section of the clay escarpment on the right bank of Naḥal Gerar. Parts of it were exposed when the riverbank was eroded; archaeological strata can be discerned over some 500 m in an east–west direction. The site extends northward about 150 m from the bank of Naḥal Gerar in the direction of Naḥal ha-Gedi. A study of the sections showed that the site was composed of ten subsidiary sites separated by sterile yellowish loess soil. This clear division permits a study of the differences between the subsidiary sites within the general framework of the entire site. This diversity is of major importance in any attempt to reconstruct the socioeconomic organization of the inhabitants.

A limited area at the eastern edge of the site (area A) was examined; it was found that the Chalcolithic remains had been destroyed by a Late Bronze Age settlement of brick buildings and an industrial installation. In the 1981 and 1982 seasons, the excavation concentrated on area B, situated about 150 m west of area A; in 1983, it concentrated on area C, some 80 m west of area B.

AREA B. The settlement in area B, of which 300 sq m have been unearthed, is a single-phase site. Below the surface layer (about 30 cm deep) lies the main settlement stratum—a blackish-gray color due to the large quantity of ash it contains. Because this settlement is characterized by numerous pits, the depth of the occupation in this stratum ranges between 30 and 100 cm, according to the depth of the pits. Several types of pits can be identified. One type is large and oval and measures 2 by 3 m and is 30 to 50 cm deep. The fill in these pits contained many finds, including potsherds, flint implements, and animal bones. Close to and in between these pits are small, rounded pits with few finds, although two burials were uncovered in one of them. Another type of pit is located at the edge of the escarpment above the riverbed. Similar in size to the pits of the first type, they are rounded and their fill is darker, probably because they have a higher ash content. These pits have also yielded rich finds. In addition to the pits, remains of the brick walls of a rectangular structure (approximately 5 by 4 m) were exposed.

The combination of types of pits and the fairly small structure suggest that most daily activities were carried out in the structure's courtyard. The pits were probably used for storage, cooking, burial, and as refuse dumps. They do not seem to have been used as dwellings, and there is no evidence that walls were built above them or that they were roofed. The brick structure may well represent the habitation unit of one family.

The pottery vessels were the most common find in every unit excavated. The range of shapes is similar to that known from other sites from the same period, such as Tuleilat el-Ghassul (q.v.), Naḥal Besor, and Beersheba (q.v.). One of the characteristic vessels in the assemblage is the cornet, of which many painted examples were recovered in every excavated area. Most cornets have a long, solid base with a rounded or an angular section. Smaller cornets, with a short, rounded base, also were found, as well as several chalices.

The flint industry was based mainly on the use of local river pebbles, and the finished products were, therefore, small or medium sized. In addition, small, gray, semitransparent flint cores, which were probably imported, were used to make bladelets (some retouched or finely retouched). Notched-denticulated tools and sickle blades were the most commonly formed implements. The sickle blades are a typical Chalcolithic type—narrow, backed with abrupt retouch, truncated or broken at their side, and with a straight or finely denticulated working edge.

Many mother-of-pearl fragments were recovered, but none bore traces of having been worked. Some trapezoid stone and clay pendants, with two holes at the upper edge, were also found, as well as loom weights of stone or clay. Of special interest is a seal impression on a lump of clay depicting an unidentifiable figure in a rhomboid-shaped frame. The back of the clay lump also bears an impression, probably of the wicker basket to which the stamped clay was attached.

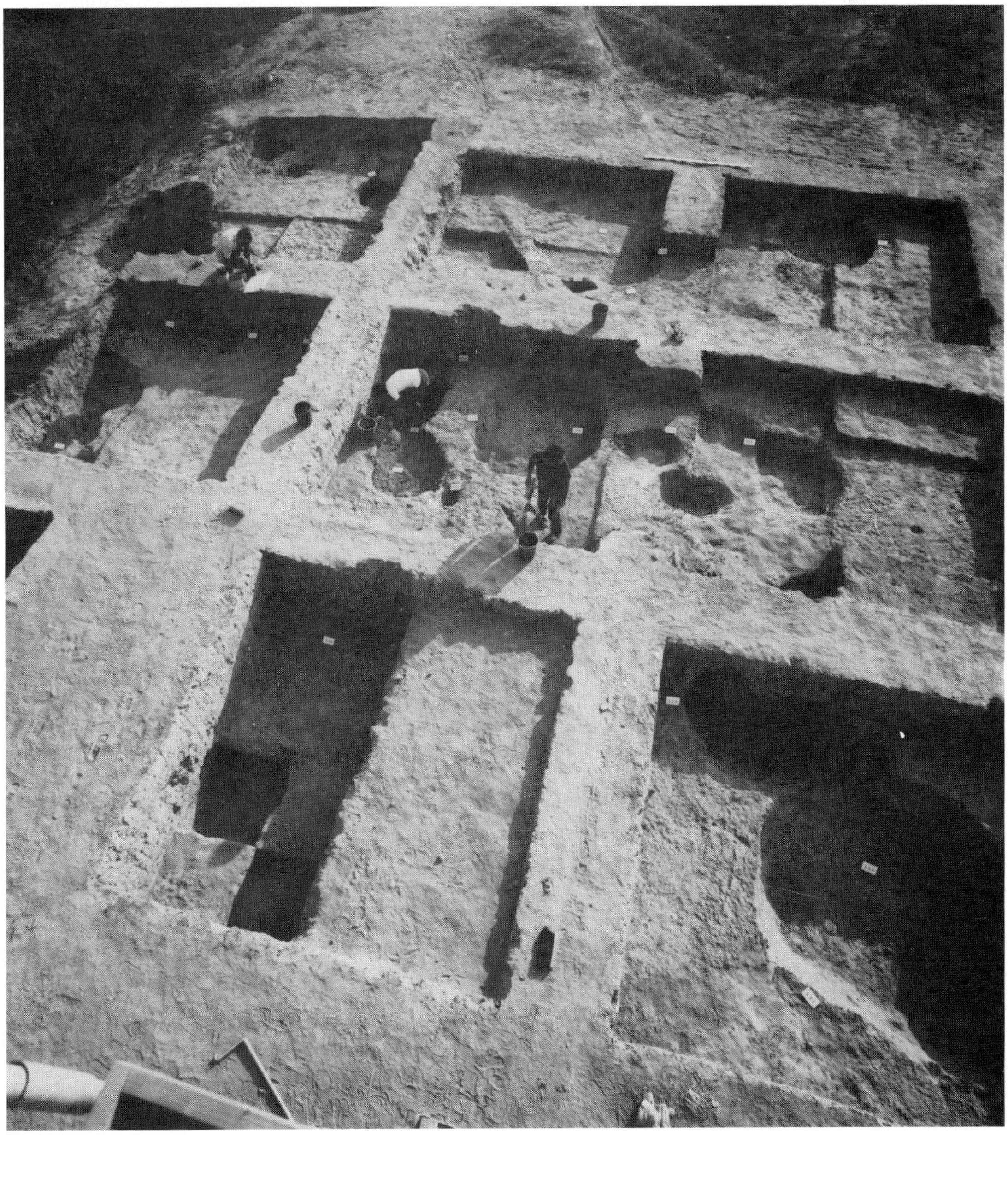

Gerar E: overview of area B.

Gerar E: pottery assemblage, Chalcolithic period.

The faunal remains found in the excavation were initially identified by C. Grigson. Half of the three hundred animal bones found were identified as sheep and goat; the other half were divided almost evenly between pig and cattle. The vertebra of a Mediterranean fish was also found.

AREA C. Areas B and C are located on the edge of the escarpment and are separated by a deep gully. During the excavation, only part of their 280 sq m was sampled. Although the excavation in these areas is only in its initial stages, it is clear that area C represents a different site type from area B. One of the chief differences is the length of occupation: while the area B site is single phased, the site in area C has at least two phases, with a deposit of up to 2 m. Because the upper phase in area C and the single phase in area B lie on the same level, they are probably chronologically close. Moreover, their pottery assemblages are similar; both include many V-shaped bowls, kraters, churns, storage jars, hole-mouth jars, and cornets. In area C, a stone button seal, with an incised spiral stamp, was found.

Although similarity is evident in the flint tools, as well, there are marked differences between the upper phase in area C and the settlement in area B. The following are the most important:

1. Area C is characterized by a horizontal settlement stratum; the pits typical of area B are absent. The material in area C is found in rich, isolated concentrations.

2. In area C, parts of field stone walls were uncovered. Although the excavated area in B is much larger, nothing of the kind has been found there to date.

3. The pottery from area C is richer in decoration than that from area B. The sherds in area C belong to vessels broken in situ; those recovered in the pits in area B are fragments thrown there before the site was abandoned.

4. In area C sickle blades, retouched bladelets, and bladelet cores are more common than in area B.

5. Pig bones, which are common in area B (about 25 percent of the identified bones), are very rare in area C.

Although the areas are close to each other, economic and perhaps also social differences are indicated between them.

I. Gilead (et al.), *ESI* 4 (1985), 33–34; id., *BASOR* Supplement 24 (1986), 75–87; id. (and Y. Goren), *BASOR* 275 (1989), 5–14; id., *JFA* 16 (1989), 377–394; E. D. Oren and M. A. Morrison, ibid., 57–87.

ISAAC GILEAD

GERASA

IDENTIFICATION

Gerasa (Greek Γέρασα) was a Greek city in Gilead, now modern Jerash, 34 km (21 mi.) north of ʽAmman, Jordan. Its identification is based on the similarity of the modern Arabic name to the ancient one and on several inscriptions found here mentioning its inhabitants as των πρότερων Γερασηνῶν. According to inscriptions and coins from the Roman period, the city's full name was "the city of the Antiochenes on the River Chrysorhoas, formerly [of] the people of Gerasa, holy and sacrosanct." Gerasa is located on a branch of the Via Traiana Nova that was built in 112 CE and links the city to Pella and lies on the banks of the River Chrysorhoas (Wadi Jerash). The river crosses the city north to south, at a height of 570 m above sea level. To the east is a large spring, ʽEin Qeruan. The city was founded at the place where the wadi widens. It is surrounded by broad stretches of arable and pasture land and woodland. The land rises gradually to the west of the valley.

The southern hill, on which the temple of Zeus stood, was apparently the original nucleus of the Hellenistic settlement. The fortified enclosure visible today belongs to the Roman-Byzantine city, which extended on both sides of the Chrysorhoas River. The city wall (3,456 m long), encloses an elliptical area of about 210 a. It dates to the end of the first century CE.

HISTORY

Stone Age sites near Gerasa were discovered by G. L. Harding; their details were published by D. Kirkbride. Stone tools of the Acheulo-Levalloisian type were found on the hill to the east of Hadrian's triumphal arch, along with remains from the Neolithic period (animal bones, arrowheads, points, chisels, scrapers, denticulated blades, and awls). In his excavations at the site, Glueck (see below) found evidence of settlement in the area: a walled enclosure on a hill 200 m from the northeast corner of Gerasa contained pottery from the Early Bronze Age I to the Middle Bronze Age I. He also found an Iron Age settlement on the hill north of the city overlooking the Valley of Birketein.

A Greek tradition held that Alexander the Great founded the Hellenistic city for his veterans (γέροντες). According to another tradition, when Alexander captured the city, all the younger men were killed and only the elderly survived, hence the city's name. More trustworthy is the information recorded in an inscription from the Roman period at the site (published by C. B. Welles in Kraeling's excavation report, no. 137), according to which a statue of Perdiccas, Alexander's general, was set up at Gerasa. It may be concluded from this that Perdiccas was regarded as the founder of the Hellenistic settlement. A Roman inscription (Welles, no. 78) reveals that a group of Macedonians was among its first inhabitants. At that time the city was known as Antiochia ad Chrysorhoam (Antioch on the Chrysorhoas River), as in 200 BCE Transjordan had passed to the Seleucid dynasty, and the new name was bestowed in honor of Antiochus III (223–187 BCE) or IV (175 BCE).

Gerasa was an important link in the chain of fortified cities erected by Hellenistic kings to defend their territory against desert tribes. Archaeological evidence of the Hellenistic city is very scanty. On the southern hill, where the temple of Zeus was built, Rhodian stamped jar handles from 210 to 180 BCE have been found. It may be that the cult of Zeus long preceded the Roman period, as the city received the titles of ἱερὰ καὶ ἄπυλος ("holy and sacrosanct"), and therefore enjoyed certain privileges. In Alexander Jannaeus' reign, Zeno and Theodorus, the tyrants of Philadelphia (ʽAmman), deposited part of their treasure in Gerasa (Josephus, *War* I, 104; *Antiq*. XIII, 393). Hence, in their time, the city was no longer within the bounds of the Seleucid Syrian kingdom. Alexander Jannaeus (103–76 BCE) captured Gerasa in the last years of his reign and died while besieging Ragaba, in Gerasene territory (*Antiq*. XIII, 398). The city remained under Hasmonean rule until Pompey's campaign in that region. It may be assumed that Pompey took Gerasa from the Jews, for in the Roman period the city counted its years according to the Pompeian era, starting with 62 BCE. It was listed among the cities of the Decapolis (the League of Ten Cities), as is attested by Stephanus of Byzantium (*Ethnika*, s.v. Γέρασα).

This association and the signs of Nabatean influence (see below) attest to its connection with the trade routes between southern Arabia, Damascus, Phoenicia, and Judea. As long as the Ptolemies ruled in Palestine, this trade went via Gaza and the Red Sea; when the Seleucids took control of the land, the merchants once again made use of the Syrian route. After Alexander Jannaeus severed this route, it was reestablished by the Romans, and the cities of Transjordan, including Gerasa, enjoyed a period of rising prosperity.

During the First Jewish Revolt against Rome (66–70 CE), the rebels attacked Gerasa, even though friendly relations prevailed between the city and the local Jews (Josephus, *War* II, 458; II, 480). The city, however, was never in the hands of the rebels. Most scholars, therefore, consider that the Gerasa captured by the Romans before the siege of Jerusalem (*War* IV, 487–488) was not the Transjordanian town. Additional evidence of this is provided by two inscriptions dated 69/70 CE (Welles, nos. 5–6), attesting to the presence of non-Jewish refugees in Gerasa at that time. Architectural fragments attributed to a synagogue and found in the fill of Hadrian's arch to the south of the city may be evidence that the Jewish community was destroyed during the revolt. However, it may equally indicate that the synagogue was destroyed in Trajan's time (cf. Welles, nos. 56 and 57 dedicated to Trajan in 115 CE). Inscription no. 50, dated 75/76 CE, as well as a Trajanic inscription from Pergamum, dated between 102 and 104 CE, attest that Gerasa belonged at the time to the province of Syria (*IG Rom.* IV, no. 374), and even the geographer Ptolemy, who wrote under Antoninus Pius (138–161 CE), reckoned Gerasa as being part of the province of Syria, like the rest of the Decapolis (*Geog.* V, 15, 23; V, 14, 18). For this, however, he must have followed an earlier, undocumented source, for inscriptions on milestones prove that already under Trajan, at least from 111 CE, Gerasa belonged to the Provincia Arabia, and probably did so from the moment of its establishment in 106 CE (Welles, nos. 252–257). Signs of Nabatean influence in the city are coins (mostly of Aretas IV, 9 BCE to 40 CE), a Nabatean inscription (Welles, no. 1), and cults of the "Arab god" as well as of Pacidas and Dionysius (Dushara; Welles, nos. 17–22, 192). The Nabatean influence disappeared with the establishment of the Provincia Arabia in 106 CE.

The city's territory extended as far west as Ragaba (Rajb). On the north it included Enganna ('Ein Jann), Eglon (Khirbet 'Ajlen), Erga, and Samta. Riḥab to the northwest was not in its territory. To the east, the border passed near the highway from Philadelphia to Bostra, and in the south close to, but south of, the Jabbok River.

EXPLORATION

Gerasa was first discovered by U. J. Seetzen in 1806. It was subsequently visited by J. L. Burkhardt (1812) and J. Buckingham (1816). Conditions for visiting improved with the settlement of a Circassian community in 1878. Between 1891 and 1902, Gerasa was explored by G. Schumacher, R. Brünnow, and J. Germer-Durand. In 1902, a German expedition under O. Puchstein investigated the ruins. Excavation and conservation work were begun by G. Horsfield under the auspices of the British Mandatory Government, in 1925. The first finds uncovered were the southern theater, the court of the temple of Zeus, the nymphaeum, the propylaea of the temple of Artemis, and the main street, or *cardo*. Work continued until 1931 under P. A. Richie, A. G. Buchanan, and G. Horsfield. Meanwhile, systematic excavation directed by J. W. Crowfoot had begun in 1928 under the auspices of the British School of Archaeology in Jerusalem and Yale University. In 1930, the American School of Oriental Research replaced the British School, and direction was assumed by C. S. Fisher. N. Glueck continued the work in 1933–1934.

In the 1940s and 1950s preservation and restoration were carried out, mainly in the southern part of the city, in the southern theater (the work was completed in the late 1960s). At that time, the lower terrace of the precinct of Zeus was cleared of its debris and partially restored. The excavation of the temple was only begun in 1987. The elliptical plaza (called the forum by the site's excavators) had already been cleared and partially restored in the 1940s. There were no excavations at in Gerasa in the 1960s. The activities of the Jordan Department of Antiquities were limited to clearing debris from both sides of the *cardo*, mainly in the area of the cathedral precinct, and partially restoring the gates in the precinct of Artemis.

Gerasa: aerial view from the late 1930s, looking southeast.

Since 1975, an Italian expedition from the University of Turin has been excavating at Gerasa.

CITY PLAN AND ARCHITECTURE

The city wall is of uniform construction. Its 101 towers are spaced at intervals of 17 to 22 m. Its offset/inset wall has a uniform thickness (3 m). There are six gates: the main gates in the north and south, two gates in the west wall, and two water gates through which the Chrysorhoas River enters and leaves. The *cardo* crosses the city in a straight north–south direction and intersects at right angles with the two *decumani*, the east–west streets—one in the southern part of the city and one in the north. The colonnaded main streets were paved with stone slabs. The two *decumani* intersect with the *cardo* at the southern and northern tetrapyla.

There were several plazas in Gerasa. One of them, elliptical in shape, is located near the city's southern gate, at the foot of the precinct of Zeus. A round plaza is located at the intersection of the *cardo* and the southern *decumanus*. A third, rectangular one, extends to the north of the northern theater, and adjoins the northern *decumanus*. This, according to some researchers, is where the forum of Gerasa was located; the city's excavators, however, have proposed that the forum should be identified with the elliptical plaza.

The valley crossing Gerasa north to south divided it in two—geographically and functionally. The eastern part of the city, which enjoyed a more inviting topography, was the residential quarter. The modern city of Jerash extends over this area, and its densely packed houses prevent exploration. The buildings in the western part filled public, ritual, administrative, and commercial functions. The separate functions of the two sections led to different planning, including the orientation of streets. This independent planning may have a chronological explanation. The orientation of the eastern city apparently sprang from earlier plans. It is possible, therefore, that it preserves the imprint of the Hellenistic city, which existed before Roman Gerasa was planned—perhaps in the first century BCE. The deep valley formed by the river aided in the separation of the two parts of the city by emphasizing the division. The parts were joined by three strong stone bridges that spanned the river with barrel vaults. The bridges were built along the routes of three east–west streets: the northern *decumanus*, the southern *decumanus*, and a processional road leading from the eastern city to the sanctuary of Artemis. Of the three bridges, only the southern one is preserved in its entirety. The middle sector of the *cardo* was lined on both sides with Corinthian colonnades, while the sector north of the northern *decumanus* was lined with Ionic colonnades. The Corinthian colonnades are generally considered to belong to a phase in which the city was replanned in the mid-second century CE.

TRIUMPHAL ARCH. The arch was uncovered in 1931, 400 m south of the city. It is dated by an inscription on it to 130 CE. It has a main passageway flanked by subsidiary passages. Both facades have four engaged Corinthian half columns carrying an architrave and pediment. Between the half columns are niches. A passage runs from side to side through the main arch. This indicates that the structure was originally designed to be a gate in the city wall to the south of its existing line. This extension of the wall, however, was never carried out. Later, pavilions were built abutting the sides of the arch.

CIRCUS. The circus, or chariot racetrack, was explored in 1933, northwest of the triumphal arch and parallel to the Roman road leading to Philadelphia. Its interior length was 244 m, and it could have held fifteen thousand spectators. It is the smallest circus known in the Roman East. At its southern end were ten compartments, from which the chariots started. The excavators differed on its date of construction. One view held that it was erected in the second or third century, another in the first century CE. Recent excavations conducted by a Polish team clearly prove that the circus was built in the middle of the second century CE.

SANCTUARY OF ZEUS. The sanctuary is situated on the city's southern hill. Adjacent to it on the west was the city's southern theater. This was apparently ancient Gerasa's cultic site: the sanctuary precinct and theater constituted a single ritual complex. The sanctuary of Zeus is situated in the area between the temple and the elliptical plaza, on a steep slope. It is on two terraces, each of which is supported on the northeast by retaining walls that form a series of barrel vaults. A staircase leads from one terrace to the other. The upper terrace was a flat and unroofed rectangle surrounded by colonnades with the temple of Zeus in the center. The temple was built from 161 to 166 CE on the site of an earlier temple that had been built between 22 and 43 CE. The temple of Zeus is a peripteral structure with eight columns in its facade and twelve along its sides, built on a podium. There is a staircase flanked by two strong pilasters in the podium's facade.

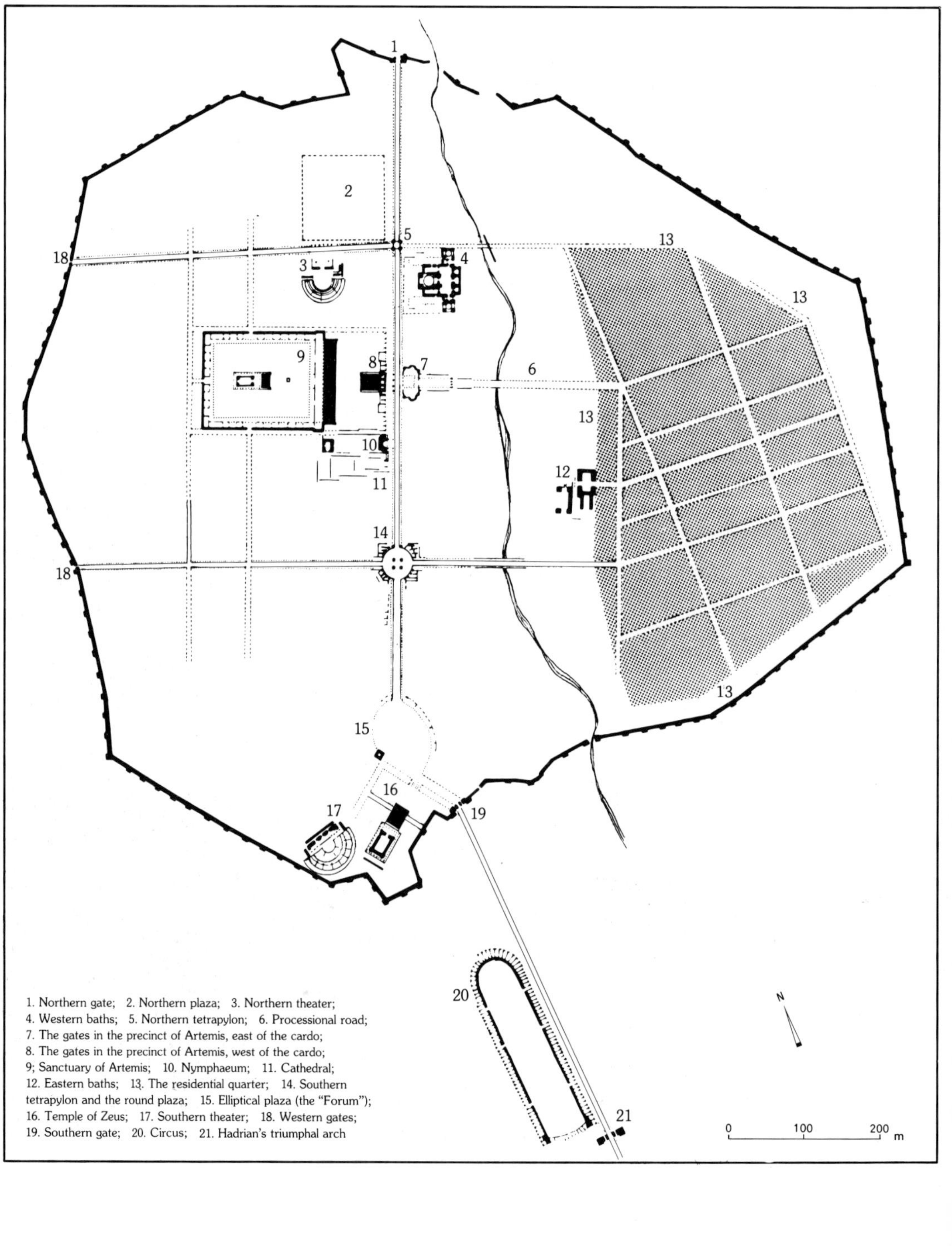

Gerasa: plan of the city.

ELLIPTICAL PLAZA. This plaza is in a natural depression extending between the hill of the precinct of Zeus to the south and the camp hill (the camp of the expedition excavating Jerash) to the north. The ellipse is 90 by 80 m. The plaza is surrounded by 160 columns with Ionic capitals and is paved with stone slabs. It was built in the first century CE. At the point where the *cardo* meets the plaza, there is a decorated gate with a broad middle entrance on the street and two narrower entrances on the sidewalks. This gate, only a small portion of which is preserved, is decorated in Corinthian style. At the southeastern end of the plaza, parallel to the retaining wall of the lower terrace of the sanctuary of Zeus, a small street connects the southern gate of Gerasa with the plaza.

SOUTHERN THEATER. This theater, situated west of the temple of Zeus, was excavated from 1925 to 1931. The lower auditorium (*ima cavea*) was divided into four segments (*cunei*), and the upper (*summa cavea*) into eight. The theater held some three thousand spectators. Four exits (*vomitoria*) issued from the gangway (*praecinctio*), and two passages (*aditus maximi*) lead into the orchestra on each flank. The facade (*scaenae frons*) behind the stage had two stories and three entrances (*aula regia*), and two *hospitalia*. Two inscriptions found in the theater commemorate the construction of parts of it under Domitian (Welles, nos. 51–52). The entire structure was built in the last decade of the first century CE.

SOUTHERN TETRAPYLON. This tetrapylon is in a circular piazza and is composed of four pedestals, each carrying four Corinthian columns bearing baldachins. It was probably erected in the middle of the third century CE. The piazza was completely surrounded by an ornamental facade of columns, behind which shops were built at the beginning of the fourth century. These were still used as dwellings in the Early Arab period.

TEMPLE C. Temple C was southwest of the Church of Saint Theodore. It was the smallest temple found in the city. It faced southeast and was surrounded by a roofed court with porticoes. The prostyle chamber is small, opening into an exedra at the rear. There was a vaulted chamber beneath the podium. The excavators believed that this building was a hero's monument, but L.H. Vincent defined it as a Nabatean temenos. The building belongs to the first half of the second century CE.

NORTHERN TETRAPYLON. The northern tetrapylon is at the intersection of the *cardo* and the north *decumanus*. It is built of four piers, with passages between them, and is roofed with a dome. It was probably built at the beginning of the third century CE.

THE EASTERN BATHS. The baths are at the edge of the city, to the east of the valley. They have not been explored.

NYMPHAEUM. The nymphaeum, or ornamental public fountain, is north of the cathedral lane (see below) west of the *cardo*. It is the most resplendent of Gerasa's ornamental buildings. It faces east and consists of a facade with two stories and a central apse, with niches and a Corinthian colonnade along its length. The first story is crowned with a lintel and the upper story with pediments; the nymphaeum is topped with a semidome. In front of it is a pool and a portico. It was built in 191 CE (Welles, no. 69).

SANCTUARY OF ARTEMIS. The sanctuary in honor of the goddess Artemis, the patroness of Gerasa, was the center of the city. Its construction continued for at least thirty years (150–180 CE; Welles, nos. 27–32), and it covered 8.4 a. Its excavation began in 1928 and is still in progress. The sanctuary of Artemis is one of the most magnificent and best preserved of the sanctuaries of the Hellenistic-Roman world in the eastern Mediterranean Basin. It is in five parts: (1) the propylaeum (complex of gates) to the east of the *cardo*, including the processional way; (2) the propylaeum to the west of the *cardo*; (3) the outer court; (4) the temple court; and (5) the temple.

The processional way begins in the eastern city, 500 m from the temple. It ends at the eastern end of the propylaeum of the temenos, after passing over the river on a strong stone bridge. Both the processional way and the bridge are aligned on the same axis as the temple and the temenos, and together form a monumental complex. The processional way (11 m wide) ends in an ornamental exedra adjoining the *cardo* on its east. At its entrance to the exedra is an ornamental gate with three arched openings. From the exedra, a broad gate (19 m wide), which seems to have had four columns, led to the *cardo*. Adjoining the *cardo* on the west was a retaining wall 120 m long and 14 m high. A staircase at its center led from the street to the outer court of the temenos. On the strip of land between the *cardo* and the retaining wall was a row of shops in two blocks—seven shops in each block—to the north and south of the staircase.

The first element of the propylaeum to the west of the *cardo* is a colonnade of extremely large columns. They replaced the columns found along the *cardo* in the section facing the temenos staircase. Behind the columns is the gate wall, in which there are three rectangular openings. The central entrance is 5 m wide and 9 m high, and each of the side entrances is 3.8 m wide.

To the west of the gate a 19.35-m-wide staircase ascends from the level of the street to that of the outer court; it is bounded on the north and the south by smooth, strong walls. The staircase and the walls enclosing it are completely preserved. Another staircase, composed of three sets of stairs, each with nine steps, led from the outer court to the temple court. The stairs were separated from the temple court by a colonnade over 100 m long and 11 m wide. On its northern and southern ends, the colonnade is bounded by two open, exedra-like buildings. It is separated from the temple court by an ornamental wall with three entrances. The court (161 by 121 m) was surrounded by colonnades, which were 14.2 m from its walls. The space between them was filled, except on the east, by alternating rows of rooms and open exedrae.

The temple of Artemis stands in a court (124 m long and 88 m wide) surrounded by colonnades. The podium on which the temple stood is 40 m long, 22.6 m wide, and 4.3 m high. The staircase in the facade of the podium is composed of two sets of stairs, each with seven steps. The stairs are flanked by two strong piers. The podium rests on a series of barrel vaults. The temple itself is a peripteral hexastylos: six columns in its facade and eleven along its length. Between the columns of the colonnade in the temple's facade and the cella wall another row of six columns was added to give the facade greater depth. The columns, which bear Corinthian capitals, are 13.2 m high. The cella is 24.15 m long and 13.37 m wide. The construction and workmanship of the architectural elements are of outstanding quality.

THE NORTHERN THEATER. This theater is situated northeast of the sanctuary of Artemis and south of the northern *decumanus*. Excavations only began here in 1987. It is smaller than the southern theater. Its cavea faces north. The orchestra's vaulted entrances (*aditus maximi*) are behind the *scaenae frons*, near the wings (*versurae*). The upper cavea has eight *cunei*; the lower four are reached by four *vomitoria*. The theater was built between 162 and 166 CE (Welles, no. 65).

WESTERN BATHS. The western baths lie between the northern tetrapylon and the Chrysorhoas River; the entrances all lead from the east into the frigidarium. A domed caldarium is on the west and there are small rooms to the south and north. The building has additional flanking rooms north and south of the frigidarium, whose ceilings are supported by piers. The plan has parallels at Timgad and Cyrene in North Africa, so the building can probably be dated to the second half of the second century CE. The pendentives used to support the dome of the hall are among the earliest known examples of this architectural device in the Roman world.

NORTHERN GATE. The city's northern gate was built in 115 CE (Welles, nos. 56–57), replacing an earlier entrance. It had a single entrance flanked by two-storied pavilions with Corinthian columns. Two trapezoidal bastions were added to its northern facade in the Byzantine or Early Arab period.

STRUCTURES OUTSIDE THE CITY WALLS. Buildings exist to the north of the town, near the Roman road to Pella, including a temple of Nemesis from the Antonine period. 1200 m north of the gate is the open-air ritual site

Marble head of Zeus-Serapis, Roman period.

Elliptical plaza (the "forum") and the temple of Zeus.

of Birketein, which contains a theater. Colonnades linked the theater with a double pool. They formed an amusement area for the celebration of the festival of Maiumas, a Syrian festival celebrated every three years by water sports and dramatic spectacles. (According to Welles, inscription no. 279, the festival was still held in the sixth century CE.) The theater accommodated about one thousand spectators. The auditorium faces east and is divided into four *cunei*. There is no stage building (*scena*). The theater was built in the Severan period (Welles, nos. 153, 197, and 198). North of it were the temple of Zeus Epicarpius (Welles, no. 42) and the tomb of the centurion Germanus, built in the Antonine period (Welles, no. 219).

CEMETERY. Gerasa's cemetery surrounded the entire city. Above-ground sepulchral structures are seen chiefly along the road running north from the city. West of the circus, twelve rock-cut tombs, dating mainly to the second to fifth centuries CE, were uncovered in 1930. Most of the finds are from the third century.

CHURCHES AND SYNAGOGUE

CHURCH OF SAINTS PETER AND PAUL. The Church of Saints Peter and Paul (Welles, no. 327) in the southwest quarter of the city was excavated in 1929. A small chapel adjoins it to its south. The first church was a basilica with three apses and an atrium at its western end. Judging from its mosaics and general plan, it was built in about 540 CE. The burial chapel was a simple hall, terminating in an apse, that opened on the south into a burial cave dating from the end of the sixth century CE.

CHURCH OF PROCOPIUS. The Church of Procopius (Welles, no. 304), which stands at the end of the southern *decumanus* in the southeastern part of the city, was excavated in 1928. It is a basilica with three internal apses. A chapel stood on its northwest side. The church was built in 525/6–527 CE.

THE CATHEDRAL OF GERASA. The cathedral of Gerasa and its associated buildings were constructed north of the southern *decumanus*, at right angles to the *cardo* and west of it. The buildings were constructed on four terraces

Southern theater.

The nymphaeum.

rising to the west. Their excavation was begun in 1928. The approach from the *cardo* was by a monumental colonnade and by steps built in the second century CE and repaired in the fourth. The structure, in its original plan, dates to the Antonine period; a temple apparently occupied the second terrace in the first century CE. The cathedral is a basilica with an internal polygonal apse and a chapel to the southwest, the fountain court to the east forming its atrium. The oldest church known in Gerasa, it appears to have been built about 400 CE.

Beneath the cathedral's remains, among construction segments from the Byzantine period, many remains were found of a ritual precinct that pre-

Temenos of Artemis: the propylaeum facade west of the cardo.

City coin of Gerasa, 2nd century CE.

Plan of the church complex of St. John the Baptist, St. George (on the south), and SS. Cosmas and Damian.

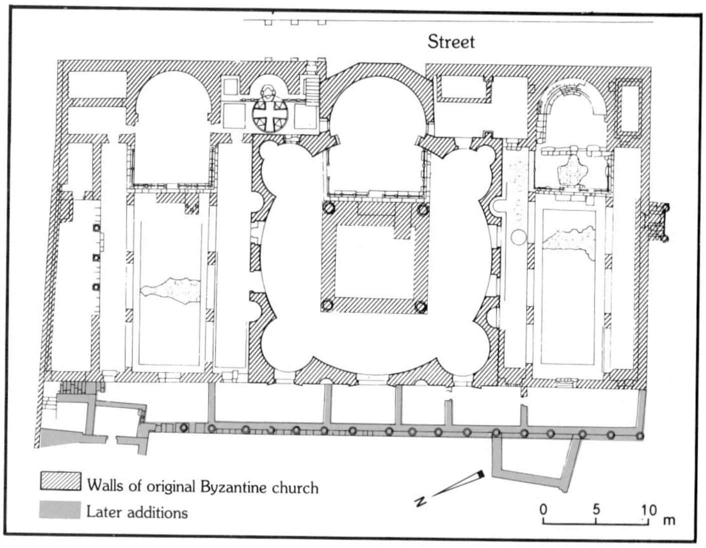

ceded the cathedral. This sanctuary was smaller and more modest than that of Artemis. The staircase leading from the *cardo* to the cathedral belongs to it. The staircase, which hardly changed over time, led from the street into the precinct. It passed along a row of shops, similar to the row flanking the staircase in the precinct of Artemis. When the sanctuary of Artemis was built in the second century CE, its dimensions and monumental magnificence overshadowed the earlier sanctuary. It is also possible, however, that the two sanctuaries existed side by side.

FOUNTAIN COURT. The fountain court was west of the cathedral, on the second terrace. A Christian festival was held here on the anniversary of the marriage at Cana. The festival is mentioned by Epiphanius, writing in 375 CE. Some scholars believe that the cathedral was originally the Temple of Dionysus (Dushara), and the miracle of Cana (Jn. 2:1) replaced the memory of some ceremony or event connected with the god of wine.

CHURCH OF SAINT THEODORE. The Church of Saint Theodore occupied the third terrace. It was erected to the west of the fountain court between 494 and 496 CE (Welles, no. 300). To its west was a rhomboid-shaped atrium. The nave is surrounded by various annexes, a chapel, baptistery, etc. The church contains magnificent mosaic pavements.

BATHS OF FLACCUS. The Baths of Flaccus were on the fourth terrace, north of the fountain court. They were built in 454–455 CE and renovated in 584 CE (Welles, no. 296). Their rooms, which are relatively small, are ranged around two courtyards. To their west was the clergy house. Erected in a third-century street, it was divided, in its first phase, into two suites. The one on the northwest was apparently used by a person of high rank. Additional rooms were later built onto the house. To its north was a residential quarter built in the fourth century CE over burial caves from the first century CE. The quarter expanded in the fifth century and existed until the seventh.

CHURCHES OF SAINTS JOHN THE BAPTIST, GEORGE, COSMAS AND DAMIAN. The churches are west of the Church of Saint Theodore, on the same axis. The three churches actually comprise one structure—that is, a central church with lateral churches. All three face west, with a narrow atrium in front of each. The Church of Saint John was built in 531 CE (Welles, no. 306). It is circular, with an exedra facing each of the cardinal points. The apse is on the east, with the chancel in front of it. The dome is supported by four columns. The plan resembles the cathedral of Bostra (512–513 CE). The two flanking churches are identical basilicas with apses in their eastern walls. Saint George's was built in 529 CE (Welles, no. 309), and Saints Cosmas and Damian's in 533 CE (Welles, no. 311). All three buildings were damaged by earthquakes. Only Saint George's continued in use in the eighth

Church of St. John the Baptist: mosaic depiction of the city of Alexandria, Byzantine period.

Church of St. John the Baptist: mosaic pavement in the northwestern exedra, Byzantine period.

Church of SS. Cosmas and Damian: the nave and mosaic pavement, Byzantine period.

century. It was excavated in 1929.

CHURCH OF BISHOP GENESIUS. The Church of Bishop Genesius, which was uncovered in 1929 to the west of the three churches described above, was erected in 611 CE (Welles, no. 335). It is a basilica with an exterior apse and a chapel on the southwest.

SYNAGOGUE CHURCH. The synagogue church was built in 530–531 CE, to the west of the temenos of Artemis and above it. It was excavated in 1929. The church's courtyard was on the west side, and the atrium was built to the east in the third or fourth century. The remains of a synagogue were found beneath the church. Its entrance was on the east, whereas the church erected on its foundations was entered from the west. Beneath the church's apse was the synagogue's narthex, whose floor had a mosaic depicting animals entering Noah's ark. From its narthex, three doors opened onto the synagogue's hall, which was divided into a nave and aisles by two rows of columns—four in

Church of SS. Cosmas and Damian: detail of the mosaic pavement in the nave, Byzantine period.

Part of the synagogue's mosaic floor, showing animals entering Noah's ark.

each row. In the western part of the floor of the nave was an inscription recording the names of its three donors: "Peace on all Israel, Amen, Amen, Selah; Phineas bar Baruch, Jose bar Samuel, and J(u)dan bar Hezekiah." The eastern floor dates to the fourth or fifth century. The western floor was sixth century in style.

CHURCHES OF THE PROPHETS, APOSTLES, AND MARTYRS. The Church of the Prophets, Apostles, and Martyrs was built in the north of the city, east of the Chrysorhoas River, and dedicated in 464–465 CE (Welles, no. 298). It was partially examined in 1929. The church's cruciform plan is unusual: each of its arms has a nave and aisles, and the angles of the cross are occupied by rooms. The central area of the cross was supported at the corners by tall Corinthian columns. The chancel is placed in the apse and nave of the eastern arm. The plan has parallels at Salona and Ephesus.

SUMMARY

The first indication of renewed prosperity at Gerasa under Roman rule is the new temple dedicated to Zeus (22/23–23/24 CE; Welles, nos. 2 and 3). There was an increase in the number of Roman coins from the reign of Claudius on. In the second half of the first century, a new street plan was prepared using the *cardo* as its main axis; it was laid out beginning in the year 75/76 (Welles, no. 50). The city wall was completed at the same time. The southern theater existed by Domitian's time (Welles, nos. 51 and 52), and in the Flavian period the first temple of Artemis was decorated and the temple of Hera built (Welles, nos. 17 and 28), apparently on the site later occupied by the cathedral. A new phase of development began under Trajan with the building of the northern gate. Among its causes was the inclusion of the city in the Province of Arabia (106 CE), when new roads were built (Welles, nos. 252–257). Hadrian stayed at Gerasa in 129–130 CE (Welles, nos. 30, 58, 143–145); the triumphal arch and the new southern gate were erected during his reign. The southern and central sectors of the colonnades on the *cardo* were apparently built during the reigns of Hadrian and Antoninus Pius. At that time, the splendid propylaeum in front of the temple of Artemis, as well as the temple itself, was built and the magnificent approach to its east was rebuilt. The focus of Gerasa was thus transferred northward. Under Marcus Aurelius (163 CE), the northern theater was added (Welles, no. 65) and the western baths were built in the second half of the second century.

Inscriptions contribute information about the city's economy and the composition of its population in the second and third centuries, by recording guilds of weavers (Welles, no. 190) and potters (Welles, no. 79). Trajanic figurines and lamps found in a tomb to the south of Gerasa attest to a local workshop. One citizen performed the duties of Phoenicarch, or president of the provincial diet in Phoenicia (Welles, no. 188), indicating that Gerasa had trade links with the cities of Phoenicia. Gerasa began to strike its own coins under Hadrian and continued to do so down to the reign of Alexander Severus. The coins usually bear the figure of Artemis, the city's Tyche, or the figure of Tyche with that of the emperor. Tyche and the river god of the Chrysorhoas appear together at the time of Lucius Verus. The city's name, Antioch, and its titles appear on coins from the time of Marcus Aurelius and Lucius Verus. In the third century, probably under Caracalla, Gerasa received the status of a Roman colony, Colonia Aurelia Antoniniana (Welles, nos. 179 and 191). Under the Severi, the festival theater at the open-air ritual site to the north of the city (Welles, no. 153) and the southern and northern tetrapylons were built; temple C was already in ruins. Gerasa began to decline in the mid-third century, and the city ceased to mint its own coins. It revived under Diocletian, when the southern tetrapylon was surrounded by shops. While fourth-century coins were numerous in the excavation's finds, the epigraphic sources record almost nothing of the city until the fifth century.

Representatives of Gerasa took part in church councils as early as 359 CE (Epiph., *Haer.* 73, 26). In the mid-fifth century, the city's fortifications were repaired. Its first church was erected in about 400, and the Church of the Apostles was built in 464. Building activity increased, and the Church of Saint Theodore and its annexes were erected in 496, reflecting the expansion of the ecclesiastical bureaucracy. The Church of Procopius dates to 562. The rest of Gerasa's churches were also built in the sixth and seventh centuries. Other public buildings were enlarged at the same time. The plans of Gerasa's churches in general resemble those of the churches in Palestine and Constantinople. They have a platform in front of which an altar and a solea (platform) are enclosed by a chancel screen. The bishop's throne stood within an apse, skirted by a semicircular bench for the priests. Semidomes decorated with glass tesserae are numerous, but the narthex is rare at Gerasa. Stones

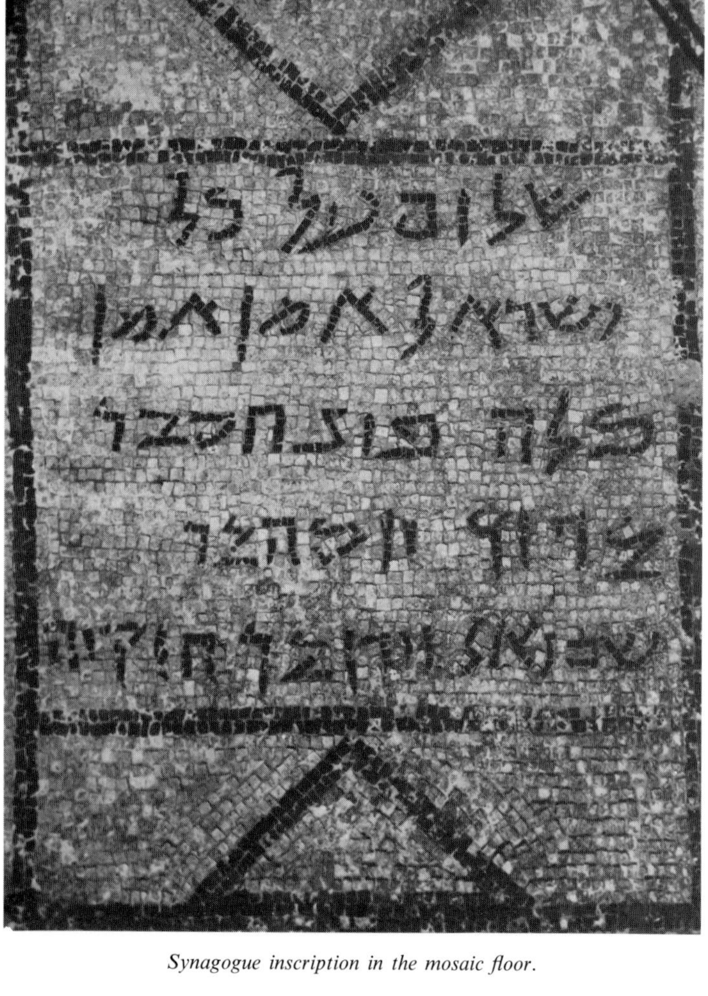

Synagogue inscription in the mosaic floor.

The cathedral of Gerasa.

and architectural items from earlier structures appear in all the churches in secondary use.

Colored mosaic floors become frequent after the fourth century, chiefly in the churches; their decorative repertoire includes human figures, animals, birds, various objects, and floral and geometric motifs. The portraits of donors and the pictures of Egyptian walled cities in the churches of Saint John and Saints Peter and Paul are unique. All human figures, however, were deliberately effaced, apparently in the eighth century, following the enactment of Muslim iconoclastic legislation. The mosaics are classical in style, but by the sixth century, the artists of Gerasa had achieved an independent style. They belonged to a school unique to Palestine and Syria that influenced Islamic mosaic art.

A great number of coins have been found that date to Justin II (565–578). By then, however, many buildings in the city were in ruins, many streets had become blind alleys, and the water system was in a state of neglect. From 614 to 628 the city was occupied by the Persians, and in 635 it fell to the Muslims. Coins testify that settlement here continued until 774, when the business center once again reverted to the southern tetrapylon. Some poorly built structures were erected in the southern elliptical plaza at that time. Most of the churches were still in use in the eighth century, but the center of gravity of economic and political life shifted away from Gerasa when the capital of the caliphs was transferred from Damascus to Baghdad in 750, and a series of earthquakes afflicted the city, hastening its ruin. In the ninth century, Gerasa was still a mixed Greco-Arab settlement. In the eleventh century, the temple of Artemis was used as a temporary fort. Baldwin III destroyed the city in 1122, and the historian William of Tyre and the Arab traveler Yaqut found the place deserted.

Glass goblet decorated with a cross and other designs, Byzantine period.

Main publications: C. H. Kraeling, ed., *Gerasa: City of the Decapolis*, New Haven 1938; I. Browning, *Jerash and the Decapolis*, London 1982; *Gerasa 1: Report of the Italian Archaeological Expedition at Jerash, Campaigns 1977–1981* (Mesopotamia 18–19, 7–134), Florence 1983–1984; R. G. Khouri, *Jerash, a City of the Decapolis*, London 1984; id., *Jerash: A Frontier City of the Roman East*, London 1986; E. Olavarri Goicoechea, *Excavaciones en el Agora de Gerasa en 1983*, Madrid 1986; *Jerash Archaeological Project* 1, 1981–1983 (ed. F. Zayadine), Amman 1986; ibid. 2, 1984–1988 (Syria 66), Paris 1989.

Other studies: C. H. Kraeling (Review), *Berytus* 7 (1942), 83–86; id., *BASOR* 83 (1941), 7–14; N. Glueck, *BASOR* 75 (1939), 22–30; L. H. Vincent, *RB* 49 (1940), 98–129; A. H. Detweiler, *BASOR* 87 (1942), 10–17; G. L. Harding, *Official Guide to Jerash*, Jerusalem 1944; id., *PEQ* 81 (1949), 12–20; id., *The Antiquities of Jordan*, London 1967, 79–105; J. H. Iliffe, *QDAP* 11 (1944), 1–26; D. Kirkbride, *BIAL* 1 (1958), 9–20; id., *ADAJ* 4–5 (1960), 123–127; E. L. Sukenik, *Rabinowitz Bulletin* 1 (1949), 11; F. S. Ma'ayeh, *ADAJ* 4–5 (1960), 115–116; id., *RB* 67 (1960), 228–229; Jordan Department of Antiquities, *Jerash*, Amman 1962; H. Bietenhard, *ZDPV* 79 (1963), 24–58; S. Mittmann, ibid. 80 (1964), 113–136; id., *ADAJ* 11 (1966), 65–87; H. Seyrig, *Syria* 42 (1965), 25–34; M. B. Steinberg, *Revista de Historia* 39/79 (1969), 197–201; G. W. Bowersock, *JRS* 61 (1971), 219–242; M. Lyttelton, *Baroque Architecture in Classical Antiquity*, London 1974, 241–247; A. Spijkerman, *LA* 25 (1975), 73–84; id., *The Coins of the Decapolis and Provincia Arabia*, Jerusalem 1978, 158–167; M. Sartre, *ADAJ* 21 (1976), 105–108; J. Pouilloux, *LA* 27 (1977), 246–254; 29 (1979), 276–278; H. Kalayan, *ADAJ* 22 (1977–1978), 163–171; 25 (1981), 331–334; id., *SHAJ* 1 (1982), 243–254; J. A. Sauer, *BA* 42 (1979), 134; H. Joyce, *AJA* 84 (1980), 215–216; R. Parapetti, *ADAJ* 24 (1980), 145–150; id., *SHAJ* 1 (1982), 255–260; 2 (1985), 243–247; id., *Mesopotamia* 18–19 (1983–1984), 37–84; E. M. Knauf, *ZDPV* 97 (1981), 188–192; A. Segal, *Journal of the Society of Architectural Historians* 40 (1981), 108–121; id., *Town Planning and Architecture in Provincia Arabia* (*BAR*/IS 419), Oxford 1988, 19–48; F. Brossier, *MdB* 22 (1982), 28–29; I. Browning (Reviews), *Berytus* 31 (1983), 161–163. — *Mesopotamia* 18–19 (1983–1984), 251–253. — *PEQ* 116 (1984), 149–150; P. L. Gatier, *ADAJ* 26 (1982), 269–275; 32 (1988), 151–155; id., *Syria* 62 (1985), 297–312; E. Will, ibid. (1983), 133–145; J. W. Hanbury Tenison, *LA* 34 (1984), 437; id., *RB* 92 (1985), 393; id., *ADAJ* 31 (1987), 129–157; R. G. Khouri, *Archaeology* 38 (1985), 18–25; id., *Jerash: A Frontier City* (Review), *ZDPV* 105 (1989), 197–198; id., *Jerash: A Brief Guide to the Antiquities* (Al-Kutba Jordan Guides), Amman 1988; M. Piccirillo, *MdB* 35 (1984), 16–21; F. Braemer, *RB* 92 (1985), 419–420, id., *Syria* 62 (1985), 159–164; id., *ADAJ* 31 (1987), 525–530; J. Seigne, ibid., 287–295; id., *RB* 93 (1986), 238–247; M. C. Bitti, *ADAJ* 30 (1986), 207–210; *Jerash Archaeological Project* (Reviews), *LA* 36 (1986), 372–374. — *ZDPV* 104 (1988), 182–183; E. de Montlivault, *Berytus* 34 (1986), 139–144; H. Stierlin, *Städte in der Wüste* (Antike Kunst im Vorderen Orient), Stuttgart 1987; R. Wenning, *Der Königsweg: 9000 Jahre Kunst und Kultur in Jordanien* (eds. S. Mittmann et al.), Mainz 1987, 256–266; A. J. 'Amr, *ZDPV* 104 (1988), 146–149; id., *ADAJ* 33 (1989), 353–356; C. Meyers, *BASOR* Supplement 25 (1988), 175–222; id., *ADAJ* 33 (1989), 235–244; J. Skurdenis, *Archaeology* 41/4 (1988), 64–66; M. Weippert and E. A. Knauf, *ZDPV* 104 (1988), 150–151; *Akkadica Supplementum* 7–8 (1989), 316–337; V. A. Clark, *ZDPV* 106 (1990), 175–176; *MdB* 62 (1990); A. A. Ostrasz, *ADAJ* 35 (1991), 237–250.

The synagogue: J. W. Crowfoot and R. W. Hamilton, *PEQ* 61 (1929), 211–219; E. L. Sukenik, ibid. 62 (1930), 48–49; C. H. Kraeling, ed., *Gerasa: City of the Decapolis*, New Haven 1938, 234–241, 318–324; Goodenough, *Jewish Symbols* 1, 259–260.

SHIMON APPLEBAUM, ARTHUR SEGAL

GERISA, TEL

IDENTIFICATION

Tel Gerisa (Tell Jerishe) is located at the end of the Coastal Plain's third *kurkar* ridge, which is crossed by the Yarkon River about 4 km (2.5 mi.) east of its estuary (map reference 1319.1665). Today, the mound lies within the borders of the city of Ramat Gan, east of Tel Aviv. The site is named after the nearby Arab village, but its ancient name is not known. B. Mazar suggested its identification with biblical Gath-Rimmon (Jos. 19:45, 21:24) and with Gath (*Knt*), mentioned in the city list of Thutmose III (no. 63). Remnants of the *kurkar* ridge near the Yarkon estuary created a small waterfall near the site, which was used to operate flour mills, giving it the additional name of "the Seven Mills." The surviving *kurkar* provided a convenient river crossing, giving the site its strategic importance. Because Napoleon's army, during the siege of Jaffa, established a blockade here the mound is popularly known as Napoleon's Hill.

The rivers along Israel's coast, especially the Yarkon, served in ancient times as natural anchorages. Because, in the early periods, there were no artificial ports, Tel Gerisa's advantageous location on the banks of the Yarkon River made it the region's main port. The *kurkar* ridge formed a barrier to boats sailing up the Yarkon estuary, so that the mound is situated at the end of the navigable stretch of the river. Until the beginning of the twentieth century, when the breakwater was built at Jaffa, dozens of fishing and trading boats anchored daily at this spot.

EXPLORATION

Five seasons of excavations were carried out at the site between 1927 and 1950, under the direction of E. L. Sukenik, assisted by S. Yeivin, E. Pinkerfeld, and N. Avigad. Another brief excavation was conducted by S. Geva in 1976 on behalf of the Institute of Archaeology at the Hebrew University of Jerusalem. In 1981, extensive excavations were resumed under the auspices of the Institute of Archaeology at Tel Aviv University, directed by Z. Herzog.

SUKENIK'S EXCAVATIONS

EARLY BRONZE AGE. Sukenik attributed the earliest remains at the site to the latest phase of the Early Bronze Age. Structural remains and pottery dating from this time were discovered in the center of the western part and in the southern part of the mound.

MIDDLE BRONZE AGE I. Only isolated sherds from the Middle Bronze Age I were found on the mound, leading the excavator to surmise that a temporary settlement existed here at the time.

MIDDLE BRONZE AGE II. The Sukenik excavations focused on examining the Middle Bronze Age II fortification system. He dated the destruction of the Middle Bronze Age settlement to the time of the Hyksos expulsion from Egypt, in the middle of the sixteenth century BCE. The conclusions were published by Geva. The 1981 and 1985 excavations have shed new light on this subject (see below). Only a few building remains from this period were found, along with weapons, jewelry, scarabs, and pottery. Several infant burials in storage jars were discovered under the floors.

According to Sukenik, only in the Middle Bronze Age II did a prosperous and fortified city arise at Tel Gerisa. The finds attest to the high level of its material culture. From the very beginning of the period, the pottery is outstanding for its fine forms, especially the vessels covered with red slip and burnished to a metal luster. A pottery kiln with unusual curved walls was also discovered on the site. Other finds include bronze weapons, scarabs and jewelry, providing much information about the daily life of the inhabitants. Building remains are scanty and yield no information about the layout of the city or the plan of the dwelling houses. In several places infant burials in jars, which were then customary, were discovered under the floors of the rooms.

Sukenik noted that the most interesting feature of the Middle Bronze Age II city is its defense system, which is based on a glacis—a form of fortification that came into use at that time in Western Asia and Egypt. Judging by the nature and strength of the glacis, Tel Gerisa was probably an important link in the chain of fortifications of the Hyksos. The complex and excellent structure of this glacis has no parallel in the country. Basically, it is formed by layers of earth and sand spread on the slopes and surrounding the whole of the mound. Only in the south and southeast were large parts of this out-

Aerial view of Tel Gerisa.

Plan and section of the MB II glacis.

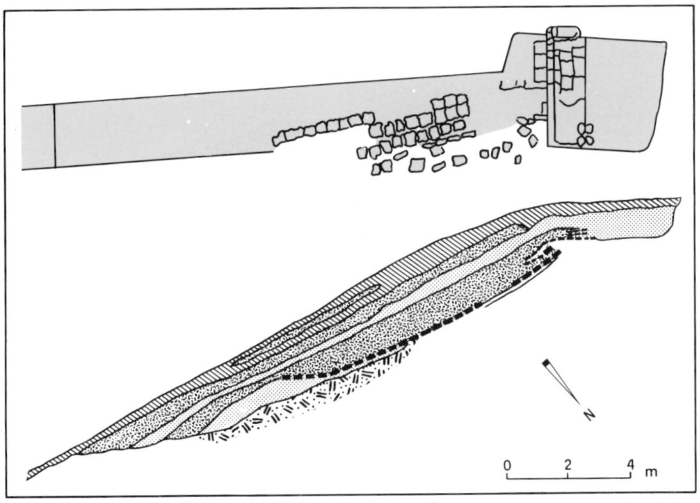

standing construction cleared. At other places the construction is simpler.

At the upper edge of the mound, along its slopes, a wall of large, sun-dried mud bricks was built (c. 3 m wide up to a height of nearly 3 m, according to topographical requirements). As could be seen after clearing, the wall was not visible from the outside, since its face was covered by the layers of the glacis sloping down from the wall to the foot of the mound. Of the upper part of the wall surrounding the city—which was exposed—no remains have survived.

Sukenik described the structure of the fortifications. The glacis proper was built as follows. The natural surface of the slope, consisting of friable *kurkar*, was covered with a layer of dark, beaten earth. On this layer sun-dried quadrangular mud bricks (40–50 cm a side) were set in one or two courses. Near the wall five to six courses were used. This layer of bricks was thickly covered with *kurkar* sand upon which were deposited several alternate layers of beaten earth and sand to a thickness of 2 to 3 m. The cross section of these layers somewhat resembles a kind of sandwich with alternating dark and light stripes. The sandy layers were probably laid for the purpose of draining off the rainwater penetrating the uppermost layers. The steep slope was intended to prevent an enemy from undermining the city walls or from breaching them by means of battering rams. It was therefore of the utmost importance to prevent the erosion of the slopes and to maintain them in perfect condition.

When the Hyksos were expelled by the Egyptians in the middle of the sixteenth century BCE, this fortress, too, fell and was destroyed.

LATE BRONZE AGE. Many Late Bronze Age buildings were found and Sukenik viewed this as a prosperous time for the city, which had now expanded over the whole mound. The finds from this period include bichrome ware, Mycenean and Cypriot vessels, weapons, jewelry, scarabs, and nude Astarte figurines. Especially noteworthy is a very large green stone scarab, of the Egyptian "heart scarab" type, on which passages from the thirtieth chapter of the Egyptian Book of the Dead are inscribed. Sukenik determined that the Late Bronze Age city had been completely destroyed in about 1200 BCE, although it is not clear who was responsible for its destruction.

IRON AGE. Sukenik identified the Iron Age city as having been concentrated in the southern part of the mound. Philistine vessels were found there above the Late Bronze Age stratum. This Philistine settlement was destroyed by fire, which Sukenik attributed to David's struggle against the Philistines. He proposed that a new Israelite city was established on top of the ruins, which was in turn destroyed by Pharoah Shishak during his campaign at the end of the tenth century BCE.

RECENT EXCAVATIONS

Three seasons of excavations were conducted between 1981 and 1983 in four areas, covering three-quarters of the mound, which extends over about 13.75 a. inside the city wall. The remaining quarter was left unexcavated, for future

Square mud bricks coating the glacis, MB II.

Pottery assemblage, MB II.

research. When the excavations began, it became clear that Sukenik had excavated much more extensively than his visible excavated areas indicated. This was due to the "canal method" he used, which filled in already excavated areas with the earth extracted from new areas. The lack of detailed plans from Sukenik's work made it difficult for the new excavators to understand the settlement at the site. Because the extent of settlement on the mound varied at different periods, each excavated area has a different stratigraphical sequence. It became apparent that only part of the southern summit had been occupied during the Iron Age, while its eastern part contained settlement remains dating from the Late Bronze Age I, with only some Iron Age I pits above them. Iron Age remains were also uncovered at the northern end of the mound, approximately 200 m from the southern summit. In the central, lower part of the mound, the last occupation layer dates to the Late Bronze Age II. In various places, traces of activity (although not occupation layers) from the Persian, Roman, and Byzantine periods were found.

EARLY AND MIDDLE BRONZE AGES. The earliest settlement on the mound was an unfortified town from the Early Bronze Age III. Above this stratum were remains of an unfortified settlement from the Middle Bronze Age IIA, and above this stratum the site's first city wall was founded (see below). The new excavations altered the previous stratigraphical picture of the Middle Bronze Age II, adding many details. Sukenik, in his numerous sections of the fortification system, concentrated on questions pertaining to the glacis that surrounded the fortifications, while the new excavations focused on the stratigraphical relationship between the fortifications and the inner-city occupation levels. It is now clear that there were three different fortification systems during the Middle Bronze Age II, not one, as was previously thought.

In an early phase of the Middle Bronze Age IIA, a brick city wall was erected above the unfortified settlement; the associated floor was covered with fallen bricks. The second phase of the fortifications was associated with two floors also dated to the Middle Bronze Age IIA. This phase was represented by two types of fortifications, uncovered in two adjacent sections in area A: one consisted of two parallel walls with a 1-m gap between them, and the other was a single brick wall. The double wall was probably part of a tower that commanded the southeastern slope of the mound. On the uppermost of the two floors associated with this fortification phase, the finds included burnished bowls with gutter rims, bowls painted with a red cross, and finely combed storage jars. These vessels are characteristic of the later stage of the Middle Bronze Age IIA.

In the third phase, the fortifications were again composed of a single wall (c. 3 m thick), that had been erected on top of the previous fortifications. Adjoining this wall on the inner, or city, side was a large brick building, five of whose rooms have so far been excavated. In the western part of this area, the floors of the buildings sloped toward the wall, as a result of the remains of the tower from the previous phase. On one of these sloping floors fragments of storage jars from the Middle Bronze Age IIB were found, evidence that the room had been used for storage. It is possible that the main residential story was above this storeroom. A pit attributed to this phase contained a storage jar, a juglet, and a bowl, underneath which was a bronze figurine of a Canaanite god (Reshef?) with his right arm raised. Because the Bronze Age remains in nearby area B are at a considerable depth (underneath the Iron Age strata), it appears that area A served as the mound's acropolis in the Middle Bronze Age II and that the brick building was part of a palace there.

LATE BRONZE AGE. The Middle Bronze Age IIB city wall was in use during the first phase of the Late Bronze Age and was abutted by poorly built structures. Remains of a small room, an oven, and chocolate-on-white and bichrome pottery were found in this phase.

The Middle Bronze Age acropolis was not occupied during the later stages of the Late Bronze Age; it appears that the administrative center was transferred to the middle of the mound, probably closer to the city gate. Late Bronze Age II–III remains were uncovered in area C. As this was the last occupation period in this part of the mound, over the millennia the Late Bronze

A very large scarab on which passages from the Egyptian "Book of the Dead" are inscribed, LB.

Bronze figurine of a god (Reshef?).

Area C: LB II stone pavement.

Age strata were badly damaged by cultivation and erosion. Area C is south of the small gully that drained the mound toward the northwest. It is possible that this marks the location of the city gate at this time. In the western part of area C, in the earlier phase, was a large courtyard (15 by 15 m), paved with wadi pebbles and crushed lime, that apparently served as a market-place. Remains of several structures surrounded it. In the later phases of this period, these structures were enlarged and the open area was reduced. Many finds from the collapsed debris (badly disturbed by frequent plowing), attest to the site's wealth and close foreign ties: sherds of Mycenean and Cypriot ware, Egyptian scarabs, and basalt weights, as well as fragments of a crucible and pipes from a bellows—evidence of local metal production.

In the center of the mound, to the east of the drainage gully, part of a monumental structure (c. 20 m long) was discovered. In its center was a floor paved with *kurkar* slabs. The floor was surrounded by a brick wall 4 m wide. The building was only partially excavated because of its great size, and its complete plan is still not clear. A Cypriot cylinder seal, a scarab set in a gold ring, and pottery vessels from the thirteenth century BCE were found on the floor.

IRON AGE. The relationship between the end of the Late Bronze Age and the beginning of the Iron Age on the mound is still not clear, as no stratigraphical sequence including both periods has yet been uncovered. The Iron Age remains are limited to areas B and D and do not continue to the center of the mound. In area D, at the northern end of the mound, five strata from the Iron Age I were uncovered. The earliest stratum contained the stone foundations of brick walls, while other two had segments of brick walls. These three strata yielded early Philistine pottery. Pits attributed to two separate phases had been dug into all the three strata. The pits were apparently first used for storage and subsequently for refuse. The pottery found in the pits included intermediate-stage Philistine vessels and collared-rim jars. Similar pits were uncovered in area A. It can be conjectured that the area at the edge of the mound was used for storage during the latter stage of the Iron Age I, while the mound's lower, central part was cultivated, but not irrigated, by the inhabitants who resided at the southern end of the site (area B).

At the southern end of the mound, three strata from the Iron Age I have so far been found, although only the latest one contained extensive remains, including three

Fragment of a rhyton in the shape of a lioness, from the Philistine settlement.

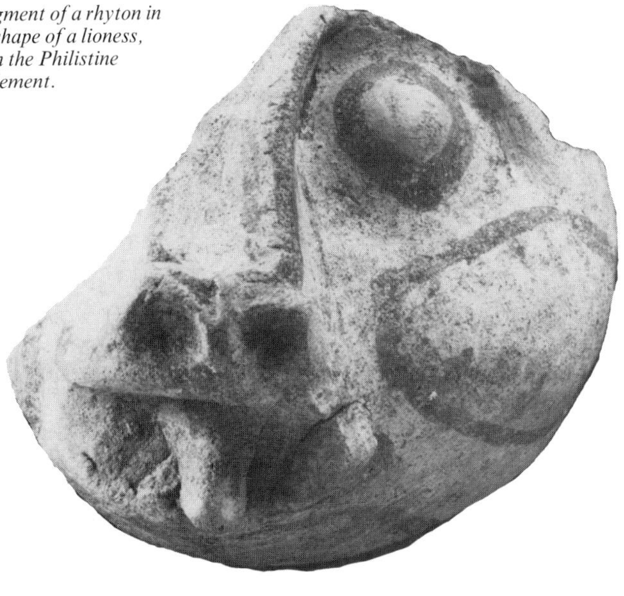

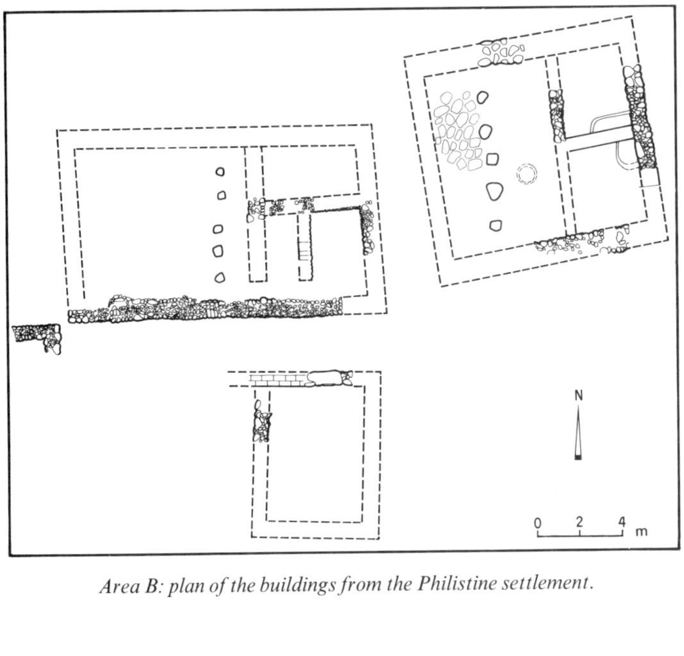

Area B: plan of the buildings from the Philistine settlement.

Clay female figurine from the Philistine settlement.

fragmentary structures. Two of these buildings had column bases dividing them into an open courtyard and a room. This stratum was destroyed in a violent conflagration; numerous pottery vessels were found in it, including several types of storage jars; a closed, globular goblet; a beer jug, a flask with a small bowl attached, and many other small bowls, some decorated with typical Philistine motifs and others red-slipped and burnished. Other finds include a strainer, bronze cymbals, a carved five-sided pyramidal seal, and a clay figurine of a woman. These finds have many parallels to finds from stratum X at nearby Tel Qasile. Judging from the scope of the structural remains, the settlement's area during this stratum is estimated at approximately three-quarters of an acre. Thus, the settlement at Tel Gerisa in this period was a small village near the central city, at Tel Qasile.

The site's water system was also partially excavated. It appears that the stone-built well Sukenik cleared had been sunk into a rounded shaft (diameter, 6 m) hewn into the *kurkar*. Steps were hewn into the sides of the shaft, sixteen of which have been uncovered so far, to a depth of 3.5 m (continuing excavation of the shaft would require dismantling the well). In the earth fill between the well's sides and the hewn shaft were pottery sherds, the latest of which date to the Iron Age I.

The area of the destroyed Philistine settlement was leveled by a gray earth fill—in preparation for the construction of a new settlement in the tenth century BCE. Foundation trenches for the new walls were dug into the fill. These walls were made of both stone and brick. The settlement had two phases, both of which contained pottery dating from the second half of the tenth century BCE—numerous cooking pots and hand-burnished bowls. This settlement was smaller than its predecessor; its area is estimated at no more than half an acre. It seems that these are the remains of a farm that was established at the southern end of the mound, whose inhabitants cultivated the area of the mound itself.

EARLY ARAB PERIOD. The tenth-century BCE stratum terminated a settlement continuum of two thousand years. The site remained unoccupied for another two thousand years, until the Early Arab period in the ninth century CE, when activity was resumed at the northern end of the mound. Among the remains in area D were large bases of small stones (diameter, c. 1 m), that served as foundations for buildings. The walls of these buildings were not preserved. Many pottery sherds made of greenish clay were found, as well as glazed bowls and closed, handmade kraters with horizontal strap handles.

Tel Gerisa: Philistine pyramidal seal.

Following this brief occupation, the site was abandoned and never resettled.

Main publication: S. Geva, *Tell Jerishe: The Sukenik Excavations of the Middle Bronze Age Fortifications* (Qedem 15), Jerusalem 1982.

Other studies: S. Tolkowsky, *JPOS* 6 (1926), 70–74; J. Ory, *Palestine Museum Bulletin* 2 (1926), 7–9; id., *QDAP* 10 (1944), 55–57; S. A. Cook, *PEQ* 61 (1929), 114–115; E. L. Sukenik, *QDAP* 4 (1935), 208–209; 6 (1938), 225; 10 (1944), 198–199; S. Geva, *IEJ* 27 (1977), 47; id., *Tell Jerishe* (Reviews), *PEQ* 116 (1984), 152. — *Syria* 62 (1985), 356; Z. Herzog, *ESI* 1 (1982), 28–31; 7–8 (1988–1989), 60–62; 9 (1989–1990), 51–52; id., *IEJ* 33 (1983), 121–123; 34 (1984), 55–56; id., *RB* 91 (1984), 406–410; Z. Herzog and F. R. Brandfon, *AJA* 89 (1985), 334; T. Clayden, *BAIAS* (1983–1984), 11–12; J. K. Eakins, *ASOR Newsletter* 35/3 (Jan. 1984), 5; F. R. Brandfon, *AJA* 91 (1987), 308; A. F. Rainey, ibid., 308; Weippert 1988 (Ortsregister); O. Goldwasser, *Göttinger Miszellen* 115 (1990), 29–32.

ZEEV HERZOG

GERIZIM, MOUNT

IDENTIFICATION

Mount Gerizim (in Arabic, Jebel eṭ-Ṭur) is located south of Shechem (Nablus), 868 m above sea level and about 500 m above the city (map reference 175.178). The mount is composed of two perpendicular ridges; the lower ridge runs east–west and the upper north–south.

HISTORY UNTIL THE HELLENISTIC PERIOD

Mount Gerizim is mentioned in Deuteronomy (11:29–31, 27:11–26) and in Judges (9:7), but the dispute that broke out between the Jews and the Samaritans during the time of Nehemiah is only related later by Josephus. In *Antiquities* XI, 321–324, Josephus reports that when Alexander the Great reached the outskirts of Tyre, Sanballat, the leader of the Samaritans, assembled his army and went to Tyre to surrender to Alexander and to request his permission to build a temple on Mount Gerizim. Josephus also relates that Ptolemy I Soter (305–283 BCE) conquered Palestine, taking captives from Samaria and Mount Gerizim and settling them in Egypt. However, the Samaritan settlers and the Jews of Egypt quarreled over where sacrifices should be sent—to Mount Gerizim or to Jerusalem (*Antiq.* XII, 7–10). A

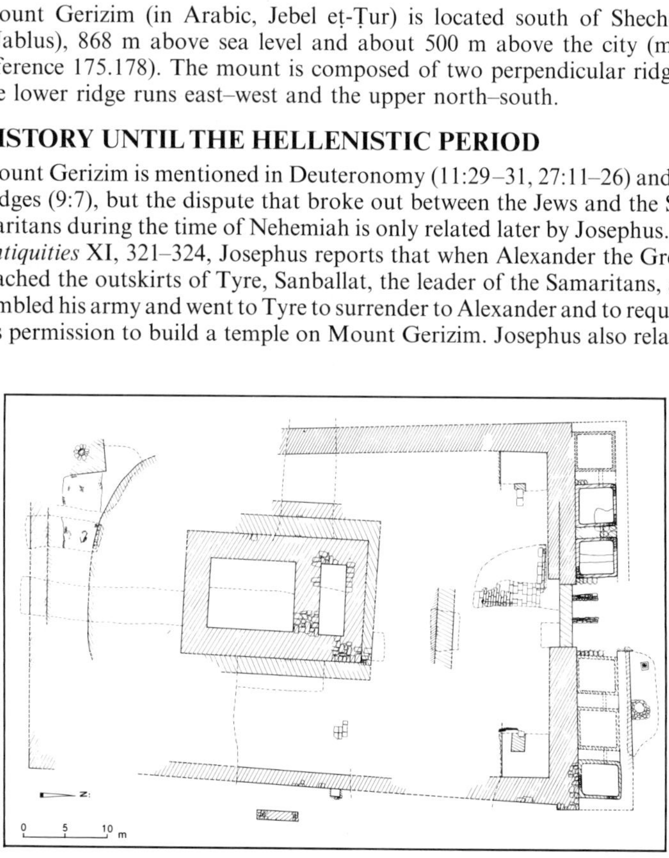

Tell er-Ras: plan of the Roman temple enclosure.

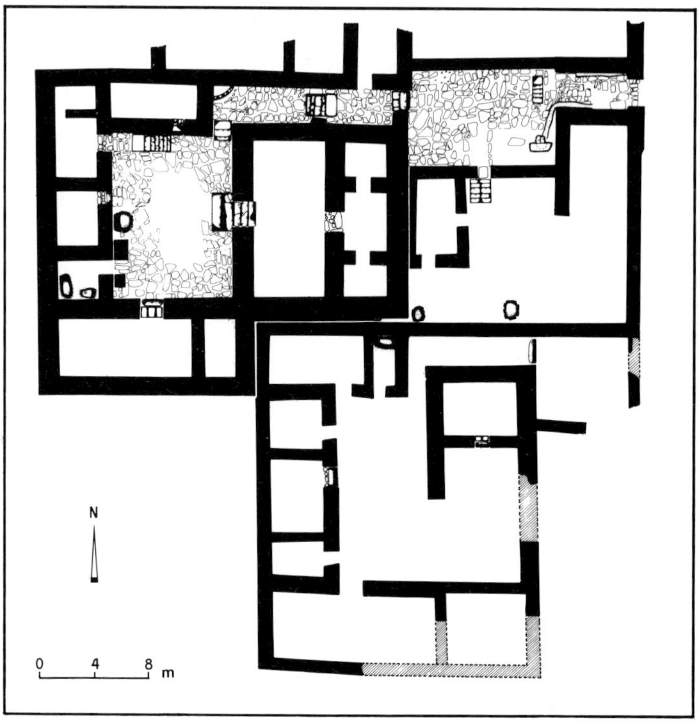

Area A: plan of building A, Hellenistic period.

Mount Gerizim and Tell er-Ras, as viewed from the city of Neapolis.

further disagreement on the same question erupted between them during the time of Ptolemy VI Philometor (180–145 BCE) (*Antiq.* XIII, 74–79). Elsewhere Josephus relates that, following the division of Alexander the Great's kingdom upon his death, the temple on Mount Gerizim was still in use (*Antiq.* XI, 346). Josephus further relates that the Samaritans were willing to name the temple after Zeus Hellenios (*Antiq.* XII, 257–264). The temple is also mentioned in the Second Book of Maccabees (6:2), where it is called Zeus Xenios (Zeus the Hospitable). Antiochus Epiphanes is said to have appointed two epistates (governors): Philip the Phrygian in Jerusalem, and Andronicus on Mount Gerizim (2 Macc. 5:22–23). According to Josephus, the temple, which was modeled after the one in Jerusalem, was destroyed by John Hyrcanus after having been in existence for two hundred years (*Antiq.* XIII, 254–256; *War* I, 63).

Area A: section of building A, Hellenistic period.

On the island of Delos two Greek inscriptions were found that refer to contributions made by the Samaritans for Mount Gerizim. One is dated to 250 BCE, and the other to 150-50 BCE (*SEG* XXXII, nos. 809–810; XXXIV, no. 786). According to *Megillat Ta'anit*, on "the day of Mount Gerizim," which falls on 21 Kislev, it is forbidden to fast or to deliver a eulogy, possibly because this was the date of the destruction of the temple on Mount Gerizim by John Hyrcanus. From that time the Samaritans were also forbidden to ascend Mount Gerizim and to rebuild the temple, or even to pray there. Josephus describes two instances in which the Samaritans were forcibly removed from Mount Gerizim by the Romans (*Antiq.* XVIII, 85–87; *War* III, 307–315).

THE HELLENISTIC CITY

A walled city, with an area of about 100 a., was built on the upper ridge of the mount in the Hellenistic period. The eastern slope of the ridge is extremely steep, while the slopes on the south, north, and west are moderate. On the southern slope a solid city wall was erected, protected by a fortress and towers. The city was divided into four residential quarters, three (in the north, west, and south) within the city wall, and a large quarter in the northwest, apparently beyond the wall. A sacred precinct was erected on the summit.

Excavations were carried out at the site continuously from 1983 to 1990, under the direction of I. Magen, the archaeology staff officer in Judea and Samaria. The excavations unearthed three buildings in area A, in the western quarter; a building and an oil press in area T in the northern quarter; three buildings in area K (the quarter outside the city wall); segments of the wall; a fortress; and the sacred precinct.

AREA A. Area A, at the southern edge of the western quarter, yielded a tripartite structure: a main building, a service building, and a western building. The main building was erected around a central courtyard (7.4 by 8.8 m) paved with irregular stone slabs. The courtyard is completely surrounded by domestic and service rooms. On its north side is a large cistern. The eastern wall contains a stairway leading to the second story, which was entered from the south through a long corridor. In the eastern wing was a large room whose floor was covered with a thick layer of ashes. The floor of the room's second story had wooden planks. The northern wing contained four rooms, the easternmost of which was divided in two. The westernmost part apparently

Area T: plan of building T, Hellenistic period.

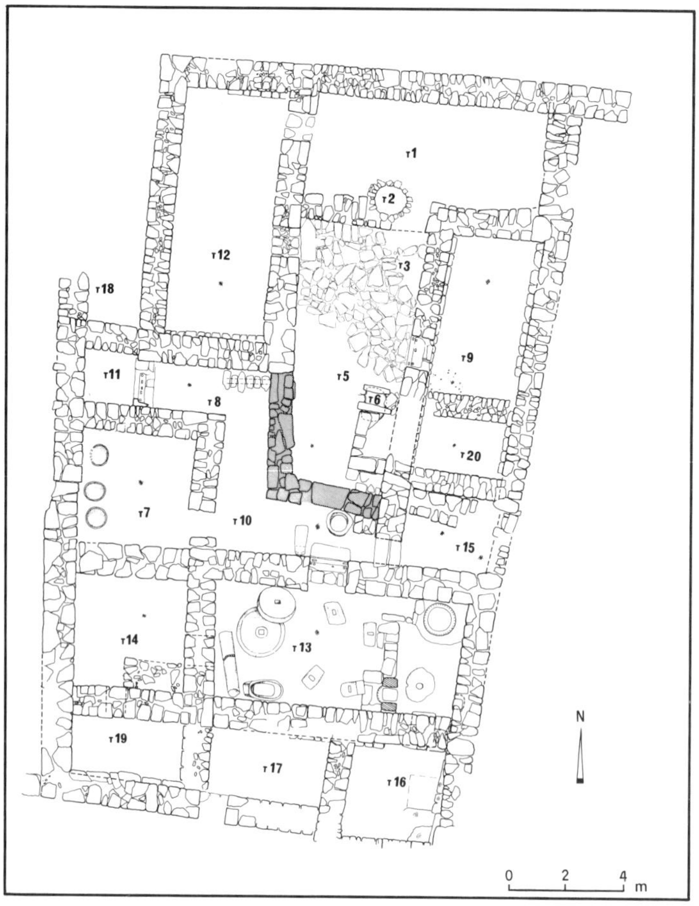

Building T: general view, looking north; note the Roman temple on Tell er-Ras and Mount Ebal in background.

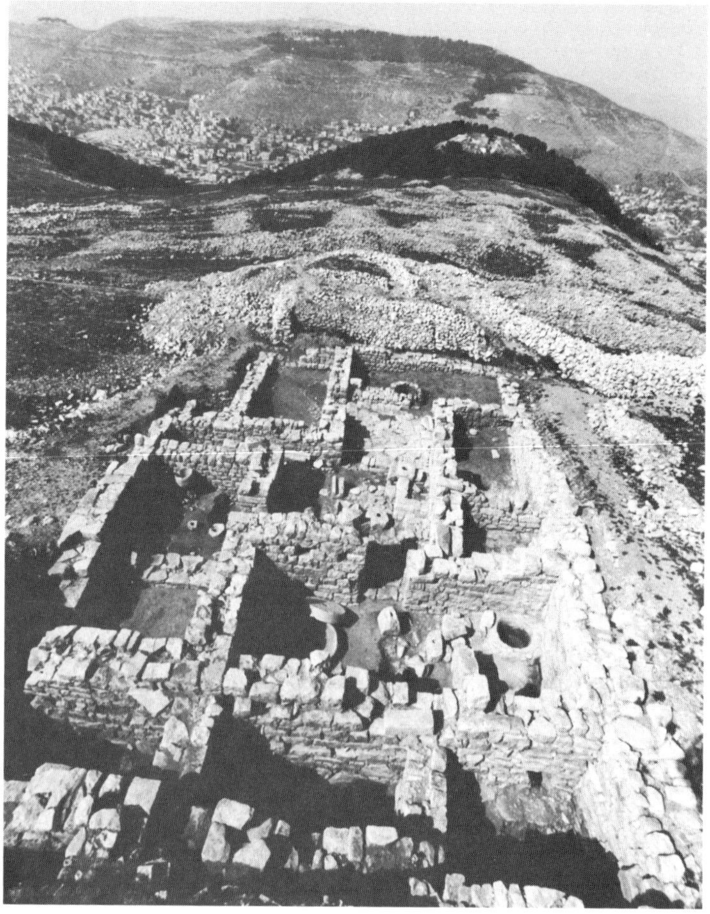

served as a bathroom, as it was equipped with a stone bathtub and a small plastered wash basin. The eastern and western rooms also had second stories. A thick layer of ash on the floor contained coins and numerous pottery, basalt and metal vessels. A reception room (triclinium) was found in the western wing. Another large triclinium, which opened onto three small interconnected rooms to its south, was uncovered in the southern wing.

The service building was erected later than the main building. It consisted of dwelling rooms and a plaza paved with stone slabs, which led down to a second plaza, with a beaten-earth floor, in which the cooking was done. To its south was a large room, entirely coated with a thick layer of plaster. The service building also contained a large cistern.

The western building was built at the same time as the service building. It was entered from the south, through a long corridor that lead to the central courtyard, whose roof was supported by lugs. This building was also identical in plan to the main building: a courtyard surrounded by rooms. In the west was a large triclinium and, to its south, another room. Three rooms in the northern wing and a large cistern in the western wing were uncovered. To the south were two large rooms and to the east, a large room and a bathroom. The bathroom had a plastered bathtub with a hole to release the water.

AREA T. Area T is north of the Byzantine church in the northern quarter. A building preserved to a height of about 4 m and identical in plan to the building complex in area A was uncovered here. Two building phases can be distinguished. In the first phase it was a residential building and in the second phase it was turned into an oil press; the latter was excavated in its entirety. A Samaritan sacrificial oven from the medieval period, built of small undressed stones, was also uncovered here.

Building T (16 by 25.5 m), oriented north–south, was entered from the north through a corridor that opens onto a central courtyard surrounded by rooms. The courtyard is paved with irregular stone slabs. Near the eastern wall is a large cistern and a south–north staircase leading to a second story with a row of rooms. A room, apparently unroofed, was uncovered in the northern wing; another room, in the west, had a thick layer of ashes on its floor that contained numerous basalt, iron, and pottery vessels and tools. A square room was found farther to the south. The building's eastern wing consisted of two rooms; its southern wing was the main wing. Its triclinium was a long room, which also included the southern room of the western wing. Behind the triclinium, toward the south, were three small rooms bearing a

Overview of building K, looking southeast.

Right: *city coin of Neapolis depicting the temple at Tell er-Ras.*
Below: *coin of Antoninus Pius from the Neapolis mint, depicting the temple at Tell er-Ras and the steps leading to it.*

second story, the entrance to which is preserved in the westernmost room (an identical plan of rooms behind a triclinium can also be discerned in building A in Area A, see above).

In the second building phase, the triclinium was reduced in size and an olive press installed. In the northwestern corner of the olive press, the vat and pressbeam were found in situ. In its southern wall was a stone bathtub that belonged to the first building phase. In the eastern wall of the olive press was the socket for the pressbeam and two posts with a platform in between, on which the bales were set. A round, plastered basin for the oil was in the southeast corner; another basin was in the entrance that led to an inner room. Four large press weights were found in the center of the room and an additional three in the courtyard. This is one of the earliest and most complete oil presses from the Hellenistic period so far discovered in Israel.

Building T yielded a large number of storage jars of different shapes, pottery, complete lamps, metal ware, and about one hundred coins of the same date as those found in building A.

AREA K. Area K, in the northwest, contains another residential quarter that apparently was built outside the city wall. Three houses, covering about half an acre, were cleared. They were built around a central courtyard, which contained an oil press. The structures are identical in plan, style, plastering, and lug construction to the buildings in areas A and T. However, the buildings differ from those within the city limits in their inferior building quality and sparse finds: there was no ash layer on their floors. About half the coins found in these buildings were of John Hyrcanus; a coin of Alexander Jannaeus was also found. This quarter may have housed John Hyrcanus's soldiers prior to the conquest of the city, and possibly garrison troops afterward.

SACRED PRECINCT. The sacred precinct, covering the entire summit (of more than 5 a.), was modeled after the Temple Mount in Jerusalem—a precinct enclosed by a wall. Worshipers ascended to it from the city's western quarter by means of a broad staircase (c. 10 m wide). Two large gates were uncovered on the eastern side. The enclosure wall is preserved for about 120 m. A large number of sheep bones, some of them charred, may have been the remains of the paschal or other sacrifices offered by the Samaritans on Mount Gerizim. Scores of building stones carved with inscriptions in Hebrew and in Aramaic were also found.

SUMMARY

The excavations have so far produced no evidence of a temple or settlement from the time of the Ptolemies. Although the nucleus of an ancient settlement from the fourth to third centuries BCE may have existed here, no signs of it have been unearthed so far. The archaeological finds, and especially the hundreds of coins recovered in the excavations, indicate that the city on the mount was established during the time of Antiochus III (c. 200 BCE) and destroyed by John Hyrcanus (114–111 BCE). All the buildings within the city wall contained a thick layer of ashes on their floors. After the destruction of the city, Mount Gerizim was not occupied until the Byzantine period, when a church was built in the Samaritan sacred precinct in the time of Zeno, in 484 CE (see below).

Tell er-Ras: part of the staircase leading from Neapolis to the temple of Zeus, Roman period.

THE ROMAN TEMPLE AT TELL ER-RAS

Tell er-Ras is on the northern ridge of Mount Gerizim, which faces the city of Neapolis (modern Shechem-Nablus). It is an artificial mound (80 by 120 m and c. 10 m high), situated about 830 m above sea level and 450 m above the city. On the east the rock descends in a steep slope, while on the north side the slope is more moderate and contains many building remains and terraces leading down to the city. To the south are the walls of the Hellenistic city of Mount Gerizim, and to the west is the main road which extends from Neapolis to Mount Gerizim.

Surveys and excavations have been carried out at the site by a number of scholars. In 1866, C. W. Wilson, on behalf of the Survey of Western Palestine, observed that this was an artificial mound surrounded by a moat. In 1930, A. M. Schneider of Göttingen conducted a survey and excavated the Byzantine church. I. Ben-Zvi discovered a portion of a staircase leading to the temple, and A. Reifenberg identified the temple and staircase by means of an

Aerial view of Tell er-Ras.

Tell er-Ras: inner foundation of the temple ("Building B"), Roman period.

aerial photograph. From 1964 to 1968 excavations were carried out by R. J. Bull, on behalf of the American Schools of Oriental Research. So far only preliminary reports have been published. The investigation of Mount Gerizim was renewed by I. Magen between 1983 and 1988; the site was reexamined, the plans were drawn anew, and Bull's dating and conclusions were reevaluated.

HISTORY OF THE TEMPLE

The temple at Tell er-Ras was first depicted on a city coin of Neapolis, minted toward the end of Emperor Antoninus Pius' reign (160 CE). More than fifty years later, the temple appears again on the coins of Caracalla (211–217 CE) and, subsequently, on the coins of Neapolis for as long as they were minted in the city (until the mid-third century). In Damascius' *Vita Isidori*, an anecdote about Marinus of Neapolis mentions a temple on Mount Gerizim dedicated to Zeus Hypositos (the supreme). The Pilgrim of Bordeaux (333 CE) reports that 1,300 steps led up to the summit of Mount Gerizim; he does not mention the temple (*Itin. Burd.* 587, 3–4, *CCSL* 175, 13). Epiphanius (315–403 CE) (*De XII gemmis*, *PG* 43, cols. 361–364) noted that there were "more than 1,500" steps leading up the side of Mount Gerizim, a fact confirmed by Procopius of Gaza (d. c. 538) (*In Deuteronomium* XI, 29, *PG* 87, col. 908). Indeed, from the height of the temple above the city, it can be assumed that this number of steps was required. The temple is also mentioned in Samaritan sources. According to the Samaritan Chronicle (Adler, 4411, *REJ* 45 [1902], 82–83) it was founded by Hadrian as a temple of Saphis (?); later it is described as abandoned (Adler, 4758, *REJ* 45 [1902], 233–234).

In the temple's depiction on the city coins of Neapolis, the staircase is shown ascending from an elaborate structure at the foot of the mountain. This was apparently the propylaeum, on which the present mosque of Rijal el-'Amud was built. From this entrance stairs led to the mount's summit, where the temple stood on a raised podium. On the coins, as well as on a pottery lamp bearing a depiction of the temple, buildings are shown close to the staircase.

EXCAVATION RESULTS

Bull distinguished two building phases at the site: building A, whose construction he ascribed to Hadrian in 130 CE; and building B, which he associated with the Samaritan temple erected by Sanballat in the fourth century BCE (*Antiq.* XI, 306–311 and 321–325). A reexamination of Bull's excavations shows, however, in the writer's opinion, that there was no Hellenistic temple at Tell er-Ras, and that both building phases belong to the Roman period.

The temple was erected on a podium consisting of an outer part and an inner one, with a fill in between. The outer part is 64 m long and 44.21 m wide. Its walls (3.5 m thick), which rest on bedrock, were only partly excavated, but they seem to have been massive. In the center of the northern wall is an opening, from which a stone block descended to the north. This was the foundation for the stairs leading to the temple. During the second phase six square cisterns were built outside the northern wall—three on each side of the stairs—to expand the sacred precinct toward the north. Above these cisterns vaults were erected to support a paved plaza.

South of the northern wall was the elaborate staircase leading to the temple. Two phases can be distinguished. In phase I, a paved plaza (c. 5 m wide) was built; from it, a staircase, of which eleven steps are preserved, ascended to the south. In phase II, the staircase and part of the paved plaza in front of it were covered with a block of fill; about 4 m north of the line of the first stairs another staircase was built. The cisterns of phase I north of the wall served as a foundation for the plaza in front of the staircase during the second building phase. The moving of the staircase clearly indicates that a new temple was constructed on the summit.

The temple (14.16 by 21.28 m) consists of a pronaos (3.3 by 18.24 m) and a naos (8.24 by 10.12 m). The temple's walls are 2.3 m thick in the north and 2.9 m thick in the south, east, and west. Stones in secondary use can be distinguished in all the walls. Above the foundation, which consists of three courses, three steps ascend toward the interior. The temple thus stood on a stepped podium and was surrounded by a plaza paved with stone slabs. This plaza was laid on solid platforms of the temple's second phase and extended to bedrock.

A deep trench dug beneath the temple (Bull's building A) in the east and west and beneath the solid platform revealed eighteen courses of stone walls descending to bedrock, to a depth of about 9 m (Bull called these walls building B). The fill of the walls contained finds Bull attributed to the Hellenistic period. The coins and the pottery were dated to the second century BCE. Bull proposed that these walls were remnants of the Samaritan temple built by Sanballat in the fourth century BCE. A reexamination of his excavation and the new excavations on Mount Gerizim, which uncovered the Hellenistic city with the sacred precinct in its center, showed that, in the writer's opinion, building B did not represent remains of the Hellenistic temple, but the inner foundation on which the temple and the surrounding plaza were built. The pottery vessels and the coins of the Hellenistic period found in the fill originated in the Hellenistic city, whose northern gate was close to the temple (c. 150 m from it).

The renewed excavations show that phase I was probably built by Antoninus Pius in the mid-second century CE, and phase II by Caracalla in the early third century, either when the temple of the first phase fell to ruins or

Tell er-Ras: mosaic in the public building north of the Roman temple of Zeus.

Church of Mary: plan of the precinct.

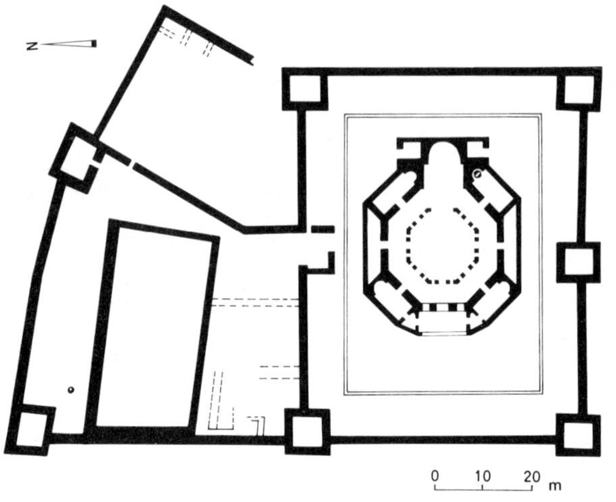

was destroyed. The temple was rebuilt in the time of Julian the Apostate and continued in use until the fourth century.

FINDS. In addition to the hundreds of coins and the pottery, many stone and marble architectural remains were found, most of them undocumented. Other finds included the head of a small statue, a hexagonal altar, and two Greek inscriptions. One inscription, "Zeus Olympius," was carved on a fragment of a limestone column, while the other, found in a cistern, was punched in a flat sheet of copper. The latter inscription is of five lines and also mentions Zeus Olympius.

REMAINS NORTH OF THE ROMAN TEMPLE

The excavations in the 1980s yielded a large quantity of building remains about 100 m north of the temple, on the mount's moderate slope. These included a section of the staircase leading from the city of Neapolis to the temple, and building remains from the first century BCE. Seven well-dressed stone steps from the staircase leading to the Roman temple (more than 10 m wide) are preserved in situ. In the stairway's continuation to the south was part of a paved street leading to the temple. The stairway was bounded by an ashlar balustrade. To its north was a plaza (10 by 18 m) whose foundation was similar in construction to that of the stairs. Its remains had served as a foundation for the stairway descending to Neapolis. Part of a large building from the first century BCE was exposed under the stairway. It may have been part of the fortification system built by the Hasmoneans to protect the ascent to Mount Gerizim.

A large structure, about 33 m wide and of greater length, was found west of the stairway. The building was constructed of large, unhewn stones laid on walls cut in the bedrock; segments of plaster painted in shades of blue, red, and green were found in its ruins. In the eastern wing of the building is a long corridor paved with a splendid colored mosaic decorated with geometrical motifs comprising intersecting circles enclosing small squares, and a guilloche frame. The corridor is entered from an elaborate gate whose jambs were in the form of pilasters. Opposite the gate is a plaza paved with uniform stone slabs. A large hall east of the corridor was divided lengthwise into three parts: an oblong hall, apparently paved with a colored mosaic and entered from the corridor; a raised bema; and a small room. A row of columns may have separated the hall from the corridor. The raised bema was paved with a white mosaic surrounded by a rectangular black frame. The front of the bema may have had columns and was a sort of chancel screen. An entrance led from the bema to a small room; opposite the entrance was a colored mosaic carpet. The small room also had a second entrance, which led to the corridor. Behind the small room, to the south, was another room with an apse oriented toward the small room and a window between them.

The many finds discovered in the building include coins, lamps, pottery vessels, tiles, and marble fragments, including fragments with relief decoration. On the basis of these finds, the building was dated to the third century CE. It probably continued in use until the end of the fourth century. The absence of figures in the mosaic pavements, the simple construction style, and the building's orientation (south) all suggest that this was a Samaritan sanctuary. It is also possible, however, that it was a pagan temple. The exact nature of the building cannot yet be determined.

CHURCH OF MARY, THE MOTHER OF GOD

EXPLORATION AND HISTORY

On the highest summit of Mount Gerizim is a large Byzantine precinct surrounded by a wall and towers. In Arabic it is known as el-Qal'ah (the fortress). In the center of the precinct is an octagonal church built of fine

Church of Mary: aerial view of the precinct, looking east.

Church of Mary: northern gate in the southern precinct.

ashlar masonry and named after Mary, the mother of God (Theotokos). The site was surveyed several times by travelers in the nineteenth century. In the 1930s, excavations were conducted in the church by Schneider. The excavations were renewed from 1985 to 1988 under the direction of Magen.

The establishment of the church on Mount Gerizim is documented in both Christian and Samaritan sources. The church does not appear on the Medeba map, even though Mount Gerizim is clearly identified on it. The details of the events leading to the construction of the church and the fortifications around it are given in the writings of Procopius (*Buildings* 1–17, V, VII). He states that the Samaritans used to ascend Mount Gerizim to pray there; their ascent to the mount was not because they had ever built a temple on the summit, but because they worshipped the summit itself. In this account, Procopius also gives a distorted version of the conversation between Jesus and the Samaritan woman (Jn. 4:20–23). He next describes a revolt of the Samaritans at Neapolis and their subsequent punishment by Emperor Zeno, who decided to drive them out from Mount Gerizim, to build a church on the summit and to dedicate it to Mary, the mother of God. Then Procopius describes the conflict between the Samaritans and the Christians following the building of the church. To protect the church Zenon fortified it with a wall and stationed ten soldiers to guard it. Procopius further relates that during the reign of Emperor Anastasius, the Samaritans ascended the mount not by the usual way, which was guarded by the Byzantine garrison, but by another route. They killed the soldiers guarding the church and apparently also damaged the church itself. In the time of Emperor Justinian, an additional wall was built around the church, and the double fortifications prevented attacks. The Byzantine author John Malalas (*Chronographia*, 382–383) relates that during the reign of Zeno, the Samaritans of Palestine rebelled against Rome, and Zeno turned their synagogue on Mount Gerizim into a house of prayer to the Mother of God Mary (Theotokos). A similar report, apparently from the same source, appears in the *Paschale Chronicle* (603–604; *PG* 92, col. 841) and a similar account is mentioned in the Samaritan Chronicle (Adler, 4876, *REJ* 45 [1902], 235–236).

CHURCH COMPLEX

The church complex (83 by 100 m) comprises two parts: in the south, a square precinct surrounded by a defensive wall and with an octagonal church in its center; and in the north a partly fortified precinct with a rectangular structure, apparently a large cistern, in its center.

SOUTHERN PRECINCT. The southern precinct has a square tower in each corner and one in the southern wall. In the northern wall, an elaborate gate house has four distinctive building phases, the later two apparently belonging to the Early Arab period. The gate (8.6 by 9.6 m) is surrounded by massive walls of fine ashlar masonry that are incorporated in the enclosure wall and form an integral part of it. The enclosure walls are built of large stones with drafted margins and a central boss. The walls, preserved in several places to a height of 4 m, were originally 7 m high. Vaulted passages can be discerned between the towers in the walls and were probably used to connect the towers. Inside the precinct are a number of rooms, some of them from a later period.

The church had a peristyle of square columns built of fine ashlars, similar to the church and the gate. The columns were uncovered in the church's northern and western wings, which suggests that the peristyle surrounded it.

The area behind the peristyle has not been completely excavated. Rooms adjoining the outer enclosure wall are visible in the northern wall. The area between the peristyle and the church is completely paved with well-fitted stone slabs that blend in well with both the walls of the church and the peristyle. It is thus evident that the peristyle, pavement, church, and gate were built as a single unit. To the west of the church is a large cistern, into which the water from the paved square drained.

Octagonal Church. The octagonal church (30 by 37.4 m) is a memorial church built on a concentric plan. It contains an open narthex, apparently paved with marble slabs. Three entrances (the middle one is the largest), led to the interior of the church. The narthex also opened onto two side chapels, two of the church's four. The two eastern chapels adjoined the cen-

Church of Mary: southern gate in the eastern wall of the precinct.

tral apse, and the two western ones adjoined the narthex and were entered through a triangular room. Between the two western chapels was a long, narrow room leading into the church. The southern chapel was faced with marble and included a hexagonal stone installation in the center of its apse.

A large central apse was elevated above the floor, and alongside it were two small square rooms. Schneider assumed that there were two additional entrances to the church, in the north and in the south, through the two rooms. The bases of the columns that supported the central dome are visible in the center of the church. Only a few fragments of the columns have survived.

NORTHERN PRECINCT. The northern precinct contains a western wall that extends from the northwestern tower in a straight line to the west. Its construction is similar to that of the southern precinct. In its northwestern corner was a square tower, from which a wall extends to the east, with another large tower in its center. This tower is situated opposite the gate of the southern precinct. A long corridor probably connected the two towers. Because no entrance has yet been found in the north wall, it may be assumed that this was a gate tower and the main entrance to the precinct.

A large structure, apparently a pool, called in Arabic Bir er-Rasas, was uncovered in the center of the precinct. It contained a large cistern; south of it the remains of walls could be seen on the ground. The pool is not compatible with the Byzantine buildings; similarly, the style of the building and the dressing of the stones are different from what is found in the rest of the precinct.

FINDS. The excavations in the 1980s uncovered relatively meager finds, including several coins and a few pottery vessels. Architectural details, such as columns, Corinthian capitals, and depictions of crosses were also found. Schneider, too, unearthed only a few finds in his excavations; these included inscriptions and an altar panel. Among the finds, seven Samaritan dedicatory inscriptions in Greek carved on stone panels are noteworthy. The inscriptions were found in secondary use and are dated to the fourth century CE.

SUMMARY

The church on Mount Gerizim was established by Emperor Zenon in 484 CE, during the struggle of the Christians against the Samaritans, which lasted for about a century. The church and the square precinct wall were built at this time. Following the Samaritans' attack on the church in the time of Anastasius and their continued rebellion in the time of Justinian, another wall was added to defend the precinct on the north. In the Early Arab and Crusader periods, the fortified precinct was again used. The discovery of seven Samaritan inscriptions and the location of the church in the center of the Samaritan sacred precinct of the Hellenistic period attest that the church was deliberately built on the area sacred to the Samaritans as part of the attempt to convert them to Christianity.

C. W. Wilson, *PEQ* 5 (1873), 69; Hill, *BMC*, XXXVIII, pls. V–VII, XXXIX; A. M. Schneider, *ZDPV* 68 (1951), 209–234; W. Schmidt, *ZDPV* 78 (1962), 89–90; J. Bowman, *EI* 7 (1964), 17*–28*; R. J. Bull, *Harvard Theological Review* 58 (1965), 234–237; id., *AJA* 71 (1967), 287–393; 74 (1970), 189–190; id., *BA* 31 (1968), 58–72; 38 (1975), 54–59; id. (with E. F. Campbell), *BASOR* 190 (1968), 4–19; 219 (1975), 29–37; id., *IEJ* 18 (1968), 192–193; id., *RB* 75 (1968), 238–243; id., *PEQ* 102 (1970), 108–110; H. C. Kee, *New Testament Studies* 13 (1967), 401–402; W. Baier, *Das Heilige Land* 102 (1970). 38–47; R. L. Hohlfelder, *5th Annual Byzantine Studies Conference: Abstracts of Papers*, Washington, D.C. 1979, 34–35; id., *City, Town and Countryside in the Early Byzantine Era*, New York 1982, 75–113; R. T. Anderson, *BA* 43 (1980), 217–221; 54 (1991), 104–107; J. Wilkinson, *Levant* 13 (1981), 156–172; H. Seebas, *Biblica* 63 (1982), 22–31; *American Archaeology in the Mideast*, 195; M. Baillet, *MdB* 43 (1986), 27–32; Y. Meshorer, *Kraay–Morkholm Essays*, Louvain-La-Neuve 1989, 173–177; *MdB* 58 (1989), 55; Y. Magen, *Christian Archaeology in the Holy Land: New Discoveries* (V. C. Corbo Fest.), Jerusalem 1990, 333–342; id., *Israel Antiquities Authority, Highlights of Recent Excavations*, Jerusalem 1990, 20–22; L. Di Segni, *Christian Archaeology in the Holy Land* (op. cit.), 343–350.

ITZHAK MAGEN

GESHER

IDENTIFICATION

The Pre-Pottery Neolithic A site and the adjoining Middle Bronze Age IIA cemetery known as Gesher are situated in the central Jordan Valley on the southern bank of Naḥal Tavor, close to Kibbutz Neveh Ur and Kibbutz Gesher (map reference 202.223), at an elevation of 235 to 247 m below sea level. The remains of the Neolithic site were found 2 to 4 m below the modern surface and the Bronze Age burials lay 1 to 3 m below the surface. Two seasons of excavations were conducted at the site in 1986 and 1987, directed by Y. Garfinkel on behalf of the Institute of Archaeology at the Hebrew University of Jerusalem.

EXCAVATIONS

THE PRE-POTTERY NEOLITHIC A SITE. The Pre-Pottery Neolithic A site was probably a small village of round huts, that extended over a few hundred square meters. It has been dated by carbon-14 tests to 7930 $\pm$ 140 BCE and seems to have been occupied for only a short period. About 40 sq m were excavated in two areas 20 m apart. In area A, a living surface was revealed from which a basalt mortar, limestone and basalt pestles, scoria items, a sandstone grinding stone, two particularly large flint axes, polished basalt axes, several flint artifacts, and a rectangular, well-made limestone bowl with a discus base were recovered. In area B, a dwelling with a rounded wall was exposed. Near the wall a hearth made of small limestone pieces with a large, well-made shallow basalt mortar next to it was found. On the structure's floor were lumps of ocher, bone tools, and fourteen long clay beads, elliptical or biconical, pierced lengthwise by a finely made hole. Inside the building was a pit (diameter, 1 m) containing grinding tools and a well-made basalt bowl. Outside the structure were dozens of basalt and limestone vessels, including pestles, grinding slabs, rounded grinding stones, and hammerstones.

The site's flint assemblage includes tools and debitage: cores, primary flakes, core-trimming elements, burin spalls, chips, flakes, blades, and bladelets. The tools include el-Khiam arrowheads, some lunates, bifacial tools such as picks and axes, awls and borers, ha-Gedud truncations, sickle blades, scrapers, burins, retouched blades, and bladelets. The flint industry is characterized by the use of light-gray flint, from wadi pebbles. The large number of hammerstones and grinding vessels made on a variety of stones (basalt, scoria, limestone, flint, and sandstone) is particularly noteworthy.

The Gesher site widens the field of information about the earliest Neolithic villages in the Levant, of which fewer than ten are known (Mureybit and Tel Aswad in Syria; Naḥal Oren, Ḥatula, Gilgal, Netiv ha-Gedud and Jericho in Israel). Its location, 242 m below sea level, is significant because it contributes to a reconstruction of the ancient landscape in the central Jordan Valley after

Area B: part of a rounded brick wall, a basalt bowl, and a cupmark, PPNA.

*Gesher: (**left**) bronze spearhead from the cemetery (note on its base the impression of the cord with which it was tied to the handle), MB IIA; (**right**) bronze duck-bill ax from the cemetery, MB IIA.*

the receding of the Lisan lake at the end of the Pleistocene.

THE MIDDLE BRONZE AGE IIA CEMETERY. At the beginning of the Middle Bronze Age IIA, a cemetery existed at the site; fourteen of its shaft tombs have been completely excavated. In other contemporary sites, shaft tombs were dug in caves or hard rock and were used over long periods for many burials. Consequently, they were often disturbed and looted. At Gesher, however, the tombs were sealed and collapsed after a relatively short period because they were dug in earth, not rock. Their contents were undisturbed because they were neither used for subsequent burials nor robbed.

Single primary burials are the most common type found at Gesher. The body was laid in a half-flexed position, with the feet touching the pelvis. The head was oriented to the east and the feet to the west; and the face was turned toward the tomb's entrance. Offerings were placed next to the body—two or three pottery vessels and sometimes bronze tools or a perforated bone. In some burials, animal bones from food offerings were also found. No tombs for infants or small children were unearthed; in this period, they were interred in jars under the floors of houses. The shafts were sealed by square or rectangular piles of stones.

The tomb offerings included thirty-seven complete pottery vessels, eight bronze items (including a decorated toggle pin, spearheads and duck-bill axes), and two perforated bones. The pottery vessels date to the beginning of the Middle Bronze Age IIA, at the beginning of the second millennium BCE.

Four of the tombs have been described as warrior burials. In them, in addition to pottery vessels, an ax and sometimes also a bronze spearhead were found. Duck-bill axes were found in three of them; a narrow, elongated, socketed ax was discovered in the fourth. On the base of one of the spearheads the impression of the cord with which it was tied to the wooden spear shaft is still evident. The three duck-bill axes form the richest assemblage of this type yet discovered in Israel. They are very similar to those found in warrior burials at the site of Baghuz in northeastern Syria, near Mari. Gesher may have been used as a cemetery by a small village in the vicinity that has not yet been discovered.

J. Perrot et al., *IEJ* 17 (1967), 201–232; Y. Garfinkel, *ESI* 6 (1987–1988), 54–55; 7–8 (1988–1989), 62–63; id., *Mitekufat Ha'even* 22 (1989), 145*; id. (and D. Nadel), *Paléorient* 15/2 (1989), 139–151; id., *L'Anthropologie* 94 (1990), 903–906.

YOSEF GARFINKEL

GESHER BENOT YA'AQOV

IDENTIFICATION

The Acheulean site of Gesher Benot Ya'aqov is located along a stretch of the course of the Jordan River, about 3 km (1.5 mi.) south of the Ḥula Basin, at an elevation of some 70 m above sea level (map reference 2090.2685–2092.2690). It is situated in the river bed and on both of its banks. The site is embedded in the Benot Ya'aqov Formation, in the northern part of the Dead Sea Rift, bordering the Golan Heights in the east and the "Korazim Saddle" in the west. The geological deposits in the site's immediate vicinity have been described by L. Picard and A. Horowitz as consisting of the fluvial-limnic sediments that form the littoral facies of the Ḥula Valley basin fill. This Middle Pleistocene formation is characterized by the presence of the gastropod species *Viviparus apameae*, which is its type fossil.

Following its discovery in the early 1930s, and until the 1960s, archaeological activities at the site were seriously obstructed by construction and extensive earthworks that disrupted the environs and resulted in serious damage to artifact-bearing strata.

EXCAVATION AND SURVEY RESULTS

D. Garrod's initial excavation of a test pit in 1935 was followed by M. Stekelis's long-term activity. Between 1936 and 1951, he conducted surveys and excavations north and south of the northern bridge. In his excavations northwest of that bridge, he observed and investigated six stratigraphic and cultural units, designated I through IV (from top to bottom). The lithic assemblages obtained were assigned to the Acheulean culture. The first basalt artifacts (hand axes, cleavers, and flakes) recorded in the Levant were found here. Stekelis selected for detailed analysis the lithic material from the well-preserved strata (V–II), having regarded the material from the abraded level (VI) as redeposited. He reported what he considered to be evidence of a change through time in the pattern of raw material preference: whereas lithic artifacts derived from the lower level (V) were made solely of basalt, in the upper units flint items became a significant component of the industry. Stekelis maintained that the high frequency of various biface types, as well as evidence of the use of an African technology and the utilization of raw materials resembling those intensively exploited in Africa, attest to a link between the Acheulean industries detected at the Gesher Benot

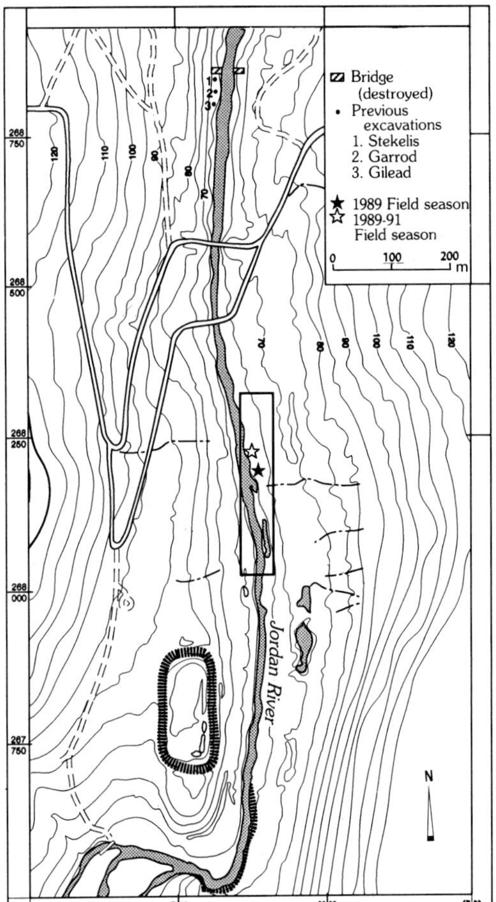

Map of Gesher Benot Ya'aqov and vicinity.

General view of the excavation site.

Ya'aqov site and Acheulean sites reported from Africa, north and south of the Sahara.

In 1967–1968, D. Gilead conducted a small-scale excavation close to one of Stekelis's test pits and surveyed the course of the Jordan south of it. He was able to discern between Middle Acheulean artifacts (derived from layer V) and Upper Acheulean ones (derived from layers IV–III) within the lithic material recovered in both his own and in Stekelis's excavations.

Following the identification (after 1981) of formerly unknown geological exposures in the Benot Ya'aqov Formation, in the previously unsurveyed region to the south of the bridges, a geological/archaeological survey was conducted for 1.5 km southward from the bridges. Geological mapping, radiometric dating, and a paleomagnetic examination established that the site extended for 3 km, considerably farther than previously estimated. Moreover, the formation's chronological span was restricted to between 730,000 and 240,000 years BP (see table). The results of the survey demonstrated that the deposits in the Benot Ya'aqov Formation had been subjected to vigorous tectonic activity characteristic of the Dead Sea Rift; it had tilted and folded strata away from their original plain of deposition.

The survey focused on a usually submerged area that became accessible because of the Jordan River's low water level in summer 1989. A barlike geological structure was detected (220 m long by 60 m across) that is composed of limnic-fluvial rocks. It was found to be rich in mollusks, including *Viviparus apameae*, that assign it to the Benot Ya'aqov Formation. The sediments are varied in composition, ranging from clay to boulders and contain faunal assemblages (including remains of elephants, cervids, and bovids) and Acheulean lithic artifacts (including hand axes, cleavers, chopping tools, cores, and flakes).

Following the survey, excavation at the site, conducted under the auspices of the Hebrew University of Jerusalem, was resumed in 1989, on the Jordan's eastern bank, south of the southern bridge. Three seasons (1989–1991) have

Fragment of a polished wooden implement.

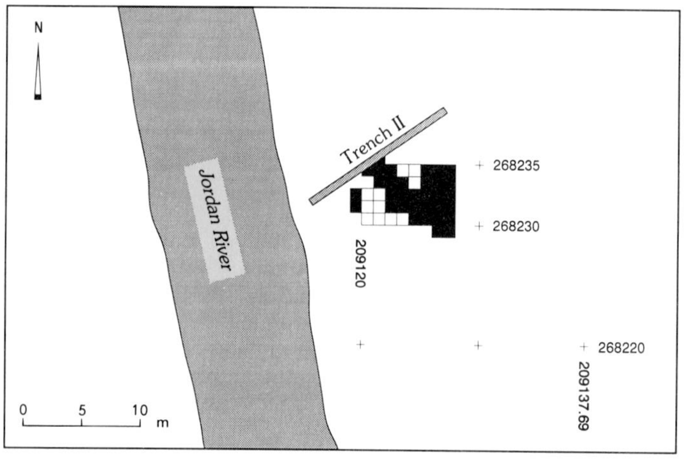

Gesher Benot Ya'aqov: map of area B and trench II.

Basalt hand ax, Acheulean culture.

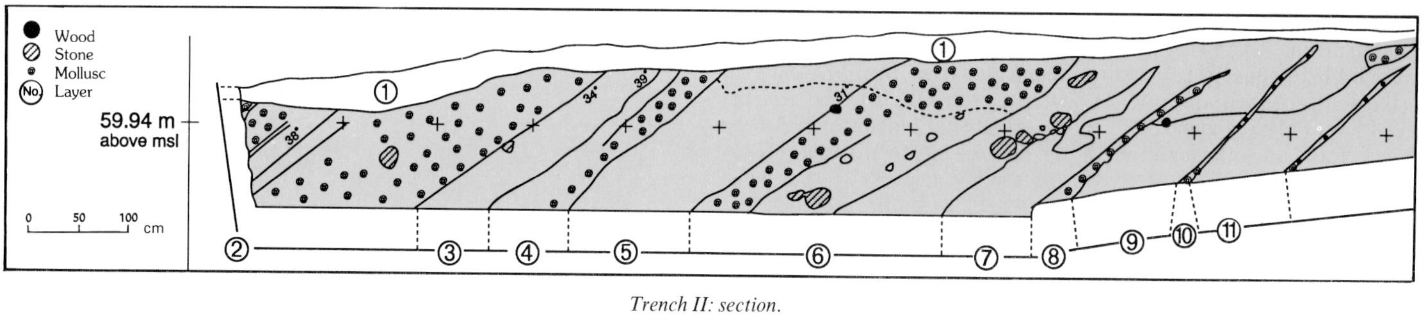

Trench II: section.

Gesher Benot Ya'aqov: elephant skull from layer II-6, level 1.

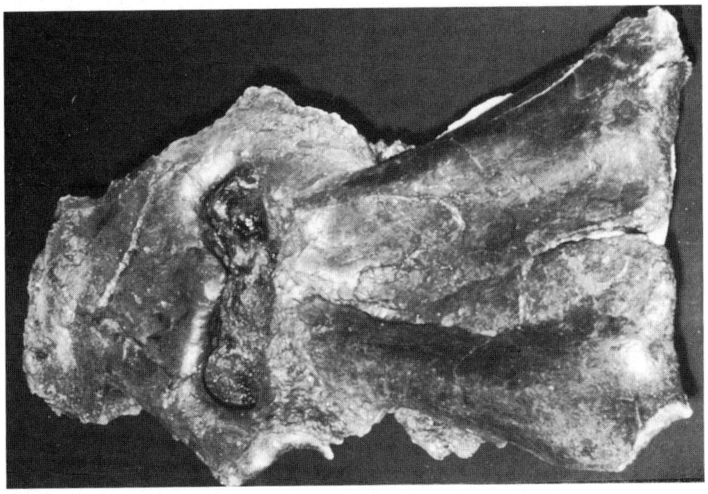

been conducted so far, within the framework of a multidisciplinary research project revolving around the site. Two trenches were excavated to facilitate recognition of the stratigraphic sequence. The sections, representing a 20-m-thick stratigraphic sequence, revealed that the geologic structure is tilted in a dip of up to 45 degrees. Excavations in two areas (A and B) adjacent to the trenches, revealed three archaeological layers: layer I-5, excavated in area A, and layers II-2/3 and II-6, excavated in area B. The lithic assemblages retrieved include typical Acheulean components (hand axes, cleavers, flake tools, flakes, and cores).

Layer II-6, identified in trench II (where it is 1.5 m thick) and laterally exposed in area B, yielded several unique finds. They demonstrate the wealth and uniqueness of the material recovered from the entire site. Up to the end of the recent excavation season (1991), five levels had been exposed within this layer, each with a distinct nature. The uppermost level yielded particularly large quantities of organic material, only rarely preserved in the Mediterranean climatic zone. Unusual (anaerobic) subterranean conditions prevailing at the site resulted in the preservation of pieces of wood, bark, seeds, and fruits. The wood, particularly the large pieces (up to 1.5 m long) are extremely well preserved. Several species have been identified so far by E. Werker, including ash, willow, oak, pistachio, and olive. Numerous knapped items of several types also were recovered from this level, among them bifaces (hand axes and cleavers) and a variety of flake tools. The knapped items are of three kinds of raw material: basalt, flint, and limestone (in descending order of frequency). The presence of limestone, which had not been reported previously from this site, may attest to the continuity of a lithic tradition based on the exploitation of a wide range of materials, available in differing frequencies.

On top of this level huge basalt cores were exposed. They bear discernible scars attesting to the removal of large flakes, most of them side-struck (their width exceeds their length), intended for the manufacture of cleavers and hand axes.

The most impressive discovery in this level is undoubtedly a cluster of associated finds that includes an elephant skull, an oak log, a large basalt core (weighing over 15 kg), and a large basalt boulder. The skull was found upside down, its occipital side resting on the log and its other, wide (premaxillar) side on the core and the boulder. Its rear part, the brain case, was absent. Large quantities of cranial bone splinters were obtained from the sediments excavated next to the spot where the skull was exposed. There are reasons to believe that this arrangment was intentional and that its preservation is owing to unique circumstances. This cluster allows insight into various aspects of the inhabitants' mode of living.

The deliberate selection of raw materials for the manufacture of specific tools (for instance, limestone to produce chopping tools and basalt to shape hand axes and cleavers), the symmetrical shapes of bifacials, and the complex knapping techniques (the Levallois and Kombewa techniques), all strongly suggest that the site's inhabitants possessed a capacity for abstract thought, which enabled a high level of planning and performance.

SUMMARY

Research at the Gesher Benot Ya'aqov site is still under way. The project is oriented toward a paleoecological reconstruction of the site's vicinity. The six distinct Acheulean layers exposed so far demonstrate the attractiveness of the Ḥula Lake region and its margins to the Middle Pleistocene Acheulean population. The assemblages recovered so far (flint, basalt, limestone, and paleontological and botanical remains) are outstanding in the Near Eastern archaeological record, contributing significantly to what is known of human development in the region of the Dead Sea Rift and its vicinity.

GEOLOGICAL SEQUENCE AND CHRONOLOGY AT THE BENOT YA'AQOV EMBAYMENT

Formation	*Previous name*	*Radiometric date (mill. years BP)*	*Paleomagnetism*
Ashmura	Upper Lacustrine series		
Benot Ya'aqov	Viviparus beds		Normal
Yarda basalt		0.64 ± 0.12	Normal
		0.90 ± 0.15	
Mishmar	Fresh-water		Reversed
ha-Yarden	tilted series		
Gadot	Gadot chalk		Normal and reversed
Unnamed		1.77 ± 0.08	Reversed
basalts		1.73 ± 0.17	

M. Stekelis and L. Picard, *QDAP* 6 (1937), 214–215; 7 (1938), 45; id., *IVe Congress Internacionale de Ciènciàs Prehistoria y Protohist. Cronica*, Madrid 1954, 391–394; id., *Bulletin of the Research Council of Israel* 9G (1960), 61–90, 104–108; D. H. Hooijer, ibid. 8G (1959), 177–199; L. Picard, *Israel Academy of Sciences and Humanities* 1/4 1–34; E. de Vaumas, *IEJ* 13 (1963), 195–207; A. Horowitz, *Israel Journal of Earth Sciences* 22 (1973), 107–139; D. Geraads and E. Tchernov, *L'Anthropologie* 87 (1983), 138–141; Weippert 1988, 75f.; N. Goren-Inbar, *ESI* 9 (1989–1990), 89–91; id. (and S. Belitzky), *Quaternary Research* 31 (1989), 371–376; id. (et al.), *Rock Art Research* 8 (1991), 133–136; S. Belitzky et al., *Journal of Human Evolution* 20 (1991), 348–353.

NA'AMA GOREN-INBAR

GEULAH CAVE

IDENTIFICATION

The Geulah Cave is situated on the eastern slope of Mount Carmel (map reference 1504.2446), 205 m above sea level. It is 2.5 km (1.5 mi.) south of the point where the outlet of Naḥal Gibborim—Wadi Rushmiya in Arabic—flows into the Mediterranean. The site now lies in the built-up area of the Geulah quarter of Haifa. The cave, and a narrow, undisturbed ledge along the face of the rocky cliff are remnants of a former, larger cave destroyed by recent quarry operations. Excavations in the two chambers of the cave and on the ledge—called a terrace by its excavator—were carried out by E. Wreschner in four seasons, 1958, 1960, 1963, and 1964.

EXCAVATIONS

Three layers were discovered, identical in archaeological content throughout the excavated area; only their thickness varied in the cave and on the terrace. In layer B two stages could be distinguished and were designated accordingly.

LAYER A: 10 to 30 cm thick, with gray dusty soil; contained Levallois-Mousterian flint implements, horn and teeth fragments; and 2,176 animal bones.

FREQUENCIES OF FLINT IMPLEMENTS

	(Percent)		
	Layer A	*Layer B1*	*Layer B2*
Levallois points	15.1	20.0	20.9
Flakes	21.2	23.4	25.7
Racloirs	12.1	—	—
Scrapersseriesseries	9.1	1.1	—
Knives	9.1	6.6	9.4
Denticulated pieces	—	—	4.6
Notched tools	—	3.3	—
Various flakes	33.4	39.0	27.9
Cores	—	3.3	4.6
Hammerstones	—	3.3	4.6

LAYER B1: 25 to 40 cm thick, with brown, powdery soil; contained Levallois flint implements, bone tools, animal bones, ocher, and Hyena coproliths.

LAYER B2: 40 to 90 cm thick, with blackish-brown soil embedded with charcoal fragments; contained Levallois flint implements of uniform size (all larger than those found in layer B1), bone tools, and animal bones.

The two B layers yielded 9,412 bones, including horns and teeth; 318 bone tools; and three small human bone fragments.

LAYER C: 5 to 20 cm thick, with light-brown powdery soil; rested on bedrock, filling cavities and crevices. The soil was sterile.

SUMMARY. A sediment analysis of layers C–A (from bottom to top) by E. Schmid showed a change from a warm, humid climate (layer C) to a warm, dry one (layers B2 to B1), followed by a change to colder, wet conditions (layer A).

A carbon-14 examination of charred bones from layer B1 gave a date of 42,000 ± 1,700 BP (GrN no. 4121).

G. Haas, in comparing the Geulah fauna with those from Tabun Cave, layer C, and el-Wad Cave, layer G, tends to believe that the Geulah fauna B2–A represents a gradual change and not a faunal break.

E. Wreschner et al., *IEJ* 10 (1960), 78–89; 13 (1963), 138; 14 (1964), 277–278; id., *Quaternaria* 9 (1967), 69–105; id., *Actes, VII Congrès Préhistorique and Protohistorique Sciences*, Prague 1970, 280–283; E. Petter and E. Heintz, *Bulletin, Museum National d'Histoire Naturelle*, 2e *Série*, 41/5 (1969–1970), 1292–1298; J. Heller, *Israel Journal of Zoology* 19 (1970), 1–49; H. Frenkel, ibid., 51–82; Y. Olami, *Prehistoric Carmel*, Jerusalem 1984.

ERNST WRESCHNER

Geulah Cave: group of flint implements.

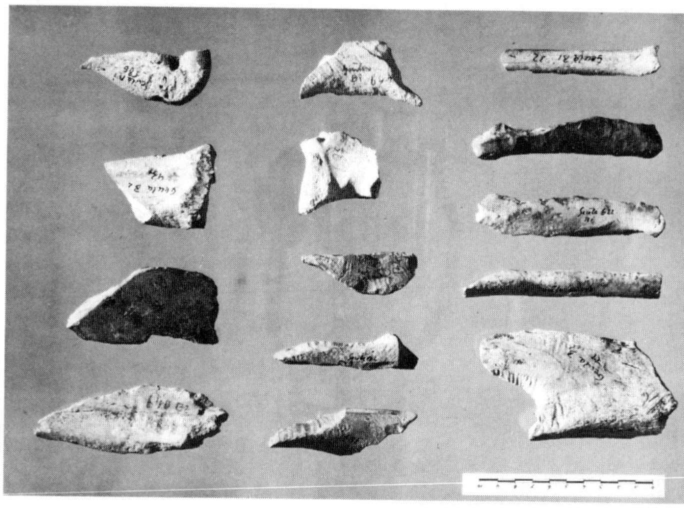

GEZER

IDENTIFICATION

Ancient Gezer has been located at Tell Jezer (or Tell el-Jazari), a 33-a. mound 8 km (5 mi.) south-southeast of Ramleh (map reference 1425.1407), since C. Clermont-Ganneau first made the identification in 1871. Just two years later, he discovered the first of the famous boundary inscriptions in the vicinity of the mound. It read "the boundary of Gezer" in an archaizing Jewish script of the Herodian period, confirming the identification (see below). Gezer is situated on the last of the foothills in the Judean Range, where it slopes down to meet the northern Shephelah. Although it lies only about 225 m above sea level, the hilltop is nearly cut off from the surrounding terrain and thus commands almost a 360-degree view. There is an especially impressive sweep across the Coastal Plain from beyond Ashdod to the southwest nearly to the Carmel promontory. Gezer guards one of the most important crossroads in the country, where the trunk road leading to Jerusalem and sites in the hills branches off from the Via Maris at the approach to the Ayalon Valley. In addition to its strategic location, Gezer possesses plentiful springs just at the base of the mound and fertile fields in the nearby valleys.

HISTORY

The earliest mention of the site is in an inscription of Thutmose III (c. 1490–1436 BCE) on the walls of the great Temple of Amon at Karnak. There, a scene commemorating this pharaoh's victories on his first campaign to Asia in 1468 BCE portrays bound captives from Gezer. A short inscription of Thutmose IV (c. 1410–1402 BCE) in his mortuary temple at Thebes refers to Hurrian captives from a city, the name of which is broken but is almost certainly Gezer. During the tumultuous Amarna period, in the fourteenth century BCE, Gezer figures prominently among Canaanite city-states under nominal Egyptian rule. In the corpus of the el-Amarna letters are ten from three different kings of Gezer. Perhaps the best-known Egyptian reference to Gezer is that of Merneptah (c. 1207 BCE) in his "Israel" stela, in which it is claimed that Israel has been destroyed and Gezer seized. The conquest of Gezer is also celebrated in another inscription of this pharaoh, found at Amada.

A relief of Tiglath-pileser III, king of Assyria (c. 745–728 BCE), found on the walls of his palace at Nimrud, depicts the siege and capture of a city called *Ga-az-ru*. This is undoubtedly Gezer in Canaan, and the background would be the campaign of the Assyrian monarch in Philistia in 734–733 BCE.

References to Gezer in the Bible itself are not as numerous as might be expected. However, that simply reflects the reality that, on the one hand, Gezer had already passed the peak of its power by the Iron Age and that, on the other, it lay on the periphery of Israel's effective control until rather late in the biblical period. In the period of the Israelite conquest, it is recorded that the Israelites under Joshua met a coalition of kings near Gezer in the famous

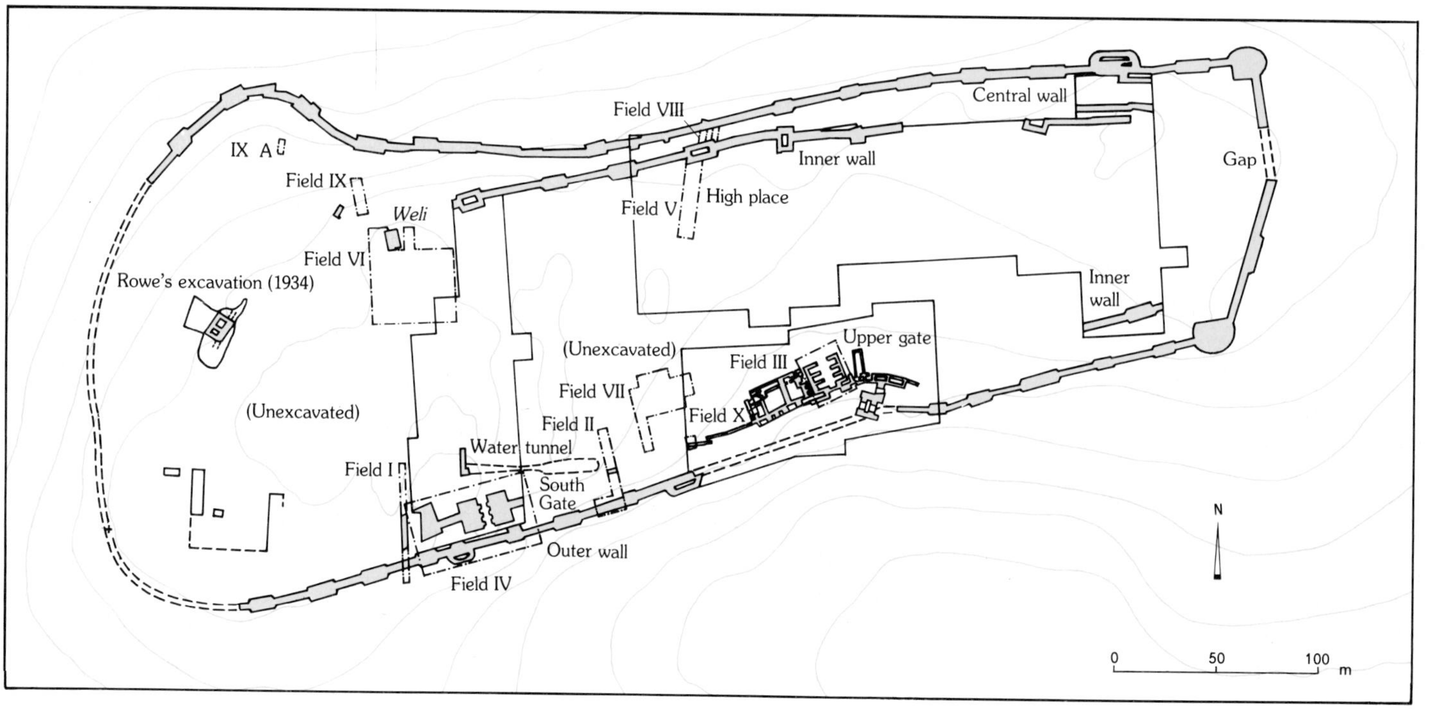

Gezer: plan of the mound, excavation fields, and principal remains.

Battle of Makkedah, in the Ayalon Valley. Although Horam, the king of Gezer, was killed, the text does not say specifically that Gezer itself was captured (Jos. 10:33, 12:12). Later, according to several passages, "Gezer and its pasture lands" were allotted to the tribe of Joseph (or "Ephraim," cf. Jos. 16:3, 10; Jg. 1:29; 1 Chr. 6:67, 7:28). However, the footnote that the Israelites "did not drive out the Canaanites, who dwelt in Gezer" makes it clear that the Israelite claim was more imaginary than real. Gezer was also set aside as a Levitical city (Jos. 21:21), but again it is unlikely that it was actually settled by Israelites. The same ambiguity is reflected in several references to David's campaigns against the Philistines, where Gezer is usually regarded as in the buffer zone between Philistia and Israel, although it is implied that it was actually the farthest outpost of Philistine influence (2 Sam. 5:25; 1 Chr. 14:16, 20:4). The most significant biblical reference to Gezer—and now confirmed as the most reliable historically—is 1 Kings 9:15–17, where it is recorded that the city was finally ceded to Solomon by the pharaoh as a dowry in giving his daughter to the Israelite king in marriage. Thereafter, Solomon fortified Gezer, along with Jerusalem, Megiddo, and Hazor.

There are no further references until postbiblical literature, in which Gezer appears to have played a significant role in the Maccabean wars. The Seleucid general Bacchides fortified Gezer (by then known as Gazara) along with a number of other Judean cities (1 Macc. 9:52). In 142 BCE, Simon Maccabaeus besieged Gezer and took it, after which he refortified it and then built himself a residence there (1 Macc. 13:43–48). His son, John Hyrcanus, made his headquarters at Gezer when he became commander of the Jewish armies the next year (1 Macc. 13:53).

Field I: section through the MB IIC glacis.

EXCAVATIONS

The first excavations at Gezer were conducted between 1902 and 1909 by R. A. S. Macalister for the Palestine Exploration Fund. The findings were published in three substantial volumes in 1912. These excavations were the largest yet undertaken by the fund or anyone else in Palestine, not surpassed in size or importance until the Germans worked at Jericho and the Americans at Samaria in 1908. Macalister began at the eastern end of the mound with a series of trenches, each about 10 m wide, running the entire width of the mound. He dug each trench down to bedrock (as deep as 13 m in some places). Then, proceeding to the next trench, he dumped the debris into the trench he had just completed. Although his notion of stratification was primitive—even judged by the standards of the day—he was able to recognize as many as nine strata. In the excavation report he combined his architectural remains into six large plans. Each purports to represent a coherent stratum but is actually a composite of elements several centuries apart. The pottery was grouped according to seven general periods, some covering as many as eight hundred years: Pre-Semitic, First through Fourth Semitic, Hellenistic, and Roman-Byzantine. The remaining material was published by categories

The inner wall and gate, MB IIB–C; (foreground) mud-brick superstructure.

Field I: inner wall, MB IIB–C; (left) the MB IIC glacis.

rather than by chronological periods—all the burials together, all the domestic architecture, all the cult objects, all the metal and lithic objects—and scarcely a single item can be related to the general strata, let alone to specific buildings.

What was to have been the beginning of a second series of excavations was sponsored at Gezer by the Palestine Exploration Fund in the summer of 1934, under the direction of A. Rowe. He opened an area just west of the acropolis, which both Macalister and he were unable to touch because of the Muslim cemetery and the shrine of a holy man, a *weli*. However, bedrock was reached in a short time, and the excavations were abandoned. The only significant exposure, apart from an Early Bronze Age cave, was a Middle Bronze Age tower that probably belongs to the inner wall (see below).

In 1964, G. E. Wright initiated a new ten-year project at Gezer, sponsored by the Hebrew Union College Biblical and Archaeological School (later the Nelson Glueck School of Biblical Archaeology) in Jerusalem and supported chiefly by grants from the Smithsonian Institution in Washington, D.C., with some assistance from the Harvard Semitic Museum. The project was directed in 1964–1965 by Wright (thereafter, he was adviser to it), from 1966 through 1971 by W. G. Dever, and from 1972 to 1974 by J. D. Seger. H. D. Lance was associate director, and Glueck was adviser to it from 1964 through 1971. Dever directed the final seasons in 1984 and 1990.

EXCAVATION RESULTS

The following brief reconstruction uses the latest excavations as a framework, but it incorporates the earlier excavations as well as the literary sources where they can be utilized.

THE CHALCOLITHIC PERIOD. The earliest occupation in stratum XXVI is represented by Macalister's cream ware, which was found in crevices in the bedrock and was evidently deposited by primitive camp sites. More of the material was recovered in the latest excavations in phase 14 of field I, again from hearths and thin deposits on the surface of the bedrock. Both the ceramic and lithic industries are similar to those of the Ghassul-Beersheba horizon and are to be dated toward the end of the Chalcolithic period, about the thirty-fourth century BCE.

THE EARLY BRONZE AGE. The beginning of the Early Bronze Age is fairly well represented, although domestic occupation was not substantial, and there is no evidence that the site was fortified at the time. (Macalister's central wall, attributed to his First Semitic period, is almost certainly nothing more than an element of the complex Middle Bronze Age ramparts.) Most of the Early Bronze Age material published by Macalister (mixed in his Pre-Semitic and First Semitic periods) came from the troglodyte dwellings—caves in bedrock that were initially used for habitation and storage and were later reused as burial places. The recent excavations cleared another of these enlarged and modified caves in the rock, from which came a variety of storage jars filled with grain, some stone vessels, and several grindstones and other implements. The grain yielded a carbon-14 date of 3040 ± 110 BCE, which tends to confirm the relative placement of this occupational phase at Gezer and elsewhere (R. de Vaux's Early Bronze IA, G. E. Wright's Early Bronze IB, K. M. Kenyon's Proto-Urban A–B), immediately following the Late Chalcolithic but preceding the development of the earliest fortifications. In addition to the cave dwellings and burials, a few straggling house walls from phase 13 in field I and slight remains just above bedrock in fields V and VI give evidence of the beginning of more substantial settlement, designated stratum XXV (c. 3300–2950 BCE).

The Early Bronze Age II (c. 2950–2600 BCE) is represented by rather meager evidence, principally from phases 12 and 11 in field I and phase 4 in field V, with their unimpressive domestic constructions. There are at least two building periods (strata XXIV–XXIII), and if most of the elements of the town plan of Macalister's First Semitic belong here, as seems likely, occupation may well have spread over most of the mound. However, the pottery and small objects from this period in the latest excavations were scant and rather poor, as they were from Macalister's excavations. (Most of the pottery from his First Semitic seems to have been Early Bronze Age I, even allowing for his tendency to publish only whole vessels from the tombs, which are indeed early.) Further evidence for the relative obscurity of Gezer in the Early Bronze Age II is that among the large, strategically located sites known from this period, it is the only one that remained unfortified (cf. the massive city walls at Tell el-Far'ah [North], Megiddo, Taanach, Ai, Jericho, and Arad).

Whether the site was destroyed or simply deserted, occupation seems to have come to an end by the Early Bronze Age IIIA at the latest. Apart from one doubtful tomb placed by Wright in the Early Bronze Age III (cave 16-I), there is no clear Early Bronze Age III material from either the early or the more recent excavations. The gap in occupation continues throughout the Early Bronze Age IV and Middle Bronze Age I and into the Middle Bronze Age IIA, although a few sherds from Macalister's publication are noted (cf., for instance, tomb 27-I, last used in the Middle Bronze Age I, and possibly also the original cutting of tomb 1). In field I, an erosion layer of rubble and occupational debris containing pottery and small objects was washed down the slope from higher on the mound, accumulating to a depth of some 1.5 m

Field I: outer wall and inner wall.

Field VI: plastered granary and stone-lined silos, MB IIA.

Field V: the high place, MB IIB–C. To the left, part of the inner wall.

Plan of burial cave 10A, field I, in LB I.

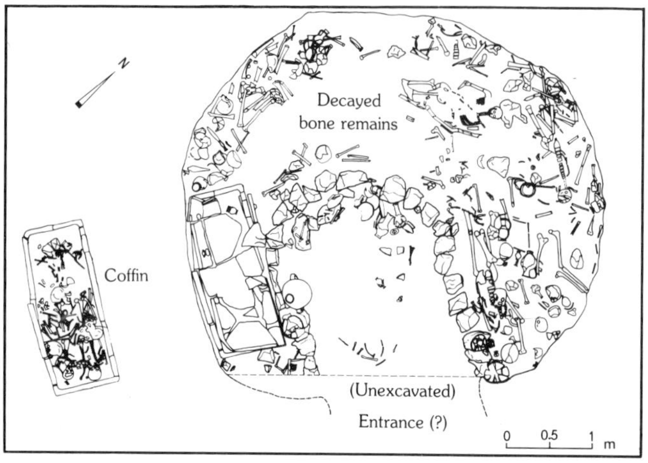

Terra-cotta coffin in situ, cave 10A, field I, LB I.

during this gap (stratum XXII, about the twenty-sixth–nineteenth centuries BCE).

THE MIDDLE BRONZE AGE. It was in the Middle Bronze Age II that Gezer enjoyed its greatest expansion and prosperity, with the main developments already underway by the end of the Middle Bronze Age IIA (stratum XXI, c. 1800 BCE). Although the city was not yet fortified, fairly elaborate domestic installations were found in phase 9-C of field VI on the acropolis. Houses and courtyards were well planned and constructed, with fine plaster floors. Rock-hewn cisterns were filled by runoff water carried from catchment areas by plastered and stone-capped drains. A partly subterranean granary was extremely well built, with substantial stone foundations, a mud-brick superstructure, and walls and floors sealed against moisture and rodents by a coat of plaster up to 15 cm thick. The pottery from stratum XXI was transitional Middle Bronze Age IIA to early Middle Bronze Age IIB. The finer vessels, especially from three infant burials, were of delicate eggshell ware turned on a fast wheel, either painted or red-slipped and beautifully burnished. These finds complemented those of Macalister from several tombs, including a cist tomb with typical Middle Bronze Age IIA pottery (tomb 30-III). A Twelfth Dynasty statuette bearing the name Heqab probably also belongs to this (or the succeeding) period.

Fortifications. Gezer reached the zenith of its power in the Middle Bronze Age IIIB–C period. To this phase (strata XIX–XVIII) belong the city's first fortifications. Macalister traced the inner wall for nearly 400 m, one third of the way around the mound. He located eight rectangular towers and Rowe

The latest burial in cave 10A, field I, LB IIA.

Egyptian glass bottle from cave 10A.

Stone vessel for kohl decorated with monkey figures from cave 10A.

Cypriot vessel in the form of a bull from cave 10A.

located one in 1934, so the wall may have had twenty-five or more such towers. The only known gate is Macalister's south gate, a typical three-entryway Middle Bronze Age city gate, reexcavated in the modern excavations as field IV. On the west, it is flanked by tower 5017, 15.6 m in width and the largest single-phase defense work known in the country.

The wall itself was constructed of large, roughly dressed stones, some of them almost cyclopean, with a mud-brick superstructure. It averaged 4 m in width and is still preserved as much as 4.5 m in height. It was set into a deep foundation trench reaching almost down to bedrock. It was this trench, when excavated in field I of the recent excavations, that provided a date for the construction of the wall. Macalister had assigned the inner wall to his First Semitic period (Early Bronze Age I–II), but renewed investigation proved that the foundation trench was cut from phase 9 surfaces and that the latest pottery in the trench was contemporary. Two clear phases, both in the Middle Bronze Age IIC, have been discerned in the connecting wall between tower 5017 and the south gate, as well as in the gate itself. Thus, the date of the initial construction must be placed early in the Middle Bronze Age IIC, in the mid-seventeenth century BCE. The suggestion of several rather complex phases of fortification within the Middle Bronze Age IIC is supported by the observation that tower 5017 and the first connecting wall were certainly freestanding for a short while before the glacis (and the second connecting wall) was added in the last phase. The latter was made up of alternating, closely packed fills of debris from the mound and freshly quarried chalk, topped with a thick plaster coating. It sloped up for about 10 m at a 30-degree angle, leveling off in places to form a horizontal platform some 3 to 4 m wide before abutting the inner wall. Its height above ground level was about 5 m.

High Place. Another piece of monumental architecture belonging to this period (strata XIX–XVIII) is the famous high place discovered by Macalister. It consists of a row of ten monoliths, some over 3 m high, erected in a north–south line just inside the inner wall in the north-central area of the mound. To the west of the alignment is a large stone block, perhaps a basin or a socket for a now-missing monolith. The surface over the area is plastered and is surrounded by a low stone curb wall. Macalister dated the main installation to his Second Semitic period (Middle Bronze–Late Bronze ages) and compared it with later biblical high places, interpreting the stelae as typical Canaanite *asheroth* and construing burial jars in the vicinity (now known to be earlier) as evidence for child sacrifice. While most of Macalister's theories must now be discarded, renewed investigation of the high place in 1968 (field V) demonstrated that it was constructed in the Middle Bronze Age IIC, with a possible reuse phase in the Late Bronze Age. A cultic interpretation still seems best, perhaps in connection with the covenant renewal ceremony of a tribal or city-state league (cf. Ex. 24:1–11).

Dwellings and Tombs. Domestic structures from the Middle Bronze Age IIB–C (strata XIX–XVIII) show continuity with the Middle Bronze Age IIA levels, especially in field VI, where an unbroken sequence extends from the Middle Bronze Age IIA–B through the late Middle Bronze Age IIC. (Elsewhere there may be a brief gap in the mid-Middle Bronze Age IIB.) There is little to distinguish this occupation anywhere, except for a series of infant jar burials and some unusual ovens situated in courtyards. These ovens are made of the necks and shoulders of large storage jars set upside down into the floors, flush with the surface. However, the prosperity and artistic development of the period are attested to by several rich Middle Bronze Age IIC tombs found by Macalister, especially tomb 28-II, with its alabaster vessels, scarabs, and gold jewelry.

The Middle Bronze Age II strata were brought to an end by a destruction that left a meter or more of burned bricks in every field investigated. Along the inner face of the city wall, just to the west of the south gate, a row of hovels and storerooms was found containing quantities of grain-filled storage jars and other vessels, crushed under an accumulation of burned beams, ash, fallen mud bricks, and collapse from the wall. Imported monochrome, local bichrome, and chocolate wares, as well as other transitional Middle Bronze–Late Bronze Age pottery, all suggest a date as late as possible for this destruction. Provisionally, it can be correlated with the first campaign of Thutmose III, in about 1468 BCE, which is when this pharaoh claims to have destroyed Gezer (see above).

A potsherd reading *klb* (Caleb) in pictographic characters of Proto-Sinaitic script belongs in all probability to the seventeenth or the sixteenth century BCE.

THE LATE BRONZE AGE I. Apart from a few hints in Macalister's material, the Late Bronze IA (early fifteenth century BCE) is scarcely represented; therefore, a partial desertion may have taken place following the Thutmose III destruction. Stratum XVII of the Late Bronze Age IB (late fifteenth century BCE) is also poorly known, except for cave I.10A in field I, cut into the bedrock outside the inner wall. Most of the bones in the several dozen burials deposited in the lower level of this cave during a generation or so show signs of advanced arthritis, probably from stooped labor, which may be an indication of the hardships of life during this period. However, im-

Field VI: schematic plan of northwestern building from stratum XII, 12th century BCE.

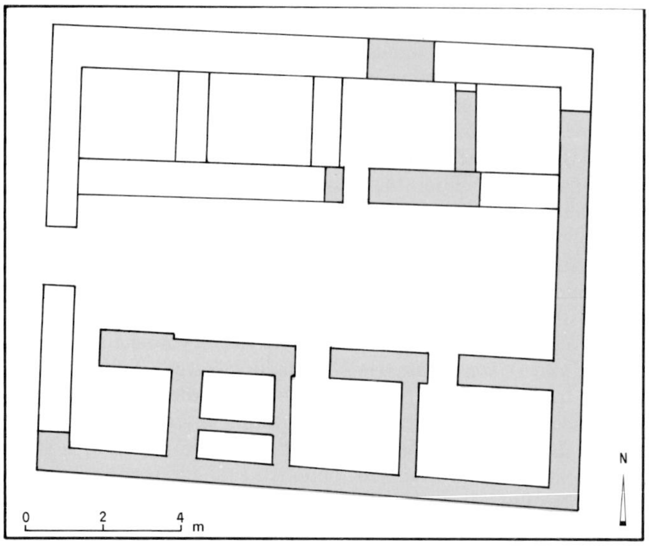

Philistine jug.

ported Cypriot pottery, Egyptian glass, alabaster and ivory vessels, and a unique terra-cotta coffin of Mycenean inspiration, all indicate international trade, even in this era. It is clear that the inner wall was for the most part too badly damaged to be repaired; it seems equally clear that construction of the outer wall that replaced it would not have been undertaken in this period of decline. Thus, Gezer was essentially unfortified (or at least undefended) for a brief period in the mid-late fifteenth century BCE. The raid by Thutmose IV (see above) may have occurred at this time.

THE LATE BRONZE AGE II. A renascence got underway with the beginning of the Late Bronze IIA (c. fourteenth century BCE), undoubtedly associated with the well-known el-Amarna period, when Canaan was under Egyptian domination. Stratum XVI, which should provide the context for the several el-Amarna letters from Gezer (see above), was exposed extensively only in field VI (phase 7), where unfortunately it had been almost entirely disturbed by later pits. There are slight remains of phase 6 in field I, and cave I.10A contains a few burials of this period in the upper level, above a silt deposit. A fragment of a cuneiform tablet that was dated by Macalister to the Assyrian period was shown by W. F. Albright to belong to the Amarna Age. I mentions a nearby site, Kiddimu (Tell Ras Abu Ḥamid?), where an Egyp tian commander is apparently demanding that the king of Gezer presen himself. Elements of the plan of Macalister's Third Semitic period probably belong here (particularly the large palacelike complex of his stratum IIIa built over the inner wall at the north end of trenches 27–28). In field VI, mere hints were preserved of what must once have been an impressive materia

Field VI: residential structure from stratum XII, 12th century BCE.

Field III: plan of the four-entryway city gate, 10th century BCE.

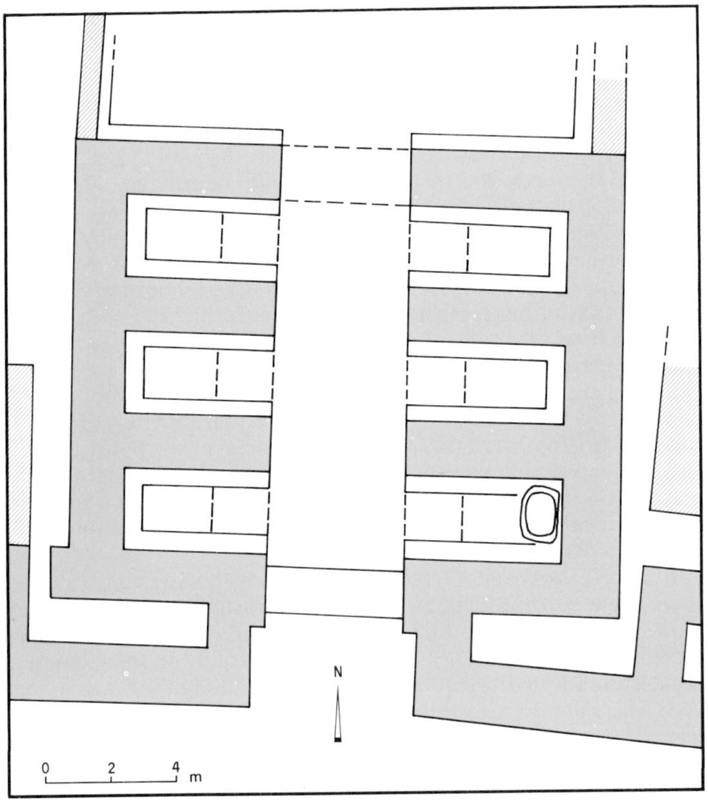

culture. House walls were as much as 2 m wide and exceptionally well constructed. Thick plaster surfaces ran across floors and outdoor courtyards and sealed, stone-capped drains. Among the small objects were quantities of Egyptian imports, especially fragments of el-Amarna glass, glass beads, faience pendants, scarabs, fragments of gold foil, and a statuette base bearing the name Sobek-nefru-ankh(?). Local objects included a clay crucible for copper smelting and a perfectly preserved bronze serpent about 15 cm long.

The Outer Wall. To this period, in all likelihood, belongs the construction and first-phase use of the outer wall, which Macalister traced for some 1,100 m, or four-fifths of the way around the perimeter of the mound (attributed to his Third Semitic period or roughly the Late Bronze Age). It supplanted the ruined Middle Bronze Age inner wall, following a line farther down the slopes and enclosing perhaps one-fourth more area, particularly on the northwest (where the lower city has never been investigated). In most places, the wall was set into a deep trench reaching to bedrock and destroying the earlier glacis. It averaged 4 m in width and is still preserved as much as 4.5 m in height. A rather crude glacis was added to the exterior. (The towers and bastions belong to later phases, as shown below.) The gateway has not been located, but it almost certainly lies below the Solomonic gate on the south slopes (field III). If this date is correct, this city wall is unique in being one of the country's few defense systems originally constructed in the Late Bronze Age and not reused from an earlier period.

The Water System. It has been suggested that the water tunnel may have been dug in this period, but the shaft was cut off from its context by Macalister and cannot now be dated. (It may belong instead, like those at Hazor, Megiddo, and Gibeon, to the Iron Age II.) A keyhole-shaped flight of steps and a round shaft about 7 m deep led to a sloping tunnel some 45 m long; groundwater was reached in an enlarged cavern at the end of the tunnel.

The Late Bronze Age IIB. The Late Bronze Age IIB (c. thirteenth century BCE) may have witnessed something of a decline at Gezer, as elsewhere in the post-Amarna age. Nevertheless, Macalister's Canaanite castle and another large building in his trenches 27–28 have been reinterpreted as Egyptian-style "residencies." No large-scale destruction took place at the end of stratum XVI, but some disturbance may be evident in the fact that in both fields I and VI almost no element of the architecture survived to be reused in stratum XV. The rather unimpressive buildings that succeeded were built on a new orientation. The ceramic repertoire of stratum XV was limited, with degenerate platter bowls, carinated bowls, kraters, juglets, and cooking pots all marking the end of a long tradition going back to the Middle Bronze Age. Imported wares virtually ceased, and among the local wares only the painted pottery showed any vitality. Kraters were decorated with crude stick figures or

Field III: overview of the four-entryway city gate, 10th century BCE.

Gezer calendar, 10th century BCE.

occasionally with geometric designs, and the series of palm-and-zigzag-panel bowls begins here, especially in the lamp-and-bowl deposits (see below).

The end of stratum XV presents a problem. In field II, domestic occupation (phase 13) was interrupted by a destruction that left quantities of smashed pottery and other objects lying about a heavily burned courtyard. This may have been a localized destruction, however, for in field I, phase 4 with Philistine pottery succeeds phase 5 after a brief, distinct gap, but there are no signs of destruction. The clearest evidence was obtained from field VI, where an interlude preceding the introduction of Philistine pottery was marked by the extensive digging of pits for stone robbing and the disposal of refuse (the post-6 phase), although there were virtually no other signs of human activity. Taken together, the evidence suggests a partial hiatus in occupation at the very end of the thirteenth and the beginning of the twelfth centuries; it is designated stratum XIV, perhaps a post-destruction period. It would be tempting to relate this to the destruction claimed by Pharaoh Merneptah, in about 1207 BCE (among Macalister's finds is a sundial bearing the cartouche of Merneptah). It would explain the curious fact that nowhere did the excavations encounter a real destruction accompanying the arrival of the Philistines, or Sea Peoples, in the early twelfth century BCE. The site may have already been partially destroyed and deserted. An alternative would be to attribute the disturbance to an Israelite destruction and brief occupation, but the literary tradition is explicit that Gezer was not taken in the conquest.

THE IRON AGE. The Philistine period at Gezer is especially well attested, with strata XIII to XI all belonging to this horizon. On the acropolis, phase 5, with its several subphases, is characteristic of the vigorous but stormy cultural history of the era. Although there is continuity in the basic architectural elements, and certainly in the typical painted pottery, no fewer than three major destructions are evident. In the first, some time in the early twelfth century BCE, a large public granary was destroyed and then rebuilt (phase 5-E–D). After the second destruction, in the mid-twelfth century BCE, it was abandoned, and the adjacent threshing floor was converted into an area of fine private houses. Two courtyard houses on the upper terrace have been excavated. Both were destroyed by fire toward the end of the twelfth century BCE, then rebuilt, destroyed again, and finally rebuilt very poorly before being abandoned (phase 5-C–A). Elsewhere, in fields I and II, two or three Philistine phases are also evident, although with less dramatic demarcations. Macalister's tombs 9 upper, 58 upper, and 59 upper may all be ascribed to this period.

The pottery of this horizon, particularly in the twelfth century BCE, is a mixture of local traditions of degenerate Late Bronze Age pottery, plus the sudden appearance of the characteristic Philistine bichrome wares. Among the former are the lamp-and-bowl deposits found under the floors of houses and near the foundations of houses in both Macalister's and the latest excavations (from strata XV–XII), in which one of the bowls is often of the palm-and-zigzag-panel design known from earlier levels at Gezer and from the Fosse Temple III at Lachish. The distinctively Philistine painted wares are relatively scarce, and they decline in number and quality toward the end of the period.

In both fields II and VI, two ephemeral post-Philistine/pre-Solomonic phases were discerned, strata X and IX. In particular, these phases were marked by a distinctive pottery that was no longer painted but was merely treated with an unburnished, thin red slip, especially on small bowls. The architecture succeeded that of the Philistine strata but was much poorer. Everywhere they were investigated, these levels came to an end in a violent destruction that may be correlated with the campaigns of the Egyptian pharaoh who, according to 1 Kings 9:15–17, had "taken Gezer and burnt it with fire" before ceding it to Solomon, probably in about 950 BCE. (It has been suggested that this pharaoh was Siamun, of the Twenty-first Dynasty, but this is uncertain on present evidence.)

IRON AGE II. The first Israelite level is stratum VIII, to which Macalister's so-called Maccabean castle belongs. This structure, only partially excavated, was first recognized by Y. Yadin as a typical Solomonic four-entryway city gate, almost identical to those previously published from Megiddo and Hazor. The excavations in field III have fully confirmed the date and have

Field III: overview of the four-entryway city gate, 10th century BCE.

Stamped amphora handle from the Hellenistic period.

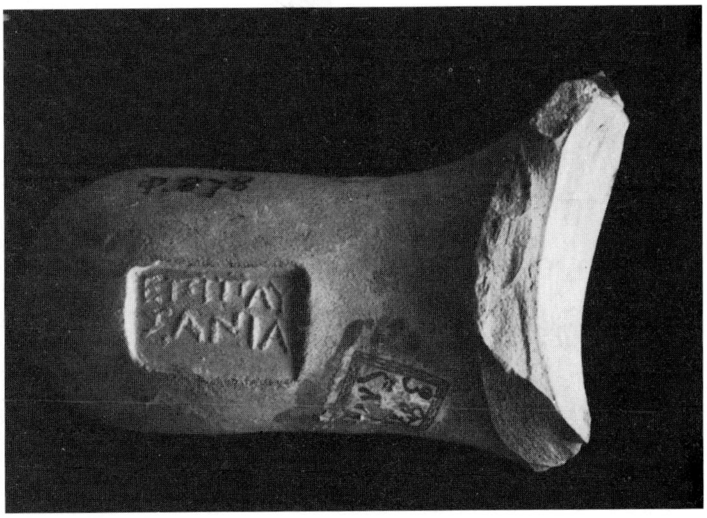

filled in many details concerning the plan and construction. The upper gate was exceptionally well built, with foundations in the guardrooms going some 2 m below the surface and with fine ashlar masonry at the jambs. Plastered benches ran around the three walls of each of the inner chambers, a feature considered so essential that each time floor levels were raised these benches were also raised and replastered. A plastered downspout drain at the rear corner of the gate structure indicates roofs over these inner chambers. Shortly after its construction, in about the mid-tenth century BCE (phase 6), the gate was altered by the raising of the street level and the addition of a large drain, over a meter wide, running down the middle of the street and under the threshold (phase 5). At this time the outer two-entry gatehouse downslope was added, along with some of the ashlar towers inserted into the then-rebuilt outer wall. Also, palace 10,000, west of the upper gate, was incorporated into the upper casemate wall.

The casemate wall connected with the upper gate has been investigated in field II; it is also Solomonic in date. In all probability, most of the towers of ashlar masonry, which Macalister demonstrated were an addition to the outer wall, are from this period. If they are, it would mean that Solomon simply repaired and reused the Late Bronze Age fortifications wherever possible, adding his own distinctive type of city wall and gateway only in the area where it is conjectured that the ruined Late Bronze Age gate had been situated. This "two-phase" theory for the outer wall has been contested by some, who would place its construction entirely in the tenth, or even the ninth to eighth centuries BCE. The work of the final seasons in 1984 and 1990, however, appears to confirm the original theory.

The domestic architecture of stratum VIII was unimpressive, indicating perhaps that Gezer under Solomonic control was little more than a token administrative center. In field VI, large ashlars identical to those in the gate were found in secondary usage in a citadel wall from about the Assyrian period—virtually all that survives here of the post-Philistine period—so it is possible that there was a Solomonic fortress or palace on the acropolis. No tombs were found in the recent excavations, but tombs 84 and 85 (middle), 96, and 138 in Macalister's excavations have good late tenth-century material. The pottery is typical of the period, with the red-slipped wares of the previous period now hand burnished. Among the small objects, a small limestone

Bilingual (Hebrew and Greek) "Boundary of Gezer" inscription.

incense altar is notable; it is inscribed with a stick figure who resembles the Canaanite storm god Baal, his uplifted arm grasping a bundle of lightning bolts. The well-known Gezer calendar also belongs to the Solomonic era. It is one of the earliest Hebrew inscriptions, perhaps a schoolchild's exercise tablet, giving a mnemonic ditty for the seasons of the agricultural year.

A destruction, particularly heavy in the vicinity of the gateway, brought stratum VIII to an end in the late tenth century BCE. This was probably the work of Shishak, in about 924 BCE—part of his well-known raid in Canaan.

Macalister's arbitrary selection and publication of the material from the Iron Age II (mixed in his Fourth Semitic period) had led most scholars, including Albright, to assume that the site had been virtually abandoned from the ninth to the seventh centuries BCE. However, Macalister's tombs 28, 31, 84 and 85 (upper), and 142 certainly belong to the Iron Age II, and the gap has been closed by strata VII to V in the recent excavations. Nevertheless, it is evident that occupation was rather sparse, and the site seems to have declined in importance following the Shishak destruction (cf. above the infrequent literary references). The total accumulation during strata VII to V was no more than 1 to 1.5 m, and even that has been almost completely eroded in fields I and VI.

In stratum VII (ninth century BCE), the Solomonic gate was rebuilt as a three-entryway gate, identical to that of Megiddo IVA. Palace 8,000 now replaced the earlier palace 10,000 west of the gate. The gate and palace survived until stratum VI was destroyed, probably by Tiglath-pileser III in the Assyrian campaigns of 733–732 BCE. Domestic levels were also brought to an end, in a conflagration that left dramatic evidence in field II.

Stratum V (late eighth–seventh centuries BCE) was of little importance, except that it provides a context for two Neo-Assyrian tablets and royal stamped jar handles Macalister found. The two cuneiform tablets belong to the period of the Assyrian conquest and dismemberment of Israel. These tablets are legal contracts from the mid-seventh century BCE and bear Hebrew and numerous Assyrian names. Slightly later in date are the several royal stamped jar handles, belonging possibly to the reign of Josiah (c. 640–609 BCE), when Gezer was part of the kingdom of Judah. Although little evidence survives, the gate apparently was converted at this time into a two-entryway gate like that of Megiddo III. Shortly thereafter, it was destroyed so badly—probably in the Babylonian invasion of 587–586 BCE—that it was never rebuilt as a chambered gate. In fields II and VIII, stratum V domestic levels were found destroyed. In the casemate of the city wall in field II, a quantity of smashed pottery was found; some of the sherds were marked by firebrands and a spill of calcined limestone. In field VII, a great collapse of burned mud brick had fallen into a storeroom, sealing in a row of early sixth-century BCE storage jars leaning against a wall.

THE PERSIAN, HELLENISTIC, AND ROMAN PERIODS. There is a gap following the end of stratum V, which stratum IV of the Persian period (fifth–fourth centuries BCE) only partially fills. As J. Iliffe has shown, Macalister's Philistine tombs, with their rich deposits of silver vessels, belong here. The recent excavations produced very scant material, although typical Persian period pottery was found in small quantities in stratum IV. Otherwise, only a few pits and some flimsy walls from the period survive. However, two phases (3 A–B in field II) can be discerned.

Strata III and II are Hellenistic, spanning the third and nearly all of the second centuries BCE but representing for the most part the Hasmonean era, as might be expected from the literary sources. From the Ptolemaic period, to which stratum III seems to belong, there is little material from the recent excavations, although Macalister's *Yhd/Yhwd* and *Yršlm* stamp impressions attest to occupation. Somewhat later, the gate in field III was rebuilt here (phase 2, Macalister's slanting building), perhaps by the Syrian general Bacchides. For the Hasmonean period, a fairly extensive exposure in fields II and VII has produced several fine courtyard houses. A coin of Demetrius II (c. 144 BCE) came from the ruins of the last phase. In fills beneath the floors was a coin of Antiochus VII (about 138–129 BCE). Rhodian stamped jar handles, lead weights, and a mass of iron tools were also found. A Greek graffito in the vicinity of the reused Solomonic city gate, if properly deciphered, reflects the disgust of one citizen, Pamphras, at the Maccabean takeover, for it reads something like "To blazes with Simon's palace!" The gate in field III had been rather hastily repaired, the threshold having been narrowed nearly a meter, and only parts of the interior structure were reused (Macalister's Maccabean castle). It seems certain that the outer wall was retrenched and reused and that Macalister's semicircular bastions were added around the towers at this time. With the destruction of stratum II sometime toward the end of the second century BCE, Gezer's long history as an important city came to a virtual end.

Stratum I belongs to about the Herodian era (late first century BCE–first century CE), as shown by material from both the earlier and the more recent excavations. The site proper was virtually deserted, and most of the known material comes from Macalister's *kokhim* (loculi) tombs in the vicinity. (However, later Roman material in some of these tombs indicates continued occupation in the second and third centuries CE). On the mound, a large wall crowning the slope in field II appears to have been a boundary wall rather than a defense wall, and the domestic remains (phase I) suggest little more than hovels or sheepfolds. The well-known boundary inscriptions, found in an arc some distance from the mound, are further evidence that in the Herodian period Gezer was no longer an independent city but merely part of a large private estate, thinly occupied and no longer of consequence. The owner or administrator, whose Greek name, Alkios, is given on the inscriptions, may have been Jewish, but that is uncertain. Macalister's Syrian bath probably belongs to this period.

THE BYZANTINE AND LATER PERIODS. The only later material consists of tombs excavated by Macalister, most of which are Byzantine (fourth–sixth centuries CE), and faint traces of occupation in the vicinity of the mound. Two coins attributed to Khosrau II (c. 614–628 CE in Palestine) attest to the era of the Persian conquest in the seventh century CE. Gezer was identified by Clermont-Ganneau with the Crusaders' Mont Gisart, but this identification lacks supporting evidence. A few coins and some vessels from the Mameluke period in reused Byzantine tombs are evidence of an occupation in the thirteenth century CE. A small *weli* was built on the acropolis in the sixteenth century CE but is now destroyed.

History: W. F. Albright, *BASOR* 92 (1943), 28–30; A. Malamat, *Scripta Hierosolymitana* 8 (1961), 228–231; R. Giveon, *VT* 14 (1964), 250; A. R. Millard, *PEQ* 97 (1965), 140–143; J. F. Ross, *BA* 30 (1967), 62–70; B.-Z. Rosenfeld, *IEJ* 38 (1988), 235–245.

Main excavation reports: R. A. S. Macalister, *The Excavation of Gezer* 1–3, London 1912; W. G. Dever et al., *Preliminary Report of the 1964–66 Seasons* (*Gezer 1*), Jerusalem 1970; id., *Report of the 1967–70 Seasons in Fields I and II* (*Gezer 2*), Jerusalem 1974; S. Gitin, *A Ceramic Typology of the Late Iron II, Persian and Hellenistic Periods at Tell Gezer* 1–2 (*Gezer 3*), Jerusalem 1990; W. G. Dever et al., *The 1969–71 Seasons in Field IV, "The Acropolis"* 1–2 (*Gezer 4*), Jerusalem 1986; J. D. Seger, *The Field I Caves* (*Gezer 5*), Jerusalem 1988 (Annuals of the Nelson Glueck School of Biblical Archeology); *Manual of Field Excavation: Handbook for Field Archaeologists* (eds. W. G. Dever and H. D. Lance), Jerusalem 1978.

Other studies: Clermont-Ganneau, *ARP* 2, 224–275; W. M. F. Petrie, *PEQ* 36 (1904), 244–245; F. L. Griffith, ibid. 38 (1906), 121–122; J. L. Myres, ibid. 39 (1907), 240–243; L. H. Vincent, ibid. 40 (1908), 218–229; R. A. S. Macalister, *PEQ* 41 (1909), 183–189; E. W. G. Masterman, *PEQ* 66 (1934), 135–140; J. H. Illife, ibid. 67 (1935), 185; A. Rowe, ibid., 19–33; id., *QDAP* 4 (1935), 198–201; G. E. Wright, *PEQ* 69 (1937), 67–78; id., *BA* 21 (1958), 103–104; id., *IEJ* 15 (1965), 252–253; id., *RB* 74 (1967), 72–73; R. Amiran, *IEJ* 5 (1955), 240–245; Y. Yadin, ibid. 8 (1958), 80–86; J. A. Callaway, *PEQ* 94 (1962), 104–117; W. G. Dever, *IEJ* 16 (1966), 277–278; 17 (1967), 274–275; 19 (1969), 241–243; 20 (1970), 226–227; 22 (1972), 158–160; 23 (1973), 23–26; 35 (1985), 64–65, 217–230; (with R. W. Younker) 41 (1991), 282–286; id., *BA* 30 (1967), 47–62; 32 (1969), 71–78; 34 (1971), 93–132; 47 (1984), 206–218; 50 (1987), 148–177; id., *Jerusalem Through the Ages*, Jerusalem 1968, 26–33; id., *Raggi* 8 (1968), 65–74; id., *RB* 75 (1968), 381–387; 76 (1969), 563–567; 77 (1970), 394–398; 78 (1971), 425–428; 79 (1972), 413–418; 92 (1985), 412–419; id., *BTS* 116 (1969), 1, 8–16; id., *AJA* 74 (1970), 192; 90 (1986), 223; id., *Gezer 1* (Reviews), *AJA* 76 (1972), 441–442. — *IEJ* 22 (1972), 183–186. — *JBL* 92 (1973), 291–293. — *PEQ* 105 (1973), 170–171. — *JAOS* 94 (1974), 277–278. — *ZDPV* 90 (1974), 78–82. — *JNES* 34 (1975), 297–299. — *Bibliotheca Orientalis* 41 (1984), 222–224; id., *Gezer 2* (Reviews), *AJA* 80 (1976), 307–308. — *IEJ* 26 (1976), 210–214. — *JBL* 96 (1977), 279–281. — *PEQ* 109 (1977), 55–58. — *BASOR* 233 (1979), 70–74. — *ZDPV* 97 (1981), 114–116; *Gezer 4* (Reviews), *BAR* 14/1 (1988), 11. — *Orientalia* n.s. 58 (1989), 435–437; id., *PEQ* 105 (1973), 61–70; id., *Journal of Jewish Studies* 33 (1982), 19–34; id., *ESI* 3 (1984), 30–31; id., *BASOR* 262 (1986), 9–34; 277–278 (1990), 121–130; H. D. Lance, *BA* 30 (1967), 34–47; id., *Magnalia Dei* (G. E. Wright Fest.), Garden City, N.Y. 1976, 209–223; A. Brunot, *BTS* 116 (1969), 3–6; N. Glueck, *Syria* 46 (1969), 186–187; J. S. Holladay, *AJA* 73 (1969), 237; id., *BASOR* 277–278 (1990), 23–70; R. G. Bullard, *BA* 33 (1970), 98–132; A. Furshpan, "The Gezer 'High Place'" (Ph.D. diss., Cambridge, Mass. 1970); id., *AJA* 75 (1971), 202; J. D. Seger, *IEJ* 20 (1970), 117; 22 (1972), 160–161, 240–242; 23 (1973), 247–251; 24 (1974), 134–135; id., *RB* 80 (1973), 408–412; 82 (1975), 87–92; id., *EI* 12 (1975), 34*–45*; id., *BA* 39 (1976), 142–144; id., *BASOR* 221 (1976), 133–139; id., *Archaeology and Biblical Interpretation* (D. Glenn Rose Fest.), Atlanta 1987, 113–128; id., *The Second International Congress on Biblical Archaeology, 24 June–4 July 1990: Abstracts*, Jerusalem 1990, 138–139; K. M. Kenyon, *Royal Cities of the Old Testament*, New York 1971; M. Avi-Yonah, *Archaeology* (Israel Pocket Library), Jerusalem 1974, 87–91; M. Hughes, *PEQ* 106 (1974), 2–3; J. M. Weinstein, *BASOR* 213 (1974), 49–57; 217 (1975), 1–16; S. Izre'el, *TA* 4 (1977), 159–167; id., *Israel Oriental Studies* 8 (1978), 13–90; D. Cole, *BAR* 6/2 (1980), 8–29; S. Gitin, *A Ceramic Typology of the Late Iron II, Persian and Hellenistic Periods at Tell Gezer* 1–3 (Ph.D. diss., Cincinnati 1979); J. N. Tubb, *PEQ* 112 (1980), 1–6; O. Borowski, *BAR* 7/6 (1981), 58–59; I. Finkelstein, *TA* 8 (1981), 136–144; id., *BASOR* 277–278 (1990), 109–119; R. Reich, *IEJ* 31 (1981), 48–52; id. and B. Brandl, *PEQ* 117 (1985), 41–54; B. Brandl, *IEJ* 34 (1984), 173–176; id., *Levant* 16 (1984), 171–172; Z. Kallai and B. Brandl, *ESI* 1 (1982), 31–32; *American Archaeology in the Mideast*, 168–171; S. Bunimovitz, *TA* 10 (1983), 61–70; 15–16 (1988–1989), 68–76; E. Pennells, *BA* 46 (1983), 57–61; H. Shanks, *BAR* 9/4 (1983), 30–42; P. A. Thomas, *BA* 47/1 (1984), 33–35; D. Milson, *ZDPV* 102 (1986), 87–92; I. Singer, *TA* 13–14 (1986–1987), 26–31; Y. Shiloh, *Archaeology and Biblical Interpretation* (D. Glenn Rose Fest.), Atlanta 1987, 209–211; Weippert 1988 (Ortsregister); A. M. Maeir, *TA* 15–16 (1988–1989), 65–67; J. K. Hoffmeier, *Levant* 22 (1990), 83–89; L. E. Stager, *BASOR* 277–278 (1990), 93–107; D. Ussishkin, ibid., 71–91; G. J. Wightman, ibid., 5–22; F. Zayadine, *RB* 97 (1990), 76; R. W. Younker, *AUSS* 29 (1991), 19–60.

Gezer Calendar: G. B. Gray, *PEQ* 41 (1909), 189–193; M. Lidzbarski, ibid., 194–195; F. M. Cross, Jr., and D. N. Freedman, *Early Hebrew Orthography*, New Haven 1952, 46–47; W. Wirgin, *EI* 6 (1960), 9*–12*; B. D. Rahtjen, *PEQ* 93 (1961), 70–72; S. Talmon, *JAOS* 83 (1963), 177–187.

Other epigraphical finds: W. M. F. Petrie, *PEQ* 34 (1902), 365; T. G. Pinches, ibid. 36 (1904), 229–236; A. H. Sayce, ibid., 236–237; C. H. W. Johns, ibid., 237–244; 37 (1905), 206–219; R. A. S. Macalister, ibid. 38 (1906), 123–124; C. J. Ball et al., ibid. 40 (1908), 26–30; P. Dhorme, ibid. 41 (1906), 107–112; W. R. Taylor, *JPOS* 10 (1930), 16–22, 79–81; E. L. Sukenik, ibid. 13 (1933), 226–231; W. G. Albright, *BASOR* 92 (1943), 28–30; N. Avigad, *PEQ* 82 (1950), 43–49; A. R. Millard, ibid. 97 (1965), 140–143; C. Graesser, Jr., *BASOR* 220 (1975), 63–66; B. Becking, *Jaarbericht Ex Oriente Lux* 27 (1983), 76–89; J. Rosenbaum and J. D. Seger, *The Word of the God Shall Go Forth* (D. N. Freedman Fest.), Winona Lake, Ind. 1984, 477–495; id., *BASOR* 264 (1986), 51–60; R. Reich, *IEJ* 40 (1990), 44–46; J. Schwartz, ibid., 47–57.

WILLIAM G. DEVER

GHASSUL, TULEILAT EL-

IDENTIFICATION

Tuleilat el-Ghassul is a large settlement (c. 50 a. in area) dating from the Late Neolithic and Chalcolithic periods. The site, c. 295 m below sea level, is made up of a group of small mounds and is situated in the lower Jordan Valley, about 5 km (3 mi.) northeast of the Dead Sea. The site was initially discovered in the 1920s, by A. Mallon and a team from the Pontifical Biblical Institute in Jerusalem. During this early phase of research, the investigators were primarily concerned with identifying the five cities of the plain mentioned in Genesis 14 and tentatively identified Ghassul with one of them. Following the first excavations, from 1929 to 1938, it became clear that Tuleilat el-Ghassul represented a new pre-Bronze Age culture in the country's archaeological history. The first to suggest ascribing this culture to the Chalcolithic period was W. F. Albright, and by the mid-1930s its distinct material culture made Tuleilat el-Ghassul the type site for this period.

EXCAVATIONS

The initial excavations by the Pontifical Biblical Institute revealed four major superimposed strata (I–IV, earliest to latest), separated from one another by layers of ash, wind-blown and other sediments. The maximum depth of the cultural deposits reached approximately 5 m. The most perplexing problem associated with these deep stratigraphic excavations was the lack of change observed in the material culture assemblage. This homogeneity led the researchers to interpret the four strata as representing a single culture, which R. Neuville named Ghassulian, a term that became synonymous with the Chalcolithic period in this country. To tackle the stratigraphic problem anew, the Pontifical Biblical Institute resumed excavations in 1960, under the direction of R. North, but was unsuccessful in demonstrating any technological development. In 1967, the third and most recent phase of excavation was initiated by B. Hennessy, under the aegis of the British School

Tuleilat el-Ghassul: plan of stratum IV on mound 1.

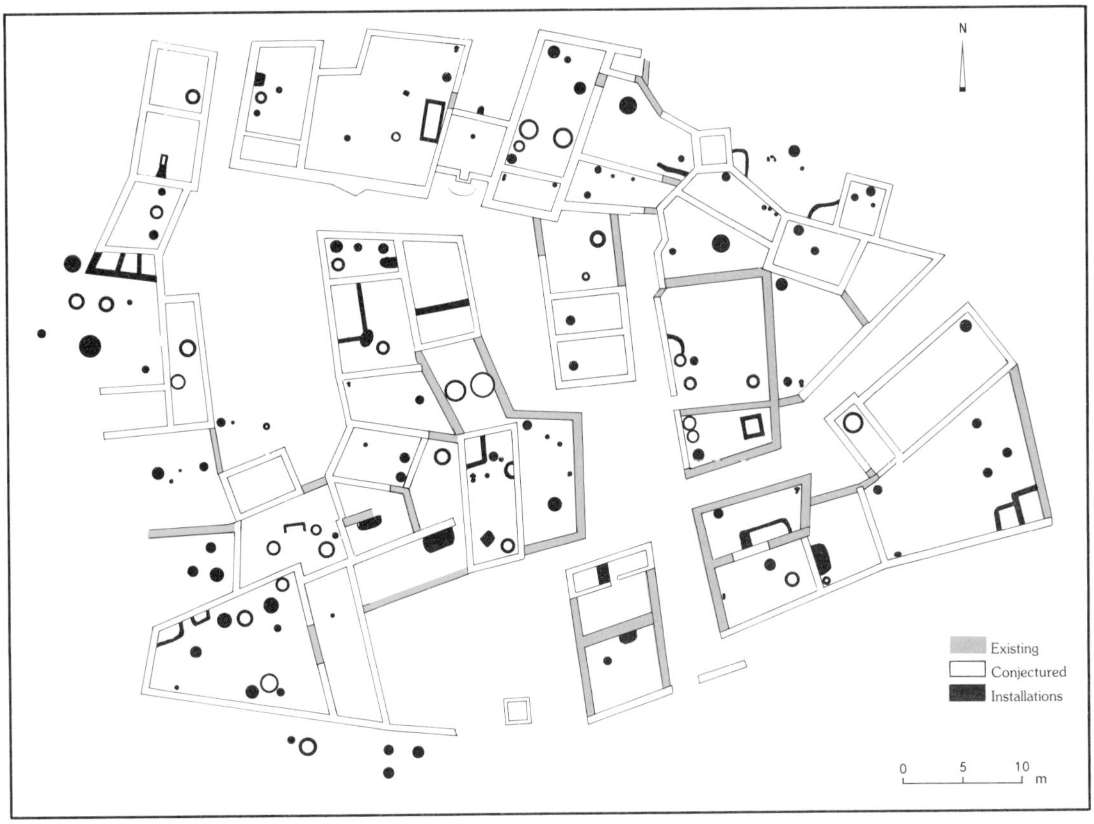

of Archaeology in Jerusalem. These excavations (1967 and 1975–1978) focused on providing a reliable stratigraphy and sequence of settlement on the site's various mounds; stratigraphically relating the individual mounds to one another; obtaining a large exposure of the earliest settlement phase; collecting paleoenvironmental data; establishing an absolute chronology for the site, using radiocarbon methods; and relating the site to surrounding settlements assumed to be contemporary. Since the early excavations, numerous regional cultures dating to the Chalcolithic period have been found in Israel and Jordan, limiting the value of the term Ghassulian to the site and its immediate environs.

STRATIGRAPHY. Through the various years of excavation, an area of over 10,500 sq m was exposed. Although the earlier excavators defined four main phases, the precision of Hennessy's more recent excavations defined ten major building phases separated by camp-floor occupations. The latter occurrences are interpreted as occupational subphases when the site was reconstructed for resettlement following periods of destruction. The entire sequence, labeled phases A through I, contains over one hundred successive floor levels. Although there is a paucity of reports concerning the recent excavations, the preliminary studies show technological development for the pottery and, to a limited extent, for the flint industries. The recent excavations also suggest that frequent seismic activity in the Jordan Valley caused the destruction of numerous settlements found in the archaeological sequence. Hennessy's excavations show no continuity for the Chalcolithic settlement into the subsequent Early Bronze Age, but there is a degree of continuity from the Late (Pottery) Neolithic period not noted by the original excavators. The following table equates the original four major phases (I–IV) with Hennessy's:

Mallon et al., 1934	*Hennessy, 1989*
IV	A+, A, B
III	C, D, E
II	F, G, H
I	I

Overview of mound 1, looking south.

Bases of pottery vessels with mat impressions.

ARCHITECTURE. Late Neolithic Buildings. The lowest phase of occupation at the site is characterized by apparently circular houses with sunken floors. Some evidence of pit dwellings also appears in this early phase. These are characterized as "half-sunk" houses surrounded by a low *pisée* wall with posts in holes to support roofs. Carefully laid pebble floors also characterize this Late Neolithic period.

Chalcolithic Buildings. The main occupation phases at the site, Ghassul IV–III (phases A–D), could be traced on most of the mounds. Because the site is composed of a number of small hillocks, its previous excavators thought it represented a group of small, closely tied settlements. Recent work has shown that these hillocks are in fact the result of erosion and represent the remains of a single large settlement. It is difficult to assess the degree of planning at the site because no single village plan has been published that incorporates all of the excavations. However, the results of excavation in mound 1 (stratum IV) do exhibit a degree of planning: alleys and public areas were constructed between the domestic buildings.

In area A I–III, between mounds 1 and 2 of the original Pontifical Biblical Institute investigation, reliable stratigraphic information about the site's architectural development became available. Above the Late Neolithic levels, there are approximately 4.5 m of deposit that display a relatively uniform domestic Chalcolithic architectural tradition. The buildings consist of large rectangular rooms that average about 5 by 15 m in length. These buildings usually have a single foundation course of large wadi stones (from the nearby Wadi Djarafa and Wadi Ghassul) with a mud-brick superstructure. The mud bricks are about 24 to 30 cm in diameter, bun shaped, and sun dried. The entrance to the rooms was usually along their broad side, through a single doorway indicated by a pivot stone. The roofs have been interpreted as pitched and built of reeds, with a mud capping over a thick timber frame. Some of the larger buildings show evidence of central posts used as roof supports.

Most floors were made of packed earth or mud. Some were found with a thick coating of lime plaster and others with a pebbled surface. In some cases, walls were plastered and painted; in some rooms, more than twenty successive replasterings were counted. A wide range of small architectural features was also found in the village, including fire pits, built hearths, ovens (*tabuns*), pits, circular silos, circular and rectangular working surfaces, paved surfaces, sunken storage pithoi, small storerooms, channels, and large in situ mortar installations.

RADIOCARBON DATING. In addition to the ceramic and lithic assemblages, the published radiocarbon determinations from Ghassul highlight the local transition from the Late Neolithic to the Chalcolithic in the southern Jordan Valley. Although precise contextual data have not been published, when calibrated these dates range from 5620 to 4880 BCE, placing them firmly at the end of the Late (Pottery) Neolithic–Early Chalcolithic sequence. A single date, 4445–4320 BCE, comes from a piece of wood found in the classic Ghassulian level (III). The wood had been in storage at the Pontifical Biblical Institute since the original 1928–1939 excavations. More dates are anticipated from the main level (IV) at the site. The following table outlines the published radiocarbon determinations from Ghassul.

Locus	*Material*	*C-14 date BP*	*CRD-1 sigma*	*Lab no.*
Area A III, 201.9, Pit A	Wood	6550 ± 160	5620–5330 BCE	SUA-732
Area A III, 201.12A	Wood	6370 ± 105	5471–5320 BCE	SUA-734
Area A II, p.107.3 & 4	Wood	6430 ± 180	5510–5320 BCE	SUA-736
Area E X, p.2.3a	Wood	6300 ± 110	5350–5210 BCE	SUA-738/1
Area E X, p.3.3b.3c	Wood	6070 ± 130	5220–4841 BCE	SUA-739
Level III	Charred	5500 ± 110	4460–4240 BCE	RT-390A

LOCAL PALEOENVIRONMENT. The available evidence indicates that Tuleilat el-Ghassul was initially settled on a sandbar surrounded by slow-moving water, perhaps in a swampy environment. Although conditions today border on arid (the site is more than 4 km [2.5 mi.] from the Jordan River), pollen collected from the site's early phases include alder (*Alnus spp.*) and sedge (*Scirpos spp.*). These species, in addition to reed mace (*Typha latifola*), water chestnut (*Trapa natans*), club moss (*Lycopodium spp.*), and fernlike plants (*Selaginella spp.*), are all found in wet environments near

Overview of mound 3.

Left: *sherd decorated with a serpent relief.*
Right: *pottery bowls with painted decoration.*

slow-moving water. This may indicate that part of the Jordan flowed near the site or that significant springs existed around it in antiquity. These data tie in with recent paleoenvironmental studies that suggest that conditions were more moist during the Late Neolithic and Early Chalcolithic periods.

AGROTECHNOLOGY. No systematic studies have been published of the floral or faunal remains from this site. However, mention has been made of the presence of domesticated sheep (*Ovis? aries*), goat (*Capra hircus*), cattle (*Bos taurus*), and pig (*Sus scrofa*) bones, as well as some samples of deer. Varieties of wheat, barley (*Hordeum vulgare*), and peas (*Lens culinaris*) have also been reported. From the perspective of farming, Tuleilat el-Ghassul provides important evidence of the earliest olives (*Olea europaea L.*) and dates (*Phoenix dactylifera L.*) in the Levant. This produce marks the beginning of the Mediterranean system of horticulture, which continues to the present. Based on the limited evidence, the Chalcolithic phases at the site can be characterized as a mixed economy based on agriculture/horticulture, village-based pastoralism, and limited hunting.

MATERIAL CULTURE. Late Neolithic Pottery. The earliest pottery from Ghassul is characterized by shallow bowls and jars with a plain rim; dark-faced coarse ware (with significant percentages of buff clays); occasional mat red slips; grass-wiped surfaces; incised decoration; flat bases, often splayed with occasional ring bases; and bases with circular mat impressions. Paint, bow rims, and burnished slips are rare—however, sometimes a thin red painted band appears around the rim of shallow bowls.

Chalcolithic Pottery. The middle phases of occupation (C–E) show the common appearance of cornet cups (plain and heavy), elaborate rim shapes, and more uniform hard-fired red and gray wares. Buff wares decline. Design patterns include chevrons, solid triangles, and loops. More geometric painted designs appear, but they are still rare. The mat impressions on vessel bases reflect a square weave. The upper levels of occupation (phases A–B) are characterized by common painted and smeared wash wares; common light cornet cups, often decorated; small multiple lug handles (they are absent in earlier phases); and a large variety of deep and shallow bowls, jars, and jugs. Churns, which are comparatively common at Chalcolithic sites in the Negev, are rare at Ghassul. Only one fragment was identified in Hennessy's excavations.

Pithos decorated with a rope relief.

Painted cornets.

"L'Oiseau" wall painting.

Sherd with a painted deer and bird.

Flint Industry. Although no quantitative information is available, information in recent reports suggests that blades with broad and fine denticulation, notched blades, and serial-flaked blades are features found only in the Late Neolithic phase. These elements seem to disappear when rectangular architecture appears at the site.

The main lithic types that characterize the industry in the Chalcolithic phase include chisels (which Neuville subdivided into *erminettes*, *hachettes*, *gouges*, and *ciseaux*); picks, generally with a triangular section; fan scrapers, a type artifact in the Ghassulian assemblage; steep, flat, and end scrapers; backed and sickle blades; and awls.

Stone Objects. The stone industry from this phase is also rich in grinding stones, mortars, and pestles made of calcareous stone and basalt. Other objects include mace heads, spindle whorls and fenestrated three-legged vessels made of basalt.

Metal Objects. Very few metal objects have thus far been found at Ghassul. In Mallon's excavations, several copper tools, including mainly axes and fish hooks, were found.

Bone and Shell Objects. Among the utilitarian objects made of bone were awls, needles, weaving shuttles, pins, and possibly gorges used for fishing. A wide range of mother-of-pearl pendants and beads was also found.

Figurines. A number of stylized violin-shaped stone figurines were found in level III that may relate to a cult. This group is characteristic of the Chalcolithic in Israel. Other figurines, made of clay, were of dogs and lambs, which may have been toys.

WALL PAINTINGS. A total of seven wall paintings were excavated at Tuleilat el-Ghassul. The first three were found between 1929 and 1932 and include the "Star of Ghassul," "*Les Personnages*" and "*L'Oiseau.*" Two more examples, found in 1960–1961, are known as the "Geometric" and "Tiger" paintings. The two most recently discovered paintings are known as the "Zig-Zag Fragment" and "Procession." The paintings are spectacular in execution. Combinations of naturalistic and geometric designs occur in combinations of black, yellow, white, red, and brown mineral paints. The most famous example is the eight-pointed "Star" that appears with terrifying masks and imaginary creatures. The star measures about 1.84 m in diameter and was painted with four rays in dark red, four in black, and overlapping white lines. "*Les Personnages*" and the "Procession" may represent cult processions that took place at the site.

SANCTUARIES. In area E, on a low mound 100 m to the west of area A, recent excavations in the upper phases have indicated the presence of a sanctuary area. It seems that only two buildings were established here, enclosed by a stone and mud-brick wall. In its general layout, the complex is similar to the sanctuaries at En-Gedi and Gilat. The continued resurfacing of the floors indicates a long period of use. The buildings (c. 4.5 by 10 m), show evidence of white plaster on the floor and an orange color on the walls. The floors in both buildings were made of large, rounded stones covered with packed mud and then sealed with lime plaster. Eight superimposed wall paintings were found in one of the buildings, as indicated by large fragments of broken plaster. Benches lined the south wall of sanctuary B, a broadroom. A wide platform built of small stones ran outside its entrance for the length of the building. Both buildings contained "cult" vessels and pottery figurines. The relationship between cult activities and the buildings

Flint fan scrapers.

"Star of Ghassul" wall painting.

Tuleilat el-Ghassul: wall painting of a mask(?).

Tuleilat el-Ghassul: jar burial.

in which wall paintings were found remains to be clarified.

BURIALS. Over twenty infant jar burials have been found at Ghassul, mostly in large pottery sherds beneath house floors. Given the extensive area excavated at Ghassul and the small number of burials, the formal mortuary grounds for the site must be located in the vicinity of the settlement. The most likely cemetery which served Ghassul is the nearby cist and grave-circle necropolis at Adeimeh (q.v. Dolmens) several kilometers to the southeast, excavated by Stekelis in the early 1930s.

SUMMARY

Tuleilat el-Ghassul is the largest Chalcolithic site in the country and provides new evidence concerning the local evolution of this culture beginning in the Late Neolithic period. Although previously viewed as the type site for the Chalcolithic, very few copper objects have been found at the site. No evidence of metal production was found in the recent excavations and only a few copper axes were recovered in the Pontifical Biblical Institute's investigations. Recent radiocarbon dates and the pottery from the earliest phase suggest an affinity to the Pottery Neolithic at Jericho, Middle and Late Neolithic Byblos, and Neolithic sites in the southern Beqa'a in Lebanon. While general similarities exist between Ghassul and the Beersheba Valley sites, the relationship between these cultures is more complex than previously thought. This is due to the lack of radiocarbon dates from the upper levels at Ghassul, the virtual absence of a metal industry at the site, and the need for more provenance studies to trace interregional relations during this period. Recent excavations at Gilat show that this site has more affinities with Ghassul. Although Tuleilat el-Ghassul has been investigated for over sixty years now, scholars have still not explained why it grew into one of the largest late fifth- to fourth-millennia sites in the Levant.

Main publications: A. Mallon and R. Köppel, annual excavation reports, in *Biblica* (1930–1938); id. et al., *Teleilat Ghassul* 1, Rome 1934; *Ghassul* 2, Rome 1940; R. North, *Ghassul 1960 Excavation Report*, Rome 1961.

Other studies: R. North, *Biblica* 40 (1959), 541–555; id., *ADAJ* 8–9 (1964), 68–74; id., *SHAJ* 1 (1982), 59–66; B. Hennessy, *RB* 75 (1968), 247–250; id., *Levant* 1 (1969), 1–24; id., *SHAJ* 1 (1982), 55–58; E. D. Stockton, *Levant* 3 (1971), 80–81; J. R. Lee, "Chalcolithic Ghassul" (Ph.D. diss., Hebrew Univ. of Jerusalem 1973); C. Elliott, *PEQ* 109 (1977), 3–25; id., *Levant* 10 (1978), 37–54; J. A. Sauer, *BA* 42 (1979), 9; P. M. Schwartzbaum et al., *Third International Symposium on Mudbrick (Adobe) Preservation*, Ankara 1980, 177–200; D. O. Cameron, *The Ghassulian Wall Paintings*, London 1981; *American Archaeology in the Mideast*, 150; G. Dollfus, *MdB* 46 (1986), 5–6; T. E. Levy, *BA* 49 (1986), 82–108; id. and A. Holl, *Archéologie Européenne* 29 (1988), 283–316; I. Gilead, *Journal of World Prehistory* 2 (1988), 397–443; id. (and Y. Goren), *BASOR* 275 (1989), 5–14; Khouri, *Antiquities*, Amman 1988, 81–85; Weippert 1988 (Ortsregister); *Akkadica Supplementum* 7–8 (1989), 230–241; Y. Goren, *Mitekufat Ha'even* 23 (1990), 100*–112*; B. Rothenberg, *University of London, Institute for Archaeo-Metallurgical Studies Newsletter* 17 (1991), 1–7.

THOMAS E. LEVY

GIBEON

IDENTIFICATION AND HISTORY

In 1838, E. Robinson identified the village of el-Jib, 9 km (5.5 mi.) north of Jerusalem (map reference 167.139), as the site of biblical Gibeon, which had been proposed previously by F. F. von Troilo (1666) and by R. Pococke (1738). A. Alt opposed this identification on the grounds of information preserved in the *Onomasticon* of Eusebius (48, 9; 66, 11). However, the discovery at el-Jib (during the excavations in 1956, 1957, and 1959) of thirty-one jar handles inscribed with the name *gb'n* has now confirmed the identification of Gibeon with el-Jib.

Gibeon is first mentioned in the account of the Israelite conquest in Joshua 9. The inhabitants of the enclave of the cities of Gibeon, Chephirah, Beeroth, and Kiriath-Jearim obtained a covenant of peace from Joshua by deception; upon the discovery of the ruse, the Gibeonites were sentenced to become "hewers of wood and drawers of water" (Jos. 9:21, 9:23, 9:27). When Gibeon was attacked by Adoni-zedek, the Amorite king of Jerusalem, for its defection to Joshua, the Israelites responded by making a forced march from Gilgal and driving the Amorite forces down the way of Beth-Horon, miraculously aided by the hailstones and the sun standing still upon Gibeon (Jos. 10:1–14). The "pool of Gibeon" is mentioned a few times in the Bible. It was the scene of the contest between the young men of Abner and those of Joab (2 Sam. 2:12–17). It was at the "great stone which is in Gibeon" (2 Sam. 20:8) that Joab slew Amasa. Seven sons of Saul were executed "at Gibeon on the mountain of the Lord" (2 Sam. 21:1–11). This was done in order to end a three-year famine thought to have been sent in retribution for Saul's slaying of the Gibeonites in violation of the ancient covenant. According to 1 Kings 3:2–5, Solomon made sacrifices and had his famous dream at the high place in Gibeon. In 2 Chronicles 1:3 and 1:13, it is asserted that the tent of the meeting was at Gibeon, and in 1 Chronicles 16:39 and 21:29, it is said that the tabernacle and the altar of burnt offering were there. Gibeon appears in the Karnak list as one of the cities taken by Shishak in the second half of the tenth century BCE. The city is mentioned as the home of Hananiah, the false prophet (Jer. 28:1); and "the great waters that are in Gibeon" are

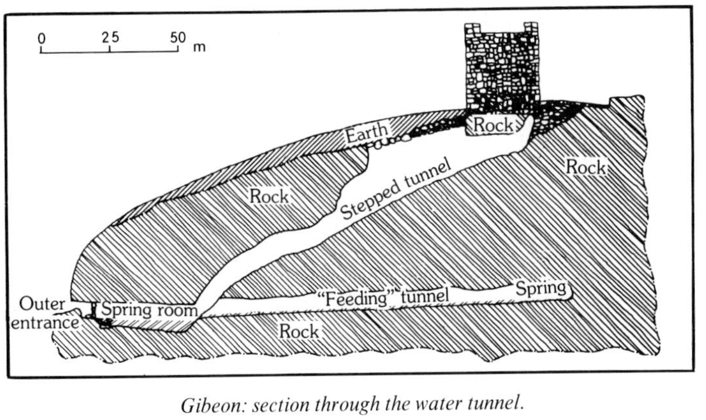

Gibeon: section through the water tunnel.

General plan of the site.

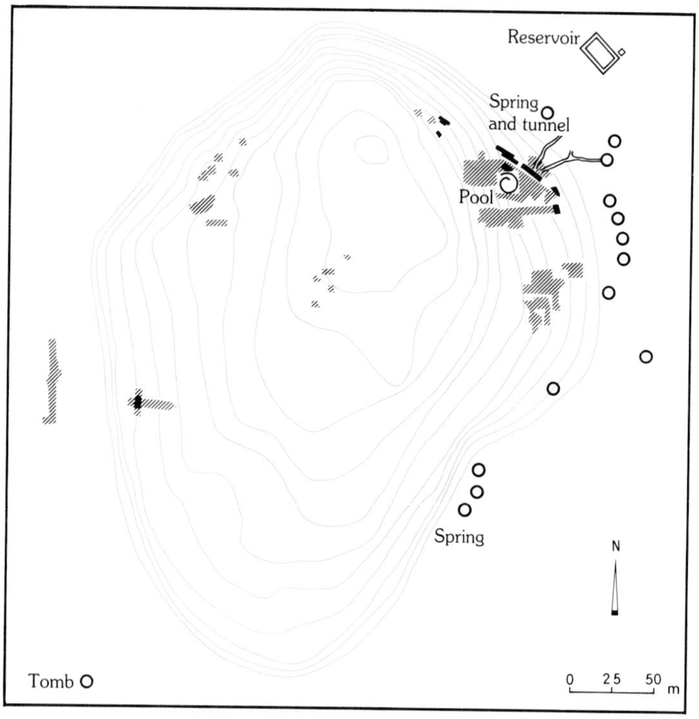

The city wall and the water system.

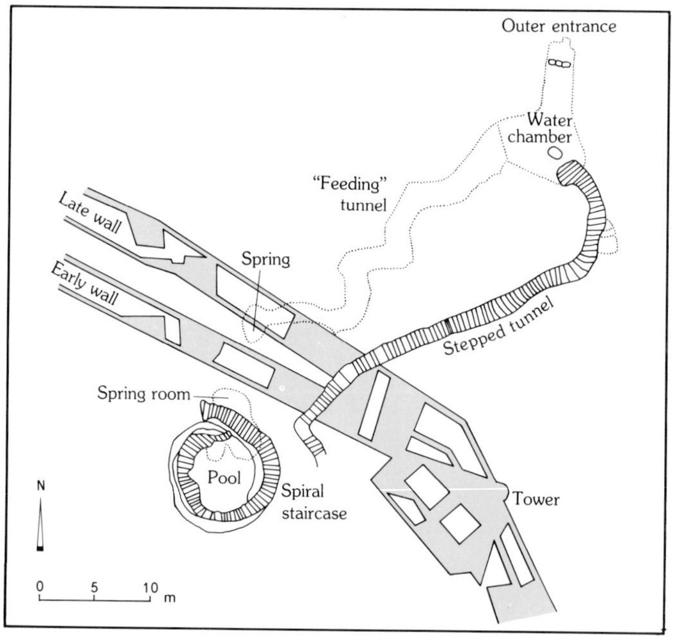

mentioned as the place where Johanan the son of Kareah met Ishmael and the Judeans whom he had seized at Mizpah (Jer. 41:12). In the postexilic period the men of Gibeon are said to have assisted in the rebuilding of the wall of Jerusalem (Neh. 3:7–8). Josephus relates that Cestius pitched his camp at Gibeon on his march to Jerusalem in October of 66 CE (*War* II, 515–516, cf. II, 540ff.).

EXPLORATION

In 1870, the site was visited by a survey expedition of the British Palestine Exploration Fund. In 1889, the rock-cut tunnel leading from the spring of the village into the hill was explored, and a rough plan was published by C. Schick. An Iron Age tomb was discovered in 1950 and published by A. Dajani. The first major excavation was undertaken in 1956 by an expedition sponsored by the University Museum of the University of Pennsylvania and by the Church Divinity School of the Pacific at Berkeley, California, with the cooperation of the American Schools of Oriental Research, under the direction of J. B. Pritchard. Subsequent excavations were carried out under the same direction and the sponsorship of the University Museum during the seasons of 1957, 1959, 1960, and 1962. A survey of burial caves near Gibeon was carried out by H. Eshel in 1983–1984. Some of the Late Iron Age burial caves that had been found by the PEF expedition were rediscovered and documented in that survey.

Part of the stepped tunnel leading from the city to the spring.

EXCAVATION RESULTS

THE WATER SYSTEM. Two systems for providing the inhabitants of the walled city with spring water in time of siege were constructed during the Iron Age. The first is a cylindrical cutting into the live rock, (diameter, 11.8 m and 10.8 m deep). A spiral staircase was cut along the north and east sides of the pool. At the bottom, the stairway continues downward into a tunnel to provide access to a water chamber that lies 13.6 m below the floor of the pool. By means of this spiral staircase of seventy-nine steps, the inhabitants of the city had access to fresh water lying 24.4 m below the level of the city. This construction, which had involved the quarrying and removal of approximately 3,000 tons of limestone, may have been the "pool of Gibeon" mentioned in 2 Samuel 2:13. The second device for obtaining water in time of siege is the stepped tunnel that leads from inside the city wall to the village spring. The construction of this passageway of ninety-three steps through the hill was made later in the Iron Age, perhaps at a time when the flow of water into the water chamber of the pool was inadequate.

THE WINERY. Gibeon was a center for the production and export of wine in the eighth and seventh centuries BCE. In the course of the 1959 and 1960 excavations, sixty-three rock-cut cellars were found for the storage of wine at a constant temperature of 18 degrees C (65 degrees F). The cellars are bottle shaped and average 2.2 m in depth and 2 m in diameter at the bottom. The opening at the top averages 0.67 m in diameter. In the same area the excavators found winepresses carved from the rock, channels for conducting the grape juice into fermentation tanks, and settling basins. The jars in which the wine was stored within the cellars had a capacity of 36 liters. It is estimated that the sixty-three cellars would have provided storage space for jars containing 95,000 liters of wine.

Smaller jars with inscribed handles were used for the export of wine produced at Gibeon. The standard formula for the inscriptions on the handles is *gb'n gdr* and one of the following proper names: *ḥnnyhw nr', 'zryhw, 'mryhw*. The proper names *dml'* and *šb'l* also appear in a slightly different formula. In the same context with the inscribed jar handles, stoppers and a funnel for filling the jars were found.

THE TOMBS. During the 1960 season of excavation, eighteen shaft tombs that had been cut into the soft limestone of the west side of the hill were found. Although the tombs had been cut in the Middle Bronze Age I, they had been reused in the Middle Bronze Age II and in the Late Bronze Age. In the area of the winery, on the top of the mound, a Roman tomb, which had been cut from more ancient wine cellars, was found. This underground

The pool.

Bowl, MB IIB.

Bronze figurine of Osiris, end of the Iron Age.

Inscribed jar handle: gb'n gdr, end of the Iron Age.

chamber had eleven loculi for burials in the floor and arcosolia cut into the wall that could accommodate four more burials. A painted mural with a bas-relief of stucco indicates a date of around 300 CE for the construction of the tomb.

SUMMARY

The first temporary occupation of the site was in the Middle Bronze Age I. This period is represented by pottery and other artifacts found in the tombs on the west side of the mound. In the Middle Bronze Age II, there was a permanent settlement at the top of the hill and the Middle Bronze Age I tombs were reused. Late Bronze Age pottery has thus far been found only in tombs, of which eight used in this period have been found. During the early part of the Iron Age, a massive city wall (3.2 to 3.4 m wide), was built around the scarp of the natural hill, and the great pool was cut into the rock to provide protected access to the hill's water table. The city apparently reached a peak of prosperity during the Iron Age IIC, when buildings covered most of the enclosed area and the Gibeonites engaged in producing and trading wine. It was during this prosperous period that the tunnel was cut from the city to the spring. There is only scant evidence of occupation from the end of the sixth century until the beginning of the first century BCE. Evidence of considerable building, including stepped baths and water conduits, has been found from the Roman period, when the city stood without a protecting wall.

Entrances to the rock-cut cellars, and winepresses.

Gibeon: burial cave 9, 7th–6th centuries BCE.

Main publications: J. B. Pritchard, *Hebrew Inscriptions and Stamps from Gibeon*, Philadelphia 1959; id., *The Water System of Gibeon*, Philadelphia 1961; id., *Gibeon: Where the Sun Stood Still*, Princeton 1962; id., *The Bronze Age Cemetery at Gibeon*, Philadelphia 1963; id., *Winery, Defenses and Soundings at Gibeon*, Philadelphia 1964.

Other studies: C. Schick, *PEQ* 22 (1890), 23; Robinson, *Biblical Researches* 1, 455; A. Alt, *PJB* 22 (1926), 11–25; 25 (1929), 14ff.; id., *ZDPV* 69 (1953), 1ff.; J. Simons, *Handbook for the Study of Egyptian Topographical Lists Relating to Western Asia*, Leiden 1937, 215; J. Muilenberg, *Tell en-Nasbeh* 1 (ed. C. C. McCown), Berkeley 1947, 40–43; A. Dajani, *ADAJ* 2 (1953), 66–74; 3 (1956), 19–22; 6–7 (1962), 121–122; 8–9 (1964), 86–87; J. B. Pritchard, *BA* 19 (1956), 65–75; 23 (1960), 23–29; 24 (1961), 19–24; id., *University Museum Bulletin* 21 (1957), 3–26; 22 (1958), 13–24; id., *Expedition* 2 (1959), 17–25; 3 (1961), 2–9; 5 (1962), 10–17; id., *Supplement to VT* 7 (1960), 1–12; id., *BASOR* 160 (1960), 2–6; id., *ADAJ* 6–7 (1962), 121–122; 8–9 (1964), 86–87; N. Avigad, *IEJ* 9 (1959), 130–133; F. M. Cross, Jr., *BASOR* 168 (1962), 18–23; W. L. Reed, *Archaeology and Old Testament Study* (ed. D. W. Thomas), Oxford 1967, 231–243; A. Demsky, *BASOR* 202 (1971), 16–23, 212 (1973), 25–31; J. Blenkinsopp, *Gibeon and Israel: The Role of Gibeon and the Gibeonites in the Political and Religious History of Early Israel* (Society for Old Testament Study Monograph Series 2), Cambridge 1972; ibid. (Review), *IEJ* 26 (1976), 60–64; id., *VT* 24 (1974), 1–7; F. S. Frick, *BASOR* 213 (1974), 46–48; R. Amiran, *PEQ* 107 (1975), 129–132; B. Bagatti, *LA* 25 (1975), 54–72; J. Halbe, *VT* 25 (1975), 613–641; C. James, *Archaeoastronomy* 5/4 (1982), 10–19; D. Pringle, *Levant* 15 (1983), 141–177; D. Cole, *BAR* 6/2 (1980), 8–29; H. Eshel, *IEJ* 37 (1987), 1–17; Y. Shiloh, *Archaeology and Biblical Interpretation* (D. Glenn Rose Fest.), Atlanta 1987, 211–214; Weippert 1988 (Ortsregister).

JAMES B. PRITCHARD

GILAT

IDENTIFICATION

Gilat is a large Chalcolithic site situated in the northern Negev desert along the eastern bank of Naḥal Patish, in the fields of Moshav Gilat (map reference 1153.0818). Located approximately 20 km (12.5 mi.) northwest of the city of Beersheba, the site extends over an area of about 25 a. It is characterized by a central mound (c. 7.5 a.) and a flat plain (17.5 a.). Chance surface finds made at Gilat by D. Alon in the early 1950s—an unusually large granite violin-shaped figurine and hundreds of cornet and other typical Chalcolithic artifacts—suggested its rich potential. Subsequent excavations produced large quantities of cult and imported artifacts identifying Gilat as a center of exchange. Its location on the border between the rich grazing land of the Negev coastal plain and the more arid inland foothill zone seems to have played a key role in its emergence as a regional cult center during the late fifth to early fourth millennia.

EXCAVATIONS

Gilat was excavated by the Israel Department of Antiquities and Museums, under the direction of D. Alon, in three seasons (1975–1977). Later excavations on behalf of the Hebrew Union College–Jewish Institute of Religion, Jerusalem, were undertaken by T. E. Levy and D. Alon in 1990 and 1991.

STRATIGRAPHY. In the early 1950s, deep plowing activities disturbed all of the site's last level of occupation (stratum I). The earlier excavations (450 sq m in area) defined four main strata. The later ones (c. 800 sq m) subdivided the sequences into seven phases. Excavation showed that deep plowing affected the top 60 to 80 cm of soil. Although stratum I is rich in artifacts, all the architectural remains have been destroyed. In some stratigraphic sections, it is possible to observe truncated stratum I pits dug into earlier strata. The more recent excavations showed that the western half of the mound is much better preserved than in the east, where work in the 1970s was carried out. While stratum II suffered from deep plowing in the east, in the west preservation was good, and it is possible to subdivide this stratum into three subphases: IIa–IIc. Below this, stratum III is consistently well preserved throughout the site. Stratum IV, the earliest stratum, was reached in only a few probes.

ARCHITECTURE. Stratum IV, the earliest occupation, was established on a Pleistocene paleosol hillock that rose above the surrounding plain. Many large pits (diameter, c. 2.5 m) were dug into the paleosol and in some cases platforms were created by carving the paleosol and adding mud bricks to achieve the desired feature.

All of stratum III was exposed in the eastern sector, where a small complex of buildings, courtyards, and silos was found associated with a rich assemblage of cult-related objects. The main structure is a rectangular unit (c. 16.25 by 14.85 m) made up of broadrooms and a large courtyard. Room A (c. 3 by 4.5 m) contained the famous Gilat lady and ram statuettes and sixty-eight other cult-related finds (see table below). In the courtyards associated with room A, a number of standing stones, fenestrated stands, torpedo jars, large violin-shaped figurines, silos, and a stone-lined basin were found.

Stratum II represents a reorganization of the building complex at Gilat after the destruction of stratum III. The establishment of stratum II marks a shift away from the earlier stratum III buildings and the establishment of a new building complex to the west. Following the stratum III destruction,

Gilat: statuette of a seated goddess holding a churn and another vessel, Chalcolithic period.

Statuette of a ram bearing three cornets, Chalcolithic period.

stratum IIc is characterized by a large open plaza with a standing stone (*maṣṣeba*) set near its center. Patches of blue mineral paint were observed on the hard-packed plaza around the *maṣṣeba*. The plaza was delineated by a number of walls with stone foundations and mud-brick superstructures.

The best-preserved architectural evidence at Gilat is found in stratum IIb. In the western sector, the architectural complex extends over an area of about 1,050 sq m. Some of the features include three broadroom buildings (c. 3.5 by 7 m); two concave mud-brick-lined basins (diameter, c. 3 m); one unusually large hearth (diameter, 1 m); one large circular mud-brick platform (diameter, 4 m), one well-built mud-brick-lined silo (diameter, 2 m; depth, 2 m); and numerous smaller silos. All these features were interconnected by a hard-packed mud-brick material surface about 10 cm thick. In the eastern sector, a large (c. 4 by 4 m) mud-brick platform was found. Numerous objects associated with cult activities were discovered throughout this complex. When stratum IIb was abandoned, the following stratum (IIa) leveled the area with a fill of mud-brick material. A number of small, ephemeral buildings were

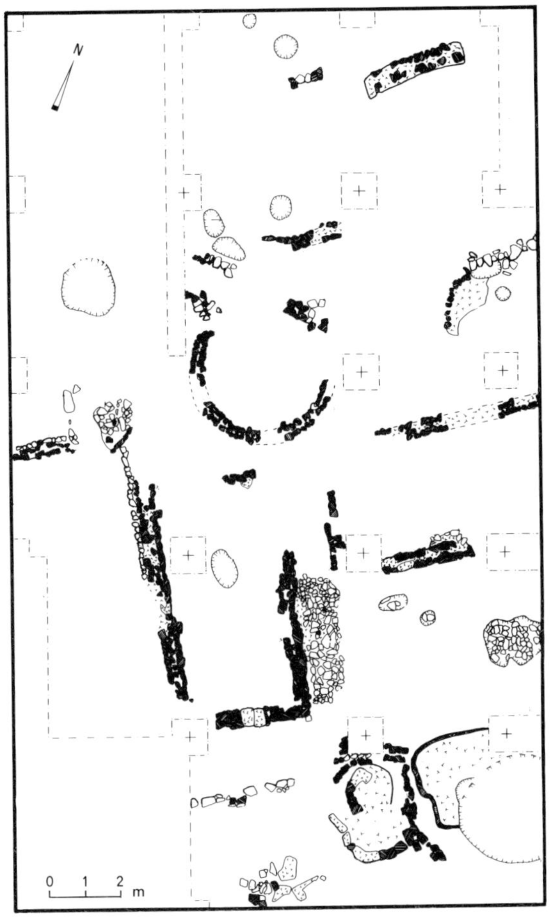

Gilat: plan of the buildings and installations in the cultic area.

Violin-shaped stone figurines.

established. At least six square, enigmatic platforms, each measuring about 1 by 1 m, were also erected.

FINDS IN ROOM A

Item	*Stratum III*	*Stratum II*
1. Violin-shaped figurines	3	2
2. Stone palettes	3	3
3. Torpedo vessels	3	2
4. Ceramic fenestrated stands	6	3
5. Stone fenestrated stands	2	—
6. Anthropomorphic statuette	1	—
7. Zoomorphic statuette	1	—
8. Female ceramic figurine	1	—
9. Animal figurine	1	—
10. Alabaster pendant	—	—
11. *Maṣṣebot* (standing stones)	1	1
12. Cornet vessels	28	8

CULT STATUETTES. The anthropomorphic and zoomorphic statuettes from Gilat are among the most important Chalcolithic cult objects in the region. The "Woman with Churn" is 31 cm high and consists of four parts: a red painted biconical stool; the nude woman's barrel-shaped body; a red-painted churn; and a fenestrated bowl under her arm. Most scholars agree that the Chalcolithic ceramic churn imitates the goat-skin churn used for making yogurt and other milk pruducts that appear in the Bedouins' ethnographic record. Like the cornet-shaped cup, the churn is one of the ceramic type fossils for the Chalcolithic in the Levant.

The "Ram Carrying Cornets" is 27.5 cm long with a total height of 23 cm to the highest cornet. Three cornets are inserted into the back of the ram and connected to its body to form a single receptacle. Like the woman, the depiction of the hollow ram with sex organs suggests that the object was

Gilat: overview of area T.

Cache of ostrich eggs found in stratum IIc.

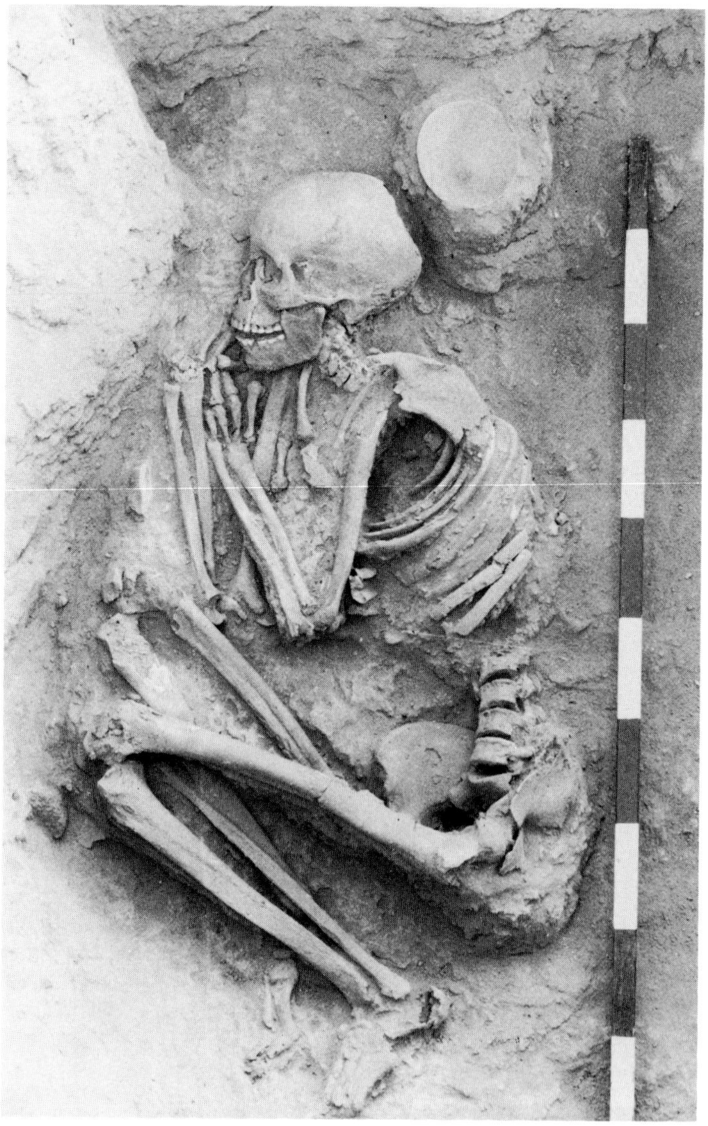
Adult burial with a V-shaped cup.

used in cultic activities concerning fertility connected with sheep/goat herds. Archaeozoological studies by C. Grigson show that sheep herding was of key importance to the economy of Chalcolithic societies in the semiarid northern Negev. Thus, the motifs of herding and milk products in the Gilat statuettes suggest that ensuring the fertility of the herd was a main concern of worshipers at this site. Another zoomorphic figure, a basalt ram's head with twisted horns (length, c. 4 cm), also reflecting a concern with herding, was found in area M. On its back a hole was carefully drilled to facilitate its use as a pendant or amulet.

VIOLIN-SHAPED FIGURINES. Violin-shaped figurines are known mainly from the Chalcolithic period. They are distinguished from "figurative" Chalcolithic statuettes and figurines by their highly abstract, geometric form. The most common type of violin-shaped figurines from Gilat have a head and neck represented in the stylized form of a narrow, rectangular thin board. Shoulders are depicted as horizontal lines and the waist as the narrowed part of the body. Sixty of these objects have been found at Gilat—the largest number from any site in the southern Levant. They are made from a wide range of materials, such as granite, limestone, and sandstone. The Gilat samples range from large (15–22 cm) to medium (8–15 cm) to small (less than 8 cm) and are exquisitely crafted. Like other imported artifacts, the violin-shaped figurines point to exchange with neighboring regions in southern Palestine.

Pottery assemblage of large vessels.

POTTERY. The pottery from Gilat represents one of the richest and most varied Chalcolithic ceramic assemblages in the southern Levant. Although located only 16 km (10 mi.) north of the well-known Beersheba Valley settlement system, the Gilat assemblage is clearly unique, with many new forms not found in the Beersheba Valley or other regions of the country. As at Tuleilat el-Ghassul, there is very little evidence of the use of a tournette, or slow wheel. A wide range of mat impressions found on pot bases indicates that some vessels were dried on straw mats.

The common vessel types include V-shaped cups, small cylindrical cups, cornets (virtually absent from Beersheba assemblages), bowls, basins, pithoi, hole-mouth jars, large and small churns, fenestrated stands, conical-base jars, and torpedo-shaped jars. Plain, painted, incised, and painted and incised design motifs are found. Some of the special vessel types include open-footed bowls with two sets of three horizontal lug handles, cone-shaped cups with vertical handles, twin-handled jars, and the Gilat torpedo jars. More than one hundred of these large pipe-shaped vessels (c. 65 cm long with 3-cm-thick walls) have been found at Gilat, but with the exception of one sherd found at Gat Guvrin, they are unknown at other contemporary sites.

Petrographic analysis of the Gilat ceramic assemblage by Y. Goren showed that of the eleven petrographic groups commonly found at Chalcolithic sites in the southern Levant, nine are represented at Gilat. This is unusual since most Chalcolithic sites in the country contain from one to three petrographic groups. While a few sherds come from as far away as the Nile Valley, the petrographic data indicate that Gilat received pottery vessels from all over southern Israel and southwestern Jordan, with significant numbers of vessels from the southern Judean Hills. Petrographic analysis of the torpedo jars shows that many were manufactured outside the vicinity of Gilat and brought to the site from areas as far as 80 km (50 mi.) away—from the northern Negev, the southern Hebron Hills, and En-Gedi. Thus, in addition to the wide range of exotic objects and materials found at Gilat, the petrographic evidence points to the production of special objects that may

Gilat: pottery assemblage of small vessels.

have been intended as offerings at the Gilat sanctuary. This highlights Gilat's role as a regional center in the Chalcolithic period.

LITHIC INDUSTRY. Like the Chalcolithic lithic industry from the Beersheba Valley, the assemblage from Gilat is based on flake production. Other items, such as celts, or core tools (axes, adzes, and chisels), are well represented, and some carefully ground Ghassulian chisels have been found. In a preliminary study of the 1987 lithic collection by Y. Rowan (based on the excavation of an 83-sq-m area), the following tool distribution was observed.

Tool type	*No.*	*Percent*
Canaanean blades (worked)	2	1.01
Notches	6	3.03
Perforators	3	1.51
Denticulates	1	0.51
End scrapers	14	7.07
Tabular scrapers	11	5.56
Sickle blades	14	7.07
Sickle blanks	3	1.51
Micro-end scrapers	3	1.51
Celts	14	7.07
Choppers	11	5.56
Retouched/utilized flakes	69	34.85
Retouched/utilized blades	2	1.01
Retouched/utilized bladelets	6	3.03
Miscellaneous trimmed pieces	39	19.70

Although only two Canaanean blades are listed here, a total of fourteen were found in clear Chalcolithic contexts at Gilat as of 1991. The discovery of these objects adds another link to the Chalcolithic-Early Bronze Age I transition in southern Palestine. Other unusual lithic objects include five pieces of Anatolian obsidian. A typical Negev micro-end scraper was manufactured from one of the obsidian blades. In addition, a wide range of mace heads has come to light. Some of these are typical Chalcolithic pear-shaped examples made of hematite; others are made of granite, are flat-topped, and resemble predynastic Egyptian Naqada I types. Other exotic stone objects include sixty fenestrated stands made of nonlocal basalt. The domestic lithic assemblage contains large numbers of grinders, hammerstones, "digging stick weights," mortars, and pestles.

HUMAN BURIALS. During the 1990–1992 excavations, twenty-five hominid specimens were found, fourteen of which were below the age of 9. Out of the eleven specimens for which the sex could be determined, six were male and five were female. All of the burials were found in pits, usually in a semiflexed position lying on one side. Only one individual was found with a burial offering. This was an adult male, 35 to 40 years old, buried in a flexed position with a V-shaped bowl placed next to his head. The burials were found scattered throughout the excavation area, usually under the floors or surfaces of courtyards. In some cases, infants were found under room floors. The possibility that a formal cemetery exists in the Gilat area cannot be ruled out.

DOG BURIALS. The earliest dog burials in their own individual plots in this country were discovered in stratum IIIb in area T. The two dogs had been carefully placed in a pit (diameter, 1.5 m). One had been disturbed by rodent activity but the other was untouched and in a perfect state of preservation. The dog had been placed on its right side, facing south, with the tail tucked between the legs. Archaeozoological determinations show that it was an old Near Eastern pariah dog who had suffered a broken leg some years before its death. Most surprising was the discovery of a burial offering with the dog: a cylindrical vessel with two handles, shaved like some examples of predynastic Egyptian pottery. The dog burial is remarkable in light of the discovery of only one human burial at Gilat with an offering. There can be no doubt that these dogs were carefully interned in a symbolic context. Dog burials from later periods (at Ashkelon, for example) have shown that dogs were associated with ancient Near Eastern healing cults. Thus, the Gilat dog burials may be one of the earliest indications of a cult involving dogs in Israel.

RADIOCARBON DATING. Only two radiocarbon determinations have been made for Gilat: RT-860A stratum III, 5440 ± 180 BP (4470–4040 BCE calibrated); and RT-860B stratum II, 4800 ± 135 BP (3774–3753 BCE calibrated). These dates indicate that Gilat and the Beersheba Valley sites were contemporaneously occupied. However, the dates are of little value for clarifying the development of Gilat because of their large standard deviations.

SUMMARY

Studies of the large numbers of cult-related artifacts and architectural features indicate Gilat's importance as a regional Chalcolithic cult center in the northern Negev. Based on the material remains, a number of cult-related activities have been identified that focus on ensuring the fertility of the herd (the assemblage from room A); the use of numerous violin-shaped figurines in worship; the association of dogs with cult; and the placement of caches of special objects, such as ostrich eggs, ceramic vessels, and stone palettes in pits around the sanctuary. The herding motifs found at Gilat and its location on the border between two distinct semiarid physiographic zones point to its importance as a gateway community that controlled access to the rich annual grazing land found on the Negev coastal plain.

D. Alon, *'Atiqot* 11 (1976), 116–118; id., *BA* 40 (1977), 63–70; id. (and T. E. Levy), *IEJ* 37 (1987), 283–284; id., *ESI* 7–8 (1988–1989), 63–64; id., *Journal of Mediterranean Archaeology* 2 (1989), 163–221; R. Amiran, *'Atiqot* 11 (1976), 119–120; id., *L'Urbanisation de la Palestine à l'Age du Bronze Ancien* (Actes du Colloque d'Emmaüs, 1986; *BAR*/IS 527, ed. P. de Miroschedji), Oxford 1989, 53–60; Y. Yadin, *'Atiqot* 11 (1976), 121; D. Frankel, *IEJ* 27 (1977), 38–39; D. Saltz, *ASOR Newsletter* (May 1977), 11–12; I. Mozel, *TA* 6 (1979), 26–27; T. E. Levy, *BA* 49 (1986), 82–108; id. and A. Holl, *La Recherche* 19/203 (1988), 1166–1174; M. Tadmor, *Israel Museum Journal* 5 (1986), 7–12; I. Gilead and Y. Goren, *BASOR* 275 (1989), 5–14.

THOMAS E. LEVY, DAVID ALON

GILGAL

IDENTIFICATION

A number of prehistoric sites were discovered south of Naḥal Peẓa'el (map reference 1933.1547) in the Jordan Valley, on a hilly ridge, about 225 m below sea level, that divides the Salibiya basin from the Jordan Valley. The sites were designated Gilgal I, II, and VI. Gilgal III, IV, and V are situated in the nearby Salibiya basin, at 230 to 240 m below sea level. Only Gilgal I was systematically excavated; trial soundings were carried out at the other sites. The excavation was directed by T. Noy, on behalf of the Israel Museum, and the staff officer for archaeology in Judea and Samaria. The sites Gilgal I, III, and IV date from the Pre-Pottery Neolithic A period; the other sites are Late Natufian.

GILGAL I. This Pre-Pottery Neolithic A site, extending over an area of about 1 acre on the ridge, is covered with pebbles accumulated on the shores of the Lisan lake, and on its west slopes. Two major phases of occupation were identified. The soil in the upper phase is light colored, while in the lower phase it is gray. So far, thirteen structures (3 to 6 m in diameter) were uncovered; they had field-stone walls covered with mud and clay and floors of light-colored, well-stamped soil. In the lowest structure thus far exposed, the light-colored floor was laid on a bed of closely packed gravel. Inside the structures concentrations of ash were exposed, as well as cup marks hewn into flat stones, grinding stones, and many tools, including well-polished axes of limestone and imported basalt. The flint assemblage consists mainly of long sickle blades, knives, small el-Khiam arrowheads and closely related types, borers, and awls. Very few flint axes, bone tools, and jewelry items were found.

Structure 11 (similar in shape to the other structures) was fully preserved and probably served as a silo. Very large quantities of barley and oat grains were found in the structure, as well as a few acorns and some terebinth seeds. Close to the area where the cereals were found, some flint, basalt, and bone tools were also recovered. Three clay human figurines and a limestone bird figurine were found next to the wall of the structure. There may be some association between these ritual objects and the grain silo. A human figurine found on the floor of another structure bears incisions suggesting a skirt made of cord. A wicker-basket imprint found on an asphalt surface in the silo is probably the earliest basketry work known thus far. A carbon-14 analysis of grain samples gave a date of from 8100 ± 150 to 7710 ± 70 BCE. These are some of the earliest known dates for the Pre-Pottery Neolithic A period in Israel.

The finds indicate that the livelihood of the inhabitants of Gilgal was based on gathering wild cereals (perhaps also some domesticated cereals), acorns, and terebinth seeds, as well as on catching crabs and turtles and hunting birds. Gazelle bones were very rare. The cereals, which were gathered in spring, and the acorns, in autumn, suggest that the site was occupied in at least two seasons and perhaps even throughout the year.

GILGAL III–IV. Sites III and IV also belong to the Pre-Pottery Neolithic A period and may either be contemporary with Gilgal I or earlier.

GILGAL II. In Gilgal II, which borders Gilgal I on the north, cylindrical mortars (about 70 cm long) are visible in the sections. The flint tools found here indicate a later stage of the Natufian culture. A stone statue of a human figure, 30 cm high, was found on the site's west slope. However, its style indicates that it belongs to the Neolithic and not the Natufian culture.

Stone human figurine, Neolithic period.

(Left) *Gilgal I: grinding stone in situ in one of the oval buildings, PPNA period.*

T. Noy (et al.), *IEJ* 26 (1976), 48; 30 (1980), 63–82; id., *Paléorient* 5 (1979), 233–238; 15/1 (1989), 11–18; id., *Israel Museum Journal* 4 (1985), 13–16; 7 (1988), 113–114; id., *ESI* 5 (1986), 41; 6 (1987–1988), 55–56; 7–8 (1988–1989), 64–66; id., *Mitekufat Ha'even* 20 (1987), 158*–159*; B. Z. Begin, *Geological Survey of Israel Bulletin* 65 (1975), 1–35; *Israel Museum News* 14 (1978), 20; O. Bar Yosef (et al.), *Paléorient* 6 (1980), 201–206; 15/1 (1989), 57–63; J. Schuldenrein and P. Goldberg, ibid. 7 (1981), 57–71; Weippert 1988, 101, 104f.

TAMAR NOY

(Above) *Gilgal I: fragment of a clay human figurine, PPNA period.*

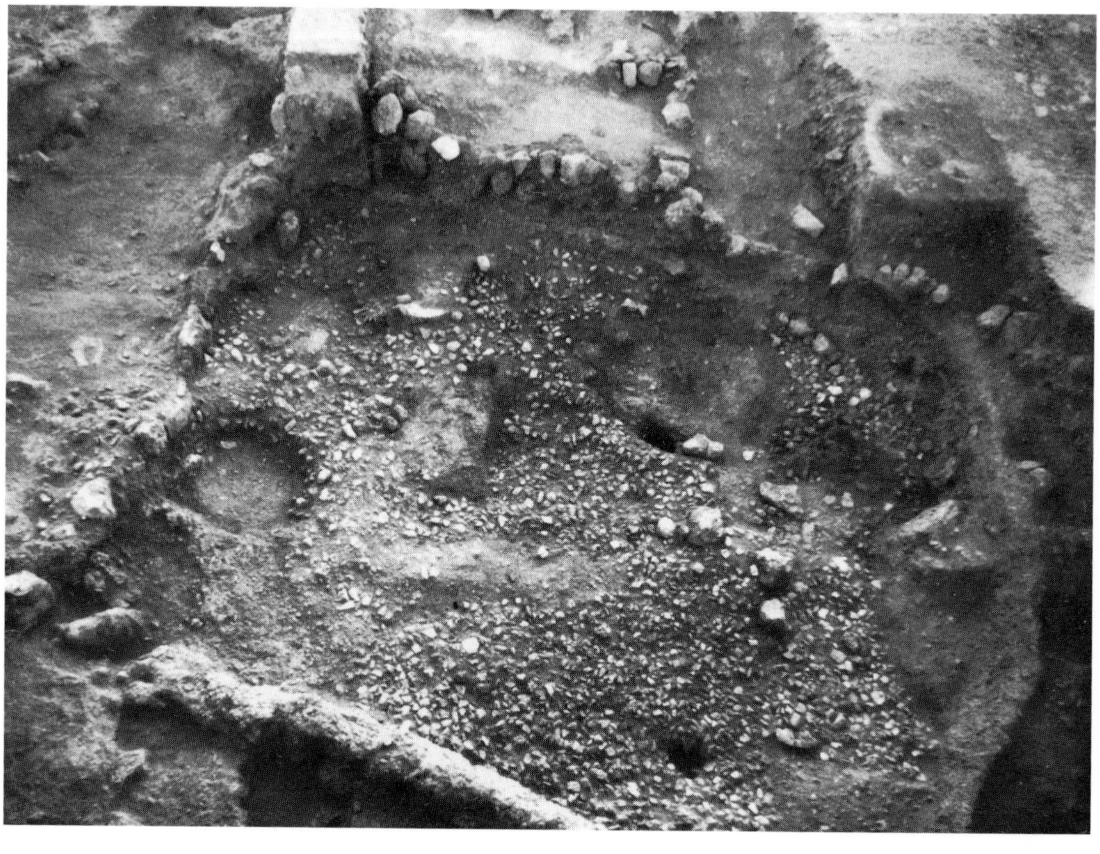

(Right) *Gilgal I: silo, PPNA period.*

GILOH

IDENTIFICATION AND EXPLORATION

The site called Giloh is located in the neighborhood of Giloh on a ridge southwest of Jerusalem, between the Valley of Rephaim to the north and the town of Beit Jala to the south. From it there is an extensive view of Jerusalem, the Judean Hills, and the Judean Desert. It is situated in barren terrain, with no local water sources. A regional survey, carried out by M. Kochavi in 1968, identified occupation levels dating to the Iron Age I and II at the site. Salvage excavations were carried out between 1978 and 1982, directed by A. Mazar, under the auspices of the Israel Department of Antiquities and Museums and the Institute of Archaeology at the Hebrew University of Jerusalem.

The site may be identified with Baal-Perazim, mentioned in the account of David's struggle against the Philistines in the Valley of Rephaim (2 Sam. 5:20). This was probably the name of one of the summits in the vicinity of this valley. The hill on which the site of Giloh is situated is near the Rephaim Valley and is so far the only summit in this area where Iron Age I remains have been found. Its fortified Iron Age II tower reinforces the possibility that this is the Mount Perazim mentioned in Isaiah 28:21; the place name (without the Baal component) may have been preserved from the settlement period. It is possible that the name Perazim is related to the Perez family, one of the most prominent in Judah (related to King David), who settled in the vicinity of Bethlehem.

EXCAVATION RESULTS

IRON AGE I. A single-phase settlement from the Iron Age I covers approximately 2 a. The southern sector was surrounded by a stone defensive wall, about 1 m wide, irregularly built of large stones. Parts of the wall are built of only one row of stones and other parts are constructed of two rows. Inside this defensive wall, remains of dwellings were found. In the center of the settlement a complete dwelling unit was excavated, including a house and a large open area that was probably used as an animal pen. The stone walls of this open area were crudely built, and its floor was bedrock. The dwelling, which was entered through the open area, included a square inner courtyard, divided by a row of three hewn stone pillars. One of the pillars is square; the other two, which had fallen, were made of long, unworked blocks quarried from nearby rocks. There was a rectangular room on the northern side of the courtyard and another room on the west.

This house can be regarded as an early attempt to construct a "four-room house," although this is not the fully developed type which appears later in the Iron Age I. Its western and southern walls were solidly built of large stones, but its other two walls were poorly constructed. It appears that the two solid walls were part of a system of main walls that divided the site into several secondary units; the flimsier walls were built as additions to these main walls. This may represent the division of the settlement into several extended family units, each with its own sheep pen and adjacent dwelling. These households may have been organized within a patriarchal framework, making their living from pastoralism rather than cultivation, which would have been extremely difficult on such barren, waterless terrain.

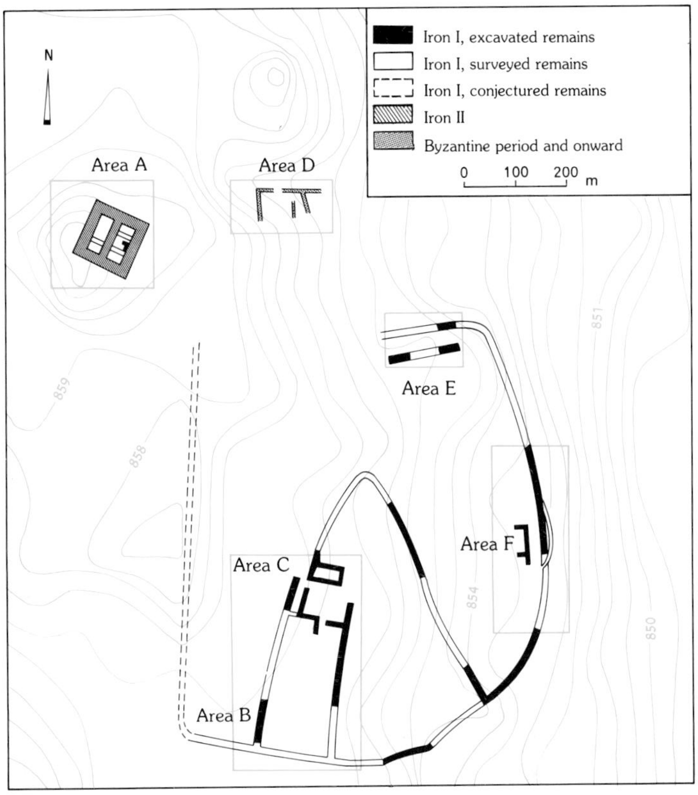

Giloh: plan of the site.

Watchtower, Iron II.

At the northern part of the site, where it overlooks the Valley of Rephaim and Jerusalem, the foundations of a square tower (11.24 by 11.58 m) were found. The structure is skillfully constructed of large, roughly worked stones; its inner part was filled with rubble. The tower is preserved to a height of one to four courses above bedrock. The pottery sherds found in the structure and on a floor abutting it to the west are identical to those found in the Iron Age I houses in the southern part of the site. A typical Canaanite bronze dagger blade was also found on this floor. The size and shape of the tower indicate advanced planning and building techniques, as well as the highly developed social organization required to erect such a formidable structure. The tower and the defensive wall surrounding the southern part of the settlement emphasize the inhabitants' need and ability to invest effort in constructing fortifications. This need, which is not apparent at most of the other contemporary sites, probably arose from Giloh's proximity to Jebusite Jerusalem.

The ceramic finds from this settlement phase were meager, consisting of a small assemblage of mostly collared-rim pithoi, storage jars, and cooking pots. These vessels are characteristic of the first stage of the Iron Age I (first half of the twelfth century BCE), when the Canaanite ceramic tradition still dominated. Different rim shapes on the collared-rim jars appear to have existed simultaneously and thus should not be used as a chronological peg, as once suggested. The nature of the ceramic assemblage, especially the small amount of vessel types represented, is characteristic of settlement sites in the hill country and can be interpreted as typical of the Israelite settlement in this region. (An opposing view, proposed by G. Ahlström, is that the settlement at Giloh was an outlying satellite village of Jebusite Jerusalem.) The site at Giloh is one of the earliest of these single-occupation sites, with no discernible building repairs or floor raisings. The site was abandoned during the Iron Age I, probably in the twelfth century BCE. This may have been the result of its location—in a barren, waterless region, that did not allow further development.

IRON AGE II. A watchtower was constructed in the Iron Age II on the highest point on the site. The square tower (11.15 by 11.15 m) was built of stones more than 1 m wide. Only its stone foundations were preserved, with four outer walls and one inner partition wall running through its center. The foundation is preserved to about 1 m above bedrock; foundations for an external flight of stairs were found on the tower's northern side. It appears that the tower was a lookout post guarding the southwestern approach to Jerusalem. A view of the Judean Hills, the Hebron Hills, and the Ramat Raḥel ridge is visible from the site. It is possible that the tower was used, among other things, to relay torch signals from points far from Jerusalem to the capital city. A similar, though larger, tower was excavated by the Department of Antiquities and Museums on French Hill, in northern Jerusalem, that may have had a similar function. The few potsherds found in and around the tower at Giloh date it to the eighth to seventh centuries BCE.

THE MIDDLE AGES. Evidence of occupation in the Middle Ages was found in the area of the Iron Age II tower. Stones from its walls were reused to construct a paved platform that may also have had a military function. Additional stones were later taken from both Iron Age towers to prepare the lime for a limekiln dug into the northern part of the site.

A. Mazar, *IEJ* 31 (1981), 1–36; 40 (1990), 77–101; id., *BA* 45 (1982), 167–178; G. W. Ahlström, *IEJ* 34 (1984), 170–172.

AMIHAI MAZAR

GINNOSAR

EXCAVATIONS

An ancient boat was discovered in the Sea of Galilee in January 1986 by M. and Y. Lufan, south of Kibbutz Ginnosar on the lake's western shore. Its discovery was made after a drought had exposed large areas of the lake's bottom. The boat was found lying perpendicular to the shore, with the bow facing east, toward the lake. Because it was listing to port, that side is better preserved.

The boat was excavated in February 1986 by S. Wachsmann, K. Raveh, and O. Cohen, on behalf of the Israel Department of Antiquities and Museums. Innovative techniques were devised by Cohen, the team conservationist, that enabled moving the hull, intact, to its conservation site at the Yigal Allon Museum at Kibbutz Ginnosar, 500 m from the discovery site. The boat is presently submerged in water in a specially built pool.

J. R. Steffy of the Institute of Nautical Archaeology, Texas A&M University, studied the boat's construction during the excavation. The boat is 8.2 m long, 2.3 m wide, and 1.2 m deep at the stern. It was built "shell first," with mortise-and-tenon joinery. It has a rounded stern and a fine bow. Both the fore and aft sections were probably decked in, although the boat was not preserved to this height.

The boat was apparently built by a master craftsman who probably learned his craft in the Mediterranean or had been apprenticed to someone who had. However, he used timber that was far inferior to what was used on Mediterranean vessels. Many of the timbers in the boat, including the forward portion of the keel, were apparently in secondary use, having been removed from older boats.

The boat must have had a long work life, for it had been repeatedly repaired. It ended its life on the scrap heap. Its usable timbers—including the mast step, stempost, and the sternpost—were removed; the remaining hull, old and now useless, was then pushed out into the lake, where it sank into the silt.

Forty-two samples of wood were submitted to E. Werker in the Department of Botany at the Hebrew University of Jerusalem. Her study indicates that the boat is built mainly of cedar strakes and oak frames, although single samples of Aleppo pine, hawthorn, willow, and redbud were represented. Based on pottery found in conjunction with the boat, Steffy's tentative dating of the construction techniques, and carbon-14 tests, the proposed date range for the boat is from 100 BCE to 70 CE.

Evidence from Josephus, the Gospels, and a first-century CE mosaic of a boat from the nearby site of Migdal (Tarichaeae) indicates that a type of large-size craft existed on the Sea of Galilee in the first century CE. This class of boat normally had a crew of five and could carry at least fifteen men inclusive of crew. It was used for fishing with a seine net but could also be used for transporting passengers and supplies. The boat uncovered near Ginnosar belongs to this class.

Slightly to the north of the immediate excavation site, remains of two other boats and various loose pieces of wood were found. These wooden remains suggest, in Steffy's opinion, that the site was an area of boat-building activities.

Ginnosar: the boat in its conservation pool.

Main publication: S. Wachsmann et al., *The Excavations of an Ancient Boat in the Sea of Galilee (Lake Kinneret)* ('Atiqot 19), Jerusalem, 1990.

Other studies: S. Wachsmann (and K. Raveh), *Israel al* 15 (1986), 6–11; id., *BAIAS* 6 (1986–1987), 50–52; id. (et al.), *ESI* 5 (1986) 42–44; id., *History from the Sea* (ed. P. Throckmorton), London 1987, 81–83; id. (et al.), *IJNA* 16 (1987), 233–245; id., *Mariner's Mirror* 73 (1987), 375–376; id., *BAR* 14/5 (1988), 18–33; id. (et al.), *The Excavations* (Review), *IJNA* 20 (1991), 181–182; O. Cohen, *BAIAS* 6 (1986–1987), 34–45; D. Manor, *Eretz Magazine* 2 (1987), 58–67; J. R. Steffy, *IJNA* 16 (1987), 325–329; D. Brown, *CNI* 28 (1988), 25–27; *Archaeology* 42 (1989), 18; G. R. Stone, *Buried History* 25 (1989), 45–54; C. Peachey, *BA* 53 (1990), 46–53.

SHELLEY WACHSMANN, KURT RAVEH

GIV'ATAYIM

IDENTIFICATION

The city of Giv'atayim is situated in a range of *kurkar* hills that rise 79 m above sea level. The top of the hill overlooks all of the Ono Valley and the Shephelah toward Gezer in the south and the Aphek area in the northeast. At the top of the ridge, burial caves from the Chalcolithic period have been found.

EXCAVATIONS

The site was first excavated by V. Sussman and S. Ben-Arieh on behalf of the Israel Department of Antiquities and Museums. The excavations uncovered thirteen damaged Chalcolithic burial caves, and one dating to the Early Bronze Age I. In 1964 and 1965, H. and J. Kaplan excavated four burial caves on behalf of the Giv'atayim municipality. In cave 1 (diameter, 3 m), the

Ḥammat Gader: the Hall of Inscriptions.

Ḥammat Gader: the Oval Hall.

walls and ceiling had collapsed and on the floor, fragments of clay ossuaries, offering vessels, and human bones were found. Among the finds was a pottery figurine of a donkey carrying two sacks. In the debris above the Chalcolithic finds were remains from the Early Bronze Age I.

Cave 2 (c. 7.5 by 5.5 m) was for the most part preserved, together with its ceiling. The cave was entered on the east side by means of steps hewn into the rock. Near the bottom step, to its left, a column was cut into the rock to support the roof. The cave had three levels of different-colored earth and contained human burials and offering vessels. In the top level (I) were human skeletons, each one marked by stones placed around it. In level II, burials of ash and charred bones were found, the bodies having been cremated and only then interred. The bottom level (III) belonged to the Chalcolithic period. Burials in ossuaries and offerings, most of them broken, were found in situ. Near the ossuaries or inside them were human bones. In several places, the ossuaries had been damaged by the burials of level I, which had penetrated the burials of level III. The cave was originally dug in the Chalcolithic period, when the clay ossuaries were placed in it. In the Early Bronze Age I, the cave was again used for burials and the settlers followed the burial practices common in the various phases of this period.

Cave 3 is very similar to cave 2, but larger, with dimensions of about 8 by 8 m. Here, too, a stepped entrance and a column supporting the roof were found. This cave also contained two Early Bronze Age levels but no level with burials in ossuaries. Such remains, however, were found in a pit in the floor to the left of the entrance steps. Several fragments of pottery ossuaries, two complete incense burners, and jugs of the Chalcolithic period were found. The entire floor was covered with ash, charred bones, offering vessels, a large number of carnelian beads, and several ornaments. All over the southern part of the walls and ceiling of the cave were signs of a great fire. These areas were both black with soot and red from the intensity of the fire. Even the carnelian beads had been turned white by the fire. In this cave, the ash and

Giv'atayim: funerary offering vessels, Chalcolithic period.

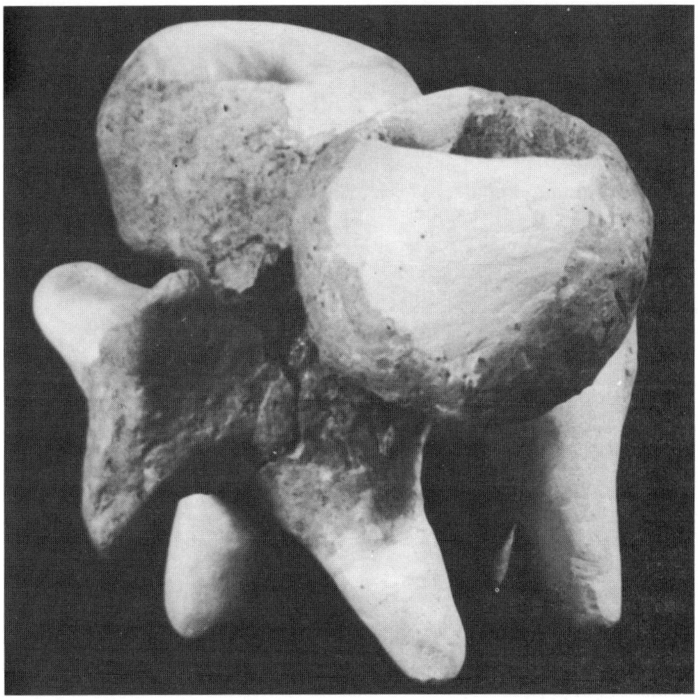

Pottery figurine of a donkey carrying two sacks, from cave 1.

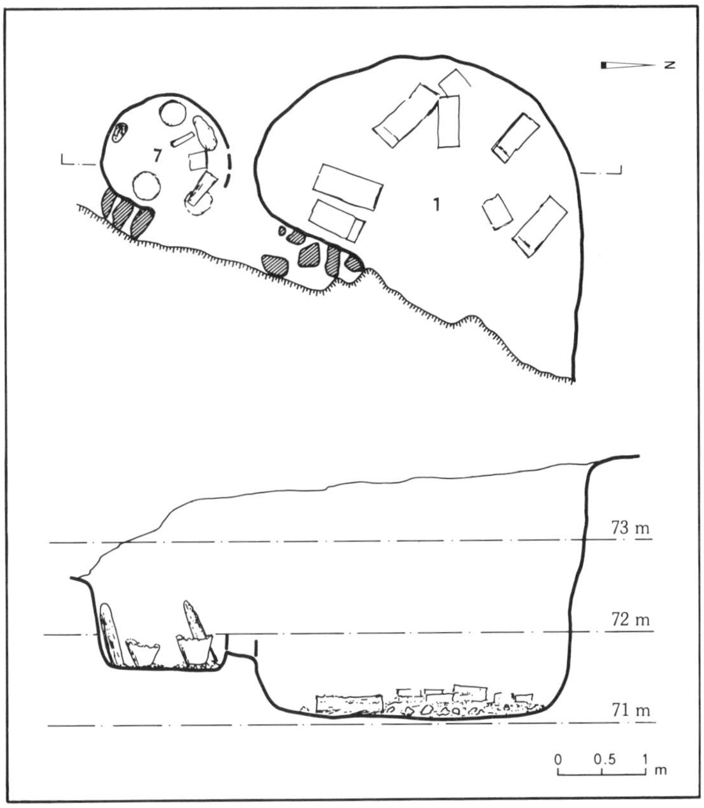

Plan and section of caves 1 and 7.

human bones were found in situ—after they had been burned but before burial. It appears that before the Early Bronze Age IA settlers turned the cave into a crematory, they cleared it of the ossuaries, bones, and offering vessels, and placed them outside it. This crematory cave is similar to the one excavated by R. A. S. Macalister at Gezer.

In plan, cave 4 resembles caves 2 and 3, but it is smaller and not as deep. It also contained a stepped entrance, a column to support the roof, and fragments of ossuaries and offering vessels from the Chalcolithic period. It appears that this cave was not used in the Chalcolithic period, but that the Early Bronze Age I settlers threw the contents of cave 3 into it. In the narrow area between caves 3 and 4, a pillar was found hewn into the *kurkar*; part of the pillar projects above the surface that had been leveled by the Chalcolithic settlers. The pillar served as a mark for the group of graves around it. It may have been this feature that led the people of the Early Bronze Age to rediscover the burial caves, which they found ready-made for their use.

Weippert 1988, 121, 127, 136.

JACOB KAPLAN

GIV'AT ORḤA

IDENTIFICATION

Giv'at Orḥa (Tell Jukhadar) is a volcanic hill in the eastern Golan, about 5 km (3 mi.) southwest of the Rafid junction (map reference 2302.2595). It lies on an important road running from Beth-Shean through the southern Golan, and north to the Bashan region and Damascus. At the foot of the hill is Khan Jukhadar, which dates to the Mameluke-Ottoman period. At its summit sherds were found belonging to the Early Bronze Age, Middle Bronze Age II, and Iron Age I. D. Urman proposed identifying the site with the biblical city of Golan in Deuteronomy 4:43, which is also mentioned in the time of Alexander Jannaeus. This proposal seems doubtful, however, both in geographical terms and due to the absence of Hellenistic finds here.

EXPLORATION

In 1967, the site was surveyed by S. Gutman; buildings roofed with stone slabs, caves with masonry entrances, and rock-cut tombs were found on the southwestern slope of the hill. The site was damaged during the construction of modern defenses. Salvage excavations were carried out at the site in 1968–1969 by D. Urman, on behalf of the staff officer for archaeology in the Golan.

EXCAVATIONS

The excavations were conducted on a flat terrace on the hill's southwestern slope. An area of about 600 sq m was exposed, revealing well-preserved building remains. The excavator distinguished four occupation strata in the buildings:

Stratum	*Period*	*Nature*
I	Mameluke (13th–14th cent.)	Small settlement, related to nearby khan; reuse of Byzantine structures
II	Byzantine and Early Arab (7th–8th cent.)	Partial reuse of earlier structures
III	Byzantine (5th–6th cent.)	Dense settlement
IV	Late Roman (3rd–4th cent.)	Main building period

In Urman's view, stratum IV was destroyed during the Gallus revolt in 351 CE, after which the site was plundered and scores of bronze coins from the first half of the fourth century were dispersed. This writer, on the other hand, is of the opinion that the fourth-century destruction did not necessarily result from the Gallus revolt, but from the earthquake that struck the Golan in 363. The end of stratum III in the eighth century may correlate with the transfer of the Arab caliphate capital to Baghdad in the Abbasid dynasty. In addition to the four strata mentioned above, the ceramic finds indicate a possible fifth stratum from the first century, although no structural remains from this period have as yet been found.

BUILDINGS. Numerous rooms, whose plan is obscure, were found in the northern part of the excavations. By contrast, the southern part of the excavated area yielded two buildings with a common wall that were surrounded by streets on the east, south, and west. The walls (c. 0.7–0.9 m thick), were founded on bedrock and built of well-dressed basalt stones, laid without mortar. The outer doorways faced the courtyards or streets and were built of ashlars. Rectangular niches found in many of the walls were used as closets. All the buildings at Giv'at Orḥa included "window walls" (q.v. Chorazin and Golan, Byzantine period); these windows, which were set about 70 cm above the floor, had jambs built of upright basalt slabs, 60 to 70 cm high. Window walls are a very common feature in the building style characteristic of the Hauran, Bashan, and Golan regions, and examples can be seen in almost every house. The windows were generally designed to provide light and ventilation in the parts of the building farthest from the entrances, but they may also have been used as feeding troughs for animals or as tombs. No troughs have been found so far at Giv'at Orḥa. One window wall built of ashlars was discovered.

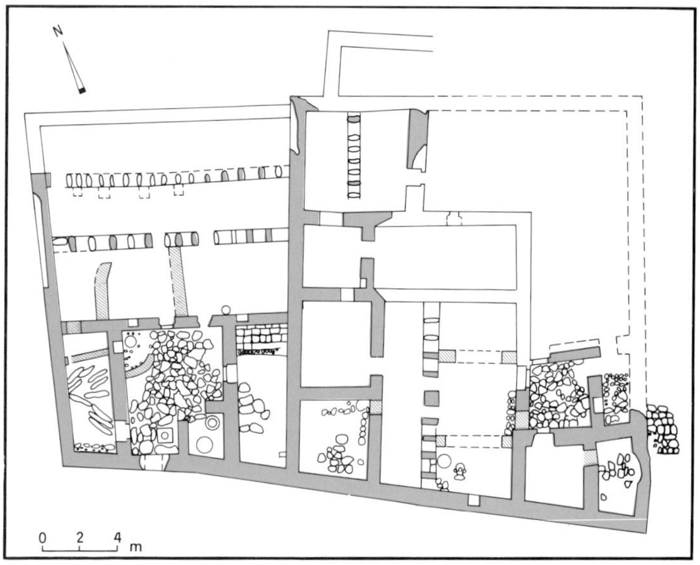

Plan of the buildings in the southern part of the excavated area.

The predominant feature in the plan of the buildings is their narrow rooms (only 2–3.5 m wide). This feature, together with in situ corbels projecting from the walls, and the narrow basalt beams found in the debris of several rooms, indicate that the roofing was mostly stone, another technique characteristic of the region.

Giv'at Orḥa: overview of the Roman-Byzantine buildings.

Buildings from the Roman-Byzantine period (detail).

Two dwellings were uncovered in the southern part of the excavations: **Western House.** This house (13 by 18.5 m) was apparently a single dwelling unit. Its entrance, which has not survived, was in the southern wall and opened onto a paved courtyard. The courtyard contained crude partition walls, *tabuns*, (clay ovens), and several basalt installations. It appears that the pavement and installations came from stratum I. The courtyard had several doors leading to narrow rooms to the west and east. In the debris of the western room (2.2 by 6.1 m) stone slabs from the ceiling were found. A shelf abutting the southern wall, with a plastered drainage channel underneath it, was also uncovered here. The room east of the courtyard measured 2.6 by 7.1 m. At its northern edge was a raised podium paved with clay rooftiles, in secondary use, inscribed with Greek letters and crosses. North of the room were three narrow halls, one behind the other, that extended along the entire width of the building. The halls had two entrances and were separated from each other by window walls. The halls were apparently used as a storehouse or as a pen for animals.

Eastern House. The northeastern part of the eastern building was destroyed, so that its dimensions (18.5 by 20.9 m) are only conjectural and its plan unclear. It seems that the building included two or three apartments, surrounding two or more courtyards. The southern apartment contained a small square courtyard (3.3 by 3.3 m) whose entrance has not survived. In a corner of the courtyard was a round stepped structure that may have provided access to the roof. The steps and pavement are apparently an addition from stratum I. Several rooms were arranged around the courtyard. The main part of the dwelling unit, whose two entrances were built of ashlars, is situated west of the courtyard. The front room (4 by 9.8 m) was the living chamber, where daily activities took place. It contained such installations as millstones, moved by a donkey, various shelves, and a round installation. Two arches resting on engaged pilasters to help support the ceiling were added to the room in stratum I, or perhaps earlier. The front chamber was separated from the middle one (2.1 by 9.3 m) by a window wall, in the center of which two entrances flanked a square pillar. The middle chamber apparently held a sleeping loft. In the rear of the house were two other rooms, one of which had an entrance to the adjacent apartment. The plan of the apartment closely resembles that of house 300 at Ḥorvat Kanaf and appears to have been one of the most common plans used in residential buildings in the Golan and Bashan regions. Three rooms, apparently built around an as yet unexcavated courtyard, were uncovered in the northern part of the building; they also contained a window wall.

Finds. An abundance of finds, generally from strata III–I and in a mixture thereof, was recovered in all the rooms. It was possible to isolate ceramic assemblages from stratum IV in only a few places. The potsherds from stratum V (first century) found in the fills included a predominance of imported red-slipped ware, as well as several fragments of "revolt lamps" (Herodian lamps), characteristic of first-century sites in Judea. The sherds from stratum IV (third–fifth centuries) include mainly Galilean bowls, cooking pots, and storage jars. Sherds of Iturean manufacture (q.v. Golan), typical of the northern Golan, are noteworthy; this type of pottery would have reached Giv'at Orḥa through its commercial ties. The pottery assemblage from stratum III included storage jars, cooking pots, casseroles, and lids characteristic of the fifth and sixth centuries. Red-slipped ware imported from North Africa and Cyprus also appears in these repertoires. Stratum II is characterized by storage jars made of dark clay, ribbed and decorated with painted white stripes ("Beth-Shean jars"). Red-on-beige painted storage jars made of yellowish clay (typical of the Umayyad period) were also found. The end of the period is marked by numerous sherds of Khirbet el-Mafjar ware (probably from the beginning of the Abbasid period). Stratum I contained large quantities of glazed pottery, as well as coarse local ware decorated in red and brown on a beige background. The small finds include an abundance of fragments of glass juglets, cups, a ring, and glass bracelets, as well as bronze objects and numerous basalt vessels. One of the rooms contained a tombstone, in secondary use, carved with a Greek inscription: "Have courage Antonia, twenty-seven years of age." More than one hundred bronze coins, mainly from the first half of the fourth century, were also recovered.

SUMMARY

The settlement at Giv'at Orḥa had its beginnings in the Early Bronze Age, on the summit of the volcanic hill, and continued into the Middle Bronze Age II and Iron Age I; no structures from these periods have as yet been excavated. The gap in finds indicates a break in settlement in the Persian and Hellenistic periods. Settlement was resumed only in the first, and particularly in the third, centuries CE; at that time the village was mainly built on the southwestern slope, near the road. Numerous buildings are preserved from the Roman-Byzantine period; they were constructed in the contemporary style characteristic of the Hauran and Bashan regions. The scope of settlement at Giv'at Orḥa is shown in its continued occupation in the Umayyad and Early Abbasid periods—similar to that at Fiq, El-'Al, and Qaṣrin—while the majority of Golan sites at the time were already abandoned. Settlement was once again resumed here in the Mameluke period, making use of the ancient structures—still another phenomenon typical of the Golan.

D. Urman, *The Golan: A Profile of a Region during the Roman and Byzantine Periods* (*BAR*/IS 269), Oxford 1985, 22 198.

ZVI URI MA'OZ

GIV'IT, ḤORVAT

IDENTIFICATION

Ḥorvat Giv'it (in Arabic, Khirbet Jib'it) is in the desert fringe region of Samaria, 1 km (0.6 mi.) south of Ma'ale Ephraim (map reference 1845.1598). The original name of the settlement was most likely Giv'it or something close to it, derived from the common root *gb'*. The site may be related to the "wilderness of Gibeon," mentioned in 2 Samuel 2:24. A Samaritan source from the Middle Ages identifies this location with biblical Gibeon. Its extensive ruins were surveyed from 1980 to 1982 by Z. Ilan, assisted by A. Izdarechet. Following the looting of the site's artifacts, excavations were conducted in 1982 under the auspices of the staff officer for archaeology in Judea and Samaria, directed by Z. Ilan and A. Dinur.

SURVEY AND EXCAVATION RESULTS

Ḥorvat Giv'it is spread over three hills that lie next to the ancient road linking the Jordan Rift Valley with the Shiloh Valley. The central hill was the site occupied by the settlement and its houses, while the hills to the west and east were covered with installations—cisterns, winepresses, graves, and a quarry. Sherds from the Early Bronze Age II, Middle Bronze Age I and IIB, Iron Age I and II, and Persian, Hellenistic-Roman, Byzantine, Early Arab, Mameluke, and Ottoman periods were found among the ruins. During the Iron Age the settlement extended over some 12.5 a.; it was thus among the largest settlements in the hills of Ephraim, and comparable in size to the settlement that occupied Khirbet Marjameh to the south. Evidently, the inhabitants made their living from cereal crops, orchards, and livestock. The Iron Age II sherds date to the sixth century BCE and belong to the Judean ceramic type, like those discovered at Khirbet Shilha to the north of Wadi Qelt. This may be evidence of the expansion of the kingdom of Judah deep into Samaria at the time of King Josiah (2 Kg. 23:8; Zech. 14:10). On the northern slope of the settlement's hill, the remains of a typical Iron Age winepress were found. The settlement was surrounded by an ashlar-built wall with a number of towers. These fortifications may have been erected in the Hasmonean period and as such may have been related to the Hasmonean fortress of Sartaba-Alexandrium, which can be seen from Giv'it. Among the remains that survived the recent looting are three fragments of "measuring cups" made of soft limestone. Cups of this type were used in the late Second Temple period.

The houses follow a uniform plan: each residential unit included a building with a cellar and an adjoining courtyard, usually with a cistern. Two residential quarters could be distinguished: one at the summit of the hill and along its eastern slope, and the other on the northern slope. An oil press, constructed of ashlars bearing unusually large brackets, was found in the summit area.

A number of subterranean chambers were surveyed in and around the settlement. One of them, to the east of the settlement hill, measures 29 by 26 m. An enormous underground cavity was found in the northern part of the settlement, as well as a subterranean network comprising several chambers—one of them particularly large—connected by rock-cut tunnels. In all likelihood, these were underground refuge systems that in peacetime were storage facilities and workshops.

THE CHURCH. In the course of the survey, a public building was uncovered at the western edge of the settlement. Once this structure was excavated, it became clear that it was a church. It was constructed on an east–west axis within a precinct surrounded by a wall built of large ashlars. Some of the ashlars bore marginal drafting. The surrounding precinct had openings facing east and west. This was a relatively small church, whose nave

Ancient road near Ḥorvat Giv'it.

Ḥorvat Giv'it: south wall of the church.

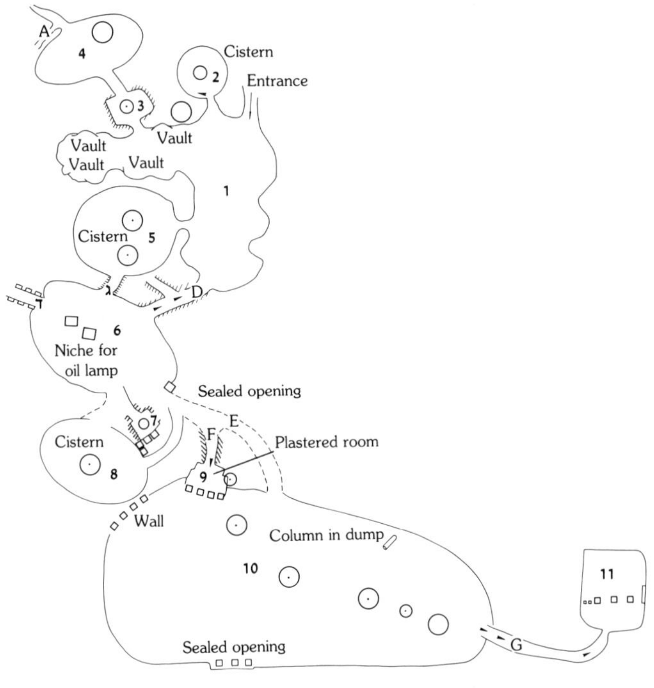

Ḥorvat Giv'it: plan of the underground refuge system.

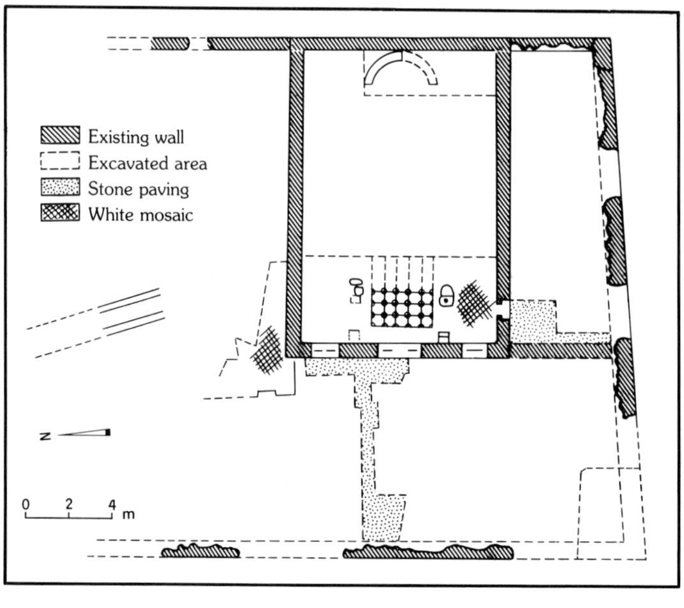

Plan of the church.

measured 10.5 by 14.7 m. It followed the typical basilican plan—two rows of columns and a single apse at the eastern end. Three openings were revealed at the western end, as well as a postern in the southern wall of the southern aisle. The church had a mosaic floor, most of which was destroyed in antiquity. Remains of this floor can be seen in the southern aisle and in an auxiliary room north of the church. The mosaic in the auxiliary room was made of white, medium-sized tesserae. In the segment of the floor uncovered in the southern part of the nave, the mosaic is in red, black, and white tesserae. The architectural details include a stone bearing a cross in relief, a carved capital, and ashlars whose upper portions are gable shaped (and whose function is unclear).

The excavations revealed that the north wall of the church precinct was erected on top of a wall consisting of ashlars with marginal drafting, and that this wall was aligned differently from the walls of the church. Apparently, this was the wall of some earlier structure, perhaps a public building, from the Herodian or Hasmonean period, and the builders of the church simply made use of some of its stones. The church was in existence from the sixth to eighth centuries CE. In the Mameluke period its stones were reused in the walls of rooms, some of which were built along the lines of the earlier walls.

ZVI ILAN

GOLAN

GEOGRAPHICAL BACKGROUND

The term Golan applies to the part of Transjordan that extends from the Yarmuk River northward to Mount Hermon and is bordered on the west by the Jordan Rift Valley and on the east by Naḥal Raqqad. The area of the Golan under Israeli rule is approximately 1,200 sq km. It drops from an altitude of 900 m above sea level in the northeast, to 250 m above sea level in the southwest. On the western reaches of the Golan, the ground falls steeply to the Sea of Galilee and the Ḥula Basin, sloping down more gently to the Jordan and the Bethsaida (Buteiḥa) valleys. A characteristic feature of the eastern Golan is volcanic cones of tuff; the volcanic cones in the south, however, have been eroded to low hills. The streams crisscrossing the basalt plateau of the Golan (known locally as *masils*) are shallow and have left little impression on the landscape; upon reaching the Rift Valley, however, they fall steeply in waterfalls into deep canyons. The rivers in the southern Golan, which drain into the Sea of Galilee and the Yarmuk, flow in wide basins.

The basalt covering most of the surface of the Golan—the "Bashan Group"—was created in volcanic eruptions that began 3.7 million years ago and continued until recent millennia. In the northeastern Golan the basalt cover is relatively young ("Golan formation"), and a layer of brown and red Mediterranean soils has developed on it. In the northwest, center, and south of the Golan, however, older formations, known as "cover basalt" and "Ortal formation," have been exposed, supporting a layer of heavy grumusols. Of particular interest is the "Dalweh member" of the Ortal formation, which erodes in large boulders—the raw material of megalithic construction in the Golan. Exposed on the slopes and in the wadis of the southern Golan are certain sedimentary rocks older than the basalt, mainly chalk and chalky limestone from the Upper Eocene, Oligocene, and Miocene, topped by colluvial, alluvial, and rendzina soils. The Golan has a Mediterranean climate, with annual precipitation varying from 350 mm in the south to 1,200 mm in the north. In antiquity the Golan was covered with Mediterranean forest vegetation, which can still be seen in a few nature reserves. In the northern Golan there are forests of two local species of oak (*Quercus calliprinos* and *Quercus boissieri*), and in the central Golan a park-forest of *Quercus ithaburensis*, rich in herbaceous vegetation; the typical vegetation of the south Golan rivers and the escarpments falling to the Sea of Galilee is a savannah of *Ziziphus spina-christi*.

The human geography of the Golan cannot be understood without considering its road network. Its main highways cross it from east to west, linking the Damascus region to the Mediterranean coast: the northernmost of these roads runs from Damascus to the Litani River by way of Banias; a central route connects Damascus to Acco (Acre) through Quneiṭra and the Benot Ya'aqov Bridge; the southern road links Damascus to Beth-Shean via Rafid, Afiq, and Ẓemaḥ. Minor east–west roads connect the Galilee to the central and southern Golan, where they turn to the Bashan; these roads ran along wadis and low ridges, such as the Roman road to Sussita and the roads from the Bethsaida Valley to the Lawiyye spur and Khushniyye. The north–south roads in the Golan are all local and confined to its eastern plains, as the terrain of the western sector is cut by deep ravines.

As far as settlement patterns, cultural territories, and administration are concerned, the Golan can be divided into three districts: the fertile plain of the southern Golan, from the Yarmuk to Naḥal Samakh and Mount Peres; the central Golan, from Naḥal Samakh to Naḥal Shu'aḥ–Kafr Nafākh, south of Quneiṭra, which is rocky terrain with an abundance of *masil*s and springs, mainly suitable for grazing but also for olive growing and some plots with irrigation by flooding; and the northern Golan, from Naḥal Shu'aḥ–Quneiṭra to Naḥal Sa'ar—a once densely forested plateau with numerous volcanoes and few springs.

Each of the three districts can be divided into distinct units, differing in landscape, geology, soils, hydrography, and floral cover. In the south, for example, there is a considerable difference between the basalt plain and the limestone escarpments, while the north and central districts can both be divided into an eastern, high region and a lower and more rugged western part. These units also differ in types of settlement, cultural landscape, and continuity of habitation.

HISTORICAL SOURCES

One of the el-Amarna letters (EA 256), from the fourteenth century BCE, mentions a "land of Gari," which, judging from the content of the letter, was situated in the southern Golan. B. Mazar suggested that Gari was a corruption (Ga-su-ri) of the biblical name Geshur (Jos. 13:11–12). The letter lists seven towns of Gari that were seized from the kingdom of Pella (Peḥal). One of these towns is ^{URU}Ha-iu-ni, identified by W. F. Albright with Khirbet 'Ayūn in the southern Golan; another is ^{URU}He-ni-a-na-bi, identified with 'Ein Nāb, near Nov. The identification of ^{URU}A-du-ri with Khirbet ed-Dūra is dubious, as it is situated far to the north. Another name in the list, ^{URU}A-ra-ra may be identified with Tell 'Ein el-Ḥariri, while the name ^{URU}U-Du-mu may have been preserved in 'Ein Umm el-Adam, at the foot of Kefar Ḥaruv. The name ^{URU}Ma-ag-da-li may be identified with Majduliyā near the spring of 'Ein es-Sufeira; pottery from the relevant period has been found nearby.

In the late group of Execration texts, from the late nineteenth century BCE, mention is made of Ma'akayw (E 62), M'ak'a (E 37), as a geographical and tribal name. Geshur and Maacah are repeatedly referred to in the Bible as enclaves left unoccupied by the Israelites west of the territory of the half-tribe of Manasseh in the district of Argob in the Bashan (Jos. 12:1–6, 13:1–13; Dt. 3:13–14). Geshur was probably in the southern Golan and Maacah in the north. By the tenth century BCE, Geshur and Maacah had become vassal kingdoms, subject to the United Kingdom of Israel. David married Maacah, daughter of Talmai, king of Geshur (2 Sam. 3:3). On the other hand, the king of Maacah, allying himself with Hanun, king of Ammon, made common cause against David with Hadadezer king of Aram-Zobah, Aram-Beth-Rehob, and the kingdom of Tob (2 Sam. 10:6; 1 Chr. 19:7). Geshur and Maacah had probably thrown off the Israelite yoke by the end of Solomon's reign—certainly after the division of the kingdom. At the beginning of the ninth century BCE, Geshur and Maacah seized sixty Israelite cities in the western Argob district of the Bashan (1 Chr. 2:23), including—in B. Mazar's opinion—the refuge city of "Golan in Bashan" (Dt. 4:43; Jos. 21:27; 1 Chr. 6:56), which has been identified with Sakhm el-Jaulan, west of the 'Alan River; according to Mazar, this city became the capital of Geshur and gave its name to the entire region of the Golan. The sixty cities were probably annexed to Geshur and Aram around the time of the expedition of Ben-hadad II, king of Aram-Damascus, to the territory of Naphtali in 886 BCE (1 Kg. 15:23; 2 Chr. 16:4); it was in this expedition that the Israelite city of 'En Gev IV was sacked and rebuilt as an Aramean settlement. Geshur and Maacah seem to have been absorbed into the kingdom of Aram-Damascus somewhere around the mid-ninth century BCE (1 Kg. 20:24), when their existence as independent entities came to an end. Near the city of Aphek, on the road to Damascus, Ben-hadad II of Aram was defeated by Ahab around the year 854 BCE (1 Kg. 20:26–30). Aphek has recently been identified by D. Ben-Ami with Tel Afiq (Soreg), a small mound in the riverbed of Naḥal 'En Gev and its springs, 1 km (0.6 mi.) west of Afiq. Surface exploration of the mound yielded sherds from the Middle Bronze, Late Bronze, and Iron ages. Excavations by M. Kochavi exposed parts of the town's fortifications dating to the ninth–eighth centuries BCE (q.v. Tel Soreg). Aphek was a fortified city in Aram-Damascus on the Israelite border until the time of Jehoash son of Jehoahaz, at the beginning of the eighth century BCE (2 Kg. 13:17). Jehoash and Jeroboam II of Israel took advantage of Aramean weakness in the mid-eighth century BCE to seize extensive territories, right up to Lebo-Hamath and Damascus (2 Kg. 14:25, 28; Am. 6:13–14). The excavations at 'En Gev have confirmed that the region changed hands at this time and was occupied by Israel. However, after Jeroboam II's death, the tables seem to have been turned, and Hazael of Aram retook the Golan, even occupying the Israelite part of Transjordan (2 Kg. 8:32–33). The Assyrian king Tiglath-pileser III's military campaign in 733–732 BCE signaled the destruction of the kingdom of Aram-Damascus, which now became an Assyrian province. The Golan was apparently included at that time in the provinces of Karnaim and Damascus; this was probably also the case later, under the Babylonians and Persians, but nothing is known of the history of the Golan during those periods.

Under the Ptolemies, in the third century BCE, the population of northern Transjordan flourished. Fortresses were erected in the region to protect the kingdom's border, such as at Pella (Peḥal), Abila, and Gadara, which were conquered in 219 BCE by Antiochus III (Polybius, V, 70). According to A. H. M. Jones, it was during the Ptolemaic period that the province of Karnaim—Hellenistic Galaaditis—was divided into four hyparchies: Hauranitis, Batanaea (Bashan), Trachonitis, and Gaulanitis (central Golan) (Josephus, *Antiq.* XV, 4, 396); others, however, believe the division to have taken place in the Roman period, at the earliest. After the Seleucids defeated the Ptolemies at Panion (Banias) in 200 BCE (Polybius, XVI, 18), they took the Golan, too, fortifying its western slopes with the fortresses of Hippos-Sussita, Seleucia—which G. Schumacher identified with Tell Seluqiyye (c. 4 km [2.5 mi.] northeast of Qaṣrin)—and Antiochia, near the Ḥula, which Z. Ma'oz has identified with the fort of 'Ateret, near the Benot Ya'aqov Bridge. During Judas Maccabaeus' war in northern Transjordan (163 BCE), two places are heard of that F. M. Abel identified in the southeastern Golan: Kaspor/Kaspon—that is, Khisfīn—and Alema, which is Kafr el-Ma' (1 Macc. 5:26). Beginning in the Hellenistic period, the Golan was divided into three administrative districts, corresponding to the region's geographical division: the district of Hippos-Sussita in the south and the district of Gaulanitis-Gaulane in the center. In the latter there was no polis, only the two fortified cities of Gamala and Seleucia (Josephus, *Antiq.* XIII, 395). The district of Gaulanitis was further subdivided into Upper and Lower Gaulanitis (Josephus, *War* IV, 3). The northern Golan—the territory of Paneas-Caesarea—was then part of the Iturean kingdom, which later belonged to Syria and Phoenicia. Alexander Jannaeus probably conquered Hippos and its environs in 101 BCE (*Antiq.* 13, 365; *Syncellus* V, 558–559). Around the year 93 BCE, Alexander Jannaeus fought the Nabatean king Aretas near Garada in the Golan (*War* I, 90; *Antiq.* XIII, 375), which Abel (and later Ma'oz) identified in the area of Skūfiyyā (Sqūpiyyā)–Bir esh-Shqūm. In 81 BCE, Jannaeus conquered Golan, Seleucia, "the Gorge of Antiochus," and Gamala, subsequently annexing the district of Gaulanitis to his kingdom (*Antiq.* XIII, 393–394; *War* I, 90–94), and Gamala seems to have become the capital of the Jewish-dominated region in the center of the Golan (Mishnah, *'Arakh.* 9:6).

The Romans Pompey and Gabinius severed Hippos from the Hasmonean kingdom in 63 BCE and incorporated it into the League of the Decapolis (*Antiq.* XIV, 75–76; *War* I, 166). In the years 30, 23, and 20 BCE, Augustus awarded Herod the districts of Hippos, Trachonitis, Hauranitis, Batanaea, and the kingdom of the Iturean Zenodorus, including the territory of Paneas (*Antiq.* XV, 215–217, 343–348, 354). Herod settled five hundred Jewish families from Babylon and three thousand Idumeans (*Antiq.* XVI, 285; XVII, 23–31) in his new territories, and he built a temple at Paneas (*Antiq.* XV, 363). After Herod's death, these territories passed to his son Herod Philip (4 BCE–34 CE), who founded Caesarea Philippi at Banias in about 2 BCE and established his capital there (*Antiq.* XVII, 319; XVIII, 28, 106). He also built Julias-Bethsaida, near the point where the Jordan River flows into the Sea of Galilee (*Antiq.* XVIII, 28). Between 37 and 44 CE, these districts were ruled by Agrippa I (*Antiq.* XVIII, 237), and from 53 to 93 by Agrippa II (*Antiq.* XX, 138; *War* II, 247; III, 56–57). Several places in the southern Golan are mentioned in the list of "forbidden towns" in the territory of Sussita, which probably dates to the time of the Second Temple: 'Einosh ('Awenish), 'En Ḥara (el-Khara el-Aret, near Moshav Ramot), Rambark-Dambar (Breik'ah in Naḥal Meẓar), 'Iyyon (el-'Ayūn), Ya'aruṭ (Khirbet el-'Arāis, south of Jibin), Kefar Ḥaruv (Kafr Ḥārib), Nov (Nāb), Khisfiya (Khisfīn), and Kefar Ẓemaḥ (Tosefta, *Shevi'it* 4:10 and parallels). During the First Revolt against the Romans, Josephus fortified three towns in the Golan (*War* II, 574; *Life* 402): Gamala and Seleucia in the Lower Golan and Sogane in the Upper Golan. Ma'oz identifies Sogane with Tell Khushniyye. Sogane and Seleucia surrendered to Agrippa II at the very beginning of the revolt, but Gamala withstood a protracted siege and fell only after a long and bloody battle with the Roman legions, in the course of which the nine thousand inhabitants of Gamala and the nearby villages died (*War* IV, 1–83). The war against the Romans probably brought about the large-scale destruction of Jewish life in the Golan, the echoes of which can be discerned in the Mishnah, "The Galilee shall be destroyed and the Golan shall be desolate" (*Sot.* 9:16).

Information about the Golan in the Late Roman and Byzantine periods is quite sparse. Contemporary Christian and Jewish sources mention only a few places: Sussita, Paneas (Banias), Kursi, and Zaydan (Bethsaida). The latter, near where the Jordan flows into the Sea of Galilee, was a Jewish settlement mentioned in connection with a few sages (*Kohelet Rab.* 2:8; Mishnah, *Git.* 7:5; *Qid.* 4:14; P.T., *Sheq.*, 6:50a; Tosefta, *A.Z.* 3:7). In the view of S. Klein and Ma'oz, the name Golan-Gablana-Yablona, which appears in fourth-century CE sources, refers to the estate of Rabbi Judah ha-Nasi in the Bashan (*Onom.* 64, 7), probably in the vicinity of Sakhm el-Jaulan, east of the 'Alan River, which was linked by a paved road to Zaydan (see below). Ḥaspin is mentioned in a Syriac-Christian manuscript from the seventh century BCE, and Aphekah is alluded to in the *Onomasticon* (22, 20), and in lists of bishops. A list of cities in Palaestina Secunda, recorded by Georgius of Cyprus, mentions the city of Hippos and the rural region Klima Gaulames, which should be identified in the center of the Golan. In the sixth century, Christian Arabs of the Ghassanid tribe penetrated the Golan and founded several settlements to its east and north. In 634 CE, the Arab army swept through the Golan on its way to Damascus; in 636, Tiberias and the Galilee were taken; and in 637 the decisive battle between the Byzantines and the Arabs took place, near Yaqusa in the southern Golan.

HISTORY OF EXPLORATION

The first archaeological investigation in the Golan took place toward the end of the nineteenth century with the work of L. Oliphant, who surveyed the region from 1879 to 1886 and recorded dozens of ruins. Of particular importance are the synagogues he discovered northeast of the Sea of Galilee, including Kanaf and Umm el-Qanaṭir. G. Schumacher conducted a detailed geographical and archaeological survey of the Golan from 1883 to 1885. His book, *The Jaulan*, which described dozens of sites, accompanied by sketches of the finds, is still considered a cornerstone of Golan exploration. Schumacher reported finds in the Golan until 1914. In 1905, H. Kohl and C. Watzinger excavated and researched the synagogues at ed-Dikkeh and Umm el-Qanaṭir. During the period of French and Syrian rule in the Golan various finds, mainly from the Roman period, were discovered, at Banias, Fiq, Khisfīn, and Skūfiyyā; they are exhibited in the Archeological Museum in Damascus.

Since the Six-Day War in 1967, several archaeological surveys and salvage excavations have been conducted in the Golan. In 1967–1968, S. Gutman and C. Epstein carried out an emergency survey, identifying dozens of sites from the Paleolithic and Chalcolithic periods, Middle Bronze Age, Late Bronze Age, Iron Age, Hellenistic and Roman-Byzantine periods, and Early Arab and Mameluke periods. From 1968 to 1972, D. Urman surveyed abandoned villages, revealing numerous sites from the Roman-Byzantine period, dozens of Greek and Arabic inscriptions, and architectural fragments from churches and synagogues. Since 1973, Epstein has been engaged in a survey of Chalcolithic villages in the central Golan (see below). From 1977 to 1982, Z. Ma'oz conducted a survey of synagogues in the Lower Golan, recording some seventeen buildings and dozens of architectural fragments. Since 1979, C. Dauphin has been surveying villages and settlement patterns from the Byzantine period. In the course of her work she has examined town plans and recorded objects and inscriptions from Na'rān, Kafr Nafākh, Farj, Ramthāniyye, and Mazra'at Quneiṭra. In 1980, Ma'oz surveyed the western slopes of the Golan down to the Sea of Galilee, discovering Hellenistic towers and milestones along a Roman road. From 1979 to 1982, D. Ben-Ami carried out a prehistoric survey of the northern Golan. From 1983 to 1988, M. Hartal conducted a survey in the northern Golan.

Most of the excavations in the Golan have been limited, salvage operations, with only a few expeditions engaging in large-scale archaeological work. From 1968 to 1972, Urman excavated at Qaṣrin; at Ḥorvat Zemel, an Iturean site from the second century BCE; at Tell Jukhadar (Giv'at Orḥa, q.v.); and (with V. Tzaferis) at Kursi (q.v.). From 1972 to 1977, M. Ben-Ari excavated dolmens at Tell el-Bazūk (Har Bazak?) and at 'Uyūn Ḥamūd, at the church at Khisfīn (Ḥaspin, q.v.), at Afiq, and in the synagogues at Qaṣrin and 'En Nashuṭ. In 1971–1972, Epstein excavated dolmens in the Yahudiyye Forest, Deir Srās, Qubbet Qar'a, Batra, Abu Fūle, and Tell el-Bazūk. In 1972, S. Barlev conducted an excavation at Fākhūra, and in 1975 he dug in the church at Khisfīn. In 1974, D. Amir excavated a bathhouse at Banias. In 1974, Gutman excavated an Iturean building at Ḥorvat Namra, and from 1976 to 1988, he was engaged in full-scale excavations at Gamala. From 1973 to 1988, Epstein excavated a number of Chalcolithic villages (see below), also carrying out soundings in the Tannūriyye fort (1975) and at Khirbet Buteiḥa (1976). In 1977–1978, E. Netzer excavated a building west of the Banias spring. Since 1978, Ma'oz has conducted excavations at the Roman fort at Ani'am; in the synagogues at Kanaf (q.v.), 'En Nashuṭ (q.v.), Qaṣrin (q.v.), and Dabiyye (q.v.); in the church at Deir Qeruḥ (q.v.); at a watchtower on the Roman road; in a tomb, a Roman villa, and since 1988, the sanctuary of Pan, in Banias (q.v.). From 1980 to 1982, prehistoric sites were excavated by N. Goren-Inbar at Berekhat Ram and in the Quneiṭra Valley (see below). Since 1985, M. Hartal has been conducting excavations at Ḥorvat Zemel, 'Ein er-Ghazlan, and Bab el-Hawa. Since 1986, M. Kochavi and P. Beck have been excavating several sites in "the land of Geshur" (southern Golan). To date, several sites have been excavated: Tel Hadar (q.v.; Sheikh Khadr), the Leviah Enclosure (q.v.), Tel Afiq (Soreg, q.v.), and Rogem Hiri (q.v.). From 1983 to 1989, A. Killebrew excavated the Byzantine village of Qaṣrin (q.v.). Since 1976, S. Dar has been surveying sites on Mount Hermon (q.v.) and excavating a sacred precinct on Mount Sena'im (q.v.). From 1987 to 1990, R. Erav excavated at Bethsaida (et-Tell). Since 1988, Tzaferis has been excavating the town center at Banias.

General: L. Oliphant, *The Land of Gilead*, London 1880; id., *PEQ* 17 (1885), 82–93; G. Schumacher, *The Jaulan*, London 1888; id., *Across the Jordan*, London 1889, 62–71, 149–152; id., articles in *ZDPV*, passim, especially 40 (1917); M. Neishtat, *Archaeology* (Israel Pocket Library), Jerusalem 1974, 175–179; S. Nemlisch and A. Killebrew, *BAR* 14/6 (1988), 54–64; Weippert 1988 (Ortsregister).

Paleoenvironment: U. Baruch, *The Palynography of a Late Holocene Core from Lake Kinneret*, Jerusalem 1983, 19, fig. 3; id., *Paléorient* 12 (1986), 37–48; W. Van Zeist and S. Bottema, *Palaeoclimates, Palaeoenvironmnets and Human Communities in the Eastern Mediterranean Region in Later Prehistory* (eds. J. L. Bintliff and W. Van Zeist), Oxford 1982, 284; J. L. Bintliff, ibid., 586.

ZVI URI MA'OZ

PREHISTORIC SITES

Research into the Pleistocene period in the Golan has advanced considerably through the study of the region's volcanics. The area's topographic features are related to several cycles of volcanic activity that occurred at different times during the Pleistocene.

The northern Golan is the only geographic unit in this general region that has been intensively surveyed for prehistoric sites. The survey resulted in the discovery of sites and find spots attributable to the Lower, Middle, and Upper Paleolithic periods. Neolithic remains were also found. The cultural sequence is incomplete, as most of the sites belong to the Acheulean and the Upper Paleolithic cultures.

It was also observed during the survey that the sites were quite varied. Most are situated near sources of raw material used in stone tool manufacture (usually near Eocene formations) and they contain exceptionally large quantities of debitage (Qela', Bir Ḥafir, and others). Sites of this type are thought to be workshops. Other sites, slightly farther away from flint sources, are relatively poor in debitage and the frequencies of the lithic elements in their assemblages are similar to those of temporary or seasonal camps.

The importance of the northern Golan sites (and find spots) is that they lie beneath hardened basalt flows or other pyroclastic materials. Basalts and pyroclastics can be dated by radiometric techniques and thus provide a key for determining the ages of prehistoric cultures in the Golan, Israel, and the Near East in general.

In the following sections, the finds from the Acheulean site of Berekhat Ram and the Mousterian site in the Quneiṭra Valley are presented. The sites were excavated on behalf of the Israel Department of Antiquities and Museums, the Israel Survey, and the Hebrew University of Jerusalem, under the direction of N. Goren-Inbar.

THE ACHEULEAN SITE OF BEREKHAT RAM. The construction of an agricultural terrace along the western edge of the Berekhat Ram crater created a section more than 6 m deep, in which the following units were exposed (from top to bottom):

A. Berekhat Ram tuff.

B. "Keramim Basalt," upper flow (c. 4 m thick).

C. "Fossil Soil" (hereafter referred to as the colluvial/alluvial unit), which contains the prehistoric site.

D. "Keramim Basalt," lower flow.

The first discovery here of a flint hand ax was made during a reconnaissance survey in 1979. During subsequent surveys, a large concentration of flint implements was found along the dirt road leading from the western edge of the crater to the water's edge. When it became clear that the artifacts had been washed from the colluvial/alluvial unit, two seasons of excavations (1980–1981) were carried out at the spot (map reference 221437. 293425). It is important to note that excavation was only possible here: other parts of the site were covered by some 4 m of basalt, which precluded exposing the archaeological horizon. Approximately 25.5 sq m were exposed in the excavation and, in addition, small pits were dug in the terraces to the north and south of the site.

Stratigraphic observations showed the exceptionally complex layering of the colluvial/alluvial unit containing the archaeological materials. The upper part of the unit (maximum thickness of about 1.5 m) is yellow, while the lower portions are dark red (Munsell, 10R 3/4). The color change is the result of the baking of the sediments by the upper flow of the Keramim Basalt. Another color change occurs at the base of the unit, which is a sandy yellow horizon deposited directly on the surface of the lower Keramim Basalt. There are also

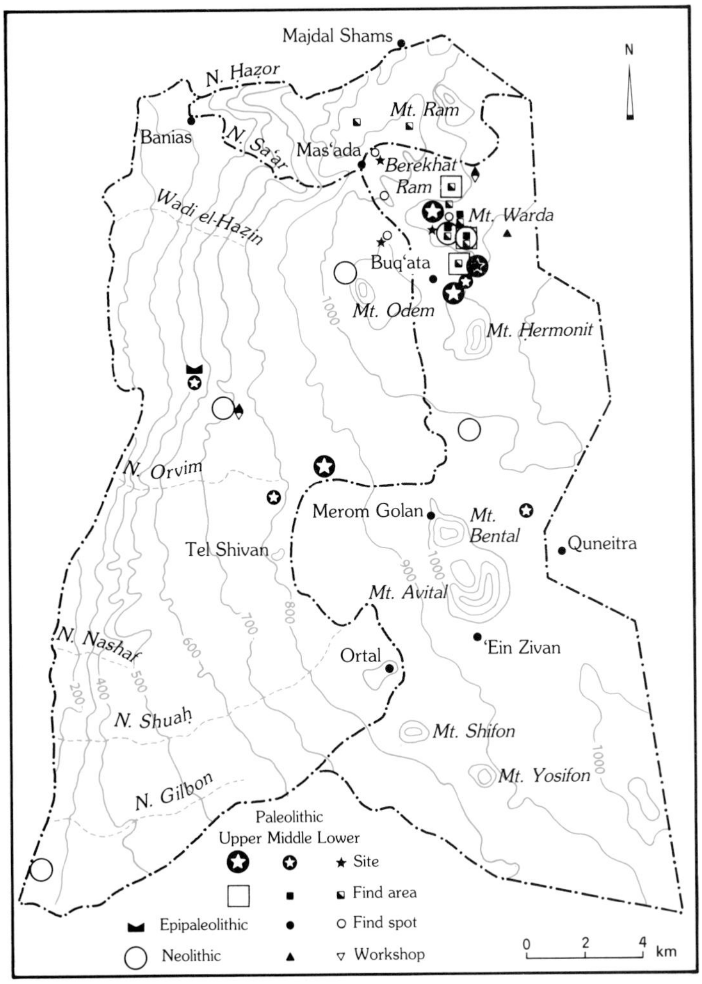

Map of prehistoric sites in the Golan.

Berekhat Ram: upper and lower flow of the Keramim Basalt and the colluvial/alluvial unit.

lateral sedimentological changes along the colluvial/alluvial unit, where a layer of blocks and cobbles overlaps the level with the worked flints. Micromorphological analysis showed that the colluvial/alluvial unit was formed during several geological events, including two stages of soil formation (between the hardening of the lower and upper flows of the Keramim Basalt).

The stone tools discovered in the excavation are flaked from flint. Their prolonged burial in the colluvial/alluvial unit resulted in the formation of a dark red patina on the pieces (10R 3/4) but did not affect the freshness of the flakes: 77.3 percent of the flakes are fresh and only a few are abraded.

The most frequent tools are Levallois flakes, side scrapers, end scrapers, burins, notches, and denticulates. The most numerous cores are Levallois and discoidal cores. Worth noting among the tools is the variety of side scrapers (14.2 percent of all tools), most of which are a simple concave type.

The Upper Paleolithic tools (20.6 percent) found here, known from most Acheulean assemblages, are mostly end scrapers and burins. The denticulates and notches (33.2 percent) form the largest group in the total tool assemblage. The number of hand axes is small (8 pieces, or 1.85 percent of the assemblage). Most of these, made on flint, were intensively worked, with an average number of 41.62 scars per tool.

Technologically, the flakes and flake tools are characterized by plain striking platforms (34 percent). Over 74 percent of all flakes were intensively worked and have no cortex; only 1.92 percent of them have more than 75 percent of their surface covered with cortex. This indicates that most of the manufacturing took place at the site but that preliminary shaping was limited. The assemblage is generally characterized by flakes, flake tools and cores made with the Levallois technique.

It is generally accepted that the Berekhat Ram crater itself is younger than the morphosedimentological units that contain the prehistoric site. Since the lithic assemblage is attributed to the Acheulean industrial complex, the age of the site should predate the last glaciation.

Absolute dates in the Golan have been determined by two radiometric techniques, potassium/argon and argon^{40}/argon^{39}. The dates discussed below were determined by the latter method. A sample taken from the upper flow of the Keramim Basalt was dated to 233,000 $\pm$ 300 BP. Two other samples, taken from the lower flow of the Keramim Basalt, gave identical dates of approximately 800,000 BP. Thus, the age of the site falls in the range between 800,000 and 233,000 years ago. These dates supplement the chronology established by carbon-14 dating of a sample taken from Berekhat Ram itself, which gave a date of 29,300 $\pm$ 4,000 BP. On the basis of the sedimentation rate in the crater, researchers estimate that it was formed some 100,000 years ago. The radiometric dates confirm the field observations that the stratigraphic units (Keramim Basalt and others) existed before the formation of the Berekhat Ram crater.

The Acheulean site of Berekhat Ram was exposed by mechanical equipment at four different localities: within the excavation area; in a section on the northern terrace; in a section on the southern terrace; and in a restricted exposure on the road to Berekhat Ram and to Mount Hermon (UTM grid 7572.6813). The stratigraphy and finds are identical in all of these. Part of the site seems to have been destroyed during the formation of the crater, and it is difficult to determine its original size. Also, the area excavated was too small to allow the collection of data concerning the nature of the occupation.

The Acheulean site of Berekhat Ram is unique from several standpoints. Stratigraphically, this is the only Acheulean site sealed between two basalt flows. In addition, this is a rare case of an in situ Acheulean assemblage which contains hand axes, cores, flakes, and debitage in an open-air site. The high frequency of Upper Paleolithic type tools should be seen as an integral component of the Acheulean industry. The absence of these tools in other Acheulean assemblages is probably the result of biased collection rather than of cultural or chronological differences.

THE MOUSTERIAN SITE IN THE QUNEIṬRA VALLEY. The Mousterian site in the Quneiṭra Valley was discovered in 1971 by D. Ben-Ami, following an excavation of trenches on the outskirts of the town of Quneiṭra. Close examination of the trench walls showed the existence of a clear Mousterian layer rich in finds. The site is surrounded by volcanic cones and ridges. They form a basin within the basaltic plateau that characterizes the northern Golan. Most of the valley's surface is covered by a volcanic tuff ("Avital Tuff") that belongs to the third volcanic cycle.

Three seasons of excavation were carried out at the site in 1982–1983 and 1985 by N. Goren-Inbar. The site is situated on the eastern side of the valley (UTM grid 7628.6694) at an elevation of 935 m above sea level. A total of 130 sq m was excavated in two different areas of the site. The archaeological horizon occurs within a series of fine-grained tuffs. The layer contains faunal remains, flint and basalt artifacts, and basalt pebbles. These pebbles do not appear in other parts of the section, either above or below the archaeological horizon. The thickness of the layer was determined on the basis of the largest pebble, bone, or other artifact found in it. The site consists of only a single occupation.

The artifacts lay directly on a horizontal layer of tuff over most of the excavated area. Different parts of this layer were either hard packed or muddy at the time of the prehistoric occupation. More than fifteen thousand artifacts, the majority of flint and a few of basalt, were recovered during the excavation. The latter material was used primarily for thick flakes, large side scrapers, and a large number of hammerstones. Flint appears to have been imported to the site from sedimentary exposures, 10 km (6 mi.) to the north. Analysis of the flint implements shows that the assemblage belongs within the framework of Mousterian industries. The retouched items are exceptionally numerous and include various types—side scrapers, points, end scrapers, burins, notches, denticulates, and a large number of composite tools. Technologically, the assemblage is characterized by the Levallois technique, as exhibited on the flakes, flake tools, and cores.

Numerous well-preserved faunal remains were also found. The bones, identified by S. Davis, represent a wide variety of species. Among the mammals were aurochs, two species of horse, deer (red and fallow), gazelle, lion, rhinoceros, wild goat, and wolf. The discovery of the remains of herbivores that lived in savannah settings, together with those of forest-dwelling animals, is an indication of the heterogeneous environment during the Upper Pleistocene.

Geological and geomorphological research has shown that the tuffs sealing the archaeological horizon were the result of a redeposition of tuff, washed away by water from its original location. This indicates that there was no volcanic activity in the region of the site during or after the period in which it was occupied. The age of this occupation, as calculated by ESR measurements, is 53,900 $\pm$ 5,900 years BP.

SUMMARY. A survey of the excavations, surface sites and find spots shows that Acheulean sites are the most numerous of the prehistoric finds in the northern Golan. Acheulean flint implements are found on the slopes of Mount Keramim, Mount Warda, Mount Ḥermonit, Tell Qaṣa'a, Tell Shu'eifri, and Tell el-Maḥfi. On the basis of geomorphological observations, it can be assumed that the Acheulean artifacts found at these places were manufactured and used there rather than having been transported from elsewhere and redeposited.

Examination of the geological formations on which the artifacts occur has shown that a developed volcanic landscape existed in the northern Golan as early as the Acheulean. Only in restricted portions of the region were there changes in geomorphological features such as those observed at the Acheulean site of Berekhat Ram.

N. Goren-Inbar, *Quartär* (1979) 29–30, 105–131; id., *Geology of the Golan Heights, Annual Meeting of the Israel Geological Society*, Jerusalem 1981; id., *Préhistoire du Levant* (eds. J. Cauvin and

Berekhat Ram: hand ax in situ.

P. Sanlaville), Paris 1981, 193–205; id., *ESI* 1 (1982), 10–11; id., *L'Anthropologie* 89 (1985), 251–254; id., *Paléorient* 11/1 (1985), 7–28; ibid., 14/2 (1988), 99–108; id. (et al.), *Mitekufat Ha'even* 19 (1986), 7*–12*; 20 (1987), 136*–142*; id., *Quneitra: A Mousterian Site on the Golan Heights* (Qedem 31), Jerusalem 1990; ibid. (Review), *Paléorient* 17/1 (1991), 169–170; id., *Investigations in South Levantine Prehistory: Préhistoire du Sud-Levant* (*BAR*/IS 497, eds. O. Bar-Yosef and B. Vandermeersch), Oxford 1989, 125–146; G. Feraud et al., *Nature* 304/5923 (1983), 263–265; A. Gopher, *ESI* 4 (1985), 77; id., *TA* 17 (1990), 115–143; E. Hovers, *Mitekufat Ha'even* 19 (1986), 30*–42*; S. J. M. Davis et al., *Paléorient* 14/1 (1988), 95–105; Weippert 1988 (Ortsregister); M. A. Courty et al., *Soils and Micromorphology in Archaeology*, Cambridge 1989, 228–234; R. Rabinovich, *Mitekufat Ha'even* 22 (1989), 141*–144*.

NA'AMA GOREN-INBAR

CHALCOLITHIC PERIOD TO THE IRON AGE

Topographical and climatic conditions in the Golan have affected the region's settlement pattern. Not only are there few tells with continuous stratigraphical sequences, but there are conspicuous gaps in the archaeological record. In periods of dense population, the dispersion pattern differed in the northern, central, and southern Golan.

THE CHALCOLITHIC PERIOD. The Chalcolithic culture appears in the Golan after a long occupational gap. Nothing has been found so far that can be assigned to the Pottery Neolithic period or to the Wadi Rabah phase that followed it. The first Chalcolithic site in the Golan (late fifth and early fourth millennia) was discovered in 1973. Between 1973 and 1988, excavations and trial soundings were carried out at fifteen Chalcolithic sites, revealing houses and a unique material culture that shares features typical of Chalcolithic sites elsewhere in the country. Concurrent with the excavations, the extensive surveys in the central Golan led to the discovery of additional sites, some of which were subsequently excavated, and it is likely that there are more. Because most of the sites were unnamed, they are called by the name of a nearby stream, waterfall, or modern village.

Of the twenty-five recorded sites dating to the Chalcolithic period (see map), all but one are in the basalt regions of the central Golan. The settlements are situated on median slopes, near streams and springs, the majority at an elevation of 455 to 555 m above sea level, in areas in which the mean annual precipitation is 500 to 600 mm. The rainfall and the impermeability of the basalt cause rapid saturation of the soil, which retains its humidity for a considerable period, especially along the banks of streams.

The results of palynological analyses indicate that no significant changes in the climate of the Golan have occurred since the fourth millennium. In the Chalcolithic period, extensive pasturage was available in the central Golan, and the water-retentive soil was utilized for field crops. This natural environment met the subsistence requirements of a population whose economy was based on sheep and goat pastoralism combined with agriculture.

In the southern Golan, only one site with a Chalcolithic stratum has been identified here to date: site 25, in Naḥal Samakh. Nothing is known of the nature of the settlement—of its economy, general layout, or house plans. Although the finds (mostly surface collected) resemble those from the central Golan, there are differences, mainly in the composition of the local clay used for pottery, due to the extensive exposures of calcareous sedimentary rocks. Much of the pottery is whitish-yellow (sometimes decorated with slashes of red paint), in contrast to the red-to-brown wares typical of the central Golan.

Settlement Layout and Architecture. All the Chalcolithic settlements in the Golan are unfortified and many are spread over a considerable area. A large village may number some forty houses and a smaller settlement up to fifteen. Smaller groups of houses and isolated farmsteads are also found. The layout of a "centralized village" consists of a series of parallel rows of rectangular structures built in chain formation, with a shared cross wall between neighboring houses. Not infrequently a settlement is concentrated on one side of a wadi with a few scattered groups of structures and isolated dwellings on the opposite bank. At site 18, a row of houses was built on the banks of a perennial stream, while others were dotted over the high ground bordering a nearby seasonal stream. In three of these houses, there was a well-built silo.

At all the sites, the structures are broadhouses built of basalt with dry-stone walls. The recurrent size of many of the houses is 15 by 6 m, but others are both larger and smaller. The long walls are oriented in a generally east–west direction, in alignment with the terrain's downward slope. The entrance is in the south, with a step down into the house. The floors are of rough stone paving, sometimes combined with patches of exposed bedrock; in some houses a low shelf (or bench) was built at the foot of the long walls.

The partitioning of the internal area accords with the widespread practice: a small narrow room, usually at the western end (inner width, 1–1.9 m), sometimes divided into two, or even three, smaller compartments; a slightly larger room (inner width, 2–4 m) usually located in the western part of the house; an internal long wall built parallel and close to the north wall to create

Map of Chalcolithic sites in the Golan.

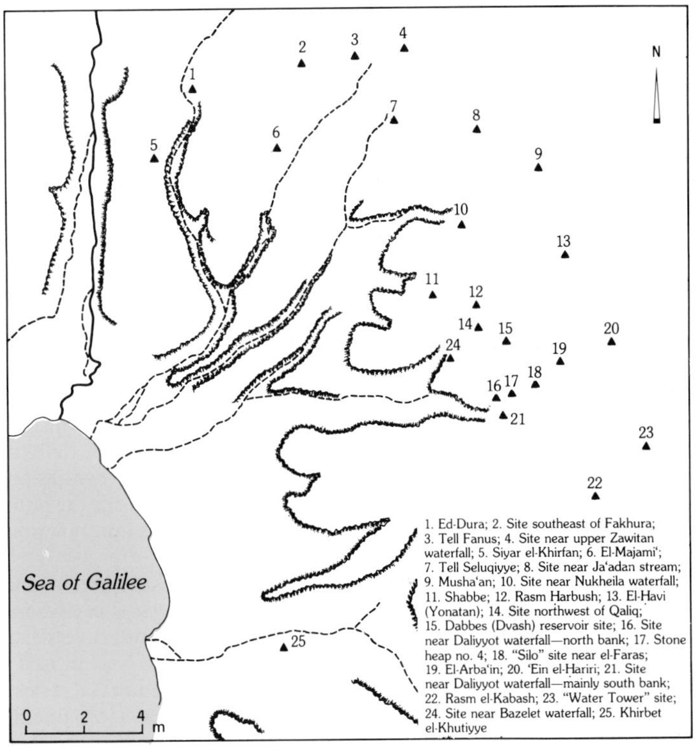

Rasm Ḥarbush: structure from the Chalcolithic period.

Basalt "pillar figures," Chalcolithic period.

a long, narrow room (inner width, 0.8–1.5 m) on that side of the house; and a short tongue of wall built out from the center of the cross wall that divides the adjacent space into two. The purpose of these forms of partitioning was to facilitate the construction of the roof; for despite the width of the walls (0.8–1 m), owing to a lack of timber long enough to span the length of the house, an attempt was made to divide up the internal space based on the average span of the available wood. In most houses the whole of the inner space was roofed, probably with branches, reeds, and skins. The roof would have rested on beams supported by a row of wooden pillars (which did not survive), set on flat paving stones along the building's axis. The well-built walls (estimated height, 2–2.5 m) were sufficiently substantial to have carried either a flat or gabled roof. In only one or two instances was there any indication of an outer courtyard adjacent to a house. The inference is that most of the daily domestic activities, including food processing and subsidiary processes connected with agriculture and stock raising, were carried out inside the house, the overall spatial area being divided by the partition walls into functional units.

The Finds. At all the sites a wide range of ceramic, basalt, and flint artifacts were discovered, some resembling those found at Chalcolithic sites elsewhere in the country and others unique to the Golan. Many of the pottery vessels are decorated with bands of impressed rope ornament; others bear incised or punctured decoration. The most common form of decoration is a series of concentric horizontal bands, but on some vessels the shoulder is ornamented with diagonal bands, circles, spirals, zigzags, or other designs. The vessels are handmade, with some use of the tournette, especially on the necks of large storage jars. The clay, whose source was the local volcanic soil, contains many grits, including basalt particles that, when fired, turn various shades of red and brown. The assemblage contains a high proportion of pithoi, used for storing crops—especially grain; their large number was no doubt due to the difficulty of digging silos into the hard volcanic basalt (although silos were found in some houses). In addition to the many storage jars, there are medium-sized vessels, including jars, bowls, hole-mouth jars, jugs, large spouted and small kraters, fenestrated footed bowls ("incense burners"), and many whorls for spinning wool. There are few utensils for daily use, such as cups and cooking pots; neither are there churns, cornets, or V-shaped bowls, common at contemporary sites elsewhere in the country, or mat impressions on any of the bases.

In a volcanic region such as the Golan it is not surprising to find basalt vessels in every house. They include variously sized bowls (in circular, oval, and flowerpot shapes), large troughlike basins, mortars, querns, and grinding stones of all kinds, as well as unworked stones set in the floor that have a smoothly hollowed cavity at the top. Many basalt tools and implements also were found, including those for use in agriculture—hammers, hoes, and digging-stick weights.

The range of flint tools is typical of the Chalcolithic period and includes axes and adzes, awls, fan scrapers, choppers, and large numbers of sickle blades. In addition, there are perforated tabular flint discoids, some of them denticulated, which are characteristic of the north.

THE PILLAR FIGURES. The hallmark of the Chalcolithic period in the Golan are the basalt pillar figures used in a domestic cult. Irrespective of size, all are circular and terminate above in a shallow offering bowl. The majority are sculpted with facial features, especially a large and prominent nose that, as the seat of the breath of life, may well have been regarded as a symbol of life and fertility. Some of the pillar figures are sculpted with horns and sometimes with a goatee. All were, no doubt, believed to be imbued with an inherent potency that could be transferred to associated objects.

Some fifty pillar figures dating to the Chalcolithic period are known from

Rasm Ḥarbush: perforated flint implement, Chalcolithic period.

Rasm Ḥarbush: krater with rope decoration, Chalcolithic period.

EB II–III seal impressions from 'Ein Quniyye.

the Golan. Although not every house contained a pillar figure, there were sometimes two, three, or as many as five in the same structure. When found, many, but by no means all, were lying close to the walls in a position suggesting that they had fallen from a shelf. Others may have been placed at the foot of the walls and been overturned when the buildings fell into ruin. Some of the features associated with the pillar figures—a nose and horns—also occur as plastic additions to different kinds of pottery vessels, especially fenestrated footed bowls, which are essentially cultic. A small, delicately modeled, pottery goat's head was also found; it had originally been attached to the wall of a vessel possibly used to process milk products.

Subsistence. Among the plant remains recovered from the houses were scattered seeds analyzed as pea, lentil, and vetch; a not inconsiderable amount of charred grains of cultivated emmer wheat (*Triticum dicoccum*) was found in one of the silos mentioned above. The most common species identified is the olive; burned pits were found in a number of houses at different sites. Among the remains of charred wood, 90 percent of thirty samples analyzed were olive wood. The high incidence of residual olive wood and fruit is good grounds for inferring domestic oil making—a suggestion endorsed by the presence of spouted kraters and the remains of a large number of spouts in the houses. This type of vessel is considered to be one of the earliest examples of a separator-vat.

Owing to the prevailing dampness and the detrimental effect of basalt on bone tissue, few faunal remains are preserved. These consisted mainly of sheep and goat bones and teeth; some fragments have been analyzed as cow, wild boar, equid, and donkey. No human bones or cemeteries were found that could be assigned to the Chalcolithic period.

Dating and the End of the Chalcolithic Period. In the absence of any indications of structural changes in the architecture or in the vessel forms, it is estimated that the Chalcolithic period in the Golan represents a single cultural phase that flourished at the end of the fifth and the beginning of the fourth millennia. This is confirmed by the results of carbon-14 dating: a specimen of burned wood (possibly a roof beam) gave a date of 4320–3980 BCE (RT 525—1979) and charred wheat from the silo in an abandoned house gave a date of 4470–4350 BCE (RT 718—1985).

The Chalcolithic culture in the Golan came to an end when the closely settled central Golan was abandoned and the inhabitants left, never to return, taking with them only such paraphernalia as were necessary for daily life. Large storage jars and other heavy equipment—including the pillar figures—were left behind in the houses. The reasons for this abandonment are unknown; there is no evidence either of an earthquake or of conquest. It is possible that a sudden, if temporary, climatic change, such as an unexpected dry period, rendered the region unable to offer conditions essential for subsistence.

THE EARLY BRONZE AGE. It appears that, following the Chalcolithic period, continuity of settlement in the northern and central Golan was interrupted. No Early Bronze Age I sites have been found to date. In the southern Golan, however, three Early Bronze Age I sites have been identified near the Yarmuk River and Naḥal Meẓar. In addition, Early Bronze Age I material has been recovered in excavations at the Leviah Enclosure (q.v.) to the east of the Sea of Galilee. At the site of Pitḥat ha-Yarmuk, limited probes revealed Early Bronze I architectural remains and an associated assemblage, including curvilinear walls and gray-burnished ware. There also are indications of an extensive Early Bronze I stratum at the site that, once revealed, will doubtless add to what is known about the period in the southern Golan.

Evidence for the Early Bronze Age II come largely from surveys. Some twenty-seven settlement and so-called enclosure sites are spread throughout the Golan: four in the south, twelve in the central region, and eleven in the north. In addition to diagnostic sherds, at some settlement sites and at all enclosure sites, the remains of fortification walls have been identified. At several of the former, sections of a surrounding defensive wall are visible with the remains of the houses within it (at Za'arta and eṣ-Ṣalabeh, in the northern and central Golan, respectively).

The "enclosure" sites are characterized by massive walls, frequently combined with naturally defensive topographical elements, such as craggy outcrops, precipitous rocks, and steep declivities. Some "enclosure" sites are built on an elongated promontory with a sheer descent on either side to the valleys below. These are further protected by huge fortification walls built across them (as at the Yitzḥaki Enclosure in the central Golan and the Leviah Enclosure [Mitḥam Lawiyye] in the southern Golan). Another enclosure site erected at the extreme end of a triangular upland above the confluence of two wadis has a massive defensive wall built across it, securing it on its open, unprotected side (el-Bardawīl in the southern Golan). Other enclosures, sited in terrain that lacks naturally defensive features, are surrounded by immense walls of heaped stones (the Sha'abaniyye and eṣ-Ṣur enclosures in the central Golan).

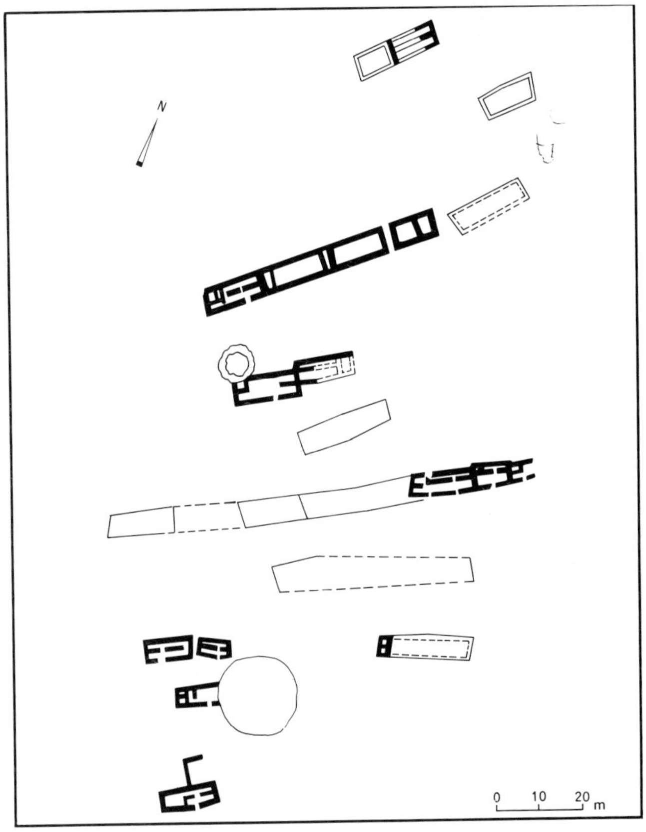

Tell 'Ein el-Ḥariri: plan of the Chalcolithic structures, erected in a chain.

EB II–III seal impressions.

For more than twenty years following their discovery in 1967, nothing was known with certainty about the possible remains of settlements and houses within enclosures. Recent excavations at the Leviah Enclosure (q.v.) revealed well-built rectilinear houses in the western sector, dated by associated pottery, including Khirbet Kerak ware, to the Early Bronze Age III. Seal impressions on pottery dating to the Early Bronze Age II–III were also uncovered. Similar seal impressions have been found at 'Ein Quniyye and at two adjacent sites near 'Ein er-Raḥman, in the northern Golan.

Surface material collected at other enclosure sites also belongs to the Early Bronze Age II and, as at Leviah, it may well be that the period's earlier and later phases will prove to be present. At eṣ-Ṣur, however, no relevant dating material has been found. It is included among the enclosure sites because of the character and similar method of construction of the surrounding fortification wall.

Another site at which reliable dating evidence has yet to be revealed is Rogem Hiri (q.v.). There are reasonable grounds for attributing the original structure here to the early third millennium.

END OF THE THIRD MILLENNIUM. Toward the end of the third millennium, there was a significant population change in the northern and central Golan, where no Middle Bronze Age I sites have been found. A very different situation prevailed in the southern Golan: some half-dozen sites belonging to the period have been identified in surveys, apportioned equally between settlements and cemeteries. In addition, a recent excavation at Tel Soreg (q.v.), in the southern Golan, has shown that the earliest open settlement there dates to this period; scattered sherds have also appeared in trial soundings at the Leviah Enclosure (q.v.).

The Dolmens. At the end of the third millennium, nomadic and seminomadic pastoral groups were to be found in the northern and central Golan; they neither built permanent houses nor established even the smallest settlement. Their presence is attested by hundreds of megalithic tombs, or dolmens, a common feature in the landscape, especially in the central Golan. The dolmens are frequently found in large concentrations, known as dolmen fields, in which one type predominates; they have been interpreted as representing tribal variations of age-old funerary customs.

More than thirty dolmens have been excavated in the Golan, and many others have been recorded in surveys. They belong to different types and the earliest material found on the paved floors—funerary offerings associated with secondary burials—dates to the end of the third and the beginning of the second millennia. The assemblages from the dolmens are distinctly northern in character, resembling deposits from contemporary shaft tombs and burial caves in northern Israel and Syria.

TYPES OF DOLMENS. The name dolmen is derived from two Old Breton (French) words: *dol* (table) and *men* (stone). They describe the simplest of these structures, which resembles a large stone table built of two unworked upright blocks, with a third placed horizontally across them. There are relatively few dolmens of this type (trilithon) in the Golan. Far more common is a medium-sized structure (c. 3.5 m long, 1.5 m wide, and 1.5 m high), surrounded by a circular tumulus. The roof consists either of a single large block, usually resting on a small roof stone over the entrance or, alternatively, it comprises a series of roof stones placed either side by side or partially overlapping one another. Dolmens have various sizes, some with an inner length of 10.5 m. Unique to the Golan is a group of dolmens found only on a broad sweep of upland northeast of the Sea of Galilee, immediately east of the Jordan River. These are the so-called Tank Dolmens, in which the well-built chamber measures about 7 by 1.5 m. The whole structure, which is surrounded by a low, elliptical tumulus, towers 3 to 4 m above the surrounding terrain. Its roof is built of large stones placed horizontally one upon the other; it rises in steplike tiers from both narrow ends toward the center (often topped by a capstone), to form a corbelled ceiling within. There can be little doubt that, in contrast to other types of dolmens, which were completely or partially covered by a surrounding tumulus, this group was intended to be seen from a distance.

Irrespective of size, most dolmens conform to a basic pattern: a rectangular (or trapezoidal) chamber, closed at one of its narrow ends and open at the other; dry-walling in unworked basalt, each stone carefully chosen in accordance with its function in a wall or roof; orthostatic blocks, placed side by side to form the lowest wall course, whose interstices were filled with smaller stones; enormous and often extremely heavy boulders for the roof, kept in position and balanced by smaller stones; a paved floor; and a capstone for the roof. Most dolmens are surrounded and partially or completely hidden beneath a tumulus (cairn) of piled stones, frequently bounded by an outer ring wall of larger stones laid in distinct courses, with spaced inner ring walls below the accumulations of stones. The size of the tumulus was determined by the size of the dolmen, but most are considerably larger. The tumulus usually has a flat upper surface and may rise 2 to 3 m above the surrounding terrain; its purpose was not only to cover and screen the dolmen, but also to stabilize the heavy pile, which was frequently built on a slope.

THE FINDS. The earliest material found on the floors of the excavated Golan

"Tank Dolmen" (type 6), near Naḥal Yahudiyye.

Dolmen (type 3), near Rasm el-Kabash.

Map of dolmens in the Golan.

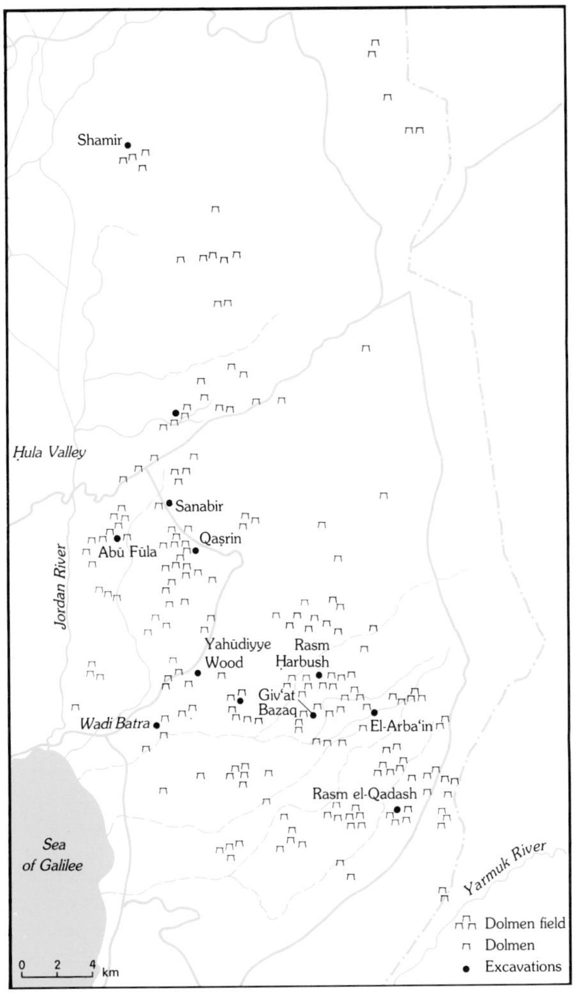

dolmens dates to the Middle Bronze I. The assemblages include jars, "teapots," *amphoriskoi*, a jug, a bottle, globular cooking pots without handles, pedestal-based lamps, and scattered carnelian beads; there were also metal objects with a high copper content, among them a long pin with a flat, curled head; a nail-headed pin; short double-pointed pins, a bracelet, and a ring; and weapons, including a diagnostic dagger, a socketed spearhead, and arrowheads with a leaf-shaped tang. Comparable pottery dating to the period has been found in shaft tombs in northern Israel, and similar metal objects are known from northern sites, especially Megiddo and Ugarit in Syria.

There were signs of the reuse of many dolmens as tombs both in antiquity and in modern times; as a result, the initial funerary deposit was pushed aside and even dispersed. There was also evidence of entry by tomb robbers in search of the valuables customarily buried with the dead. The original burial was, thus, disturbed and the skeletal remains scattered. The bones, adversely affected by dampness and contact with the basalt, tended to disintegrate. As is usual with secondary burial, only a scattering of disarticulated bones and a few grave goods had been placed in the dolmen, near its closed end.

The building techniques used to construct the dolmens were no doubt dictated by the volcanic nature of the terrain in the Golan and in adjacent regions in which basalt predominates. The moving and positioning of huge stone blocks (some weighing more than a ton) to build a dolmen required enormous physical effort and technical skill. This expenditure of effort to construct a tomb reflects the importance attached to preparing a final resting place for the dead in a society that did not build permanent houses for the living. Moreover, the indications are that when these nomadic (or seminomadic) tribes, whose tradition it was to erect a dolmen-type tomb, reached areas of softer rock, the burial chamber was adapted to local conditions: a shaft tomb was cut below ground (recalling the tumulus-covered dolmen). This is borne out by the Middle Bronze Age I shaft tombs found in the southern Golan (and q.v. Dolmens).

MIDDLE AND LATE BRONZE AGES. At the end of the Middle Bronze Age I, the population of the Golan became substantially reduced. It was only after an interval of some 150 years that settlement was resumed, in the second quarter of the second millennium. The intervening period is equivalent to the Middle Bronze Age IIA, from which no sites have been identified in the Golan to date. The only artifacts that can be attributed to this period were found in assemblages from dolmens reused for later burials. A fenestrated bronze axhead was, however, found out of context in the southern Golan. In addition to this sparse evidence, in a dolmen reused as a tomb throughout most of the second millennium BCE, several juglets were recovered—some of them painted—that are typical of the transitional phase between the Middle Bronze Age IIA and IIB. They resemble comparative material from tombs at Ginnosar, Hazor, Dan, and other northern sites.

In the Middle Bronze Age IIB, the Golan witnessed a renewal of settlement. About forty-five sites (including burials) have been identified. While the majority were discovered in the course of surveys, at one or two that were excavated a stratum dating to this period was revealed in a deep sounding. The marked growth in the pattern of settlement is paralleled by a similar expansion throughout the country. In the Middle Bronze Age IIB, the focus shifted to the southern Golan; the number of sites recorded was twice that for either the northern or central Golan.

The preference for the southern Golan as a settlement area may have been due in part to its sedimentary rock. It is very much easier to cut and contrive water-tight cisterns from it for storage purposes than from hard basalt. Most of the sites were first settled in the Middle Bronze Age IIB and in many instances continued in use through subsequent periods. Many are fortified; small forts were erected at strategic locations. Some burial caves with grave goods characteristic of the period were uncovered, but without a corresponding stratum on the adjacent tells. The settlement distribution pattern points to a predilection for sites on the broad upland plateau stretching between the Sea of Galilee and Naḥal Raqqad and on the slopes bordering the valleys of Naḥal Samakh and its tributaries.

The finds belonging to this period resemble assemblages typical of contemporary sites throughout the country. In the southern Golan, however, there are, in addition, large coarse-ware storage jars decorated with bands incised in a coil motif, short lines and combing, that resemble storage jars from the northern part of the country, especially from Hazor.

In the Late Bronze Age, the number of identified settlements decreased by half. The majority of them represent the uninterrupted settlement of sites first occupied in the Middle Bronze Age II that continued into the Iron Age. This is especially true in the southern Golan, where 50 percent of the known sites are located. There is also every likelihood that sites identified on the basis of surface material as having been settled both before and after the Late Bronze Age, but not during it, will eventually be found to have continued throughout the intervening period. This was the case at Tell Abu Mdawwar where plentiful Middle Bronze Age II material was collected on the surface, but none from the Late Bronze Age; some years later, a burial cave was discovered at the foot of the tell containing complete vessels from the Late Bronze Age. Another burial cave, in use from the Middle Bronze Age IIB onward and containing a sizable Late Bronze deposit, was discovered at the foot of Tel Afiq (Tel Soreg, q.v.), where excavation has shown that the site was occupied for most of the second millennium into the Iron Age.

Typical of the Late Bronze Age, especially in the southern Golan, are light

Red-painted storage jar, from a tomb in the southern Golan, LB.

colored coarse-ware jars decorated in red with linear motifs; a small fragment of Late Bronze Age I bichrome ware, showing a bird eating a fish, was collected on the surface. Additional indications of settlement in the Late Bronze Age are the Cypriot imports found in assemblages at several sites, including Tel Afiq (Soreg), and among funerary offerings associated with a later burial in a dolmen in the central Golan. In the upper layer of another dolmen, an Astarte plaque figurine wearing a Hathor wig was found; it belongs to a type characteristic of the fourteenth century BCE. A pilgrim flask and bronze arrowheads dating to the end of the Late Bronze Age were also found in a dolmen that was reused as a tomb over a long period of time. All of these artifacts point to a Late Bronze settlement in the Golan, the full extent of which has yet to be determined.

THE IRON AGE. Following the reduced overall population of the Late Bronze Age, there was a renewal of settlement in the Golan in the Iron Age, comparable to that of the Middle Bronze Age IIB, when many of the sites had been founded. Several of the Iron Age sites already existed in the Late Bronze Age.

The majority of the Iron Age sites were identified in surface surveys, while excavations at ʿEn Gev (q.v.) revealed five successive phases. At other excavated sites, where the main levels excavated date to much later periods, Iron Age material has also been found (Qaṣrin and Ḥorvat Kanaf). The possibility that levels dating to this period will eventually also be found at other sites, where nothing has so far been found intimating the existence of an Iron Age stratum, should not be ruled out. The site distribution map for the period would then prove to be far more extensive than at present, especially in the central Golan, where far fewer sites are known than in the south. As for the northern Golan, a recent survey has shown the existence of more than thirty Iron Age sites—albeit many of them of small size—few of which were known previously.

In the central Golan, fourteen sites (including material from a late dolmen burial) have been identified; in the southern Golan twenty-two sites are known. Several of those first settled in the Iron Age are fortified and some are small forts erected at strategic points (Tannūriyye, in the central Golan). To this category belong fortified strongholds set up at the heads of valleys through which vital approach roads passed, especially in the southern Golan (Tell Duweir at the head of the Yarmuk Valley and Khirbet Dajājiyye at the head of Naḥal Samakh). Sites on the eastern shore of the Sea of Galilee, such as Tel ʿEn Gev and Tel Hadar, commanded the important road around it. Recent excavations at Tel Hadar (q.v.) revealed remains dating to the Iron Age I and II.

Excavations at Tel Afiq (Tel Soreg, q.v.) have revealed that although earlier settlement there was in small open villages, in the Iron Age II, in the wars between Israel and Aram, the site was fortified. This was doubtless in order to secure the road that ran below it—further evidence of the struggle for domination of the region well known from biblical sources.

W. F. Albright, *BASOR* 89 (1943), 7–15; B. Mazar et al., *IEJ* 14 (1964), 1–49; C. Epstein, ibid. 22 (1972), 209–217; 23 (1973), 109–110, 239, 241; 24 (1974), 254–257; 25 (1975), 193–201, 255–257; 27 (1977), 43–45; 28 (1978), 116–119; 29 (1979), 225–227; 31 (1981), 112–116; 32 (1982), 141–144, 252–254; 33 (1983), 255–257; 35 (1985), 53–57, 293–295; 37 (1987), 274–275; 38 (1988), 205–223; 39 (1989), 91–93; 40 (1990), 69, 71; id., *Israel Land and Nature* 2 (1972), 97–100; id., *RB* 79 (1972), 404–407; 80 (1973), 560–563; 82 (1975), 77–79; id., *BA* 40 (1977), 57–62; id., *Archaeology in the Levant* (K. M. Kenyon Fest.), Warminster 1978, 22–35; id., *BASOR* 229 (1978), 27–45; 258 (1985), 53–62; id., "Dolmens" (*Interpreter's Dictionary of the Bible*, Supplement, 1978), 245–247; id., *EI* 15 (1981), 78*–79*; id., *Antike Welt* 13/2 (1982), 34–38; id., *Bolletino del Centro di Studi Preistorici* 19 (1982), 60–82; id., *BAIAS* (1982–1983), 41–45; id., *ESI* 2 (1983), 35–37; 3 (1984), 33–35; 4 (1985), 36–38; 6 (1987–1988), 56–58; 7–8 (1988–1989), 67–69; id., *ʿAtiqot* 17 (1985), 20–58; id. (and T. Noy), *Paléorient* 14/1 (1988), 133–141; J. Weinstein, *Radiocarbon 26* (1984), RT 525, 306; M. Hartal, *ESI* 4 (1985), 82; L. E. Stager, *Palestine in the Bronze and Iron Ages* (ed. J. N. Tubb), London 1985, 177; T. E. Levy, *BA* 49 (1986), 92, 94–95; P. Beck and M. Kochavi, *ESI* 6 (1987–1988), 75–78; I. Carmi, *Radiocarbon 29* (1987), RT 718, 105; Weippert 1988 (Ortsregister); M. Kochavi, *ESI* 7–8 (1988–1989), 110–113; id., *IEJ* 39 (1989), 1–17; 41 (1991), 180–184.

CLAIRE EPSTEIN

HELLENISTIC PERIOD TO THE MIDDLE AGES

The results of archaeological surveys and excavations already conducted in the Golan indicate, in most cases, that the region was not populated during the Babylonian, Persian, and Early Hellenistic periods (sixth–third centuries BCE); there are a few exceptions in the southern Golan, such as Tel Afiq (Soreg). The earliest sherds from the later periods discovered in surveys and excavations date to the second century BCE—that is, after Palestine was conquered by the Seleucids (in 200 BCE). From that time onward, until the Byzantine period, there is impressive growth in the number of sites in the Golan, the amount of built-up area, and the population: from seventy-eight sites in the second century BCE (thirty-three of them Iturean settlements), to 108 in the first century CE, and to 173 and more in the sixth. The number of sites and settlements in the Byzantine period amounts to six times the figure for the Middle Bronze Age. This settlement activity is particularly prominent in the central and northern Golan, which had almost no permanent agricultural settlements during the earlier periods. There were several causes for this occupational revolution: (1) Under the Seleucids, and later under Alexander Jannaeus and Herod, factors of defense and economics made it imperative to populate the Golan, a frontier region in Palestine. (2) Various technological developments, such as the introduction of olive presses, winepresses, and aqueducts, made it possible to develop such industries as oil and wine production, thus providing a sufficient economic basis for a more intensive settlement of the Golan; no less important were agricultural planning and the ready availability of markets in the enlarged political-economic entity. (3) Population growth encouraged migration and settlement in Palestine's frontier areas.

HELLENISTIC PERIOD

According to survey and excavation results, which are supported by historical sources, the earliest settlements in the Hellenistic period were established at the beginning of the second century BCE, mainly in the southern Golan, with its fertile plains and rich springs. Agricultural settlements were established at the edges of these plains, above the springs and in the nearby river valleys: Khisfīn and el-Maʿ (both mentioned in the time of Judas Maccabaeus), ʿAyūn, ʿEinosh (ʿAwenish), Kefar Ḥaruv, Jibin, and others. In addition to agricultural villages, the survey also revealed a system of fortresses and towers built to defend and control the region and its roads at the following locations, all of which command highways: Antiochia-Hippos (Sussita), Seleucia (Quṣbiyye el-Jdeideh), and the Gorge of Antiochus (Meẓad ʿAteret). Judging by their Seleucid dynastic names and the pottery found, the citadels were probably built by Antiochus IV and Seleucus IV (187–163 BCE). Toward the end of the second century BCE, their numbers were reinforced by the addition of Gamala, probably built by a local tyrant, perhaps Demetrius (Josephus, *Antiq.* XIII, 394). These fortresses are typical products of Hellenistic military doctrine—strongholds built on high hills, isolated from their surroundings, and out of range of artillery fire. Water was supplied through aqueducts; if necessary, when the aqueduct had to cross a low saddle, a

Khirbet el-Khutiyye: stones with dressed margins from the Hellenistic period, in secondary use.

Map of sites from the Hellenistic and Early Roman periods in the Golan.

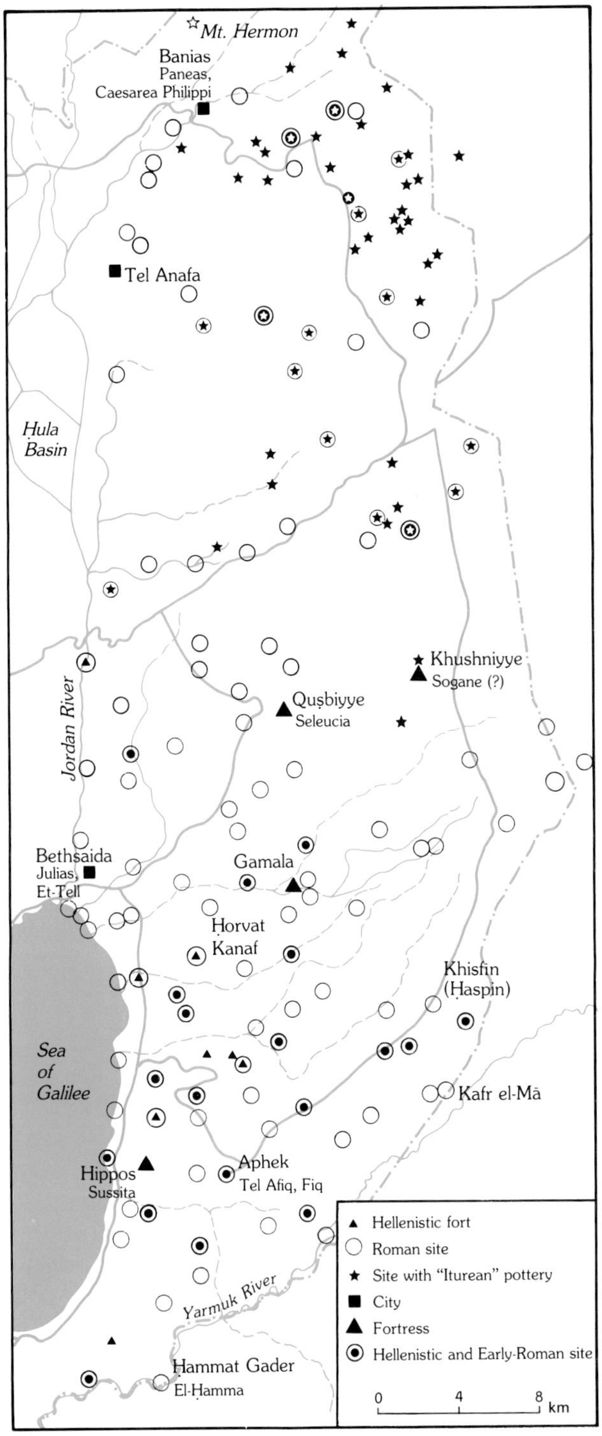

siphon was installed. Surveys have identified the aqueducts carrying water to Hippos (Sussita) and Gamala. The major fortresses controlled the main highways, while ascents and secondary roads were defended by towers. The survey has identified about six such forts, built of the margin-dressed ashlars typical of Hellenistic fortifications. The northernmost fort was at Mashrafāwī, near Moshav Ramot, the southernmost was at Khan el-'Aqabeh (Khirbet Tawāfiq el-Fawqā). They were probably part of the fortification system built to defend the territory of Hippos (Sussita) when the latter was established by Antiochus IV.

In the central Golan, too, the beginning of this phase of settlement has been dated to the second century BCE. The black-slipped pottery typical of this period was found at various sites and in the excavations at Qaṣrin and Ḥorvat Kanaf. An occupation level from this period has only come to light so far in the excavations at et-Tell (Julias-Bethsaida) and at Ḥorvat Kanaf, where it includes the foundations of a watchtower.

THE ITUREANS IN THE NORTHERN GOLAN. The first Iturean settlements were established in the northeastern Golan in the second century BCE. The Itureans were a tribe of Arab stock that gained control of Trachonitis, the northern Golan, Mount Hermon, and the Beqa'a in Lebanon. They settled at various localities and in the first (or late second) century BCE formed the Iturean kingdom, whose capital was at Chalcis in the Beqa'a. Iturean settlements in the Golan and on Mount Hermon are identified by their distinctive pottery, which is a prominent element among the finds at their sites. This pottery, also known as Golan ware, consists primarily of large handmade pithoi of a pinkish to light-brown clay, with a considerable admixture of grits. Sixty-seven Iturean sites, at which almost all the sherds collected on the surface were of Golan ware, have been identified in the northeastern Golan, all at an altitude of 700 m or more. Thirty-three of these sites have been dated to the Hellenistic period (with a small proportion of imported ware). In addition, pottery from the Early Roman period has been discovered at thirty-eight sites.

The Itureans generally built their villages on low hills, at the edge of the fertile valleys of the northeastern Golan. Settlement in this region necessitated clearing the area of the Mediterranean forest that until then formed a dense cover. The Iturean sites are unwalled, small in area (c. 1 a. or less), and comprise a few isolated buildings, constructed of roughly hewn field stones. The walls were generally one stone wide. The population seems to have subsisted mainly on agriculture. The large pithoi so prominent in their pottery repertoire were probably used to store water. The distribution of Iturean pithoi in the Roman-Byzantine period goes beyond Iturean territory proper, extending southward to the central and southern Golan and even reaching the Rosh Pinna plateau; this may be evidence of commercial contacts.

Based on the results of the survey, only fifty of the sixty-seven Iturean sites remained populated through the Late Roman and Byzantine periods. There was a general tendency to abandon smaller sites and move to larger, central settlements. The settlement pattern and history of the Itureans recall the process of Israelite settlement during the Iron Age I. To date, excavations have been conducted on a limited scale at only three Iturean sites in the Golan—Ḥorvat Zemel, Ḥorvat Namra, and Bab el-Hawa.

Ḥorvat Zemel. Ḥorvat Zemel (map reference 2241.2890) is an Iturean site southeast of Tell Shu'eifri (Buq'ata). Over an area of approximately half an acre, remains of about five buildings, mostly standing one course above the surface and built of unhewn basalt stones, are visible. Salvage excavations were conducted in a building in the north of the site in 1971, directed by D. Urman; excavations were completed there from 1985 to 1987 by M. Hartal. The building (12 by 24 m) consists of five rooms. The walls have survived to a height of two or three courses (0.8 m). The rooms had beaten-earth floors, laid directly on bedrock. Two work areas were paved with field stones. The roofs were probably supported by wooden pillars standing on flat stones—the latter were found lying lengthwise in the three largest rooms.

The excavations revealed two phases of occupation, separated by a short interval. The first phase consisted of a residential structure of the broadhouse type—a main living space and a small annex with a courtyard in front. In the second phase, the courtyard floor was elevated and subdivided. East of the courtyard was another, larger room, in which, again, two phases of occupation were identified. The finds included a large quantity of Iturean pithoi, four of which were intact and found in situ. Some bore brief inscriptions in Greek. The pottery also included some fine ware, mostly local but some imported, such as "fish plates" and hemispherical bowls. Inside one of the intact pithoi was a unique pear-shaped jug; it is covered with spiralling rhomboids in relief that make it resemble a pine cone, its pointed base perforated. Various other artifacts were found in the building, including iron tools and bronze arrowheads. Three Tyrian silver tetradrachms, minted in 146–145 BCE by two Seleucid kings—Alexander Balas and Demetrius II—and some bronze coins from the same period date the building to the second half of the second century BCE. The building seems to have been abandoned in an orderly fashion. Almost all the small utensils were removed; only the large and less portable pithoi were left behind. Some of the doorways to the building were blocked with masonry. Based on the numismatic finds, the excavators have suggested that the Golan ware at Ḥorvat Zemel should be dated to the second century BCE. Finds at other sites in the northern Golan, where Golan ware has been found together with imported pottery from the second century BCE, indicate that its production indeed began simultaneously with the Iturean settlement in the region. However, finds elsewhere indicate that this distinctive pottery continued to be manufactured (with some typological modifications) throughout the Roman and Byzantine periods.

Ḥorvat Namra. Ḥorvat Namra is another Iturean site, 1 km (0.6 mi.) south of Berekhat Ram (map reference 2214.2921). Several buildings and courtyards, most of which were destroyed when the land was prepared for cultivation, were found here on the surface, as well as a large quantity of Golan ware. In 1974, S. Gutman conducted a salvage excavation in a building at the center of the site that revealed two rooms separated by a "window wall," a characteristic feature of Hauran architecture. A window wall is a wall whose lower section consisted of a row of windows framed by vertical basalt slabs standing on a low shelf 60 to 70 cm high; the lintels were formed by a pair of joined beams or a broad slab.

The walls at Ḥorvat Namra were 0.8 m thick and built of large, unhewn basalt stones laid in rough courses that are preserved to a height of six or seven courses. The stone-paved western room (2.15 by 5.9 m) had an entrance on the west and another opening in the window wall on the east. The window wall between the two rooms was comprised of a shelf to a height of approximately 0.6 m, above which were found three basalt slabs (0.25 by 0.45 by 0.75 m) that originally framed a window. The floor of the main chamber (5.5 by 5 m) was paved with stone. Two columns were found here, built of roughly dressed rounded stone drums. One of the columns was found in situ, near the northern wall. The estimated height of both is similar to that of the "windows," and they presumably supported an upper sleeping loft, some 1.5 m above the floors in the western part of the building. The preserved parts of the house were probably used as storerooms for the residential quarters above (5.6 by 8 m). Near the southern wall was a small kitchen area that held a stone table, fragments of an oven, and a large quantity of ashes. Large quantities of potsherds were found on the floor—mainly of the thickly lined pithoi with spiral-scraped, pointed bases and shaped rims that are particularly characteristic of Golan ware (from the Roman period onward). Other items of local ware were roof tiles, kraters, and a strainer jug. A second group of pottery included storage jars, cooking pots, large and small bowls, juglets, frying pans, and a pestle and mortar. This group is dated to the Late Roman period, the pottery recalling finds at Banias and probably produced by a workshop at Khirbet el-Ḥawarith on Mount Hermon. The finds also include coins, mainly from the second and third centuries CE. The excavator was therefore inclined to date the building and its distinctive Golan ware to that period. However, a coin of Demetrius from the second century BCE found at the site, as well as other data, implies, in this writer's opinion, that the manufacture of this ware began in the second century BCE and continued into the Roman and Byzantine periods.

EARLY ROMAN PERIOD (66 BCE–67 CE)

Sherds from 143 sites throughout the Golan indicate the magnitude of the settlement in the Early Roman period; many additional sites from the Byzantine period were probably settled in the Early Roman period as well, but their remains have disappeared beneath the massive construction of later periods. Some sites, on the other hand, were not occupied after the Early Roman period, such as Jumeizeh in Naḥal Daliyyot, Sada el-Fakhūri in Naḥal Samakh, and, of course, Gamala. Knowledge of the material culture of this period in the Golan derives primarily from the excavations at Gamala and Ḥorvat Kanaf. Gamala provides an example of a planned city, adapted to the topography as dictated by the steep slopes; the few streets that have been excavated follow contour lines or climb steeply up the hill. The construction at Gamala is of an exceptionally fine quality, heralding the beginnings of a typical style of construction in the basalt areas of Palestine known as the Hauranite style (see below). Among the most notable finds at Gamala are the magnificent synagogue, private houses, streets, an oil extraction installation, and the remains of the city's eastern defensive wall. A number of artifacts attests to the battles that raged through the city during the First Revolt against Rome (q.v. Gamala). The overwhelming majority of the coins found in the excavations at Gamala and at Ḥorvat Kanaf were minted at Tyre, and it may be assumed that the economy of the settlements and the marketing of their agricultural produce—mainly olive oil—were dependent on that important port city. Fragments of stone vessels, made of Jerusalem chalk, found at Gamala and Ḥorvat Kanaf, attest to socioeconomic contacts with the metropolis of Jerusalem.

Occupation levels from this period in the northern and southern Golan have been excavated only at Banias (q.v.), where remains of temples, monumental *horrea* (storage buildings) and other structures were uncovered. **The Aftermath of the First Revolt Against Rome in the Jewish Settlements in the Golan.** The excavations at Gamala confirmed that the site was abandoned after its conquest by the Romans and the massacre of all its inhabitants, never to be resettled. A similar picture emerges from the excavations at Ḥorvat Kanaf—the occupation level from the first century CE precedes a hiatus of two or three centuries in the site's occupation. The Kanaf villagers probably sought refuge at nearby Gamala and met their fate there. Excavations of the synagogues at 'En Nashuṭ, Qaṣrin, and Dabiyye also testify to an archaeological gap, lasting from the late first to the early fourth centuries CE. Moreover, there is almost no mention of places in the Golan in the Mishnah or the Talmud. It would seem, therefore, that its Jewish population was almost completely obliterated in the First Revolt, following which there was a drastic decline—if not a complete halt—of Jewish settlement in the region. An echo of this catastrophe can be discerned in a redemption homily dating to the time of the sages of Yavneh: "And the Galilee shall be destroyed and the Gaulan desolate and the people of the border [of the Galilee] shall wander from city to city and none shall pity them ..." (Mishnah, *Sot.* 9:16). Moreover, the Roman authorities may have forbidden the renewal of Jewish settlement in the rebellious Golan, as they did in the area of Jerusalem, with the prohibition remaining in effect until the beginning of the Byzantine period. A similar pattern of destruction, followed by a palpable gap in Jewish presence, has been detected in other districts that took part in the revolt, such as Peraea and Narbata. The disappearance of the Jewish population of the villages in the territory of Sussita (Hippos), mentioned in the *Baraita di-teḥumin*, may also be linked to the aftermath of the First Revolt. The remains identified by the archaeological survey at the locations figuring on that list, such as Khisfīn, Nov, and Kefar Ḥaruv, among others, did not include synagogues—only evidence of Christian occupation in the Byzantine period.

MIDDLE AND LATE ROMAN PERIODS

As the surveys have produced almost no pottery from the Middle and Late Roman periods, information about the settlement pattern then is vague. The excavations at Qaṣrin and Dabiyye exposed occupation levels from the fourth century CE. The most impressive finds have come from the Roman cities of Hippos (Sussita) and Banias. In the former, part of the *cardo maximus* was exposed, from the imposing east gate, which was flanked by a semicircular tower with a molded base, to a postern gate (from the Byzantine period) at its west end. Sections of a stone-pipe siphon, incorporated in the aqueduct that conveyed water to the city from a distance, were found in the saddle to the east. A section of the pipe was found beneath the

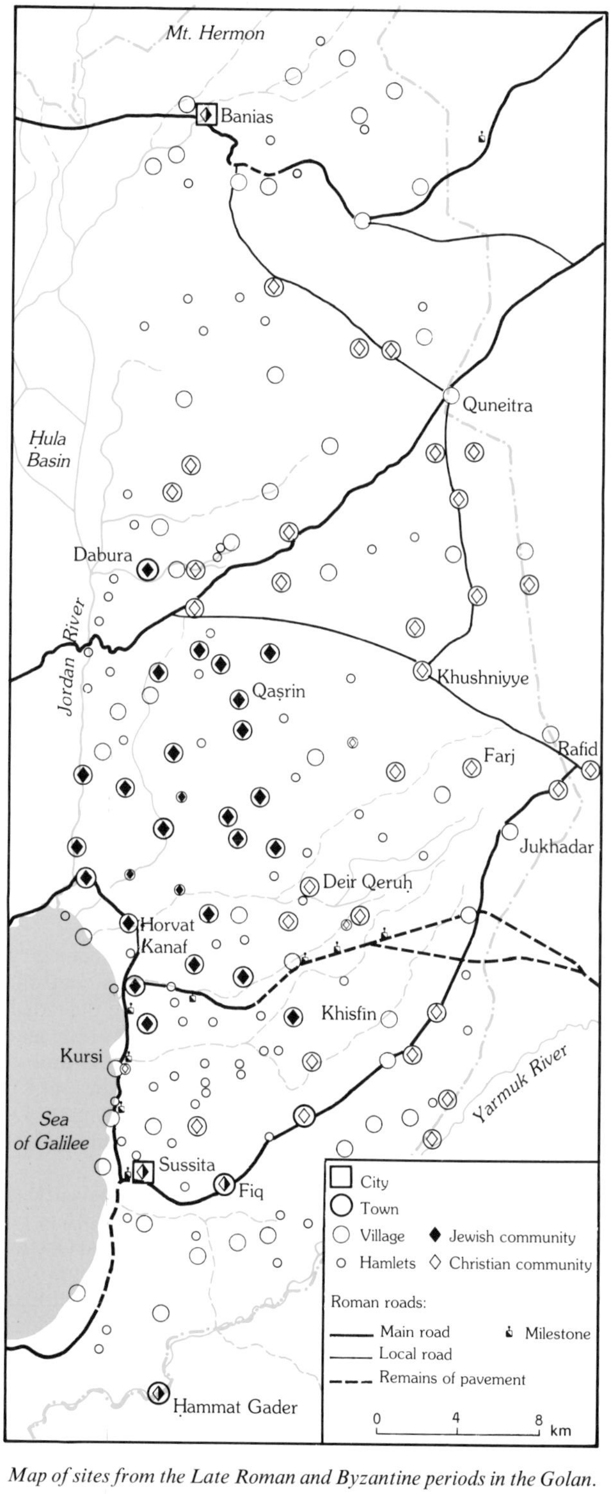

Map of sites from the Late Roman and Byzantine periods in the Golan.

Ḥammat Gader: the spring area.

Herodium: mosaic floor in the central bathhouse in Lower Herodium.

Tel Haror: incense stand and large goblet from the MB II temple in area K.

Tel Haror: overview of Late Iron Age remains in areas D and G; (center) a sheikh's tomb.

Plan of part of a Roman road and milestone station.

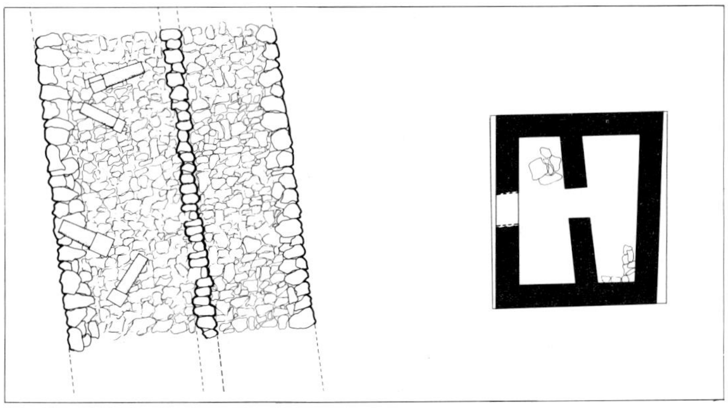

basalt-paved *cardo* inside the east gate. The water system continued to a basalt nymphaeum with a sunken apse in its facade and a subterranean stone-vaulted reservoir (5.2 by 18 m in area and 8.5 m high) at its foot. The remains of monumental basalt buildings and other architectural moldings were found scattered about the site. These fragments, as well as marble and granite columns, bases, and ornate Corinthian capitals, incorporated in secondary use in Byzantine churches, attest to the wealth and magnificence of the city in the Middle Roman period (q.v. Hippos).

The principal features of the remains at Banias from the Middle Roman period are a sanctuary to the god Pan, with niches hewn in the rock escarpment above the spring, a monumental public building in the town's center, and a gigantic vaulted *horreum* (q.v. Banias).

In some Golan villages, private houses built of basalt ashlars with stone ceilings have been preserved (sometimes up to the ceiling). A survey conducted by C. Dauphin in the village of Na'rān found a nymphaeum (which had already been identified by Schumacher) and an aqueduct, probably from the time of the emperor Philip the Arab (third century). In Na'rān, Kafr Nafākh, and Farj, Dauphin identified the villas of wealthy farmers that were built in the Hauranite style (see below) and, in her opinion, date to the third and fourth centuries CE. The villas in Farj had ashlar mangers in stables, probably intended for horse breeding, similar to the finds in the southern Bashan and in northern Gilead (Umm el-Jimal). According to the conclusions of the above-mentioned survey, such villages were not pre-planned but developed from scattered villas that sprang up, depending on the topography, around a hillock or on the banks of a stream. In some sites in the southern and eastern Golan, finds associated with cults from the Roman period have been discovered: statues of Tyche (at Kafr Nafākh, Khushniyye, and El-'Al) and altars (at El-'Al and Kefar Ḥaruv). Architectural fragments from temples were found at El-'Al and es-Safūriyye. A particularly notable find is the statue of a griffin found at es-Safūriyye, which has parallels in the Nabatean temples at Seeia and Qanawat. Tombs excavated at Khisfīn and Skūfiyyā before 1967 contained small objects of silver, gold, glass, and ivory from the Roman period; they are on exhibit in the Damascus Museum.

ROMAN ROADS IN THE GOLAN. Schumacher identified numerous remains of Roman roads in the Golan, but many of them have not been preserved. Gutman has identified additional paved roads, but not all of them can be definitely attributed to the Roman period. Remains of pavements, milestones, and watchtowers characteristic of Roman roads, which were examined toward the end of the 1980s, attest to the existence of the following roads:

1. A Roman road was traced from Banias, running below Qal'at el-Mghara through the Odem Forest and Buq'ata Valley, on toward Damascus. The road is 6.6 m wide, with two rows of large curbstones and a central spine also built of large stones. The space between the three rows was filled with small stones. Two watchtowers have been identified along the road. One stood at Manq'a ez-Zeyat (west of Mas'ada); it was 4 by 4 m square and surrounded by a courtyard (9 by 7 m). The other, a mile away, in the Odem Forest, was 5.4 by 5.4 m in size and surrounded by a courtyard (15 by 10 m). This road is listed in the *Tabula Peutingeriana* as part of the Tyre–Banias–Damascus road. Along this road two milestones were found, one, south of Tel Dan, from the reign of Gordian III, and the other, near Taranje (outside the Golan), from the reign of Marcus Aurelius. Josephus mentions a road running in a similar course (*War* III, 10, 7): "And this pool (Ram) is located on the way to Trachonitis at a distance of 120 miles from Caesarea (Philippi), and it is near the King's Highway on the right."

2. The remains of a paved Roman road were discovered in the 1940s at the foot of the Ha-On cliffs, from the vicinity of Ḥorvat Samra to Wadi Jamusiyye on the way to Hippos. Several milestones without inscriptions also were found along this line. A number of milestones bearing inscriptions from the second century CE were later discovered, although not in situ, at the foot of Khirbet Tawāfiq el-Fawqā. These remains may be associated with the Scythopolis–Hippos road mentioned on several Hadrianic milestones found in the Beth-Shean Valley.

3. Some milestones were discovered on the eastern shore of the Sea of Galilee, north of 'En Gev: at Ḥorvat Mei Ḥamma, in the fields of Kursi, and near Sheikh Khadr. They attest to a branch of a Roman road linking the road to Sussita (Hippos) with the road coming from Zaydan (Bethsaida).

4. Impressive remains of a paved road extending from the Lawiyye spur eastward to the Syrian border were found. The course of the road can be followed from 'Amrat el-Fureij for 7 km (4.5 mi.), up to the road junction to the west of Rasm Baluṭ. At this junction the road forks, both branches running to 'Ein Dhakhar in Syria—one in a straight line and the other through Bjūriyye. The lengths of the branches within Israel are 7 and 8.5 km, respectively. The road was built in straight lines, and low-lying areas, swamps, and streams are crossed on elevated ramps. Its width is 5.7 to 6.5 m and it has two rows of large curbstones, a central spine (also of large stones), and fills of small stones that provide a bed for a layer of soft earth (which has eroded). Clusters of milestones were found along the road at four locations (north of Ramot, at UTM map references 7564.6404 and 7582.6409, and west of Rasm Hudhud). At two of these locations groups of uninscribed milestones were found; nearby were small buildings that measured some 6 by 6 m.

One of the buildings, a watchtower near the Roman road, and a group of milestones (UTM grid 7582.6409) were excavated in 1981 on behalf of the Israel Department of Antiquities and Museums and the Golan Field School, under the direction of Z. Ma'oz and R. Lavi. On the northern side of the road the excavations revealed a building (5.9 by 5.4 m), preserved to a height of one or two courses above its foundations. The walls are 0.7 m thick and built of squared, carefully laid stones on a broad foundation. The interior of the building was divided by a partition wall into two narrow rooms, which were linked by a doorway. The entrance to the building, which no longer exists, may have been in the southern wall, which faces the road; it may have provided access to the upper story only, which was the case with similar towers in the Hauran. An earthen floor on a stone bedding was cleared, and on it were restorable vessels—bowls, cooking pots, jars, flasks, and a cosmetic juglet. Based on three coins from the reigns of Commodus and Elagabalus found here, the structure has been dated to the second or early third century CE. These remains probably belong to a Roman road that ran from the direction of Capernaum, through Bethsaida, toward the city of Naveh and the Bashan. A milestone found near Capernaum dates the road to the time of Hadrian (q.v. Capernaum), but the section between Bethsaida and Naveh may only have been built at the end of the second century CE. This road also linked the estates of Rabbi Judah ha-Nasi in the Bashan with the Galilee. It is known in the Palestinian Talmud (*A.Z.* 4, 44d) as "Istratia beZaydan" (the Bethsaida road.)

5. Along the Benot Ya'aqov Bridge–Quneiṭra–Damascus thoroughfare—perhaps a branch of the Via Maris—is a typical paved stretch south of 'Aweinat esh-Shimaliyah. A complex of buildings at the highest point in the village of Na'rān is thought by Dauphin to represent a *mansio* (horse-changing inn) from the third century CE.

ANI'AM: THE ROMAN FORT. On the outskirts of Moshav Ani'am, near a gushing spring (map reference 2197.2624), Khirbet el-'Amudiyye sits on a cliff overlooking Wadi Marawi. Excavating in 1978 on behalf of the Israel Department of Antiquities and Museums, Z. Ma'oz exposed a square structure (7.1 by 7.1 m) that he identified as a fort from the Late Roman period. It consists of an anteroom and two additional chambers. In the anteroom (2.5 by 2.4 m) a square pillar supported a staircase tower; doors led from the anteroom to another small room (2.3 by 2 m) and to a room that extended for the entire width of the fort (5.4 by 2.1 m). The fort was built in dry masonry of solid basalt blocks on stone foundations. The walls are 0.85 m thick. Reused ashlars were found incorporated in the north wall.

The building was probably both paved and roofed with stone slabs. Evidence to that effect is provided by the ends of paving stones found bonded into the walls and by the stone brackets found at the top of one wall. The stones were robbed and replaced in the Late Arab period, when the building was reused. Coarse pavements, earthen floors, and ancillary rooms were added then. A large quantity of pottery from the thirteenth and fourteenth centuries was found on the floors; the fill for the foundations beneath the floors yielded pottery from the third to fifth centuries CE.

In plan, the fort resembles the corner towers of Roman fortresses in Transjordan dating to the reign of Diocletian, such as Qaṣr el-Bashir; the tower of the Byzantine Qaṣr el-Banat in the Bashan; and some fourth- to fifth-century forts along the eastern border road of Mount Hebron, such as Rujm el-Qaṣr, Kheleifeh, and Ras Jurjis. Judging from these similar plans and the limited pottery finds, the building should be assigned to the late third or fourth century CE. Its function may have been to defend the spring or, perhaps, a local road.

BYZANTINE PERIOD (365–636 CE)

The Byzantine period was a time of great prosperity in the Golan, as in other parts of the country. Evidence of the intensification of settlement is provided by the increase in the number of sites (173) and in the extent of the built-up area. However, not all parts of the Golan were settled with the same density, as the varying geographical conditions offered different prospects for settlement. Examination of the settlement patterns for this period shows that the southern Golan was the most densely populated. The southern district included the city of Hippos and, along the road to the Bashan and Damascus, a chain of small towns, each with a built-up area of 25 a. or more, such as Fiq, El-ʿAl, and Khisfīn. By contrast, the area of a typical village in the central or northern Golan did not exceed 2.5 to 7.5 a. (mainly because of the sparse springs), and there was only one town—Dabūra. On the other hand, the city of Banias, at the northern end of the Golan, enjoyed great prosperity at the time, in part because of its abundant water sources and its location on the road from Tyre and Sidon to Damascus. Banias reached the peak of its prosperity in the fifth century CE, when its walls extended beyond Naḥal Saʿar in the south. The walled area covered some 250 a. (q.v. Banias).

VILLAGE AND HOUSE PLANS. According to the surveys and excavations conducted in the Golan, the village layouts followed one of three basic patterns. Such villages as Givʿat Orḥa, Qaṣrin, ʿAssaliyye, Dabūra, and Beidarus were orthogonal. Narrow streets and parallel lanes run between the buildings, crossing one another at right angles; however, the orthogonal plan was not rigidly adhered to and the buildings are of different sizes. At Ḥorvat Kanaf, which is built on the slopes of an elliptical spur, the village streets ascending the slope converge toward the center, like the spokes of a wheel. Elsewhere, as at Farj, Kafr Nafākh, and Naʿrān, no regular plan could be identified: the villages were made up of villas built here and there, depending on the topography. The space around and between the villas was then gradually filled in with a conglomeration of randomly placed buildings and annexes, among which ran narrow, sharply winding lanes. Village streets were unpaved (at Qaṣrin and Bab el-Hawa, layers of gravel and pebbles were used as the bedding for the street). All the houses were built of the local basalt. Because an abundance of this raw material was available in the fields and on the banks of streams, no basalt quarries were found. Walls were generally built of hewn stones, laid fairly precisely, using the dry-stone technique. Some walls were built of unhewn stones, but they were mainly internal partition walls and late additions. Ashlar masonry was always used to frame external entrances of private houses and sometimes in the facade of a villa or in rooms intended for some special function. The prevailing architectural style in the Golan during the Roman-Byzantine period, the Hauranite style, is known from southern Syria and northern Transjordan. The principles that dictated its features are attributable to a lack of limestone to manufacture cementing materials and to the great abundance of basalt inter alia—in the form of natural colonnettes (hexagons) in the canyons. The latter were particularly convenient for use as strong stone beams (generally 1.3 to 2.5 m long). Much of the basalt was in the form of large boulders, from which solid slabs were readily made. A distinctive feature of the Hauranite style is thus the use of stone ceilings—basalt beams resting side by side on stone brackets (corbels) projecting from the walls or from arches, with spans of from 2 to 3.5 m. Another characteristic feature of Hauranite building, the window wall, supported the weight of walls and ceiling because of the natural strength of the basalt. The window walls fulfilled a variety of functions: they were sometimes used as mangers in stables (Farj, Buṭmiyye, Rafid, Deir Qeruḥ) or as wall cupboards for storage. Their main function, however, was to illuminate and ventilate the rear sections of a house. The combination of stone ceilings, brackets, and arches made it possible to build spacious halls, for use either as storage space or as stables; a similar technique was used in churches (Deir Qeruḥ, Duer el-Lōz). At Kafr Nafākh, Schumacher reported "windows" being used as loculi in a stone-built burial cave. A tomb of this type was also uncovered at Bab el-Hawa.

In some villages in the eastern and southern Golan, villas with well-dressed ashlar walls were found. The typical plan of such a villa (which was common in the Bashan) was rectangular. It consisted of a central chamber, whose high stone ceiling rested on two parallel arches, flanked by rooms in two stories, one above the other. Sometimes the rooms were separated by window walls. A more complex unit might consist of a combination of several characteristic subunits and halls whose ceilings were supported by a series of cross arches. The domestic structures in the villages in the central Golan, such as Qaṣrin and Kanaf, are of lower quality, with scarce use of arches and ashlar masonry. The usual domestic unit there included a living room with a window wall at the rear that supported a low stone ceiling. The rear section of the house was thus divided into two levels: the upper one served as sleeping quarters and the lower as storage space. The Hauranite style was already being used in the Second Temple period, as evidenced by finds at Gamala; apparently its beginnings can be traced to the third century BCE in eastern Transjordan and southern Syria. Some of its elements were common in the Bashan and the Golan as late as the Mameluke period and even up to the twentieth century; the distinctions between architectural styles in the different periods are in some cases difficult to detect.

HOUSEHOLD VESSELS. The pottery repertoire of the Byzantine period in the southern and central Golan (in the districts of Hippos and Gaulanitis) is basically similar to that common in the country as a whole, particularly in the north. The most common household vessels are storage jars, cooking pots, kraters, and bowls—as well as jugs, juglets, and a variety of lamps. An archeometric study conducted by D. Adan has shown that, despite the typological similarity to other parts of the country, most of the pottery was manufactured in the Golan itself, with only a small amount imported from the Galilee. A potter's workshop was found at Khirbet el-Ḥawarith, at the foot of Mount Hermon, that supplied its distinctive products to Banias and the northern Golan. Red-slipped tableware, imported from North Africa and Cyprus, has also been found in the Golan. Finds other than pottery include numerous glass vessels, glass bracelets, and carved bone plaques.

ETHNIC MAKEUP: CHRISTIANS AND JEWS. The archaeological data from the Byzantine period has made it possible for the first time to determine the ethnic and religious identity of the population of the Golan. Public buildings, such as synagogues and churches; inscriptions in Hebrew, Aramaic, and Greek; and artistic and religious symbols, such as seven-branched candelabra and crosses, provide clear guidelines to the ethno-religious map of the Golan in this period.

The main impetus for the renewal of Jewish settlement in the Golan—after it was interrupted in the Middle Roman period—was provided by migration from the Galilee during the fourth century CE. The dense Jewish population northeast of the Sea of Galilee was simply a territorial extension of the Jewish presence in the eastern Galilee. Z. Maʿoz surveyed some forty sites in this region, in twenty-five of which there were synagogue remains or architectural fragments that had originated in synagogues. Jewish settlement in the Byzantine period extended from Naḥal Gilbon in the north to Naḥal Samakh in the south and from the Jordan River and the Sea of Galilee in the west to the 400-m contour line (approximately) in the east.

The northern Golan was still populated at this time by descendants of the Itureans; at any rate, the Golan ware typical of this ethnic group in the Hellenistic period continued to appear in Byzantine times, with some typological variations (in the shape of the rims, handles, and bases); it has, in fact, been discovered in Late Byzantine strata at Givʿat Orḥa and Qaṣrin. Churches and Christian symbols have been found only in a few villages in the Iturean territory of the northern Golan, and then usually along the main roads from Banias to Quneiṭra and from the Benot Yaʿaqov Bridge to Quneiṭra. This may indicate that the conversion to Christianity of the Iturean population—which in the sixth century also included Arabs from the Ghassanid tribe—was slow and was not completed even to the end of the Byzantine period. However, the eastern and southern Golan have yielded numerous remains of churches and Christian symbols (twenty-two sites).

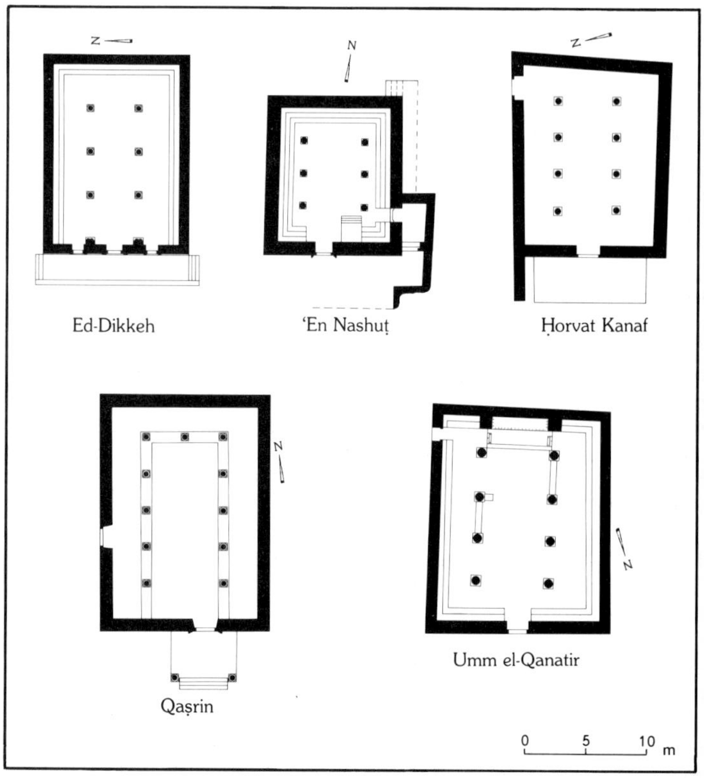

Plans of synagogues in the Golan.

and Hippos (Sussita) was apparently entirely Christian. There were bishops' seats at Hippos, Afeca (Fiq), and Khisfīn.

CHURCHES. In surveys and excavations in the Golan, churches of two main architectural types have been found at er-Ramthāniyye, Deir Qeruḥ, Khisfīn (Ḥaspin), Hippos, Kursi, and Duer el-Lōz. The church buildings at Hippos, Kursi, and Khisfīn are basilicas with distinct architectural features: walls built of stones and mortar; two rows of arcades on columns that divide the building into a nave and two aisles; a semicircular apse; mosaic floors; and tiled roofs laid on wooden truss beams. This type of church is the most common in the coastal and valley regions of Palestine. The churches at Deir Qeruḥ and Duer el-Lōz (as well as architectural fragments from Ramthāniyye, Deir Srās, and other villages) are of the type common at the time in the Bashan: their ceilings, of basalt slabs, rest on large arches supported by square pillars. The apse in this church is sometimes square, and the floor is generally paved with stone slabs or (rarely) with mosaics. Dozens of Greek dedicatory and funerary inscriptions have been discovered in churches and Christian villages in the Golan; most of them, now in the Museum of Antiquities of the Golan at Qaṣrin, have yet to be published.

SYNAGOGUES. Surveys carried out in the western part of the central Golan (the Lower Golan) identified remains of seventeen synagogues; at eight other sites, architectural fragments were found from synagogues whose exact locations are unknown. Four of those synagogues have been excavated: at Ḥorvat Kanaf, 'En Nashuṭ, Qaṣrin, and Dabiyye (qq.v.). The synagogue was generally the only public building in the typical Jewish village in the Golan. It was built on the best site available, which, given the topographical and climatic conditions of the Golan, was not necessarily the highest or most central point in the village. Rather, it was the highest point on a slope or somewhere near a spring. The Golan synagogues constitute a regional architectural group, sharing certain common features: basalt ashlar masonry, thick (0.8–1 m) dry-stone walls, a single entrance in an ornamental facade, columns and stone architraves, an internal division by two rows of columns, and gabled roofs made of tiles laid on wooden trusses. At the same time, different subgroups of buildings, the work of different masons' "schools," can be discerned, each with its distinctive plan, elevation, and carved decorations. The differences between these schools may be attributable in part to the date of construction (fifth as opposed to sixth century CE), but also to the different economic constraints on the builders.

The Chorazin–'En Nashuṭ "School." The Chorazin–'En Nashuṭ "school" includes the synagogues at Chorazin (q.v.), Khirbet Shura, and Khirbet Tuba west of the Jordan, and 'En Nashuṭ (q.v.), ed-Dikkeh, Rafid, Khirbet Khawkha, Ḥorvat Bet Lavi (Wakhshara), and Khirbet Zumeimira in the Golan. These synagogues have richly decorated facades, and the gables are surrounded by convex friezes with floral scrolls in relief and decorated cornices. The facade is pierced by windows whose frames are carved with a gable with colonnettes, and sometimes also with conches and animal reliefs. The outer walls are decorated with pilasters crowned by diagonal Ionic capitals. The columns in the synagogue hall stand on pedestals: the lower order of columns has Doric or Ionic capitals and the upper story has Corinthian capitals (or sometimes Doric columns without bases). The architraves resting on the columns are of the "'En Nashuṭ type": an abundance of sculpture in relief, with subjects taken from the world of flora and fauna. Miniature animals carved in relief on architectural elements, such as capitals and parts of windows, are very common.

Based on the excavations at 'En Nashuṭ and on some specific architectural details, the date of this group has been assigned to the mid-fifth century CE. The ornate decoration on the synagogues mentioned above is an artistic parallel to the "Byzantine baroque" characteristic of fifth-century churches on the Aegean and Levantine coasts, as well as inland Syria. The school includes synagogues that face west, as at ed-Dikkeh and Zumeimira, and south, as at 'En Nashuṭ and Bet Lavi (see below).

The Kanaf "School." The Kanaf "school" includes the synagogues at Ḥorvat Kanaf (q.v.), Deir 'Aziz, and probably also Ṭaiybeh. This school lacks the ornate decoration of the preceding school. What decoration there is in its generally simple style is concentrated mainly on the outer facade, usually around the portal. The columns in the prayer hall have no pedestals and their capitals are Doric (Deir 'Aziz, Ḥorvat Kanaf) or schematic Ionic (Ṭaiybeh). The architraves are of the 'En Nashuṭ type. Based on the Kanaf excavations, the school has been dated to the beginning of the sixth century CE. It is apparently a local continuation and simplifying development of the Chorazin–'En Nashuṭ style. Syrian churches from the sixth century also lack baroque ornamentation.

The Qaṣrin "School." The Qaṣrin "school" includes the synagogues at Qaṣrin (q.v.), 'Assaliyye, Quṣbiyye, and Yahudiyye. The decoration in these buildings is concentrated on the outer entrance. All of them have the same type of frame around the main entrance: a convex frieze merges at the bottom of the doorposts with a kind of engaged pillar on an Attic base, and the cornice is decorated with an egg-and-dart motif. The lintels are carved in different designs: Qaṣrin has a central wreath, amphorae, and pomegranates; at Yahudiyye, a central wreath is flanked by trailing ivy and vine branches, pomegranates, and an amphora; and at Quṣbiyye, an eagle with outspread wings is featured. Within the hall the plan is uniform—two rows of columns stand on Attic bases. The columns have Ionic capitals whose design is specific to this school. No stone architraves were found in the synagogues in this subgroup. Judging from the excavations at Qaṣrin, these synagogues had an elevated clerestory rather than galleries. Based on the Qaṣrin excavations, this school, too, is to be dated to the beginning of the sixth century CE. Its architectural style is not a local development but a new fashion that originated in western Palestine.

In addition to reflecting these well-defined architectural "schools," synagogues in the Golan exhibit a distinctive architectural design within the general "Golan" style, such as those at Umm al-Qanaṭir, Ṣalabeh, and Dabiyye.

Mashrafāwī: basalt head of a lion, Roman-Byzantine period.

Location of the Entrance and the Direction of Prayer. In some Golan synagogues—at Zumeimira, Dabiyye, Bet Lavi, Umm el-Qanaṭir, and 'En Nashuṭ—the main entrance in the facade of the building was not aligned with the axis of symmetry but was displaced from the center. The explanation for this can be bound in the 'En Nashuṭ synagogue, where it is apparent that the displacement was to accommodate the Ark of the Law, which was built on the inside of the facade. It solved the problem of locating the entrance and the ark in the same wall.

The orientation of the Golan synagogues and the direction of prayer in them are still open questions. The Golan survey found some synagogues built along an east–west axis, with the facade oriented west (ed-Dikkeh, Ḥorvat Kanaf, Deir 'Aziz, Zumeimira, Ṣalabeh, Batra, Yahudiyye, and Zawitan). The displacement of the entrance from the center at Zumeimira, as at 'En Nashuṭ, to make room for the Ark of the Law, seems to indicate that in the synagogues listed above the congregation prayed facing west. However, other Golan synagogues were aligned north–south, with their facades facing south ('Assaliyye, Dabiyye, Bet Lavi, 'En Nashuṭ, and Ṭaiybeh). The facade of the Qaṣrin synagogue is in the north, but the Ark of the Law was installed in the southern wall, so that here, too, the congregation faced south. Excavations in some synagogues with facades facing west and south indicate that both types were probably built about the same time. Possibly, therefore, some *amoraim* (Talmudic sages) may have ruled that congregants should face west in prayer, in order to distinguish Jews from Christians. In addition, one tradition may have originated in Transjordan, where, according to E. L. Sukenik, it was customary to pray in the direction of Jerusalem—hence, to face west (as in the synagogue at Gerasa); another tradition was that in the Galilee, where synagogues are oriented south, toward Jerusalem. Yet another explanation is the geographical proximity to the Jordan River and the Sea of Galilee of the synagogues that face west, whereas those farther away from these bodies of water face south. Finally, the source of the discrepancy may lie in some as yet unknown halakhic ruling, traces of which may nevertheless be discerned in Talmudic works.

Artistic Reliefs. As in the synagogues in the Galilee, the major decorative element in the Golan synagogues is the reliefs carved on various parts of the building: on lintels, capitals, cornices, windows, Arks of the Law, and even

Basalt tombstone from Ṣurman in the Golan with the Greek inscription: "Be strong, Monimousa daughter of Philippus. No one is immortal. She lived sixty years. The year 367" (of the Banias era, or 365/366 CE).

Ghadriyya: stone engraved with a menorah and a Torah ark(?).

walls. The repertoire of patterns includes formal Roman ornamental designs, such as meanders, wreaths, Hercules' knots, vine branches, amphorae, pomegranates, rosettes, and seashells. The variety of animals depicted in the reliefs is particularly rich—mainly lions, eagles, and other birds. These are familiar from synagogue decorations in the Galilee, but in the Golan Egyptian vultures, snakes, and fish are also found, which are not at all common in the Galilee. Of particular interest is a basalt orthostat discovered in the village of 'Ein Semsem, which probably came from the synagogue at 'En Nashuṭ. Carved in three dimensions on its narrow face are the head and forelegs of a lion; the long side bears a scene carved in bas-relief of a male figure raising his hands in supplication, flanked by a lion and a lioness, the latter suckling her cub. At both ends of the scene are eagles with outspread wings, one of them pecking at a cluster of grapes. Traces of painting are visible on the relief (the space was filled with a network of red lines). The scene depicted here is Daniel in the lions' den, a subject also treated in the medium of mosaic in the synagogues at Na'rān and Susiya. Fragments of lions sculpted in three dimensions—like those at Capernaum, Chorazin, and Bar'am—have also been found in some synagogues in the Golan, such as at 'En Nashuṭ, Bet Lavi, and er-Rafid; they probably adorned the Ark of the Law.

A common Jewish symbol in synagogue art in the Golan is the menorah (candelabrum), with varying numbers of branches—three, five, seven, and even nine. The bases also exhibit different designs. The menorah is generally carved on the lintels of side entrances or windows (Qaṣrin, Dabiyye, Ghadriyya, and 'Assaliyye), on capitals ('En Nashuṭ and Kanaf), on arch stones (Yahudiyye), and in one case on a column (Fiq). Rarely, the menorah is accompanied by an incense shovel and a shofar (Yahudiyye and Fiq). Another Jewish symbol is the aedicula, or Ark of the Law, featured on lintels at 'Assaliyye and Ghadriyya. No mythological motifs are found in Golan synagogues, with the exception of the lintel at ed-Dikkeh, which shows two winged Victories (Nike) bearing a wreath (like the lintels of the synagogues at Rama and Bar'am). The artistic style is generally flat and schematic, and sometimes the carving is of high quality. The depictions of animals and the composition of the various motifs adhere to the conventions of eastern Mediterranean Byzantine art. The architectural and artistic style of the Golan synagogues is influenced both by that of the Galilee synagogues, whose influence is evident in the overall design of the buildings, and by the style of construction in the Bashan, particularly that in the Jewish city of Naveh. The latter influence is evident in the constructive elements of the raw material (basalt), the style in which the reliefs are sculpted, and the choice and execution of motifs.

Ed-Dikkeh. Ed-Dikkeh is situated on the east bank of the Jordan River, approximately 3 km (2 mi.) north of the Sea of Galilee (map reference 2087.2588). The remains of the synagogue here were discovered by L. Oliphant in 1884. In 1889, G. Schumacher surveyed the site, and in 1905 the remains of the synagogue were partly cleared by H. Kohl and C. Watzinger. In 1932 an expedition from the Hebrew University of Jerusalem, led by E. L. Sukenik, visited the site. In 1967, it was surveyed by C. Epstein. Some additional architectural remains were recorded in 1979 by Z. Ma'oz.

The synagogue is oriented east–west and its highly decorated facade faces west. The facade has three entrances, the central one broader and higher than the two flanking it. The frame of the central entrance is decorated with a plain

Ghadriyya: fragment of a gable.

molding including faciae, a convex frieze, and a cornice. Above the lintel is a relieving arch decorated with a vine branch. The lintels at the side entrances are also decorated with vine branches and convex friezes. From both corners of the front wall and between the doors project two pilasters topped by diagonal Ionic capitals. Parts of a window found here belong to the facade of the building's second story. On either side of the window are pairs of colonnettes with spiral fluting; the lintel is shaped like a pediment, with reliefs of a vine branch, a dolphin(?), lions, and an eagle. The lintels above other windows have arched pediments. The facade of the building is topped by a Syrian gable, its base decorated with a convex frieze featuring floral scrolls and a cornice with rows of dentils, astragal and egg-and-dart motifs, or meanders.

The prayer hall (10.8 by 13.8 m) is divided into a nave and two aisles by two rows of columns, each consisting of four columns and a double half column projecting from the western wall. The lower order features columns on pedestals with Corinthian capitals; the upper order columns have Doric capitals. There probably were galleries above the aisles. In the walls of the upper story the windows were decorated with Corinthian half columns. The floor of the hall was paved with basalt slabs and double benches ran along three of the walls. Stylistic considerations prompted G. Foerster to date the synagogue to the third century CE. However, on the basis of its stylistic association with the Chorazin–'En Nashuṭ "school" and on certain details—such as the Corinthian capital with eagles carved on its corners—this writer is of the opinion that the date of construction is the mid-fifth century CE.

Khirbet er-Rafid. Khirbet er-Rafid is a large ruin overlooking the east bank of the Jordan River, approximately 7 km (4.5 mi.) south of the Benot Ya'aqov Bridge (map reference 2092.2625). The site was discovered by G. Schumacher in 1889 and surveyed in 1932 by E. L. Sukenik and again in 1979 by Z. Ma'oz, but it has not been excavated. Protruding from the ground on the eastern side of the site—not necessarily in situ—is a molded doorpost, part of the entrance to the synagogue. Near the doorpost were found two pedestals, column drums, and fragments of windows decorated with a pediment and a conch with lions in relief. Among the other fragments found here were a richly ornamented cornice and pieces of a three-dimensional sculpture of a lion. A notable find was a fragment of a frieze with a palmette and two crossed fish in relief. Sukenik believed that the fish frieze was part of a depiction of the zodiac, similar to the one in the synagogue at Bar'am. On the western side of the site there was a concentration of columns and Ionic and Doric capitals that had been reused in a building from the Mameluke period. The synagogue was probably located in the eastern sector of the site, but its walls were completely robbed and its architectural elements scattered.

Khirbet Khawkha. Khirbet Khawkha is a ruin on the southern bank of Naḥal Daliyyot, approximately 1 km (0.6 mi.) northeast of Moshav Ma'ale Gamla (map reference 2153.2556). The site was surveyed in 1976 by Z. Ilan and S. Barlev and in 1979 by Z. Ma'oz. Standing in the center of the village is a long wall, built of reused ashlars; this was the site of a synagogue. A few fragments from the synagogue were found in secondary use in the village: a stone from a console with a lion in relief, part of a convex frieze with scrolls of leaves and a rosette, Ionic and Doric capitals, and a fragment of a pedestal.

Ḥorvat Bet Lavi (Wakhshara). Ḥorvat Bet Lavi is located northeast of the peak of Qubbat Qar'a, near the source of Wadi Nukheile (map reference 2187.2588). The site was discovered and surveyed in 1979 by Z. Ma'oz. At the southwestern edge of the modern village were the remains of a building built of ashlars, whose facade, facing south, was preserved to a height of two courses; the other walls had mostly been robbed. The building measured 10.8 by 13.1 m; its central entrance (1.6 m wide) was flanked by molded doorposts. To the north of the building, a lintel was found, broken at both ends, that depicts a lion in relief, its body viewed from the side and its face from the front. Only the outline of the body and the mane have been preserved; the head has been mutilated. To the right of the lion's head was a *tabula ansata* containing a badly worn Aramaic inscription that has not been deciphered. Scattered around the building and in village houses were other fragments from the synagogue, including a pedestal, parts of Ionic and Corinthian capitals, part of a conch, parts of a convex frieze with floral scrolls and rosettes, a cornice decorated with floral motifs, and a relief of a wreath around a rosette.

Khirbet Zumeimira. Khirbet Zumeimira is a small site north of Naḥal Zawitan (map reference 2138.2612). It was discovered in 1970 by C. Epstein and surveyed in 1978 by Z. Ma'oz. At the western end of the ruin was a structure (14.4 by 18.9 m) built of ashlars and oriented east–west. The only entrance (1.58 m wide) was in its western wall. It was placed slightly off-center (to the north) to accommodate the installation of the Ark of the Law on the inside of the wall. The doorposts were molded and above the entrance was a relieving arch with a carved Ionic architrave. In front of the entrance was an ashlar-paved square or portico. At the two corners and along the facade were engaged pilasters with diagonal Ionic capitals, similar to those in the synagogues at ed-Dikkeh and Chorazin. Scattered around the building were architectural fragments from the synagogue, including column drums, an Attic base, and Doric capitals. Particularly worthy of note is a rectangular stone carved with a column in relief, complete with base and capital. A small lion (whose head has been mutilated) is shown climbing, which was, presumably, part of the decoration of the Ark of the Law or of the facade. In secondary use in a nearby (modern) building was a stone with a roughly incised drawing of a seven-branched menorah and two circles. It probably came from a private house.

Aḥmadiyye. Aḥmadiyye is a ruin and an abandoned village northeast of Qaṣrin, on a slope overlooking four springs (map reference 2160.2679). The site was discovered in 1884 by G. Schumacher, who recorded most of the fragments from the synagogue, some of which have since disappeared. In 1978, the site was resurveyed by Z. Ma'oz. The ancient site occupied the summit and slopes of the southwestern hill. A lintel decorated with a Hercules' knot was found protruding from the ground on the slope. Farther up the hill, in a modern house, columns and Doric capitals were found in secondary use. In the courtyard of the house was a stone fragment of an architrave engraved with a vine branch emerging from an amphora. Along the fascia ran part of a Hebrew inscription of unknown meaning: *tmwšmšmr*. A fragment of a Greek inscription and a carving of a seven-branched menorah were also found. At the foot of the hill were a fragment of a pedestal and a column base. Among the items recorded by Schumacher were two fragments of a lintel with a wreathed bull's head and a central eagle with outspread wings flanked by fish. Among Schumacher's other finds were two fragments of a lintel with incised depictions of seven-branched menorahs and a Greek burial inscription translated: "Simeon son of Justinus." The actual location of the synagogue is still unknown.

Batra. Batra is a small site at the end of a spur north of the confluence of Naḥal Daliyyot and Naḥal Batra (map reference 2138.2567). The site was discovered by C. Epstein in 1967 and surveyed by Z. Ma'oz in 1978. The village houses are built on a steep slope facing south, at the top of which stood the synagogue. Only a small section of the western wall has survived to a

Khirbet er-Rafid: part of a window lintel in the synagogue's facade.

Aḥmadiyye: architrave from the synagogue bearing the Hebrew inscription תמושמשמר (tmwšmšwmr).

Ṭaiybeh: lintel of the synagogue.

height of one course, but its extent is discernible from the marks hewn in the rock. The building, 10 by 12.9 m, was aligned on a northeast–southwest axis, its facade facing southwest. In several of the modern houses there were fragments of cornices, half of an engaged Ionic capital, and Doric capitals. To the west of the building a broken lintel was found that depicts a wreath tied in a Hercules' knot, its ends developing into vine branches with leaves alternating with rosettes. Z. Ilan discovered a few additional fragments from the synagogue, including a capital with a relief of a vine branch emerging from an amphora, a bird, and acanthus leaves.

Ḥuseiniyye (Ḥuseiniyyat Sheikh 'Ali). Ḥuseiniyye is a ruin at the mouth of Naḥal Yahudiyye (map reference 2114.2560). The site was discovered by L. Oliphant in 1884 and surveyed by G. Schumacher in 1885, D. Urman in 1968, and Z. Ma'oz in 1985. The synagogue stands at the northern end of the ruin, where the badly damaged remains of its hard plaster floor were found. Alongside the floor, protruding from the ground, was a carved doorpost from the entrance and part of a richly ornamented cornice. In addition, a few Doric capitals of unknown provenance were scattered about the site. Oliphant reported that Bedouin digging in the ruin had unearthed two lion reliefs, which he recorded. Schumacher recorded some other elements from the synagogue, such as a fragment of a lintel with a wreath tied below in a Hercules' knot, vine branches, and grape clusters.

Jarābā. Jarābā is an abandoned Syrian village on a spur west of Naḥal Meshushim (map reference 2113.2618). The site was surveyed by S. Gutman in 1967; by D. Urman, S. Barlev, and M. Hartal in 1969; and by Z. Ma'oz in 1979. The ancient remains are at the top of the eastern slope of the spur—presently the location of a Muslim cemetery. In the northwestern part of the cemetery are the remains of an ashlar-built wall with a doorpost in situ, probably the original location of the synagogue. The plan of the building is unclear. Various architectural fragments from the synagogue were found in secondary use in the village, including column drums, an Attic column base, Doric capitals, and part of a bench. A notable find is an eagle sculpted in three-dimensional relief, its head mutilated; it probably adorned the top of the pediment, as in the synagogue at Chorazin.

Deir 'Aziz. Deir 'Aziz is a large ruin on the southern bank of Naḥal Kanaf, some 2.5 km (1.5 mi.) east of Ḥorvat Kanaf (map reference 2170.2525). The synagogue was discovered in 1885 by L. Oliphant; at that time its eastern part still stood quite high. The site was surveyed again by C. Epstein and S. Gutman in 1967 and by D. Urman in 1969 but the synagogue was mistakenly identified with an ashlar building at the summit of the hill. In 1978, Z. Ma'oz rediscovered Oliphant's synagogue on the southern slope, a short distance below the summit. It measures 10.7 by 17.9 m and oriented east–west. The main entrance (in the west) has not been preserved, but the lintel was found nearby, with a wreath and Hercules' knot in relief. Oliphant recorded a second entrance in the east (1.41 m wide), with a plain lintel. In the synagogue, two columns were preserved in situ, and it would appear that it was divided by two rows of four columns each into a nave and two aisles. The columns supported architraves of the 'En Nashuṭ type, one of which can be seen projecting from the rubble. Scattered over the slope below the synagogue are column drums, Doric capitals, and capitals of pilasters. The remains indicate that the synagogue was very similar to that excavated at Ḥorvat Kanaf, and the probable date of construction was therefore the beginning of the sixth century CE.

Deir 'Aziz: synagogue's western wall, built of large ashlars.

Ḥorvat Zawitan. Ḥorvat Zawitan is a small ruin on the bank of Naḥal Zawitan, near its confluence with Naḥal Meshushim (map reference 2130.2596). The site was discovered by M. Inbar and Y. Gal in 1968 but was not identified as a synagogue. In 1979, the site was surveyed by Z. Ma'oz and identified as a synagogue. It consists mainly of the remains of an ashlar structure that has been partly eroded by the waters of the stream and buried under rock falls. Aligned along an east–west axis, it is approximately 13.1 m long. There is a small doorway in the southern wall flanked by engaged pilasters with Attic bases. A few Doric capitals were found in the bed of the stream, downstream from the ruin.

Ṭaiybeh. Ṭaiybeh is an abandoned Syrian village on the banks of Naḥal Yahudiyye, near its confluence with Naḥal Ṭaiybeh (map reference 2178.2614). The remains of the synagogue were discovered by H. Ben-David and G. Peli in 1977, and the site was surveyed in 1979 by Z. Ma'oz. In the center of the village, standing on the foundations of the synagogue, is a recent building of reused ashlars. Its southern wall contained the synagogue's complete lintel. It bears a wreath in relief, with a rosette in its center; projecting from either side are medallions containing geometrical rosettes. The lintel had palm branches (the tree of life?) at its ends and a band of egg-and-dart motifs around its edges. The location of the lintel and the orientation of the recent building indicate that the synagogue was originally built on a north–south axis, with its facade on the south. Near the lintel two stone consoles with carved acanthus leaves were found, like those in the synagogues at Capernaum and Bar'am. In the village an Ionic capital, molded cornices, pilaster bases, and architraves of the 'En Nashuṭ type were found.

Umm el-Qanaṭir. Umm el-Qanaṭir is built on a limestone ledge under the basalt escarpment of the Golan, near a northern tributary of Naḥal Samakh (map reference 2195.2506). The Arabic name of the site means "Mother of the Arches," after a nymphaeum with two arches built over the spring to the south of the synagogue. The site was discovered by L. Oliphant in 1884 and surveyed by G. Schumacher in 1885. A limited excavation was conducted in 1905 by H. Kohl and C. Watzinger, who published a very accurate plan of the remains; however, their reconstruction of the building was faulty. In 1932, the site was surveyed by E. L. Sukenik and in 1980 by Z. Ma'oz.

Umm el-Qanaṭir: capital decorated with an eagle and rosettes, detail from the Torah ark(?).

Umm el-Qanaṭir: facade of the synagogue.

The synagogue (13.8 by 18.8 m) is preserved to a height of several courses of ashlars, particularly in the southern wall. The structure is oriented north–south, with its facade in the south. Outside the entrance is a small portico with a stone floor that is reached by three steps. The porch has two columns, topped by corbel capitals. The main entrance (1.63 m wide) was slightly to the east of the building's central axis, probably in order to leave room for the Ark of the Law inside. The doorposts were diagonally molded. The lintel was not found, but nearby was a stone from a relieving arch, decorated with bands of circular, zigzag, and bud patterns. At the top of the arch was a decoration resembling a three-branched menorah(?). The facade had decorated windows with lintels in the form of Syrian pediments, as well as pilasters with capitals decorated with bands of meander, egg-and-dart, and dentil motifs. Found in the debris of the synagogue were two similar stones, each of which bore a three-dimensional depiction of the forepart of a lion (of which only the legs have survived). Kohl and Watzinger suggested that these stones had stood on either side of a window, but it seems more probable that they adorned the base of the Ark of the Law. The unmutilated head of one of these lions was later found at the site. Its face is schematic and naively rendered. The building was crowned with a gable topped by an eagle with outspread wings. A side entrance to the hall, 1.55 m wide, was found in the western wall. There were three rows of columns in the prayer hall: two rows of five columns each, parallel to the long walls, and an additional row at right angles, parallel to the northern wall. The columns supported architraves of the 'En Nashuṭ type, one of them decorated with egg-and-dart motifs and a vine branch. Worthy of mention is a capital consisting of a pair of colonnettes with a relief featuring an eagle with outspread wings and rosettes; it was probably part of the stone-built aedicula of the ark.

The synagogue building probably collapsed in an earthquake; most of its walls and architectural elements were found in the debris among the remains. Kohl and Watzinger, as well as Ma'oz, identified an ancient repair: the gaps between the columns in the western row were sealed to form a wall incorporating various architectural elements. The modification was probably necessary because of the apparent earthquake damage to the building. The synagogue at Umm el-Qanaṭir is unique among the Golan synagogues for its architectural style and decoration, being so far unparalleled by anything revealed by the Golan survey. Kohl and Watzinger believed it had been built in the fifth century CE, but M. Avi-Yonah, F. Hüttenmeister, and G. Reeg dated it to the third century CE. A comparison of its artistic style with that of other synagogues in the Golan indicates, in this writer's opinion, a date in the second half of the fifth century CE, however.

Ṣalabeh. Ṣalabeh is a large ruin on an elevated tongue of land between Naḥal Batra and Wadi Nukheile that is steep on three sides (map reference 2168.2594). The site was discovered by Y. Gal in 1969 and the synagogue identified and measured by Z. Ma'oz in 1979. The village houses were built along the ridge of the spur and the synagogue on its northwestern slope. It is a small building (8.5 by 11 m) built on a terrace formed by large boulders and incorporating parts of olive presses. Only the facade of the building, in the southwest, was built of ashlars; it has survived to a height of five courses. In the center was a single entrance (1.7 m wide) with plain doorposts and a lintel. The prayer hall was divided by two rows of three columns each into a nave and two aisles. An unfinished Ionic capital and a Doric capital are visible in the building's debris. In the northwestern wall were traces of a doorway leading into a narrow space running along the entire length of the hall. The synagogue at Ṣalabeh is a small, unadorned building; such simple synagogues, which are difficult to identify in ruins, were probably more common than once believed.

'Assaliyye. 'Assaliyye is an abandoned village and large ruin, some 3 km (2 mi.) west of Qaṣrin (map reference 2136.2635). The site was discovered by G. Schumacher in 1885, but he failed to identify the synagogue. The latter was discovered by T. Eshel in 1976 and surveyed by M. Ben-Ari, S. Barlev, H. Ben-David, and others. Z. Ma'oz carried out a detailed survey and recorded the plan in 1978. Built on a terrace near the summit of the slope on the western side of the village, the synagogue was rectangular (16 by 18 m), aligned along a north–south axis. The western part was almost completely

'Assaliyye: lintel of the entrance to the synagogue decorated with two menorahs and a Torah ark.

'Assaliyye: Aramaic inscription.

destroyed, while the eastern part is incorporated in a modern house, in whose lower parts the walls of the synagogue were visible. One column, found in situ, hinted at the partition of the hall into a nave and two aisles by two rows of four columns each. The interior walls were plastered with herringbone patterns. Architectural fragments of the building are scattered in the rubble on the slope below the synagogue. The column capitals were Ionic, very similar to those in the Qaṣrin synagogue. The doorposts of the main entrance, which were found near the southern wall, were also molded like those at Qaṣrin. Fragments of an arch, carved in the style of an architrave, probably came from a relieving arch above the entrance. Ashlar blocks from a pediment and various cornices were also found. Incorporated in a modern house in the southwest of the village was a lintel that undoubtedly came from the synagogue; it may have belonged to a side entrance. Carved on the lintel in relief was an aedicula, symbolizing the Ark of the Law, flanked by two incised seven-branched menorahs. Another stone with an incised seven-branched menorah was found in the village, as was a stone with an as yet undeciphered Aramaic inscription. The evident architectural similarity between this synagogue and that at Qaṣrin, in respect to size, plan, and artistic elements, indicates that it was built at around the same time, probably at the beginning of the sixth century CE.

Yahudiyye. Yahudiyye is a village on a narrow spur north of Naḥal Yahudiyye (map reference 2161.2603). Although the site was discovered by G. Schumacher in 1885, he did not identify the remains of the synagogue. Since 1967, various molded fragments that originated in the synagogue have been found in the village; but it was only in 1979 that D. Ben-Ami located the building.

The synagogue at Yahudiyye was built on the outskirts of the village, on the cliff overlooking Naḥal Yahudiyye. One course of ashlars (8.25 m long) has survived from the southern wall, incorporated in secondary use in the foundations of a modern house. One column projects from the ground, but the data are insufficient to reconstruct the plan of the synagogue. Various fragments originally in the synagogue were found in secondary use in the village houses. Among the finds was a lintel with a frame carving similar to that at the entrance to the Qaṣrin synagogue (convex frieze, astragal and egg-and-dart motifs). There is a relief in the center of the lintel of a rosette alongside an amphora and branches of vine and ivy surrounded by a wreath. Two of the column capitals are Ionic; they are identical to those in the Qaṣrin synagogue. Also found at the site were a cornice with a meander design, a pedestal and a column, a lintel with a geometric relief, and an arch stone with a relief showing a nine-branched menorah, a shofar, and an incense shovel. Some of the fragments may have belonged to a second synagogue. The similarity in the design of the lintel and the capitals indicates that this synagogue, too, was built by the Qaṣrin school at the beginning of the sixth century CE.

Yahudiyye: voussoir decorated with a menorah, shofar, and incense shovel, from the synagogue.

Khirbet Quṣbiyye. Khirbet Quṣbiyye is a small abandoned village built on an ancient site, on a hill west of the Yahudiyye–Khushniyye road, 1.3 km (0.7 mi.) southwest of Quṣbiyye el-Jdeida (map reference 2171.2645). The site was discovered in the 1967–1968 survey and surveyed again between 1969 and 1971 by D. Urman, S. Barlev, Z. Ilan, and others. The location of the synagogue was later identified by Y. Kentman, at the highest point in the village. Only a small portion of its foundations has survived in situ. Among the village houses were a few fragments from the synagogue, among them part of a lintel in the style of the Qaṣrin synagogue, with a relief depicting an eagle with outspread wings. A second relief of an eagle with outspread wings was found that was probably originally at the apex of the gable. Among the other fragments were column drums and cornices. An eleven-branched menorah was found incised on a stone.

Dabūra. Dabūra is an abandoned village on the northern bank of Naḥal Gilbon, approximately 5 km (3 mi.) northeast of the Benot Ya'aqov Bridge (map reference 2124.2725). West of the village on the slope is a large ruin. Dabūra is mentioned in Targum Jonathan as the translation of the city "Golan in Bashan" in Deuteronomy 4:43: *Dabūra be-Botnin*. This may imply that Dabūra was identified with Golan in Bashan in the fourth century CE. The site was surveyed in 1885 by G. Schumacher. From 1967 to 1970, S. Gutman, A. Druks, S. Barlev, M. Hartal, and Z. Ilan discovered inscriptions and architectural elements that had originated in Jewish public buildings. In 1982, Z. Ma'oz identified the location of the synagogue or school (*beth midrash*).

Dabūra, with more than thirty buildings, was the largest Jewish village in the Golan. Six olive presses were discovered in the industrial sector in its western sector. Several Jewish inscriptions and dozens of architectural fragments were found in the village, probably all originally from two public buildings, perhaps a synagogue and a school. Both stood at the top of the slope, in the eastern part of the ancient village. Their remains were found in secondary use in the houses in the modern village. One building stood at the southeastern corner of the village; only a round depression in the ground remains, which contains architectural fragments, including pedestals and column drums. The second building apparently stood at the northeastern corner of the village; this follows from the concentration of ashlars and molded stones abundantly found in secondary use in the vicinity. The following architectural elements are particularly worthy of mention.

1. A lintel, in the center of which two snakes form a wreath and are tied below in a Hercules' knot; two Egyptian vultures flank the wreath, each holding a snake in its beak. Inscribed in and around the wreath is a Hebrew inscription: "This is the school of Rabbi Eliezer ha-Kappar."
2. The left half of a broken lintel, in the center of which an eagle with outspread wings holds a small wreath in its beak. Beside it are two fish and an Aramaic inscription: "*tr'h* made the gate."
3. Three fragments of an architrave with two fasciae and a cornice, with an Aramaic inscription: "Eleazar son of . . . the great made the columns that are above the arches and the beams." The inscription records a contribution to the columns above the arch and the beams, testifying to the existence of an upper story of columns in the Golan synagogues.
4. A lintel, at the center of which a wreath encloses a four-petalled rosette that is flanked by Egyptian vultures holding snakes in their beaks.
5. A part of a lintel with a relief of an eagle with outspread wings.
6. A doorjamb with a relief of a double meander containing a rosette.
7. A doorjamb with a fish, in relief.
8. A stone with a relief of a goblet with a heraldic pair of birds on its rim.
9. A building stone with a schematic relief of a bird.
10. A doorjamb with a schematic relief of a human figure with a stela at his side; he is carrying unidentifiable objects. Also found at the site were numerous architectural elements, such as lintels, bases, capitals, and cornices. Among the other inscriptions found at Dabūra are ". . . they made the house . . . may it bring him blessing" and ". . . son of Judah . . ."

The artistic style of the rich remains at Dabūra and the pottery found there, as well as the Phoenician-style olive presses, may imply that the village was not affected by the First Jewish Revolt against Rome. It may well have been the capital of the Jewish Golan during the Late Roman and Byzantine periods (qq.v. Dabiyye, Ḥorvat Kanaf, 'En Nashuṭ, Qaṣrin).

CONCLUSION. The literary sources do not attest to a Jewish population in the Golan during the Late Roman and Byzantine periods. Only the

Dabūra: fragment of a lintel decorated with an eagle holding a wreath in its beak, two fish, and the inscription "tr'h *made the gate.*"

archaeological data enable a reconstruction of its size, history, material culture, and artistic achievements. It seems that after the destruction of most of the settlements during the First Revolt and their subsequent abandonment, Jewish settlement in the Lower Golan was interrupted until the end of the third century CE. It was only in Dabūra that a Jewish village survived up to the time of the Mishnah and the Talmud. This explains why the sages of the Talmud identified it with the biblical "Golan in the Bashan."

Jews returned to the Golan in the fourth century CE, migrating from the Galilee. The economy of the region was based on agriculture, particularly the extraction of olive oil. Villages were generally small—not more than twenty to thirty buildings—owing to the scarcity of water. It appears that the first synagogues were built in the second half of the fifth century CE, and a few buildings were added in the sixth century. The excavations at Ḥorvat Kanaf, 'En Nashuṭ, and Qaṣrin indicate that these synagogues were damaged by earthquakes in the sixth century CE and repaired in the sixth and seventh centuries. The architectural and artistic level of the Golan synagogues is high, revealing influences from the Galilee and the Bashan (particularly from the Jewish metropolis of Naveh), as well as the culture of the eastern Mediterranean coastal region. The Aramaic and Hebrew inscriptions point to the congregants' familiarity with the Torah, as well as the presence of such sages as Rabbi Abun of Qaṣrin, Rabbi Eliezer son of Esther from Kanaf, and the school of Rabbi Eliezer ha-Kappar at Dabūra. The excavations at Ḥorvat Kanaf and 'En Nashuṭ reveal that many of the villages were abandoned as early as the end of the sixth and beginning of the seventh centuries CE, probably because of the continuing state of war between the Persians and the Byzantines. In Qaṣrin, however, the Jewish community persisted until the Early Arab period, probably coming to an end only at the end of the Umayyad period.

EARLY ARAB PERIOD (636–745 CE)

The Early Arab period witnessed a sharp decline in the population of the Golan, which was already underway by the end of the Byzantine period. Of the 173 Byzantine sites in the Golan, only fourteen yielded pottery from the Early Arab period. Occupation levels from this period have come to light as yet only in the excavations at Giv'at Orḥa and Qaṣrin—and even there the area occupied by the village during the Early Arab period is relatively small, and many buildings were uninhabited. The causes of this extreme decline were probably economic: the ravages of war and changes in government, and the loss of markets for olive oil exports, previously the major branch of the economy in the central Golan. In the southern Golan, which subsisted mainly on field crops, the damage to the economy was less serious, and settlement along the Ẓemaḥ–Damascus road continued without interruption to the present day.

An Arabic inscription found near Ẓemaḥ commemorates the building of the road to Fiq in 692 CE by Yahyye Ibn el-Hakim, governor of Palestine. Fiq became the capital of the Golan after Hippos-Sussita was abandoned following the earthquake in 749 CE. Dozens of (as yet undeciphered) Arabic inscriptions have been found in the Golan villages. Judging from some synagogue fragments found in Fiq—including a lintel with a medallion containing a menorah, a shofar, and an incense shovel, as well as a column with an incised menorah and the inscription, "I, Judah the Ḥazan"—there must have been a Jewish community in Fiq in the eighth century CE. A Christian document mentions a monastery near Afeca in the tenth century CE. The excavations at Giv'at Orḥa and Qaṣrin indicate that buildings from the Byzantine period remained occupied. The material culture, in general, as represented by the pottery, glass, and metal ware found at these sites, continues that of the previous period. The original (Christian and Jewish) population probably remained in those settlements that had survived the crises of the early seventh century CE. They were subsequently reinforced by nomadic Arab elements, then undergoing a process of permanent settlement. A large occupational gap was also revealed by the excavations at Giv'at Orḥa and Qaṣrin (and by the findings of the surveys) in levels from the Abbasid, Fatimid, and Crusader periods—from the mid-eighth to the end of the thirteenth centuries. This gap may be attributable to the neglect of Palestine by the central Arab authorities, after the center of the caliphate moved to Baghdad.

AYYUBID AND MAMELUKE PERIODS (THIRTEENTH AND FOURTEENTH CENTURIES)

The Mameluke period was a time of renewed prosperity for the population of the Golan. Pottery from this period was found at 139 or more sites. At most of them the Byzantine buildings were renovated or rebuilt: their walls were raised and their ceilings replaced with stone slabs on arches, after the fashion of Hauranite architecture. The occupation levels from this period that were exposed in the excavations at Ḥorvat Kanaf, Giv'at Orḥa, and Qaṣrin provide evidence of this rebuilding and of new construction and changes in village plans. There is an abundance of glazed pottery in green, brown,

Dabūra: lintel decorated with two Egyptian vultures holding snakes forming a wreath and inscribed "This is the school of Rabbi Eliezer ha-Kappar."

Fiq: column from the synagogue, decorated with a menorah and Aramaic inscription: "I, Judah the Ḥazan."

Fiq: a menorah, shofar, and an ethrog carved in relief on the synagogue's lintel.

and yellow, as well as imported "frit ware." The local pottery is handmade and painted with geometric patterns in reddish-brown on a creme background. A few inscriptions (as yet undeciphered) from this period have been discovered in the southern Golan.

Khans. A feature of this period is the network of khans built along the Mameluke mail routes from Egypt to Damascus. Well-preserved buildings of this type are situated at Khan el-'Aqabeh (Tawāfiq), Khan Jukhadar, Khan Jisr Bint Ya'qub (Benot Ya'aqov Bridge), and Khan Duweir. The khans are built like forts, with a fortified gate in a tower (sometimes with a monumental inscription on the gate). The khan was built around a large central courtyard, with vaulted halls and rooms.

Hellenistic period and Iturean settlement: Schürer, *HJP* 1, Edinburgh 1973, 564–573; Z. Ma'oz, *ESI* 4 (1985), 79–80; S. Gibson and D. Urman, *BAIAS* 10 (1990–1991), 67–72.
Early Roman period: Conder–Kitchner, *SWP* 1, 109–131; R. Arav, *IEJ* 38 (1988), 187–188; A. Negev, *Personal Names in the Nabatean Realm* (Qedem 32), Jerusalem 1991, 108–112.
Middle and Late Roman periods: Y. Aharoni, *'Atiqot* 1 (1955), 109–114; E. M. Meyers et al., *BASOR* 230 (1978), 1–24; D. Urman, *The Golan during the Roman and Byzantine Periods*, Ann Arbor 1979 (Ph.D. diss., New York Univ. 1979); id., *IEJ* 22 (1972), 16–23; id., *The Golan: A Profile of a Region during the Roman and Byzantine Periods* (*BAR*/IS 269), Oxford 1985; ibid. (Review), *AJA* 91 (1987), 156–157; Z. Dulab et al., *Scripta Classica Israelica* 6 (1981–1982), 98, 109; C. M. Dauphin, *IEJ* 29 (1979), 223–225; 31 (1981), 239–240; 33 (1983), 112–113, 189–206; 34 (1984), 268–269; 36 (1986), 273–274; (with S. Gibson), 41 (1991), 176–179; id., *PEQ* 112 (1980), 68; 114 (1982), 74–75, 129–142; id., *ESI* 2 (1983), 37; 3 (1984), 35–36; 5 (1986), 44; 9 (1989–1990), 6–7; id., *Archaeological Survey in the Mediterranean Area* (*BAR*/IS 155, eds. D. R. Keller and D. W. Rupp), Oxford 1983, 353–355; id., *Proche-Orient Chrétien* 304 (1984), 233–245; Z. Ma'oz, *ESI* 4 (1985), 38–39; P. Porat, *Scripta Classica Israelica* 10 (1989–1990) 130–133.
Roman roads: D. Urman, *The Golan during the Roman and Byzantine Periods*, Ann Arbor (op. cit.), 193–215; Z. Ma'oz, *ESI* 1 (1982), 32–33; C. M. Dauphin and J. J. Schonfield, *IEJ* 33 (1983), 203–204.
Byzantine period: D. Urman, *The Golan during the Roman and Byzantine Periods*, Ann Arbor 1979 (op. cit.); ibid. (*BAR*/IS 269), Oxford 1985; C. M. Dauphin, *PEQ* 114 (1982), 129–142; id., *IEJ* 33 (1983), 189–206; id., *Archaeological Survey in the Mediterranean Area* (*BAR*/IS 155, eds. D. R. Keller and D. W. Rupp), Oxford 1983, 353–355; id., *Proche-Orient Chrétien* 304 (1984), 233–245; id., *RB* 91 (1984), 231–239; id., *BAIAS* 8 (1988–1989), 82–85; J. J. Schonfield, ibid. (1982–1983), 17; Z. Ma'oz, *PEQ* 117 (1985), 59–68; P. Porath, *Scripta Classica Israelica* 8–9 (1985–1988), 166–170.
Churches: see Deir Qeruḥ, Ḥaspin, Hippos, Kursi.
Synagogues: Z. Ma'oz, *ASR*, 98–115; id., *Jewish Art in the Golan* (Reuben and Edith Hecht Museum Cat. 3), Haifa 1987, 15–20; id., *BA* 51 (1988), 116–128.
Aḥmadiyye: G. Schumacher, *The Jaulan*, London 1888, 70–72; id., *ZDPV* 8 (1885), 333f.; Goodenough, *Jewish Symbols* 1, 222; Hüttenmeister–Reeg, *Antiken Synagogen*, 5.
Dabūra: D. Urman, *IEJ* 22 (1972), 16–23; Z. Ma'oz, *ASR* 109–112.
Khirbet ed-Dikkeh: L. Oliphant, *PEQ* 17 (1885), 82–86; G. Schumacher, *The Jaulan*, London 1888, 120–123; id., *ZDPV* 13 (1890), 70ff.; Kohl–Watzinger, *Synagogen*, 112–124; Goodenough, *Jewish Symbols* 1, 205–206; 3, 520–521; Hüttenmeister–Reeg, *Antiken Synagogen*, 524–528; Z. U. Ma'oz, *BA* 51 (1988), 116–128.
Deir 'Aziz: L. Oliphant, *PEQ* 18 (1886), 76–78.
Khirbet Zumeimira: Hüttenmeister–Reeg, *Antiken Synagogen*, 517.
Ḥuseiniyye: L. Oliphant, *PEQ* 17 (1885), 82–83.
Yahudiyye: G. Schumacher, *The Jaulan*, London 1888, 270–272; Hüttenmeister–Reeg, *Antiken Synagogen*, 482f.
Umm el-Qanaṭir: L. Oliphant, *PEQ* 17 (1885), 89–91; G. Schumacher, *The Jaulan*, London 1888, 260–265; Kohl–Watzinger, *Synagogen*, 59–70, 125–134; Goodenough, *Jewish Symbols* 1, 199, 206–208; E. L. Sukenik, *The Ancient Synagogue of el-Hammeh*, 85–87; id., *JPOS* 15 (1935), 172–174; M. Avi-Yonah, *QDAP* 14 (1950), 57; Hüttenmeister–Reeg, *Antiken Synagogen*, 465–468; Z. Ilan, *ESI* 6 (1987–1988), 110; Z. U. Ma'oz, *BA* 51 (1988), 116–128.
Khirbet Quṣbiyye: Goodenough, *Jewish Symbols* 1, 211; 3, fig. 528–541; Hüttenmeister–Reeg, *Antiken Synagogen*, 365.
Khirbet er-Rafid: G. Schumacher, *ZDPV* 13 (1890), 71–73; E. L. Sukenik, *The Ancient Synagogue of el-Hammeh*, Jerusalem 1935, 91–93; id., *JPOS* 15 (1935), 178–180; Goodenough, *Jewish Symbols* 1, 211.
(See also Gamala, Dabiyye, Ḥaspin, Ḥorvat Kanaf, 'En Nashuṭ, Qaṣrin.)

ZVI URI MA'OZ

GUSH ḤALAV

IDENTIFICATION AND HISTORY

Gush Ḥalav (in Arabic, el-Jish) is about 8 km (5 mi.) northwest of Safed in Upper Galilee (map reference 191.270). It is mentioned in the Mishnah (*'Arakh.* 9:6) as a fortified city from the time of Joshua. Its walls were rebuilt in 66 CE, when Josephus fortified many cities and villages in the Galilee (Josephus, *War* II, 575, 590; *Life* 189). However, the city surrendered to Titus without a fight in 67 CE (*War* IV, 92–120). The town was the home of John of Gischala, one of the prominent Zealot leaders in the revolt and a bitter enemy of Josephus, who had survived the siege of Jerusalem to be led in chains in Titus' triumphal procession. According to Jerome (*De Viris Illustritus*, 5), Gischala was also the home of Paul's parents. Gush Ḥalav (Fat Soil) produced fine olive oil (*War* II, 591–592; *Life*, 74–75; Tosefta, *Men.* 9: 5; B.T., *Men.* 85b). According to Jewish tradition of the Middle Ages, the town was famed for its graves of rabbis and ancient synagogue.

The Gush Ḥalav settlement and the entire Meiron area were clearly oriented north, toward Tyre, into whose economic orbit both Khirbet Shema' and Gush Ḥalav fell. The high percentage of coins minted in Tyre found at Gush Ḥalav and Khirbet Shema' attests to the fact that regional trade was directed north, and that the cultural affinities were also northern—that is, southern Syrian. Ancient sources cite fine silk as well as olive oil among the products of Gush Ḥalav. The presence of imported fine wares at the site indicates that the eastern Mediterranean world was very much a part of everyday life here.

EXPLORATION

Although the site received considerable attention in the nineteenth century by such notables as E. Renan, C. Wilson, V. Guérin, and H. H. Kitchener, the first scientific survey was completed by the Germans H. Kohl and C. Watzinger in 1905. Excavations were carried out at the site in 1977 and 1978 under the auspices of the American Schools of Oriental Research, under the direction of E. M. Meyers. C. L. Meyers and J. F. Strange served as associate directors. All other modern work at Gush Ḥalav has been conducted at sites in el-Jish itself, including the site's upper synagogue on which the village's church was later built.

ASOR EXCAVATION RESULTS. The ASOR excavations were limited to the area of the lower synagogue itself, except for several meters on each side, because the ancient site is located in private orchards. It was soon learned that the results of the German survey were both misleading and inaccurate. The major surprise, however, was that the synagogue structure sat on an ancient subterranean tell, which became evident only after weeks of digging. The following are the four phases of the synagogue's history:

Period I	250–306 CE	Middle–Late Roman
Period II	306–363 CE	Late Roman
Period III	363–460 CE	Byzantine I
Period IV	460–550 CE	Byzantine IIA

In addition, the following other periods are represented in the material remains excavated: Iron Age II, Persian, Early and Late Hellenistic, Early Roman, Late Byzantine (IIB), and Early and Late Arab periods.

THE SYNAGOGUE. The earliest synagogue structure is significantly different from the one proposed by Kohl and Watzinger. They noted that the building was an almost square structure whose interior space is 17.5 m north–south by 17.5 m east–west. The ASOR excavations revealed that the Germans had mistaken the exterior walls on the east and west for load-bearing walls defining interior space. After excavating the two newly discovered north–south walls, the internal space was verified as 13.75 by 10.6–11 m. The main room is rectangular, with two stylobates supporting two rows of columns parallel to the two north-south load-bearing walls.

The remains of the earliest bema are to be associated with this first building period. The bema is in the southwest corner, just west of the central entrance in the southern wall, oriented toward Jerusalem. There is no archaeological trace of a fixed Ark of the Law in this phase or in any other. The central entrance was in the southern facade. It was decorated with an eagle and a garland cut into the underside of the lintel stone, a very unusual but not unique feature of Hellenistic-Roman decorative style. A small outer stairway led to a second entrance in the northwest corner. Apparently these were the only two entrances to the synagogue, which maintained the same basic ground plan in all four building periods (see below).

The most unusual features of the basilical building are the attached corridor on the western side, the two storage rooms on the eastern side, and the gallery area for extra seating, to the north. The rooms on the east and west are well preserved and are still standing. They were not noted by Kohl and Watzinger. The space on the north, however, is hypothetical. It is justified on the basis of the remains of several heart-shaped columns found outside the north wall and other architectural fragments found nearby. It is clear from stratified deposits at foundation levels in each of these areas that the synagogue building, from its inception, included these areas as major architectural features.

Gush Ḥalav: plan of the synagogue.

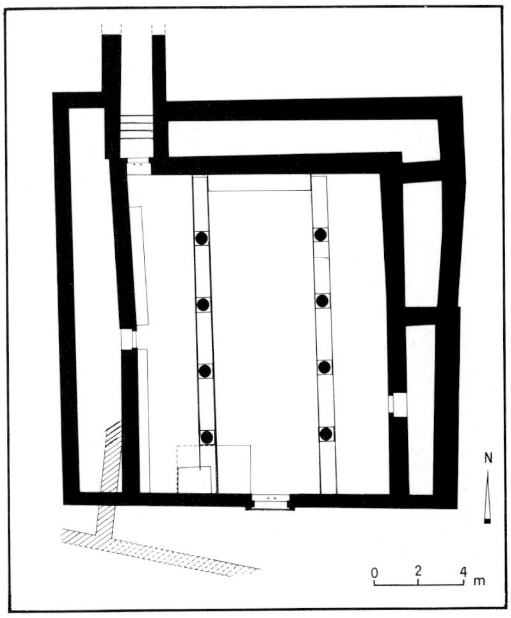

The clarification of these features enabled the resolution one of the major questions that had plagued modern researchers of the Gush Ḥalav synagogue: the spanning distance between the stylobates and the exterior walls. A reasonable distance between the columns and the internal walls could be postulated following the discovery of the interior load-bearing walls on the east and west. Although the earthquake of 306 CE apparently did a great deal of damage to the structure, the stylobates were shored up and other repairs undertaken to make the period II building sturdier. Lying on the direct line of the Safed epicenter, Gush Ḥalav is especially susceptible to earthquakes and tremors. The foundations at each of the four corners betray the extensive measures that were undertaken by the original builder to stabilize the building. It is not at all clear to which building period the inscription on the southeast column belongs. The inscription, in Aramaic, reads: "Jose son Naḥum built this. A blessing be on him."

Benches were attached to at least the western walls in all four building periods, but it was the northern gallery, set slightly back from the interior, that enabled the small basilica to accommodate more people. What appears to be a bench along the north wall is actually a step to the gallery platform.

The first building period was undoubtedly the most ambitious, for it was

Bema in the southwestern part of the synagogue.

Overview of the synagogue, looking west.

then that the building took definitive shape. The eagle lintel (see above) undoubtedly dates to the original structure and was repeatedly used. The all-ashlar southern facade wall is so well built, it is possible that it survived the repeated destruction of the building by earthquakes and that the eagle lintel survived antiquity still in place.

The second building period thus witnessed no major modification in the plan of the building. However, stratigraphic assessment of the data indicates quite clearly that great effort was made to reinforce corners, stylobates, and walls. The debris buildup in the western corridor in particular demonstrates how soon after the great 363 CE earthquake the basilica was reused. Many architectural fragments were then reused, and a smaller bema replaced the earlier and larger one on the southwest interior of the southern facade wall. The final Byzantine phase (period IV), is basically attested through the buildup of floors, which were renewed regularly over time. A coin hoard of some 1,953 specimens was discovered in the western corridor. Although the latest coins do not extend to the great earthquake of 551 CE, the collapse of 19 m of molding in the western corridor testifies to the building's collapse in a single event.

Two architectural features of the Gush Ḥalav synagogue underscore the importance of the building's southern, sacred orientation. The persistence of the bema along the shorter southern wall in several phases not only attests to the importance then of orienting prayer toward Jerusalem, but also to the central importance of the reading of scripture in ancient Jewish liturgy: it was on the bema that the *ḥazan* (precentor) read and interpreted scripture.

The construction of a single southern wall of finished ashlar masonry has been doubted by some, but there are enough parallels in the immediate area and in the Golan to confirm that it was not at all unusual. At Gush Ḥalav, a single door is cut into this finished wall. On the underside of its lintel, a well-incised eagle has been carved into the stone so that it seems to hover above the double-hung doorway leading to the sanctuary. Elsewhere, at the Meiron basilical synagogue, for example, finished ashlar masonry appears only on

Hoard of coins inside a cooking pot, from the synagogue, Byzantine period.

Synagogue lintel decorated with an eagle and a wreath in relief.

the portico and on the wall of orientation. To be sure, it is somewhat difficult to imagine how such a building would have looked, but there can be little doubt that someone approaching from the south would immediately have been aware of the facade's very elaborate nature. In contrast, those arriving from the north faced a rather modest entryway (in the northwest) and stepped up a darkened alley, climbing five stairs into the main hall.

ERIC M. MEYERS

THE MAUSOLEUM. In the spring of 1973, a sarcophagus lid was unearthed while work was in progress on the foundations of a building on the western slope of el-Jish. Excavations were carried out at the site from 1973 to 1975, directed by F. Vitto and G. Edelstein, under the auspices of the Israel Department of Antiquities and Museums.

The lid was revealed to be part of a double sarcophagus, that was resting on a large, magnificent mausoleum preserved to a height of about 5 m. The mausoleum was part of a complex of tombs arranged around a courtyard paved with dressed and fitted slabs. Bordering the courtyard are two ashlar-built walls; the eastern wall leans on a steep stone scarp and the western wall rises parallel to it at a distance of 6 m. The paved courtyard was reached via a flight of stairs between the courtyard's and the mausoleum's western wall. Only the foundations of the stairs have survived, but the impressions in the mausoleum's western wall indicate that they were built of large ashlars, which were robbed over time.

The excavations were confined to the southern part of the tomb complex. The mausoleum is at the southern end of the courtyard, built against the stone scarp. It is a rectangular building (4.2 by 3.5 m), built of ashlars. The walls are preserved to a height of 5.5 m above the courtyard pavement, and the foundations are at least 1.5 m deep.. The mausoleum consists of three parts: a rock-hewn burial cave; a vaulted anteroom leading into the cave; and a room built above the anteroom, where the sarcophagus was found.

Burial Cave. The burial cave (8 m long and 2.5 m wide) has a vaulted ceiling and a standing pit dug in its floor. Its two long walls contained ten hewn loculi (*kokhim*), five in each wall. Circles, rosettes, lines, and other patterns whose significance is unknown are incised on the walls. The loculi contained several skeletons in a good state of preservation, which had been laid there intact. The finds from the loculi and the pit were poor—a few oil lamps and a glass bottle from the fourth century CE.

Antechamber. The vaulted antechamber leading into the cave is built of well-dressed and fitted ashlars. Its interior is 2.9 m high. Three long ashlars placed along the walls functioned as benches. The entrance to the cave is in the rear wall of the antechamber. A limestone door, which still revolves on its hinge, opens into the cave. The deceased's relatives could move the door by means of an iron ring. It was sealed with a bolt, which fit into two holes hewn in the side of the door and in the doorjamb. The mausoleum's facade, which faces

Overview of the mausoleum.

Antechamber of the mausoleum.

Glass vessels found in one of the sarcophagi in the mausoleum.

the courtyard, consists of an arch supporting a cornice, which separates the structure's lower and upper floors.

Room above the Antechamber. A room above the antechamber, identical in size to it, is built of well-dressed stones; the entire room is taken up by a double sarcophagus. The wall of the room facing the courtyard was built of only one course of stones, which afforded a view of the sarcophagus from the courtyard. It is impossible to determine whether the upper story was roofed.

The sarcophagus was carved from hard limestone and covered by two gabled lids with four horns. It contained two burial cells, each of which is 2.2 m long, 1.8 m wide, and 1 m high. Fifteen skeletons, four in one cell and eleven in the other, were found in it. It also contained two glass bottles, a bronze oil lamp, gold earrings, a necklace of gold beads, a glass ring, bone and ivory pins, and bronze kohl sticks. Particularly noteworthy is a bronze bucket found in the sarcophagus, that is engraved with four running animals alternating with stylized trees. These finds have been dated to the fourth century CE.

The excavators also unearthed a rock-hewn burial complex on the eastern side of the courtyard. Its facade was marked by two pillars that originally supported a broad arch that had collapsed in antiquity. The tomb consists of a single hall (c. 3.5 by 3.5 m) with a slightly vaulted ceiling. Two tiers of loculi were cut in the walls. A bench built of large ashlars was placed along each of the three walls (excluding the wall with the entrance). The loculi contained skeletons and a few burial goods, such as oil lamps and glass bottles. The identity of the individuals buried in the complex is unknown, as no inscriptions or other identifying information were discovered.

The complex is part of Gush Ḥalav's large necropolis, which extended mainly down the western slope; it was used for burial during the Mishnaic and Talmudic periods. Associated with this necropolis are some other burial caves, similar in shape to that beneath the mausoleum; these, too, have stone doors that turn on hinges. The necropolis of ancient Gush Ḥalav also contained sarcophagi similar to the one found above the mausoleum. The unique feature of the mausoleum is its combination of different elements: a burial cave with a large antechamber and a double sarcophagus above it. These elements are found individually in other tombs at Gush Ḥalav and its environs; their unique juxtaposition in this mausoleum may have been influenced by burial complexes in the north, perhaps in Asia Minor.

FANNY VITTO

The Synagogue

Main publications: E. M. Meyers et al., *Excavations at the Ancient Synagogue of Gush Halav* (Meiron Excavation Project 5), Winona Lake, Ind. 1990.

Other studies: Kohl–Watzinger, *Synagogen*, 107–111; Goodenough, *Jewish Symbols* 1, 205; E. M. Meyers, *IEJ* 27 (1977), 253–254; 28 (1978), 276–279; id., *RB* 85 (1978), 112–113; 86 (1979), 439–441; id. (et al.), *BASOR* 233 (1979), 33–58; id., *BA* 43 (1980), 97–108; id., *Ancient Synagogues: The State of Research* (ed. J. Gutmann), Chico, Calif. 1981, 61–77; id., *ASR*, 75–77; id., *The Synagogue in Late Antiquity* (ed. L. Levine), Philadelphia 1987, 127–137; D. Chen, *LA* 38 (1988), 249–252.

The mausoleum: F. Vitto, *IEJ* 24 (1974), 282; id., *RB* 82 (1975), 277–278.

Miscellany: N. Makhouly, *QDAP* 8 (1938), 45–50; H. Hamburger, *IEJ* 4 (1954), 201–226; M. Avi'am, *ESI* 3 (1984), 37; 5 (1986), 44–45; I. Stepanski, ibid. 4 (1985), 39–40.

H

HADAR, TEL

IDENTIFICATION

Tel Hadar (Sheikh Khadhr) is located on the eastern shore of the Sea of Galilee, about 7 km (4 mi.) north of 'En Gev (map reference 2122.2507). The mound is rounded in shape and about 2.5 a. in area.

EXCAVATIONS

Tel Hadar was first discovered and surveyed in the 1968 Golan Survey (site 140). Excavations were carried out here beginning in 1987, on behalf of the Land of Geshur Project of the Institute of Archaeology at Tel Aviv University, under the direction of M. Kochavi and P. Beck. The field director was E. Yadin; the excavations were also supported by several American institutions: Cornell University (1987) and the Archaeological Consortium of New Jersey Colleges represented by T. Renner and I. Spar (since 1988). Excavations in the southeastern part of the site revealed two Iron Age levels: stratum I (ninth and eighth centuries BCE) and stratum II (eleventh century BCE). Sherds from the Middle and Late Bronze Ages also came to light, although the strata of these periods have not yet been exposed.

STRATUM II. Two concentric stone walls assigned to stratum II created the present surface of the mound. The thickness of the outer wall reached 4 m and that of the inner wall, 2.5 m. No architectural remains were uncovered in the excavated area in the 25-m-long space between the walls, which was found to contain only stone-lined silo pits about one meter in diameter. The inner wall was pierced on the eastern side of the mound by a gate, the wall reaching it from the north made a 45-degree angle with the wall reaching it from the south. The passageway within the gate was finely paved. A large basalt basin, basalt tripod bowls, and two orthostats were found near the gate but not in situ. The legs of a basalt bowl, shaped like an animal's legs, attest to a very high artistic level.

Not far from the gate, a public building was found against the inner wall, which served as its southern wall. The building had one main entrance but was divided into two wings, one a pillared building and the other a granary. The pillared building is one of the earliest examples of this architectural type, but in addition to the three parallel halls it also had a narrower back room. Some of the stone pillars were monoliths, others were made of stone drums. Most of the pillars and walls were preserved to their original height (2 m).

A large and varied quantity of pottery was found on the floor of the pillared building and in the brick debris that filled the rooms. The most common vessels were egg-shaped jars, clearly of local manufacture. Also found were three-handled jars and jars with handles attached to the rim—both types foreign to local assemblages. Together with cooking pots, bowls, and jugs of types typical of the eleventh century BCE in this country, there was also imported ware from the Phoenician coast (bichrome flasks and jugs), as well as bowls with incised rims, of a type known from Tell el-Ḥammah in the central Jordan Valley and Irbid in Gilead. The pottery dates the destruction of stratum II to the eleventh century BCE.

The granary was entered through a doorway in the wall between the building's two wings; the doorway had been walled up with bricks. The granary was square, with 1-m-thick stone walls; it was divided into six square, paved cells, each approximately 3 by 3 m, with plastered walls and floors. In the corner of each cell, 80 cm above the floor, was a passage to the adjoining cell. The structure's unique form, the fact that it had been burned at a temperature of 1,200 degrees C and, mainly, its contents—thousands of charred grains of wheat—indicate that it was a royal granary. It is quite unique in the context of Iron Age architecture in this country, although similar structures have been found in Egypt, where they date to the Middle Kingdom. It was destroyed by a tremendous conflagration sometime in the eleventh century BCE.

STRATUM I. A gap of several centuries separates stratum I from its predecessor. By the Iron Age II, almost nothing remained of stratum II's royal citadel. An ordinary settlement developed on the ruins of stratum II that reused its outer wall. Within the walls there were now private houses, with broad or square rooms and walls one-stone thick, without pillars, as was the rule then in all parts of the country. The houses were built quite close together, with many common walls. The builders made good use of the stone founda-

Public building from stratum II.

Tripartite pillared building—eastern wing of stratum II public building.

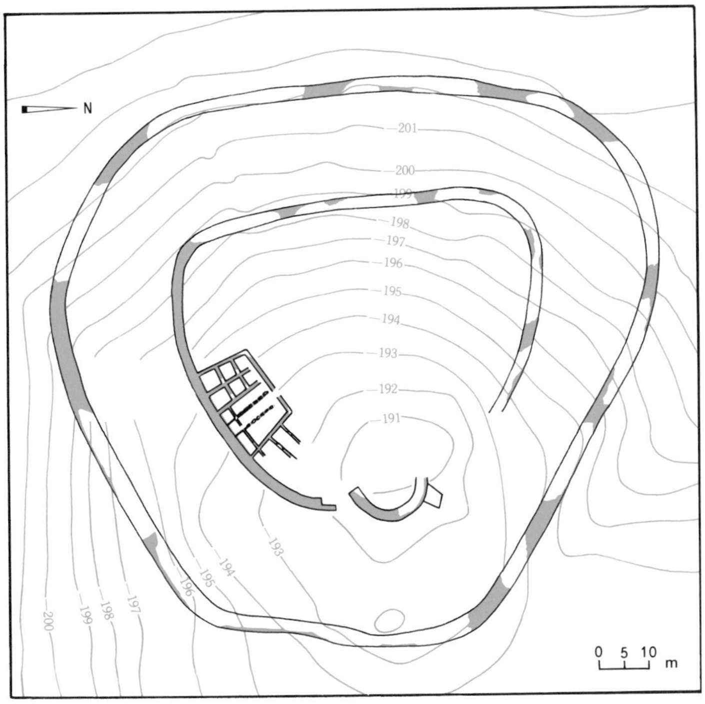

Tel Hadar: general plan of stratum II.

tion of the stratum II inner wall, using it as a floor. Along the outer wall, however, they left a kind of street unbuilt, with a beaten-mud surface. The stratum I houses in the central, elevated part of the mound were damaged because they were relatively close to the surface; their remains indicate that they were better built than the houses along the periphery.

The finds date the final phase of stratum I to the eighth century BCE. The more noteworthy among them were basalt anchors with a hole drilled through them, a figurine of a woman holding a tambourine, and a fragmentary inscription on a sherd.

SUMMARY

Tel Hadar II was not an ordinary city. It was a royal citadel that fulfilled some kind of defensive, economic, and commercial function—an integral part of a political and economic system that comprised the entire district. In view of the site's location and the high level of its unique material culture, it is to be identified as one of the seats of government of the kingdom of Geshur, whose king, Talmai son of Ammihud, was related by marriage to King David. Tel Hadar I, in contrast, was merely a small farming village, a "satellite" of the new fortified city built at nearby 'En Gev. When the Golan and the Galilee were destroyed by Tiglath-pileser III in 733–732 BCE, this town also fell into ruins and was never resettled.

Tel Hadar: multihandled krater, stratum II.

Tel Hadar: jug and brick material from stratum II conflagration.

B. Mazar, *JBL* 80 (1961), 16–28; P. Beck and M. Kochavi, *ESI* 6 (1987–1988), 75–78; M. Kochavi, *IEJ* 39 (1989), 1–17; 41 (1991), 181–182; id. et al., *AJA* 94 (1990), 299.

MOSHE KOCHAVI

Tel Hadar: pottery from stratum II, 11th century BCE.

ḤADERA

IDENTIFICATION

In the summer of 1934, in the course of quarrying *kurkar* near the Naḥli'el neighborhood school in Ḥadera, fragments of pottery ossuaries and decayed human bones were discovered at the foot of a hillock called Giv'at Bilu. Under the 1.5-m-thick *kurkar* layer was a layer of sand from which fragments of ossuaries protruded. Some ossuaries were broken by the workers, but others had been damaged in antiquity.

EXCAVATIONS

In December 1934, E. L. Sukenik carried out excavations on the site on behalf of the Hebrew University of Jerusalem. With the removal of part of the *kurkar* layer, two complete ossuaries and many fragments were uncovered. Because the quarry workers had not dug at that spot, the discovery confirmed that some of the ossuaries had been broken in antiquity, either when they were deposited or while being moved aside to make room for more ossuaries. In the course of the excavations, many specimens were recovered. One contained

Ḥadera: fragment of an ossuary shaped like a human face.

Ḥadera: house-shaped ossuary, Chalcolithic period.

human bones covered with sherds from a large vessel. Pottery vessels were found near the ossuaries—bowls, incense burners, and jugs. Of special interest was an ossuary with a pointed, arched roof standing on four legs. A few chalices and bowls were found beneath it, apparently arranged in some defined order. Behind the ossuary the sherds of a large vessel were covered with bones. From the condition of the ossuaries and from the geological data, Sukenik inferred that the *kurkar* layer had formed after the chests were deposited.

The bones found inside and around the ossuaries clearly show that these receptacles were used for secondary burial. Visible on numerous ossuaries were decorations in red paint or in a pattern of parallel lines. Sukenik distinguished three main types of ossuaries:

1. A rectangular type, open at the top like a box.

2. An oblong type, with a vaulted roof and a rectangular opening in one of the short sides. This was the most common type. One specimen was found somewhat apart from the others. It had no opening and no bones inside. A fragment of the front part of another ossuary had the shape of a human face with a protruding nose and round eyes.

3. A second rectangular type, but with a pointed, arched roof, standing on four legs. A square opening in one of the narrow sides was flanked at mid-height by lug handles. The other narrow side (at the rear) had three small openings at the top, arranged in the shape of a triangle with the point upward.

DATE AND NATURE OF THE FINDS. At the time of excavation, no comparable sites were known. Owing to the similarity of the pottery with Ghassulian ware, Sukenik dated the finds to the Ghassulian Chalcolithic—that is, to the fourth millennium BCE. The shapes of the ossuaries, reminiscent of house models, led Sukenik to conclude that they were meant to represent the houses of that period. He compared the ossuaries—the oblong type with an opening on the narrow side—with similar house plans discovered at Tuleilat el-Ghassul, Megiddo (stage V), Jericho, and other sites. He also found common features with the shape of Egyptian "soul houses" and especially European "house urns," where the ashes (not the bones) of the deceased were kept.

From the study of the legs on one of the ossuaries, Sukenik suggested, although with reservations, that, at least in that area, the houses of the period had rested on stilts because of climatic conditions. Since the discovery of the Ḥadera ossuaries, similar objects have been found at other sites in the country, confirming Sukenik's main conclusions about the date of the finds.

E. L. Sukenik, *JPOS* 17 (1937), 15–30; B. A. Mastin, *PEQ* 97 (1965), 153–160; A. Ronen and D. Kaufman, *TA* 3 (1976), 16–30; D. Kaufman, "Typological and Technological Comparisons of Two Epi-Palaeolithic Assemblages from the Coastal Plain of Israel" (Master's thesis, Tel Aviv Univ. 1976); E. C. Saxon et al., *Paléorient* 4 (1978), 253–266; E. Steigelmann, RB 85 (1978), 103–104; id., *ESI* 6 (1987–1988). 113; *Scripta Classica Israelica* 6 (1981–1982), 102; Weippert 1988 (Ortsregister); T. Schioler, *PEQ* 121 (1989), 132–143.

YIGAEL YADIN

HA-GOSHERIM

IDENTIFICATION

The prehistoric site of Ha-Gosherim is located at an altitude of 120 m above sea level on a wide terrace that declines southward toward the Ḥula Valley. The terrace is divided by two perennial streams. The abundant water sources and the fertile alluvial soil enabled the establishment of a large settlement, covering an area of about 2.4 a. Most of the numerous objects collected on the surface of the site over many years are now on display in the Museum of Prehistory of the Ḥula Valley at Kibbutz Ma'ayan Barukh. From the nature of some of the finds, it is evident that the site resembles prehistoric sites in northern Syria, Anatolia, and Lebanon.

EXCAVATIONS

The finds from Ha-Gosherim were first studied by J. Perrot, who attributed them to the Pottery Neolithic period contemporaneous with the Amuq B period. In 1978 and 1980, exploratory excavations were conducted at the site by T. Noy, on behalf of the Israel Department of Antiquities and Museums and the Israel Museum. Stone-built walls were exposed in two soundings to a depth of 0.6 m. Enlargement of the excavation area revealed a straight stone wall (c. 8 m long and 0.4 m thick) and a circular stone wall (c. 1.5 m thick). The straight wall, built of two rows of basalt stone, forms part of a structure on whose floor flint artifacts, animal bones, and a human burial were found deposited on a large number of flint flakes. Two other occupation levels were unearthed in another sounding next to the structure. They are about one m deep, but the finds do not enable a clear chronological determination.

The artifacts unearthed in the various sections did not contribute any information to support determinations of a specific Neolithic phase. Short, wide denticulated sickle blades appeared, but there were no pottery sherds. It is therefore assumed that the lower part of the sections belongs to the Pre-Pottery Neolithic B or C. In the museum collection at Ma'ayan Barukh additional items support this thesis. Moreover, in the northern Ḥula Valley, a few small satellite sites have been discovered that belong to the same Neolithic period.

From the surface collection in the museum another two cultural phases can be identified: one belonging to the Late Neolithic, including stamped seals with a geometric design, oval gray and green small bowls, pottery with very few decorations, and many flint artifacts, stone vessels, and stone querns. Obsidian blades and cores, some from eastern Anatolia, are numerous.

A large number of grinding stones, most of them rectangular and about 60 cm long, were also recovered. They are shaped with low and high grinding surfaces, which are known from the Pre-Pottery Neolithic B period, but some have only one grinding surface. There is also a large number of upper grinding stones. The site's proximity to areas rich in basalt accounts for the frequent use of the stone. The numerous grinding stones undoubtedly testify to the existence of advanced agricultural practices in this fertile region.

The last phase at the Ha-Gosherim site is from the Chalcolithic period.

G. Foerster, *RB* 74 (1967), 90–92; J. Perrot, *Supplément au Dictionnaire de la Bible* 8 (1968), 286–446; id., *MUSJ* 45 (1969), 136–145; G. D. Weinberg, *Journal of Glass Studies* 15 (1973), 35–51; *Israel Museum News* 14 (1978), 20; T. Noy, *'Atiqot* 14 (1980), 93–94; Weippert 1988, 111, 114; I. Hershkovitz and B. Arensburg, *Hagoshrim Anthropological Report* (unpublished).

TAMAR NOY

ḤALIF, TEL

IDENTIFICATION

Tel Ḥalif (Tell Khuweilifeh) is a prominent, 3-a. mound on the southwestern flank of the Judean Hills. It overlooks the Shephelah and the plain of Philistia to the west and borders the Negev desert to the south (map reference 1373.0879). Its importance derives from its strategic position commanding the route from Egypt and the seacoast into the Judean Hills toward Hebron and Jerusalem. From its vantage point, Tel Ḥalif guards the agricultural lands and water resources in the southeastern Shephelah. Moreover, its special geomorphological location—at the juncture between the coastal, mountain, and desert regions—supports a unique variety of flora and fauna. As indicated by the Paleolithic remains found at nearby Beer Faḥer, the region's special potential for habitation has been recognized since prehistoric times.

Tel Ḥalif: map of the mound and excavation areas.

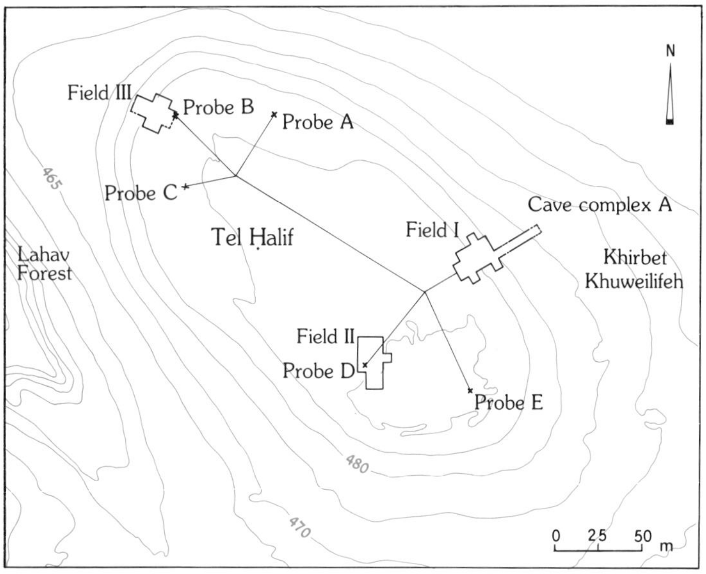

Egyptian-style jug from site 101.

For many years, Tel Ḥalif was identified with biblical Ziklag, the city ceded to David by the Philistines and the headquarters for many of his exploits while in exile from the court of King Saul (1 Sam. 27:6 ff.). This suggestion, made by F. M. Abel in 1938, was based on the proximity of Tel Ḥalif to its neighboring site, Ḥorvat Rimmon (Khirbet Umm er-Rammamin), which is less than a kilometer to the south. C. R. Conder and H. H. Kitchener, who surveyed and mapped this area for the British Palestine Exploration Fund in the second half of the nineteenth century, proposed the identification of Khirbet Umm er-Rammamin (Arabic for "Mother of the Pomegranates") with the biblical city of Rimmon or En-Rimmon. This city is mentioned in the territorial lists of Judah in Joshua 15:32 and as part of the inheritance of the tribe of Simeon in Joshua 19:7. Abel supplemented this hypothesis by stating that Ziklag, also mentioned in the Simeonite town list (Jos. 15:31), should accordingly be identified with nearby Tell Khuweilifeh (Tel Ḥalif). Following Conder and Kitchener, Abel also identified the Tel Ḥalif ruins with the later Byzantine settlement called Tala or Tilla. According to the *Onomasticon* of Eusebius, two large Jewish villages, named Tala and Rimmon, were located just 26 km (16 mi.) south of Beth Guvrin. Geographically, this brings us exactly into the area around Tel Ḥalif.

More recently, utilizing this same data, A. Biran and R. Gophna, A. Kloner, and O. Borowski have argued that Tel Ḥalif was the biblical city of Rimmon, and that the name was coopted by residents at Ḥorvat Rimmon when the area was resettled in the Late Roman/Byzantine period. At the same time, E. D. Oren has proposed that Ziklag be identified with Tel Sera' in the Philistine plain, 15 km (9 mi.) to the west. N. Na'aman has also suggested identifying Tel Ḥalif with biblical Hormah.

EXPLORATION AND EXCAVATION

Although visits to the Khuweilifeh area were made by various early travelers, deliberate archaeological exploration at and around Tel Ḥalif only began in the 1950s, following the establishment of Kibbutz Lahav on its eastern slopes. These first investigations consisted of informal survey work by members of the kibbutz, with intermittent salvage operations in 1970 by A. Biran and R. Gophna, in 1972 by Gophna, and in 1974 by D. Alon for the Israel Department of Antiquities and in 1972 by J. D. Seger for Hebrew Union College. These explorations provided evidence of ancient settlement both on the tell and on its lower eastern terrace. An Iron Age cemetery was also discovered on the hillside opposite the tell to the south. Traces of occupation from the transitional Chalcolithic/Early Bronze Age I (c. 3200 BCE) through the Late Byzantine and Arab periods were found, along with remains of nineteenth- and early twentieth-century CE Arab dwellings.

Beginning in 1976, the Lahav Research Project, formed by a consortium of American scholars and institutions under J. D. Seger's direction, launched an integrated study of the Tel Ḥalif region. Phase I of the project included field seasons in 1976, 1977, 1979, and 1980. Phase II was initiated in 1983, with summer seasons in 1986, 1987, and 1989. Supplementary field work was also conducted in the spring of 1985, under the direction of P. F. Jacobs.

Principal excavation efforts in phases I and II were concentrated in three fields on the mound's summit (fields I–III), with satellite projects in cave complex A, just below field I on the north; at sites 101 and 301, on the lower terrace area to the northeast; and at cemetery site 72, to the south. In addition, the research program included an extensive site survey of the region immediately around the tell and within 5 km (3 mi.) to the north of it.

EXCAVATION RESULTS

The following stratigraphical sequence was determined:

Stratum	*Period*	*Date*
I	Modern Arab	1800–1948 CE
II	Early Arab-Crusader	700–1500 CE
III	Roman-Byzantine	100–600 CE
(Gap)	Early Roman	100 CE–100 BCE
IV	Hellenistic	300–100 BCE
V	Persian	500–300 BCE
(Gap)	Late Iron II	650–500 BCE
VIA	Iron II	700–650 BCE
	DESTRUCTION	
VIB	Iron II	900–700 BCE
VII	Iron I	1200–900 BCE
VIII	LB IIB	1300–1200 BCE
IX	LB IIA	1400–1300 BCE
	DESTRUCTION	
X	LB IB	1475–1400 BCE
XI	LB IA	1550–1475 BCE
(Gap)	MB II	1850–1550 BCE
(Gap, traces)	EB IV (site 101)	2300–1850 BCE
XII	EB IIIB	2400–2300 BCE
XIII	EB IIIB	2450–2400 BCE
XIV	EB IIIA–B	2500–2450 BCE
	DESTRUCTION	
XV	EB IIIA	2600–2500 BCE
(Gap)	EB II	2900–2600 BCE
XVI	EB I (sites 101, 301)	3200–2900 BCE
XVII	Chalcolithic? (site 101)	3500–3200 BCE

LATE CHALCOLITHIC AND EARLY BRONZE AGE I (STRATA XVII–XVI). Investigations on the lower terrace area immediately northeast of the tell (sites 101 and 301) produced clear evidence of transitional Chalcolithic and Early Bronze Age I occupation and revealed that Ḥalif steadily developed as a major village center between 3500 and 2900 BCE. At site 101, four separate phases (stratum XVI, phases a–d) of the Early Bronze Age I settlement were identified, and probes reached a fifth phase (stratum XVII, phase e) with transitional Chalcolithic/Early Bronze Age I materials. Evidence suggests that the earliest (phase e) dwellers were troglodytes whose occupation ended when the roofs of their caves collapsed. Settlement was resumed in the beginning of Early Bronze Age I and reached its greatest prosperity during the latest phases (b and a). The occupation of phase a is represented by the addition of a well-constructed rectangular house with mud-brick walls built adjacent to an established complex of phase-b circumlinear houses. The special architecture of this rectilinear structure, along with the presence of imported Egyptian potsherds and typical Egyptian-type bread molds on its floors, suggests linkage with a regional network of Early Bronze Age I sites, including 'En Besor, Arad, and Tel 'Erani, that traded with Egypt.

Two distinct phases of the Early Bronze Age I occupation were also found at the adjacent site (301). They included a substantial complex of storage silos. From the upper phase, parts of five adjacent mud-brick bins (each c. 2 m in diameter) were identified. Fills within these also contained examples of imported Egyptian jars. This silo complex lay just inside a meter-wide set o

South section across the EB IIIA fortifications in field I.

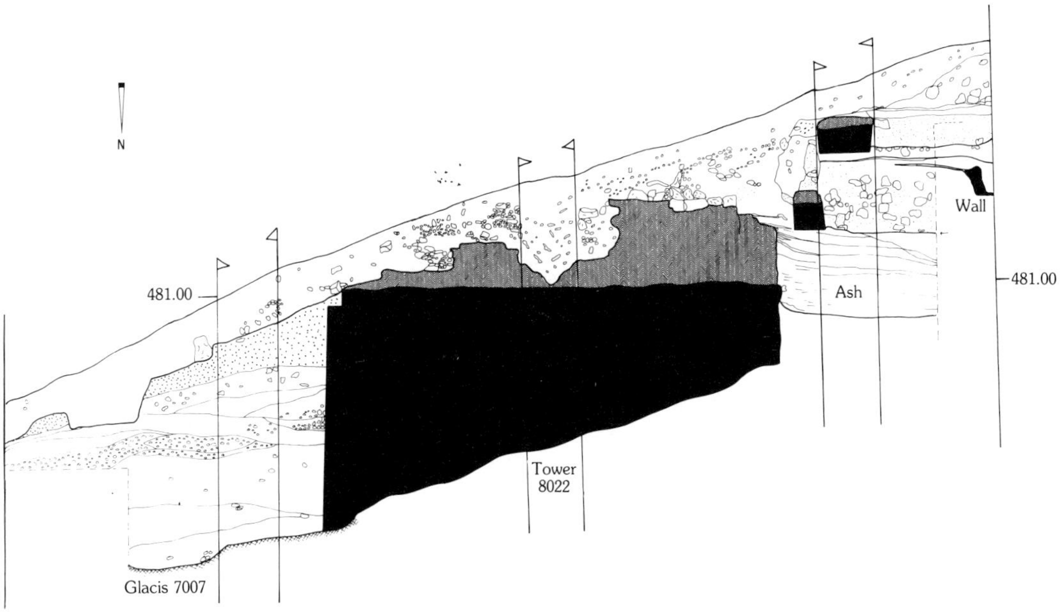

terrace walls. The walls sealed several stone-lined bins (c. 1.2 m in diameter) that belong to the earlier occupation phase. Together with evidence from site 101, these structures indicate that Ḥalif was a well-developed village of more than an acre in size in the Early Bronze Age I. The presence of public storage facilities indicates centralized sociopolitical organization. The Early Bronze Age I village at Ḥalif most likely served as a regional economic center that in its later phases enjoyed regular commercial contact with early dynastic Egypt.

THE EARLY BRONZE AGE III (STRATA XV–XII). The village occupation at Ḥalif came to an uncertain end at the close of the Early Bronze Age I. During the Early Bronze Age II, when settlement flourished at the neighboring site of Arad, Ḥalif was apparently unoccupied. However, with the decline of Arad in late Early Bronze Age II, a vigorous resettlement took place at Ḥalif above the terrace area to the southeast, where the present tell is located. Here, significant Early Bronze Age III remains were revealed, representing four separate architectural strata.

Stratum XV. The first Early Bronze Age III settlement was defended by substantial fortification walls. In field I, exposed remnants of this defensive system included a 15-m-long section of a 3.5-m-wide wall, built with a mud-brick superstructure set on deep stone foundations. This wall connected on the east with a similarly constructed fortification tower that was 7.5 m wide. Outside, and fronting this defensive line, a sloping glacis was discovered. This revetment was constructed of compacted layers of crushed limestone and chalk. At 8 m downslope, this chalk fill was retained by a 2.5-m-wide stone footing wall. In a narrow downslope section in field III, at the western end of the tell, elements of this same double wall system were also exposed. These fortification elements were founded directly on bedrock.

The end of the stratum XV city is marked dramatically by a 3.5-m-deep layer of water- and wind-transported ash debris. This debris covered a stairway and several adjacent intramural rooms. It also filled two small guardrooms built within the wall's mud-brick superstructure. The outlines of the wall and these room structures suggest that they may lie adjacent to, or be part of, a gateway to the city. The accumulated ash debris yielded a large collection of Early Bronze Age IIIA pottery sherds, as well as numerous chert blades of the "Canaanean" type. Several miniature ceramic animal figurines also were recovered. Based on these materials, the destruction of stratum XV is dated to about 2500 BCE.

Below the stairway surface, three earlier subphases of stratum XV were identified. The first of these was associated with the construction phase of the tower and wall and lay immediately above bedrock. Ceramic indicators related to this first phase belong to the transitional Early Bronze Age II/Early Bronze Age IIIA, placing construction of the fortifications somewhere in the late twenty-seventh century BCE.

Stratum XIV. The destruction of the stratum XV city did not mark the end of the Early Bronze Age III occupation at Ḥalif. Above and upslope in field I, evidence of three subsequent phases of the late third-millennium BCE settlement were encountered. The stratum XIV reoccupation began after a brief hiatus of fifteen to twenty years. Its architecture was founded directly on and into the deep deposit of ash associated with the end of stratum XV. Surfaces in several room areas produced midden deposits, indicating domestic use. From one of these middens came a fine example of an Early Dynastic Egyptian-style green-slate cosmetic palette, an artifact apparently curated from earlier Early Bronze Age I occupation levels. Within an adjacent courtyard, a section of a cobblestone cooking platform was exposed. The stratum XIV occupation established a pattern of terraced architecture on the northeastern slope. The settlement was unfortified and suffered a major destruction in about 2540 BCE.

Stratum XIII. The stratum XIII rebuilding efforts included the reuse and further development of the terrace system supporting house foundations along the slope of the tell. The most notable architectural change involved the creation of a 1.5-m-wide street curving from the north along the contours of the mound and then upslope to the west. On both sides of this street, new room areas were formed. From surfaces in one of these rooms in area B9, an unusual number of beads and small stone pendants were recovered. These included a still-articulated necklace of over forty tiny faience beads. The same room produced evidence of an active flint-knapping industry. The surface scatter included a number of freshly struck "Canaanean"-type blades and a tubular fan scraper, along with three large, well-prepared flint cores. The end

General view of the stratum XV, EB IIIA fortifications in field I.

of stratum XIII was, again, clearly marked by a disruption that produced a considerable ash and debris layer. However, the site seems to have recovered fairly swiftly from this disruption and many areas, including the street, were completely cleared for reuse in stratum XII.

Stratum XII. The architectural evidence of stratum XII is less well preserved than in other strata because of the prolonged gap in occupation between the Early Bronze Age IIIB and Late Bronze Age I and because of intrusions by the stratum XI, Late Bronze Age IA, settlers. Downslope, architectural development concentrated on consolidation work involving the construction of smaller room areas within remnants of stratum XIII foundations. In area B9, the earliest stratum XII surface within such a redesigned room produced further evidence of the flint industry, including ten more fresh blades, another fan scraper blank, and a goat horn, as well as other flakes and flint debitage. Close continuity with the stratum XIII occupants is thus clearly suggested.

Along the slope to the south, architectural changes were more dramatic, involving the formation of new room areas. A surface in area A9 produced a good occupation assemblage, including a large spouted vat. This vat form is typical of the Early Bronze Age IIIB and was used in connection with olive oil production. An incised potter's mark near its spout is illustrative of a tradition of such signs and markings found on numerous jar and pot fragments at Ḥalif throughout the Early Bronze Age III.

Like its predecessors, the stratum XII settlement ended with a general destruction. Its final-phase surfaces were buried under a considerable layer of brick and ash debris. Above this no evidence of subsequent Early or Middle Bronze Age occupation was found. The site lay abandoned until the mid-second millennium BCE, when stratum XI resettlement began. While it is tempting to associate the fortunes of Early Bronze Age III Ḥalif with the forays of the late Fifth and Sixth Dynasty Egyptians into the area, no evidence is available to clarify explicitly the nature of such linkage.

LATE BRONZE AGE (STRATA XI–VIII). Immediately above the Early Bronze Age levels in field I were several substantial occupation phases belonging to the Late Bronze Age. The earliest of these, stratum XI, can be dated to the Late Bronze Age IA in the late sixteenth century BCE.

Stratum XI. Stratum XI is a transitional occupation phase; however, during the Late Bronze Age IA, Ḥalif developed rapidly into a more substantial settlement. Excavations show five subphases of occupational use and remodification of structures before a more generalized redevelopment is initiated in stratum X. Stratum XI ceramic evidence includes the presence of both gray-burnished and Late Bronze bichrome fabrics. Also indicative of this chronology was the recovery of a typical Hyksos-style scarab from a surface in area 10.

Stratum X. With Stratum X (c. 1475 BCE), major architectural renovation was initiated. In the upslope areas of field I, the remains of a large, well-founded, residency building from this period, with a 6-by-6.5-m central courtyard surrounded by adjacent rooms, was exposed. Evidence provided by the earth and plaster resurfacings in its courtyard indicates that this structure passed through three distinct subphases of use before a massive destruction marked the end of its occupation (c. 1400 BCE). On the courtyard's surface, sealed beneath the ash and brick debris of this destruction, were numerous ceramic vessels, stone tools, and other objects indicating domestic use by an extended family of moderate wealth. All of the storage jars and one of the pitchers found here had potters' marks of differing types on their handles. In addition to a large assemblage of smaller stone blades and tools, there were also four major installations housing large querns and mortars. Among the courtyard's special architectural features is a low stone bench along its southern and eastern walls. Within the stonework of its northern wall foundations was a series of six sockets for wooden roof supports. Several of these sockets still contained charred remnants of the beams. A large wood sample found nearby was identified as *Quercus sp.* (oak).

Stratum IX. The architecture of stratum X was partially reused in the succeeding stratum IX occupation of the Late Bronze Age IIA. Although two distinct subphases of occupation can be discerned for stratum IX, the latter of these seems to have been only a modest squatters' occupation following the general destruction that ended the main phase. Remains covered by debris from this destruction date the stratum to the early el-Amarna period, with a terminus near the end of the fourteenth century BCE. Among the more interesting items recovered from the surface of the courtyard area was a small collection of faience jewelry, including several beads, a scarab, and a rectangular stamp seal.

Stratum VIII, LB IIB storage jar handle with Proto-Canaanite letters from field I, area 11.

Stratum VIII. The Late Bronze Age IIB, stratum VIII occupation in field I introduces an entirely new architectural perspective. The structures in stratum IX are deeply buried beneath the preparation materials for a massive platform developed to support a large storage complex. Throughout the area, successive layers of clay and compacted loess were deposited to create a fill that, in places, reached a depth of 2.5 m. From the uppermost stages a number of deep, stone-lined pits were cut into the fill. In all, nine such pits were excavated. This stratum VIII storage complex was used throughout the thirteenth century BCE. It passed through several phases of redevelopment with intermittent additions of layers of clay and loess and some redesign of the pit structures. The largest pit had initially been cut well down into the platform to serve as a deep storage silo. During its final stage of use, however, the bottom

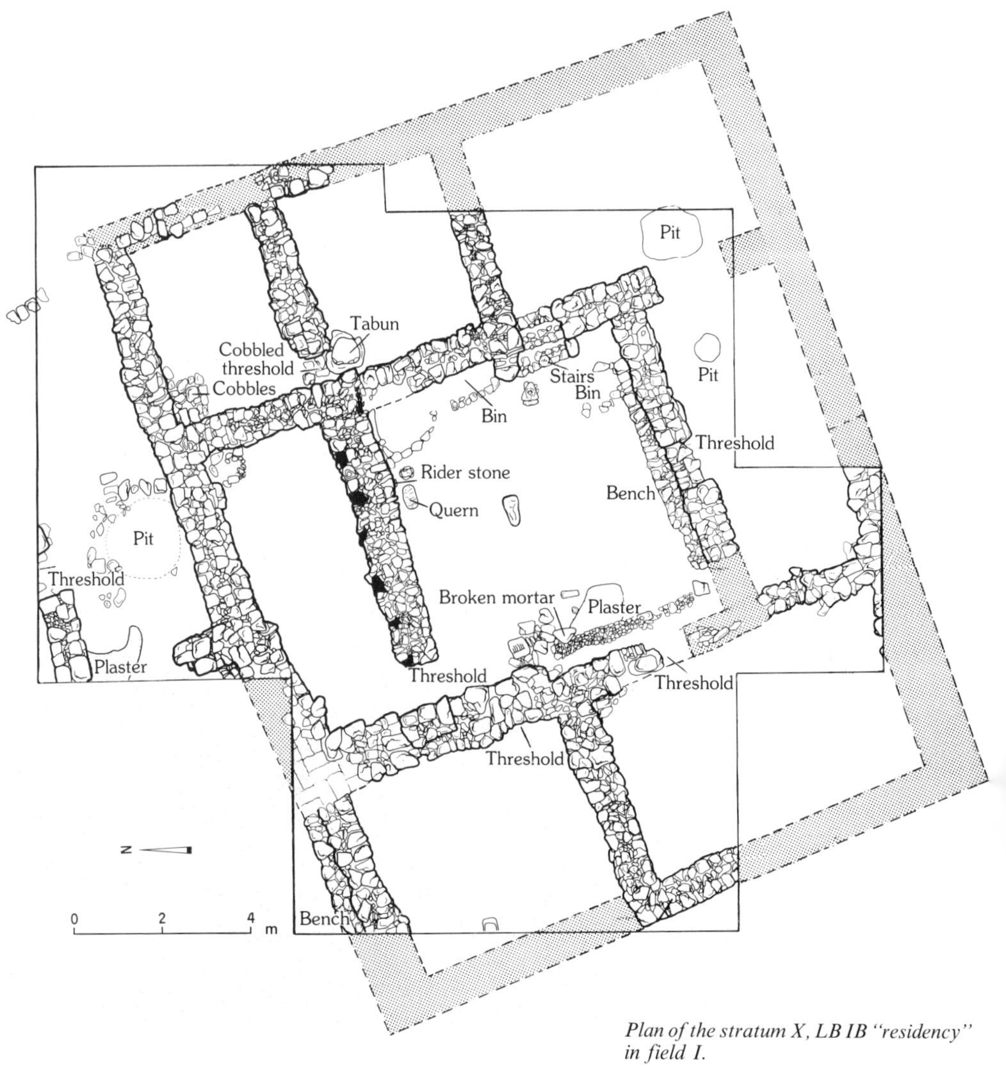

Plan of the stratum X, LB IB "residency" in field I.

2 m were filled in, making it only a shallow structure. Within this later bin, excavations uncovered more than a dozen large storage jars, one of which had a handle bearing several letters in Proto-Canaanite script. This collection of storage vessels and other accompanying pottery evidence dates the end of the stratum VIII occupation to about 1200 BCE.

The remains of the stratum VIII domestic occupation in field I were encountered only in area B10. In this area, a series of walls and surfaces extended north from the storage platform to the very edge of the mound. Three subphases of cobble and earth floors belonging to these structures were found, further demonstrating the intensity of the Late Bronze Age IIB phase of settlement. The latest of these provided an especially fine assemblage of late thirteenth-century BCE pottery.

Throughout its history, the Late Bronze Age city at Ḥalif was apparently unwalled. As with the founding of settlement on the high mound in the early Early Bronze Age III, resettlement in the mid-second millennium BCE also occurred in the wake of the demise of a neighboring site, in this case the destruction of city D at Tell Beit Mirsim to the north. During the Late Bronze Age IB occupation, it is probable that Ḥalif was a "special-use site," probably a trading station maintaining connections between the coastal highway and areas in the Judean Hills. With the upheavals of the el-Amarna age in the Late Bronze Age IIA, this stratum X outpost was destroyed and briefly abandoned. The stratum IX resettlement was much less imposing, and by about 1300 BCE the massive stratum VIII redevelopment had been effected. Throughout the thirteenth century BCE, Ḥalif functioned largely as a storage center.

IRON AGE I (STRATUM VII). In field I, area B10, immediately above the latest stratum VIII surface, another surface provided evidence of the earliest Iron Age I, stratum VII occupation. Along with the Iron Age I sherds on this surface was an almost complete early style pyxis. Only a modest shift in architecture marked this transition. The northern boundary wall of the stratum VIII storage platform continued in use, and three subsequent Iron Age I surface phases continued to be associated with it. From one of these surfaces came an impressive array of stone tools and pottery. Ceramic items included a pilgrim flask and the head of a bull from a kernos vessel.

Evidence of the Iron Age I occupation was also found in deep probes in fields II and III. In field III, stratum VII levels were reached only in a limited section cut through areas A4 and B3. However, work in area F6/1, at the extreme northwest corner of field II, provided good evidence linking the field-II stratigraphy with that in field I. The deepest excavations uncovered two

Clay female figurine, Iron I (front and back views).

clear Iron Age I phases. The latest of these was represented by remains of a shallow, stone-lined bin, filled to a depth of over 35 cm with an accumulation of ash and animal bone fragments. From the midst of this debris came several special objects, including an unusual clay female figurine, as well as a small group of late eleventh- to tenth-century degenerate-style Philistine potsherds. Some connection with coastal Philistine centers during the Iron Age I is thus demonstrated, although the extent of Philistine influence at the site is still in question.

IRON AGE II (STRATUM VI). The Iron Age II was clearly an era of growth and expansion at the site. Traces of occupation from this period have been found in almost every area excavated. This includes areas 1–3, downslope in the lower part of field I, as well as in probe areas off the tell on the site-101 terrace. The most significant remains, however, were found in fields II and III, on top of the mound itself, and in the site 72 cemetery on the hillside opposite the tell to the south.

Stratum VIB. The most extensive stratum VI evidence was found in field III, along the western periphery of the mound. Remains of the Iron Age II city's fortification system were discovered here. Excavations show the complex to have consisted of a modified casemate-wall system, with rooms formed be-

Overview of the stratum VI architecture in field III.

Field III: plan of the Iron II casemate wall.

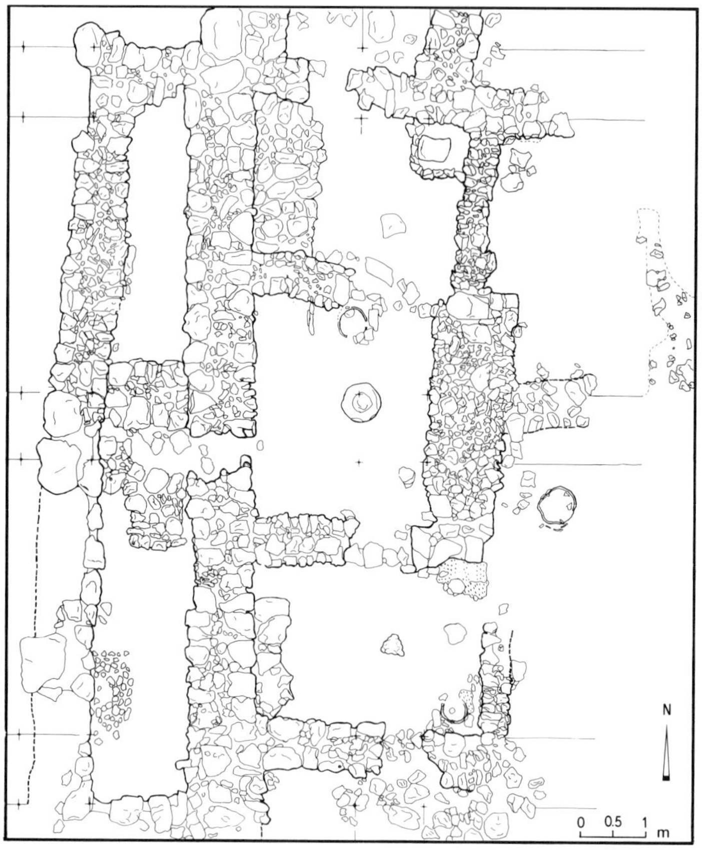

"Rimmon bowl" from tomb 6, Iron II.

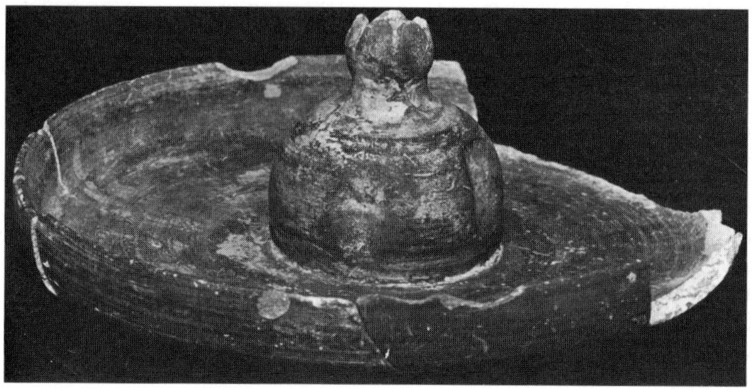

tween a double wall line, and an outlying glacis with a paved flagstone facing extending about 15 m down the steep western slope. In addition, the architecture included an offset defensive screening tower, protruding beyond the main wall line. A doorway leading through the main outer wall into this tower area suggests that it may have protected a postern at this point in the western city defenses. Additional structures in this fortification complex were exposed in areas excavated at both the north and south ends of the field. Here the main "casemate" walls combined with other inner-city walls to form elements of typical Israelite three- and four-room house patterns.

The initial construction of this architectural complex took place in the early ninth century BCE. The scope of the site's redevelopment at this time is illustrated by excavations in downslope areas A5 and A6. Here the elaborate preparation stages used in the construction of the outlying glacis system were evident. Great quantities of diverse fill materials were laid directly on top of the Early Bronze Age wall foundations to create a steep, 30-degree sloping rampart. These fills were held in place by intermittent retaining walls and stone piles. Finally, the face of this slope was paved with a layer of tight-fitting flagstones. This paving extended all the way upslope, to abut the foundation courses of the offset tower and outer city walls. The foundations of the casemate fortification walls were themselves also laid directly above earlier Early Bronze Age and Iron Age I walls.

The most demonstrative evidence of the stratum VIB occupation was found inside the wall line in areas A3 and B3, at the northeast corner of the field, and in areas N3 and N4, to the south. On surfaces in areas A3 and B3, a large assemblage of domestic artifacts was found buried under a thick layer of destruction debris. More than a dozen whole and restorable cooking pots, jars, and bowls were recovered, as well as a collection of over 300 sun-baked clay loom weights. These loom weights were loosely contained in a shallow, plastered bin near a large stone mortar or vat (65 cm in diameter and 37 cm deep) that was sunk to its rim in the floor. Special objects from these areas included part of a delicately carved stone cosmetic palette and a bone comb, as well as numerous sling stones and metal arrowheads. Also recovered was a significant collection of paleofloral samples, including olive pits, cereal grains, grape pits, and charred, whole pomegranates.

Stratum VIB destruction remains were also encountered at the southern end of the field, in areas N3 and N4. Elements of two more rooms and a large courtyard were exposed. In an adjacent "pantry" area, a special group of domestic stone tools, including numerous pestles and small querns, was uncovered. All of the evidence now in hand indicates that the destruction of the stratum VIB city took place very late in the eighth century BCE, probably in association with the Assyrian invasions of Sennacherib in 701 BCE.

Stratum VIA. The stratum VIA evidence shows that for a brief period immediately following this destruction the structures in field III were partially reoccupied. This resettlement involved the reuse of several of the casemate room areas immediately adjacent to the offset tower. In these rooms, destruction debris was cleared and clean fill imported to create new surfaces. A number of features were added in this phase, including several ovens, a large stone vat, a stone-lined storage pit, and a grinding platform supporting a large saddle quern. The pattern suggests that the site was abandoned at some point in the first half of the seventh century BCE.

In field II, excavations in area F6/1 and in adjacent areas in the northern part of the field, and in areas F6/4 and F6/14 on the south, provided additional good evidence of the widespread stratum VI occupation. Three distinct phases of Iron Age II habitation were identified. The latest of these, belonging to stratum VIA, was the most widely exposed. It consisted of well-defined domestic architecture with in situ occupational remains, including large grinding installations similar to the one found in field III, and a good collection of pottery and stone implements. Special finds in area F6/12 included two fenestrated ceramic incense stands. No evidence of fire or willful disruption was found in association with these remains. As was the case for the stratum VIA remains in field III, the general disposition of the materials suggests that this phase ended with abandonment rather than in destruction.

The density of Iron Age II settlement is also witnessed by the extensive cemetery from this period located at site 72 on the slopes across the valley just south of the tell (see below). From tomb 6 came a beautiful bowl in the Samaria ware tradition, decorated in the center with a molded pomegranate (*rimmon* in Hebrew). This find reopened speculation concerning the identification of the Iron Age settlement at the site with the biblical city of Rimmon.

THE PERSIAN AND HELLENISTIC PERIODS (STRATA V–IV). Stratum V. Evidence of Persian period occupation was encountered in a number of pits and bins in both fields I and III, and in area F6/1 in the northern part of field II. However, substantial architectural remains came only from the southern part of field II. There, excavations uncovered elements of a large building, with walls one meter wide. The building directly overlay the latest Iron Age II structures of stratum VIB and was below the Early Hellenistic architecture of stratum IV. The surfaces associated with the stratum V walls were generally sterile, but clear evidence of a Late Persian period date was recovered from foundation trenches. The substantial size of the walls suggests that they may have been part of a large storehouse, barrack, or military building erected on the summit of the tell during the Persian administration of the region.

Stratum IV. Architectural remains from the succeeding stratum IV Hellenistic settlement were only found in areas across the southern perimeter of field II. Above the Persian period remains, two distinct subphases of a large building were found. Each had stone foundation walls 80 cm wide. The domestic nature of this occupation was indicated by the presence of several ovens on room

Stratum V walls in field II, Persian period.

surfaces. Sherd evidence dates the initial construction of the stratum IV buildings to the mid-fourth century BCE. Assistance in dating the stratum's terminus was provided by a bronze coin with the head of Alexander the Great, symbolizing Heracles, found in a grave in area F6/26. The coin derives either from the reign of Ptolemy II (c. 267 BCE) or from the second coinage minted in Egypt by Ptolemy III Euergetes (247–222 BCE). The grave's capstones were sealed by the resurfacing for the final phase of the building's use.

THE ROMAN-BYZANTINE PERIOD (STRATUM III). A hiatus in occupation occurs at Ḥalif in the Early Roman period. However, a dramatic recovery takes place in the second and third centuries CE. Remains from the Late Roman and Byzantine periods are very much in evidence at and around the site. The primary locus of resettlement seems to have been at the foot of the tell, along the northeast slopes, where large natural caves were used for habitation. During the 1976 and 1977 seasons, several limited probes were carried out in this area in connection with the investigation of cave complex A. In areas 1–3, at the lower end of field I, a cobbled area and terrace walls were uncovered, apparently built to support structures upslope. From observations of these and other architectural traces, sherd evidence produced in surface clearance, and additional probes conducted across site 101 by Jacobs in 1985, it seems clear that the Byzantine settlement was quite substantial. This concurs with evidence from the cemetery belonging to this period, which was investigated at site 66 by the Israel Department of Antiquities in 1962. Located to the west, below the northern slopes of the tell near the settlement, this cemetery produced goods to indicate that the community in the second and third centuries CE was prosperous and enjoyed lively trade. The identification of this Byzantine settlement with Ḥorvat Tilla, mentioned in Eusebius's *Onomasticon*, is almost certainly correct.

The same profile of intensive Late Roman/Byzantine occupation is reflected in the results of the Lahav Research Project's regional survey efforts. All of the major sites within a 4-km (2.5-mi.) range to the north of Tel Ḥalif either were established or reoccupied in the second to fifth centuries CE. Included are substantial remains at Khirbet Za'aq, Khirbet Abu 'Amud, and Khirbet Bureida, along with numerous outlying winepresses, cisterns, caves, and basins. The picture in the region to the south of the tell is similar. Project survey work at Ḥorvat Rimmon (q.v.) in 1976 and 1977, and excavations there by the Israel Department of Antiquities in 1978 and 1979, suggest that it may have been the regional center in the period. Extensive Jewish and Christian remains from the Late Roman and Byzantine periods have also been discovered by the Israel Department of Antiquities at Khirbet Abu Ḥof several kilometers to the southwest of Tel Ḥalif.

Plan of cave complex A at the foot of field I.

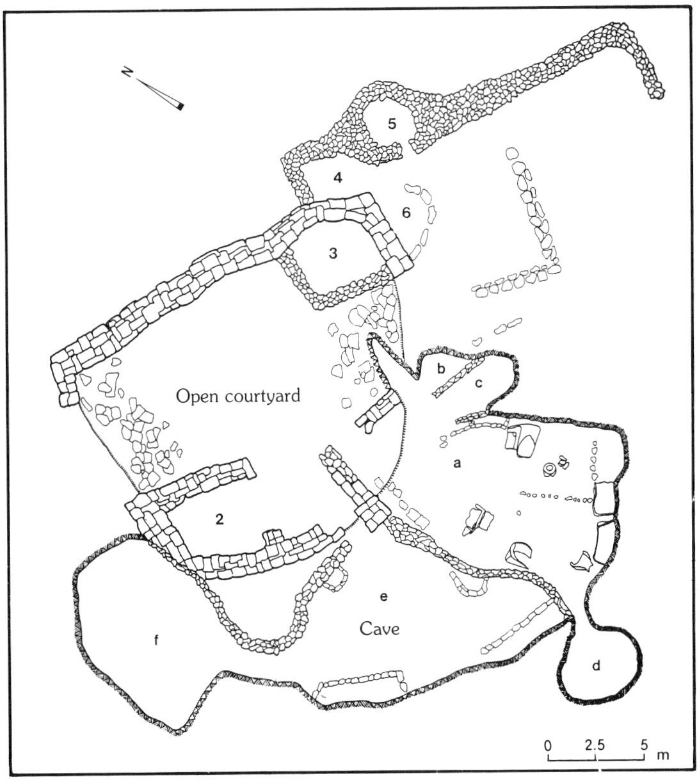

THE EARLY ARAB AND MODERN ARAB PERIODS (STRATA II–I). The Lahav Project's archaeological work related to these periods was concentrated on explorations at site 101 and in the excavation of remains in cave complex A, part of the ruins of Khirbet Khuweilifeh, just below field I. Probes in the outer courtyard area of this complex revealed a sequence of Arab occupation phases reaching back at least to about 700 CE. The predominant remains, however, belonged to the more recent, late nineteenth- and twentieth-century Khuweilifeh settlement.

JOE D. SEGER

THE IRON AGE CEMETERY

IDENTIFICATION AND EXPLORATION

The Iron Age cemetery at Tel Ḥalif consists of several rows of tombs cut in the limestone, on the slope of a hill that faces the southwest side of the tell (map reference 137.088). The size and extent of the cemetery are still unknown. The first Iron Age tomb belonging to this cemetery was excavated by A. Biran and R. Gophna for the Israel Department of Antiquities and Museums in 1965, after its discovery during construction work. The cave was found sealed by a blocking stone.

A second salvage excavation was directed in 1972 by J. D. Seger, following the discovery of three tombs (nos. 1–3) during road construction. Additional tombs (nos. 12–13) reused by Bedouin were excavated by B. Arensburg and others by R. Gotthart (nos. 7, 12) in 1974, D. Alon (nos. 15–20) in 1976, O. Borowski (nos. 4–6) in 1977 for the Lahav Research Project, and again in 1988 (nos. 8, 16–20) for the Israel Department of Antiquities and Museums.

1988 EXCAVATIONS

In 1988, six tombs were examined, all of which had been disturbed in antiquity; tomb 20 had been reused in the Roman period and tomb 8, by Bedouin. For the most part, the pottery, which includes fragments of and whole bowls, oil lamps, black juglets, cooking pots, necks and handles of jars, dates to the ninth and eighth centuries BCE, and possibly also to the first quarter of the seventh century BCE. No later Iron Age pottery was found.

All the tombs are of the Judahite type but differ one from the other in details. All display the typical elements: an entrance court, a narrow entrance

Entrance to burial cave no. 7.

Burial cave no. 7, Iron II.

with steps, a square burial chamber, one to three burial benches, and one or two repositories. The differences suggest that they were carved as variations on a basic theme. Contrary to Loffreda's proposal that the differences among Judahite burials represent an evolution beginning in the Iron Age I, the cemetery at Tel Ḥalif contains all subtypes in simultaneous use.

The relatively large number of iron arrowheads in tomb 20 suggests a link between the burials here and the destruction by fire of stratum VIB at Tel Ḥalif in the late eighth century BCE where many arrowheads and sling stones were found. The numerous beads of various materials and the silver earrings and rings found indicate that women were also buried here.

Tomb 8. Tomb 8 contains several peculiar elements such as a rock-cut stand on either side of the steps which could have been used for placing certain items. The three benches are cut into arcosolia with two rectangular repositories in the corners opposite the entrance. The rear bench has dividing walls on each end from the ceiling to the bench, with an opening in one of them enabling clearance of bones into the southwest repository.

Tomb 16. Access to tomb 16, which is comprised of two chambers, is through a more than one-meter-deep court with a large square blocking stone. Standing in the southwest corner of the antechamber was a platform 1.5–1.95 by 1.25–1.35 m and 15–20 cm high. This room was probably used for ceremonies accompanying the burial. East of and at right angle to the antechamber was a burial chamber with one bench and a bell-shaped repository, which was probably cut at a later stage. The plan suggests that originally the tomb was cut for one, possibly important, individual.

Tomb 19. Tomb 19 was apparently never completed because the stonecutters hit hard rock. Its state of incompleteness enables a reconstruction of the stages in the cutting of burial caves. First, the entrance court was cut out in rough form, and then the entrance. A large stone threshold protected the entrance floor from possible damage during cave hewing and rubble removal. The stone also prevented soil and rainwater from entering while work was in progress. When necessary, it could be replaced and was removed entirely when the tomb was completed. In the next stage the burial chamber was cut. First, a space big enough for someone to work in was hollowed out; this space was then expanded in all directions until it was large enough. Then the floor of the standing pit in the middle of the chamber was deepened while steps at the entrance were cut and the height of the ceiling was fixed. Next, the benches, repositories, and niches for lamps were cut into the walls. When all these elements were cut and smoothed, the stone threshold was removed.

Tomb 20. Tomb 20, a few meters west of and above tomb 19, was originally cut and used in the Iron Age II. In the Roman period, it was renovated by constructing a new entrance resembling a window and a corklike blocking stone. Three ossuaries and three covers found in the tomb belonged to this secondary phase. The tomb had three benches cut in arcosolia, a niche for an oil lamp in the west wall near the ceiling, and two circular repositories. Most of the finds were made in the pits and include beads, rings, silver earrings, and iron arrowheads. Thick pottery fragments suggest the use of clay coffins. A crude stone seal with a figure resembling a four-legged animal (ass, horse?) on a straight line (land?) beneath an inverted V shape (house, stable?) was also found. The finds from the Roman period are similar to those from neighboring Ḥorvat Tilla and Ḥorvat Rimmon.

ODED BOROWSKI

Abel, *GP* 2, 318; A. Biran and R. Gophna, *IEJ* 15 (1965), 255; (et al.), 20 (1970), 151–169; id., *RB* 74 (1967), 77–78; R. Gophna, ibid. 77 (1970), 578; id., *Museum Ha'aretz Bulletin* 14 (1972), 47–52, id. (and V. Sussman), *'Atiqot* 7 (1974), 69–76; id., *TA* 3 (1976), 31–37; J. D. Seger, *IEJ* 22 (1972), 161; 27 (1977), 45–47; 28 (1978), 119–121; 29 (1979), 247–249; 30 (1980), 223–226; 37 (1987), 192–195; id., *RB* 79 (1972), 585; 84 (1977), 393–398; 85 (1978), 423–425; 88 (1981), 573–577; 92 (1985), 404–406; 96 (1989), 220–222; id., *ASOR Newsletter* (Nov. 1977), 1–4; id. (and O. Borowski), *BA* 40 (1977), 156–166; 44 (1981), 183–186; 47 (1984), 47–53; id., *Archaeology* 32/3 (1979), 50–52; id., *BASOR* 252 (1983), 1–23; id., *ESI* 2 (1983), 38–39; 5 (1986), 45–46; 7–8 (1988–1989), 69–71; 9 (1989–1990), 67–68; id. (et al.), *BASOR* Supplement 26 (1990), 1–32; id., *L'Urbanisation de la Palestine à l'Age du Bronze Ancien* (Actes du Colloque d'Emmaüs, 1986; *BAR*/IS 527, ed. P. de Miroschedji), Oxford 1989, 117–135; D. N. Freedman, *ASOR Newsletter* (Nov. 1976), 1–3; O. Borowski, *BA* 40 (1977), 99; id., *BASOR* 227 (1977), 63–65; id., *BA* 49 (1986), 210–215; 51 (1988), 21–27; id., *BAIAS* 7 (1987–1988), 66–67; id., *ASOR Newsletter* 39/3 (1988), 10–11; C. Cole, *BAR* 3/2 (1977), 32–36; D. P. Cole, *IEJ* 28 (1978), 119–121; id., *AJA* 84 (1980), 200–201; 85 (1981), 190; W. H. Shea, *BASOR* 232 (1978), 78–80; A. Kloner, *IEJ* 30 (1980), 226–228; N. Na'aman, *ZDPV* 96 (1980), 136–152; (with H. O. Forshey), 38 (1988), 278–281; id., *ASOR Newsletter* 36/4–5 (1985), 4–5; 37/1 (1985), 7; id., *ESI* 4 (1985), 40–41; id., *Archaeology and Biblical Interpretation* (D. Glenn Rose Fest.), Atlanta 1987, 67–86; J. D. Currid and A. Navon, *ASOR Newsletter* 37/2 (1986), 7; id., *BASOR* 273 (1989), 67–78; J. D. Currid and J. L. Gregg, *BAR*/IS 14/5 (1988), 54–59; N. Porat, *Bulletin of the Egyptological Seminar* 8 (1985–1987), 109–129; J. D. Berry, "A Preliminary Study of Ceramics from the Northern Negev" (Ph.D. diss., Fullerton 1986); H. O. Forshey, *ASOR Newsletter* 38/3 (1987), 2–4; J. P. Dessel, *BASOR* 269 (1988), 59–64; id.., "Ceramic Production and Social Complexity in Fourth Millennium Canaan: A Case Study from the Halif Terrace" (Ph.D. diss., Univ. of Arizona 1991); Weippert 1988 (Ortsregister); E. Braun, *PEQ* 121 (1989), 1–43.

ḤAMADYA

IDENTIFICATION

The Neolithic site on the lands of Kibbutz Ḥamadya is located in the Jordan Valley east of the Beth-Shean–Ẓemaḥ road (map reference 2000.2141). The site lies on an ancient terrace in the valley, about 200 m below sea level. The soil is a dark-brown alluvium, which covers an area extending from the foot of the hills on which the kibbutz is situated to about 150 m west of 'Ein es-Suda. The ancient remains were discovered in a shallow depression in the brown soil that overlaid the basalt bedrock. In the center of the depression was a vein of basalt tuff with a diagonal incline. Into this tuff the Neolithic settlers managed to cut pits and depressions.

Ḥamadya: Yarmukian occupation floor.

EXCAVATIONS

In 1964, J. Kaplan carried out excavations on behalf of the Israel Exploration Society near Khirbet es-Suda (west of the spring 'Ein es-Suda). Immediately below the surface, a Neolithic settlement of the Yarmukian stage was unearthed that extended over an area of about 100 sq m. No remains of buildings were found. The inhabitants apparently found shelter in huts or tents. Ovens and fireplaces were uncovered in a few places in the floor, as were a number of depressions and pits that probably had been dug for storage purposes.

Among the objects found were a large number of potsherds of cooking pots, cups, and bowls. Some were decorated with the incised herringbone pattern common in Yarmukian pottery. This pattern encircles the outside of the body and forms zigzag lines. It is sometimes marked at the ends by two bands in red paint. The flints found included a large number of deeply serrated sickle blades that showed a gloss from use, axes, chisels, awls, arrowheads,

Two stone fertility figurines of the Yarmukian culture.

ɔears, and many other implements, as well as the waste of the lithic industry ·pical of the Yarmukian culture. Also found were basalt grindstones and ·ımerous animal bones, spindle weights, and two fertility figurines incised ı stone, one of them apparently depicting childbirth.

A workshop for the production of flint sickle blades was of special interest. ı the workshop, located outside the excavated area, were more than three ·ındred sickle blades ready for use, together with thousands of chips of ·ıdustrial waste. Among the sickles were a great many that had apparently been brought there to have their blunt or broken serration reworked.

Trial trenches dug around the excavated area produced only sterile earth. Thus, it seems that the small area excavated was inhabited by a single household or, at most, a camp. This household was probably one link in the chain of similar small settlements scattered nearby.

N. Tzori, *PEQ* 90 (1958), 44–45; J. Kaplan, *RB* 72 (1965), 543–544; Weippert 1988, 112.

JACOB KAPLAN

ḤAMMAH, TELL EL-

DENTIFICATION

'ell el-Ḥammah (map reference 1973.1977) stands at the southern entrance to ɪe Beth-Shean Valley, 16 km (10 mi. south of Tell Beth-Shean and 2 km (mi.) north of the junction formed by the Jordan Valley and Wadi Malikh.

The mound today rises 30 m above the surrounding plain and covers an area f about 1 a. at the summit and approximately 7 a. at the base. The site's ncient topography has been altered by heavy erosion, however, resulting in :eeply sloping sides and the partial destruction of each archaeological stra-ım uncovered thus far. Consequently, the size of the ancient settlement uring many periods of antiquity cannot be precisely determined. The site ; watered by two springs, one of which is thermal, giving it both its ancient ame Hamath (see below) and its Arabic name—Tell el-Ḥammah, or The ⁄Iound of the Thermal Spring.

W. F. Albright identified Tell el-Ḥammah with ancient Hamath, a city ppearing in the list of towns vanquished by Pharaoh Seti I on a campaign o Canaan conducted during his first regnal year, about 1291 BCE, to quell an ·prising in the Jordan Valley. Details of Seti's campaign are recorded on a ·asalt victory stela found at Beth-Shean. An additional account of this ampaign is preserved in Egypt on the walls of the Great Temple of Amon t Karnak. There, too, the town of Hamath appears together with Pella, Beth-Shean, Rehob, and Yeno'am in the list of cities vanquished by Seti's troops.

:XPLORATION

ʖurface surveys of the site conducted by W. F. Albright (1925–1926), N. Zori 1977), R. Gophna and Y. Porath (1967–1968), and these writers (1984) have ·ielded pottery from the Early Bronze Age I–II, the Early Bronze Age IV/ ⁄Iiddle Bronze Age I, the Middle Bronze Age II, the Late Bronze Age I–II, the ron Age I–II, as well as from the Persian and Byzantine periods. Fragments ɔf Egyptian or Egyptianlike "beer bottles" dating to the Nineteenth or Twentieth Dynasty were discovered in the 1984 survey.

Excavations at the site began in 1985 under the direction of J. Cahill, ɜ. Lipton, and D. Tarler, on behalf of the Institute of Archaeology at the Hebrew University of Jerusalem, in association with the Israel Exploration Society and the Society for Mediterranean Studies, New College, The University of Toronto. To date, three seasons of excavations (1985, 1987, 1988) ıave been conducted within a single area (area A) that comprises approximately 360 sq m within the site's southeastern quadrant. The steep, 30-degree ·lope in the area necessitated excavating along consecutive terraces in a ·tepped trench that ranges in width from 3 to 20 m.

EXCAVATION RESULTS

M TERRACE. Excavations along the M terrace (squares M6, M7), located just below the summit of the site, have yielded a number of pits from the Early Arab period, one pit from the Persian period, and at least six occupational phases ascribable to the Iron Age IIC (about the eighth to seventh centuries BCE). The preliminary stratigraphical analysis of the Iron Age material from this terrace indicates that its eighth- to seventh-century BCE stratum is characterized by substantial stone and mud-brick structures. Prominent among these is the northeastern corner of a large stone building whose walls are almost one m wide. Although only a small section of the building's plastered interior floor was uncovered, it held ceramic vessels in situ. A cobbled pavement with stone steps was laid against the outer face of the building's eastern wall. This wall was also found preserved on the lower L terrace and serves as a stratigraphical link between it and the M terrace. East of this stone building lies a mud-brick structure with a standing monolith and a cobbled floor.

Beneath these buildings of the eighth to seventh centuries BCE is a level ascribable to the eighth century BCE. It is characterized by open courtyards containing ovens (*tabuns*), hearths, and other installations associated with modest architectural features. These courtyards and installations were built directly on top of a mud-brick collapse. The collapse is associated with structures destroyed by fire—and tentatively ascribed to the ninth to eighth centuries BCE—that were largely excavated along the lower L terrace.

Miscellaneous finds ascribable to the Iron IIC from the M terrace include one fragment of a wedge-impressed "Cuthian" bowl, Judahite pottery, spindle whorls, and large numbers of unbaked clay loom weights.

L TERRACE. Excavations along the L terrace (squares L5–L7) have revealed two destruction levels tentatively dated to the tenth and ninth to eighth centuries BCE. The upper destruction level is characterized by a thick layer of mud-brick collapse similar to that reached at the lowest levels of excavation on the M terrace. This brick collapse was found covering the remains of structures characterized by brick walls built on stone foundations; the walls are preserved to approximately 1.2 m in height. Two nearly complete rooms as well as parts of three others, all belonging to a single structure, have been cleared along this terrace. One room contained two limestone installations set into the floor and a large basalt quern surrounded by cobblestones. A large assemblage of restorable ceramic vessels, more than one hundred doughnut-shaped, unfired clay loom weights, and the remains of fossilized cloth adhering to a restorable storage jar have been recovered from this structure.

Between the destruction layer of the ninth to eighth centuries BCE just

Aerial view of Tell el-Ḥammah, looking southeast.

Bowl with eight handles, 10th century BCE.

Decorated kernos.

described and that of the tenth century BCE, a thick layer of brown soil contained large pieces of broken hole-mouth jars. As this layer of brown soil could not be related to a living surface, it may best be understood as a fill laid over the tenth century BCE destruction debris to level the area for construction. A similar layer of soil and broken hole-mouth jars was also found in square L5. Immediately beneath this layer of broken hole-mouth jars lay building remains ascribable to the tenth century BCE that extended over both the L and the K terraces.

Thus far, two mud-brick building complexes separated by an open courtyard have been excavated within this stratum. The walls of each complex are built of sun-dried bricks laid on stone foundations. Their interior faces bear remnants of the mud plaster with which they were originally coated. The intense heat of the fire that destroyed this stratum caused the upper courses of these brick walls to crumble and collapse. This created a thick layer of vitrified brick and plaster debris that sealed both the lower courses of the walls and the contents of the rooms they enclosed.

Clearance of the burnt-brick debris covering the western complex revealed portions of four units, the largest of which comprised a rectangular space measuring 3.95 by 2.28 m, paved with round limestone cobbles. This large room yielded more than forty restorable ceramic vessels, including at least three complete ceremonial objects: a kernos with five projectiles, a multi-handled krater with horned animal appliqués, and a zoomorphic vessel. In addition, this western complex produced the upper half of a female plaque figurine cast from a mold; a number of "Cypro-Phoenician" black-on-red juglets; several gypsum pyxides with lids; a large collection of knucklebones (astragali); a faience cat amulet; and a stone stamp seal with a pyramidal top that depicts a human figure with upraised arms flanked by two animals. Large pieces of carbonized wood and fibrous matting were also found lying on the cobbled pavement of this room.

East of this complex were the remains of a beaten-earth floor that has been identified as an open courtyard. Within the eastern complex, two adjacent rooms of almost identical size (2.2 by 3.45 to 3.55 m; 2.3 by 3.6 m) have been excavated. Here, too, the fire that destroyed the building created a deep layer of collapsed mud-brick that sealed the contents of the rooms. Among the items recovered from the floor surfaces was a large assemblage of complete and restorable ceramic vessels, including a number of storage jars filled with carbonized grain. At least one of the storage jars was sealed with a pierced, unbaked clay ball of the type commonly identified as a loom weight; another jar was found sealed with a ceramic stopper shaped like a truncated cone. In addition, pieces of unbaked clay bearing cloth impressions on one side suggest that some objects—probably the mouths of ceramic vessels—had first been covered with cloth and then sealed with clay. A pair of large, two-handled, poorly fired ceramic containers and a polygonal installation built into the northwest corner of one of the rooms were also found filled with carbonized contents. Other finds from this complex include a number of "Cypro-Phoenician" black-on-red juglets; several gypsum pyxides, including one whose lid was fused in place by the intense heat of the conflagration; a basalt bowl resting on top of a decorative tripod base; a variety of iron tools, including a trident; a cache of over one hundred beads of various shapes and sizes fashioned from carnelian, rock crystal, faience, glass, and silver; an assortment of stone weights of various materials, including hematite; three seals bearing figurative motifs—two scaraboids (one of stone and one of bone) and one stone conoid seal; three clay bullae, or sealings, bearing stamped seal impressions—including one depicting a geometric design and another portraying a horned quadruped alongside a second figure; and a small lidded, round ivory box containing swatches of fabric.

Carbonized wooden spindles and spindle whorls, remains of thread wound around spindle fragments, a large number of bone spatulae, and a number of gypsum and unbaked clay loom weights uncovered within the building provide evidence of spinning and weaving at the site.

The conflagration that ended this stratum is dated to the tenth century BCE and is tentatively attributed to the military campaign of Pharaoh Shishak (Sheshonk I) in the fifth regnal year of Rehoboam, king of Judah, about 918 BCE (1 Kg. 14; 2 Chr. 12). Alternatively, however, the possibility that this destruction level occurred earlier in the tenth century BCE, perhaps as a result of Israelite efforts to expand and consolidate the territories under their dominion during the period of the United Monarchy, cannot be overlooked.

Iron pitchfork, 10th century BCE.

TERRACES K AND J. Excavation along the K and J terraces has revealed at least three architectural phases ascribable to the Iron Age I. The uppermost of these three phases comprises the remains of four parallel units bounded by a single wall on the south. At some point during this phase, a mud-brick building was added to the parallel units. A beaten-earth floor excavated in square K6, and tentatively dated to the eleventh to tenth centuries BCE, served all of the units ascribed to this level.

An even earlier phase from the eleventh century BCE is represented by three walls of a rectangular structure at least 6.5 m long that was excavated in squares K8, J6, and J7. A beaten-earth floor associated with these walls in squares J6 and J7 (locus 384) bore traces of destruction by fire and yielded the remains of restorable vessels, some of which retained their carbonized contents. Five storage jars were recovered from this floor; two stood in stone circles and one stood in a shallow depression. Additional finds from this floor include several flint pounders, basalt grinding stones, and unbaked clay loom weights.

The earliest phase reached in squares K8, J6, and J7 has not been completely excavated.

TRENCH: SQUARES I6–F6. Immediately south of square J6, the surface debris overlying an area approximately 3 m wide and 20 m long was scraped in order to discern the extent and sequence of archaeological deposits along the mound's southeastern slope.

Square H6 yielded the southern face of a massive mud-brick wall at least 2.8 m wide, with an offset at least 0.4 m wide and 1.75 m long. The wall's northern face has yet to be found. Its uppermost courses were cut by a pit containing very few sherds, none of which postdate the Middle Bronze Age IIB–C. Running up to and south of the wall—in squares H6, G6, and F6—is a series of striated layers consisting, alternately, of brown soil with few stones and of stone chips with small quantities of brown soil. At the southernmost edge of the trench, in square F6, the layers of stone chips were found to rest on a layer of compacted earth that, in turn, rested on bedrock. Investigation of the trench ended when bedrock was reached at the –120-m contour. The small amount of pottery retrieved from the stone chips at the southern edge of the trench contained nothing that could be dated later than the Middle Bronze Age II.

The massive brick wall revealed in square H6 is identified as a fortification wall; the alternating layers of soil and stone chips running up to it are identified as a glacis or rampart associated with it. Although both of these fortification elements can be dated to the Middle Bronze Age II, a more precise date within that period is precluded by their limited area of exposure. Extrapolating the line of the fortification wall along the –115-m contour on which it is located suggests an intramural area of approximately 3 a. during the Middle Bronze Age II.

W. F. Albright, *AASOR* 6 (1926), 13–74; J. A. Wilson, *ANET*, 253–254; D. Tarler et al., *ESI* 4 (1985), 41–42; 6 (1987–1988), 58–60; 9 (1989–1990), 134–135; J. Cahill et al., *IEJ* 37 (1987), 280–283; 38 (1988), 191–194.

JANE CAHILL, DAVID TARLER

ḤAMMAM, KHIRBET EL-

IDENTIFICATION, EXPLORATION, AND HISTORY

During the Mount Manasseh Regional Survey of 1978, a fortified mound called Khirbet el-Ḥammam (map reference 1628.2017) was discovered in the northwestern Samarian hills, about halfway between the Dothan Valley and the Sharon Plain and 5 km (3 mi.) west of the large village of 'Arabeh (which may preserve the ancient biblical name Arubboth). The site stretches over two hilltops and the saddle between them, at the southern end of a narrow spur that drops into the deep Wadi Jiz. This wadi drains most of the Dothan Valley to the west, into Naḥal Ḥadera and the Mediterranean Sea. The northern hilltop is naturally fortified by steep slopes on its west, north, and east sides; the only easy access is from the saddle to the south.

From 1978 to 1984, excavations were carried out at the site under the direction of A. Zertal, on behalf of Tel Aviv University and the Israel Exploration Society. Based on the excavation results, Zertal suggests identifying the site with Arubboth-Narbata.

For many years, scholars have been divided over the identification of Arubboth, the capital of Solomon's third district (1 Kg. 4:10), and Narbata, a Jewish city whose inhabitants participated in the First Jewish Revolt (66–70 CE) (Josephus, *War* II, 291, 509). In 1 Kings 4:7–14, which describes the twelve districts of the United Monarchy created by Solomon for tax purposes, each district's definition is comprised of the name of its commissioner and a short geographical description, either according to its tribal affiliation or by listing the settlements within its boundaries. The telegraphic brevity of the third district's description—"Ben-Hesed, in Arubboth (to him belonged Socoh and all the land of Hepher)" (1 Kg. 4:10)—made its identification, and Arubboth's, enigmatic. Another problem is presented by the difficulty in understanding "the land of Ḥepher." According to A. Alt and B. Mazar, Arubboth was on the Sharon Plain, where both the third district and the land of Hepher were located. In Alt's view, all the districts defined by their towns were originally Canaanite areas annexed by King David. On the basis of this supposition, Alt identified Arubboth with Tel Esur (Tell el-Asawir) at the effluence of Naḥal 'Iron (map reference 1521.2098); Mazar, following Alt's lead, identified Narbata of the Second Temple period with Khirbet Beidus (map reference 1532.2066). However, no archaeological remains from the United Monarchy have been uncovered at Tel Esur, and its identification with Arubboth was not accepted.

W. F. Albright and G. E. Wright suggested alternative identifications. Albright recommended locating Arubboth and Narbata in the northern region of the central highlands, without being more specific. He suggested that the third district was in the highlands and not in the Sharon, and concluded, based on the Samarian ostraca, that the clans and districts of the tribe of Manasseh were to be located in the northern Samarian hills. Other researchers dealing with the problem have made little progress resolving it.

Apparently, the site was first established as an administrative center on the northern hilltop alone. Based on ceramic criteria, the earliest date for this settlement is the end of the eleventh century BCE. The fortification wall, however, seems to date to the tenth century BCE—that is, during Solomon's reign.

Arubboth is not mentioned in the Bible after 1 Kings but probably continued to exist as a district capital. In later periods, the name appears in 1 Maccabees 5:23. Some scholars, such as J. M. Grintz, see a connection between the name Nabrakhta (noted in the tractate *Ta'anit* as indirect evidence for Jewish settlement in Samaria) and Arubboth-Arbata. In 1 Maccabees, the name Arbata appears in Greek ('Αρβάττα) as the name of a Jewish region whose inhabitants, together with Galilean Jews, joined Simon Maccabaeus in aiding Jerusalem. It can therefore be surmised that the settlement and the region continued to be occupied by Jews in the Hellenistic period—an assertion demonstrated by the excavations, as well.

Somewhat later, Josephus relates how the Jews of Caesarea moved to Narbata when the Jewish Revolt broke out in 66 CE (*War* II, 291). The town

Aerial view of Khirbet el-Ḥammam showing the Hellenistic city wall around the mound's summit, with the line of the Roman dike in the background.

Map of the site and the Roman siege system.

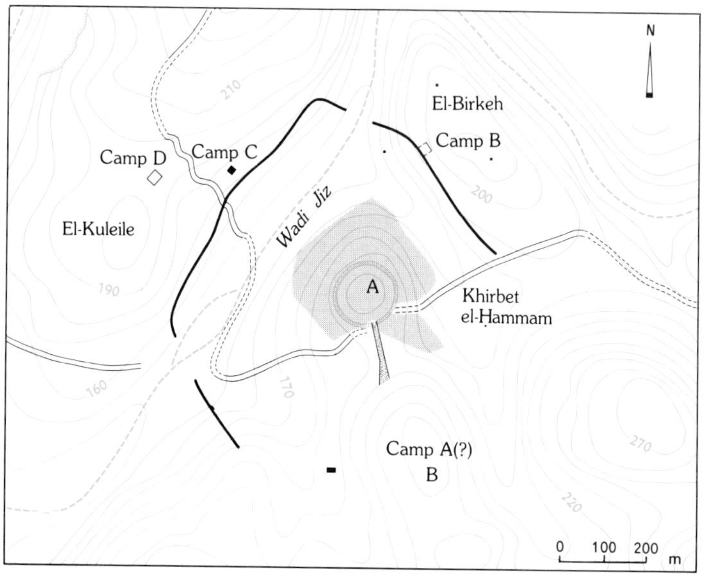

Khirbet el-Ḥammam: ashlar-built corner of the Hellenistic city wall, which was also in use in the Jewish Revolt.

is described as belonging to the Jews of Caesarea and the two places must have been closely connected. According to Josephus, the Jewish Revolt began as a result of riots in Caesarea, and six months later Cestius Gallus sent a cavalry cohort to the district of Narbatene, resulting in widespread looting and destruction (*War* II, 509). In the Jerusalem Talmud (*Ber.* 6, 10b), reference to the Inn of Nabrakhta may be the same place. The citing of the Narbaton region in the writings of the Byzantine historian Cedernos is problematic and may be out of context. Later sources do not mention the town.

EXCAVATION RESULTS

The earliest material found at Khirbet el-Ḥammam is datable to the eleventh century BCE, although no definite stratum from this period has yet been uncovered. Four strata were discerned: stratum 4—Iron II (950–530 BCE); stratum 3—Persian to Hellenistic periods (530–102 BCE); stratum 2—Late Hellenistic and Herodian periods (c. 100 BCE–66 CE); stratum 1 (after 66 CE). The site was destroyed and abandoned in the first or second century CE.

AREA A: THE CENTRAL SECTION AND FORTIFICATION SYSTEM. Area A was opened at the southern slope of the mound. Two city walls were discerned. The earlier one, dated to about the tenth century BCE, was founded on bedrock. It is 3 to 4 m wide and seems to have surrounded the whole northern hill, 7.5 a. in area. In the Late Hellenistic perod, changes were made in the city's fortifications. The Iron Age wall was lowered to become a base for an outer "ring road," encircling the town and entering into a city gate on the north. Beyond this "ring road" a new city wall was erected in the Late Hellenistic period, which was preserved to a height of 3 to 4 m. This wall was constructed in the "teeth" method—that is, a projection was built, mostly of ashlar stones, at 10-to-20-m intervals on the line of the wall.

AREA B: THE RESIDENTIAL QUARTER. Area B was opened on the highest part of the city, where two dwelling complexes with a street in between were unearthed, both from stratum 2 (Late Hellenistic and Roman periods). They consist of a central court with rooms, cisterns, and other installations. In the southern complex a possible bath (mikveh) was unearthed. The houses seem to have been abandoned and not destroyed, and in spots where deeper trenches were cut, Persian and Iron Age II walls were revealed.

AREA C: THE WATER SYSTEM. The water system of the mound is located on the northern slope, below the Iron Age city wall line. It consists of three large cisterns, with a capacity of from 600 to 1,000 cu m each. All three are elongated underground halls, well plastered, with one or two openings and without stairs. Their depth from the slope's surface varies from 6 to 9 m. The cisterns, similar in shape to the northwestern cisterns at Masada, were fed by a built and quarried aqueduct, some 0.6 m wide and 0.4 m deep. This aqueduct, running along the slope at the same height as the cisterns' openings, collected the rainwater from the city's roofs and streets, and the water from the ramp below the Iron Age city wall. This ramp, with its heavily plastered surface, was presumably meant to collect the water and channel it into the aqueduct and cisterns. This type of water system differs from those already known in the deserts of Israel in that it uses the city itself as the catchment area rather than collecting water from neighboring wadis, an arrangement suited to the Mediterranean climate of Khirbet el-Ḥammam. The water system was probably built in the Herodian period (stratum 2) and continued in use until the end of the Second Temple period.

THE SIEGE SYSTEM. The excavations carried out in 1980 revealed that the site was surrounded by Roman siegeworks, probably from the beginning of the Jewish Revolt. Although it is not mentioned by Josephus, this siege system points to the site's identity as Narbata, the only place in Samaria cited in connection with Roman military activity during the Jewish Revolt. While it is true that Josephus gives a distance of only 60 *ris* (c. 12 km, or 7.5 mi.) between Caesarea and Narbata (the distance between Caesarea and Khirbet el-Ḥammam is 25 km, or 15.5 mi.), he may have been referring to the distance between Caesarea and the Narbata toparchy's border (as M. Avi-Yonah has suggested), and not the town of Narbata itself.

The siegeworks, only the fourth Roman system of this type identified in Israel and Jordan (the others are at Masada, Bethar, and Machaerus), include a wall, three small camps, and a possible siege ramp. The stone-built siege wall is 2.2 m thick, with a known length of 1,516 m. It encloses the site on the west, north, and east; the southern flank seems to have been deliberately omitted. The wall is well preserved, except where it crossed Wadi Jiz and was washed away. Several small towers were discerned in it. The camps are relatively small and square (c. 20 by 20 m). Two were constructed along the wall on its eastern and northern stretches (camps B and C), while the third was set up in the saddle to the northwest. The latter was reached by a paved road from the main highway that connected Caesarea and Ginae (modern Jenin). The remains of what may have been another camp were found on the southernmost of the site's two hilltops.

Overview of Khirbet el-Ḥammam, looking north; note the rampart in center.

On the saddle connecting the two hilltops, a possible siege ramp (130 m long and 4.5 m wide) constructed of stone with an earth fill was discovered running perpendicular to the northern hilltop's fortification wall. The ramp's southern part broadens into a triangle. A section dug through the ramp shows that it was not built uniformly: the eastern retaining wall is constructed of well-dressed stones and was probably in place before the ramp was built. In contrast, the western wall was hastily constructed of large stones and was added later, to form the ramp. The ramp abuts a terrace wall (wall 2), above which the main road ran at the base of the city wall; however, there is a height difference between the ramp and the terrace wall. When the siege began, the ramp was constructed and siege engines were brought up to the wall, but the excavations have revealed only scant testimony of the ensuing battle.

On the northern slope and under the Iron Age city wall, three large, plastered, rock-hewn cisterns were uncovered, each with a capacity of 800 to 1,000 cu m. Their openings all lie on the same contour. A wall in the same location may have carried an aqueduct, used to fill the cisterns. Dozens of private cisterns were also found within the town's structures.

Camp B, whose western half was excavated in the course of two seasons in 1980, is a square structure on the steep slope of the el-Birkeh hill to the east of the mound. It has a fine view of the town's eastern slope. Its exterior dimensions are 20.5 by 23.5 m and the interior is 16 by 19 m (304 sq m). Like the siege wall, camp B's surrounding wall is 2.2 m thick. The eastern siege wall, the walls of camp A at Masada, and the siege wall at Machaerus have the same thickness. The walls are well built, with two stone faces and a rubble fill. Two gates provided access to the camp: the northern gate (1.68 m wide) has especially large corner stones and a paved passageway. The southern gateway (1.75 m. wide) was also paved, but its opening was blocked by a stone wall 0.8 m wide. The significance of this is obscure, but it is clear that the wall was built over the gate's pavement.

The entire camp was constructed on a platform raised one meter above the uneven level of the hilltop. Parts of the camp were paved. Two rooms and a passageway were uncovered in its southwestern part, which is connected to the siege wall. The few sherds found here were mostly of cooking pots like those found at Masada, dating to the first and second centuries CE. A coin of Herod Archelaus (4 BCE–6 CE) found in a sealed locus on the floor of the camp is of value in dating the siegeworks. This coin, together with architectural and historical criteria, enable the dating of the siegeworks to the First Jewish Revolt. The remaining camps are as yet unexcavated. The siege wall was excavated in several places, including its juncture with camp B. It is a finely constructed stone wall (2.2 m thick) with towers. Its circuit was determined by military considerations, which required that it be located beyond firing range of the besieged on a contour that would hinder counterattacks.

SUMMARY

Excavations have revealed that Khirbet el-Ḥammam was first settled in the eleventh or tenth century BCE and fortified in the time of the United Monarchy. No other architectural remains from this period or from the Iron Age II and Persian period have been found, although ceramic evidence points to continuity of settlement. The excavator suggests identifying the site with biblical Arubboth. In the second or early first century BCE, the town was refortified and rebuilt on an impressive scale. Its acropolis was fortified with an ashlar wall, while many structures were erected on the slope outside the fortifications. During this time, the town (identified as Narbata) seems to have been a toparchic capital and the main settlement in northwest Samaria. It was either destroyed or abandoned during the First Jewish Revolt and was never resettled.

A. Zertal, *ESI* 2 (1983), 39–41; 3 (1984), 38–39; id., *IEJ* 34 (1984), 52.

ADAM ZERTAL

ḤAMMAT GADER

IDENTIFICATION AND HISTORY

The site is on the Yarmuk River, 7 km (4.5 mi.) east of the Sea of Galilee (map reference 212.232), in a valley 1,450 m long, 500 m wide, and 180 a. in area. The name Ḥammat Gader and its baths is preserved in the Arabic place name, el-Ḥammeh, and in the name of the mound on which the ancient synagogue was discovered, Tell Bani (the mound of the bath). There are five hot springs in the valley: two, 'Ein el-Jarab and 'Ein Bulos, to the north of Tell Bani (a corruption of the Greek word βαλανεῖον, meaning "bath"); two in the southern part, 'Ein er-Riḥ and 'Ein el-Maqle (Ḥammat Selim); and one, 'Ein Sakhneh, to the northeast of the valley of Ḥammat Gader. The site identified with Ḥammat Gader was first mentioned, although not by name, by the geographer Strabo (XVI, 2,45), who described the hot springs near the city of Gadara toward the end of the first century BCE.

The baths are mentioned by Origen (mid-third century CE) in his Commentary on John 6:41; however, the appearance of the name of the emperor Antoninus Pius (138–161 CE) in the Eudocia inscription discovered in the excavations (see below) invites the supposition that they were built before Origen's time. They are also mentioned by Eusebius at the beginning of the fourth century (*Onom*. 22:25–27, 74:11–13). At the end of the fourth century the Greek biographer Eunapius, who visited the site, wrote in his *Life of Jamblichus* that the baths of Ḥammat Gader were second in beauty only to those of Baia in the Bay of Naples. The colorful crowds of people who filled the place were described by his contemporary, Epiphanius (*Haer*. 30, 7). According to Talmudic sources, many sages visited Ḥammat Gader, from Rabbi Meir (mid-second century CE) onward: Judah ha-Nasi, Ḥanina, Jonathan, Ḥamma bar Ḥanina, and Ami, the latter with Judah ha-Nasi II. These scholars discussed the problems of the Sabbath boundaries between Gadara and Ḥammat, located below Gadara (Reeg, *Ortsnamen*, 258–259). The synagogue inscriptions also testify to the numbers of foreign visitors (Naveh, nos. 32–35).

In the fifth to seventh centuries, the baths building was at its most glorious. The complex was extensive and ramified. Evidence of this is found in the Hall

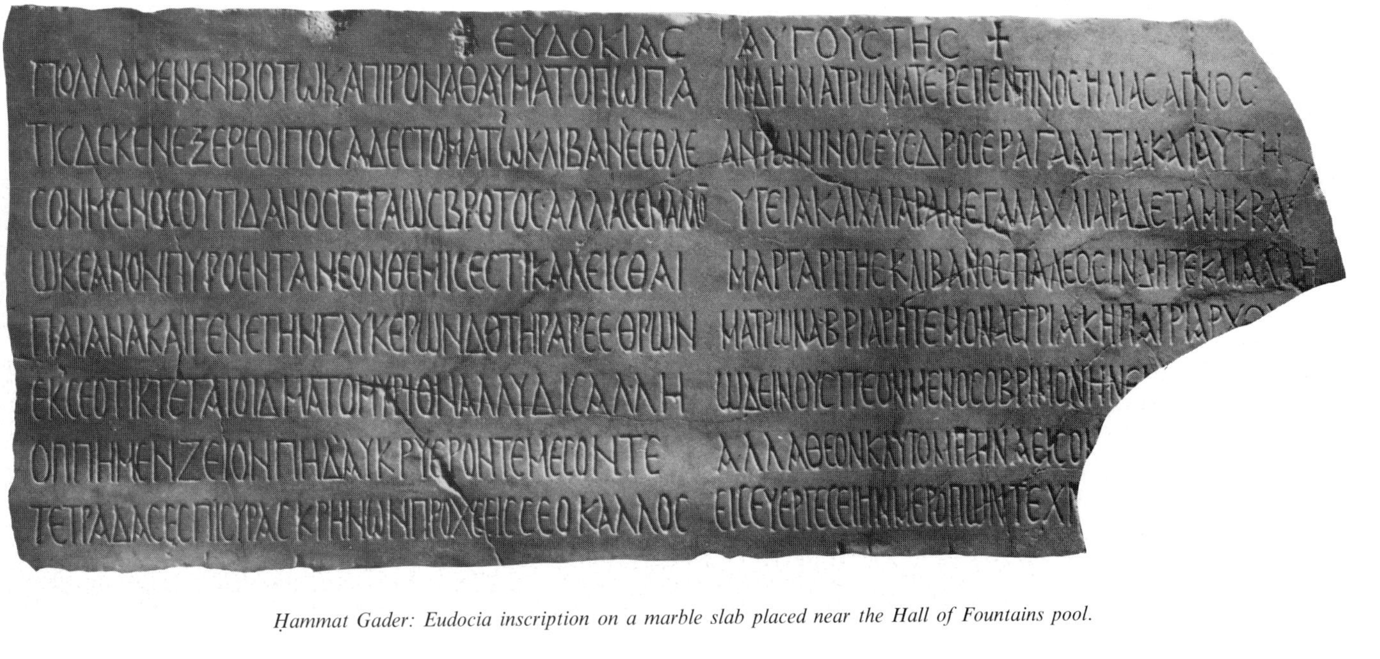

Ḥammat Gader: Eudocia inscription on a marble slab placed near the Hall of Fountains pool.

of Fountains (see below) in which the six building inscriptions found were written in a Greek rhetorical style. In these inscriptions mention is made of Empress Eudocia (421–460), Emperor Anastasius I (491–518), and the Caliph Mu'awiya (661–680), founder of the Umayyad dynasty in Damascus. The Eudocia inscription is a paean to the hot springs and baths of Ḥammat Gader. The inscription lists sixteen names of different parts of the baths building—halls, pools, and fountains—on a marble slab (71 by 181 cm) laid in the pavement beside the bathing pool in the Hall of Fountains. In the inscription, flanked by two crosses, the name of the authoress appears, Empress (Augusta) Eudocia. The name of Emperor Anastasius is mentioned in two inscriptions as having granted a money gift (λῶρον) to the place. In these and in two other inscriptions, mention is made of a figure unknown from other sources, Alexander of Caesarea, the governor of Palaestina Secunda, who resided in Beth-Shean (Scythopolis), the capital of the province. According to the inscriptions, Alexander built (or restored) various portions of the structure—the bathing pools, tholos structures, and others. These building inscriptions attest to the fame of the baths at Ḥammat Gader and to the crowds who streamed to them for cures. The wealthy and powerful also sought to perpetuate their names in magnificent construction projects here.

In the second half of the sixth century CE, Ḥammat Gader was visited by the pilgrim known as Antoninus of Placentia. He testifies that the inhabitants of Ḥammat Gader named the medicinal baths after the prophet Elijah (*Thermae Heliae*). According to Antoninus, the baths were a center for the healing of lepers, who were accommodated in a hostel supported at public expense (*Itinerarium Antonium*, 7).

Nothing is known of the history of the baths at the end of the Byzantine period. It may be assumed, however, that they suffered damage or neglect during the troubled times in the first half of the seventh century, because they were completely renovated by Caliph Mu'awiya shortly after he ascended the throne in Damascus. The sixth building inscription in the Hall of Fountains—which was found in situ, in the wall of the hall's central alcove, 2.1 m above the floor—commemorates the renovation in Greek. The marble slab (50 by 80 cm) apparently was laid on the day the baths opened in 662 CE. The Umayyad restoration was carried out by the governor Abdullah Ibn Abu Hashem and under the care of a local alderman of Gadara, Iohannes.

The last phase of the baths is attested by several graffiti in Kufic script found on the paving slabs and walls. One of the inscriptions contains the word 'Allahuma, an early form of address to 'Allah, in use until the mid-eleventh century, at the latest. In addition, the Muslim geographer el-Muqaddasi (tenth century) speaks of the baths in the past tense. The bath complex was probably destroyed in the earthquake of 749. The fallen debris was eventually covered with earth, and the building was abandoned; however, the place continued to be visited by sick people until modern times.

YIZHAR HIRSCHFELD

TELL EL-ḤAMMEH

In 1932, N. Glueck made soundings at Tell Bani (Tell el-Ḥammeh) and found sherds from the Early Bronze Age I–III. Sherds with band-slip decoration were particularly plentiful. Although Khirbet Kerak sherds were not found, in Glueck's opinion this was accidental. However, the absence of sherds from the Early Bronze Age IV and Middle Bronze Age indicates that this settlement, like those in Transjordan, was destroyed at the end of the Early Bronze Age. The site remained unoccupied until the Roman period.

THE SYNAGOGUE. In the spring of 1932, the Mandatory Department of Antiquities uncovered the remains of a synagogue on the summit of Tell Bani (unoccupied during Roman times). In the fall of the same year, the Department of Antiquities granted a license to the Hebrew University to complete its excavations. Some 700 sq m were excavated, and the synagogue hall and a few buildings in the vicinity were uncovered. Additional excavations were undertaken in 1982 by the Israel Department of Antiquities and Museums.

There were two entrances to the synagogue hall, both indirect. One was through a narrow corridor (3.2 m wide) on the western side, which led to an opening in the wall of the hall. At the end of the corridor, another opening led to the western of the two rooms behind the apse (on the south side). The entire complex was surrounded by a wall 32.5 m long. The main entrance was from

Overview of the synagogue.

Panel of the chancel screen from the synagogue.

the east. Here, too, access was through a narrow passage (3.5 m wide). The entrance was divided into two rooms (5.45 and 6.9 m long). In the second room, remains of a mosaic pavement with a geometric pattern of intersecting lines were discovered. There was an entrance from the first room in this eastern entrance to two side rooms (4.9 by 4.7 m and 4.7 by 5.5 m). Between them and the hall complex was a third corridor (2.6 m wide). To the west of the corridor, two rooms adjoined the synagogue hall. From the small room (3.1 by 2.8 m), the second, larger room (4.65 by 3.65 m), paved with stone, was entered on the north. The small room could be entered either from the corridor or from the synagogue hall. Along the larger room's eastern wall was a bench. This room was used for study or teaching or as a prayer hall for women. Opinions are divided as to the existence of a women's gallery in this synagogue.

The hall was almost square (13.9 by 13 m) and was divided by three rows of columns into a nave (7.8 m wide) and two long aisles (the eastern one 3 m wide and the western one 2.4 m wide) and a transverse aisle (1.8 m wide) opposite the apse. The longitudinal rows had four columns each and the transverse rows only two. At the corners of the rows were two plastered columns, L-shaped in section. The columns stood on foundations under the mosaic pavement. There were no bases. Along the walls were the remains of benches.

In the center of the southern wall, facing Jerusalem, was a platform (bema). It was the same length as the apse (4.55 m) and was 1.2 m wide. Two steps flanked by marble screens led to its center. Remains of chancel posts and a panel from one of them were also found. (After the excavations were completed, a fragment of a panel from the screen bearing a menorah within a wreath was found accidentally.) The apse itself was 1.18 m below the level of the bema. The thickness of its back wall was 1.45 m.

The entire hall had been paved with mosaics. In the aisles, the mosaics were in simple geometric patterns (squares, flowers, circles, intersecting lines in guilloche). On both sides of the bema there were lozenges, in the center a flame pattern; in the corners there were jugs with plants coiling out of them. The floor of the nave had a complex border in crow-step, guilloche, and wave-crest patterns. The center of the mosaic was divided into three panels, each bordered by a guilloche. In the northern panel there was a pattern of intersecting lines, and between them large squares with guilloches inside and smaller ones with checkerboard patterns inside. In this part of the mosaic the first inscription was found (see I, below), a little west of the axis of the pavement in a *tabula ansata*. There was most likely a matching inscription east of the axis, but it is not preserved. The central panel of the mosaic in the nave was ornamented with patterns of fleurons in intersecting lines—with roses or pomegranates in the center of each lozenge. At the southern end of this panel, two inscriptions (see II and III, below) were found side by side, each in a *tabula ansata*. Only in this section, closest to the bema, was the dominant abstract geometric pattern abandoned and a representational design adopted. Two cypresses stand at the edges of the panel. Between them, facing the viewer, are two lions with tongues protruding and tails rising above their backs. Inscription IV was placed within a wreath with ribbons, between the lions. Another inscription once existed in the western aisle, but nothing was left of it except the edge of the *tabula ansata*.

Inscriptions. I. "[And remembered be for] good Ada, the son of Tanḥum, who has contributed one tremissis and Yoseh, the son of Qrw'h and his child, who has contributed one-half denarius toward this [mos]aic. May theirs be the blessing. Ame[n. Se]lah. Peace."

II. (Right) "And re[membered be for] good Rav Tanḥum the Levite, the

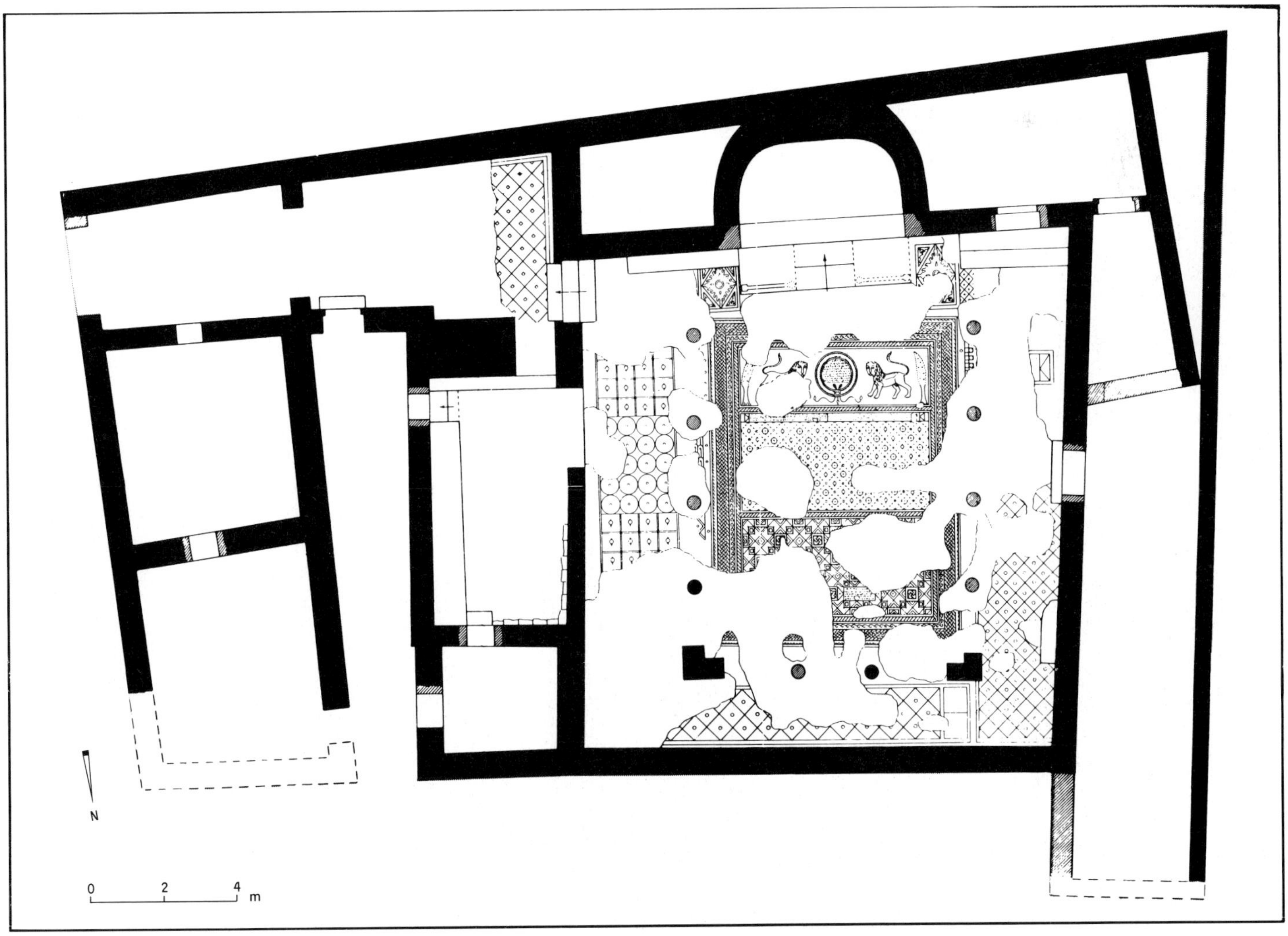

Plan of the synagogue.

Inscription I in the synagogue's mosaic floor: "[And remembered be for] good Ada, the son of Tanḥum . . . and his child . . ."

Inscription IV in the synagogue's mosaic pavement: "And remembered be for good Lord Oples . . ."

so[n of Ḥ]alfa, who has donated one tremissis; and remembered be for good the son of Sisiphus(?) the [Se]pphorite and [Lord Pa]tricius, of Kefar 'Aqabyah and Yoseh, the son of Dositheus, of Kefar Naḥum, who have, all three, donated three *grmyn* (scruples?). May the King of the U[niverse best]ow the blessing upon [their] works. Amen. Amen. Selah. Peace. And remembered be for good Yudan the architect(?) of Emmaus who has donated three [scruples?]. And remembered be for good the people of Arbela who have donated the cost(?). May the King of the Universe bestow blessing upon their work. Amen. Amen. Selah."

III. (Left) "And remembered be for good Lord Leontius and Lady Kalinike, who [have donated . . . denarii in h]onor of the synagogue. May the King of the Universe bestow blessing upon his work. Amen. Amen. Selah. Peace. And remembered be for good a righteous woman(?), who has donated one denarius in honor of the synagogue. May the King of the Universe bestow blessing upon her work. Amen. Amen. Selah. Peace. And remembered be for good the inhabitants of the town/others(?) who have donated one tremissis."

IV. "And remembered be for good Lord Oples and Lady Protone, and Lord Sallustius his son-in-law, and *Comes* Pheroros his son and Lord Photios his son-in-law, and Lord Ḥaninah his son—they and their children—whose acts of charity are constant everywhere and who have given here five coins of gold. May the King of the Universe bestow the blessing upon their work. Amen. Amen. Selah."

Date of the Synagogue. The excavator dated the synagogue to the first half of the fifth century CE, on the basis of the names of the coins in the inscriptions, which occur from the fourth century onward, and also on the basis of the title *comes*, which he believed Jews could not hold after 438. The plan of the synagogue has elements possibly characteristic of the transition between early and late types. The transverse row of columns and the square hall are characteristic of early synagogues, whereas the apse and mosaic pavement are typical of the later types. Because of the absence of human images and the paucity of faunal and floral representations, this synagogue should be assigned either to the earliest period of the laying of mosaic pavements in synagogues, or to the time when resistance to images and figures was beginning and interest in geometric patterns was again on the increase (after the mid-sixth century). In comparison with the mosaics in the synagogue in Hammath-Tiberias, a later date should perhaps be assigned.

During the 1982 excavations, two earlier phases were discovered. The first was a rectangular building paved with plain white mosaics, 1.4 m below the mosaic floor of the third phase. The second phase, which collapsed during the

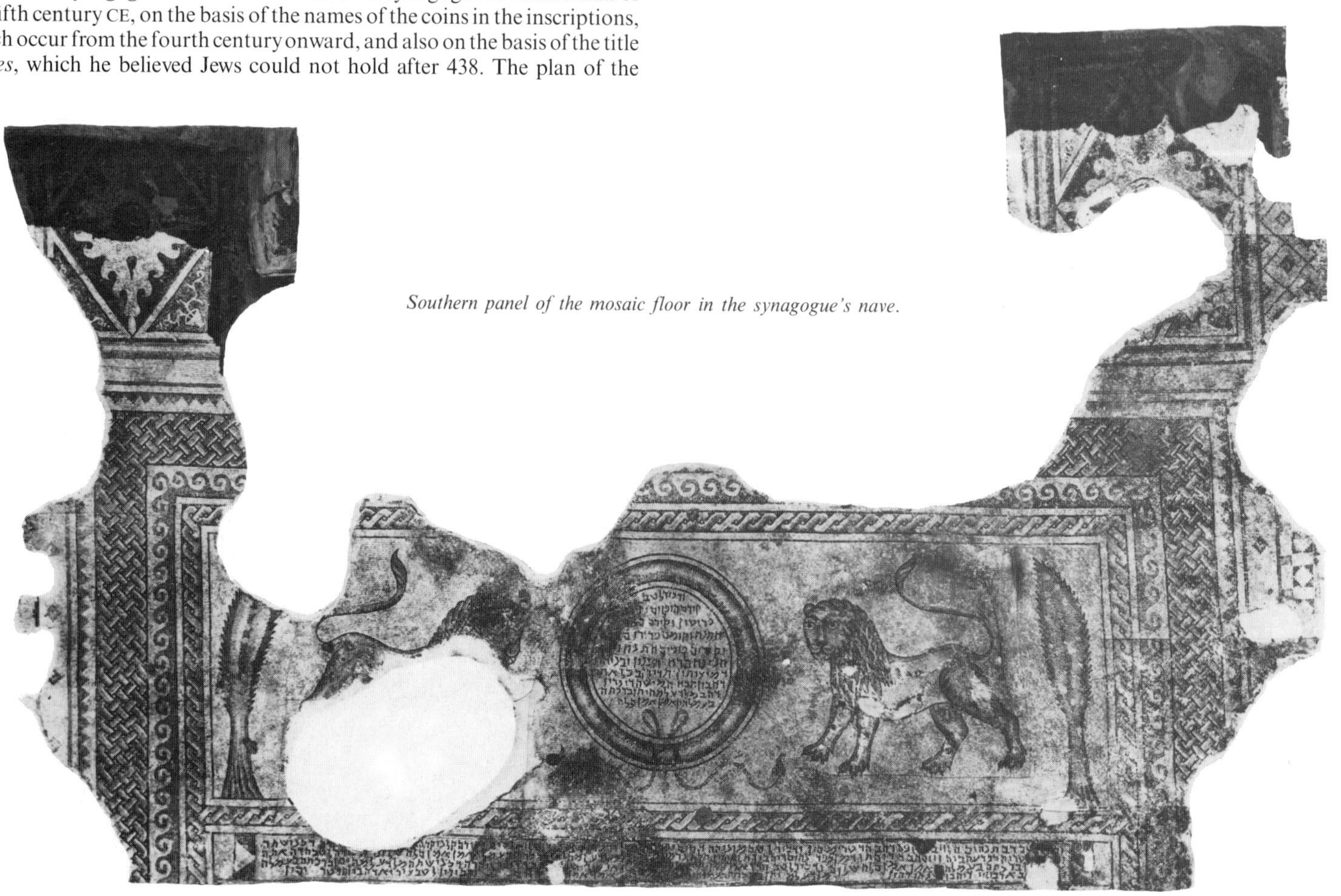

Southern panel of the mosaic floor in the synagogue's nave.

second half of the fourth century CE, was a building with a distinctive floor, laid in opus sectile. The last phase of the synagogue was uncovered by Sukenik (see above).

THE THEATER

In 1932, the Institute of Archaeology at the Hebrew University of Jerusalem, under the direction of E. L. Sukenik, made a few soundings in the ruins of the baths. That expedition also made soundings in the artificial mound (11 m high) built to support the theater. The cavea had fifteen rows of seats, each 60 to 70 cm high, and a seating capacity of 1,500 to 2,000. The highest row was 6.6 m above the orchestra (diameter, 13 m). The side entrances (parodoi) were about 3.6 m wide. The stage was 1.5 m higher than the orchestra and was 5.8 m deep and 29.6 m long.

MICHAEL AVI-YONAH

The theater.

THE ROMAN BATHS

The Roman baths are located in the southern portion of the recreational site of Ḥammat Gader, between the Roman theater and the Yarmuk River (map reference 2125.2320). The baths were built around the hot springs of 'Ein el-Maqle, whose waters reach a temperature of 51 degrees C and to which great curative powers were attributed in ancient times.

EXPLORATION

Systematic excavations in the baths began in 1979 and continued for seven seasons, until large parts of the complex were completely cleared. The excavations were conducted on behalf of the Hebrew University of Jerusalem, the Israel Exploration Society, and the Israel Department of Antiquities, under the direction of Y. Hirschfeld and G. Solar.

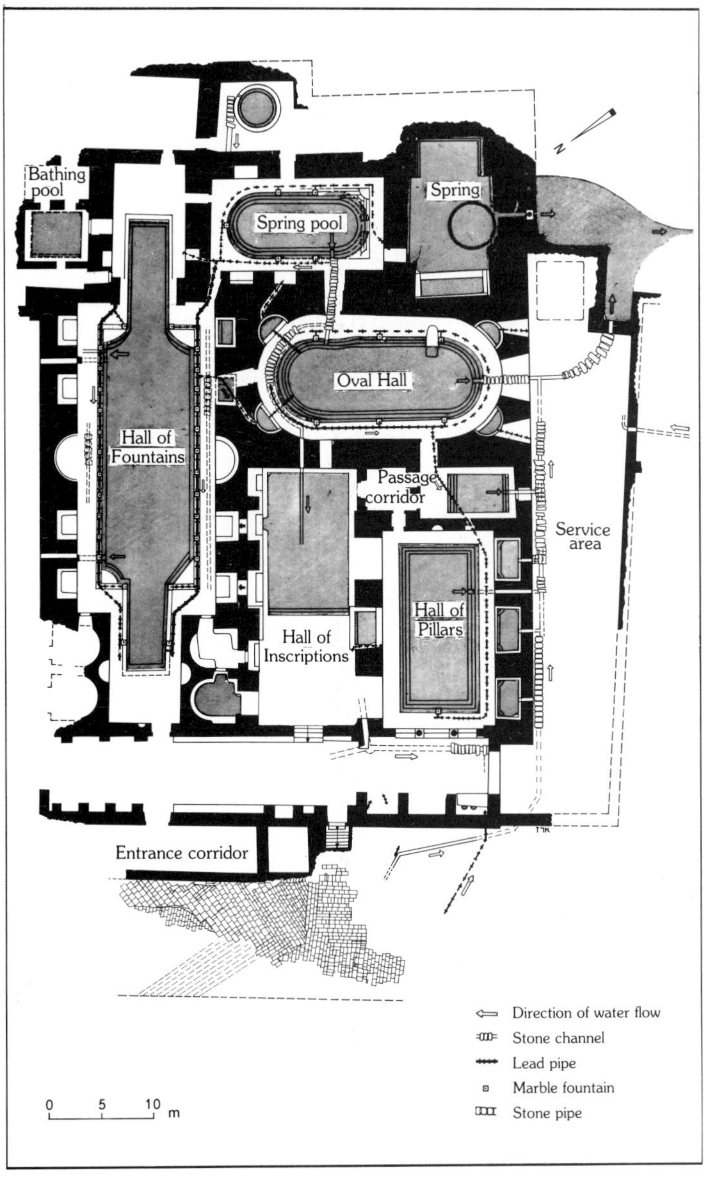

Plan of the baths.

DESCRIPTION OF THE REMAINS

The baths were built around the hot mineral springs. Water was channeled to a row of bathing pools from an elevation pool at the edge of the spring. So far, seven of the pools have been cleared, each in a hall with a different size and shape. Graded levels of heat in each of the pools enabled a bather to become accustomed gradually to the heat of the water as he passed from one bathing hall to the next, eventually reaching the pool built next to the hot springs.

The shape of the bath halls was determined by a long wall containing a series of windows facing southwest. The windows provided the structure with light and ventilation. Their direction was intentional: they provided the bathers with sunlight during the hours Romans preferred for bathing—from noon until evening (Vitruvius, *De Architectura* V, 10, 1).

The total area of the baths cleared in the excavations was about 5,200 sq m. Most of the structure was built of coarsely dressed basalt stones, except for the Hall of Fountains (area D), whose walls were finely hewn limestone. The basalt walls were faced with courses of stones; their core was medium and large undressed stones, cemented with high-quality "Roman cement." Masons marks are hewn in the outer face of most of the stones, more frequently either Greek letters or geometric symbols. The limestone walls were built without mortar. The floors were paved with slabs of clayey limestone that could be buffed and polished; most of the ceilings of the various halls were made of limestone that could be dressed easily.

THE ENTRANCE CORRIDOR (AREA H). Visitors to the baths began their tour in a wide corridor flanked with stone benches. The corridor (7.3 m wide) led directly into the building. The pavement was well-smoothed basalt stones. Engaged pillars, which supported the ceiling, adjoined the walls. The walls are preseved to a height of 2.3 m. To date only about 30 m of the corridor have been uncovered (its northeast end is not yet completely cleared). It is assumed that the entrance gate, or a staircase descending from the street to the baths complex, stood here.

To the north of the baths building a length of the Roman road led directly to

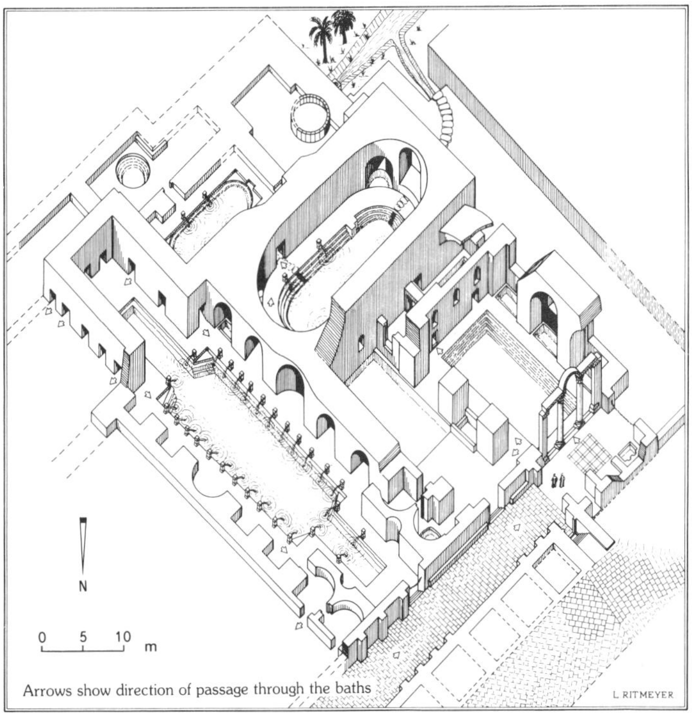

Partial reconstruction of the Roman baths.

the theater, about 200 m to the northeast. The road is paved with smooth basalt stones. Half its width (over 6 m) and a row of shops alongside the road have been cleared. Judging from the road's width and its location between the baths and the theater, it was probably the main street of Ḥammat Gader in the Roman-Byzantine period.

From the level of the street, a secondary staircase of seven steps (2.2 m wide and 25 cm high), preserved in their entirety, descended to the western end of the entrance corridor. These steps made it possible to exit from the side of the baths building to the street. On the corridor pavement, next to the southern wall, several marble fragments were found, fashioned either in the image of a human face or a lion. Examination of the fragments showed that some of them belonged to the marble fountains in the Hall of Fountains. The faces on the fountains were probably removed by the iconoclasts who destroyed the decorations depicting human and animal figures.

THE HALL OF PILLARS (AREA C). The entrance corridor in area H ends in a large hall (10.5 by 22.6 m), bounded by two rows of large pillars. The pillars in the eastern row are 2.6 by 3 m, and those in the western row 3 by 3.5 m. The western row of pillars is preserved to a height of 8 m. Between the pillars were arches, which apparently supported an upper row of pillars. The many glass pane fragments found in the excavations attest to the existence of windows in the upper portion of the walls, in the spaces between the pillars. Many vault stones from the hall's ceiling were also found in the debris on the pavement. The vault was probably cruciform, resembling those found in public baths in Rome from the time of the emperors Caracalla and Diocletian (third century CE). The hall's ceiling can be reconstructed to a height of about 18 m above the floor, based on the vault remains found in the adjoining Hall of Inscriptions (see below). The many broken sections of glass mosaics found on the pavement attest to the magnificence and wealth of decoration of the hall's upper parts.

In the hall's southern wall, preserved to a height of 6.7 m, are three niches that held statues. The niches are preserved entirely. Each base is about 2.5 m above the pavement and is aligned to the symmetrical axis of the hall. Under each niche was an entrance (1.1 m wide and 1.9 m high) to area B. In the central part of the hall, a walkway (1.5 m wide and 1.9 m high) paved with marble surrounds a stepped bathing pool (7.6 by 15.9 m and 1.4 m deep). Three additional baths were installed in the spaces between the pillars in the western row. The baths (2 by 4 m) have an average depth of 0.8 m. Their sides are made of a layer of fired bricks. The temperature of the water in those baths probably differed from that in the central pool. A platform in the northern part of the hall is 0.6 m higher than the walkway in the center of the hall. Its pavement, of colored marble tiles (white, gray, and red), is laid in geometric patterns; there is a pair of semicircular fountains in the corner, in a niche sunk in the pavement. The fountains received water through a lead pipe, the remains of which were found next to the hall. The fountains may also have provided drinking water for the bathers.

The two parts of the hall were separated by a magnificent pillared passageway that constituted a monumental gate at the beginning of the bathing course. The passageway was built on a stepped stylobate located between two of the hall's columns. The lower portion of the columns was found in situ; their upper parts, capitals, and all of a richly decorated arched lintel were found in the piles of debris to their south. One side of the lintel was decorated with acanthus leaves and palmettes, and the other with a meander pattern containing animal figures. The discovery of these parts enabled the reconstruction of the passageway to a height of 7.8 m.

In the mid-fifth century, the Hall of Pillars ceased to be used for bathing and the central pool was filled in and covered with a handsome marble pavement; in its center a marble slab (1 by 1.1 m) with a dedicatory inscription was laid. The inscription attests to the violent destruction of the pool and the transformation of the hall into a "place of games." Similarly, the three baths in the western part of the hall were filled in and paved over. Later, in the Early Arab period, the entrances in the walls were blocked with inferior masonry. The defacing of the figures on the lintels of the pillared passage should also be attributed to this period.

THE HALL OF INSCRIPTIONS (AREA E). The more than thirty-five dedicatory Greek inscriptions found in the floor of one hall gave it its name: The Hall of Inscriptions. It is rectangular (c. 10 by 25 m) and has its main entrance in its northern wall. It is also possible to enter directly from the entrance corridor (area H). The main entrance (c. 3 m wide) has three basalt steps. The bathers could also use two passages in the space between the pillars separating the Hall of Inscriptions from the Hall of Pillars (area C).

In the hall's eastern wall two more entrances led to a pair of apsidal rooms. In these rooms (3.9 by 4.7 m), semicircular alcoves faced in the direction of the Hall of Fountains (area D). The southern room served as a passage; stone benches were built around its walls. The northern room had an apsidal bath similar to the shape of the room. Another entrance in the southern wall of the Hall of Inscriptions connected it with the Oval Hall (area A). The entrance (1.3 m wide and 1.9 m high), judging from an examination of the wall, is a smaller version of the earlier one.

General view of the Hall of Pillars (area C) and the Hall of Inscriptions (area E).

The walls of the Hall of Inscriptions are preserved to an average height of about 3 m, with the exception of the southern wall, which is 8.1 m above the floor, up to the beginning of the vault. Judging from the remains of the vault, it was originally about 12 m above the floor. One end rested on the row of pillars in area C, and the other end on the wall bounding area D (the Hall of Fountains). Three engaged basalt pillars of different sizes abutted the wall bounding area D. Between them were well-dressed stone benches. In this wall, 2.4 m above the floor, are two windows, each of which is 1.4 m wide. Two of the alcoves in area D (see below) can be seen through them. There were probably more windows in the wall's upper portion.

The hall was originally divided into two parts: a spacious paved platform on its north and a large bathing pool south of it. The paved platform (9.9 by 11 m) provided direct access to the pool or passage to one of the adjoining halls. This pool (c. 8 by 14 m and 1.1 m deep), unlike the others, was coated with dark gray plaster. Three steps appear to have been built along its entire breadth. The pool received water from a subterranean channel, which led directly from the hot spring. This channel (1.35 m high and 50 cm wide) branched off from the water pipe supplying the central pool of the Oval Hall (area A). When it was cleaned, a rich collection of glass vessels, including whole vessels, was found in it.

Another bath (2 by 3.2 m and 1.6 m deep) was found between two of the pillars separating areas C and E. The railing in front of it is revetted with smooth marble slabs. In the bath, many pieces of magnificent glass mosaics were found.

In its second phase, the hall ceased to be used for bathing; the central pool was filled in and covered with marble slabs that now covered the floor of the entire hall. In this phase (dating from the second half of the fifth century), the practice of engraving dedicatory inscriptions on the floor began. The inscriptions were not engraved in the floor in any special order. Most of them begin with the formula: "In this holy place remembered be . . .," followed by personal names and sometimes titles—probably of visitors who sought to commemorate their names in the building. Several of the inscriptions are enclosed in a frame, and a few are decorated with various symbols—crosses, goblets, and olive and palm branches.

In the Early Arab period, changes were made in the hall, as in other parts of the building, that chiefly reduced the size of the chambers by blocking entrances and adding walls. The inferior quality of construction suggests that these changes were made during the Abbasid dynasty (eighth–ninth centuries). A water channel was installed under the floor that damaged several of the original paving slabs. To this phase is to be attributed the defacing of several of the crosses decorating the inscriptions and the engraving of two pairs of feet facing south, toward Mecca.

THE PASSAGE CORRIDOR (AREA B). The Passage Corridor is a long, narrow space separating the Oval Hall to the south of it (area A) from the Hall of Pillars to its north (area C). A partition wall divides the corridor into two chambers: a western room (5 by 9 m), containing a bathing pool and a smaller eastern room (4.1 by 4.1 m) that served as a passage. The excavators completely cleared two rooms, to reveal the original walls and parts of the vaults (maximal height, 6.5 m). The Passage Corridor thus had a relatively low ceiling, hidden by the high walls of the adjoining halls (areas A, E, and C). Windows were installed for illumination in the walls abutting it, attested by the many glass fragments found when the pool was uncovered. The bathing pool (5.9 m long; 3.6 m wide and 1.25 m deep) is almost completely preserved. The bathers entered it via four steps on its eastern side and three on its western side. At the foot of the western steps was an opening for draining the water from the pool. The pool contained rich finds, sealed by a later floor—many coins, glass vessels, pottery vessels, and a fragment of a marble statue. Scores of clay oil lamps also were found, of a type attributed to the fourth and fifth centuries CE.

All the entrances to the room containing this pool could be closed by doors, which made it a separate unit. This, and the oil lamps found in the pool, match the details in the description by Antoninus of Placentia of the lepers' bath at Ḥammat Gader. This leper's bath may have existed until the pool was blocked in the mid-fifth century. The pool fell into disuse in the Byzantine period, and the two rooms were repaved and used as a passage. During the Umayyad dynasty, various installations were built into the floor, including a bath, a system of lead and clay pipes, and benches along the walls. In a later phase, probably in the Abbasid period, most of the entrances to this hall were blocked.

THE OVAL HALL (AREA A). The Oval Hall is the best preserved of all the halls in the baths building. It is 11.9 m wide by 23.8 m long, equivalent to 40 by 80 Roman feet. The walls of the hall are preserved to an average height of about 8 m. It was roofed with a vault, flanked by two semidomes. The courses of the base of the vault are preserved in situ, to 5.3 m above the floor. These dimensions enable the estimate that the height of the top of the vault was about 10 m above the hall's floor.

The Oval Hall (area A).

An entrance (1.5 m wide and 2.3 m high) led the bathers from the Passage Corridor (area B) to the Oval Hall. In the center of the hall was a stepped bathing pool (8.1 by 20.3 m and 1.15 m deep) surrounded by a walkway (average width, 1.5 m.) The waters of the hot spring were brought to it via a channel (c. 1 m deep and 30 cm wide), from which another channel branched off, circumventing the pool to the east and supplying the pool in area E. At the western end of the pool, a channel drained the water into the streambed of the hot springs, in the direction of the Yarmuk (see below, area F). The pool's water was cooled by the surrounding lead pipes and marble fountains, through which cold water flowed to the pool from another spring at the site.

There were four semicircular alcoves in the hall's rounded corners, each of which contained a bath. Above each bath is the opening of a narrow tunnel that passes through the structure's narrow walls. These channels apparently carried lead pipes through which cold water was directed to the baths. The water from the baths was channeled into the central pool through lead pipes, as well, some of which were found in situ.

The hall received light from the gigantic windows set in the western wall. The three central windows were built in the form of a Roman triumphal arch (the middle window is 3.5 m wide and 4.8 m high). The side windows are shaped like a funnel, becoming progressively narrower, and ending in the bathing alcoves. Above the side windows, the sills of two more ventilation windows were preserved. The bathers entered and left the hall through two entrances in the southern and eastern walls. The southern entrance (1.5 m wide and 2.3 m high) led to the area of the Hot Spring (area G), and the eastern entrance (1.3 m wide) led to the Hall of Fountains (area D).

The Oval Hall, in use until the end of the Umayyad period, underwent many renovations and repairs. In the Abbasid period, the bath's final phase, the pool fell into disuse and was covered with a pavement of coarse stone. The debris from the vault and the thick layer of alluvium on the floor attest that shortly afterward the hall was abandoned and fell into disrepair.

THE HOT SPRING (AREA G). The Hot Spring was the very heart of the baths. An elevation pool was built around it, to create enough pressure so that water flowed to all parts of the complex. The bathing hall was built to the east of the spring—the culmination of the circuit followed by the bathers. In antiquity, great sanctity was attributed to natural phenomena such as the hot springs of Ḥammat Gader, and bathing in the pool adjoining the hot springs was both a religious and a medicinal experience. Because of its nearness to the fountainhead, the water in this pool was probably hotter than that in the other pools. The northern wall of the structure erected around the mouths of the springs is preserved to a height of about 8 m; its southern walls were severely damaged, and some were almost completely destroyed. Nonetheless, it is possible to reconstruct the missing portions of the southern half of the hall on the basis of its northern half.

The hall was entered from the east through the doorway connecting it with the Oval Hall (area A). This is a vaulted entrance, 2.1 m wide and about 3 m high. There is a smaller entrance (1.7 m wide) in the hall's southern wall leading to another bathing chamber. Two entrances in the eastern wall led to the Hall of Fountains (see below). There was a fifth entrance (1.5 m wide), in the western wall, in the direction of the springs pool. The hall is rectangular (9 by 15.5 m). In the original building phase, a stepped bathing pool (6.8 m wide and c. 14 m long) was built in its center. In a later phase, apparently in the second half of the fifth century, the hall underwent a basic change, and the rectangular pool was replaced by a new oval pool, surrounded by four steps for sitting. Five marble fountains at the pool's edges cooled the water. The pool is paved with diagonally set tiles. A Greek dedicatory inscription in its center marks the completion of the building project by "Petrus son of Romanus." The inscription was probably laid to commemorate the construction of the new pool, which seems to have been in constant use until the destruction of the baths building in the ninth century. In both phases of its existence, the pool was fed directly from the springs through an upper water channel. This may be the "bath of the lepers" seen by Antoninus in front of the hot spring (the *clibanus*, in Greek). There was a walkway (1.2 m wide) around the pool, and two alcoves containing benches in the northern wall.

Another bathing chamber (6.7 by 7.4 m) containing a round pool was built to the south of this hall. The pool (4.4 m in diameter and 1.1 m deep) contains two steps for sitting and is walled with fired clay bricks. From the round pool, a corridor (c. 2 m wide) led in the direction of the spring (its walls were destroyed, and its function cannot be determined).

The area from which the spring flows is surrounded by solid basalt walls between 3.5 and 4.5 m thick. Even before the excavations, two massive pillars were visible here; they constituted part of the wall enclosing the spring on the north. These pillars bore a large barrel vault (in photographs from the 1930s, the complete vault could still be seen). The vault was 7.5 m wide and its top was about 9 m above the present water level. Judging from the building's symmetry, it is probable that a similar vault faced it on the southern side of the springs. The central part above the springs was probably roofed as well, perhaps with a dome.

At some stage, far-reaching changes were made in the area of the spring; the

The Spring Area (area G).

original pool was damaged in an earthquake, and parts of its walls collapsed. It was replaced by a circular elevation pool (diameter, c. 4 m), surrounding the mouth of the spring. Various measures were taken by the builders to ensure the pool's stability: its sides were made of long basalt slabs placed on its muddy bottom; the slabs were joined to one another with tongue-and-groove drafting. Small butterfly-shaped sockets, into which bronze clasps were cast (one of which remained in situ), were hewn on the outer side. It may be assumed that the "tholos" mentioned in the inscriptions was this rounded pool of the Hot Spring.

The original installation for regulating the flow of the spring water was found in the spring pool's western wall. It contained a sluice and an opening to release excess water. Two vertical slots that faced each other were hewn in the sluice installed at the opening of the channel that drained the spring water into the Yarmuk. It was possible to insert a wooden or metal slab into it, thereby sealing the opening and raising the water level in the spring pool. Above the sluice was a large stone block (80 by 90 by 60 cm) with a round opening in it for the release of excess water.

THE HALL OF FOUNTAINS (AREA D). The Hall of Fountains is one of the largest chambers from the Roman period discovered in this country. The central part is 13.9 by 29.7 m; with its two wings, it is 53.3 m long. In its center was a large cold-water swimming pool. Thirty-two marble fountains along the edge of the pool fed it with water conveyed through a system of lead pipes. When the hall was excavated, it became clear that its upper part had fallen to the bottom of the pool and onto the walkway surrounding it. However, it is not known whether the stones in the debris are from the hall's walls or ceiling. It was probably an open hall, with the swimming pool (*natatio*) under the open sky, as was common in public baths in the Roman period. The imperial inscriptions may have been placed here because there was sufficient light to read them.

Five niches were found in each of the hall's long walls (preserved to an average height of 5 m): a semicircular niche in the center, flanked by two rectangular niches on each side. The central niches were roofed with semi-domes, while the rectangular ones were roofed with barrel vaults. Four vaults of this type are preserved in their entirety. Two wings were built against the hall's transverse walls, a northern and a southern one, each about 7 m wide. They are roofed with semicircular stone vaults, which have been reconstructed to a height of 6.5 m. The hall has no fewer than twelve entrances. Two connected it with the Spring Area (area G): one (1.1 m wide and 2.2 m

The Hall of Fountains (area D).

Marble fountainhead.

high) led to the center of the hall; the second, narrower and lower than the first, led to the back of the southern wing. Facing it, in the eastern wall of the same wing, were five entrances, in which changes took place over the course of time. Originally, however, they were meant to enable the bather to leave the Hall of Fountains in the direction of the dressing and service rooms in the east (see below). The other entrances in the Hall of Fountains connected it with the adjoining bathing halls: one entrance was set between this and the Oval Hall (area A), and two other entrances were located in the sides of the apsidal chambers at the end of the hall's northern wing (see above, area E). Another entrance (1.8 m wide) was located in the northern wall of the hall, between the hall and the entrance corridor to the baths (area H).

The plan of the Hall of Fountains resembles that of the building's other bathing halls: that is, it is a large central pool (9 by 24.2 m) surrounded by bathing alcoves. The central pool had an average depth of 1.3 m. Steps were built in its corners, for the convenience of the bathers. At the edges of the pool are thirty-two marble fountains. They differ from each other in size (average height, 0.6 m) but are uniformly designed to resemble an altar; on the side facing the pool, water flows from the mouth of a human or animal head. The fountains were supplied with water by a central lead pipe that passed under them. It was 22 cm in diameter and composed of sections whose average length was 2.2 m. Thirty-two vertical pipes were welded along the pipe, each 10 cm in diameter, on which the marble fountains were fitted. On the east side of the pool, near one of the vertical pipes, Greek letters are found impressed in the lead. They were probably made by the Roman plumbers who installed the system of pipes.

Small baths (1.4 by 2.3 m) were installed in the alcoves surrounding the central part of the Hall of Fountains. In the Byzantine period, they were filled in and benches were built above them. In the building's last phase, several changes were made, mainly the blocking of openings and the installation of elevated water channels. The figures that decorated the marble fountains surrounding the pool were systematically defaced then.

THE SERVICE AREA (AREA F). In antiquity, area F was outside the limits of the bathing area. During the excavations, various water installations were found here—pipes, drainage channels, and pools—that had been necessary to ensure the proper functioning of the baths. The area was bounded by the western wall of the baths building. This wall is more than 60 m long; facing it was a parallel wall, and beyond it were portions of the houses of Byzantine Ḥammat Gader. On the south, the service area ends in a block of buildings that separates the baths building from the stream running from the springs to the Yarmuk River.

At the foot of the western facade, a central drainage channel (45 cm wide and c. 1.5 m deep) is covered with heavy stone slabs. The channel is built next to the wall as far as the drainage point of the Oval Hall (area A). It then turns in an arc toward the stream running from the spring. The central channel drained the pool in area B and probably the pool in area C. Above the presumed continuation of the line of the channel, a section of a stone pipe 9 m long was discovered in situ; its external diameter is 0.8 m and its internal diameter is 0.4 m. Similar pipes were found in the systems supplying water to Jerusalem, Tiberias, and Hippos, dated to the second to third centuries CE. This pipe probably brought cold water from one of the springs in the area of Ḥammat Gader (possibly from 'Ein Bulos, whose water temperature is 25 degrees C).

In a later phase, at the end of the Byzantine or beginning of the Early Arab period, the area was paved with white mosaic. In this period staircases, various chambers, and baths were built in the service area. The service area is bounded on the west by a well-built wall coated with white plaster, preserved to a height of 2.2 m. The line of the wall is more or less parallel to the western facade of the baths building, with an average distance of 9 m between them. On the west, the wall is adjoined by two channels whose starting point and purpose are unknown. Above the channels remains of houses were found, paved with mosaics typical of the Byzantine period. This seems to have been a residential area next to the baths building. The southern part of the Service Area is bounded by a block built with mortar and bricks. It was meant to keep the spring's water from penetrating and seeping into the baths building. The sides of this block were built in a unique manner: courses of basalt were laid in a stepped fashion, and the stones in each course were joined to each other by means of a tongue and groove in the shape of an inverted trapezoid. These connections apparently were meant to strengthen the walls, to withstand the pressure of the built block behind them.

AREA J. Area J extends east and south of the Hall of Fountains. The excavators have begun to clear bathing chambers and additional halls here, most of which have not yet been excavated. The walls of the structure in this area are preserved to heights of 3 to 5 m. To the east of the southern wing of the Hall of Fountains (area D), two rooms were divided by a wall. In the northern room (5 by 6.2 m) was a small bathing pool revetted with marble. The southern room (3.4 by 6 m) has not been completely cleared. In the dividing wall between the two rooms, a broad arch (whose span reaches 4.4 m) with a column in its center bisected the passage below the arch. To the north of the two rooms was a corridor (about 2 m wide) whose roof is completely preserved. It is a travertine vault that stands on a basalt cornice protruding from the wall. Its top is 2.6 m above the floor. This corridor leads to the various rooms and halls in area J. To the north of the corridor was another rather large hall paved with basalt. Its walls are preserved to a height of about 5 m. Area J is bounded on the north by the wide entrance corridor of the complex (area H). There may have been dressing rooms for bathers in the area between the two corridors.

YIZHAR HIRSCHFELD

General: N. Glueck, *BASOR* 49 (1933), 22–23; id., *AJA* 39 (1935), 321–330; id., *AASOR* 25–28 (1951), 137–140; J. Blau, *IEJ* 32 (1982), 102; I. Hasson, ibid., 97–101.

The Synagogue

Main publication: E. L. Sukenik, *The Ancient Synagogue of el-Hammeh*, Jerusalem 1935.

Other studies: E. L. Sukenik, *JPOS* 15 (1935), 101–180; id., *Rabinowitz Bulletin* 1 (1949), 13–14; N. Makhouly, *QDAP* 6/2 (1936), 59–62; Goodenough, *Jewish Symbols* 1, 239–241; G. Foerster, *ESI* 2 (1983), 41.

The baths: Y. Hirschfeld and G. Solar, *IEJ* 29 (1979), 230–234; 31 (1981), 197–219; id., *ESI* 1 (1982), 35–38; id., *BAR* 10/6 (1984), 22–40; Y. Hirschfeld, *ZDPV* 103 (1987), 101–116; J. Green and Y. Tsafrir, *IEJ* 32 (1982), 77–96; L. Di Segni and Y. Hirschfeld, ibid. 36 (1986), 251–268

HAMMATH-TIBERIAS

IDENTIFICATION

The remains of Hammath-Tiberias extend from the hot springs (el-Ḥammam) to the southern boundary of ancient Tiberias, on the western shore of the Sea of Galilee (map reference 2019.2417). In the Talmud, the place is identified with Hammath (Jos. 19:35), a fortified city of the tribe of Naphtali: "Hammath-Hammatha" (J.T., *Meg.* 1, 70a). This identification is not certain, however, because the excavations and a survey of the Hammath area uncovered no remains earlier than the Hellenistic period. Hammath is mentioned many times in the Mishnah. Tiberias and Hammath were originally two separate cities, each surrounded by a wall of its own ("Rabbi Jeremiah said . . . from Hammath to Tiberias—a mile" [J.T., *Meg.* 2:1–2]). Subsequently, however, they were united, apparently in the first century CE: "Now the children of Tiberias and the children of Hammath again became one city" (Tosefta, *'Eruv.* 7:2). In the liturgical sources (*Mishmarot* 24), Tiberias was known as Ma'uziah after the priestly order that had settled in Hammath. Tiberias was forbidden to the priests because it contained a cemetery. When Tiberias became the seat of the Great Yeshiva and the Sanhedrin in the third century CE, and the spiritual center of the Jews of Palestine and the Diaspora, the suburb of Hammath shared its prominence. With the abolition of the patriarchate in about 429 CE, Hammath began to decline, but it continued to exist as a city, supporting itself with its profitable hot springs. The Jewish community remained in the city throughout the Arab period until its decline in the Middle Ages.

EXCAVATIONS

Two excavations have been carried out at the site. The first was undertaken in 1921 (two seasons) under the supervision of N. Slouschz. It was the first excavation by a Jewish resident of the country and the first on behalf of the Palestine Exploration Society and the Department of Antiquities. The second (two seasons in 1961–1962 and 1962–1963), under M. Dothan, assisted by I. Dunayevsky and S. Moskowitz, was on behalf of the Israel Department of Antiquities. The site was earlier explored by the Mandatory Department of Antiquities in 1947.

SLOUSCHZ'S EXCAVATIONS. About 500 m north of the city's southern wall, Slouschz uncovered a synagogue in the form of a square basilica (12 by 12 m), divided by two rows of columns into a nave and two aisles. The three entrances to the building were on the north. East of the building was a courtyard that was entered from the east, and from there a doorway led to the eastern aisle. At the southern end of the nave was a partition consisting of four small columns. The enclosed area behind it probably held the Ark of the Law. In the eastern aisle stood the "seat of Moses" (cathedra). The various levels of pavements, the mosaics, and the alterations in the structure indicate that there were several phases in the construction. However, the excavators did not succeed in tracing them. In the opinion of L. H. Vincent, there were two building phases. In the first, the entrance to the building was on the south, facing Jerusalem. Two building phases are also confirmed by the pavements, one of which is a stylized mosaic.

Slouschz identified the synagogue with the *kenishta de-Hammatha* (synagogue of Hammath) mentioned in the Jerusalem Talmud (*Sot.* 1, 16d), and assigned it to the Early Roman period. Vincent, however, disputed this identification, on the basis of a comparison with other ancient synagogues and the building's small size. In his opinion the main, late phase of construction should be attributed to the fourth to fifth centuries CE. Synagogue research since Slouschz's identification attributes this synagogue, which lacks an apse but whose entrance (according to Dothan) faces Jerusalem, to the fourth century CE. Near the synagogue the excavators uncovered part of a cemetery containing sarcophagi from the third and fourth centuries CE with the names of the deceased written in Greek—Isidorus, Symmachus son of Justus (*SEG* VIII, nos. 9–11)—as well as several graves dating from the Early Arab period. Among the finds are a capital decorated with a menorah, a fragment of a chancel screen with a menorah in relief, and a seven-branched menorah carved in limestone. In addition to Slouschz's investigations, M. Narkiss and Z. Eshkoli published architectural details and a number of objects found in the synagogue and its vicinity.

DOTHAN'S EXCAVATIONS. An area of approximately 1,200 sq m was excavated near the hot springs, about 150 m west of the Sea of Galilee. The ancient buildings had been erected on an artificial terrace running parallel to the seashore from southeast to northwest, closely following the contours of the terrain. Beyond the southern limit of the main excavation area the remains of the city wall and one of its towers were uncovered. These were found to date not earlier than the Byzantine period, although they appear to rest on the remains of walls of an earlier city.

Hammath-Tiberias: plan of synagogue IIA.

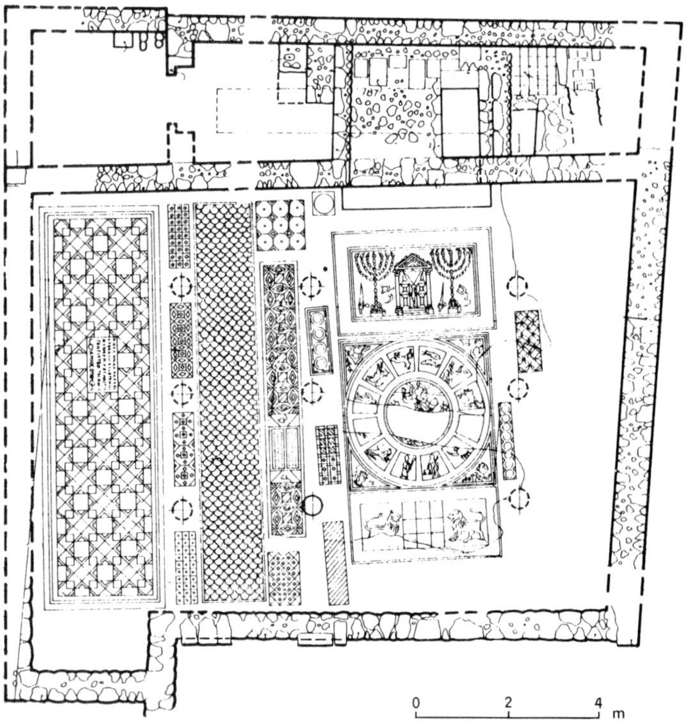

Three main construction levels were revealed, dating from the first century BCE to the eighth century CE. The numismatic evidence showed that remains from the first century BCE lay beneath level III.

Level III. The main building (60 by 40 m) in level III dates from the first century or first half of the second century CE. This building, only half of which was excavated, consists of a central court with halls and rooms along at least

Remains of synagogues II and I, looking west.

Southern panel of the mosaic floor in the nave of synagogue IIA: a Torah ark, menorahs, shofars, incense shovels, and the four species.

three of its sides. Two entrances to the building were found on the south side. Its plan resembles that of a public building, such as a gymnasium, and it may have already been a synagogue in that early period. All the later structures (above the building), except perhaps those of the intermediate phase III–II, were synagogues. Among the meager finds from this building is a unique glass goblet in the shape of a cantharus, silvered on the inside and outside and decorated with floral reliefs below the rim. Level III seems to have been destroyed in the middle of the second century, and the few remains above it (intermediate phase III–II) do not appear to belong to a public building.

Level II B–A. The synagogue in level II was erected on these remains. The last stage of the synagogue (IIA), which was the better preserved, is based, for the most part, on the earlier phase, IIB. It is a broadhouse (15 by 13 m), oriented southeast to northwest, and is separated from the structures around it. Three rows of columns, each containing three columns, divide the building into four halls, the widest of which (the second from the west) is the nave. Attached to the building on the south is a corridor paved with mosaics with an entrance on the east. Although no other entrances to the building are preserved, there may have been more than one. On the north side of the building was a room that may have contained stairs leading to the roof or to a second story.

Building IIA does not differ greatly from its predecessor. The corridor, however, was divided into cells and closed off as a passage. In this writer's opinion the direction of the entrance to the synagogue was also changed. Henceforth, the entrance seems to have been through three openings in recesses in the northern wall. The stairwell was no longer in use, and access to the second floor may have been from a small room adjoining the corridor. From the southern end of the nave, a step led to a raised niche in the corridor where the Ark of the Law, which in the previous stage had no permanent place, was probably kept. The walls of the building were decorated with colorful paintings, remains of which were found in the debris.

The nave and aisles were paved with magnificent mosaics in thirty hues, which have survived in a fine state of preservation. The most important is the mosaic pavement in the nave, which is divided into three panels. In the southern panel the Ark of the Law is depicted, flanked by seven-branched menorahs with flames and a lulab, ethrog, shofar, and incense shovel. The middle panel represents the zodiac surrounding the figure of the sun god Helios riding in his chariot (the chariot was partly destroyed when the wall of level I was built). Helios has a halo above his head, one hand raised in benediction and the other hand holding a globe of the universe. The corners of the panel display female busts, each with a Hebrew name beside it, symbolizing the four seasons of the year. The northern panel contains a dedicatory inscription in Greek of the founders of the synagogue. It is flanked by two lions. The two eastern aisles contain mosaics in geometric design and three inscriptions, one in Aramaic and two in Greek.

The main builder of the synagogue, according to the Greek inscription, was Severus, called "the pupil of the most illustrious patriarchs," evidently the title bestowed on high officials in the court of the presidents of the Sanhedrin in Tiberias ("Severus . . . completed [the work of construction]. Praise be to him and to Julius the *parnas* [synagogue official]"). Another Greek inscription mentions Profuturos, who built one of the porches. The Aramaic inscription refers to the place as "a holy site"—that is, a synagogue.

The remains of the floors, as well as the coins and lamps, date the synagogue to the fourth century CE. The plan of the building, which is a broadhouse divided into four halls, differs from all the known ancient synagogues of the second to third centuries CE.

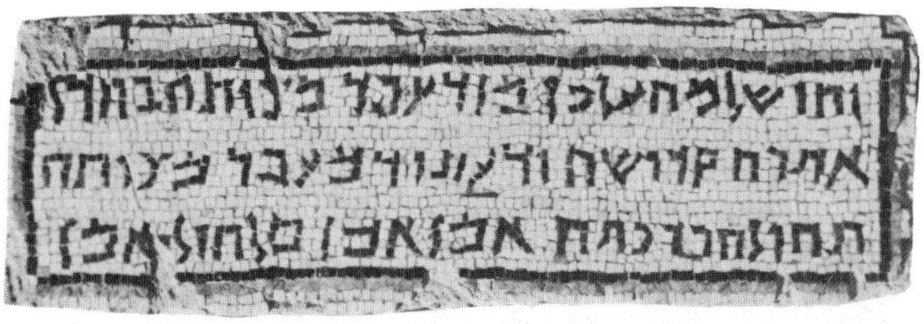

Aramaic inscription in the mosaic floor of synagogue IIA.

Mosaic floor in the eastern hall of synagogue IIA.

Middle panel of the mosaic floor in the nave of synagogue IIA: Helios on his chariot surrounded by a zodiac.

Hammath-Tiberias: capital decorated with a menorah in relief.

Stone-carved menorah, c. 3rd century CE.

Menorah carved on a column.

The artistic level of the mosaics is high. In the individual treatment of the figures, they strongly resemble the Constantinian mosaics at Antioch. Evident here is the strong influence exerted by Hellenistic-Roman art at the beginning of the fourth century on the Jewish capital at Tiberias. The free artistic expression displayed in the nude representations of the signs of the zodiac, the frequent use of Greek, as well as the various finds, all accord with the spirit that prevailed in the period when the heads of the Sanhedrin flourished in Tiberias and confirm a date in the first half of the fourth century CE for the construction of synagogue IIA. Level IIA was evidently destroyed in the fifth century, and the great synagogue IB was erected in its place.

Level IB–A. The new synagogue, IB, was oriented in the same direction as its predecessors. Unlike them, however, it was not isolated from the other buildings, which were attached to it on the north and south, whereas streets skirted the building on the east and west. The synagogue was built in the form of a basilica, as was common in synagogue and church construction in the fifth and sixth centuries CE. It was divided by two rows of columns into a nave and two aisles. A third row of columns divided the nave transversely, thus creating an entrance hall (pronaos). The three rows of columns supported a gallery on the second story that ran along three sides of the building. The three main entrances were on its north side. Three steps led from the nave to an interior apse. East of the apse was a room with stairs ascending to the second story; to the west was another room, where the synagogue's "treasury" was hidden in the floor. From the western aisle, three doorways opened onto a courtyard paved with flagstones. Its walls are well preserved. A small apse was discovered on the southern side of the courtyard and beyond it were plastered rooms that had served as cisterns (mikvehs?). The mosaic in the hall was made of tiny colored tesserae; the preserved fragments indicate that it depicted figures of animals in addition to geometric and floral designs. Level IB was apparently destroyed in the first half of the seventh century, perhaps when the Byzantines reconquered the country from the Persians. The new synagogue (level IA), probably built at the beginning of the reign of the Umayyads, is not markedly different from its predecessor except that the small apse was no longer in use. Part of the courtyard was covered with a roof, supported by a column, thus creating a room in which one of the stairs of the apse was used as a bench. This may have served as a *beth midrash*, or study hall. A new mosaic pavement was laid that was decorated mainly with geometric designs, but at the entrance to the nave there were other motifs, such as a menorah. The rich finds included pottery of the type found at Khirbet el-Mafjar and many clay lamps, some bearing Arabic inscriptions. A long Aramaic inscription on a jug has been partly deciphered. It concerns a gift of oil from Sepphoris.

In this level, a segment of a paved street was also found (which was constructed in level IB). It ran from the city gate along the western wall of the synagogue's courtyard. The evidence furnished by the coins makes it clear that all the structures in this level were destroyed at the beginning of the Abbasid period, in approximately the middle of the eighth century, and never rebuilt. The ruins were used as dwellings and silos by squatters in the twelfth to the fifteenth centuries.

SUMMARY

The prominent features of the southern synagogue may be summarized as follows.

1. At Hammath several superimposed synagogue buildings were found, beneath which was a public building whose function is not clear. The synagogues were built from the fourth to the middle of the eighth centuries.

2. A unique type of synagogue was uncovered here—a broadhouse with four rooms (IIA, B). The entrance was on the side facing Jerusalem (IIB) and there was a permanent place for the Ark of the Law in a rectangular room that preceded the apse in Palestinian synagogues (IIA).

3. The mosaic pavement in synagogue IIB was constructed in the spirit of the Hellenistic-Roman art of the fourth century. The zodiac depicted in the mosaic is the earliest found in the country.

4. The Greek inscriptions referring to this synagogue's builders are the first to mention the patriarchs of the Sanhedrin. They contribute greatly to what is known about Judaism in the fourth century CE in Tiberias.

5. The uppermost synagogue (IA) is an instructive example of Jewish architecture at the beginning of Arab rule in Palestine. It sheds light on the customs practiced in syagogues then.

Main publication: M. Dothan, *Hammath Tiberias: Early Synagogues and the Hellenistic and Roman Remains* (Final Excavation Report 1), Jerusalem 1983.

Other studies: L. H. Vincent, *RB* 30 (1921), 438–442; 31 (1922), 115–122; Goodenough, *Jewish Symbols* 1, 214–216; B. Lifshitz, *ZDPV* 78 (1962), 180–184; id., *Journal for the Study of Judaism* 4 (1973), 43–45; M. Dothan, *IEJ* 12 (1962), 153–154; id., *RB* 70 (1963), 588–590; id., *ASR*, 63–69; id., *Hammath Tiberias* (Reviews), *BAR* 10/3 (1984), 32–44. — *IEJ* 34 (1984), 284–288. — *JAOS* 104 (1984), 577–578. — *Syria* 62 (1985), 362–364. — *Bibliotheca Orientalis* 45 (1988), 401–402; Hüttenmeister–Reeg, *Antiken Synagogen* 1, 436–461; *Archives of Ancient Jewish Art: Samples and Manual* (eds. Y. Yadin and R. Jacoby), Jerusalem 1984, 1–38; D. Milson, *LA* 37 (1987), 303–310.

Early Arab period: E. D. Oren, *Archaeology* 24 (1971), 274–277; id., *IEJ* 21 (1971), 234–235; id., *RB* 78 (1971), 435–437.

MOSHE DOTHAN

ḤARIF, MOUNT

IDENTIFICATION

Mount Ḥarif is located at the western edge of the central Negev Highlands, adjacent to the Sinai Peninsula, at elevations of between about 900 and 1,000 m above sea level. The region comprises a series of narrow plateaus and rolling hills sharply dissected by deep wadis and the escarpment overlooking Sinai. The high elevations result in relatively abundant precipitation. In the past, it enabled a relatively diverse and marginally Mediterranean flora to thrive, present today in relic form. Water is not available locally—only some 10 km (6 mi.) away, at 'Ein Qadis, where a cluster of other sites is also present. However, it is likely that water may have been available once, near Bor Ḥoresha.

HISTORY OF RESEARCH

An area of approximately 15 sq km was systematically surveyed between 1969 and 1974 by an expedition from Southern Methodist University in Dallas, Texas, under the direction of A. E. Marks. Subsequently, between 1979 and 1982, and again in 1989, further investigations were conducted, under the

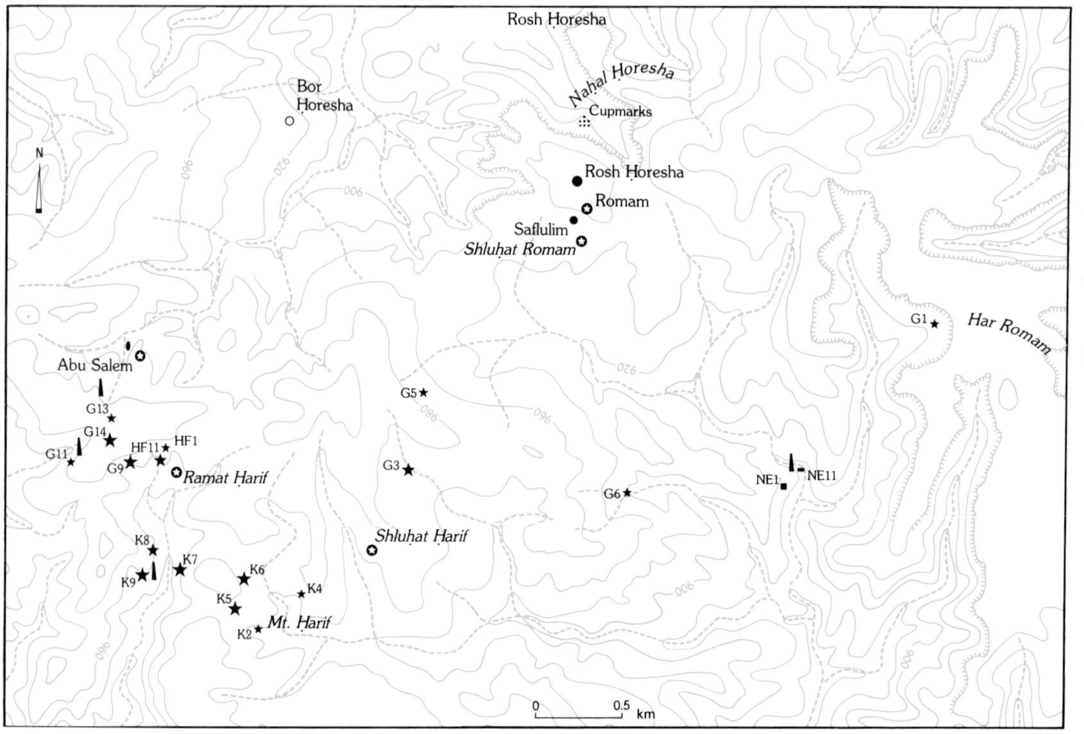

Map of the Mount Ḥarif area, showing the location of the main prehistoric sites.

auspices of the Emergency Archaeological Survey of the Negev, by A. N. Goring-Morris and A. Gopher. Although the research indicated occupation of the area from at least the Middle Paleolithic through the Late Neolithic periods, the most intensively investigated, and apparently the most intensively occupied, were the Upper Paleolithic and Epipaleolithic periods.

THE UPPER PALEOLITHIC. Several exposed, Upper Paleolithic surface sites were discovered and systematically collected from deflated loess surfaces on top of the plateau adjacent to Mount Ḥarif, including K9A and G11, and, several kilometers farther north, at Har Ḥoresha I. At least two other occurrences, both in situ, have been noted in the area but are untested. Because of the surface nature of the sites, no organic remains were recovered.

The lithic assemblages from the collected sites all display flake technologies, with scrapers, burins, and retouched pieces comprising the main tool categories. The assemblages have thus been assigned to the Levantine Aurignacian complex. However, in light of recent investigations elsewhere, it is possible that part, if not much, of the scraper component of the assemblage from K9A may in fact be Epipaleolithic. Marks has proposed dating sites K9A and G11 to a more humid period—to about 30,000 BP—although others believe they may be considerably later, during the final millennia of the Upper Paleolithic. Of some interest, however, is the apparent absence of evidence for occupation from the other Upper Paleolithic tradition, the blade-based Ahmarian (Lagaman).

THE EPIPALEOLITHIC PERIOD. The Ramonian. A series of completely deflated sites (G9, K9, G14, K5, K6, K7, and G3) at the top of Mount Ḥarif and the adjacent plateaus formed the basis for the techno-typological definiton of the Epipaleolithic Ramonian entity—the same as that earlier termed Negev Kebaran by Marks and A. H. Simmons. The latter appellation has been abandoned as a consequence of the demonstrable absence of connections with the Kebaran complex focused in the central and northern parts of the country. The Ramonian is a microlithic industry featuring high frequencies of distinctive straight or concave backed and distal oblique truncations achieved using the microburin technique—the Ramon point. The presence in some assemblages of small numbers of Helwan-backed lunates was interpreted as having chronological implications and led to the widely accepted proposal for a later phase within the Ramonian. Other tool groups commonly represented include scrapers and notches. The origins of the Ramonian as a whole are believed to lie in the more lowland, Sinai-based Mushabian complex. It thus appears likely that the Ramonian can be dated to the interval 13,000 to 12,000 BP. The specific, exposed site locations appear to indicate summer occupation of the region and movement to lower elevations in the Negev and Sinai in the winter months.

LATE NATUFIAN. The huge in situ site complex of Rosh Ḥoresha and Saflulim is located in a shallow valley 3 km (1.5 mi.) northeast of Mount Ḥarif. Rosh Ḥoresha alone extends for at least 4,000 to 5,000 sq m, while Saflulim, some 200 m away, on the other side of a small wadi, is less extensive. To date, only limited testing has been conducted at the sites. These revealed two structures on the surface at Rosh Ḥoresha, one composed of massive slabs; Marks and P. Larson concluded that they had been an integral part of the Natufian occupation, although doubts have been raised about their dating. At Saflulim, part of a lime-plastered floor was exposed, indicating that architectural features are present, in addition to various terrace walls. Immediately adjacent to the site are dozens of bedrock mortars and cupmarks, smaller numbers of which have also been noted at Rosh Ḥoresha.

One of the test pits at Rosh Ḥoresha exposed part of what seems to be a large fire pit filled with burned stones and abundant faunal remains of gazelle, ibex, and some onager, as well as wild sheep. Smaller prey included hare, lizard, and partridge. The rich marine mollusc assemblage comprised mostly species from the Mediterranean, but also from the Red Sea. The many beads recovered were dominated by dentalia but included numbers of limestone beads and malachite spacers. Bone tools, including points and a fragment of a bone handle, occurred in small numbers.

Pollen samples indicated 9.5 percent arboreal pollen together with 6 percent cereal grasses. This indicates a marginal Mediterranean maquis-type vegetation at the time of occupation.

The lithic assemblage from Saflulim is fully compatible with other Late Natufian assemblages in the Negev: locally available translucent chalcedony was the preferred raw material for fabricating abruptly backed lunates, notches and denticulates, scrapers, burins, small numbers of borers, and items with sickle sheen. Massive tools are rare but distinctive, usually on cherty flint. The microburin technique was extensively employed in manufacturing the geometrics. The Rosh Ḥoresha assemblage is similar, but also contains small numbers of trapezes and rectangles; the size of the lunates displays a bimodal distribution in contrast to Saflulim, however. It thus appears likely that Rosh Ḥoresha at least was composed of a series of partially overlapping sequential occupations. Several carbon-14 dates have been obtained on charcoal:

Rosh Ḥoresha	13,090 BP ± 200 (I-5496)
	10,880 BP ± 280 (SMU-10)
	10,490 BP ± 430 (SMU-9)
Saflulim	11,150 BP ± 100 (OxA-2869)
	10,930 BP ± 130 (OxA-2136)

The Saflulim dates appear consistent with a Late Natufian occupation, while only the middle date at Rosh Ḥoresha appears reliable. The other two dates, combined with the anomalies in the lithic assemblage, have been used to argue that Rosh Ḥoresha contains, in addition, an admixture of earlier, Geometric Kebaran and later, Ḥarifian components, a view rejected by others.

Ramat Ḥarif: semisubterranean structure with worktable, grinding slabs, and mortar.

The Rosh Ḥoresha-Saflulim site complex is nevertheless by far the largest Late Natufian site documented to date and was clearly repeatedly occupied. Its slightly protected location, together with faunal evidence, indicated that it was most likely occupied in the winter and, as such, may have been a regional aggregation locale for Late Natufian groups in the Negev. This may have been facilitated by the relative profusion of readily available resources, such as the pistachio, as well as other vegetal foods and medium-sized game.

Ḥarifian. Several large, in-situ occupations with architectural remains were also investigated in the area, forming the basis for the definition of the terminal Epipaleolithic Ḥarifian culture. Included are the sites of Abu Salem (G12), Ramat Ḥarif (G8), and Shluḥat Ḥarif (K3), and the more ephemeral occurrences at Romam (G20) and Shluḥat Romam.

A series of carbon-14 dates is available from Abu Salem and Ramat Ḥarif. These are presented with those from two other Ḥarifian sites in the Makhtesh Ramon investigated by A. N. Goring-Morris and S. A. Rosen:

Ramat Ḥarif	L3/280	10,500 BP ± 100	Pta-3009
	L3/275–280	10,380 BP ± 100	Pta-3284
	L3/220–225	10,300 BP ± 100	Pta-3001
	L3/210–220	10,390 BP ± 100	Pta-3285
	L7/220–225	10,250 BP ± 100	Pta-3288
	L7/180–185	10,100 BP ± 100	Pta-3286
Abu Salem	L22/180–190	10,550 BP ± 90	Pta-3292
	L24/190–200	10,420 BP ± 100	Pta-3293
	L22/120–130	10,140 BP ± 80	Pta-3291
	L22	11,660 BP ± 90	Pta-3080
	L21/120–130	10,340 BP ± 90	Pta-3290
	L1/155–160	10,300 BP ± 100	Pta-3289
	Trash pit 45–55	10,230 BP ± 150	I-5500
	Trash pit 25–30	10,230 BP ± 150	I-5499
	Trash pit 15–25	9,970 BP ± 150	I-5498
Ma'ale Ramon East	L1/30–35	10,530 BP ± 100	Pta-3371
	L1/25–30	10,430 BP ± 80	Pta-3483
Ma'ale Ramon West		10,400 BP ± 100	Pta-3483
		10,000 BP ± 200	RT-1068N

These dates are for charcoal. On the basis of the stylistic attributes of Ḥarifian lithic assemblages, there are grounds for believing that the Ḥarifian began slightly earlier than the dates indicate. It is thus estimated that the Ḥarifian may have lasted from about 10,750 to 10,100/10,000 BP.

Pollen samples from Abu Salem included 5.6 percent arboreal pollen and 2 percent cereal grains, indicating a somewhat more humid environment than at present. Charcoal samples from Abu Salem and Ramat Ḥarif were all identified as *Pistacia atlantica*.

Allowing for subsequent erosion, the original extent of the three main sites seems to have been on the order of 600 sq m. Architectural remains were preserved at three of the sites. The structures are circular and commonly semisubterranean, dug into the loess surface of the plateau (Ramat Ḥarif) or utilizing natural dips in the bedrock (Abu Salem and Shluḥat Ḥarif); they are 3.5 m in diameter and lined with slabs. Only two or three of these larger structures are documented at each site. They are accompanied by smaller structures (diameter, 2 m), sometimes as separate units; in other instances, they are appendages to larger structures. The general plan is of a loose alignment of independent units. Large work surfaces of wadi slabs or bedrock protrusions covered with shallow cupmarks and incised cutmarks were a standard feature, particularly of the larger structures. One or two large, deep mortars are also a characteristic feature of several of these structures. Because pestles are almost absent, it can be assumed that they were of wood. Grinding and pounding stones and cobbles are, however, common. Bell-shaped pestles on green magmatic rock were found at Abu Salem and Shluhat Ḥarif. Unlined hearths are also present in several structures, as well as in open areas at the sites.

Shallow trash pits were used for discarded bones at Abu Salem and Ramat Ḥarif. The faunal remains include gazelle, ibex, and wild sheep, as well as occasional onager and aurochs. Bone points are limited to a few points and awls and a decorated spatula.

Exotic items, each of which have been discovered at more than one site, include shaft straighteners on flat basalt pebbles, sandstone whetstones, polished spatulas on red micaceous sandstone, turquoise beads, malachite spacers, fossil teardrop pendants, and large quantities of red ocher. They derive from the Makhtesh Ramon area, Timna', and/or western Sinai.

Shluḥat Ḥarif: pestle on green magmatic stone.

The abundant marine mollusc assemblages include large quantities of dentalium. Among the other species, a clear Red Sea orientation can be detected, as well as some from the Indo-Pacific. Of note are the large Mediterranean trumpet shells—*Charonia sp.* and Red Sea *Pecten sp.*—that likely served in stationary contexts as opposed to the smaller, more mobile shells.

The lithic industry was microlithic, with quantities of very small lunates (22 percent). Other characteristic forms include scrapers (11 percent), many of which are crudely denticulated. Micrograveties and other pointed microliths are quite common. Sickle blades are rare but noteworthy, as are numbers of backed knives and massive denticulates. Most distinctive, however, is the Ḥarif point and its derivatives, which constitute an early arrowhead form. Although the lithic densities are great, marked intrasite and intersite patterning in the frequencies of the main tool groups is discernible.

The location, contents, and internal spatial organization of the sites indicate that they represent spring-to-autumn residential base camps of small bands (two to three families) of hunter-gatherers: the economy was probably based on collecting nuts (pistachio and almonds), legumes, roots, tubers, and cereals (barley). In addition to hunting game locally available in the region's various micro-habitats, they would have shifted, probably in smaller groups, to lower elevations in the Makhtesh Ramon, northern Sinai, and western Negev in the winter. Thus their annual round was probably on the order of 25,000 to 30,000 sq km.

Although well adapted to the region, there is some evidence that this system operated under stress: that ongoing desiccation resulted in a critical threshold being reached. Their adaptation was no longer viable and the area was abandoned.

PRE-POTTERY NEOLITHIC B. The Mount Ḥarif region was subsequently reoccupied in about 9,000 BP, when a small (c. 125 sq m) settlement was founded on the northern side of Abu Salem. The excavations revealed a honeycombed arrangement of small, interlocking circular-to-oval structures (diameter, 1–2.5 m). Although no organic remains are preserved, a few grinding stones were found. The lithic assemblage, however, was knapped on different raw material from that of the Ḥarifian, enabling a separation of the two elements. Cores are commonly bipolar for the production of blade blanks. Helwan, Jericho, and Byblos points are the common arrowhead forms. Sickle blades are also present. Given differences in the proportions of the arrowhead forms through the depth of the sediments, it seems likely that this locale was repeatedly occupied for short periods in the spring and/or summer months by a small hunter-gatherer band and perhaps by groups based more permanently at the edge of the highlands.

A possible Late Neolithic site with architecture was also noted in the area but is as yet uninvestigated.

A. E. Marks et al., *IEJ* 22 (1972), 73–85; id., *Paléorient* 1 (1973), 97–99; id. (and T. R. Scott) *JFA* 31 (1976), 43–60; *Prehistory and Paleoenvironments in the Central Negev, Israel* 2/2 (ed. A. E. Marks), Dallas 1977, 173–354; P. Lawson, *JFA* 5 (1978), 120–121; A. N. Goring-Morris and A. Gopher, *IEJ* 31 (1981), 133–134; 32 (1982), 71–73; id., *ESI* 1 (1982), 38–39; A. N. Goring-Morris, *Mitekufat Ha'even* 22 (1989), 48*–60*; id. *At the Edge: Terminal Pleistocene Hunter-Gatherers in the Negev and Sinai* (*BAR*/IS 361), Oxford 1987; id., *Proceedings of the 1986 Shell Bead Conference* (Rochester Museum and Science Center Research Records 20, eds. C. F. Hayes III and L. Ceci), Rochester 1989, 175–188; id., *Proceedings of the 2nd Symposium on the Upper Palaeolothic Mesolithic and Neolithic Population Around the Mediterranean Basin* (*BAR*/IS 508), Oxford 1989, 7–28; id., *Paléorient* 14/2 (1990), 231–244; id., *The Natufian Culture in the Levant* (International Monographs in Prehistory, Archaeology Series 1, eds. O. Bar-Yosef and F. R. Valla), Ann Arbor 1991, 173–216; S. Davis et al., *Paléorient* 8 (1982), 87–93; A. Belfer-Cohen and A. N. Goring-Morris, *Mitekufat Ha'even* 19 (1986), 43*–57*; N. Lipschitz, ibid., 80*–85*; S. A. Rosen, *Paléorient* 10/2 (1984), 111–121; id., *ESI* 4 (1985), 60; Weippert, 1988, 88, 95, 104.

NIGEL GORING-MORRIS

HAROR, TEL

IDENTIFICATION

Tel Haror (Tell Abu Hureireh) is located in the western Negev desert, on the northern bank of Naḥal Gerar (map reference 08795.11257), approximately 20 km (12.5 mi.) west of Beersheba and 7 km (4.5 mi.) from Tel Sera', on the main road from Gaza to the Beersheba Valley. The ancient site consists of two superimposed mounds: the lower tell, a trapezoidal compound of about 40 a.; and the upper tell, in its northern corner. The upper tell is shaped like a rhombus with sides approximately 100 m long, its surface area is nearly 4 a. The upper tell rises 10 to 15 m above the surrounding terrain, to an altitude of 130 m above sea level. Early identifications of Tel Haror with cities in the territory of Simeon, such as Beth-Merkaboth (Jos. 19:4 and 1 Chr. 4:31, proposed by W. F. Albright) relied on the assumption that the site had not been inhabited until the Iron Age. However, surface surveys by D. Alon and Y. Aharoni in the 1950s concluded that Tel Haror had been inhabited continuously in the Bronze and Iron ages, which enhanced its identification with Canaanite and Philistine Gerar, the city of Abimelech (Gen. 10:9, 20, 22, 26; 2 Chr. 4:39–41, 14:9–15).

EXCAVATIONS

The Land of Gerar expedition, under the auspices of Ben-Gurion University of the Negev and in cooperation with the French Centre National de la Recherche Scientifique in Jerusalem, directed by E. D. Oren, conducted six seasons of excavations at Tel Haror between 1982 and 1990. Excavations indicated that the site had been occupied since the Chalcolithic period. The main periods of occupation discerned are:

Period	*Date*	*Area*
Iron III–Persian	8th–4th cent. BCE	D, E, G, and K
Iron I	12th–11th cent. BCE	B, D, K, and L
LB III	13th cent. BCE	B and K
LB I–II	16th–14th cent. BCE	L
MB II	18th–16th cent. BCE	B, K, and L

MIDDLE BRONZE AGE. The Middle Bronze Age settlement extended over an area of about 40 a., making it one of the largest sites in southern Canaan. It was fortified by an elaborate system of earthen ramparts and defense walls similar to the defense systems at neighboring Tell el-'Ajjul and Tell el-Far'ah (South).

In the 1986–1990 excavation seasons, area K yielded the architectural remains of a well-preserved cultic complex that was exposed for 500 sq m. The building shows two clearly defined architectural phases (K4a–b), involving repairs and floor raising. In the northwestern part of area K, a thick, mud-brick wall (1.2 m across), built on a stone foundation, enclosed a spacious courtyard and various structures and installations. Sections of the wall were coated with thick white plaster. A small chamber (10 sq m) constructed against the northern enclosure wall included niches and low mud-brick benches, presumably to receive offerings. The floor and benches were found covered with ash mixed with animal bones and many cultic vessels; new benches were built on top. A large concentration of vessels was found at the entrance to the chamber, including cylindrical incense stands topped by large bowls and decorated with bands of red and blue paint on a white background.

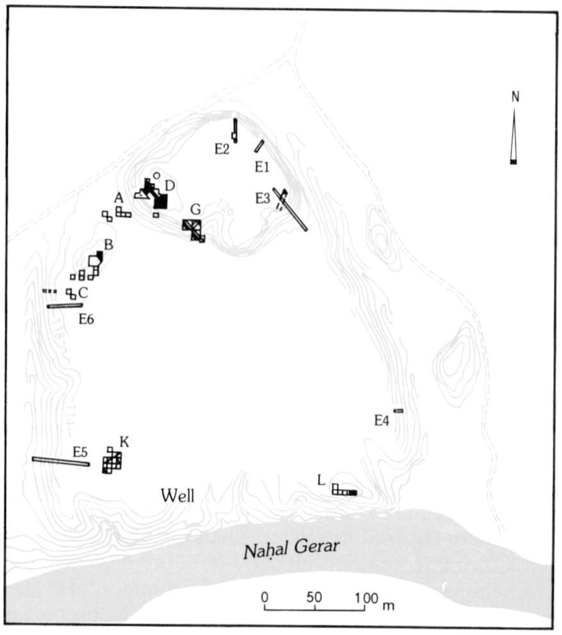

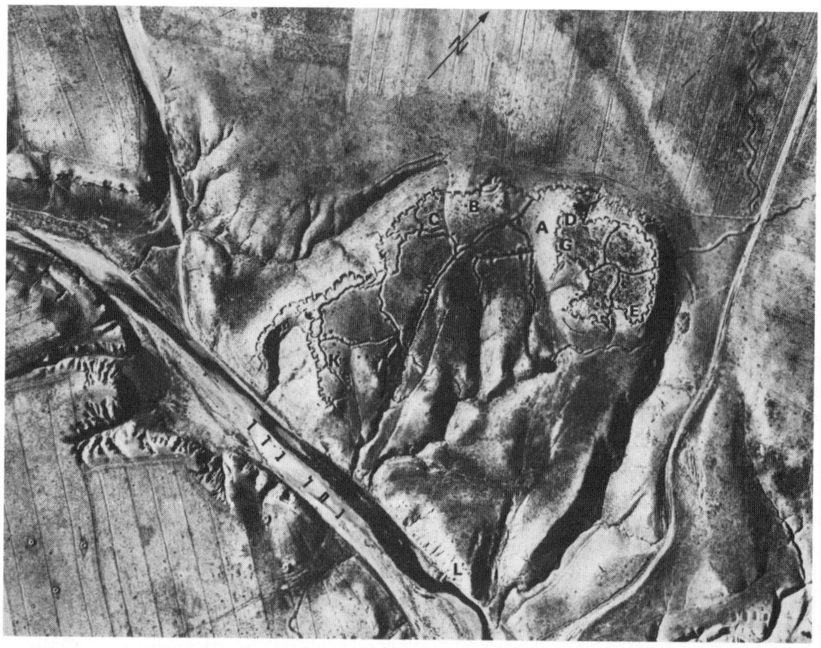

*Tel Haror: **(above)** map of the site and excavated areas; **(above right)** 1949 aerial photograph (note the Turkish communication trenches).*

*Area K: **(below)** plan of the MB II temple; **(right)** one of the temple's rooms, containing benches and niches.*

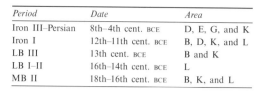

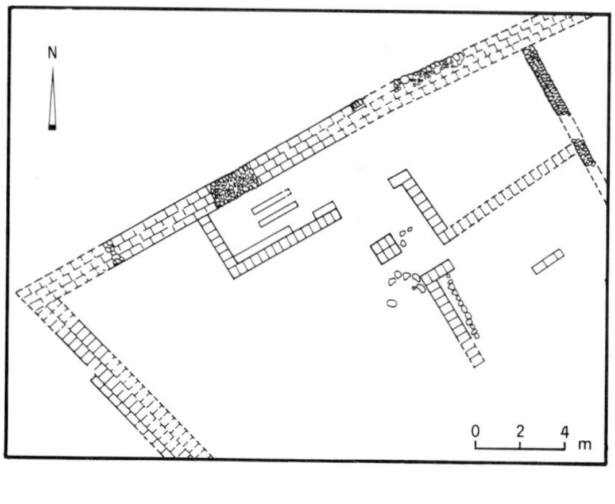

Tel Haror: aerial view, looking southeast.

In the eastern wing of the courtyard, a complex of structures was excavated that included a low partition wall with a niched recess for offerings at its northern end. Opposite the niche a square block of bricks, probably used as an offering table or an altar, had been erected on the *kurkar*-filled and leveled area; a number of *favissae* were cut into the floor around it. This area is represented by many hearths, ash pockets, and large collections of cultic vessels, implying that ceremonies, such as the burning of offerings, were performed in this part of the temple. North and west of the building were *favissae* containing large quantities of ash, bone, and offering vessels; one also contained a fragment of the red-painted arm of a large statuette. Various alterations were noted in the last phase of the temple that involved the raising of the floors. In the process, the floor level in the northern chamber was also raised and the original benches were covered entirely by the remains of offerings—animal bones, particularly the jaw bones of sheep and goats, and various vessels—and new benches were constructed on top. In the courtyard area, the brick block and *favissae* were buried under heaps of animal bones and offering vessels. The new *favissae* in this section contained complete skeletons of birds and puppy dogs, as well as many miniature (votive) vessels and clay objects with seal impressions. The large collection of cult vessels included cylindrical stands topped with large bowls, seven-mouthed lamps, hundreds of miniature vessels, vessels applied with snakes in relief, a bowl with bull's protomes attached to the rim; and imported Cypriot wares. East of the altar a number of chambers were excavated, with hundreds of miniature offering vessels and an elegant carinated chalice on a high foot with Minoan-type tall handles. The collection of animal bones in the temple area consists largely of sheep and goats (62 percent), fowl (28 percent), and dogs (5 percent). Analysis of the bones supports the conclusion that sacrificial slaughter, mainly of young sheep and goats, took place in the temple area. The sacrifice of dog puppies is attested by contemporary records from Mari, in northwest Syria. The last phase (K4a) of the sacred precinct at Tel Haror was not destroyed by a conflagaration. The uppermost floors were covered by heaps of fallen brick walls whose orientation suggests destruction by an earthquake.

In area L sections of a massive building (9028) whose size indicates a palace or an upper-class building were preserved to the east of building 9094 (see below) which it resembles in plan and architectural details. Stratigraphic considerations suggest a date in the late Middle Bronze Age IIB for stratum L4. Buildings 9094 and 9028 also resemble the Middle Bronze Age palace (stratum 12) at nearby Tel Sera', as well as palace I at Tell el-'Ajjul.

At the southern edge of the site, overlooking Naḥal Gerar, a well (diameter, 3 m) was excavated to a depth of 11.5 m—2.5 m below the present water table. Perhaps as much as one-third of its original height has been eroded. The upper 7 m were built of carefully dressed large blocks of local sandstone; the remainder was cut through bedrock. For some reason the well was intentionally filled with brick material, *tabun* fragments, animal bones, and domestic pottery, including Middle Cypriot imports.

In area B, under the Iron Age I settlement strata and evidently at the foot of the inner slope of the Middle Bronze Age rampart, a burial was excavated.

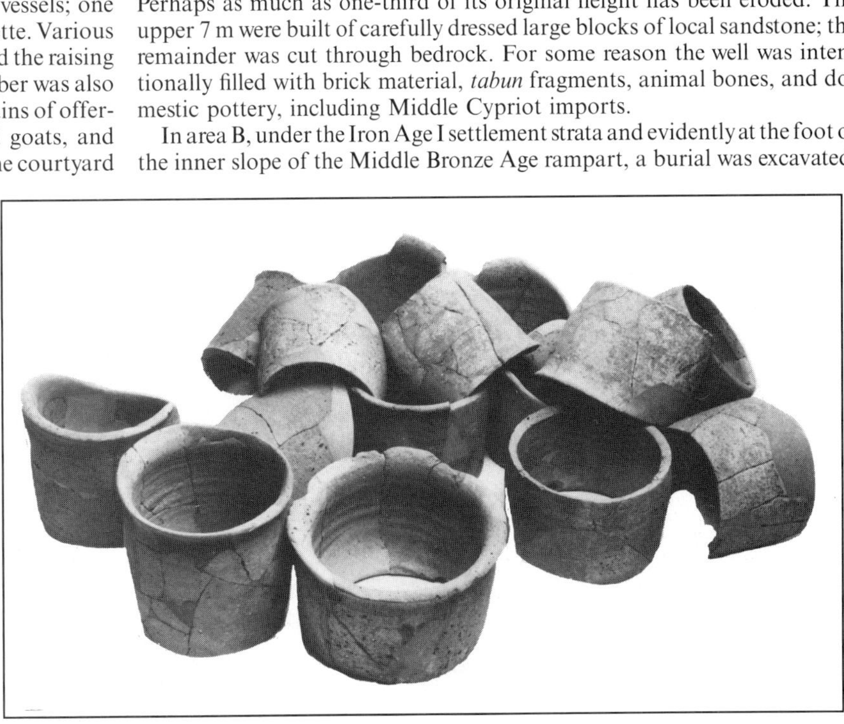

Pottery stands from the temple.

Cylindrical stands topped with decorated bowls.

***Right:** cult stand and a huge goblet from the temple.*

The shallow grave was lined with stone slabs and sealed with mud plaster. In it were the fragile remains of three infants lying next to each other and an adult, with only its legs preserved, opposite them. The grave goods included two storage jars, a deep bowl with handles, a juglet, and a typical Hyksos scarab.

Four wide sections cut along the western and northern flanks of the lower compound provide detailed information on the massive defense system that surrounded the Middle Bronze Age city at Tel Haror. The fosse was first dug 5 to 7 m deep and at least 15 m across. The various materials in its makeup—*kurkar*, sand, soil, and loess—were used to construct the rampart, a trapezoidal enclosure. At its base, the rampart was, on average, 20 m wide; it was 8 to 10 m high. Its core included alternating layers and lenses of *kurkar* and clean sand. The entire structure was finally capped with flat *kurkar* stones and coated with thick mud plaster. Evidence from the section on the northern flank indicates that, at the initial stage of construction, a massive belt of *kurkar* stones was built on the outer edge of the fortification to prevent the enormous rampart from eroding into the fosse. Because the superstructure of the fortifications has long been eroded, it is impossible to ascertain the existence of a city wall on top of the ramparts. On the other hand, excavations in the southeastern section revealed that at some stage in the Middle Bronze Age IIB, the rampart went out of use. Large refuse pits were cut into it and a massive mud-brick city wall was constructed at the base of the disused rampart. The considerable accumulation in area K of settlement debris (as much as 4 m thick) suggests a lengthy occupation in the Middle Bronze Age. Judging from the evidence in area K, Tel Haror did not experience violent destruction at the end of the Middle Bronze Age.

LATE BRONZE AGE. The evidence retrieved thus far suggests that the Late Bronze Age settlement at Tel Haror was considerably smaller than that of the Middle Bronze Age, totaling only a few acres. The main Late Bronze Age settlement was restricted to area L in the northeastern corner of the lower tell, overlooking the springs of Naḥal Gerar. Excavations in the 1986 and 1990 seasons over an area of some 250 sq m exposed occupational remains (depth, c. 2 m) overlying the disused Middle Bronze Age fortification system. To stratum L2 (Late Bronze Age II) belongs a large, well-planned building (9106) whose stone foundations were constructed directly on earlier walls of a buttressed building from stratum L3, as well as on the much deeper foundations of walls from the Middle Bronze Age stratum L4. Building 9106 may have been a patrician's house, as it comprised spacious pebbled courtyards provided with stone-built installations, a square water reservoir lined with a thick layer of plaster, and various chambers for storage and other domestic functions. The floors of this building yielded a large quantity of imported Cypriot pottery, as well as a bronze bowl with an omphalos base.

Ostracon with a fragmentary hieratic inscription, LB.

The impressive buttressed building (9094) in stratum L3 was most likely a public building or palace. Unfortunately, its northern section was completely destroyed when a road was constructed nearby. The outer wall of the building (width, c. 1 m) is based on a massive stone foundation and has accurately disposed stone buttresses protruding inward. At the junctions of the walls, the foundations were as much as 2 m deep. The mud-brick walls of building 9094 were destroyed to below floor level by a building operation in stratum L2. In a few places it was possible to discern two floor phases with finds that would be dated to the Late Bronze I period, including a Cypriot white-painted VI clay rattle and a cylinder seal with a geometric pattern.

The last phase of the Late Bronze Age III in the thirteenth century is represented in area B (stratum B7), below the occupation strata of the Iron Age I, as well as in area K (stratum K3), directly overlying the remains of the Middle Bronze Age temple. The latter included sections of poorly preserved mud-brick walls on stone foundations, various domestic installations, and a number of sizable refuse pits (as much as 5 m across and 2.5 m deep) cut into the temple structure. Nearby were large, shallow pits full of ash and organic remains. The rich ceramic assemblage from stratum K3 included Egyptian style cups and bowls, Cypriot white-shaved, base-ring II, and white-slip II imports, Mycenean IIIB and decorated "Levanto-Helladic" wares, decorated chalices, and a vessel shaped like a pomegranate. A refuse pit from this period excavated in area D, on the southern slope of the upper tell yielded an ostracon inscribed in hieratic script with some illegible toponym completed with the determinative for a foreign country. Stratum B7 had witnessed a devastating fiery destruction at the end of the Late Bronze Age.

EARLY IRON AGE. The main settlement in the Iron Age I is represented in area B at the northwestern part of the lower tell. Its location on the inner slope of the Middle Bronze Age rampart and the absence of data on the ancient topography of this area make it impossible at this stage of the research to determine accurately the size of the Early Iron Age site. Limited excavations in 1982–1983, 1988, and 1990 over an area of some 250 sq m yielded a series of building phases (strata B7–1) extending from the Late Bronze Age III to the end of Iron Age I or the beginning of the Iron Age II, overlying burial remains from the Middle Bronze Age II (stratum B8).

Strata B6–5 have so far been reached in only a very limited area. In 1990, a section of an impressive building with 1-m-wide mud-brick walls and a nicely paved stone courtyard was exposed. The pre-Philistine ceramic evidence from the floors of the building provides an early twelfth-century date for its use.

To strata B4–2 belong a series of carefully planned and well-constructed buildings with stone foundations, as well as stone-lined grain silos. The southern part of area B was occupied by large refuse pits, the largest of which was 5 m across and 3.5 m deep, containing stones and hearths, kitchen waste, bones, and ash. The abundant ceramic collection includes richly decorated Philistine pottery, both monochrome and bichrome (twelfth–eleventh centuries BCE). The amount of decorated Philistine pottery in the pits exceeded 25 percent of the total ceramics. Of special interest are two beautiful stone seals, one schematically representing a figure of a lion and the other a horned animal suckling its kid and fronted by a tree. The rich assemblages of

Philistine pottery at Tel Haror, coupled with complementary data from neighboring Tel Sera', testify to the dynamic expansion of Philistine culture from the southern coast of Philistia and its establishment in the western Negev in the twelfth to eleventh centuries BCE.

Immediately below surface stretches of a massive mud-brick wall (width, 6.5 m) were recorded that belong to a substantial defense wall, perhaps remnants of a citadel partially built on the upper slope of the Middle Bronze Age rampart, that guarded the stratum B1 settlement. South of it were sections of a large building with a cobbled courtyard. Evidence of intensive activities in the same period also has been found in nearby area D, as well as in distant areas K and L. They include domestic installations, ash pits covered with a layer of stones, probably some working surfaces for processing agricultural products, and many ash and refuse pits. The ceramic repertoire includes Cypro-Phoenician wares and black juglets, hand-burnished vessels, and characteristic storage jars that help date stratum B1 to the end of the Iron Age I or the beginning of the Iron II (c. 1000 BCE).

LATE IRON AGE. Excavations in areas D, E, and G on the upper tell uncovered the well-preserved remains of a highly organized town or fortified citadel from the Late Iron Age with an elaborated defense system and carefully designed public architecture. The fortification system—a rampart, defense wall and glacis, watchtowers, and perhaps also a corner fort—determined the overall shape of the upper tell. The defense wall was traced immediately under the surface of the tell and exposed for some 60 m. Approximately 4 m wide, it was coated with a thick layer of plaster and preserved to a height of about 4 m. In area D, a massive mud-brick tower (c. 9 by 7 m) projected from the wall and a complementary buttress was added against it on the interior. Nearby, a massive mud-brick platform (c. 150 m) was constructed, apparently to support a corner tower that stood at this strategic position. Excavations within the wall uncovered a series of gravel floors with various cooking and storage installations attesting that the area had been part of an open courtyard. A thick deposit of burned brick and ash found on the upper floor (phase D3) implies the wholesale destruction of the settlement toward the end of the Iron Age. A section of the inner face of the enclosure wall was incorporated with courses of well-dressed, margin-drafted ashlars laid in the headers and stretchers technique. The method in which the blocks were laid and the mud-filled gaps between the ashlars indicate that the ashlar masonry was in secondary use, probably originating in an earlier phase. The integration of ashlar masonry in mud-brick walls has been noted in stratum VI (eighth century BCE) at neighboring Tel Sera'. Excavations outside the defense wall in the area of the southern tower revealed that its foundations were reinforced by a glacis-like structure built of bricks, *kurkar* stones, *terre pisée*, and ash heaped up irregularly against the wall and the tower. The fill material included a handful of Late Iron Age sherds alongside a large collection of Middle Bronze Age pottery and a Hyksos-type scarab.

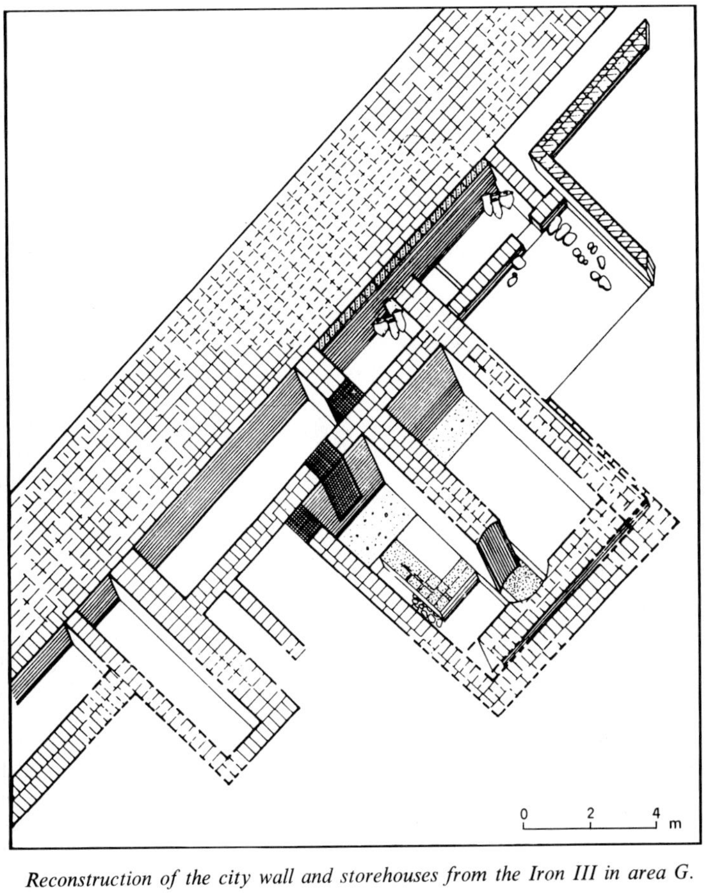

Reconstruction of the city wall and storehouses from the Iron III in area G.

Section of the storehouse. The block of bricks in the center was used to elevate the building.

A wide stratigraphic section in area E (length, 50 m; width, 6 m; depth, 6–8 m) enabled a detailed study of the defense system to establish the sequence of construction. The wall of the Late Iron Age town or citadel was partially founded on the enormous Middle Bronze Age rampart that, at this point, formed the northeastern corner of the fortified enclosure. The foundation courses were laid on top of the rampart construction and were supported by a massive embankment of brick material and soil. An impressive glacis was then constructed against the town wall and over the embankment. It was faced with flat *kurkar* stones affixed in, and coated with, gray clay. The glacis underwent a major repair and was raised some 1.5 m above the level of the stone capping. It is likely that the improvised glacis in area D represents the last repair of the defense system. Systematic excavations inside the walled area encountered a series of floors, fill material, and buildings constructed against the wall. The earliest floor abutting the wall and on top of the earthen rampart belonged to a large building. It was associated with a rich ceramic assemblage of eighth-century BCE types. A major phase of repair was followed by the construction of a courtyard house with stone bases for wooden pillars. The latter was destroyed by fire in the seventh century BCE and apparently soon restored, with new cobbled floors and cooking facilities added. It is thus suggested that this enormous defense complex at Tel Haror was constructed in the eighth century BCE. Soon after some unknown event, the settlement underwent a major phase of restoration. It was subsequently destroyed in a great conflagration in about the mid-seventh century BCE.

Excavations in area G uncovered a complex of well-planned storehouses with symmetrical magazines with long halls (averaging c. 6.5 by 3 m) constructed against the defense wall and erected on mud-brick platforms. The construction was of high quality; the walls are generally preserved with their plaster coating, in some places up to 3 m or more. Prior to construction, the area was raised and leveled. The platform structure consisted of a network of massive foundation walls (height, c. 1 m); the space between them was packed with stones, broken bricks, and *kurkar*. The earliest floors (G6–5) were assigned to the late eighth century BCE. For reasons not yet clear, soon after construction was completed, both the fortification system and the build-

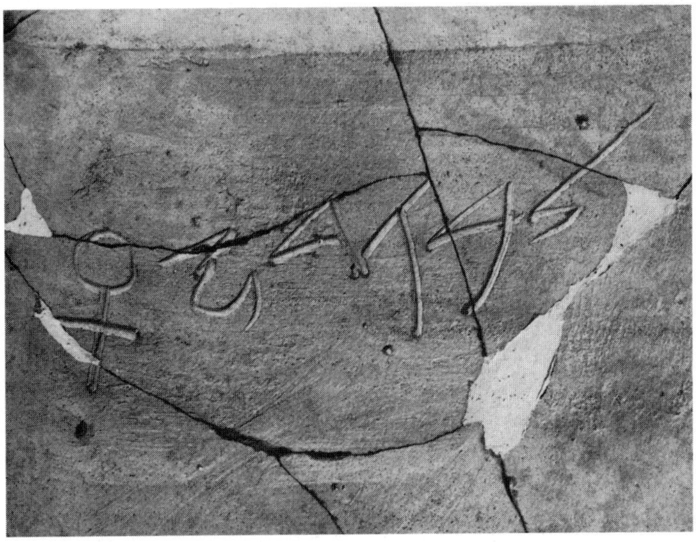

Storage jar inscribed with the word lbgd, *the hieratic numeral "8," and the Egyptian ankh symbol, Iron III.*

ings inside underwent a major renovation (phase G4). It involved raising the floors some 2 m, blocking the windows and doorways of phases G6–5 structures to accommodate for the enormous amount of fill, and adding new sections of glacis in some places. The last fortified settlement on the upper tell (phase G3) essentially follows the original town plan of phases G6–5. This implies that there was no abandonment of or hiatus in the Late Iron Age settlement. The settlement in phase G3 came to a violent end, evidence of which was visible in all the areas of excavation. The burned debris (thickness, c. 1 m) contained heaps of broken bricks, remnants of charred beams, and large quantities of pottery vessels that had been left standing against the walls and inside installations. The ceramic repertoire recorded on the floors of phase G3 is represented by wares typical of the southern coast and the western Negev toward the end of the Iron Age: Phoenician-type transport amphorae, wide-bellied storage jars, red-burnished dipper juglets, spiral-burnished bowls, Phoenician-type mushroom-lipped jugs, and globular perfume bottles with tiny handles. The storage jars were often incised with potter's marks—such as a palm branch or pentagram—before firing. One storage jar was inscribed with the word *lbgd* (belonging to *bgd*) alongside an Egyptian ankh and the hieratic numeral 8 incised four times, one above the other. One room adjacent to the defense wall contained a heap of some thirty loom weights placed against a low stone partition; nearby was a pillar figurine. Worthy of note are diagnostic Edomite sherds and a broken clay weight with the word *pym* inscribed in ink.

The results of the excavations on the upper tell, particularly the evidence of the comprehensive planning of the settlement and its defenses as a single integrated architectural system, suggests that it was a state enterprise. The building of the fortified settlement at Tel Haror may have been part of the Assyrian administration's overall military and economic organization in southern Philistia and on the border with Egypt. The fortified town appears to have been established as an administrative center in the late eighth century BCE (Sargon II?) and destroyed in the middle or second half of the seventh century BCE, probably by an Egyptian military expedition of the Saite kings to Philistia.

PERSIAN PERIOD. Following the destruction of the Late Iron Age fortified town, the site was occupied in the fifth–fourth centuries BCE by one or two settlement phases (stratum G1) represented in area G by a large building, cobbled floors, and grain and refuse pits. The finds included Greek and Cypriot imports, clay figurines, bone spatulae, and an Aramaic ostracon. Excavations in area D exposed the remains of a large structure based on stone foundations and attached to a courtyard paved with stone slabs. As in area G, the construction of the Persian period settlement involved a large-scale leveling of the Iron Age site. A probe square in area K yielded a badly preserved burial associated with Egyptian pottery and a Greek fibula. The settlement at Tel Haror is in line with the densely populated map of the western Negev in the Persian period.

E. D. Oren et al., *ESI* 2 (1983), 33–35; 3 (1984), 27–30; 4 (1985), 31–33; 9 (1989–1990), 69–73; E. D. Oren and M. A. Morrison, *BASOR Supplement* 24 (1986), 57–87.

ELIEZER D. OREN

HARTUV

IDENTIFICATION AND EXCAVATION

The Early Bronze Age I site of Hartuv (er-Rujum) is located on a shallow hill in the inner Shephelah, south of Beth-Shemesh, at the junction between Naḥal Sorek and Naḥal Kesalon (map reference 149.129). The site was excavated on behalf of the Institute of Archaeology at the Hebrew University of Jerusalem and the Centre de Recherche Français de Jérusalem, under the direction of A. Mazar and P. de Miroschedji, in three short seasons between 1985 and 1988. The site's estimated area is 7.5 a. The main area of excavation (area A) is located on a hillock of about 600 sq m at the center of the site. A secondary area (B) is located on a smaller hillock, southwest of the main area.

EXCAVATION RESULTS

The excavations in area A revealed three occupation levels: stratum 1—a circle of large stones dated to an undefined period, later than the Early Bronze Age I; stratum 2—a public building complex from the Early Bronze Age I; and stratum 3—an occupation level from a previous phase of the Early Bronze Age I.

Hartuv: general view of the EB I public building in area A, stratum 2; note the circle of stones from stratum 1 on top of it.

PUBLIC BUILDING COMPLEX. A unique public building complex in the Early Bronze Age I village probably occupied the entire hillock of area A, but only its southern part, in an area of 350 sq m, was exposed. The excavated parts of the complex include two large broad halls (134 and 152); two narrow, elongated rooms; an open courtyard; and a street or a piazza. The two halls stand perpendicular to one another. Both were entered from the central courtyard. One of the narrow rooms separates the two halls, while the other, directly opposite it, on the other side of the courtyard, was probably attached to another large hall, as yet unexcavated.

It is suggested that hall 152 is a sanctuary. It was a broad hall (c. 15 by 5.8 m) with five pillar bases, made of flat stones, along its central long axis. An outstanding feature of this hall is a row of finely worked stone slabs, some over one meter high, standing on their narrow side along the inner face of the southern wall, opposite the entrance. Nine such stones were preserved, but there were probably more, as the eastern end of the wall is missing. A narrow bench was built along part of the row of stones. It appears that the vertical stones should be interpreted as a line of ritual standing stones (*maṣṣebot*). There is evidence that the stones once stood free and only in a later phase were

Row of maṣṣebot *in the temple.*

incorporated into the building. Similar standing stones, dated to the fifth and fourth millennia, are known from eastern Sinai, the southern Negev, and Transjordan. These finds demonstrate the use of standing stones for cultic purposes in protohistoric periods in this country. The plan of the hall recalls broadroom temples known from the end of the fourth millennium (the Chalcolithic temple at En-Gedi and the stratum XIX temple at Megiddo).

The inner dimensions of hall 134 are 11.7 by 4.3 m. Two flat stones along its long axis probably served as pillar bases. The entrance was from the courtyard, on the east, and was located in the northern part of the eastern wall. The construction of the entrance is monumental and unique for the period: each of its two jambs was made of one well-worked monolithic stone, more than 2 m high and square in section.

The quality of the architecture, the size of the main halls, and the construction techniques indicate that this was the community's main public complex. The temple in hall 152 was probably just one component of this multifunctional architectural unit. Hall 134 may have served administrative purposes, or it may have been the main reception hall of a community leader. The only public buildings known from the Chalcolithic and Early Bronze I periods are temples, so that it can be assumed that priests were also community leaders and administrators. The public complex can thus be explained as the location of both the temple and civil administration.

DWELLINGS. Fragmentary dwellings were excavated in area B. However, the remains were too fragmentary to suggest the house plans.

Stratum 3 is known only from two small probes. In both there was about a 1-m-thick accumulation of gray earth containing a lot of organic material, without any building remains. The nature of the debris may indicate that life in stratum 3 was in temporary or seasonal dwellings.

FINDS. The empty floors in stratum 2 revealed that the site had been abandoned peacefully. The stratum 2 pottery is characteristic of a regional variation in the Early Bronze Age I that spread over the central and southern parts of the country. The number of vessel forms is limited; some vessels (mainly closed forms) are decorated with parallel reddish-orange stripes, sometimes on a white wash. Also common are incised decorations found mainly around the necks of closed vessels and on loop handles. Almost none of the sherds had red slip or burnish. Among the pottery were some sherds that may be of Egyptian types produced in the southern Coastal Plain, in the region of Tel Erani. The stratum 3 pottery is very similar to that from stratum 2, except that there are more small, rounded bowls, decorated with a red band along the rim.

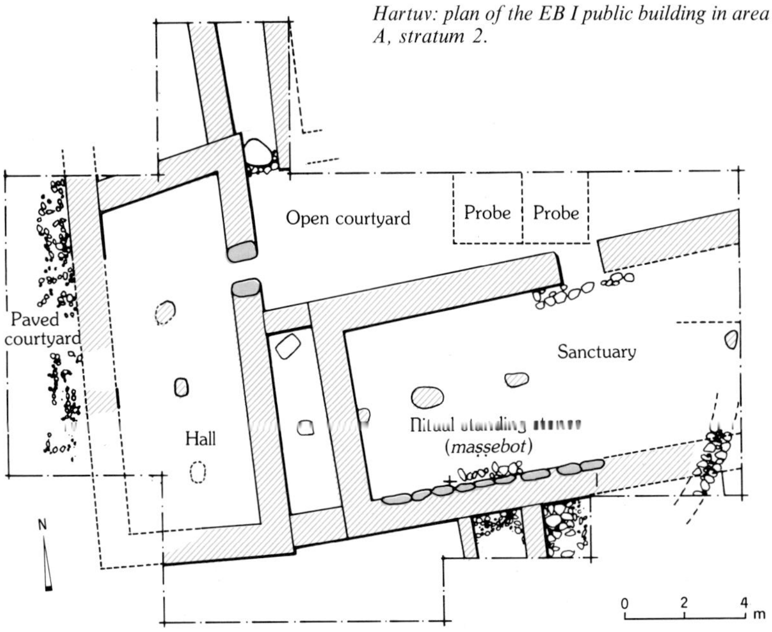

Hartuv: plan of the EB I public building in area A, stratum 2.

CONCLUSIONS

The excavations at Hartuv exposed a village site that was founded on virgin soil, developed, and abandoned in the Early Bronze Age I. Its founding at this particular location demonstrates a divergence from the preceding period, as two Chalcolithic (Ghassulian) sites are known from surveys a few kilometers away, in Naḥal Sorek. The public building complex exposed in the center of the site is an important contribution to the study of architectural forms of the period, building techniques, aspects of ritual and religious architecture, and perhaps social structure. The abandonment of the site may be related to the emergence of urban life in Canaan in the Early Bronze Age I.

C. Schick, *ZDPV* 10 (1887), 131–159; P. S. Malky, *JPOS* 20 (1946), 43–47; A. Mazar and P. de Miroschedji, *ESI* 4 (1985), 45; 7–8 (1988–1989), 79; id., *IEJ* 36 (1986), 109; 38 (1988), 84; 39 (1989), 110–112; id., *RB* 95 (1988), 215–217; 96 (1989), 214–217.

AMIHAI MAZAR, PIERRE DE MIROSCHEDJI

ḤASHAVYAHU, MEẒAD

IDENTIFICATION AND EXPLORATION

The fortress now called Meẓad Ḥashavyahu was discovered approximately 1.7 km (1 mi.) south of Yavneh-Yam (Minet Rubin, map reference 120.146). Its remains were excavated in 1960 by J. Naveh on behalf of the Department of Antiquities and the Israel Exploration Society. The fortress was found to contain an abundance of East Greek pottery dating to the last third of the seventh century BCE and several Hebrew ostraca. The ancient name of the fortress is unknown; its modern name was taken from one of the ostraca, which was read "Ḥashavyahu ben Ya . . ." In 1986, a limited salvage excavation was carried out at the site under the direction of R. Reich, on behalf of the Israel Department of Antiquities and Museums.

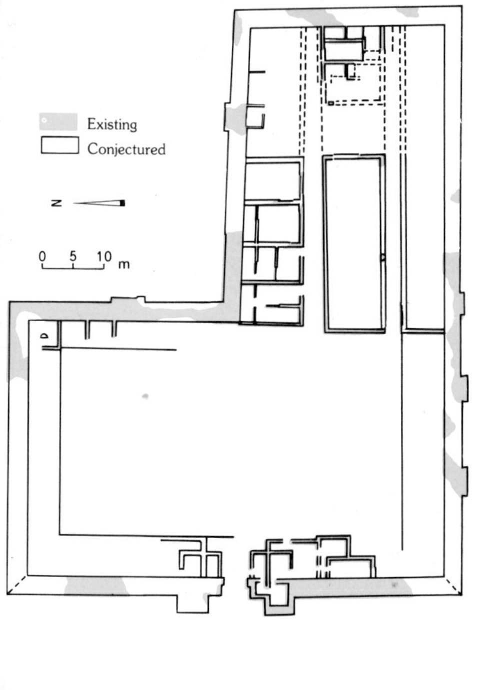

Meẓad Ḥashavyahu: plan of the fortress.

EXCAVATION RESULTS

The fortress covers an area of 1.5 a., and its form follows the natural contour of the *kurkar* hill on which it stands. The fortress is L-shaped and composed of two rectangles: the larger one (1 a.) contains a courtyard and rooms adjacent to the fortress wall; the smaller one (0.5 a.) consists of three rows of houses that flank two streets. The wall (3.2 m wide) of the fortress was built of bricks on a

Meẓad Ḥashavyahu: view of the rooms adjoining the eastern wall of the fortress (1986 excavations, looking east).

stone foundation with buttresses along its facade (projecting about 0.7 m from the wall). The gate complex, including the guardrooms and towers, was built of dressed *kurkar*.

The excavations in 1960 uncovered the southern wing of the gate and the buildings adjacent to it. Six test pits were also dug within the fortress area. Each pit showed the same picture: a floor and, below it, either the natural *kurkar* bedrock or the sand fill used in leveling the area. No structural changes were distinguished in the fortress. All the evidence found indicates that it was only in existence for a very short period. The 1986 excavations were conducted next to the eastern wall of the fortress. Part of a side street and most of an additional building, belonging to the central block of buildings in the east of the fortress, were cleared.

The pottery found on the fortress' floors included the local ware common in the seventh century BCE, together with coarse bowls and jars that, prior to the excavations, were considered to date to the Persian period. The site must therefore be considered to have been occupied during the final decades of the seventh century BCE. Included among the finds was East Greek pottery, originating from the eastern islands of Greece and Asia. Much of it is decorated in the Middle Wild Goat style dated to 630 to 600 BCE. At Meẓad Ḥashavyahu, East Greek pottery appeared in large quantities and included ordinary household ware such as amphorae, cooking pots, lamps, and cups. On the basis of this pottery, Naveh concluded that the site had been occupied by settlers of Greek origin, probably mercenaries, who preferred to use their own pottery, to which they were accustomed. Herodotus (II, 152, 154) relates that Pharaoh Psamtik I (664–610 BCE), the founder of the Twenty-sixth Dynasty, hired Greek and Carian mercenaries. It seems likely that other contemporary rulers used Greek mercenaries as well. Thus, the soldiers stationed at Meẓad Ḥashavyahu may have been employed by Josiah, king of Judea.

Because the ostraca were written in biblical Hebrew, and because of their contents and the names mentioned—Hoshayahu, Obadiahu, Ḥashavyahu—it is clear that the site was under Judean control. Apparently, Josiah not only controlled the north and south of the country, but expanded his rule westward (2 Chr. 34:6). Pieces of a fourteen-line Hebrew ostracon were discovered inside the guardroom and on the paved square. It is the letter of a worker employed in the harvest, who complains that his garment was confiscated. He pleads his innocence and entreats the governor to return his property. Five other fragmentary ostraca and a four-shekel stone weight (44.82 g) with the sign 1X were found in the vicinity of the gate.

The fortress may have been abandoned during Pharaoh Necho's campaign in 609 BCE, the year he defeated Josiah at Megiddo.

Hebrew ostracon from Meẓad Ḥashavyahu: letter of a worker employed in the harvest who complains that his garment was confiscated; he entreats the governor to return his property.

J. Naveh, *IEJ* 10 (1960), 129–139; 12 (1962), 27–32, 89–113; 14 (1964), 158–159; id., *Archaeology* 15 (1962), 108–111; F. M. Cross, Jr., *BASOR* 165 (1962), 42–46; S. Yeivin, *Bibliotheca Orientalis* 19 (1962), 3–10; I. S. Shifman, *Epigrafika Wostoka* 16 (1963), 21–28; J. D. Amusin and M. L. Heltzer, *IEJ* 14 (1964) 148–157; H. Donner and W. Röllig, *Kanaanäische und Aramäische Inschriften* 1, 2, Wiesbaden 1962–1964 no. 200; S. Talmon, *BASOR* 176 (1964), 29–38; H. Tadmor, *BA* 29 (1966), 102; R. M. Cook, *Annual of th British School at Athens* 64 (1969), 13–15; A. Lemaire, *Inscriptions Hebräiques 1: Les Ostraca*, Paris 197 259–269; id., *VT* 38 (1988), 220–230; D. Pardee, *Maarav* 1 (1978), 33–66; id., *BASOR* 239 (1980), 47–48 id., *Handbook of Ancient Hebrew Letters: A Study Edition*, Chico, Calif. 1982, 15–24; V. Sasson, *BASO* 232 (1978), 57–63; id., *Journal of Northwest Semitic Languages* 12 (1984), 115–120; Y. Suzuki, *Annual o the Japanese Biblical Institute* 8 (1982), 3–49; R. Wenning, *Vom Sinai zum Horeb* (ed. F. L. Hossfeld) Würzburg 1984, 169–196; T. Booij, *Bibliotheca Orientalis* 43 (1986), 642–647; J. Hoftijzer, *Tradition an Re-interpretation in Jewish and Early Christian Literature* (J. C. H. Lebram Fest.), Leiden 1986, 1–6 R. Reich, *ESI* 5 (1986), 68–69; K. A. D. Smelik, *Amsterdam Cahiers voor Exegese en Bijbelse Theologie* (1986), 114–122; Weippert 1988 (Ortsregister); Y. Young, *PEQ* 122 (1990), 56–58; A. Kuyt and J. W Wesselius, *Bibliotheca Orientalis* 48 (1991), 726–735.

JOSEPH NAVE

ḤASPIN

IDENTIFICATION

Ḥaspin is a deserted Syrian town in the Golan founded on a Byzantine ruin, on the road leading from Beth-Shean to Fiq and Damascus (map reference 2266.2507). It is identified with Casphor/Casphon, in the time of Judas Maccabaeus (1 Macc. 5:2), and with Hisfiya, a Jewish town in the territory of Sussita (Hippos) mentioned in Second Temple sources (*Baraita de-Teḥumin*, Tosefta, *Shevi'it* 4:10). The absence at the site of ceramic finds from the Hellenistic period raises the possibility that Hellenistic Ḥaspin was not here, but at Tell edh-Dhahab, about 1.5 km (1 mi.) to the southeast. A large quantity of pottery was found there, from the Hellenistic period, as well as from the Iron and Middle Bronze ages. The settlement at Ḥaspin apparently moved to the present site when the Roman road to the Bashan was built, in the Late Roman period. An early Syriac manuscript on the life of the emperor Maximianus states that the emperor was born to a Jewish father and a Samaritan mother who fled from Tiberias to Ḥaspin at the beginning of the third century CE. Arab historians have also mentioned Ḥaspin; in the ninth century, el-Ya'aqubi spoke of Ḥaspin as being in the district of Damascus, and in the thirteenth century, the historian Yaqut described the site as being on the road to Damascus.

EXPLORATION

In 1884, Ḥaspin was surveyed by G. Schumacher. He identified a fortified structure (40 by 48 m), in the western part of the site, whose entrance (3.5 m wide) was on the south. The structure consisted of an outer wall (2 to 3 m thick), corridors or rooms 6 m wide, and a large central courtyard. The building apparently served as a khan or fortress in the Early Arab period or the Middle Ages. No traces of the building remain. From 1943 onward, several tombs were uncovered that contained rich finds from the third century CE, presently exhibited in the National Museum in Damascus. The finds include a silver bowl, an elephant-shaped bronze juglet, a bronze figurin of Venus, bronze surgical instruments, an incense shovel, and several glas vessels, including bowls and trays of millefiori glass and light opaque glas amphoriskoi and juglets. Among the jewelry found, gold earrings shaped lik a ring bearing a disk and pearl pendants are especially noteworthy. Severa ivory jewelry boxes were found with such scenes as the three Graces carved o a pyramidal lid, and depictions of Venus, Eros, and two animals.

Since 1967, the remains of Byzantine buildings roofed with stone slabs an of mosaic pavements have been found at the site in surveys conducted b S. Gutman, D. Urman, S. Barlev, and M. Ben-Ari. Dozens of carved a chitectural remains and Greek inscriptions from public buildings and tomb were reused in the modern village houses. These include a basalt lintel bearin a triglyph relief, a vine scroll, a garland, a Hercules knot, rosettes, a palm tre and a bird. Another lintel contains a garland with a cord, rosettes, and tw *tabulae ansata*. Still another is decorated with a double meander with ge metric patterns. Chancel-screen posts and limestone slabs originally from church were found in the center of the town. The slabs are decorated wit elaborate geometric motifs and crosses. Some of the Greek inscriptions th have been deciphered include: "Eternal Christ! Christ save us!"; "The gift c Velans the priest"; "Live in the eternal light"; "Julius the son of Domitia built..."; "Be strong, Porphyrius, twenty years old"; and "Be strong, Nuric . . . years old."

EXCAVATIONS

Salvage excavations following public works carried out at the site uncovere two churches and yielded parts of several dwellings.

THE WESTERN CHURCH (CHURCH OF GEORGIUS). The Church c Georgius is at the northwestern end of the town. A salvage excavation wa conducted here in 1972 by Urman and Barlev, on behalf of the staff officer fc

Ḥaspin: plan of the western church.

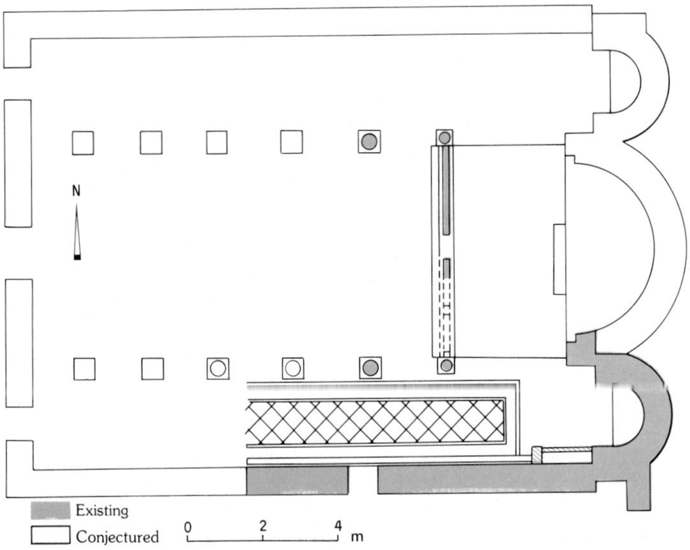

archaeology in the Golan. Column bases, drums and unique capitals (see below), on which Greek letters were incised, were found reused in the courtyard of a Syrian house. No traces of the building's walls were found on the surface. About 10 sq m of the southeastern part of the church were excavated, revealing the southern apse and part of the central apse, the bema, and parts of the southern aisle and the nave, together with their mosaics. To the south of the church, at right angles to the southern wall, parts of rooms were found, apparently built around a courtyard next to the church. The courtyard was entered through an opening in the church's southern wall. The entire complex may have been a monastery. The church, as indicated by the excavated area and by a column protruding from the ground, was rectangular (20.5 by 14.2 m), with its long axis oriented east to west; the church had three apses in the east. The walls (0.8–0.9 m thick) are built of stones hewn on both faces and a stone core bonded with white mortar. The inner face of the walls is coated with white plaster and bears traces of decoration in red paint.

Prayer Hall. The prayer hall (12.5 by 17 m) was divided by two rows of six columns each into a nave (6.6 m wide) and two aisles (2.8 m wide from the column centers). The excavations revealed the place of four of the column bases. The columns stood on square pedestals (0.5 by 0.5 m, 0.65 by 0.65 m) with Attic bases and Ionic capitals carved in an unusual and extremely fine design. Three capitals (46 cm in diameter) were found on the surface prior to excavation. One side of each capital was left undecorated, while the other was carved with two large flowers with twelve leaves, alternately protruding and receding, instead of the usual spirals. The large flower has a smaller flower in its center. From it, a bud emerges and extends over the echinus, in which only the central egg was carved. A relief of an amphora and an incised cross were found on one of the column drums discovered prior to excavation.

The southern apse is 1.85 m wide and 1.4 m deep. A platform, 0.45 m above the church floor, was built inside it. The central apse is 4.25 m wide and an estimated 2.6 m deep; its outer wall was not found. The plastered floor of the central apse is 0.15 m higher than the level of the bema. The bema (3.4 m deep) in front of the central apse is the entire width of the nave (6.1 m) and had a mosaic floor (see below) with several repairs in plaster. The bema stood 0.5 m higher than the nave and was reached by two limestone steps. The upper step contained mortises and a groove for the chancel-screen posts and slabs. The center of the groove allowed for a 0.7-m-wide opening, permitting passage from the nave to the bema. Parts of the chancel-screen slabs, made of imported marble, were found in the area of the bema. One fragment was decorated with carved borders that surrounded a Maltese cross. Another fragment of a chancel screen bore a depression with a hole in the center. A circle and a small Maltese cross were depicted on other fragments.

Mosaics. Small sections of mosaics are preserved in the nave, the bema, and between the columns. The well-preserved mosaic in the southern aisle was uncovered for a length of 7.2 m. Small green-glass tesserae, many coated with gold paint, were found scattered on the bema. This attests to there having been splendid wall mosaics either in the dome of the apse or on the walls of the clerestory. The mosaic floors were also of high quality and display many colors.

Most of the bema's mosaic was destroyed in antiquity and consists mainly of plaster repairs. The remains of its pattern include a border (0.5 m wide) with black bands, a band of red triangles, and a guilloche in red, blue, gold, purple, brown, and other colors. The central carpet (4.75 by 2.6 m) is divided into a network of lozenges, each of which contains such depictions as a cyclamen leaf, a flower, a vine scroll, and unidentified parts of plants and fruit.

Most of the mosaic in the nave was similarly destroyed. In one section, part of the carpet border, which resembles the bema's, survived; here, however, the pattern consists of interlacing lozenges with four red-tesserae flowers in their center. Judging from the preserved parts of the central carpet, the mosaic was decorated with small black and red flowers. Small carpets containing geometric motifs and scales were found between the columns.

The eastern part of the mosaic in the southern aisle (close to the apse) is a coarse carpet made of large tesserae, apparently the result of later repairs. This carpet, whose tesserae were placed obliquely, has no border, and the pattern is of alternating rows of flowers and squares. The original mosaic in the southern aisle is well preserved; only its bird motifs are defaced. The carpet's border is black and white bands and a guilloche motif that resembles the bema's. The carpet's interior (1.2 m wide) is divided into a network of lozenges. The border is made of small red and blue flowers. Twenty-one alternating rows of a single lozenge and a double lozenge were uncovered. Each lozenge contains a different motif: a pair of fowl facing each other; three pomegranates hanging from a branch; an ethrog(?); a bird pecking at a bunch of grapes; citrus fruit; a flower; the branch of a plant; wicker baskets holding six loaves of bread; cyclamen leaves; a pomegranate tree with three branches; a cluster of grapes; and a vine scroll. In the center of one lozenge is a Greek inscription: "For the salvation of Georgius Aplata." The mosaic patterns in the nave and aisles closely resemble the mosaics in the church at Kursi but are of better quality.

Phases of Repair and Additions. Other architectural phases were discerned in the excavation, such as a coarse pavement laid in the southern aisle, in front of the apse (see above). Additions to the church were made at a later stage. In front of the central apse, a bench made of tiles and cement was added, with a cross carved on one tile. In one corner of the southern aisle, a plastered trough was built, from which a plastered channel ran along the south wall. This channel damaged the original mosaic, which was repaired with plaster. The plastered installation may have been used for baptisms. In the later, perhaps modern, phases, poorly built walls were added in several places in the church.

Date of the Church. The church floor contained numerous clay tiles that had fallen from the roof, as well as small fragments of oil lamps and a few sherds from the sixth and seventh centuries CE. One of the rooms to the south of the church is paved with white tesserae and contains many tiles and pottery from

Mosaic in the southern aisle of the western church; the depictions of fowl were defaced by iconoclasts.

the sixth and seventh centuries. Judging from the style of the mosaic, the church was erected in the first half of the sixth century; it continued in use, with repairs and additions, until the seventh century.

THE EASTERN CHURCH (CHURCH OF THOMAS). The digging of a trench near the road, about 200 m east of the western church, uncovered two mosaic pavements, laid one above the other. Barlev's limited salvage excavation in 1975 revealed that the mosaic belonged to a church 12.75 m wide and at least 8.7 m long. The church's walls, not visible on the surface but shown by the trench section, were built of stone hewn on both faces with a core of stones bonded with white mortar. The mosaics were discovered in two areas, apparently near the (unexcavated) apses. A cluster of grapes, a basket within medallions, and a guilloche border were depicted in one area; a Greek inscription, deciphered by V. Tzaferis, was found in the other. The five-line inscription is surrounded by a black border (0.6 by 3.5 m) and reads: "The gift of Olympus for the salvation of the sons Leontis and Eugenius. And for the memory and repose of the father Varus, the brothers Vasilius and Eugenius, and the son Varus. In recognition, they restored the holy house, on the command of Thomas, the priest and head of the monastery, in the month of July, the seventh year of the indiction, the year 667" (in 604 CE, according to the Era of Hippos).

Inside the trench section, another mosaic pavement, laid about 20 cm below the upper mosaic, can be discerned. Masonry debris was found on the lower mosaic. The church was apparently damaged in the earthquake of 551. Beneath the church is a row of hewn-stone buildings. The sherds collected in the trench are all from the Byzantine period, indicating that the church was built in the late fifth or early sixth century and restored after the earthquake, in 551.

DWELLINGS. The digging of the trench also revealed the remains of dwellings, about 400 m south of the eastern church. In 1972, in Ben-Ari and Barlev's short rescue excavation, portions of hewn-stone dwellings, a white mosaic pavement, and a wealth of pottery from the sixth and seventh centuries CE were recovered.

SUMMARY

Ḥaspin was an important center of settlement in the Golan in the Late Roman and Byzantine periods. Survey and excavation results reveal a town whose center consisted of ashlar-built dwellings and villas roofed with stone slabs, typical of the Hauran region (q.v. Golan). The chancel screens found in the survey attest to the existence of an additional church in the center of the town. The strength of Ḥaspin's economy, which was based on agriculture and trade along the Damascus route, was expressed in the rich tomb finds. Ḥaspin's population at the time was apparently Christian. In the sixth century, two magnificent churches, probably belonging to monasteries, were built at the edge of the town. The excavations revealed that the town located at this site, close to the road, was probably not established before the Late Roman period, when it moved here from nearby Tell edh-Dhahab. According to the ceramic finds, settlement at Ḥaspin came to an end in the seventh century CE. However, it may have continued in later periods in the central part of the settlement which has not yet been excavated.

G. Schumacher, *The Jaulan*, London 1888, 184–186; P. S. Brock, *Analecta Bollandiana* 91 (1973), 314ff.; V. Tzaferis and S. Bar-Lev, *'Atiqot* 11 (1976), 114–115.

ZVI URI MA'OZ

ḤATULA

IDENTIFICATION

Ḥatula is situated on the southern bank of Naḥal Naḥshon, near where it enters the Ayalon Valley, about 200 m above sea level. The site derives its name from Khirbet Ḥatula, located on a hill some 2.5 km (1.5 mi.) east of the prehistoric site. Prehistoric remains were found in an alluvial stratum overlying an ancient stream terrace of unknown age, about 15 m above the present streambed. The site extends over a strip, about 100 m long from east to west and some 25 m wide, at the foot of the escarpment. It was discovered by Père Claude from the Trappist monastery at Latrun. Since 1980, six seasons of excavations have been conducted by A. Ronen and M. Lechevallier, under the joint auspices of the Department of Archaeology at Haifa University and the Centre de Recherche Préhistorique Français de Jérusalem. The site comprises two layers, one of which is Natufian and the other from the Pre-Pottery Neolithic A period. Some 130 sq m of the upper Neolithic layer have been cleared; the underlying Natufian layer has been exposed only in a few soundings, in a total area of about 20 sq m.

EXCAVATIONS

THE NATUFIAN LAYER. The Natufian layer (up to 1 m thick) which forms the lower half of the alluvial stratum overlying the ancient stream terrace, is dark brown, rather compact, and contains no gravel. The archaeological remains are dispersed throughout the layer; however, in area G, a particularly dense concentration was recovered. The Natufian occupation level (c. 10 cm thick) contained an abundance of flint implements and faunal remains. As most of the items recovered from the occupation level are larger than those retrieved from the layer's upper part, it can be assumed that all the finds originated in the occupation level. Some were, however, eventually pushed upward, as a result of the movement of the clayey soil and burrowing by animals. It thus seems that the Natufian occupation and the superimposed Neolithic one are separated by a lengthy time gap.

Flint Tools. The flint tools recovered include mostly microliths (57 percent), among which lunates are common. Awls (8.7 percent) are of a peculiar type, with a needlelike point. Of all the Natufian assemblages exposed in Israel, this one had the most awls. The large number of cores and the presence of waste flakes indicate that knapping was done at the site. By contrast, the exceedingly small number of flint nodules recovered suggests that the cores were prepared at the place where the flint was obtained—apparently the conglomerate strata in the upper reaches of Naḥal Naḥshon. The lunates' dimensions and their type of retouch indicate that the Ḥatula assemblage belongs to the Late Natufian phase.

Other Finds. Other finds include a fragment of a bone sickle haft with a groove 2.5 mm deep, several long bone awls (one of which had an eye), and several decorative objects, including beads, perforated seashells, and dentalia. No structures or grinding tools were found. A burial containing a skeleton of a twelve-to-fourteen-year-old girl, in a flexed position with no offerings, can be attributed to the Natufian period.

Ḥatula: oval structure, PPNA period.

Ḥatula: burial in a flexed position, PPNA period.

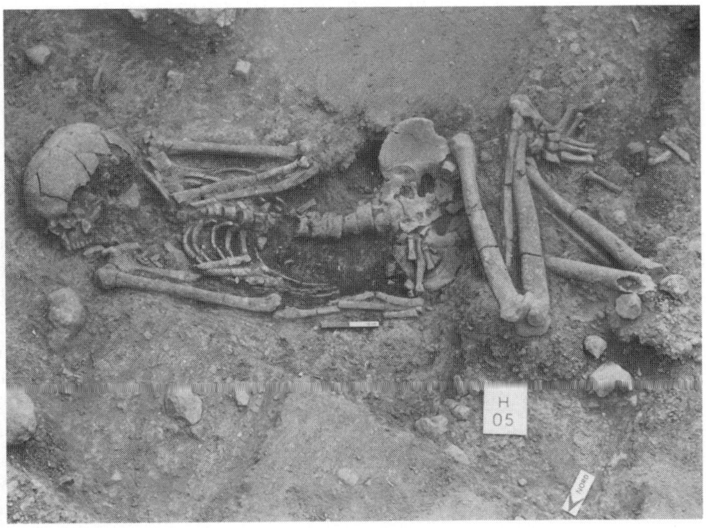

THE NEOLITHIC LAYER. The layer with the Neolithic finds differs from the Natufian. It is about 0.5–0.7 m thick, friable, and light brown interspersed with patches. The layer contains a considerable amount of gravel—mostly pebbles (5–10 cm in diameter), many of which were broken, presumably intentionally. Both the composition and contents of the Neolithic layer (which resembles that at Tel Qadum) furnish evidence of intensive human activity.

Structures. Two phases of occupation have been recognized: the first one, the Khiamian, contained an oval structure (3 by 4 m) dug into the underlying Natufian stratum. It contained a yellow, fine-grained, friable sediment, as well as concretions that seemed like remnants of bricks or mud walls. The 20-cm-thick yellow fill was covered by a 30-cm-thick deposit of gray, friable ash. It contained numerous pebbles like those described above, as well as animal bones, some of them large.

A few other shallow depressions were found, filled with yellow sediment like that described above. They were at places overlaid by an ashy layer containing concentrations of broken pebbles, as well as animal bones—including cranial fragments and gazelle horn cores. These concentrations mark function-specific areas, perhaps for dismembering animals and preparing food.

In the second, Sultanian, phase two stone oval houses were excavated. One of them (6 m by 3.5 m) was preserved to a height of 20 cm. The southern end, facing the slope of the hill, is built of large, heavy stones; the rest of the wall is built of small stones, set in two or three courses, at most. The building does not seem to have been much higher originally. It is still unclear how the remaining walls were constructed—whether of perishable materials (such as hides or plant material) or mud. The structure has an entrance (1.4 m wide) in the middle of its eastern wall. Various installations were found on the floor: an ash pit, a pit containing pebbles, and a block with a cup-hole.

Stone Tools. Numerous stone pestles and mortars were unearthed in and next to the Sultanian structures. The mortars are heavy stone slabs (c. 20 by 30 by 30 cm) with central depressions 10 cm in diameter and 10 cm deep. The majority of the pestles are limestone, and the rest are basalt. They are 7 to 15 cm long; their rounded end is worn; the flat end was designed to be gripped for applying pressure.

Flint Tools. The flint tools resemble their Natufian counterparts, both in shape and in method of manufacture, but the Neolithic assemblage includes axes and el-Khiam points. The proportion of awls is also considerably higher (29 percent in the Neolithic layer, as opposed to 9 percent in the Natufian); typologically, however, they are identical.

El-Khiam points (4 percent) are arrowheads with notches next to the tang. They are made on thin blades that average 10 mm in width, with truncated, concave tangs. The presence of el-Khiam points establishes this industry as Khiamian, but in and around the stone structures several axes attributed to the Sultanian phase of the Early Neolithic—as well as ha-Gedud truncations and more delicate el-Khiam arrowheads—were also found. It is currently agreed that the Khiamian phase preceded the Sultanian. However, the two cultures may have been contemporaneous, with their tool kits differing for functional reasons.

Other Finds. Bone awls of the type prevalent in the Natufian layer were recovered in the Neolithic layer as well, although in larger numbers. Beads, limestone and greenstone pendants with 40-mm-long biconical perforations, and several pierced shells and dentalia (in the Natufian layer) were also found. Four burials were uncovered in the Neolithic layer, all with skeletons in a flexed position. Several skeletons were found without skulls; near the chest of one of them a round, perforated limestone bead was found. (The burial attributed above to the Natufian layer may also be Neolithic.)

Fauna. The vast majority of the animal remains consumed at the site are gazelle. In the Natufian layer, these constitute 95 percent of all faunal remains, with a slightly lower proportion in the Neolithic layer. Bones of wild cattle and boar are abundant, as are those of avifauna, particularly waterfowl. In both layers a small amount of fish bones was found, which must have been brought (possibly in dried form) to the site from the Mediterranean Sea, some 30 km (19 mi.) away. Considerable amounts of mole and reptile bones were recovered, some of them charred, as well as single specimens of deer, fox, hedgehog, polecat, and badger. Although no dog bones were recovered, their existence at the site was deduced by S. Davis from the presence of small bone fragments corroded in a peculiar way, indicative of partial digestion by a dog. The bone assemblages from the Natufian and Neolithic layers do not differ significantly from one another, although in the Neolithic layer the proportion of avifauna and fish is higher and that of gazelle somewhat lower. Gazelle populations may have diminished during the Neolithic, perhaps due to an increase in human population.

SUMMARY

The site of Ḥatula was occupied throughout the Late Natufian (Gif Tan 91138: 11,020 ± 180 BP) and the Early Neolithic (Gif Tan 91139 and 91141: 10,170 ± 120 BP and 10,030 ± 140 BP) periods. The Pre-Pottery Neolithic A layer seems to be a direct continuation of the Natufian one. The remains of game from both periods attest to a very sparse forest coverage (deer remains are quite rare) and a dry climate. By contrast, the large amounts of waterfowl remains suggest a perennial pond in the vicinity of the site.

DISTRIBUTION OF MAIN TOOL TYPES (IN PERCENT)

Tool types	*Natufian*	*Neolithic*	
		Khiamian	*Sultanian*
	(N=517)	(N=705)	(N=610)
End scrapers	1.7	2.1	1.3
Burins	6.3	2.5	2.9
Awls	8.7	17.4	28.6
Backed and truncated	1.9	0.1	0.6
Truncated	2.9	2.6	2.6
Notches and denticulates	5.4	2.6	3.6
Sickle blades	0.19	1.4	1.8
Retouched items	13.0	18.8	27.9
Backed bladelets	22.0	8.8	9.1
Geometric bladelets	35.3	36.0	7.2
El-Khiam points	—	3.1	4.2
Axes	—	—	0.8

Main publication: M. Lechevallier and A. Ronen, *Le site natoufien: Khiamien de Hatoula près de Latroun, Israël, fouilles 1980–1982, rapport préliminaire* (Les Cahiers du Centre de Recherche Français de Jérusalem 1), Jerusalem 1985.

Other studies: Centre de Recherche Français de Jérusalem, *Lettre d'Information* 1 (1982), 17; ibid. 2 (1982), 19; M. Lechevallier and A. Ronen, ibid. 6 (1984), 23–24; id., *ESI* 1 (1982), 39–40; 4 (1985), 46; 5 (1986), 48–49; id., *Quartär* 35–36 (1985), 141–164; id., *Investigations in South Levantine Prehistory: Préhistoire du Sud-Levant* (*BAR*/IS 497, eds. O. Bar-Yosef and B. Vandermeersch), Oxford 1989, 309–321; M. Lechevallier et al., *Paléorient* 15/1 (1989), 1–10; A. Ronen, *Mitekufat Ha'even* 19 (1986), 93*; A. Ronen and M. Lechevallier, *The Natufian Culture in the Levant* (International Monographs in Prehistory, Archaeology Series 1, eds. O. Bar-Yosef and F. R. Valla), Ann Arbor 1991, 149–160; O. Bar-Yosef, *Paléorient* 15/1 (1989), 57–63; S. J. M. Davis, *Investigations in South Levantine Prehistory* (op. cit.), Oxford 1989, 43–59; P. C. Edwards, *Journal of Mediterranean Archaeology* 2 (1989), 5–48; F. Le Mort, *People and Culture in Change* 1 (*BAR*/IS 508, ed. I. Hershkovitz), Oxford 1989, 133–140; R. Unger-Hamilton et al., *Quartär* 39–40 (1989), 141–149.

AVRAHAM RONEN, MONIQUE LECHEVALLIER

HAYONIM CAVE

IDENTIFICATION

Hayonim Cave is located in a cliff on the right bank of Naḥal Meged, a tributary of Naḥal Yosef, in the western Galilee (map reference 1707.2588). Systematic excavations in the cave were initiated in 1965, under the direction of O. Bar-Yosef, E. Tchernov, and B. Arensburg, on behalf of the Institute of Archaeology at the Hebrew University of Jerusalem. The terrace fronting the cave, where Natufian occupational remains were detected overlying a Geometric Kebaran complex, was excavated in 1974–1975 by D. Henry of Tulsa University, Oklahoma. Since 1980 F. R. Valla, of the French Archaeological Mission in Israel, has been excavating here.

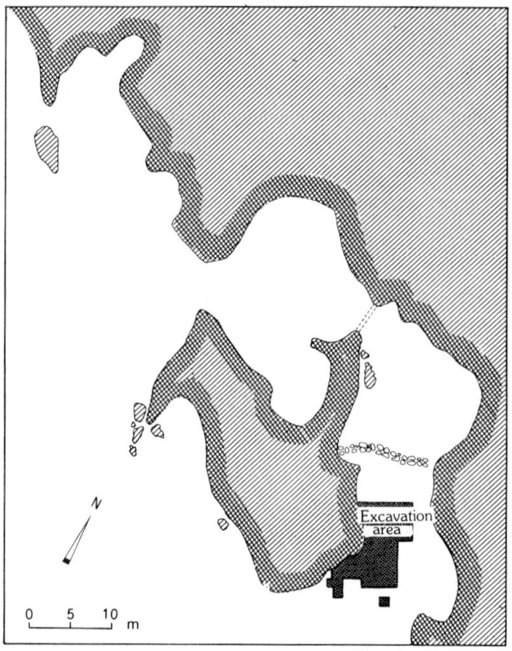

Hayonim Cave: plan of the cave and excavated area.

Grave no. 8: two bodies laid in a flexed position, one above the other; (right) another skull, Natufian culture.

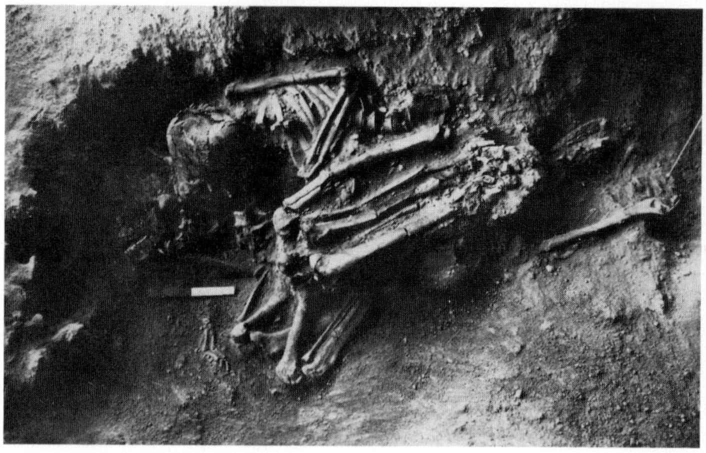

EXCAVATIONS

Excavations in the cave have exposed the earliest layers; bedrock has not yet been reached. The excavated area's stratigraphy follow:

Layer A: black and white ash accumulations from annual burnings by shepherds, from the second century BCE onward. A glass furnace was unearthed at the base of this layer.

Layer B: a 1-m-thick layer, comprising a series of Natufian occupational remains and burials.

Layer C: a 2.3-m-thick layer, accumulated near the cave's entrance. It contains mainly flint assemblages attributed to the Kebaran culture.

Layer D: a layer accumulated to 0.45 m, at most, in a depression and formed by the erosion of the upper part of the Mousterian strata. This layer contains hearths, an abundance of faunal remains, and flint, as well as bone-tool assemblages, that ascribe it to the Aurignacian culture.

Layer E: a complex of Mousterian layers, hitherto exposed to a maximal depth of 3 m.

NATUFIAN OCCUPATION. The remains of an early circular structure, erected at the cave's entrance, can be distinguished in layer B. This structure was eventually ruined and replaced by a series of closely adjacent circular structures, each some 2 to 3 m in diameter. Although still not completely excavated, they seem to have been arranged in two rows of three structures each. In three of the four structures that had been cleared to the bottom, fireplaces containing white ashes were found. Once these structures had ceased to serve as dwellings or for other uses, they gradually filled with rockfall. Some of them later served other purposes: in one of them, for instance, a lime-kiln was installed that was replaced at a later stage by a bone-tool workshop.

After the structures had filled with rockfall and debris, another occupational stage appeared on top of them. Each stage in the use of the cave seems to have been linked in a yet unclarified manner with the Natufian occupation on the terrace. The latest occupation in the cave was largely ruined, in the second century BCE, by leveling activities and by construction work on the glass furnace.

Burials. Several burials were exposed alongside or in the structures, depending on the various occupational stages. The earliest are mostly communal and display a variety of burial styles: the skeletons were placed in an extended, semiflexed, or flexed position, with their knees next to their chins. Among the uppermost graves containing single burials, a constructed grave containing the remains of several skeletons in secondary burial was found. Secondary burials of individuals were found in most of the graves containing primary burials; it seems that in the course of grave digging, earlier graves were penetrated and their bones mixed with the later inhumations. Several adult skeletons were found with the skull removed and the mandible left intact—a practice that was to become widespread in the Pre-Pottery Neolithic A period.

A few of the skeletons were adorned with strings of dentalium shells on their necks and occasionally on their hands. On one skeleton were the remains of a garment or belt decorated with polished-bone pendants. Another skeleton was adorned with a sort of belt decorated with fox canine teeth, perforated for stringing. Other funerary goods include a necklace of partridge bones and a bone dagger.

The large number of child and infant burials constitutes about 30 percent of the analyzed population (the remains of fifty skeletons). This seems to attest to a higher death rate than in hunter-gatherer communities and may point to a phenomenon of "demographic stress."

Flint- and Stone-Tool Assemblages. The Natufian flint assemblage from the cave is characterized by a high frequency of burins, lunates (which in the lower part of the Natufian occupation were Helwan-retouched and in its upper part were mostly the backed variety), an absence of a systematic use of the microburin technique, and the presence of elongated picks (mostly triangular or lenticular in cross section), seemingly heralding the future appearance of axes. Flint was knapped in situ, as attested by the abundance of cores and debitage. The exploitation of flint was thorough, which suggests that the Natufian cave occupants had limited quantities of that raw material available to them. The lithic industry attests to the presence of a Natufian occupation in the Hayonim Cave throughout both the early and late stages of this culture.

The most common stone implements are basalt and limestone pestles, as well as mortars of various sizes. A large gobletlike basalt mortar, some 60 cm high, was found broken. Fragments of "stone pipes," of the kind found intact on the terrace (see below), were collected within the rubble. The basalt items seem to have been brought from a distance, as part of the ongoing exchange

General view of Hayonim Cave, looking west.

with other Natufian communities.

Bone- and Horn-Tool Industries. The Natufian site in the Hayonim Cave is characterized by an abundance of bone tools and pendants. Noteworthy among the former are gorgets, awls, bone points, spatulae (some decorated with a net pattern), hide burnishers, and certain rounded implements of unknown use that were shaped from the bones of large animals. The bone pendants were shaped, polished, and subsequently perforated, as indicated by those items that were broken in the process of manufacture. No pendants or beads made of gazelle phalanges, common at other contemporary sites, were found here.

Among the unique items were broken sickle hafts made from the long bones or ribs of bovids. A cache of cut ribs was found in the upper layer. The primary shaping of a haft had been completed on one of them, except for the groove into which the flint blades were to be inserted. Another cache yielded a large number of burned gazelle horn cores.

Art Objects and Decorations. Only a very few ornaments have so far been discerned in the Hayonim Cave. An engraved net pattern on bone tools and an arrangement of two columns of almost evenly spaced, parallel holes and rows of holes extending laterally on large bone items are quite unique. Engravings were also found on a series of stone slabs, one of them apparently depicting a large fish. Numerous other slabs are engraved with a ladder pattern. Additional decorative items include a large number of seashells; the most common species is *Dentalium*. The majority of the shells came from the Mediterranean coast.

Economy and Nature of Occupation. The site's faunal material suggests that gazelle was the most common game. An abundance of bird and fish remains were recovered, as well as a few bones of other species. Several legume seeds, dated to the second half of the eleventh millennium, were recovered from the Natufian layer. Grinding tools indicate the consumption of plant food, as yet undetermined.

The question of whether the occupation of the cave and the terrace was permanent was resolved by analyzing the bird and rodent remains, the most common among the latter being those of the house mouse. The high frequency of the house sparrow and the house rat, both of them commensal species that multiply only under conditions of almost year-round human occupation, suggests that, at least on the terrace, occupation was permanent.

Finds from the Terrace. The excavations yielded the remains of two circular structures, a well-built silo of stone slabs, an abundance of flints, a few bone tools, and a plethora of faunal remains, of which gazelle is the most common game. Age-distribution analysis of the gazelle indicates that about 30 percent were young when they were killed. This percentage, which is characteristic of an annual mean age distribution within a gazelle herd, implies that gazelle was hunted by the Natufian occupants throughout the year.

The lithic assemblages collected from the various layers belong, for the most part, to the later phases of the occupational stage in the cave. The exposed graves usually contain a single skeleton in a flexed position. Two joint man-dog burials were discovered as well.

KEBARAN LAYER. The Kebaran layer contains mainly flint-tool assemblages, characterized by a high frequency of microliths. The upper levels display a decidedly higher proportion of obliquely truncated backed bladelets, whereas the lower levels are dominated by arched micropoints and retouched bladelets. The scarcity of bone tools, shells, and faunal remains, as well as the smallness of the occupied area, all indicate that the site was camped in only by a small group, probably in summer.

AURIGNACIAN LAYER. The Aurignacian layer yielded the remains of several encampments, attributed, on the basis of the most frequent flint-tool types (carinated and nosed scrapers and Aurignacian blades), to the Aurignacian culture (or stage), some 28,000 years BP. Among the various levels, one is outstanding: it contains an abundance of bones, among which the remains of over 120 gazelles, a few fallow deer, red deer, and boar were identified inter alia. The early level contained hearths with white ashes that were dug into the Mousterian layer. One hearth, bowl-like in section, contained a large number of stones. Another hearth, at a higher level, was constructed of two stone slabs.

The lithic assemblage is characterized by the use of local flint. Part of the knapping seems to have been done elsewhere; a considerable proportion of the items was brought to the cave in finished form. A scarcity of raw material drove the Aurignacian occupants to remodify previously shaped items, which were scattered on the ground.

The notably rich assemblage of bone and horn tools includes awls, points, double points (reminiscent of the horn spearheads, familiar from Western Europe), spatulae, and pendants made of teeth with perforated roots.

Among the stone objects are slabs bearing red ocher remains and a shaft straightener, of a type documented only since the Natufian culture. Two stone slabs bear intentional engravings: one seems to depict an animal, reminiscent in outline of a horse; the second is not as clear. These slabs are instances of the artistic ritual expression familiar from the Upper Paleolithic, particularly in Western Europe.

MOUSTERIAN LAYER. Excavations of the Mousterian layers have hitherto yielded only meager finds. Apart from the flint assemblages, discernibly dominated by Levallois flakes and side scrapers, single human bones (a vertebra or a skull fragment, for example) were found. Of major significance is the rodent-bone collection, in which two stages are discernible: the later stage, comprising most of the excavated layers, resembles that identified at sites such as the Tabun (layers B and C), Kebara, and Geulah caves; the early stage is akin to that found in layer D in the Tabun Cave and in the early layers in the Qafzeh Cave. Tchernov's division of the Mousterian rodent inventory into an early and a later stage (q.v. Qafzeh Cave) is based on this classification.

Main publications: A. Belfer-Cohen, "The Natufian Settlement at Hayonim Cave: A Hunter-Gatherer Band on the Threshhold of Agriculture" (Ph.D. diss., Jerusalem 1988); *The Natufian Culture in the Levant* (International Monographs in Prehistory, Archaeology Series 1, eds. O. Bar-Yosef and F. R. Valla), Ann Arbor 1991 (passim).

Other studies: O. Bar-Yosef (and E. Tchernov), *Israel Journal of Zoology* 15 (1967), 104–140; id., *IEJ* 20 (1970), 141–150; O. Bar-Yosef, *RB* 78 (1971), 411–412; id. (and N. Goren), *Paléorient* 1/1 (1973), 49–68; E. Tchernov, *Succession of Rodent Faunas during the Upper Pleistocene of Israel*, Hamburg 1968; id., *Préhistoire du Levant* (CNRS Colloque 598, eds. J. Cauvin and P. Sanlaville), Paris 1981, 67–97; P. Smith, *Paléorient* 1/1 (1973), 69–72; S. Davis, ibid. 2/1 (1974), 181–182; D. O. Henry (and S. Davis), ibid., 195–197; id. (and A. Laroi-Gourhan), *JFA* 3 (1976), 391–406; id. (et al.), *Journal of Archaeological Science* 8 (1981), 33–58; P. Goldberg, *Catena* 6 (1979), 167–181; A. Belfer-Cohen (and O. Bar-Yosef), *Paléorient* 7/2 (1981), 19–42; id., *Paléorient* 14/2 (1988), 297–308; A. Sillen, ibid. 81–85; F. R. Valla, *RB* 88 (1981), 563–565; id., *IEJ* 32 (1982), 144–145; id., *ESI* 5 (1986), 49; 6 (1987–1988), 60; 7–8 (1988–1989), 80–81; 9 (1989–1990), 103; id., *Mitekufat Ha'even* 19 (1986), 90*–92*; 23 (1990), 171*–175*; id. (et al.), *Paléorient* 15/1 (1989), 245–257; id., *Investigations in South Levantine Prehistory* (*BAR*/IS 497, eds. O. Bar-Yosef and B. Vandermeersch), Oxford 1989, 255–273; D. S. Reese, *Paléorient* 8/2 (1982), 83–89; *Préhistoire en Israel* (Dossiers Histoire et Archéologie 100), Paris 1985, passim; M. Hopf and O. Bar-Yosef, ibid. 13/1 (1987), 117–120; Weippert 1988, 76f., 87–92; P. C. Edwards, *Journal of Mediterranean Archaeology* 2 (1989), 5–48; J. Pichon, *Investigations in South Levantine Prehistory* (op. cit.), 61–74; B. Arensburg et al., *Paléorient* 16/1 (1990), 107–109; D. E. Lieberman, ibid. 17/1 (1991), 47–57.

OFER BAR-YOSEF

ḤAYYAT, TELL EL-

IDENTIFICATION

Tell el-Ḥayyat is located in the Jordan Valley (map reference 205.203), 5 km (3 mi.) southwest of Tabaqat Faḥl (ancient Pella). It is a small (1.2 a.), unfortified agricultural settlement 2 km (1.2 mi.) east of the Jordan River on the first terrace above the present floodplain, at an elevation of 240 m below sea level. Although abundant Early Bronze Age IV pottery suggests the initial presence of an Early Bronze Age IV village on the site, the architectural sequence dates to the Middle Bronze Age IIA–IIC periods.

EXPLORATION AND REGIONAL BACKGROUND

Prior to the 1980s, only fragments of a stratigraphically controlled Early Bronze IV/Middle Bronze I through Middle Bronze IIA sequence were available for the Jordan Valley. Archaeological surveys in the Jordan Valley, notably those published by N. Glueck and later by M. Ibrahim, J. Sauer, and K. Yassine, indicated that Tell el-Ḥayyat had the potential to bridge the Early Bronze Age–Middle Bronze Age gap in what was known of the region. Thus, the major impetus for excavation at Tell el-Ḥayyat came from the identification of Early Bronze IV/Middle Bronze I, Middle Bronze IIA, Middle Bronze IIB/C, and Persian surface pottery by Ibrahim, Sauer, and Yassine (their site 56).

EXCAVATIONS

S. E. Falconer and B. Magness-Gardiner conducted three seasons of excavation here for the University of Arizona (Tucson) from 1982 to 1985. Excavations exposed approximately 400 sq m (8 percent of Ḥayyat's surface area) through 4.5 m of cultural deposition. Six phases of occupation are present:

Phase	*Period*
6	EB IV
5	Early MB IIA
4	MB IIA
3	MB IIB
2	MB IIC
1	Late MB IIC

Tell el-Ḥayyat: map of the site and excavation areas.

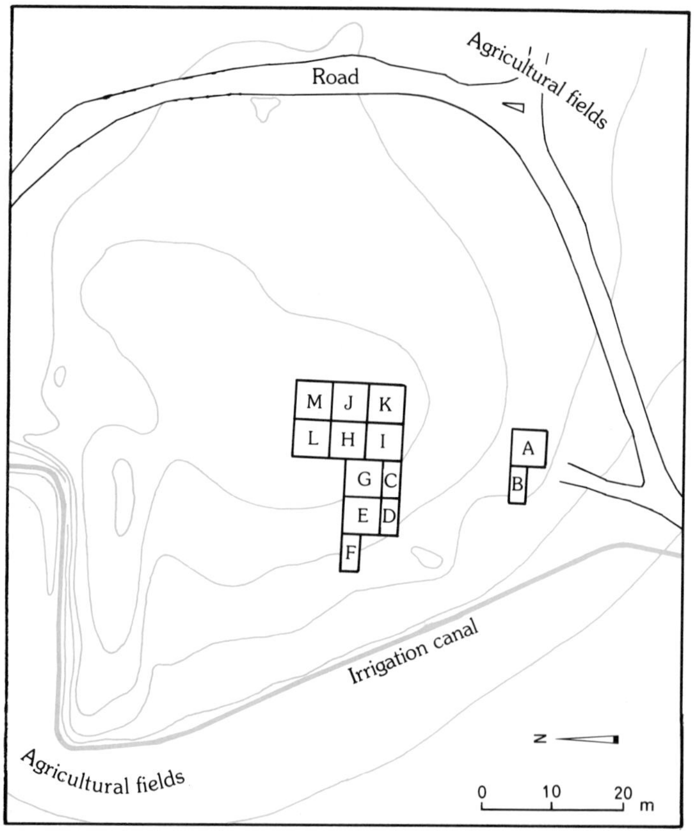

PHASE 6. Phase 6 is a shallow debris stratum with Early Bronze IV/Middle Bronze I pottery immediately above virgin soil in squares H and J. Early Bronze Age IV pottery includes the envelope ledge handle; "trickle-painted" decoration on cups, bowls, and jars; and thumb-impressed and incised wares and ware with applied rope molding, typically found in the Jezreel Valley and on the Transjordanian Plateau. Stratified remains from an Early Bronze Age IV agricultural village are present at Tell Abu en-Niaj, 1 km (0.6 mi.) to the southwest of Tell el-Ḥayyat. Soundings directed by Falconer and Magness-Gardiner were carried out at Niaj in 1985.

PHASE 5. Phase 5 is the basal stratum in every area except H and J. The first temple was built during this phase. Constructed of *terre pisée*, it has a simple rectilinear plan (7.6 by 7.6 m) and two projecting "buttresses" flanking the entrance. The temple is surrounded by a *terre pisée* enclosure wall. Outside the enclosure wall no buildings were found in the excavated area to house the local population. Only ash, cobbles, abundant animal bones, and ceramic debris attest to the occupation of areas outside the temple. The pottery from phase 5 is typically Middle Bronze Age IIA. Carinated bowls, straight-sided handmade cooking pots with thumb-impressed applied decoration, deep bowls with heavy rims (the so-called kraters), and jars of all shapes and sizes comprise the assemblage. The fabric is quite coarse and there is little red slip and burnish. All the pottery except the cooking pots are wheel-made.

Pottery kiln, MB IIA.

PHASE 4. Phase 4 saw the rebuilding of the temple on the same site with the same orientation and a similar plan. Constructed of mud brick, the exterior shows elaborate inset-offset niching around the sides of the temple and framing the entrance. Interior features include benches and a stepped mud-brick altar just inside the door. Just outside and to the north of the door, a series of stones 0.5–1 m high stand upright in a group. Stones found lying flat in front of each of the standing stones may have served as receptacles for offerings. Metal objects (points, figurines, tools, and jewelry), as well as the equipment to cast them, were found in the temple interior and courtyard. Abundant animal bones (primarily sheep and goat) and numerous cooking pots found within the temple enclosure suggest that offerings included cooked meats. Outside the temple, one- and two-room mud-brick houses with a courtyard and lane accommodated the village population. On the southern slope (square A), a kiln attests to local pottery production. The pottery for phase 4 included a higher proportion of red slip and burnish and finer fabrics than for phase 5. Otherwise, the assemblage is still clearly Middle Bronze Age IIA in date.

PHASE 3. In phase 3 the temple was rebuilt again, but with a stone foundation, which is all that remains of it. The standing stones no longer occupy the position near the entrance's northern side but are arranged in groups in a shallow arc in front of it. Both the temple and the arrangement of stones recall the temple and standing stones at Tel Kitan, also in the Jordan Valley. Outside the enclosure, the mud-brick houses were rebuilt (without stone foundations), following the same orientation as the phase 2 structures. The ceramic assemblage is characteristic of the Middle Bronze Age IIB and includes both handmade and wheel-made cooking pots, large jars with incised decoration, and dipper juglets.

PHASE 2. In phase 2, the temple underwent its most radical expansion and modification. Substantial subfoundations were dug into the phase 3 temple (removing most of it) and filled with rubble to provide a base for a five-course stone foundation for the phase 2 temple. The temple plan was enlarged to 11 by 10 m, and the enclosure wall was moved 1 m to the south, to accommodate the expansion. The interior walls and floor were plastered and the exterior walls were plastered and painted red. Only a basalt "column drum," or pedestal, was set into the plastered courtyard surface. Outside the temple enclosure, the mud-brick houses are slightly larger and have one or two courses of stone as a foundation. The high proportion of disc and ring bases, the necked bowls, and a few pieces of chocolate-on-white ware from the end of this phase date it to the Middle Bronze Age IIC.

PHASE 1. The latest phase at the site probably should be dated to the Middle Bronze Age IIC/Late Bronze Age I, on the basis of the chocolate-on-white ware that occurs in undisturbed contexts. Modern pits, plowing, and other

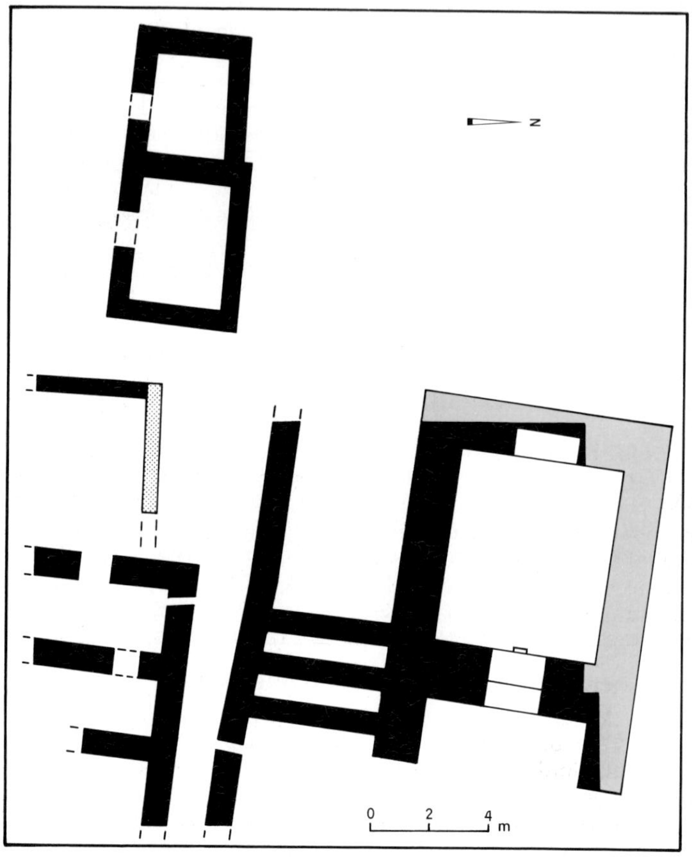

Plan of phase 2, MB IIC.

Tell el-Ḥayyat: foundations of a house from the MB IIB–C.

activities have left only ephemeral traces of walls and floors. No trace of destruction exists at this or any other level at the site. At the end of its occupation, Tell el-Ḥayyat was probably abandoned rather than destroyed.

FLORAL AND FAUNAL EVIDENCE. Plant macrofossils were recovered via flotation. Ash samples from the kiln suggest that dung was used as fuel. Wheat and barley made up the bulk of all plant material. Legumes (peas and lentils) are next in abundance to cereals and were probably of equal dietary importance. Fruits and nuts, wild and cultivated, also contributed to the diet. Domesticated species of animals made up over 95 percent of the assemblage (sheep/goat—63 percent; pigs—21 percent; cattle—11 percent). While the frequencies generally persist between phases, the proportion of sheep to goat does change over time. Sheep and goat are present in approximately equivalent numbers in the early phases of occupation; sheep predominate over goat in the later phases. M. C. Metzger explains this shift by the increased importance of raising animals for a market economy—sheep produce more secondary products (wool and milk) than goats.

N. Glueck, *AASOR* 25–28 (1951), 259; M. Ibrahim et al., *BASOR* 222 (1976), 49; W. G. Dever, ibid., 237 (1980), 35–64; id., *AJA* 87 (1983), 231–232; S. E. Falconer and B. S. Magness-Gardiner, *ADAJ* 27 (1983), 87–104; id., *Archaeology of Jordan* 2 (1989), 254–261; id., *National Geographic Research* 5 (1989), 335–347; S. E. Falconer, *Syria* 60 (1983), 306–310; id. (with M. C. Metzger), *BASOR* 255 (1984); 49–74; id., *SHAJ* 3 (1987), 251–259; M. C. Metzger, *ASOR Newsletter* 37/4 (July 1986), 5; Khouri, *Antiquities*, 32–35; A. B. Knapp et al., *Journal of Mediterranean Archaeology* 1/2 (1988), 57–113; id., *IEJ* 39 (1989), 128–148; B. S. Magness-Gardiner, *AJA* 92 (1988), 278; *Akkadica Supplementum* 7–8 (1989), 255–261.

STEVEN E. FALCONER, BONNIE MAGNESS-GARDINER

ḤAẒEVA, MEẒAD

IDENTIFICATION

Meẓad Ḥaẓeva (map reference 1734.0242) was established on a hill adjacent to the southern bank of Naḥal Ḥaẓeva, close to ʿEn Ḥaẓeva in the northern Arabah. Researchers who toured the area in the nineteenth century discovered remains near the spring. A. Musil, on a visit to the site in 1902, prepared a sketch of the fortress and determined that its plan was square, each of its sides being about 90 m long, with protruding corner towers. He observed another building, adjoining the fortress on the south, that contained several rooms and the remains of a bathhouse to the east. The fortress was severely damaged in 1930, and its original plan could no longer be discerned. In 1932, the site was visited by F. Frank. Subsequently, A. Alt concluded that the large structure at Ḥaẓeva was a Roman fortress. N. Glueck, who visited the site in 1943, was of the opinion that the building was a khan established by the Nabateans that the Romans continued to use. He identified Ḥaẓeva with Eiseiba (Είσειβα), which appears on a list of settlements in the Negev and the amount of the annual tax imposed on them by the Byzantine authorities (the so-called Beersheba edict; Alt, *GIPT*, no. 2). B. Mazar and M. Avi-Yonah, who visited Ḥaẓeva in 1950, found several Iron Age sherds in addition to decorated Nabatean potsherds and sherds from the Roman-Byzantine period. Following this discovery, Y. Aharoni proposed identifying Ḥaẓeva with biblical Tamar and Roman Tamara. This view was opposed by B. Rothenberg, who noted that no Roman coins earlier than the fourth century CE had been found at the site; he therefore located Roman Tamara at Meẓad Tamar (q.v.).

EXCAVATIONS

In 1972, excavations were conducted at Meẓad Ḥaẓeva under the direction of R. Cohen, on behalf of the Israel Department of Antiquities and Museums. The excavations were renewed from 1987 to 1990, on behalf of the Israel Antiquities Authority, under Cohen's direction.

Five occupation strata were distinguished at the site. The uppermost stratum (1) contains remains from the Early Arab period. In stratum 2, remains of a fortress from the Roman period (second–fourth centuries CE) were found. The fortress is square (46 by 46 m); four towers protrude 4 m from it that were entered through a narrow corridor. On the floors of the tower were fragments of glass vessels, bronze bracelets, fragments of pottery vessels—oil lamps, jars, and jugs characteristic of the fourth century CE—and many coins from the reign of Constantine. The remains of a staircase leading to an upper story were found inside the fortress, east of the entrance to the southwest tower.

Remains from the Nabatean period (first–second centuries CE) were found in stratum 3, beneath the remains of the Roman fortress. A thick layer of ashes contained painted Nabatean bowls, a bowl of the terra sigillata type, oil lamps, cooking pots, jugs, and jars. Many coins from the first century CE were also found, including bronze coins from the time of the procurator Valerius Gratus (15–26 CE) and of the emperor Trajan (98–117 CE) from the foundation of the Provincia Arabia in 106.

The recent excavations revealed that the Roman fortress was built on the

Aerial view of Meẓad Ḥaẓeva.

Meẓad Ḥaẓeva: plan of the Roman fortress and the two Iron Age fortresses.

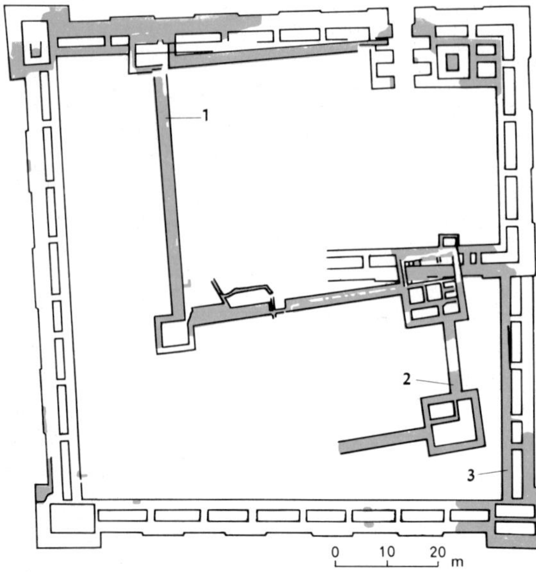

ruins of fortresses from the end of the Iron Age. Only the eastern side (c. 36 m long) and protruding towers of the stratum 4 Iron Age fortress were uncovered. Its southeast tower, which is square (11 by 11 m), was completely excavated; the wall here is about 2.25 m thick. The northeast tower is buried under the walls of the later strata (1–3), so that its dimensions have not yet been determined. This fortress was probably established in the reign of King Josiah and destroyed close in time to the destruction of the First Temple in 586 BCE.

Stratum 5 also includes a fortress. In some sections, its walls are destroyed almost to their foundations, while in others they are preserved to a height of 2 m. It was apparently square (100 by 100 m), with four protruding towers. The parts of the fortress that have been uncovered so far are (1) the southeast and the northwest towers, which protrude about 3 m from the line of the wall; (2) the line of the fortress's casemate wall, for almost its entire length and width. The outer wall is about 2.5 m wide; the parallel wall, about 2 m wide; and the casemate room north of the tower is 2 by 9.25 m; and (3) the area of the entrance gate to the fortress, which is situated near the fortress's northeast corner. The pottery finds on the floor of the stratum 5 fortress are too sparse to establish its exact date of construction. It probably existed in the eighth and seventh centuries BCE, in the reign of King Uzziah and his successors.

SUMMARY

In the excavator's opinion, the excavation results at Meẓad Ḥaẓeva strengthen the identification of the site with biblical Tamar. In his view, this was a central fortress on the southeastern border of the kingdom of Judah. Its specific role in the fortification system of Judah and Edom has yet to be established.

Musil, *Arabia Petraea* 2, 207–208; N. Glueck, *AASOR* 15 (1935), 17–20; F. Frank, *ZDPV* 57 (1934), 254.

RUDOLF COHEN

Stratum 5: eastern part of the fortress near the gate.

Stratum 5: entrance gate of the fortress.

HAZOR

IDENTIFICATION

Hazor, a large Canaanite and Israelite city in Upper Galilee, was identified by J. L. Porter in 1875 with Tell el-Qedaḥ (also called Tell Waqqas), some 14 km (8.5 mi.) north of the Sea of Galilee and 8 km (5 mi.) southwest of Lake Ḥula (map reference 203.269). This identification was proposed again in 1926 by J. Garstang, who conducted trial soundings at the site in 1928. Today, Kibbutz Ayelet ha-Shaḥar lies at the foot of the mound.

HISTORY

Hazor is first mentioned in the Egyptian Execration texts (published by G. Posener) from the nineteenth or eighteenth century BCE. It is the only Canaanite city mentioned (together with Laish-Dan) in the Mari documents of the eighteenth century BCE that point to Hazor having been one of the major commercial centers in the Fertile Crescent. The caravans plying between Babylon and Hazor passed through other large centers, such as Yamkhad and Qatna. Hazor is also mentioned frequently in Egyptian documents of the New Kingdom, such as the city lists of Thutmose III's conquests, the Leningrad Papyrus 1116–A, and city lists of Amenhotep II and Seti I.

The role of Hazor in the fourteenth century BCE, as reflected in the el-Amarna letters, is of particular significance. The kings of Ashtaroth in the Bashan and of Tyre accuse 'Abdi-Tirshi, king of Hazor, of having taken several of their cities. The king of Tyre furthermore states that the king of Hazor had left his city to join the Ḥabiru. The king of Hazor, on the other hand, one of the few Canaanite rulers to call himself king (and to be called so by others), proclaims his loyalty to Egypt. In the Papyrus Anastasi I, probably dating from the time of Ramses II, the name of Hazor occurs together with that of a nearby river.

Hazor is first mentioned in the Bible in connection with the conquests of Joshua. The Bible relates that Jabin, king of Hazor, was at the head of a confederation of several Canaanite cities in the battle against Joshua at "the waters of Merom." Especially noteworthy are the verses: "And Joshua turned back at that time, and took Hazor, and smote its king with the sword; for Hazor formerly was the head of all those kingdoms. . . . and he burned Hazor with fire . . . . But none of the cities that stood on mounds did Israel burn, except Hazor only; that Joshua burned" (Jos. 11:10–13). Here, then, is a direct reference to the role of Hazor at the time of the Israelite conquest. Hazor is also indirectly mentioned in the account of Deborah's wars in the prose version preserved in Judges 4, in contrast to the "Song of Deborah," which describes a battle in the Valley of Jezreel without mentioning Hazor. In 1 Kings 9:15, it is related that Hazor, together with Megiddo

Hazor: aerial view of the mound and the lower city, looking east.

and Gezer, was rebuilt by Solomon. According to 2 Kings 15:29, Hazor, among other Galilean cities, was conquered in 732 BCE by Tiglath-pileser III, king of Assyria.

The city is again mentioned indirectly in 1 Maccabees 11:67, which relates that Jonathan and his army marched northward from the Valley of Ginnosar in his campaign against Demetrius. Jonathan camped on the plain of Hazor (Το πεδίον Ἀσωρόν) near Cadasa. Josephus describes Hazor as situated above Lake Semachonitis (*Antiq.* V, 199).

TOPOGRAPHY

The site comprises two distinct areas: the mound proper, covering 30 a. (at the base) and rising about 40 m above the surrounding plain, and a large rectangular lower city of about 170 a. (1,000 by 700 m) to the north of the high mound. On the west the lower city is protected by a huge rampart of beaten earth and a deep fosse, on the north by a rampart alone, and on the east by a steep slope reinforced by supporting walls and a glacis. On the south, a deep fosse separates the lower city from the mound.

EXCAVATIONS

The results of Garstang's trial soundings (1928) on the mound and in the lower city (the "enclosure") were not published in detail. He concluded, inter alia, that the enclosure, which he called the camp area, was a camping ground for infantry and chariotry, rather than an actual dwelling area. As no Mycenean pottery was found, Garstang dated the final destruction of the site to about 1400 BCE, the period to which he assigned Joshua's conquest. On the west side of the mound proper stood a structure that he dated to the Israelite and Hellenistic periods (see below, area B). In the center of the mound (see below, area A), he found a row of pillars and assumed they were part of a stable from the time of Solomon.

From 1955 to 1958, the James A. de Rothschild Expedition, under the direction of Y. Yadin, conducted excavations on the site on behalf of the Hebrew University of Jerusalem in conjunction with PICA, the Anglo-Israel Exploration Society, and the Government of Israel. Among the members of the expedition were Y. Aharoni, C. Epstein, M. Dothan, T. Dothan, R. Amiran, I. Dunayevsky, J. Perrot, and E. Stern. During the first four seasons of work, several areas were excavated, both on the mound and in the lower city. Because of the great distances between the areas, separate stratum numbers were assigned to each. The dating of the strata at Hazor and the correlation between the lower and upper cities are presented in the table at the end of this article.

Excavations were resumed in the summer of 1968 (the fifth season), under the direction of Y. Yadin, with A. Ben-Tor and Y. Shiloh as the main field directors and I. Dunayevsky as the team's architect. Excavations were renewed in 1990 as a joint project of the Hebrew University of Jerusalem and the Complutense University at Madrid, in cooperation with Ambassador College at Big Sandy, Texas, and the Israel Exploration Society, under the direction of A. Ben-Tor.

EXCAVATION RESULTS: FIRST FOUR SEASONS (1955–1958)

THE LOWER CITY

During the four seasons of excavations in the lower city, areas C, D, E, 210, F, H, and K were cleared. Five strata were distinguished in each area; moreover, the stratigraphical sequence in all the areas was identical. It became evident that the whole area had been inhabited. The following is the order of the levels from bottom to top:

Stratum 4	MB IIB, 18th cent. BCE
Stratum 3	MB IIC, 17th–16th cent. BCE
Stratum 2	LB I, 15th cent. BCE
Stratum 1-b	LB IIA (el-Amarna period), 14th cent. BCE
Stratum 1-a	LB IIB, 13th cent. BCE

The results of the excavations in each area are briefly presented below.

AREA C. Area C is located at the southwestern corner of the lower city, adjoining the earthen rampart. The buildings excavated in this area provided the first evidence that the enclosure was in fact the lower city.

Stratum 4, the lowest level, is assigned to the beginning of the Middle Bronze Age IIB—that is, the mid-eighteenth century BCE—when the first fortifications and the ramparts of the lower city were constructed. A jar bearing an Akkadian inscription, incised before firing and bearing the name of the owner of the vessel, most probably belongs to this period.

Stratum 3, which was destroyed by a conflagration, belongs to the end of the Middle Bronze Age IIC. Many infant burials in jars were found beneath the floors of the houses of this stratum.

Stratum 2, above a thick layer of ash, represents the city inhabited during the Late Bronze Age I. Various dwellings were excavated in this level.

Stratum 1-b represents the peak of Hazor's prosperity in the Late Bronze Age II. A small broadhouse temple was discovered on the inner slope of the

Pottery mask from area C, 14th–13th centuries BCE.

Map of the mound, the lower city, and excavation areas.

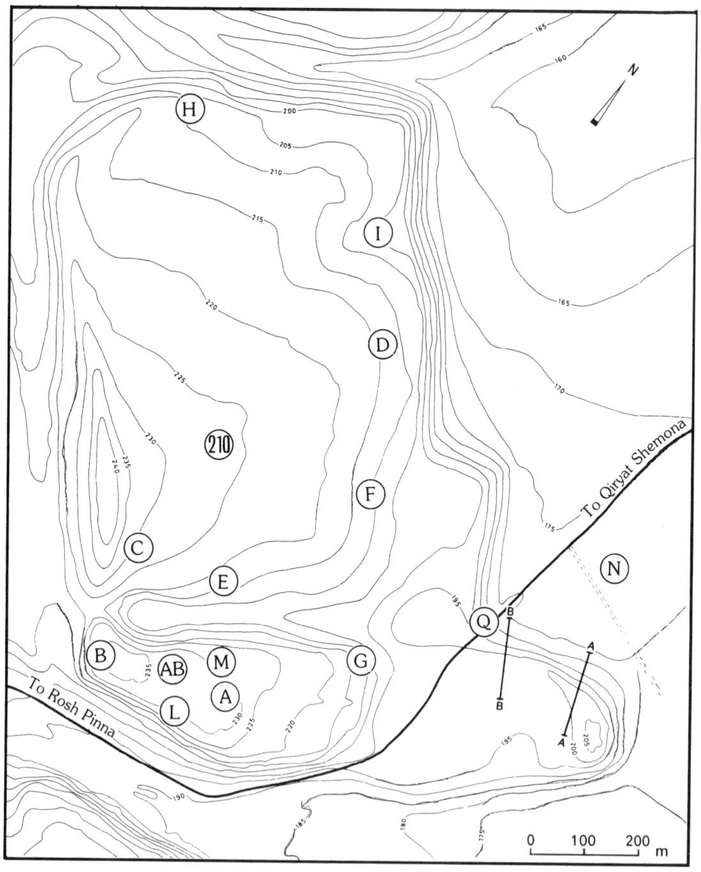

Area C: "stelae temple" containing a row of basalt stelae and a statue of a seated figure, 13th century BCE.

rampart. In a niche in its western wall were a number of small stelae and statuettes that were reused in the next stratum. Benches for offerings line the walls. Nearby are several large houses, including potters' workshops, complete with their installations. These evidently served the temple. The local and imported (Mycenean IIIA) pottery place the city in the el-Amarna period (fourteenth century BCE). Noteworthy finds include a pottery cult mask, discovered in a potter's workshop and similar to another mask found in area D, and a bronze standard plated with silver that bears a relief of a snake goddess. The standard was apparently attached to a wooden pole by means of a tang and was used in religious processions. The city was destroyed, but the circumstances of the destruction are not clear (possibly it was during Seti I's campaign).

Silver-plated bronze cult standard, 14th–13th centuries BCE.

Basalt stela decorated with a pair of hands raised in prayer toward a crescent and a disc.

Stratum 1-a is a reconstruction of the city of stratum 1-b. The structures of stratum 1-a are essentially similar to those of 1-b. Because they were quite close to surface level, they have been poorly preserved. The temple was also reconstructed in this stratum, and all the accessories of the former stratum were found in situ—a row of small basalt stelae, one with two hands stretched toward a divine lunar symbol (crescent and circle), and a statuette of a seated male figure. The head of the male figure had been deliberately broken off and was found lying on the floor. Mycenean IIIB sherds, together with the local pottery, indicate that this city came to an end before the close of the thirteenth century BCE, when occupation ceased in the lower city.

Basalt statue of a seated figure.

AREAS D, E, AND 210. Areas D, E, and 210 are located at various points in the lower city. Aside from their many finds, their main importance was to confirm that the entire area of the enclosure had indeed been inhabited and that their stratigraphical sequence corroborated with that of area C. In area D, at the eastern edge of the lower city, rich Middle Bronze Age II graves were uncovered, as well as Late Bronze Age I–II building remains. Among the finds was part of a sherd inscribed in paint in Proto-Canaanite script (thirteenth century BCE): [*'*/*b'*]*lt*. Area E, at the southern edge of the lower city, considerably enriched the knowledge of the pottery at Hazor. A number of vessels were found that have no parallels in Canaan but resemble Late Bronze Age I ceramic types from Anatolia. Area 210, a trial sounding (measuring 5 by 5 m) in the center of the lower city, proved that the sequence of strata here is similar to that found in area C. As in area C, a large number of infant burials in jars were found beneath the floors of stratum 3.

AREA F. Area F is located in the eastern section of the lower city, south of area D. Buildings and installations from all phases of occupation in the lower city were uncovered.

Stratum 4. A remarkable find, attributed to stratum 4, was rock-cut tombs with an elaborate network of connecting tunnels. As a rule, these tombs consisted of a large rectangular shaft, with caves hewn in varying shapes branching from its base. The eastern extension of the tunnel network, which was not cleared, may have also originally served to drain water that had collected in the shafts. Except for a few pottery vessels, the tombs were empty. They probably had been rifled in antiquity.

Stratum 3. In stratum 3 (Middle Bronze Age IIC), a large building with very thick walls was found, constructed on a rectangular plan. It was perhaps a double temple, consecrated to two deities. A sewage network ran from the structure and connected with the ancient tunnels that, in this phase, served as classical drainage tunnels.

Stratum 2. In stratum 2 (Late Bronze Age I), part of the temple from stratum 3 was reconstructed, while other parts remained in disuse. The building is square in plan and divided into chambers around a central area. It, too, is perhaps a temple similar in plan to the one discovered in Amman. A number of burials nearby contained a large assortment of bichrome ware.

Area F: plan of the MB IIC "palace" and MB IIB tunnel system.

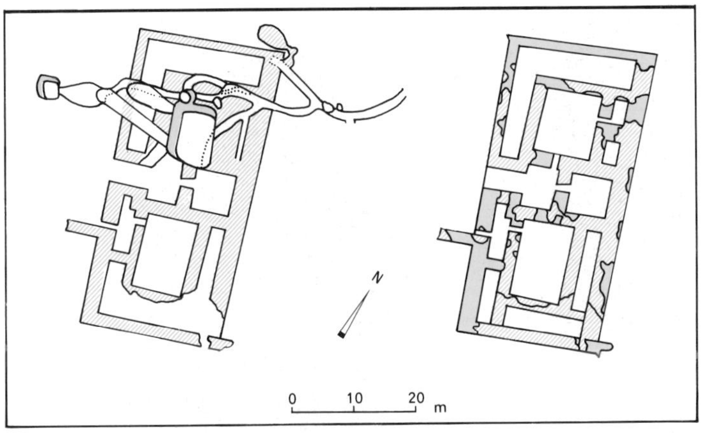

Stratum 1-b. Stratum 1-b (el-Amarna period) has a clear cultic nature. A stone altar—a huge ashlar taken from the Middle Bronze Age II building—with depressions for draining the sacrificial blood, stood in the southwestern part of the area. A drainage canal leading from the altar joined the earlier drainage and tunnel systems. Around the altar were a number of structures (evidently of a cultic nature), in which alabaster incense burners and other ritual vessels were found. A large tomb belonging to this stratum contained hundreds of vessels, including much Mycenean IIIA ware. The tomb served as a burial place during the entire period of stratum 1-b, the fourteenth century BCE.
Stratum 1-a. Most of the buildings surrounding the altar in stratum 1-b were renovated. Many incense burners and Mycenean IIIB vessels were also found in stratum 1-a, which was completely destroyed in the thirteenth century BCE.
AREA H: THE TEMPLES. Area H lies at the northern tip of the lower city. A series of four superimposed temples was unearthed here against the inner face of the earth rampart, similar to the location of the temple in area C.
Stratum 4. No remains of buildings were uncovered in stratum 4. This was the phase in which the rampart was erected. We know that because in the course of constructing the earliest of the temples—that of stratum 3 (Middle Bronze Age II)—the entire area had been leveled and filled up to the edge of the rampart. A number of stone structures found within the fill may have been part of the fill itself. It has been established, however, that the large rampart also found in this area was constructed during stratum 4—that is, in the Middle Bronze Age IIB.
Stratum 3. The temple of stratum 3 consisted of a broad hall, with a small rectangular niche, a sort of holy of holies, on the north side. The remains of two basalt capitals, or bases, indicate that two columns supporting the roof stood in the center of the room. This was necessary because of the dimensions of the hall. Two square areas on either side of the wide entrance on the south were evidently the foundations of two towers that flanked the entrance to the hall. South of the hall was a raised platform that was reached by several steps made of finely dressed basalt. The entire area around the temple was paved with very small cobblestones. In several respects, this temple is similar in plan to those found at Shechem and Megiddo (stratum VIII), except that here the temple consists of a broadhouse rather than a long hall.
Stratum 2. The temple plan of stratum 2 is identical with that of the one above. The floor, however, had been raised and paved with large cobblestones. These stones were plastered with a white, limey clay, typical of the Late Bronze Age I constructions at Hazor (see below, area A). The major modifications were made around the temple. South of it was a closed court paved with cobblestones, and farther to the south was a large open court, paved in a similar manner. The closed court was entered through a broad propylaeum, the threshold of which

Area H: aerial view of the temple in its various phases, looking southwest.

*Plan of the temple in area H: **(above)** stratum 1-b; **(below)** stratum 2.*

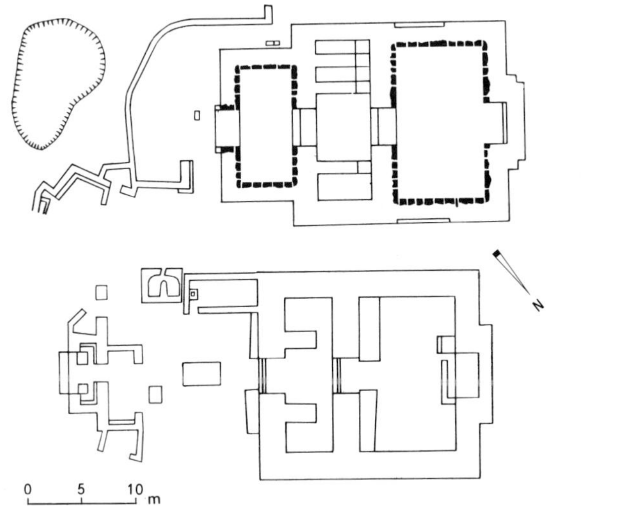

consisted of dressed basalt slabs (taken from stratum 3?). A large rectangular *bamah* (high place) and several smaller altars were found in the court. Near the *bamah*, where the sacrificial animals were slaughtered, a single drainage channel was discovered, consisting in part of discarded incense stands. On the other side of the court was a pottery kiln that still contained a large number of votive bowls. To the east of the main *bamah* was a heap of broken ritual vessels, including fragments of clay models of animals' livers for priestly divination. One of the fragments bore an Akkadian inscription that mentioned various evil omens. Another noteworthy find in the court was a delicately hammered bronze plaque of a Canaanite dignitary enveloped in a long robe. It is possible that the orthostats mentioned below originated in this temple.
Stratum 1-b. The temple of stratum 1-b was constructed during the fourteenth century BCE, the el-Amarna period, when ties between Egypt and the northern kingdoms were close. The plan of the temple in stratum 1-b is essentially different from that of the two earlier structures, although it was built partly on their foundations. Only on the northern side was the later temple influenced by the plan of the earlier ones. The temple comprised three main elements built in succession from north to south, with the doorways on a single axis leading into each chamber.

THE PORCH. Situated on the southern side of the temple, the porch constituted the main innovation in the previous plan. It is somewhat narrower than the hall and served as a sort of entrance hall to the temple proper; unlike that of stratum 2, however, it was attached directly to the main structure.

THE HALL. The hall was identical in its basic features with the porch of the previous temples.

Area H: clay liver models bearing Akkadian inscriptions, 15th century BCE.

Area H: bronze plaque of a Canaanite nobleman.

THE HOLY OF HOLIES. The holy of holies was a broadroom, similar to that in the previous temples, with a rectangular niche in its northern wall. In the center of the room were two bases of columns that supported the roof.

In its general plan, this temple resembles several of those found at Alalakh, as well as Solomon's Temple. From an architectural point of view, the most important feature in temple 1-b is the row of well-dressed basalt orthostats forming a dado around the lower part of the interior of the porch and the holy of holies. This feature clearly reflects a northern influence and has close parallels at Alalakh and other sites. On either side of the entrance to the porch stood a basalt orthostat with a lion in relief. One lion was found buried in a pit deliberately dug for the purpose near the entrance. The lion is similar in style to those found on the small orthostats, one in the temple of area C, and the other in area A (see below). No traces of fire were evident in this temple, and the finds were relatively scarce. It is very likely that most of the ritual vessels found in stratum 1-a originally belonged to this temple.

Stratum 1-a. The temple of stratum 1-a is identical with the previous one, with only minor repairs and alterations. The floor of the holy of holies was raised and two new column bases were found resting on it, one of them still bearing the lower part of a stone column. The hall was widened at the expense of a side room on the east. The porch was reconstructed in such a manner that it is difficult to establish whether it was roofed. In front of the entrance leading from the porch into the hall, two round bases were found in situ. Their location indicates that they had a cultic significance similar to that of the pillars Jachin and Boaz in Solomon's Temple. Of particular interest in this temple are the cultic furnishings. These were found in a thick layer of ash, especially in the holy of holies, showing that stratum 1-a was brought to an end by a conflagration. Among the ritual vessels that probably originated in the temple of stratum 1-b, the excavators discovered a basalt altar in the form of a square pillar. On one side it has the divine symbol of the storm god in low relief—a circle with a cross in its center. As indicated by the traces of fire on its upper part, this altar was used for burning incense. A large round basin made

Area H: the lion orthostat in situ, as found in the pit next to the temple entrance.

Area H: pottery and basalt cultic vessels in situ, in the temple's holy of holies, stratum 1-a, 13th century BCE.

Area H: basalt incense altar from the temple's holy of holies, stratum 1-a, 13th century BCE.

of basalt, somewhat like the "sea" of Solomon's Temple, was found next to the altar, as were several libation tables, a deep basalt bowl with a running-spiral design in relief on its exterior, a statuette of a seated figure, a large group of cylinder seals of the Late Mitannian type, and a scarab with the name of Amenhotep III (similar to scarabs discovered in other temples of the thirteenth century BCE, such as those at Beth-Shean and Lachish). Outside the area of the temple proper, fragments of a statue of a deity were found. This statue, which stood on a bull-shaped base, had a divine symbol on its chest, similar to the one on the incense altar described above. A basalt table for offering was found in situ in the hall near the entrance to the holy of holies.

AREA K: CITY GATES. Area K is situated on the eastern edge of the lower, city not far from the northern corner. In this area, which is lower than its surroundings, the excavators uncovered a series of city gates, whose dates range from the founding of the lower city down to its final destruction.

Stratum 4. Very little was found of the gate of stratum 4, which dates to the beginning of the lower city and was built on virgin soil, although enough has survived to indicate its general plan. A simple gate passageway was flanked on either side by a solid brick tower on stone foundations that measured about 8 sq m. This gate, which is similar to the southern gate at Gezer, apparently had a number of pilasters in the passageway. The city wall near the gate stood on lower ground and consisted of two parallel walls, each of which was about 1.5 m thick and was also built of brick on stone foundations. The space between the walls was filled with beaten earth, similar to the Middle Bronze Age fortress found in area B. On both sides of the gate, the wall joined the rampart and the glacis at the point where it reached the natural, higher level of the lower city. The gate was situated slightly to the rear of the natural slope and was approached by means of a gradual ascent constructed of beaten earth laid in alternate layers of basalt flakes and clay, crushed yellowish chalk rock, and brown brick clay.

Stratum 3. The gate of stratum 3, built at the end of the Middle Bronze Age II, is completely different from the gate of stratum 4, both in plan and in position. It is patterned after the "classical" gate plan of this period. Three pairs of pilasters narrowed the width of its passageway to 3 m. The entrance to the gate was flanked by two large towers. The southern tower (the only one excavated) is divided into two interconnected chambers. To this gate belongs the adjoining true casemate wall—one of the earliest of its type thus far found in Canaan. The wall evidently continued for only a short distance before joining

Area K: plan of the city gate in stratum 3, MB IIC.

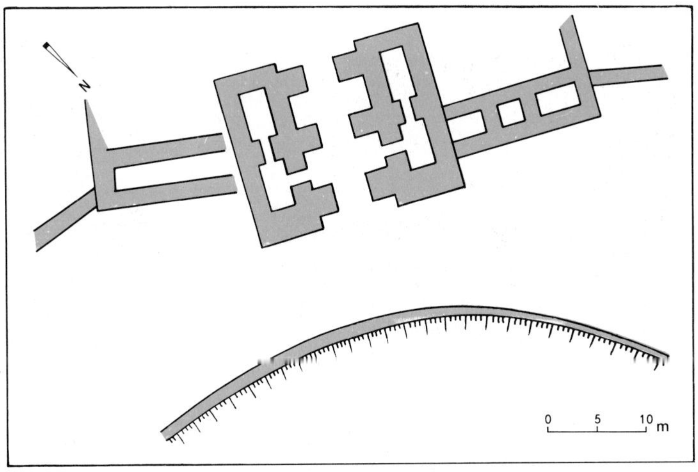

the rampart of the lower city. The great revetment wall built of large basalt boulders discovered on the slope east of the gate probably belongs to this phase. This wall supported the causeway leading up to the gate from the north along the slope. In front of the gate, the road made a right turn at an angle of 90 degrees on a large platform supported on the east by the revetment wall. This wall has been preserved to a height of more than 5 m and is one of the finest examples of Middle Bronze Age IIC fortifications in the country.

Stratum 2. The gate of stratum 2, built during the Late Bronze Age I, is identical with that in stratum 3. The structure is composed of very large, well-dressed, ashlars. The casemate wall was strengthened in this period by the construction of additional upper courses.

Stratum 1-b. The gate of stratum 1-b, which dates from the Late Bronze Age II (fourteenth century BCE), is that of stratum 2, with several modifications and the addition of a cobblestone floor of the type found in areas A and H in the parallel strata. South of the gate are a number of workshops and a small cult installation containing several stelae similar to those discovered in area C. The section of the wall adjacent to the gate was rebuilt, and the casemate wall of the previous stratum was replaced by a brick wall 3 m thick.

Stratum 1-a. In stratum 1-a, the gate is identical with that of stratum 1-b, except for minor repairs and additions. A thick layer of ash and rubble on the cobblestone floor of the passageway contained the fallen brickwork of the gate and towers. The excavators differ as to the date of this layer. In Dunayevsky's opinion, the gate of stratum 1-b was no longer in use. It was not newly renovated in stratum 1-a and the conflagration is, therefore, to be assigned to stratum 1-b. This theory is based on the fact that a flimsy structure, apparently constructed on the city wall, was found south of the gate, thus proving that the fortifications had ceased being used. In this writer's opinion, however, the destruction of the gate is to be attributed to stratum 1-a, paralleling the conflagration in the temple of stratum 1-a in area H. The nature of the small structure mentioned above was not satisfactorily established during the excavations, nor did a trial sounding in 1961 succeed in proving that it was indeed built upon the wall.

THE UPPER CITY

Three main areas were excavated in the upper city in the 1955–1958 seasons: area A in the center, area B on the western edge, and area G on the eastern edge.

AREA A. Area A, at the center of the mound, was the site of Garstang's trial excavation. He found a row of pillars, which he identified as a stable from the time of Solomon (see below, stratum VIII). In one section of area A, the 1955–1958 excavations reached bedrock and obtained a clear section of the levels of occupation in the upper city from the first settlement onward.

Strata XXI–XIX. Immediately above bedrock, building remains of three Early Bronze Age strata were found. Stratum XXI contained some pottery datable to the end of the Early Bronze Age II. In strata XX–XIX, a large number of sherds of Khirbet Kerak ware (Early Bronze Age III) was found.

Stratum XVIII. No buildings were uncovered in the small sector cleared (see, however, the next stratum). The pottery found here is typical of the Middle Bronze Age I.

Strata XVII–XVI. Strata XVII–XVI, which parallel strata 4–3 in the lower city and represent the Middle Bronze Age II-B–C, are separated from one another by two floors of a large building originating in stratum XVII. Although only a small part of this structure was uncovered, it is clear from its size, the thickness of its walls, and its building technique that it was either a palace or a citadel. another building of the Middle Bronze Age II found in area A and most probably originating in stratum XVI was a rectangular temple (16.2 by 11.6 m) that was reused and rebuilt in stratum XV (see below).

In a sectional trench dug east of the excavated area, a massive wall attrib-

Map of the excavation areas and principal remains in the upper city.

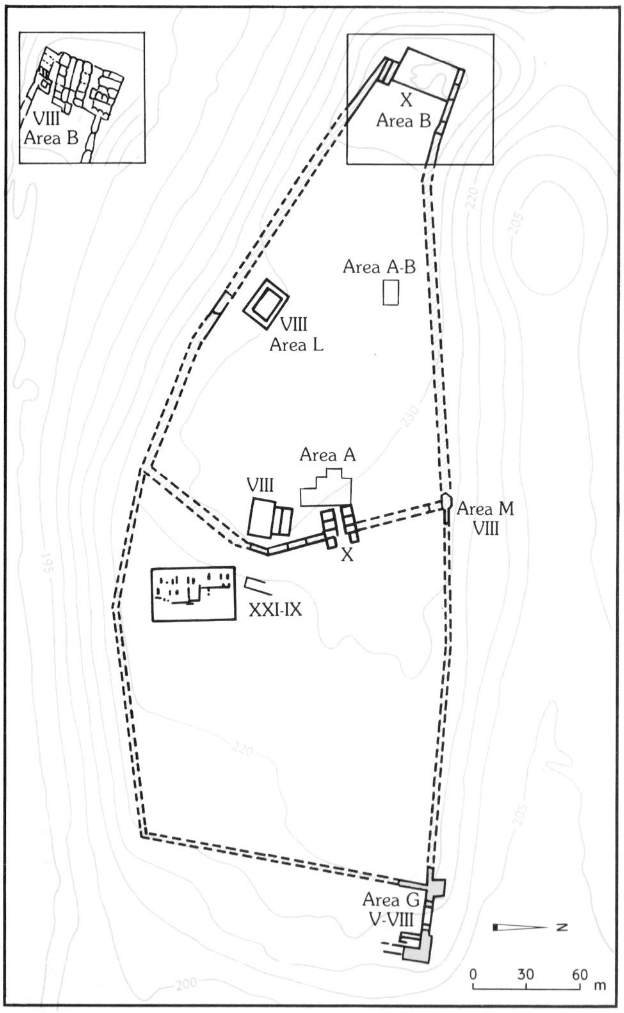

uted to these two strata was discovered. This wall, which is 7.5 m thick and built of plastered bricks on a stone foundation, probably protected the inner part of the upper city. A good part of the wall survived into the Late Bronze Age. It was again used, together with its moat, in Solomon's fortifications (see below), apparently as a sort of outer defense.

Stratum XV. Stratum XV parallels stratum 2 in the lower city. The rectangular temple was reconstructed in this stratum and an impressive orthostat entrance added to it (see below). Several sherds of bichrome ware were found among the Late Bronze Age I pottery.

Stratum XIV. Stratum XIV parallels stratum 1-b in the lower city, the fourteenth century BCE. The orthostat temple was not rebuilt, although many shrines and cult installations were found in its vicinity.

Stratum XIII. Stratum XIII, the last Late Bronze Age level on the mound, parallels stratum 1-a in the lower city. With the destruction that occurred in this level, Canaanite Hazor was brought to an end in the thirteenth century

Area A: plan of the LB I temple.

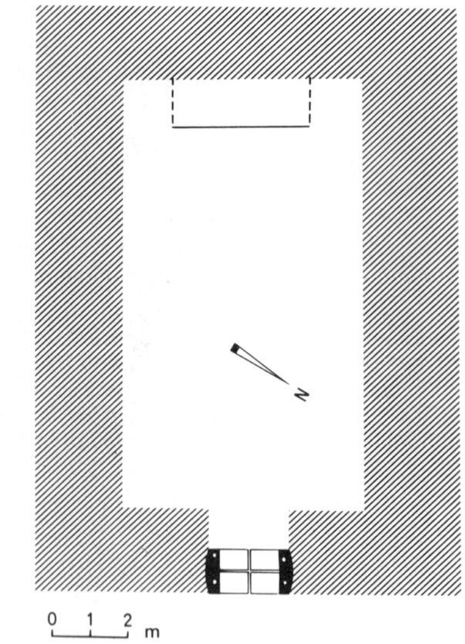

BCE. As in the lower city, few new houses were built; the ruins of the previous stratum were reconstructed and some structures were erected here and there around the reservoir. A small cult installation, including stelae, found near the derelict temple, may be assigned to this stratum.

Stratum XII. After a certain gap, a small settlement rose at the beginning of the Iron Age on the ruins of stratum XIII. This settlement, which can hardly be called a city, consisted mostly of deep silos, hearths, and foundations for tents

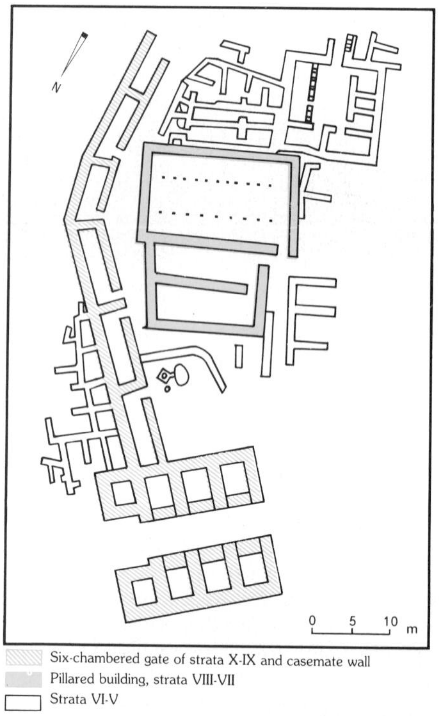

Plan of the principal Iron Age remains in area A.

MB II mud-brick city wall in the large trench east of area A.

Area A: LB I temple entrance built of orthostats.

Herodium: view from Lower Herodium of the mountain palace-fortress.

Herodium: overview of Lower Herodium.

Hazor: basalt statuette of a seated figure, from the stratum 1-a temple in area H, LB IIB.

Hazor: overview of the stratum 1-b temple in area H, LBII, looking northwest.

and huts. The pottery is typical of the twelfth century BCE and closely resembles that found in similar poor Israelite settlements in Upper Galilee (see also the summary below).

Stratum XI. No definite structures of stratum XI were uncovered in area A.

Stratum X. Stratum X represents Hazor rebuilt as a fortified city. Its main features are a casemate wall and a large gate with six chambers—three on either side—and two towers flanking the passageway. On the basis of both the stratigraphy and pottery, these fortifications are to be attributed to Solomon, as related in the Bible (1 Kg. 9:15). The resemblance of the plan of the gate and the wall to similar Solomonic structures at Gezer and Megiddo confirm this conclusively. This stratum has been subdivided by the excavators into two phases (X-a and X-b).

Stratum IX. Stratum IX, which is also divided into two phases (IX-a and IX-b), shows a certain decline in the quality of the buildings. This stratum is assigned to the period between Solomon and the rise of the Omrid dynasty. It was destroyed by fire.

Stratum VIII. The main discovery in stratum VIII, in which extensive building activity is evident, is a large storehouse with two rows of pillars along its center and two halls attached to the north side. The rooms of the earlier casemate wall now served only as storerooms. The northern row of pillars was that uncovered by Garstang and mistakenly attributed by him to Solomon. In their general plan, these buildings differ completely from the structures of strata X–IX. The construction of this city by the Omrid dynasty represents a definite turning point in the history of Israelite Hazor (for a description of the city fortifications, see area B below).

Stratum VII. The pillared storehouse continued in use in stratum VII, although the floor was raised and laid over the debris of the fallen roof of stratum VIII. More basic changes occurred in the structures around the storehouse. This stratum was completely destroyed, and the pillared storehouse and other buildings were not reconstructed in the following strata.

Stratum VI. The public buildings of the stratum VII were not reused in stratum VI, and the entire area became a residential quarter with workshops and stores. There are clear signs that this city was destroyed by the earthquake in the days of Jeroboam II, which is mentioned by Amos. In one of the houses, a sherd was found bearing an incised inscription למכבדם, "belonging to the food servers." An ivory cosmetic palette was also found here.

Stratum V. In stratum V, most of the buildings of the previous stratum were reconstructed. The city was destroyed by a conflagration, traces of which were evident throughout the area. With this destruction, which is ascribed to the conquests of Tiglath-pileser III in 732 BCE—as recorded in 2 Kings 15:29—Hazor, as a fortified Israelite city, came to an end.

Strata IV–I. With the exception of several burials of stratum II (see below, area B), little was found in strata IV–I in this area.

AREA B. Area B is located at the western edge of the mound. Most of this area was occupied in the Israelite period by a large citadel, which was not removed. Most of our knowledge of the older periods, therefore, derives from the excavation of a small sector east of the citadel. Only poorly preserved remains from the Bronze Age were revealed here.

Strata XVII–XVI. In stratum XVII–XVI the remains of a large citadel constructed of brick were found; the spaces between the foundation walls were filled with beaten earth, as in stratum 4 in area K. The citadel is attributed to the Middle Bronze Age IIB.

Strata XV–XIII. Remains were found in strata XV–XIII indicating the existence of a settlement during the Late Bronze Age, but there were not enough to ascertain their nature. The local pottery and imported wares point to the Late Bronze Age I and IIA–B.

Stratum XII. As in area A, in stratum XII, remains were found of the first poor Israelite settlement built on the ruins of the last Canaanite occupation of the thirteenth century BCE. It resembles the settlement in area A and consists of silos, tent and hut foundations, and the like. The pottery is homogeneous and identical with that found in the small Israelite settlements of the twelfth century BCE scattered throughout Upper Galilee.

Stratum XI. Stratum XI was uncovered mainly in area B. The remains indicate that another unfortified settlement existed in several parts of the mound after the first Israelite settlement but before Solomon established a city at Hazor (stratum X). Unlike stratum XII, which still had a seminomadic character, stratum XI shows definite traces of a permanent settlement. The most important find in this level is a sort of *bamah*, alongside

Area A: aerial view of the main Iron Age remains.

Ivory spoon from area A, stratum VI, 8th century BCE.

Bronze figurine of Ba'al(?), area B, Iron I.

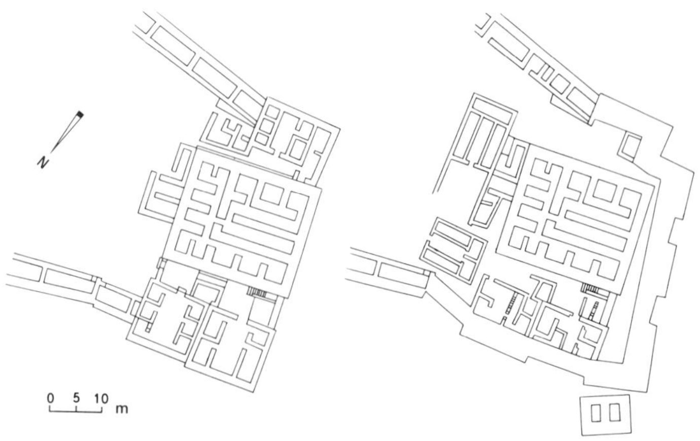

Plan of the fortifications and Israelite citadel in area B: ***(left)*** *stratum VIII;* ***(right)*** *stratum VA.*

Area B: Proto-Aeolic capitals from the stratum VIII citadel, in secondary use as a shelter for an oven in stratum VII.

which were found incense vessels and a jar containing a cache of bronze objects, as a foundation deposit. Among these were a number of weapons and a statuette of a deity. The stratigraphy and pottery date this stratum to the eleventh century BCE.

Stratum X. The remains of the Solomonic city, in particular the casemate wall surrounding the mound, are also well preserved in this area. At the western edge, the fortifications were expanded to form a type of citadel; however, because the later citadel of stratum VIII was built on it, it was impossible to ascertain its exact plan.

Stratum IX. Very few traces of stratum IX were found in area B, and no plan could be established with certainty.

Stratum VIII. The main feature of stratum VIII was a large citadel that covered practically the entire excavated area. The erection of this edifice marks a turning point in the character of Israelite Hazor (see also area A below). It has a rectangular plan and measures 21 by 25 m, with walls about 2 m thick. Two long halls, running from west to east, are surrounded by a series of rooms on three sides (north, south, and east). It is probable that these remains represent the cellars of the citadel and that the upper parts, reached by means of stairs (discovered intact), were built of brickwork that has not survived. Nearby was a number of buildings that evidently were used in the administration of the citadel. Because this fortress occupied almost the entire width of the mound in area B, its walls also formed, in effect, the city wall at this spot. The city wall, which extended from the east, was the earlier casemate wall. It had been filled with earth and stones to form a solid construction typical of many Israelite city walls from the ninth century BCE. A similar change is evident in the Solomonic

General view of the Israelite citadel in area B.

fortifications at Megiddo. The large citadel, built in the first half of the ninth century BCE, continued in use throughout the Israelite period until (in stratum V) it was destroyed to its very foundations. Of special interest is the entrance to the open area between the adjoining buildings and the citadel. This was a monumental entrance adorned with proto-Aeolic capitals and a monolithic lintel—all found near the citadel in secondary use in a later level (end of stratum VII).

Stratum VII. In stratum VII, several additions are plainly evident in the citadel, although the general plan was not altered.

Stratum VI. The citadel continued in use for the duration of stratum VI, with some changes and additions to the surrounding buildings.

Stratum V. Drastic changes are evident in the first phase of stratum V. To meet the imminent Assyrian menace, the citadel was strengthened by an additional offset-inset wall on the west, north, and south. Some of the adjoining buildings had to be sacrificed in the process, and the wall was constructed directly on their ruins and joined to the older wall. At the northwest corner, a single tower was erected that commanded the terrain to the north. In this phase, two buildings of the four-room type were constructed east of the citadel and evidently replaced the buildings destroyed.

The citadel met its final, complete destruction at the end of this level (the conquest of Tiglath-pileser III). The entire area was covered with a layer of ash and rubble about 1 m thick. The most noteworthy finds in this citadel are an ivory pyxis and several Hebrew inscriptions, including one incised on the shoulder of a storage jar, לפקח סמדר "belonging to Pekaḥ, *semadar* (a type of wine), and another לדליו "belonging to Delayo."

Stratum IV. After the destruction of the citadel, a temporary unfortified settlement arose. Its remains were found directly above the foundations of the fortress and the city wall. This occupation, stratum IV, from the end of the eighth century BCE, is probably to be ascribed to the Israelites who returned after the city fell.

Stratum III. Stratum III also contains a large citadel, evidently constructed by the Assyrian conquerors. It consists of an inner courtyard surrounded by halls and rooms on all four sides. On the east side another large courtyard was enclosed by a wall.

Stratum II. Stratum II is ascribed to the Persian period. The citadel of stratum III continued to be used, although it had undergone many alterations. The pottery—which includes Attic ware—indicates a span over the fourth century BCE.

Stratum I. The remains of another citadel attributed to the second century BCE—that is, to the Hellenistic period—were found in stratum I.

AREA B–A. East of area B, a small trial trench, 5 by 5 m, was excavated. Its finds confirmed the stratigraphical sequence obtained in areas A and B from the Middle Bronze Age II onward.

AREA G. Area G, located on the northern edge of the eastern terrace of the mound, furnished important information regarding the extent of the upper city in various periods and the fortifications in this sector.

Bronze Age. An important find from the Middle Bronze Age II were the fortifications in the northeastern corner of the terrace, centered around a large, rounded stone bastion whose battered outer walls were protected by a deep, narrow fosse. The abundant pottery shows an occupation throughout the Middle and Late Bronze ages.

Iron Age. There is not enough evidence to establish the character of the settlements before stratum VIII. But from this level onward, the remains clearly indicate that the city defenses were expanded to include area G as well. There they formed a sort of outer citadel to protect the terrace and the approach to the main gate (not yet excavated) on the south. The main city wall passed along the western edge of the terrace, which was, in turn, enclosed by another casemate wall. All the phases of the Israelite occupation are represented here. Especially noteworthy is a four-room building originating in stratum VIII, found to the west of the terrace, and a huge silo, whose walls were lined with stone, dug into the center of the terrace. A postern in the northern part of the wall led from the outer citadel to the fields on the north. At some time during stratum V, this gate was apparently blocked in the course of strengthening the fortifications against the Assyrians (see above, area B). Traces of the fire that destroyed the city in 732 BCE are also clearly visible in this area. As in area B, remains of an unfortified Iron Age settlement (stratum IV), built over the ruined fortifications, were uncovered. Above these, the traces of buildings from the Persian period (stratum II) indicate that in this phase settlement was not limited to the citadel alone.

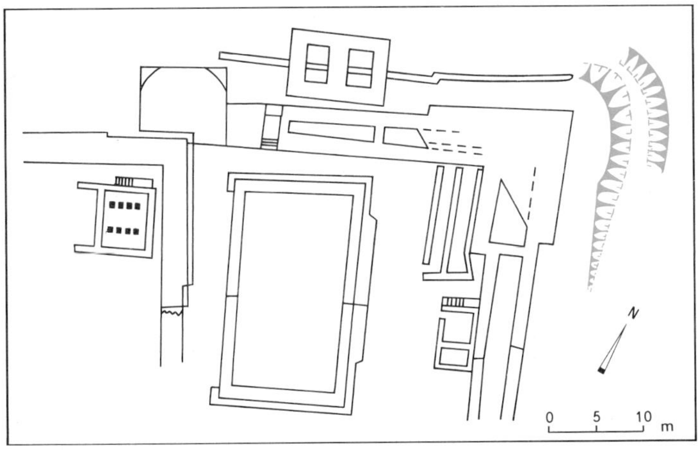

Area G: plan of the MB II and Iron Age remains.

Area G: view of the MB II fortifications.

SUMMARY

The results of the excavations at Hazor enable us to reconstruct the history of the site and the nature of its settlement. In the third millennium BCE, the city was confined to the mound. At the end of this period there was a gap in occupation until the Middle Bronze Age I, when the mound proper was resettled.

The great turning point in the development of Hazor started in the Middle Bronze Age IIB (mid-eighteenth century BCE), when the large lower city was founded. Excavations in all the areas of the lower city proved that it should not be termed an enclosure or a camp but that it was a built-up area with fortifications, constructed by a new wave of settlers too numerous to settle within the upper city alone. Unlike the mound with its natural fortifications, here it was necessary to dig a large, deep fosse on the west; the excavated material was used to construct a rampart on the west and north. The slopes of the eastern side of the lower city were strengthened by the addition of a glacis. Thus, a fortified area came into being, within which the various structures of the lower city were built—the temples, public buildings, and private houses.

Because the mention of Hazor in the Mari documents presumably refers to the city only after the large lower city had been established, the results of the excavations lend support to the lower chronology for dating these documents—that is, to the end of the eighteenth century BCE.

The lower city flourished throughout the Late Bronze Age, being alternately destroyed and rebuilt. Hazor reached its peak in the fourteenth century BCE, the el-Amarna period, at which time it was the largest city in area in the whole land of Canaan. The final destruction of Canaanite Hazor, both of the upper and the lower cities, probably occurred in the second third of the thirteenth century BCE, by conflagration. This destruction is doubtless to be ascribed to the Israelite tribes, as related in the Book of Joshua.

Important evidence for understanding the process of Israelite settlement is the remains of stratum XII. These remains, which clearly belong to the twelfth century BCE, when Hazor ceased to be a real city, are essentially identical with the remains of the Israelite settlements in Galilee. This indicates, in the opinion of this writer, that the Israelite settlement, which was still seminomadic in character, arose only after the fall of the cities and provinces of Canaan.

Only from the time of Solomon onward did Hazor return to some extent to its former splendor, although on a smaller scale than in Canaanite times. Occupation was henceforth limited to the upper city.

In 732 BCE, Hazor was destroyed by the Assyrians. It remained uninhabited thereafter, except for occasional temporary occupations—lonely forts overlooking the Ḥula Valley and the important highways that passed it.

YIGAEL YADIN

FIFTH SEASON OF EXCAVATIONS (1968–1969)

The aim of the fifth season of excavations was to elucidate certain details that had not been sufficiently clarified in previous seasons: (1) the nature and date of the building whose imposing entrance, flanked by orthostats, was discovered beneath the gate from the Israelite period in area A, (2) the precise extent of the so-called Solomonic city, (3) whether the topographical depression clearly visible near the southern edge of the upper city, halfway between areas A and B, indicates the location of a subterranean water system, and (4) whether there was a gate to the lower city at the corner between the eastern edge of the lower city and the northern edges of its eastern spur.

More limited excavations were undertaken to solve problems relating to the stratigraphy of the Bronze Age remains, the structure of the rampart, and the nature of the drainage channels discovered while the foundations were being dug for the Hazor Museum, close to the mound.

AREA A. By extending the excavated area to the west, beyond the area covered by the Solomonic gate, it was possible to conduct a more detailed examination of the levels preceding the gate's construction and, in particular, to expose the building with the basalt orthostat entrance (see below). It became clear that the building was a rectangular temple with thick walls. It was entered from the east, and opposite the entrance, built up against the rear wall of the building, was a *bamah* built of brick and plastered. In plan, the building resembles the temples discovered at Megiddo VIII and, to a certain extent, at Shechem, as well as certain Syrian temples, and is clearly classifiable as a temple of the *migdol* type. Its proximity to the large building to the south, which was apparently a palace (but has been only partially excavated), seems to indicate that it was a royal temple—that is, a temple serving a royal palace. Judging from the finds in the building, it was destroyed at some time in the Late Bronze Age I; hence, its construction should be dated to this period (no later than stratum XV), or perhaps to the end of the Middle Bronze Age IIB (stratum XVI).

It should be noted that the orthostat entrance was not built at the same time as the temple but was incorporated at some later stage. In any event, the date of the building and, in particular, the fact that it was destroyed at some time during the Late Bronze Age I and not restored, implies that the use of orthostats at Hazor dates to the beginning of the Late Bronze Age I, at the latest, and perhaps even earlier.

After its destruction, the temple was left in ruins; all that remained was an immense heap of rubble in the center of the settled area. Throughout this period, intense cultic activity continued all around it—for example, stelae and other cultic installations were erected—but no use whatsoever was made of the area of the ruined temple itself.

Area L: shaft of the water system and the entrance to the tunnel.

AREA L. It was already suspected during the first season of excavations that the great depression near the southern edge of the mound, opposite the natural springs at the foot of the mound in Wadi Waqqas, marked the location of the water system that supplied the city's needs under siege. Approximately one year of excavations, during which hundreds of tons of stones and debris were removed, revealed this water system, which consists of three parts.

A. Entrance Structure. The water system could be entered at its south-eastern corner, near the edge of the mound, via two ramps made of crushed limestone, which slope down gently toward the shaft. The entrance to this structure and the exit from it to the shaft were built of huge ashlar blocks.

B. Vertical Shaft. The upper part of the shaft was cut through the strata of the mound and was revetted by retaining walls, which have been preserved to a height of 4 m. The lower part was quarried out of the rock. The total depth of the shaft is approximately 30 m; its length and width taper off gradually toward the bottom. Steps 3 m wide, cut into the rock on a relatively gentle gradient, provide a convenient means of descent. At the bottom of the fifth flight of stairs, the steps merge with those descending into the tunnel.

Area L: aerial view of the water system and entrance structure.

Area L: section of the water system.

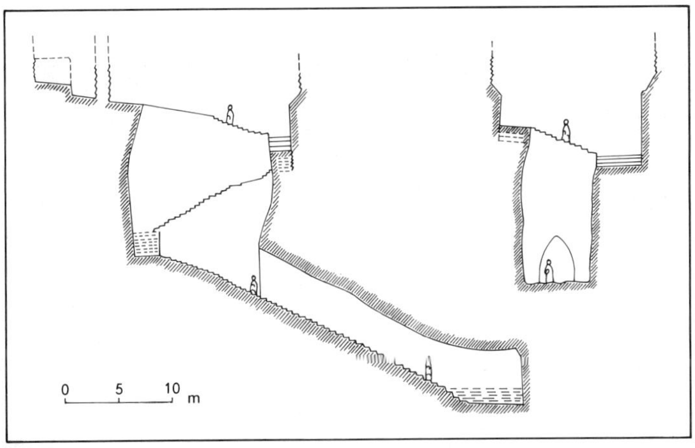

C. Tunnel. The entrance to the tunnel is situated at the western edge of the shaft bottom. The tunnel itself runs west–southwest for approximately 25 m, sloping down gradually to a pool of fresh water. The vaulted ceiling of the tunnel is some 4 m high. The fact that the tunnel was cut running westward, rather than southward, toward the springs, reduced by approximately 75 m the length that had to be quarried; moreover, the entire water system lies within the precincts of the mound, unlike the one at Megiddo, for example. This was an extremely important factor when the city was under siege; it testifies to the geological expertise of the builders of the Hazor water system, who directed the tunnel toward the aquifer rather than the springs.

It became evident that the latest level through which the builders of the water system cut is stratum X, which is contemporaneous with the Solomonic casemate wall. Thus, the system was built after Solomon's reign, possibly under the reign of Ahab (stratum VIII), when Hazor was reconstructed as a large fortified city. Other proof of this date is that the four-room building associated with the entrance structure to the shaft is also dated to stratum VIII.

When Iron Age Hazor was destroyed in the eighth century BCE (stratum V), the water system also went out of use; this is evident from the rubble and conflagration debris filling the shaft, as well as the date of the pottery found in it.

After the water system fell into disuse, a large depression was left that was used to collect rainwater. Sherds from the Persian and Hellenistic periods date this pool to the fifth to second centuries BCE. The earliest use of the depression to collect rainwater may, however, be attributable to the time of strata IV–III—that is, the Iron Age levels postdating the destruction of the city.

AREA M. During the 1957–1958 season, it became clear that the casemate wall attributed to the Solomonic period cuts across the upper city approximately at its center, whereas the solid wall dated to Ahab's reign was exposed only along a short section of area G, at the northeastern corner of the upper city. In order to ascertain that the casemate wall and gate discovered in area A are indeed part of the outer wall (toward the east) of the Solomonic city, rather than an inner wall enclosing only the western half of the acropolis, a trial sounding was conducted in the middle of the northern edge of the high mound. This confirmed the hypothesis that the Solomonic city occupied only the western half of the upper city, whereas Ahab's city (stratum VIII) extended over the entire area of the upper city: it became evident that when the casemate wall reached the northern edge of the mound it swung westward at an acute angle, not continuing to the east at all. Moreover, the builders of Ahab's fortifications built the western end of the solid wall up against the northeastern corner of the Solomonic city.

AREA P. The superimposed remains of five gates, dating from the Middle to the Late Bronze ages were exposed in area P. The gates were badly damaged by the construction of the Rosh Pinna–Qiryat Shemona road, which cut through their eastern halves; the surviving remains nevertheless provide sufficient evidence of their nature. Like the gates in area K, they were of the direct-access type, flanked by two large towers; three pairs of piers narrowed the width of the passageway. Each tower had two chambers and two pairs of doors, one pair at the outer piers and a second at the inner piers.

The remains of a large, imposing building from the Late Bronze Age, of an undetermined nature, were uncovered near the gate and to its west. The numerous fragments of orthostats found scattered in the area indicate that the walls of this building, like those of the gates from the Late Bronze Age, were probably covered with orthostats.

THE RAMPART. The structure of the rampart was examined both in area P, in the region east of the Rosh Pinna–Qiryat Shemona road, and in two exploratory trenches cut across the northern rampart of the eastern spur of the lower city. It was found that the area P gate linked up with the rampart via a series of stone-built terraces rising from the gate to the top of the rampart. The terraces provided the foundations for a thick mud-brick wall, so that the gate and the parts of the wall flanking it served as a kind of "stopper," plugging the breach created by the gate in the rampart. The trenches cut in the rampart itself revealed various technical details of its construction, such as that the brick-built core was divided into "boxes" (*kastenbau*). The excavators were also able to determine the nature of the layers of earth and clusters of stones constituting the main part of the rampart.

AREA N: THE CHANNELS SYSTEM. Of the additional soundings carried out at the site, some of the most significant were those directly associated with various aspects of the Early and Middle Bronze Age occupation of Hazor. A subterranean system of channels, parts of which were discovered northeast of the mound, drained water from the city and irrigated the surrounding fields. The potsherds found in the channels date this system to the Middle Bronze Age IIB, making it one of the earliest subterranean irrigation systems to be discovered in the country.

EARLY AND MIDDLE BRONZE AGE LEVELS. The excavations in areas A and L revealed several details that were of importance in rounding out our picture of the sequence of levels from the Early and Middle Bronze ages in the upper city. In area L, the excavators uncovered remains of structures ascribed to Early Bronze Age levels. These remains were badly damaged by the construction of the shaft of the water system in the Iron Age. Of particular interest is part of a structure dating to the Early Bronze Age IIIA, with abundant pottery of the Khirbet Kerak type and two cylinder seal impressions featuring geometric patterns typical of the period. The finds in area A assign the latest level in the Early Bronze Age sequence of the mound, stratum XIX (which produced a rich assemblage of pottery similar to that discovered at various sites in Syria), to the period known as post–Khirbet Kerak (Early Bronze IIIB). This conclusion refutes the previous attribution of the two strata XX–XIX to the Early Bronze Age IIIA, which is characterized, inter alia, by the appearance of Khirbet Kerak ware in the ceramic repertoire.

Some modifications were also introduced in the sequence of Middle Bronze Age IIB levels. As early as the end of the 1958 season, it was suggested that this period should include more than the two strata originally ascribed to it, XVII–XVI. In anticipation of this possibility, the strata beginning from XVIII were marked with an asterisk (for example, XVIII*). It indeed transpired that structures of stratum XVII overlay the remains of walls and structures, also dating to the beginning of the Middle Bronze Age IIB (or, at the earliest, the end of the Middle Bronze Age IIA). It was also realized that after the destruction of stratum XVI, but before the reconstruction of the city early in the Late Bronze Age I (stratum XV), the mound was used as a necropolis; evidence to that effect was discovered in several areas. In order to avoid confusion in the numbering of the sequence of strata at the site, as established in previous seasons, the stratum immediately preceding XVII is now called pre–XVII, while that following XVI is called post–XVI.

An important discovery, assigned according to its rich ceramic material to stratum pre–XVII, is a rock-hewn burial cave, in area L, very near the southern edge of the mound. This discovery seems to have some bearing on the problem of dating the first construction of the Middle Bronze Age II fortifications of the upper city (that is to say, the brick-built wall on a stone foundation uncovered in previous seasons, its thickness being as much as 8 to 9 m). The entrance to the burial cave was from the south, through a shallow shaft; the length of the entire cave (together with the entrance shaft) was approximately 8 m. Collation of all these data implies that the entrance to the cave must have lain beneath the above-mentioned wall (nonexistent at this point), which is impossible. It follows that in stratum pre–XVII—that is, as stated above, in the transitional period between Middle Bronze Age IIA and Middle Bronze Age IIB—the upper city of Hazor was not fortified at all: the upper city of the Middle Bronze Age II was first fortified during the Middle Bronze Age IIB.

No changes occurred in the numbering of the strata of the Late Bronze and Iron ages.

AYELET HA-SHAḤAR

In 1950, within the bounds of Kibbutz Ayelet ha-Shaḥar, a public building was partly excavated by P. L. O. Guy and attributed by him to the Persian period. Although the structure is preserved in fragmentary form and only a small part has been excavated, as indicated by R. Reich, the remains reveal a close similarity to the plan of Assyrian palaces, such as the one in Arslan-Tash.

In all likelihood, the structure which Guy associated with the Persian period is an Assyrian palace contemporary with stratum III of the upper city. It is similar to the strata III–II citadel of area B in the upper city and, like the latter, continued in use in the Persian period. If this is indeed the case, it may be assumed that during the Assyrian period the citadel alone existed in the upper city, while the settlement and the palace were located on the plain northeast of the mound.

AMNON BEN-TOR

STRATIFICATION AT HAZOR

Upper City	*Lower City*	*Period (BCE)*	*Remarks*
I	No longer settled	Hellenistic (3rd–2nd cent.)	Citadel
II		Persian (4th cent.)	Citadel, graves
III		Assyrian (7th cent.)	Citadel
IV		8th cent.	Unfortified settlement
V		8th cent.	Destruction by Tiglath-pileser III, 732 BCE
VI		8th cent.	City of Jeroboam II, destruction by earthquake
VII		9th cent.	Reconstruction of parts of stratum VIII
VIII		9th cent.	Omrid dynasty
IX		End 10th–beginning 9th cent.	Conflagration (Ben-hadad I)
X		Mid-10th cent.	City of Solomon
XI		11th cent.	Limited Israelite settlement
XII		12th cent.	Temporary Israelite settlement, seminomadic
XIII	1-a	13th cent.	Destruction in second half of 13th cent. by Israelite tribes
XIV	1-b	14th cent.	El-Amarna period
XV	2	15th cent.	Thutmose III–Amenhotep II
Post–XVI		16th cent.	Graves in the ruined city
XVI	3	17th–16th cent.	Destruction by conflagration (Ahmose)
XVII	4	18th–17th cent.	Lower city founded in mid-18th cent. BCE (Mari documents)
Pre–XVII	Not yet founded	Beginning 18th cent.	Unfortified; many burials and some structures
XVIII		22nd–21st cent.	Small quantity of pottery
XIX		25th–24th cent.	Remains of structures (post–Khirbet Kerak culture)
XX		27th–26th cent.	Remains of structures
XXI		29th–28th cent.	Khirbet Kerak culture; poorly preserved remains of structures

General publications and identification: J. L. Porter, *Handbook for Travellers in Syria and Palestine*, London 1875, 414–415; J. Garstang, *PEQ* 59 (1927), 224–225; Y. Yadin, *Antiquity and Survival* 2 (1957), 165–186; id., *Archaeology* 10 (1957), 83–92; id., *Guildhall Lectures* 1962, 7–26; id., *The Biblical Archaeologist Reader* 2 (eds. E. F. Campbell, Jr., and D. N. Freedman), Garden City, N.Y. 1964, 191–224; id., *Archaeology and Old Testament Study* (ed. D. W. Thomas), Oxford 1967, 244–263; id., *Hazor: The Head of All Those Kingdoms* (Schweich Lectures 1970), London 1972; id., *BTS* 156 (1973), 8–14; id., *Hazor: The Rediscovery of a Great Citadel of the Bible*, New York 1975; O. Tufnell, *PEQ* 91 (1959), 90–105; J. Gray, *VT* 16 (1966), 26–52; Weippert 1988 (Ortsregister).
Early reports: Y. Yadin, *BA* 19 (1956), 1–12; 32 (1969), 49–71; id., *IEJ* 6 (1956), 120–125; 7 (1957), 118–123; 8 (1958), 1–14; 9 (1959), 74–88; 19 (1969), 1–19; (with Y. Shiloh) 21 (1971), 230; id., *RB* 67 (1960), 371–375; 76 (1969), 550–557; 78 (1971), 584–585.
Main publications: Y. Yadin et al., *Hazor* 1–4, *An Account of the First Season of Excavations*, Jerusalem 1955. — Second Season, 1956. — Third and Fourth Seasons, 1957–1958, pls. (The James A. de Rothschild Expedition at Hazor), Jerusalem 1958–1961; Third and Fourth Seasons 1957–1958, text (ed. A. Ben-Tor), Jerusalem 1989.
Late Bronze Age: P. Bienkowski, *PEQ* 119 (1987), 50–61; G. C. Grindstaff, "An Analysis of Five Late Bronze Age Cities in the Ancient Mediterranean World" (Ph.D. diss., Oklahoma 1988).
Iron Age I: J. Garstang, *Joshua–Judges*, London 1931; B. Mazar, *HUCA* 24 (1952–1953), 80ff.; F. Mass, *Von Ugarit nach Qumran* (ZAW Beiheft 77), Berlin 1958, 108ff.; Y. Aharoni, *BAR* 1/4 (1975), 3–4, 26; Y. Yadin, ibid. 2/1 (1976), 3ff.; 8/2 (1982), 25–36; id., *ASOR Symposia* (ed. F. M. Cross, Jr.), Cambridge, Mass. 1979, 57–68; W. E. Rast, *EI* 20 (1989), 166*–173; W. G. Dever, *BASOR* 277–278 (1990), 121–130; G. J. Wightman, ibid., 5–28.
Iron Age II–III: Y. Yadin, *IEJ* 8 (1958), 80–86; W. G. Dever, *BA* 32 (1969), 71–78; K. M. Kenyon, *Royal Cities of the Old Testament*, London 1971, 53–58; R. Reich, *IEJ* 25 (1975), 233–237; D. Cole, *BAR* 6/2 (1980), 8–29; D. Milson, *ZDPV* 102 (1986), 87–92; Y. Shiloh, *Archaeology and Biblical Interpretation* (D. Glenn Rose Fest.), Atlanta 1987, 207–209; S. Geva, *Hazor, Israel: An Urban Community of the 8th Century B.C.E.* (*BAR*/IS 543), Oxford 1989; O. Lipschitz, *TA* 19 (1990), 69–99; E. Stern, *IEJ* 40 (1990), 12–30.
Temples and cult: W. F. Albright, *VT Supplement* 4 (1957), 242–258; K. Galling, *ZDPV* 75 (1959), 1–13; Y. Yadin, *NEAT*, 200–231; H. Shanks, *IEJ* 23 (1973), 234–235; M. Ottosson, *Temples and Cult Places in Palestine* (Uppsala Studies in Ancient Mediterranean and Near Eastern Civilizations 12), Uppsala 1980; P. Beck, *IEJ* 33 (1983), 78–80; id., *TA* 17 (1990), 91–95.
Epigraphical finds: W. W. Hallo and H. Tadmor, *IEJ* 27 (1977), 1–11; H. Tadmor, ibid., 98–102; J. Naveh, *EI* 15 (1981), 85*; *Buried History* 27 (1991), 91–93.
Hazor in ancient documents: A. Malamat, *JBL* 79 (1960), 12ff.; id., *BA* 46 (1983), 169–174; id., *2nd International Congress on Bibilical Archaeology 24 June–4 July 1990: Abstracts*, Jerusalem 1990, 17; id., *Mari and the Early Israelite Experience* (Schweich Lectures of the British Academy 1984), Oxford 1989, 55–69; id., *Reflets de Deux Fleuves* (A. Finet Fest.), Leuven 1989, 117–118.

HEBRON

IDENTIFICATION AND HISTORY

Hebron is the capital of the part of the Judean Hills that lies south of Jerusalem and was the major city of the region during most of its history. Its association with the patriarchs and King David's choice of it as his first capital have made it a major biblical site.

The only information about ancient Hebron comes from the Bible, where it is also called Kiriath-Arba and Mamre. These names are commonly considered evidence that the town was divided into quarters (*arba'*, or "four," in Hebrew) or clans. Various locations are mentioned as being in the Hebron region: Elonei (oaks of) Mamre, the Eshcol and Hebron valleys, and the Cave (field) of Machpelah. Hebron and the Cave of Machpelah play a central role in the patriarchal narratives, particularly in the traditions about Abraham (Gen. 13:18, 14:13, 18:1, 23:1–20, 25:9–10), but scholars differ as to the periods reflected by these narratives. The ancient formulation of the Caleb tradition mentions the inhabitants of Canaanite Hebron, "Ahiman, Sheshai, and Talmai, the descendants of Anak" (Num. 13:22). These persons were probably members of a tribal unit, associated by some scholars with the Amorite unit *y'nq*, mentioned in sources from the second millennium BCE. The statement in the second part of Numbers 13:22, "Hebron was built seven years before Zoan in Egypt," was once thought to indicate that the founding of Hebron was contemporaneous with the Hyksos period in Egypt; more recently, it has been suggested that the verse refers to David's choice of Hebron as his capital, at approximately the same time as the establishment of the Egyptian city of Zoan during the Twenty-first Dynasty.

The conquest of Hebron is attributed variously to Joshua and the Israelites in general (Jos. 10:36–37), to the tribe of Judah (Jg. 1:10) or to Caleb (Jos. 14:13–15); the Calebite tradition is apparently the most authentic. After the Calebites had defeated the Anakites and settled in the Hebron region, they played a major role in the consolidation of the tribe of Judah. Levites were also among those who settled at Hebron: the Hebronites were one of the most important Levite families, and Hebron was a city of refuge and a Levitical city (Jos. 21:11–13; 1 Chr. 6:55–57).

David was crowned king of Judah at Hebron, which served as his royal capital for seven years, until he moved to Jerusalem (2 Sam. 2:3–4, 5:5). It was in Hebron that Absalom rebelled against his father. The biblical account seems to imply that there was a temple at Hebron (as Absalom's excuse

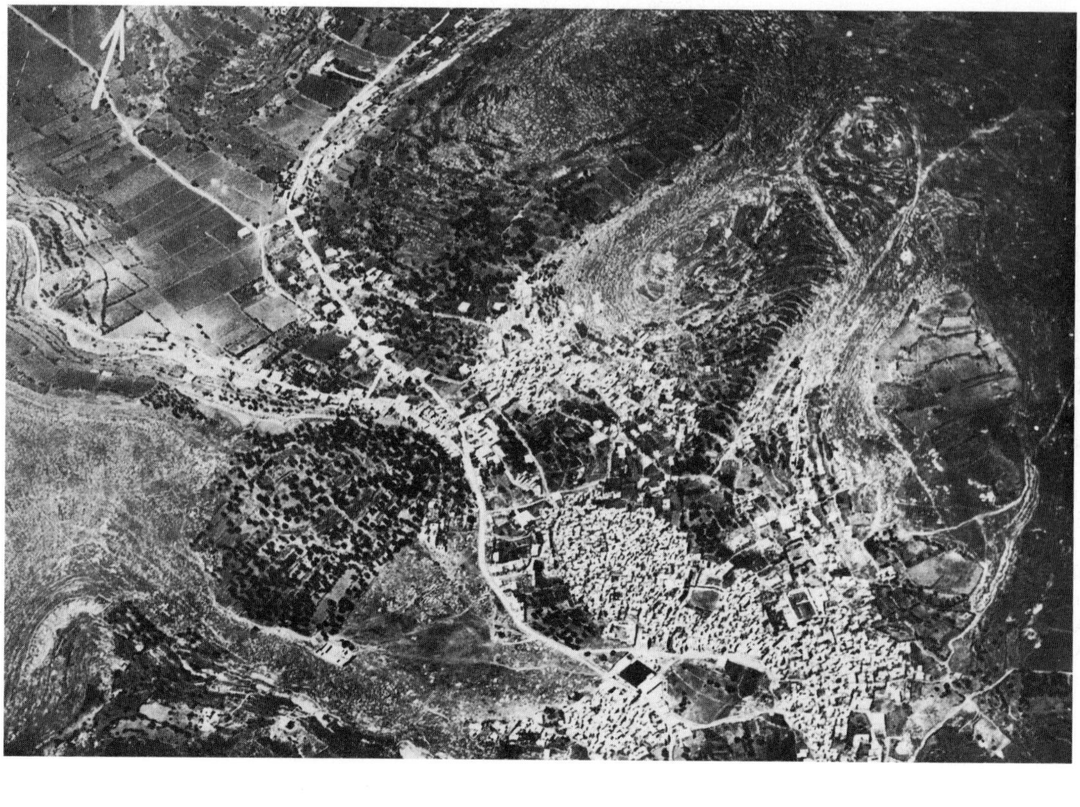

Hebron: 1918 aerial photograph; the mound is seen at the bottom left.

for going to Hebron was the need to "pay his vow" (2 Sam. 15:7–12). Hebron is mentioned again in the list of "cities for defense" whose fortification is attributed to Rehoboam (2 Chr. 11:5–12), but it should probably be dated to a late phase in the period of the monarchy. Hebron is mentioned in Hezekiah's time in the *lamelekh* seal impressions, and some scholars consider this evidence that the city was at that time an administrative and economic center. It appears once again in the list of cities of Judah (Jos. 15:54), which is commonly dated to the reign of Josiah. The last biblical reference to Kiriath-Arba is in the list of cities in the Book of Nehemiah (11:25), but the significance and date of that list are unclear.

Hebron is referred to again in sources from the time of Judas Maccabaeus, who occupied it in the course of his war in Idumea (1 Macc. 5:65). During the Jewish Revolt against the Romans, Simeon Bar Giora conquered Hebron, but Vespasian reoccupied the city and burned it to the ground (Josephus, *War* IV, 529, 554). Eusebius describes Hebron as a "very large village" (*Onom.* 6:8). In the Byzantine period, both Christian and Jewish pilgrims visited Hebron. The pilgrim of Placenta describes the basilica containing the tombs of the patriarchs, and the religious ceremonies held by the Jews and the Christians on opposite sides of a partition wall (Antoninus Placentinus, *Itinerarium* 30, *CCSL* 175, 144). The bishop Arculf, who visited Hebron after the Arab conquest (in c. 680), describes the town as having been half destroyed: it had no wall and its inhabitants lived in scattered clusters of houses. The houses of the partriarchs, however, had not been damaged (Adamnanus, *De Locis Sanctis* II, VIII–X; *CCSL* 175, 209–210). Thereafter, the city is frequently mentioned in various sources from the Early Arab period, the Crusader period (when it was the seat of the Latin bishop), the Mameluke period, and the Ottoman period.

THE MAJOR SITES: THEIR IDENTIFICATION AND EXPLORATION

There are several archaeological sites in the vicinity of the ancient nucleus of Hebron.

1. Tel Hebron, located on a low spur of Jebel Rumeida, is the main site of the Bronze and Iron Age city. Biblical Hebron should be identified here.

2. Ḥaram el-Khalil is a monumental structure from Second Temple times, built on a slope opposite Tel Hebron, on a site commonly identified with the Cave of Machpelah. A variety of evidence indicates the presence of several shaft tombs, dating to the Middle Bronze Age I and perhaps also the Iron Age, beneath the Ḥaram and in its environs. The structure itself is undoubtedly from the Second Temple period, but its construction is unattested in the sources. It is commonly attributed to Herod the Great, although some scholars date it even earlier. Over the years the building has undergone various modifications and additions; it has served at different times as a church and as a mosque.

3. The city of Hebron lies in the Valley of Hebron, between Tel Hebron and Ḥaram el-Khalil. This is probably the site of Hebron from the Second Temple period onward.

4. A large building from the Persian period stands on Jebel Nimra, which some believe preserves the name of ancient Mamre.

Farther away from the ancient nucleus, although still within modern Hebron, are the following sites:

5. Ḥaram Ramet el-Khalil, a monumental enclosure, identified by some authorities with Mamre (q.v.).

6. Khirbet en-Naṣara (Ruin of the Christians), a site whose beginnings are dated to the Iron Age, but whose main occupation occurred during the Byzantine and Early Arab periods (its old Arabic name was apparently Majdal Bani Fadil).

7. Jebel Baṭrak (Patriarch's Hill) is another Byzantine and Early Arab site.

Tel Hebron (erroneously called Tell er-Rumeida) was identified and surveyed in the 1920s by W. F. Albright, A. E. Mader, and F. M. Abel. From 1964 to 1966 an American expedition led by P. C. Hammond excavated at the site. Since 1984 the mound has been excavated by the Judean Hills Survey Expedition, directed by A. Ofer with the assistance of G. Suleimani. Ḥaram el-Khalil has been described by many excavators, but no systematic examination of the remains under the building has ever been possible, nor a fortiori any excavation at the site. Neither have any proper excavations been conducted within the city of Hebron itself. The sites of Jebel Nimra and Mamre have recently been excavated by I. Magen on behalf of the Israel Department of Antiquities and Museums.

Hebron: Ḥaram el-Khalil (Cave of Machpelah).

TEL HEBRON

Tel Hebron lies on a secondary spur of Jebel Rumeida, overlooking the city of Hebron from the south. The first settlement was established near a spring ('Ein Judeida) and near an area of cultivated plots in the Hebron Valley. Topographically, the mound is not easily defensible, as it is dominated on the southwest by Jebel Rumeida. The debris on the mound covers an area of some 17 a., but the area of the ancient city was probably not more than 12 a.

The renewed excavations at Hebron were based on a central section (area S), intended to cut through the entire mound and determine its stratigraphical sequence. Thanks to the Middle Bronze Age city wall, it is possible to associate the other excavated areas, as well as some of the areas excavated by Hammond, with the section and its strata.

Area S. A stratigraphical sequence from the Early Arab period, Byzantine period (two phases), Roman period, Hellenistic period, Iron Age II (two phases), Iron Age IIA–IB (two phases), Iron Age I, and Middle Bronze Age has so far been exposed in area S. The excavators have reached the top of an as yet unexcavated stratum, that dates to the end of the Early Bronze Age.

The most important structure in this area, ascribed to the Middle Bronze Age, is situated near the city wall. One room was used to collect ashes, animal bones, and potsherds. Also discovered in this room was document TH1: a well-baked clay tablet, inscribed in Akkadian cuneiform, including a list of animals, most probably offered as sacrifices. Also mentioned in the tablet are the names of four people and possibly also a king. The animals listed include only sheep and goats; this complies with the great quantity of bones found at the site, most of which are from sheep and goats. The pottery uncovered here appears to represent a broad range of phases of the Middle Bronze Age. Discovered near the document was a bulla with scarab impressions from the time of the Twelfth Dynasty in Egypt; the finds in a nearby room included a socketed ax from the same period.

Area I3 (Southern City Wall). Exposed in area I3 was the Middle Bronze Age city wall, which rose to a height of more than 2 m above the surface even before excavations began. Outside the wall the excavators reached bedrock, on which an Early Bronze Age I stratum was found. Incorporated in the wall from the

Tel Hebron: Akkadian cuneiform tablet with a list of animals, 17th–16th centuries BCE *(front and side views).*

inside was a fortified tower that exhibited evidence of repairs and repeated use during the Iron Age.

Area G. In area G, in the western part of the mound, a large building, whose beginnings go back to the Hellenistic period, was uncovered. Its outer wall was excavated by Hammond as area I7 and first mistakenly identified as part of the Middle Bronze Age wall. The structure continued in use in the Roman period, during which it was destroyed twice, probably in the first and second centuries CE. Its walls were reused in the Byzantine period. Also exposed here was the outer face of the Middle Bronze Age wall, against which a stone glacis was later built. Area G presents the easiest access to the mound. The excavators found indications of a rock-hewn fosse, and the city gate may have stood here as well.

Area F (Northern City Wall). Area F yielded the continuation of the Middle Bronze Age wall. Outside the wall was a revetment, which should probably be dated to the eleventh and tenth centuries BCE. If that is indeed the case, it would prove that the Iron Age city expanded beyond the limits of the Middle Bronze Age walls.

Area W. Hebron's water source, 'Ein Judeida (New Spring), is in area W (in the eastern and lowest part of the mound). The spring, whose water remains very cold throughout the year, was originally a surface groundwater spring. As the area of the spring was buried under debris accumulating from the mound, a domed structure was built over the site (in the Middle Ages?). Debris continued to accumulate on top of the dome, to the extent that today the spring seems to be flowing from a cave. A massive wall built at the inner end of the spring pool may be concealing a water system hewn inside the mound, but this is a conjecture that requires further research.

Area I1. Hammond excavated area I1 (east of area S), uncovering levels from the Early Bronze Age I, Middle Bronze Age, Iron Age I, and Iron Age II. He reported the discovery of a well-built pillared house from the Iron Age II.

Area I4. One terrace below area I1 is area I4. Here Hammond reported the presence of Arab buildings, overlying earlier remains, down to the Early Bronze Age I.

Area I6. The only area excavated to date on the acropolis of the mound is area I6. It presented the stratigraphical sequence regularly found at Tel Hebron. Particularly noteworthy is the rich and dense occupation during the Iron Age. Hammond also found here a scarab of Ramses II, but until his excavations become fully published, the level to which the scarab should be assigned remains unknown.

Area I2. A group of buildings which Hammond ascribed to the Early Arab period belongs to area I2 (the eastern part of the mound). He also reported a complete sequence (at least in terms of pottery) of the other known periods of the mound, and similarly in area I5 (in the southwest of the mound).

Hammond's expedition also exposed some burial caves, mainly in the southeastern part of the mound. Some of them date to the Early Bronze Age I. (Hammond also reported a dwelling cave from this period.) He reported continuous occupation for one burial cave from the Middle Bronze Age through the Late Bronze Age (including Cypriot pottery) and perhaps also the Iron Age I.

Also noteworthy is Deir el-Arba'in, a building at the summit of the mound, built on Byzantine foundations; the superstructure is probably later, perhaps from the Crusader period. Since the Middle Ages, popular tradition has identified the building with the tombs of Ruth and Jesse (David's father), but there is no basis for this identification.

SUMMARY. The earliest known occupation of the mound was in the Early Bronze Age I, as part of a wave of settlement that occurred throughout the entire hill region. However, the only remains of this stratum exposed so far are a few sections of walls and rock shelters that apparently also served as dwellings.

Settlement continued through the Early Bronze Age II–III, but no remains have been excavated as yet. It is not clearly understood whether the site was completely abandoned during the Intermediate Bronze Age (Middle Bronze Age I). In any event, the shaft tombs within the modern city limits testify that the area was at the very least a tribal-nomadic center, like other sites in the hill region.

During the Middle Bronze Age II the site was occupied by a fortified city, some 6 to 7 a. in area, surrounded by a cyclopean wall. This city was the major settlement in the Judean Hills during the Middle Bronze Age. The cuneiform tablet dated to this period testifies to the city's central role in the administration, apparently as the capital of a kingdom. The list of animals in the tablet, together with the bones found in the area, indicate that the local inhabitants were shepherds. The proper names on the tablet indicate a West Semitic (Amorite) population, with a Hurrian minority.

During the Late Bronze Age, the city of Hebron was abandoned; however, a tribal population continued to bury its dead in the environs, and even on the outskirts of Tel Hebron. It is possible that a small part of the site itself, besides serving as a necropolis, was also used for residential purposes. However, it would seem that during the Late Bronze Age there was no large, permanent

Jar handle stamped with the inscription למלך חברן *([belonging] to the king / Ḥbrn).*

settlement on the site. The permanent occupation of Hebron was resumed in the first phase of Iron Age I, apparently by the tribal unit known as the Calebites. Judging from the finds, it is unlikely that Hebron was a fortified town on the eve of the Israelite settlement. This detail in the Calebite tradition is probably etiological, a conjecture on the part of a late writer, who was probably familiar with the ancient cyclopean walls of Hebron and associated them with the tradition telling of the war with the Anakites. In fact, parts of these walls are still visible on the mound; in the Iron Age they rose to an even greater height and were probably a familiar sight and may well have been reused. The glacis (if such existed) was partly destroyed before the Iron Age.

The next occupational level at Tel Hebron represents the zenith of the city's history, between the eleventh century and the end of the tenth century BCE. During that time the city probably extended beyond the line of the Middle Bronze Age walls. The latter were presumably used as fortifications for the upper sector of the city. Historically speaking, this golden age at Hebron reflects the city's position as a tribal and religious center for the people of the Judean Hills and the first royal capital of King David.

In the later part of the Iron Age, Hebron's importance declined; the remains exposed from this phase are fragmentary. Hammond's excavations probably exposed more abundant evidence from the period of the monarchy, but it has not been published. The precise history of Hebron during that period, including the date of its final destruction, is unclear. An important find from the time of the monarchy are five *lamelekh* seal impressions on storage jar handles. All five feature the two-winged symbol, and the two inscribed ones include the name Hebron. Notably, of the four cities named in the *lamelekh* seal impressions, Hebron is the only one that has also been confidently identified and excavated; hence, the considerable significance of the find.

During the Persian period Tel Hebron was completely abandoned; in subsequent periods the city shifted to its present location in the valley, at the foot of the mound. As the city of Hebron has not been excavated, it cannot be determined whether occupation of the area actually began during the Persian period.

Occupation of the mound was resumed in the Hellenistic period, but most probably as a suburb of the city now located in the valley. During the Roman period, settlement in this area flourished; to this period are dated pool installations of an as yet undetermined (industrial?) nature. Two violent destruction levels belong to this period. The first should probably be associated with Vespasian's burning of Hebron, the second perhaps with the Bar-Kokhba Revolt. The remains from the Byzantine period comprise two phases, and occupation continued into the Umayyad, Crusader, and Mameluke periods. Only in the Ottoman period was the mound completely abandoned.

A. Ofer, *ESI* 3 (1984), 94–95; 5 (1986), 92–93; 6 (1987–1988), 92–93; M. Anbar and N. Na'aman, *TA* 13–14 (1986–1987), 3–12.

AVI OFER

ḤEFER, TEL

IDENTIFICATION

Tel Ḥefer (Tell el-Ifshar) is situated on the northern side of the Alexander River breach through the eastern *kurkar* ridge in the central Sharon Plain, about 4 km (2.5 mi.) from the Mediterranean coast (map reference 1976.1415). The site is strategically located on one of the coastal routes and at the farthest inland point navigable for river traffic. In this region, the flood plain of the Alexander River Valley broadens, so that the site is surrounded by rich alluvial soils. There was also a number of small freshwater springs in the vicinity that have dried up as a result of modern water usage. Together, these natural resources enabled its inhabitants to make it one of the largest and most important sites in the central Sharon Plain. The mound is more than 11 a. in area and consists of a high terrace on the south and a lower, narrower terrace on the north. The highest point on the mound is 22.5 m above sea level and approximately 15 m above its surroundings.

Tell el-Ifshar was first mentioned by the surveyors of the British Palestine Exploration Fund when they investigated the area in 1872. In the early 1930s, B. Mazar surveyed the area; he was followed, three decades later, by R. Gophna. Since 1979, the mound has been excavated by the 'Emeq Ḥefer Archaeological Research Project, on behalf of the State University of New York at Buffalo and the Israel Antiquities Authority, joined in various seasons by The Brooklyn Museum (New York), The Jewish Museum (New York City), Rutgers University (Newark, New Jersey), and the College of DuPage (Glenn Ellyn, Illinois). The project is directed by S. M. Paley and Y. Porath.

The ancient name of the site is unknown. Mazar suggested that it could be identified with the kingdom of Hepher conquered by Joshua (Jos. 12:17), as part of the Solomonic administrative district (1 Kg. 4:10), or as one of the Manassehite clans (Num. 26:33; Jos. 17:2–3, passim). He later identified the area with the "Land of Hepher" (1 Kg. 4:10). Other researchers (W. F. Albright and, more recently, A. Zertal and Y. Porath) do not place the biblical Hepher in the Sharon Plain but on the mountain of Manasseh. S. Applebaum suggested that the mound's Roman-Byzantine remains were of Kefar Parshai, a Samaritan village mentioned in the Talmud (B.T., *A.Z.* 31a, 71a). The modern name of the site remains in archaeological literature as a courtesy to current popular usage.

The only extra-biblical textual source that may mention the area in the Late

Tel Ḥefer: general view of the mound, looking west.

Tel Ḥefer: map of the mound and excavation areas.

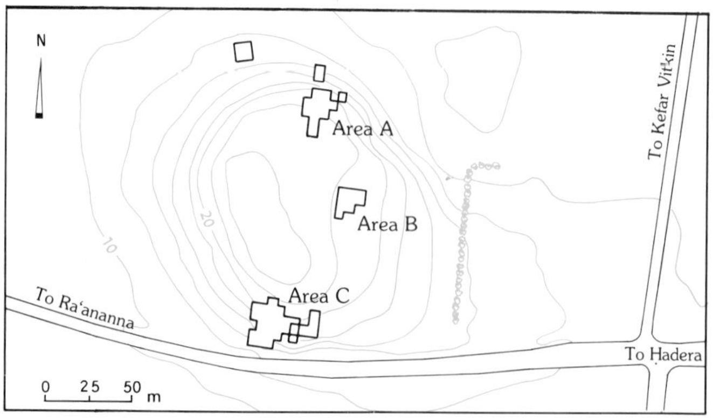

Ma'barot: pottery assemblage, MB I.

Bronze Age is in the account of a military campaign by Pharaoh Amenhotep II (1447–1421 BCE) in the ninth year of his reign. The text describes a raid by the Egyptian army from its camp at Yaḥam (Khirbet Yamma, north of Tulkarm), into the region of the settlements Khttjen and Mepsen, where booty was seized. However, there is no proof that either of the two names is to be located at Tel Ḥefer.

EXCAVATIONS

Excavations were conducted in three areas on the mound: area A on the southwest slope; area B in the center of the mound, at the juncture of the upper and lower terraces; and area C on the eastern slope. During the course of the excavations, it became clear that the present-day slopes on the southwest and east were inside the boundaries of the ancient settlement at its greatest extension. Natural erosion as well as soil quarrying, principally during the Byzantine period, reduced the overall size of the site.

THE EARLY BRONZE AGE. The earliest settlement was established on the crest of the southeastern part of the *kurkar* ridge on which the mound later took form. Its remains, found only in area C, include foundations of walls, fragments of floors, and concentrations of broken pottery. Bowls, platters, jugs and juglets, hole-mouth jars, and pithoi, all dating to the Early Bronze Age IB, were discovered. Burnt sherds of several large, flat-based pithoi, crescent-shaped mud bricks (fired in the destruction), and a significant amount of charred lentil were found in a pile of settlement debris. It seems that the debris belonged to an Early Bronze Age IB storage installation (round silo?/apsidal building?) that had been pushed down the slope by later inhabitants of the mound. Finds from the later stages of the Early Bronze Age have not been revealed.

THE MIDDLE BRONZE AGE I. Between the Early Bronze Age IB and Middle Bronze Age II remains a few pottery sherds were found from the Middle Bronze Age I, proof that some sort of human activity (burial or small settlement) occurred at the site during that time. It is somehow related to that of other Middle Bronze Age I sites in the vicinity. A Middle Bronze Age I cemetery, cut into the *kurkar* ridge 1 km (0.6 mi.) south of the mound, was investigated at Kibbutz Ma'barot by S. Dar and R. Gophna. Another Middle Bronze Age I burial cave was a chance find made at Moshav Eliashib, north of the mound. There are two Middle Bronze Age I settlements 5 km (3 mi.) east of the site; the one on the left bank of the Alexander River was investigated by S. Dar, and the one on the right bank of its tributary, Naḥal 'Omeẓ, was surveyed by E. Yannai.

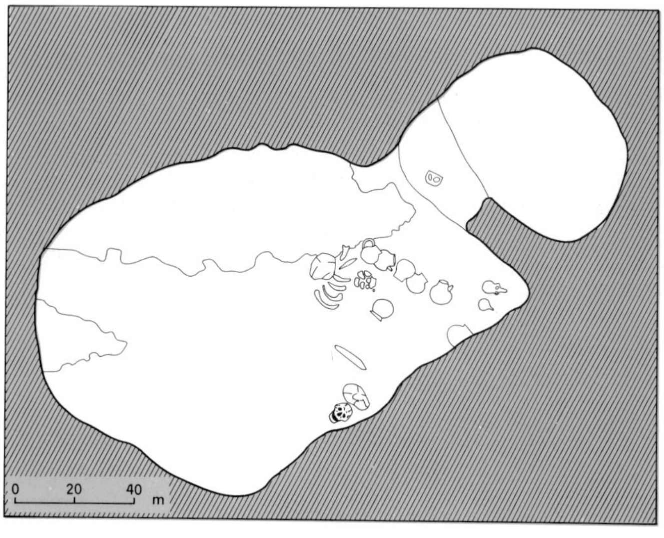

Ma'barot: plan of the tomb.

THE MIDDLE BRONZE AGE IIA. The Middle Bronze Age IIA is the best represented on the mound. Well-stratified remains have been excavated on both the western and eastern parts of the mound (areas A and C, respectively).

The remains of eight distinct phases of this period (C/A–H) are superimposed in area C. They can be dated from the very earliest stages of the Middle Bronze Age IIA in Canaan. These remains are partly disturbed by Late Bronze Age II and Byzantine pits. In some cases, burials of children and youths below the floors of later Middle Bronze IIA buildings interfere with earlier phases. In area A, four distinct phases were discovered (A/16–13), but there is as yet no real point of contact between the two areas for stratigraphic comparison.

The characteristic construction materials of the period were sun-dried mud bricks, about 60 by 40 by 11 cm in size, made in a form. Some of the bricks bear manufacturers' marks made with a finger while the bricks were still soft (a circle, "shepherds' crook," or lines). The bricks are made either out of a sandy soil and are brownish in color or out of alluvium and are blackish in color. There are three categories of wall widths—about 0.4 m, 0.6 m, and 1 m—relating to the arrangement of the bricks in the construction. The wider walls and some of the narrower ones were built on stone foundations. The walls were covered with mud plaster, sometimes painted over with a thin coat of red "paint" made from the local *ḥamra* soil or a white paint made from lime plaster. The floors were usually of beaten earth, but some were plastered, especially in the larger buildings. Courtyards were also built of beaten earth, although work stations could have been paved with flagstones or crushed *kurkar* mixed with sherds. Roofs were made of layers of mud and straw on a bed of reeds and branches laid across rafters that spanned the rooms. The roofs seem to be flat and pitched slightly, possibly to carry off rainwater. A typical residence consisted of a courtyard with one or two adjacent rooms. A *tabun* (cooking oven) was found in the courtyard, next to a wall, along with grinding and pounding stone tools used for preparing food.

Area C. The excavations in area C uncovered Middle Bronze Age IIA building remains over a 600-sq-m area. Eight superimposed phases were recorded, as follows:

PHASE C/A. This is the earliest phase of the Middle Bronze Age IIA. It

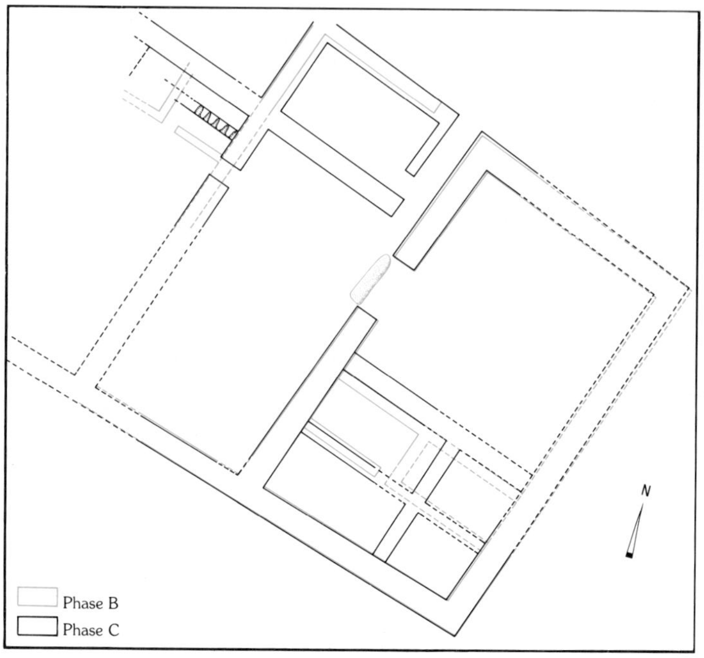

Plan of the public building, MB II.

Egyptian jar, MB IIA.

Painted vase from the pottery cache in area A, LB.

Hemispherical bead incised with Egyptian hieroglyphs, LB.

included short wall segments high on the slope, with a few associated patches of flooring and refuse pits together with the rest of the settlement's dump farther down the same slope. The wall segments are built into the virgin soil, as well as into soil mixed with sherds of Early Bronze and Middle Bronze Age I deposits. The finds in this phase can be dated to an early stage of the Middle Bronze Age IIA.

PHASE C/B. In phase C/B, a large building complex was constructed on the northeastern edge of the settlement. The complex has not yet been completely uncovered. The area excavated to its east and southeast was open and used as a dump into which many broken vessels, quantities of animal bone, and much other organic material were thrown. North of the building a broad space paved with crushed *kurkar* and sherds was discovered, perhaps a street. A paved area (alley?) to the south separated the building from other construction not yet excavated.

The building complex consists of an east and a west wing, each subdivided into rooms and courtyards. A grand courtyard separates them. The entrance to the complex was through a wide opening in the northern wall of the grand courtyard. A thick wall closed off the grand courtyard on the south. In front of the entrance to the east wing was a large *kurkar* block, about 2.2 by 0.65 by 0.2 m, used as a stepped threshold. The block is flat on one end and tapers on the other; its shape resembles the Middle Bronze Age IIA stelae at Gezer and Byblos. It may be in secondary use here and the possibility that it originated in a sacral context of phase C/A cannot be excluded.

The building was destroyed in a fire. Piles of debris from this destruction, 30 to 50 cm thick, which included charred wooden rafters from the roof, burnt bricks, and shattered ceramics, covered the floors of the courtyards and rooms. The remains of this structure and the quantity of finds in it suggest that it might have been a public building—either a "palace," a fort on the edge of the settlement, part of a cultic establishment, or a villa belonging to an important member of the community.

PHASE C/C. The building complex was rebuilt in phase C/C on a similar plan, except that the grand courtyard was divided by a wall across its northern end. Two rooms were excavated north of this wall: a large one oriented east–west and a small one oriented north–south. The smaller room served as an entrance corridor to the now smaller, grand courtyard, bypassing the larger room.

The west wing was only partially excavated. Its principal room, which was entered from the courtyard through a doorway, had a plastered floor 2 to 3 cm thick. This carefully prepared surface recalls the plastered floors in Middle Bronze Age II palaces, such as at Aphek and Kabri. The floor was repaired several times and then covered with successive layers of beaten earth. During the course of the use of these successive earthen floors, some pits were dug into them that penetrated the plastered floor. A round hole was also cut through the floor and a flat stone placed on its bottom. The hole was probably made to hold a wooden column.

A stepped installation was built next to the northern wall of the principal room. This installation belonged to a later stage in the use of the room because it rests above its plastered floor on a thin layer of beaten earth and later floors come up to it. Five depressions are preserved in the top of the lower step. The purpose of this installation is not clear, but it could have served as a platform at the northern end of the room for a bench, a "royal" seat, an offering table, or a plinth for one or more images.

The alley south of the large building that originated in phase C/B continued to be used. A few wall fragments and associated living surfaces excavated south of this alley can be attributed to this phase. Phase C/C was destroyed by fire, the signs of which could be seen everywhere on its latest living surfaces: collapsed roofs and mud brick from the walls, charred wooden rafters from the ceilings, and quantities of pottery broken in place.

PHASE C/D. After the destruction at the end of phase C/C, the large building was not rebuilt. In the destruction debris of phase C/C the hearths and storage and refuse pits from phase C/D were discovered, but no architecture. This phase is not yet represented in the excavation outside the limits of the building's site.

PHASE C/E. The phase C/E buildings were along the upper part of the eastern side of the mound. New construction encroached on the alley that once separated the large building from the rest of the settlement to the south. Parts of the thick walls of the large building were now rehabilitated. The southeast corner of the courtyard of the large building of phase C/C was transformed into a brick-built granary. Private houses existed to the south of the granary. The buildings of phase C/E were also destroyed by fire. The fire in the area of the granary was so intense that the sun-dried mud-brick walls were partially baked. A deposit of charred grains of emmer wheat remained on the floor of one compartment of the granary.

PHASES C/F AND C/G. The houses and living quarters of phase C/F now cover the whole eastern slope of the site. In phase C/F, the granary of phase C/E was turned into a courtyard with a *tabun*. The transition between phases C/F and C/G was not drastic. Generally, the plans of the buildings in these two phases are similar. The main changes were the rebuilding of collapsed walls, the raising of floors, the replacement of installations, and the repositioning of some of the doorways. In phase C/F, a schematized human figure made out of limestone was discovered on the floor of a courtyard, next to a broken *tabun*. Also, the grave of a young man, belonging to phase C/G, was found under the floor of one of the phase's jar-filled storage rooms.

In several places, above phase C/G, fragmentary wall sections, patches of living surface, and *tabun*s from another Middle Bronze Age IIA phase were discovered. This phase (C/H) is poorly preserved because of the damage caused by Late Bronze Age II and Byzantine period pits. No meaningful plans could be pieced together from these fragments of architecture.

Area A. Four phases were recorded in area A, as follows:

PHASES A/16 AND A/15. Phase A/16 was built on virgin soil. Both phases were uncovered in a stratigraphic test trench, 5 m wide, in which some living surfaces and fragments of walls were preserved. On the floors many broken storage jars and cooking pots and a few bowls were found, all of which can be dated to the early part of the Middle Bronze Age IIA.

PHASE A/14. Portions of a large building were discovered in phase A/14, constructed on top of the remains of phases A/16 and A/15. The building leaned against a thick brick wall built on the western edge of the mound. The wall's outer face had been destroyed when the slopes of the mound were eroded and mined in later periods.

PHASE A/13. Portions of another large building were discovered in phase A/13. The walls were built of dark-colored clay bricks, made of the soil at the bottom of the mound, and have no stone foundations. At the northern end of the building was a courtyard, at whose north side was a flight of stairs leading down toward an exit to the adjacent street. The sherds found on the floors of the rooms of the building were mostly bowls and pitchers, red-slipped and burnished, that belong to the "classical" stage of the period. It seems that phases A/16 and A/15 were characterized by regular houses, whereas the structures in A/14 and A/13 were larger and more splendid, perhaps public buildings or the houses of the well-to-do.

The Finds. In the excavations of the Middle Bronze Age IIA settlements, many finds were discovered on the floors of buildings and in the refuse on the flanks of the mound: pottery, stone tools, food remains, and a small number of metal objects.

It is possible to follow the development of the pottery types and their decoration in the Middle Bronze Age IIA. In the early phases, the surface decoration of most vessel types was confined to combing. Some storage jars had relief or incised rope decoration. Red-slip and burnishing—the classic decoration of the period—became common only in phase C/D and remained characteristic thereafter. Also, in the earliest phases (C/A to C/C), some of the jars were burnished but without slip. Some jars, jugs, and juglets from the early phases were painted with bands, circles, spirals, and net patterns in dark brown and red (sometimes on a white background). By phase C/E painted decoration gives way to a red-slipped, burnished surface treatment.

There were two different types of cooking pots: handmade, with a flat base and straight sides, and wheelmade, with a tall, ovoid body and molded rim. The shape of the handmade cooking pots changed very little throughout the period. The rims of the wheelmade pots were modified from simple, outturned, or gutter rims, into tube, or folded rims. (The axe-shaped rim developed from the latter to become the characteristic cooking pot rim in the Late Bronze and Early Iron Age.)

In the earliest phases (C/A and C/B), deep bowls were hemispherical and combed on the surface. The red-slipped and burnished hemispherical and carinated bowls started in phase C/C and became the characteristic bowl of phases C/E–C/H and A/14–A/13.

In the early phases, there were two major storage jar shapes, one rounded (and sometimes painted) and the other conical (and occasionally without handles). In the later phases, they were usually ovoid and with two handles. In the large building in phase C/B, three examples of a squat onion-shaped jar type were discovered. This shape, which is represented only in this phase, is a new form in the early Middle Bronze Age IIA assemblage and at this site. There was one burnished and painted jug in phase C/B with bands of cross-hatching and lozenges with net patterns. A vessel similar in shape and decoration was discovered in a tomb at Ras Shamra (Ugarit) and dated by C. F. A. Schaeffer to the Middle Bronze Age I. Neutron activation analysis showed that the Tel Ḥefer jug was not necessarily an import.

A bottle of Egyptian origin was discovered in a brick collapse in phase C/C. This was a typical vessel from the Twelfth Dynasty, of the so-called Qena ware. Many of them were found at el-Kab and Thebes in Egypt, with an ancestry dating back to at least the end of the Eleventh Dynasty. This bottle can be dated typologically to the first half of the nineteenth century BCE, during the reigns of either Senusert II (1897 to 1878 BCE) or Senusert III (1978 to 1843 BCE). Sherds of other Egyptian vessels of the same ware were found in dumps in phases C/B and C/C.

Summary. A comparison of the material culture recovered in the excavation of areas A and C suggests that phases C/A to C/C are similar to phases A/16 and A/15, and that C/E to C/H are similar to A/14 and A/13. The Middle Bronze Age IIA settlement on the mound increased in size in each succeeding phase (except for a local recession in phase C/D). The large public building in area C, phases C/B and C/C, went out of use before the large building in A/13 (and possibly A/14) was constructed. Comparisons with published, stratified material—specifically painted jars, jugs, and juglets—from other sites in Canaan show that phases C/A and C/B at Tel Ḥefer are contemporaneous with strata X-20 and X-19 (pre-palace) at Tel Aphek. The existence of imported pottery in phases C/B and C/C, if used as chronological indicators, suggests that the Middle Bronze Age IIA settlement at Tel Ḥefer was founded during the middle of the twentieth century BCE, if not earlier.

THE MIDDLE BRONZE AGE IIB. The Middle Bronze Age IIB is not well represented on the site. A few sherds from the early stages of the period were recovered (only a few Tell el-Yehudiyeh ware sherds and no Cypriot imports were found) but no building remains in either area.

THE LATE BRONZE AGE. Several strata of settlement from the Late Bronze Age were revealed in area A. In the earliest of them (phase A/11), only pits and dumps were preserved in the excavated area. In the next phase (A/10), dating to the end of the sixteenth or beginning of the fifteenth century BCE, a group of rooms was discovered adjoining a courtyard. In the courtyard were a silo and an oven. A storage room was the main structure in the succeeding phase, A/9. The room was built and destroyed three times (phases A/9–7) before the end of the period, about 1200 BCE. The last phase of the storeroom was destroyed by fire.

Many sherds were found from jars, cooking pots, bowls, lamps, juglets, including base-ring jars and "milk bowls" imported from Cyprus. Silver earrings and beads were among the finds. One bead, a hemispheroid, was incised with an Egyptian hieroglyph. It is possible that the loop in its center can be read as the *s3* or the *sn* sign, "protection." This would give the piece amuletic value. By combining *sn* with the letter *t*, it is also possible to read *snwt*, "granary." However, the latter writing would be highly unusual alone either on a seal or on an amulet. Bone inlays that had decorated a box were also unearthed in these Late Bronze Age levels, in addition to three Astarte figurines in terra cotta, two in area A and one in area C. A rich cache of pottery, dated to the middle of the fifteenth and fourteenth centuries BCE (Late Bronze IIA), was found at the bottom of a deep pit (*favissa*?). The Late Bronze Age is represented in area C only as homogeneous refuse pits (phase C/Y) and individual sherds that were mixed into the refuse pits of the Byzantine period.

The finds have not revealed either the perpetrators who brought the last phase to an end or the exact time: the campaigns of one of the Egyptian kings at the end of the Nineteenth or during the Twentieth Dynasty, the Sea Peoples, Israelite raiders from the hills of Manasseh, or a more local catastrophe.

THE IRON AGE. The Iron Age I is represented only in disturbed contexts and in a few pits and silos dug in the destruction of the Late Bronze Age (phase A/6). The vessel shapes found were cooking pots and collared-rim jars; a few sherds of Philistine pottery also were recovered. The Iron Age I pits were sealed from above by a thick fill (phase A/4) of Iron and Bronze Age detritus. This fill may have been spread to prepare a base for constructing buildings. The latest sherds from the fill date to the end of the tenth and the beginning of the ninth centuries BCE. The settlement (phase A/5) whose sherds were discovered in this fill has not been located. A house belonging to the settlement that prepared the fill was built on top of it (phase A/4). On its floors were typical eighth-century BCE sherds of juglets, decanters, and cooking pots. A silo was discovered beside the house, on the bottom of which were five basalt grinding stones and some charred grains of wheat.

THE PERSIAN AND HELLENISTIC PERIODS. No building remains from the Persian and Hellenistic periods were discovered. Nevertheless, many sherds dating to those periods were found in pits on the western slope (A/3 and A/2) and in disturbed contexts in areas A and C. These remains suggest that a small settlement in both periods existed on the unexcavated portions of the mound.

THE ROMAN AND BYZANTINE PERIODS. The settlements in the Roman and Byzantine periods are represented over a wide area of the mound. Their centers seem to have been on the mound's lower step. In the Byzantine period, the settlement also spread north and east outside the boundaries of the mound. The most important remains from these periods were revealed in area B, where a deep sounding uncovered two superimposed building phases (strata B/V and B/IV) dating from the late second to the early fourth centuries CE. Above them were three Byzantine strata, in the earliest of which (stratum B/III) were remains of a large residence and fragments of additional buildings. The foundations of these buildings were built of dressed stones and their floors were paved with stone slabs. On the floors were found fifth-century CE pottery, including oil lamps; objects made of wood, bone, and metal; and food remains, especially animal bones. Like the bones from the Roman levels, these were mostly of large and small cattle. This stratum was destroyed in the late fifth or the early sixth century CE.

General view of the Byzantine stratum.

Kefar Monash hoard: 1. spearheads; 2. daggers; 3. saw; 4. scales; 5. knives; 6. axes; 7. horn-shaped implement, EB II–III.

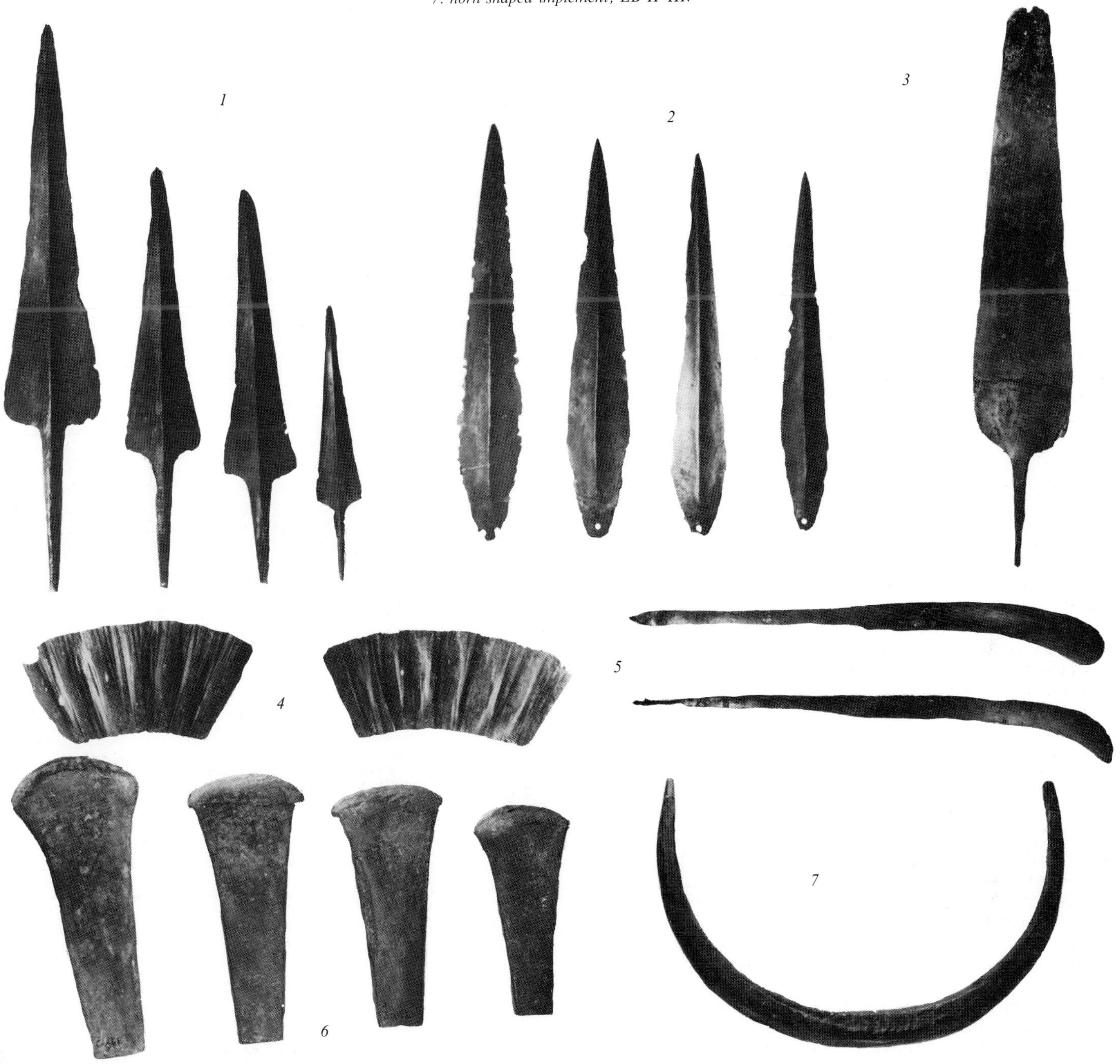

Most of the remains of the following phase (stratum B/II) are large pits that were dug into earlier Roman and Byzantine ones. A large quantity of pottery (mostly storage jars painted with white lines typical of the sixth century CE) were found with construction rubble and a large number of bones of domesticated animals, especially pigs. Many of the animals were killed between the ages of ten and fourteen months. In the latest Byzantine phase (stratum B/I), immediately below the surface, fragmentary walls were revealed that had been built above both the pits of stratum B/II and the building remains of stratum B/III not damaged by the pits. The characteristic remains found in the buildings in the latest stratum are similar to those from stratum II.

Northwest of the mound the remains of a winepress and a bathhouse were discovered. A second winepress was discovered on the southern slope of the mound. These can be dated to the Byzantine period but cannot be attributed to any one specific stratum.

Differences in diet between the inhabitants of strata B/I and B/II and strata B/III–B/V suggest that there was a change of population at the site. People who restricted their diet to kosher animals (Samaritans and Jews) seem to have been replaced by a Christian community in the sixth century CE. It could be that the change is somehow connected with the Samaritan revolt in 529 CE, in the wake of which many Samaritan settlements were destroyed. This is a well-documented phenomenon in the Sharon Plain. Occupation on the mound ended in the first half of the seventh century CE, when the latest Byzantine settlement was destroyed, possibly in a revenge raid mounted by the Samaritans at the time of the Persian conquest in 614, or as a result of the Arab conquest in 638.

COMPARATIVE TABLE—STRATIGRAPHY/CHRONOLOGY

Period/Level	*Area A*	*Area B*	*Area C*
Byzantine	1a: Pits, fills, and dumps	I: Wall fragments	Z: Pits, fills, and dumps
		II: Pits	
		III: Buildings	
Roman	1b: Pits, fills, and dumps	IV: Buildings	Y: Pits, fills, and dumps
		V: Buildings	
Hellenistic	2: Pits and fills		X: Sherds only
Persian	3: Pits and fills		W: Sherds only
Iron II	4: Buildings		V: Sherds only
	5: Fill/buildings		
Iron I	6: Pits and silos		U: Sherds only
LB II	7: Settlement		S: Pits, sherds
	8: Settlement		
	9: Settlement		
	10: Settlement		
LB I	11: Poor settlement		P: Pits, sherds
MB IIB	12: Few sherds		M: Few sherds
MB IIA	13: Public building		H: Dwellings
	14: Building (wall?)		G: Dwellings
			F: Dwellings
			E: Dwellings
			D: Pits, domestic installations in area of public building
	15: Dwellings		C: Public building, dwellings
	16: Occupation on virgin soil		B: Public building
			A: Squatters, dwellings(?)
MB I			Few sherds
EB I	17: Sherds		O: Squatters

Conder–Kitchener, *SWP* 2, 143; ibid., *Name List*, 176; W. F. Albright, *JPOS* 5 (1925), 17–54. B. Maisler (Mazar), *ZDPV* 58 (1935), 82; A. Malamat, *Scripta Hierosolymitana* 3 (1961), 218–231; Y. Porath and S. Paley, *IEJ* 29 (1979), 236–239; 30 (1980), 217–219; 32 (1982), 66–67; (and R. Stieglitz); 259–261; 33 (1983), 264–266; 34 (1984), 276–277; 35 (1985), 299–301; id., *ESI* 1 (1982), 42–43; 2 (1983), 46–47; 3 (1984), 44–45; 4 (1985), 49; 9 (1989–1990), 135–136; id. (et al.), *The History and Archaeology of Emek Hefer* (1985), 163–175; M. C. Chernoff, *The Archaeobotanical Material from Tell el-Ifshar, Israel* (Ph.D. diss., Brandeis Univ. 1988; Ann Arbor 1989); Weippert 1988, 147, 173, 229, 704.

SAMUEL M. PALEY, YOSEF PORATH

THE KEFAR MONASH HOARD

A hoard of thirty-seven copper tools and weapons from the Early Bronze Age II–III was discovered in the fields of Kefar Monash, about 3.4 km (2 mi.) southeast of Tel Ḥefer. The tools included axes, adzes, chisels, and a saw. The weapons include daggers and spearheads. In 1967, a rare crescentic copper axhead was discovered, 200 m north of the hill where the hoard was found.

R. Hestrin and M. Tadmor, *IEJ* 13 (1964), 265–288; C. A. Kay, ibid., 289–290; R. Gophna, ibid. 18 (1968), 47–49; S. Yeivin, *JNES* 27 (1968), 40–48; A. Ben-Tor, *IEJ* 21 (1971), 201–206; T. F. Watkins, *PEQ* 107 (1975), 53–63; S. Dar, *BAIAS* 9 (1989–1990), 46–52.

EDITORIAL BOARD

Arrowheads from the Kefar Monash hoard.

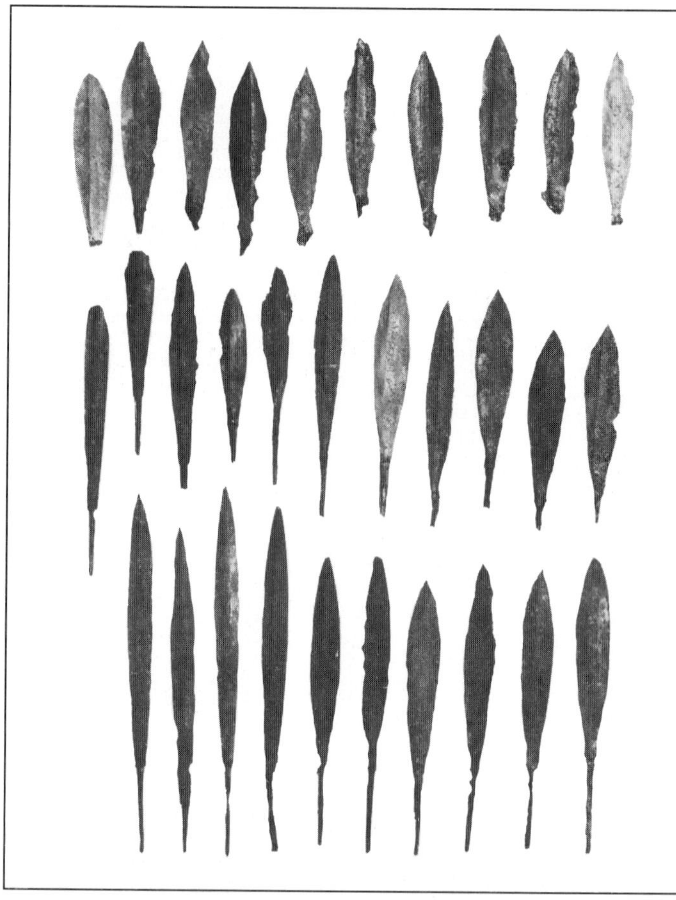

HEPTAPEGON ('EN SHEVA'; EṬ-ṬABGHA)

IDENTIFICATION

Heptapegon on the northwestern shore of the Sea of Galilee (map reference 2017.2532) is the site of the multiplication of loaves and fishes (Mt. 14:13–21; Mk. 6:34–44; Lk. 9:11–17; Jn. 6:1–14) The Arabic name eṭ-Ṭabgha derives from the Greek 'επτάπηγον, "(Land of) the Seven Springs." The area is first mentioned by the pilgrim Egeria in the late fourth century CE, who mentions a church on the site (Peter the Deacon, *De Locis Sanctis* V3, *CCSL* 175, 99). At the end of the fifth century St. Sabas made a pilgrimage to the holy place (Cyril of Scythopolis, *Life of St. Sabas*, ch. 24). Further mention of the site was made in Byzantine times in the intineraries of Theodosius (who visited Palestine in about 530) and Antoninus Placentinus (c. 570; *CCSL* 175, 115, 133). In the second half of the seventh century Arculf saw only ruins of the church of Heptapegon (Adamnanus, *De Locis Sanctis* II, XXIV; *CCSL* 175, 218). Later references to the site, in ninth century sources, seem to be to a different spot (Baldi, nos. 405–406).

The discoveries and the Arabic name are reliable evidence for the identification of the site. It appears that a chapel was erected here in the fourth century and a church built toward the middle of the fifth. The church probably was destroyed in the seventh century, at the time of the Persian or the Arab invasion, and soon forgotten (see Adamnanus).

EARLY EXCAVATIONS

The property, belonging to the Deutscher Verein vom heiligen Lande, was explored by Z. Biever at the end of the nineteenth century and by P. Karge in 1911. In 1932, A. E. Mader, assisted by A. M. Schneider, cleared the main remains. In 1936, the latter explored the earlier chapel.

CHURCH. The length of the church, court, and hospice complex was 56 m from north to south, 33 m on the west, and 24.3 m on the east. The church (25 by 19 m) was a basilica with a transept. The level of the prayer hall was 0.3 m above the narthex and 0.5 m above the atrium. The walls (0.6–0.95 m thick) are built on foundations 0.8–0.95 m wide and preserved to a height of 1.45 m. Except for the sills and stylobates (which were of white *mizzi* limestone), the complex was built of local, roughly dressed basalt, covered on the interior with mortar (a mixture of cement and lake sand), in which ribbed potsherds were set. The top layer was plaster mixed with straw and was painted red.

The church had a straight eastern wall. Between the eastern wall and the rear wall of the apse (1.2 m wide with a radius of 3.3 m) was a narrow corridor. The

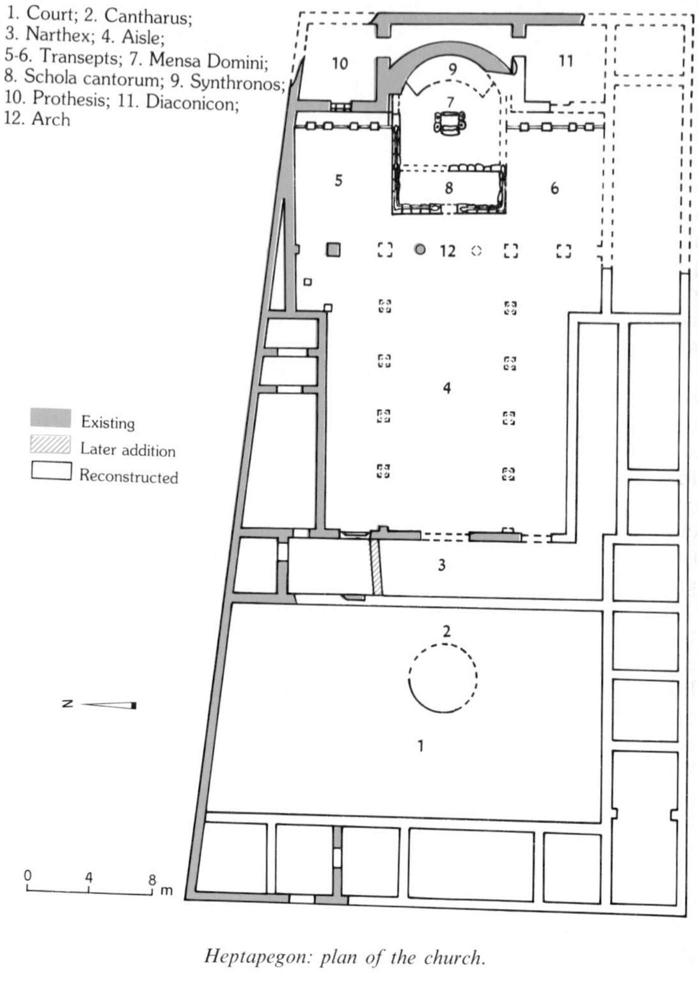

Heptapegon: plan of the church.

apse was flanked by two rooms. The presbytery (6.9 by 6 m) extended in front of the apse and was separated from the nave and transept by a chancel screen. The altar stands in front of the chord of the apsidal arch. It was shaped like a table, resting on four square legs. According to Peter the Deacon (who reports Egeria's description), the stone on which the Lord placed the bread had been made into an altar. People who went there took away small pieces of the stone to bring them prosperity. Below the table was a block of undressed limestone (1 by 0.6 by 0.14 m). Traces of a metal cross and the limestone's chipped appearance mark it as the traditional "mensa (table) of the Lord." Behind the altar, a semicircular seat (1.1 m wide) served as a synthronos for the clergy.

A transept projected 1.75 m on either side of the front of the presbytery. A row of four pillars separated the transept from the nave (7.9 m wide). The central two pillars bore an arch that collapsed in an earthquake. The central pillars were reset, with a narrower range for the two supporting the arch in the nave. This, and the enlarged chancel screen, were the main later additions.

Two aisles (each 3.58 m wide) were separated from the nave by two rows of five columns each, set 3.3 m apart. The main entrance was probably 3.2 m wide, and the aisle entrances, 1.85 m. A narthex (3.3 m wide) led to an atrium in the form of a rough trapezoid (23 by 13 m) surrounded by the rooms of a hospice on the east, south, and west. A diagonal wall, slightly below the level of an ancient road, closed the complex on the north. A cantharus (diameter, 5 m) stood in the center of the atrium.

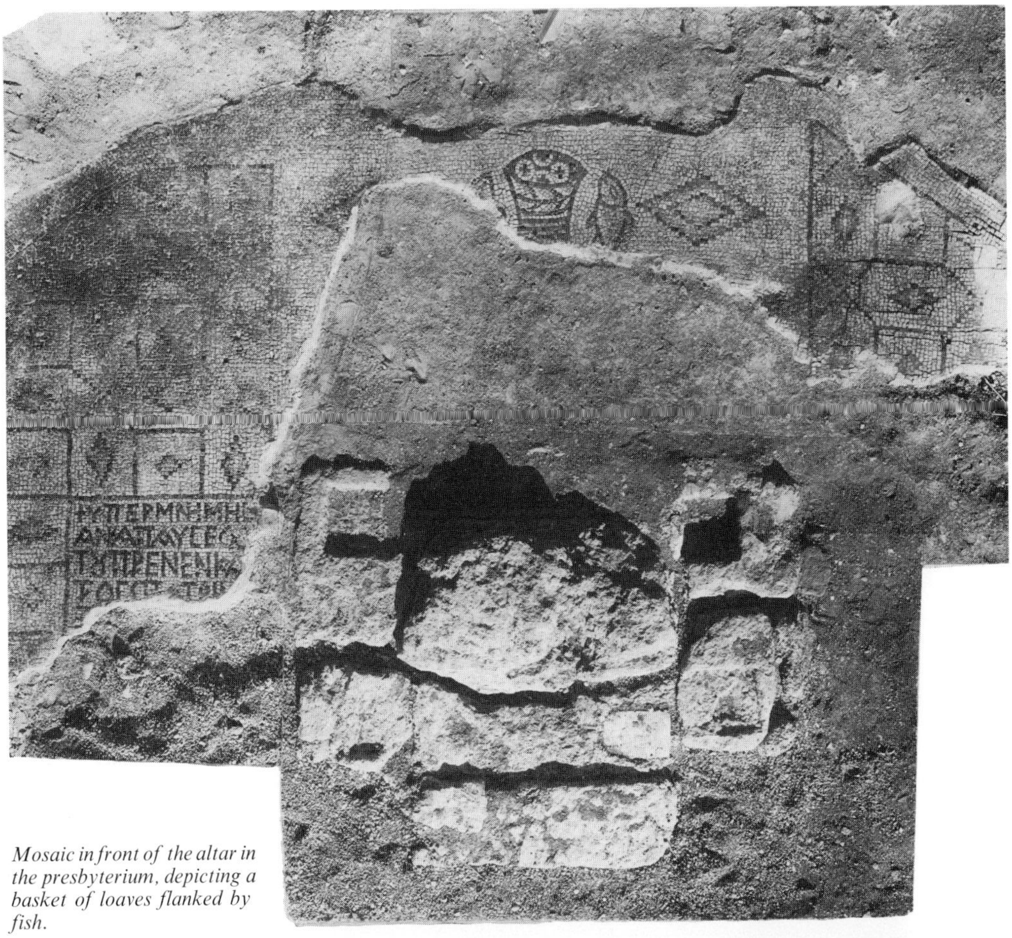

Mosaic in front of the altar in the presbyterium, depicting a basket of loaves flanked by fish.

An earlier chapel, orientated 28 degrees more to the south, was found below the basilical church. It measured 15.5 by 9.5 m, with an apse 2.6 m deep. This single room was roofed with beams from attached pillars 3 m apart and 1 m wide. Smaller finds included coins of Justin II (from 565 and 578), a fragment of a chancel screen, sixth-century clay lamps, and a reused Jewish epitaph of a certain Joseph.

MOSAICS. Of principal interest in the Heptapegon church are its mosaic pavements. The atrium, narthex, aisles, the area between the transept pillars to the west, the presbytery, and the side rooms were all paved with ordinary geometric patterns. In the northern intercolumnary spaces (those on the south are lost) two birds (*Francolinus vulgaris*) holding garlands, two herons, two barnacle geese, and a bird fighting a badger are represented. In the northern transept, in the space between the pillars, are two peacocks. In the presbytery, the altar is surrounded by a representation of a basket with loaves of bread (marked with crosses) that is flanked by two fish. An inscription nearby commemorates a "holy father" (whose name is missing); another mentions a certain Saurus.

The two principal mosaics are in the left and right transepts. Each consists of a rectangular panel bordered by lotus flowers turned alternately inside and out. Within each field (6.5 by 5.5 m) are strewn—seemingly irregularly but actually arranged in long lines—representations of plants and animals, with a few buildings interspersed. The faunal and floral elements are depicted with considerable naturalism, so that each species is identifiable. The unrealistic element in Byzantine art is apparent in the various figures' lack of proportion (houses, birds, and plants are all the same size) and the lack of shading and ground lines.

In the north panel a red-crested duck is poised on an Indian lotus flower, then there is a snipe, and, farther to the right, two ducks, a red oleander bush, a heron, and then a barnacle goose. Below, from left to right, a dove on an Indian water lily, bulrushes and a duck, another heron, a stone curlew and a *Spatula clypeata*, and, farther to the right, a mountain duck are depicted. Returning to the left, there is a swan with two cormorants below it, a flamingo killing a water snake, and a bearded titmouse poised on a lotus bud. The pavement also depicts bulrushes and thistles that could not be identified. The buildings include a city gate, a pavilion, and a (tomb?) tower. There are many restored areas and traces of fire on the floor.

The parallel panel in the southern transept is less well preserved. It shows a duck (*Anas boschas*), and then an *Anthropoides virgo* attacking a young water snake springing out of a leaf. A crane stands to the left of a tower marked with stories numbered 6 to 10 in Greek (a type of nilometer, that also could be used

Mosaic in the northern transept.

Mosaic in the southern transept.

to measure the water level of the Sea of Galilee). A stork is perched on top of the tower. In the lower left two ducks and a crane are depicted.

The colors used include two hues of blue, light gray, three hues of red, and two of yellow. All the tesserae are of local limestone. The number of tesserae in a square decimeter is 100 to 105 in the transept, 105 to 107 in the intercolumnia, 76 in the presbytery, 105 in the original part of the nave, 53 in the rest of the church, 23 in the narthex, and 17 in the atrium.

SUMMARY. The existence of the earlier chapel (which cannot antedate the second quarter of the fourth century) is a terminus ante quem for the later church. The excavators suggested a date in the late fourth or early fifth century, basing their estimates on stylistic grounds. In view of the stylistic similarity with the mosaics in the Great Palace in Constantinople, dated to the mid-fifth century, a similar date seems reasonable for the upper church at Heptapegon. The presbytery mosaics and inscription seem to belong to a sixth-century repair.

Apart from their intrinsic artistic value (and they are the work of a great master), the mosaics are interesting from two aspects: they mark the introduction of the figurated pavement into the repertoire of church pavements in Palestine, which until then, as far as is known, was exclusively geometric. This new freedom was of course limited by symbolic considerations. The other characteristic is the adaptation of a Nilotic landscape, popular in Hellenistic and Roman art, to the fauna and flora of the Sea of Galilee and its shores.

MICHAEL AVI-YONAH

RENEWED EXCAVATIONS

In 1968, excavations were carried out at Heptapegon by B. Bagatti and S. Loffreda, on behalf of the Studium Biblicum Franciscanum, in order to examine the site's stratigraphy. The following results were obtained:

1. Near the modern chapel of the Primacy of Peter a large quarry was found that operated in the early centuries CE.
2. Water from the abundant springs was stored in large water towers at the beginning of the Byzantine period.
3. A church was erected on the site in the seventh or early eighth century. Three superimposed floors, the latest dating to the Crusader period, were uncovered here.
4. A fortress, apparently from the Crusader period, was built on the northern side of the church.
5. A few water mills, most of which postdate the Crusader period, were found.

In 1979 and 1980, trial excavations were conducted in the Church of the Multiplication of Loaves and Fishes by R. Rosenthal and M. Hershkovitz, on behalf of the Israel Department of Antiquities and Museums, the Institute of Archaeology at the Hebrew University of Jerusalem, and the Dormition Abbey in Jerusalem. These excavations showed that the step crossing the bema from north to south was apparently not from antiquity, but was created when the mosaics were extracted from the church. In clearing the apse of the earlier chapel, it became evident that the holy rock on which the altar of the later chapel was built was not part of the bedrock. The excavation of the atrium was also completed; only its northern part and the rooms next to it were preserved. The northern half of the north portico was paved on the east with black and white mosaics, in a geometric pattern, and on the west with basalt stones. The two entrances set in this portico were apparently the main ones to the church. The pottery finds indicate that the later chapel was built in the second half of the fifth century—a date previously determined by comparing the basilica's floor with the mosaics in the Great Palace in Constantinople.

AVRAHAM NEGEV

Main publications: A. M. Schneider, *Die Brotvermehrungskirche von Et-Tabga am Genesarethsee und ihre Mosaiken*, Paderborn 1934; id., *The Church of the Multiplying of the Loaves and Fishes*, London 1937; S. Loffreda, *Scavi di et-Tabhah: Relazione Finale della Campagna di Scavi 25 Marzo–20 Giugno 1969* (Pubblicazioni dello Studium Biblicum Franciscanum—Collectio Minor 7), Jerusalem 1970; id., *The Sanctuaries of Tabgha*, 2d ed. (Holy Places of Palestine), Jerusalem 1981.

Other studies: A. E. Mader, *Das Heilige Land* 78 (1934), passim; A. M. Schneider, *Oriens Christianus* 34 (1937), 59–62; B. Gauer, *JPOS* 18 (1938), 233–253; UNESCO, *Israel Ancient Mosaics* (introd. M. Shapiro and M. Avi-Yonah), New York 1960, 9, 16–17, 20–22, pls. 1–30; J. Meysing, *BTS* 77 (1965), 6–16; id., *Das Heilige Land* 98 (1966), 1–16; A. Biran, *CNI* 20/3–4 (1969), 40; S. Loffreda, *LA* 18 (1968), 238–243; 20 (1970), 370–380; id., *Biblia Revuo* 5 (1969), 39–46; id., *Scavi di et-Tabhah* (Review), *BTS* 124 (1970), 22; id., *Les Sanctuaires de Tabgha* (Lugares Santos de Palestina), Jerusalem 1975; ibid. (Review), *Syria* 53 (1976), 349–350; R. Rosenthal and M. Hershkovitz, *IEJ* 30 (1980), 207; id., *BA* 45/3 (1982), 188; A. Niccacci, *Bibbia e Oriente* 26 (1984), 227–230; D. J. Shenhav, *BAR* 10/3 (1984), 22–31; U. Hüber, *Near East Archaeological Society Bulletin* 25 (1985), 29–34; V. Mora, *MdB* 38 (1985), 32–36, 40–42; 72 (1991), 30–33; B. Pixner, *BA* 48 (1985), 196–206; id., *CNI* Special Issue (June 1985), 18–26.

HERMON, MOUNT

IDENTIFICATION AND HISTORY

The so-called Hermon Slopes, the southwestern part of the Hermon Massif, under Israeli control since the 1967 Six-Day War, occupies an area of approximately 70 sq km. The first archaeological survey, carried out between 1969 and 1972, revealed settlements and a material culture of a type not previously encountered in western Palestine. A small part of the Syrian Hermon was surveyed in 1973–1974; the survey was extended to the Lebanese part of the Hermon in 1982–1983. Since 1983 an archaeological expedition from Bar-Ilan University, directed by S. Dar, has been working on the Hermon.

The Hermon Slopes is a general geographical term for the Arabic *'Arqub*. The area is divided into three parallel spurs, between which run Naḥal Si'on (Wadi 'Asal) and Naḥal Guvtah. The western spur is known as the Si'on Shoulder, the middle one the Siryon Ridge, and the eastern one the Hermon Shoulder. In antiquity, permanent settlements were established at altitudes not exceeding 1,600 m above sea level, although evidence of seasonal pastoral settlements has been found at altitudes of up to 2,000 m above sea level.

The written sources, and now the archaeological finds from the Hermon, indicate that during the Hellenistic period the Hermon was part of the Iturean kingdom of Chalcis, the center of which was located in the Lebanon Beqa'a. The Iturean tribes, who were of Arab stock, settled in the northeastern districts of the region and established a well-developed material culture on the Hermon, which provided the basis for the prosperity of their settlements. The Iturean kingdom of Chalcis fell to the Romans in the mid-first century BCE, and the whole region was later ceded to the Herodian dynasty. It subsequently belonged to the Phoenician cities and finally became part of the Roman province of Syria. Throughout this period, the Iturean tribes and local inhabitants of Phoenician and Syrian origin continued to live in the area, maintaining their ancestral traditions. The local cult survived the rise of Christianity, and stone worship was still common on the Hermon during the Byzantine period. Some sites furnish archaeological evidence of settlement during the Middle Ages, as well.

Hazor: shaft of the Iron II water system, viewed from the tunnel.

'Iraq el-Emir: the Qaṣr el-'Abd.

'Iraq el-Emir: feline relief from the Qaṣr el-'Abd.

SETTLEMENTS AND THEIR ECONOMIES

The harsh climate of the Hermon, its plentiful precipitation (up to 2,000 mm of rain annually), and the snow and strong winds characteristic of the region all obliged the local inhabitants to develop appropriate construction techniques. Buildings in the ancient settlements on Mount Hermon were built of hard limestone, with the thickness of the walls sometimes exceeding 1 m. The roofs were made of thick layers of stone, wood, and plaster made of beaten clay. To compensate for the lack of natural springs and streams, the inhabitants built rock-hewn cisterns and unroofed pools, faced with stone and clay; there also are indications that they collected snow and stored it in special underground silos for refrigeration.

The economy of the ancient Hermon settlements was based on horticulture, mainly olive groves, vineyards, and nut and fruit trees—apples, pears, and plums. Olive- and winepresses have been discovered at altitudes of up to 1,500 m, and literary sources mention special wines manufactured locally. Herds and flocks were probably also an important economic factor, as evidenced by the animal pens found here. Pens have been found at an altitude of some 2,000 m above sea level. Among the special trades practiced in the Hermon area were the mining of lead, kohl, bitumen, and clay (for the manufacture of pottery). Iron may also have been produced on the northern Hermon, as evidence of the forging of iron ingots has been discovered at many sites.

NATURE OF THE SITES

Approximately sixty sites have been surveyed to date in the part of the Hermon under Israeli control. Most can be classified as isolated farmhouses; clustered farmhouses; nucleated towns and villages; temples and cult sites; seasonal agricultural plots; or military enclosures.

ISOLATED FARMHOUSES. An example of an isolated farmhouse (site 43) is situated on the southern bank of Naḥal Guvtah. The central structure is a rectangular building (c. 5.4 by 9 m), in the rear of which is a cell paved with a coarse mosaic. Attached to the building are two courtyards used for farm work, an animal pen, and an agricultural tower at the edge of one of the courtyards. A trial sounding produced pottery from the Roman-Byzantine period and the Middle Ages. The farmhouse was probably owned by a local family of farmers, who made their living by working plots of cleared land in the vicinity and tending flocks. The Hermon survey also located farms belonging to wealthy owners. Two large farmhouses were surveyed above Mughar Shab'a; they were built of ashlar blocks and comprised dozens of rooms, courtyards, olive presses, and cisterns. A similar farmhouse was surveyed at Qal'at Busṭra.

CLUSTERED FARMHOUSES. Upstream in Naḥal Si'on, south of Jebel Ḥawarta, the survey identified several clusters of ancient farmhouses (sites 50–53). The number of houses in each cluster is not fixed—it may vary from isolated houses to a dozen or so. Each house is a few dozen meters from its nearest neighbor, and the distances are sometimes even greater. Such clusters may have belonged to an extended family or to some other kin group.

NUCLEATED TOWNS AND VILLAGES. Numerous settlements, such as Dura, Bir an Suba, and Sena'im are nucleated towns or villages on the Hermon. Khirbet Dura (site 44) is approximately 7 km (4 mi.) up Naḥal Si'on, on the steep eastern bank of the deep wadi. The remains of the settlement consist of about two dozen stone houses, rock-hewn cisterns, a workshop for the manufacture of dyes(?), and a small temple. A trial sounding conducted in the temple unearthed evidence that the structure had been in use from the Hellenistic to the end of the Byzantine periods.

TEMPLES AND CULT SITES. The peaks of the Hermon Massif, like other mountains in Israel, were considered sacred in antiquity—the Bible mentions Baal-Hermon (1 Chr. 5:23). In later periods, the sun god Helios and his consort were worshiped on the Hermon among other deities. Many Hermon sites include shrines and temples, built according to a local tradition that exploited the natural rock as an integral architectural element (the Sena'im temple, the temple at Khirbet Dura, and other northern temples). At other sites, pairs of round *maṣṣebot* (stelae) were found scattered around residential areas, apparently pertaining to the local stone worship. Similar stelae were found in situ at Sena'im, Bir an Suba and Ḥawarith. At Bir an Suba, a decorated shrine was discovered at the top of a rocky scarp overlooking the houses in the settlement. At the foot of Mount Agas (Jebel Sumaq), at the edge of the ancient settlement, a pair of megaliths was found. Stone worship, in its various forms, was quite widespread in the Hermon region, and the tradition apparently continued throughout the Byzantine period.

Khirbet Dura: rock-cut reservoir.

The ancient road at the foot of Bir an Suba.

AGRICULTURAL PLOTS. Recent agricultural plots belonged to seasonal settlements of Muslim and Druze farmers from the villages at the foot of the Hermon. They came up the mountain to work their fields and stayed a few months each year. Frequently a plot of this type was established on the site of an ancient settlement and made use of the old buildings and installations, such as at Dura. At many agricultural plots established in modern times, ancient cisterns were used by herders.

MILITARY ENCLOSURES. A stone-built enclosure with a tower at its end was found in the region of the agricultural plot at Jebel Siri (site 47). Among the finds in the enclosure were coins from the Hellenistic, Roman, Ayyubid, and Mameluke periods. North of the hill of Sheikh 'Uthman Hazuri, a medieval enclosure was discovered (site 58). Judging from the numismatic finds, this was a Muslim administrative center between the eleventh and the end of the fifteenth centuries.

S. Dar, *ESI* 5 (1986), 78–82; id., *PEQ* 120 (1988), 26–44; S. Dar and A. Kindler, *Israel Numismatic Journal* 10 (1988–1989), 129–136.

SHIMON DAR

HERODIUM

IDENTIFICATION

Herodium lies about 12 km (7.5 mi.) south of Jerusalem as the crow flies (map reference 1731.1192). The fortress of Herodium is situated on a hill 758 m above sea level. Its position and appearance accord with the evidence provided by Josephus, who locates the fortress 60 stadia from Jerusalem and describes the hill, which is in the form of a truncated cone, as being shaped like a woman's breast (*Antiq.* XV, 324). The Arabic name of the hill, Jebel Fureidis, evidently preserves the name Herodis, as it was called in documents from the time of Bar-Kokhba. Excavations at the site have confirmed the identification of Jebel Fureidis with Herodium.

HISTORY

The main literary source for the history of Herodium are the writings of Josephus. The fortress is also mentioned by Pliny (*NH* V, 70) and in several documents from the time of the Bar-Kokhba Revolt. Herodium was built on the spot where Herod, when retreating from Jerusalem to Masada in flight from Matathias Antigonus and the Parthians in 40 BCE, achieved one of his most important victories over the Hasmoneans and their supporters (*Antiq.* XIV, 359–360; *War* I, 265).

Herodium appears to have been built after Herod's marriage to Mariamne, the daughter of Simeon the Priest of the House of Boethus. It was probably not constructed before 24 BCE, but it was prior to Marcus Agrippa's visit to Judea, which included Herodium, in 15 BCE (*Antiq.* XV, 323; XVI, 12–13). According to Josephus, Herodium was built to serve as a fortress and the capital of a toparchy, as well as a memorial to Herod (*Antiq.* XV, 324; *War* I, 419; III, 55). Josephus also gives a full description of Herod's funeral procession to his burial place at Herodium (*War* I, 670–673; *Antiq.* XVII, 196–199). During the First Jewish Revolt, Herodium was the scene of some of the internal strife among the Zealots (*War* IV, 518–520). It is listed together with Masada and Machaerus as one of the last three strongholds, in addition to Jerusalem, remaining in the hands of the rebels on the eve of the siege of Jerusalem (*War* IV, 555). Herodium was the first of these strongholds to be captured by the Romans after Jerusalem fell (*War* VII, 163). According to documents found at Wadi Murabba'at from the time of the Bar-Kokhba Revolt, Simeon, Prince of Israel (Bar-Kokhba), had a command post at Herodis, where, among other things, land transactions were carried out and a treasury was kept—perhaps storehouses of grain.

EXPLORATION

In the fifteenth century, the Italian traveler F. Fabri gave the name Mountain of the Franks to Herodium, the place where, he assumed, the Crusaders made a stand after the Arab conquest of Jerusalem (*PPTS* X, 403). It retained this name until the nineteenth century. The first sketch of Herodium's plan was made by E. Pococke during a visit in 1743. E. Robinson, in 1838, gave a detailed description of its buildings, dating them to the Roman period and noting their resemblance to Josephus' description. In 1863, the French explorer and traveler F. de Saulcy recorded important site details and drew sketches and plans of the buildings at the foot of the hill, especially of the pool. In his opinion, the round structure in the pool was Herod's burial place. Several years later, V. Guérin accurately described the outer wall with its three semicircular towers and eastern round tower. Until the modern excavations, the fullest account of the remains was made in 1879 by C. Schick, with plans and cross sections. He noted that the lower part of Herodium was a natural hill and the upper part was artificial. Schick traced the staircase leading to the structure on the summit of the hill; his assumption that the steps led to the courtyard of the building through a tunnel-like passage dug in the artificial fill was later confirmed. His further assumption that cisterns had been dug in the lower part of the hill was also later verified. In addition, Schick was correct in his belief that the upper structure had been designed as a grandiose mausoleum and not merely a stronghold. In 1881, C. R. Conder and H. H. Kitchener prepared the first accurate plan of the site with the two circular walls, three semicircular towers, and a round eastern tower.

From 1962 to 1967, V. Corbo conducted four seasons of excavations at the site on behalf of the Studium Biblicum Franciscanum. At that time, most of the main buildings on the summit from the Herodian period, the period of the two wars with Rome, and the Byzantine period were uncovered.

Preservation and restoration works were carried out in 1967 and 1970 by G. Foerster for the National Parks Authority. The entrance room to the palace was uncovered, as well as a complex network of cisterns and an elaborate system of tunnels dug in the hill that apparently dated to the time of the Bar-Kokhba Revolt.

Excavations were resumed in 1970 by an expedition headed by E. Netzer, on behalf of the Institute of Archaeology at the Hebrew University of Jerusalem (see below).

The investigations at Herodium have, to a great extent, confirmed Josephus' detailed description of the place in the Herodian period (*Antiq.* XV, 324–325): "This fortress, which is some sixty stades distant from Jerusalem, is naturally strong and very suitable for such a structure, for reasonably nearby is a hill, raised to a (greater) height by the hand of man and rounded off in the shape of a breast. At intervals it has round towers, and it has a steep ascent

Herodium: general plan of the site.

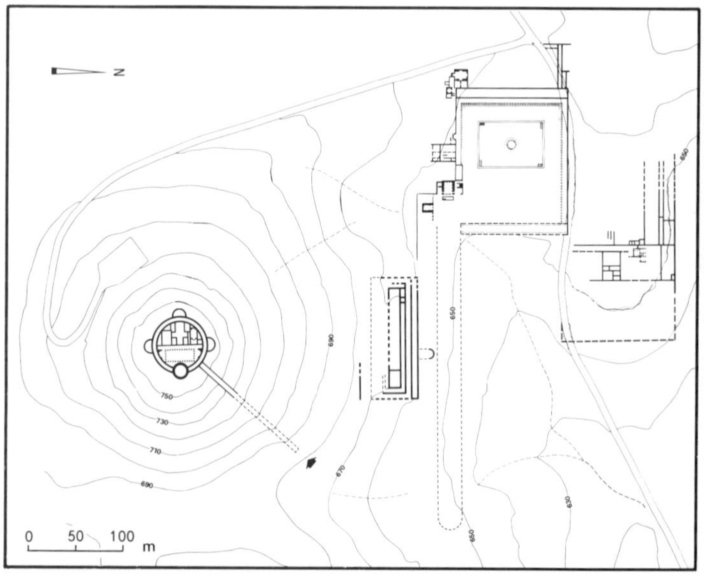

Herodium: aerial view of the mountain palace-fortress, looking east.

Herodium: general plan of the mountain palace-fortress.

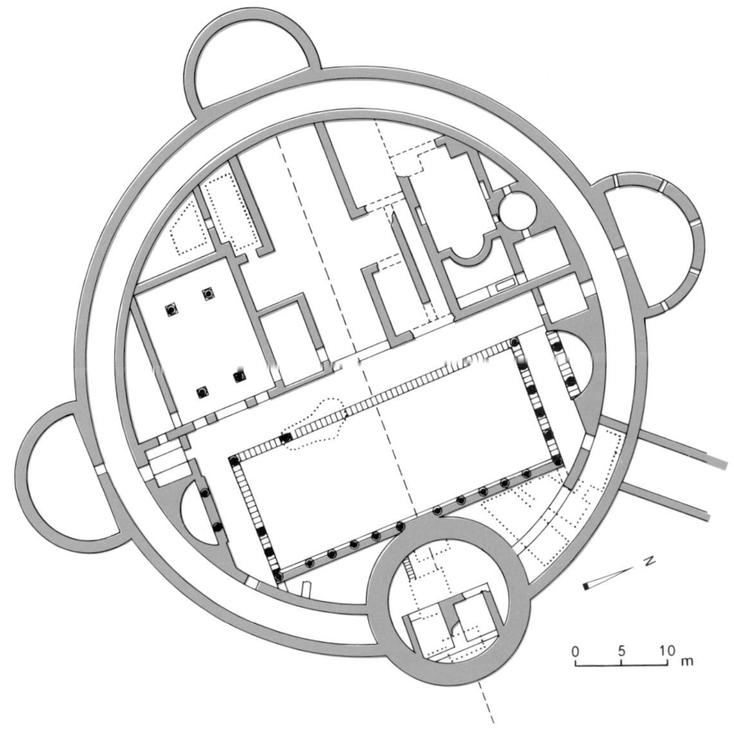

Mountain fortress: exedra and part of the peristyle in the circular palace.

formed of two hundred steps of hewn stone. Within it are costly royal apartments made for security and for ornament at the same time. At the base of the hill there are pleasure grounds built in such a way as to be worth seeing, among other things because of the way in which water, which is lacking in that place, is brought in from a distance and at great expense. The surrounding plain was built up as a city second to none, with the hill serving as an acropolis for the other dwellings."

THE MOUNTAIN PALACE-FORTRESS

HERODIAN PERIOD. On the summit of the hill, which rises 60 m above its surroundings, a round building was erected that is defined as a fortified palace or royal fortress. It consists of two parallel circular walls (diameter of the outer wall, 62 m). The walls start on the east side, at the monumental tower, which, according to its surviving remains, has an external diameter of 18 m and is 16 m high. A corridor (3.5 m wide) between the two walls extended up to the eastern tower, which protruded from the outer wall. Three semicircular towers also protruded due west, north, and south from the wall. The outer wall and the towers were built on a series of vaults (found in the excavations) designed to level the top of the natural hill. An earth and stone rampart was apparently poured over the towers and the outer wall (which rises at least 12 m) immediately after they were constructed, leaving only their tops projecting from the fill. This is indicated by the abundant amount of building debris found in the fill of the rampart. Sections of a well-built, sloping retaining wall were discovered in the lower southeastern side of the rampart that probably supported it. It is this rampart that gives the hill its distinctive conical shape and turns it into a giant tumulus—Herod's monument and grave.

An imposing entrance passage was built inside the artificial rampart. The passage rises gradually from the base of the hill to a 5-m-high vaulted entrance in the outer wall north of the eastern tower. The entrance leads into a gate chamber that opens onto the palace garden. The entrance passage (3.5 m wide) apparently had two hundred marble steps (mentioned by Josephus but not yet found). It was formed by two strong walls supported by a series of arches to counteract the pressure exerted by the artificial fill. Because the nature of the fill is homogeneous, it appears that the passage was deliberately sealed after Herod's burial.

Circular Palace. The circular palace area is divided into two main sections. The eastern half of the area below the round tower was occupied by a garden (12.5 by 33 m), enclosed by columns on the north, south, and west. The east side of the garden was bounded by a wall with pilasters. To the south and north of the peristyle garden were two symmetrical exedrae, both with two columns in their facades. Below the eastern tower on the south side was a third exedra. West of the southern and northern exedrae two identical rooms led from the garden to the corridor between the double wall of the palace. Two entrances east of the exedrae also led to the corridor.

The western half of the area contains dwellings and service rooms and was divided into two parts by a cross-shaped courtyard. A well-built bathhouse occupied the northern part. In the middle of the southern part was a rectangular triclinium (10.6 by 15.15 m), with four columns supporting the roof

Mountain palace-fortress: caldarium in the bathhouse.

(only one column base was found in situ). Its entrance was in the center of the facade and was flanked by two windows. Doorways in its north and south walls led to additional rooms. The floor was laid in opus sectile, but only its base has survived. The triclinium is surrounded by four smaller rooms that also abut the inner circular wall on the south and west sides. Two well-plastered cisterns with barrel vaulting were found beneath the two western rooms. Another room was attached to the triclinium on the north. Signs of at least one more story, used as living quarters, were found above these rooms and also above the bathhouse. Traces of upper stories (three?) were also noted in the corridor between the walls and in the northern tower, where there were slits in the top of the walls for inserting wooden ceilings beams.

Bathhouse. The elaborately decorated bathhouse is situated northwest of the palace. The apodyterium (dressing room) had a mosaic pavement, of which only fragments of two black borders on a white background survive. The walls are ornamented with crustae in the Pompeian First Style. The tepidarium (warm room) is circular (diameter, 4.15 m) and is topped with a hemispherical dome (height, 5 m). Three doors led from this room to the apodyterium, caldarium (hot room), and frigidarium (cold room). The tepidarium had a floor of white mosaic with a black band. The decoration in the center is not preserved. The walls were decorated with frescoes in a geometric pattern in the Pompeian First Style in red, brown, blue, yellow, and black. Waterfowl were also depicted on the walls. The frigidarium, a small chamber abutting the inner wall of the palace, had a plastered pool in the center. The rectangular caldarium terminates in an apse on the east. It, too, is decorated with rectangular panels in the Pompeian First Style, in white, black, green, red, and yellow. Beneath its floor is the hypocaust. The hot air passing through its pipes was also conveyed to the north and south walls. East of the caldarium was a small chamber with a black and white mosaic pavement and a fleuron design within a black border.

Cisterns. In addition to the cistern found on the summit, within the palace proper, a network of huge cisterns was also discovered dug into the interior of the hill. Thus far, four cisterns with hydraulic plaster have been excavated about 15 m below the floor of the palace in the northeast. A number of staircases hewn in the rock led directly from the palace to the cisterns so there was no need to leave the palace area for water. Because these cisterns were situated well above the aqueduct that brought water to Herodium from the springs of Artas, they could not have received water directly from the aqueduct or from the pool at the foot of the palace. It can be assumed, therefore, that these cisterns were filled with water carried by pack animals from the lower pool (see also below).

Building Method. Herod's palace was built wholly of medium-sized ashlars, partly having drafted margins. All the walls, except perhaps the outer face of the exterior wall, were coated with plaster, and their lower part was painted in various colors and in various geometric panel designs in the Pompeian First Style. The upper part of the walls was generally white stucco molded to imitate architectural details. The column bases, Corinthian capitals, and the parts of the entablature found were also coated with a thin colored plaster. A number of Ionic capitals were also found. Some of the architectural fragments had stonemasons' marks in Greek or Hebrew and numerals. Several partly ruined mosaic pavements were uncovered with geometric patterns in black and white alone. Some of the floors were laid in opus sectile.

REMAINS FROM THE PERIOD OF THE TWO WARS WITH ROME. Many traces of settlement were found from this time (First Jewish Revolt, 67–70 CE) and the Bar-Kokhba Revolt (132–135 CE). Settlement then is also known from literary sources. The new inhabitants occupied various parts of the palace, altering them to suit their needs. Signs of construction were found in the area of the peristyle garden on the east and in the bathhouse and triclinium on the west. The new settlers' building activities were not extensive, being generally limited to the addition of walls in dry construction and the reuse of stones from the decaying palace. Many ovens for domestic use were found, some of which may have been used to smelt iron for making weapons. More basic changes of a religious and cultic nature were made in the triclinium, where rows of stone benches, constructed of building materials taken from the palace, were added along three of the walls. It apparently was used as a synagogue by the rebels who had taken refuge here. A mikveh, found in front of the hall, appears to have been added when the building became a synagogue.

In Corbo's opinion, the intersecting walls in the three semicircular towers on the north, south, and west were also built at this time. Building activities were also noted on the upper part of the eastern tower. One of the vaults beneath the corridor near the eastern tower was used as a cistern. A network of subterranean passages was dug into the northern part of the hill, clearly for defensive purposes. These passages, which are later than the cisterns from the Herodian period, contain traces of habitation—walls, pottery, and signs of

*Mountain palace-fortress: **(left)** entrance to one of the lower cisterns; **(right)** cistern from Herodian period.*

Mountain palace-fortress: area of the triclinium that may have served as a synagogue in the period of the First Revolt, looking west.

fire—and may be confirmation of Dio Cassius' description of the defensive measures taken by the rebels during the Bar-Kokhba Revolt (*Roman History* LXIX, 12).

Corbo emphasizes the difficulty of differentiating between the two strata from the First and Second revolts. The important finds from this period include large rolling stones, ballista stones, arrowheads, some scores of coins of the First Revolt, and an unusual hoard of about eight hundred bronze coins from the three years of the Bar-Kokhba Revolt found near the southern exedra of the palace.

BYZANTINE PERIOD. The small monastic settlement at Herodium in the Byzantine period is not mentioned in the ancient sources, but it left its mark on several parts of the destroyed palace. The monks lived mainly in the parts of the bathhouse that were still roofed, building cells and ovens there. They also erected a small chapel in one of the palace rooms south of the bathhouse. They apparently abandoned the place in the seventh century.

INSCRIPTIONS. The written material found at Herodium comprises graffiti scratched on the stucco coating of the palace walls, ostraca, and inscriptions on jars. The inscriptions, which were written in Greek, Aramaic, and Hebrew, belong to the three main periods of settlement. It is difficult to differentiate paleographically inscriptions from the time of Herod and from the two revolts. Graffiti from the various periods were found mainly on the walls of the bathhouse and in its vicinity. One, written in Greek, mentions Herodium as a βασίλειον (*basileion*, or palace). In the bathhouse were several erotic inscriptions written by soldiers. One Hebrew ostracon mentions Herod; others contain personal names, and several contain the Hebrew alphabet.

General

F. de Saulcy, *Voyage en Terre Sainte* 1, Paris 1865, 171–176; 2, 332–335; Guérin, *Judée* 3, 122–132; C. Schick, *ZDPV* 3 (1880), 88–99; Conder–Kitchener, *SWP* 3, 315, 330–332; Benoit et al., *Discoveries* 2, index, 296; Y. Yadin, *IEJ* 11 (1961), 51–52; A. Segal, ibid. 23 (1973), 27–29; Y. Hirschfeld, *Map of Herodium* (Archaeological Survey of Israel 108/2), 11–17, Jerusalem 1985; ibid. (Review), *BAIAS* 7 (1987–1988), 56–57; E. Netzer, *Herodium: An Archaeological Guide*, Jerusalem 1987.

The Mountain Palace-Fortress

Main publications: V. Corbo, *Herodion 1: Gli Edifici della Reggia Fortezza* (Studium Biblicum Franciscanum Collectio Maior 20), Jerusalem 1989; A. Spijkerman, *Herodion: Catalogo delle Monete* (Herodion 3), Jerusalem 1972; E. Testa, *I Graffitie gli Ostraca* (Herodion 1), Jerusalem 1972; E. Netzer, *Greater Herodium* (Qedem 13), Jerusalem 1981.

Other studies: V. Corbo, *LA* 13 (1962–1963), 219–277; 17 (1967), 65–121; id., *BTS* 60 (1963), 6–10; id., *CNI* 18 (1967), 33–36; id., *RB* 75 (1968), 424–428; id., *Herodion* 1 (Reviews), *PEQ* 122 (1990), 68–69. — *Qadmoniot* 89–90 (1990), 64–65 (Hebrew); E. M. Lapperrousaz, *Syria* 41 (1964), 347–358; id., *Revue des Études Juives* 144 (1985), 297–304; id., *Archéologie, Art et Histoire de la Palestine: Colloque du Centenaire de la Section des Sciences Religieuses, École Pratique des Hautes Études, Sept. 1986*, Paris 1988, 149–165; G. Foerster, *IEJ* 19 (1969), 123–124; id., *RB* 77 (1970), 400–401; id., *Journal of Jewish Art* 3–4 (1977), 6–11; id., *ASR*, 24–29; id., *MdB* 57 (1989), 9–14; E. Netzer, *Greater Herodium* (Reviews), *Phoenix* 28 (1982), 41–43. — *Syria* 62 (1985), 73–80, 195–196; id., *MdB* 17 (1981), 17–21; id., *Jerusalem Cathedra* 1 (1981), 48–61; id., *ESI* 1 (1982), 40–42; 2 (1983), 47–49; id., *Recherches Archêologiques en Israël*, 190–199; id., *Epistemonike . . .* 28 (1985), 523–547; id., *BAIAS* 6 (1986–1987), 57–60; id., *Judaica* 45 (1989), 21–44; E. J. Vardaman, *IEJ* 25 (1975), 45–46; A. Segal, *Antike Welt* 8 (1977), 21–28; J. F. Strange, *BASOR* 226 (1977), 65–73; 233 (1979), 63–69; D. Chen, *BASOR* 239 (1980), 37–40; Y. Tsafrir, *Jerusalem Cathedra* 1 (1981), 68–72; 2 (1982), 120–145; *Biblia Revuo* 20 (1984), 32; D. M. Jacobson, *ZDPV* 100 (1984), 127–136; id., *BAIAS* 5 (1985–1986), 56–68; J. Zias, *BA* 49 (1986), 182–186; *The Times Atlas of the Bible* (ed. J. B. Pritchard), London 1987, 159; G. Garbrecht and J. Peleg, *Antike Welt* 20/2 (1989), 2–20; M. T. Shoemaker, *BAR* 17/4 (1991), 58–59.

GIDEON FOERSTER

LOWER HERODIUM

Excavations in the lower part of Herodium were initiated in 1970 by an expedition from the Hebrew University of Jerusalem, with the participation of the Israel Exploration Society and the archaeology staff officer for Judea and Samaria. By 1987, ten seasons of excavations had been carried out under the direction of E. Netzer (with E. Damati serving as co-director in the first two seasons). The excavations were concentrated in the area on the north side of the hill, where remains from the Herodian period extend over an expanse of about 37.5 a. This area is known as Lower Herodium. Aerial photographs, a

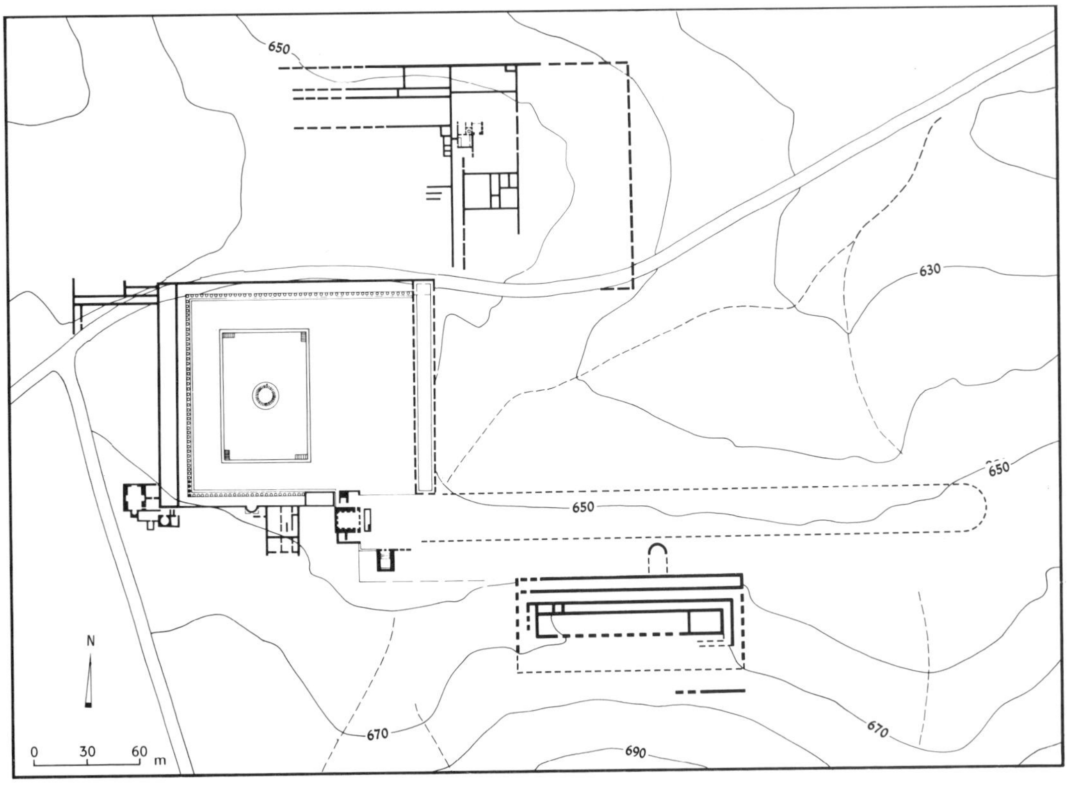

Lower Herodium: plan of the main structures from the Herodian period.

Lower Herodium: general view, looking northwest.

survey of the remains, and the excavations revealed that the structures of the Herodian period, including the round building on the summit (the mountain palace-fortress), were all constructed at the same time, as part of a single plan, and were oriented in the same direction (north–south and east–west).

SECOND TEMPLE PERIOD. Pool Complex. In the center of Lower Herodium, a large pool (46 by 70 m and c. 3 m deep) was uncovered (that had been reported in the surveys). The pool received water from the Artas spring by means of an aqueduct from the Herodian period (its remains had been surveyed initially by C. Schick and later by A. Mazar and Y. Cohen). Built mainly of courses of large field stones, the pool was dug into bedrock on its

Lower Herodium: (restored) columns in the pool complex.

southwestern side. Its entire surface had originally been plastered with hydraulic lime mortar with an ash base, large segments of which were visible. In the interior of the pool, on its southern side, remains of a bench were uncovered that probably once extended for the length of the pool. Four stairways (each 2.3 m wide) led to the bottom of the pool, one in each of its corners.

In the center of the pool were the foundations of a round structure (diameter, 13.5 m). A row of sixteen deep piers surrounded it, whose function has not yet been clarified. The round structure may have been the foundation of a pavilion built in the middle of the pool and surrounded by columns, similar to the building that probably stood on the middle terrace of the northern palace at Masada. The entire complex may have been a kind of artificial lake for swimming and for sailing small boats, as well as a reservoir and an architectural focal point.

A rectangular area, bounded on the east and southeast by retaining walls, surrounded the pool; it also had been located in early surveys. Examination of this area revealed that a large ornamental garden (110 by 145 m) had encompassed the pool. To create this garden it had been necessary to fill in the part of the valley that extends east from the area of the pool and the garden. A massive retaining wall was erected there, a kind of earthen dam whose base was about 13 m wide. On top of this base were two superimposed halls (c. 110 m long and 9 m wide). The lower hall, which lay below the garden, is partially preserved (most of it has not yet been excavated). The upper hall was almost entirely destroyed. At the southern end of the lower hall (the garden's southeastern corner), two rooms from the Byzantine period were uncovered. The easternmost room had served as a stable and contained a trough extending the length of the eastern wall (see below). Trial soundings exposed all the walls encircling the vast garden (the pool complex) and the remains of porticos on three sides. Like the pool, a corner of the garden, on its southwestern side, had also been partially cut into bedrock—to a height of about 6 m. The porticos were about 6 m wide and extended along the western side of the garden and along two-thirds of the southern and northern sides—in all, over a distance of about 250 m. The porticos were raised about 1.2 m above the gardens and were reached by stairs, running along their full length, that were preserved in the two western corners. Only a few fragments of the columns themselves—in Ionic style—survive.

West of the garden, a hall was uncovered whose length equals the width of the garden and whose width was about 9 m, like the hall east of the garden. (It, too, was partly cut into bedrock.)

Most of the Herodian buildings in Lower Herodium are concentrated at the southern, western, and northern parts of the pool complex. Evidence accumulated in the numerous trial trenches and excavations indicates that most of the buildings in this area were wings or auxiliary buildings of the palace. Part of the wing situated north of the pool complex was uncovered north of the Bethlehem–Tekoa road. The buildings examined stood mostly on a level tract north of the pool complex and partly on two parallel, stepped terraces (each c. 15 m wide), found in the northern part of the wing. These terraces were created in Herod's time, during the construction of the substantial infrastructure. Among the remains uncovered here were two small Roman-style bathhouses.

Service Building. Northwest of the pool complex, adjoining the Bethlehem–Tekoa road and its junction with the road ascending the hill, part of a large service building was excavated. It contained a long, narrow storeroom that seems to have been destroyed in an earthquake. On the floor lay tens of identical storage jars. Part of another long, narrow storeroom uncovered nearby may have been used as a stable.

The South Wing. The wing south of the pool complex was investigated in a large number of soundings that exposed remains of buildings, some of which were decorated with frescos. Two stone windows with latticework were preserved in their entirety.

Bathhouse. Excavations in the south wing also revealed the remains of a large bathhouse close to the southwestern corner of the pool complex but at a higher level. The corner of the bathhouse and the base of several of its rooms were cut into bedrock. This bathhouse, which was built in typical Roman style, is the largest of its kind discovered so far in any of Herod's palaces. It was entered through a peristyle, only a small part of which has been excavated. The dressing room and entrance (apodyterium) to the bathhouse measured 6.2 by 7.5 m. A bench extended along at least one of the walls of the courtyard. Three rooms that formed a passageway served as warm rooms (tepidaria); the largest measured 5.8 by 7.5 m. The bathhouse was equipped with two hot rooms (caldaria), the larger of which (7.8 by 12.8 m) had niches in all of its walls (the niche in the southern wall was semicircular). The smaller room was round (diameter, c. 4 m), and also had niches in all its walls. The round room may have been the laconicum. The cold room (frigidarium) has not yet been located with certainty. Of the two furnaces that heated the caldaria, the furnace in the round caldarium was located and excavated in its entirety.

This large bathhouse was decorated with a wealth of mosaic floors and the frescoes are similar to those found at Masada, Jericho, and Cypros. The mosaic carpets in the center of some of the rooms were decorated with geometric designs. The round room was decorated with a mosaic circle in a floral pattern and had the most outstanding frescos. In the debris of the bathhouse, a fragment was found of a large marble wash basin ornamented with a figure from Greek-Roman mythology (apparently Silenus).

Storage Building. During the excavations, the remains of a huge building were examined at the foot of the mountain palace-fortress. The building (130 m long and about 55 m wide) was on the same axis as the round elevated building. Only its foundations are preserved, mostly for its northern half. These included the remains of two cellars (each c. 5 m wide) that extended along its length and were most probably used as storerooms (at least one had a vaulted ceiling). The capacity of the two cellars alone is equal to about half of the capacity of the storerooms near the northern palace at Masada. On the eastern side of the building, a narrow room, built above a stone vault from the Herodian period, is preserved in its entirety. The room has been used by the local inhabitants until the modern times as a sheepfold. It may be for this reason that the British Survey termed it the stable. Its vast size and location, at any rate, indicate that it was the main wing of the palace of Greater Herodium (the "large palace").

The Monumental Building and Artificial Course. A large artificial course (c. 350 m long and 30 m wide) extended west–east along the northern foot of

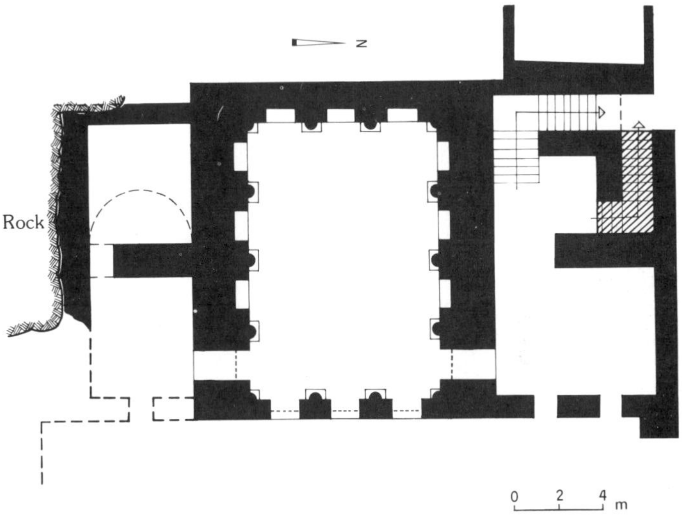

*Lower Herodium: monumental building from Herodian period; **(above)** plan; **(below)** interior view of the hall.*

the large palace. It was built when Herodium was constructed and was too narrow to serve as a hippodrome (as was initially proposed by the excavators). At the western end of this long tract an elaborate building was completely exposed. Rectangular in plan (14 by 15 m), it was preserved on its west side to a height of about 7 m. This impressive building was partly cut into the bedrock, but was otherwise built of ashlars. It consisted of a single hall (8.8 by 12 m), surrounded by niches with half columns set on pedestals between them. The building had three entrances on the east (from the initial course), one on the north, and one on the south. The hall's side walls were about 3 m thick, and they probably supported not only a vaulted ceiling, but also a monumental roof (pyramidal?). This elaborate building, called the monumental building by its excavators, faces the course. The two were built on the same axis and there was undoubtedly a close connection between them.

In view of the possibility that the monumental building was Herod's mausoleum, a theory already proposed at the end of the first season of excavations, work in this section of Lower Herodium was expanded. On the building's north and south sides, small courtyards were uncovered (one on each side) with a small room adjoining each. The room on the north was used as a stairwell and a passageway leading from the course and the monumental building to the pool complex. About 20 m southeast of the monumental building was a rectangular building with a stepped immersion pool, apparently a mikveh (6 by 8.5 m), in its center. The pool was entered through a pair of doors. The mikveh resembles structures uncovered from this period in the Jewish Quarter in Jerusalem and at other sites. South of the monumental building was a large group of excellent quality ashlars (with drafted margins and smooth, slightly projecting bosses), some of them decorated with floral patterns. Also discovered here were several fragments of a Doric frieze, similar to the friezes adorning many funerary monuments from the Second Temple period in Jerusalem and its vicinity. These stones (found in secondary use in the Byzantine church, see below) might have originated from a mausoleum that probably stood nearby, crowning Herod's tomb or in its facade, and whose location has not yet been discovered. If the fragments belong to the mausoleum, the "course" should probably be viewed as a special route that was built for Herod's funeral procession—the funeral described at great length by Josephus. If Herod's burial place is discovered close by, it will also be possible to determine the function of the monumental building. Its hall, in any case, closely resembles an elaborate triclinium found in one of the large tombs at Petra. Another structure in the vicinity that may have belonged to the tomb complex is the mikveh described above.

Most of the remains uncovered in Lower Herodium from the Herodian period belong to a single building stage. Some, however, come from a later, greatly inferior phase, apparently following the site's partial destruction in the earthquake that struck in about the first half of the first century.

The excavations and the survey carried out in Lower Herodium enabled the excavators to arrive at a fresh evaluation of the dimensions and functions of Greater Herodium. It is now evident that a vast complex was constructed (c. 60 a. in area), not only to commemorate the name of Herod and the fateful battle he waged here at the beginning of his reign and to serve as his burial place, but also to function as a great countryside palace, probably a summer palace. The role of the mountain palace-fortress as a stronghold was only secondary to the other functions of Greater Herodium. It was fortified to protect the king during his residence here because there was a lack of fortified sites in the immediate vicinity—in contrast to Jericho, where several forts were situated near the unfortified winter palaces. Herodium was also apparently the district capital in Herod's time. Herodium was one of the great palaces in the Roman world; it was certainly the largest at the time of its construction in the early days of the Roman Empire.

The Tunnels. A ramified network of tunnels was surveyed and partly excavated from 1973 to 1975 inside the hill of Herodium, mainly at its northeastern edge. The survey and excavation of the tunnels were carried out with the participation of S. Arzi and a team from the Kefar Eẓyon Field School. The network connected the main courtyard on the hill with the cellars of the palace (located beneath the round structure encircling the hill) and the cisterns of the Herodian period on the northeastern slope (see above). The tunnels branched off in all directions, apparently to form hidden escape hatches across the slopes.

Some 300 m of tunnels have so far been investigated (some of them were also excavated). All the tunnels were found to be dug high enough for an individual to walk upright through them. In the steep sections, steps were hewn into the rock to facilitate passage. Several of the tunnels were dug through the Herodian fill; there was evidence that the sides of the tunnels had been reinforced with wooden frames to prevent their collapse. The four cisterns on the mountain slope became the junctions and convergence points for the tunnels; the debris from the quarrying was also thrown into them. Isolated remains from the Bar-Kokhba period (132–135) found in the tunnels (mainly oil lamps) and evidence of an earlier tunnel leading to the cisterns, apparently dug during the First Jewish War (66–70), date the network of tunnels to the time of the Bar-Kokhba Revolt. One of the escape exits, at one end of the branches of the network, was uncovered in the excavations.

Excavation of the tunnels clarified how the cisterns from Herod's period functioned. The three cisterns uncovered so far at the base of the cone, on the northeastern slope, were filled with rainwater that ran down the slopes; in times of need, they were probably also filled with water brought from the large pool in Lower Herodium. The water from the pool was carried up the stairway and poured into a "funnel" (c. 5 m below the entrance), from which it entered a channel whose end was uncovered in another cistern (the "intermediate" cistern), located directly below the entrance to the hill. From here the water was drawn directly into the inner courtyard through a round, rock-cut opening in the roof of the intermediate cistern. This arrangement also enabled water to be brought to the building without entering it.

BYZANTINE PERIOD. Numerous remains from the Byzantine period were uncovered at Lower Herodium. Some were found above or alongside remains from the Herodian period, and some were found inside the Herodian buildings, which had been cleared of debris and their remains and reused. Most of them were concentrated in the area of the monumental building, the large palace, and the earthen dam east of the pool complex. The new occupants restored the buildings and made use of the same floors, sometimes also constructing new floors. Among the ruins uncovered here were three fairly small churches, similar in size and plan. In all three, the main hall was divided into three aisles by rows of columns; small chambers—one on each side—flanked the apse. All three churches were provided with baptismal fonts; in two of the churches, they were found in the room south of the apse, and in the third, adjoining the hall.

Northern Church. The first church, which was excavated in 1973 and 1978, was erected north of the Bethlehem–Tekoa road, above remains from the Herodian period. The church is well preserved and paved throughout with mosaics, most of which survived in a good state of preservation. Three, almost

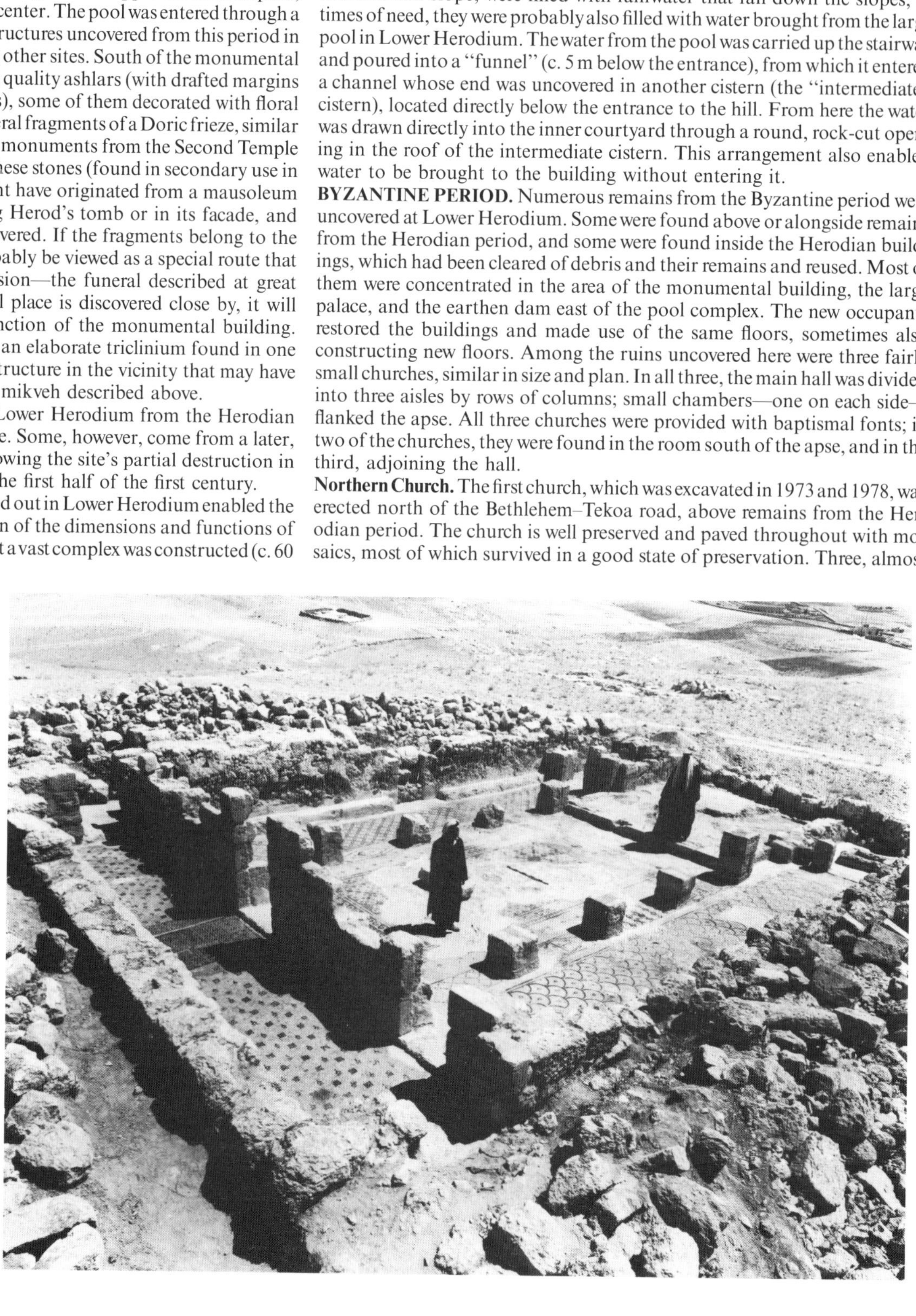

General view of the northern church, looking northeast.

Mosaic in the nave of the northern church.

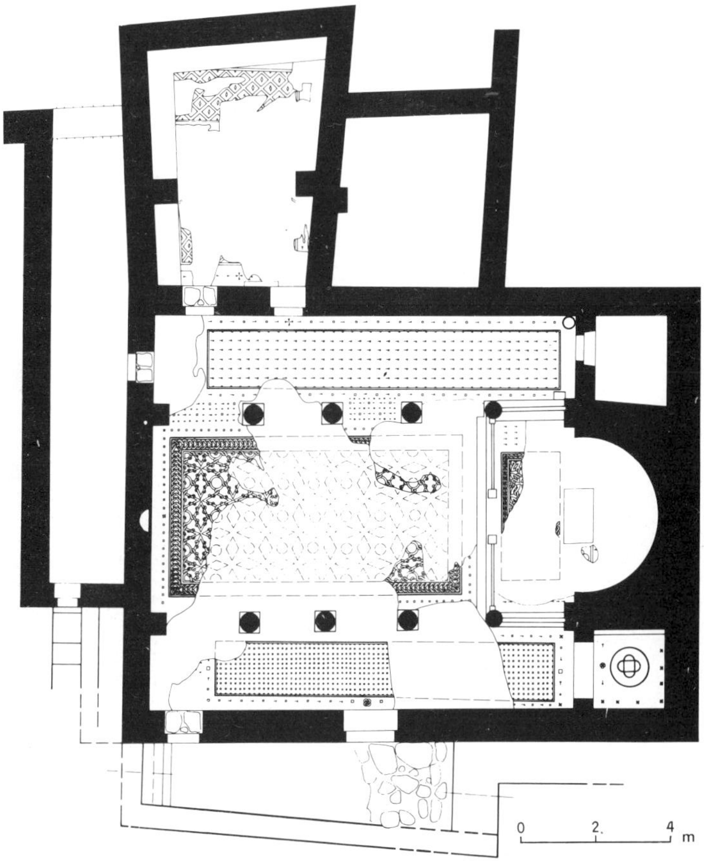

Plan of the central church.

Lower Herodium: plan of the northern church.

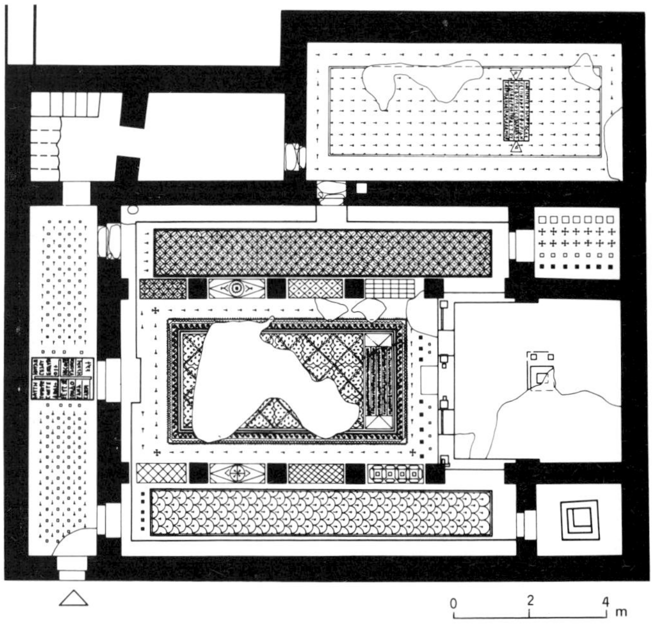

complete, dedicatory inscriptions were found here. One was laid in the narthex, another in the hall, and the third in a side room north of the hall. According to the inscription in the main hall (8.8 by 10.6 m), the church was dedicated to Saint Michael. Two unusual features of this church are the apse, which was rectangular and not semicircular, as in the other two churches, and a bench that extended along the entire length of the walls in the nave.

Eastern Church. The second church, which was uncovered in 1979–1980, was

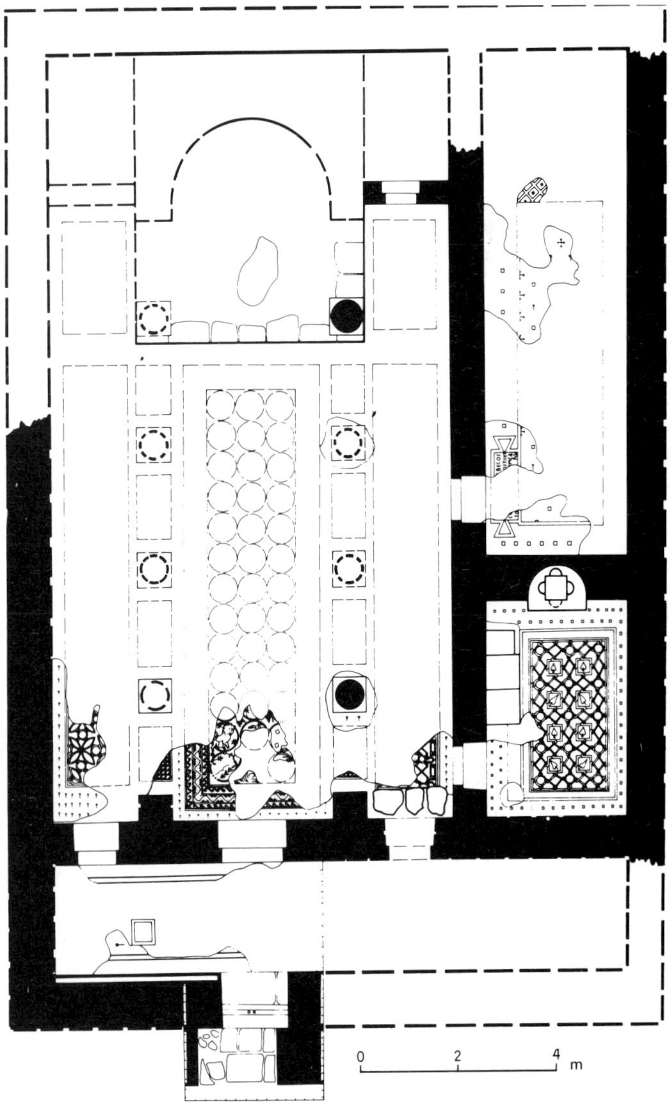

Plan of the eastern church.

built above the remains of the foundations of the large palace, on its eastern side. It, too, was paved throughout with mosaics. The main mosaic floor in the nave was decorated with medallions enclosing figures of animals. It resembles the mosaics in the Ma'on (Nirim) synagogue, and the Shellae church, among others. The nave's mosaic floor was not well preserved; only one medallion, containing the figure of a lioness, survives in its entirety. In two other medallions, the partially preserved figures of birds can be distinguished. Two rooms were added to the church on its southern side: one contained a baptismal font inside a niche in the eastern wall and a tomb dug beneath the floor; the tomb was found plundered. A partially preserved inscription was found in the floor of the second room.

Central Church. The third church, which was excavated from 1980 to 1983, is situated south of the monumental building and close to it. It is cut into the bedrock in its southwestern corner. Unlike the other two churches, the main entrance here was not in the narthex on the west side, but in the southern wall of the hall (10.5 by 11.5 m). Instead of a narthex on the west, there was a narrow corridor that contained an entrance leading to the aisle on the north. This entrance was sealed sometime later. The church's ornamented mosaic floor was only partially preserved, even though the church as a whole had survived. In the room adjoining the apse on the south was an elaborate baptismal font, made of a monolithic stone block (diameter, 1.1 m). In this church, as in the other two, there was evidence of a second story (with a coarse white mosaic pavement) built above the side aisles. In the central church, however, the second story also extended above the narthex or side corridor.

The walls of the central church, and of the auxiliary rooms on the north side, were built mainly of well-dressed ashlars (some of which were ornamented) that had been taken from Herod's "missing (funerary?) monument." No stones of this type were found anywhere else in Lower Herodium (or in the mountain palace-fortress). It is thus reasonable to assume that the plundered Herodian monument had stood close by and its stones integrated into the church building.

The site's identity in the Byzantine period is not yet known, nor is it clear whether Lower Herodium was an ordinary or monastic settlement then.

Main publication: E. Netzer, *Greater Herodium* (Qedem 13), Jerusalem 1981.

Other studies: E. Netzer, *IEJ* 22 (1972), 247–249; id., *RB* 80 (1973), 419–421; id., *MdB* 17 (1981), 17–21; id., *BAR* 9/3 (1983), 30–51; 14/4 (1988), 18–33; id., *ESI* 5 (1986), 49–50; id., *Christian Archaeology in the Holy Land* (V. C. Corbo Fest.), Jerusalem 1990, 165–176; A. Rabinovitch, *MdB* 9 (1979), 51–53; C. Patrick, *SRI Journal* 3/6 (1983), 2–3; D. Milson, *LA* 39 (1989), 207–211; L. Di Segni, V. C. Corbo Fest. (op. cit.), Jerusalem 1990, 177–190.

EHUD NETZER

HESHBON

IDENTIFICATION

For both geographical and linguistic reasons, Heshbon is identified with Tell Ḥesbân, an 895-m-high, 15-a. mound guarding the northern edge of the rolling Moabite plain. Here, a southern tributary to Wadi Ḥesbân begins to cut sharply down toward the Jordan River, about 25 km (15.5 mi.) to the west (map reference 226.134). Eusebius locates "Hessebon, now called Hesbous" 20 Roman miles (c. 30 km) east of the Jordan River, in the mountains opposite Jericho (*Onom.* 84:5). A ground course from the Jordan River would place the approximate location of Tell Ḥesbân here. Several milestones along the Roman road from the Jordan Valley and the Bible's reference to Heshbon's location confirm this identification. It is about 60 km (37 mi.) east of Jerusalem, 20 km (12 mi.) southwest of 'Amman, 9 km (5.6 mi.) north of Medeba, 8 km (5 mi.) northeast of Mount Nebo, and 3 km (2 mi.) southeast of (and 200 m higher than) 'Ain Ḥesbân, the perennial spring with which it is associated.

The excavations at Tell Ḥesbân have so far produced no evidence for an occupation earlier than the twelfth century BCE. This poses a problem for locating Sihon's capital (see below) here. It may not have been found because it is elsewhere on the site, which is unlikely, or, which is more likely, because its seminomadic (impermanent) nature left no trace to be discovered. More extreme options are to consider the biblical account unhistorical or at least anachronistic (now favored by such scholars as J. M. Miller, H. O. Thompson, and others) or to seek the Amorite capital at another location—for example, Jalul (an identification favored by S. H. Horn) or 'Umeiri (a view favored by R. D. Ibach). Most, at least, would identify Tell Ḥesbân with Greco-Roman Hesbus, based on numismatic and milestone evidence coupled with the geographical specifications as provided by Ptolemy and Eusebius. If F. M. Cross's reading of the Ammonite ostracon (A.3), found at the site in 1978, is accepted, it would support such an identification for Iron Age Heshbon, as well.

HISTORY

Heshbon is first mentioned in the Bible in Numbers 21:21–30 (cf. Dt. 2:16–37), where it is referred to as the city of Sihon, king of the Amorites, whose

Heshbon: map of the mound and excavation areas.

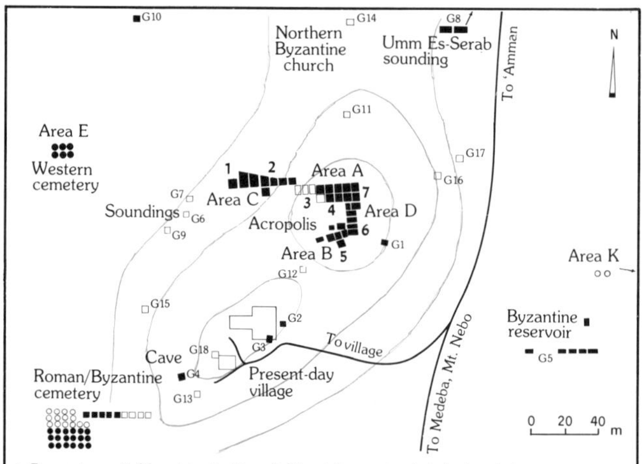

1. Roman tower; 2. Mameluke dwellings; 3. Mameluke courtyard; 4. Arab period bathhouse; 5. Iron Age reservoir; 6. Roman buildings; 7. Byzantine church

Heshbon: general view of the mound, looking southwest.

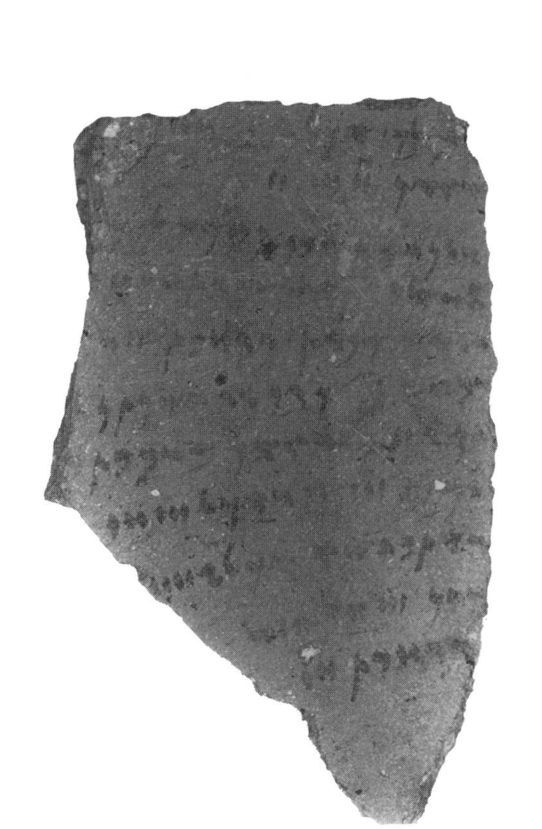

Ammonite ostracon documenting the distribution of supplies and money to court officials, 7th–6th centuries BCE.

ingdom extended "from Aroer, which is on the edge of the valley of Arnon, ınd from the middle of the valley as far as the river Jabbok, the boundary of he Ammonites, that is, half of Gilead" (Jos. 12:2; cf. Jos. 13:10, Jg. 11:22). Numbers 21:26–31 may be—in the writer's opinion—an attempt to justify srael's occupation, under Moses, of territory claimed at various times by Moab. This passage claims that at least the southern half of Sihon's kingdom, he tableland known in Hebrew as the Mishor (Dt. 3:10, 4:43), had indeed een Moabite but that Sihon had earlier wrested it from Moabite control Num. 21:26). As proof, the so-called Song of Heshbon (Num. 21:27–30), stensibly an Amorite war taunt, was inserted in the narrative. This claim was gain made in Judges 11:12–28, where Jephthah denies the Ammonites wnership of the region between the Jabbok and Arnon on the basis that srael originally took it from the Amorites and not the Ammonites.

The tribes of Reuben and Gad requested the territory that had been encompassed by Sihon's kingdom for their tribal allotment on the basis of its eing good for their cattle (Num. 32:1–5). It was, however, actually Reuben hat built Heshbon and other nearby towns (Num. 32:37) which, according to he difficult and cryptic next verse, "changed as to name . . . and they called by other?) names the names of the cities which they built." Joshua 13:15–23 onfirms the allotment of Heshbon to Reuben, although the next few verses 24–28) indicate it was contiguous with Gad's allotment. When Heshbon ecame a Levitical city, it was considered a city of Gad (Jos. 21:34–40; cf. 1 Chr. 6:81)—apparently because Reuben lost its tribal identity and was absorbed by Gad.

Although Heshbon is not mentioned by name in connection with the istory of the United Monarchy, 1 Kings 4:19 puts "the land of Gilead, he country of Sihon king of the Amorites" in Solomon's twelfth district.

The Mesha Stone (ninth century BCE) does not mention Heshbon, but ecause Medeba, Nebo, and Jahaz all came back into Moabite hands at that me, presumably Heshbon did as well. At least by the close of the eighth entury and into the seventh century BCE, Heshbon appears to be under firm Moabite control, for it figures in both extant recensions of a prophetic oracle gainst Moab (Is. 15:4, 16:8–9; Jer. 48:2, 48:34–35), where its fields, fruit, and arvest are mentioned. In Jeremiah 49:3, Heshbon appears again in the oracle gainst the Ammonites; perhaps it had changed hands again. Heshbon's final iblical mention is in Nehemiah 9:22, where it is part of a historical allusion to he Israelite conquest.

In the postbiblical literary sources, Heshbon is commonly called Hesbus ılthough there are many variant spellings). Josephus relates that in he second century BCE, Tyre of the Tobiads was located "between Arabia nd Judea, beyond Jordan, not far from the country of Hesebonitis Εσεβωνῖτις)" (*Antiq.* XII, 233). Further on he lists Heshbon among the ities (perhaps the capital) of the Moabites (*Antiq.* XIII, 397). The Maccaean John Hyrcanus captured the cities of Medeba and Samaga in 129 BCE Antiq. XIII, 255). Even though Hesbus is not specifically mentioned, it robably came into the hands of John Hyrcanus at this time because it is listed among the Jewish possessions in Moab during the reign of Alexander Jannaeus (103–76 BCE), not as a city captured by him (*Antiq.* XIII, 397).

Josephus includes Hesebon among several fortresses and fortified cities built by Herod the Great to strengthen his kingdom (*Antiq.* XV, 294); he populated it with veterans, probably to protect his border with the Nabateans. Under Herod's son, Antipas (4 BCE–39 CE), Jewish Peraea was on the south "bounded by the land of Moab, and on the east by Arabia, Hesebonitis, Philadelphia, and Gerasa" (*War* III, 47). At the beginning of the Jewish War (66 CE), the Jews sacked Heshbon (*War* II, 458). When the Roman province of Arabia Petraea was created in 106 CE, Hesbus was certainly a part of it; at least it is assigned to Arabia in Ptolemy's *Geography* (V, 17, 6).

W. Vyhmeister has summarized the evidence with regard to the Roman road: "Around 129–130, in preparation for the visit of the Emperor Hadrian, a road was built to connect Esbus with Livias, Jericho, and Jerusalem. . ." Three milestones (5–7) recording distances from Hesbus have been discovered. Two bear inscriptions naming several emperors and are so dated to the years 219, 307 and 364–375 (no. 5) and 162, 236 and 288 (no. 6). The mention of Hesbus as *caput viae* in Greek and Latin is an indication of its relative importance in this period.

Elagabalus (218–222 CE) raised Hesbus to municipal status, and in the early third century it minted its own bronze coins inscribed "Aurelia Esbus" (*BMC Arabia*, XXXIII, 29–30). At the turn of the century the town is frequently mentioned in Eusebius' *Onomasticon* as a reference for locating other towns in its district. In the next century, Hesbus appears for the first time as an episcopal see in the Acts of the Council of Nicaea. Again Hesbus sent its bishop to the Councils of Ephesus (431) and Chalcedon (457). Some correspondence of Pope Martin I (649) shows that Hesbus was still an important bishopric in the middle of the seventh century (R. Le Quien, *Oriens Christianus*, II, cols. 863–864).

A number of Greek Christian inscriptions were discovered at Heshbon (*IGLS, Jordanie*, nos. 58–62). Moreover, the town is represented in two eighth-century mosaic pavements featuring cities of Palestine, Arabia and Egypt, at Ma'in and Umm er-Rasas.

After the eighth century, the name Hesbus disappears from literary and epigraphic sources, reappearing only in its Arabic form, Ḥesbân. It is mentioned in the Abbasid period by the Arab geographer, Yaqut—who says there was a strong fortress here in the early ninth century—and Abu Dja'far Muḥammad at-Ṭabari (839–923). The next clear reference to Ḥesbân as an inhabited place comes in 1184, in connection with a campaign of Saladin recorded by Beha ed-Din. In the fourteenth century, Ḥesbân became the capital of the Belqa district and is mentioned by Ibn Fadl Allah al-'Umari (1301–1348), Dimishqi (d. 1327), Abu el-Feda (d. 1331), and several others. Finally, several Western travelers and explorers visited Ḥesbân, particularly in the nineteenth and twentieth centuries, from U. J. Seetzen in 1806 to N. Glueck in the early 1930s.

EXCAVATIONS

Six seasons of excavations have been carried out at Tell Ḥesbân, the first five by the Andrews University, Berrien Springs, Michigan, and the last by the Baptist Bible College, Clarks Summit, Pennsylvania, both with the cooperation of the American Schools of Oriental Research and the Jordan Department of Antiquities. The first three seasons (1968, 1971, 1973) were directed by S. H. Horn, and the fourth and fifth (1974 and 1976) by L. T. Geraty; R. S. Boraas provided continuity throughout as chief archaeologist. In 1978, J. Lawlor directed the continued excavation of the northern Byzantine church (found two years earlier), with the assistance of Geraty as senior advisor and L. G. Herr as chief archaeologist.

In the first season of excavation, the site was marked off by a major north–south and east–west pair of axes centered on the summit. The initial strategy was to cut a series of squares along the west and south lines of the intersection, providing a continuous stratigraphic connection from the west perimeter of the mound up to the center of the summit, then down the south slope to the edge. Eventually this was accomplished through the gradual expansion of four work areas (areas A–D, with 32 squares). These were carried down to bedrock and augmented in later seasons by investigations scattered around the perimeter of the site (22 squares), by tomb research carried out in four widely separated cemeteries (43 tombs), by a sounding at Umm es-Sarab to the north, and by a survey team seeking sites within a 10-km (6-mi.) radius of Tell Ḥesbân (155 sites). On the mound itself, a series of nineteen superimposed, distinguishable strata was identified. These covered a period from about 1200 BCE to 1500 CE, with only two primary gaps in occupation in evidence: Persian and Early Hellenistic (c. 500–250 BCE) and Ottoman (c. 1500–1870).

IRON AGE. The Iron Age remains (c. 1200–500 BCE) are very fragmentary due to the periodic removal of earlier strata on the top of the hill by later builders. Nevertheless, evidence for at least four strata remains.

Stratum 19 (twelfth–eleventh centuries BCE) probably represents a small, unfortified village dependent on an agrarian-pastoral economy. In its earliest

Heshbon: aerial view of the mound, looking west; (foreground) the large trench to the east of the acropolis.

phase, the most notable installation was a long (15 m exposed), 4-m-deep trench crudely carved out of bedrock on the mound's southern shelf. There is no real clue as to its purpose, although suggestions include a moat for defense, storage, cultic activity, subterranean habitation, or a water channel, if not a narrow reservoir itself. In its later phase, this installation was filled with soil and both the cobbled floor of a room and a 2.5-m-wide "filler" wall were built in it. An egg-shaped cistern may also be associated with this phase, which produced so many loom weights there may have been a cottage industry here. The Iron Age I at the village of Heshbon was characterized by mixed farming, much cattle, and many neighboring farming communities.

Stratum 18 (tenth century BCE) left no in situ remains, but its pottery was found in deep dump layers outside the contemporary settlement on the western slope. It may have been a continuation of the stratum 19 village.

Stratum 17 (ninth–eighth centuries BCE) is also represented by sloping debris layers dumped to the west, but it may be better remembered for the initial construction of a reservoir, 17.5 m to a side and 7 m deep. Its eastern wall was plastered three times and supplemented a header-stretcher retaining wall cut into the bedrock. Although several channels carved out of the adjoining bedrock funneled rainwater to the reservoir, its capacity appears to exceed the amount of winter rain that would normally fall in the catchment area; the intention may have been to transport the extra water up to the reservoir from below the mound. If so, perhaps this stratum is what is left of Mesha's attempt to fortify his northern border with Israel. This might also be the pool referred to in the Song of Songs (7:4).

Stratum 16 (seventh–sixth centuries BCE) was the best-preserved Iron Age stratum. Its remains indicate a general prosperity and continued growth that probably clustered around a fort. A few scattered domestic units came to light on the western slope, and the reservoir continued in use, perhaps as part of a way station or supply depot on the King's Highway. It was probably controlled by the Ammonites, judging from the pottery and several ostraca found in the reservoir fill. Stratum 16 may have come to a violent end, considering the great quantity of ash in the debris that was scraped from the abandoned town into the reservoir by its (Hasmonean?) rebuilders in the second century BCE.

In general, the Iron Age II/Persian period town at Heshbon is characterized by central government planning (the reservoir) and mixed farming with a small tree and vineyard dependency.

HELLENISTIC AND ROMAN PERIODS. After it had been abandoned for nearly 300 years, Tell Ḥesbân was reoccupied in the Late Hellenistic period. The remains from the Hellenistic and Roman periods (c. 200 BCE–365 CE) comprise at least five strata.

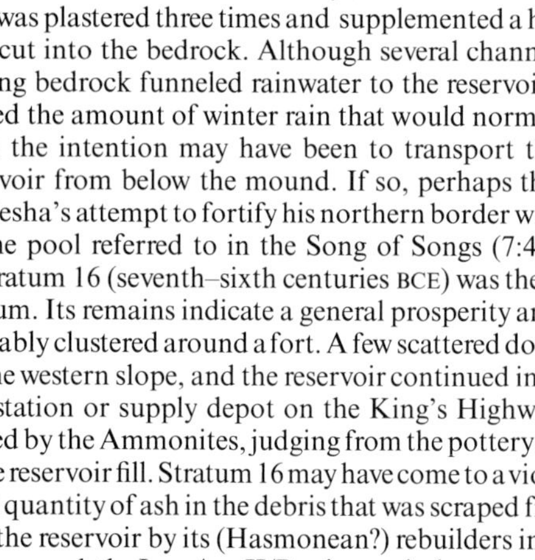

Coin of Elagabalus, minted in Heshbon.

Stratum 15 (c. 200–63 BCE) consisted primarily of a rectangular military fortress at the summit, probably surrounded by the dwellings of dependents (in which luxury goods were occasionally found), often in association with bell-shaped subterranean silos. Thus, there is evidence for a transition from a nomadic to a semisedentary existence at Hesbus.

In stratum 14 (c. 63 BCE–130 CE) Hesbus came under the control of Herod the Great, probably as a border fort against the Nabateans. There is abundant evidence for extensive subterranean dwellings on the mound and characteristic Herodian period family tombs in the cemetery. Two such tombs, which are indications of moderate wealth, were found sealed with rolling stones. Stratum 14 was destroyed by an earthquake.

Stratum 13 (130–c. 193 CE) contained much new building. South of the fort, a new inn with an enclosed courtyard testifies to the increased traffic past the road junction (Via Nova and Hesbus–Livias) at which Roman Hesbus was located. A mixed-farming food system prevailed.

In stratum 12 (c. 193–284), the inn was partially rebuilt and saw frequent use. On the acropolis, earlier masonry was incorporated into what has been interpreted as a small temple—perhaps the one depicted on the Elagabalus coin minted for Hesbus, a very fine example of which was found at the site in 1973. Access to the temple from the south was via a ramp.

Stratum 11 (c. 284–363) continued to demonstrate a modest level of prosperity; there was a decrease in the use of cattle for food, but an increase in the use of horses and donkeys for farming. There was also evidence for an increase in cultivated trees and vines. A porch was added to the temple and a double colonnade built eastward from it. The inn to the south of the acropolis platform was demolished and a wide monumental stairway replaced the earlier earth ramp. The stratum came to an abrupt end with the severe earthquake of 363.

BYZANTINE AND EARLY ARAB PERIODS. Apart from the earthquake, the transition from the Roman to the Byzantine period was a gradual one. The Roman cemetery continued to be used. There was intensive food production to support an ever-growing population that required careful water management (a reservoir 70 by 50 m was partially excavated in the eastern wadi) and practiced a market economy. At least six strata encompass the Byzantine and Early Arab remains (365–c. 1000) at Tell Ḥesbân.

In stratum 10 (365–408), the growing Christian community was apparently significant enough to prevent the rebuilding of the temple that had been destroyed by the earthquake, but not quite strong enough to construct a church immediately. A bone carving of Prometheus is a choice find from this period.

Stratum 9 (408–551) saw the construction of a slightly asymmetrical basilica-type church on the acropolis. Its plaster apparently came from a large subterranean lime kiln to the south. The stratum may have been brought to a close by the earthquake that affected Palestine and Arabia in 551.

In addition to reconstruction activity, possibly necessitated by the 551 earthquake, stratum 8 (551–614) also witnessed the construction of another basilica-type church, with well-preserved mosaic floors, to the north of the

Byzantine church on the acropolis, looking east.

acropolis. The reconstructed acropolis church had a much less ornate mosaic loor than its predecessor.

The close of stratum 8 was probably brought on by the invasion of the Sassanid Persians. The remains from stratum 7 (614–661) are very scant. Occupation seems to have centered south of the acropolis church within he acropolis circumvallation wall.

The coming of Islam in the Jmayyad period coincided with a light increase in activity in stratum 6 (661–750). A large oven was contructed on the mosaic floor of one of the anterooms in the Late Byzantine acropolis church, which by then was probably already in ruins because here is no evidence for an Umayyad destruction. With the move of the center of Islamic rule to the east in the Abbasid period, there was a sharp decline in population in stratum 5 (750–1000) and a reversal of the processes hat had peaked in the Byzantine period. No architectural remains from the Abbasid period were uncovered. Unless it was abandoned, the mound may eventually have been occupied by a seminomadic population.

Bone carving depicting Prometheus in chains, Early Byzantine period.

AYYUBID AND MAMELUKE PERIODS. Although it was a village of no particular significance in the early periods of Islamic rule, after a gap in sedentary occupation, Ḥesbân flourished again immediately after the Crusades. It even replaced 'Amman as the capital of the Belqa district in central Transjordan. Its remains comprise at least three strata (c. 1200–1500), which were relatively well preserved compared to the earlier remains. Stratum 4 (c. 1200–1260) represents the occupational surfaces of an Ayyubid village and terracing around two cisterns on the summit.

Stratum 3 (c. 1260–1400) is characterized by food-production intensification, a water-collection system, and a large number of soil and architectural loci that reflect extensive new Early Mameluke construction activity using the existing Roman-Byzantine ruins as a base. At the mound's summit an elaborate, U-shaped building complex (including a bathhouse) was reached by a stairway from the south. A number of vaulted rooms opened onto a central courtyard created by clearing the debris of the collapsed Byzantine church. Because the postal route from Kerak to Damascus passed through the town, these remains may be an inn complex in which wayfarers and their animals were cared for. The mound at that time was surrounded by domestic quarters and cisterns that covered large parts of the slope above the terraces.

Stratum 2 (c. 1400–1500), at the end of the Mameluke period, witnessed the city's decline, apparently as a result of plagues or wars; it was eventually abandoned. The gap in occupation that followed lasted until the end of the nineteenth century. Stratum 1 shows a gradual return to the mound and limited occupation from the Ottoman period to modern times.

(Most of the publications on Heshbon appear in *Andrews University Seminary Studies.*)
History: W. Vyhmeister, *AUSS* 6 (1968), 158–177.
Excavations
Main publications: O. S. LaBianca, *Hesban 1: Sedentarization and Nomadization*, 1990; *Hesban 2: Environmental Foundations* (eds. O. S. LaBianca and L. Lacelle), 1986; *Hesban 3: Historical Foundations* (eds. L. T. Geraty and L. G. Running), 1989; O. S. LaBianca, *Hesban 4: Ethnoarchaeological Foundations* (in prep.); R. D. Ibach, Jr., *Hesban 5: Archaeological Survey of the Hesban Region*, 1987; *Hesban 6: Iron Age Strata* (ed. L. T. Geraty, in prep.); L. A. Mitchell, *Hesban 7: Hellenistic and Roman Strata* (in prep.); J. B. Storfjell, *Hesban 8: Byzantine and Early Islamic Strata* (in prep.); B. DeVries, *Hesban 9: Ayyubid-Mamluk Strata* (in prep.); *Hesban 10: Cemetery Remains* (ed. O. S. LaBianca and L. T. Geraty, in prep.); J. A. Sauer, *Hesban 11: Ceramic Finds* (in prep.); *Hesban 12: Small Finds* (ed. L. T. Geraty, in prep.); *Hesban 13: Faunal Remains* (ed. O. S. LaBianca, in prep.); *Hesban 14: Hesban and Biblical History* (ed. L. T. Geraty, in prep.) (all published in Berrien Springs, Mich.).
Other studies: *ADAJ* 12–13 (1967–1968), 51–52; 17 (1972), 15–22; 18 (1973), 87–88; 19 (1974), 151–163; id., BA 32/2 (1969), 26–41; id., *RB* 76 (1969), 395–398; 79 (1972), 422–426; 82 (1975), 100–105; id., *ASOR Newsletter* (Nov. 1971), 1–4; (Sept. 1973), 1–4; id., *Heshbon in the Bible and Archaeology*, Berrien Springs, Mich. 1982; R. S. Boraas, S. H. Horn et al., *AUSS* 7/2 (1969); 10 (1972); 11/1 (1973); 13/1–2 (1975); 14/1 (1976); id., *Heshbon 1968* (Andrews University Monographs 2), Berrien Springs, Mich. 1969; id., *Heshbon 1971* (Andrews University Monographs 6), Berrien Springs, Mich. 1973; id., ibid. (Reviews), *PEQ* 106 (1974), 91. — *IEJ* 29 (1979), 257; id., *Heshbon 1973* (Andrews University Monographs 8), Berrien Springs, Mich. 1975; id., ibid. (Reviews), *JBL* 96 (1977), 578–580. — *PEQ* 109 (1977), 55; R. S. Boraas and L. T. Geraty, *Heshbon 1974* (Andrews University Monographs 9), Berrien Springs, Mich. 1976; id., *Heshbon 1976* (Andrews University Monographs 10), Berrien Springs, Mich. 1978; id., *Archaeology* 32 (1979), 10–20; A. Terian, *AUSS* 9 (1971), 147–160; 12 (1974), 35–46; 18/2 (1980), 173–178; E. N. Lugenbeal and J. A. Sauer, *AUSS* 10 (1972), 21–68; J. A. Sauer, *Heshbon*

Pottery 1971 (Andrews University Monographs 7), Berrien Springs, Mich. 1973; id., ibid. (Reviews), *AJA* 78 (1974), 434–435.— *PEQ* 106 (1974), 91.— *BASOR* 227 (1977), 78–79; L. T. Geraty, *ASOR Newsletter* (Nov. 1974), 1–8; (Jan. 1977), 1–16; id., *ADAJ* 20 (1975), 47–56; 21 (1976), 41–53; 27 (1983), 646–647; id., *RB* 82 (1975), 576–586; 84 (1977), 404–408; L. T. Geraty and O. S. LaBianca, *SHAJ* 2 (1985), 323–330; id., *Proceedings of the Second International Conference on the Archaeology of Jordan*, Oxford 1985; H. Mare, *Near East Archaeology Society Bulletin* 5 (1975), 21–46; W. H. Shea, *AUSS* 15 (1977), 217–222; J. I. Lawlor, *ASOR Newsletter* (Jan. 1979), 1–8; id., *RB* 86 (1979), 115–117; id., *ADAJ* 24 (1980), 95–105; id., *AUSS* 18 (1980), 65–76; O. S. LaBianca, *AJA* 84 (1980), 219; id., *ADAJ* 28 (1984), 269–287; id., *The Archaeology of Jordan and Other Studies* (S. H. Horn Fest.), Berrien Springs Mich. 1986, 167–181; id., "Sedentarization and Nomadization Food System Cycles at Hesban and Vicinity in Transjordan" (Ph.D. diss., Brandeis Univ. 1987); L. A. Mitchell, *AJA* 84 (1980), 224; id., "The Hellenistic and Roman Periods of Tell Hesban, Jordan," Ann Arbor 1981 (Ph.D. diss., Andrews Univ. 1980); J. B. Storfjell, *AJA* 84 (1980), 234–235; id., "The Stratigraphy of Tell Hesban, Jordan, in the Byzantine Period" (Ph.D. diss. Andrews University 1983); *American Archaeology in the Mideast*, 190–195; J. M. Miller, *ZDPV* 99 (1983) 123–124; G. V. Foster, *AJA* 88 (1984), 243–244; R. Althann, *Biblica* 66 (1985), 568–571; F. M. Cross, Jr. *The Archaeology of Jordan and Other Studies* (S. H. Horn Fest.), (op. cit.) 475–490; R. A. Coughenour *MdB* 46 (1986), 24; B. de Vries, (S. H. Horn Fest.) (op. cit.), 223–235; P.-L. Gatier, *Inscriptions de la Jordanie 2, Région Centrale* (Bibliothèque Archéologique et Historique 114), Paris 1986, 76–77 U. Hübner, *ZDPV* 104 (1988), 68–73; H.-C. Schmitt, ibid., 26–43; Weippert 1988 (Ortsregister) *Akkadica Supplementum* 7–8 (1989), 262–268; E. A. Knauf, *ZDPV* 106 (1990), 135–144; D. Merling *Archaeology in the Biblical World* 1/2 (1991), 10–17.

LAWRENCE T. GERATY

ḤESI, TELL EL-

IDENTIFICATION

Tell el-Ḥesi is located on the southeastern Coastal Plain, 26 km (16 mi.) northeast of Gaza and 7 km (4 mi.) south of Qiryat Gat (map reference 124.106). The site occupies a cluster of barchan sand dunes on the west bank of Wadi Ḥesi (Naḥal Shiqma) and is composed of a 25-a. lower city with a 4-a. acropolis at its northeast corner. The natural dune on which the acropolis sits was originally 17 m high, and the occupational remains have added 21 m to its height. Occupational deposits in the lower city are a maximum of 3 m deep; in the low-lying portions of the site they have been removed by erosion and modern deep plowing.

Ḥesi's ancient identity remains unknown. C. R. Conder was the first to identify Ḥesi with Lachish. W. M. F. Petrie also accepted this identification, particularly because of the proximity of a small site with a similar name, Khirbet Umm Lakis, 4.5 km (3 mi.) northwest of Ḥesi. This identification was supported by F. J. Bliss's discovery in 1891 of an el-Amarna tablet that mentions Lachish. However, discoveries at Tell ed-Duweir have led most scholars to conclude that this site is to be identified with Lachish. In the 1920s, W. F. Albright proposed that Ḥesi was to be identified with Eglon, a Canaanite city-state conquered by the Israelites (Jos. 10:34, 15:39). No conclusive evidence for this has yet come to light. Biblical accounts place Eglon in the Shephelah, and Ḥesi's location several kilometers west of these foothills makes the identification unlikely.

EXPLORATION

Ḥesi holds a unique place in Near Eastern archaeology as the first site to have been excavated by scientific archaeological methods. Petrie conducted a brief six-week season in 1890 under the auspices of the British Palestine Exploration Fund. In this excavation he developed the foundations of modern archaeological method through the application of the principles of stratigraphic excavation and ceramic chronology. His publication of this work was the first to correlate pottery and artifacts with stratigraphy and to illustrate pottery in section drawings. Petrie carried out soundings in the lower city and excavated along the slopes of the acropolis because the summit was under cultivation. When the PEF continued its work from 1891 to 1893, Bliss, the new director, was able to arrange excavation of the summit. In his four seasons of work, he removed the entire northeast quadrant of the acropolis down to virgin soil and attempted to provide a detailed picture to complete the investigation begun by Petrie.

After an interval of almost eighty years, work resumed at Ḥesi in 1970 when the Joint Archaeological Expedition, affiliated with the American Schools of Oriental Research, began its investigation. Eight seasons of field work took place between 1970 and 1983. The Joint Expedition investigated the acropolis to the west and south of Bliss's excavation area (field I), the southern slope of the acropolis (field III), and the lower city (fields II, IV–IX).

THE PALESTINE EXPLORATION FUND EXCAVATIONS

Petrie and Bliss placed a total of seventy-nine probes in the lower city. Petrie identified the remains, which were up to 3 m deep, as belonging to the site's earliest occupation. He dated this to about 1700 BCE and named it the Amorite period. In the northwest quadrant of the lower city, Petrie uncovered a very thick mud-brick city wall from this early period, and Bliss found a mud-brick wall with a tower in the northeast quadrant. More recent excavations have shown that the occupation in the lower city can be dated to the Early Bronze Age.

The focus of Petrie's work was the eastern slope of the acropolis, where erosion and the water from Wadi Ḥesi had cut away some of the mound and produced a fairly steep slope. Probes along the eastern face revealed portions of several walls and buildings. Petrie traced one thick wall around the north, west, and south sides of the acropolis. He attributed this wall to Manasseh. He also identified a "long range of chambers" whose eastern portion had been washed away. This consisted of a mud-brick wall with cross walls that formed chambers. The chambers had been filled with rubbish, according to Petrie. Covering this structure was a crushed-stone glacis and above the glacis, the so-called Manasseh wall. Petrie attributed these structures to his Phoenician period, which encompassed the Late Bronze and Iron ages. The Joint Expedition has shown that these architectural elements were part of a large construction project in the Iron Age II (see below).

Bliss's excavation, which removed almost one-third of the acropolis, produced eleven layers of features that he grouped into eight "cities." Bliss followed Petrie's chronology of the site and his pottery analysis. Bliss's pub-

Tell el-Ḥesi: general view, looking northwest.

Reconstruction of a doorjamb in the Pilaster Building found by Petrie.

lication focused on the architecture and the artifacts and provided detailed descriptions and plans of the major structures in each city.

CITIES I-B AND I. In the earliest levels excavated by Bliss, there were poorly preserved and fragmentary building remains. The very thick mud-brick wall found by Petrie to the northwest belongs to this stratum, as do the wall and tower found by Bliss. A collection of bronze vessels and tools found in a sounding at the southeast part of the acropolis was dated by Bliss to this stratum. These bronze implements date to the Early Bronze Age III, but because their location was separated from the main excavation, it is difficult to determine their stratigraphic relationship.

CITIES II-B AND II. Here again it was difficult to provide a plan of coherent structures. It is not clear whether the wall and tower of cities I-b and I may in fact belong to cities II-b and II. The pottery from city II is Late Bronze Age I, so Bliss's dating of the fifteenth century BCE was fairly accurate. A significant find was a kiln discovered by Bliss that still contained large amounts of slag. He determined that this was not from iron smelting and attributed it to an undetermined industrial activity.

CITY III. A portion of a large building filled nearly half of the excavation area. It consisted of a wall with a row of rooms adjoining it. A cuneiform tablet of the el-Amarna type was found in bricky debris adjacent to this building. On the basis of the tablet, city III was dated to the fourteenth century BCE. The letter was written by an Egyptian official to his superior. The official, who apparently was writing from Lachish, complained that the Canaanite rulers in the area were leading their own groups of followers in defiance of Pharaoh and were contributing to the region's instability.

City III was covered by a thick ash layer previously noted by Petrie. The ash layer, from 1 to 2.5 m deep, covers a large part of the site. Petrie attributed it to alkali burners, whereas Bliss attempted to relate it to the kiln of city II. This is not possible stratigraphically, although Bliss's interpretation of extensive industrial activity at the site may be correct. The thick ash layer is still visible in the vertical face of Bliss's trench; it is actually made up of many very thin lenses of ash that may well be the result of industrial activity.

CITIES IV-B AND IV. City IV-b was built on the ash layer covering city III. A large, thick-walled building measuring about 18 by 18 m filled the excavation area. Bliss placed Petrie's pilaster building in this city. Because, however, the pilasters are of the Proto-Aeolic style of the ninth century BCE, Bliss's dating of this structure to city IV is incorrect. Bliss dated city IV to 1400 to 1300 BCE. The pottery, cylinder seals, and scarabs confirm this dating, as does a sherd with a fourteenth-century incised Canaanite inscription *bl'* (בלע).

Petrie and Bliss believed that there was a gap in occupation following city IV. Petrie stated that there was no evidence present at the site from the period of the Judges, and Bliss's evidence showed nothing between 1300 BCE at the end of city IV and city V with its tenth- to ninth-century dating. Recently, however, the Joint Expedition has uncovered Iron Age I material in a probe.

CITY V. The chief structure of city V was parallel rows of stone pillar bases with brick walls between them. This structure covered an area of 15 by 37 m. Bliss was uncertain about the purpose of this construction, although it is likely to have been a typical Iron Age storehouse. Petrie's Pilaster Building probably belongs in this city. Pottery found by Petrie inside the building suggests a date of tenth or early ninth century BCE.

CITIES VI–VIII. Beginning with city VI, Bliss's plans are fragmentary and probably represent composites. His plans show many pits, which are now known to have typified the site during the Persian period. Between cities VI and VII there was a depth of over 3 m of earth without structural remains. Bliss did not explain this feature, but it was likely fill between some of the walls composing Petrie's "long range of chambers." In city VII there was a residential area with portions of two houses preserved. Pottery within the houses dates to the eighth to seventh centuries BCE. City VII was destroyed by fire. Little can be said about city VIII from the meager information given by Bliss. He dated cities VI–VIII from 800 to 400 BCE. Today these strata are known to represent the ninth to third centuries BCE.

THE JOINT ARCHAEOLOGICAL EXPEDITION

The Joint Expedition began its work on the acropolis and opened areas to the west and south of Bliss's trench and along the southern slope of the acropolis, where correlations with Petrie's excavation were anticipated. Excavation on the acropolis reached the level of the Iron Age I period. A series of probes and extended excavation in the lower city were also carried out in order to expand upon the conclusions of Petrie and Bliss. The Joint Expedition established Ḥesi's almost continuous occupation from the Chalcolithic through the Hellenistic periods. Unstratified Roman-period pottery was also found. After a hiatus of several centuries, Ḥesi was again in use during the seventeenth to nineteenth and the twentieth centuries CE. A surface survey also identified a Middle Paleolithic occupation in the vicinity of Ḥesi.

CHALCOLITHIC PERIOD. Chalcolithic pottery has been found both on the acropolis and in the lower city. The only stratified material found by the Joint Expedition was the lower portion of two pits located at the base of the southern slope of the acropolis. The find spots of unstratified sherds suggest that additional stratified Chalcolithic material may exist at the unexcavated base of occupation on the acropolis.

EARLY BRONZE AGE. During the Early Bronze Age, occupation at Ḥesi covered the site's 25 a. The Early Bronze Age inhabitants lived first on the sand dune of the acropolis, where remains of seven Early Bronze Age phases were associated with Early Bronze Age I and Early Bronze Age II pottery.

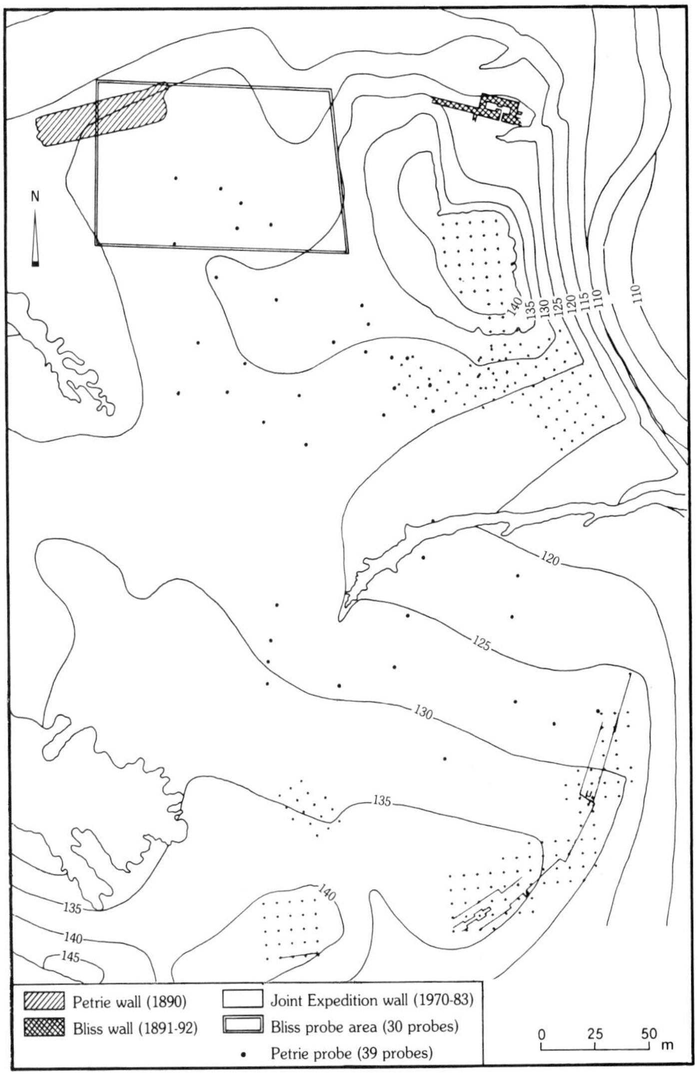

The EB city at Tell el-Ḥesi, as excavated by Petrie, Bliss, and the Joint Expedition.

*Section in the mound's northern slope: **(A)** top of the lower city wall, Iron II; **(B)** EB remains cut by the foundation trench of the lower city wall; **(C)** stepped slope and fill, Iron II; **(D)** upper city wall, or "Manasseh wall," Iron II.*

Section through the lower city wall, Iron II.

These phases have not been excavated but were identified in the course of excavating the foundations of the Iron Age city wall. In the late Early Bronze Age II/Early Bronze Age III the population increased and the site expanded to the full 25 a. The remains in the lower city contain this later pottery.

Probes in the lower city by the Joint Expedition confirmed the shallow depth of occupation noted by Petrie and Bliss. Much of the evidence for occupation in the lower city, especially at the lower elevations, has been removed by erosion and modern plowing. On the ridge of dunes at the southern perimeter of the site, the Joint Expedition found the Early Bronze Age city wall in fields V, VI, and IX. The wall was traced for 82 m along the south and 95 m along the eastern edge of the site. This mud-brick wall was about 5 m wide and it had towers spaced along it. A tower was found in field VI that was more than 20 m long, although its western end had been eroded. The tower contained two chambers connected by a corridor. On the floors of the chambers basalt grinding stones and smashed Early Bronze Age III pottery were found sealed by a black ash layer. The plan of this tower strongly resembles that of the tower found by Bliss on the northern edge of the acropolis, with which it is very probably contemporary.

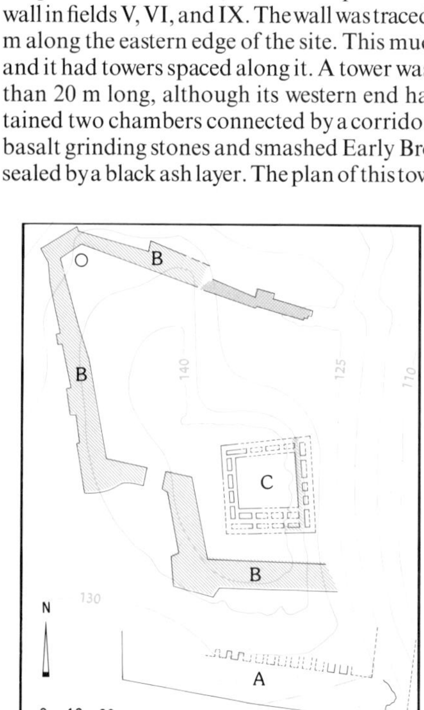

Petrie's excavations (1890)
Bliss's excavations (1891-1892)
Joint Expedition's excavations (1970-1983)
Conjectured walls
Well (Petrie, 1890)

Plan of stratum VII-d, Iron II.

Along the outer face of the Early Bronze Age city wall a thick layer of ash contained large quantities of Early Bronze Age III sherds, ceramic animal figurines, and other artifacts. This was not destruction ash; it was wind and water sorted, with a heavy organic content, and it may represent a local garbage dump. At the southeast corner of the site the city wall turns to the north; a glacislike deposit of crushed limestone had been placed against its outer face. This construction had a horizontal exposure of 9 m before it sloped down toward the wadi, which suggests that its primary purpose was erosion control. This crushed limestone construction was traced for 60 m to the north, along the outside of the city wall.

Within the Early Bronze Age city and adjacent to the city wall were remains of domestic and industrial activity. These included a drainage channel, a courtyard work area containing ovens and a variety of tools, and residential dwellings. Five phases of occupation were identified here, and all can be dated to the Early Bronze Age III. A few ceramic forms are reminiscent of the Early Bronze Age II, although they occur alongside classic Early Bronze Age III vessels.

Ḥesi appears to have been abandoned at some time during the Early Bronze Age III. There is no evidence of destruction at the site. The mold-made bricks of the city wall were rich in organic materials no longer available. The bricks contained a humus-filled clay no longer present, as well as the snail *Gryaulus piscinarum*, which inhabits sluggish streams and swamps. Organic material from the ash deposits revealed pistachio and emmer wheat, along with a range of animal bones suggestive of an economy based on cattle, sheep, and goat raising and the cultivation of emmer wheat. The overuse of natural resources to accommodate a growing population may have combined with a slight climatic shift to lead to the demise of Ḥesi. Progressive desiccation moving northward from Egypt late in the third millennium BCE has been documented. Ḥesi most likely became part of the trend of abandonment experienced by its southern neighbors.

MIDDLE BRONZE AGE. There is meager evidence for a Middle Bronze Age occupation at Ḥesi. None of the excavators has identified any structural remains from this period, although some Middle Bronze Age II sherds have been found. The focal point of occupation in the area during the period appears to have been at Tel Nagila, located 5.5 km (3 mi.) from Ḥesi. Apparently, occupation at Ḥesi was not resumed until the Late Bronze Age.

LATE BRONZE AGE. Although the Joint Expedition did not reach the Late Bronze Age levels in its excavation, some Late Bronze Age materials were encountered in the removal of later strata on the acropolis. Fragments of both mud-brick and stone walls accompanied by Late Bronze Age pottery were identified as belonging to three phases of occupation. Excavation in the lower city in field V revealed significant quantities of Late Bronze Age pottery, but these sherds were not well stratified, and any associated structures had been eroded.

IRON AGE I. The Iron Age I period (stratum VIII) was reached in only one probe. The probe revealed a mud-brick wall about 1.5 m wide, with an interior plaster floor to its east and an exterior sandy surface to its west. The plaster floor was covered by a heavy layer of destruction debris made up of bricky material and charcoal. The few sherds found have been dated to the eleventh century BCE.

IRON AGE II. During the ninth century BCE, a massive engineering project was undertaken at Ḥesi. Petrie had found portions of this construction in his so called Manasseh wall and in the "long range of chambers." Bliss also had excavated a small part of the Iron Age II construction along the north side of the acropolis as part of his city VI. Identified by the Joint Expedition as stratum VII-d, this construction project produced a double wall system

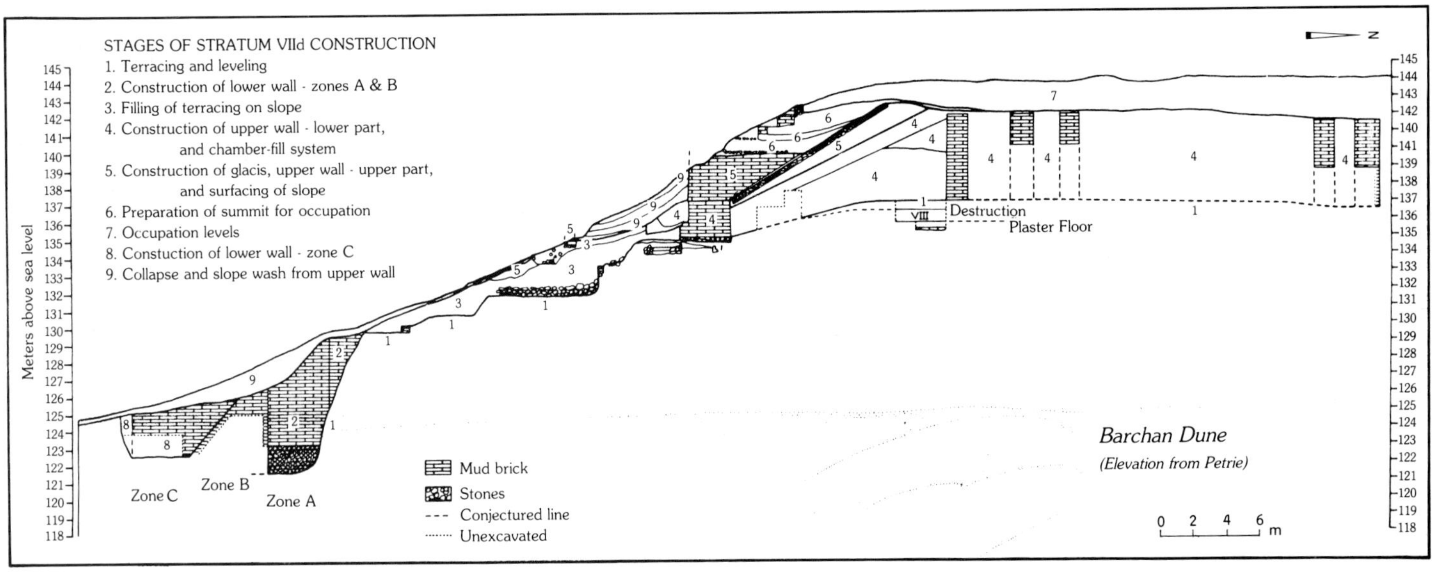

Schematic section of the Iron II (ninth century BCE) constructions at Ḥesi, excavated by the Joint Expedition.

around the acropolis and a platform at its summit on which occupational structures could be built. This platform raised the height of the southern half of the acropolis by 6 to 7 m. The wall system surrounded the acropolis on all sides; erosion has removed most of the eastern portion.

The 12-m-wide outer wall, at the base of the acropolis, formed the foundation of the system. A series of four terraces consolidated the slope between the lower and upper walls. The upper wall (Petrie's Manasseh wall) was 3 m wide. Between the upper wall and platform on the summit, the slope was filled with consolidating material that was secured in place by means of a pebble and lime-plaster glacis. The platform on the summit of the acropolis (Petrie's long range of chambers) consisted of a system of chambers and fill. A series of double walls connected by cross walls formed the limits of the platform. The space between the walls and the area enclosed by the walls was filled with earth to form the platform that supported the structures built above it.

The first structure built on the platform was a ninth-century BCE courtyard building (stratum VII-c). Above it were several smaller residential structures dating to the eighth to sixth centuries BCE (strata VII-b and VII-a). The sixth-century BCE occupation of stratum VII-a was covered with a heavy layer of ash and destruction debris, probably the result of the Babylonian/Edomite destruction of the site. Stratum VI consisted of a poorly built mud-brick house that was dated to later in the sixth century BCE.

Ḥesi's location dominates the surrounding plain and provides an excellent view of all the roads in the area. It is one of a group of small Iron Age sites that runs along the inner Shephelah. This group includes Bornat, 'Erani, Sheqef, Ḥesi, Queiṭra and Muleiḥa, and together they may have served as border outposts along the outer perimeter of defense for Lachish and southwestern Judah. The contemporary Iron Age fortress at Lachish is very similar in plan to that at Ḥesi. These outposts and defensive systems may be those established by Rehoboam to protect the southern and western borders of Judah from Egyptian raids (2 Chr. 11:5–12). The defensive system established by Rehoboam continued in use throughout the eighth century BCE until the Assyrian conquest of Judah. This correlates with the dates of strata VII-d and VII-c at Ḥesi. Ḥesi's occupation during the seventh and sixth centuries BCE was residential and industrial rather than military.

PERSIAN PERIOD. During the Persian period Ḥesi once again served a military or governmental function. In the first half of the fifth century BCE, the result of another massive building project was a large platform on which a small citadel was constructed (stratum V-d). The citadel was formed by casemate walls surrounding a central courtyard with a hard-packed earthen floor. No residential dwellings were found in the excavation area, although there were some signs of domestic activities, including the production of flour from grain. In stratum V-d, as well as in the later Persian period phases, there were significant quantities of imported Attic Greek ceramics that aided in dating the stratum. On this basis, stratum V-d may be dated to roughly 500 to 460 BCE. Taking into account the artifactual and ceramic materials, it is likely that the citadel of stratum V-d functioned as a semipermanent governmental grain storehouse and/or a depot under the control of the Persian Empire.

In the mid-fifth century BCE, stratum V-c was occupied for a short time. A building of simpler construction than that of V-d was located roughly above

Round tower in the city wall, Persian period.

Bes jug, Persian period.

the V-d citadel. Again, a hard-packed earthen floor covered much of the excavation area. The ceramics and artifacts strongly resembled those from stratum V-d, with the exception of a high proportion of transport jars. Transport jars were less common in stratum V-b, while the architectural evidence showed fragmentary walls of several buildings. The Greek ceramics from stratum V-b indicate that occupation occurred over a number of years in the last third of the fifth century BCE. A small cemetery from the Persian period was found on the southern slope of the acropolis in field III and is probably contemporary with strata V-c and V-b. This cemetery contained simple graves of men, women, and children, which suggests that some people remained at the site year-round to oversee the grain business.

Stratum V-a, dated to the end of the fifth century BCE, was structurally a renovation of the preceding phase. Characteristic of this phase were large, brick-lined pits 1 to 2 m wide and up to 2 m deep. These pits were probably used as grain silos. They were a rich source of broken pottery, seeds, bones, and a variety of implements and weapons. The botanical evidence indicates a preponderance of wheat over barley within the pits. The general absence of fourth-century BCE Greek ceramics suggests that the stratum V-a occupation probably did not continue into the fourth century BCE. Between 404 and 401 BCE, the Persian military engaged in raids into Egypt, and it is probable that stratum V-a at Ḥesi served as a staging ground and supply dump during those years.

HELLENISTIC PERIOD. The Joint Expedition identified three phases of Hellenistic material on the acropolis (stratum IV). Bliss's city VIII plan was a composite of all three phases. Although mud-brick construction characterized the site throughout its history, during the Hellenistic occupation the use of stone was common in walls, in foundations for mud-brick walls, and in stone-lined drains and basins. The Hellenistic structures were quite fragmentary because burials from the Muslim cemetery (stratum II) had been dug down into the Hellenistic levels. There was little architecture in the latest Hellenistic phase, and the excavation area was filled with pits containing pottery, artifacts, and faunal and botanical material.

LATE ARAB PERIOD. Some time after the Hellenistic period, the summit of the acropolis was leveled and was perhaps used sporadically for agriculture. The site has produced hardly any evidence for the Roman, Byzantine, or Early Arab period. Stratum III appears to belong to the Ottoman period. It consists of a few remains of pits, hearths, surfaces, and fragmentary walls, which were probably associated with agriculture and stock raising.

Arab Cemetery. Bliss's workers encountered burials immediately below the modern surface of the site, both on the acropolis and in the lower city. Bliss suggested that these burials were two hundred to three hundred years old. This dating has held up, and the burials of stratum II have been dated by the Joint Expedition to about 1600 to 1800 CE. The Joint Expedition discovered these burials on the acropolis and along the dunes on the southern rim of the lower city. These dunes were probably used for burials because there was a shrine there of a minor Muslim saint. Altogether, the Joint Expedition removed over eight hundred burials. The scientific study of these remains has provided important data about the Bedouin population of the seventeenth to nineteenth centuries. Bodies were placed in simple earth graves primarily with jewelry but generally with few grave goods. Stone slabs were sometimes used as capstones or to line the bottom of the grave pit. The bodies were placed so that the eyes were directed toward Mecca.

Main publications: W. M. F. Petrie, *Tell el Hesy (Lachish)*, London 1891; F. J. Bliss, *A Mound of Many Cities*, London 1898; J. A. Blakely and L. E. Toombs, *The Tell el-Hesi Field Manual* (Joint Archaeological Expedition to Tell el-Hesi 1), Cambridge, Mass. 1980; L. E. Toombs, *Tell el-Hesi: Modern Military Trenching and Muslim Cemetery in Field I, Strata I–II* (Joint Archaeological Expedition to Tell el-Hesi 2), Waterloo, Ontario 1985; W. J. Bennett, Jr., and J. A. Blakely, *Tell el-Hesi: The Persian Period, Stratum V* (Joint Archaeological Expedition to Tell el-Hesi 3), Winona Lake, Ind. 1989; *Tell el-Hesi: The Site and the Expedition* (Joint Archaeological Expedition to Tell el-Hesi 4, eds. B. T. Dahlberg and K. G. O'Connell), Winona Lake, Ind. 1989; *PEQ* 122/2 (1990).

Other studies: W. M. F. Petrie, *PEQ* 24 (1892), 114–115; W. F. Albright, *BASOR* 15 (1924), 2–11, id., *Archiv für Orientforschung* 5 (1928), 150–152; id., *AJSLL* 55 (1938), 345; id., *BASOR* 87 (1942), 32–38; G. E. Wright, *AJA* 43 (1939), 462; id., *BA* 34 (1971), 76–86; id., *Harvard Theological Review* 64 (1971), 437–448; J. Obermann, *AJA* 44 (1940), 93–104; K. M. Kenyon, *Annual Report*, Institute of Archaeology, University of London 11 (1955), 1–9; J. E. Worrell, *ASOR Newsletter* (Apr. 1970); (Dec. 1970), 1–4; L. E. Stager, *BA* 34 (1971), 86–88; id., *Harvard Theological Review* 64 (1971), 448–450; L. E. Toombs and J. E. Worrell (later with D. G. Rose and K. G. O'Connell), *IEJ* 21 (1971), 177–178, 232–233; 24 (1974), 139–141; 25 (1975), 172–174; 27 (1977), 197–199, 246–250; 30 (1980), 221–223; 32 (1982), 67–69; id., *RB* 79 (1972), 585–588; 82 (1975), 268–270; 83 (1976), 257–260; 85 (1978), 84–89; 91 (1984), 272–277; L. E. Toombs, *PEQ* 106 (1974), 19–31; 108 (1976), 41–54; 110 (1978), 75–90; 112 (1980), 73–91; 115 (1983), 25–46; 122 (1990), 101–113, id., *ASOR Newsletter* (Nov. 1977), 4–7; 35/3 (1984), 7–9; id., *Tell el-Hesi* (Review), *American Journal of Physical Anthropology* 71 (1986), 381–383; id., *Classical Views* 33/N.S. 8 (1989), 125–146; id. *Second International Congress on Biblical Archaeology, 24 June–4 July 1990, Abstracts*, Jerusalem 1990, 136–137; M. D. Coogan, *BASOR* 220 (1975), 37–46; D. G. Rose and L. E. Toombs, *AASOR* 43 (1976), 109–149; M. Bennett and W. J. Bennett, Jr., *JFA* 3 (1976), 97–101; W. M. Hammond, "The Raw and the Chipped: An Analysis of Correlations between Raw Material and Tools of a Lithic Industry from Tell el Hesi, Israel" (Ph.D. diss., Columbia Univ.), Ann Arbor 1977; V. M. Fargo (and K. G. O'Connell), *BA* 41 (1978), 165–182; id., *BASOR* 236 (1979), 23–40; id., *ESI* 2 (1983), 49–50; id., *The Answers Lie Below* (L. E. Toombs Fest.), Lanham, Md. 1984, 77–96; id., *Archaeology and Biblical Interpretation* (D. Glenn Rose Fest.), Atlanta 1987, 157–164; J. F. Ross, *BASOR* 236 (1979), 11–21; J. A. Blakely and L. E. Toombs, *The Tell el-Hesi Field Manual* (Reviews), *BASOR* 242 (1981), 87. — *BIAL* 19 (1982), 214–215; J. A. Blakely and F. L. Horton, *Levant* 18 (1986), 111–119; K. G. O'Connell (and D. G. Rose), *BA* 43 (1980), 254–256; id., *PEQ* 122 (1990), 83–86; J. W. Betlyon, ibid. 45 (1982), 124–126; 54 (1991), 36–43; id., *PEQ* 118 (1986), 66–69; E. D. Oren, *Journal of the Society for the Study of Egyptian Antiquities* 14 (1984) 46–47; R. W. Doermann and V. M. Fargo, ibid. 117 (1985), 1–24; R. W. Doermann, *Archaeology and Biblical Interpretation* (D. Glenn Rose Fest.), (op. cit.), 129–155; Weippert 1988 (Ortsregister); J. D. Seger, *L'Urbanisation de la Palestine à l'Age du Bronze Ancien* (Actes du Colloque d'Emmaüs, 1986; *BAR*/IS 527, ed. P. de Miroschedji), Oxford 1989, 117–135; R. C. Steiner, *BASOR* 276 (1989), 15–23; *PEQ* 122 (1990), 83–132.

VALERIE M. FARGO

HIPPOS (SUSSITA)

IDENTIFICATION AND HISTORY

Hippos, a Greek city, known in Arabic as Qal'at el-Ḥuṣn, is situated some 2 km (1 mi.) east of the Sea of Galilee on a promontory rising 350 m above the sea (map reference 212.242). It was founded by the Seleucids in the Hellenistic period, possibly on the site of an earlier settlement. The town, known by its Greek name, Antiochia Hippos (*hippos*, "horse"), continued to exist until the Arab conquest. In Aramaic it was known as Sussita. It was conquered in one of the campaigns of Alexander Jannaeus (*Syncellus*, ed. Dindorf, I, 559). Pompey took it from the Jews (Josephus, *Antiq*. XIV, 75); according to Pliny (*NH* V, 74), it was one of the cities of the Decapolis (League of Ten Greek Cities). Augustus gave the city to Herod, much to the dissatisfaction of the inhabitants. After Herod's death it became part of the Province of Syria (Josephus, *Antiq*. XV, 217; XVII, 320; *War* I, 396; II, 97). During the First Revolt against Rome, the Jews attacked Hippos (*War* II, 459, 478). Jews from the city were among the defenders of Taricheae (Magdala) (*War* III, 542). The territory of Hippos extended down to the Sea of Galilee (Josephus, *Life* 31, 153), and the city was the sworn enemy of Jewish Tiberias on the opposite shore of the lake (*Lam. Rab.* 19), despite the trade connection between them (J.T., *Shevi'it* 8, 38a). Jewish villages east of the lake were included in the territory of Hippos and were exempt from tithes in the time of the patriarch Judah I, being considered beyond the frontiers of the land of Israel proper (Tosefta, *Shevi'it* 4:10; Tosefta, *Ohal.* 18:4). Remains of ancient synagogues have been found at Fiq (Aphek) and at Umm el-Qanatir, both of which lay within the territory of Hippos. In the Byzantine period, Hippos was the seat of a bishop being one of the sees of Palaestina Secunda. Like many other towns in the Byzantine period, it enjoyed great prosperity, and many churches and public buildings were erected. The city was probably abandoned after the Arab conquest at the beginning of the seventh century. Isolated buildings were erected on its ruins in later times.

City coin of Hippos-Sussita, 2nd century CE.

In the nineteenth century Hippos was identified with the neighboring village of Sussiya, which preserved the city's ancient name (Sussita), while Qal'at el-Ḥuṣn, whose natural shape resembles a camel's hump, was considered to be the site of ancient Gamala. However, following recent surveys of the ruins at Qal'at el-Ḥuṣn, its identification with Hippos is now generally accepted.

THE SURVEY

With the settlement at 'En Gev in 1937, surface surveys were again carried out at Hippos by members of the kibbutz. These owed much to the earlier thorough studies made by G. Schumacher during the latter part of the nineteenth century. However, the new information from observation on the spot as well as from aerial photographs, made possible a reliable reconstruction of the city plan, on which the positions of its chief public buildings were correctly plotted.

Although Hippos is known to have been founded in the Hellenistic period few remains from that time have been found, probably because of the comparatively small size of the Hellenistic town. The inhabitants were entirely dependent on a natural water supply, which was inadequate for a large population. After its conquest by Pompey in 63 BCE, Hippos, as one of the cities of the Decapolis, was rebuilt in accordance with standard contemporary town planning. The town plan, which had been preserved, is essentially that of the Roman period, although many buildings were erected later

General plan of the site.

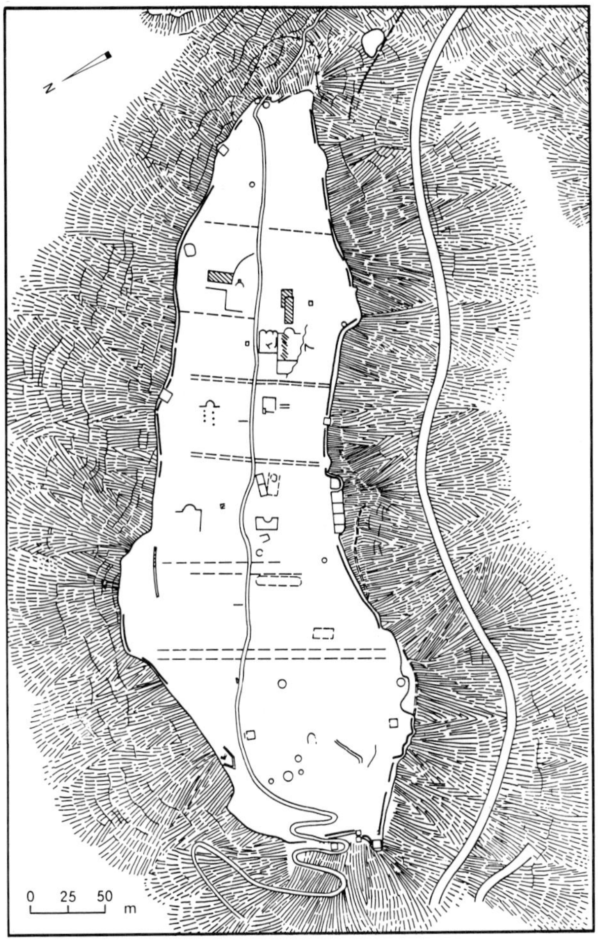

The streets of the city ran at right angles to one another over the length and breadth of the town, forming the characteristic insulae. The public buildings stood at the intersections of the important streets. Of these, the main street is easily distinguishable. It is paved with large basalt flagstones and runs from north-northeast to south-southwest through the center of the town. It is still in use today as a path. Halfway along the main street was the nymphaeum. Close to it was a large subterranean cistern with a vaulted roof and plastered walls and a flight of steps leading down to the water level. After the water had been brought to the nymphaeum and used in its ornamental fountains, it was collected in the cistern for further use. In Hippos, water was a valuable commodity; the main water supply was brought from some distance by a specially constructed aqueduct (see below). Not far from the cistern are Byzantine baths that also required a considerable amount of water.

Evidence that this town of the Decapolis had imposing buildings in Roman times can be seen in the many architectural remains strewn over the surface: massive red-granite column shafts, numerous capitals (Corinthian and Ionic), decorated pilasters, molded lintels, and carved cornices, many of which were reused in the Byzantine period. Most of these lie along the main street or in the center of the city.

Section of the main street in the western part of the city.

The town wall has also been well preserved. It is provided with a number of towers at strategic points. The wall follows the contours of the hill and makes use of the natural cliff wherever possible. On the south side, sectors of the wall still stand to a considerable height, providing an excellent view of the Roman road that ascends from the lakeside through Wadi Jamusiyeh (Naḥal Sussita). It is very likely that there was a harbor of some kind at the point where this valley opens upon the lake and where the Roman road coming from the city turned south to continue along the eastern shore of the Sea of Galilee. Evidence of such a harbor may be seen in the heaps of stones extending for some distance into the water at this spot.

At the eastern end of Wadi Jamusiyeh is a small promontory or bluff in which there are caves containing niches, stone sarcophagi, ornamented tomb doors, and other evidence of burials. This was doubtless one of the places the people of Hippos used as a cemetery, other graves having been found in the west, also outside the city walls.

EXCAVATIONS

Excavations were carried out at Hippos by C. Epstein (1950–1955), M. Avi-Yonah (1951), A. Shulman (1951), and E. Anati (1952), on behalf of the Israel Department of Antiquities. North of the main street, buildings dating to the Byzantine period were found, including houses and a small church with an apse and a mosaic floor. This is one of four churches discovered so far at Hippos, the largest and most impressive of them (20 by 40 m) having been excavated from 1951 to 1955. The latter was probably the cathedral. It is situated to the south of the main street, not far from the nymphaeum at the center of the city. Like many churches of the period, it was built as a triapsidal basilica (with an inscribed apse). Two rows of nine columns (average preserved height, 5 m) of differently colored marble and granite separated the nave from the aisles. The columns were found lying on the floor of the building in the same direction, having been thrown there during an earthquake. Close by were the pink and white marble Corinthian capitals the columns had originally supported. The floor was laid in an opus sectile pattern of colored marble (parts were executed in a lozenge-shaped flower pattern). It is almost certain that the walls, as well as the apse itself, were lined with marble. Many marble slabs of various colors were found on the floor, and a number of copper clamps to hold them in position were still in situ in the apse wall. Around the main apse, where the altar had stood, the sockets for the chancel screen and for the posts that supported its panels were found set into the floor. One of these panels (of white marble) was found broken. It was decorated with a relief showing the entrance to an ornate public building. From its architrave hangs a large circular object, perhaps a basket commemorating the Miracle of the Loaves and Fishes. Above the molding of the surrounding frame is an inscription in Greek: "In the time of Procopius, Presbyter." The back of the panel was decorated with a large dolphin in relief, apparently dating from the time of its original use, since attempts to efface the outlines of the dolphin are clearly visible.

Entrance to the cathedral was through three doorways in the western wall. They were approached through a paved corridor that gave on to a colonnaded atrium beyond. The southern aisle was not completely excavated. It appears to have matched the northern one in all respects, except that in the latter the external wall served as a partition for the adjacent baptistery building. The baptistery was also triapsidal. Its nave was separated from the aisles by two rows of four white marble columns (two of them with unusual fluting). In the central apse a cruciform font with rounded ends was set into the floor, with a mosaic around it. The floor of the baptistery was completely covered with colored mosaics laid in a variety of geometric designs. These mosaics include three inscriptions in Greek and the monogram of Christ (north apse). In the southern aisle there was an intact dedicatory inscription to Saints Cosmas and Damian in a *tabula ansata.* These were two Syrian brothers who, as physicians, gave free service to the poor and were martyred in the early fourth century. The remains of another inscription, framed in a medallion, of which only a few words remain, was found in a central position in the nave. This fragment, however, does contain the date of the building of the baptistery—January 654, according to the Pompeian era of 63 BCE used in Hippos (= 591 CE). In the northern aisle, a third inscription was found, also framed in a circular border. Here, the end of most of the lines is missing. The name Procopius, mentioned also on the cathedral chancel screen, is still legible. He was apparently responsible for the building of the baptistery and the laying of its mosaic floor. Here, too, the date, which is the same as that in the nave inscription, can be made out.

The Hippos baptistery is unusual because it is built in a triapsidal plan and divided into a nave and aisles and because it is dedicated to special patron saints. All these characteristics are more often associated with mother churches, to which baptisteries served as annexes.

MOUNT SUSSITA. In the east, a rocky saddle links the hill on which the city was built to the north–south range beyond it. The road to the city passed over this natural ridge, branching off from the main highway, which ascended from the lakeside through Wadi Jamusiyeh and continued eastward into the Golan

Hippos: the cathedral's northern aisle, looking west.

hills. The approach to ancient Hippos was by way of this saddle. Over it also ran a massive basalt aqueduct that conveyed water into the city by gravitation from the 3.5 km distant spring at Fiq. Sections of this aqueduct can still be seen at various points within the city itself, as well as on the saddle ridge. During the 1952 excavations, twenty-four sections were found in situ below the main street pavement near the east gate. Each section is square outside but circular and hollow inside (average internal diameter, 30 cm). The sections are joined by spigots and sockets reinforced with plaster. Some had a venthole in the upper wall to enable the air bubbles caused by the uprushing of the water to escape. The aqueduct entered the city at the east gate and continued beneath the main street to the nymphaeum.

The east gate, which was the main gate into the city, had a paved area within. Its southern pier was built as an integral part of the city wall (it is well preserved at this point). The wall was strengthened here by a well-built circular tower (external diameter, 9 m) that commanded the road leading into the city from the east. Built into the rocky slope of the hillside, the lower part of the tower contained a stone fill coated with a thin layer of plaster—probably the floor. In the round tower and the gateway, two building phases could be distinguished from the Roman and Byzantine periods (but no trace of the Hellenistic). On the northern side, only the foundations of the gate pier have survived (giving a probable internal width of 3.1 m). From here, the wall, which follows the contours of the hill, turns abruptly west at a point not far from the gate. At this corner position a two-storied square tower was erected that commanded the northeastern approaches to the city. Its lower section appears to have been used as a plastered cistern, probably by the garrison manning it.

In the west, the main street terminated at a much smaller city gate, whose chief purpose was to provide easy access into and out of the town for those of its inhabitants who cultivated the terraces on the western slopes of the hill. Remains of a well-preserved city wall were also found in the west. Below it, the hillside falls away steeply, making a hostile approach from this direction extremely hazardous. A little below the west gate is a group of large rocks that in an emergency could undoubtedly be used for defense purposes (as is borne out by the signs of building found between them). Not far from these graves were found cut into the rock face that can be dated by their contents to the Byzantine period.

G. Schumacher, *ZDPV* 9 (1886), 327ff.; id., *The Jaulan*, London 1888, 194ff.; Schürer, *GJV* 2, 155ff.; E. Anati, *IEJ* 3 (1953), 133; J. Leibovitch, *CNI* 4/2–3 (1953), 31; A. Ovadiah, *PEQ* 113 (1981), 101–104; Weippert 1988, 6, 65; J. Peleg, *Mitteilungen des Leichtweiss-Institut füur Wasserbau*, 103 (1989), 325–336; V. Tzaferis, *BAR* 16/5 (1990), 50–58; C. Epstein and V. Tzaferis, *'Atiqot* 20 (1991), 89–94; M. Nun, *The Sea of Galilee: Water Levels Past and Present*, Ein Gev 1991, 11.

CLAIRE EPSTEIN

ḤOLON

IDENTIFICATION

A prehistoric site was discovered in Ḥolon in 1960 in the city's industrial zone, on the border with Azor. Today, the site's landscape is composed of hillocks and small gullies, most of them covered by red *ḥamra* soil and occasionally by dune sand or *kurkar*. The site lies 38 m above sea level (map reference 1312.1581). The settlement remains lie between two layers of *ḥamra*, with the lower one resting on the third coastal *kurkar* ridge from the Mediterranean Sea. A broad alluvial valley extends east of the site. In antiquity, Naḥal Ayalon probably flowed close to the site. The layer in which the archaeological remains were found is formed of a light-colored clay soil, attesting that a swamp formed here due to high groundwater and drainage problems caused by the proximity of the ancient shoreline. Two seasons of excavations were carried out at the site in 1963–1964, directed by T. Noy, on behalf of the Israel Department of Antiquities.

EXCAVATION RESULTS

An area of 20 sq m was excavated (in 2-by-2-m squares) and the following phases uncovered:

Phase A: *ḥamra* soil, up to 2 m deep;
Phase B: dark-colored clay soil, up to 0.5 m deep;
Phase C: light-colored clay soil, 0.3 to 1.7 m deep;
Phase D: *ḥamra* soil, up to 0.7 m deep;
Phase E: *kurkar* rock, indicating the top of the third coastal *kurkar* ridge.

The light-colored clay soil in phase C contained Acheulean material. The

Ḥolon: elephant tusk, Middle Acheulean period.

layer of densely clustered finds does not exceed 0.7 m. The finds included animal bones, flint implements, and a few bone tools. Of the animal bones, mainly long bones and teeth are preserved. Despite systematic sieving, no bones of small animals were found. The animals identified were elephant, horse, hippopotamus, deer, cattle, and gazelle. The flint implements included hand axes, flakes, and chopping tools. Triangular, rounded and pointed hand axes were found in equal proportions, in addition to truncated and other hand axes. The hand axes were worked with both hard and soft hammers and were similar in size to specimens found at other Acheulean sites in the country. The flakes were debitage produced in the manufacture of hand axes, but some were flaked-off cores resulting from use of the Levallois technique. The flaked tools include retouched flakes, end scrapers, occasional burins, and notches. The choppers were made on small, flat river pebbles; several hammerstones were also found.

Ḥolon: hand ax, Middle Acheulean period.

SUMMARY

The picture presented at the Ḥolon site is similar to that at other sites from the Early and Middle Acheulean period in the region. Hunter-gatherer communities camped alongside freshwater sources in the vicinity of the Mediterranean forest that must have covered parts of the Coastal Plain at the time. The stratigraphic position of the site on the third *kurkar* ridge, which is dated to the first Tyrrhenian marine incursion, may be connected with the sea withdrawal in the Riss pluvial. Judging from the lithic assemblage, the site should be attributed to either the Middle Acheulean or to the later part of this culture.

T. Yisraeli-Noy, *IEJ* 13 (1963), 137; 17 (1967), 144–152; 20 (1970), 221–222; id., *RB* 78 (1971), 581–582; A. Issar, *Israel Journal of Earth Sciences* 17 (1968), 16–29; O. Bar-Yosef, *After the Australopithecus* (eds. K. W. Butzer and G. Isaac), The Hague 1975, 571–604; Weippert 1988, 75f.

TAMAR NOY

ḤUSIFAH

IDENTIFICATION

Ḥusifah was a Jewish settlement in the Roman-Byzantine period in which the remains of a synagogue were discovered. It is identified with the site of the modern village of ʿIsfiya on Mount Carmel, about 12 km (7.5 mi.) southeast of Haifa (map reference 156.236). The existence of this early settlement is also attested by ancient graves within the boundaries of the village and by coin finds. The latter include a hoard of 4,560 silver coins, the latest among them dating to 52–53 CE. The destruction of the Jewish settlement of Ḥusifah is mentioned in a Hebrew elegy discovered in the Cairo Genizah. Most scholars accept the suggestion of S. Assaf that this Ḥusifah be identified with ʿIsfiya.

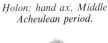

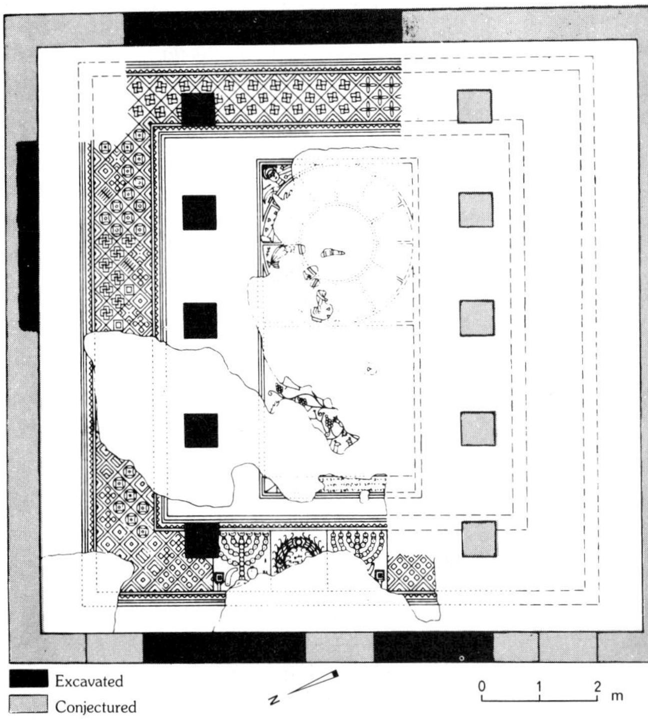

Ḥusifah: plan of the synagogue and its mosaic pavement.

THE SYNAGOGUE

In 1930, a mosaic floor with the representation of a seven-branched candelabrum (menorah) was discovered in one of the village streets in ʿIsfiya. In 1933, excavations were conducted at this spot under the direction of N. Makhouly and M. Avi-Yonah, on behalf of the Mandatory Department of Antiquities. Because part of the remains lay beneath one of the village houses, little more than half of the synagogue could be uncovered. A floor and the foundations of a hall (probably square) were discovered. The northern wall was cleared for its full length (10.1 m), but the eastern wall and the foundations of the western wall could only be partially uncovered (for 6.2 and 5.5 m, respectively). In the mosaic floor in the hall there were square gaps, the traces of a row of five pillars or columns, set at unequal distances. The second row of columns apparently stood in the unexcavated part. In the western wall, remains of a threshold were noted, and west of it, the bed of a mosaic pavement. These finds point to the existence of a narthex.

THE MOSAIC PAVEMENT. Along the walls of the hall there was a broad band of mosaics (width, c. 1 m) containing geometric motifs: steps, double diagonal lines, stylized guilloche, rhombuses, and meanders. This border terminated on the western side (in front of the threshold but not on the axis of the building) in three square panels, each 1 sq. m. In the middle panel a wreath was depicted composed of three rows of elongated flowers with leaves and intertwined branches. The wreath surrounds an inscription, partially preserved: שלום [ע]ל ישראל [אמן], "Peace upon Israel, Amen" (Naveh, no. 38). The lateral panels were occupied by two seven-branched candelabra, or menorahs. The menorah on the left had a trunk consisting of squares and circles and alternating branches of circles (knobs) and heart-shaped "flowers." The lamps at the top of the branches have a triangular base and a handle. The lamps are depicted in profile, and at the top of each, a flame burns (on the left side, the three flames incline to the right; on the right side, the single surviving flame inclines to the left). The central lamp, above the trunk, shows two flames. The menorah is made of red, orange, and golden (yellow) tesserae. In the center of each link is a cube of green glass (representing

Ḥusifah: part of the mosaic pavement depicting a seven-branched menorah, an ethrog, a lulab, and the inscription שלום [ע]ל[ישראל [אמן] *(Peace upon Israel, Amen) within a garland.*

Figure of one of the four seasons depicted in the zodiac in the mosaic pavement.

a precious stone?). Beneath the branches of the menorah are depicted, from right to left, a lulab (only its tip survived), an ethrog (with a green glass mosaic cube in its center), a shofar, and an incense shovel. The trunk and branches of the menorah on the right are made of alternating square and round links, with a green tessera in the center of each. At the top of each branch a flame rises out of a square. Near the menorah an incense shovel and the end of a shofar can be seen.

A band of geometric designs, similar to the one along the walls, surrounds the main field of the mosaic floor in the center of the hall. This field is divided into three parts (from west to east):

1. An inscription in three lines, 2.8 m long (of which 1.3 m is preserved) and 0.27 m wide, which reads "[. . .] and blessed be [all the mem]bers of the city, the elder[s and the young . . . who pro]mised and gave their donation. [They] shall be [blessed . . .] Honored be the memory. Honored be the memory of Josiah who gave [. . .]" (Naveh, no. 39).

2. A vine trellis (of which only a narrow diagonal band is preserved) presented in a naturalistic manner, with bunches of grapes, leaves, and tendrils. At the western end are the heads of two peacocks. A bird is standing among the branches of the vine, facing in the opposite direction to that of the peacocks.

3. A zodiac. The diameter of the inner circle of the zodiac is 0.6 m, and of the outer circle, 1.38 m. The center of the circle was almost completely destroyed. Of the twelve signs of the zodiac, fragments of only the five signs from Sagittarius to Aries have survived. Sagittarius is pictured as a nude figure with a yellow mantle thrown over one shoulder, like Hercules' lion skin. Only the ends of Capricorn's horns have survived. The sign of Aquarius is depicted as an amphora with water flowing out of it. Pisces was apparently represented by two fish swimming in opposite directions. Of Aries, only the hind legs are left. In the corner of the square field, the head of a woman (one of the Seasons) is preserved. She wears a necklace of green tesserae and a yellow and white head covering. There are pomegranates and other symbols (possibly a cluster of dates or a sickle) near her head. The head apparently symbolized autumn (*Tequfat Tishri*), although the zodiac signs near it are those of spring. A similar discrepancy appears in the synagogue mosaic at Na'aran.

The mosaic is of fine quality—sixty-five tesserae to 10 sq cm. Most of the material is local red, yellow, white, pink, brown, and orange limestone. Bluish marble and an abundance of green glass are also employed. Its artistic level is reasonably good. In one place, the mosaic was repaired with coarse red tesserae.

SUMMARY

The synagogue at Ḥusifah represents a mixture of early and late features. Like the early synagogues, it did not seem to have had an apse, but like some of the late synagogues it is built in the form of a basilica without a row of cross columns. It is oriented toward Jerusalem; its entrances are in the west, on the side opposite Jerusalem (like the other synagogue remains on Mount Carmel), and it is paved with mosaics. Judging by the quality of its mosaic, the synagogue at Ḥusifah was later than that at Hammath-Tiberias, which also has no apse. It is, however, earlier than the synagogue at Ma'on (Nirim), where representations of vines and animals were found but no human images. The synagogue is thus dated to the early sixth century CE. The structure bears obvious signs of conflagration. Parts of the mosaic had faded because of heat, and a layer of ash had accumulated in its southeastern corner. It seems that the building was destroyed during Justinian's actions against the Jews. Perhaps the lament found in the Cairo Genizah elegy should be attributed to that event.

The synagogue was built according to halakhic rules—that is, on the highest spot in the village. This modest building can be associated, on the one hand, with a group of synagogues in which the zodiac is depicted—Beth Alpha, Na'aran, Hammath-Tiberias, and Japhia—or, on the other, with such later synagogues as Ḥammat Gader and Ma'on (Nirim). The mosaic bears no traces of iconoclasm, which would seem to indicate that it was destroyed before those tendencies appeared among the Jews of Palestine.

N. Makhouly and M. Avi-Yonah, *QDAP* 3 (1934), 118–131; Goodenough, *Jewish Symbols* 1, 257–259; *Archives and Ancient Jewish Art—Samples and Manual* (eds. Y. Yadin and R. Jacoby), Jerusalem 1984, 39–72.

MICHAEL AVI-YONAH

EL-ḤUṢN

IDENTIFICATION AND EXCAVATION

A dwelling and burial cave near the town of el-Ḥuṣn in Gilead, about 1 km (0.6 mi.) south of Tell el-Ḥuṣn and 22 km (13.5 mi.) north of Gerasa, was discovered during construction work and excavated by G. L. Harding. As a result of collapses inside the cave, its original form was not preserved. In the course of the excavations, a shapeless cavity was discovered in the soft limestone that contained a mixture of implements and skeletons.

The examination of the finds showed that they represented two periods of occupation, about a thousand years apart. To the first period belong sherds and fragments of large, coarse storage jars with flaring rims, simple ledge handles, and band-slip decoration. Pottery without a slip was also discovered, made of a very gritty material, similar to cooking pot ware—mostly holemouth jars and storage jars with slightly flaring rims. In Harding's opinion, these finds are to be dated to the Early Bronze Age II. J. Isserlin, on the other hand, assigned them to the Early Bronze Age I.

During the second period, the cave was probably used for burials. Most of the pottery vessels were preserved in good condition. They were probably placed in the cave, together with copper pins, as burial offerings. More than fifty pottery vessels were discovered, including storage jars with flared rims and folded ledge handles, storage jars with globular bodies (some of them with incised decoration on the shoulders), *amphoriskoi* (comprising more than half of the objects found, some of them decorated like the storage jars and others with red-painted decoration) and jugs with handles joining the rim to the shoulder (some of them painted in the style of the *amphoriskoi* and some red slipped). Other finds included a lamp of the four-pinch type, a "teapot" with a loop handle and two copper pins with convoluted heads. In the opinion of Harding, these finds belong to the period from the Early Bronze Age IV to the Middle Bronze Age I. Isserlin ascribed them to the beginning of the Middle Bronze Age I, as represented in stratum I at Tell Beit Mirsim.

El-Ḥuṣn: selection of pottery from the later period, MB I.

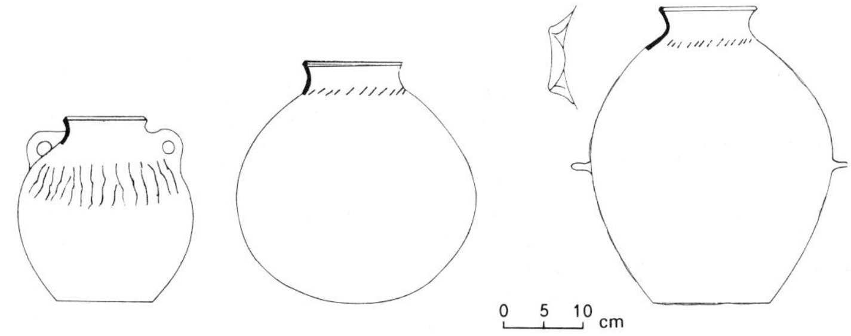

The objects from the earlier period are similar to the Early Bronze Age I finds from the north of the country, especially from the Jordan and Jezreel valleys. Cave dwellings were not unusual in the Proto-Urban period (as defined by K. M. Kenyon). People then lived in the open country, in caves and impermanent structures. The pottery repertoire from the later period is also characteristic of the culture of that time in the north of the country, with analogies at Megiddo and Ma'ayan Barukh. The pottery belongs to families B and C, according to R. Amiran's classification.

G. L. Harding and J. B. S. Isserlin, *PEFA* 6 (1953), 1–13; R. Amiran, *IEJ* 10 (1960), 209–213; K. M. Kenyon, *Amorites and Canaanites*, London 1966, 32–33.

MOSHE KOCHAVI

HYRCANIA

IDENTIFICATION

Hyrcania is a Hasmonean fortress in the Judean Desert, built on an elongated hilltop isolated from its surroundings. It is situated at a height of 248 m above sea level, some 200 m above the Hyrcania Valley (q.v. el-Buqei'a). The fortress is on the western edge of the valley (map reference 1847.1252). Its approach from the west is along a saddle that was narrowed by rock cutting. The saddle carried an aqueduct. The identification of el-Mird with Hyrcania and Castellion was first suggested by K. Furrer in 1880 and was accepted by all scholars. The Arabic name of the fortress, el-Mird, is a corruption of the Syrian-Aramaic word *marda*, meaning "fortress." Castellion, the name of the Byzantine monastery built on the site, is derived from *castellum*, the Latin term for fortress.

HISTORY

Hyrcania is first mentioned by Josephus (*Antiq.* XIII, 417) as one of the three fortresses retained by Queen Alexandra Salome (Shelomṣiyyon, 76–67 BCE). It may have been erected by Alexander Jannaeus, or perhaps even in the time of his father, John Hyrcanus, after whom the fortress was named. It was destroyed by Gabinius in 57 BCE (*Antiq.* XIV, 89; *War* I, 160–170); Herod captured the fortress in 31 BCE, rebuilt it, and made it into a detention site for his political opponents, many of whom were executed and buried here, including his son Antipater (*War* I, 364, 664; *Antiq.* XV, 365–367; XVI, 13). The name Hyrcania does not appear in the literary sources after the death of Herod. Monks settled among its ruins in the Byzantine period, and in 492 CE a coenobium, called Castellion, was erected on the site by Saint Sabas. This monastery was a dependency of the Great Laura of Saint Sabas (today Mar Saba) in the Kidron Valley. The monastery is mentioned in the eighth-century *Life of Stephen the Sabaite*. Papyri dating from the seventh to tenth centuries discovered at the site attest to its continued occupation after the Persian invasion and the Arab conquest. It was abandoned in the fourteenth century CE. In 1923, the site was reoccupied by monks from the Mar Saba monastery. They cleared the ruins of the church and set up a chapel in an

Aerial view of Hyrcania, looking northwest.

Map of the principal remains at Hyrcania and in its vicinity.

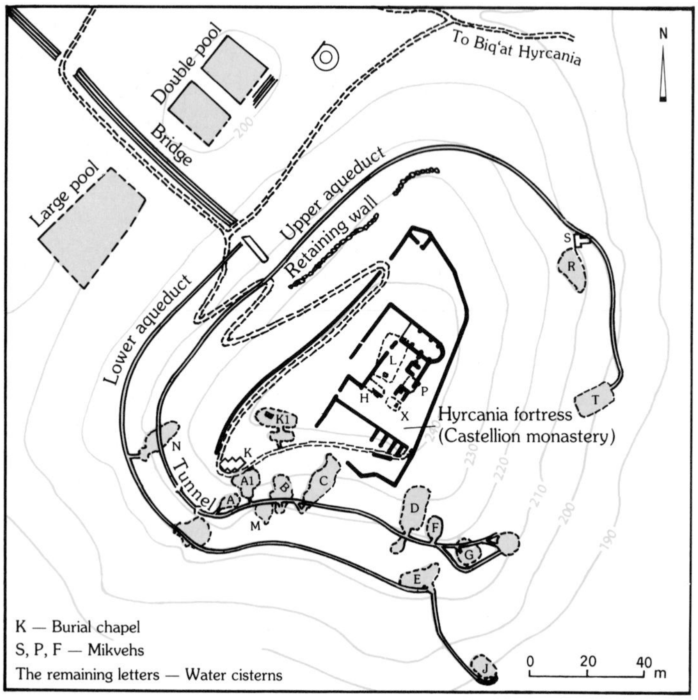

Section of a mosaic floor in the monastery of Castellion, from the room south of the chapel.

ancient burial cave. They, in turn, abandoned the site in 1939 because of security problems and their buildings were destroyed by Bedouins.

EXPLORATION

Hyrcania has not yet been excavated. Data concerning its ruins are based on surveys and mapping. The site was first surveyed by the British Palestine Exploration Fund in 1873. In 1877, C. Schick prepared a map of the site and its surroundings. A. E. Mader studied the frescoes in the Christian burial cave during five visits to the site between 1913 and 1927 and also published various finds discovered here. Following the discovery by Bedouins in July 1952 of inscribed papyri, a Belgian expedition from Louvain University, headed by R. de Langhe, arrived at the site in spring 1953. The expedition discovered texts written on papyrus and parchment in Palestinian Aramaic, Greek, and Arabic. In April 1960, an expedition headed by G. R. H. Wright investigated the site, measured the structures on the hilltop, and excavated some of the burials found at the foot of the hill east of Hyrcania, as well as a watchtower incorporated into the fortress's circumvallation. This circumvallation was reidentified and surveyed in 1973 by Z. Meshel, on behalf of the Institute of Archaeology at Tel Aviv University. The water supply system was studied in 1971 by Y. Feldman, on behalf of the Israel Society for the Preservation of Nature. The site and the water supply system were further investigated and the structures on the hilltop resurveyed by J. Patrich, as part of the survey of the Mar Saba region, on behalf of the Archaeological Survey of Israel.

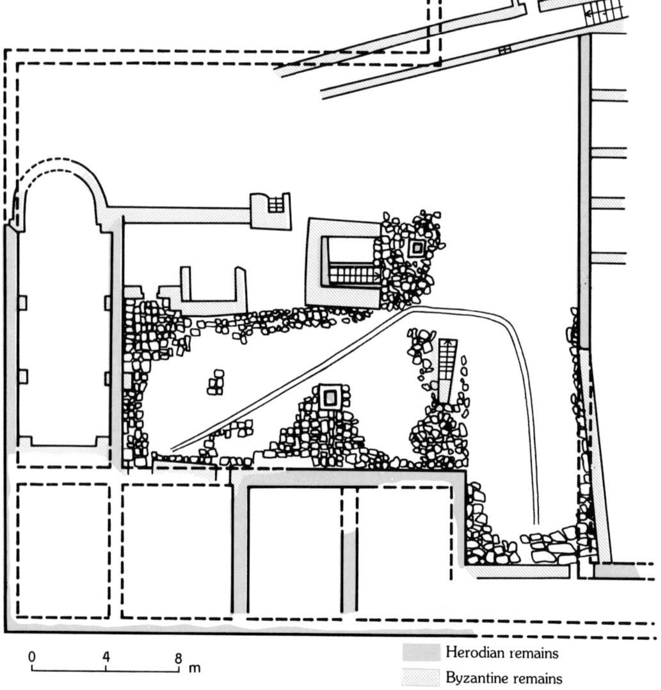

Plan of the remains on the summit.

DESCRIPTION OF THE REMAINS

The structure on the hilltop was erected on a leveled area (25 by 40 m) supported by subterranean vaults used as cisterns. The structure consists of rooms around a central courtyard on the north, east, and west. The bottom courses of the walls, preserved in the east and north, were ashlars with drafted margins and a smoothed face laid as headers and stretchers. These features are typical Herodian construction techniques. Some stones also have a prominant central boss characteristic of Hasmonean masonry. The base of a heart-shaped column was also found. On the south, the boundary is a Herodian retaining wall, with several monastic cells abutting its eastern edge. The fence enclosing the hilltop today is from a later period, but under it a mass of stones set into mortar is visible, especially on the west. These stones probably belong to a glacis that was part of the fortress defenses. A cemetery from the Herodian period was found at the foot of the hill on the east, and the Aramaic inscription, published by J. Naveh, may have come from there. The circumvallation is well preserved, especially on the south, west, and east. Meshel is of the opinion that it was built during Herod's siege of Hyrcania, which had been seized by a sister of Antigonus (Josephus, *War* I, 364).

The Byzantine monks settled in the structure on the hilltop and transformed its northeast part into a chapel (5.5 by 16 m) with a white mosaic floor and a roof supported by two arches. The room south of the chapel was paved with a colorful mosaic. The western wing is full of debris. A Byzantine burial cave was excavated on the west side on a lower level. Eight pit graves were recorded under its white mosaic floor. The cave's plastered walls are covered with frescoes depicting thirty-six saints—most of them monks from the Judean Desert. Twenty-seven can be identified by Greek inscriptions. Identified on the west wall were Saints Euthymius, Athanasius, Thalelaeus, and Martyrius; on the south wall: Lazarus, Basilius, Arsenius, Timotheus, Simeon, Palladius, Johannes, Theoctistus, Georgius Chosibites; on the east wall: Abramius, Marcianus, Theoctistus, Macarius, Moises, Theodosius, Paulus, Stephanus, Isidorus, and Arcadius; on the north wall: Johannes and Xenophon. Mader suggested that these frescoes should be dated to the twelfth century CE, but the cave itself may be older.

The finds in the monastery included a baptismal font that was discovered south of the chapel, along with three marble columns decorated with vine tendrils issuing from an amphora (formerly part of the chapel's chancel screen) and a Byzantine stone sundial. An icon kept in the Mar Saba monastery depicts the twelve apostles and bears an inscription on the back which records that it was brought here in 1355 from the Castellion monastery by a monk named Paulus. This is the latest evidence attesting to the existence of the monastery. Schick's map shows monastic cells west of the hill of Hyrcania.

Of the papyri found in pit K1, only those written in Arabic have been fully published. They consist of approximately one-hundred texts from the first two centuries *anno Hegirae*, most of them fragmentary, including a fragment from the Koran. Of the Syriac papyri, only a letter written in the seventh century by a monk named Gabriel to the head of the Mar Saba laura, and two fragments from the Acts of the Apostles (10:28–29, 10:32–41) were published. Among the other texts reported are fragments from the Gospels of Luke (3:1, 3:3–4) and Matthew (21:30–35); the Acts of the Apostles (10:36–42); the Epistle to the Colossians (1:15–18, 1:20); and the Book of Joshua (22:9–11). The last

Monastery of Castellion: chancel screen post from the chapel.

three fragments were hitherto unknown in Syriac. The papyrus and parchment fragments inscribed in Greek include parts of the Gospels of Mark and John and the Acts of the Apostles. These texts have not yet been published.

THE WATER-SUPPLY SYSTEM. Of the twenty-one rock-cut cisterns, six are on the hilltop, three on the eastern slope, and twelve on the southern slope—eight on the upper level and four on the lower level. Two open water reservoirs are situated at the foot of the fortress to the west, north of the aqueduct bridge. Another reservoir may have been dug south of the bridge. The cisterns and reservoirs are plastered with white lime and gravel plaster laid directly on bedrock. Rows of rock-cut benches above the east side of the northernmost reservoir suggest that it may also have functioned as a swimming pool. Water was supplied from the west by two aqueducts, plastered along their entire length, that collected runoff water. The course of both aqueducts followed the contours of the hill—some parts were rock-cut and some were masonry—built or supported by retaining walls. The shorter aqueduct, coming from the northwest, was probably built in the Hasmonean period. It issued from a dam

Eastern bridge of the aqueduct. The lower courses are from the Hasmonean period and the upper courses from the Herodian period.

in Wadi Abu Shu'ala that drains the eastern slope of el-Muntar and is approximately 1,950 m long. The longer aqueduct, arriving from the southwest, begins in the Kidron Valley and meanders 9 km (5.6 mi.), crossing some deep ravines on high bridges on its way. Both aqueducts merge into a single channel on a saddle 750 m west of Hyrcania; beyond that point, the aqueduct runs along another three bridges crossing three saddles. The most impressive and highest of these is the eastern one, which is built in isodomic technique and graded upward. The four lower courses, which are visible on the north side and date to the Hasmonean period, are built headers above stretchers and have drafted margins and a central boss. The upper courses, laid as alternating headers and stretchers, have drafted margins and a smoothed face, typical of Herodian masonry.

The Byzantine aqueduct is identifiable by its reddish plaster. Sections of this aqueduct were exposed next to the westernmost of the three bridges west of Hyrcania and at the head of the easternmost bridge (which in the Byzantine period was lower by 6.3 m than in the Second Temple period). Between these two points, the aqueduct runs along a course parallel to the earlier one, but on a lower level and to the north of it. Thus, the Byzantine aqueduct could only fill the cisterns of the lower level. Indeed, in the excavation carried out next to the steps in cistern C on the upper level, fragments of Herodian jars and lamps were recovered, together with a coin of the same period, but no later sherds were found.

Conder–Kitchener, *SWP* 3, 212; K. Furrer, *ZDPV* 3 (1880), 234–236; C. Schick, ibid., 19–24; A. E. Mader, *JPOS* 9 (1929), 122–135; id., *Oriens Christianus* 34 (1937), 27–58, 192–212; O. Plöger, *ZDPV* 71 (1955), 148–151; G. R. H. Wright and J. T. Milik, *Biblica* 42 (1961), 1–21; J. T. Milik, *RB* 60 (1953), 529–539; id., *Biblica* 42 (1961), 21–27; J. Briend, *MdB* 17 (1981), 27; Y. Tsafrir, *Jerusalem Cathedra* 2 (1982), 120–145; G. Garbrecht and J. Peleg, *Antike Welt* 20/2 (1989), 2–20.

The papyri: J. T. Milik, *RB* 60 (1953), 533–539; C. Perrot, ibid. 70 (1963), 506–555; A. Grohmann, *Arabic Papyri from Khirbet el-Mird*, Louvain 1963; M. J. Kister, *Jerusalem Studies in Arabic and Islam* 3 (1981–1982), 237–240; id., *Studies in Judaica, Karaitica and Islamica presented to L. Nemoy*, Ramat Gan 1982, 163–166.

JOSEPH PATRICH

I

'IRA, TEL

IDENTIFICATION

Tel 'Ira (in Arabic, Khirbet Ghara) is situated in the Beersheba Valley, in the Negev desert, on a tablelike chalk hill 514 m above sea level (map reference 1487.0713). This hill is the south end of a spur of the Hebron Hills. The site, whose area is slightly more than 6 a., covers the entire hill, which is quite steep and isolated. It is surrounded by an Iron Age stone wall, whose entire length has been exposed.

The site's biblical identification is unclear. Y. Aharoni suggested identifying it with Kabzeel, which heads the list of Judahite cities in the Negev (Jos. 15:21—the equivalent of Jekabzeel in Neh. 11:25). A. Lemaire, N. Na'aman, and A. F. Rainey suggest Ramah of the Negev (Jos. 19:8), in view of the site's high altitude, and B. Mazar suggests Eltolad (Jos. 15:30). It is noteworthy, however, that excavations have not revealed an occupation level from the tenth century BCE, when Ramoth (pl.) of the Negev is mentioned as one of the towns to which David sent some of the spoil taken from the Amalekites (1 Sam. 30:27). However, this suggestion is noteworthy in view of the following facts: one of the rock-cut tombs (see below) contained vessels dating to the tenth to ninth centuries BCE. Several irregularly hand-burnished sherds were found on the eastern slope of the site and in the fills of stratum VII. There are no finds from later cities that occupied the site—from the Hellenistic to the Byzantine periods—that might contribute to a more confident identification.

The site was first surveyed in the early 1950s by D. Alon. In 1956 Aharoni conducted a thorough survey. He favored the view that Tel 'Ira had been the capital of the Negev province during the Iron Age II.

Tel 'Ira: plan of the mound and excavation areas.

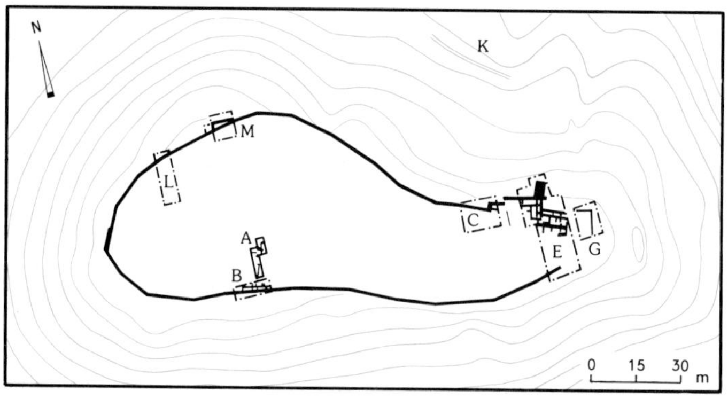

EXCAVATIONS

Seven seasons of excavations were conducted at Tel 'Ira from 1979 to 1987. The first season was held under the auspices of the Israel Department of Antiquities and Museums, as part of the emergency surveys and rescue excavations in the Negev. It was carried out by an expedition from the Institute of Archaeology at Tel Aviv University, under the direction of M. Kochavi, and an expedition from Hebrew Union College, directed by A. Biran and R. Cohen. Subsequent seasons were carried out under the auspices of the Institute of Archaeology at Tel Aviv University, with the participation of Bar-Ilan University and Baylor University, Rice University, and the University of California, Fullerton. The first season was directed by M. Kochavi, the third by I. Beit-Arieh and I. Finkelstein, and the others by Beit-Arieh.

The Tel Aviv University expedition excavated areas C, D, E, and G in the eastern part of the site; areas A and B in the south center; area K, an agricultural terrace at the northern foot of the hill; and area T, a cemetery on the eastern slope. The Hebrew Union College excavated areas L and M, in the northwestern part of the site.

THE TEL AVIV UNIVERSITY EXCAVATIONS

The Tel Aviv expedition exposed nine occupation strata, from the Early Bronze Age III to the Early Arab period. The most extensive levels, and the richest in architectural remains, were the Iron Age and the Byzantine period levels. The following table presents the stratigraphical sequence of the site:

Stratum	*Period*	*Nature*
IX	EB III (27th–23rd cent. BCE)	Unfortified; pottery widely scattered
VIII	Iron II (late 10th–early 9th cent. BCE)	Pottery in fill of stratum VII and in one tomb; unfortified(?)
VII	Iron II (late 8th–early 7th cent. BCE)	Fortified city
VI	Iron II (late 7th cent. BCE)	Fortified city
V	Persian (5th–4th cent. BCE)	Settlement in Iron Age buildings
IV	Hellenistic (4th–2nd cent. BCE)	City, use of Iron Age wall
III	Early Roman (1st cent. CE)	City, use of Iron Age wall
II	Byzantine (5th–7th cent. CE)	City and monastery, use of parts of Iron Age wall
I	Early Arab (7th–8th cent. CE)	Settlement in Byzantine buildings

STRATUM IX: EARLY BRONZE AGE III. The only architectural remains from the Early Bronze Age III (stratum IX) were found in area E, where part

Tel 'Ira: aerial view, looking north.

View of the site at the summit of the flat hill, looking south.

of a wall was uncovered. In area A, intact pottery vessels were found in situ, and sherds from this period were found in the fills of floors in the Iron Age strata and elsewhere on bedrock. The presence of contemporary sherds everywhere on the site and the nature of this stratum suggest that the Early Bronze Age III population lived mostly in hutlike structures. No other aspects of this settlement were exposed by the excavations, but the difference between it and the Canaanite city at Arad during the Early Bronze Age II is striking.

STRATUM VIII: IRON AGE II. Occupation of the site was apparently renewed in the late tenth or the early ninth century BCE. No masonry has yet been discovered in this level, only sherds. The sherds were found in various parts of the site—in the fill under the floors of strata VII and VI, in debris cleared from the site toward the slope, and in a tomb in area T, where intact vessels were also found. It is only possible to conjecture that at this time the site was partly occupied and unfortified. Its precise nature cannot be determined.

Plan of the eastern part of the Iron Age city and the northern wing of the gate.

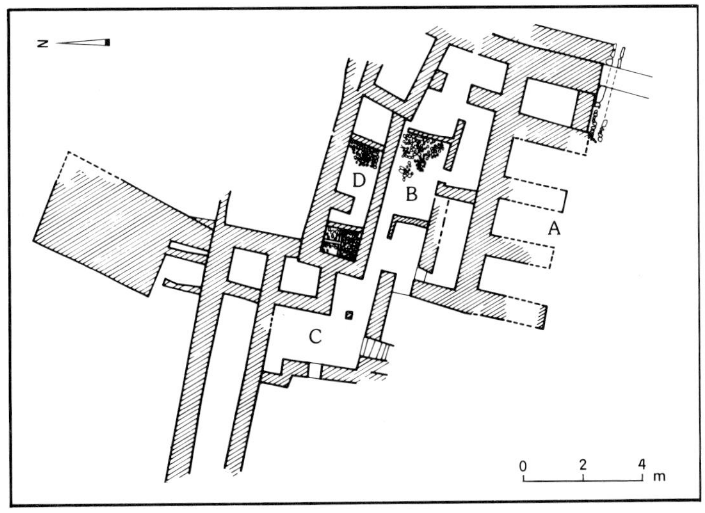

Storeroom building, Iron Age.

STRATUM VII: IRON AGE II. In stratum VII (Iron Age II), which is dated on the basis of its pottery to the late eighth or early seventh century BCE, a fortified city was erected over the entire site. In its eastern part, the city gate and some public buildings were uncovered; private houses were found in the other areas. The city's strategic position, its considerable area, and its powerful fortifications testify to its great importance among the cities of the eastern and central Negev; it presumably was an administrative center for the kingdom of Judah and a major fortified city on its southern border. The stratum VII structures were built directly on bedrock, or on earth fills (in a relatively thin layer), with a mixture of sherds from strata IX and VIII.

Fortifications and the City Gate. Most of the city is surrounded by a solid wall, preserved in several places to a height of more than 2 m. The wall (1.6–1.8 m thick) is built of local flint and hewn limestone set in straight segments, one

Iron Age rooms built against the city wall in area B.

Interior of tomb T16; three biers are cut in the vaulted niches.

Hebrew ostracon with the inscription מפקד ברכיהו גבה מוקר שלמיהו*, probably a list of individuals residing in one of the city's houses.*

against the other. The foundations rest on bedrock, and the wall's outer face is supported by revetments up to 1 m thick. In some places in the north of the city, the wall had offsets that may have been used as watchtowers guarding the valleys and the road to the gate. Part of the city gate area is surrounded by a thick casemate wall, indicating the probable citadel. Parts of the wall were also exposed in the north and east of area E. The north wall has a total thickness of about 5 m, including a 1.5-m-thick outer wall and a 1-m-thick inner wall. Along the wall on the outside was an earthen glacis covered with plaster. A stone tower (6 by 9 m), built outside the wall, also was found in this area; it seems to have been used as a strong forward outpost protecting the gate and its approaches.

The city gate in the east wall consists of six chambers and two towers (building A). The northern wing and parts of the passageway have been cleared. Its total length is 18 m, the width of one wing is 6.5 m, and the thickness of its outer wall is 1.6 m. Judging from these data, the total width was 17 m. Within the passageway, part of a stone-lined drainage channel was uncovered. Access to the gate was by way of a broad natural terrace on the eastern side of the hill. A stone wall ran along the terrace's eastern edge. It is impossible to determine whether there was here an outer gate.

Structures in Areas A, B, C, and E. Two large structures were discovered in area E. One structure (building B), which consists of four rooms and a paved courtyard, was built between the gate's outer wall and the casemate wall. Some of its walls are set on a platform covered with beaten lime ascribed to stratum VII. The building was destroyed by fire and a significant amount of pottery was discovered on its floors. The second structure, a storehouse (building C), is built on a natural terrace some 1.5 m below the level of the gate area. It includes two rooms and, possibly, another wing, as yet unexcavated, at its western end. The entrance was on the south, with six steps leading to the threshold. Two floors were found in area E's casemate rooms (building D) and in the casemate area C's offset wall. The earlier floor, assigned to stratum VII, was founded on a low ledge of bedrock, leveled by an earth fill. In the part that was cleared, two rooms were divided by a thick partition wall that was "sealed" by the stratum VI floor. The eastern part of the casemate wall collapsed when the city was still standing.

In area B, a row of rooms abutting the city wall was uncovered. The front wall of these rooms was parallel to the city wall. To the north, part of a peripheral street was uncovered. Remains of contemporary houses were also uncovered in area A. The city was destroyed in a conflagration.

STRATUM VI: IRON AGE II. The remains of the Iron Age II level, dated to the late seventh century BCE, were found mainly in the casemates in areas B, C, and E—but not in area E's storehouse and large building (building B). A striking change occurs in area E's casemate wall: its northeastern section, which had collapsed in the previous period, was rebuilt, but along a new line, at an angle of 12 degrees farther into the city. The floor level in the casemates in areas C and E was raised 80 cm from the previous level, and the internal division of the casemates between the two walls was altered. Stratum VI was destroyed in a conflagration that left numerous pottery vessels and other finds on the floors.

Biran's excavations at the site revealed a number of rooms near the city wall and a rectangular tower surrounded by an inclined stone glacis from the late seventh to the early sixth centuries BCE. The finds included an intact Cypro-archaic amphora.

THE IRON AGE CEMETERY. The necropolis lies at the foot of the eastern slope of the hill. Approximately twenty-five tombs were discovered hewn in the chalk, eight of which were cleared by the expedition. Most had been robbed. The tombs held the supine burials common in the Iron Age in the country's hilly areas: each tomb consisted of one, two, or three chambers, with one, two, or three burials in each room, some of them in vaulted niches.

AREA K'S AGRICULTURAL TERRACE. Area K is located in a small valley at the foot of the site, on the north. A few terrace walls were identified here and probes were carried out; the sherds produced indicate that the terrace

Pottery assemblage found in the destruction layer from the end of the Iron Age.

Right: *Cypriot amphora from the early 6th century BCE.*

was built in the Iron Age, but it cannot be assigned to either stratum VII or stratum VI. Botanical analysis of the pollen collected in the area showed that the crops grown here were mainly cereals.

STRATA VII AND VI: IRON AGE II. The pottery from strata VII and VI is quite varied and includes types common in Judah. The pottery assemblage found in the large building and storehouse in area E, assigned by the excavators to stratum VII, includes vessels commonly dated to the late eighth century BCE and some typical of the seventh century BCE. A few vessels and decorated fragments of Edomite origin, as well as bowls imitating Assyrian palace ware, are noteworthy; another important find was a group of marked shekel weights and a single inscribed Hebrew *pym* weight. The epigraphic material includes an ostracon with the inscription מפקד ברכיהו גבח מוקר שלמיהו, probably a list of individuals residing in one of the city's houses, and two jar fragments probably inscribed with personal names: one אחקֹ[ם] (*'ḥq̊[m]*) and the other רבתמגן (*rbtmgn*). A fragment of a letter was also found, consisting only of the opening phrase: . . . עבדך אמר (Your servant said . . .). Metal objects—a plow point, a sickle, and arrowheads—were also found. The rock-hewn tombs yielded silver earrings and bronze bracelets, in addition to pottery.

STRATUM V: PERSIAN PERIOD. Following the destruction of the Iron Age city, occupation was resumed at the site, as it was in other places in the Negev—one of the regions resettled by the exiles returning from Babylon (Neh. 11:25–30). This level is represented in areas B and C, where the houses in the Iron Age stratum abutting the city wall were rebuilt and silos were erected near them. The settlement appears to have been smaller than the Iron Age city. The finds include pottery, equestrian figurines, and an Aramaic ostracon.

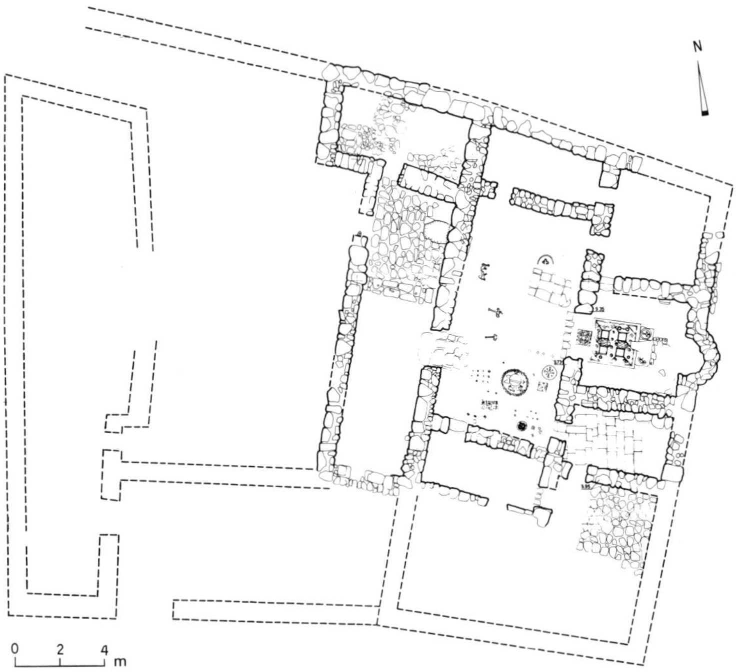

Plan of the Byzantine monastery.

STRATUM IV: HELLENISTIC PERIOD. Judging from the excavation results, the site was occupied in the Hellenistic period by a large fortified city, whose remains were found in most of the excavated areas. New houses were built in areas B and C, abutting the Iron Age city wall. They overlaid the Iron Age houses and had a similar plan. The houses in area A rested on bedrock. No public buildings were found here, apparently because of the limited extent of the excavation in relation to the size of the site. Pottery typical of the fourth to second centuries BCE was found, as well as "fish plates," decorated lamps, and coins from the reigns of Ptolemy II, Antiochus III, Antiochus IV, and John Hyrcanus.

STRATUM III: EARLY ROMAN PERIOD. In the Early Roman period only a small part of the site seems to have been occupied. The remains were concentrated in area C—a few structures abutting the wall, part of a street, and drainage channels. At this time, the offset in the wall was still in existence, but its western wall was rebuilt over the early wall and its thickness doubled. This construction testifies to the fortified nature of the settlement in the period in question; perhaps it was part of the Herodian limes. The finds consist primarily of objects of daily use.

STRATUM II: BYZANTINE PERIOD. The occupation of Tel 'Ira in the Byzantine period was extensive and dense, covering an area at least equal to that of the Iron Age city. Houses abutted the city wall in areas B and C and most of the wall served as a fortification and was restored and made higher. The rooms of some of the above-mentioned houses rested on the walls of the Hellenistic structures, and their plans were identical. The casemate rooms in area E, near the storehouse, were cleared of the conflagration layer and debris from the Iron Age destruction and were reused. Two large structures were found and excavated in area D, as well.

On the eastern part of the site, among ruins whose walls survive to a considerable height, a large monastery, with a church, was discovered. The monastery (c. 800 sq m) was built around a large courtyard paved with limestone slabs and furnished with a plastered cistern. The monastery building had three wings. The central wing contained a church paved with a mosaic featuring geometric and floral patterns and various figures and an eight-line intact inscription describing the dedication of the place to Saint Peter. Two crosses are depicted in the mosaic in front of the screened altar, and the eastern wall contained an external apse. Clay vessels were found on the floor along with some sherds from the bases of burnished bowls that were engraved with crosses.

A large Byzantine building (11 by 16.5 m), comprising two halls and a room, was found in area G, on the lowest terrace of the site and at its eastern edge. The eastern wing is divided into two: the southern part is paved with stone, and north of it is a beaten chalk floor with two large cooking hearths (or other installations) in its center. This was probably a public building, perhaps belonging to the city's administration. It was founded in the fifth century CE. The Byzantine finds include a variety of pottery—storage jars, bowls, cooking pots, and decorated lamps—coins, and metal artifacts—bronze knives and spatulae.

STRATUM I: EARLY ARAB PERIOD. Arab occupation of the site was observed mainly in areas C and E. In area C, new rooms were built opposite the city wall, which was still in use. The monastery was also reused in this period, although with major alterations: doorways were sealed, new inner walls were erected, and the apse became the main eastern entrance; the

Overview of the Byzantine monastery, looking north.

mosaic floors were buried under a layer of beaten earth; and benches, coated with a thick layer of white plaster, were built on the new floor.

SUMMARY

Although it is still not possible to propose a confident biblical identification of the site, it seems clear that during the Iron Age II Tel 'Ira was occupied by one of the major cities in the Negev. It may have been the region's administrative center, particularly in the seventh century BCE. One of the reasons for this was undoubtedly the site's strategic position controlling the Beersheba Valley and its routes. It provided a convenient outpost for the defense of the kingdom's southern border. The last Israelite city to occupy the site was destroyed in the late seventh century BCE, perhaps in an Edomite attack. The site's unique location was probably also a decisive factor in the erectior of later cities here—in the Hellenistic, Early Roman, and Byzantine periods They, too, appear to have been major cities and fortified outposts in the southern defenses of Palestine.

Y. Aharoni, *BA* 39 (1976), 55–76; 42 (1979), 133–134; A. Biran (and R. Cohen), *IEJ* 29 (1979), 124–125 id., *RB* 86 (1979), 464–465; M. Kochavi, *BAR* 6/1 (1980), 24–27; N. Na'aman, *ZDPV* 96 (1980), 136–152; I. Beit-Arieh, *IEJ* 31 (1981), 243–245; 32 (1982), 69–70; 41 (1991), 1–18; id., *PEQ* 115 (1983), 105–108; id., *ESI* 4 (1985), 51; 9 (1989–1990), 74–75; A. G. Baron, *ASOR Newsletter* 35/7 (1984), 2–3; J. D Berry, "A Preliminary Study of Ceramics from the Northern Negev" (Ph.D. diss., Fullerton 1986; Anr Arbor 1990); Y. Garfinkel, *PEQ* 119 (1987), 19–23; A. Lemaire, *VT* 38 (1988), 220–230; Weippert 198 (Ortsregister); G. J. Wightman *BASOR* 277–278 (1990), 5–22; N. Avigad, *IEJ* 40 (1990), 263

ITZHAQ BEIT-ARIEH

'IRAQ EL-EMIR

IDENTIFICATION

'Iraq el-Emir is located on a nearly direct line between Jericho and 'Amman, Jordan—29 km (18 mi.) east of Jericho and 17 km (10.5 mi.) west of 'Amman (map reference 221.147). The site includes a partly inhabited mound on which some of the architectural fragments of the ancient site are being reused. Situated on the heights above the west bank of Wadi eṣ-Ṣir, it commands a view of the spectacular plunge of that valley southward into the Wadi Kafrein. Two hundred meters northwest of the mound are cliffs with natural and hewn caves. Down a fairly steep slope, some 500 m southwest of the mound, is the megalithic Qaṣr el-'Abd (Fortress of the Servant) with retaining walls and gates. Between the Qaṣr and the cliffs lies the Square Building, near which, in antiquity, the area was irrigated by a canal. The canal can be traced northward to the base of the cliffs and toward a source beyond. The source ensures a year-long flow of water through the site.

'Iraq el-Emir is probably to be identified with the Ramath-Mizpeh of the Bible (Jos. 13:26) and Birtha (stronghold) of the Ammonites in the land of Tobiah mentioned in the Zenon papyri (P Edgar 59003–59004). It is certainly the Tyros fortress built by the Tobiad Hyrcanus in the early second century BCE (Josephus, *Antiq.* XII, 230–233). Of the sites proposed for Ramath-Mizpeh (Khirbet Jel'ad, Khirbet eṣ-Ṣar and Khirbet eṣ-Ṣireh), only 'Iraq el-Emir has both a geographically satisfactory position and evidence of ar Iron Age I occupation. The two "Tobiah" inscriptions on the facades of the two large halls carved in the cliffs and the name Fortress of the Servant (ar obvious reference to "Tobiah the servant, the Ammonite" mentioned ir Neh. 2:10) stamp the site as a Tobiad center. The family and land of Tobiah have been traced in biblical and other sources to the eighth century BCE However, the archaeological evidence available so far indicates that there was no substantial occupation at the site between the eleventh century unti about 200 BCE. This situation is probably best explained by considering the site as the country estate from which the land of Tobiah was administered Birtha perhaps consisted of a manor at or near the mound, with the nearby caves offering a defensive stronghold. A few coins and sherds from the early

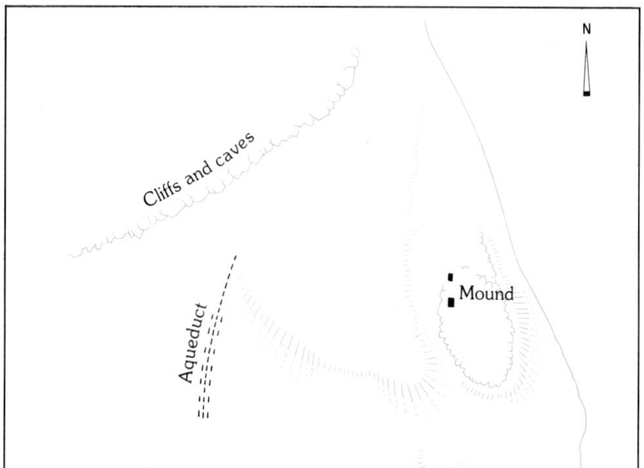

'Iraq el-Emir: plan of the site.

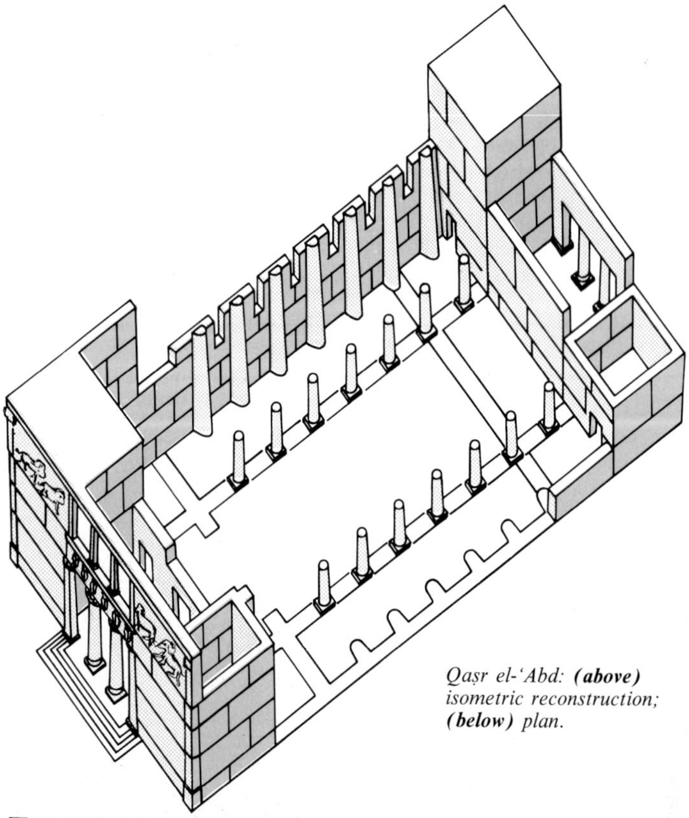

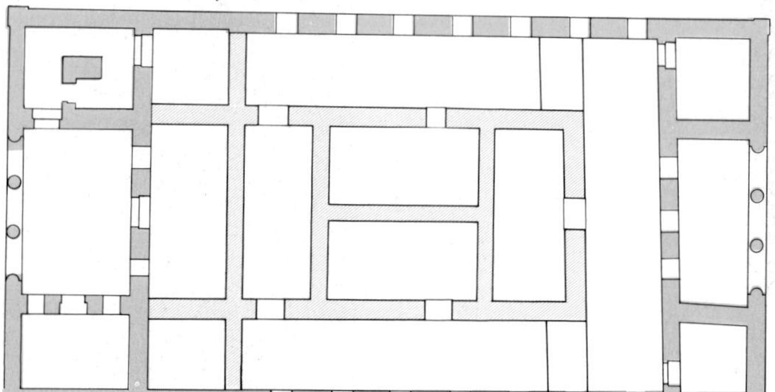

Qaṣr el-'Abd: ***(above)*** *isometric reconstruction;* ***(below)*** *plan.*

Northeastern corner of the Qaṣr el-'Abd.

third century BCE may be associated with the estate. It seems dubious, however, that 'Iraq el-Emir had been the center of the Tobiad dominions since the eighth century BCE.

Josephus' description of the building of Tyros may be of construction on a previously unimportant site. There are so many links between Josephus' description of Hyrcanus' Tyros and 'Iraq el-Emir that the identification has never been seriously contested. The name Tyros itself is still preserved in the name Wadi eṣ-Ṣir. The Qaṣr el-'Abd can hardly be dissociated from the "strong fortress" Hyrcanus "constructed entirely of white marble up to the very roof, and had beasts of gigantic size carved on it, and he enclosed it with a wide and deep moat" (Josephus, *Antiq.* XII, 230). The two large halls with the two Tobiah inscriptions correspond to the chambers carved in the rock with narrow entrances "so that only one person and no more could enter at one time" (*Antiq.* XII, 232). The Plaster Building, excavated in 1962, is almost certainly one of Hyrcanus' "large enclosures" (*Antiq.* XII, 233). Excavation has undermined the attempts of many scholars to attribute to the Qaṣr a date before Hyrcanus' operations in the first quarter of the second century BCE. The Qaṣr is now clearly dated by archaeological evidence to Hyrcanus' time, and the Plaster Building is contemporaneous with it. The dating of the cave inscriptions has been much disputed—a fifth-century BCE date having been accepted by a majority of scholars of paleography for many years. F. M. Cross, Jr., has proposed a date of about 300 BCE, on epigraphic grounds. The epigraphic evidence is not clearly decisive, however, and the excavator has proposed that the reliability of Josephus' account be accepted in this matter, too. He even suggested the revival of an early view that the "Tobiah" of the inscriptions is the Jewish name of Hyrcanus.

EXPLORATION

The environs of the Qaṣr were described by early travelers and scholars, beginning with C. L. Irby and J. Mangles, in 1817. The visits of E. M. de Vogüé in 1864, F. de Saulcy in 1868, and C. R. Conder in 1881 resulted in publications that were superseded only by those of H. C. Butler, whose Princeton expedition survey team spent six days at the site in October 1904. Little attention was paid to the mound by these explorers, and Conder was the only one who provided detailed plans of the caves. Little was added to Butler's amazingly complete descriptions of the Qaṣr, except that a number of his conclusions were refuted in a dissertation by M. Etchemendy in 1960.

EXCAVATIONS AND STRATIGRAPHY

Three campaigns were undertaken at 'Iraq el-Emir in 1961 and 1962, under the direction of P. W. Lapp, with most of the budget supplied by the American Schools of Oriental Research. Most of the staff members were appointees and residents of its Jerusalem school. In 1976, excavations at the site were resumed under the direction of E. Will, assisted by F. Larché, J. M. Dentzer, and F. Zayadine, on behalf of the Institut Français d'Archéologie du Proche Orient, in collaboration with the Jordan Department of Antiquities.

Lower course of the eastern wall of the Qaṣr el-'Abd with a feline carved in relief.

The stratigraphic history of the mound indicates six main strata of occupation. A few Chalcolithic sherds have been found, but always in later contexts. Small patches of undisturbed Early Bronze Age occupation have been discovered on the site (stratum VI), and a contemporary stratum has been excavated in the Square Building. A second series of layers (stratum V) produced pottery from an occupation on the mound from the beginning of the eleventh century BCE until close to its end. Its major feature was a 17-m segment of a 1.5-m-wide defensive wall. This could have been part of a Gadite fort at Ramath-Mizpeh abandoned at the end of the eleventh century BCE, when Ammon is presumed to have eliminated the Gadites from the area. Stratum IV follows a long gap and belongs to an occupation in the early second century BCE, the period when Hyrcanus was building Tyros. There is scattered evidence of occupation in the third century BCE, but as yet it cannot be isolated as a separate stratum. Hyrcanus began building Tyros about 182 BCE, perhaps as early as 210 BCE. Pottery in the fill under the floors of stratum IV belongs to the beginning of the second century BCE, and pottery in the ash layer on the floor, marking the destruction of the Plaster Building, belongs to a ceramic horizon of about 175 BCE. Unfortunately, except for the Plaster Building, Hyrcanus' major construction on the mound was cleared to floor level by the next major rebuilding at the site. It seems likely that there was a break in occupation from the time of Hyrcanus' death in about 175 BCE until near the end of the century.

In about 100 BCE, at least in the northwest quarter of the mound, where excavation has taken place, there was a major rebuilding of the site (stratum IIIB). It established the town's defensive limits with a casemate-style construction with a large plastered court inside it. Except for importing 0.5 m of fill for the floors of the casemate rooms in the early first century CE, the occupants of this part of the town made few changes in their quarters before abandoning them in about 50 CE.

About the end of the first century, a complete renovation of the stratum III structures was undertaken, involving changes in entryways, new partition walls, and a fill that raised the floor level another 0.5 m. This occupation (stratum II) seems to have continued without interruption until close to the end of the second century when, judging from the burned destruction layer, the occupation was brought to a violent end. This destruction seems to have been followed by immediate reoccupation, for the stratum I sherds are only slightly later than those in the stratum II destruction. In stratum I, the floor level was raised 0.8 m with an imported fill, and rooms were further partitioned, indicating an expanding population. The floor level of this stratum was approximately at the surface level of the mound; the surface remains failed to indicate any further occupation of the site from the end of the stratum I occupation, just after 200 CE, to the present.

The Qaṣr environs were inhabited in the Early Bronze Age (stratum IV), the early second century BCE (stratum III), and in the Byzantine period (strata II and I). Stratum IV consisted merely of debris into which foundations for Hyrcanus' buildings were cut. No Hellenistic layers related to the Qaṣr were found. The Byzantine occupants had cleared the environs of the Qaṣr to below the Hellenistic floor level, and the earlier stratum II floors rested directly on stratum IV debris. Some sherds from the early second

Qaṣr el-'Abd: restored western wall.

century BCE were mixed with the Byzantine debris. The Byzantine occupation could be quite closely dated by coins and pottery. The occupation of stratum II, which ended in a violent destruction of much of the Qaṣr, belongs to the mid-fourth century and probably ended with the major earthquake that rocked Transjordan in 363 CE. In the final occupation of the site, a 2-m fill was required to level the quake debris. This level lasted through the fifth century CE. The stratigraphy of the Square Building is identical with that of the Qaṣr, except for two pits that contain pottery from about 200 CE. It was built with reused architectural fragments from Hellenistic buildings.

The results of the 1962 excavation included the elucidation of the plan and dimensions of the Plaster Building. The walls surrounding its large inner court were covered by thick plaster with a fine, dark red surface, beveled edges, and white borders. The plaster and carefully dressed rectangular blocks at the doorways contrast strikingly with the bricky dirt core of the wall, the thin plaster layers in the corridor around the court, and the small stones used to build the outer walls. The structure belongs stratigraphically to the early second century BCE and can be identified as one of the large enclosed courts that Josephus attributes to Hyrcanus.

THE QAṢR EL-'ABD

Excavations at the Qaṣr involved a trench through the main hall; trenches against the east, west, and north walls; and scattered probings. The results have shed light on the date, function, unfinished state, and a number of architectural details of this megalithic building. The only precise evidence for the date of the Qaṣr's construction comes from a group of early second-century BCE sherds found in the Byzantine fill. Because this was the only occupation in the vicinity of the Qaṣr between the Early Bronze Age and the Byzantine period, it provides clear support for Josephus' attribution of the Qaṣr to Hyrcanus.

Until the 1962 excavations, scholars had interpreted the Qaṣr as a fortress, a temple, a palace, or a mausoleum. The architectural details of the stairwell located in the northeast tower were studied by the architect M. Brett during the third campaign. The five flights of the gradually rising staircase gave access to a gallery at the north end of the main hall; the stairs led to a tower above the frieze course and presumably also to a terrace roof that (as the large interior half-columns indicate) covered all or part of the main hall. These elements—stairway, terrace, and tower—have been convincingly associated by R. Amy with a temple-cult function. The opisthodome and megalithic voussoir blocks found in the adytum area also support the temple interpretation. The Qaṣr emerges as a unique, indigenous example of the old Syrian temple type in the Hellenistic period. It provides a link between the stair temples at Ugarit and Jerusalem and those characteristic of the Roman East. It has a striking contemporary parallel in the temple of Onias IV at Leontopolis, mentioned by Josephus (*Antiq.* XIII, 62–73; *War* VII, 421–436) but not located with certainty.

A number of architectural fragments point to the incomplete state of the building. The frieze blocks in the eastern towers, still in situ, bear weathered reliefs of what are usually considered lions. One of the frieze megaliths unearthed near the southwest tower, which had probably fallen during the fourth-century CE earthquake, displayed only the roughed-out head, back, hind leg, and tail of the beast that was to have been sculptured in place. A fragment of the string course (lower cornice), with its dentils still uncut, and the only partial removal of the bosses on the lowest course in the

Qaṣr el-'Abd: the monumental gate.

east wall further indicate that, although the building's main walls had been erected, its architectural details were never completed. There is no evidence that there was a terrace roof over the main hall, but it could have been entirely obliterated by Byzantine operations.

The most interesting discovery of the 1962 excavations was a fountain, with a feline sculptured in high relief on a large block of mottled red-and-white dolomite. It was located in the lowest course of the east wall of the Qaṣr on a line with the spur by which the moat was crossed to the Qaṣr from a gate to the east. A study by D. Hill concludes that this is a unique example of provincial Greek sculpture from the early second century BCE. The stone used in the relief is local (the quarry for the Qaṣr megaliths was discovered at the very top of the hills directly west of it).

The Byzantine reuse of the Qaṣr involved a major building operation, and the series of piers unearthed in some of the large rooms, together with related artifacts, suggests that it may have been used by a monastic group.

PAUL W. LAPP

RECENT EXCAVATIONS

The architectural conclusions of E. Will, the director of the Institut Français, like those of the preceding excavators, are that a Hellenistic building, the Qaṣr, constructed by Hyrcanus, was left unfinished at the beginning of the second century BCE. After several seasons of work, and with the use of heavy equipment, he and his assistant, F. Larché, were able to uncover and analyze architectural elements and theoretically reconstruct the probable structure planned and partially executed by Hyrcanus. Detailed plans are now available for the north facade, including the evidence that the lion frieze continued from the east to west walls, and for the reconstruction of the corner towers recognized by Lapp and others. When the west side was cleared, walls were uncovered lying face down, the way they had collapsed, outward. Long slabs

Inscribed weight from 'Iraq el-Emir.

in the first course of stones laid horizontally held second-course blocks set vertically. This left spaces for windows; small blocks of stone were used as sills between them. Some lintel and cornice blocks above the windows have been reconstructed. Corrections have been made in Butler's earlier plan, most notably in the elimination of the half columns he thought had filled the spaces (windows) between the vertical block. The accuracy of this reconstruction is more certain for the lower courses, revealed through excavation, than for the top courses with the lion frieze.

Especially significant was the discovery in 1962 of another animal fountain. It had been placed symmetrically in the Qaṣr's west wall, but unfortunately it was greatly mutilated. Adding to information about the lion frieze was a block found face down. It had fallen before it was defaced and weathered unlike those still standing. The feline is carved in high relief and there is a small cub between her fore- and hind legs.

Inside the Qaṣr, Will concluded, as Lapp had before him, that Hellenistic foundations can be determined, even though they were reused and added to by the Byzantines. Stratigraphical excavations with the Jordan Department of Antiquities uncovered a Hellenistic surface in at least one place. However, as already discovered by earlier excavations, even though the Hellenistic level could be determined in most places, the floor had either been removed by the Byzantines or never been completed. Although Will's reconstruction of the Hellenistic building differs considerably from Butler's, Will's internal reconstruction is close to Lapp's.

Excavations of the remains of the monumental gateway were undertaken in 1976, in order to understand the Qaṣr, much as the Square Building had been excavated in 1961. The gateway's architectural affinities with the Qaṣr did become clear: it was also decorated with eagles and felines. Its orientation is not toward the Qaṣr or cave area, but toward a road that, with the dam, contained the artificial lake.

The clearance and reconstruction of the Qaṣr has led its French investigators to consider that it was the center of a palatial estate—a château or manor. The interior Qaṣr rooms on the lower floor were meant for storage or animals, while the incomplete upper story would have been used for living—as can still be seen in homes in some Near Eastern villages today. The Qaṣr may have been only one part of a huge country estate, planned and partially executed by Hyrcanus. There is evidence throughout the area—obvious to the early explorers here, as well—of irrigation canals and ancient terraces. The wadi still flourishes with vegetation and the natural surroundings are ideal for gardens and parks. Investigations point to a lake, rather than the moat as Josephus described (see above), held back by an earth dam. An expanded study of the environs has led to further excavations on the village mound. More Hellenistic occupation has been uncovered, including what may be a city wall, but the Roman settlement was the most widespread.

NANCY L. LAPP

Main publication: N. L. Lapp, *The Excavations of 'Araq el-Emir* 1 (AASOR 47), Cambridge, Mass. 1983; E. Will, *'Iraq al Amir: Le Chateau du Tobiade Hyrcan* (Texte et Album), Paris, 1991.
Other studies: H. C. Butler, *Syria*, div 2, sect. A, Leyden 1919, 1–22; G. Dalman, *PJB* 11 (1920), 14; L. H. Vincent, *JPOS* 3 (1923), 55–68; N. Glueck, *AASOR* 18–19 (1939), 154–156; O. Ploger, *ZDPV* 71 (1955), 70–81; C. C. McCown, *BA* 20 (1957), 63–76; B. Mazar, *IEJ* 7 (1957), 137–145, 229–238; M. Etchemendy, "Le Site d'Araq el-Emir" (Ph.D. diss., Jerusalem 1960); P. W. Lapp, *ADAJ* 6–7 (1962), 80–89; 10 (1965), 37–42; id., *BASOR* 165 (1962), 16–34; 171 (1963), 8–39; id. (et al.), *The Tale of the Tell*, Pittsburgh 1975, 39–65; M. J. Brett, *BASOR* 171 (1963), 39–45; D. K. Hill, *BASOR* 171 (1963), 45–55; J. M. Dentzer, *ADAJ* 22 (1977–1978), 102–107; 26 (1982), 301–321; id., *MdB* 22 (1982), 19; id., *SHAJ* 1 (1982), 201–207; R. M. Brown, *ADAJ* 23 (1979), 17–30; E. Will, *CRAIBL* (1977), 60–85; id., *ADAJ* 23 (1979), 139–149; id., *RB* 86 (1979), 117–119; id., *MdB* 22 (1982), 12–18; id., *SHAJ* 1 (1982), 197–200; N. L. Lapp, *ADAJ* 23 (1979), 5–15; id., *Archaeology and Biblical Interpretation* (D. Glenn Rose Fest.), Atlanta 1987, 165–181; J. A. Sauer, *BA* 42 (1979), 135; F. Larché, *ADAJ* 25 (1981), 327–330; id. et al., *LA* 31 (1981), 333–342; *Akkadica Supplementum* 7–8 (1989), 280–297.

ISKANDER, KHIRBET

IDENTIFICATION

Khirbet Iskander is a 7.5-a. site lying on the northern bank of the perennial Wadi el-Wala, approximately 24 km (15 mi.) south of Medeba in Jordan (map reference 2233.1072). The site is situated near the bridge where the Medeba–Dhiban road crosses the wadi. This highway follows closely the Via Traiana Nova, probably the ancient King's Highway. Iskander, therefore, was strategically located at a crossing point for caravans traversing the Transjordan between 'Aqaba and Damascus. The site is 484.46 m above sea level and rises about 20 m above the surrounding area. Its average annual precipitation is about 250 mm a year.

The site is on a mountain tableland, designated in the biblical text as *hammishor* (Dt. 3:10, 4:43). Its southern and northern boundaries, respectively, are the Wadi Mojib and Wadi Ḥesbân. About 2 km west of the site, the Wadi el-Wala enters the Wadi Ḥeidan, which ultimately empties into the Dead Sea. To the east is the desert. N. Glueck described the ruins as "located partly beyond two small *wudyan* (wadis in Arabic) which, coming from the north, join the Wadi el-Wala." The walled area on the west was the more important. Today, the area to the east of the walled site, between the *wudyan*, is mostly under cultivation, although remains can be seen of what Glueck described as a field of menhirs and circles of stones. Ceramic evidence and a menhir immediately to the south across the wadi may indicate that the limits of the site were more extensive in antiquity. Indeed, Glueck even noted house foundations north and east of the walled area.

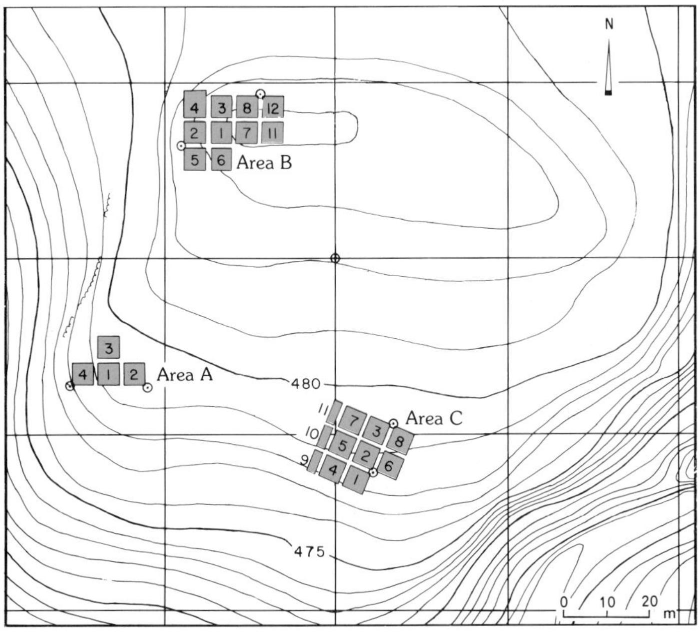

Khirbet Iskander: map of the site and excavation areas.

HISTORY

The ancient name of this site is unknown, although K. H. Bernhardt attempted to connect Iskander with the biblical site of Jahaz (Num. 21:23; Dt. 2:23; Jg. 11:20). Jahaz is one of the sites mentioned in connection with the movement of the Israelites up the King's Highway prior to their battle at Heshbon. On the basis of past and present surveys and excavations at Khirbet Iskander, none of which has uncovered evidence for stratified occupation at the site later than the Early Bronze Age IV, this identification seems unlikely. The site was abandoned following the Early Bronze Age IV, at some time after 2000 BCE.

EXPLORATION

C. Schick in 1879, R. E. Brünnow and A. von Domaszewski in 1904, and A. Musil in 1907 explored and described the site. Glueck, in 1939, was the first to publish material culture from Iskander. He described a well-fortified site with extensive domestic occupation, the pottery of which was exclusively "Early Bronze IV/Middle Bronze I." In 1955, P. Parr excavated two trenches on the perimeter of the mound, one at the northeast, the other on the east. These soundings revealed stratified Early Bronze Age IV layers, as well as an earlier stratified layer thought to date to the Late Chalcolithic/Early Bronze Age I. There were few sherds from other periods. In trench I, Parr found massive fortifications in period 1; destruction debris, particularly ashy layers and mud-brick debris, in period 2; and a walled, cobblestoned courtyard in period 3. Similar findings came to light in trench II, except that four building phases were exposed in the upper level.

Since 1981, S. Richard has directed excavations at the site: a pilot season in 1981, and three full seasons of excavations in 1982, 1984, and 1987. R. S. Boraas was associate director in 1982 and 1984. A survey of the vicinity within 5 km (3 mi.) of the site generally confirmed Glueck's survey, except for the addition of several new sites. Following the 1984 season, a two-week salvage dig sponsored by the Jordan Department of Antiquities was conducted in cemetery D across the wadi, to the south of the site. The Khirbet

Area B: inner wall of phase E and the outer wall of phase D, including a square tower and buttress.

Iskander Expedition is sponsored by the American Schools of Oriental Research and has been affiliated with Drew University, Madison, New Jersey; Upsala College; and Seton Hall University. The project's primary focus has been to test the hypothesis that sedentism—that is, permanent agrarian settlement—was an alternative subsistence choice to pastoralism in the Early Bronze Age IV (Middle Bronze Age I, c. 2350–2000 BCE). Four seasons of work have underscored the validity of this hypothesis.

EXCAVATIONS

The areas investigated by the current expedition are summarized here: area A, squares 1–4, at the southwestern crest; area B, squares 1–8 and 11–12, at the northwestern corner; area C, squares 1–11, at the southeastern crest; cemetery D, tombs 1–9 south of the site, across the wadi; cemetery E, tombs 1–3, east of the site; cemetery J, tombs 1–3, west of the site; and soundings G, I, K and L, at various points around the perimeter of the site. Thus far, only two periods of stratified occupation have been discovered: a multiphased Early Bronze Age IV stratum overlying a (thus far) one-phase Early Bronze Age I stratum. Discoveries in the cemeteries corroborate these findings on the tell. The current expedition's work has clarified and in many ways affirmed Glueck's observations and Parr's excavations. Surface survey and fill layers have yielded an insignificant number of sherds from the Late Chalcolithic, Early Bronze Age II–III, Iron Age, Roman, and Arab periods. The following stratigraphic analysis represents a preliminary phasing of the site by area prior to additional excavation and final publication.

AREA A. The area A and contiguous sounding G squares provide a good picture of domestic occupation in the latest phases along the southern crest of the mound. Surface clearance of wall lines linking this area with area C (see below) revealed an unbroken but slightly meandering wall line (1.25 m high and 0.8 m wide). It had served as a southern boundary to a series of rectangular domestic structures sharing common walls (also 1.25 m high). These walls linked areas A and C stratigraphically in phase B; they were reused in phases A1–2. This type of building construction contrasts sharply with the houses in later levels, where three-row, three-course, well-constructed walls are characteristic. A *tabun*, the usual grinding stones and querns, fire pits, and bins illuminate the domestic activities that occurred in these houses. The material is all Early Bronze Age IV. Glueck's photograph and description of a (surmised) fortification bisecting the site in the middle, from east to west, compare favorably with these findings.

AREA B. The most extensive stratigraphical profile on the tell comes from area B. There the expedition has so far discerned seven occupational layers. Phases A–G encompass an inhabitational sequence covering a prefortification, fortification, and postfortification stage.

Prefortification Stages. From the bottom, phase G dates to the Early Bronze Age I. It is the lowest stratified layer reached in the deep probe in the area B4 extension; the layer included a red-slipped omphalos base and several sherds of line-group painted ware. The site was probably an open village at this time, given the location of these materials at the edge of the mound, beyond the line of the later fortifications. The subsequent six phases date to the Early Bronze Age IV. Phase F, a surface with an associated fragmentary wall, lies beneath the level of the fortifications. This prefortification stage illumines the site as an open village in its first Early Bronze Age IV phase of occupation.

Fortification Stages. In the fortification stage, the sequence of defenses at the site appears to encompass four separate and distinct phases: a founding phase (E), an extensive rebuild (D), plus two subsequent phases of use (C–B). The founding of a substantial stone wall (the inner wall) with a mud-brick superstructure designates phase E. Excavation revealed its inwardly collapsed state at a 30-degree angle. In phase D, there were constructed an outer wall (including a square tower with steps); buttresses against the northern face of the inner collapsed wall; a rubble fill in between the two walls; and a stone layer covering the whole stone structure. The resulting defense line was the 2.5-m-wide defenses articulated for 20 m in B4, B3, B8, and B12. Early Bronze Age IV sherds, as well as a piece of painted Syrian "caliciform" black-on-white ware discovered in the foundation trench assured the date.

The degree of reuse and construction and the extent of the mud-brick debris associated with the fortifications have thus far severely complicated the search for stratified interior occupational evidence of these early levels.

Although it remains to be determined, the earliest surface and house wall excavated thus far in association with the 2.5-m-wide defense line appears to postdate the founding of the phase D wall. This level has thus been designated phase C. These remains came to light in a restricted section of areas B7–8, below the surface of the phase B "storeroom" (see below). The number of whole and restorable vessels found in phase C prompted the team to call it the lower storeroom.

Phase B is the most complete level of occupation excavated within the fortifications. In it, a cluster of architectural features and ceramic, botanical, and zoological remains combined within clearly defined structures to present an almost complete picture of activity-specific occupation areas. Excavation has exposed a two-room broadhouse with very fine wall construction running parallel to the defense line. Unfortunately, the destruction of the structure's northern wall rendered a definitive stratigraphical link with the outer fortifications problematic. However, other lines of evidence strongly support the view that the fortifications were still in use in phase B.

The western room in this structure contained benches on the three extant sides, on top of which sat a number of pithoi (1 m high). Many other vessels including lamps, jugs, "teapots," and bottle *amphoriskoi*, were discovered in situ on the floor, encased in what appeared to be plaster roofing material. The exceedingly large number of vessels, particularly storage jars, some with

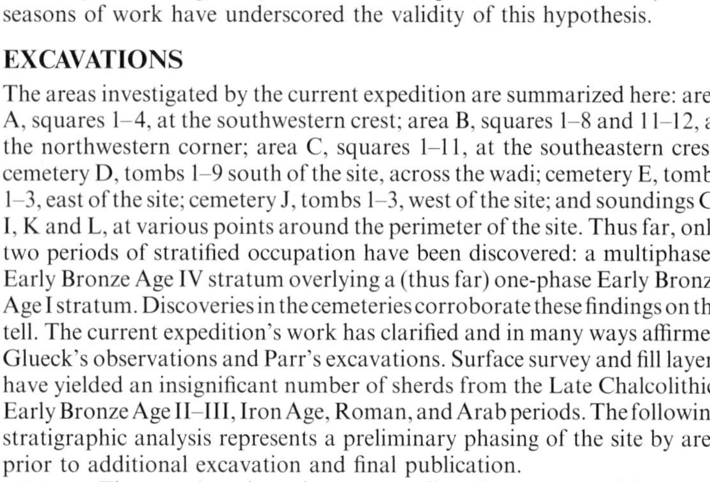

Area B: square tower (phase D) built against an earlier collapsed (phase E) inner stone and mud-brick wall.

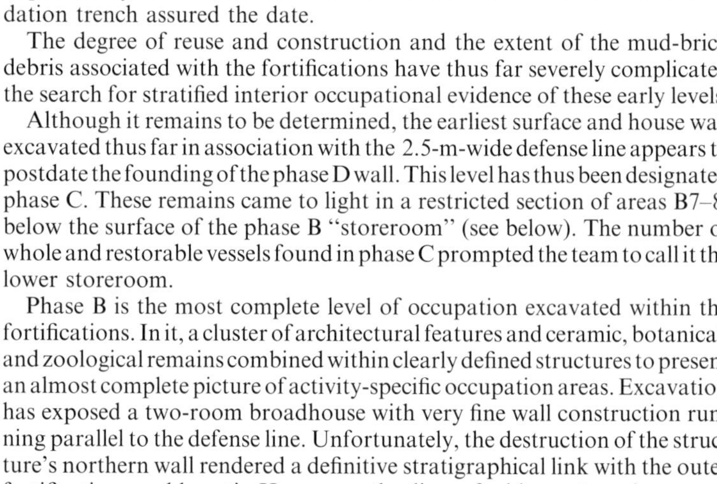

Area B: inner wall (phase E) and outer wall (phase D).

Area B: stone-lined pit found in the phase B "storeroom."

grain still inside, suggests a storeroom of some kind. It is doubtful that this cache represents a typical domestic store of food vessels. In any case, this is probably the largest and most important cache of Early Bronze Age IV pottery found in a domestic rather than a tomb context.

On the east, a doorway led to an adjacent room appointed with an extremely well-constructed bin of finely hewn stone slabs. Plaster lined the bin, the floor, and the lower wall. In dimension and construction, this feature parallels quite closely the bin found in the Early Bronze Age II sacred area at Arad. The Iskander bin is 1 m deep, with a hewn slab of 0.8 m in diameter at the bottom. In association with this bin were a fire pit, a hearth, two goat horns, miniature vessels, and a painted (offering?) dish in which lay the hoof of a bovine. Excavation here, as in the western room, yielded vast numbers of whole and restorable vessels. Botanical remains from the bin were extensive and multivariate, suggesting a range of offerings, if indeed it is a *favissa*. It is, however, conceivable that the inclusions came from the general destruction that brought phase B to an end. The cumulative evidence strongly suggests that this was a public structure, possibly part of a larger complex that included not only a storage area, but a cultic area, as well.

Postfortification Stage. Finally, the reuse of phase B walls following the destruction of that level implies that an immediate rebuilding occurred. The layout and construction of the structures, however, are totally different, as are the activities associated with them. The latest settlement (phase A) in area B, the so-called domestic complex, was exposed across ten squares and has provided an excellent perspective on Early Bronze Age IV domestic activities, community organization, and architectural traditions. Phase A house walls cover the fortifications. Although the excavators call this a postfortification stage, several lines of evidence converge to suggest that a defense line—albeit vastly less substantial than the 2.5-m-wide fortification—protected the site. In the north balk of the B4 extension, a substantial wall line was discovered; an additional remnant appeared north of square B8. Evidence for a gateway in area C must also be taken into consideration (see below). A wealth of food preparation and general domestic paraphernalia distinguished the nature and function of these structures, including, among other things, three *tabuns*, saddle querns, grinding stones, mortars, unusual stone tables, and benches.

This conversion of a probable public area to a domestic area of houses and courtyards includes an interesting change in settlement planning, as well. Now, in addition to the broadhouse form, there is a series of longhouses with shared walls running perpendicular to and above the earlier fortification line. Of particular note is their constructional history. The houses in B7 and B11 included pillared walls. There is significant stratified evidence to support the conclusion that these pillars were freestanding in phase A3, blocked except for a doorway in phase A2, and finally turned into solid walls in phase A1. This discovery of the use of either monolithic or multiple drums as roofing supports unveils a link in addition to ceramics between Khirbet Iskander and Negev sites—particularly Mount Yeroḥam and Be'er Resisim—but including numerous Early Bronze Age IV (and II) sites known from surveys. Following phase A1, the site was abandoned and never reoccupied.

AREA C. The Gateway. In area C, at the southeastern crest, there are three building phases (A–C), top to bottom. Termed the gateway, area C has yielded significant new information concerning the level of complexity in the Early Bronze Age IV, in addition to the fortifications, public buildings, storerooms, and a possible cultic area already noted in area B. Here, there is clear evidence in the latest levels (phases A1–2) of an Early Bronze Age IV entryway at the southeastern corner of the site, an entryway that leads, up a series of steps, into a bench-lined, 2.5-m-wide plastered passageway. The northern end of the passageway ended in steps leading into an open courtyard and to the town beyond. Flanking this entranceway are similar, but not totally symmetrical, rooms—the western one paved and the eastern partitioned. Bounding this entranceway on the south is a massively proportioned two-course, two-row wall. This massive wall had clearly been set in an earlier wall line, for on both sides of the gate it abuts a 1.25-m-high wall whose construction is entirely different. It is this latter wall (Glueck's presumed fortification) that the expedition has traced some distance to the east and as far west as area A.

The 1987 season turned up another massive building (11 m long) connected to the gateway on the west. Associated with the gateway on the east is a series of interconnected rooms, all reusing 1.25-m-high walls from an earlier phase (phase B). In these rooms, a large number of unusual stone platforms was found, presumably worktables, given the stone implements nearby and the vast quantities of flint debitage collected. Some of these rooms, at least, were very likely workshops.

As for the constructional history of the gateway, probes in the eastern half of the passageway have revealed domestic occupation lying immediately below. Notably, the house discovered was a well-constructed broadroom exhibiting an unusual wall of alternating mud brick and stone. It has been assigned to phase B, even though its construction is not characteristic of that phase. Several of the walls belonging to this house were reused in the construction of the gateway. Below, yet another domestic structure, aligned differently, presented evidence for an earlier level (phase C) of domestic occupation in this area.

It is thus possible to ascertain definitively that the transformation of area C into a gateway occurred in phase A2, and it is, of course, tempting to connect this transformation with the events that brought about the destruction of the fortifications observed in area B (at the end of phase B).

Left: *juglet with strap handles, rilled neck, and two bosses decorating the shoulder;* ***(right)*** *hybrid jug, red-slipped with band-combing and vertical burnish, EB IV.*

THE CEMETERIES. Except for one Early Bronze Age I tomb discovered in 1987, all the tombs excavated at Iskander belong to the Early Bronze Age IV. While there are some distinctive forms, the bulk of the pottery generally can be compared with the Early Bronze Age IV tomb repertoire known from Bab edh-Dhra' (tombs A51 and A54). There is a high percentage of red-slipped and burnished forms. Preliminary study hints at a close correlation in form and decoration between tell and tomb pottery at Iskander. Characteristic forms include large rilled-rim platter bowls, small to medium carinated or incised bowls, "teapots," four-spouted lamps, and a great range of small to medium jars and jugs. There is a great variety of incised, rilled, punctate, slashed, and band-combed techniques decorating the tomb pottery.

The tombs are all of the round-shaft, single-chamber variety. All the burials were secondary. There were indications that some of the shaft tombs were originally natural caves. The best-preserved tombs were in cemetery D, in the hillside to the south. Architectural features included blocking stones, steps carved near the bottom of the shaft, and in one tomb two small monoliths at the entrance and a bench at the rear. Several of these tombs were distinguished by unusual quantities of pottery. Exploration across an extremely wide expanse of this hillside uncovered evidence for shaft tombs. It is reasonable to infer that hundreds of tombs were cut into this mountainside.

Glueck's descriptions of menhirs and circles of stone between the two *wudyan* to the east of the site have proved to reflect accurately the nature of this area wherever the present expedition was able to explore. In particular, bulldozer cuts made in the construction of a roadway through that area have exposed rows of shaft tombs or the partial remains of chambers. This is the expedition's cemetery E. Only one tomb gave a glimpse of what was perhaps a cemetery with somewhat different burial traditions than those found in cemetery D. This particular tomb contained the remains of three disarticulated, but mostly complete skeletons, six vessels, and a pounding stone. In the small number of ceramic offerings, and in the fairly intact nature of the skeletal remains, there is a contrast with cemetery D. Unfortunately, additional corroborative evidence is lacking. In another tomb chamber, two skulls with bones between and over them had been placed just inside the opening. Three bowls and a juglet shielded the interments from the opening.

A bulldozer cut in the mountainside immediately to the west of the site, in cemetery J, had broken through a chamber (J1), at the rear of which the team found two Early Bronze Age IV vessels and a scattering of bones. In the same cemetery, the team discovered the first evidence for burials predating the Early Bronze Age IV. That tomb (J2–3), dated to the Early Bronze Age I, included two false-spouted jars and two dipper juglets. When combined with the omphalos base and band-slipped fragments found in phase G in area B, this tell and tomb data underscore the gap in occupation at Khirbet Iskander in the urban Early Bronze Age II–III.

The Early Bronze I tomb consisted of two rooms separated by a wall. On one side lay the remains of fifteen skulls, as well as pottery; in what appeared to be an antechamber, only pottery was found. The end of the 1987 season effectively terminated further exploration of what appeared to be a second phase below the floor of the tomb. In many ways, this tomb parallels tombs K2 and A13 at Jericho, where "Proto-Urban B" pottery lay above and "Proto-Urban A" pottery below.

CONCLUSIONS

Khirbet Iskander joins the ranks of a category of sites in Transjordan occupied in the Early Bronze Age I and, after a lengthy gap, again in the Early Bronze Age IV (Middle Bronze Age I). The peculiarities of habitation at Khirbet Iskander should offer some insight into cultural episodes when nonurban features are ascendant: shifts to despecialized economies, downsized sociopolitical structures, and two rather than three-tier settlement-pattern configurations.

The conditions that necessitated the construction of fortifications following phase G remain enigmatic. However, the results of recent surveys in Transjordan show that the Iskander Early Bronze Age IV defenses, although the first to be excavated, are not unique to that period. Iskander's location on a major thoroughfare at a crossing point hints at the importanc of the King's Highway at a time when the major trade routes west of th Jordan River were in eclipse. The operation of the Wadi el-Feinan coppe mines in this period is only one indication (amid a pattern of sites along it length) that the King's Highway was an important interregional thorough fare for trade in the Early Bronze Age IV.

The causes of the destruction at the end of phase B and subsequent re organization and change in the settlement pattern in phase A are beyond th reach of the existing research. Whatever the reason for the diminution in are B of a highly fortified public area to a quite typical Early Bronze Age ar rangement of domestic houses around a courtyard, the phase A so-calle domestic complex hardly reflects a squatter occupation. On the contrary well-built houses partitioned into separate domestic activity areas are th standard. Based on the monumental structures associated with the gatewa in area C, the focus of the public sector had clearly shifted in phase A. Thu far, it appears that phases A1–2 from areas A and C can be correlated with th phase A domestic complex in area B—a phase that clearly postdates th fortifications.

What remains to be clarified is the stratigraphical relationship of the 1.25 m-high wall of phase B (in areas A and C) to the 2.5-m-wide fortifications Glueck's description and original aerial photographs of the mound strongl suggest a contemporaneous date. Unfortunately, well-placed probes at th eastern and western edges of the mound encountered severe erosion an ambiguous results.

Thus, all indications are that Khirbet Iskander was a medium-sized tow exhibiting a level of complexity comparable to a similar-sized town in a urban milieu. Indeed, owing to its strategic location, Iskander appears t have been a regional center, very probably an important node in a trad network along the King's Highway. Its specialized occupation areas (de tailed above), fortifications, multiple continuous occupation, monumenta public buildings, gateway, storage areas, possible cultic area, and cache o whole vessels give some indication of a hierarchical, complex society. Si milarly, these data (as well as corroborative paleoethnobotanical/zoologica remains) concretely demonstrate that permanent, agrarian settlement was feasible alternative level of subsistence to pastoralism in the Post-Urba Early Bronze Age IV.

C. Schick, *PEQ* 11 (1879), 187–192; Brünnow–Domaszewski, *Die Provincia Arabia* 1; Musil, *Arabi Petraea*; N. Glueck, *Explorations in Eastern Palestine* (AASOR 19), New Haven 1939; K. H. Bernhard *ZDPV* 76 (1960), 136–158; P. J. Parr, *ADAJ* 3 (1956), 81; 4–5 (1960), 128–133; S. Richard, *BASOR* 23 (1980), 5–34; (with R. S. Boraas), 254 (1984), 63–87; id., *Expedition* 28 (1986), 3–12; id., *BA* 50 (1987), 22 43; id. (with R. S. Boraas), *BASOR* Supplement 25 (1988), 107–130; id., 26 (1990), 33–58; J. C. Long, Jr "Sedentary Adaptations at the End of the 3rd Millennium BCE: Khirbet Iskander and the Excavate Settlement Sites of Early Bronze IV Palestine-Transjordan" (Ph.D. diss., Drew Univ. 1988); *Akkadic Supplementum* 7–8 (1989), 301–309.

SUZANNE RICHARI

‘IZBET ṢARṬAH

IDENTIFICATION AND EXPLORATION

‘Izbet Ṣarṭah is situated on a gently sloping hill on the western fringes of the hill country northeast of Rosh ha-‘Ayin, southwest of Kafr Qasim and about 16 km (10 mi.) east of Tel Aviv (map reference 14675.16795). The hill lies at the end of a spur overlooking the Coastal Plain, bordering on the alluvial plain. Approximately 3 km (2 mi.) to the west, across the Aphek Pass, lies Tel Aphek, which dominates the sources of the Yarkon River. The natural shape of the hill was damaged by quarrying during the British Mandate. The site drew its water supply from cisterns hewn in the hillside.

The site was discovered in 1973 by an archeological survey team from Te Aviv University, directed by M. Kochavi. Excavations continued for fou seasons, from 1976 to 1978, under the auspices of the Institute of Archaeology at Tel Aviv University and the Department for the Land of Israe Studies at Bar-Ilan University. The excavations were directed by M. Kochavi, with I. Finkelstein serving as field director.

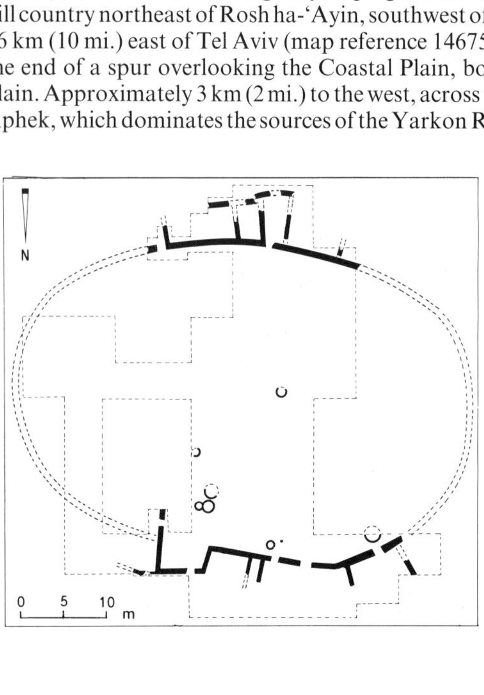

‘Izbet Ṣarṭah: plan of stratum III.

EXCAVATION RESULTS

Three strata were distinguished at ‘Izbet Ṣarṭah: the two earliest date to the Iron Age I and the latest to the beginning of the Iron Age II. Not far from the site, and similarly located on the borderline between the hills and the Coasta Plain, the survey identified six other Iron Age I sites. Various considerations—the general pattern of occupation presented in the region, the architectural features of all levels at the site, and the pottery—imply that the occupants belonged to the population which settled at that period in the heart of the hill country.

STRATUM III. The earliest level, stratum III, was established at the end of the thirteenth or beginning of the twelfth century BCE and abandoned at the beginning of the eleventh century BCE. The settlement at that time was oval in shape, with an area of about half an acre. At its center was a large courtyard surrounded by a wall, to which (from the outside) a row of rooms was adjoined to form a kind of casemate wall. The wall and rooms were excavated in two segments, for a total length of 55 m. The rooms, which were not uniformly wide, could only be entered from the courtyard and lacked interconnecting doorways. The outer wall of the site was not continuous. The walls, which were preserved to a height of one course, were built of large stones; the floors in most of the rooms were the bedrock. The entrance to the site was on its northeastern side—a narrow opening between two monolithic doorjambs that led to an open space paved with stone slabs. Inside the courtyard were several stone-faced silos. Wherever this level was excavated, the excavators found light-colored mud-brick material that was later leveled to make the foundations for the houses of stratum II.

'Izbet Ṣarṭah: aerial view of the site at the completion of the excavations, looking southeast.

The stratum III settlement was abandoned in an orderly fashion; it therefore yielded only a few complete vessels (including three collared-rim jars). Because this was the first occupation on the hill, its sherds reflect the accumulation of the entire period of activity of stratum III. Among the earliest finds, mention should be made of a small fragment of a stirrup jar fashioned in the Mycenean Simple Style, a fragment of a krater of the "ibex and palm" type, a fragment of a krater featuring a "palm" ornamentation in applied relief, bases of "Canaanite" jars, cooking pots with an everted rim, and various bowls reflecting the pottery tradition of the Late Bronze Age. Some rims of red-slipped bowls and fragments of jars with plain, unshaped rims date the end of activity in stratum III. The pottery repertoire indicates contacts between the inhabitants and the nearby plain. Because the site lies at the border between the hill country and the Coastal Plain, its history reflects the political fluctuations typical of the region. The expansion of the hill country population to the edge of the Coastal Plain may be ascribed to the period just after the destruction of nearby Aphek and just before the Philistines consolidated their control of the region. The site was abandoned because of heightened tension between the Israelites and the Philistines, at the beginning of the eleventh century BCE—the same tension that soon broke out in the battle at Ebenezer, apparently located nearby.

STRATUM II. After a gap in occupation, activity at the site was renewed at the end of the eleventh century BCE, when conditions ripened for Israelite expansion westward from the hill country, perhaps under Saul. Stratum II is quite different in plan from stratum III, and there are signs of some planning. The area of the site was now almost one acre; in its center was a large four-room house, around which were dozens of silos, hewn in close proximity to one another into the light-colored mud-brick material and the buildings of the previous level. A series of small houses was built at the edge of the hill. The central house was 16 by 12 m in size and was preserved to a height of two or three courses of stone. The thickness of its outer walls reached 1.4 m. Stones from these walls were robbed at a later date and the larger ones were reused. The three long rooms of the house were separated by two rows of column drums. The side rooms were paved with stone slabs, but in the rest of the house the floors were bedrock and beaten earth. The entrance to the building was at one end of the long walls. A small room abutted the house from the outside.

The average capacity of the silos at 'Izbet Ṣarṭah is approximately 1.3 cu m. They rest on the bedrock or on small stones. The walls were lined with small and medium-sized stones. Some silos leaned on the walls of the building; some touched one another. A total of forty-three silos was cleared in stratum II. In some areas a beaten-earth floor was exposed between the silos.

Worthy of note among the smaller structures on the perimeter of the hill are two four-room houses. As these houses were not built in contiguity, they were clearly not intended to bolster the defenses of the settlement toward the slope of the hill.

Stratum II survived for a short time—one or two decades. Its abandonment may be associated with the Philistines' consolidation of power in their war with Saul.

STRATUM I. Shortly thereafter, at the beginning of the tenth century BCE, activity at the site was resumed, once again for only a short time (stratum I). The settlement was now smaller: the four-room house was rebuilt and some new silos replaced the ones in disuse. In the process, houses built around the perimeter of the site in stratum II were damaged. Additions to the four-room house included partitions between the columns, two rooms on the north of the building, and a few installations in the rooms. The pottery of stratum I is of the same types as stratum II; only statistical analysis of the quantitative variance between the different types can differentiate the two levels. The renewed occupation of the site may be attributable to a resumption of Israelite expansion to the west under David. After a short time, however, when the fertile plain of the Yarkon Basin opened up to Israelite settlement, 'Izbet Ṣarṭah was abandoned and never resettled.

BYZANTINE REMAINS. During the Byzantine period there was some

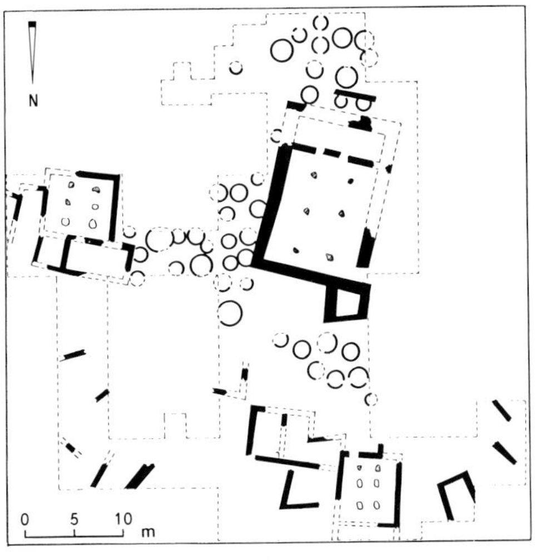

Plan of stratum II.

Silos in stratum II, north of the four-room house.

agricultural activity at the site. A stone wall was erected around the top of the hill, using stones apparently looted from the ancient structures; a few other walls were built to mark off heaps of stones cleared from the site.

Main publication: I. Finkelstein, *'Izbet Ṣarṭah: An Early Iron Age Site Near Rosh Ha'ayin, Israel* (*BAR*/IS 299), Oxford 1986.
Other studies: M. Kochavi (and A. Demsky), *BAR* 4/3 (1978), 19–22; id. (and I. Finkelstein), *IEJ* 28 (1978), 267–268; id., *RB* 86 (1979), 114–115; M. Garsiel and I. Finkelstein, *TA* 5 (1978), 192–198; J. M. Miller, *ZDPV* 99 (1983), 125–128; Weippert 1988 (Ortsregister).

ISRAEL FINKELSTEIN

THE OSTRACON. The 'Izbet Ṣarṭah ostracon was found in one of the silos (no. 605). It bears a finely engraved inscription, written on two fragments of a jar; the inscription comprises five lines, including eighty-three letters in Proto-Canaanite script. Most of the letters in the lowest line are engraved more deeply and are in fact larger and more legible than the others. Most of the letters are written from left to right. Only the lower line is decipherable: it includes a Proto-Canaanite alphabet, read from left to right. This ostracon is the longest Proto-Canaanite inscription found in the country to date.

Buried History 12 (1976), 157; A. Demsky, *TA* 4 (1977), 14–27; id. (and M. Kochavi), *BAR* 4/3 (1978), 23–30; M. Kochavi, *TA* 4 (1977), 1–13; A. Lemaire, *Journal Asiatique* 266 (1978), 221–235; J. Naveh, *IEJ* 28 (1978), 31–35; id., *BA* 43/1 (1980), 22–25; J. Teixidor, *Syria* 56 (1979), 353–354; F. M. Cross, Jr., *BASOR* 238 (1980), 1–20; A. Dotan, *TA* 8 (1981), 160–172; W. H. Shea, *AUSS* 28 (1990), 59–86.

MOSHE KOCHAVI

Proto-Canaanite ostracon from 'Izbet Ṣarṭah.

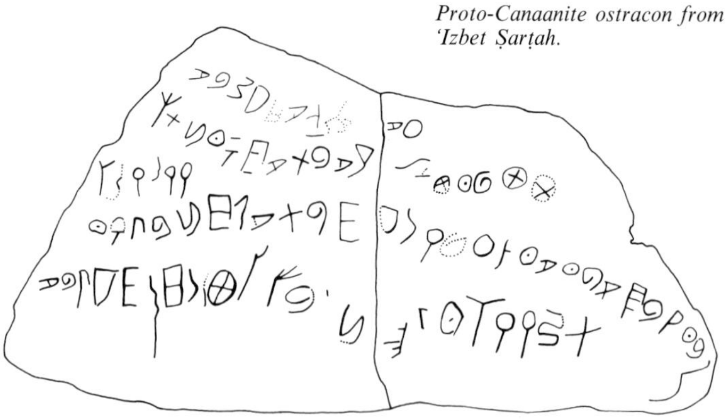

J

JAFFA

IDENTIFICATION AND HISTORY

Ancient Jaffa, situated just south of Tel-Aviv, was built on a high promontory jutting into the Mediterranean Sea. In Arabic it was called Yafa el-'Atiqa (ancient Jaffa) or el-Qal'a (the fortress). The ancient harbor, protected by a chain of large rocks which formed a kind of breakwater, was situated at the foot of the promontory.

Jaffa is first mentioned in Egyptian sources as one of the cities conquered by Thutmose III in the fifteenth century BCE. The Harris Papyrus describes his capture of the city: Thutmose III sent the governor of Jaffa a present of baskets, in which were hidden soldiers who conquered the city from within. The city is mentioned in the el-Amarna letters as an Egyptian stronghold sheltering royal granaries. The Papyrus Anastasi I provides additional information about the city in the thirteenth century BCE. Jaffa and the surrounding towns—Azor, Bene-Berak, and Beth-Dagon—are mentioned later in the prism stela of Sennacherib, the king of Assyria, who conquered the towns in his campaign of 701 BCE.

Jaffa is mentioned in the Bible in the description of the boundaries of the tribe of Dan (Jos. 19:46). Cedars from Lebanon were brought by sea to the port of Jaffa for building the First and Second temples (2 Chr. 2:15; Ezra 3:7). The prophet Jonah sought to flee from the Lord via Jaffa (Jon. 1:3). The Greek legend of Perseus and Andromeda was located in the sea of Jaffa, where the heroine was chained on rocks to be devoured by a monster from the sea. According to the inscription of Eshmunazar of Sidon (probably fifth century BCE), the "Lord of Kings" (king of Persia) presented him with Dor and Jaffa. The Sidonian occupation of Jaffa in the Persian period is also known from the description of the coastal towns of Syria and Palestine attributed to Scylax.

In the Hellenistic period, Jaffa was colonized by Greeks. The papyri of Zenon, an Egyptian treasury official who visited the country in 259–258 BCE, during the reign of Ptolemy II, throw some light on the history of the city in his time.

In the Hasmonean period, the city was captured from the Seleucids and became the port of Judea. During the war with the Romans, it was destroyed first by Cestius Gallus and then by Vespasian (in 67 CE) but was quickly rebuilt. Tombstones from the Jewish cemetery of Jaffa (at Abu Kabir), dating from the first to the fifth centuries CE, provide information about the inhabitants of the city and their occupations.

EXCAVATIONS

In 1937–1938 and from 1950 to 1954 a number of crumbling buildings were cleared in old Jaffa, making possible the beginning of archaeological exploration in some areas of the mound.

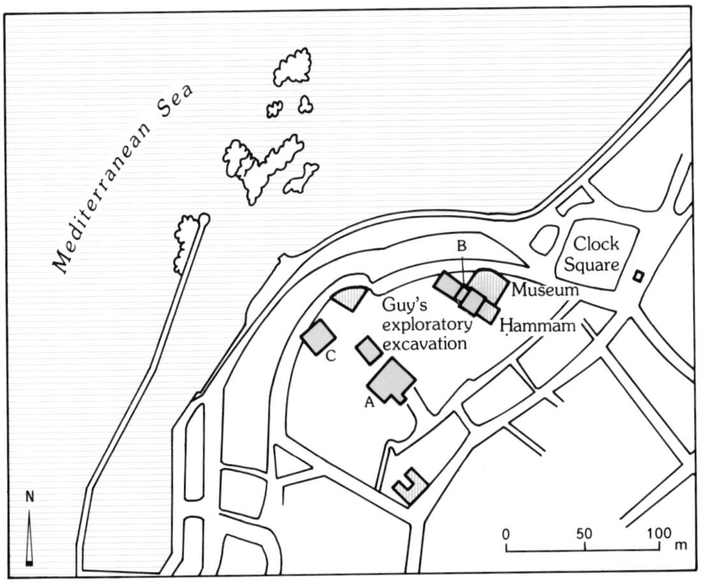

Jaffa: map of the main excavation areas.

From 1948 to 1950, P. L. O. Guy carried out the first exploratory excavations in Jaffa on behalf of the Israel Department of Antiquities and Museums. In 1952, Guy's excavations were continued down to virgin soil by J. Bowman and B. S. J. Isserlin, on behalf of the University of Leeds. The excavators established that the earliest remains at that spot were sherds dating from the fifth century BCE and that the site had been uninhabited prior to that date. They also discovered a structure from the fourth or third century BCE, of which only the floor of one of the rooms was preserved. The walls of the building were repaired in the second century BCE, and in the following century

Area A: fragment from the jamb of the fortress gate, inscribed with the name of Ramses II.

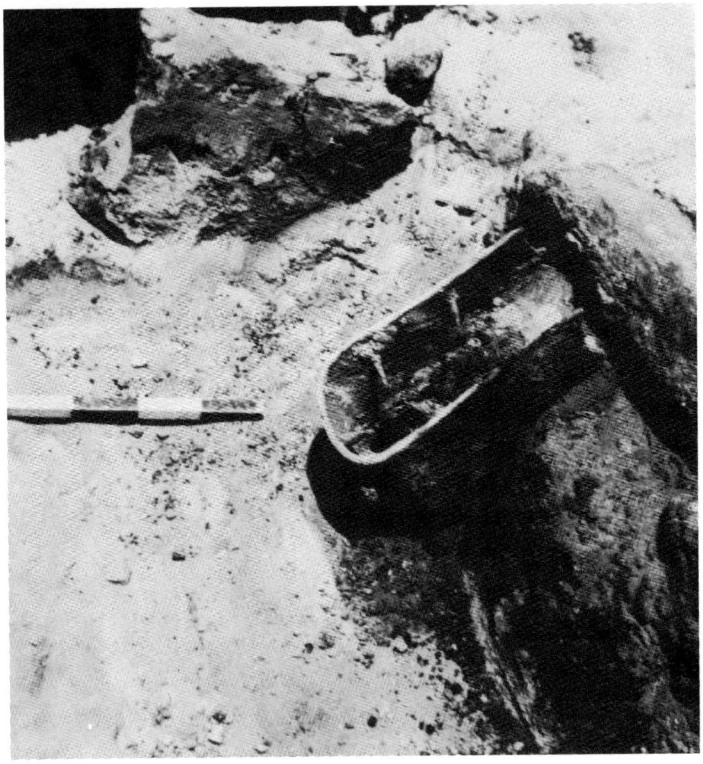

Bronze hinge of the door of the fortress gate, LB II.

Pottery plaque figurine of a goddess, LB.

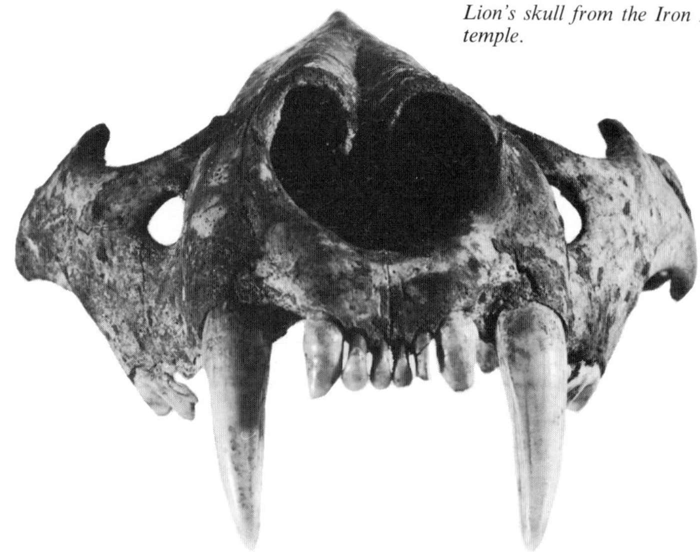
Lion's skull from the Iron I temple.

the level of the floor was raised. During the Byzantine period the area was settled anew.

In 1955, J. Kaplan undertook a systematic excavation of ancient Jaffa on behalf of the Museum of Antiquities of Tel Aviv–Jaffa. By 1964, three areas (A, B, C) in different sections of the mound had been excavated in six seasons. Limited soundings were also carried out in Jaffa's Clock Square, where part of the cemetery of the city's pagan population in the Late Hellenistic and Roman periods was uncovered. In 1964 and 1968 excavations were also conducted in area Y, near Saint Peter's Church.

AREA A: THE 1950s EXCAVATIONS. Seven occupation levels, the latest dating from the first century BCE, were excavated in area A in the 1950s. The following stratification was established:

Level I (Hellenistic Period). Level I is divided into two sublevels, IA and IB. Level IA contained a section of an ashlar wall, 2.2 m wide, joined to a casemate construction. They date from the first century BCE—that is, from the Hasmonean period. In level IB, the corner of a fortress, also built of ashlars, was uncovered, with a wall 2.5 m wide. The fortress is dated to the third century BCE. To this level are also assigned a group of five round stone floors, 0.8 to 1.2 m in diameter, each with a small, stone basin. These floors were found in the southern section of the excavation and had no connection with the walls.

Level II (Persian Period). A section of an ashlar wall, 2.5 m wide, and some adjacent structures were cleared in level II. The wall dates to the second half of the fifth century BCE and was apparently built by the Sidonians.

Level III (Iron Age). Level III, like level I, is divided into two sublevels. Remains of sublevel IIIA were preserved at the eastern edge of the excavation, and remains of IIIB were found at the western edge. In sublevel IIIA a rough stone wall, approximately 0.8 m thick, was found adjoining a stone floor that sloped eastward. These constructions were assigned to the eighth century BCE. Level IIIB contained a section of a courtyard with a beaten-earth floor and an ash pit nearby. The floor and pit contained Philistine sherds from the eleventh century BCE.

Level IV (Late Bronze Age IIA). Level IV also was divided into two sublevels. Sublevel IVA contained the threshold of the citadel gate and two entrance walls, 18 m long and 4 m apart, built of gray mud bricks. The walls run in an east–west direction from the gate into the citadel. The passageway between the walls was paved with stones and pebbles. The walls and gate were destroyed by fire, apparently late in the thirteenth century BCE. A bronze hinge from the gate was discovered in situ near the bottom of the left jamb.

Beneath the structures of sublevel IVA the remains of sublevel IVB were revealed. These included the lower part of an earlier gate, fallen stone doorjambs, and two entrance walls, all on the same line as the structures of sublevel IVA. It is thus clear that sublevel IVA had been built on the ruins of a previous occupation, level IVB, which had also been burned, apparently in the third quarter of the thirteenth century BCE (in the first reports, sublevel IVB appears as level V). The entrance walls are built of yellow-red mud bricks, whereas the doorjambs of the gate were of hard, dressed sandstone. Inscribed on four of the stone jambs were the five titles of Ramses II and part of his name. It seems that the inscriptions were originally set symmetrically on both sides of the gateway.

The gate and the entrance walls dating from the time of Ramses had been dug deep into the eastern part of the ruined citadel of Jaffa. As a result, remains from the eighteenth to fourteenth centuries BCE, situated to the north and south of the entrance walls, lay at a higher level than the threshold of Ramses' gate. These strata were only partially cleared.

Level V (Late Bronze Age IIB). Some building remains were found in level V, as well as a small silo built of rough stones and set between the southern entrance

A view of the Iron I temple.

Reconstruction of building M from the Persian period.

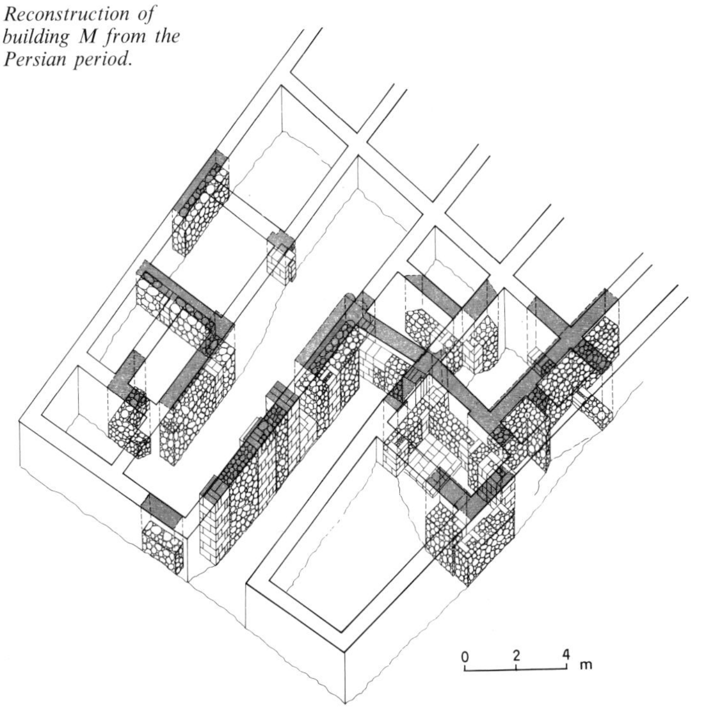

Fragment of a stone door from a burial cave, c. late 2nd–early 3rd centuries CE.

wall of Ramses' gate and parts of the structures of level VI south of it. Quantities of potsherds from the fourteenth century BCE were found in the silo and its vicinity.

Level VI (Late Bronze Age I). Level VI contained some remains of mud-brick buildings on stone foundations on both sides of the entrance walls of Ramses' gate. North of the northern entrance wall, a locus of pottery vessels was uncovered, including bichrome and gray-burnished ware. South of the southern entrance wall was a heap of sherds probably thrown there when the inhabitants cleared an adjacent area. These broken vessels are of Cypriot origin and include base-ring and monochrome wares. Level VI is dated from the second half of the sixteenth to the second half of the fifteenth centuries BCE.

Level VII (Middle Bronze Age IIC). Sections of two brick walls were found in level VII at the northern and southern edges of the excavated area. It seems that, subsequently, occupation levels VI–IV were concentrated in the space between those two walls. The outer face of the northern wall did not join any visible glacis, the southern wall was set on a rampart of beaten earth and *kurkar*. This rampart belongs to an earlier, unexcavated layer, probably level VIII. Level VII is tentatively dated to the period between the second half of the seventeenth and the first half of the sixteenth centuries BCE.

AREA A: THE 1970S EXCAVATIONS. The excavations in area A were resumed in 1970, and the area was extended on the south and west sides. As in the excavations in the 1950s, settlement levels for the Early Arab, Byzantine, and Roman periods were absent. Some scattered remains attest the destruction and damage caused to those levels in recent generations. The same is true for the remains from the Late Second Temple and Hasmonaean periods found in Jaffa.

Level I (Hellenistic Period). Reasonably well-preserved levels begin in the early part of the Hellenistic period. The remains consist mainly of sections of walls built of brick-shaped, ashlar blocks set on their narrow ends. In most cases, these walls were constructed on top of walls from the Persian period. Of special interest is an altar (2.4 by 2.4 m) built of field stones uncovered in square L-4. It stood in a room whose measurements were only 3.9 by 5.3 m. This type of cult hall is also known from the same period in Cyprus.

Level II (Persian Period). Remains from the Persian period in level II cover almost the entire excavated area. They date from the second half of the fifth century BCE to the Macedonian conquest—that is, to the period in which, in the excavators' opinion, the Sidonians held Jaffa.

Several building stages of this period were discovered, notably sections of walls of a large store building for keeping imported goods, extending from east to west across the entire area. Fragments of a mud-brick floor were found in its western part and the entrance was paved with large stones. The walls were built of regularly spaced ashlar piers with a fill of field stones between them, and several coins of stratum I were found among the stones. In the excavations in the 1950s, great heaps of blacksmith's waste had been discovered in various places apparently above the Persian level; this waste was also found in the subsequent excavations, along with part of a forge. Two coins of Alexander

Part of an ashlar building, constructed using headers and stretchers, 3rd century BCE.

Wall from building M: alternating ashlar piers (headers and stretchers) and field-stone fill, Persian period.

the Great were found in one heap of the waste. The floor of the forge, black from the soot mixed into it, was cleared near one of the store building's walls; a container was set against the wall, an iron sickle lay on its bottom, and a knife lay nearby. It was apparently the remains of a furnace for heating the metal to be worked. All the evidence suggests that this iron smithy was in use when the large store building was already in ruins.

In square K-3, an early Persian level with the foundations of a pre-fifth-century building was discovered. The structure was found under the ashlar walls. The level was designated IIB; the ashlar structures were designated level IIA.

Level III (Iron Age). The Iron Age II is represented by layers of earth mixed with ashes but no building remains. At the bottom of this level two cattle burials were found dug into the Iron Age I level. The burial of the cattle whole, and accompanied by stone markers, clearly points to some religious ritual. Indeed, this was a sacred site hundreds of years earlier (see below). A different picture emerged under the ashlar blocks of the Persian level in squares I-2 and I-3. Here an Iron Age II level was found and underneath it a level from the Iron Age I. In depressions and pits belonging to this last level, eleventh century BCE Philistine pottery was found. The pits and depressions were partly dug into a layer of rubble and clay bricks that had fallen from a nearby structure.

Pre-Philistine Temple. Under these levels the foundations of a long hall were cleared. A citadel with mud-brick walls was attached to it on its south side. The temple's hall measured 4.4 by 5.8 m and was entered from the north. The floor was covered with a coat of white plaster. On the floor were the bases of two wooden columns that had supported the beams of the roof. The pottery finds were meager—only two bowls and some fragments of other vessels. On the floor, however, the skull of a lion was found with half of a scarab seal near its teeth. This find suggests that the building was a temple in which a lion cult was practiced. Evidence for such a cult is found in the city names Laish (Dan), ha-Kefira, and Beth Leva'ot. Despite the paucity of the pottery finds, the building could be dated from the end of the thirteenth to the beginning of the twelfth centuries BCE. The reconstruction of the inscription on the half-scarab found near the lion's teeth produced the name of Queen Tiy, wife of Amenḥotep III. However, scarabs of kings of the Eighteenth and Nineteenth dynasties continued in use as talismans or jewelry for generations afterward, and therefore they cannot serve as evidence for dating.

AREA B. Excavations in area B were concentrated in the premises of the Ḥammam (bathhouse) building adjoining the Jaffa Museum and on the slope to the west of it. In the Ḥammam, a sandwich-built glacis was uncovered that sloped from west to east. The external revetment was made of thin stone slabs resting on layers of sandy soil. Beneath them were courses of mud bricks laid in a layer of gray soil. The potsherds unearthed in the gray soil layer indicated that the glacis is not later than the eighth century BCE. This would make it contemporary with level IIIA in area A.

Beneath the mud-brick and soil layer, the excavation revealed another thick layer of *kurkar*, indicating that there must have been an earlier glacis here. Indeed, layers of beaten earth and *kurkar* were also found on the slope of the tell west of the Ḥammam. These are situated at a lower level than the glacis of the eighth century BCE and rest on the eastern slope of a rampart of beaten earth, trapezoidal in section, running south to north. This rampart dates to the eighteenth century BCE—that is, to the beginning of the Hyksos period. It probably enclosed Jaffa in a square area.

AREA C. The excavation of area C revealed six occupation levels and a catacomb built of ashlars. The levels of this area are later than those excavated in area A and in effect continue them.

The first (upper) level contained a rough mosaic floor from the sixth to seventh centuries CE. The second level had structures from the fifth century CE situated immediately beneath the mosaic floor. In the third level, a section of a fourth-century CE building of large proportions was found built on thick rubble foundations and containing a floor made of large stone slabs. The fourth level, dating from the third century CE, contained a section of foundations lying under the stone floor slabs of the large building of the previous occupation level. The fifth level dates from the beginning of the second century. It contained a two-room structure whose foundations were sunk deep into the earlier levels. In this level pottery, a stone bowl, a bronze jug, and a hoard of bronze and silver coins were found, none later than the reign of Trajan. The sixth level contained a section of a private dwelling from the first century CE with a courtyard and cistern. A doorway, approximately 2 m high, of which two jambs had survived, was situated in the wall facing the courtyard. Numerous pottery vessels and oil lamps were found on the floor of the courtyard.

Behind the eastern wall of the fifth occupation level part of the courtyard of a catacomb of extremely fine construction was uncovered—ashlar blocks laid as headers and stretchers. The catacomb consisted of three chambers. The first to be found had been damaged by the collapse of the ceiling, and its entrance was blocked with ashlars. The ceiling of the second chamber also was destroyed; the third, the front chamber, had been rebuilt after its ceiling collapsed. It was fitted with a new roof supported by ashlar arches. The arches supported stone slabs that formed the floor of a private dwelling erected above the chamber.

Among the finds excavated in area C, two Greek inscriptions deserve special mention. One of them, engraved on limestone, mentions, in three identical versions, that during the reigns of Nerva and Trajan, a man named Judah was the *agoranomos* of Jaffa. The second is a fragment of a votive inscription from the third century BCE that mentions Ptolemy IV Philopator. Many jar handles with Greek and Latin stamps also were found, as well as a tile fragment with the stamp of the Tenth Legion and a pyramidal seal engraved with the name Ariston.

AREA Y. Area Y is located near Saint Peter's Church in Jaffa. Some remains were found beneath the square in front of the church. The site is located west of the edge of the glacis of the Jaffa citadel. The area was not inhabited prior to the Persian period. The finds consisted mainly of tombs and various installations. Two strata of settlement were uncovered in area Y: Hellenistic IB and Persian IIA. Beneath the latter virgin clay soil contained tombs and other installations from the Middle Bronze Age II.

The Hellenistic remains were found immediately below the ruins of modern buildings. In the southern part of the area, a section of an ashlar structure was uncovered with walls preserved to a height of 1 m. The northern part of the area contained the corner of a large building, also of ashlar construction, in which several square rooms were side by side. This building may have been part of the agora, or marketplace, of Hellenistic Jaffa. The Persian period is represented only by layers of ash. There were no building remains. Many fragments of Attic pottery were found. An infant burial in a jar, dating from the seventeenth century BCE, was discovered in the virgin soil. In addition to the remains of the body, the jar contained a red-burnished juglet; outside, near the burial, was a scarab seal. In the northern part of the site, two furnaces were dug into the loam. One of the furnaces was intact, except for its vaulted roof. It had been constructed over a Middle Bronze Age II tomb. The tomb contained funerary offerings and a scarab seal. Pits dug into the loam in the eastern part of the area were found filled with ash and animal bones. These remains date to the Late Bronze Age I. In one of the pits the leg bones of domestic beasts were found, preserved from the upper end to the hoof. These finds suggest a cult place nearby.

City coin of Jaffa from the time of Elagabalus (218–222 CE).

B. S. J. Isserlin, *PEQ* 82 (1950), 101; A. Kindler, *IEJ* 4 (1954), 170–185; J. Bowman et al., *Proc. Leeds Philosophical Society* 7 (1955), 231–250; J. Kaplan, *IEJ* 6 (1956), 259–260; 10 (1960), 121–122; 11 (1961), 191–192; 12 (1962), 149–150; 14 (1964), 285–286; 16 (1966), 282; 20 (1970), 225–226; 21 (1971), 174; 24 (1974), 135–138; 25 (1975), 163; id., *RB* 67 (1960), 376–377; 72 (1965), 553–554; 74 (1967), 87–88; 80 (1973), 415–417; 82 (1975), 257–260; 83 (1976), 78–79; id., *Archaeology* 17 (1964), 270–276; id., *Archaeological Discoveries in the Holy Land*, New York 1967, 113–118; id., *BA* 35/3 (1972), 66–95; J. H. Landau, *'Atiqot* 2 (1959), 186–187; B. Lifshitz, *Euphrosyne* n.s. 6 (1973–1974), 29–32; R. Kark, *ZDPV* 97 (1981), 93–108; S. Derfler, *AJA* 88 (1984), 242; H. E. Mayer, *IEJ* 35 (1985), 35–45; S. Applebaum, *Scripta Classica Israelica* 8–9 (1985–1988), 138–144; Weippert 1988 (Ortsregister); M. Burdajewicz, *The Aegean Sea Peoples and Religious Architecture in the Eastern Mediterranean at the Close of the Late Bronze Age* (*BAR*/IS 558), Oxford 1990, 45–46.

JACOB KAPLAN, HAYA RITTER-KAPLAN

JAPHIA

IDENTIFICATION AND HISTORY

Japhia was a city in Lower Galilee identified in the region of the Arab village Yafa, about 2 km (1 mi.) southwest of Nazareth (map reference 1763.2326). In the Bible, Japhia is mentioned as one of the cities of Zebulun (Jos. 19:12). The place is apparently mentioned in the el-Amarna letters (fourteenth century BCE), where it is called Iapu. During the Jewish War against Rome, Josephus Flavius strengthened the defenses of the city, whose inhabitants took an active part in the revolt. Titus captured the city in the summer of 67 and killed most

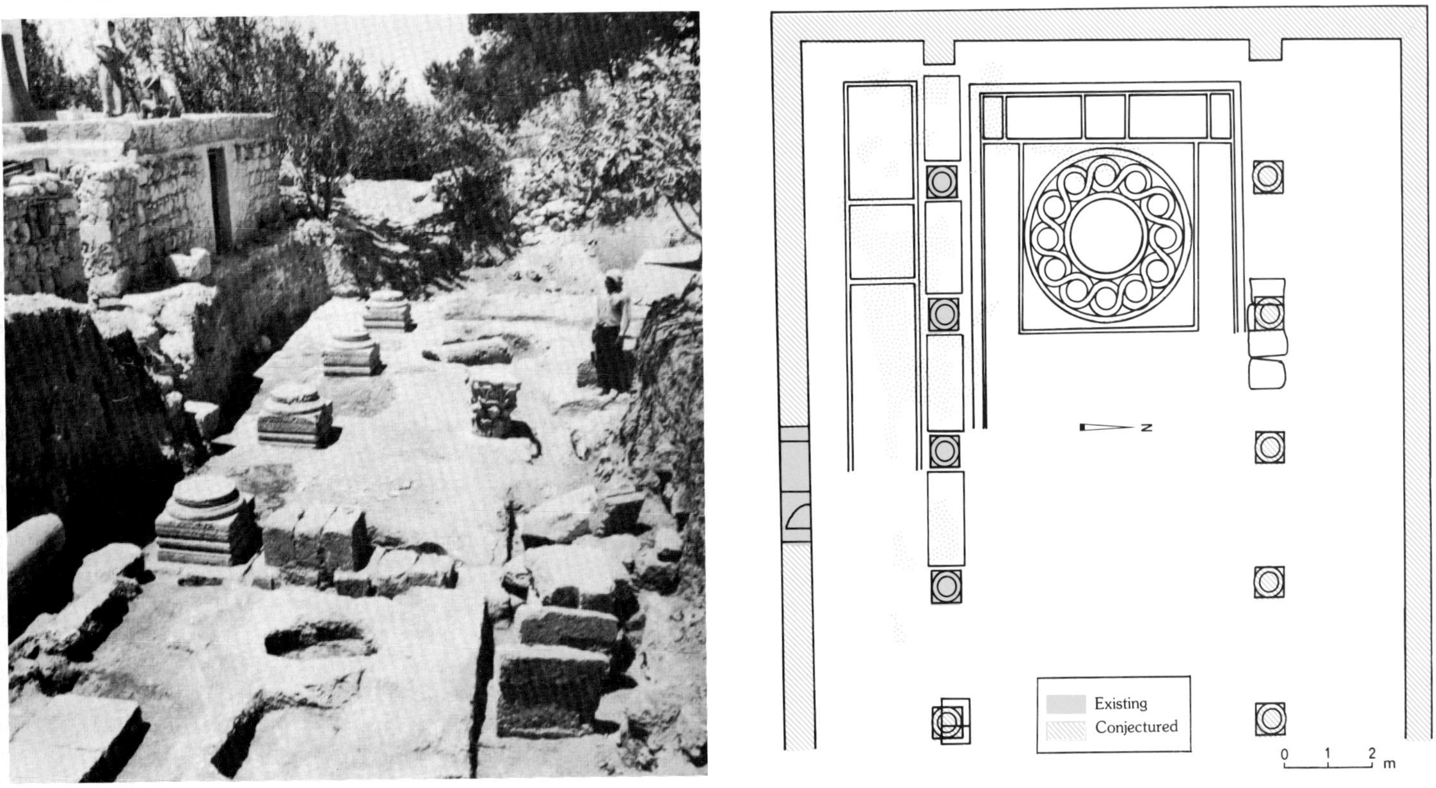

Japhia: the synagogue. ***Left:*** *general view;* ***(right)*** *plan.*

of its inhabitants (*War* II, 573; III, 289–306; *Life* 188, 230, 270). According to a late Christian tradition, the apostle James, son of Zebedee, was born here. The location of the Roman-Byzantine city is certain, but the site of the ancient settlement of the Bronze and Iron ages is not known.

EXPLORATION

In 1921, L. H. Vincent published two lintels that had been found in the village. A menorah with a rosette on either side is carved on one and, on the other, a wreath flanked by eagles with outspread wings holding small wreaths in their beaks. These finds indicated that the remains of a synagogue of the Galilean type, datable to the third to fourth centuries CE, should be sought here. In the summer of 1950, E. L. Sukenik excavated the remains of the synagogue on behalf of the Hebrew University of Jerusalem.

EXCAVATION RESULTS

The excavations established that the synagogue had stood on a peak to the north of the village and that only few remains survived. A segment of the southern wall (2.7 m long and 0.65 m thick) was discovered. At a distance of 2.9 m north of the wall, a row of four column pedestals, with Attic bases attached, and the foundation stones of a fifth pedestal were found. Seven m north of them were several foundation stones that apparently belonged to a second row of columns. It became evident, therefore, that the synagogue had been built as a basilica, slightly more than 15 m wide. The eastern and western ends of the building had been destroyed, and it proved impossible to establish its original length. However, it is clear that it was at least 19 m long.

Only a few fragments of the synagogue's mosaic pavement were preserved. It was multicolored (black, brown, red, gray, and white—thirteen different hues altogether). In the southern aisle, the pavement was decorated with squares, rectangles, and simple geometric patterns, surrounded by bands of guilloche. The few remains of faunal and floral decorations in the nave indicate that its floor had been richly decorated. The mosaic depicted a circle (diameter, 3.8 m) with twelve circles in it, all enclosed in an interlocking guilloche. The pattern is similar to the zodiacs in the synagogues at Na'aran, Beth Alpha, Ḥusifah, and Hammath-Tiberias. While E. R. Goodenough believed that the signs of the zodiac are presented here, the excavators believed that the symbols of the twelve tribes are portrayed. Of the symbols, only two are extant: a buffalo, with the fragmentary legend [אפ]רים ([Eph]raim?) beside it, and an ox, the symbol of Manasseh. These are not in keeping with the Midrash (*Num. Rab.* 82), however, where the ox is the symbol of Ephraim, and the buffalo the symbol of Manasseh. At the southwestern end of the nave, one panel of the pavement was preserved in its entirety. On it an eagle with outspread wings is depicted, standing on two pairs of volutes. Between the volutes is the head of Helios (in the opinion of Goodenough, the head of Medusa). On the basis of style, the pavement may belong to the fourth century CE, but it is not known if it was part of the original building.

The orientation of the synagogue is west–east; its facade apparently faces east. This differs from other early Galilean synagogues, whose facades are oriented south, toward Jerusalem. Sukenik claimed that this change of orientation could be explained by the fact that Japhia was in Zebulun, presumed (according to Gen. 49:13) to be located on the sea—that is, west of Jerusalem. It is not known whether the synagogue had a permanent place for the Holy Ark, because there was probably no apse. This synagogue displays a mixture of features of the "early" synagogue—the pedestals of columns and perhaps the lintels published by Vincent—as well as the "late types"—the mosaic floor. M. Avi-Yonah was therefore of the opinion that it was a transitional type (q.v. Syn-agogues).

G. M. FitzGerald, *PEQ* 53 (1921), 182–183; L. H. Vincent, *RB* 30 (1921), 433–438; E. L. Sukenik, *Rabinowitz Bulletin* 2 (1951), 6–24; Goodenough, *Jewish Symbols* 1, 216–218.

DAN BARAG

An eagle spreads its wings over volutes and the head of Helios (?) in the mosaic pavement in the southwestern part of the nave.

Fragment of mosaic floor depicting the zodiac or the symbols of the twelve tribes—an ox and a buffalo.

JARMUTH, TEL

IDENTIFICATION

Tel Jarmuth (in Hebrew, Yarmut; in Arabic, Khirbet el-Yarmûk) is situated in the central Shephelah, about 25 km (15.5 mi.) southwest of Jerusalem and 5 km (3 mi.) south of Beth Shemesh (map reference 147.124). The site extends over a natural hill overlooking Naḥal Yarmut (Wadi Bulus), a seasonal tributary of Naḥal Sorek fed by several springs, one of which is located at the foot of the mound.

An identification of Tel Jarmuth with the "Land of Yarmuth" referred to in several el-Amarna letters is doubtful, as the latter was probably located somewhere along the Syrian coast north of Byblos. But the equation with the biblical Jarmuth, mentioned first as a Canaanite city in the story of Joshua's conquest (Jos. 10:3–5, 10:23, 12:11) and later as a city in Judah (Jos. 15:5; Neh. 11:29), is generally accepted by scholars and has given its modern Hebrew name to the site. At the present state of research, the identification cannot be confirmed nor dismissed on archaeological grounds. More secure is the identification of the site with a Byzantine village by the name of Ἱερμοχῶς, which gave the Arabic form of the toponym. Located about 10 Roman miles from Beth Guvrin on the road to Jerusalem, this village is mentioned by Eusebius, who equates it with Ιερμοῦς, or Jarmuth.

The site attains a maximal length of 640 m and a width of 420 m. It covers about 40 a. in area and is comprised of a small acropolis of almost 4 a., culminating at 405 m above sea level, and a large lower city, whose lowest point is at 290 m. Both parts of the city are fortified, the line of the fortifications being marked by a slope several meters high. The topography of the lower city is characterized by a succession of large terraces distributed around a deep, funnel-shaped depression, that could have been used to channel runoff water toward a reservoir.

EXPLORATION

In their description of the site, early scholars referred to the acropolis only, to which the name Khirbet el-Yarmûk applies strictly. The existence of the lower city remained unsuspected until the 1960 survey by the Israel Department of Antiquities and Museums. By revealing the site's true dimensions, this discovery gave the impetus for further research. The first trial excavations were undertaken in 1970 by A. Ben-Tor, on behalf of the Hebrew University of Jerusalem. Three areas (A, B-north, and B-south), located in the west corner of the lower city, were excavated. Early Bronze Age structures, both public and domestic, were uncovered right below the present surface, together with the remains of a large construction tentatively ascribed to the Byzantine period.

Excavations were resumed in 1980 by P. de Miroschedji, on behalf of the Centre de Recherche Français de Jérusalem and the Institute of Archaeology at the Hebrew University of Jerusalem. Eight seasons of excavation have taken place so far (December 1990). Investigations were continued in Ben-Tor's area A and B, six additional areas (C–H) were opened in the lower city, and two small soundings were carried out on the acropolis. Extensive geomagnetic and resistivity surveys were also conducted in the lower city by A. Kermorvant.

EXCAVATION RESULTS

HISTORY AND STRATIGRAPHY. Both the acropolis and the lower city of Jarmuth were first settled in the second half of the fourth millennium (Early Bronze Age I) and continuously occupied until the end of the Early Bronze Age (IIIB), about 2300 BCE, when the entire settlement was quietly abandoned. Reoccupation apparently took place no earlier than the Late Bronze Age II, and only on the acropolis and in its immediate vicinity. This restricted area remained inhabited until the Early Byzantine period, when the site was finally abandoned.

The investigations have concentrated so far on the lower city, mainly its western corner, where impressive architectural remains from the Early Bronze Age were traced on the surface. Here, the archaeological deposit is about 4 m thick and corresponds to the following periods.

Early Bronze I: sherds in later fills and a thin stratum (?) on bedrock. The remains suggest that this part of the site was on the periphery of the fourth-millennium settlement.

Early Bronze II: about 2 m deep, with several building levels.

Early Bronze IIIA and IIIB: up to five building levels.

Early Byzantine: some agricultural terraces and sherds in the top soil.

On the acropolis, there is evidence of occupation in the Early Bronze Age II–III, and from the Late Bronze Age II to the Early Byzantine period. However, as the major stratigraphic sounding is still in progress, a complete sequence of occupation is not yet available.

Topographic plan of Tel Jarmuth, showing excavated areas and remains of fortifications traced on the surface.

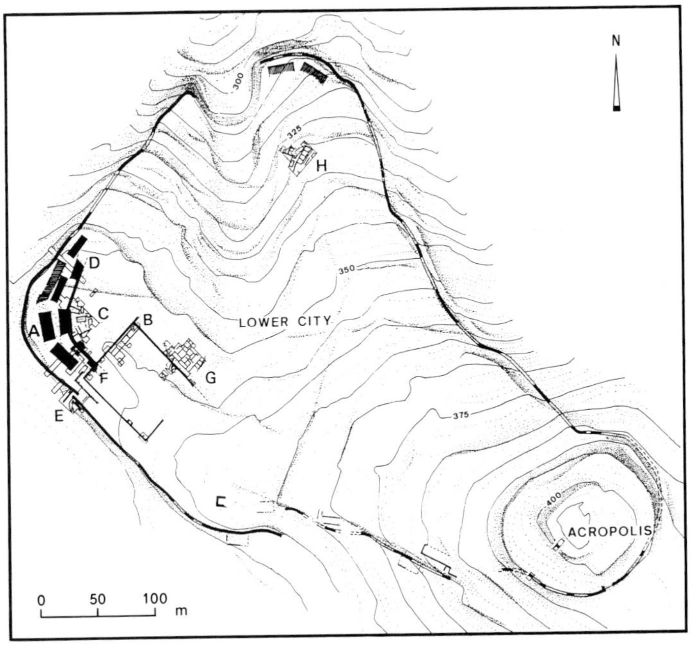

General view, looking south.

Southwestern outer wall of the EB III building complex, looking northwest from the southern corner. Note the square inner buttresses.

The city gate, view of the entryway at the end of phase 2.

City gate, looking east.

EARLY BRONZE AGE

The size of the settlement, its fortifications, public constructions, and town planning suggest that Jarmuth ranked among the major Early Bronze Age cities in this country.

FORTIFICATIONS. The Early Bronze Age city was protected by a fortification system of exceptional size and complexity. In use for a period of about six centuries, it underwent successive changes and rebuildings. Three major phases and several subphases were distinguished in this long history.

The first city wall (wall A = phase IA) was built sometime in the Early Bronze Age II over the leveled remains of an unfortified early Early Bronze Age II settlement. In area A, it consisted of a stone wall (5.6 m thick) with large buttresses placed equidistant from a massive stone bastion (25 by 13 m) in the western corner of the city. This rampart was reinforced by an earthen glacis along its northwestern face and by glacislike stone buttresses along its southwestern face (phase IB).

A second line of defense (wall B = phase IIA), erected at the end of the Early Bronze Age II some 20 to 30 m in front of wall A, brought the total thickness of the fortification system to nearly 40 m in area A and about 26 m in area D. Built with cyclopean masonry, and still preserved in places to a height of almost 7 m, this wall (3–3.6 m thick) can be traced all around the site, for a distance of nearly 1.8 km (1 mi.). The area between the two walls was later subjected to a terracing operation involving the construction of a series of small stone terraces (phase IIB). Subsequently, it was progressively filled with layers of ash, earth, and stones and used for domestic activities (phase IIC).

Finally (phase III), monumental stone platforms (30–40 by 10–12 m) were built with deep foundations in this intermediate space along the corner of the city in the Early Bronze Age III. These huge and enigmatic constructions, which probably had a brick superstructure, are reminiscent of the so-called "citadel" at Ai and the "rectangular towers" at Early Bronze Age III Taanach.

CITY GATE. Access to this part of the site was through a monumental offset single entryway established in the outer city wall (wall B). This structure underwent several changes and rebuildings in the Early Bronze Age II–III. It was reached indirectly from the outside by means of a U-shaped, ascending ramp limited on both sides by retaining walls. Because the floors inside the entryway were raised as a result of successive filling operations, the ramp and the associated retaining walls were rebuilt and raised several times, rising eventually to more than 7 m above bedrock. Later in the Early Bronze Age III, the approach to the gate was protected by a small rectangular "bastion" measuring 12 by 2 m.

URBANISM. A prominent feature at the site is a terrace system with strong retaining walls, over the slopes of the entire lower city. The excavations in area H suggest that, at least in the Early Bronze Age III, all or many of these terraces were artificial, built with a fill of stone containing inner partition walls. Each terrace supported a series of constructions that, once destroyed and leveled, became foundations for new buildings. Should these observations apply to the entire site, the external appearance of Jarmuth in the Early Bronze Age III may have been comparable to that of traditional settlements in present-day Judea and Samaria.

BUILDING REMAINS. Extensive architectural remains were cleared in several areas in the lower city. None are dated to the Early Bronze Age I.

Early Bronze Age II. Building remains from the Early Bronze Age II have been cleared on a limited scale in area C. Most remarkable is a large and massive platformlike construction built prior to the erection of the first city wall and assumed to have been the foundation of a building of some importance, possibly a public building. Remains of a large building associated with the first city wall should also be mentioned.

Early Bronze Age III. Building remains dating to the Early Bronze Age IIIA

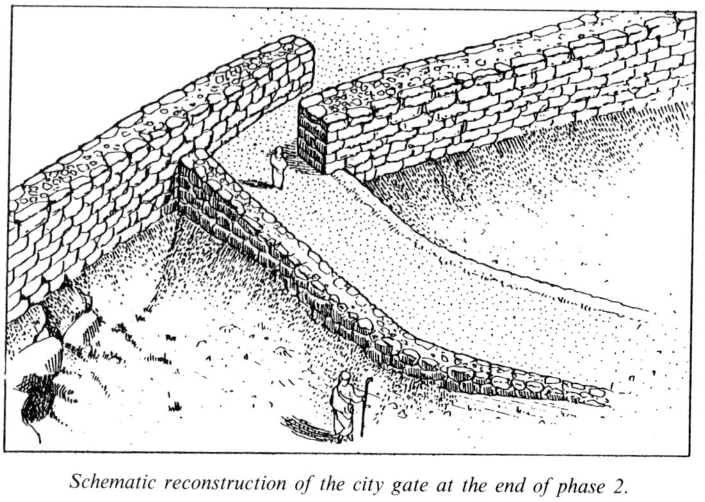

Schematic reconstruction of the city gate at the end of phase 2.

Area G, stratum G-II, partial view looking east.

and IIIB include "industrial" installations, private houses, and public constructions.

"INDUSTRIAL" INSTALLATIONS. In area H, on the far side of the lower city, an area where specialized activities were performed was identified. A row of six small rooms and courtyards were cleared on the edge of a terrace; they contained only coarse pottery (pithoi, vats, coarse platters, bowls, and double vessels), large mortars, stone-lined and pottery vats sunk in the floor, and three kilnlike structures. Comparable finds at Beth Yeraḥ suggest that this installation might have been used for processing olive oil.

PRIVATE HOUSES. The best exposure of private architecture was obtained in area G (stratum G-II), where private houses, grouped in an insula surrounded by a street, were excavated over an area of 500 sq m. The insula apparently resulted from the progressive agglutination of several dwelling units that had been modified, enlarged, and finally linked together. The typical dwelling was composed of one or two rooms and a courtyard with several domestic installations. Some rooms contained a central row of stone pillar bases. Other rooms are long and narrow (up to 8.5 by 2 m) and could be subdivided into smaller units to create storerooms. The underlying stratum G-III has revealed a curved street with a paved floor sloping down to the north and bordered by houses.

PUBLIC BUILDINGS. An interesting discovery made in area C (strata C-V and C-IV) is that of a large structure called the White Building, which probably was a sanctuary. It is a rectangular hall of the broadroom type (inner dimensions 11.5 by 4.75 m), whose roof was supported by four pillars resting on large stone bases arranged on an axial line. Its floor is about 80 cm lower than the contemporary floors adjacent to it. The walls are one meter thick and covered on their inner face, from top to bottom, with white plaster that also covers the floor. The main entrance was through a door situated in the middle of the southern facade; another narrow door is located near the southwestern corner. Both doors were followed by stone steps to reach the hall's low floor.

This building seems to have been part of a larger complex. Reached by means of a paved street, it included a chamber built around the southeastern corner of the main building, a courtyard established in front of it, and two adjacent rooms to the south. The courtyard (10 by 6 m) contained a fireplace and a sunken vat. One of the two adjacent rooms to the south contained a rectangular stone platform (c. 3.5 by 2.3 m), at least one meter high, that might have been connected to the activities in the White Building at the other end of the courtyard. The interpretation of the White Building as a sanctuary is not suggested by the rare finds made in it, but by its plans, typical features, careful construction, and especially by comparisons with other, similar cultic buildings: the temples at En-Gedi (Chalcolithic), Megiddo XIX (Early Bronze Age I), Ai and Tel Arad (Early Bronze Age II), Megiddo XV, Bab edh-Dhra', and Khirbet ez-Zeraqun (Early Bronze Age III).

Another major construction (85 by 70 m) with a public character, initially dated to the Byzantine period, has been identified in area B, where it turned out to be contemporary with stratum G-II (Early Bronze Age IIIB). Located

Area C, the White Building (with overlying remains of stratum C-II), looking east.

Area C: axonometry of the White Building.

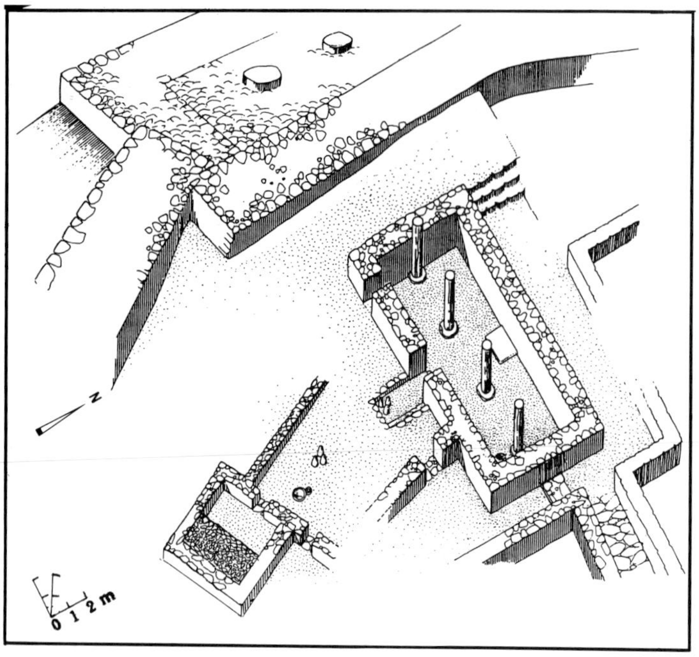

Stone seal, probably EB.

on sloping ground, it covers nearly 6,000 sq m. It was part of the terrace system that characterizes the planning in this sector of the Early Bronze Age city and is itself composed of two terraced levels. This structure is probably responsible for the outer and the inner walls of the complex being built differently. The outer walls are almost 2 m thick and have solid foundations (up to 3 m deep). Except for the southeastern wall, which has not yet been cleared, the outer walls display, along all or part of their length, inner stone buttresses that measure 1.9 m on each side and are placed at 2-m intervals. These buttresses are reminiscent of a similar feature on Early Bronze Age walls at Byblos that are related to courtyards or open spaces. The inner walls either have no foundations or shallow ones. Some are 1.3 to 1.4 m thick and others are only 1 to 1.1 m thick. Their state of preservation varies with the topography from one course of stone to a height of almost 2.5 m. The walls and floors are plastered.

It is on the basis of the buttresses along the outer walls that a large courtyard occupying the southwestern half of the complex and a secondary courtyard to the northeast have been tentatively identified. The built-up areas seem to occupy the northeastern half. Concentrated to date near the northern corner, the excavations have revealed a corridor along the northwestern outer wall and a series of perpendicular walls. These suggest that this zone was occupied by several loci, each with a square or rectangular plan. The function of this complex cannot be determined on the basis of the observations made so far. What is significant here is the amount of urban and architectural planning invested in this construction, which is presently without parallel at contemporary sites in the country.

ECONOMY AND FOREIGN RELATIONS. Given its size and the density of its construction, the Early Bronze Age III city of Jarmuth may have had a population of about three thousand. Its inhabitants were mainly engaged in agriculture (cereals, vegetables, grapes, and especially olives) and animal husbandry (mostly sheep and goat, but also cattle for traction and transport). Relations with Egypt are indicated by a palette in steatite(?) and several

Fragmentary bone bull's head, EB II.

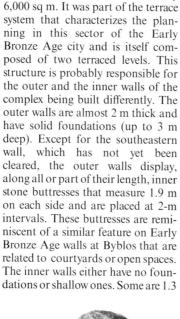

***Above:** fragment of a cultic object in the shape of a building with a human figure decorating the facade.*
*Human terra-cotta figurines, EB II (**right**) and EB III (**below**).*

Tel Jarmuth: ***(left)*** *pottery platter;* ***(right)*** *basin, EB.*

fragments of vessels in alabaster and diorite; exchange with local regions is indicated by basalt objects from the Golan, bitumen fragments from the Dead Sea, flint fan scrapers from the Negev, copper tools (mainly chisels and awls with a square section), and rare sherds of Khirbet Kerak ware from the northern part of the country.

POTTERY AND SMALL FINDS. A large corpus of Early Bronze Age pottery was recovered from the excavations. It is especially rich for the Early Bronze Age III phase, in which almost every known pottery shape can be seen. Most interesting is the Early Bronze Age IIIB pottery, represented mainly by large pithoi, deep spouted vats with a combed surface, and an unusual range of vessels with a highly burnished red slip—notably jars, jugs, bowls, and very large platters whose diameter commonly reaches 80 cm. Among the small finds are an interesting series of animal and human terra-cotta figurines, a piece of a carved bone representing a bull's head, a stone palette, a stone seal, and a fragment of a ceramic object in the shape of a building, probably a temple, whose facade is decorated in relief with a human figure (a dancer?) and an animal (of which only the rear legs are preserved).

LATER REMAINS

The small acropolis represents the site of the post–Early Bronze Age settlement, established after a period of complete abandonment of about one millennium. Survey and soundings have revealed traces of more or less continuous occupation from the Late Bronze Age II to the Early Byzantine period, including three Iron Age I strata. The uppermost Iron Age IB stratum (stratum III), which shows evidence of destruction by fire, is dated to the mid-eleventh century by pottery similar to Beth Shemesh III and Tell Qasile XI–X. Surface finds include an Early Hellenistic jar handle stamped with a pentagram and the letters *yršlm* and a coin of Herod the Great. The northeastern side of the acropolis is occupied by the ruins of a small village dating from the third to the fourth centuries CE, to be identified with Eusebius' Ἰερμοχὼς (see above). Several earlier or contemporary cisterns and rock-cut tombs are located on the slope of the acropolis and to the southwest.

Identification: Guérin, *Judée* 2, Paris 1869, 371 ff.; P. Thomsen, *Loca Sancta*, Halle 1907 (rev. ed. Hildesheim 1966), 71–72; W. F. Albright, *JPOS* 8 (1928), 243; id., *BASOR* 77 (1940), 31; 87 (1942), 32–38; R. Tonneau, *RB* 38 (1929), 426; J. Garstang, *Joshua–Judges*, London 1931, 171–172, 386; F. M. Abel, *GP* 2, 356; H. N. Richardson, *BASOR* 192 (1968), 12–16; M. Avi-Yonah, *Qedem* 5 (1976), 68; E. Nodet, *Yarmouth* 1 (ed. P. de Miroschedji), 97–104.

Excavations

Main publications: A. Ben-Tor, *Qedem* 1 (1975), 55–87; P. de Miroschedji, *Yarmouth 1: Rapport sur les trois premières campagnes de fouilles à Tel Yarmouth (Israël), (1980–1982)* (Editions Recherche sur les Civilisations, Mémoire 76), Paris 1988.

Other studies: A. Ben-Tor, *IEJ* 21 (1971), 173–174; P. de Miroschedji, *Paléorient* 6 (1980), 281–286; id., *IEJ* 31 (1981), 121–124; 32 (1982), 159–161, 190–194; (with A. Kermovant), 34 (1984), 194–196; 35 (1985), 71–73; 38 (1988), 84–88, 194–199; 41 (1991), 200–205, 286–293; id., *RB* 88 (1981), 568–571; 92 (1985), 394–404; 95 (1988), 217–226; id., *Archéologia* 165 (1982), 9–10; 252 (1989), 52–66; id., Centre de Recherche Français de Jérusalem, *Lettre d'Information* 1 (1982), 21; 2 (1982), 20–24; 6 (1984), 25–27; id., *ESI* 1 (1982), 112–113; 3 (1984), 108–111; 7–8 (1988–1989), 184–187; id., *11th Archaeological Conference in Israel: Abstracts*, Jerusalem 1985, 35; id., *CRAIBL* 1988, 186–211; id., *Yarmouth 1* (Reviews), *Paléorient* 15/2 (1989), 153–154. — *Qadmoniot* 87–88 (1989), 118 (Hebrew). — *Syria* 67 (1990), 523–524. — *Bibliotheca Orientalis* 48 (1991), 651–653; id., *EI* 21 (1990), 48*–61*, id., *MdB* 70 (1991), 55–59.

PIERRE DE MIROSCHEDJI

JEBEL QA'AQIR

IDENTIFICATION

In September 1967 a necropolis and settlement from the Middle Bronze Age I (c. 2200–2000 BCE) was discovered at Jebel Qa'aqir, a ridge 12 km (7.5 mi.) west of Hebron in the southern Judean Hills (map reference 1457.1034). Attention had been drawn to the area after several dozen distinctive pieces of pottery and copper implements had been purchased from Jerusalem antiquities dealers. The artifacts were subsequently traced to a large cemetery that tomb robbers were digging illicitly. Thereafter, the Nelson Glueck School of Biblical Archaeology in Jerusalem sponsored three seasons of excavation, a total of twenty weeks, in the fall of 1967 and 1968 and the spring of 1971.

EXCAVATIONS

Excavations began in the partially robbed cemetery B, which was situated on the southern slope of an S-shaped ridge nearly 2 km (1 mi.) long. The ridge had signs of burials all around the slopes and considerable evidence of human occupation along the crest. Eventually, other cemeteries—A to the west and C, D, and E to the east—were investigated, as well as groups of tombs found by chance in all directions, as far as 2 km (1.2 mi.) or more from the ridge. In all, thirty-eight undisturbed tombs were located and excavated, and forty-one partially robbed tombs were excavated and drawn and part of their material salvaged or retrieved from the robbers.

THE CEMETERIES. Cemetery B accounted for fifty-nine of the seventy-nine tombs investigated. The tombs were cut into the bedrock near the valley floor, now covered by more than 2 m of eroded topsoil. Set off from the settlement above by a boundary wall, the tombs had been carefully laid out along five natural rock terraces and regularly spaced from 1 to 2 m apart. A round vertical shaft, 1 to 1.7 m in diameter and up to 2 m deep, led to a single or occasionally a double round chamber about 2 m in diameter. The doorway was normally blocked by a large boulder, although sometimes it was choked with small stones and sealed with plaster. Adze and chisel marks, often perfectly preserved, showed how carefully some of the tombs had been finished, especially around the doorways. A shallow recess for the body was frequently found cut into the chamber floor, and in several tombs lamp niches were cut into the walls. Some tombs had elaborate geometric designs scratched around the doorways. Two had miniature doorways a few centimeters high, adjacent to the main entrance.

The typical tomb contained from two to four human burials and occasionally the headless carcass of a sheep or goat. In every case the burials were secondary, and the bones, even those of the animals, were disarticulated and completely disarrayed. Analysis of forty-one well preserved skeletons showed that 17 percent were children, 17 percent adolescents, and the rest adults. All the skeletons were of the gracile Mediterranean type, very close to the Late Chalcolithic–Early Bronze Age skeletons already analyzed from ancient Palestine, but somewhat different from the more robust Middle Bronze Age

Jebel Qa'aqir: overview of cemetery B and openings to the shaft tombs.

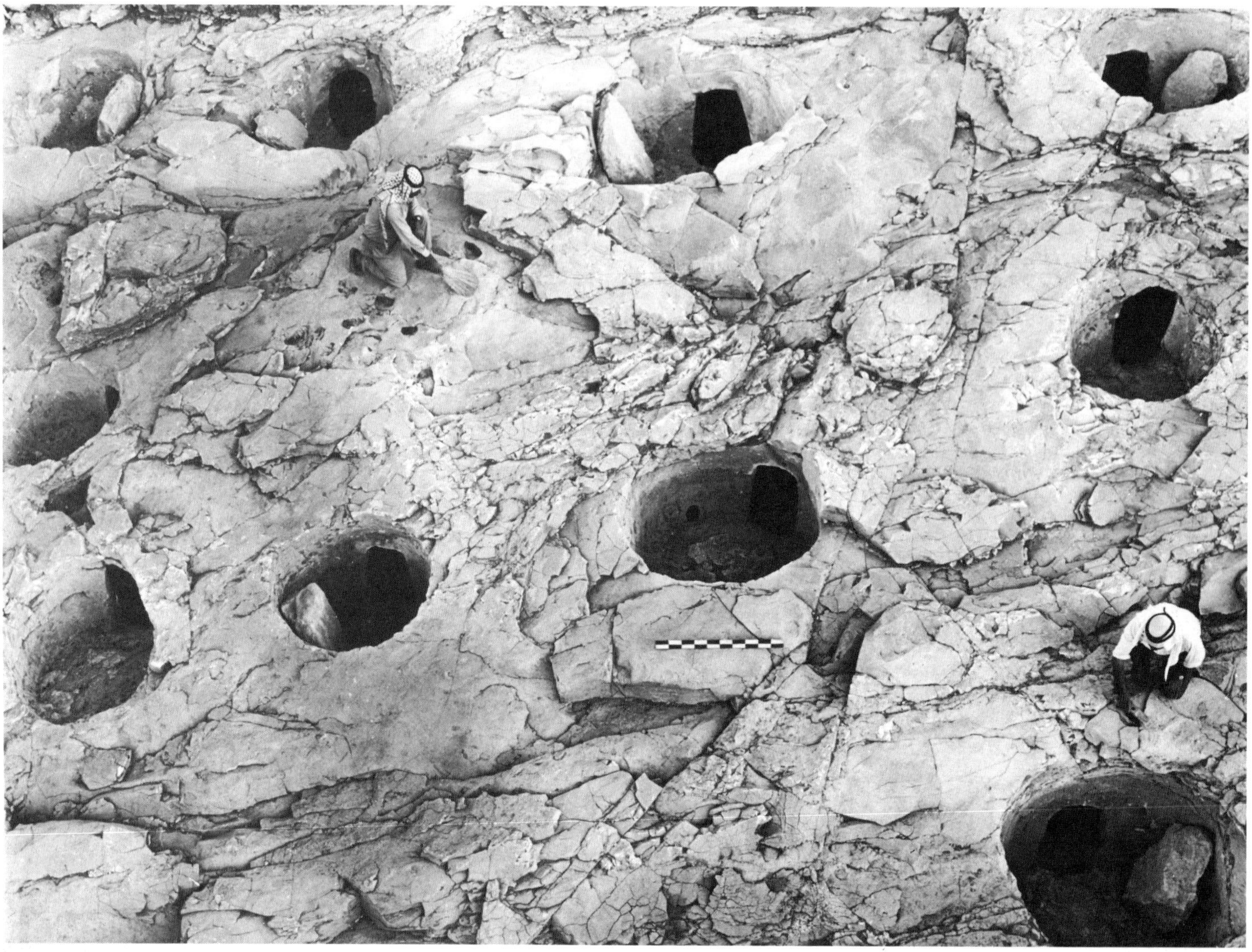

II type. This population group was remarkably free of the diseases often associated with urban populations.

Although many tombs contained a piece or two of pottery (sometimes up to eight pieces) and occasionally a copper dagger, javelin, or pin, more than half had no grave goods. The evidence of the skeletal material and the poor offerings suggest these were the remains of seminomadic groups of people, probably pastoralists who roamed a seasonal circuit and carried their dead with them for burial at an ancestral burying ground. The evidence of the Jericho tombs and many other Middle Bronze Age I cemeteries in the Hebron Hills points to the same conclusion.

The distinct differences between the cemeteries in the cutting of the tombs and in the grave goods, even though the tombs must have been nearly contemporary, are further evidence of tribal groups, some seminomadic. Tombs of a single type are always grouped together. Their careful layout—none was dug into another—indicates that all the shafts had been open and visible at one time. The tool marks were as fresh as though cut yesterday. The tombs must have been dug, used, and then the shafts filled in during a single summer season, between the rains. This was confirmed by the excavators' observations of how the soft chalk bedrock weathered after exposure for only one winter.

Burials in tomb B54.

THE SETTLEMENT. A settlement was discovered on the ridge above the cemeteries shortly after work began. Six large stone cairns, strung out along the crest of the ridge, are located at each end of the site. As the site's most obvious feature, they must have given it its modern (and perhaps its ancient) name, for Jebel Qa'aqir in Arabic means "Mountain of the Cairns." A wall encompassing both groups of cairns was traced nearly all the way around the ridge's crest. Clearly too flimsy to have served for defense, the wall must be considered simply an enclosure wall. Trenches dug against the wall confirmed its Middle Bronze Age I date but yielded little else.

Three cairns from the southern group were excavated. One, cairn 4, was nearly 16 m in diameter and 3 m in height. It had an outer curb wall, an inner chamber wall, and, in the center, a mysterious "tower" filled with wood ash. The cairn had been built over an earlier Middle Bronze Age I rectangular structure that had domestic pottery smashed on its earthen floor. While the sherds give a probable Middle Bronze Age I date for cairn 4, a few Byzantine sherds were found at the bottom of a smaller cairn. The use of the three cairns remains unknown. In the Middle Bronze Age I such cairns are paralleled at Mount Yeroḥam, Be'er Resisim, and many other sites in the Negev desert, but most of those contain human burials, unlike those at Jebel Qa'aqir.

The ridge has dozens of caves. Many have the cupmarks around the entrance that have long been noted as characteristic of Middle Bronze Age I settlements. Several caves were excavated and found to have considerable evidence of human habitation; many had apparently been used for storage. Cave G23 produced 198 buckets of pottery with nearly 1,800 partially restorable vessels, all characteristic of Dever's "Family S," or southern/sedentary group. Cave G26 showed signs of domestic use: several stone storage bins were on the terrace, and there were two large inner chambers, apparently for sleeping. Some twenty-five completely restorable pottery vessels, as well as chert pounders and blades and ground-stone implements, were recovered from the earthen living surface of the terrace. Cave H19 was a "split-level" dwelling, with a cupmark and a fire-blackened hearth on the upper level and a group of storage jars and other domestic vessels on the lower one. Occupation at Jebel Qa'aqir seems to have been almost exclusively in caves because the only other habitation found was the structure under cairn 4. The caves would have been ideal for summer occupation, when they are cool and pleasant. They thus provide further evidence for a pattern of seasonal settlement, exhibited also in occupied caves at nearby Tell Beit Mirsim and Lachish.

A pottery kiln was discovered just outside the boundary wall on the eastern end of the ridge. Oval-shaped and about 1.65 m in diameter, it had terra-cotta side walls preserved some 70 cm high. These hollow walls communicated with an external firing chamber on each end, oriented to catch the prevailing winds and utilize them as a forced draft. (It is likely that a primitive bellows was also used, but no trace was found of any.) The kiln had been frequently repaired, perhaps with nearly every firing, and at least nine phases of use could be detected. The abundant pottery in and around it made its Middle Bronze Age I date indisputable. There is no parallel known from this period.

On the ridge was also a large "dolmen" that seemed to have consisted originally of a single standing monolith with several smaller stelae surrounding it, all now collapsed. Exhaustive excavation produced nothing more than a handful of Middle Bronze Age I sherds, although Late Chalcolithic sherds were found on the floor of a cave in the bedrock below the dolmen. Another feature was a curious complex of several large standing stones, erected in striking fashion on a flat outcrop of bedrock, that was dubbed (perhaps facetiously) the "high place." Nothing could be learned about it, except that it probably belonged, like almost everything else at the site, to the Middle Bronze Age I.

SUMMARY

It may be suggested that Jebel Qa'aqir—along with Khirbet Kirmil and many other isolated shaft-tomb cemeteries in the area—represents the summer encampments of pastoral nomads. They may have migrated seasonally between the Hebron Hills and the Negev, where at Be'er Resisim and elsewhere several hundred small Middle Bronze Age I villages have been found.

W. G. Dever, *RB* 76 (1969), 572–576; 78 (1971), 595–597; id., *NEAT*, 132–163; id., *IEJ* 21 (1971), 229–230; id., *Harvard Theological Review* 64 (1971), 197–226; id., *Archaeology* 25 (1972), 231–233; id., *BASOR* 237 (1980), 35–64; id., *EI* 15 (1981), 22*–32*; E. M. Meyers, *BA* 33 (1970), 1–29; S. Gitin, *EI* 12 (1975), 46*–62*; P. Smith, *BASOR* 245 (1982), 65–73; G. A. London, *ASOR Newsletter* 35/7 (1984), 5; 36/1 (1984), 5; id., *BA* 50 (1987), 70–74; id., "Decoding Designs: The Late Third Millennium B.C. Pottery from Jebel Qa'aqir" (Ph.D. diss., Univ. of Ariz. 1985); L. Kolska Horwitz, *IEJ* 37 (1987), 251–255; id., *BASOR* 275 (1989), 15–25; Weippert 1988, 187.

WILLIAM G. DEVER

JEMMEH, TELL

IDENTIFICATION

Tell Jemmeh (Tel Re'im), is in the northwestern Negev desert about 10 km (6 mi.) south of Gaza, on the southern bank of Naḥal Besor (Wadi Ghazzeh), map reference 097.088. It was the site of a flourishing town in the Middle Bronze Age II, the Late Bronze and Iron ages, and the Persian and Hellenistic periods. There is also evidence of a small Chalcolithic occupation on the east side of the site and of a large Byzantine city in the field directly south of the mound. The site was originally identified with ancient Gerar (Gen. 20:1, 26:1–12, for example) by W. J. Phythian-Adams, an identification accepted by W. M. F. Petrie. Subsequently, B. Mazar proposed identifying the site with ancient Yurza, an equation now accepted by most scholars. Yurza was a Canaanite city-state mentioned in the Egyptian topographical lists of the New Kingdom and in the el-Amarna letters. Thutmose III describes Yurza as the southernmost city to have rebelled against Egypt, which corresponds with the location of Tell Jemmeh. Jemmeh is almost certainly the "Arṣa (or Arza) near the Brook of Egypt" mentioned in texts of Esarhaddon, because ex-

Tell Jemmeh: aerial view after the 1971 season, looking west.

Tell Jemmeh: map of the mound and excavation areas.

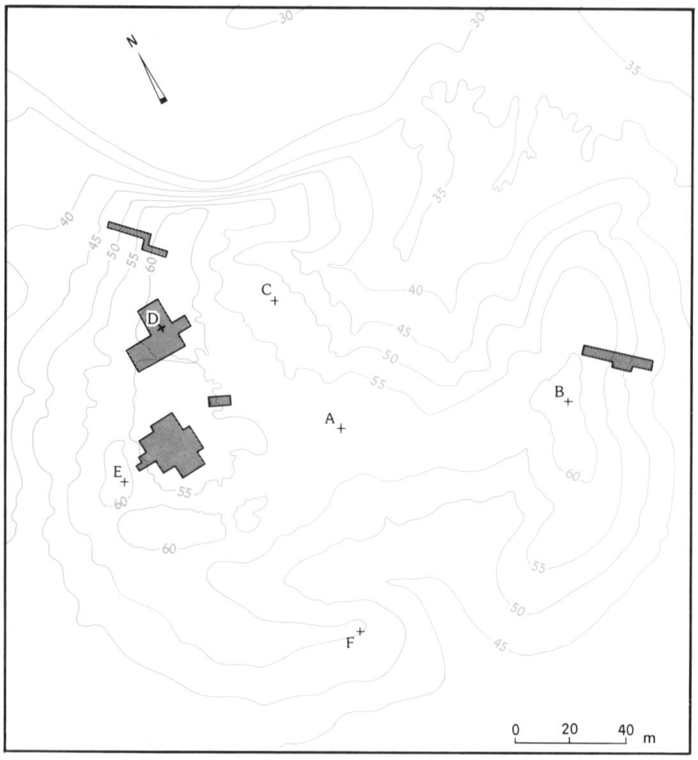

cavations have shown that the site was extremely important in the time of Assyrian domination. It is also probable that the Byzantine city immediately south of the mound is to be identified with Orda.

EXPLORATION

In 1922, Phythian-Adams dug a trial step trench. In 1926–1927, Petrie spent six months excavating a large area along the western sector of the site. This was the first of three mounds in the northwestern Negev excavated by Petrie in the 1920s and 1930s (the other two were Tell el-Far'ah [South] and Tell el-'Ajjul). Since 1970, a Smithsonian Institution expedition, directed by G. W. Van Beek, has been excavating the site.

EXCAVATION RESULTS

The area of the mound—at virgin soil—originally consisted of 12.15 a., according to recent estimates. The north side of the site has been partially cut away by Naḥal Besor, entirely removing about 45 m of the mound and deeply eroding the northeastern sector. The south side is similarly eroded, so that the present surface has the shape of the Roman numeral I. All major excavations have focused on the western side of the mound where, as Petrie correctly surmised, the most important buildings were to be found. This area faces the fresh sea breeze prevailing in the late mornings and afternoons. Phythian-Adams's step trench was located on the southwestern slope of the northern eroded area of the site and is now covered by one of Petrie's dumps. Petrie excavated about 2,300 sq m near the western perimeter, gradually stepping the area inward from the east and south sides. In the 15-m accumulation of debris, he reached a depth of about 10 m over most of this area and continued down to virgin soil only in a small area in the northwest corner of his excavation. He distinguished six strata, five designated by letters, plus the topmost granary phase. Van Beek opened several areas in the site: (1) an area immediately north of Petrie's excavation, to coordinate with his stratigraphy; (2) a large area at the bottom of Petrie's dig, to ascertain the date of his lowest occupation, designated field I; (3) a step trench on the northwest slope near the escarpment, to examine defense systems, field II; (4) a step trench on the east slope, to examine the history of occupation on this previously unexcavated side of the mound, field III; and (5) a trench on the south slope, to search for Middle Bronze Age defenses, the south trench.

There were serious technical flaws in Petrie's excavation methods and in his assignment of material to strata; only room or structure assemblages from approximately the same level in feet can be dated, and even then caution must be used because the relationship of floors to walls was not uniformly established. Subsequent studies by W. F. Albright, G. E. Wright, and others indicated a number of necessary revisions, but ultimately, however, reexcavation of the site, employing newer and more precise methods, was required.

CHALCOLITHIC PERIOD. Appearing only in field III, the Chalcolithic period is represented by a series of pits—huts or silos—sunk into virgin soil, some with plastered bottoms, and similar to Khirbet Abu Matar levels I–II. Pottery and other artifacts are typical of the Beersheba culture. Following this period, the site, like others in the northwestern Negev, was abandoned until the Middle Bronze Age II.

MIDDLE BRONZE AGE II. Jemmeh was reoccupied in the Middle Bronze Age IIB, apparently over the entire site; in fields I and III, deposits from the Middle Bronze Age IIB–C accumulated approximately 2 m in depth with four domestic building phases. The south trench yielded the remains of a Middle Bronze Age II rammed earth revetment, preserved to a height of 1.6 m, with a thickness of more than 6 m. It was built on virgin soil and consists of flat, sandy layers varying from 20 to 28 cm in thickness, each separated from adjacent layers above and below by thin, clayey layers, about 1 to 1.5 cm thick. After it was no longer used, the revetment was sealed by at least eight debris layers, with a minimum depth of 2.15 m. Of these, layers 1 to 8 contain only Middle Bronze Age II sherds, whereas Middle Cypriot White-Painted VI and Tell el-Yahudiyeh ware were confined to layers 1 to 4B.

From the last phase of the Middle Bronze Age IIC in field III came a Tell el-Yahudiyeh ware zoomorphic vessel in the form of a bull head—with muzzle, eyes, horns, and probably ears added in relief—standing on a high trumpet foot, and with a pouring spout rising from the top of the head. Features such as folds of skin, eyelashes, and mouth are incised and filled with white paint. Imports from Cyprus in the Middle Bronze Age II period include fragments of White-Painted VI vessels—primarily globular jars of buff clay painted with vertical groups of three, four, and five thick bands rising from the base and with horizontal bands separated by single wavy lines around the shoulder—and Pendent Line Style III–IV juglets. In field III, a small cylinder seal of baked clay, with five vertical rows of geometric designs and two vertical lines of cuneiform, was also found. A foundation deposit of a small equid was buried beneath the lowest Middle Bronze Age wall in field I, and the skull and two leg bones of another equid were discovered in a pit in field III. They probably relate to contemporary equid burials at Tell el-'Ajjul. A tomb from this period was found by Petrie southwest of the mound.

LATE BRONZE AGE. The Late Bronze Age I is represented by shallow deposits in both fields I and III. The Late Bronze Age II is, however, the most intensively occupied period at Jemmeh, with debris accumulating to

Tell Jemmeh: general view, looking south.

Scarab depicting an Egyptian king (Ramses II?) worshiping the god Ptah.

about 6 m in eight building phases in only 250 years. The most noteworthy structure, which belongs to the thirteenth century BCE, is a large residence in field I—possibly a palace—consisting of a courtyard with an adjacent suite of rooms. The building measures 19.2 by 16.5 m, as excavated; the western portion remains buried under Petrie's balk, and the northern end was probably cut away by Petrie's probe to virgin soil. The large open courtyard was paved with carefully laid cobblestones and had two entrances, one from the outside and one from the domestic quarters. In one corner of the courtyard was an enclosed bathroom with plaster on its walls and floor and a plastered drain that emptied through the wall into a sump outside. In another corner a large bread oven stood on the remnant of an earlier cobblestone floor and was surrounded by a mud-brick bench circumscribing a quarter circle. A flight of three stone steps led down to the domestic suite, which consisted of a series of small rooms and a small courtyard with an earthen floor and successive bread ovens. These rooms were also entered through an outer doorway, which showed traces of a wooden threshold; outside the doorway was a small cobblestone-paved area and two mud-brick benches built against the adjacent walls.

South of the building and separated by a narrow lane, were three rooms of another building: a bathroom with plaster on its walls and floor and a drain leading to another external sump; a courtyard with an earthen floor, an almost completely preserved bread oven, and an outside entrance; and a larger room with a mud-brick bin built against one wall.

Objects from this period were numerous and diverse. Notable locally made pottery included substantial fragments of two unusual vessels. One, a deep bowl on a ring base, features a scene in red paint of deer or goats running to the right, with a stylized tree(s) between them. The second, a tankard, is decorated with red and black painted designs above the carination, divided into three bands: the upper consists of birds—perhaps swans—facing one another; in the middle a scene of two birds facing a tree and feeding on black fruit is repeated; and the lower band features alternating triangular panels, each with a single bird or a fruit-laden tree. The imported pottery includes many fragments of Cypriot white-slip ware bowls and base-ring ware jugs and bowls, as well as several fragments of a Late Helladic III octopus vessel and numerous Mycenean sherds.

Three scarabs were found, all with variations of the same motif: a king, probably Ramses II, paying homage to the god Ptah, and in one instance, also to the uraeus, standing behind Ptah. Bone objects include the wing and tail of a duck-shaped cosmetic container with incised feathers above and a scale design below. Among the faunal remains two were unexpected: the vertebrae of an African ostrich and the horn core of a hartebeest. Overall, the proportions of mammals and especially bird bones in the faunal sample suggest climatic changes between the Middle Bronze Age and the Iron Age.

On the northwest slope (field II), a mud-brick fortification system protected this occupation. The only gateway discovered at Jemmeh pierced the wall at this point. Although it was not possible to examine it in depth, it was found to be paved with a fine cobblestone floor, identical in type and construction to the floor of the courtyard in the large Late Bronze Age II building described above.

IRON AGE I. Petrie's lowest continuous stratum—JK—substantially belongs to the beginning of the Iron Age I and represents the earliest Philistine occupation. Parts of three buildings were discovered, the most noteworthy of which is the series of rooms around courtyard JF and the irregularly shaped enclosure JA. In Van Beek's excavations, Philistine deposits were found east of Petrie's area in field I and also in field III, accumulating to about 2.5 m. They also were reached in the area north of Petrie's excavations, adjacent to and deep below the eastern wall of the Assyrian vaulted building (see below).

The principal structure found in the recent excavations is a large, technologically sophisticated ceramic kiln, the largest Philistine kiln yet found in Israel. The kiln is ovoid in plan, with an interior length of 3.7 m and a maximum width of 2 m; it is preserved to a height of 1.35 m, just above the level of the floor separating the firebox and baking chamber. The firebox was lined with mud plaster that had baked to a greenish-white color. The chamber floor, made of large, specially shaped bricks, with as many as four holes 10 cm in diameter in each to conduct heat to the baking chamber, was carried by a series of four arches. These arches, springing from the sides of the kiln, were constructed with mud bricks laid radially—with faces adjacent to one another and narrow edges exposed on all sides—and with potsherds and stones embedded in the mortar between the outer edges, to force the bricks into an arc. The preserved springer of one of the arches established the height of the firebox at 1.05 m. With a minimum ratio of 1:3, this indicates a minimum height of 3 m for the baking chamber. A series of flues, one between each arch, had been scooped in the side walls. In the best-preserved example, the flue led to two square earthen pipes that conducted heat to the upper area of the tall baking chamber, providing a more uniform baking temperature. The stoking hole at the pointed end of the ovoid kiln was found blocked by irregularly laid bricks and brick fragments. The kiln belongs to the twelfth

Pottery figurine from the Iron Age.

Iron mattock and plow blade.

Bronze bull head, 8th century BCE.

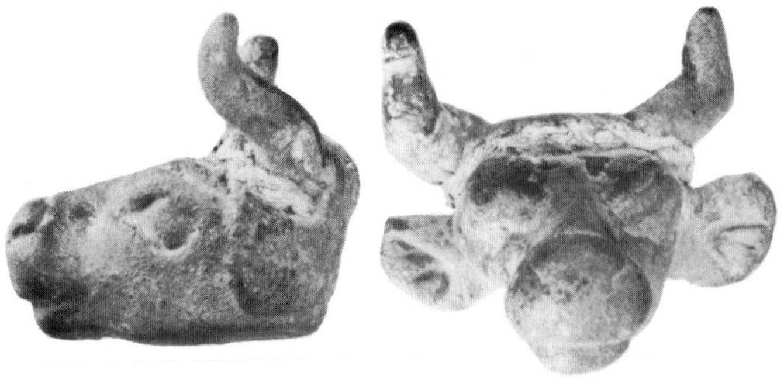

century BCE. It is possible that Petrie's JA enclosure was associated with the kiln operation, perhaps serving as the potter's yard. During the eleventh century BCE, two walls forming the corner of a room were built over the destroyed kiln.

A considerable quantity of Philistine sherds—predominantly of bowls with characteristic spirals—was found in the kiln. Curiously, neither Petrie's nor Van Beek's excavations have yielded a single sherd painted with the common Philistine motif of a bird preening its feathers.

Several successive fortification systems were partially cleared in field II, but none could be examined in detail, owing to the adjacent collapse of the mound. At least three separate construction phases are distinguished, dating between the twelfth and eighth centuries BCE.

IRON AGE II. Petrie's strata GH and EF can be assigned to the Iron Age II. The chronological division between them is not clear, but GH can be roughly dated to the tenth to ninth centuries and EF to the eighth to seventh centuries. In stratum GH, two of the buildings (HA and GC) are probably four-room structures. The largest of the four furnaces discovered by Petrie belongs to this occupation. Petrie thought that the furnaces were used for smelting iron. This seems probable, owing to the fact that the mud walls of the furnaces were vitrified, a process requiring temperatures above 1100 degrees C, even though no trace of iron has been found inside the furnaces.

The Tenth and Ninth Centuries BCE. The tenth to ninth centuries are meagerly represented in Van Beek's excavations. Thus far, all the tenth-century walls are built entirely of crumbly brown brick with foundation trenches and bedding layers of clean sand. From the ninth century, a substantial portion of a large room with a lime-plastered floor and walls and an adjacent room were found; the latter contained a storage jar and a jug, both finished with a vertically burnished, rich red slip, augmented by black and white painted bands around the shoulders and neck. Imported Cypriot pottery includes a black-on-red barrel jug and a bichrome jug, both with handle ridges. A number of clay figurines of animals and humans from this period were recovered, including one found by Petrie featuring a man sitting in a wheeled vehicle, probably a chariot. A number of gold earrings also were found.

The Eighth Century BCE. The eighth century BCE is represented by a series of three building phases east of the vaulted building (see below). To this period belongs the earliest known casemate fortification system at Tell Jemmeh. Found on the northwest slope, it consists of an outer wall at least 2 m thick, erected 2 m from the inner wall (whose thickness was not determined), with narrow connecting cross walls. Noteworthy objects from the period include a small, solid bronze bull head, which was probably used as a weight. It had been worn around the neck on a string, as evidenced by its original linen string, preserved beneath the corrosion and below the horns. A fine bronze chisel was also discovered.

The Seventh Century BCE. Substantial parts of Petrie's stratum EF and probably much of CD can be assigned to the seventh century BCE. In EF, a series of buildings (ET-EW-EY, EC-ED, EB-EG-EK-Et-Es-Ew, and FE-FF-FG-FH) share a plan characterized by three or four parallel long rooms with a transverse room across one end and sometimes across both ends; the transverse room is often divided into three small rooms, each connected by a doorway to the adjacent long room. The same plan was utilized in the Assyrian vaulted building excavated by Van Beek. It is similar to plans used at Nineveh, Khorsabad, and Calah (Nimrud) in Assyria during the eighth and seventh centuries BCE.

The Assyrian Vaulted Building. This is one of the most remarkable structures ever found in Israel because it preserves vaulted mud-brick ceilings that were erected with keystone-shaped bricks, or voussoirs, marking the earliest known use of voussoirs in world architecture. It consisted of at least six rooms, of which five were excavated (A, B, C, E, F); E and F were long parallel rooms (maximum preserved length, 6.8 m), and A–C were short rooms (average length, 3.2 m) dividing the transverse end room.

All of these rooms must have been basement storerooms because the

Overview of the Assyrian vaulted building.

Isometric reconstruction of the Assyrian vaulted building, 7th century BCE.

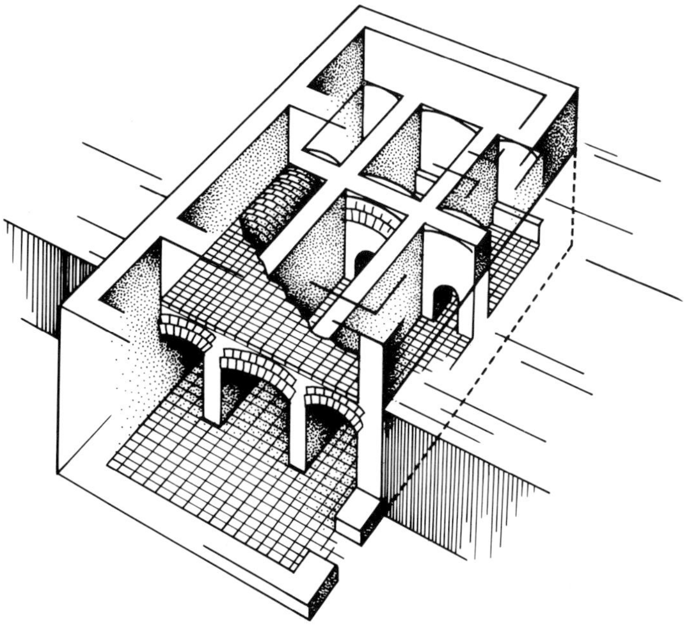

Assyrian-style bowl.

Assyrian vaulted building, room C.

Assyrian-type palace ware.

building was constructed in a large hole 2 m below ground level. The rooms were all floored with mud bricks, and against the rear wall of each of the short rooms—A, B, and C—was a mud-brick ledge, probably to hold lamps when the rooms were dark. All of the walls were constructed of rectangular bricks laid in English bond with sand-filled bedding and rising joints—without mud mortar. To prevent the sand from falling out of the joints, the walls were immediately covered with a thick coat of mud plaster. The vaults, portions of which were preserved in all five rooms, carried the floor of the rooms above, and, where fully preserved, were 60 cm thick. They were erected in the "pitched-brick" technique, in which the successive rings of vault brick are based on the side walls and lean obliquely against an end wall already constructed to its full height. The lower face of each vault brick is scored with a series of deep parallel grooves to key the mud mortar used in the vaults. This type of vault is constructed without any form of support or centering. The use of voussoirs not only makes stronger vaults, but also permits the arc, or curvature, of the vault to vary, as is the case in this building. Voussoir vault bricks are a significant technological development out of the Mesopotamian square vault-brick tradition; they cannot be derived from the rectangular vault-brick tradition of Egypt. Between rooms A-F and B-E are arched doorways, each formed by six pairs of rib, or strut, vault bricks, a style of vaulting otherwise found only in Iran, and best known at Nush i-Jan, a contemporary site in northwestern Iran.

In room A, where a large part of the vault had fallen, a mass of Assyrian palace ware was found resting in the debris above the collapsed vault, having dropped from the room above. Many sherds were also found in other rooms as well as in rubbish pits outside the building. Petrie first identified this type of pottery at Jemmeh, where he, too, found hundreds of fragments in rubbish pits. In the basement storerooms, a number of local storage jars were also found.

The typical Assyrian building plan, the style of vaulting, and the great quantity of palace ware suggest that the building was built by Assyrians as the residence of the Assyrian king, military governor, or other ranking official. Assyrian cuneiform texts of Esarhaddon (about 680 to 669 BCE) relate that he captured a town known as Arṣa on the Brook of Egypt. Because Esarhaddon undertook three campaigns to conquer Egypt—in 674, 671, and 669 BCE—and because the Jemmeh region was the border zone between Philistia and Egypt, it is likely that the site was a major staging point for those of his armies involved in these operations. Immediately east of the vaulted building, three phases of seventh-century BCE constructions were found, one earlier than the vaulted structure and two later. A substantial section of vaulting broken from a building—but not from the vaulted building discussed above—was found in the debris. A casemate fortification system, built almost directly on top of the destroyed eighth-century BCE casemate walls in one area, protected the settlement in this period. In field II, no later defense walls were found, and it seems likely that Jemmeh was not circumvallated from about 600 to 200 BCE.

Among the finds other than pottery are a fine silver earring, an ivory furniture inlay in the form of a palmette, a cache of 150 carnelian beads in the corner of room A of the vaulted building, and two ostraca. Of the latter, one has four lines and the other six; they are apparently Philistine and contain lists of northwest Semitic and non-Semitic names. Faunal remains from the seventh century BCE and later show that the relative proportions of the major food animals (sheep, goat, cattle, and pig) changed in response to shifts in the site's economic foci from an agricultural town to a military installation to a storage facility.

The Sixth Century BCE. Petrie's buildings CA-CT and rooms DG-DH, as well as those surrounding DT, can be assigned to the sixth century BCE. From Van Beek's excavations, the sixth to fourth centuries BCE are represented by only a few walls, none of which form a coherent plan. During the late sixth and early fifth centuries BCE, a pit was dug that cut into the north wall of the Assyrian vaulted building. The pit contained a round, saucer-like lamp with a central tube and two opposing nozzles that was imported from the Aegean area.

Plan of the Persian period fortress.

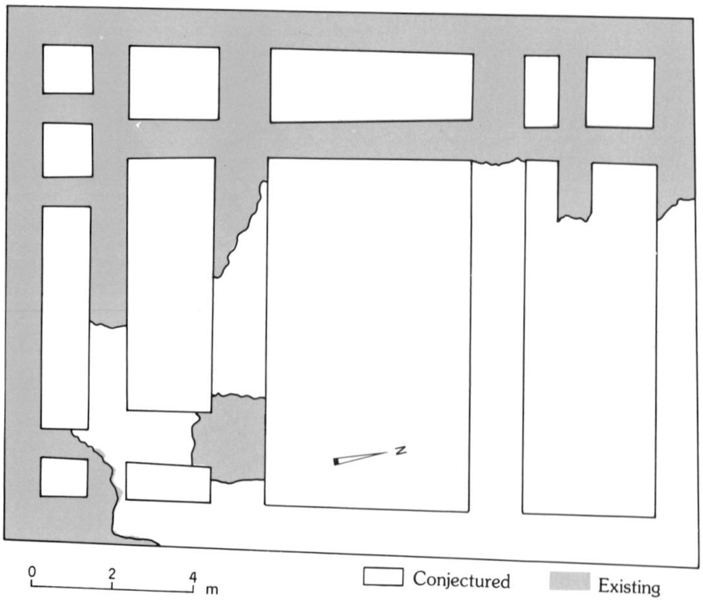

PERSIAN PERIOD. Petrie's best-preserved stratum, AB—especially the large building BAA-BY with later additions, as Petrie observed, and the enormous fort with corner rooms AF-AK-AD—can be assigned to the fifth to late fourth centuries BCE. This dating is based both on stratigraphic considerations and the notable finds of Greek imported pottery, some pieces of which were found under buildings of the period. Among the Aegean pottery is a large red-figured lekythos (about 450 BCE), two smaller lekythoi, and substantial fragments of amphorae. The fort is the largest structure yet found at Jemmeh, measuring approximately 38 by 29 m. Its walls are slightly more than 2 m thick, and it features a central courtyard with a double range of rooms on the south and north sides and a single row of rooms on the west and probably the east sides. Apart from the imported pottery, the local pottery of this period included mortaria, small juglets, and storage jars with heavy vertical loop handles, through which a pole was passed for carrying. A number of small limestone incense burners was also found in this stratum, decorated with lightly incised animals—camels, cattle, and probably gazelle—as well as simple geometric designs. In this period, Jemmeh produced the earliest known zoological evidence of major camel caravan activity.

Red-figured Attic lekythos, 5th century BCE.

HELLENISTIC PERIOD. During the Ptolemaic occupation, Jemmeh was apparently converted

Base of round silo, Hellenistic period.

from its function as a typical town to a vast grain-storage depot. While some families no doubt continued to live on the site, it seems likely that most of the population was housed off the mound in surrounding fields. The entire western sector of the site appears to have been occupied by large, circular, mud-brick granaries; altogether, eleven have been excavated in this area, ten by Petrie and one by Van Beek. That identical structures were also built in the eastern sector was established by Van Beek with the finding of a granary immediately below the surface in field III.

In spite of the cursory publication of Petrie's granaries, where design and construction details are limited to compass-drawn circles and two schematic cross sections, it is clear that the granaries differed somewhat in construction. In interior diameter, there are three sizes: the largest range from 8 to 9 m; the majority range from about 5.5 to 6 m; and the smallest range from about 4.5 to 5 m. The largest ones have at least one stairway built in the inner wall; none of the others have obvious entries. The type of roofing also seems to differ. Based on granary BFF, where the superstructure wall was inclined inward, Petrie assumed that all had high conical roofs; however, the granary Van Beek completely excavated, with a diameter identical to that of BFF, had a flat roof supported by an arched cross wall. There are similarities in design and construction. All the granaries were erected in deep, excavated holes that, on the west side, penetrated into deposits from the seventh century BCE and, on the east side, where later Iron Age deposits are nonexistent, into debris from the twelfth century BCE. Most, and perhaps all, had an interior ledge at ground level formed by offsetting the superstructure, so that it rested in part on solid ground.

The only granary completely excavated by Van Beek is in the western sector, to the north of Petrie's granaries; it was not removed. It belongs to the middle size range, with an interior diameter of 6.1 m at the base, and is preserved to a height of 2.64 m. Its foundation hole reached a depth of 1.8 m. It has two successive floors: the earliest was composed of square bricks laid in straight rows on a northwest–southeast axis; the latest, separated from the earliest by a debris layer about 25 cm thick, was made of square bricks randomly laid. Two opposed, pierlike structures bonded into the circular wall project into the interior; these are the bases of an arched cross wall—the arch bricks of which were laid radially—that was flat on top in order to carry the beams of a flat mud roof. Based on the probable height of the arch, the interior height of the granary would have been about 5.5 m. This estimate suggests that the granary's capacity would have been about 155.78 cu m, capable of containing approximately 132.23 tons of grain. This granary was destroyed quickly, probably in a matter of minutes, but whether by warfare or earthquake is not known, although the latter seems much more likely.

The granary was filled with a mass of broken brick from the superstructure and several tons of potsherds. Whole vessels were limited to small pieces, such as lamps and juglets; not a single storage jar was found intact or crushed in one place, although sherds of such jars amounted to about 75 percent of all pottery. When reconstruction is complete, more than twenty storage jars will have been reassembled. Ostraca from within the granary indicate that grain, collected through government taxation, was stored there, while the smaller granary on the east slope (field III) stored wine. The local pottery dates to the Late Persian and Hellenistic periods (late fourth to third centuries BCE) and includes several new forms, especially a storage jar with a hollow, cuplike base, the most common storage jar form in the granary. One of these jars bears a South Arabic monogram reading *'bm* (*'abum*), a name known in both Sabean and Minean inscriptions. This suggests that South Arabian caravans stopped at Jemmeh, probably to purchase grain for making bread on their long journey back to Yemen. They would have already delivered their cargoes of frankincense and myrrh to the Mediterranean incense port of Gaza (Pliny, *NH* XII, 32, 63–64). Imported pottery includes late fourth to third century BCE lamps, small black-ware bowls with incurving rims but without stamping or rouletting, and amphorae, probably from the western Mediterranean.

Settlement on the mound ended about the beginning of the second century BCE, and the site was never reoccupied. Bedouin encampments and a few late burials, as well as occasional travelers, are attested by finds of later date. Someone during Crusader times apparently lost his money while visiting the site: in the surface layer, a heavily corroded copper lump was recovered that contained eleven silver coins, nine of which bear the inscription "AMAIRICUS REX DE IERUSALEM" and belong to the second half of the twelfth century CE. An impression of cloth preserved on the corroded lump contained actual cotton fibers, indicating that the coins had been in a bag or tied in cloth.

Identification: K. Galling, *ZDPV* 52 (1929), 242–250; B. Maisler (Mazar), *PEQ* 84 (1952), 48–51; Y. Aharoni, *IEJ* 6 (1956), 26–31; N. Na'aman, *TA* 6 (1979), 68–90.

Excavations and finds: W. J. Phythian-Adams, *PEQ* 55 (1923), 140–146; W. M. F. Petrie, *Gerar*, London 1928; G. E. Wright, *AJA* 43 (1939), 458–463; W. F. Albright, *AASOR* 21–22 (1943), 23f., 144; B. Maisler, *PEQ* 84 (1952), 48–51; G. W. Van Beek, *IEJ* 20 (1970), 230; 22 (1972), 245–246; 24 (1974), 138–139, 274–

275; 27 (1977), 171–176; id., *RB* 79 (1972), 596–599; 80 (1973), 572–576; 82 (1975), 95–97, 573–576; id., *Archaeology* 36 (1983), 12–19; id. *National Geographic Research Reports* 16 (1984), 675–696; id., *BA* 49 (1986), 245–247; (with O. Van Beek), 53 (1990), 205–209; id., *ESI* 5 (1986), 54–55; id., *EI* 20 (1989), 12*–29*; id., *2nd International Congress on Biblical Archaeology, 24 June–4 July 1990: Abstracts*, Jerusalem 1990, 140–141; L. Y. Rahmani, *IEJ* 21 (1971), 158–160; D. N. Freedman, *ASOR Newsletter* (Nov. 1976), 8–9; G. L. Mattingly, *Near Eastern Archaeology Society Bulletin* 15–16 (1980), 33–49; J. Schaefer, *AJA* 84 (1980), 230–231; id., *BASOR* 274 (1989), 33–60; P. Wapnish, *Journal of the Ancient Near East Society of Columbia University*, 13 (1981–1983), 101–121; P. Wapnish and B. Hesse, *JNES* 47 (1988), 81–94; E. D. Oren, *Journal of the Society for the Study of Egyptian Antiquities* 14 (1984), 46; J. Naveh, *IEJ* 35 (1985), 8–21; N. Na'aman, *12th Congress of the International Organization for the Study of the Old Testament: Program and Abstracts*, Jerusalem 1986, 95; id. and R. Zadok, *JCS* 40 (1988), 36–46; A. Kempinski, *IEJ* 37 (1987), 20–24; Weippert 1988 (Ortsregister).

GUS W. VAN BEEK

JERICHO

IDENTIFICATION

The town of Jericho is situated on the wide plain of the Jordan Valley, about 10 km (6 mi.) north of the Dead Sea and close to the steep cliffs that fringe the valley to the west (map reference 193.142). At a depth of 250 m below sea level, it is the lowest town on the surface of the earth. This location, shut in by mountain walls to the east and west, has a climate that is tropical in summer and usually mild in winter. The amount of rainfall is small, about 140 mm a year, most of which falls in a few violent downpours—in some years there is virtually none. The flourishing agriculture of which the area is capable is dependent on the spring known as Elisha's Well, or 'Ein es-Sultan. With irrigation based on the spring, the valley's alluvial soil can produce crops of almost every kind, tropical and temperate in habitat—dates, green vegetables, or wheat. In times of expansion, the waters of 'Ein es-Sultan can be supplemented by those of 'Ein ed-Duk (Na'aran), some 3 km (2 mi.) to the northwest, which, as in the Early Arab period and today, can be brought to Jericho by aqueduct. With irrigation, an extensive oasis can be created; but when it is neglected, the area reverts to the parched scrub of the adjacent valley, as is seen in nineteenth-century photographs taken in the immediate neighborhood of 'Ein es-Sultan. Destruction of the irrigation system by enemies, or the interruption of the water supply as a result of the earth movements to which the Jordan Valley is liable, may account for the periodic abandonments of the ancient site that excavation has revealed.

TELL ES-SULTAN

HISTORY

Jericho enters written history as the first town west of the Jordan River to be captured by the Israelites approaching from the east. Joshua's instruction to his spies to "Go, view the land, especially Jericho" (Jos. 2:1) is an illustration of the position of Jericho in the age-long process of penetration by nomads and seminomads from the desert area in the east into the fertile coastal lands. It stood near the Jordan fords between a good valley route down the eastern side of the Jordan Valley and another going up the western mountains. As it dominated one of the few routes leading directly from east to west, it was liable to attack by successive invaders.

The identification of the main mound of the oasis, Tell es-Sultan (map reference 192.142), with the oldest city is generally accepted. The mound rises to a height of 21.5 m and covers an area of about one acre. It stands quite near 'Ein es-Sultan (Elisha's Well). As regards the Jericho of the Book of Joshua, there are some chronological difficulties, as will be seen below. Following its destruction by Joshua, the Bible states, Jericho was abandoned for centuries until a new settlement was established by Hiel the Bethelite (1 Kg. 16:34), in the time of Ahab, in the ninth century BCE. Other biblical references do not suggest that Jericho ever recovered its importance. The archaeological evidence shows that occupation on the ancient site came to an end at the time of the Babylonian Exile. The centers of the later Jerichos were elsewhere in the oasis.

EXPLORATION

Soundings at Tell es-Sultan were first made by C. Warren in 1868 as part of the early campaigns of the British Palestine Exploration Fund. Warren sank a number of shafts into the mound and concluded that there was nothing to be found. Two of his shafts were identified in the 1957–1958 excavations, one of them penetrating the Early Bronze Age town wall and the other missing the great Pre-Pottery Neolithic stone tower by only one meter.

The first large-scale excavations were those of an Austro-German expedition, from 1907 to 1909, under the direction of E. Sellin and C. Watzinger. The expedition cleared the face of a considerable part of the Early Bronze Age town wall and traced the line of about half of the revetment at the base of the Middle Bronze Age defenses. Within the town, a large area of houses was cleared at the north end and a great trench was cut across the center. Re-excavation in 1953 showed that it had penetrated well into the Pre-Pottery Neolithic levels. The excavations were conducted and published by the best standards of the time. Unfortunately, at that time, there was no accepted chronology, so that the usefulness of this early work is limited.

By the time new excavations were undertaken by the Neilson expeditions, directed by J. Garstang, from 1930 to 1936, the knowledge of pottery chronology had greatly increased. Excavation technique lagged, however, and the absence of detailed stratigraphy still often made the dating of the structures mere guesswork. The dating of the successive Bronze Age defensive systems by Garstang has, in fact, proved to be wrong. No Late Bronze Age wall survives. Also, as knowledge of pottery chronology increased, the dating given to the scanty Late Bronze Age levels from the mound and the tombs was shown to be incorrect. Garstang's most important discovery was that beneath the Bronze Age levels there was a deep Neolithic accumulation, usually of the Pre-Pottery stage. He believed that there was a transition to the use of pottery at the site, but this was a mistake. A third major series of excavations was

Tell es-Sultan: general view after the Sellin and Watzinger excavations, looking east.

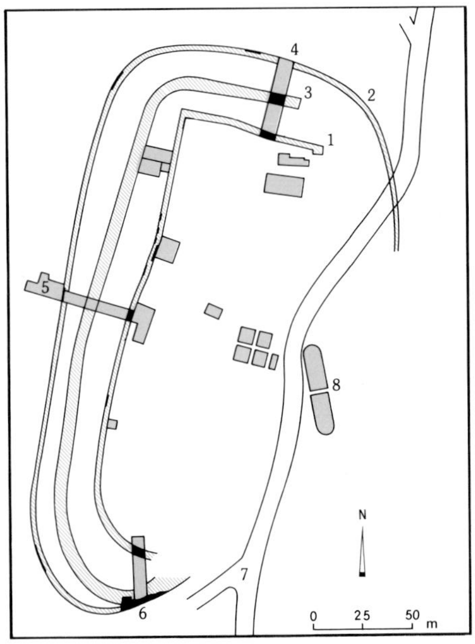

Tell es-Sultan: plan of the site and excavation areas.

1. City wall from Early Bronze Age; in west it is built directly above Neolithic wall; 2. Retaining wall of glacis from Middle Bronze Age II; 3. Glacis; 4. Kenyon's trench I; 5. Trench II; 6. Trench III; 7. Road; 8. Pools near spring

carried out between 1952 and 1958, directed by K. M. Kenyon on behalf of the British School of Archaeology in Jerusalem. The results are described below.

EXCAVATION RESULTS

Although extensive excavations have been carried out by Kenyon at Tell es-Sultan, the great depth of deposit in the lowest levels has allowed their examination only in limited areas. The mound rises to a maximum height of 21.5 m above the surrounding plain, and to an average height of 17 m. Bedrock has been reached in a sufficient number of places to show clearly that all of this height was built up by human occupation. The original settlement was on a surface sloping gently to the east. Its position was doubtless dictated by the position of the spring, the actual source of which is now buried beneath the accumulation of the mound.

THE EPIPALEOLITHIC PERIOD. The earliest remains, found in an area near the north end of the mound, belong to the Natufian culture. Carbon-14 dates for the deposit range from 9687 BCE $\pm$ 107 to 7770 BCE $\pm$ 210. The nature of the remains is not clear, but an oblong structure enclosing a clay platform, with a group of sockets for uprights set in a wall, too close together to be structural, may represent a sanctuary. The associated flint and bone industries, including a harpoon head and a lunate, found in layer K, are clearly related to the Lower Natufian of Mount Carmel. It is possible that this was a sanctuary set up by hunters near the spring of Jericho.

THE NEOLITHIC AND CHALCOLITHIC PERIODS. Definite Epipaleolithic levels were found only at one spot in the limited area excavated to bedrock. However, in a number of other places, levels were found that link these first Natufians of Jericho with the subsequent Neolithic stage. The most important of these areas was square M. At this spot, the very lowest deposit consisted of a layer 4 m thick, composed of a close succession of surfaces bounded by slight humps. The humps clearly represent the bases of flimsy

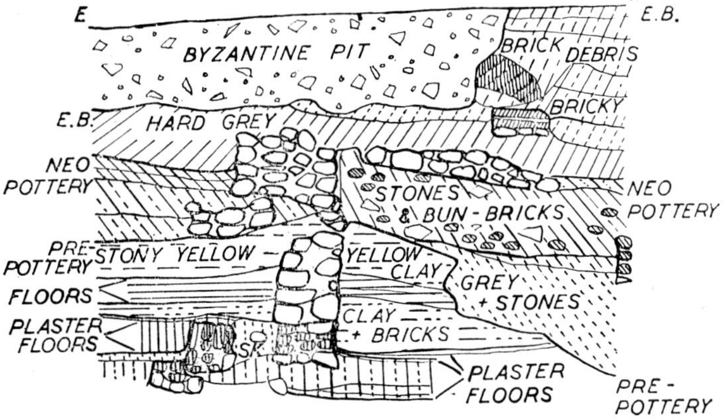

Sample section from Kenyon's excavations.

City fortifications, PPN: ditch, city wall, and tower.

Tell es-Sultan: the round tower, PPN.

walls, perhaps little more than the weighting down of tents of skins, although rudimentary mud bricks were present in the form of balls of clay. The area excavated was so limited and the traces so slight that no plan could be established.

The surfaces that made up this 4 m of deposit represent the remains of a succession of slight structures, huts, or tents seemingly suitable to the needs of a nomadic or seminomadic group. But the creation of this great depth of deposit indicates that these people were no longer nomadic, or at least that they returned to Jericho at regular and frequent intervals, perhaps practicing some form of transhumance. It is a truly transitional stage of culture, and the flint and bone industries are clearly derived from the Epipaleolithic Natufian. Although in square MI there is no preceding Epipaleolithic stage, it is reasonable to presume that the stage represented is that of Neolithic hunters, of whom evidence was found in area E, settling down to a sedentary way of life.

From such slight shelters, the first solid structures are clearly derived. The actual transitional stages were not found. In square MI they may even have been destroyed, for a thickish deposit containing fragments of clay-ball bricks intervened between the earlier succession of surfaces and the first solid structures, probably representing the leveling over of a nucleus mound that had become too small and steep. Above this deposit, the solid structures appear already fully developed, but their circular plan, usually single roomed, is clearly derived from that of a primitive hut. These circular structures are built with solid walls of plano-convex mud bricks, often with a hog-backed outline. The walls are inclined somewhat inward and the amount of brick in the debris of collapse suggests that the roofs were domed. The interiors of the houses were sunk below the level of the courtyard outside, and there were porches with a downward slope, or steps of stone or wood, projecting into the room. Rich industries of flint and bone were found in the houses: many axes and adzes, with polished or partially polished cutting edges, pestles, mortars, hammerstones, and other stone implements, which are clearly derived from the Lower Natufian. Limestone dishes and cups represented the only surviving utensils. The construction of these solid houses marked the establishment of a fully sedentary occupation, and the expansion of the community was rapid. Over all the area occupied by the subsequent Bronze Age town, and projecting appreciably beyond it to the north and south, houses of this type have been identified. The total area covered was almost 10 a.

The expansion of the settlement was soon followed by a step of major importance, the construction of a town wall. This is best preserved in trench I on the western side, where the first of a succession of defensive walls still stands to a height of 5.75 m. At the south end, a structure that was probably the same wall survived to a height of 2.1 m; at the north end, however, although the line could be identified, only one course survived. In each case, the foundations of the wall cut through the remains of preexisting houses, but not of a long succession, so the enclosing of the site by a defensive wall followed soon after the growth of the settlement.

On the west side, the first town wall was associated with a great stone tower (8.5 m in diameter and preserved to a height of 7.75 m) built against the inner side of the wall. The tower was constructed solidly of stone, except in the center, where a staircase provided access to the top of it from the interior of the town. The tower is not only a monument to remarkable architectural and constructional achievement, but tower and wall together furnish evidence of a degree of communal organization and a flourishing town life wholly unexpected at a date that, as will be seen, must be in the ninth millennium BCE.

In all the areas excavated to this level, there was a long succession of structures belonging to this first Neolithic stage. In the house areas, the ruins of successive houses were built up on a deposit of up to 6.5 m. In trench I at the western side of the mound, there was a sequence of four stages of the town wall, each incorporating the tower. The second stage was associated with a rock-cut ditch (9.5 m wide and 2.25 m deep). At the north and south ends of the town (trenches II and III), these later walls lie farther out, obscured by the Middle Bronze Age revetment. The carbon-14 datings obtained for different stages in the deposits of this period range from 8340 BCE ± 200 to 6935 BCE ± 155. However, the majority suggest a date for the beginning of the period in the late ninth millennium.

In all the areas excavated, the town of the period seems to have been fairly closely built up. In its area of about 10 a. there may have been two thousand or so occupants. A sedentary population of this size must have been largely dependent on agriculture. The favorable conditions provided by the perennial stream, the warm climate, and fertile land must have led to a very early development in food production. Organized agricultural activity already began in the Proto-Neolithic stage and increased with the growth of the town. It is also possible to assume that the developing agriculture was accompanied by developing irrigation, for the spring in its natural state could not have watered an area large enough for the fully grown town. The urban society, which succeeded in solving its defensive problems, was able to provide the manpower and the organization needed to create an irrigation system.

This Pre-Pottery Neolithic A culture of Jericho came to an abrupt end, the exact time of which could not be determined, and was succeeded by a second,

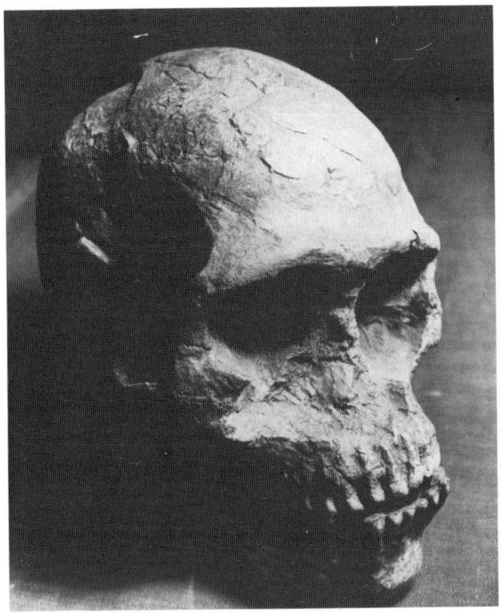

***Left:** plastered human skull, PPNA; **(below)** clay human head, PPN; **(right)** plastered human skull, PPNB.*

Pre-Pottery Neolithic B. Between the two there was a period of erosion, although it is uncertain whether it was caused by destruction wrought by the newcomers, or whether natural causes such as disease or an interference in the water supply caused its inhabitants to abandon the site. The Pre-Pottery Neolithic B culture arrived at Jericho almost fully developed and differed from its predecessor in almost every respect. The most immediately obvious contrast was the architecture. The houses were far more elaborate and sophisticated. The rooms were comparatively large, rectangular in plan, and grouped around courtyards. The plan seems to have been stereotyped, with central suites divided by cross walls in which there were entrances at either end and in the center, with smaller rooms adjoining. No complete house plan was recovered, as the size of the houses was such that in no case was an entire building within an excavated area. The walls were of elongated handmade mud bricks with a herringbone pattern of thumb impressions on the top. Floors and walls were covered with a continuous coat of highly burnished, hard lime mortar. It is presumed from the rectangular plan that the roofs were flat. There was no evidence of upper stories. There were fireplaces in the courtyards, whose floors were usually of mud mortar, and there was often an innumerable succession of charcoal spreads.

The material equipment was also almost completely different from that of Pre-Pottery Neolithic A. The flint industry was distinct and is not derived from the Natufian. The bone industry was very poor, being confined to simple implements such as pins and borers. Polished axes and adzes were rare, and in fact there were very few heavy stone implements. A very characteristic object was a trough-shaped quern with the grinding hollow running out to one edge and a flat border around the other three sides. This type was never found in Pre-Pottery Neolithic A. The types of grinding stone were also distinct. Bowls and dishes of white limestone, some of them very well made, became very common.

Two structures were found that probably served religious purposes. In one, a room had been cut off from part of the usual suite of rooms. In its end wall was a small niche with a rough stone pedestal at its base. In the debris nearby was a carefully trimmed stone pillar, which must be interpreted as a representation of a deity. The plan of the other structure was unique—a large central room with a burnished plaster floor, at each end of which were annexes with curvilinear walls. At the center of the large room was a rectangular plastered basin. It is likely that this structure had a ceremonial use.

The most remarkable evidence bearing on religious practices was the discovery of ten human skulls with features restored in plaster, sometimes with a high degree of skill and artistic power. Flesh-colored tinting, eyes inlaid with shells, and delicately modeled ears, nose, and eyebrows combined to make the heads extraordinarily lifelike. These plastered skulls were most likely associated with a cult of ancestor worship. The normal practice was to bury the dead beneath the floors of the houses, and many of the bodies had the cranium removed, presumably to ensure that the wisdom of the individual was preserved for the benefit of the descendants. The skulls were found in three groups, two close together, but the tenth skull came from a house some distance away, so the practice must have been followed by a number of separate families.

The Pre-Pottery Neolithic B settlement seems originally to have been undefended, for the earliest town wall found was later than a long series of house levels. Like the Pre-Pottery Neolithic A wall, it was built of rough stones, some of them very large. It was traced only on the west side of the site (trench I), where it overlay the earlier wall, although it was separated from it by a considerable depth of fill. Its probable continuation was found in area M. At the north and south ends (trenches II and III), the houses of the period were truncated by the Middle Bronze Age revetment, and the contemporary town wall must have been farther out.

The town of this period had a long existence, for the houses were rebuilt many times. Usually, the houses were rebuilt in approximately the same position and on the same plan, but there was nearly always evidence that the preceding destruction had been very severe, and the walls had to be rebuilt almost from floor level. The carbon-14 datings range from 7379 BCE ± 102 to 5845 BCE ± 160. Whereas Pre-Pottery Neolithic A had every appearance of being an indigenous development, this was not the case with Pre-Pottery Neolithic B. The latter arrived at Jericho with a fully developed architectural tradition and an industry that owed nothing to its predecessor on the site. Other related sites have since been found in the country (for example, Wadi Beidha). In 1961, at Çatal Hüyük, in Anatolia, J. Mellaart excavated a site that must also be related to this culture. The plans of the houses have the same rectangular layout, the same abundant use is made of burnished plaster, the dead are buried beneath the floors of the houses, and there are other similarities. The relationship, however, is probably indirect. The material culture of the Anatolian site, with molded plaster decoration and elaborate wall paintings, is much more sophisticated than that at Jericho, and pottery is found, although in the lower levels it is not common. The earliest period is dated by carbon-14 to about 6700 BCE. It is very probable that the cultures of the Anatolian and local sites are derived from a common ancestor.

Thus, there were two successive and quite separate Pre-Pottery Neolithic cultures at Jericho, and in each case the settlement assumed the character of a walled town. Of the first indigenous culture, all the stages of development can be traced on the spot. The second had evolved elsewhere.

Like Pre-Pottery Neolithic A, its successor, Pre-Pottery Neolithic B, came to an abrupt end. In all the areas excavated, the buildings and surfaces of the period are eroded on an angle sloping down to the exterior of the town, often very steeply. The terrace walls, which were an essential part of the layout on the slopes of the mound, had collapsed in whole or in part, and the fill and floors behind them had been washed out, often to a depth of several layers. It is impossible to estimate the length of the period of abandonment that produced this erosion. Once an earthquake or violent rains had made breaches in the terrace walls, the washout process could have proceeded rapidly if there was a series of heavy rains, but less violent conditions might have slowed down the erosion over a long period.

The evidence for the next period of occupation appears in the form of pits cut into this eroded surface. These pits, which often were as deep as 2 m and about 3 m across, and in one instance as deep as 4 m, were at first interpreted as quarry pits sunk to obtain material for brickmaking. It was suggested that the characteristic fill of angular stones represented material sieved out in the brickmaking process. Subsequently, however, it became clear that the pits contained a series of floors and occupation levels, including, in one case, a well-constructed oven; it was also observed that the stones originated from walls revetting the edges of the pits. It is therefore clear that these were occupation pits, or the emplacements of semisubterranean huts. Closely similar phenomena, including the angular stones, were observed at Tell el-Far'ah (North) in the levels that preceded the Early Bronze Age structures. The use of subterranean dwellings may also be compared with those of the Chalcolithic period, with a culture allied to the Ghassulian, at Tel Be'er Matar and Tel Be'er Ṣafad near Beersheba (q.v.).

The first pottery appears in these pits at Jericho. Analysis of it suggests that two different and successive groups are represented, called Pottery Neolithic

A and Pottery Neolithic B. The A pottery, consisting of vessels decorated with burnished chevron patterns in red, and also of extremely coarse, straw-tempered vessels, corresponds with that ascribed to stratum IX by Garstang. The B pottery, consisting of jars with bow rims, jars and bowls with herringbone decoration, and vessels with a mat red slip, corresponds with that ascribed to stratum VIII. The former was believed to appear as an indigenous development out of the Pre-Pottery Neolithic. A reexamination of Garstang's trench and fresh evidence from other parts of the mound, however, make it quite clear that this is not so. It was a conclusion arrived at only because the pits containing the pottery were not observed, and it was believed that the pottery belonged to the latest plastered-floor houses instead of being intrusive. With the appearance of pottery there was a change in the flint industry, most noticeably the use of coarse, instead of fine, denticulation for the sickle blades. By far, the greatest amount of finds from the period came from the pits. Above the pits, however, there were some scanty remains of buildings. Too little was found to establish any house plans, but their characteristic feature was the round and the plano-convex bricks, not found at any other period. The relation of the two types of pottery to the successive stages is not yet clear.

Scattered examples of the characteristic Neolithic A pottery have been found at a number of local sites—Lachish, Megiddo, and Teluliyot Batash—but usually only in mixed groups found at the lowest levels, with a range from the Neolithic to the Early Bronze Age. Such finds indicate that the people who used this pottery were fairly widespread in the country at this time, but tell little about them.

Objects comparable with the finds of Pottery Neolithic B are found over a wide area. Pottery and flints, particularly the former, can be closely paralleled at Sha'ar ha-Golan on the Yarmuk River. Similar pottery is also found in the Enéolithique A at Byblos, with the additional link of incised pebbles, so common at Sha'ar ha-Golan. It would appear, therefore, that this element in the Pottery Neolithic of Jericho had Syrian or at least northeastern connections. However, this period in the life of the site is at present rather obscure.

Between the Pottery Neolithic and the next stage at Jericho there is another gap, perhaps covering the period of the Ghassulian culture. The gap is indicated by the usual erosion stage and by a complete break in the artifacts, particularly the pottery.

THE EARLY BRONZE AGE. Toward the end of the fourth millennium, a completely new people arrived in the country. It is probable that some of the earliest evidence of their arrival is to be found at Jericho. Both groups of Pre-Pottery Neolithic people buried their dead beneath the floors of the houses. There is no evidence for how the Pottery Neolithic people buried theirs. The newcomers, for the first time, buried in rock-cut tombs, a practice that was to become standard at least until the Roman period. They brought with them pottery in simple forms—bag-shaped juglets and round-based bowls. These vessels had been found in earlier excavations—at Ai, Tell el-Far'ah (North), and Megiddo—together with vessels more elaborate in form or decoration. The Jericho tombs showed that such combinations represented a later stage because at Jericho the components could be shown as separate entities. The Jericho evidence suggested that the newcomers could be divided into A, B, and C groups. The A group, with the bag-shaped juglets and the round-based bowls, was the first to arrive at Jericho. Upon this group the B group supervened, which decorated vessels in elaborate patterns of grouped lines. Elsewhere, at Tell el-Far'ah (North) and Megiddo, for instance, the A group

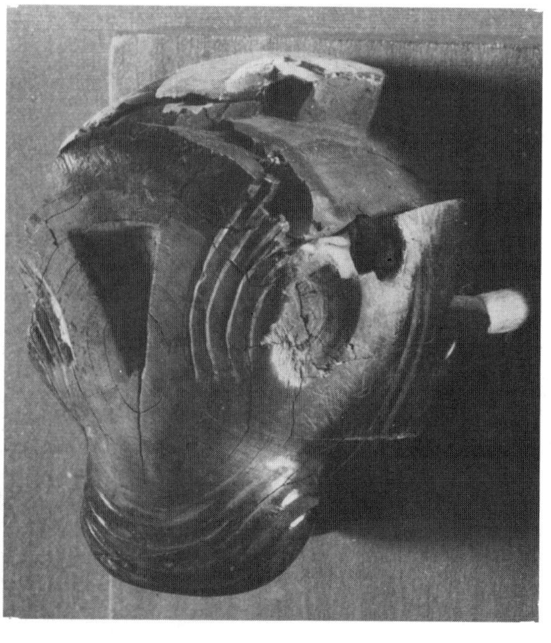

Ivory head of bull, EB.

Tell es-Sultan: plan and section of MB I tomb.

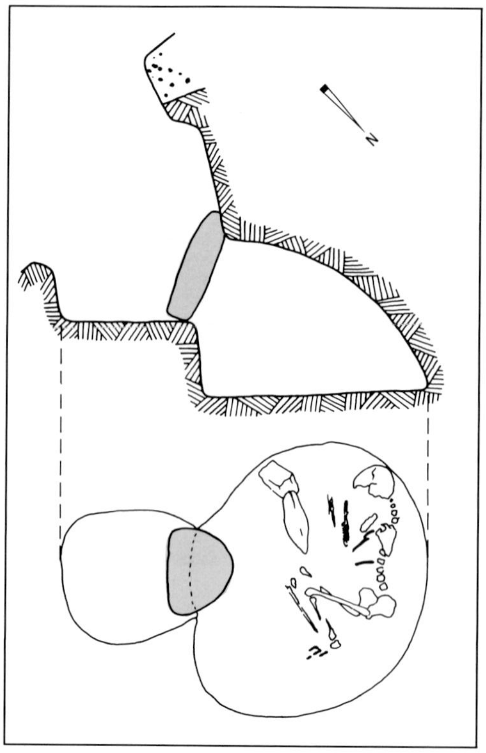

was mingled with a C group not found at Jericho, with vessels characteristically gray burnished and known as Esdraelon ware.

These combinations and permutations suggest immigrant groups arriving successively and mixing differently in the various areas. Nowhere is there evidence that they were responsible for true urban development, for almost all the evidence concerning them comes from tombs. However, at sites where there is evidence of them, urban development subsequently took place (unlike the sites at which the people of the Ghassulian culture are found). It is for this reason that the classification Proto-Urban is suggested.

The Proto-Urban phase at Jericho, with the combination of the A and B elements, developed into the urban civilization of the Early Bronze Age. The process was clearly a gradual one, and other immigrant groups may have provided the impetus toward urbanization. From the amalgamation of influences emerged a culture responsible for the walled towns that at Jericho, as elsewhere, are the country's characteristic feature for the greater part of the third millennium BCE. Jericho at this stage had grown into a steep-sided mound beside the spring responsible for its continued existence. Around its summit can be traced the line of mud-brick walls by which the Early Bronze Age town was defended. The line is uncertain only on the east side, due to the intrusion of the modern road. This line was traced in the earlier excavations. Sections cut across and into it during the 1952–1958 excavations showed that the history of the walls was complex. The section that was cut completely through the walls on the west provided evidence of seventeen stages. The walls were completely destroyed, by earthquakes, by enemies, or merely through neglect. It is impossible to estimate a time scale for the successive events, and it is impossible to correlate the succession observed in one area with that in another, for one length of wall might have collapsed or have been destroyed while other sections remained intact. It was also impossible to relate the detailed history of the defenses with the successive building stages within the town. In the areas in which the interior of the town has been investigated, there was a sequence of building periods, although not the same number of destructions found in the defenses. The remains, however, showed a succession of solidly built and spacious structures that confirms the impression that this was a period of full urban development.

A number of tombs was found covering the same period. All were large and rock cut and contained numerous burials. The interpretation of the evidence was complicated by the fact that in almost every case erosion had removed the roof of the chamber and the greater part of the shaft by which the chamber presumably was approached. It is clear, however, that in each tomb there were multiple successive burials (about a hundred skulls were found in one of the tombs). At intervals the tombs were cleared, and in many cases most of the bones were discarded, leaving mainly the skulls and the pottery vessels and other objects that had accompanied them. Many successive burials were therefore made in the tombs, but it is not known whether they represent family vaults covering a long period, or simply the current burial site for all the members of the community.

The end of Early Bronze Age Jericho was sudden. A final stage of the town wall, which in at least one place shows signs of having been hurriedly rebuilt, was destroyed by fire.

THE MIDDLE BRONZE AGE. The next building stage consisted of houses quite different from those of the Early Bronze Age—more slightly built, of irregular plan and distinctive greenish bricks. These houses, however, did not immediately succeed those of the Early Bronze Age. Between the layers associated with the two types of houses was an accumulation of a new type of pottery associated with newcomers who apparently were not yet building houses but must still have been living in tents. The stage (elsewhere called Middle Bronze Age I) is best called the Intermediate Early Bronze–Middle Bronze period, for it represents an intrusion between the Early Bronze and Middle Bronze ages, differing from both in every important respect. The newcomers were nomads and pastoralists. Even when they started to build houses, they did not develop a true urban center. The houses straggle down the slopes of the mound and over the surrounding country, and there is no evidence of a town wall. The tribal and nomadic character of the population is shown by its burial customs. The dead were buried individually in separate tombs, a feature that sharply distinguishes this period from the preceding and succeeding ones. But within this general practice there are distinctive variations, grouping the tombs into seven categories. The variations cover disposition and state of the body, form and size of the tomb and shaft, and type of offerings. These differences may represent the practices of separate tribal groups. One feature occurring in several of the groups is the very careful burial— in large, deep tombs—of skeletons that are largely disintegrated and often incomplete. This must be taken as evidence of a nomadic way of life, in which those who died during seasonal migrations were brought back for burial when the tribe returned to some focal spot.

The appearance of the Intermediate Early Bronze–Middle Bronze period people is part of the great expansion of the Amorites, to which reference is made in Sumerian records as early as the time of Sargon of Akkad (2371–2316 BCE) and the Third Dynasty of Ur (2113–2004 BCE), and who were responsible for the destruction of Byblos at about the end of the Sixth Egyptian Dynasty. It thus seems clear that it was at this stage that the Amorites, who formed an important element of the population both in this country and in Transjordan at the time of the entry of the Israelites, arrived on the scene.

Tomb from MB IIB: (right) skeleton lying on burial bed; (left) offering table with a wooden bowl, basket, and pottery.

An abrupt cultural break marks the beginning of the Middle Bronze Age (according to Kenyon's terminology, it is more often called the Middle Bronze Age II). The evidence at Jericho is very clear. The break is again in type of settlement, burial customs, tools and weapons, and pottery. Unfortunately, very little survives of the town from that period. The greater part of the summit of the mound suffered very severe erosion during periods in which the site was unoccupied. As a result, with one exception, the latest houses to survive in all the areas excavated within the line of the Bronze Age defenses belong to the Early Bronze Age. Those of the Intermediate Early Bronze–Middle Bronze period that survived did so because they were protected by the Middle Bronze Age rampart. The exception to this considerable erosion was in the center of the east side of the town, immediately adjacent to the spring. Here, there was a crescent-shaped hollow, presumably because access to the spring prevented the accumulation of the earlier levels. The Middle Bronze Age levels have survived in the hollow. Only a limited area in the lower levels has been excavated, but the evidence is sufficient to show that from the earliest stages the buildings were substantial. In this respect and in the regularity of their plans, they resemble those of the Early Bronze Age and not those of the Intermediate Early Bronze–Middle Bronze period. Like the Early Bronze Age houses beneath them, they were built in terraces on the side of the mound. A brick-built tomb found in one of the earliest stages contains multiple burials. Other burials were found in graves nearby. These burials appear to be earlier than any found in the cemetery. It may be that the position of the new inhabitants was not yet very strong, and fear of desecration by enemies kept them from burying outside the walls.

Associated with these earliest Middle Bronze Age levels was a succession of town walls of the same brick-built type as those from the Early Bronze Age. Very little of them was exposed, as to the north they were cut by the modern road and to the south they were buried by a modern water point. It seems that immediately adjacent to the south there had been a gate, with the rear of a gatehouse just on the edge of the excavated area, but it was impossible to explore this further. It is probable that elsewhere the line of these early Middle Bronze Age walls followed approximately that of the Early Bronze Age walls that had created a crest around the edge of the mound. However, for the greater part of the circuit, the earlier walls alone survived. The destruction of the summit of the later Middle Bronze Age rampart (see below) showed that there had been much erosion on the line of the walls.

It appears that the first Middle Bronze Age occupation at Jericho does not belong to the beginning of the period. No evidence was found of anything comparable with the Middle Bronze Age I remains at Aphek, in the Tell el-'Ajjul courtyard cemetery, or at Megiddo. Only one tomb in the cemetery area in Jericho is likely to belong to the Middle Bronze Age I. It is probable, therefore, that the site was first occupied at the end of the Middle Bronze Age I (more commonly referred to as Middle Bronze Age II), perhaps toward the end of the nineteenth century BCE.

For the final stage of the Middle Bronze Age, something more of the town plan can be established. The houses excavated in the 1930–1936 and 1952–1958 expeditions were small dwellings, with small and rather irregular rooms, lining two roads that in parts had shallow cobbled steps going up the slopes. These houses were called the palace storerooms by the earlier expedition, for at the time of their final destruction many of them contained a large number of jars filled with grain. However, this interpretation is improbable, both because the roads show that it was an ordinary quarter of the town, and because the building called the palace is quite obviously later in date. The houses were, in fact, of the type common then and up to the present time: the living rooms were on the first floor and storerooms and shops were on the ground floor. There were clear examples of the little one-room shops found in modern *suqs* that have a door onto the street and no connection with the rest of the house. This quarter of the town may have been one in which corn millers lived, for in one house that had grain stored on the ground floor, no fewer than twenty-three grinding querns were found in the debris that had fallen from the upper story.

Remains of a chair and its reconstruction, from an MB IIB tomb.

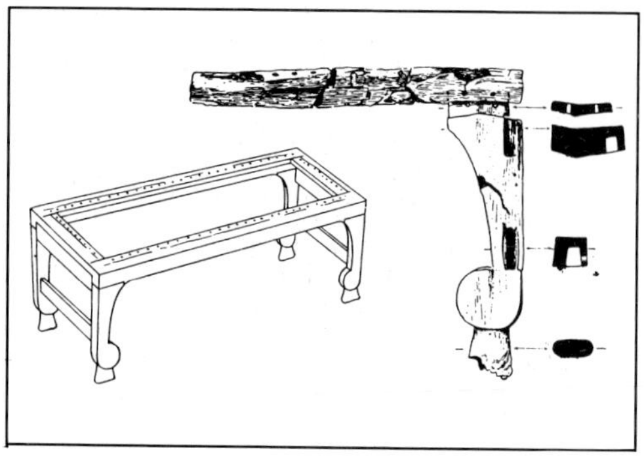

Anthropomorphic vessel, from Garstang's excavations, MB II.

This final Middle Bronze Age building phase, and several of the preceding ones, is later than the town wall described above, and extends over its top to the east, where it is truncated by the modern road and the water installations beyond. It is reasonably certain, however, that these building phases belonged to the new type of defenses that appear at Jericho, as at many other sites in the country—the type in which the wall stands on top of a high glacis. The surviving portion at Jericho consists of a revetment wall at the base (without the external ditch found at some sites), an artificial glacis overlying the original slope of the mound and steepening the slope to an angle of 35 degrees, and the face of the glacis surfaced with hard lime plaster. On the summit of this glacis was the curtain wall, at a height of 17 m above the exterior ground level and set back 26 m from it. Inside the wall was a lesser slope down to the interior of the town. Only in one place, at the northwest corner of the town, did the glacis survive to its full height, with the foundations of the wall above it. Elsewhere, erosion had removed some 6 m of it and, with them, all traces of the previous Middle Bronze Age walls. Those walls are presumed to have existed beneath the glacis and can probably be identified beneath its surviving high point.

Three stages of this glacis can be traced. The final one had a very massive revetment wall placed in front of earlier and less massive walls. This wall can be traced around nearly two-thirds of the circuit of the mound, swinging out at the north end well to the east of the present road. Here, the glacis had left the crest of the sloping edge of the mound and must have formed a freestanding rampart on level ground, as it does at some other sites with such defenses—at Qatna and Tell el-Yahudiyeh, for example.

Evidence of the Middle Bronze Age at Jericho was considerably supplemented by that from the tombs. Once more there was the practice of multiple burials, additional evidence of a break with the preceding period. From the evidence of a succession of forms of pottery and other objects, it is possible to establish a series covering the whole period of the Middle Bronze Age II. The normal practice was to provide each burial with food, furniture, and personal toilet articles. As new burials were made, the skeletal remains and associated offerings of previous ones were pushed to one side, thus creating a heap of bones and objects in the rear of the chamber. Some property in the Jericho tombs arrested the total decay of the organic material, and objects of wood and basketry often survived in recognizable form. In the pushing-aside process, many of the larger objects were broken. However, a number of tombs were found in which groups of simultaneous final burials remained undisturbed. Most of these belonged to the latest stage of Middle Bronze Age Jericho. They are probably evidence of a period of high mortality so soon before the final destruction of the town that the tombs were never reused.

From these tombs, therefore, it was possible to obtain evidence of the full normal equipment in tombs of the period. Almost without exception there was a long narrow table, usually found laden with food. The structure of the table, with two legs at one end and one at the other, presumably was designed to enable it to stand on an uneven floor. Stools and beds were also found, but these were rare and only occurred in tombs of apparently important persons. In other tombs, the dead person lay on rush mats, leading to the conclusion that beds and stools were luxury articles. Most adults were provided with baskets containing toilet articles, alabaster vessels, wooden combs, and boxes with applied bone decoration. Wooden vessels—from huge platters to small bowls, cups, and bottles—clearly supplemented the pottery vessels. In most cases, the dead were buried clothed. The garments were not well preserved, but textile fragments, usually of a rather coarse texture, were found extending at least to the knees and held in place by toggle pins on the shoulder, chest, or at the waist. Personal ornaments were not numerous. From the position of a number of wooden combs, it appears that they were worn in the hair. There were a few beads that in some cases may have belonged to necklaces. A considerable number of scarabs were found, sometimes worn on finger rings but more often apparently as pendants. It is reasonable to assume that the equipment provided for a dead person in a tomb was the same equipment to which he or she was accustomed in life.

The final Middle Bronze Age buildings at Jericho were violently destroyed by fire. Thereafter, the site was abandoned, and the ruins of two buildings on the lower part of the slope gradually became covered with rain-washed debris. The date of the burned buildings would seem to be the very end of the Middle Bronze Age, and the destruction may be ascribable to the disturbances that followed the expansion of the Hyksos from Egypt in about 1560 BCE.

THE LATE BRONZE AGE. The site was abandoned during most of the second half of the sixteenth century and probably most of the fifteenth. The conclusion formed during the 1930–1936 excavations—that there was continuous occupation in this period—was due to a lack of knowledge of the pottery from the beginning of the Late Bronze Age. The significance of its complete absence was not appreciated.

Only very scanty remains survive of the town that overlies the layers of rain-washed debris. These include the building described by Garstang as the middle building, the building he called the palace (although there is no published dating evidence and it could be Iron Age), and fragments of a floor and wall in the area excavated from 1952 to 1958. Everything else disappeared in subsequent denudation. The small amount of pottery recovered suggests a fourteenth-century BCE date. This date is supported by the evidence from five tombs excavated by Garstang that were reused in this period. It is probable that the site was reoccupied soon after 1400 BCE and abandoned in the second half of the fourteenth century. The pottery on the mound and in the tombs is certainly later than 1400 to 1380 BCE. A calculation based on biblical evidence led Garstang to suggest this date for the destruction of the site. It is probably not as late as the thirteenth century, which is the date supported by other scholars for the entry of the Israelites into the country after the Exodus.

Of the defenses of the period, nothing at all survives. The double wall ascribed to the Late Bronze Age in the 1930–1936 excavations is composed in part of two successive walls from the Early Bronze Age. For most of the circuit, only stumps survive. Even of these walls and of the Middle Bronze Age glacis that buried them, only the part on the slopes of the mound was intact. At the highest preserved point of the mound, the northwest corner, the glacis was intact, but of the wall that crowned it, only the bare foundations were still in position. There is not the slightest trace of any later wall.

Jericho, therefore, was destroyed in the Late Bronze Age II. It is very possible that this destruction is truly remembered in the Book of Joshua, although archaeology cannot provide the proof. The subsequent break in occupation that is proved by archaeology is, however, in accord with the biblical story. There was a period of abandonment, during which erosion removed most of the remains of the Late Bronze Age town and much of the earlier ones. Rainwater gulleys that cut deeply into the underlying levels have been found.

THE IRON AGE AND PERSIAN PERIOD. According to the biblical account, Hiel the Bethelite was responsible for the first reoccupation of Jericho in the time of Ahab (early ninth century BCE). No trace of an Iron Age occupation as early as this has so far been observed, but it may have been a small-scale affair. In the seventh century BCE, however, there was an extensive occupation of the ancient site. Evidence of this does not survive on the summit of the mound but is found as a thick deposit, with several successive building levels, on its flanks. On the eastern slope, a massive building from this period was found, with a tripartite plan common in the Iron Age II. The pottery suggests that this stage in the history of the site lasted until the period of the Babylonian Exile. A few finds, including jar handles with the seal impression יהד (Yehud), the name of the satrapy of Judea, belong to the Persian period. Thereafter, the site near 'Ein es-Sultan was abandoned. Later periods are represented only by some Roman graves and a hut from the Early Arab period.

Early Periods

Main publications: E. Sellin and C. Watzinger, *Jericho*, Leipzig 1913; J. Garstang, *The Story of Jericho*, rev. ed., London 1948.

Other studies: Conder–Kitchener, *SWP* 3, 224–226; J. Garstang, *AAA* 19 (1932), 3–22, 35–54; 20 (1933), 3–42; 21 (1934), 99–136; 22 (1935), 143–168; 23 (1936), 67–76; I. Ben-Dor, ibid., 77–90; G. M. Fitzgerald, ibid., 91–100; E. B. Banning and B. F. Byrd, *Paléorient* 15/1 (1989), 154–160; O. Bar-Yosef, ibid., 57–63.

Kenyon Excavation Reports

Main publications: K. M. Kenyon, *Excavations at Jericho* 1, *The Tombs Excavated in 1952–1954*, London 1960; ibid. 2: *The Tombs Excavated in 1955–1958*, London 1965; ibid. 3: *The Architecture and Stratigraphy of the Tell* (text and pls.), London 1981; id. and T. A. Holland, ibid. 4: *The Pottery Type Series and Other Finds*, London 1982; id., ibid. 5: *The Pottery Phases of the Tell and Other Finds*, London 1983; K. M. Kenyon, *Digging up Jericho*, London 1957; H. J. Franken, *In Search of the Jericho Potters: Ceramics from the Iron Age and from the Neolithicum* (North Holland Ceramic Studies in Archaeology 1), Amsterdam 1974; P. Bienkowski, *Jericho in the Late Bronze Age*, Warminster 1986.

Other studies: K. M. Kenyon, *PEQ* 83 (1951), 101–138; 84 (1952), 62–82; 85 (1953), 81–96; 86 (1954), 45–63; 87 (1955), 108–117; 88 (1956), 67–82; 92 (1960), 88–113; id., *Jericho* 1–3 (Review), *Bibliotheca Orientalis* 41 (1984), 486–489; id., *Jericho* 4–5 (Reviews), *ZDPV* 83 (1967), 88–89. — *BIAL* 19 (1982), 205–206. — 23 (Review Supplement 1986–1987), 38–42. — *Antiquity* 57 (1983), 222–223. — 61 (1987), 341–343. — *Biblica* 64 (1983), 573–574. — *IEJ* 33 (1983), 144–146. — *Syria* 60 (1983), 189–190. — 63 (1986), 161–163; id., *Archaeology* 20 (1967), 268–275; id., *Archaeological Discoveries in the Holy Land*, New York 1967, 19–28; id., *Archaeology and Old Testament Study* (ed. D. W. Thomas), Oxford 1967, 264–275; id., *ADAJ* 16 (1971), 5–30; F. E. Zeuner, *PEQ* 86 (1954), 64–68; 87 (1955), 70–86, 119–128; 90 (1958), 52–55; I. W. Cornwall, ibid. 88 (1956), 110–124; P. C. Hammond, *BASOR* 147 (1957), 37–39; id., *PEQ* 89 (1957), 68–69; M. Wheeler, *Walls of Jericho*, London 1958; D. Kirkbride, *PEQ* 92 (1960), 114–119; R. L. Cleveland, *BASOR* 163 (1961), 30–36; K. Branigan, *PEQ* 99 (1967), 99–100; M. Hopf, *The Domestication and Exploitation of Plants and Animals* (eds. P. Ucko and G. Dimbleby), London 1969, 355–359; J. Kaplan, *JNES* 28 (1969), 197–199; R. North, *Proc., 5th World Congress of Jewish Studies, 1969*, Jerusalem 1971, 35–49; id., *SHAJ* 1 (1982), 59–66; J. Clutton-Brock, *Levant* 3 (1971), 41–55; id. (and H.-P. Verpmann), *Journal of Archaeological Science* 1 (1974), 261–274; id., *Proceedings of the Prehistoric Society* 45 (1979), 135–157; J. D. Frierman, *IEJ* 21 (1971), 212–216; E. B. Smick, *Orient and Occident* (C. H. Gordon Fest.), Kevelaer 1973, 177–180; E. Strouhal, *Paléorient* 1 (1973), 231–247; N. Avigad, *Archaeology* (Israel Pocket Library), Jerusalem 1974, 113–121; H. J. Franken, (Reviews), *PEQ* 109 (1977), 58. — *Antiquity* 54 (1980), 62–63; D. P. Williams, "An Examination of Middle Bronze Age II Typology and Sequence Dating in Palestine, with Particular Reference to the Tombs of Jericho and Fara (South)" (Ph.D. diss., Univ. of London 1975); H. M. Weippert, *ZDPV* 92 (1976), 105–148; J. A. Callaway, *Sunday School Lesson Illustrator* 3 (1977), 24–32; P. Dorell, *Archaeology in the Levant* (K. M. Kenyon Fest.), Warminster 1978, 11–18; F. Godfrey, *Holy Land Review* 4 (1978), 35–47; J. Bury, *Kadath* 43 (1981), 21–29; J. A. Soggin, *EI* 16 (1982), 215*–217*; J. Zias, *BASOR* 246 (1982), 55–58; J. R. Bartlett, *Jericho* (Cities of the Biblical World), Guildford 1982; id., ibid. (Reviews), *Antiquity* 57 (1983), 160–162. — *BA* 47 (1984), 60–62. — *BAR* 10/6 (1984), 9; R. G. Boling, *BA* 46 (1983), 115–116; *American Archaeology in the Mideast*, 125–128; E. Pennels, *BA* 46 (1983), 57–61; T. Shay, *TA* 10 (1983), 26–37; id., *BASOR* 273 (1989), 85–86; G. R. H. Wright, *MDOG* 115 (1983), 9–14; id., *Journal of Prehistoric Religion* 2 (1988) 51–56; D. B. Merkes, *Near East Archaeological Society Bulletin* 23 (1984), 5–34; O. Bar-Yosef, *Current Anthropology* 27 (1986), 157–162; P. Bienkowski (Reviews), *PEQ* 119 (1987), 72. — *AJA* 92 (1988), 444–445. — *BIAL* 25 (1988), 99–102. — *JNES* 47 (1988), 189–190. — *VT* 38 (1988), 490–492. — *Bibliotheca Orientalis* 48 (1991), 649–651; id., *Levant* 21 (1989), 169–179; id., *BAR* 16/5 (1990), 45–46; K. Prag, *BASOR* 264 (1986), 61–72; G. Palumbo, ibid. 267 (1987), 43–59; R. Chapman, *BAIAS* 6 (1986–1987), 29–33; Y. Garfinkel, *Paléorient* 13/1 (1987), 69–76; M. Broshi, *BAIAS* 7 (1987–1988), 3–7; B. F. Byrd and E. B. Banning, *Paléorient* 14/1 (1988), 65–72; T. Noy, *The Israel Museum Journal* 7 (1988), 109–112; Weippert 1988 (Ortsregister); D. Gheva and M. Louhivouri, *BAIAS* 8 (1988–1989), 49–63; D. Ussishkin, ibid., 85–90; id., *BASOR* 276 (1989), 29–53; E. Braun, *PEQ* 121 (1989), 1–43; P. T. Crocker, *Buried History* 26 (1990), 100–104; 27 (1991), 5–11; M. Roaf, *Cultural Atlas of Mesopotamia and the Ancient Near East*, New York 1990, 32–35; L. E. Stager, *EI* 21 (1990), 83*–88*; B. G. Wood, *BAR* 16/2 (1990), 44–58; 16/5 (1990) 45–49; *MdB* 69 (1991), 3–28; P. R. S. Moorey, *A Century of Biblical Archaeology*, Cambridge 1991, 94–99; R. Sparks, *Mediterranean Archaeology* 4 (1991), 45–54.

KATHLEEN M. KENYON

HELLENISTIC TO EARLY ARAB PERIODS

IDENTIFICATION

Although the evidence available at present is not sufficient to establish the size of the town of Jericho in the Second Temple period, it can be assumed that at the beginning of the period it lay within the confines of the modern town. At that time the town received its water supply mainly from the spring of 'Ein es-Sultan. Like the modern town, Jericho then also probably spread out as far as the gardens and plantations.

In the Hasmonean period and in the time of King Herod, the area of cultivated lands was greatly enlarged around Wadi Qelt. This followed the construction of a network of aqueducts that carried the waters of the springs of 'Ein Duk, 'Ein Nu'eima (Na'aran), and Wadi Qelt.

Because of the rich agricultural land, the mild winter climate, and the relatively short distance to Jerusalem, a number of winter palaces were erected at the site called today Tulul Abu el-'Alayiq. The rich and upper classes of Judea also built winter homes here. The entire valley of Jericho was protected by a chain of fortresses built by the Hasmoneans on the hills around the valley. Herod continued this practice and, like the Hasmoneans, combined the fortresses with palaces.

In the Late Roman and Byzantine periods, the town was again reduced to the area of modern Jericho. A number of synagogues and churches from the Byzantine period have been found in the vicinity (see below).

EHUD NETZER

HISTORY

Historians of the Hellenistic-Roman period (Strabo, Pliny, and Josephus) stress Jericho's economic and military importance. In the tropical climate prevailing in the vale, the groves of Jericho produced high-quality dates and various medicinal plants and spices, particularly balsam, which thrives on intensive irrigation. Because of these products, famed throughout antiquity, Josephus considered the valley a veritable paradise (*War* IV, 469).

Because it was situated at the eastern approaches to Judea, the Jericho district was also of great strategic importance. This was the main reason fortresses were established here at various times. These served also to defend the plantations that constituted an important source of revenue for all rulers of the area. Jericho was a district headquarters during the Persian period. Later rulers retained this administrative pattern. It seems that the Jericho district already constituted a portion of the private domain of the ruler at the time of Alexander the Great's conquest. It became the property of the conqueror and his heirs, being "spear-won" land, according to Hellenistic custom. Consequently, the Jericho area was not urbanized and thus did not prejudice either the king's revenue or his estates.

The Syrian general Bacchides fortified Jericho (1 Macc. 9:50; Josephus, *Antiq.* XIII, 15). On the basis of the excavations at Tulul Abu el-'Alayiq, these fortifications are identified with the remains of two towers from the Hellenistic period. These are probably the forts of Threx and Taurus that were destroyed by Pompey during his Jerusalem campaign (Strabo XVI, 2, 40). The two mounds of Tulul Abu el-'Alayiq were mistakenly considered by scholars to be the remains of these forts. Under Gabinius (58 BCE), Jericho had the administrative status of a district headquarters (*Antiq.* XIV, 91; *War* I, 170). According to Talmudic sources, a large number of priests resided here. In the struggle between Herod and the last Hasmoneans, the Vale of Jericho played a prominent role. It was here that Antigonus concentrated the bulk of his military force and waged a bitter campaign against Herod and his allies (Josephus, *Antiq.* XIV, 448, 454–458; *War* I, 323, 331–335). Herod was extremely active in building Jericho and developing its environs.

It was only natural that Antony should consider Jericho a present fit for Cleopatra, who thereafter leased it to Herod. Octavian (Augustus Caesar), however, restored Jericho to Judean rule in 30 BCE (*War* I, 361–362, 396). Herod built his winter residence there (*War* I, 407; II, 57), as well as an amphitheater (*Antiq.* XVII, 194) and a hippodrome (*War* I, 659). He also erected the fortress Cypros, named for his mother, on the spot called Tell 'Aqaba today (map reference 190.139) (*Antiq.* XVI, 143; *War* I, 417). In the area between the fortress and the palace, Herod had residences built for his courtiers (*War* I, 407). Both he and Archelaus, his successor, developed the

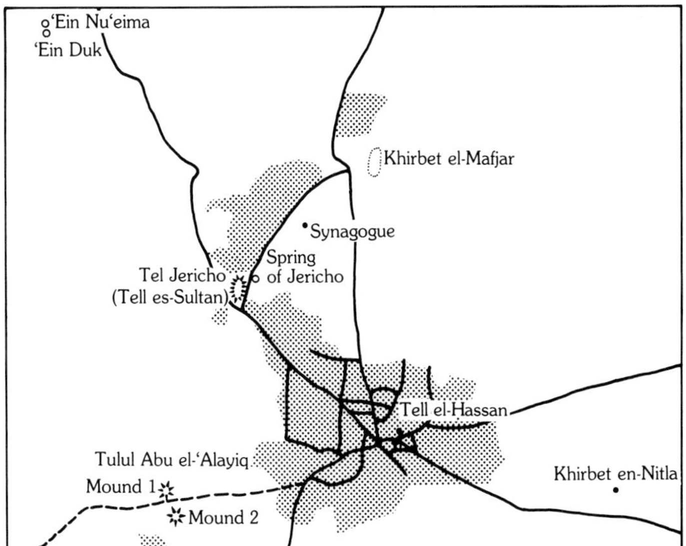

Map of the main sites at Jericho and its environs, Roman-Byzantine period.

irrigation installations until the valley was replete with ponds and gardens. Surveys and excavations have brought to light five aqueducts that distributed water throughout the city and the valley.

Upon Herod's death, his slave Simeon declared himself king and set fire to his master's palace and other edifices (*War* II, 57). Archelaus, after succeeding to power, reconstructed the palace magnificently (*Antiq.* XVII, 340). Apparently, no alteration occurred in the status of Jericho when, on the extinction of the Herodian dynasty, it became an estate of the Roman emperor. Throughout the Second Temple period, Jericho was occupied by a Jewish community, which, as may be concluded from Talmudic sources, continued to exist there in the postdestruction period. In the fourth century CE, Jericho contained a Christian community with a bishop. Christian literature, in accounts up to the sixth century, mentions five local bishops by name. The city quarreled perpetually with its Jewish rival at Na'aran (*Lam. Rab.* 1:17).

GIDEON FOERSTER

TULUL ABU EL-'ALAYIQ

EXPLORATION UNTIL 1951

In 1838, the site was first discovered by E. Robinson, at the debouchment of Wadi Qelt from the hills. In 1868, C. Warren conducted excavations at the two mounds of 'Alayiq (map reference 191.139) as part of his examination of nine mounds in the Jericho area. He cut large trenches (3 m deep) in an east–west direction and ascribed his finds to the Roman period. On mound 1, south of Wadi Qelt, many glass fragments and a Roman amphora with a seal impression on its handle were found; and on mound 2, north of the wadi, walls of sun-dried brick, some of them decorated with painted plaster, were exposed.

In 1909, an expedition headed by A. Nöldeke, C. Watzinger, and E. Sellin conducted a small excavation in the vicinity of Tulul Abu el-'Alayiq. In 1911, they conducted another (unpublished) excavation and surveyed the entire area. The excavators identified the site with Herodian Jericho; the settlement's remains—aqueducts, pools, and a crescent-shaped mound (perhaps the theater mentioned by Josephus)—were uncovered along Wadi Qelt, mostly in the north. The excavations on mound 1 yielded the remains of opus reticulatum walls (0.8–1 m wide), whose continuation was later traced by the American expedition in 1950. The remains of additional walls using the same method were found all along the wadi, as were remains of stucco and of columns grooved with stucco.

Excavations at Roman Jericho were renewed in 1950–1951. The 1950 campaign was conducted by a joint expedition of the American Schools of Oriental Research and the Pittsburgh-Xenia Theological Seminary. The work was directed by J. L. Kelso and D. C. Baramki. In 1951, the American Schools conducted another season of excavations, first directed by A. H. Detweiler, and then by F. V. Winnett and J. B. Pritchard, who supervised the field work.

Both excavations were conducted within the same complex of buildings but were published separately (by Kelso and Baramki and by Pritchard). Kelso's expedition concentrated mainly on the southern mound (1); they also probed the northern mound (2) and uncovered the remains of the opus reticulatum walls north of mound 1, on both sides of Wadi Qelt. On the top of the southern mound remains of an Early Arab fortress from the eighth and ninth centuries were found. The fortress is oval (31 m long and 27 m wide) and its outer walls are 1.05 to 1.1 m thick; it contains a polygonal courtyard surrounded by a row of rooms. The most important discovery in the fortress was that of a marble slab inscribed with twenty-six lines from the Koran. Twenty-three types of pottery from this period were distinguished; the absence of glazed and molded pottery was especially noted. Only two Umayyad coins from the eighth century were recovered. Under the fortress the excavators found remains which they mistakenly ascribed to three periods. At the center of the mound a structure, built of field stones, with a square outer face (c. 20 by 20 m) and a round inner face, was uncovered; the excavators viewed it as a Hellenistic ruin—one of the two towers of Threx and Taurus. Overlying this structure were field-stone and ashlar-built walls that had been incorporated with wooden beams. Several walls covered with opus reticulatum were also found, as was a pile of large blocks of Roman "cement," faced in similar fashion. From E. Netzer's excavations, and according to Z. Meshel's proposal, as well, it became clear that the remains under the Early Arab fortress all belonged to a single structure from the Herodian period.

North of the mound, adjacent to the southern bank of Wadi Qelt, Kelso and Baramki uncovered the remains of a magnificent structure that they called the sunken garden. In their opinion, it was part of Jericho's civic center. A broad facade, with an exedra in its center flanked by twenty-five alternating rectangular and round niches, was also uncovered here. To its north lay the "sunken garden," bounded on the north by Wadi Qelt and on the east and west by revetment walls. Alongside these walls were remains of painted plaster and stucco, as well as fragments of columns. At both ends of the facade were rooms. A set of steps (50 m long and c. 4 m wide) in front of the eastern wing led to a building on the top of mound 1. Because of the building's poor state of preservation, a reconstruction could not be made.

Fragmentary remains of a building (or buildings), also covered with opus reticulatum, were found north of Wadi Qelt. On mound 2 walls built of field stones, surrounding a square (11 by 11 m), were exposed; alongside them were sun-dried brick walls, some coated with painted plaster (like the ones previously found here by Warren). The excavators attributed some of the remains to a Roman guardpost from the second and third centuries, and others to a tower from the Hellenistic period.

Pritchard's expedition concentrated mainly on clearing a large structure (46 by 87 m) that was identified by him as a gymnasium; this identification, however, was opposed by R. de Vaux, K. M. Kenyon, and others, who suggested that it was Herod's palace, or part of it. Its northeastern corner is situated about 117 m from the sunken garden. The structure, whose walls are one meter thick on average, consists of a large courtyard apparently surrounded by columns and rooms on three sides. A passage on its west led to the remains of a structure enclosed by rows of pedestals on three sides; the excavators identified this structure with a courtyard, but it appears more likely to have been a roofed hall. A hypocaust, which was found amid the rooms, was adjoined by two rooms with floors of white mosaic within black rectangular borders. The apodyterium was flanked by well-plastered bathrooms, similar to those found at Khirbet Qumran. The building had a sophisticated water-supply and drainage system. A group of 122 pyriform

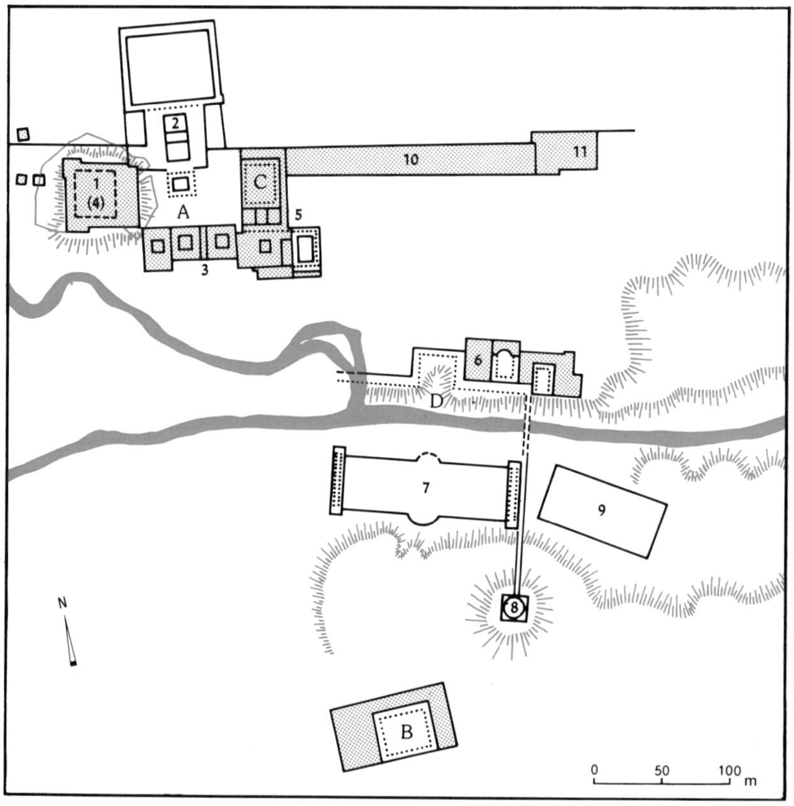

A. Hasmonean palace
1. Central building
2. Pool complex
3. Southern wing ("the twin palaces")
4. Fortified palace, on artificial mound surrounded by fosse
B. Herod's first palace
C. Herod's second palace
5. East wing
D. Herod's third palace
6. North wing
7. Sunken garden
8. Southern mound
9. Large pool, adjacent quarters
10. Dwellings/Service wing
11. Industrial installations

Tulul Abu el-'Alayiq: general plan.

Aerial view of the Hasmonean palace complex.

unguentaria for oils or spices was found—further evidence, according to Pritchard, that this building was a gymnasium.

Among the ruins of the building, 266 coins from the Early Arab period—most of them Umayyad and a few Abbasid—were found. Coins later than the ninth century are rare, probably left here by wayfarers. The few changes made in the northwest corner of the building probably date to this period.

EHUD NETZER

THE CHALCOLITHIC SETTLEMENT. The various excavations at Tulul Abu el-ʿAlayiq found Chalcolithic objects. Undisturbed Chalcolithic layers with pottery implements were first uncovered in 1951 when, under the supervision of W. H. Morton, an exploratory pit was dug south of the large Herodian facade (see above) in an area 3 by 5 m, to a depth of 3.75 m, to virgin soil. Thirteen layers were encountered. The excavators found no evidence of a typological development of the pottery in the different strata. Because there were no structural remains and the strata were rather thin layers, the excavators suggested that this was not stratification in the ordinary sense, but rather superimposed alluvial deposits from the Chalcolithic settlement that apparently had been located at the top of the cross section. It is possible, however, that these strata are linked to a yet undisclosed structure because the area of the cross section was a limited one. Among the pottery was gray-burnished ware. This ware seems to date from the Late Chalcolithic, a period paralleling part of the chronological gap between strata VIII and VII (according to Garstang's stratigraphy) at Tell es-Sultan.

GIDEON FOERSTER

EXPLORATION SINCE 1973

Excavations were carried out from 1973 by a Hebrew University expedition headed by E. Netzer, with the assistance of the Israel Exploration Society and the staff officer for archaeology in Judea and Samaria. The excavations were conducted annually from 1973 to 1983 and in 1986–1987. Mounds 1 and 2 were reexamined and large areas to the west and east of mound 2 and to the north of mound 1 were cleared; these were the most extensive excavations ever conducted at the site. In addition, the extensive system of aqueducts west and north of the site (originally surveyed by the British Palestine Exploration Fund) was resurveyed and investigated; numerous agricultural installations were discovered in the vicinity of this water-supply system.

HASMONEAN AND HERODIAN WINTER PALACES AT THE MOUTH OF WADI QELT. The extensive excavations carried out since the beginning of 1973 in the valley of Jericho and on the hills to its west have produced a considerable amount of new information that has virtually transformed scholars' conceptions of Second Temple period Jericho. The most important discoveries affect the vicinity of Tulul Abu el-ʿAlayiq, which was used as a winter resort by the Hasmonean and Herodian rulers who resided in Jerusalem. Another discovery was that the two towers referred to by Strabo (XVI, 2, 40) as Threx and Taurus (destroyed by Pompey in 63 BCE) stood not at Tulul Abu el-ʿAlayiq but on the hills to the west. Contrary to the previously accepted view that Second Temple period Jericho was concentrated in the vicinity of Tulul Abu el-ʿAlayiq, it is now certain that in the Second Temple period the city's houses extended throughout the entire valley of Jericho, which received its water supply from the springs at ʿEin es-Sultan, Naʿaran, Wadi Qelt, and ʿAuja et-Taḥta.

The area to the south of the palaces and Wadi Qelt yielded evidence of dozens of homes of the wealthy, surrounded by orchards and vegetable gardens from the end of the Second Temple period. At that time, Jericho was probably a garden city adjoining the royal estates. The location of the winter palaces in the western part of the valley, near the mouth of Wadi Qelt, was apparently chosen because of its proximity to Jerusalem. The palaces, and indeed the entire valley, were defended by a series of fortresses built on the hilltops to the west: Cypros, Nuseib-ʿUsheira, and the Dagon (Duq) fortress on Mount Qarantal.

HASMONEAN WINTER PALACE COMPLEX. The recent excavations have shown that the Hellenistic remains discovered by Kelso and Baramki on mound 2, as well as all the mud-brick walls decorated with colored plaster, were the remains not of a tower but of a palace extending over an area exceeding that of the mound proper (about 6 a.). The mound itself contained the central building of the palace, which was the original core of the Hasmonean structure. Most of the area has still to be cleared. As will be explained below, the mound under which the palace was buried is artificial and dates

Tulul Abu el-'Alayiq: plan of the Hasmonean palace.

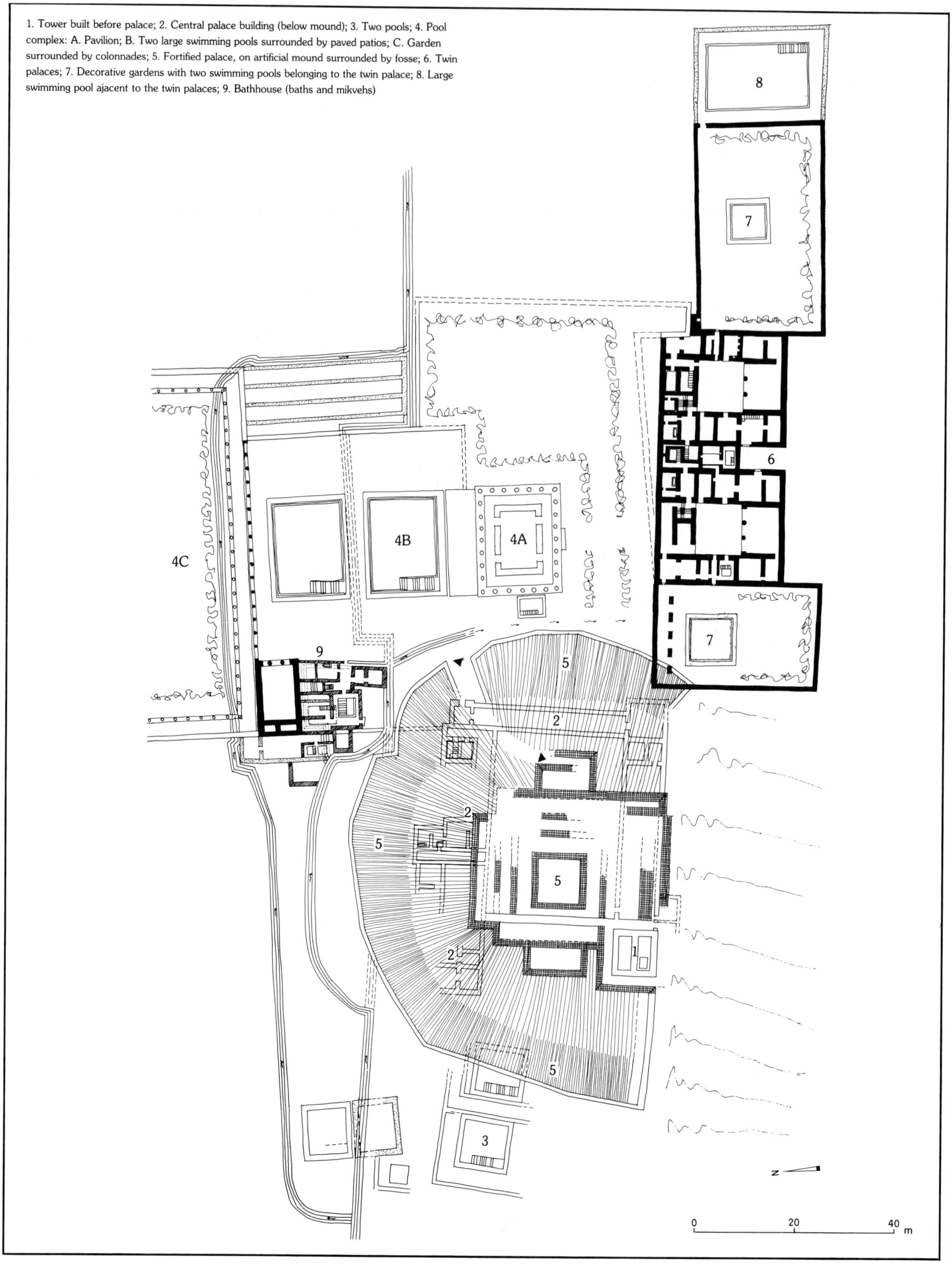
1. Tower built before palace; 2. Central palace building (below mound); 3. Two pools; 4. Pool complex: A. Pavilion; B. Two large swimming pools surrounded by paved patios; C. Garden surrounded by colonnades; 5. Fortified palace, on artificial mound surrounded by fosse; 6. Twin palaces; 7. Decorative gardens with two swimming pools belonging to the twin palace; 8. Large swimming pool ajacent to the twin palaces; 9. Bathhouse (baths and mikvehs)
8
7
6
4B
4A
4C
9
5
2
1
3
N
0
20
40
m

from the Hasmonean period—contrary to the view of the excavators before the 1986–1987 season, when it was believed to be the work of Herod.

The Hasmonean palace complex was built in stages. First to be erected was the central building (c. 50 by 55 m). This building has so far been only partially excavated. Among the several rooms exposed in the southeast of the building is a room or hall decorated with frescoes. This part of the building was in fact already excavated by Kelso and Baramki, but they erroneously dated it to the second and third centuries CE. Patches of plaster with frescoes were found in various places here during the excavation, and it is likely that other rooms were similarly decorated. In the northwest corner of the building a large mikveh (ritual bath) was discovered. It consisted of two pools, one with and the other without steps, connected by a pipe (perhaps in accordance with halakhic prescriptions regarding the communication between a mikveh's two parts). The silt at the bottom of the pools contained hundreds of small bowls that had been dropped into the mikveh while it was in use. Remains of other rooms were found nearby, including a washroom with a bathtub, next to which was an installation for heating water. Remains of rooms were also found in the northwest corner of the building. One room had walls decorated with stucco in imitation of marble slabs; similar walls were exposed at Masada, mainly in the guardrooms.

An interesting structure was uncovered at the southwest corner of the building. It was probably the site of a tower (c. 12 by 12 m) whose walls were built of ashlars, unlike the other walls of the building, which were built of sun-dried mud bricks. The original height of the tower is unknown; the walls in the center of the mound were preserved to a height of 6 or 7 m, indicating that the tower was probably one or two stories higher. In the center of the building was an inner courtyard, whose exact dimensions have not yet been determined.

Baths in the "twin palaces," Hasmonean period.

Two pools (each c. 8 by 9 m) for swimming and bathing were found side by side to the west of the building. These should probably be associated with the first stage of the building, which the excavators are now inclined to date to the time of John Hyrcanus I (134–104 BCE). At that time, the palace received its water through a clay pipe from the Wadi Qelt aqueduct.

A radical change occurred in the palace area when an aqueduct was built, probably in the first years of Alexander Jannaeus' reign (103–76 BCE), to bring water to the palace from the Na'aran springs. East of the central building (buried inside mound 2) a large complex was built, centered on two large swimming pools (each 13 by 18 m and c. 3 m deep). Shallow steps (2.3 m wide) descended to the bottom of each pool. South of the pools was a rectangular building (17 by 20 m), of which only the foundations have survived in situ. From the debris of columns and beams found in a small pool nearby, a reconstruction of a hall surrounded by colonnades in Doric style is possible. This was probably a pavilion for the enjoyment of the bathers in the pools. The two large pools were surrounded by spacious patios, paved and covered with lime plaster; beyond the patios there presumably were ornamental gardens. Whereas in the west and east there was easy access between the gardens and the adjoining patios, the northern garden (60 by 72 m) was closed off by thick walls, and probably also by colonnades. The wall that separated the garden from the pool area was eventually removed and replaced by a row of columns. The entire pool complex—pavilion, swimming pools, paved patios, and large garden in the north—was built along a single axis, attesting to a sophisticated overall plan.

Under Alexander Jannaeus, probably from 92 to 83 BCE, when the Hasmonean kingdom was in the throes of a political and military decline, another significant change occurred in the palace. In order to provide the winter palace complex with a fortress, or at least a fortified wing, the central building was filled in. To this end, foundation walls of large field stones were constructed within the building and massive fills were deposited. An artificial mound was

Pair of swimming pools in the "pool complex," from the time of Alexander Jannaeus.

created—a kind of platform on which a new building was erected. Its floor level was some 8 to 10 m higher than that of the earlier structure. Simultaneously, the mound was surrounded by a fosse, dug some 7 m deep into virgin soil. The outer bank of the fosse, which surrounded the mound on three sides—north, east, and west—was formed by a vertical stone wall, built partly of ashlar; its inner bank was a steep, earthen slope, incorporating the sloping sides of the mound. On the fourth, southern side there was no need of a fosse, as the palace overlooked the deep canyon of Wadi Shaq ed-Dabi. The digging of the fosse had cut one of the swimming pools west of the palace, causing it to be abandoned, as was the aqueduct from Na'aran running north of the new mound. The paved patios around the pool east of the mound were also slightly reduced in size. Nevertheless, the bathing and entertainment facilities around the palace seem to have continued to function.

Practically no walls or floors have survived from the fortified superstructure, which was accessible only from the pool complex on the east. The fortified building seems to have been surrounded by towers on all sides. An exception was the southwestern corner tower that was originally part of the abandoned palace. This tower was not filled with earth like the other rooms in the central building; instead, its walls were thickened, probably to increase its height. Judging from the hundreds of jars (some still with stoppers) found in the two rooms in the tower, it was used to store liquid commodities. The state of these sherds when unearthed indicated that a violent conflagration had taken place here. Also worthy of note are two clay pipes found on the slope of the mound—remnants of a siphon that pumped water to the building at the top. Although, as stated, nothing is preserved of this structure, its location at the heart of the winter palace complex indicates that it functioned as a fortified palace—despite the proximity of several other fortresses, such as Cypros and Duk.

The last important stage in the development of the Hasmonean palace complex should be attributed, in the excavators' view, to the reign of Queen Salome Alexandra (76–67 BCE). During this stage, a large new wing was built to the south of the pavilion and the large swimming pools. When it was built, however, the eastern part of the fosse between the mound and the pavilion was already in disuse. At the center of the southern wing, the excavators cleared two square palaces (each c. 25 by 25 m) almost entirely. The palaces were built side by side, as mirror images of one another, and were thus nicknamed the twin palaces. In the center of each palace was an inner courtyard (9 by 10 m), surrounded by rooms. Separating the southern room (7 by 9 m) and courtyard of each palace were two pillars in the center and piers on either side. This exedralike room probably served as a triclinium. Each palace had a main and a side entrance, as well as a staircase, attesting to the existence of a second story. Three staircases were found in the western palace. Both palaces contained bathhouses, consisting of a bathroom and an immersion pool, as well as other pools for immersion. Some of the rooms were decorated with frescoes, and there was evidence of other decorated rooms, mainly on the second story. The twin palaces were built on the southern slope, on an artificial ledge leveled off for the purpose. The northern edge of the leveled area cut 5 m down into the mound, necessitating the erection of a stone revetment along the whole of the southern wing. The buildings' other walls were mud brick. The masons undoubtedly took great pains to build the palaces in this way, partly embedded in the mound, despite the considerable technical difficulties, in order

General view of the "pool complex" in the Hasmonean palace.

to avoid blocking the view of the landscape from the higher-standing pavilion to the north.

Two spacious courtyards, each abutted to one of the buildings, were partly cleared on either side of the twin palaces. In the center of each courtyard was a swimming pool; the pool in the western court measured 8 by 8 m and that in the eastern court, 7 by 7 m. The pools were surrounded by decorative gardens; there was apparently a small building (pavilion?) next to each pool for the bathers' use. Some years later, a second, larger pool (12.5 by 20 m) was built in the eastern court (only partially excavated). This pool became part of Herod's palace (see below). It is dated to the period immediately following Salome's death.

Over the years, the water systems of the palace complex underwent many modifications. For example, when the pool complex was built, the main aqueduct ran between the two pools, but it was later diverted to a new position, leading into the garden, north of the pools. The excavators were not always able to determine the order of such changes. Changes also occurred on either side of the two large swimming pools, which were combined into a single pool during Herod's reign (see below). East of the pools, in the garden, three long, narrow storehouses (each c. 2.7 by 32 m) were built.

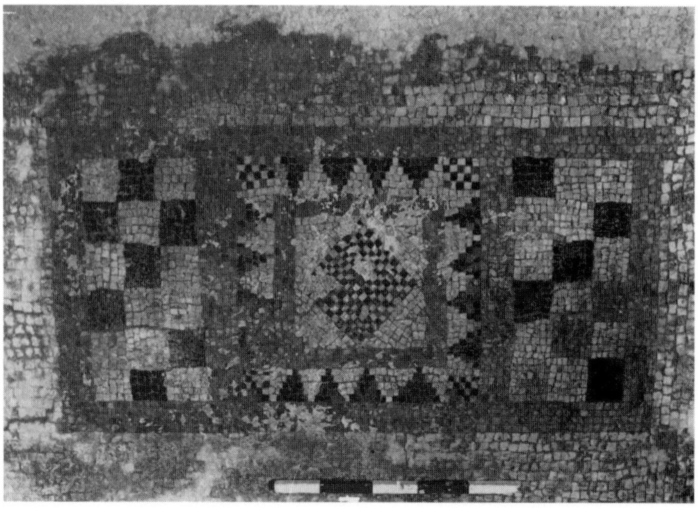

A mosaic in the bathhouse in the Hasmonean palace.

West of the pools, in an area originally occupied by a garden, there was a stepped pool that was later replaced by a bathhouse. A mikveh with two pools was built nearby, similar to the mikveh found at the northeast corner in the central building. A large hoard of objects had been thrown into the mikveh, including an alabaster mortar and a vessel resembling a rhyton (or a cornucopia). The bathhouse contained a bathroom and two stepped immersion pools, one smaller than the other (the water was heated by a furnace and a special installation). These pools were undoubtedly used ritually. Two rooms in the bathhouse had mosaic floors, as well as frescoes in the bathroom. The addition of the mikvehs and the bathhouse west of the pools may be attributed to the difficult location (and the problems of water supply) created by the fortified palace built on the artificial mound during Alexander Jannaeus' reign. The excavators are inclined to date these additions to the period from Queen Salome to the reign of Mattathias Antigonus (40–37 BCE). A hoard of twenty coins of that king was found near the bathhouse, on the paved patio around the swimming pools.

Remains of buildings from the Hasmonean period were exposed east of the palace complex, as well—particularly along the aqueduct from Na'aran, which runs through the palace area and continues eastward. At the end of the row of buildings along the aqueduct (to its south) a workshop area was found, built in the Hasmonean period (see below). The finds from the Hasmonean palace were uniform and characteristic of the Hasmonean period. As already mentioned, the origins of the palace and the building of the farm to its north (together with the aqueduct from Wadi Qelt) should be dated to the time of John Hyrcanus I.

The Hasmonean palace was still in use during the early days of Herod's reign; Aristobulus III was drowned in a pool at Jericho on Herod's orders (Josephus, *Antiq.* XV, 50–61; *War* I, 435–437). This dramatic event undoubtedly took place in one of the two pools east of the central building. The Hasmonean kings of Judea probably occupied the palace until the battle of Actium (30 BCE). At the time, Jericho was under the rule of the Egyptian queen Cleopatra, who maintained close relations with the Hasmonean dynasty. From the evidence found in the pavilion and the twin palaces, the palace was probably damaged in the earthquake of 31 BCE.

The hypocaust in the bathhouse in Herod's second palace.

Herod's Winter Palaces. FIRST PALACE. The first palace built by Herod at Jericho was excavated in 1951 by J. B. Pritchard, who identified it as a gymnasium, an interpretation that was rejected by some scholars. With the resumption of excavations at the site and the continued flow of information from excavations already conducted at Herod's other palaces, it became clear that the rectangular building (46 by 87 m) had functioned as a palace from the start. It was built on both sides of Wadi Qelt, using Roman construction techniques (opus reticulatum and opus quadratum). Netzer interpreted the complex as a palace added to the first palace and referred to it as an extended palace. As excavations progressed, however, other Herodian buildings and remains came to light in most of the area of the Hasmonean palace. Another Herodian palace took shape, built over the ruins of the Hasmonean palace and, in fact, reusing some parts of it (mainly the swimming pool). The history of Herod's winter palace can now be divided into three stages: (1) the first palace—the "gymnasium"; (2) the second palace—the structures superimposed on the Hasmonean palace; and (3) the third palace—the extended palace—comprising the luxurious palace built on both sides of Wadi Qelt. The first palace is rectangular, built facing inward, around a peristyle court; the second and third are multiwinged structures, partly open to the surrounding landscape.

SECOND PALACE. The excavations in the area of the Hasmonean palace complex revealed substantial changes, ascribed to Herod's reign. All the remains unearthed in this area belong to a single complex, which the excavators referred to as Herod's second palace at Jericho.

The final fate of Alexander Jannaeus' fortified palace, built on the artificial mound in the heart of the Hasmonean complex, is still unclear. The building was probably damaged in the earthquake of 31 BCE, but whether it was repaired, rebuilt, or simply excluded from the palace precincts cannot be determined. In any event, if Herod built a structure of his own on the high mound, it was probably residential.

While the second palace was being built, it was apparently decided to combine the two large swimming pools of the Hasmonean palace into a single pool. This was done by cutting away the strip of ground (6 m wide and c. 2 m high) separating them. This produced a pool 18 by 32 m in area. The rest of the Hasmonean pool complex (such as the pavilion) was found in ruins. The plastered patios around the pools were covered with soil and converted into a garden, as attested by the flowerpots found in situ, embedded in the ground and arranged in parallel rows alongside the pool. Similar flowerpots were found by Kelso and Pritchard south of Wadi Qelt, mainly in the sunken garden.

Southeast of the double pool with its surrounding gardens, and northeast of the by-then ruined twin palaces, a new, two-level wing was built. This new wing, referred to by the excavators as the east wing, is as large (in area) as the entire first palace. On the upper level in the northern part of the wing, the excavators exposed a large court (28 by 34 m) that was actually a garden surrounded by colonnades. This court's construction was rather unusual: its floor level was about 80 cm higher than the floors of the surrounding colonnades—rare in such courts. The elevated location of the garden demanded a special system of irrigation: two siphon systems channeled the water through clay pipes beneath the colonnades into small pools in the court's northwest corner.

The court was surrounded by rooms on three sides—north, east, and south. Particularly noteworthy was a hall (7.5 by 10 m) with frescoes on the southern side. This hall and the rooms flanking it apparently adjoined a large portico, which looked out onto the landscape to the south—to Wadi Qelt and the northern tip of the Dead Sea. The difference in height between the two parts of the east wing was as much as 6 m. It necessitated the construction of high retaining walls, backed by fills, beneath the broad portico and the rooms flanking it. A clear view of the landscape, unobstructed by the buildings on the lower level, was achieved.

Access to the east wing's lower level was by way of a staircase, of which only the lowest part has survived. This level incorporated the two Hasmonean swimming pools. The larger pool (12.5 by 20 m) was then probably surrounded by stoas, while the smaller pool became part of a garden under the portico. South of the garden, a Roman-style bathhouse was built, consisting of a row of rooms: apodyterium, tepidarium, frigidarium with a stepped pool, and a caldarium (4 by 5 m). In the caldarium, the furnace and most of the hypocaust columns are preserved in situ. Most of the bathhouse rooms had mosaic floors (mostly destroyed); evidence was also found of fresco and stucco decoration on the walls. Several rooms were built south of the Hasmonean swimming pools; to the west was a closed courtyard or hall for the bathers' use.

Herod's second palace was amply provided with gardens. Apart from the gardens around the double swimming pool, another garden was planted over the ruins of the twin palaces, as attested by the terraces and water channel discovered there. This palace, unlike the third (see below), did not follow high architectural standards. The incorporation of Hasmonean remains probably created architectural constraints; thus, while the upper level of the east wing was aligned along a symmetrical axis, the lower part was not based on a coherent architectural plan.

THIRD PALACE. Kelso and Baramki excavated mound 1 and exposed the northwestern part of the sunken garden. The garden had a magnificent facade with forty-eight niches and an exedra at its center. They also excavated some sections of walls north of Wadi Qelt. The recent excavations concentrated on the area north of Wadi Qelt, but trial soundings were also cut south of the wadi. These not only produced further details about the results of Kelso and Baramki's excavations, but revealed an enormous pool (42 by 90 m). This pool belongs to the building complex of mound 1—the sunken garden and the large wing uncovered north of the wadi. Common to all these wings is the use of Roman "concrete" coated with opus reticulatum and opus quadratum. Moreover, they were built on the same architectural plan: all the buildings (except for the large pool) are parallel to each other and to the course of Wadi Qelt where it flows between them.

The excavators referred to the extensive remains uncovered in the recent excavations north of Wadi Qelt as the north wing. It consists of entrance rooms and a passageway, two courtyards surrounded by colonnades on three sides, a luxurious bathhouse, a few small reception rooms, and two reception halls, one medium sized and the other very large. This great hall (19 by 29 m), which could accommodate hundreds of guests, is one of the most impressive structures in the entire site. Three rows of columns ran parallel to three of the walls; a broad opening in the fourth wall provided a view out to Wadi Qelt and the sunken garden. Most of the hall was paved with colorful stone slabs in intricate opus sectile patterns; some of the stones were imported (marble), while others had been quarried locally.

In the center of the hall there was originally a mosaic carpet, which is not preserved. The paving stones in most of the hall floor have also disappeared, but nearly all of the floor retains their impressions. The walls in the hall, like the walls in other rooms and courtyards in the north wing, were decorated with frescoes, usually fashioned in panels, like those at Masada. This great hall, the palace's central triclinium, was designed for banquets, ceremonies, and receptions. The wooden beams in the ceiling must have been some 15 m long (the distance between the rows of columns is c. 13 m). The reconstruction of the original floor and the ceiling's enormous beams recalls Josephus' detailed descriptions of Herod's palace in Jerusalem, which included two gigantic halls. Another connection with the halls in Jerusalem is in their

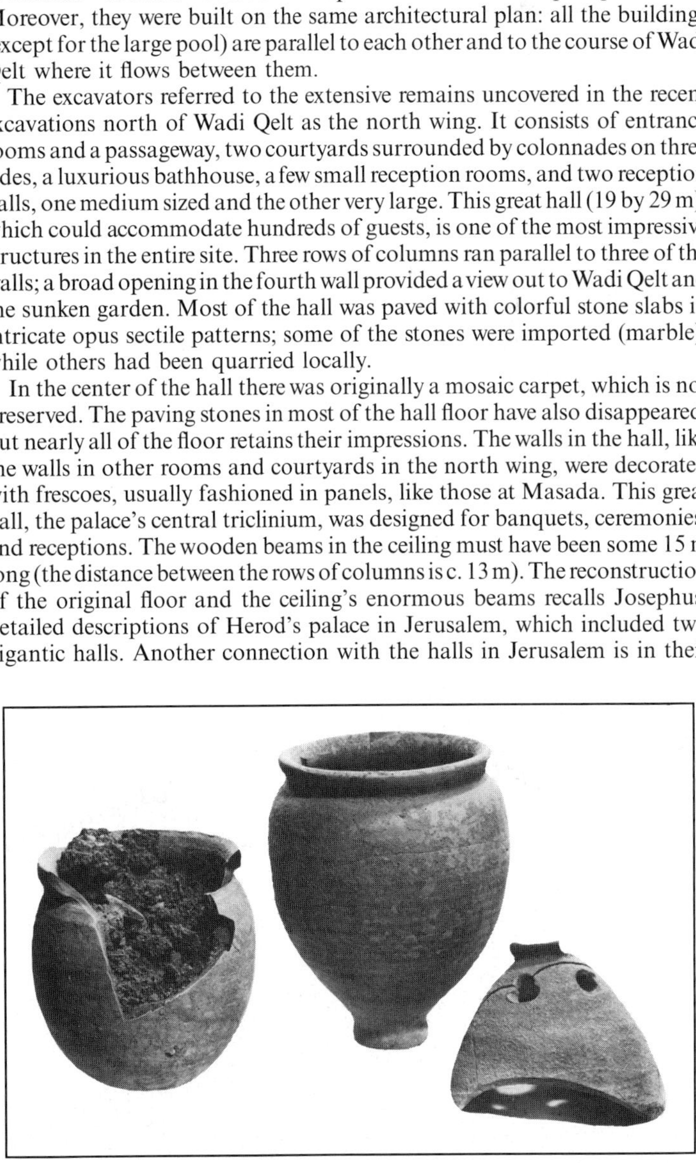

Flowerpots from the area of Herod's third palace.

names: the halls in Jerusalem were called Caesarium and Agrippium, while those in the palace at Jericho (according to Josephus) were named for Octavianus Augustus and Marcus Agrippa (*War* I, 402–407; *Antiq.* XV, 318). It is to be assumed that at Jericho, too, these names actually referred to the halls—the hall just described and another, presumably at the top of mound 1 (see below).

Adjoining the great hall was a courtyard (c. 19 by 19 m) with a semicircular exedra (diameter, 9 m) at its northern end. A garden adorned the middle of the courtyard; here, too, flowerpots were found embedded in the ground. Several reception rooms opened onto the court; the most luxurious of them was accessible from the semicircular exedra. This room (4 by 5 m) may have been a throne room. The second hall (8 by 13.5 m) was built on the other (eastern) side of the wing. Its front section, adjoining its broad entrance, was wider than its rear (its width reached 11 m). This hall also opened onto a courtyard (14 by 20 m) surrounded on three sides by colonnades and with a garden in its center. All the courtyard columns were found in the debris, evidence perhaps of an earthquake that destroyed parts of the palace. Several rooms were found between the two courts, some of them entrance rooms and passageways, others reception rooms. Preserved in one of the passageways were fresco decorations (in floral and geometric patterns), some of the most exquisite found in any of Herod's palaces.

The east courtyard contained the entrance to the bathhouse, which extended along the northeastern side of the north wing. This Roman-style bathhouse, built mainly of Roman "concrete," contained six rooms, mostly

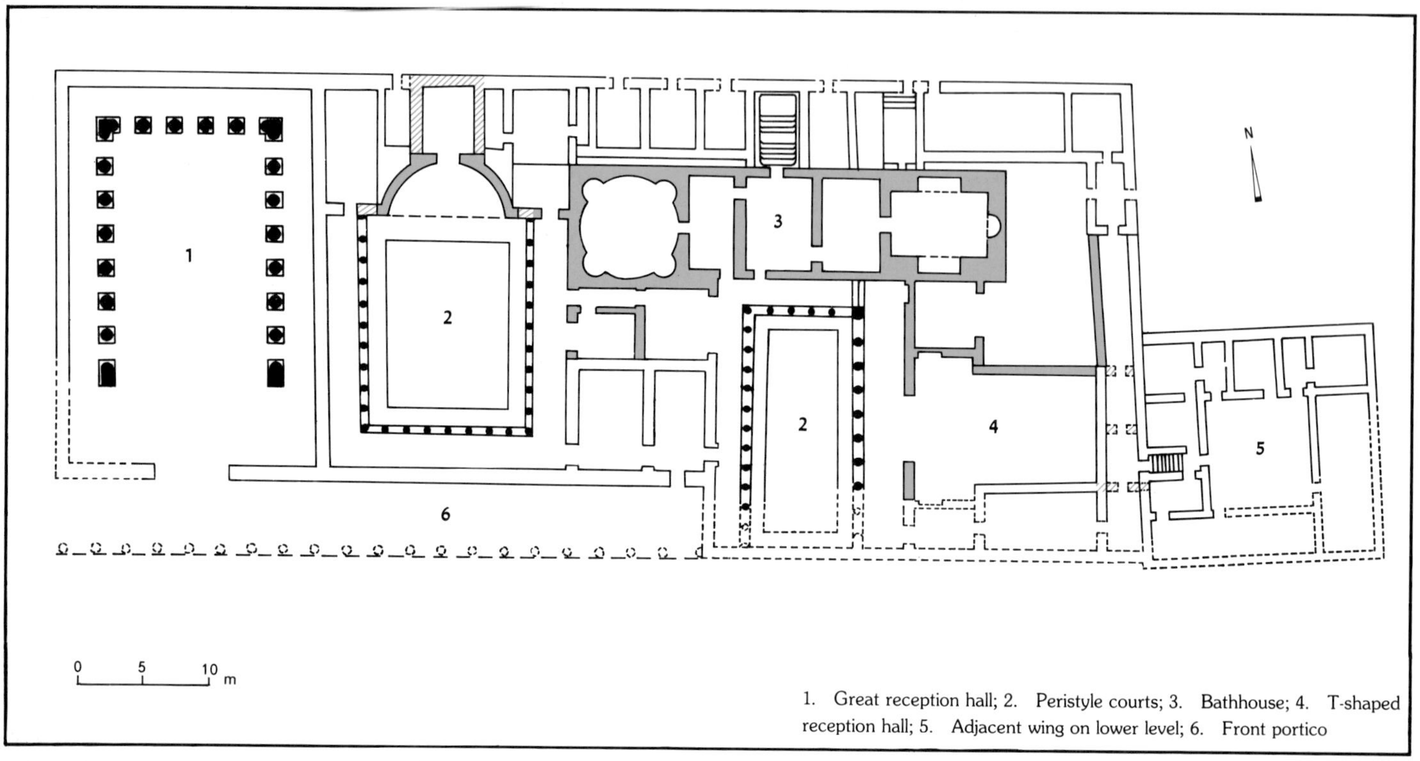

Tulul Abu el-'Alayiq: the northern wing of Herod's third palace. ***Above:*** *plan;* ***(below)*** *aerial view.*

Left and right: the circular room in the bathhouse in Herod's third palace.

in a row. The most striking room was circular (diameter, 8 m), with four semicircular niches equally spaced in its walls. This room probably had a domed roof and a large basin in its center. All that remains is the substructure that originally lay under its now nonexistent floor. This room may have served as a laconicum (sweating room). Similarly shaped rooms have been found in Roman bathhouses at Pompeii, Baia, and elsewhere. The caldarium (5 by 7.3 m) also had niches—one of them semicircular—in its walls. The adjoining room was heated by a hypocaust, as well, and may be considered an additional caldarium, or perhaps a tepidarium. The frigidarium, which contained a stepped pool, was north of the other five rooms. It was in a group of rooms that had originally been part of a large Herodian building constructed earlier than the north wing of the third palace. Another room in this group accommodated the furnace that heated the two caldaria. Another group of rooms was exposed east of the north wing. This group, too, belongs to the earlier building stage and was incorporated into the new third palace. Other remains from the earlier building, obliterated when the third palace was built, were exposed beneath the floor of the north wing. Among these were a large mikveh, industrial installations (on the eastern side of the wing), and a magnificent mosaic floor with geometric designs in black and white (on the western side of the wing, beneath the central triclinium). Judging from these remains, the earlier building may have been a villa with a service wing.

A broad, imposing colonnade can be reconstructed along the greater part of the north wing. Its continuation was discovered on the high ground west of the north wing, on the other side of a narrow gulch. The two parts of the colonnade, together with the gulch between them, in which a garden was planted, created a mirror image of the sunken garden south of the wadi. This reflects the intimate architectural relationship between the two wings of the palace north and south of Wadi Qelt.

The north wing of the palace was built mostly of mud bricks on rough stone foundations and partly of Roman "concrete" (the five rooms of the bath-

The great hall in the northern wing of Herod's third palace; the imprints of the opus sectile paving stones are clearly visible.

Opus recticulatum and opus quadratum in the facade of the "sunken garden."

house, the eastern hall, and the semicircular exedra at the end of the western court). The two construction techniques were used here in combination. It is apparent that the palace was built by a team of local builders and an additional team of builders from Rome, working simultaneously. All the walls were covered with fine lime plaster, giving the building a uniform appearance. Almost all the rooms were decorated with frescoes, and some rooms preserve evidence of stucco decorations, as well. The columns in the western court were Ionic, whereas those in the eastern court, and probably also those in the great hall, were Corinthian. The style of the columns in the portico along the facade of the north wing cannot be determined. The floors of the rooms in the north wing are mostly lime plaster on a bedding of coarse gravel. In two rooms, grooves had been cut in the plaster floor, as if in imitation of paving stones.

Thanks to the exposure of the north wing and the trial soundings cut south of Wadi Qelt, it is now possible to reexamine the conclusions from Kelso and Baramki's excavations. Mound 1 was undoubtedly artificial, built all at once as part of the third palace and not in three stages (the earliest of them Hellenistic), as surmised by Kelso and Baramki. The top of the mound was probably occupied by a circular hall (diameter, 16 m) built of Roman "concrete" and similar to the circular hall in the north wing bathhouse. Access to this hall was by means of a staircase on an arched bridge, whose remains were exposed by Kelso and Baramki. Presumably, mound 1 was also intended to raise the building standing on it to a level overlooking the tops of the surrounding palm trees.

The Hasmonean aqueduct.

Examination of the sunken garden showed that it was flanked on the east and west by double colonnades, standing some 2 m above the level of the garden itself. In front of the colonnades was a portico from which the garden could be viewed. The garden itself has not been excavated.

The third palace was planned and executed following high architectural standards. It was built on both sides of Wadi Qelt, probably to permit its residents to enjoy the seasonal flow of water in winter—just as wealthy citizens all over the Roman Empire often built their homes and palaces alongside lakes or seas. As already stated, Roman builders probably participated in the construction of this palace.

Herod's three palaces at Jericho should be viewed as a single unit that developed in stages; all three palaces probably coexisted in the last years of his reign. The first was apparently built while Cleopatra of Egypt still ruled Jericho (35–30 BCE). At the time, the Hasmonean palace was probably still standing and in the possession of the Hasmonean family. After the earthquake of 31 BCE and the death of Cleopatra following the battle of Actium, Herod took control of the Hasmonean palace and built his second palace over it (c. 30–25 BCE). The third palace is to be dated to 15 to 10 BCE. Netzer has associated the building of this magnificent structure with Marcus Agrippa's visit to Palestine in 15 BCE; in appreciation of Herod's building projects, he may have sent the monarch a Roman construction team to take part in constructing the palace at Jericho. Evidence of this team's work has also been unearthed in a building with opus reticulatum at Banias and in a similar circular building near the Damascus Gate in Jerusalem.

In theory, the third palace may have been built by Archelaus, as Kelso and Baramki indeed suggested at the start of their work. This view rests on Josephus' report that Herod's slave, Simeon, burned Herod's palace at Jericho after his master's death, and that the palace was rebuilt by Archelaus (*War* II, 57; *Antiq.* XVII, 340). However, Kelso and Baramki could not decide on a definite date; Netzer is inclined to attribute the building to Herod's extensive building projects. In Netzer's view, the conflagration in the great triclinium was Simeon's work. When this hall was repaired, the surrounding area was cleared and the hall itself separated from the palace precincts by a wall built at the edge of the peristyle court to its east.

HASMONEAN AQUEDUCTS AND FARM. The region at the foot of the western hills of the valley of Jericho, north of Wadi Qelt, received its water supply from two long aqueducts: one from the springs in Wadi Qelt and the other apparently from Na'aran. Studies have shown that the first aqueduct to be built was from Wadi Qelt, which ran along the foot of the hills and ended some 750 m north of the palaces. The waters were used to irrigate the flat area of more than 110 a. north of the palaces. This area was surrounded by walls whose foundations were exposed on the south, west, and north. These walls were built mostly in a straight line, sometimes in stretches of several hundred meters. The irrigated enclosure was a royal farm, that probably grew the date palms and persimmon and balsam trees mentioned in contemporary sources (Strabo, XVI, 2, 41; Pliny, *NH* XII, 111–123; Josephus, *War* IV 459–475).

The irrigation system was later augmented by another aqueduct that brought water from Na'aran. Northwest of the farm this aqueduct divided into two, one branch skirting the farm from the north and the other from the

A columbarium on the farm from the Hasmonean period.

Winepresses on the farm, Hasmonean period.

south. Both branches were apparently designed to enlarge the irrigated area to the east of the farm; the southern branch, in addition, increased the water supply to the winter palaces, which, in the early years, seem to have received their water through an underground clay pipe. This pipe (c. 400 m long) issued from the Wadi Qelt aqueduct and ran parallel to the south wall of the farm. The southern branch of the aqueduct crosses over the Wadi Qelt aqueduct to the west of mound 1 (near the southwest corner of the farm). The excavations exposed the point of intersection of the two aqueducts, which resembled a sophisticated modern road junction.

Two large, intact winepresses were uncovered near the Wadi Qelt aqueduct, close to the western edge of the farm. They may have been used to produce date wine and date honey. The larger winepress contains three treading vats (each 5.5 by 5.5 m), two sinking vats (each 1 by 1 by 1 m), and a collecting vat for the finished product (3 by 3 by 3 m). It is possible that these presses were located near the aqueduct because water was needed at some stage in the manufacture of date wine. Two other winepresses from the Herodian period were uncovered near the winter palaces.

At the western edge of the farm, near the ancient road that ascends from the valley of Jericho to the Bethel region, a round tower (diameter, c. 13 m) was found. It is identical in plan to the circular columbarium at Masada, and probably also to a Hasmonean tower whose foundations were discovered at Cypros. In the excavators' opinion these towers were used simultaneously as columbaria and watchtowers.

The correlation between the aqueduct system and the Hasmonean winter palace complex makes it possible to date the aqueducts and enclosure walls to the Hasmonean period. The farm was probably in use until the end of the Second Temple period.

WORKSHOP AREA. Some 150 m north of Herod's third palace, at the edge of the large Hasmonean farm, an extensive area was discovered that was mostly filled with workshops. The excavators found interconnected systems of pools, ovens, treading pavements, and drainage channels there. Also found was a square building (c. 12 by 12 m) used mainly to store liquids. The industrial installations were in use from the Hasmonean period to the first half of the first century CE. They were associated with the cultivation of persimmon and balsam reported in many contemporary sources.

LATE REMAINS. It is still unclear whether the palaces at Jericho were abandoned after Archelaus' death (6 CE) or only after the reign of Agrippa I (44 CE) or II (c. 92 CE). They may have been partly ruined in an earthquake in the mid-first century CE. In either case, by the time of the destruction of the Second Temple, in 70 CE, most of the palace areas had been destroyed and abandoned. There was only evidence of scattered habitation up to the beginning of the Early Arab period. Among these remains is a private house from the end of the first to the beginning of the second century CE. It was built on the northern bank of Wadi Qelt, on the portico of Herod's third palace (facing the sunken garden). The house was destroyed by fire (during the Bar-Kokhba Revolt?). Among the many finds in the ruins was a remarkable circular lamp with seventeen wick-holes, decorated with vine patterns. The latest remains in the area are a few isolated Byzantine structures and, on the summit of mound 1, a small fortress from the beginning of the Early Arab period.

EHUD NETZER

General: R. Beauvery, *RB* 64 (1957), 72–101; A. Spaer, *Numismatic Chronicle Series* 7/10 (1970), 23–28; 142 (1982) 140–142; P. D. C. Brown, *Levant* 3 (1971), 95–96.

History: Schürer, *GJV* 2, 3–4; 380 n. 67, 382; L. Mowry, *BA* 15 (1952), 33–42; M. Avi-Yonah, *The Holy Land*, Grand Rapids 1962; id., *The Jews of Palestine*, Oxford 1973, passim; A. Schalit, *König Herodes*, Berlin 1969.

Tulul Abu el-'Ala'iq

Main publications: J. L. Kelso and D. C. Baramki, *Excavations at New Testament Jericho and Khirbet en-Nitla* (AASOR 29–30), New Haven 1955; J. B. Pritchard, *The Excavation at Herodian Jericho 1951* (AASOR 32–33), New Haven 1958; G. Garbrecht and E. Netzer, *Die Wasserversorgung des geschichtlichen Jericho und seiner königlichen Anlagen (Gut, Winterpaläste)* (Leichtweiss-Institut für Wasserbau der Technischen Universität Braunschweig, Mitteilungen 115), Braunschweig 1991.

Other studies: J. L. Kelso, *BASOR* 120 (1950), 11–22; 121 (1951), 6–8; id., *BA* 14 (1951), 34–43; A. Augustinovic, *Gerico e Dintorni: Guida*, Jerusalem 1951; J. B. Pritchard, *BASOR* 123 (1951), 8–17; E. Netzer, *IEJ* 23 (1973), 260; 25 (1975), 89–100; id., *RB* 82 (1975), 270–274; id., *Archéologia* 110 (1977), 70; id. (with E. M. Meyers), *BASOR* 228 (1977), 1–14, 15–28; id., *BTS* 189 (1977), 8–16; id., *BAR* 4/4 (1978), 10–15; id., *ASR*, 49–51; id., *MdB* 17 (1981), 28–31; id., *ESI* 1 (1982), 44–49; 2 (1983), 50–51; 5 (1986), 55; id., *Jerusalem Cathedra* 2 (1982), 106–119; id., *Leichtweiss-Institut für Wasserbau der Technischen Univ. Braunschweig Mitteilungen* 82 (1984), 1–12; id., *Recherches Archéologiques en Israël*, 190–199; id., *Judaica* 45 (1989), 21–44; id., *Akten des XIII Internatzionalen Kongresses für Klassische Archäologie Berlin 1988*, Mainz 1990, 37–50; S. F. Singer, *BAR* 3/2 (1977), 1, 6–17; V. Tzaferis, *CNI* 26 (1976–1978), 29–31; K. L. Gleason, *BAIAS* 7 (1987–1988), 21–39; id., *AJA* 94 (1990), 299–300; J. Schwartz, *Jewish Quarterly Review* 79 (1988), 23–48; F. Brossier, *MdB* 69 (1991), 33–37; Y. Yellin and J. Gunneweg, *IEJ* 39 (1989), 85–90.

TELL ES-SAMARAT

Tell es-Samarat (map reference 1917.1413) is located approximately 600 m southwest of Tell es-Sultan, the site of ancient Jericho. The mound was first examined in 1868 by C. Warren, who cut a narrow trench from west to east but found nothing of interest. In the 1970s, evidence from aerial photographs suggested that this was the site of the hippodrome mentioned by Josephus in connection with the events in Jericho just before Herod's death (*Antiq.* XVII, 175, 178, 193). In order to clarify the situation, several exploratory excavations were conducted in 1975–1976 by the expedition digging at the winter palaces, under the direction of E. Netzer. It transpired that Tell es-Samarat is an artificial mound—the podium of a structure of which only the foundations have survived, among them the foundations of a theater built at the southern edge of the mound. Another discovery was that the level area south of the mound (c. 320 m long and 85 m wide), was surrounded by walls whose direction matched that of the structure at the top of the mound. This area in the south was probably a track for horse and chariot races (henceforth referred to as the racecourse); the surrounding walls (of which only sections of the foundations—west and south of the racecourse—have survived) were 1.6 m thick.

Adjoining the racecourse on the north was a theater, the only surviving elements of which are a circular mud-brick wall (c. 4.4 m thick) around the rear and the foundation of the artificial fill on which the seats were built; the seats themselves had been robbed. The sole indications of the seats are plastered surfaces, apparently the foundations of a horizontal aisle running around the theater approximately halfway up its height, between the seats. The diameter of the theater was approximately 70 m. Nothing whatsoever remains of the orchestra or the stage; moreover, there was probably no permanent structure behind the stage, so that the audience seated in the theater could also watch the races taking place on the track. In any case,

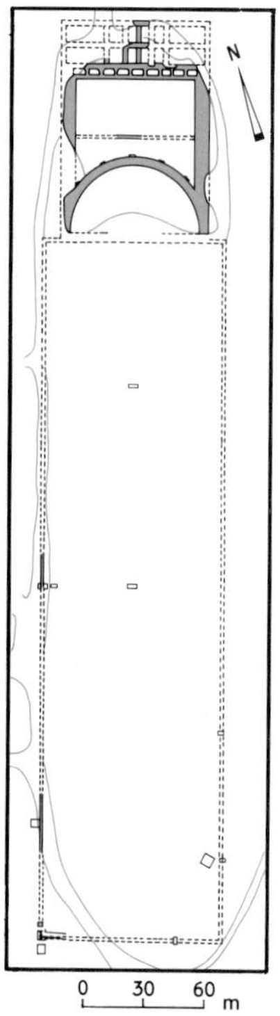

Hippodrome at Tell es-Samarat: ***(left)*** *plan;* ***(right)*** *aerial view.*

no evidence has yet emerged of seats around the racecourse, like those usually found in Roman hippodromes.

Adjoining the theater at its rear was a square structure (c. 70 by 70 m)—the artificial podium of a building of which almost nothing has survived. The podium rose some 8 to 12 m above the surrounding area and was bounded on the west and east by retaining walls (c. 7 m thick). The south side of the podium was bounded by the semicircular wall of the theater; in the north it abutted two rows of "rooms," built, like the walls, of mud bricks and containing a fill. An examination of the center of the podium revealed almost no foundations, indicating that the superstructure was probably built around an open courtyard. This courtyard was presumably surrounded by stoas on three sides. Of the building itself, only a small section of a plastered floor survives in situ; found beside it was a group of ashlar blocks, including two column drums, one of which (diameter, c. 60 cm) was adorned with frescoes resembling veined marble. The outer walls of the podium, originally built on a gradient, were probably faced with ashlars, unlike the two artificial mounds incorporated in Herod's third palace at Jericho (see above).

The scanty finds at the site, as well as isolated fragments of capitals and friezes, indicate that the complex was built and used during the Herodian period. In the excavators' view, the structure is to be associated with various events described by Josephus in connection with Herod's last days (*Antiq.* XVII, 161, 173–179, 193–195). The combination of the building that originally stood on the podium and the racecourse is unique in the Hellenistic-Roman world: a racecourse combined with a theater and a magnificent superstructure. The building on the podium may well have been used as a residence for those participating in the racing events, or even as a gymnasium. The rectangular racecourse at Jericho is similar in shape to that of the Herodian stadium discovered by the Joint Expedition at Samaria-Sebaste.

J. H. Humphrey, *Roman Circuses*, London 1986, 530–532.

EHUD NETZER

Tell es-Samarat: remains of the brick foundations at the northwestern part of the site.

Tell es-Samarat: remains of the west wall that enclosed the racetrack.

THE SECOND TEMPLE PERIOD JEWISH CEMETERY AT JERICHO

IDENTIFICATION AND EXPLORATION. In the course of a survey and salvage excavations conducted west of Jericho, a Jewish cemetery from the Second Temple period was discovered. The excavations were carried out from 1975 to 1977 under the direction of R. Hachlili, on behalf of the Israel Department of Antiquities and Museums and the staff officer for archaeology in Judea and Samaria. Some 120 tombs, spread over seven hills, were surveyed and excavated. Because of the region's arid climate, organic remains were preserved in many of them.

EXCAVATION RESULTS

THE TOMBS. The tombs are hewn in the limestone rock, following a uniform plan: a square burial room with loculi—from one to nine loculi in each. Most of the tombs have a pit in the center of the burial chamber, to enable a person to stand. The tombs' openings were blocked with hewn sealing stones or brick, stone, and earth masonry. Wall paintings and charcoal drawings are preserved in two of the larger tombs. Inscriptions were found only on ossuaries.

Burials and Burial Customs. Various methods of burial were used in the Jericho cemetery.

PRIMARY BURIAL IN WOODEN COFFINS. Many remains of wooden coffins used for primary burial (sometimes for more than one person) were preserved in the tombs. Only one coffin was laid in each loculus or on each shelf. The coffins were rectangular boxes (c. 1.9 m long) with four feet and usually a gabled lid. They were painted with red and black geometric designs and were made entirely of wood, including the hinges and nails; eleven kinds of wood were used in their manufacture.

SECONDARY BURIAL IN OSSUARIES. Some of the loculi contained secondary burials of bones collected and deposited in ossuaries (c. 60–70 cm long) hewn out of soft limestone that are similar in shape and ornamentation to the ossuaries from Jerusalem. Most of them were decorated with an incised square frame, within which incised rosettes were painted red. Inscriptions in Aramaic, Hebrew, and Greek, specifying the deceased's name and family relationship, were incised or written on some of the ossuaries.

SECONDARY BURIAL IN LOCULI AND ON SHELVES. In four tombs heaps of skulls and bones had been placed in loculi or on shelves, without ossuaries.

Two basic burial customs can be distinguished:

BURIAL IN WOODEN COFFINS. As mentioned, burial in wooden coffins was primary: the deceased was placed in the coffin, the head inclined sideways, and the arms extended alongside the body. In most of these burials, personal objects for everyday use were placed in the coffins or beside it. The tombs contained cooking pots, and small vessels were found in the pits, on the shelves, and on the floor. Many of these funerary objects were already damaged when they were placed in the tombs; quite possibly, this was intentional, for economic reasons; alternatively, the damaged objects may have had some symbolic funerary significance. It is noteworthy that funerary objects were mostly found in women's and children's tombs, and only once in men's tombs.

SECONDARY BURIAL IN OSSUARIES. Burial customs underwent a radical transformation in the early first century CE. The transition was quite sudden and comprehensive—from primary burial in wooden coffins to secondary burial in ossuaries. The procedure of secondary burial was long and complex: first the deceased was temporarily interred in a primary grave; after about a year, the bones were collected and placed in a stone ossuary. The bones were deposited in the ossuary in a fixed order, and the ossuary was placed in a loculus or on a shelf in a tomb. Funerary and other objects were placed next to (not inside) the ossuaries. Particularly noteworthy is the so-called Goliath Tomb, which contained the remains of three generations of one family, nicknamed Goliath on the evidence of the inscriptions on the ossuaries (see below). The upper chamber of this tomb was decorated with wall paintings.

Inscriptions. Some of the ossuaries bore inscriptions in Hebrew, Aramaic, and Greek, mostly incised. The majority of the inscriptions were found in two tombs. In one tomb two ossuaries, placed side by side, were found with a bowl beside them. The bowl was inscribed in Jewish script in ink on the interior and exterior with a genealogical list of three generations: "Ishmael son of Shimeon son of Palta from Jerusalem." The inscription states that the ossuaries contained the remains of this Ishmael's father and grandfather. The inscrip-

Bowl bearing a genealogical list of three generations: "Ishmael son of Shimeon son of Palta from Jerusalem."

General view of the Jewish cemetery west of Jericho.

Wooden coffin in a loculus.

tion also specifies the family's origin—"from Jerusalem"—the first reference to Jerusalem in connection with a family that lived in Jericho but proudly preserved the memory of its Jerusalem origins.

A second group of Greek and Aramaic inscriptions was found on fourteen of the twenty-two ossuaries preserved in the Goliath Tomb. Four ossuaries, found in one loculus in the tomb's lower room, provide the root of the family tree. The inscriptions on the four refer to the father of the family, Yeho'ezer son of Eleazar, his wife Shelomṣion, their son Yeho'ezer son of Yeho'ezer Goliath and his wife Salome and their sons Ishmael and Yeho'ezer. The name Goliath is appended to the names of some family members; it was probably a nickname, inspired perhaps by the physical stature of the father and some of his sons. Other inscriptions found in the tomb throw additional light on the family. The inscription on one ossuary refers to Theodotus. This Theodotus, whose Hebrew name was Nethanel, was a slave who had received his freedom—probably in Rome—from Agrippina, the wife of the emperor Claudius (50–54 CE). He returned to Jericho and was interred in his family tomb. Two inscriptions were found on children's ossuaries; the name of one child was Yeho'ezer, that of the other, 'Akavia (or 'Azabia). It is of interest that sons in several successive generations bore the same name Yeho'ezer. Another inscription, written in charcoal on the inside of an ossuary lid in the pit in the Goliath Tomb, contained eight letters of the Greek alphabet.

Wall Paintings. The remains of wall paintings are preserved on the walls of the upper chamber in the Goliath Tomb. The northern and southern walls bore drawings of vine scrolls and birds above the loculi; all that remains of the painting on the western wall is an architectural structure and floral motifs. The paintings probably date to the last stages of the hewing of the tomb, at the beginning of the first century CE.

Monument for the Dead. On one of the hills in the cemetery the excavators found a grave marker, a *nefesh*—a stone carved in the shape of a fluted column, topped by a cone. This column recalls a charcoal drawing on the wall of one tomb of three fluted columns on a square base, bearing Ionic capitals and cones.

The Finds. Four coins were found in the cemetery, three in skulls and one in the debris at the entrance of one of the tombs. Pottery and glass vessels were found in the tombs, most of them on the shelves and in the standing pits. Some tombs contained the remains of wooden coffins and vessels. Sandals were found under the skulls of women and children. Leather mattresses filled with twigs were preserved in some of the wooden coffins.

Dates of the Burials. Primary burials in wooden coffins were common in the Jericho cemetery at the end of the Hasmonean period and in the early Herodian period; this is attested by the coins and pottery found in the wooden-coffin tombs. This burial practice has been dated to the first century BCE. In this cemetery, the custom of placing bones in ossuaries replaced burial in wooden coffins during the first century CE.

*"Tomb of Goliath": **(above)** the upper chamber; **(below)** the lower chamber. Four Goliath family ossuaries were found in situ in a loculus.*

The cemetery: R. Hachlili, *BASOR* 230 (1978), 45–56; 235 (1979), 31–65; (with P. Smith), ibid., 67–72; id., *BAR* 5/4 (1979), 28–35; (with A. Killebrew), 9/1 (1983), 44–53; id., *BA* 43 (1980), 235–240; (with A. Killebrew), 46 (1983), 147–153; (with A. Killebrew), 49 (1986), 59–60; id. (et al.), *Current Anthropology* 22 (1981), 701–702; id., *PEQ* 113 (1981), 33–38; (with A. Killebrew), 115 (1983), 109–139; 117 (1985), 112–127; id., *Jewish Ornamented Ossuaries of the Late Second Temple Period* (Reuben and Edith Hecht Museum, Cat. 4), Haifa 1988; M. Rimon, *BASOR* 235 (1979), 71–73; D. Shenhav and D. Biegelaijzen, *Israel Museum Journal* 1 (1982), 75–78; L. Y. Rahmani, *BA* 49 (1986), 60–61; id., *PEQ* 118 (1986), 96–100.

RACHEL HACHLILI

THE SYNAGOGUE AT TELL ES-SULTAN

A synagogue was found north of Tell es-Sultan, indicating that in the Byzantine period the settlement here included a Jewish community. It is not altogether clear, however, whether this settlement is identical with Byzantine Jericho. Today, the latter is identified with the site occupied by modern Jericho, some 2 km (1 mi.) southeast of the mound.

In 1936, D. C. Baramki excavated the synagogue on behalf of the Mandatory Department of Antiquities. The rectangular building (10 by 13 m) is divided into a nave and two aisles by two rows of square pillars. The apse, facing southwest, in the direction of Jerusalem, is semicircular. Two steps lead to it from the nave. On the northeastern side of the structure a doorway could be identified, in front of which two columns once stood. The synagogue pavement was a mosaic with stylized geometric and floral patterns. The nave mosaic is surrounded by a guilloche border and divided into two sections. The southern one was laid in lozenges, containing a pattern of heart-shaped leaves (ivy), alternating with rhomboid-shaped plain lozenges. On the northern side, the mosaic is laid in alternating interwoven squares and circles. Along the aisles and in the spaces between the pillars are simple geometric motifs. In the southern portion of the nave, the mosaic is decorated with the image of the Ark of the Law standing on four legs, with a stylized conch above it. This is one of the few instances of a mosaic in which the ark is represented with a shell ornament, rather than a gable motif above it. The front of the ark shows two locked doors decorated with panels, the latter crossed by diagonals to give an impression of lighter and darker triangles. Beneath the Ark of the Law is a medallion containing a seven-branched menorah with a lulab on its left side and a shofar on its right. Beneath it is the Hebrew inscription: "Peace upon Israel." In this mosaic pavement, decorated mainly with geometric patterns, there is a strong tendency, then prevalent throughout Palestine, to exclude human and animal figures from synagogue mosaics.

Near the entrance is a six-line Aramaic inscription that reads: "Remembered for good be the memory of the entire holy community, the old and the young, whom the Lord of the Universe aided and were of strength and made the mosaic. He who knows their names and those of their children and of their families, may He inscribe them in the Book of Life [together] with all the pious, friends to all Israel. Amen."

Noteworthy among the finds are three glass vessels, fragments of bronze

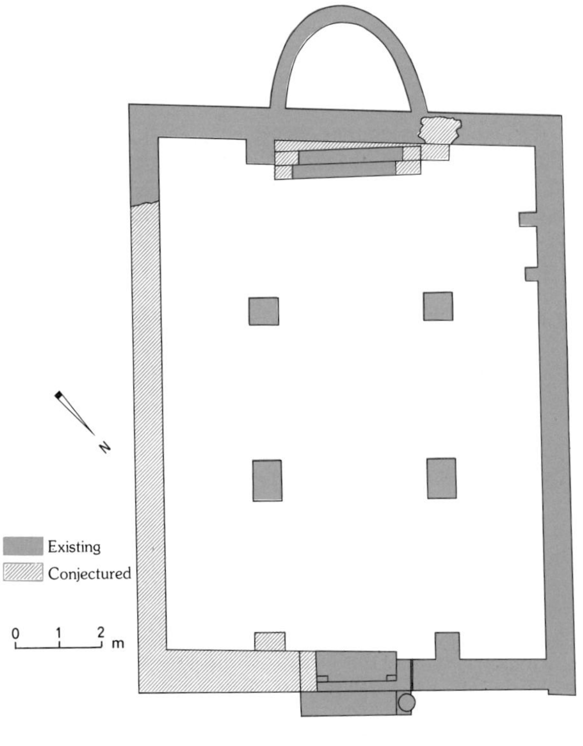

Plan of the synagogue.

Mosaic pavement in the synagogue.

lamps and other objects apparently dating to the fifth to seventh centuries CE. Three Early Arab coins found among the rubble indicate that the synagogue was in use as late as the eighth century. Baramki suggested that the synagogue was constructed at that time. It is more likely, however, that it was erected during the seventh or at the end of the sixth century.

Tell es-Sultan: Aramaic inscription in the mosaic floor of the synagogue.

TELL EL-ḤASSAN

After the accidental discovery at Tell el-Ḥassan of a section of a mosaic floor belonging to a basilica, Baramki excavated at the site in 1934, on behalf of the Mandatory Department of Antiquities. Two strata of settlement were encountered, one from the Early Byzantine and the second from the Arab period.

THE BYZANTINE PERIOD STRATUM. This stratum revealed a basilica with a nave and two aisles and, attached to the north side, two additional chambers and a portico. Two rows of arches separated the nave from the aisles. The floor is paved with mosaics. All the walls had been completely destroyed and the plan of the basilica was reconstructed solely on the basis of gaps in the flooring left by the original walls. The plan of the apse was similarly reconstructed. It apparently contained two altars separated by a row of pillars supported by a stylobate built of black stone. Except for a small section, the mosaic floor in the nave was destroyed but in the aisles, the mosaic floors, decorated with geometric patterns, were well preserved. Adjoining the wall of the northern aisle was a portico flanked by two chambers. All have mosaic floors. The area south of the basilica has not been excavated.

IDENTIFICATION. Procopius related that the emperor Justinian (527–565 CE) restored the Church of the Holy Virgin in Jericho. It can therefore be inferred that a church dedicated to the Virgin Mary had previously existed at Jericho. Procopius gives no details about the repairs ordered by Justinian. However, on the basis of the other buildings the emperor constructed throughout the country, it is reasonable to assume that this church, too, was built in a grandiose style. No information is available in the literature on the early church, either. Mosaic portions found between the pillars of the southern aisle of the basilica resemble the mosaic in the Church of the Nativity at Bethlehem, which has been assigned to the fourth and fifth centuries CE. It is therefore possible that these portions belonged to the earlier church mentioned by Procopius, whereas the basilica belongs entirely to the time of Justinian, in the sixth century.

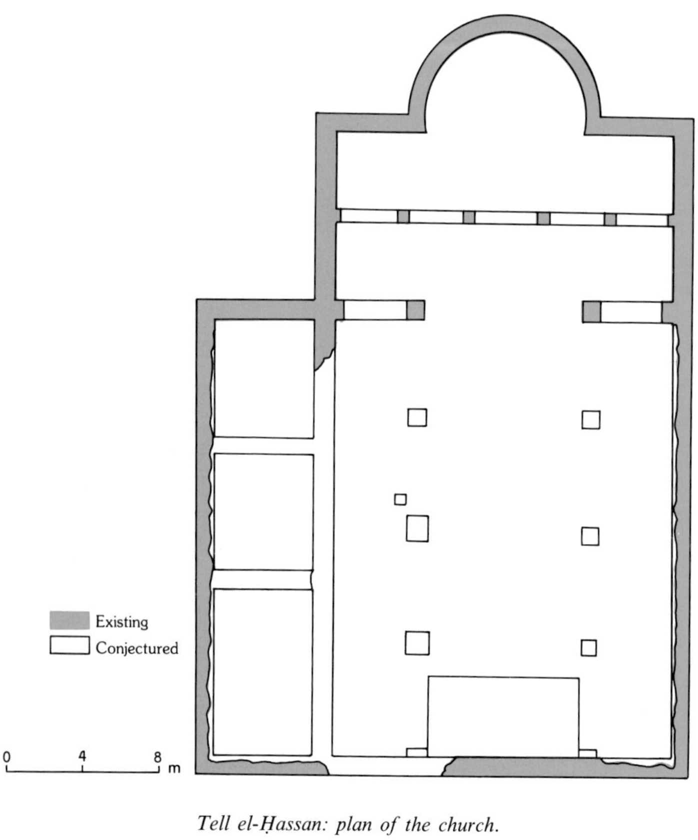

Tell el-Ḥassan: plan of the church.

THE ARAB PERIOD STRATUM. Stones taken from the walls of the Byzantine basilica were used to construct the building dated to the Arab period. During its construction, the basilica's mosaic pavement was damaged. The plan of the chambers and the position of the walls are slightly different. The pavement remained on the same level, and the mosaic floor, where undamaged, continued in use throughout.

KHIRBET EN-NITLA

The excavation undertaken by Kelso and Baramki at Khirbet en-Nitla in February 1954 was restricted to five small exploratory pits. In four of these Byzantine or Early Arab walls were revealed. The kind of buildings the walls belonged to could not be determined. In the fifth pit, a church was unearthed that apparently had existed from the fourth or fifth century until the ninth century CE. During this period, the structure underwent many architectural modifications.

The First Church. The first church was a basilica built of ashlars. Sections of the south wall, parts of a rectangular apse, fragments of a mosaic pavement, part of the foundations of the atrium, and parts of the monastery and diaconicon were excavated. Most of the foundations of the nave and of the northern aisle had been destroyed. The width of the rectangular apse indicated that the nave had been wider than the aisles. The mosaic floor of the apse, which had been severely damaged, was decorated with a pattern of hexagons and squares and with a six-line Greek inscription in the center. At the facade of the church foundations for pillars and a stylobate were discovered. This church was erected in the fourth or fifth century and possibly was destroyed at the time of the Samaritan revolt in 529.

The Second Church. The second church contained a single hall that covered approximately the area of the southern aisle of the first church. The diaconicon of the first church became the apse of the second. This church may have been smaller than its predecessor because of insufficient financial support. The church may have been destroyed during the invasion of the Persian king Khosrau II in 614.

The Third Church. The third church was constructed immediately after the destruction of the previous church. Nothing remains of its walls, so the reconstruction of its plan was based on foundation trenches and extant fragments of a mosaic floor. The third church was smaller than its predecessor. In fact, it was only a small chapel with a narthex, apparently built of dried, plaster-coated brick. The narthex was paved with white mosaic with an inscription at the entrance. The church apparently was destroyed by the earthquake of 749.

The Fourth Church. Erected a short time after the destruction of the previous church, the fourth church was also only a chapel. It was built of dried brick overlaid with a thin coating of plaster. Its area was enlarged somewhat to the north and south (roughly 30 cm in either direction), although the overall plan was similar to that of the previous church, and the earlier mosaic pavement was also reused. The small chambers adjacent to the southern side of the church testify to the existence of a small monastery. This church was not destroyed but was converted into a storage room for the fifth church, which was built on top of it.

The Fifth Church. The fifth church was a small chapel built as a second story over the previous church. This additional story was supported by a row of six square-shaped pillars set in the mosaic floor and running east–west along the building's central axis. The chapel was entered by means of an exterior stairway built against the northern wall of the fourth church. The walls of the chapel were also dried brick, and its area was equivalent to that of the fourth church. Architectural fragments and the debris of a mosaic floor that had fallen from the upper story were found above the ground-floor level. The fifth church, as well as the fourth, was erected at the end of the

'Iraq el-Emir: hall with Tobiah inscription carved in cliff.

Jericho: medallion containing a menorah, lulab, shofar, and the inscription "Peace upon Israel"; part of the mosaic floor in the synagogue.

Jericho: the triclinium in the northern wing of Herod's third palace; the impressions of the opus sectile floor are clearly visible.

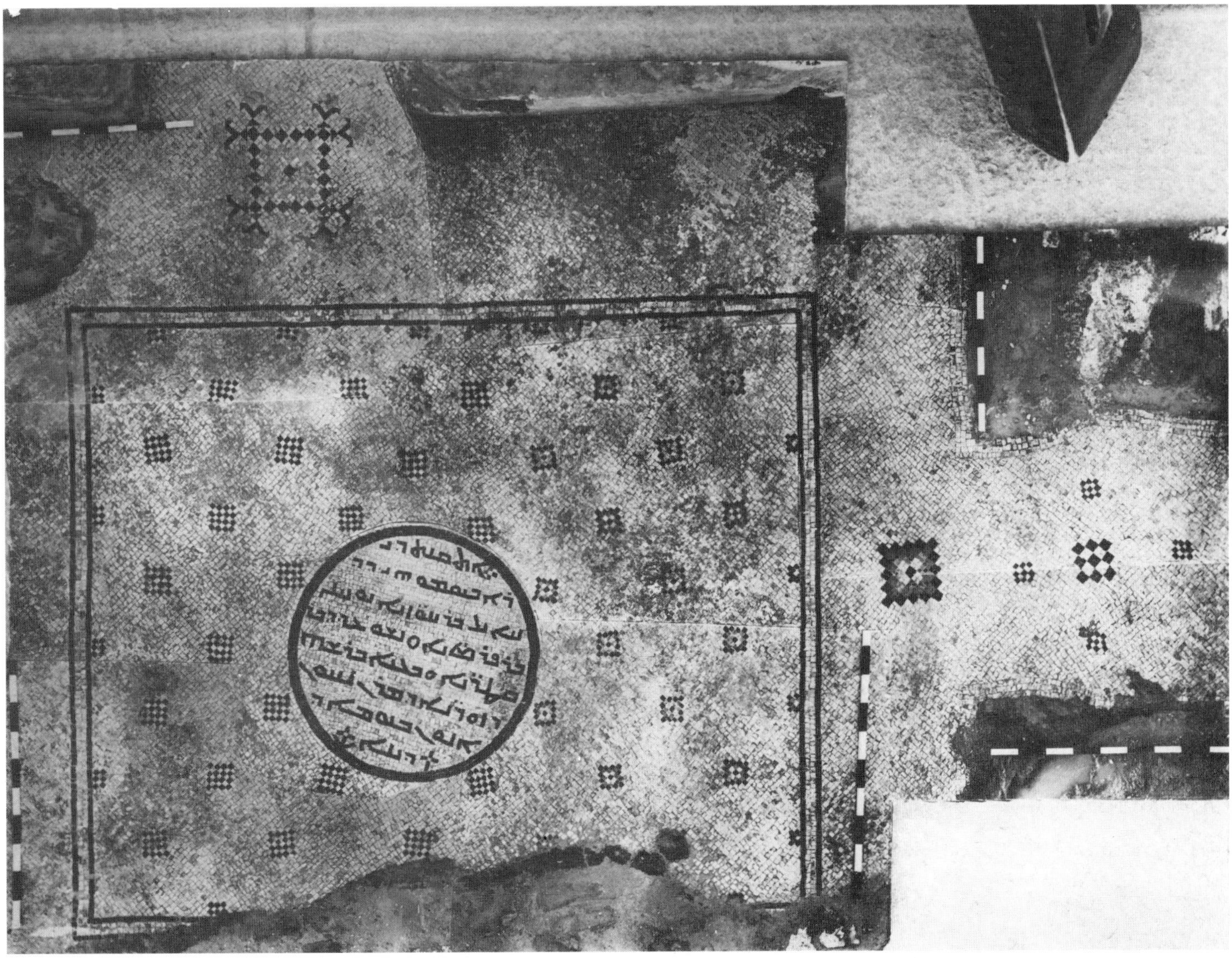

Jericho: mosaic floor in the Nestorian monastery. (The builders are mentioned in the Syriac inscription in the circle.)

eighth or beginning of the ninth century—the period of Charlemagne. At that time, the country was already under Islamic rule, a fact that may explain the poverty of its construction. The church seems to have collapsed of its own accord, in the ninth century. Ceramic finds confirm the building's existence until that time. In addition to the architectural remains, a small altar pillar of bituminous limestone, glass fragments from windowpanes, doornails, pieces of a bronze shovel, and a small pottery incense burner were recovered.

In the vicinity of the church the ruins of modest dwellings were found contemporaneous with the various churches. Ceramic finds in the area prove the existence of a settlement after the buildings at Tulul Abu el-ʿAlayiq were deserted. The finds at both sites testify to a continuity of settlement from the end of the Hellenistic until the Arab period.

The synagogue: D. C. Baramki, *QDAP* 6 (1938), 73–77; E. L. Sukenik, *Rabinowitz Bulletin* 1 (1949), 14–15; M. Avi-Yonah, ibid. 3 (1960), 35; Goodenough, *Jewish Symbols* 1, 260–262; D. Chen, *Jahrbuch des Deutschen Evangelischen Instituts für Altertumswissenschaft des Heiligen Landes* (1990), 83–88.
The churches: D. C. Baramki, *QDAP* 5 (1936), 82–86; J. L. Kelso and D. C. Baramki, *AASOR* 29–30 (1955), passim.

GIDEON FOERSTER

JERUSALEM

THE EARLY PERIODS AND THE FIRST TEMPLE PERIOD

NAME

The name of the city appears as early as the Egyptian Execration texts in the twentieth and nineteenth centuries BCE, in a form probably to be read *Rushalimum*. In the fourteenth century BCE el-Amarna letters, it appears as *Urusalim* and in the Sennacherib inscriptions (seventh century BCE), as *Uruslimmu*. The early Hebrew pronunciation was apparently *Yerushalem*, as is evidenced by the spelling in the Hebrew Bible and by its form in the Septuagint. As for the meaning of the name, it can be assumed to be a compound of the West Semitic elements *yrw* and *šlm*, probably to be interpreted as "Foundation of (the God) Shalem" (cf. Jeruel, 2 Chr. 20:16 and the usage of the word *yrh* in Job 38:6). Shalem is known from an Ugaritic mythological text as one of the two "beautiful and gracious gods," Shaḥar and Shalim (Dawn and Twilight, respectively). Salem, the shortened form of the name occurring in Genesis 14:18 and Psalms 76:2, as well as in later sources, also seems to be quite early.

The city was known also as Jebus, an ethnic name denoting the population of the city and its land in the period of the Israelite settlement down to its conquest by David. Araunah (*'wrnh, 'rwnh*), apparently the last pre-Israelite ruler of the city, is thus called Araunah the Jebusite. In the narrative of David's conquest, it is related that "the king and his men went to Jerusalem against the Jebusites . . . David took the stronghold of Zion, that is, the city of David" (2 Sam. 5:6–7). The name City of David was given to the citadel of Zion by the king himself: "And David dwelt in the stronghold, and called it the city of David" (2 Sam. 5:9, 1 Chr. 11:7).

The early name Zion specified the eastern hill of the city, with its northern summit (Mount Zion), known also as the Temple Mount, the "mountain of the house of the Lord," where Solomon built the Temple and the royal palace. Over the generations, the name Zion took on poetic connotations as an appellation for the entire city. The Temple Mount is also identified as Mount Moriah (2 Chr. 3:1) and the holy mountain in the "land of Moriah" (Gen. 22:2), vestiges of some early, obscure tradition.

There are still other early names for Jerusalem, such as the "city of Judah" (2 Chr. 25:28) denoting its status as the capital of the kingdom of Judah, and "The City" (in the Lachish letters).

HISTORY

THE PRE-DAVIDIC CITY. The archaeological finds and epigraphic and biblical evidence do not provide a well-founded basis for reconstructing the development and history of Jerusalem from its founding until its establishment as the capital of the Israelite kingdom. Even so, archaeological research has been able to determine precisely where the city was located in earliest times—on the southeastern spur below the Temple Mount (see below).

The many changes in the city's history and never-ceasing construction and destruction have largely obliterated the remains of the early settlement. Even so, various finds point to the continuity of settlement on this historical site from the Chalcolithic period. Painted ware from the Early Bronze Age I was discovered here, as early as the Parker expedition (c. 1910). Remains from the Chalcolithic period, the Early and Middle Bronze ages, as well as from the Late Bronze Age, have been found in the various excavations carried out on the southeastern spur and its slopes (see below).

Also indicative of the early settlement are cemeteries from the Middle and Late Bronze ages on the western slopes of the Mount of Olives and in the Kidron Valley, opposite the eastern hill. In one group of burials, excavated by the Franciscan Fathers on the site known as Dominus Flevit, a very rich assemblage of pottery was discovered, along with a number of alabaster and faience vessels and Egyptian scarabs, mostly from the Middle Bronze Age IIC and the Late Bronze Age I–IIA. Especially instructive are the numerous vessels from the fourteenth century BCE, mostly from the first half of that century (the Amarna period). They generally are of the same types found in a tomb with a rich pottery collection in the Naḥalat Aḥim neighborhood near Reḥavia, and in a pit on the grounds of the former Government House south of the city. These discoveries suggest sporadic settlement outside the fortified city. There is a surprisingly large number of imported pottery and

City of David, looking north: (rear) the Old City and the Temple Mount; (right) Kidron Valley.

Topographical map of Jerusalem.

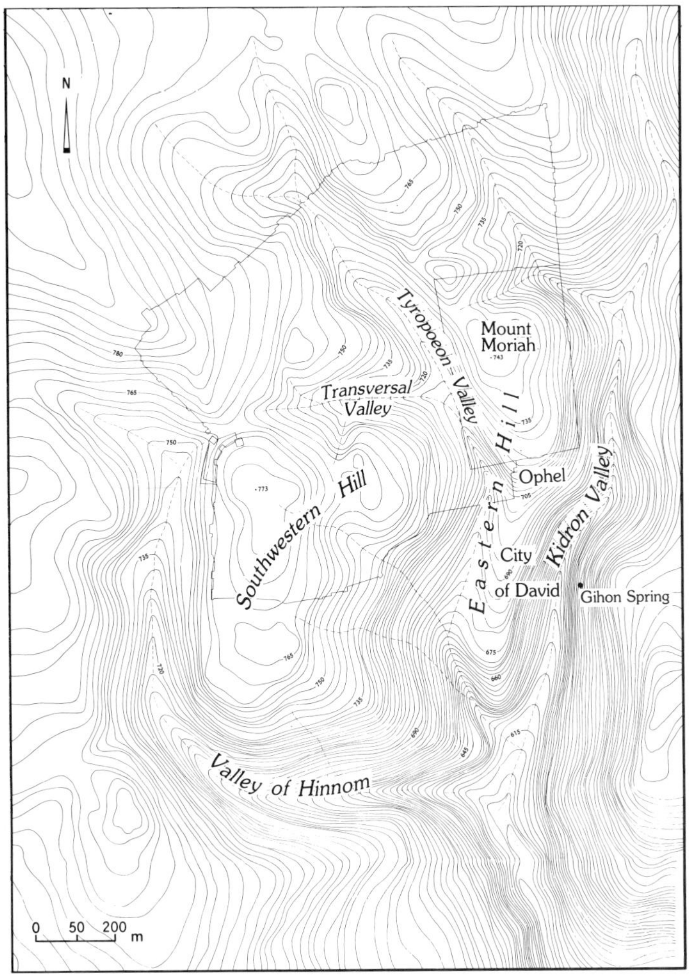

other objects, especially from Cyprus, the Aegean, and Egypt.

Information about Jerusalem in the days of Egyptian rule in Canaan, in the fourteenth century BCE, is found in the el-Amarna letters—diplomatic correspondence between the kings of various Canaanite cities and their overlords, Amenḥotep III and Amenḥotep IV (Akhenaten). They include six letters sent by the ruler of Jerusalem to the Egyptian king, confirming the allegiance of the "Land of Jerusalem" (*mât Urusalim*). This ruler, ARAD-ḪI-pa "Servant of Ḫipa" (a Hurrian goddess), wrote in the lingua franca of that period, Akkadian. However, the peculiarities of usage indicate that the language spoken in Jerusalem at this time was a West Semitic dialect (Canaanite), closely related to the Hebrew of the Bible. The ruler of Jerusalem describes the situation in Canaan, requesting assistance in repelling Egypt's enemies—disloyal Canaanite rulers and their allies, the Ḫabiru—and writes of the rebelliousness of the locally stationed Nubian troops, part of the Egyptian garrison in Canaan. Another letter, sent by Shuwardata, the ruler of a city in the Shephelah, informs the Egyptian overlord of the great danger posed by the Ḫabiru, especially after all his colleagues had abandoned him, and only he and ARAD-ḪI-pa remained to fight them. These ties between local kings, as mentioned here and in other letters, fully reveal the importance of Jerusalem in the fourteenth century BCE. It seems that the "land of Jerusalem" extended in this period over a large area in the southern hill country.

The biblical sources treating the early population of Jerusalem and its neighbors to the south (Jos. 10) use the term Amorite; toward the end of the period of Israelite settlement and at the beginning of the monarchic period, however, the term Jebusite appears in this context. It seems that Jerusalem was not Jebusite until the time of the Israelite conquest—more specifically until the conquest of the city by the tribe of Judah. Some clue of the ethnic affiliation of the Jebusites may be hinted at in Ezekiel 16:3: "Thus says the Lord God to Jerusalem: Your origin and your birth are of the land of the Canaanites; your father was an Amorite, and your mother a Hittite." And we may note that a well-known inhabitant of the city was Uriah the Hittite, who possessed a house in the City of David. Equally of interest is the name of the owner of the site of the Temple Mount, who was probably the ruler of the city when David conquered it: Araunah (or *the* Araunah, as the Hebrew has it in 2 Sam. 24:16) seems not to have been a personal name but rather the Hurrian word *ewrine* (lord), found in Hittite (and as a personal name in Ugaritic). Thus, the Jebusites are related to the Hittites, and they came to control the Land of Jerusalem, remaining a foreign enclave surrounded by the Israelites during the twelfth and eleventh centuries BCE (cf. Jg. 19:10).

City of David, area E: bone inlays, MB II.

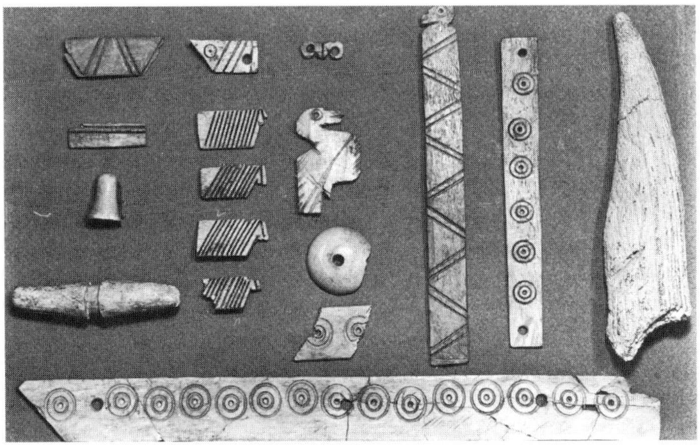

THE CITY OF DAVID AND THE TEMPLE MOUNT. The conquest of the stronghold of Zion and its becoming the City of David are described in 2 Samuel 5:6–9 as a daring deed on the part of the king, but in 1 Chronicles 11:4–7 it is ascribed to Joab, who thus gained his lofty position under David. It can be assumed that David took Jerusalem early in his reign, prior to the events around the pool at Gibeon (2 Sam. 2:12–32) and the death of Abner (2 Sam. 3:20–27). Joab was already the commander of the Judean army, and the foreign enclave between Judah and Benjamin had already been eliminated. The Jebusites were not wiped out but rather continued to live "with the people of Benjamin in Jerusalem to this day" (Jg. 1:21).

David seems to have transferred his seat from Hebron to the new capital at Jerusalem some seven years after he had conquered the stronghold of Zion.

City of David, area E: remains of a broadhouse built on bedrock, EB.

During this period several events occurred that led to the strengthening of David's kingdom. The new capital became the royal estate, thus forging a bond between the City of David and the Davidic dynasty. This bond was a decisive factor in the history of the kingdom for many generations.

There are few references in the Bible to David's building activities. His principal efforts—"And he built the city round about from the Millo in complete circuit" (1 Chr. 11:8; 2 Sam. 5:9)—should be ascribed to his early years in the city. The construction of the House of Cedar (apparently on the Millo) by craftsmen sent by Hiram, king of Tyre, apparently took place later (2 Sam. 5:11). It is assumed that David extended the fortified city on the north, toward the Temple Mount. This seems to have led to the breaching of the older city wall north of the stronghold of Zion, until Solomon "closed up the breach of the city of David his father" (1 Kg. 11:27), strengthened the Millo, and began to erect his new acropolis, including the magnificent structures on the Temple Mount itself.

The Valley Gate apparently stood on the west of the spur, in the vicinity of the later gate in the western wall of the City of David discovered in J. W. Crowfoot's excavations. The term Millo may have designated the terraces on the eastern slope of the southeastern spur that formed retaining walls for the structures above. It seems to have been here that the more splendid of the buildings in the City of David were built, such as the "house of the mighty men" (Neh. 3:16), the "house of cedar" (2 Sam. 7:2), and the "tower of David" (Song 4:4). Both man and nature worked toward the obliteration of these structures, and even in the period of the monarchy it was necessary to repair the Millo from time to time. Finds from the zenith of the period of the monarchy were discovered in the excavations carried out in the City of David by K. M. Kenyon and Y. Shiloh (see below).

David brought the Ark of the Covenant, symbol of the unity of the tribes and of the covenant between the people and God, to Jerusalem when it became the royal city of Israel, and high officials and a permanent garrison were stationed here. Thus, he established Jerusalem as the metropolis of the entire people and the cultic center of the God of Israel. In the latter years of his reign, David built an altar on the Temple Mount; according to the tradition recorded in the Bible, David purchased the threshing floor of Araunah the Jebusite, upon God's command, for this purpose. It is clear that this site was held sacred even prior to David, for an elevated, exposed spot at the approaches to a city often served as the local cultic spot. The sanctity of Jerusalem, atop the Temple Mount, is already inferred in the Book of Genesis (Mount Moriah), although this is anachronistic. The tale of the connection between Abraham and Melchizedek, king of Salem and "priest of God Most High"—who blessed the patriarch and assured him of victory over his adversaries, receiving "a tenth of everything" (Gen. 14:18–20)—is the outstanding example. Psalm 110 indicates the importance placed by tradition upon Melchizedek as an early ideal ruler. It uses his prestige to strengthen the claim on the city and the legitimacy of his successors here, the Davidic line. The story of the sacrifice of Isaac (Gen. 22) is also revealing. The spot on one of the mountains in the land of Moriah, where Abraham built his altar, was the place called "the Lord provides," the site on which David built his altar much later. Thus, David is regarded as having rebuilt the altar of Abraham on this sacred spot.

ROYAL TEMPLE AND THE ROYAL PALACE. The acropolis of Jerusalem, which included the Temple and the royal palace, had apparently already been planned during the coregency of David and Solomon, under the inspired guidance of Nathan the Prophet (2 Sam. 7). The actual construction, however, began only after the death of David, in the fourth year of Solomon's reign. The craftsmen, recruited from Tyre, labored for about twenty years, and the buildings were built according to the typical plan of Neo-Hittite and Aramean royal cities in that period. The plan kept the acropolis—the royal precinct, with the military command and the civilian government, along with the priesthood—separate from the city proper. Solomon built the Temple first, for it was not his intention merely to build a house for God and for the Ark of the Law, but to establish the central Temple of Israel under the patronage of the Davidic dynasty, to forge a perpetual bond between the royal line and the Temple, a bond that lasted throughout the period of the First Temple.

Construction of the Temple lasted for seven years. The palace complex—the palace proper, the House of Pharaoh's Daughter, the throne room, the Hall of Columns, and the House of the Forest of Lebanon—was built immediately to the south, over a thirteen-year period. Phoenician craftsmen were employed in both projects. They left their imprint on the architecture, on the actual construction work, and on the decoration and furnishings. Solomon was also active in the City of David and its fortifications, and it has been suggested that the small segment of a casemate wall located near the top of the eastern slope of the spur (discovered by Kenyon, see below) should be ascribed to his reign. At this time the city included within its walls not only the acropolis, but also markets, which were of considerable importance in international trade. It may even have been at this time that the city began its spread westward and northward, outside the walls.

CITY OF JUDAH. From the time of the splitting of the monarchy, following Solomon's death (c. 930 BCE), Jerusalem remained the capital of Israel. At the end of Solomon's reign, factional differences arose between the royal family and the priesthood over the division of authority between the secular and the religious powers. These differences recurred throughout the period of the divided monarchy, with varying foreign influences—at first Phoenician, later Aramean, and finally Assyrian. This finally led to the strengthening of the purist faction and to religious reforms. Throughout, the Temple continued to serve as the focal point of the national-religious feelings of the people.

The historiographical sources in the Bible provide considerable information on the persistent efforts of the kings of Judah to fortify and glorify Jerusalem. Special importance seems to have been attached to the establishment of the High Court in Jerusalem by Jehoshaphat (2 Chr. 19). Of interest also are the descriptions of the repairs carried out in the Temple, such as those of Joash, as well as of the fortification work carried out on the city's defenses. Uzziah and his son and coregent Joram seem to have done much to reinforce the fortifications of the city in the difficult days of Assyria's rise in the mid-eighth century BCE (2 Chr. 26:9). Great attention was then given to the new citadel (the Ophel) built to the south of the Temple Mount, between the royal palace and the City of David. At the same time, the city probably began expanding westward.

A new phase in the history of Jerusalem began under Hezekiah, when the destruction of the kingdom of Israel and its capital, Samaria (722 BCE), led to renewed ties between Judah and the remnant of the population of the Northern Kingdom. The new political and economic conditions created in the days of Sargon II of Assyria (722–705 BCE) again raised Jerusalem to the status of the entire nation's national-religious and economic center. This enabled Hezekiah to achieve a strong position for his country between Assyria and Egypt, to extend the political borders of Judah in the Negev and in Philistia ("till Gaza"), to take an important role in the trade with Egypt and Arabia, and to carry out religious reforms. However, the struggle of the Assyrian empire for hegemony over the lands of the West and its conflict with Egypt brought Judah, too, into the maelstrom of war. Among the projects of Hezekiah in Jerusalem, on the eve of Sennacherib's campaign (701 BCE), was the strengthening of the Millo and of the city wall with its towers, the construction of a new wall (2 Chr. 32:5), and the blocking of all sources of water outside the

City of David, area G: remains of Iron Age walls on the slope.

city. This also involved the diversion of the waters of the Gihon Spring through the Siloam Tunnel.

Another phase in the city's history began toward the end of the reign of Manasseh (698–642 BCE), when that king was allowed to restore the autonomy of Judah, under Assyrian tutelage. Manasseh saw to the refortification of Jerusalem, the strengthening of its citadel, and the building of a new outer wall (2 Chr. 33:14). The city reached new heights, however, in the reign of Josiah (639–609 BCE), when Judah threw off the Assyrian yoke, expanding its borders and influence and undergoing an economic revival. In the reign of Josiah, the walled city of Jerusalem already included much of the area of the present Old City, with the Makhtesh (apparently in the Tyropoeon Valley) and the Mishneh (the western hill), undoubtedly its new residential and commercial center. The city's expansion to the west has been indicated clearly by the various excavations on the southwestern hill, and especially by the discovery there of a section of a solid city wall (see below). The height of Josiah's efforts was reached in his concentration of the cult in the Temple in Jerusalem, basing it on the Scroll of the Law—apparently the nucleus of the Book of Deuteronomy—discovered during repairs he made in the Temple (622 BCE). With the restoration of the glory of the Davidic line, the status of the Zadokite family of High Priests, which had served in the Temple in the days of Solomon, was restored. This dynasty of priests played an important role in Second Temple times also, in religious and political spheres.

After the destruction of Jerusalem and the Temple by the Babylonians (586 BCE), the city continued to be the focal point of the national aspirations of the exiles and those who had remained in the country. Pilgrimages to the Temple Mount continued, not only from Judah, but also from Samaria (Jer. 41:5). The decree of Cyrus, king of Persia, in 538 BCE, gave expression to the reawakening of the Babylonian exiles. With the movement of the return from exile, the establishment of an altar, and the beginning of work on a new Temple, Jewish settlement in Jerusalem was renewed.

BENJAMIN MAZAR

TOPOGRAPHY

Ancient Jerusalem extended over several hills or spurs. Its eastern border is marked by the Kidron Valley, which separates it from Mount Scopus and the Mount of Olives. Its western border is the Valley of Hinnom, which then turns east, skirting Mount Zion, to form the southern border of the ancient city up to its confluence with the Kidron Valley near the spring of En Rogel. The city's northern border is less well-defined, for in that direction the hills on which ancient Jerusalem was built merge with the hilly areas to the north, without a clear-cut topographical demarcation. The city is divided by the Central Valley (the Tyropoeon Valley), which begins in the north, near the present-day Morasha neighborhood, north of the Damascus Gate. The valley runs south then through the Damascus Gate and along ha-Gai Street in the present-day Old City, separating the Temple Mount from today's Jewish Quarter and the spur of the City of David from Mount Zion. It was this Central Valley that separated the so-called western hill, now occupied by the Armenian and Jewish quarters and Mount Zion farther to the south, which was known in Second Temple times as the Upper City; and the main part of the eastern spur—the City of David and the Temple Mount at its crest. The area south of the Temple Mount was included in the Lower City in the Second Temple period. Josephus named the Central Valley the Tyropoeon—that is, the Valley of Cheesemakers—and the eastern ridge, the Ophel. The Gihon Spring, the city's major source of water throughout its history, gushes at the foot of the eastern slope of the City of David and still waters the orchards and other cultivated land in the Kidron Valley. Most probably, the spring and the cultivable areas in its vicinity were a major factor in encouraging permanent settlement in Jerusalem, at the end of the fourth millennium BCE, and also subsequent settlement of the City of David ridge.

EXCAVATION RESULTS

The area of the City of David, excluding the Temple Mount, is small: the width of the crest of the ridge varies from 60 to 100 m, amounting to a little more than 12 a. The inhabitants therefore needed the slope of the eastern hill for additional building. Shiloh's excavations revealed that this slope was used for building as far back as the Early Bronze Age, and that it continued to be part of the Canaanite and Israelite city up until the destruction of Jerusalem in 586 BCE. This added almost three more acres to the available area on the hill, for a total urban area of approximately 15 a. The topography of the hill, in obliging town planners, from the Middle Bronze Age IIB onward, to utilize the steep eastern slope, also necessitated building the city's defenses some way down the slope, determining the location of its eastern fortifications. This line of defenses served the city for some 1,200 years.

For several centuries, until the end of the Iron Age, the natural rock was exposed over many parts of the City of David hill, particularly on the eastern slope. In view of the steep proclivity, builders of all periods endeavored to utilize the rock as a foundation and to take advantage of walls surviving from earlier periods. These practices complicated the stratigraphical and chronological interpretation of the findings, mainly in those early excavations, which did not adapt their techniques to the hilly conditions. As a result, archaeological exploration of the area up to the 1960s involved a continuous series of errors. The following table summarizes information about continuity of settlement, including the numbering of strata, based on the finds in all areas of excavation of the Shiloh expedition.

THE STRATIFICATION OF THE CITY OF DAVID

Stratum	*Period*	*Date*	*Comments*
1	Medieval and later	14th–20th cent. CE	
2	Arab–Ayyubid	7th–13th cent. CE	
3A	Byzantine	6th–7th cent. CE	
3B	Byzantine	4th–6th cent. CE	
4	Late Roman	1st–4th cent. CE	After 70 CE, few finds
5	Early Roman	From Herodian period to 70 CE	Destruction debris
6	Early Roman		
7A	Hellenistic (Hasmonean)	First half of 1st cent. BCE to 37 BCE	
7B	Hellenistic (Hasmonean)	Second half of 2nd cent. BCE	
8	Early Hellenistic	4th–2nd cent. BCE	
9	Persian	6th–4th cent. BCE	
10A	Iron II	6th cent. BCE	Mainly destruction rubble, to 586 BCE
10B	Iron II	Second half of 7th cent. BCE	Subdivided as 10B–C in area G only
11	Iron II	7th cent. BCE	Mainly mid-7th cent. BCE
12	Iron II	8th cent. BCE	Mainly time of Hezekiah
13	Iron II	9th cent. BCE	
14	Iron II	10th cent. CE	
15	Iron I	12th–11th cent. BCE	
16	LB II	14th–13th cent. BCE	
17	MB IIB	18th cent. BCE	
18A	MB IIB	18th cent. BCE	
18B	MB IIB	18th cent. BCE	
19	EB II–III	First half of the 3rd mill. BCE	
20	EB I	31st cent. BCE	
21	Chalcolithic	Second half of 4th mill. BCE	

CHALCOLITHIC PERIOD TO IRON AGE I (STRATA 21–15). The earliest occupational level at the site produced sherds from the Chalcolithic period (stratum 21), that were washed into natural cavities in the rock. In area B of Shiloh's excavations, at the foot of the eastern slope, a deposit was found containing sherds from this level only. In most of the other parts of the slope, sherds from this stratum were found mixed with sherds from the Early Bronze Age I (stratum 20), which were also washed into cavities. In the middle of the slope, in area E1, an Early Bronze Age I–II broad building was unearthed. It was built on bedrock and had benches built along the inside of its walls (as in the Arad type houses). This building and other deposits with sherds from stratum 20—sherds that mostly accumulated in low places and in rock cavities—are the first evidence of permanent settlement in the City of David in this country's pre-urban period. In 1909, Parker excavated some tombs from the Early Bronze Age I at the summit of the hill, unearthing a few complete red-painted pottery vessels. These finds were published by L. H. Vincent. Early Bronze Age II and III sherds were found in various places, out of stratigraphical context, by Macalister, Kenyon, and Shiloh. In 1965, Kenyon cleared a shaft tomb from the Middle Bronze Age I on the eastern slopes of the Mount of Olives.

The city was first surrounded by an upright wall at the beginning of the Middle Bronze Age IIB (strata 18–17). Kenyon exposed a portion of this wall (c. 12 m long and c. 2 m thick) at the bottom of her site A. Shiloh's expedition exposed 30 m of this wall in its area E. Parts of it undoubtedly formed the nucleus of the Iron Age II wall and were buried under it (see below). The wall was built on the summit of a steep outcrop of rock, approximately 25 m above the foot of the slope. It consisted of particularly large stones and was built as a vertical wall (thickness, 2.5 m). In the next phase (stratum 18A), the wall was reinforced from the inside in several places by the addition of narrow buttresses. It rested directly on bedrock or on the remains of stratum 20. Kenyon interpreted the portion exposed in her excavations, above the spring, as a tower projecting east, probably near the Water Gate above the Gihon Spring. Shiloh revealed three phases of the city wall; they indicated that the wall's construction and earliest use date to the eighteenth century BCE. Because Shiloh exposed fragmentary construction remains from this period farther up the eastern slope, in his area E, it can be assumed that utilizing the slope by building terraces and this specific line of defense were characteristic of the City of David as far back as the Middle Bronze Age IIB.

Six of the el-Amarna letters, which date to the fourteenth century BCE, were sent from Jerusalem by its king ARAD-ḪI-pa to the pharaoh in Egypt (see above, The Pre-Davidic City), but prior to Kenyon's excavations the only evidence of Late Bronze Age settlement in Jerusalem had been found in tombs, which produced rich finds of local and imported pottery from the fourteenth to thirteenth centuries BCE. These tombs were exposed not far from the City of David: near Dominus Flevit on the western slope of the Mount of Olives, near the Government House south of the city, and in the modern Naḥalat Aḥim neighborhood to the west.

The first evidence of actual settlement in the city at this time was located by Kenyon at the top of her site A. She interpreted some retaining walls from this period as part of terraces that had been used for residential buildings. In 1978, Shiloh's expedition began to clear area G, at the top and north of Kenyon's site A. The work revealed that the fourteenth and thirteenth centuries BCE (stratum 16) had been periods of extensive construction activity. A dense network of retaining walls, built in a crisscross pattern to form, as it were, rectangular receptacles for stone fills, was found adjoining the rock

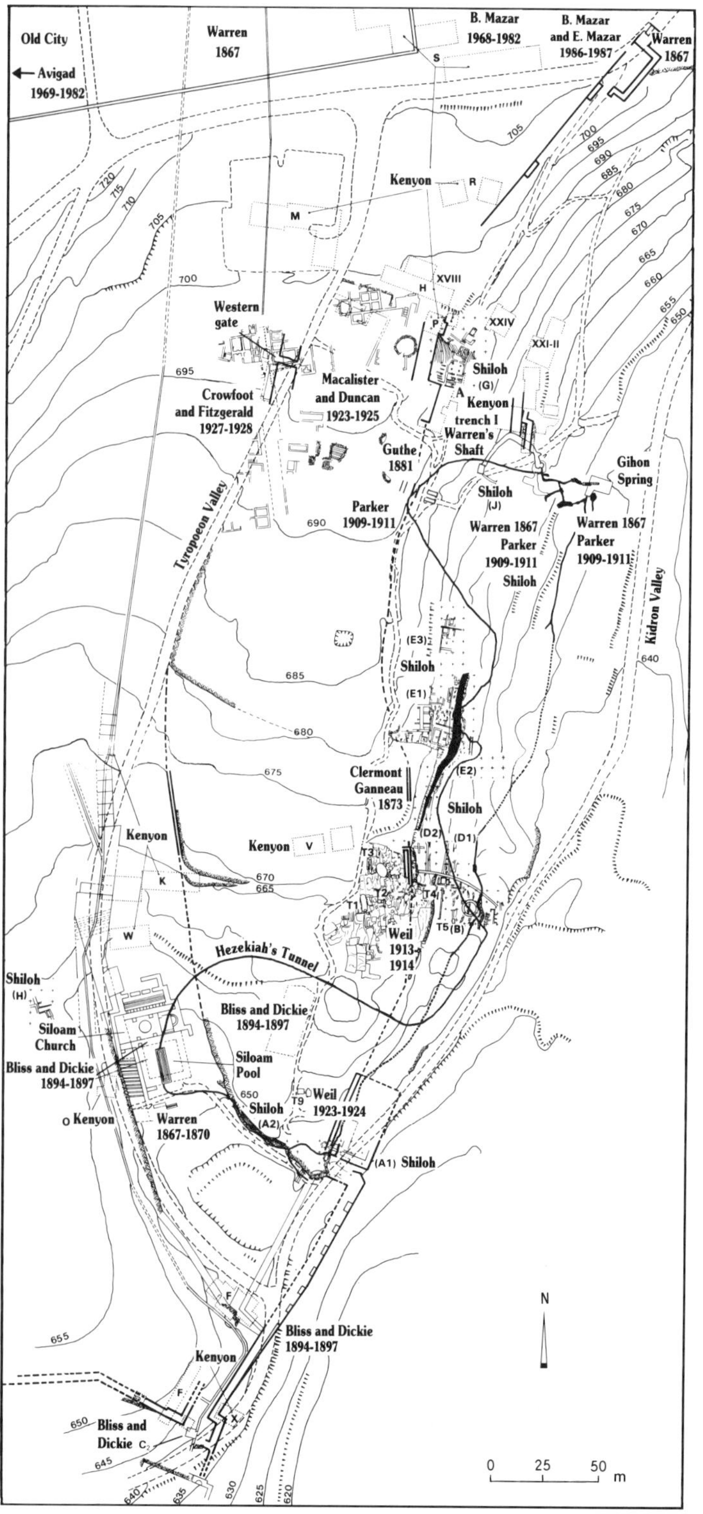

City of David: map of the excavated areas.

City of David: the excavation areas on the eastern slope.

scarp at the summit of the eastern slope. This network overlies a leveled, terraced area of some 250 sq m, which enlarged the area on the summit of the ridge on the east. The eastern edge thus descends in terraces, clinging to the slope, while its southern edge forms a steeper proclivity. The height of some of the retaining walls and terraces reaches some 8 m. This massive construction created a broad platform—different in size, building technique, and plan from the terraces which were intended for ordinary residential building—that was probably the Bronze Age fortress. It would have been at the highest point in the Canaanite city—the acropolis of Jerusalem in the fourteenth and thirteenth centuries BCE. In this writer's opinion, its first stages were probably in the early Middle Bronze Age.

There is little archaeological evidence for the Jebusite town of the twelfth and eleventh centuries BCE. Shiloh's excavations produced—for the first time in Jerusalem—an orderly stratigraphical sequence of layers dated, on ceramic evidence, to the Iron Age I. The layers in this stratum (stratum 15) were found in areas E1 and D1. Most of the finds, which were sparse and poor in quality, were characteristic of the eleventh century BCE; they do not as yet provide significant information about Jerusalem's role in the Iron Age I process of the conquest and settlement described in the Bible (Jos. 10; 2 Sam. 5:6–8).

Recently, after Shiloh's untimely death, it was realized that the terrace system ascribed by him to the Late Bronze Age contained pottery resembling that at Giloh—namely, fragments of collared-rim jars commonly dated to the Iron Age I or, at the earliest, to the transition from the Late Bronze Age to the Iron Age I. Shiloh's dating and interpretation for the terrace system throughout this entry should thus be revised. [Editors]

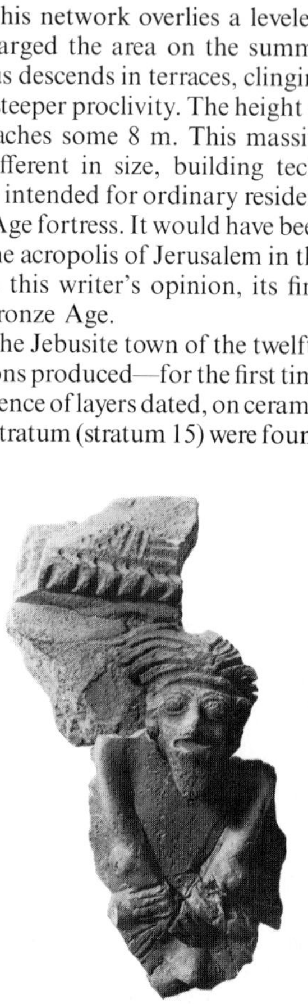

City of David, area G: decorated fragment of a cultic stand, Iron Age.

THE PERIOD OF THE MONARCHY (STRATA 14–10). The Bible describes in detail how Jebus became the capital of

City of David: remains in area G; (center) the stepped stone structure, looking west.

the kingdom of Judah and Israel in the tenth century BCE. It became a major political center and parts of it were rebuilt or annexed to the existing city to enable it to fulfill its function: "And this is the account of the forced labor which King Solomon levied to build the house of the Lord and his own house and the Millo and the wall of Jerusalem . . ." (1 Kg. 9:15). This and other biblical passages specify several architectural units built by David and, in particular, by Solomon: the Temple, the royal palace and its annexes, the city wall, the Ophel, and the Millo.

Tenth Century BCE (Stratum 14). The data now available permit a reconstruction of the contours of the city in the tenth century BCE. These data pertain to such things as town planning, public building, residential areas, defenses, and subterranean water-supply systems in Jerusalem in the tenth to sixth centuries BCE, up until the city's destruction by the Babylonians in 586 BCE.

Remains from stratum 14 (tenth century BCE) were found in areas D1 and E, on the eastern slope; here, for the first time in Jerusalem, excavators exposed a building dating to this period, and in its vicinity pottery vessels such as chalices and a ritual stand. It is known from the literary sources that most of the new building activity in this period took place in what became the acropolis in First Temple times, in the northern part of the City of David spur. (This area has been excavated by Macalister, Crowfoot, Kenyon, Mazar, and Shiloh, see below).

The first remains ascribed to the Jebusite city and to the time of David and Solomon were found by Macalister, who interpreted the walls and structures he found on the crest of the spur as fortifications from the early period of the monarchy. The impressive remains on the summit of the eastern slope, above the spring, are particularly prominent: a stepped stone structure, resembling a stone glacis, or ramp, that Macalister interpreted as part of the fortifications of the Jebusite city; and a large square tower to its south, which he explained as one of David's additional fortifications. However, Avigad has argued that the walls and structures on the summit of the ridge, inside the fortification, could not be any earlier than the Second Temple period. This was then proved by Kenyon in her excavations in sites H, M, and R. She found that the square tower was built partly on the rubble of ruined buildings from the seventh and sixth centuries BCE, and so it could not have been built before the Second Temple period. At that time, the tower was part of the fortifications of the so-called First Wall of Jerusalem. Kenyon had assumed that the stepped stone structure also belonged to this late system of fortifications. It is now understood that her revised date for the square tower was correct, but not her dating of the stepped stone structure.

Shiloh's expedition continued to expose the lower part of the stepped stone structure, right up to the eastern edge of the excavated area (area G). The structure, only the northern half of which survives, is preserved to a height of some 18 m. As more of its lower part was excavated, it was found to fit into a well-defined stratigraphical sequence: part of its base rests on the remains of the stone-filled podium of the Canaanite city fortress, which was still standing to a considerable height when the stepped stone structure was built. On the other hand, parts of its base are buried under masonry and thin earth layers dating to the ninth century, perhaps even to the end of the tenth century BCE. In the seventh and sixth centuries BCE, all of the lower half was buried under a row of well-built structures that were destroyed at the end of the First Temple period (see below). In view of this information, Shiloh dated the impressive structure to the tenth century BCE. He interpreted it as a massive retaining wall and solid platform for the fortifications of the Jerusalem acropolis at the time. In order to stabilize the basis of the new citadel—which was not built on bedrock but on Late Bronze Age II ruins—its builders had sealed the terrain by burying the ruins under the stepped structure. Its terraced construction indicates that its primary function was technical: it was a constituent of the platform supporting the buildings, rather than part of the fortifications. The upper part of this structure, as well as the area to its west on the summit of the ridge, had already been excavated by Macalister. An analysis of his findings shows that construction dating to the Second Temple period, and later, obliterated almost any trace of earlier buildings.

Proto-Aeolic capital discovered in Kenyon's excavations in the northern part of the City of David.

An analysis of the relative position of area G in the plan of the Israelite city implies that it bordered on the area rightly defined by previous excavators as the administrative-public sector of the city, between the Upper City to the south and the Temple compound to the north. There are further, secondary proofs of this assertion: Kenyon, in her site H, at the northwestern corner of the stepped stone structure and inside it, exposed a fragment of a fortification wall turning west. In view of its construction, she interpreted it as part of a tenth-century BCE casemate wall. In the nearby rubble, in Kenyon's square A-XVIII, northeast of the stepped stone structure, there was a large quantity of ashlar blocks and a proto-Aeolic capital. These two architectural elements, both common in important buildings at other Iron Age II administrative centers (Samaria, Megiddo, Hazor, and Ramat Raḥel), suggest that such an administrative building stood here, too. Further confirmation for this hypothesis comes from the proximity of the entrance to Warren's Shaft (see below). It is thus assumed that the stepped stone structure was part of the southeastern corner of the city citadel—David's stronghold—which rose above the Lower City to the south and stood between it and the Temple Mount. The builders of the new capital maintained the fragment of the Canaanite city within the Lower City and the citadel, rebuilding it as David's stronghold. The main alteration in the city plan took place to the north, when the Temple Mount was annexed to the Upper City.

The question of Jerusalem's western defenses has yet to be settled. In 1927–1928 J. W. Crowfoot, working to the west of Macalister's excavations and at

The Ophel: stone seal bearing the image of a griffin, Iron Age.

the head of the eastern bank of the Central Valley, exposed a stretch of wall 27 m long, about 8 m thick, and 7 m high. Built in this wall, which defended the western part of the City of David ridge, was a gate known as the Western Gate or Valley Gate. Both the wall and gate were still in use under the Hasmoneans but had presumably been built a good deal earlier. They may have been part of the fortifications on the western side of the City of David in the tenth to eighth centuries BCE, before the city spread westward to the western hill.

David's citadel, which remained standing from the time of David and Solomon until the destruction of the First Temple, is architecturally well suited to the definition of the term Ophel, the biblical equivalent of "acropolis" (Is. 32:14; 2 Chr. 27:3, 33:14). The term probably denoted the citadel of the Israelite city, built in Jerusalem on top of the remains of the Canaanite city fortress.

The location and nature of the Millo (2 Sam. 5:9; 1 Kg. 9:15; 2 Chr. 32:5) have also been a subject of considerable debate. Kenyon interpreted the term as denoting terraces and stone fills built in the Iron Age II to support houses. However, because these terraces fulfilled different functions in the city from the Middle Bronze Age IIB onward, their construction in the Iron Age constituted no innovation. It may be worth reexamining the theory that the Millo (fill?) was located between the Temple Mount and David's citadel. The rock-elevation data from Mazar's excavations to the north of the City of David and Shiloh's excavations in area G in the center of the city imply the existence of a shallow saddle between these regions. This saddle may have been filled in and leveled in the tenth century BCE, to create a topographical and conceptual link between the location of the old citadel and the annexed area to the north. In the southeastern corner of the excavations of B. Mazar and E. Mazar, impressive remains of massive walls were found. Some of the walls, approximately 1.4 m wide, had been part of a monumental complex destroyed at the end of the Iron Age. In view of the solidity and location of these remains, B. Mazar suggested that they might represent "the house of Millo" (2 Kg. 12:21, see below, The Ophel).

The remains of those buildings are the only masonry from the Iron Age II found in proximity to the Temple Mount. No excavation in Jerusalem has yet produced finds relating to the Temple itself; all reconstructions of it and of its environs rely on the details in the biblical description, as well as on comparative studies of construction techniques and architectural constituents known from other, contemporary administrative centers in this country and in Syria.

Ninth Century BCE (Stratum 13). Remains belonging to stratum 13 (ninth century BCE) were meager, in comparison with the remains antedating and postdating this stratum. The remains of this century must have been destroyed between the massive building activities in the tenth century BCE and the building boom during Hezekiah's reign.

Eighth to Sixth Centuries BCE (Strata 12–10) and the City's Expansion Westward. In the eighth century BCE (stratum 12), the city reached the peak of its development. It seems that refugees flocked to Jerusalem from Samaria and the surrounding countryside, which was conquered by the Assyrians in 722 BCE. Hezekiah, then reigning as king in Jerusalem, prepared his kingdom and its capital for the next, predictable step by the Assyrians, who were clearly about to turn south and invade Judah (2 Chr. 32:5). Presently available excavation results provide ample evidence for the growth of Jerusalem's population and concomitant increase in area: the city's residential section spread to the western hill; the fortifications around both the old and new areas of settlement were rebuilt on a large scale; and the water-supply system was reinforced by the digging of Hezekiah's Tunnel to supplement the existing water system—Warren's Shaft and the Siloam Tunnel (see below).

Strata 12 to 10, excavated by Shiloh in areas D and E, produced an abundance of finds from the eighth to sixth centuries BCE. The city wall on the eastern slope (of which Kenyon, in her site A, had already exposed 20 m) was now exposed for a length of some 120 m. The width of the wall is not uniform: in some places it reaches about 5 m; in some places it is preserved to a height of about 3 m. In parts of areas E1 and E3, there was clear evidence of the builders' use of the previous city wall, which had protected the city in the Middle Bronze Age IIB and later, as a basis for the eastern slope's last stage of fortifications. On this side, the wall served both as an element in the city's defenses and as a massive retaining belt for a system of four terraces built on the slope above. The walls of the lowest terrace and the structures on it were an integral part of the wall's fill. In area E1 several large residential units were defined, including "the lower terrace house" which abuts the city wall, and "the Ashlar House"—a building impressive for its thick walls and the ashlar blocks built into its corners—dated to stratum 11 (seventh century BCE). Similar houses were found in areas E2 and E3. In some of these houses, but especially in "the lower terrace house," three superimposed floors were identified; the finds on these floors assign them to strata 12, 11, and 10. The general plan of the houses was maintained through all three strata, except for a few minor modifications, mainly internal. They were destroyed at the end of stratum 10.

A feature specific to stratum 12 was detected in Shiloh's excavations in areas B, D, and E2. In the eighth century BCE, a few structures with simple plans

City of David, area E: general view, looking west.

City of David, area E: remains of buildings; (foreground) the eastern city wall, Bronze and Iron ages.

were built on the rock ledges on the slope, outside the city walls. The sparse finds they produced indicated their date. Most of them fell into disuse in the seventh century BCE, which may be associated with Sennacherib's siege of Jerusalem in 701 BCE. The masonry and caves found by Kenyon at the bottom of her site I (squares A-XXI and A-XXII) may be connected with this stage of settlement outside the walls. In the seventh century BCE, when the overflow population of Jerusalem settled on the western hill, the extramural area on the eastern slope was abandoned.

Since the earliest archaeological exploration of Jerusalem, scholars have been divided into minimalists and maximalists regarding the boundaries of ancient Jerusalem. While the maximalists held that the city occupied both the western and eastern hills ever since the tenth century BCE, the minimalists, relying on the location of archaeological material from the Iron Age II available to them, argued that the city was confined to the eastern ridge—to the City of David and the Temple Mount above it. Kenyon was the last in a series of minimalists. In her view, based on her research on the eastern slope of Mount Zion (her sites B, D, and E), the western hill, beyond the Central Valley, could not have been settled before the time of Agrippa I (first century CE). This was the prevalent view at the close of Kenyon's excavations in 1967.

Jewish Quarter: fertility figurines, First Temple period.

Today, as a result of the abundant information about the Iron Age II from the new excavations, a clearer picture of the development of Jerusalem's urban area between the tenth and sixth centuries BCE has emerged. The Jebusite city that David conquered stood within the confines of the City of David spur, with the citadel on its crest. In the tenth century BCE, the city expanded to the north; the area of the early city (15 a.) was almost doubled by the addition of the Temple Mount.

From the tenth to the middle of the eighth centuries BCE the city was still limited to these borders. The rock-cut caves discovered by B. Mazar at the foot of the eastern slope of the western hill, opposite the Temple Mount, were interpreted by him as tombs. They demonstrate that this area then served as a necropolis for the city's wealthy residents, as did the necropolis discovered in the village of Silwan, across the Kidron Valley from the City of David. The quarries discovered by Kenyon and Broshi in various parts of the western hill apparently supplied stone for large-scale Iron Age building projects, mainly those of Solomon.

Jerusalem's urban area expanded in the eighth century BCE. Many simple buildings went up in the area outside the city wall on the eastern slope. N. Avigad found abundant evidence of a similar, but even more extensive phenomenon in his excavations in the Jewish Quarter.

In most of the excavation areas in the Jewish Quarter that were taken down to bedrock, remains of walls and floors, as well as pottery, from the Iron Age II were found in the terra rossa soil. The disappearance of most of the building remains from that period can be attributed to later construction. Among the small finds were the common fertility and zoomorphic figurines of the period; jar handles with *lamelekh* seal impressions and impressions of "personal seals"; and a few ostraca, one of which includes the divine designation [אל] קנה ארץ (['*l*] *qnh 'rṣ*, [El] the creator of earth). Taken in combination,

Jewish Quarter: the Broad Wall, end of the First Temple period, looking northeast.

the finds indicate that the western hill (the biblical *Mishneh*) was occupied from the first half of the eighth century BCE to the end of the First Temple period.

Thus, there is no doubt that the city expanded westward, across the Central Valley, in the eighth century BCE, taking advantage of the terrain on the western hill because it was easy to build on. One of Avigad's most important discoveries was the so-called Broad Wall. This wall was built during Hezekiah's reign as part of the expanded city's new fortifications. The wall is about 7 m wide; a stretch approximately 65 m long was exposed. Judging from its direction, the wall ran west from the Temple Mount, aiming at the northwestern corner of the southwestern hill, apparently up to the present location of the Citadel ("Tower of David") near the Jaffa Gate. During the construction of the wall, eighth-century BCE private houses standing in its way were cut through and destroyed. The Broad Wall is evidence of deliberate, comprehensive state planning of the fortifications in this area (Is. 22:9–11).

The Amiran–Eitan and Solar–Sivan excavations in the Jerusalem Citadel ("Tower of David") near the Jaffa Gate revealed evidence of Iron Age II masonry, which should be combined with Broshi's similar evidence as well as the evidence from the excavations of D. Chen, S. Margalit, and B. Pixner on Mount Zion (see below, The Citadel, Mount Zion). In the area of the Transversal Valley, slightly north of the line of the Broad Wall, Avigad found more fragmentary fortifications, including a corner of a massive tower, preserved to a height of approximately 8 m, and interpreted by him as belonging to a gate. These were all part of the northern defenses of the expanding Jerusalem. The walls of the tower are about 4 m deep. Avigad suggested identifying the gate with the "middle gate" mentioned in Jer. 39:3. It seems, therefore, that the "First Wall" of the Hasmonean period (see below) reused the course and some parts of Hezekiah's wall in the area of the Jewish Quarter, the vicinity of the Citadel, and the southern extremity of the City of David. Confirmation for this hypothesis may be Josephus' statement that the First Wall was the "most ancient . . ., David and Solomon and their successors having taken pride in the work" (*War* V, 4, 2).

Plan of the fortification remains discovered in the Jewish Quarter.

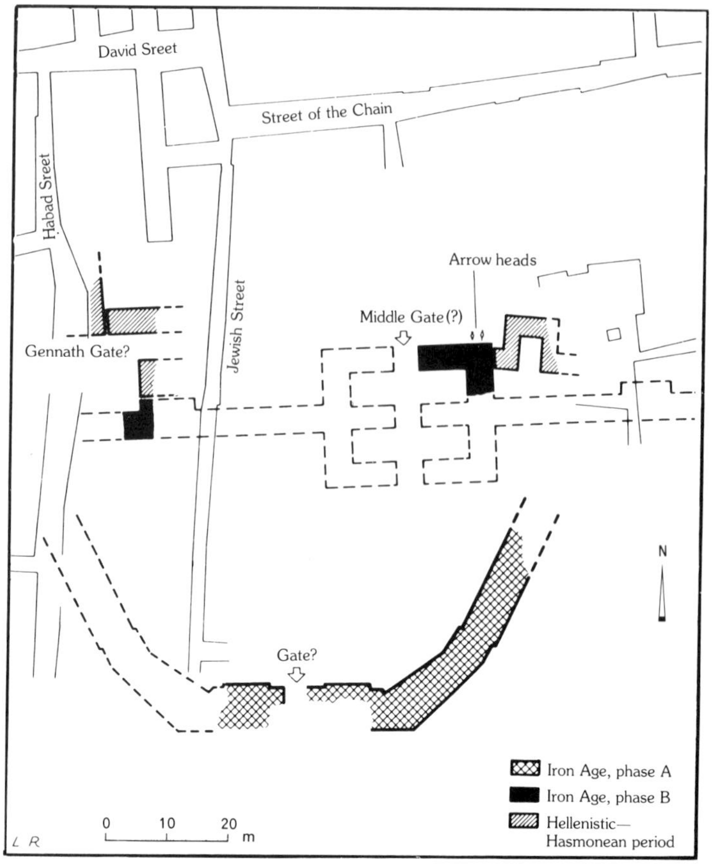

It is significant that the tombs from the end of the First Temple period, mainly from the seventh and sixth centuries BCE, built outside the fortified limits of the city, were found (by A. Kloner, A. Mazar, and G. Barkay) north of the line of defenses, north of the present-day Damascus Gate. Kloner discovered a necropolis from this period on the eastern bank of the Valley of Hinnom, beneath Mount Zion. Similar tombs were discovered by Barkay on the hill of the Scottish Church, southwest of the valley. Amiran published an assemblage of vessels from a contemporary tomb in the Mamilla area. Tombs continued to be dug in the area of the present-day village of Silwan; on

Jewish Quarter: tower from the end of the First Temple period, adjoined on its left by a Hasmonean tower.

Map of Jerusalem at the end of the First Temple period.

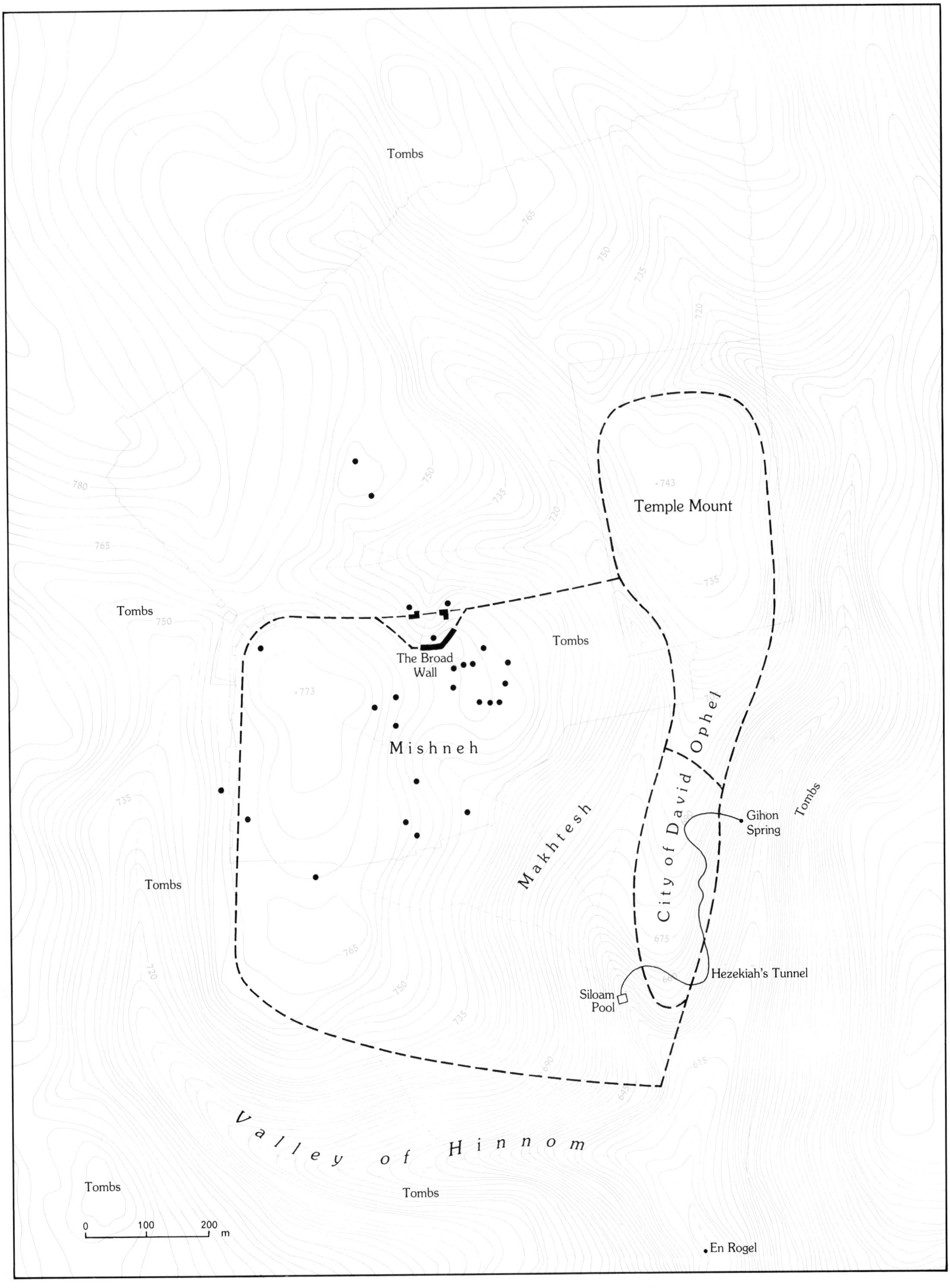

the other hand, the necropolis discovered by B. Mazar west of the Temple Mount was not used in the seventh and sixth centuries BCE, as the area was then within the walls (see below, the description of the tombs). Examination of the distribution of necropolises in Jerusalem, in the ninth to sixth centuries BCE, provides further proof of the extent of the built-up and fortified area of Jerusalem from Hezekiah's reign to the destruction of the First Temple.

Presumably—as proposed by Avigad, Barkay, and H. Geva—the wall of the Late Iron Age city encircled the western hill along the line of the "First

City of David: remains in area G with the reconstructed House of Ahiel in the center.

Wall," whose continuation was located by F. J. Bliss at the south and southeast of Mount Zion. This wall linked up with the southern end of the City of David, thereby blocking the issue of the Central Valley. This was a topographically convenient location for the construction of water reservoirs (see below). This raises the issue of what the point was of cutting Hezekiah's Tunnel to transport the waters of the Gihon Spring to the area of the Siloam Pool, which, in the minimalists' position, was undefended. According to the above interpretation, the logic underlying the expansion of the city, its refortification, and the enlargement of its water system is understandable. The planning of Hezekiah's Tunnel fits quite well into this scheme, as it delivered its water to a reservoir "between the two walls" (Is. 22:11)—an area that henceforth would be within the city walls. Clearly, then, Jerusalem reached the zenith of its expansion in the First Temple period toward the end of the eighth and in the seventh centuries BCE. Its residential quarters were spread over an area of more than 110 a. Such new quarters as the Mishneh—the "Second Quarter"—and the Makhtesh—"the Mortar" (2 Kg. 22:14; Zeph. 1:10–11)—should be sought on the western hill. This should put an end to the dispute between the minimalists, whose theory has proved correct only with regard to the city limits in the tenth to eighth centuries BCE, and the maximalists, whose view conforms to the boundaries of the city from the end of the eighth to the sixth centuries BCE.

City of David, area G: selection of pottery, bullae, and stone objects from the House of the Bullae.

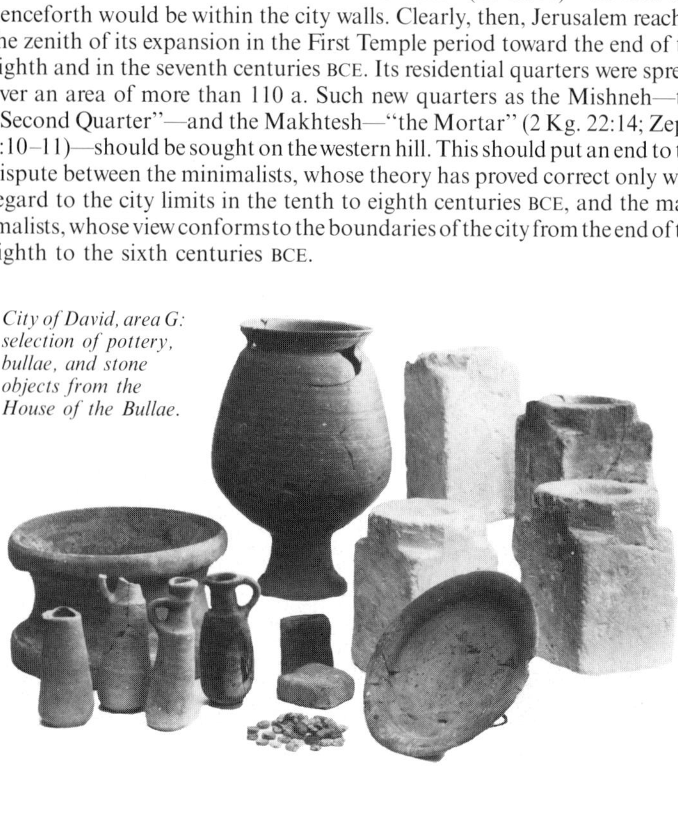

Evidence of construction activity in the seventh century BCE, especially in the latter half of that century, probably under Josiah, was found in the City of David, in Shiloh's area G. Between the lowest part of the stepped stone structure and the outer wall of the city, above the spring, several stepped terraces had been built to serve as a solid platform for the buildings of stratum 10. The main terrace exposed by Shiloh was about 12 m wide and 27 m long. Three main structures were identified in the two upper terraces cleared. The area in the southern part of the middle strip was occupied by the so-called House of Ahiel, built along the lines of a four-room house. The main building (8 by 12 m) had attached storerooms and service rooms, in which a large collection of small finds and dozens of pottery vessels were found. The name Ahiel appeared twice on ostraca found in and near the house. To the north was the Burnt Room, so called because of the fierce conflagration that raged there during the destruction in 586 BCE. It contained, inter alia, pottery, stone and bone vessels, and a metal spoon. The charred wooden remains included pieces of roof beams and possibly furniture, of wood imported from northern Syria, carved in palmette patterns.

On the second terrace, some 5 m lower than the uppermost one, a narrow section of a building, known as the House of the Bullae, was cleared. Among other finds, the destruction layer above the conflagration layer produced a collection of fifty-one bullae with seal impressions featuring various Hebrew names: "[belonging] to Benayahu son of Hoshaiah," "[belonging] to Azaryahu son of Hilkiahu," "[belonging] to Azrikam Michyahu," and "[belonging] to Elishama son of Samachiah." The most significant of these names—identifiable with a personality mentioned in the Bible—was "Gemariah son of Shaphan," a scribe or secretary who had chambers in the court of Jehoiakim king of Judah, in the fifth year of his reign—604 BCE (Jer. 36:9–12). This seal impression suggests the nature of the bullae collection, whose documents were burned in the conflagration, and may explain its location: the House of the Bullae, which is situated on the border between the Upper City and the Ophel, may have been an archive or public office.

Kenyon cleared an additional building from this period, on a lower terrace, in her square A-XXIV. According to the photographic record of the finds in her site A and trench I, the entire slope, from the base of the citadel to the city wall, consisted of stepped terraces with buildings on them, which are what Shiloh found in his area E in the southern part of the Lower City. These finds represent an unambiguous stratigraphical and chronological sequence: stratum 12 must be assigned to the late eighth century BCE, stratum 11 to the early seventh century BCE, and stratum 10 to the late seventh and mainly the sixth centuries BCE. A gap begins with the destruction of Jerusalem in 586 BCE. The

City of David, area G: selection of bullae from the end of the First Temple period, found in the House of the Bullae.

pottery assemblages of complete vessels from these strata have parallels at other sites in Judah: Lachish III–II, En-Gedi V, Ramat Raḥel V, stratum A at Tell Beit Mirsim, and Arad VII–VI, for example.

The Babylonians' destruction of Jerusalem in 586 BCE is well documented in the biblical sources (2 Kg. 25:8–10; 2 Chr. 36:18–19), which describe the destruction, burning, and collapse of houses and walls. The archaeological evidence for this phase in Jerusalem's history, which rounds out the historical account, can be counted among the most dramatic at any biblical site. Alongside the Israelite tower cleared by Avigad in the north of the city was a thick conflagration layer, in which arrowheads were found, that may have been fired when the city's northern defenses were being breached. In addition, many of the buildings excavated by Shiloh, mainly in areas E and G, were also destroyed in a fierce conflagration: the Ashlar House, the House of Ahiel, the Burnt Room, and the House of the Bullae. Their walls collapsed and buried abundant and rich finds, including large quantities of pottery; dozens of metal and stone vessels; and bone implements, and considerable epigraphic material. The dozens of flat iron arrowheads of the local type and triangular bronze arrowheads of the so-called Scythian type found in the houses bear mute witness to the battle for the city on the eve of its destruction, as the inhabitants amassed ammunition in their homes. The destruction of these residential quarters, which resembles that on the western hill and in one section of the "house of Millo" cleared by B. Mazar, was total. The rubble was preserved in some of the buildings up to the height of their first-story ceiling. Perhaps the most graphic telling of the story is Nehemiah's description of the ruins in the City of David as he found them in his tour of the city, some 140 years later (Neh. 2:13–14).

City of David, area G: carved wood fragments from the destruction layer, end of the First Temple period.

PERSIAN PERIOD (STRATUM 9). During the postexilic period, the returnees settled in the older part of Jerusalem, on the spur of the City of David. Zerubbabel built the Temple overlooking it, on the north (Ezra 3:8–10). Although the books of Ezra and Nehemiah have much to say about Jerusalem in the Persian period, it is difficult to locate actual finds from that time, except for a few small items that were not found in situ. The Persian stratum in Jerusalem may be less well preserved because it was nearly obliterated between the destruction of the Israelite city and the extensive construction in the Hasmonean and Herodian periods. The eastern slope was in such a ruinous condition, so covered with rubble from its buildings and retaining walls, that for the first time in its history no attempt was made to build and resettle it. The city developed on the crest of the narrow spur of the City of David, over an even smaller area than in the tenth century BCE. The fortified area no longer included the eastern slope. Only a few traces have survived of the city wall Nehemiah rebuilt along the course described in the Bible (Neh. 3:1–32). A segment of a wall excavated by Macalister on the summit of the eastern slope—reexamined by Kenyon and Shiloh at the higher, western edge of Kenyon's site A and Shiloh's area G—should, however, be assigned to this period. If Crowfoot's Valley Gate did indeed provide access to the western part of the City of David as early as the Iron Age, it would also have been incorporated in Nehemiah's wall.

For the first time, in several places on the eastern slope, the Shiloh expedition was able to locate layers of stratum 9, from the Persian period, in a regular stratigraphic context. These layers were found above the debris of stratum 10, underneath the fills and retaining walls of strata 8–7 from the Hellenistic-Hasmonean period. Only a few building remains were found, but there was a large quantity of small finds, mainly assemblages of pottery and seal impressions on jar handles, representing the whole range of known types of such impressions: *Yehud* impressions of various kinds, names of satraps such as Ahazai and Hananiah, a seal featuring the figure of a standing animal, and a Lycian silver coin from the fifth century BCE. It follows, therefore, that in the Persian period the City of David spur was again the center of Jerusalem's settled area, the nucleus from which the city would develop to the north and west under the Hasmoneans, just as it had in the Iron Age II.

No remains from the Persian period were uncovered in the Jewish Quarter excavations. Directly overlying the remains from the First Temple period are Hellenistic strata. This gap in occupation after the Babylonian destruction of Jerusalem in 586 BCE and the deportation of its inhabitants indicates that the Mishneh on the western hill remained abandoned. The same negative evidence remains valid for the Early Hellenistic period (fourth and third centuries BCE).

Recently, Barkay excavated some tombs, rich in finds, dated by him to the sixth century BCE, on the hill of Saint Andrew's Church southwest of the Valley of Hinnom (see below).

THE WATER-SUPPLY SYSTEMS. The City of David's primary source of water was the Gihon Spring, which surfaces in the Kidron Valley at the foot of

City of David: the Gihon Spring in the Kidron Valley.

City of David, Warren's Shaft: the vertical shaft.

Hezekiah's Tunnel.

the eastern slope. The spring is abundantly filled with water year round, but in hydrogeological terms it does not resemble the groundwater springs commonly found near the mounds of ancient cities in this country. The Gihon Spring is an intermittent spring, whose waters gush forth several times a day and flow into the Kidron Valley. In order to exploit these waters, it is necessary to capture them in pools while the spring is flowing. Such pools were apparently built along the Kidron Valley and at the issue of the Central Valley in the southwestern part of the City of David. This is the lowest terrain in the vicinity of the spur, where the topographical layout makes it easy to construct reservoirs, channel the water into them, and efficiently defend the system.

There are three ancient subterranean water systems in the City of David spur: Warren's Shaft, the Siloam Tunnel, and Hezekiah's Tunnel. Warren's Shaft was discovered by C. Warren in 1867 and named after him. Parker examined parts of the system from 1909 to 1911. The Shiloh expedition cleared all of the system, which is in its area J. The entrance chamber is in the middle of the eastern slope, not far from and below the city's ancient acropolis. It leads down to a rock-hewn tunnel, extending, first by steps and then horizontally, for about 41 m and a descent of about 13 m, to the top of a vertical shaft. The depth of the shaft to the level of the Gihon Spring and Hezekiah's Tunnel is approximately 12.3 m. Before Hezekiah's Tunnel was cut, an earlier tunnel delivered the waters of the Gihon to the base of the shaft, from which they were pumped by the people of the city, who had access to the top of the shaft, through the upper tunnel. Until Kenyon's excavations, scholars were puzzled about the location of the entrance to the system, which is beneath (and outside) the city walls, as defined by Macalister (1923–1925). The Canaanite and Israelite city walls exposed in Kenyon's trench I and Shiloh's areas D and E, both describing a line farther down the slope, below the entrance chamber, solved the problem. It is now clear that the entrance to the water-supply system lay within the fortified area of the Lower City, beneath the Ophel (the acropolis of the biblical city). A hydrogeological survey carried out by D. Gil on behalf of the Shiloh expedition showed that the vertical shaft and much of the horizontal tunnel were originally natural karstic tunnels that the planners were able to adapt by cutting the rock further where necessary. The unique feature of Warren's Shaft is thus the exploitation of a vertical shaft to prevent penetration into the city from without, via the system of water supply (which was possible at other Iron Age administrative centers, such as Megiddo, Gibeon, and Ibleam).

The Siloam Tunnel was built to solve a specific hydrogeological problem of the Gihon Spring. It carried the water for a distance of some 400 m along the foot of the western bank of the Kidron Valley; part of it was an open channel and the other part was cut in the rock as a tunnel. Windowlike openings

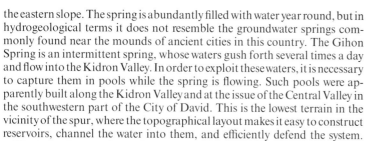

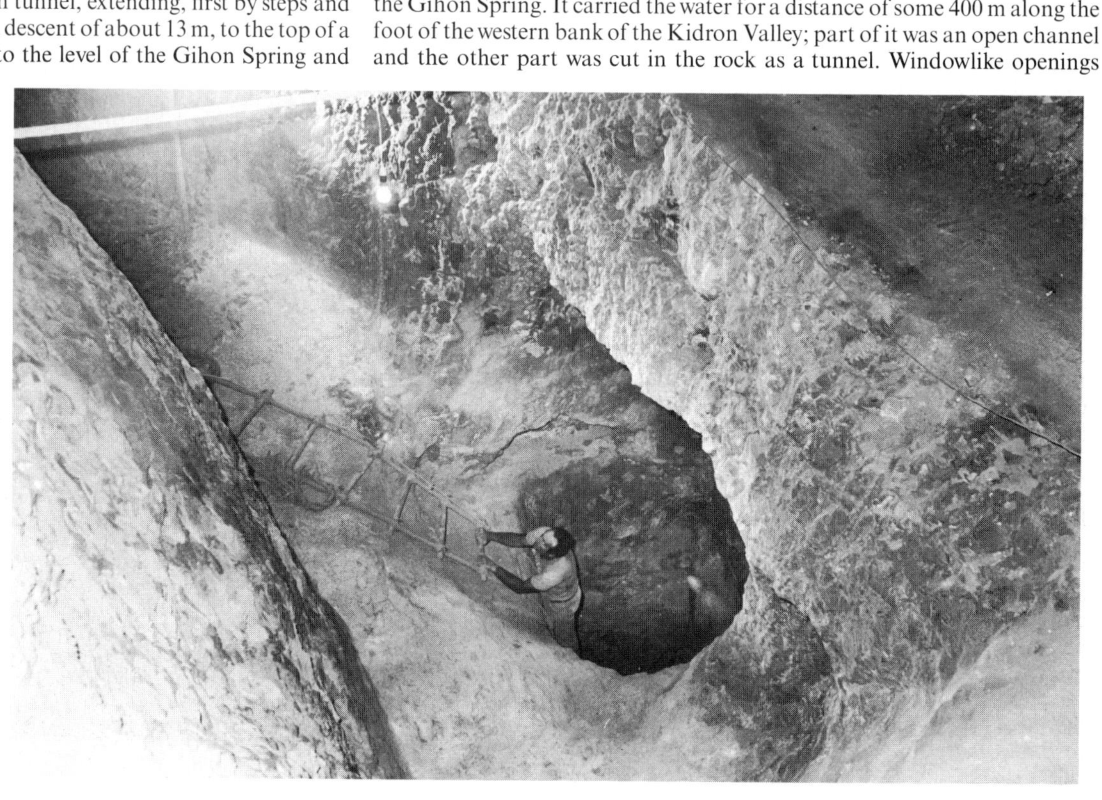

City of David, Warren's Shaft: the top of the vertical shaft where it joins the horizontal tunnel.

City of David, Siloam Inscription: photograph and facsimile.

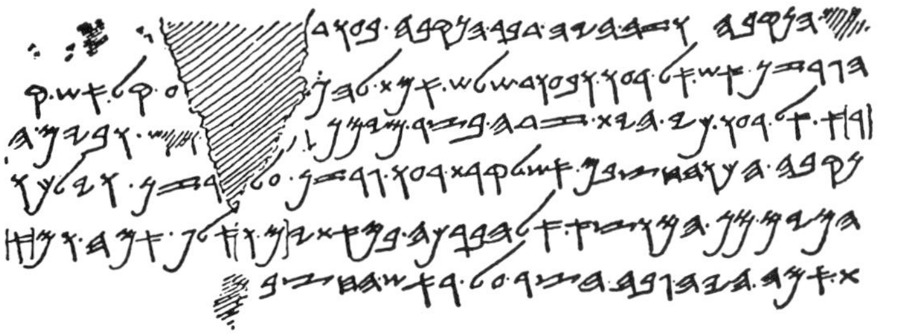

pierced in the eastern side of the channel permitted the diversion of water to irrigate plots of cultivated land in the valley. The Shiloh expedition reexcavated and cleared the Siloam Tunnel for a distance of approximately 120 m in its areas A1, B, and J. The tunnel carried the Gihon waters to the vicinity of the Siloam Pool, where they could be stored and their use regulated. Rainwater runoff on the hill's exposed rock drained into the channel through openings in its roof. The main disadvantage of this system was that it was entirely outside the city's defenses and highly vulnerable in times of war and siege. This was the motive for cutting Hezekiah's Tunnel, which is essentially an aqueduct that winds through the Cenomanian rock. Its entire length (c. 533 m from the spring to the reservoirs at the issue of the Central Valley) is enclosed. The levels of the tunnel floor were carefully calculated: the height differential between the point of issue in the spring and the end of the tunnel is at most 35 cm, a very moderate gradient. The cutting of the tunnel was described by the workers in the famous Siloam Inscription, which was incised in the tunnel wall near its southern end. The tunnel is mentioned several times in the Bible in connection with Hezekiah's construction projects in Jerusalem, which are now confirmed by the abundant archaeological evidence (2 Kg. 20:20; 2 Chr. 32:3–4, 32:30). Hezekiah's Tunnel was planned and executed as part of a comprehensive design by Hezekiah's town planners: the western hill was encompassed by the Broad Wall, which skirted Mount Zion up to the southern extremity of the City of David, also sealing and fortifying the issue of the Central Valley and bringing the reservoir area into the fortified limits of the city. Hezekiah's Tunnel thus supplanted the Siloam Tunnel and permitted an uninterrupted flow of water in a closed aqueduct into a defended reservoir, both in times of peace and war.

The dating of these three water-supply projects relies on the biblical data, the stratigraphical relationships among them, the connection between them and the city plan, and a comparative study of similar water-supply systems elsewhere in the country. According to the biblical sources, Hezekiah's Tunnel was cut during his reign, at the end of the eighth century BCE. It probably took over one of the important functions of the Siloam Tunnel: to deliver water to the reservoirs in the Central Valley. The ground at the southern end of the Siloam Tunnel (area A1 in Shiloh's excavations) was lowered about 3.5 m, to reverse the direction of flow. After this modification, the relevant part of the channel merely drained excess water from the reservoirs, bringing it eastward to the floor of the Kidron Valley, where there may have been additional reservoirs outside the city. There can, thus, be no doubt that the Siloam Tunnel predates Hezekiah's Tunnel.

Hezekiah's Tunnel at first made use of the earlier supply channel at its northern end, which had brought water from the spring to the base of Warren's Shaft. Thus, this system, too, predates the eighth century BCE. W. F. Birch (1878) and later L. H. Vincent (1911) suggested that Warren's Shaft might be the *ẓinnor* mentioned in the biblical account of David's occupation of

City of David: Siloam Tunnel.

Jerusalem (2 Sam. 5:6–8; 1 Chr. 11:4–7). However, this identification means that Warren's Shaft must be interpreted as a Canaanite (Jebusite) water system, which is unsubstantiated by any concrete archaeological evidence. The suggestion has been rejected for various reasons—textual, architectural, and archaeological—by most scholars (W. F. Albright, Y. Yadin, Y. Aharoni, B. Mazar, M. Ben-Dov, and Shiloh). Such water systems are one of the most characteristic constituents in the plans of Israelite administrative centers in Judah and Israel—Megiddo, Hazor, Gezer, Gibeon, and Ibleam.

Thus, Warren's Shaft, sunk near the acropolis, served the royal city of Jerusalem in the tenth century BCE. In the main, it represents the most common type of water system, with tunnels providing the townspeople with access to the vicinity of a water source outside the city. The Siloam Tunnel delivered the Gihon waters to a reservoir area and provided a regulated supply of water to irrigate the fields on the floor of the Kidron Valley. It, too, presumably was in use throughout the Iron Age, until it was blocked at the end of the period. Its southern part had already gone out of use, at the end of the eighth century BCE, when Hezekiah's Tunnel was cut. Since then the latter has been the main route by which water flows from the Gihon Spring to the Siloam Pool. Most probably, all three systems functioned simultaneously from the end of the eighth century until 586 BCE. In the Second Temple period, the residents of the Lower City continued to use the waters of the Gihon; however, the municipal water-supply system underwent various alterations and expansions in the Hasmonean and Herodian periods. In particular, new aqueducts were built to bring plentiful water from the springs in the Hebron Hills and the vicinity of Bethlehem to the upper sections of the city. Thus, for the first time in the history of Jerusalem, some of the city's more important residential sections no longer depended on the Gihon Spring.

YIGAL SHILOH

Tomb from the First Temple period, hewn into the eastern slope of the southwestern hill. It was converted into a mikveh in the Second Temple period.

TOMBS

All excavators of the remains of the First Temple period in Jerusalem were eager to find the tombs of the kings of Judah which, according to the Bible, were located in the City of David. In his excavations on the Ophel, R. Weill discovered three rock-cut tombs, which are of special interest because of their size and form. The best preserved of these tombs has the form of a vaulted tunnel, resembling a huge loculus, reached by several steps. It is 16 m long, 2.5 m wide, and 4 m high in front and 1.8 m high in the rear, where the floor level is elevated to form a shelf. In this shelf a shallow rectangular pit was cut, probably to hold a coffin. Slots in the walls indicate that the tomb was divided by beams into two stories. Weill ascribed these tombs to the kings of Judah, and at the time his opinion was shared by other scholars. Today, however, it is no longer accepted, especially since no other evidence has been found to confirm that they belong to the Israelite period.

Across the Kidron Valley in the Siloam (Silwan) village are the remains of a necropolis from the period of the First Temple. The most outstanding and best known of these tombs is the so-called Tomb of Pharaoh's Daughter, situated on a rock scarp, at the northern end of the village. It is hewn from the rock in the form of a cube (5 by 5.8 by 4 m). At the top, the tomb terminates in an Egyptian cornice, which is surmounted by a pyramid of which very little remains. Its general aspect is that of a small Egyptian chapel. Inside the tomb is a small corridor and a single chamber with a gabled ceiling. An inscription was cut above the entrance in ancient Hebrew script, of which only the last two letters have been preserved.

In the rock scarp—which continues along the Kidron Valley—several burial chambers are cut, which have gabled roofs like that of the "Tomb of Pharaoh's Daughter." Within the village another rock-cut tomb, consisting of two chambers, was found above ground level. Two inscriptions in ancient Hebrew script were carved on its facade. This is the tomb of an official of the royal court whose title was "Steward of the House" and his maidservant (*amah*). The inscription contains a curse against anyone who dare open the tomb. It is dated to the beginning of the seventh century BCE. The fragment of a similar inscription was found on a monumental rock-cut tomb nearby.

Another group of tombs from the First Temple period was uncovered in Mazar's excavations on the eastern slope of the southwestern hill opposite the Temple Mount. These were rock-cut shaft tombs that contained material from the eighth to seventh centuries BCE.

NAHMAN AVIGAD

Tomb from the First Temple period, hewn into the eastern slope of the southwestern hill.

Jerusalem: excavations in the Jewish Quarter, Herodian period.
***Above:** frescoed wall from the Palatial Mansion.*
***Right:** mosaic with an interlacing meander motif, area F.*

Jerusalem: painted pottery from the Upper City, Second Temple period.

Jerusalem: southwestern corner of the Temple Mount and the remains of Robinson's Arch.

Jerusalem: flight of steps in front of the southern wall of the Temple Mount, Herodian period.

Silwan village: general view, looking east. The left arrow indicates the site of the "Tomb of Pharaoh's Daughter"; the right arrow the "Tomb of the Royal Steward."

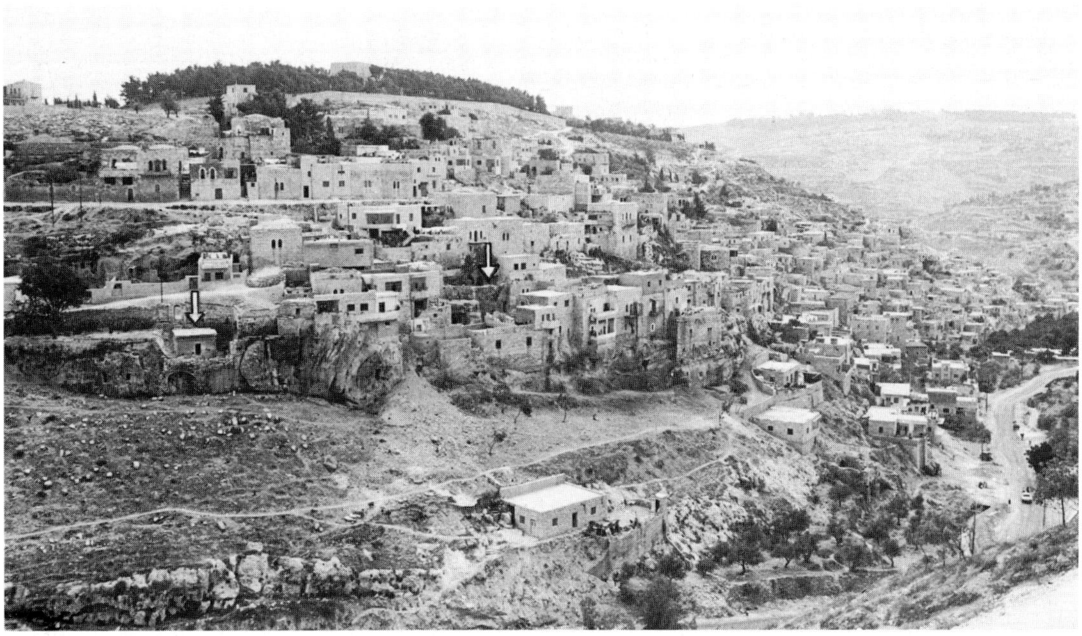

Since 1967, further tomb caves belonging to the necropolises of Jerusalem in the First Temple period have been discovered and surveyed. To date there are about 130 tombs, concentrated in the village of Silwan, the Valley of Hinnom, and north of the Damascus Gate. Many of the tombs were of types previously unknown in this country, featuring architectural details indicative of foreign influence—Anatolian (Urartu and Phrygia), Phoenician, and Egyptian. These cemeteries, particularly those north and west of Jerusalem, are of great importance to the research of the city's topography and the extent of the built-up area at the end of the First Temple period (eighth–seventh centuries BCE).

VILLAGE OF SILWAN. From 1968 to 1970, D. Ussishkin conducted a detailed survey of the necropolis in the village of Silwan. The necropolis included about fifty tombs, some previously unknown. The tomb caves were cut into the steep, rocky eastern bank of the Kidron Valley, facing the City of David. All were found empty; some had been damaged by use and quarrying in later periods. The area was used for burial mainly in the eighth and seventh centuries BCE, although the earliest burials in the necropolis probably date to the ninth century BCE.

The tombs discovered in Silwan fall into several categories, differing in architectural details and in their location on the slope. Their architectural design is unique and the workmanship of the rock-cutting is of high quality. One group of tombs consists of an elongated, single chamber with a gabled ceiling. The chambers contain a burial trough and a stone "pillow" to support the deceased's head. Another group consists of two or three large rock-cut chambers, arranged one behind the other. Most of these chambers had no burial installations, except for a few troughs in some tombs. A third, smaller group consists of above-ground rock-cut monuments with a burial chamber and inscriptions. Two examples of this group are known from earlier excavations—the "Tomb of Pharaoh's Daughter" and the "Tomb of the Royal Steward" (see above).

NECROPOLIS NORTH OF THE OLD CITY. The tombs of this necropolis were cut in the rock scarp of the upper stretches of the Tyropoeon Valley (the Central Valley) north of the Damascus Gate. Fifteen tombs dating to the First Temple period have so far been found here; some have been known since the end of the nineteenth century. Several burial caves were recently reexamined

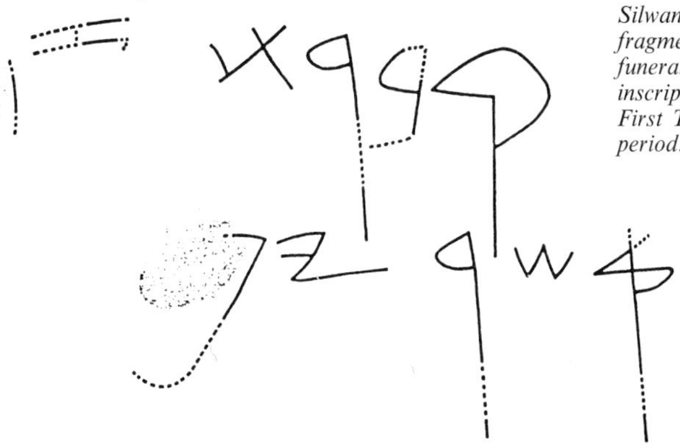

Silwan village: fragmentary funerary inscription, First Temple period.

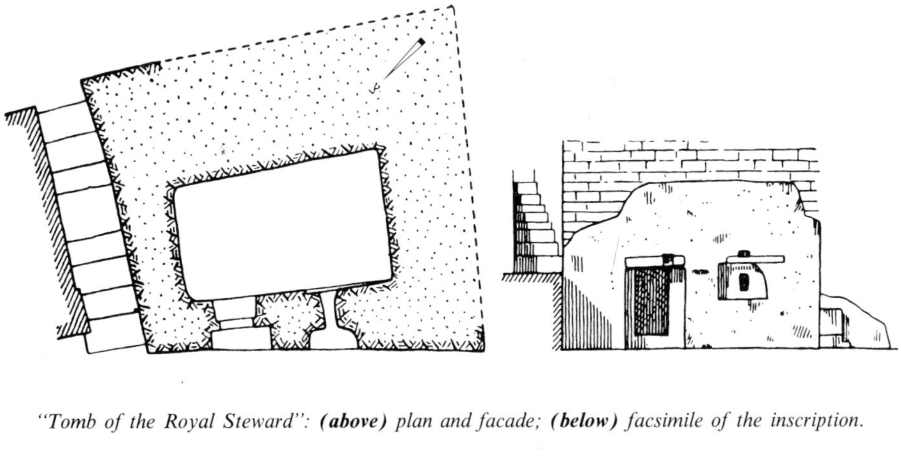

*"Tomb of the Royal Steward": **(above)** plan and facade; **(below)** facsimile of the inscription.*

***Above:** "Tomb of Pharaoh's Daughter": reconstruction of the facade.*

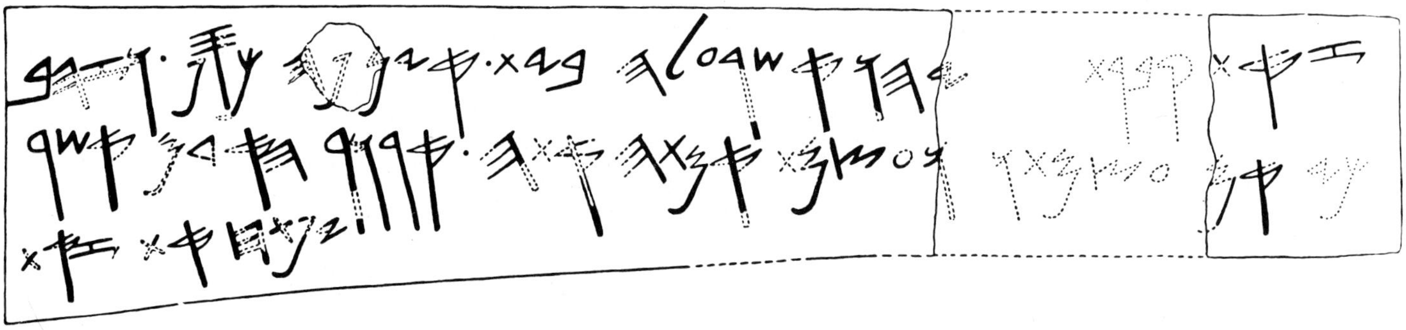

Monastery of St. Etienne: burial cave 1, First Temple period.

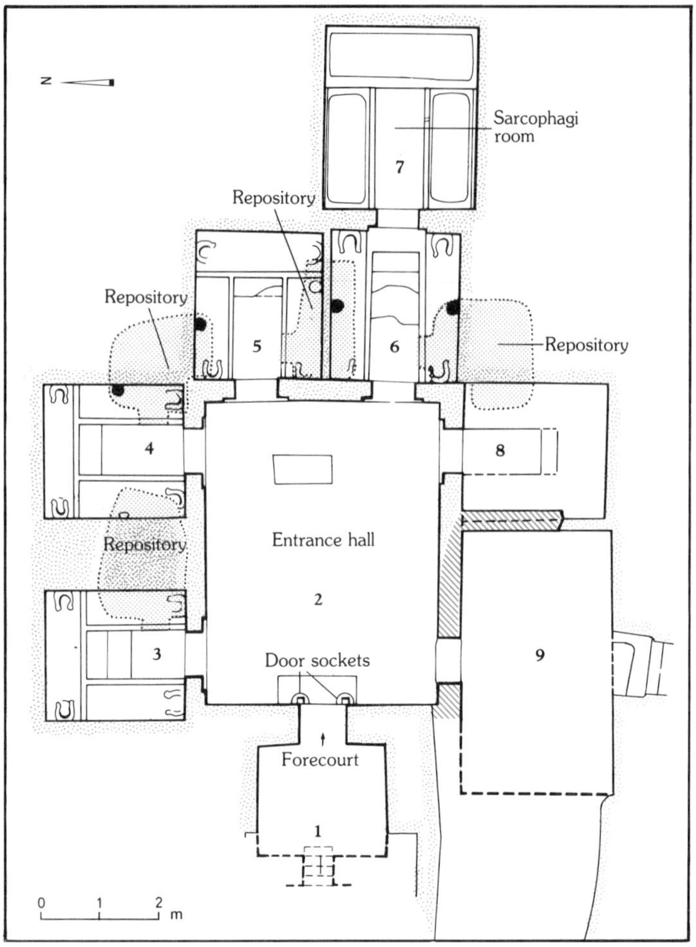

and published by Barkay and Kloner; a careful analysis of the architectural remains dated them to the end of the First Temple period (eighth–seventh centuries BCE).

The Garden Tomb. The Garden Tomb, also known as Gordon's Calvary, consists of two chambers cut side by side in the rock. Still visible along the walls of the inner room are the remains of three burial benches, a typical feature of First Temple period tombs.

Tombs on the Grounds of Saint Etienne's Monastery. In this area there were two rock-cut tombs, which are among the largest and most elaborate discovered to date in this country from the time of the kingdom of Judah. The plan of cave 1 included a forecourt and a particularly large entrance hall with a high ceiling. The entrance to the hall has an inner step with two protruding door sockets—a typical feature of Assyrian architecture. The walls were decorated with concave rectangular panels, and a double angular cornice at the juncture of the walls and ceiling. Openings in the walls led to five burial chambers of similar size and plan, containing burial benches with raised edges and horseshoe-shaped headrests; the sides of some of the headrests flared out in a shape recalling the hairstyle of the Egyptian goddess Hathor. In the floor of each chamber was an irregularly shaped repository pit. One of the two inner (back) chambers of the tomb differed from the others in plan, being decorated in a style similar to that of the entrance hall. Behind it was another chamber—the most important of the entire burial complex—lined with three rock-cut sarcophagi hewn along its walls. Cave 2 resembled the first in plan and architectural remains, except for a few minor differences.

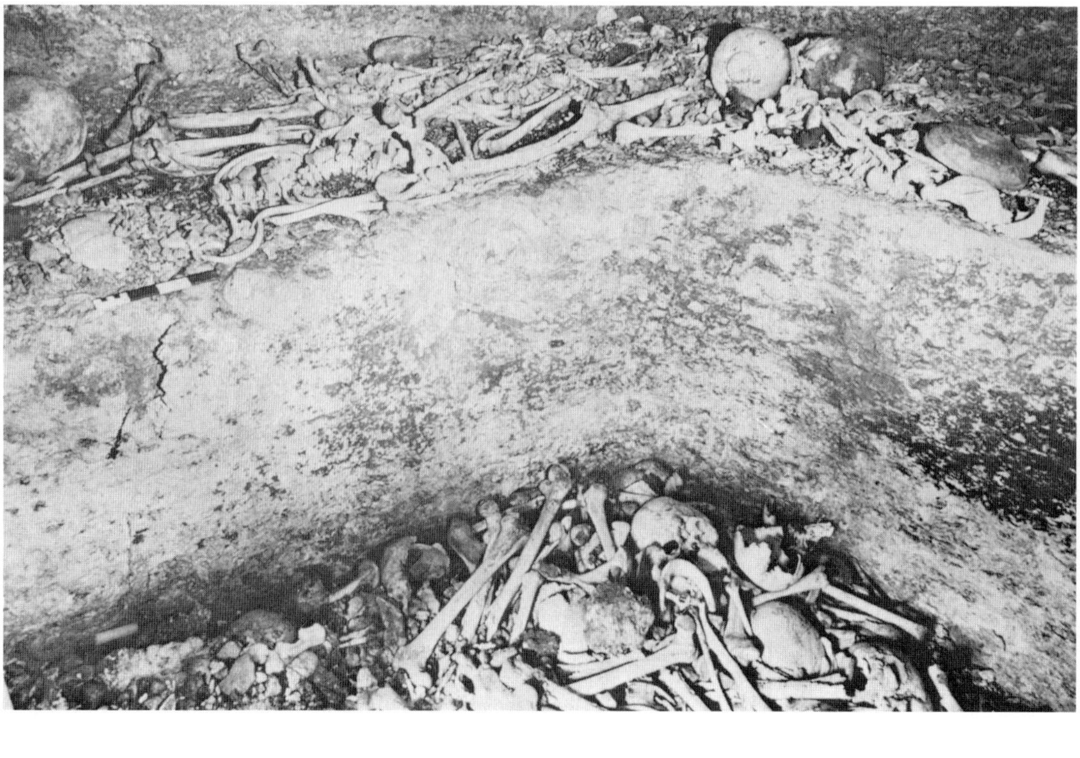

Mount Zion: burial cave on the western slope, First Temple period.

Mount Zion: plan and section of a burial cave on the western slope, First Temple period.

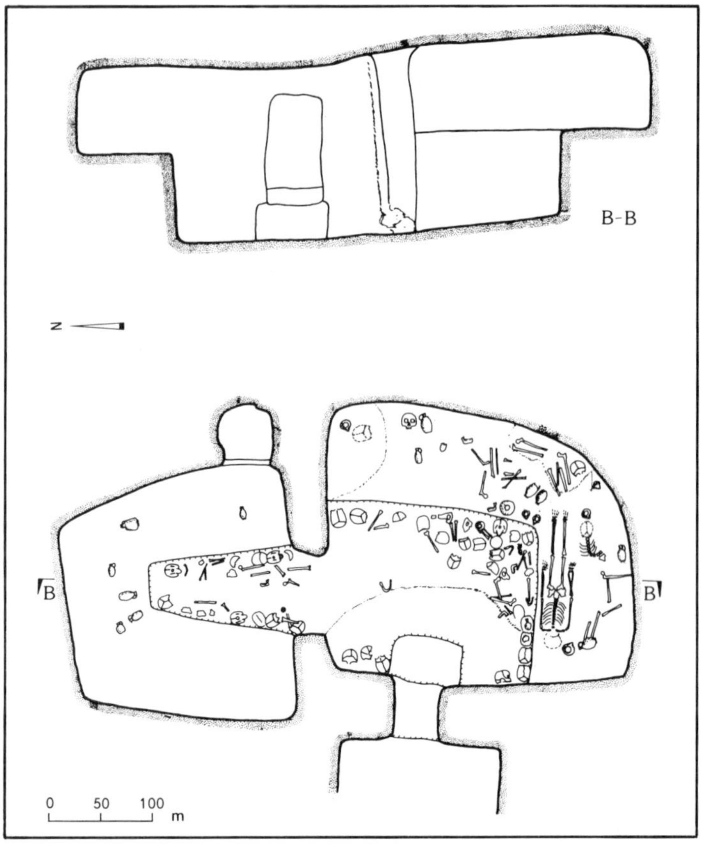

Suleiman Street. Two additional burial caves from the end of the First Temple period, originally discovered in 1937 near Damascus Gate, were recently published by A. Mazar. One cave was unusually shaped; it included a central hall and five burial chambers. A pottery assemblage from the end of the First Temple period (eighth–seventh centuries BCE) was found in situ. The second cave was beautifully and precisely hewn; it had two chambers containing burial benches with raised edges and horseshoe-shaped headrests.

VALLEY OF HINNOM. The southern and western cemetery of Jerusalem toward the end of the First Temple period extended along the Valley of Hinnom, skirting the southwestern hill of Jerusalem. In 1900, R. A. S. Macalister surveyed and recorded several caves in the high southern scarp of the valley.

Western Slope of Mount Zion. In 1975, D. Davis and A. Kloner examined several burial caves on the lower part of the western slope of Mount Zion. One cave, found sealed and undisturbed, included two chambers side by side, with

Ketef Hinnom: plan of burial cave 24, end of First Temple period.

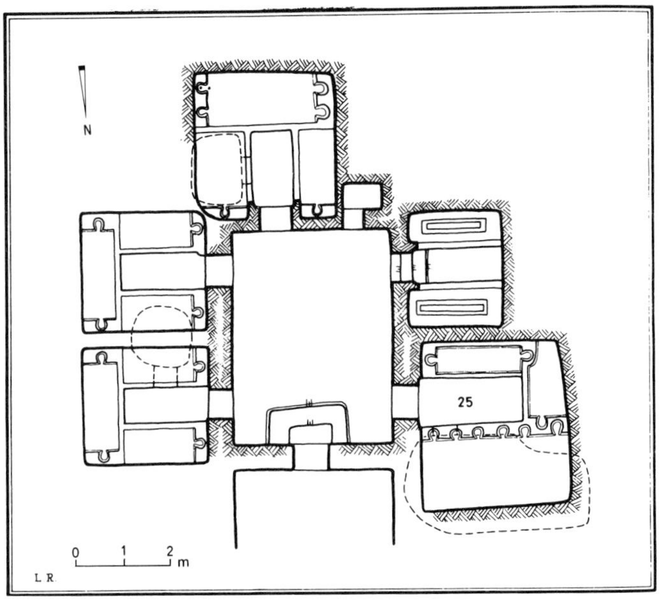

Reconstruction of room 25 in burial cave 24.

rock-cut benches along the walls. It contained dozens of skeletons, a pottery assemblage from the end of the First Temple period (eighth–seventh centuries BCE), and a bone seal with an engraved representation of a fish and the name of the owner, "[Belonging to] Ḥamiahel daughter of Menaḥem." In 1976, M. Broshi discovered two adjoining tomb caves just outside the western city wall of the Old City, south of the Citadel and the Jaffa Gate. Each cave had a forecourt and a small entrance leading to a single burial chamber. One cave had two entrances. In the center of the burial chamber was a rock-cut sarcophagus, with a headrest; at the rear of the chamber was a similar sarcophagus, perpendicular to the first. The finely-hewn facade of the second cave was decorated with a pair of smoothed pilasters. Hewn in the walls on both sides of the burial chamber were benches, behind each of which was a niche on the same level, thus creating a broad bench in which was a shallow double depression with two headrests, accommodating two bodies.

Ketef Hinnom. Between 1979 and 1988, G. Barkay excavated nine tomb caves from the end of the First Temple period on the high scarp of the southwestern bank of the Valley of Hinnom. The caves were found disturbed and in an advanced state of ruin, due to late quarrying activities. Five of the caves were similar in plan: a single burial chamber with three burial benches along the walls.

Cave 20 included a forecourt and an entrance hall, with a decorative cornice where the walls and ceiling meet. A long, unusually broad bench that could accommodate several bodies side by side was cut in one wall of the hall. Beneath the bench was a burial chamber, so that the tomb could be used for burial on two levels. Cut in the walls of the entrance hall were the entrances to further burial chambers and a repository.

Cave 24 consisted of a forecourt and a large central hall. The hall led to five burial chambers with rock-cut benches and headrests arranged in various ways. The chambers to the right of the hall differed from the others. One chamber contained only two benches, with a long, deep groove along the center of each. The other room on the right contained an unusually broad bench along which a raised pillow with six depressions used as headrests was carved. Beneath this bench was a repository filled with hundreds of finds, including pottery, jewelry and various other artifacts from the end of the First Temple period (eighth–seventh centuries BCE). The most important find consisted of two rolled-up silver plaques that had been used as charms. They were incised with benedictory formulas in ancient Hebrew script, including parts of the biblical priestly blessing (Num. 6:24-26).

Ketef Hinnom: priestly benediction on a silver plaque, from burial cave 24.

Mamilla Neighborhood. In 1990, R. Reich began to excavate a cemetery containing dozens of tombs in the Mamilla area, in the broad upper part of the Valley of Hinnom opposite the Jaffa Gate. Most of the caves were found disturbed and destroyed because of later quarrying. Two of the caves, found undisturbed, had similar plans: a forecourt, a small entrance, and burial chambers with benches and a repository in the walls. The finds in these caves included many pottery vessels and other artifacts from the end of the First Temple period (eighth–seventh centuries BCE). Finds from two other tombs in this area were published previously by R. Amiran.

SUMMARY. The distribution of cemeteries around Jerusalem at the end of the First Temple period provides important evidence about the built-up area of the city at the time, supplementing what is known from finds within the city itself. It indicates that at some time in the eighth century BCE, when Jerusalem's population was spreading from the City of David to the southwestern hill, the Valley of Hinnom began to be used as the city's principal necropolis, mainly for the lower classes; at the same time, the nobility of Jerusalem, as well as high-placed officials, continued to be interred in the traditional cemetery, in the area now occupied by the village of Silwan. It is unlikely that the tombs discovered on the grounds of Saint Etienne's—the most elaborate known to date from the end of the First Temple period in Jerusalem and Judah—are those of the last kings of Judah; nevertheless, the latter's tombs were probably designed along similar lines. The cemetery north of the Damascus Gate probably attests also to the existence of a residential quarter outside the city's northern wall at the end of the First Temple period. Another interesting point is that finds from some of the tombs in the Valley of Hinnom indicate that they were used for burial in the Second Temple period (sixth to first centuries BCE), as well.

RECENT DISCOVERIES WITHIN THE CITY. Since Shiloh's summary of the First Temple period Jerusalem was written, the following important discoveries relating to that period have been made.

The Ophel. In 1986 to 1987, B. Mazar and E. Mazar continued to excavate the complex of Iron Age II public buildings in the southeastern part of the Ophel. The buildings were partially unearthed in B. Mazar's 1970 excavations; he identified them as remains of the biblical "house of Millo." The renewed excavations revealed many additional remains that add up to a complex of several interconnected, but well-defined building units. The quality of the construction is impressive, featuring thick walls founded on bedrock, sometimes preserved to a height of some 4 m. The first stages of these buildings date to the ninth century BCE, at the earliest; they were destroyed, together with the rest of Jerusalem, in 586 BCE, as the visible signs of destruction and conflagration indicate.

The remains of building C consisted of the walls of two rooms, the foundations of the walls of other rooms, and sections of floors. They have been identified as belonging to a four-chamber gatehouse of the type characteristic of the Iron Age II. The earlier excavations had exposed dozens of vessels, including many storage jars, in the gate's southwestern chamber. Building D, which adjoins building C on the east, consisted of several rooms, in which pithoi were found, suggesting that the building was a storehouse.

The various building units combined to form a dense complex whose outer walls created a continuous line of fortifications along the eastern side of the Ophel, overlooking the Kidron Valley. The gate may be associated with the large tower (building B) to the south, discovered by Warren in the Ophel wall between 1867 and 1870, and with another, smaller tower (building A) whose eastern side Kenyon exposed in 1967 in her site SII.

The gate has been identified with the biblical "Water Gate" (Neh. 3:26) that was part of the complex known as the "upper house of the king." The excavators believe that it was a gate in the western section of the Jerusalem city wall, providing access to the separate royal quarter, which stood on the Ophel until the end of the First Temple period.

Plan of the public building complex on the eastern part of the Ophel.

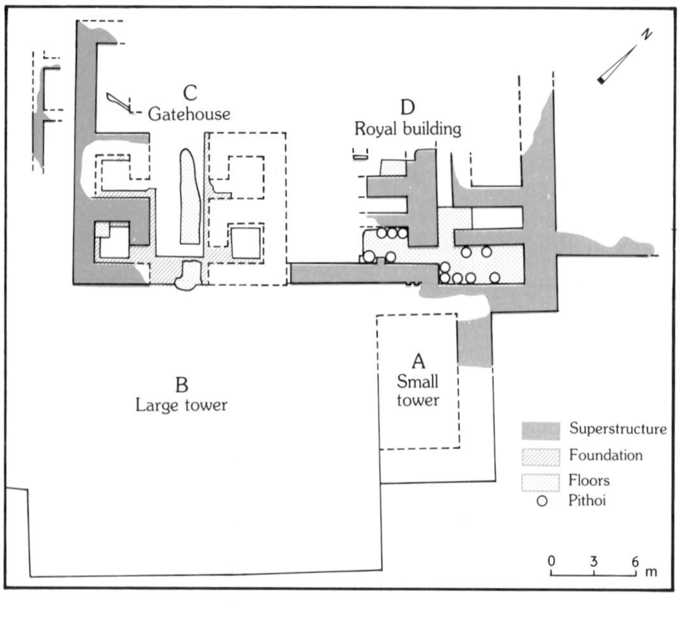

The Citadel ("Tower of David"). Solar and Sivan, excavating in the eastern moat of the Citadel between 1984 and 1988, found remains of quarries in the bedrock. Overlying them were the foundations of walls and earth fills from the Iron Age II (eighth–sixth centuries BCE). Particularly impressive for the quality of its masonry was a segment of a broad wall, built of large field stones, possibly part of the western section of the city wall that encircled the southwestern hill of Jerusalem toward the end of the First Temple period.

Mount Zion. In 1988, Chen and Margalit discovered remains of Iron Age II fortifications, made of large field stones, in the foundations of the First Wall from the Second Temple period, in the southwestern sector of Mount Zion. This was part of the wall that skirted the southwestern hill of Jerusalem on the south toward the end of the First Temple period.

SUMMARY. The most recent discoveries in the city have furnished significant new evidence in favor of the view, now widely accepted by scholars, that the city wall of Jerusalem at the end of the First Temple period enclosed all of the southwestern hill. The city wall at that time ran along the northern part of the hill, above the Transversal Valley, and continued west to the Citadel ("Tower of David") and the modern Jaffa Gate. At that point the wall turned south and ran above the Valley of Hinnom along the course of the present Old City wall, to Mount Zion; it then descended the southern slope of the hill, toward the issue of the Tyropoeon Valley, and continued south to the City of David.

HILLEL GEVA

Chalcolithic Period: L. H. Vincent, *Jérusalem sous terre*, London 1911, pl. 7:1–2; R. P. J. Nasralleh, *JPOS* 16 (1936), 293–315; Y. Shiloh, *Excavations at the City of David I, 1978–1982: Interim Report of the First Five Seasons* (Qedem 19), Jerusalem 1984, 7, 11, 25.

Bronze Age: C. Warren, *Excavations at Jerusalem, 1867–1870*, London 1884, passim; V. Scheil, *RB* 1 (1892), 113–117; F. A. Dieber, ibid. 11 (1902), 441–442; H. Gressman, *PJB* 3 (1907), 72–75; H. Haensler, *Das Heilige Land* 53 (1909), 33–36; L. H. Vincent (op. cit.), passim; id., *RB* 13 (1914), 438–441; id., *Jérusalem, Recherches de topographie, d'archéologie et d'histoire*, 2, Paris 1926, passim; id. (with A. M. Stève), *Jérusalem de l'Ancien Testament*, Paris 1954–1956, passim; R. Weill, *La Fin du Moyen Empire Egyptien* 2, Paris 1918, 736–737, 740; R. A. S. Macalister and J. G. Duncan, *Excavations on the Hill of the Ophel, 1923–1925* (PEFA 4), London 1926, 21–25, 34, 175–178; A. Mallon, *JPOS* 8 (1928), 5–6; J. W. Crowfoot and G. M. Fitzgerald, *Excavations in the Tyropoeon Valley, 1927 (*PEFA 5), London 1929, 20–22, 65–66; B. Mazar, *JPOS* 10 (1930), 181–191; id., *AJSLL* 49 (1932–33), 248–253; id., *The Mountain of the Lord*, Garden City, N.Y. 1975, 40–50, 153–166; id., *Jerusalem Revealed* (ed. Y. Yadin), Jerusalem 1975, 1–4; W. F. Albright, *Jewish Quarterly Review* 21 (1930–31), 164–166; D. C. Baramki, *QDAP* 4 (1935), 165–167; K. Galling, *PJB* 32 (1936), 91; A. Rowe, *Catalogue of Egyptian Scarabs etc. in the Palestine Museum*, Cairo 1936, 291; J. Nougayrol, *Cylindres sceaux et empreintes du cylindres trouvés en Palestine*, Paris 1939, 50–51; R. Maxwell-Hyslop, *Iraq* 8 (1946), 26–28; 11 (1949), 115; N. Avigad, *IEJ* 2 (1952), 230–235; J. S. Simons, *Jerusalem in the Old Testament*, Leiden 1952; S. J. Saller, *Excavations at Bethany*, Jerusalem 1957, 372; id., *LA* 12 (1961–1962), 146–176; id., *The Excavations at Dominus Flevit (Mount of Olives, Jerusalem) 2: The Jebusite Burial Place*, Jerusalem 1964; K. M. Kenyon, *PEQ* 95 (1963), 11–12; id., 97 (1965), 13; 100 (1968), 29, 106; id., *Jerusalem: Excavating 3000 Years of History*, London 1967, 76–97; id., *Digging up Jerusalem*, London 1974, 76–97; Y. Saad, *ADAJ* 8–9 (1964), 77–80; T. H. Busink, *Der Tempel von Jerusalem*, Leiden 1970, 77–89; R. H. Smith, *ADAJ* 15 (1970), 17–20; S. Loffreda, LA 24 (1974), 142–169; 34 (1984), 357–370; D. L. Saltz, *Report of the Department of Antiquities of Cyprus* 1977, 52; A. Ben-Tor, *Cylinder Seals of Third Millennium Palestine*, Cambridge 1978, 61; J. J. Schmitt, *Scripture in Context: Essays in the Comparative Method* (ed. C. D. Evans et al.), Pittsburgh 1980, 101–121; R. S. Merrillees, *Report of the Department of Antiquities, Cyprus* 1981, 50–52; T. Watkins, *Levant* 13 (1981), 122–126, 130; L. E. Stager, *JNES* 41 (1982), 111–121; B. Brandl and B. Sass, *ZDPV* 101 (1984), 111–113; Y. Shiloh, *Excavations at the City of David 1, 1978–1982: Interim Report of the First Five Seasons* (Qedem 19), Jerusalem 1984, passim; id., *IEJ* 35 (1985), 66–67, 302–303; R. Gonen, *BAR* 11 (1985), 44–55; W. H. Mare, *The Archaeology of the Jerusalem Area*, Grand Rapids 1987; R. Reich, *IEJ* 37 (1987), 163–164; M. Steiner, ibid. 38 (1988), 203–204; A. Maeir, *Göttinger Miszellen* 110 (1989), 35–40; E. Mazar and B. Mazar, *Excavations on the South of the Temple Mount, Jerusalem* (Qedem 29), Jerusalem 1989; D. T. Ariel, *Imported Stamped Amphora Handles, Coins, Worked Bone, and Ivory and Glass: Excavations at the City of David 1978–1985* 2 (Qedem 30), Jerusalem 1990, passim; D. Bahat, *The Illustrated Atlas of Jerusalem*, New York 1990; K. Prag, *PEQ* 123 (1991), 129–132; S. Wimmer, *Studies in Egyptology presented to Miriam Lichtheim* 2 (ed. S. Israelit-Groll), Jerusalem 1990, 1073.

Iron Age: C. Warren, *Underground Jerusalem*, London 1876, passim; id., *Excavations at Jerusalem, 1867–1870*, London 1884, passim; id. (with C. R. Conder), *SWP* 5, 1884, passim; C. R. Conder, *PEQ* 13 (1881), 201–205; E. Flecker, ibid. (1884), 178–181; C. Schick, *ZDPV* 8 (1885), 170–173; id., *PEQ* 19 (1887), 154–155; 24 (1892), 120–124; W. M. F. Petrie, ibid., 28–35; F. J. Bliss and A. C. Dickie, *Excavations at Jerusalem 1894–1897*, London 1898, 260–265; C. Clermont-Ganneau, *Les Tombeaux de David et des rois de Juda et le tunnel-aqueduc de Siloe*, Paris 1897; id., *ARP* 1, passim; R. A. S. Macalister, *PEQ* 32 (1900), 248; (1901), 145; L. H. Vincent, *Jérusalem sous terre*, London 1911, passim; id., *Jérusalem: Recherches de topographie, d'archéologie et d'histoire* 1, Paris 1912, passim; id. (with F. M. Abel), ibid. 2, Paris 1914–1926, passim; id., *RB* 33 (1924), 357–370; id. (with A. M. Stève), *Jérusalem de l'Ancien Testament*, Paris 1954–1956, passim; W. F. Albright, *JPOS* 2 (1922), 286–290; id., *BASOR* 10 (1923), 1–3; R. Weill, *La Cité de David* 1, Paris 1920; ibid. 2, Paris 1947; id., *PEQ* 58 (1926), 171–175; E. Sukenik, *JPOS* 8 (1928), 12–16; R. Hamilton, *PEQ* 67 (1935), 142–143; K. Galling, *PJB* 32 (1936), 73–101; G. E. Wright, *BA* 4 (1941), 17–31; G. Bressan, *Biblica* 25 (1944), 217–224; 35 (1954), 217–224; S. Yeivin, *JNES* 7 (1948), 30–45; P. L. Garber, *BA* 14 (1951), 2–24; C. N. Johns, *QDAP* 14 (1950), 129; J. Simons, *Oudtestamentische studien* 7 (ed. P. A. H. de Boer), Leiden 1950, 179–200; id., *Jerusalem in the Old Testament*, Leiden 1952, passim; N. Avigad, *IEJ* 2 (1952), 230–235; 3 (1953), 137–152; 5 (1955), 163–166; 20 (1970), 5–6, 8, 129–134; 22 (1972), 193–197,200; 25 (1975), 260–261; 27 (1977), 55–56; 29 (1979), 123–124; id., *Jerusalem Revealed* (ed. Y. Yadin), Jerusalem 1975, 41–44; id., *Discovering Jerusalem*, Nashville 1983, 23–60; id., *Biblical Archaeology Today*, Jerusalem 1985, 469–475; id., *Israel Museum Journal* 8 (1989), 7–16; M. Avi-Yonah, *IEJ* 4 (1954), 239–248; 21 (1971), 168–169; A. Parrot, *The Temple of Jerusalem*, London 1957; R. Amiran, *IEJ* 8 (1958), 205–227; (with A. Eitan), ibid. 20 (1970), 9–10, 16; id. with A. Eitan, *Jerusalem Revealed* (ed. Y. Yadin), Jerusalem 1975, 52–53, 75–78; M. Burrows, *ZAW* 70 (1958), 221–227; H. J. Katzenstein, *IEJ* 10 (1960), 152–155; G. Fohrer, *Theologisches Wörterbuch zum Neuen Testament* 7 (1961), 291–318; R. de Vaux, *Ancient Israel: Its Life and Institutions*, New York 1961, 312–330; K. M. Kenyon, *PEQ* 94 (1962), 76–83; 95 (1963), 9–23; 96 (1964), 8–11; 97 (1965), 11–14; 98 (1966), 85, 74–81; 99 (1967), 66–69; 100 (1968), 104–109; id., *Jerusalem: Excavating 3000 Years of History*, New York 1967, passim; id., *Near Eastern Archaeology in the Twentieth Century* (N. Glueck Fest., ed. J.A. Sanders), Garden City, N.Y. 1970, 232–253; id., *Mélanges offrets à M. Maurice Dunand*, 2, Beirut 1972, 137–149; id., *Cities of the Old Testament*, London 1971, passim; id., *Digging up Jerusalem*, New York 1974, passim; J. Prignaud, *RB* 71 (1964), 372–383; 77 (1970), 50–67; id., *Archaeology in the Levant* (K. M. Kenyon Fest., eds. P. R. S. Moorey and P. J. Parr), London 1978, 136–148; S. Loffreda, *LA* 16 (1965–1966), 8–9; 32 (1982), 59–72; D. R. A. Thomas, *Archaeology and Old Testament Study* (ed. D. Winton-Thomas), Oxford 1967, 276–295; G. Levi Della Vida, *In Memorium Paul Kahle* (eds. M. Black and G. Fohrer), Berlin 1968, 162–166; D. Ussishkin, *BASOR* 196 (1969), 16–22; id., *BA* 33 (1970), 34–38; id., *Jerusalem Revealed* (op. cit.), 63–65; id., *Levant* 8 (1976), 93–95; id., *IEJ* 16 (1966), 104–110; 29 (1979), 137–142; T. A. Busink, *Der Tempel von Jerusalem*, Leiden 1970, passim; B. Couroyer, *RB* 77 (1970), 248–250; U. Lux, *ZDPV* 88 (1972), 193–194; E.-M. Laperrousaz, *IEJ* 132 (1973), 465–474; 134 (1975), 3–30; H. Shanks, *The City of David: A Guide to Biblical Jerusalem*, Tel Aviv 1973; M. Broshi, *IEJ* 24 (1974), 21–26; 26 (1976), 81; (with G. Barkay), 35 (1985), 119; id., (op. cit.), 57; id., *Israel Museum Journal* 1 (1982), 5–10; J. Wilkinson, *PEQ* 106 (1974), 36–51; id., *Levant* 10 (1978), 116–125; D. Bahat and M. Broshi, *Jerusalem Revealed* (op. cit.), 56; B. Mazar, *The Mountain of the Lord*, Garden City, N.Y. 1975, passim; id., *Jerusalem Revealed*, 1–8; G. Barkay (with A. Kloner), IEJ 26 (1976), 55–57; *IEJ* 26 (1976), 58; id., *Biblical Archaeology Today*, Jerusalem 1985, 476–475; id., *BAIAS* (1985–1986), 32–43; id. (with A. Kloner), *BAR* 12 (1986), 22–39, 40–53; A. Issar, *IEJ* 26 (1976), 130–136; A. Mazar, ibid., 1–8; S. Singer, *BAR* 2 (1976), 7–10; M. Hoberman, *Levant* 9 (1977), 174–175; T. A. Holland, ibid. 9 (1977), 121–155; N. Shaheen, *PEQ* 109 (1977), 107–112; 111 (1979), 103–108; A. Lemaire, *Levant* 10 (1978), 156–161; id., *RB* 88 (1981), 236–239; id., *BAR* 10 (1984), 24–29; id., *IEJ* 28 (1978), 274–276; 29 (1979), 244–246; 30 (1980), 220–221; 32 (1982), 157–158; 33 (1983), 129–131; 34 (1984), 57–58; 35 (1985), 65–67; 301–303; 36 (1986), 16–38; id., *Excavations at the City of David* 1, *1978–1982: Interim Report of the First Five Seasons* (Qedem 19), Jerusalem 1984, passim; id., *Archaeology in the Land of Israel* (eds. H. Shanks and B. Mazar), Washington, D.C. 1984, 149–157; id., *Biblical Archaeology Today*, Jerusalem 1985, 451–462; id., *The Land of Israel: Crossroads of Civilizations* (ed. E. Lipinski), Leuven 1985, 113–146; id., *PEQ* 119 (1987), 9–18; id., *AASOR* 49 (1989), 97–105; G. Brunet, *VT* Supplement 30 (1979), 73–86; H. Geva, *IEJ* 29 (1979), 84–91; 33 (1983), 56–58; A. D. Tushingham, *ZDPV* 95 (1979), 39–55; id., *Excavations in Jerusalem* 1, Toronto 1985; id., *Biblical Archaeology Today*, Jerusalem 1985, 440–450; id., *Levant* 19 (1987), 137–143; id., *PEQ* 120 (1988), 142–145; D. Bahat, *IEJ* 31 (1981), 235–236; id., *The Illustrated Atlas of Jerusalem*, New York 1990; L. Y. Rahmani, *BA* 44 (1981), 229–235; V. C. Corbo, *Il Santo Sepolcro di Gerusalemme*, Jerusalem 1981–1982, passim; M. Ben-Dov, *In the Shadow of the Temple: The Discovery of Ancient Jerusalem*, Jerusalem 1982, 31–55; J. Naveh, *IEJ* 32 (1982), 195–198; V. Sasson, *PEQ* 114 (1982), 111–117; L. E. Stager, *JNES* 41 (1982), 111–121; R. Wenning and E. Zenger, *Ugarit-Forschungen* 14 (1982), 279–294; A. Kloner, *BAIAS* (1982–1983), 37–40; D. Cole, *BAR* 9 (1983), 73; A. Kaufman, *BAR* 9 (1983), 40–59; J. R. Abercrombie, *BASOR* 254 (1984), 61–62; G. Barkay, *Israel Numismatic Journal* 8 (1984–1985), 1–5; H. J. Franken, *Newsletter of the Department of Pottery Technology* 3 (1985), 24–42; id., *Levant* 19 (1987), 129–135; 21 (1989), 197; id. (with M. L. Steiner), *Excavations in Jerusalem 1961–1967*, 2, Oxford 1990; S. Gibson (and G. Edelstein), *Levant* 17 (1985), 139– 155; id., *PEQ* 119 (1987), 81–96; H. D. Lance, *Biblical Archaeology Today*, Jerusalem 1985, 481–483; M. L. Steiner, *PEQ* 118 (1986), 27–32; H. E. Lagro and D. Noordhuizen, *Newsletter of the Department of Pottery Technology* 5 (1987), 1–24; W. H. Mare, *The Archaeology of the Jerusalem Area*, Grand Rapids 1987, passim; R. Reich, *IEJ* 37 (1987), 158–160; A. J. 'Amr, *Levant* 20 (1988), 185–196; T. Schneider, *IEJ* 38 (1988), 139–141; E. Mazar and B. Mazar, *Excavations on the South of the Temple Mount, Jerusalem* (Qedem 29), Jerusalem 1989, passim; A. Maeir, *Göttingen Miszellen* 114 (1990), 63–69; B. Sass, *PEQ* 112 (1990), 59–61; J. Nadelman, *IEJ* 40 (1990), 31–41; D. Gill, *Science* 254 (1991), 1467–1471; J. Cahill et al., *BAR* 17 (1991), 64–69.

Iron Age tombs: K. Galling, *PJB* 32 (1936), 73–101; A. Mazar, *IEJ* 26 (1976), 1–8; B. Arensburg and Y. Rak, *PEQ* 117 (1985), 30–34; G. Barkay (with A. Kloner), *BAR* 12/2 (1986), 22–39, 40–57; id., *BAIAS* (1985–1986), 37–40; R. Reich, *Highlights of Recent Excavations*, Jerusalem 1990, 16–17.

For additional bibliography, see, for example: P. Thomsen, *Die Palästina-literatur* 1–7, Leipzig 1911–1969, passim; L. A. Mayer and M. Avi-Yonah, *QDAP* 1 (1932), 163–193; M. C. Salzman, *'Atiqot* Supplement 4 (1965), 12; 8 (1969), 18; 9–10 (1973), 32–37; R. P. Goldschmidt-Lehman, *Jerusalem Cathedra* 2 (1982), 328–351; J. D. Purvis, *Jerusalem the Holy City: A Bibliography* 1–2 (American Theological Library Association Bibliography Series 20), Metuchen, N.J. 1988–1991.

(comp. Aren Maeir)

THE SECOND TEMPLE PERIOD

HISTORY

BABYLONIAN AND PERSIAN PERIODS. After Jerusalem had been destroyed by the Babylonians in 586 BCE and its inhabitants deported, only the "poorest of the land" were left in the city and its environs (2 Kg. 25:8–12). This situation, although consistent with the archeological finds, is at odds with Jeremiah 52:29-30, in which the number of exiles who left Jerusalem after the destruction is small—832 persons, and 745 more after the assassination of Gedaliah son of Ahikam. Possibly, many Jerusalemites had abandoned the city even before the siege, and many others escaped during the fighting.

After the Babylonians lost Judah and Jerusalem to the Persians, Cyrus published his celebrated proclamation (538 BCE) permitting the Jews to rebuild Jerusalem and the Temple (Ezra 1:2–3). The returning exiles settled mainly in Jerusalem (in the City of David) and in the nearby villages to the north. Under the leadership of Sheshbazzar, who was appointed governor of Judah, the Temple altar was repaired and the Temple implements restored. It is quite possible that even at this early stage preparations were begun to rebuild the Temple itself (Ezra 5:16); this would have been a first, symbolic step, heralding the inception of a new period in Jerusalem's history. However, the small population of Jerusalem at the time, the hostility and interference of gentile neighbors, and the difficulty of financing the construction put an end to any such effort.

In the year 521 BCE a new, larger wave of returnees reached Jerusalem, led by Zerubbabel son of Shealtiel, a scion of the royal dynasty who had been appointed governor of Judah, and Joshua son of Jehozadak, one of the leading priests in Babylon. The returning exiles, encouraged by the prophet Haggai, set about completing the construction of the Temple, but they encountered the same difficulties as their predecessors. The work dragged on, and only in 515 BCE, after the text of Cyrus' original proclamation had been located, was the building of the Temple crowned with success. Preparations may have been undertaken at the same time to repair the walls of Jerusalem, which had been in ruins since the Babylonian occupation. This act signified the immigrants' renewed political independence.

The history of Jerusalem in the first half of the fifth century BCE is shrouded in darkness; the written sources offer no information for the period. The country's relative calm at the time presumably encouraged the Jews to continue to settle in Jerusalem. In 458 BCE, Ezra the Scribe came to Jerusalem at the head of yet another group of returnees. He concentrated his efforts in Jerusalem on consolidating the legal and religious identity of the city's Jewish community. Possibly, a further failed attempt was made in Ezra's time to repair the city's fortifications—a plan of far-reaching political significance; this may be inferred from the Aramaic letter of accusation sent to the king of Persia to thwart the plan (Ezra 4:7–16).

In the wake of Ezra's failure, a new governor, Nehemiah, arrived in Jerusalem in 445 BCE. His first and most urgent concern was to rebuild the wall around Jerusalem, as related in Nehemiah 2–4. Nehemiah describes the ruins of the city and relates how he organized the people into construction teams, finally completing the walls in fifty-two days. Once again, the neighboring nations were bitterly opposed to the project and actively tried to sabotage it.

The city wall, described in the book of Nehemiah in considerable detail, with all its gates and towers, probably encircled only the City of David and the Temple. According to the biblical account (Neh. 2:8), "the fortress (*birah*)" was still standing near the Temple and Nehemiah in fact used it as his headquarters. Nehemiah's account is a most important and detailed documentation of the topography of the city and its wall before the city expanded westward to occupy the southwestern hill. The wall, in addition to its obvious defensive function, also played a social role: the mere fact of its construction symbolized the Jews' aloofness from their gentile neighbors. Nehemiah also issued an official decree that compelled part of the Jewish rural population to settle in Jerusalem (Neh. 11:1). Through his efforts, the city's Jewish community grew in numbers and increased its economic and social stability;

The Jewish Quarter and southern part of the Old City, looking west.

Map of Jerusalem at the end of the Second Temple period.

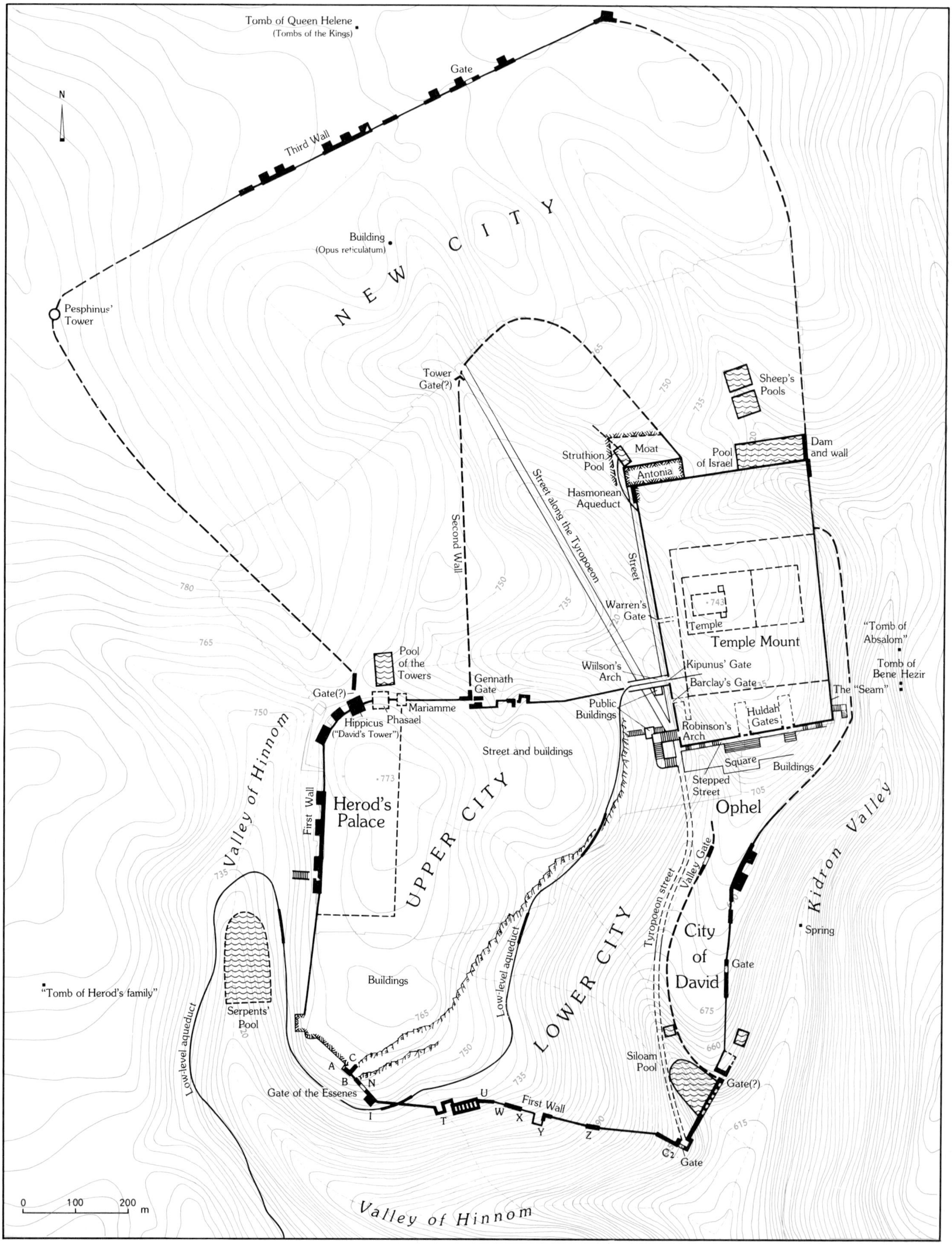

nevertheless, Jerusalem was still only sparsely populated: "The city was wide and large, but the people within it were few and no houses had been built" (Neh. 7:4).

The two centuries between the close of Nehemiah's activity in Jerusalem and the beginning of the Hellenistic period are also wrapped in obscurity.

HELLENISTIC AND HASMONEAN PERIODS. In 332 BCE, Judah and Jerusalem were conquered by Alexander the Great and came under Greek rule. After his death, Jerusalem changed hands several times (during the

Diadochi's wars of succession), until 301 BCE, when it finally became part of the Ptolemaic kingdom of Egypt. The Ptolemies ruled Jerusalem and Judah for a long time. There is very little information about the city in this period. It seems that Jerusalem, whose economic infrastructure had been badly damaged by long years of instability, benefited from the prolonged period of political calm. The city's ruins and its walls were rebuilt, perhaps as far back as the time of Simeon the Just, in the early third century BCE, and a pool was built (*Ecclesiasticus* 50:1–4). In the mid-third century BCE, the city's population grew as a result of the political stability and economic development in the area under the Ptolemies. According to Hecataeus (cited by Josephus in *Against Apion* I, 197), the population of Jerusalem was then 120,000. This figure is certainly exaggerated, but it attests, at the very least, to a steady increase in population.

Upon the accession to the throne of Antiochus III (223 BCE), military initiative in Palestine was taken over by the Seleucids, who ruled Syria. The struggle between the Seleucid and Ptolemaic kingdoms at the end of the third century BCE and the consequent unrest cut short Jerusalem's economic and urban development. During one of those clashes, the city was apparently occupied by King Ptolemy of Egypt, reportedly because he attacked the city on the Sabbath, when its Jewish defenders refused to fight (*Antiq.* XII, 4–6; *Against Apion* I, 209–210).

In 200 BCE, Palestine and Jerusalem fell to the Seleucids. The Jews of Jerusalem welcomed the rule of Antiochus III and in fact helped him wrest the city fortress from its Ptolemaic garrison (*Antiq.* XII, 138).

In the early years of the second century BCE, the municipal administration of Jerusalem, encouraged by the Seleucid kings and supported by Hellenized elements among the city's wealthier Jews and the aristocratic priestly families, was organized along the lines of a Greek polis. In 175 BCE, as part of the endeavor to give Jerusalem the character of a Greek polis, the high priest Jason received permission from Antiochus IV Epiphanes to build a gymnasium (2 Macc. 4:9). The Jews were allowed "to live according to their ancestral laws," and the authorities in fact assisted in repairing Jerusalem and the Temple, probably damaged when the city was occupied. The Letter of Aristeas provides details about the Temple, its walls and towers, as well as the mighty fortress that protected the northern approaches to the Temple in the Hellenistic period.

With the appointment of Menelaus as high priest in Jerusalem in 171 BCE, the Seleucid authorities intensified their intervention in the city's affairs. In 168 BCE, upon his return from an unsuccessful military sortie to Egypt, Antiochus IV looted the Temple treasures. That same year, inspired by a rumor that the king had died in another military expedition to Egypt, the Jews of Jerusalem rebelled, reappointing Jason as high priest. Menelaus and his supporters were forced to take refuge in the fortress until Antiochus reconquered the city. In order to buttress his control of the city, Antiochus IV now brought foreign settlers to Jerusalem and erected a new fortress, known as the Acra, in which he stationed a hostile mercenary garrison.

The Seleucid ruler's attempts to prohibit observance of the commandments and interfere with the sacrificial rites in the Temple, even installing a graven image in the sanctuary, aroused vehement opposition on the part of the Jews, who finally rose in armed revolt. After a series of Hasmonean victories at the very beginning of the revolt, Judas Maccabaeus entered Jerusalem in 164 BCE and cleansed the Temple. In the coming years, however, the Hasmoneans were unable to maintain continuous control of Jerusalem, in particular owing to the presence of a Seleucid garrison in the Acra. Repeated attempts to displace this garrison were successful only under Simeon the Hasmonean, in 141 BCE (2 Macc. 13:49–52). The whole of Jerusalem was now finally under Hasmonean control and the constant Seleucid threat was removed.

Some sections of Jerusalem's fortifications had already been repaired under Judas Maccabaeus and the first Hasmonean rulers, in order to enhance the defenses of what was then the capital city of their kingdom. Hasmonean initiative also furthered population growth, as a result of which the city spread to the southwestern hill. The foundations were laid for a high-class residential section that ultimately became known as the Upper City. Under Simeon the Hasmonean, the conqueror of the Acra, and his successor, Hyrcanus I, the "First Wall" around the southwestern hill was rebuilt.

In 134–132 BCE, Antiochus VII Sidetes laid siege to Jerusalem but failed to penetrate its defenses. The treaty he signed with John Hyrcanus I required the Hasmonean king to demolish parts of Jerusalem's fortifications in return for lifting the siege and Seleucid recognition of his kingdom. The subsequent years of John Hyrcanus' reign and those of his successor, Alexander Jannaeus, were marked by rapid development in Jerusalem, which was now the capital city of a large kingdom. New residential sections were built in the northern part of the city and encircled by the "Second Wall." In order to satisfy Jerusalem's burgeoning needs for water, the so-called Low Aqueduct was built in the Hasmonean period, to bring water to the Temple from the distant springs in the hills far to the south.

The wars of succession that broke out among the Hasmoneans after Salome Alexandra's death (67 BCE) hastened the end of their rule in Jerusalem. In 63 BCE the city was occupied by Pompey, who besieged it at the head of a Roman army to aid the pretender Hyrcanus II. The supporters of the latter's rival, Aristobulus II, retreated from most of the city and shut themselves up in the Temple. After a three-month siege, during which parts of the city around the Temple were systematically destroyed, the Temple Mount was overrun and the independent rule of the Hasmoneans in Jerusalem came to an end (*Antiq.* XIV, 58–71; *War* I, 421–152). In subsequent years, Aristobulus' son, Alexander, in fact planned to restore the fortifications, but his attempt to implement this plan (in 57 BCE) was foiled by the intervention of Gabinius, the Roman procurator in Syria (*Antiq.* XIV, 82–85; *War* I, 160–163).

HERODIAN PERIOD. In 48 BCE, Antipater the Idumean, who ruled Judea as regent on behalf of the Romans, repaired the breaches in Jerusalem's defenses that had been made during the Roman conquest. He appointed his sons Phasael and Herod as tetrarchs of Jerusalem and Galilee, respectively (*Antiq.* XIV, 156, 158; *War* I, 199, 203).

In 40 BCE, when the Parthians invaded Syria and Palestine, Mattathias Antigonus the Hasmonean seized the opportunity to march on Jerusalem at the head of his supporters, forcing Herod to flee the city. Mattathias Antigonus, the last of the Hasmonean kings, ruled Jerusalem for the next three years. In 37 BCE Herod, with Roman support, returned to Judea at the head of an army and laid siege to Jerusalem. After five months he took the city from the north, breaching both walls. The defenders of Jerusalem and their leader, Mattathias Antigonus, were thrust back into the Temple and the Upper City but were soon ousted from there, too (*Antiq.* XIV, 468–486; *War* I, 345–357).

Herod, having consolidated his hold over Jerusalem and the country as a whole, embarked on several ambitious building projects that utterly transformed the architectural face of the city; within the span of a single generation, Jerusalem became one of the most beautiful capitals in the ancient Near East. Whole sections of the city were rebuilt and impressive public buildings erected; luxurious palaces went up in the Upper City, and to the west the royal palace was built, defended by three huge towers. Crowning Herod's achievements in Jerusalem was the reconstruction of the Temple on an artificial elevated platform that was impressive both for the technology employed to make it and for its size (*War* V, 184–237). The Temple Mount and the Temple itself are described in detail, from the point of view of Jewish law, in the Mishnaic tractate *Middot*.

Herod's construction projects not only beautified Jerusalem, they also ushered in a period of great economic prosperity. They both provided employment for thousands of inhabitants over a period of many years and made the city an attraction for myriads of pilgrims who thronged to the Holy City from the rest of the country and all over the Diaspora.

Upon Herod's death in 4 BCE, the kingdom was divided among his sons. Archelaus inherited the bulk of his father's dominions and became the ruler of Jerusalem. In the wake of his failure to respond to popular demands to alleviate various oppressive measures, riots broke out in the city, and he was obliged to leave immediately for Rome to give an account to the emperor. The Roman official Sabinus, left in command in Jerusalem, tried to gain control of the city; he invaded the Temple, set fire to the stoas, and looted the Temple treasures. These events only intensified the violence of the people's reaction, and Sabinus and his troops were forced to take refuge behind the wall of the royal palace. The uprising was finally suppressed by Varus, the Roman procurator in Syria, who occupied the city and put many of its inhabitants to death (*Antiq.* XVII, 250–264, 286–297; *War* II, 39–50, 66–79).

PROCURATORS' PERIOD. Archelaus was sent into exile in 6 CE, and his kingdom was made a Roman province, under the direct rule of a Roman procurator. This change in the political status of Judea as a whole also adversely affected Jerusalem, which lost its position as the administrative capital of the country; in addition, a Roman garrison was permanently stationed in the city, based in the Antonia fortress, which controlled the Temple area.

Up until the Jewish Revolt in 66 CE, a total of fourteen Roman procurators ruled Jerusalem. Their policies and behavior, which ignored the feelings of the Jewish residents, aroused tensions that erupted on occasion as violent clashes. Friction with the Roman authorities peaked under the procurator Pontius Pilate (26–36 CE), who used Temple monies to build an aqueduct to Jerusalem (*Antiq.* XVIII, 60–62; *War* II, 175–177).

Jerusalem in the first century CE was in the throes of expanding its territory north, where the so-called New City sprang up. In 41–44 CE, Agrippa I began to build the Third Wall to defend the new section of the city. However, the Roman emperor forbade him to continue, and the new wall was only completed during the revolt. At this time, too, construction work on the Temple came to an end, and the many laborers who thus became unemployed were set to work paving the streets of Jerusalem.

The Sanhedrin, which held jurisdiction over religious and civil affairs, was then the central institution in Jerusalem—the concrete expression of the internal autonomy of Judea. In addition, positions of considerable influence were held by a few of the senior priestly families, from which the high priests were chosen. Jerusalem attracted residents in large numbers, from near and far; among the best known of the foreigners who came was Helena, queen of Adiabene, who built an impressive family tomb north of the city (*Antiq.* XX, 95).

By the end of the Second Temple period Jerusalem had the largest Jewish community in Judea and was a focus of Jewish spiritual creativity and a major economic center in the country. The historical sources estimate the city's population at the time in exaggerated numbers, reaching hundreds of thousands (Tacitus, *Historiae* V, 13) and even more (Josephus, *War* II, 280; VI, 420–425).

The most important written sources for information about Jerusalem in most of the period in question are the works of the contemporary historian Josephus Flavius, who had firsthand knowledge of the city. His most important work in this regard is *The Jewish War*, which devotes two entire chapters to a detailed, systematic description of Jerusalem, its fortifications, buildings, and Temple, as they were on the eve of the destruction in 70 CE (*War* V, 136–183; 184–247).

Jerusalem's significance and renown at the end of the Second Temple period transcended the narrow boundaries of Judea; in Philo's words, "Jerusalem [was] the metropolis not only of Judea but of many other countries" (*Legatio ad Gaium* 281). So great was its splendor at this time that Pliny the Elder called it "the most illustrious city in the East" (*NH* V, 70).

The last days of the Second Temple period were marked by the emergence of Zealot movements in Jerusalem, fueled by growing resentment of Roman government and religious, economic, and social tensions among the various classes in the populace. Further complicating the situation were deep religious convictions and messianic expectations, popularized by numerous visionaries and prophets, who promised the people speedy redemption from the oppressive Roman yoke.

One of these was undoubtedly Jesus of Nazareth, who was active in Jerusalem during the 30s of the first century CE; he was brought there to trial before the Roman procurator Pontius Pilate, who sentenced him to death by crucifixion.

THE FIRST REVOLT AND THE DESTRUCTION OF THE SECOND TEMPLE. In 66 CE, disturbances erupted in Jerusalem and soon reached the proportions of a full-scale rebellion against the Roman authorities. The rebels took over Jerusalem and evicted the Roman procurator Florus and his troops from the city; at the same time, they abolished the sacrifice regularly offered in the Temple for the emperor's welfare—an act tantamount to declaring war on Rome. The civil war that broke out among the rival factions and between them and the advocates of peaceful compromise with Rome devastated entire sections of Jerusalem, including the palaces in the Upper City. The Zealots finally prevailed. The Roman army that had been dispatched to quell the revolt conquered the Antonia, and the remnants of this army shut themselves up in the royal palace in the Upper City. When the rebels conquered the palace and the three towers that defended it, the whole of Jerusalem was in their hands. An attempt by Cestius Gallus, the Roman procurator in Syria, to suppress the uprising failed. After occupying some parts of Jerusalem, he was driven back by the rebels and retreated.

The leaders of the Zealot factions that had gained control of Jerusalem—John of Gischala, Simeon bar Giora, and Eleazar ben Simeon—imposed a reign of terror on the population. As a result of their internecine struggle to control strategic sections of the city, many houses were destroyed and food stores burned. This weakened Jerusalem's ability and the resolve of its residents to withstand the imminent Roman attack.

In the spring of 70 CE, Titus besieged Jerusalem at the head of an army consisting of the Fifth, Tenth, Twelfth, and Fifteenth legions, assisted by numerous auxiliary forces. After bitter fighting, the city was conquered from the north, in several stages. The Romans first breached the Third Wall; immediately thereafter, the Second Wall fell. The Romans then reared two siege mounds over against the Antonia in the north of the Temple Mount and two other siege mounds west of the city, threatening the wall of the Upper City. These mounds were partly damaged by the defenders' attacks. Unable to breach the wall of the Upper City, Titus ordered a circumvallation to be constructed in order to block escapes from the city and cut off food supplies. A further effort, in the course of which the siege mounds were repaired, finally resulted in his occupation of the Antonia fortress. In the fierce battles that then ensued, the northern and western stoas of the Temple Mount burned down and the sacrificial rites were discontinued. On the ninth of the Hebrew month of Av, the Temple was occupied and destroyed. One month later, on the eighth of Elul, the Romans overran the Upper City and burned it to the ground. The next day "the dawn . . . broke upon Jerusalem in flames" (*War* VI, 407). The deliberate and systematic destruction of the city and the Temple continued for some time after its occupation by the Roman legions. Most of the inhabitants and refugees who had sought shelter in Jerusalem perished in the fighting and the siege; the survivors were sold into slavery. After the revolt, the Tenth Roman Legion erected its camp on the ruins of the city, in the shadow of the three great towers that Herod had built in its western part (*War* VII, 2).

*Silver shekel from the First Jewish Revolt against Rome: **(left)** "Jerusalem the Holy"; **(right)** "Shekel of Israel, year 3" (68 CE).*

TOPOGRAPHY

Josephus' description reveals that during most of the period in question Jerusalem was essentially built on two hills (*War* V, 136–137.) The first, known on the map of ancient Jerusalem as the southwestern hill, was the site of the Upper City; it included the present-day area of the Jewish and Armenian quarters of the Old City and Mount Zion to their south. The second hill, known as the Acra, on which the Lower City stood, mainly consisted of the spur of the City of David and the Ophel, as well as parts of Mount Moriah—the site of the Herodian Temple Mount. At the time of the Second Temple, the urban area of the Lower City undoubtedly included most of the Tyropoeon Valley and the low southeastern slope of the hill of the Upper City. Between the two hills, says Josephus, ran the Tyropoeon Valley—the Valley of the Cheesemakers—extending south as far as the Siloam Pool. The upper part of the Tyropoeon followed the same course as the present-day el-Wad Street, which runs south from the Damascus Gate to the Dung Gate. The southern continuation toward the Siloam Pool, as well as the spur of the City of David and the Ophel, are today outside the Old City walls to the south. A third hill, which, according to Josephus, was leveled by the Hasmonean kings, is today occupied mainly by the northwestern corner of the Temple Mount and a small area north of that corner. Toward the end of the Second Temple period the hill of Bezetha, which is higher than the rest of the city, was annexed to Jerusalem in the north; it was here, according to Josephus, that the New City was built (*War* V, 149–151, 246). East of the city, on the other side of the Kidron Valley, rose the Mount of Olives, and north of that, Mount Scopus (*War* V, 67–70). The fortified area of urban Jerusalem in the Second Temple period was delimited on the south and west by the Valley of Hinnom.

EXPANSION OF THE CITY

The latest archaeological evidence indicates quite definitely that Jerusalem's urban development in Second Temple times essentially resembles its development during the First Temple period. In both, the residential area was initially limited to the City of David, with the Temple towering above it to the north. In time, the inhabited area expanded dynamically toward the southwestern hill, which ultimately became the city's municipal and political center. By the end of this evolution, additional residential neighborhoods had been established north of the southwestern hill; by the end of the Second Temple period these neighborhoods were also surrounded by a wall.

Judging from the most recent excavation results, as well as previous ones, it is clear that the exiles who returned from Babylon after a seventy-year absence confined their settlement to the traditional limits of the City of David. In the first years of the restoration the city was small, unwalled, and sparsely populated; it was built on the ruins of the city that had been destroyed in 586 BCE by the Babylonian armies. The safety of the newly settled Jerusalemites was assured only after Nehemiah rebuilt the ruined walls, at about the end of the fifth century BCE. Recent excavations have shown that the new line of the city's eastern defenses was shifted to the crest of the ridge, thus reducing the area of the city on that side. This wall, later incorporated in what Josephus called the First Wall, protected Jerusalem from the east and was repeatedly restored and strengthened in the Second Temple period.

The archaeological evidence indicates that at the end of the Persian period, in the fourth century BCE, the development of the city was quite slow and gradual; this was also the case in the Early (pre-Hasmonean) Hellenistic period, in the third and second centuries BCE—the city remained within the fortified but narrow bounds of the City of David, for the time being. North of the City of David, on Mount Moriah, stood the newly rebuilt Temple.

At this time the city occupied an area of no more than 30 a., and its population is estimated at only a few thousands. However, by the eve of the Hasmonean period, some settlement had already been attempted in the western outskirts of the City of David and the Temple Mount, although its precise nature is difficult to determine. At this time, too, the Seleucid Acra, frequently mentioned in the books of the Maccabees, was erected; its precise location is still a mystery, however (see below).

By the beginning of the Hasmonean period, urban Jerusalem occupied the whole of the southwestern hill, which had been uninhabited since the destruction of the city at the end of the First Temple period. Traces of this new occupation have been identified by excavators in a great many areas. The finds indicate the nature of the occupation in these early stages and provide striking evidence of the hill's intensified population then. It was probably the Hasmonean revolt and its outcome, with all its ramifications, that brought about this dramatic expansion. The extensive building activities of the Hasmonean kings are reported in the books of the Maccabees. Part of the process was the refortification of the southwestern hill at the very beginning of the Hasmonean period. This was the strong city wall known to us from Josephus' detailed account as the First Wall. Recent excavations have shown that the Hasmonean kings only restored the fortifications, following the same line as the original wall from the late First Temple period.

The occupation of the southwestern hill, which dates, as already mentioned, to the Hasmonean period, developed rapidly in the first century BCE and soon became an exclusive residential area known as the Upper City. This new section, which was protected by the First Wall, increased the city's fortified area all at once to approximately 160 a.; the population of the new walled area is estimated to have been more than thirty thousand. As the Hasmonean period progressed, the population of Jerusalem continued to spread northward, moving up the Tyropoeon. Finally, probably in the later part of the period, it was surrounded by the Second Wall. However, the limited excavations that have hitherto been possible in the northern part of the Old City have not located any definite remains of this wall. Thus, a satisfactory answer to the question of the line of the Second Wall or the time of its construction is still needed. It would seem that by the end of the Hasmonean period, the fortified area of Jerusalem had increased to more than 220 a., with an estimated population of more than forty thousand.

Herod, at the end of the first century BCE, radically transformed the architectural face of Jerusalem. A great many public buildings and luxurious private homes were built, in the best traditions of Hellenistic-Roman architecture. The most impressive and monumental structure was the Temple Mount enclosure, with its retaining walls and the Temple itself. Excavations west and south of the walls of the Temple Mount have unearthed impressive evidence of the magnificence and strength of the walls and the enormous efforts invested by Herod in artificially raising the level of the sacred enclosure. Remains of streets and houses indicate the public character of the immediate environs of the Temple Mount. Another outcome of the intensive building activities in Herodian Jerusalem was the erection of some particularly luxurious residential buildings in the Upper City, some of whose remains are exposed in the present-day Jewish Quarter. The magnificence of the remains and the nature of the finds point to the wealth of the residents and the luxury of the entire Upper City, corroborating Josephus' account. Also preserved among the remains excavated in the Jewish Quarter are some dramatic and poignant evidence of the city's destruction by the Romans in 70 CE (see below). One of the most prominent structures in the Upper City was Herod's palace, which commanded a view of the entire city from its location at the northwestern corner of the hill. The palace was protected on the north by three high towers—Phasael, Hippicus, and Mariamme—which Josephus describes in detail. The sole remnant of these towers is the massive base of one of them, which was incorporated in later construction as part of what is now known traditionally as David's Tower.

As Jerusalem developed and its built-up area expanded—a process that continued throughout Herod's long reign—new residential sections sprang up in the northern part of the city. The new residential quarter known as the New City, established on the hill of Bezetha, was surrounded by the Third Wall during the reign of Agrippa I. Remains of that wall were exposed a short distance north of the Old City.

Jerusalem reached the zenith of its expansion and magnificence toward the end of the Second Temple period. The walled area of the city amounted to nearly 450 a., encompassing areas no longer in the Old City today. A cautious estimate puts the population at about eighty thousand. Water conduits supplied the city from far-distant springs.

CITY OF DAVID

FORTIFICATIONS. The most definite vestiges of the Second Temple period discovered to date in the City of David are a few segments of a city wall running along the eastern crest of the ridge. The missing lengths of this wall, between the parts actually excavated, were reconstructed by the excavators according to the present features of the rock and the surface in general. It was once believed that this was the eastern wall of the City of David in the Bronze and Iron ages. However, the excavations conducted since the 1960s in the northeastern part of the City of David (by Kenyon and Shiloh) have proved definitively that the earliest stage of these fortifications dates to the Second Temple period and that the city's eastern defenses in earlier periods were built at a lower topographical level (see above). The eastern fortifications of the City of David constitute the eastern section of the First Wall of the Second Temple period, as described in detail by Josephus (*War* V, 142–145): the First Wall ran round the southwestern hill and climbed northward along the City of David and the Ophel, until it reached the eastern wall of the Temple Mount.

As it turns out, the most outstanding remains of the eastern line of fortifications (now dated to the Second Temple period) were excavated by R. A. S. Macalister and J. G. Duncan (1923–1925) near the top of the eastern slope of the City of David, above the Gihon Spring. The remains consisted of a wall (c. 30 m long) with two projecting towers. It was built of roughly hewn stones. North of the southernmost of the two towers is a stepped, stone structure. The southern tower (16 m long) was built in pairs of recessed courses. The tower projects 9 m from the wall on its southern side, but only 6 m on its northern side; the thickness of the wall between the two towers reaches 8 m. From the southern tower, the wall runs north approximately 20 m up to the second, smaller tower. The northern tower is 6 m long; it projects 3 m from the wall on the south, but only 2 m on the north. Macalister and Duncan mistakenly dated these fortifications to the time of Jebusite Jerusalem (Bronze Age) and the reigns of David and Solomon (Iron Age), with the exception of the northern tower, which, they believed, was added only in Second Temple times, probably under the Hasmoneans.

From 1961 to 1967, K. Kenyon continued the excavation in this area (squares A-I–III), going down to the foundations of the towers. She found that the foundations of the southern tower had been laid on a loose earth fill and ruins of walls from the First Temple period. In the tower itself she identified two building phases. The first was dated to the Hasmonean period (Jonathan—152–142 BCE), in which repairs had already been made. North of the northern tower (square A-XVIII) Kenyon discovered an earlier length of wall, founded on a rock scarp, that she dated to the time of Nehemiah. The northern tower, which she dated to the Hellenistic (probably Hasmonean) period, was built against this early wall. She suggested that the City of David's eastern defenses were reestablished at the time of the postexilic period on the crest of the ridge, abandoning the earlier and strategically inferior line of the wall placed lower on the hill. The two towers were incorporated in the wall by the Hasmoneans, as was the stepped stone structure built to buttress the unstable terrain north of the southern tower.

Y. Shiloh's excavations in the City of David (1978–1985) continued to examine this site (area G). It turned out that the stepped stone structure had originally been built during David's reign, in the tenth century BCE. Shiloh believed that most of the city wall at this point had been built by the Hasmoneans (stratum 7), incorporating the top of the First Temple period stepped stone structure, as well as the remains of fortifications built during the postexilic period, which are not in evidence in this area. During the Hasmonean period (stratum 7B, end of second century BCE), the southern tower was added. The northern tower was a slightly later structure (strata 7–6), probably built against two earlier building phases in the line of the wall itself. At the same time an earthen glacis (3–4 m thick) was built on the slope farther down to the east. Founded on the First Temple period stepped stone structure, it was intended to buttress the unstable, steep terrain and the weak foundations of the fortifications at this point.

In area R, slightly to the north of the remains just described, Kenyon had discovered only remains of terrace walls from the first century CE. She associated them with the city wall that in her view ran slightly to their east and descended the slope. To the north of these remains, on the eastern part of the Ophel, C. Warren had discovered a segment of the Byzantine wall, generally known as the Ophel Wall (see below, the Byzantine Period). Judging from the dispersal of the buildings from the Second Temple period unearthed in B. Mazar's excavations on the eastern Ophel, it is quite possible that the First Wall of Second Temple times was also built along this line, but farther down the eastern slope of the Ophel; it was along this line that the First Wall ran north, probably circumventing the southeastern corner of the Temple Mount, to a point near the present-day Golden Gate, where it joined the eastern wall of the Temple Mount. It is noteworthy that no remains of Jerusalem's defenses from the Second Temple period were discovered to the north of area G, so that the line of the First Wall in this sector is necessarily a matter of conjecture.

Some distance to the south of the fortifications discovered in Shiloh's area G, H. Guthe (1881) and M. Parker (1909–1911) discovered massive masonry remains that may be additional segments of the First Wall. Farther south along the crest of the ridge, C. Clermont-Ganneau (1873) identified the remains of a massive wall (20–25 m long) built of large stones; this is now considered to be yet another part of the eastern fortifications of the City of David. However, because sufficient archaeological data is lacking for these fortifications and because they were not properly published, conjecture as to

The First Wall from the Second Temple period, in the southern part of the City of David.

their nature and time of construction is based mainly on their location along the estimated line of the First Wall of the Second Temple period, along the crest of the eastern slope of the City of David.

To the south of these fortifications, R. Weill (1913–1914) discovered another fortified element of the eastern wall of the City of David from the Second Temple period on a rock-cut scarp. Shiloh continued to excavate the northern end of this structure (area D1). Its total length was 20 m, and it survived to a height of 3 m. It consisted of two walls built against one another, of dressed stones, for a total thickness of 3.5 m. An opening at the northern end was found deliberately blocked with stones. The width of this opening was 1.5 m and a section of a stepped stone pavement was found in it. Shiloh assigned the whole structure to the Hasmonean period (stratum 7B), implying that some of the stone quarries on which the fortification was built had been in use in the Hellenistic period and possibly even earlier, in the First Temple period. This conclusion is an important complement to Kenyon's view that the stone quarries in the southern part of the City of David were active throughout the period of Aelia Capitolina and the Byzantine period.

The entire eastern slope of the ridge of the City of David, beneath and parallel to the line of fortifications described above, was transformed in the Second Temple period by the building of a system of agricultural retaining walls (terraces). The southern part of this system was discovered early in this century by Weill, and its northern continuation was excavated by Shiloh. One of the retaining walls was founded on the remains of the ancient wall of the City of David from the Bronze and Iron ages; farther to the east a section 51 m long was exposed of an additional retaining wall. The terrace system is bounded on the south by a wall at right angles to the city wall, which descends to the Kidron Valley. Farther to the south Weill discovered a circular stone structure, founded on bedrock, of as yet undetermined nature and date. Beneath the terrace system Shiloh discovered the remains of a circular stone structure that resembles a columbarium (diameter, 4.8 m). Its interior was divided into two by a partition wall and there were eight small niches in the inner face of the circular wall. The structure was probably built in the Persian period (stratum 9). The system of retaining walls (terraces) was built in the Hasmonean period, at the end of the second century BCE (stratum 7B). It continued in use, with some additions being made in the first century CE (stratum 6), up to the end of the Second Temple period. The city wall from the Second Temple period and the system of retaining walls at its foot were found buried under an enormous quantity of earth spills and rubble (stratum 5), mute evidence of the destruction of Jerusalem in 70 CE.

In the area of Weill's and Shiloh's excavations (area D), the First Wall of the Second Temple period, which ran to that point along the crest of the eastern spur, joined the line of the earlier wall of the City of David, which was built at a lower topographical level. The wall of the City of David probably ran south from this point at all times, along the vertical rock scarp that extends southward to the tip of the spur. At this point the First Wall turned west, cutting across the issue of the Tyropoeon in a system of dams (see below, The First Wall in the southwestern hill). The wall of the City of David left the First Wall south of the City of David, to run north probably along the rock scarp that circumvents the southern end of the City of David on the west and continues north above the Siloam Pool. In 1923–1924, Weill discovered the remains of a square tower of unknown identity on this scarp, south of the Siloam Pool; from this tower a double wall ran north. Excavations in Shiloh's area A found no traces here of fortifications predating the Byzantine period.

The estimated line of the western wall of the City of David in the Second Temple period is marked by the rock scarp still visible north of the Siloam Pool. The most prominent and best known remnant of these fortifications is the gate unearthed by J. W. Crowfoot and G. M. Fitzgerald (1925–1927), in the northwestern part of the ridge of the City of David, opposite the fortification discovered by Macalister and Duncan in the northeastern part of the spur. The surviving remains consisted of ten courses (total height, 6 m) of particularly large, coarsely dressed square stones. The gate (3.5 m wide) was flanked by particularly massive towers (8.4 m wide); the southern one was 19 m long. The excavators dated the gate to the Jebusite (Bronze Age) and Israelite (Iron Age) period, identifying it as the Valley Gate—that is, the western gate of Jerusalem referred to in Nehemiah 3:13. A trove of some three hundred Hasmonean coins was discovered in the gate, indicating that it was in use in the Hasmonean period. Most scholars now date this gate to the time of the Second Temple, probably the Hasmonean period, with the foundations possibly dating to the postexilic period, or perhaps even earlier.

South of the gate Crowfoot (1928) found an earlier wall (30 m long) of which two courses survived of large, smoothed stones, laid in headers and stretchers. Crowfoot dated the wall to the second century BCE (he suggested that it might have been part of the Seleucid Acra). This wall was undoubtedly part of the western fortifications of the City of David in the Hellenistic-Hasmonean period and should be associated with the gate to its north.

According to Kenyon, the line of the City of David's western fortifications was slightly altered under the Hasmoneans. In her site K, northwest of the Siloam Pool, she exposed a wall (3.5 m thick) she identified as a terrace wall and part of the city wall in the Hasmonean period. She considered this proof that, during that time, the city had expanded somewhat toward the west in the southern part of the City of David. North of the Valley Gate, in her site M, Kenyon unearthed another fortification wall (3.25 m thick) whose outer (western) face was built of well dressed stones. Based on this, she conjectured that the City of David's western wall in this area had been built by the Hasmoneans, slightly farther east than the earlier, traditional line of the wall, thus somewhat reducing the northern area of the city.

Summary. Of the fortification remains excavated up to the present along the eastern and western flanks of the City of David, there are only a few that can be confidently dated to Second Temple times. It is particularly interesting that the City of David's eastern defenses should have been displaced farther up the ridge in the early part of the Second Temple period, abandoning the earlier, inferior line, which remained outside the city limits and became quite useless. The operation, which considerably limited the already small area of the City of David in the Second Temple period—in comparison with its size in the Bronze and Iron ages—was probably motivated by a combination of reasons—in particular, the insecure nature of the slope, which was strewn with ruins from the end of the First Temple period. The remains confirm the biblical account, according to which Nehemiah did not actually restore the eastern fortifications of the City of David but built a new wall, probably at the top of the ridge. However, despite this commonly held view, the recent excavations along the line of the First Wall from Second Temple times have revealed no unequivocal archaeological evidence that these fortifications were first built during the postexilic period.

Those of the fortified remains unearthed in the area of the City of David that have been dated to the Second Temple period reveal no uniform style of masonry. This indicates that the wall around the City of David was not built all at once, but repaired and strengthened on various occasions during the Second Temple period. The style of the masonry in these fortifications and the dressing of the stones differ considerably from the high quality characteristic of contemporary remains of the First Wall around the southwestern hill. These remains are of ashlars with marginal dressing, one of the most characteristic hallmarks of Hasmonean and Herodian masonry in Jerusalem. This may indicate that the segments of Second Temple period walls discovered in the City of David predate the remains of the First Wall that was built around the southwestern hill, beginning only in the early Hasmonean period.

OTHER REMAINS AND FINDS. Excavations have revealed very little about the buildings in the City of David in the Second Temple period. The most concrete evidence of occupation in the area in the Persian period comes from a few dozen *Yehud* seal impressions in Aramaic script, as well as seal impressions featuring the inscription *phw'* or representations of various animals, typical of the Persian period, found mainly in the northern part of the City of David. Kenyon, in her squares A-I–III and A-XVIII, in the northern part of the eastern slope of the City of David, found archeological levels containing finds from the Persian period. Shiloh, in his areas E1 and G, identified a Persian period layer (stratum 9) east of the line of fortifications, containing remains of retaining walls and earth fills, including various finds from the Persian period. He was, in fact, able to identify, for the first time in the City of David, an occupational level from the Persian period in a clear-cut stratigraphical context (see above). The significance of this level in the layout of the city in the Persian period is still unclear, as the area in question falls outside the walled city, which was confined at the time to the crest of the ridge.

A collection of more than seventy bullae and two seals from the Persian period, published by N. Avigad, may be associated with Jerusalem as the capital of the province of Yehud. The circumstances surrounding its discovery are unclear, but the provenance was reportedly the vicinity of Jerusalem. It includes a group of bullae inscribed with the name of the province of Yehud and names of various officials, some with their titles specified, as well as a group of bullae inscribed with proper names only. In view of the quantity and nature of the bullae it has been suggested that they belonged to a state archive for official documents, which probably existed at the time in Jerusalem.

The most notable finds from the Early Hellenistic (pre-Hasmonean) period in the City of David are a few dozen *Yehud* seal impressions in Hebrew script, and in particular many hundred Rhodian seal impressions on handles of amphorae, discovered in the various early excavations conducted in the northern part of the site; in addition to these, hundreds of similar seal impressions were unearthed by Shiloh's excavations. In area E he also discovered part of a building on whose floor was an assemblage of vessels from the third century BCE (stratum 8).

The quantity of finds from the Persian and Early Hellenistic periods discovered in the City of David is particularly striking, considering the absence of any settlement on the southwestern hill in those periods. This is further support for the assumption that Jerusalem's population at the time, up until the second century BCE, was concentrated mainly within the rather constrained limits of the City of David. Presumably, the returnees from Babylon were too few in number to rebuild the ruins on the southwestern hill; they were therefore content merely to restore the City of David and its fortifications, a situation clearly reflected in Nehemiah 7:4.

Only poor and fragmentary remains of buildings from the time of the Hasmoneans and the Herodian dynasty (mid-second century BCE to 70 CE) have been discovered up to now in the City of David excavations. Worthy of mention are sections of walls, cisterns, and a few stepped ritual baths (mikvehs), typical of the period, found mainly in the Macalister-Duncan excavations in the northern part of the site. Weill's excavations at the southern tip of the ridge exposed remains of a building and of nearby water installations. The parts of the ruined building were found deposited in an orderly fashion in a nearby cistern: carved stones, column fragments, and a Greek inscription testifying to a complex of buildings around a synagogue founded by Theodotus son of Vettenus. A translation of the inscription reads as follows: "Theodotus (son) of Vettenus, priest and / Archisynagogus, son of Archisynago/gus, grandson of Archisynagogus, bui/lt the synagogue for read/ing the Law and teaching the commandments, and / also the hospice and rooms and water installations for accommodation of the / needy guests from abroad, which / (synagogue) was founded by his ancestors and the el/ders and Simonides."

The Ophel: Greek inscription from the synagogue of Theodotus son of Vettenus, end of the Second Temple period.

THE ACRA

It is known from the written sources that the fortress called the Acra was built by Antiochus IV in 168 BCE, to control the city and permit close surveillance of the Temple Mount and the Temple (1 Macc. 1:30–36; *Antiq.* XII, 5, 4). The fortress was destroyed by Simeon the Hasmonean in 141 BCE (1 Macc. 13:49–51). The location of the site of the Seleucid Acra is the key to reconstructing the Jerusalem city plan in the Early Hellenistic (pre-Hasmonean) period. Lacking concrete archaeological evidence, the debate on this question was, until recently, mainly theoretical, relying on different interpretations of the sources that refer to the fortress and the local topography. Over the years, numerous scholars have offered a wide variety of sites in ancient Jerusalem as the preferred location of the Acra. Most notable among these sites are the southwestern hill; the northwestern corner of the Temple Mount—the site of the Antonia fortress; the Temple Mount itself, particularly its southern part; and the area of the Ophel, including the City of David. More recently scholars have attempted to relate various archaeological remains to the Acra fortress.

The archaeological evidence that the southwestern hill was uninhabited at the beginning of the second century BCE places it out of the discussion. Thus, M. Avi-Yonah's suggestion must be rejected that the fragments of monumental columns unearthed by Avigad in the Jewish Quarter were the remains of the temple that Antiochus IV had intended to build in honor of the Olympian Zeus, but was prevented from completing by the Hasmonean revolt. This temple was supposed to beautify the new residential section—the Acra fortress—which, Avi-Yonah conjectured, had been built on the southwestern hill.

Y. Tsafrir has suggested that a section of an early wall, built of large ashlar blocks with drafted margins, incorporated in the southern part of the Herodian eastern wall of the Temple Mount enclosure, is a remnant of the Acra fortress. He thus believed that the fortress had been built in the southeastern corner of the Temple Mount and its remains were later incorporated in the eastern wall, which Herod extended southward.

M. Ben-Dov located the Acra in the region of the Ophel, south of the Huldah gates in the southern wall of the Herodian Temple Mount. He identified the remains of the fortress in a rock-cut cistern (15 by 20 m) that has a system of rooms connected to it on the north.

B. Mazar and L. Ritmeyer placed the fortress south of the Temple Mount enclosure as it was at the beginning of the Second Temple period. They suggested that the ruins were later buried under the southern, Herodian extension of the Temple Mount. They associated a cistern (no. 11) in that area with the remains of the Acra.

J. Schwartz suggested that the "cistern of Acra" appearing in the written sources is an echo of the Acra fortress. Following Mazar and Ritmeyer, he identified cistern no. 11 in the southern part of the Temple Mount enclosure with the cistern mentioned above. He, too, considered the cistern indirect evidence that the Acra fortress was located in the southern part of the Herodian Temple Mount.

Material evidence of the existence of the Acra comes from a fragmentary Greek inscription, discovered by chance in the vicinity of the Old City and published by S. Applebaum. It reports an oath taken by soldiers stationed at the Acra and associated with the Gymnasium.

Despite progress in research and new finds, it still seems impossible to settle the question of the precise location of the Seleucid Acra in Jerusalem. On the evidence of the sources and the archaeological finds, it seems most probable it was built in the Second Temple period in the Lower City, somewhere near the Temple Mount. This lends support to the hypothesis, advanced long ago by some scholars, that the Acra was simply one of a series of fortresses built on the hill overlooking the northwestern corner of the Temple Mount area, beginning in the Ptolemaic period (perhaps even earlier, in the First Temple period), that culminated in the Herodian Antonia.

THE SOUTHWESTERN HILL

Excavations conducted in all parts of the southwestern hill of ancient Jerusalem (the area now occupied by the Jewish and Armenian quarters of the Old City and Mount Zion outside the walls to the south) have produced incontestable archaeological evidence that a fortified residential quarter developed here from the mid-second century BCE onward.

Only a few artifacts from the Persian period have been found on the southwestern hill—mainly a small quantity of sherds. Worthy of mention is a silver coin from the fourth century BCE, unearthed by M. Broshi on Mount Zion. There is also evidence that the late First Temple period cemetery on Ketef Hinnom, where G. Barkay conducted five seasons of excavations (1975–1989), was still in use, albeit on a limited scale, in the Babylonian and Persian periods. Found in one of the tombs (no. 25) was a tiny Archaic Greek coin from the sixth century BCE—one of the earliest coins discovered in Israel. Identical evidence emerged from two of the Iron Age tombs excavated by R. Reich in the upper Hinnom Valley opposite the Jaffa Gate (the Mamilla neighborhood). Nothing in these finds alters the general pattern revealed by the excavations throughout Jerusalem. Following the destruction of the First Temple, the city's population was largely confined to the ridge of the City of David.

It is significant that the frequency of finds from the Early Hellenistic (pre-Hasmonean) period on the southwestern hill increases steadily toward the end of the period. Apart from sherds, this trend is obvious in small artifacts: a few *Yehud* seal impressions in Hebrew script; a few dozen Rhodian seal impressions—a considerable number of them date to the second century BCE; and coins. There is, thus, clear evidence for the formation of a poor, unwalled residential area on the hill, whose exact nature and extent of occupation have yet to be determined. The main part of Jerusalem's population, however, was still confined at the time to the City of David.

From the mid-second century BCE there is archaeological evidence of a more significant occupational level on the southwestern hill, including—for the first time in the Second Temple period—architectural remains and many finds. The new inhabitants presumably settled here in the wake of the Hasmoneans' victory and the liberation of Jerusalem from Seleucid rule. In time, a wealthy residential quarter, known as the Upper City, was built here; it was protected by the First Wall, which was restored around the hill by the Hasmonean kings.

THE FIRST WALL

The history of the First Wall, which circumvented the southwestern hill and the City of David, is more complex than that of the other two walls that defended Jerusalem in Second Temple times. Nevertheless, more is known about this wall than about the other fortifications from a variety of sources: the information provided by Josephus (*War* V, 142–145) about the line of the wall, its towers, and gates; present-day topographical conditions; and, above all, the many fortification remains that have come to light.

According to Josephus, the line of the First Wall began at the Hippicus Tower, at the northwestern corner of the southwestern hill, in the area now occupied by the Jerusalem Citadel ("David's Tower"). From there, the wall continued to the east, crossing the Chamber of Hewn Stones (the Xystos) and the Council Building toward the western stoa of the Temple precincts. On the other side of the Hippicus Tower, the wall ran south and east along the edge of the southwestern hill, overlooking the Valley of Hinnom. On its way, it passed Bethsoh and the Gate of the Essenes, in the southern part of Mount Zion, and then descended toward the Siloam Pool. After skirting the southern tip of the City of David, the First Wall began to ascend again, along the eastern slope of the City of David, through the Ophel, until it once again reached the eastern

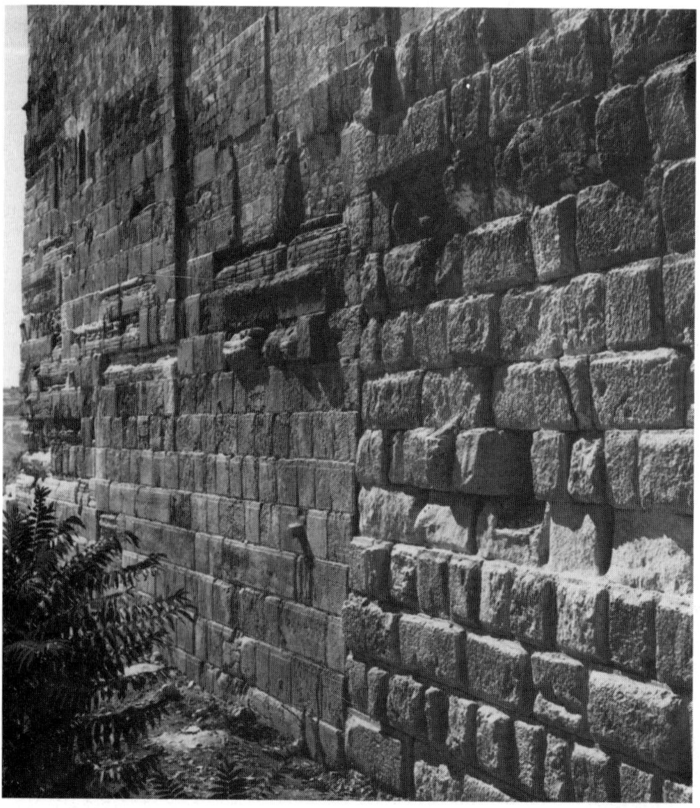

Eastern wall of the Temple Mount: (right) the early wall; (left) addition from time of Herod.

The Citadel: plan of the First Wall and its towers.

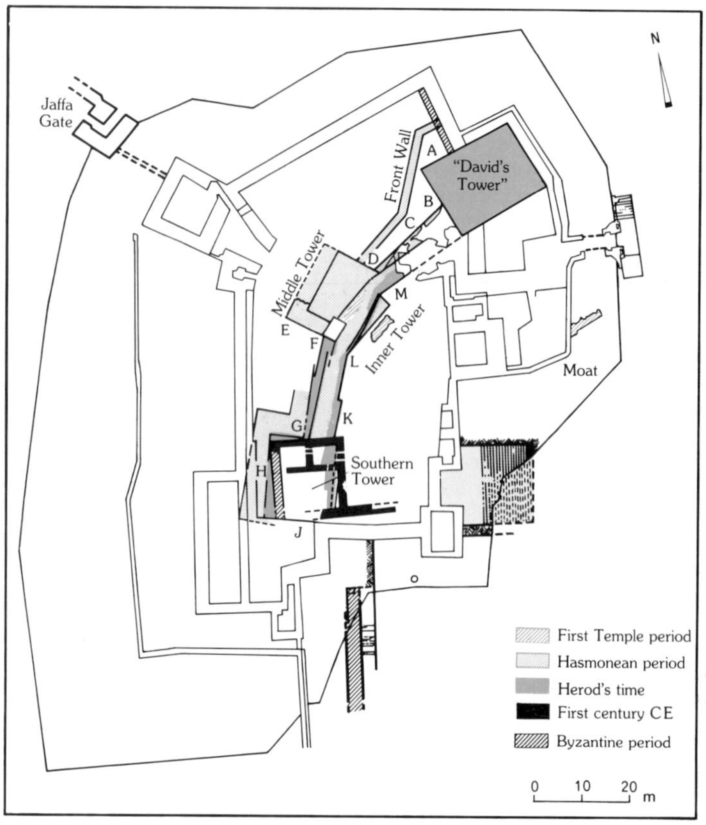

side of the Temple enclosure (see above, description of the eastern part of the First Wall in the City of David). Sixty towers were built along the First Wall (*War* V, 158). The many fortified remains excavated along the course of the First Wall around the southwestern hill indicate that it was built high above the surrounding valleys: in the north it overlooked the shallow bed of the Transversal Valley; in the west and south, it overlooked the steep, rocky banks of the Valley of Hinnom.

REMAINS OF THE NORTHERN PART OF THE WALL. As early as the mid-nineteenth century, various remains of masonry were discovered by chance within the Old City, along the conjectured line of the First Wall. They were identified as remains of the wall's northern section. As these discoveries are not adequately documented, their precise nature and dates cannot be determined today and so they cannot confidently be listed as remains of the First Wall. Nevertheless, as they are constantly referred to in studies of the fortifications of ancient Jerusalem, they will be briefly described here.

In 1864, C. Wilson discovered an impressive arch (now known as Wilson's Arch) just north of the Western Wall plaza, at the estimated juncture of the First Wall with the western wall of the Temple Mount enclosure. The place of the presently existing arch, which, according to the commonly held view, postdates the Second Temple period, was occupied then by an even more impressive arch, which was part of a pedestrian bridge. In Warren's opinion, the bridge was incorporated in the First Wall where the latter crossed the Tyropoeon Valley. In 1931, R. W. Hamilton discovered a massive wall west of Wilson's Arch and identified it as a dam and wall built across the Tyropoeon. An ancient arch, incorporated in a residential building that still stands at the northern end of the Jewish Quarter, at the junction of Ḥabad and Saint Mark streets, was previously misidentified as the Gennath Gate, described by Josephus in the northern section of the First Wall. Avigad has proven once more, following Warren, that this arch is later than the Second Temple and was not a part of a gate in the city wall. In 1862, a section of a massive wall (18 m long), with two towers projecting from it on the north, was exposed to the west of this arch, in the area of the Lutheran Hospice on Saint Mark's Street. The discovery was first reported by C. Schick and has since been discussed repeatedly. From the scanty published details and from the existing remains it seems that the masonry in question included a large number of reused stones with drafted margins and protruding bosses—these typical elements of the Hasmonean First Wall apparently misled nineteenth-century scholars. Contemporary scholars now believe that this masonry postdates the Second Temple period and in fact cannot be confidently identified as the remains of fortifications at all.

The only unambiguous remains along the northern line of the First Wall were exposed by Avigad in the mid-1970s in two excavated areas in the northern part of the Jewish Quarter.

HILLEL GEVA

Aerial view of the Citadel; (foreground) the Jaffa Gate.

Built against the eastern face of the Israelite tower (see below) was another tower, dated to the Hasmonean period (no. 4 in the plan). Shaped like the letter U—that is, a square open to the south—it measured 9 by 9 m and its walls were 2.5 to 3 m thick. The outer faces of the walls were built of soft ashlar stones with dressed margins and a projecting central boss—the same style as the stones in the lengths of Hasmonean walls discovered along the west and south of the southwestern hill. The outside of this tower and the Iron Age (Israelite) tower are abutted by a beaten-lime floor dated, according to the ceramic finds, to the second century BCE. This indicates that both systems of fortification, Israelite and Hasmonean, were in use simultaneously.

The abutting of the two towers indicates that, when the Hasmoneans decided to refortify Jerusalem, they returned to the old defensive line from the First Temple period, the remains of which were still visible. When the masons discovered parts of the old wall in a good state of preservation and still usable, they repaired and incorporated them in the new defensive wall. A similar pattern emerges in area X-2, some 45 m west of area W, at the northern end of the Street of the Jews. Beneath the paving stones of the Byzantine Cardo the remains of fortifications from the First Temple and Hasmonean periods (nos. 3 and 5–7 in the plan) were found. Two parallel massive walls (nos. 6–7; 4.6 m thick and 6.5–8 m high) were built of hard field stones that had probably been taken from the ruined fortifications of the First Temple period. The pottery points to a second-century BCE date for these remains; they were probably part of a gate in the Hasmonean defenses of the city. This gate is to be identified with the Gennath Gate that Josephus mentions as the point in the First Wall from which the Second Wall began (*War* V, 4, 2). Section 5 differed from section 6 in its direction and in being built of soft, dressed stones. Some of these stones were reused in the construction of section 6.

The Hasmonean gate (7 m high) adjoining section 3 of the First Temple period wall provides yet another illustration of how the Hasmoneans incorporated the remains of the old wall into their fortifications. This is highly significant in terms of the conjectured course of the northern part of the First Wall to the west where it connects with its other part, which encircled the city from the west and south.

NAHMAN AVIGAD

REMAINS OF THE NORTHWESTERN CORNER. The northwestern corner of the First Wall was first exposed as far back as the 1930s in the courtyard of the Jerusalem Citadel ("David's Tower"), south of the Jaffa Gate; it has since been investigated in a long series of excavations. A length of a fortification wall is preserved here to the impressive height of more than 10 m, including three projecting towers. The remains show evidence of several building phases, with additions and repairs dating to the Second Temple period. This wall links up with the tower traditionally named David's Tower, which was actually built in Herod's reign and today forms part of the walls of the Citadel. The ancient system of fortifications exposed in the Citadel courtyard presents the most complicated stratigraphic sequence in any part of the First Wall, or of Jerusalem's walls in general. The remains and the excavators' conclusions will be described here in the order of their discovery.

From 1934 to 1947, C. N. Johns excavated in the Citadel courtyard. His main finds related to the outer face of the fortifications, in which he identified four successive building phases ("builds," following his terminology), characterized by different styles and dates of construction.

Johns's First Build was preserved in wall segments D–F, L–M, and the lower part of wall segment C–D. Their characteristic masonry consisted of dressed stones, laid mainly in courses of headers. Johns dated this fortification to Jonathan the Hasmonean (152–142 BCE). Incorporated in the southern part of wall segment D–F was a stretch of earlier masonry, consisting of

The Citadel: (right) the First Wall; (left) foundations of buildings associated with Herod's palace.

The Citadel: remains of the southern tower, 1st century CE.

unhewn stones, dated by the excavator to the time of Judas Maccabaeus (164–161 BCE) or slightly earlier. It seems fairly clear that this was, rather, another remnant of the wall from the First Temple period, incorporated in the new system of fortifications by the Hasmoneans.

In the Second Build, the upper part of wall segment C–D was built and reinforced by the construction of the "middle tower" (DEF). The foundations of this tower were filled with densely packed masonry; the remains of a narrow opening were found on its northern side. The typical masonry of this phase consists of ashlar blocks with drafted margins and a coarse protruding boss, laid in alternating courses of headers and stretchers; masons' marks were found on many stones in wall C–D. Johns dated the beginning of this stage of construction to the reign of Hyrcanus I (134–104 BCE) and its end to the time of Alexander Jannaeus (103–76 BCE)—the stage as a whole being assigned to about 100 BCE.

In the Third Build, the inner face of the fortification in section K was repaired with additional masonry. The wall was breached from point C eastward, and "David's Tower" was built in the breach. Subsequently, the remainder of the foundation trench of the wall in section B–C was sealed. Typical of the wall in this phase is the use of ashlar blocks with precise marginal drafting and a flat, well-smoothed boss. It is dated to Herod's reign (37–4 BCE).

In the Fourth Build, according to Johns, the wall segment F–G and the "southern tower" GHJ were added. A characteristic feature of this stage is the reused stones from the previous building stages; Johns dated the construction work to the time of the First Jewish Revolt against the Romans (66–70 CE) or immediately thereafter and attributed it to the Roman army then stationed here. Further excavation in the Citadel ascertained that the elements assigned by Johns to a Fourth Build actually belong to the earlier phases.

The first three phases of construction, as identified by Johns, provide an architectural and chronological framework for the entire history of the First Wall around the southwestern hill in the Second Temple period. All the other remains of the First Wall fit into this framework.

In 1968–1969, R. Amiran and A. Eitan excavated in the Citadel courtyard and exposed part of the eastern, inner face of the Second Temple period fortifications and the occupational levels adjoining it on the east. In an early phase, contemporaneous with Johns's First Build, an inner tower was built on the line of the wall. Under Herod the inner side of the fortification was repaired by additional construction founded in the north on the earlier wall but built against its inner face farther to the south.

In 1979–1980, H. Geva examined a segment of the outer face of the fortification in the Citadel courtyard, exposing most of the remains of the southern tower and revealing its various stages of construction. A trial sounding opposite Johns's point D proved that the lower part of wall segment C–D was only a foundation of the city wall, built of roughly hewn stones laid in alternating courses of headers and stretchers; it was, thus, not an earlier phase of the fortifications, as Johns had supposed. The construction along this section as a whole—the foundations and the overlying masonry, which consists of stones with drafted margins and a coarse protruding boss (Johns's Second Build)—has proven to be an outer thickening of the wall from the First Build. The total thickness of the wall thus reached approximately 6 m. The excavator dated both constituents of Johns's Second Build to the early first century BCE; the middle tower (DEF) was built somewhat earlier than wall C–D, as John had already determined.

The northern part of the southern tower, part of which was cleared by Johns, was then exposed in the southern part of the Citadel courtyard. The remains indicate that there were actually three successive towers, each built on the foundations of its predecessor at various times in the Second Temple period. The first tower was built in the Hasmonean period, its walls constructed of ashlar blocks with drafted margins and a coarse protruding boss—features typical of Johns's Second Build; the construction as a whole was not uniform, and some of the stones may have been reused. The tower was filled with densely packed stones, incorporating a stepped ritual bath (mikveh)—mikvehs were located along other sections of this wall. In Herod's reign, the remains of the Hasmonean tower served as the foundations for a smaller tower. The outer face of this tower and, in particular, its northern corner

The Citadel: northwest corner of the First Wall and the Hasmonean middle tower.

Western and northern sides of "David's Tower" built in Herod's time.

were built of large ashlars, with drafted margins and smoothed bosses, similar to the typical stones in Johns's Third Build. Reused stones from the previous tower were built into the walls. The stretch of the wall cleared here by Johns at point H is actually part of the western side of the Herodian tower. At the beginning of the first century CE the southern tower was rebuilt, on an alignment and plan different from those of the previous structures. It included several rooms and also extended to the east of the city wall and the earlier towers in this area. The tower walls, which have survived in the north to a height of 2.5 m, were built of ashlars, mostly taken from the earlier, Herodian tower. The inner side of the tower still has traces of white or colored plaster. The tower was probably built by one of the Roman procurators or by Agrippa I when he took over Herod's palace in the first century CE. It was completely destroyed with the rest of Jerusalem in 70 CE, as shown by the debris of masonry, plaster, and charred wooden beams from the ceiling that was found on the floor.

From 1980 to 1984, Solar and Sivan excavated along the outer face of the line of fortifications in the Citadel courtyard, clearing away all the earth fills that had covered it. In their view, the various constructive elements that make up the fortifications in this area should be divided into three main building periods, not necessarily identical with Johns's Builds; each of these periods presents several different styles of construction, reflecting several secondary building phases. In the first building period—the time of Simeon the Hasmonean or John Hyrcanus I—the first fortifications were erected here. Their clearest remains are Johns's First Build in wall D–F and the early tower whose remains were exposed by Solar and Sivan beneath Johns's middle tower (DEF). The early tower, which was founded on bedrock, was smaller than the middle tower (DEF): its length was 14.35 m, its width 8.9 m and its walls were preserved to a maximum height of 11 courses. The walls were built of ashlar blocks with drafted margins and protruding bosses, laid in alternating courses of headers and stretchers; the tower was filled with closely packed stones. Found on bedrock opposite the face of the tower and the wall to its east were concentrations of hundreds of round ballista stones of different sizes, a few dozen characteristically Hellenistic arrowheads, scores of slingstones, and iron spearbutts shaped like elongated, hollow cones. The excavators agree with Johns's attribution of similar finds to the siege of Jerusalem by Antiochus VII Sidetes in 134–132 BCE. In the second building phase, under Alexander Jannaeus, the western and southern sides of the early middle tower were thickened by 3.5 m (this was Johns's middle tower, DEF). This thickening was also done with drafted masonry, most of it apparently in secondary use. At the same time the southern, Hasmonean tower—whose western and northern sides were then cleared for their entire length—was built. This tower was about 24 m long and 11 m wide; running up to it on the north was a wall, only a small segment of which was exposed. In the second building period, another wall was built parallel to and in front of the outer face of the fortification system, a few meters away—along the stretch between the middle tower and running east to beyond the northern side of "David's Tower." The wall (1.6 m thick) was built of small field stones and had an entryway. In the third, Herodian building phase, "David's Tower" was built. The defensive line between "David's Tower" and the middle tower was thickened by adding masonry (this is Johns's wall segment B–D). The thickening amounted to 1.1 m in the west (D), widening out in the east (B) near "David's Tower" to an estimated thickness of 3.5 m. Visible in the face of the wall near "David's Tower" (segment B–C) is a repaired segment, later than the Second Temple period. In Herod's reign the stretch of the fortified line between the middle tower and the southern tower was also repaired.

During the various excavations in the Citadel courtyard, and in particular those of Solar and Sivan, the enormous earth fills, which had been heaped to a considerable height over the outer face of the fortifications, were examined and cleared; they were found to contain finds mainly from the first century BCE. Having been buried under these fills, the original construction of wall segment B–D was preserved to a particularly impressive height.

"David's Tower." Prominent in the defenses of the southwestern hill were the three towers—Phasael, Hippicus, and Mariamme—built by Herod at the northwestern corner of the First Wall, north of his palace. Details of their construction and their exact measurements are given by Josephus (*War* V, 161–175). The sole remnant of these towers is the lower part of one of them, traditionally known as "David's Tower."

"David's Tower" is rectangular; its base on the north is 22.6 m long, the base narrows at the top to 21.4 m. The width of the base on the east is 18.3 m; it narrows to 17.1 m at the top. The tower is founded on bedrock and survives to a maximum height of 19 m. It is built of sixteen courses of ashlars with dressed margins and smoothed, protruding bosses. The stones are on the average 2.5 m long, 1.25 m wide, and more than 1 m high. Each course is recessed a few centimeters, compared with the underlying course, and after the first eight courses from the bottom the recess forms a ledge some 20 cm wide. C. Schick, who carefully charted the building at the end of the nineteenth century, proved that the entire structure is filled with densely packed masonry, consisting of large, hewn stones laid in layers.

Since the mid-nineteenth century it has been clear to excavators of Jerusalem that "David's Tower" was one of Herod's three towers. Johns, who excavated along the northern side of the structure, proved, on the basis of the archaeological data, that it is indeed of Herodian construction and was built into the already existing Hasmonean First Wall. As the measurements of "David's Tower" agree in general with Josephus' figure for the Phasael Tower in *War* V, 166 most scholars have identified the existing structure as the remains of Phasael, which was the largest of the three towers; a minority prefer to identify it as the remains of Hippicus. Recently published studies by D. Bahat and H. Geva seem to confirm the identification with Hippicus, the westernmost of the three, which played a key role in the defensive system formed by the towers on this side of the city. In this three-tower system, Phasael was exceptional for its size; this pattern of one tower rising high above the others is characteristic of other Herodian construction, such as the Antonia fortress in Jerusalem and the fortress at Herodium.

Avi-Yonah arranged the three towers in a triangle: the Phasael Tower ("David's Tower") on the west and Hippicus Tower on the east formed the base—both along the line of the First Wall—and Mariamme, at the apex of the triangle, stood to their south. However, Josephus' description, which places the three towers along the First Wall, should probably be given greater weight. Thus, the towers should be arranged consecutively along the estimated line of the First Wall in this area, with Hippicus ("David's Tower") in the west, Phasael in the center, and Mariamme to their east, near the so-called Gennath Gate, which Avigad has reconstructed in the middle of the northern line of the First Wall. Thus arranged in a tight, linear pattern, the three towers created a solid defensive line, compensating admirably for the lack of sufficient natural protection along this part of the southwestern hill.

"David's Tower" has survived because it was integrated, in later periods as well, in the western line of Jerusalem's defenses. The disappearance of the other two towers may be attributable to the construction of the Third Wall and later stretches of the city wall (see below) farther to the west. Left within the city limits, they lost their original strategic significance. An interesting point in this connection was the discovery, in the mid-nineteenth century, when Christ Church was being built southeast of the Citadel, of an impressive length of masonry that, as reported by E. Pierotti, consisted of stones similar in size and dressing to those in "David's Tower." It has been conjectured that these were the remains of another of Herod's three towers.

REMAINS OF THE WALL IN THE WEST. To the south of the Citadel, additional remains of the First Wall are buried under the foundations of the Old City wall. In recent years, the outer face of the First Wall has been exposed for its entire length up to the southwestern corner of the Old City wall, and in some places the inner face has also been exposed.

A short stretch of the inner face of the First Wall was excavated in 1962–1967 by A. D. Tushingham (in cooperation with the Kenyon expedition) in area L, in the southern part of the Armenian Garden. He exposed the inner corner of a tower built in Herod's reign, which extends farther to the west beneath one of the towers in the Old City wall.

In 1970–1971, D. Bahat and M. Broshi excavated another stretch of the inner face of the First Wall in the northern part of the Armenian Garden. It was built of ashlars with drafted margins and central bosses.

The outer, western face of the First Wall south of the Citadel was exposed and examined by Broshi from 1973 to 1978. Remains of the early wall, amounting to 200 m, were discovered beneath the Old City wall, with four projecting towers. Two main building phases were identifiable in this part of the fortifications. Predating them was a single, isolated tower, built of ashlar blocks with drafted margins; only part of its entrance was found, preserved to a height of several courses. The excavator dated its construction to the time of Antiochus IV (Epiphanes) or to one of the first Hasmonean rulers. During the Hasmonean period, the First Wall was built here, with four projecting towers, one of which blocked the entrance to the earlier tower. The wall in this phase (c. 5 m thick), was built of ashlar blocks with drafted margins and coarse protruding bosses, identical to the stones in the Hasmonean fortifications in the Citadel. Under Herod the line of the First Wall and three of the Hasmonean towers were strengthened by the addition of external fortification. Most of the outer wall was built of stones dressed like those in the Hasmonean wall, although some parts were built of field stones. The excavator suggested that the outer wall had been built along this segment to support the foundations of the First Wall, compensating for the construction of Herod's palace on an artificial elevated platform inside the wall. A gate was built in the wall. The existence of this gate in Herod's time is suggested by a broad, impressively built staircase whose remains were found west of the fortification.

The southwestern corner of the First Wall was a rock scarp, first exposed by H. Maudslay in 1874–1875, in the precincts of the Bishop Gobat School in the southwestern part of Mount Zion. The eastern part of this scarp was reexamined by Bliss and Dickie in their excavations in the southern part of Mount Zion; the northern part was reexamined by R. W. Hamilton in 1933. The vertical rock scarp was exposed for a length of over 200 m and a height of 6 to 15 m; it runs northwest–southeast. Two towers, also hewn from the rock, project from it. A large quantity of ashlars with drafted margins found strewn in the area indicates that the scarp served in Second Temple times as the base of the city wall and its towers.

REMAINS OF THE WALL IN THE SOUTH. From 1894 to 1897 Bliss and Dickie used tunnels to trace the extensive fortifications along the southern line of the First Wall, on the southern slope of Mount Zion. They believed that this part of the wall had been built originally in the First Temple period and continued in use, subject to some modifications, until the Middle Ages. Essentially, what they discovered was two separate superimposed lines of fortifications, both descending to the east down the steep slope of the southwestern hill to the bed of the Tyropoeon Valley: an upper wall, sometimes built on top of and sometimes alongside the earlier, lower wall. The lower wall is now identified with the First Wall of Second Temple times, whereas the upper, later wall is dated to the Byzantine period (see below, Byzantine Period). Some stretches of the lower wall, amounting to approximately 700 m, have been exposed. Its average thickness is approximately 4 m, and several towers project southward from it. It is built mainly of ashlars with the typical drafted margins and coarse bosses of the Hasmonean phase in the First Wall, as discovered in the Citadel and elsewhere. Many stretches of different masonry are evident along the line of this wall, testifying to different stages of later restoration and repair throughout the Second Temple period.

At the highest point of the southwestern corner of Mount Zion, Bliss and Dickie completed the excavation of tower ABC, the easternmost of the two rock-cut towers that Maudslay had discovered a few years before. The face of the tower was approximately 13 m long. Its base was cut out of the rock, and some of the original ashlars with drafted margins were still in place. Surrounding the tower on its south and east was a deep, rock-cut trench, identified as a moat, that ran northeast, along the tower, for a distance of a few dozen meters. The width of the moat was 12–20 m, and its maximum depth, 6 m. Along the western side of the moat Avi-Yonah (following Wilson) reconstructed the line of an inner wall that, he believed, protected the eastern approaches to the Upper City at the end of the Second Temple period. This conjecture has now been disproven. None of the various excavations along the northward continuation of this hypothetical line have revealed evidence of such fortifications. The moat had apparently been cut later than the Second Temple period.

Beyond tower ABC, the line of the First Wall continues on to the southeast along 45 m, up to tower I. This tower presents two building phases, the earlier of which Bliss and Dickie dated to the Second Temple period. In this stretch of the wall they discovered four phases of a gate from the Byzantine period. The gate and tower I complex was reexamined again in 1979 to 1986 by B. Pixner, D. Chen, and S. Margalit, who dated the gate's earliest phase to Second Temple times. The gate, under whose threshold was a drainage channel, was incorporated in the already extant wall. Some scholars identify this gate with the Gate of the Essenes, used by Josephus as a reference point in his description of the First Wall.

After tower I, the wall turned eastward; no further remains from the Second Temple period survive in that segment, until the point where it reaches tower T—a tower shaped like the letter "U," about 14.6 m across. A short stretch of the wall runs from this point down to an elongated tower composed of six narrow chambers arranged in a row. Beyond this tower the Second Temple period wall runs east for some distance, disappearing at point U, beneath the late (Byzantine) wall. It reappears a little farther to the east, at point W, and runs on continuously until point X, where it begins to descend the steep southeastern slope of Mount Zion. In this area two additional segments of the wall were exposed: segment Y, which forms a tower corner, probably similar in shape to tower T, and segment Z to the east. These fortified segments were also built of masonry characteristic of the Hasmonean constructions elsewhere along the First Wall.

Another part of the city wall (C2), including a gate protected by a tower whose masonry resembles that in the preceding sections, was exposed at the foot of the slope of Mount Zion, near the issue of the Tyropoeon Valley. Three phases of use were identified in the gate, the earliest dated by the excavators to the Second Temple period. The gate was mainly used in the Byzantine period, however. Some scholars identify this, rather than the gate exposed farther up the slope of Mount Zion, as the Gate of the Essenes. Others consider it the Dung Gate referred to in Nehemiah 3:14.

From 1961 to 1963, Kenyon, in site F, reexcavated the gate that Bliss and Dickie had exposed in area C2. She also exposed the inner (northern) face of the city wall to its west for a length of some 24 m. Kenyon concluded that the gate had been built in the reign of Agrippa I (41–44 CE). This conclusion is in accord with the nature of the finds in her sites D1, D2, B1, and E on the eastern slopes of Mount Zion, which provided no evidence for occupation prior to the time of Agrippa I. She thereby inferred that the southern, lower part of the Tyropoeon Valley and most of the eastern slope of Mount Zion had not come within the fortified area of Jerusalem before the time of Agrippa I. In her view, therefore, the southern line of Jerusalem's fortifications in the Hasmonean period, and even in Herod's time, only rounded the summit of Mount Zion

Foundations of the First Wall from the Hasmonean period, south of the Citadel.

and ran on from there to the northeast until it reached the southern end of the Temple Mount enclosure. This view has been rejected by most scholars—suffice it to point out the clearly Hasmonean style of the masonry of the gate in the fortified segment (C2) southwest of the Siloam Pool and in segments Z and Y on the slope of Mount Zion. In addition, Shiloh's excavations in his area H, at the foot of the eastern slope of Mount Zion, revealed remains of Hasmonean masonry.

From the gate in area C2 the wall continued to the east, cutting across the broad, southern issue of the Tyropoeon Valley in a series of dams, along the line of the southern dam wall of the present-day Birket el-Ḥamra. The southernmost of this ancient system of dams detected by Bliss and Dickie is the so-called buttressed wall, commonly believed to have served as the city wall in this area. Its total length is more than 100 m; the foundation is about 6 m thick; and it survives to a considerable height. A series of seven buttresses projected from the outer (southern) face of the wall; each buttress is approximately half as thick as the wall. Most of the upper part of the wall is ashlar masonry with drafted margins. To the north, 15 m away, is a parallel wall, some 3 m thick; other walls connect the two parallel walls. The system of dam walls was dated by Bliss and Dickie to the First Temple period, a date accepted by early scholars of Jerusalem archaeology. In her site F, Kenyon discovered an additional Hasmonean dam wall, also part of the system of dams at the mouth of the Tyropoeon Valley. In 1978–1979 Shiloh, in his area A1, exposed and reexamined the southeastern corner of the buttressed wall and the wall running north from it to the rock scarp. He concluded that the buttressed wall already existed in the first century CE and might have been built even earlier, under the Hasmonean rulers (stratum 7B). After crossing the issue of the Tyropoeon Valley, the First Wall skirted the southern tip of the City of David on the rocky scarp visible there. From that point on, it continued along the crest of the eastern slope until it reached the Temple Mount enclosure (see above The City of David, The Fortifications).

DATE OF THE FIRST WALL'S CONSTRUCTION. The new archaeological data produced by the recent excavations in the Jewish Quarter and the Citadel date the original construction of the First Wall around the southwestern hill to the end of the First Temple period. This conclusion is in agreement with Josephus' account (*War* V, 142–145): he attributes the building of the First Wall to David and Solomon (that is to say, the First Temple period) and therefore refers to it as the Old Wall. This new conclusion runs counter to the previously held view: scholars hitherto believed, based on previously excavated fortification remains, that the First Wall was erected in the Hasmonean period. It is now possible to be more precise: the Hasmonean rulers only restored the fortifications of the First Wall along the line already laid down by the original builders toward the end of the First Temple period. The exact date of these operations is difficult to determine. Some scholars place it in the reign of one of the first Hasmonean rulers, in the mid-second century BCE; others prefer a later date, in the time of Hyrcanus I (end of the second century BCE) and Alexander Jannaeus (beginning of the first century BCE).

The archaeological finds on the southwestern hill clearly testify to intensive occupation on the hill in the Second Temple period, beginning in the second half of the second century BCE. The abundance of ballista stones and arrowheads discovered in what was originally the foreground outside the fortifications in the Citadel courtyard demonstrate that when Antiochus VII Sidetes laid siege to Jerusalem (in 134–132 BCE), the southwestern hill was already surrounded by a massive wall with towers, which the attackers were unable to breach. It would appear, therefore, that the rebuilding of the First Wall was carried out mainly in the time of Simeon and John Hyrcanus I, after the conquest of the Acra in 141 BCE—but before the beginning of the siege in 134 BCE.

An examination of the architectural features of the various sections of fortified city walls from the Second Temple period discovered along the line of the First Wall on the southwestern hill indicates that there were three principal building phases, as already detected by Johns in the fortifications he found in the Citadel. In the First Build—from the beginning of the Hasmonean period—the First Wall—originally built in the First Temple period—was rebuilt with smoothed stones, laid mainly as headers, incorporating surviving elements of the earlier fortifications. In the Second Build—which lasted for most of the Hasmonean period—the wall was thoroughly restored, with a concomitant change in its architectural features. The construction of this phase is characterized by the use of ashlar masonry with drafted margins and a coarse protruding boss, generally laid in alternating courses of headers and stretchers. The fortifications belonging to this Second Build are the most characteristic of the First Wall on the southwestern hill. In the Third Build—which can be assigned to the span of time from Herod's reign to the destruction of Jerusalem in 70 CE—several segments of the wall were restored using ashlar blocks with drafted margins and a smooth, flat boss.

The three main building phases, which are accompanied by a long series of repairs and local additions, visible at various places along the line of the First Wall and its towers, testify to the long and complex history of this wall in the Second Temple period. Its most characteristic features are its nonuniform thickness and the nonuniform size and plan of the towers along its course. Also noteworthy is the difference between the high-quality masonry in the bulk of the First Wall on the southwestern hill and the simpler masonry of the wall segments discovered on the eastern slope of the City of David (see City of David).

THE UPPER CITY. The many excavations carried out in the area of the Upper City, within the part of the southwestern hill enclosed by the First Wall, have revealed evidence of particularly elaborate buildings from the late Second Temple period. As already stated, the beginnings of massive settlement in this area should be dated to the Hasmonean period. The Upper City reached the zenith of its importance and magnificence during Herod's reign, when it was redesigned and rebuilt; this is indicated by the luxurious residential houses unearthed in Avigad's excavations in the Jewish Quarter.

HILLEL GEVA

HASMONEAN PERIOD. Fragmentary remains of buildings from the Hasmonean period were found scattered in many areas, particularly overlying the First Temple period Broad Wall (see above). These buildings were sacrificed to the intensive building activities in the Herodian period. Some of the remains, mainly rock-cut structures, such as mikvehs (ritual baths) and cisterns, were discovered for the most part beneath Herodian buildings. One such example, a cistern discovered beneath a Herodian house in area E, contained an important pottery assemblage from the second century BCE. It seems very probable that the Hasmonean city was less well developed than the later Herodian city. A point of interest is the construction of the Hasmonean buildings, for the most part, on top of ruins from the First Temple period, without an intermediate layer (there was a gap in the occupation of the area in the Persian and Early Hasmonean periods, see above).

The small finds from the Hellenistic-Hasmonean period include pottery of various types, including imported ware; Rhodian jar handles stamped with Greek inscriptions; jar handles stamped with the inscription יהד-ט (*yhd-ṭ*) in paleo-Hebrew script; jar handles stamped with a pentagram with the paleo-Hebrew inscription ירשלם (*yršlm*); and Hasmonean coins, mainly of Alexander Jannaeus but including a hoard of coins of Mattathias Antigonus, the last Hasmonean king.

HERODIAN PERIOD. The Herodian period was one of general prosperity in Jerusalem, a time of growth, development, and intensive construction in the Upper City, which became the center of the city. No buildings associated with Herod's public construction projects were discovered in the excavations in the Jewish Quarter. Although parts of particularly large Ionic columns and a Corinthian capital of excellent workmanship were discovered, attesting to the presence of monumental buildings, they cannot be associated with any one building. On the other hand, there are particularly abundant remains of private houses from the Herodian period, showing an impressive state of preservation and providing, for the first time, a faithful picture of house plans and living conditions in Jerusalem toward the end of the Second Temple period.

Despite the buildings in the Upper City having been built quite close together, the spacious conditions and comfort offered by many of these homes give them the character of luxurious villas. It seems clear that the area housed wealthy, aristocratic families, who built their homes in conformity with the taste and style of the Hellenistic-Roman period.

Among the most common installations in all the Upper City houses were mikvehs. Each house contained at least one, and some had two or more. This implies a high degree of observance of the laws of ritual purity. The typical plan of a mikveh is a stepped pool, hewn in the rock, with a vaulted ceiling built of ashlars. The water came from the many cisterns on the hill. Only one or two houses contained a mikveh with an *oẓar* (store) which supplied pure,

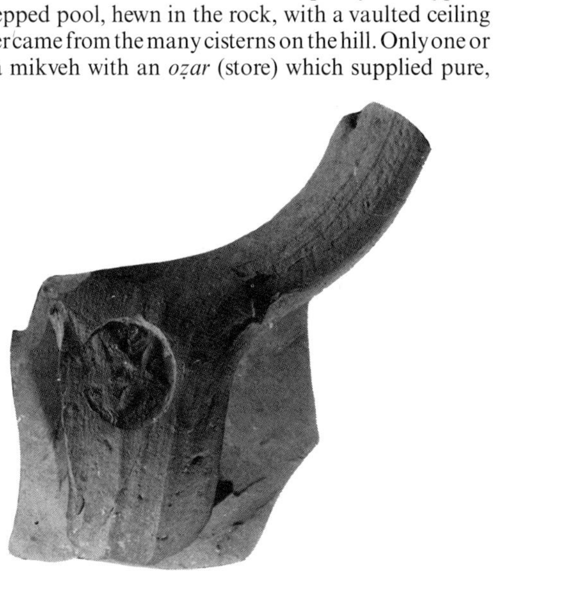

Jewish Quarter: upper fragment of a jug stamped with a pentagram and the name yršlm.

Jewish Quarter: plan of the excavation areas and principal remains.

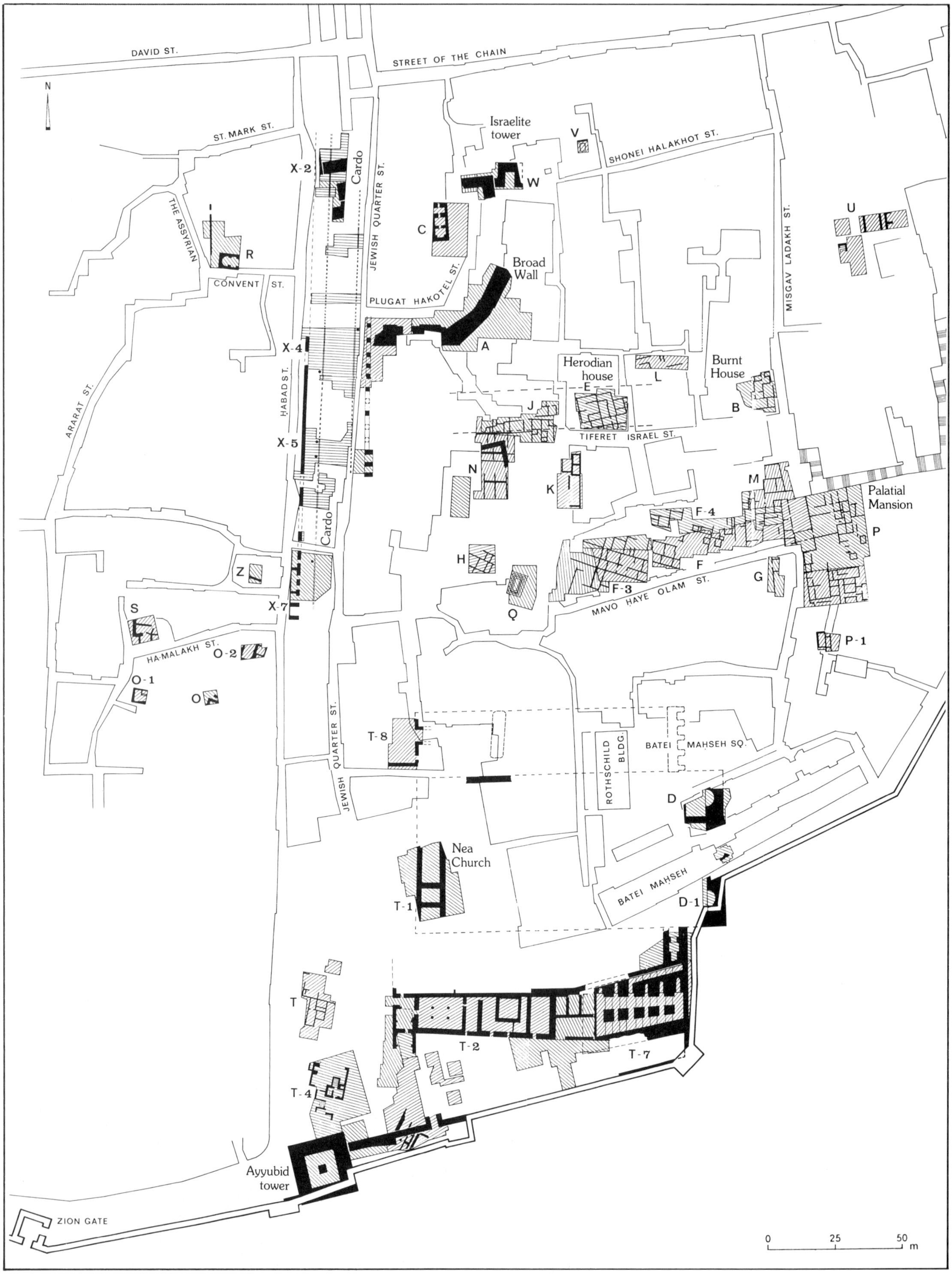

undrawn water (area T-4). Evidence that the baths were used for ritual immersion only is the bathrooms, complete with bathtubs, found adjoining them. The bathrooms were paved with colored mosaics, as were some of the rooms.

The mosaic floors discovered in the Upper City are the earliest of their kin in Jerusalem, dating from Herod's reign to the destruction of Jerusalem in 7 CE. Contemporary mosaics laid in the same style were found in Herod's palac at Masada. Common to all of them is the total absence of animal or huma

Jewish Quarter: mosaic with an interlacing meander motif, area F.

figures, as Jews at that time strictly avoided figurative art. The mosaics are decorated with geometric and floral motifs. The central motif is most often a schematic rosette, carefully drawn with a compass—a very common element in Second Temple period Jewish art. Other motifs are interlacing meanders, wavy lines, and pleated bands.

Jewish Quarter: mosaic floor in the bath courtyard (no. 8) in the Palatial Mansion.

Jewish Quarter: seven-branched menorah, shewbread table, and an altar incised in plaster.

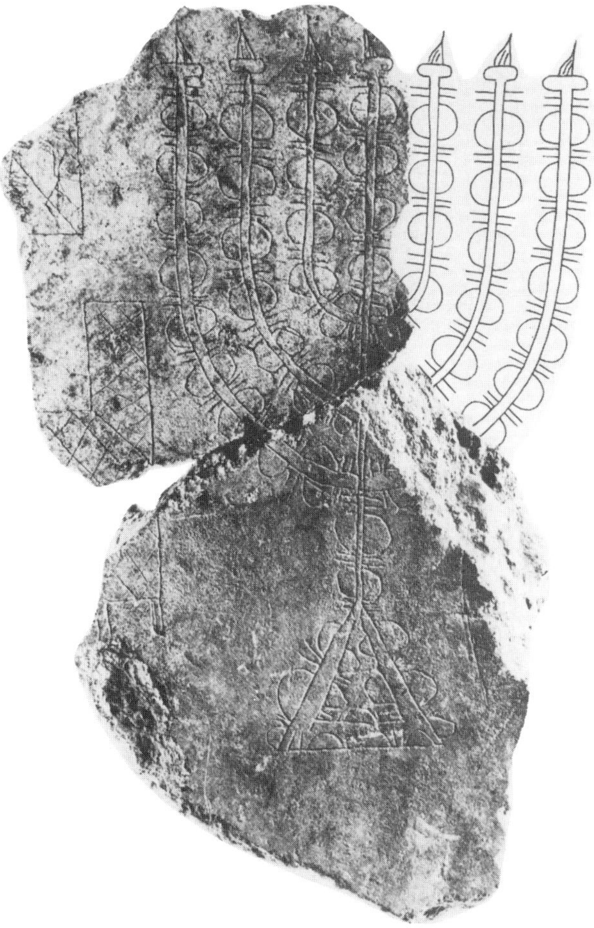

The residents of Jerusalem decorated their walls in the Hellenistic-Roman style, with frescoes. The painted plaster was found mostly in fragments. The decorative motifs used were colored panels, imitation marble, architectural patterns (columns and dentils), and floral patterns, some similar to the frescoes at Pompeii. Representations of animals and humans were also avoided in the wall paintings. Stucco also decorated walls, but less commonly. This molded plaster was used to imitate ashlar blocks; floral and architectural motifs in stucco were also found.

The houses in the Upper City yielded the first pieces of furniture from the Second Temple period—stone tables. These impressive products of Jerusalem's stone industry were common in wealthy homes. There were two types: high (80 cm) tables, made of a rectangular slab on a central leg shaped like a column; and low (c. 50 cm) tables made of a circular stone slab and three wooden legs (which have not survived).

Jewish Quarter: bronze vessels on a decorated stone table and under it, two large stone vessels.

Jewish Quarter: red-slipped Eastern terra sigillata ware.

Jewish Quarter: Corinthian capital.

Below: Jewish Quarter, area E: plan of the house from Herod's time.

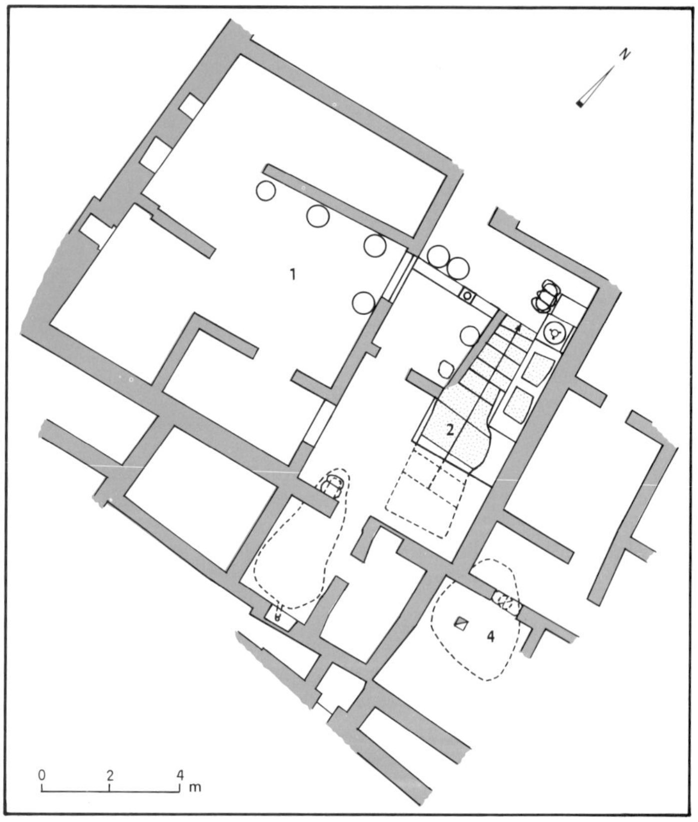

Particularly striking was the abundant use of stone vessels of various types: bowls, plates, cups, trays, lids, and large, gobletlike jars. All show fine workmanship; most were trimmed on a lathe, a few were handmade. This abundance of stone vessels may have been in response to Jewish law, which says that stone vessels cannot become impure (Mishnah, *Kel.* 10:1; *Par.* 3:2).

Other small finds in these houses include painted pottery bowls, red-slipped imported terra sigillata ware, stone sundials, and an elaborate glass decanter signed by Enion of Sidon. A unique find was waste material from a glass factory.

The House from Herod's Time (Area E). Based on the numismatic and ceramic evidence, this house, excavated in area E, was built in the mid-first century BCE on the ruins of an earlier building. A sealed cistern beneath the house contained a pottery assemblage from the second century BCE. The house was destroyed at the beginning of the first century CE, when a road was built through it and its remains were buried under the paving stones. The house (c. 200 sq m) was comprised of several rooms around an inner courtyard (1). Broken vessels were found in three niches in the western wall that were used as cupboards. The walls were coated with white plaster, remains of which were also found on the floor. A mikveh (2) with broad steps was a significant element in the house's plan. Near the entrance to the mikveh, a stone basin, with a projection in the center of its bottom, was pierced with three holes; it may have been used for washing the feet.

The finds—red-slipped imported Eastern terra sigillata ware and a group of Italian wine-storage jars bearing Latin inscriptions—suggest that the house belonged to a wealthy family. Among the local vessels, a group of asymmetric pilgrim flasks is noteworthy. There was, curiously, a total absence of the so-called Herodian lamp among the many lamps discovered in the house. This may indicate that those lamps were in use only after Herod's reign. On the floor coins of Alexander Jannaeus and Herod were found; beneath it there were only Hasmonean coins.

Herodian Quarter. The excavated, restored part of the site that includes all of areas F, M, and P is referred to by its excavators as the Herodian Quarter. Covering an area of approximately 2,700 sq m, it contains the remains of six or seven houses from the Herodian period. During the excavation of these areas, fragmentary remains of both earlier and later periods emerged. The site's unique feature is the continuous series of buildings from the Herodian period discovered over its length (c. 120 m). Part of the residential area of the Upper City of Jerusalem, it provides evidence of an urban plan for a residential neighborhood, house plans, domestic architecture and art, the living conditions of the city's inhabitants, and various aspects of everyday life in the city in the Second Temple period.

Jewish Quarter, area E: the house from Herod's time.

Jewish Quarter, area F-3: system of bathrooms in a private house.

Jewish Quarter: plan of the Palatial Mansion.

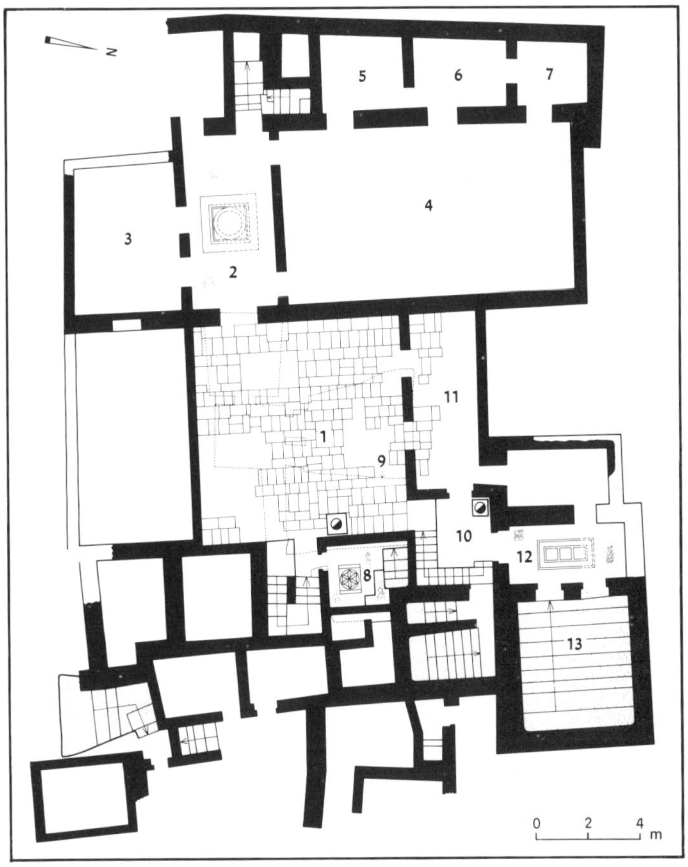

Western House (Area F-3). Only the basement of this house, at the western edge of the Herodian Quarter, survived; it illustrates the nature and layout of the wealthy quarter's basements in private houses. They usually held the water installations and service rooms. A network of bathrooms was preserved in this western house that comprised a vestibule (A2), a room with a bathtub (A3), two mikvehs (A4, A5), and a number of cisterns. The bathrooms were paved with colored mosaics. One mikveh (A4) was preserved intact: the lower part, with a flight of wide steps, was hewn in the rock; the vaulted ceiling was built of ashlars. The vault of the second mikveh (A5) was not preserved. This rich array of bathing and ritual immersion installations attests to the great importance that was attached to this aspect of life.

Palatial Mansion (Area P). The houses at either end of the Herodian Quarter were built on the slope of the hill, which descends to the east. Thus, the basement floor of the Palatial Mansion at the eastern edge of the site was 9 m lower than the floor of the building at the western edge. The Palatial Mansion, occupying an area of some 600 sq m, was the largest and most magnificent of the buildings discovered in the Jewish Quarter. Remains were found of two stories: the ground floor, which contained the living quarters, and the basement, which contained the water installations and service rooms. The ground-floor rooms were grouped around a central courtyard paved with stone tiles (1). The courtyard communicated with the various wings in the house, the best preserved of which was the west wing, a well-built ashlar structure. The west wing consisted of a vestibule, paved with a (mostly destroyed) colored mosaic (2), from which doorways led in all directions. Stairs in the west led to a narrow lane. One room contained numerous charred remains of wooden beams, evidence of the violent conflagration that had raged here and in the adjoining room (3), where a whole wall, decorated with red-painted frescoes, was preserved intact.

North of the vestibule was a large hall (6.5 by 11 m), plastered with white molded stucco (4). The stucco on the hall's northern wall was preserved almost up to the ceiling. Three small rooms on the west were originally decorated with frescoes that were later replaced by white plaster. Beneath the northern room (7) the excavators discovered a mikveh from an earlier house; it contained fallen stones and Hasmonean pottery. In the east wing of the house, all that remained of the ground floor was a bathroom (8); it was paved with a colored mosaic featuring a rosette pattern. On this side of the courtyard two flights of stairs led to the basement. Most of the rooms seen on the plan belong to the basement. Worthy of note is the large number of mikvehs, which were even found beneath the courtyard. Most striking was a magnificent vaulted mikveh with a double entrance and a mosaic-paved corridor.

The residents of this house must have been a particularly notable and wealthy family, and the exceptional number of mikvehs may indicate that they were a family of high priests. The numismatic and other evidence reveals that the building was erected during Herod's reign on the ruins of a Hasmonean house and destroyed when the Upper City was overrun by the

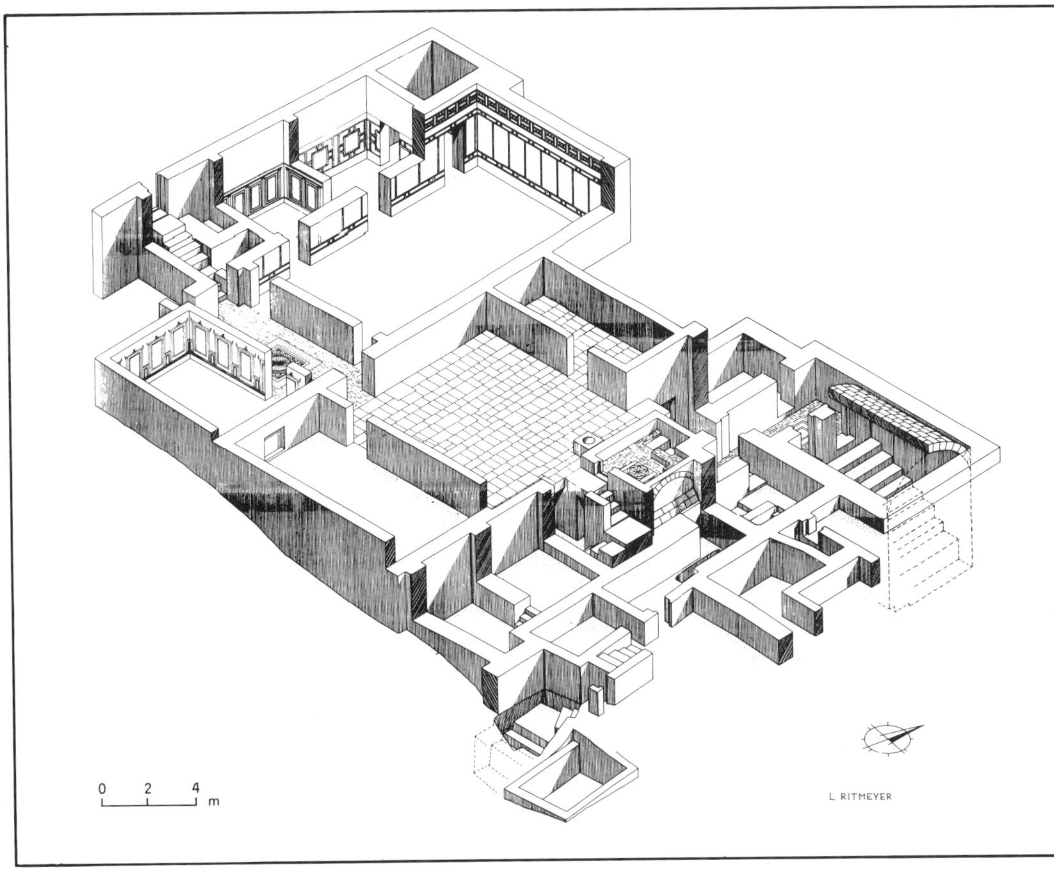

Jewish Quarter: reconstruction of the Palatial Mansion.

Jewish Quarter: reconstruction of the large hall (no. 4) in the Palatial Mansion.

Romans and Jerusalem was destroyed in 70 CE.

House of Columns (Area M). The House of Columns, exposed north of the Palatial Mansion, is unique because it is the only house in the Herodian Quarter in which columns were used. However, the exact plan of the house could not be confirmed. The excavators unearthed a stylobate, which retained a few column fragments, probably from six columns. A narrow passage ran between the columns and the parallel wall. Adjoining the wall were two rooms paved with colored stone tiles (opus sectile), most of which had been plundered. The columns probably formed part of a peristyle in the manner of luxurious contemporary Roman villas.

Jewish Quarter: wall coated with stucco from the Palatial Mansion's large hall.

Jewish Quarter: general view of the Palatial Mansion.

Burnt House (Area B). The Burnt House was uncovered north of the Palatial Mansion, at the corner of Tiferet Israel and Misgav Ladakh streets. It consisted of a small courtyard, four rooms, a kitchen, and a small mikveh, near which was a small space, probably used as an *oẓar* (storage pool). Only the basement could be excavated. It had been used as a workshop or laboratory, as indicated by the type and quantity of finds recovered from a thick conflagration layer. That layer had not been disturbed by later building and had therefore preserved objects exactly as they had been at the time of the destruction: numerous stone vessels, stone tables, basalt mortars, stone weights, cooking pots, oil juglets, and perfume bottles. One of the stone weights was engraved with the name [ד]בר קתרס ([belonging] to the son of Katros). The house of Katros is mentioned in the Talmud as a priestly family that served in the Temple (B.T., *Pes.* 57a; Tosefta, *Men.* 13:21). The debris that filled the rooms also included fallen stones, badly scorched by fire, and charred wooden beams.

Stone weight from the Burnt House inscribed "(belonging) to the son of Katros."

Many coins from the years of the

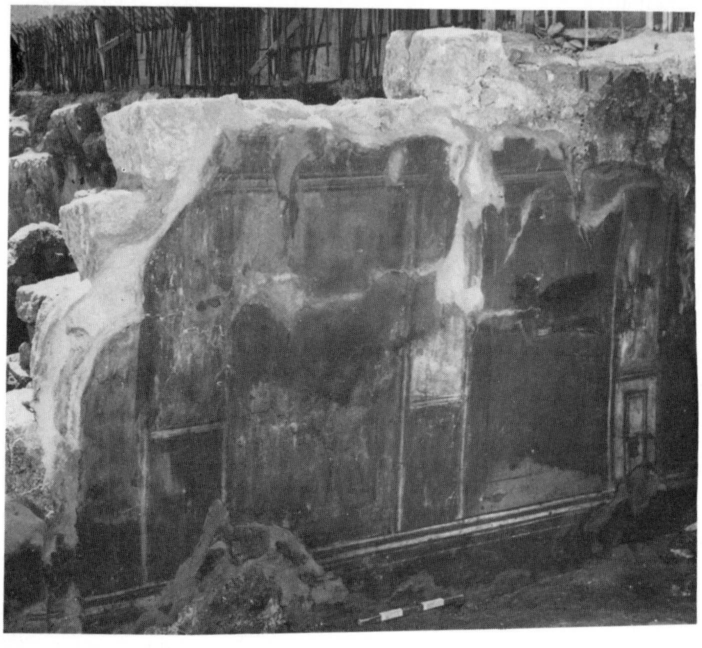

Jewish Quarter: frescoed wall (room 3) from the Palatial Mansion.

Jewish Quarter: plan of the Burnt House.

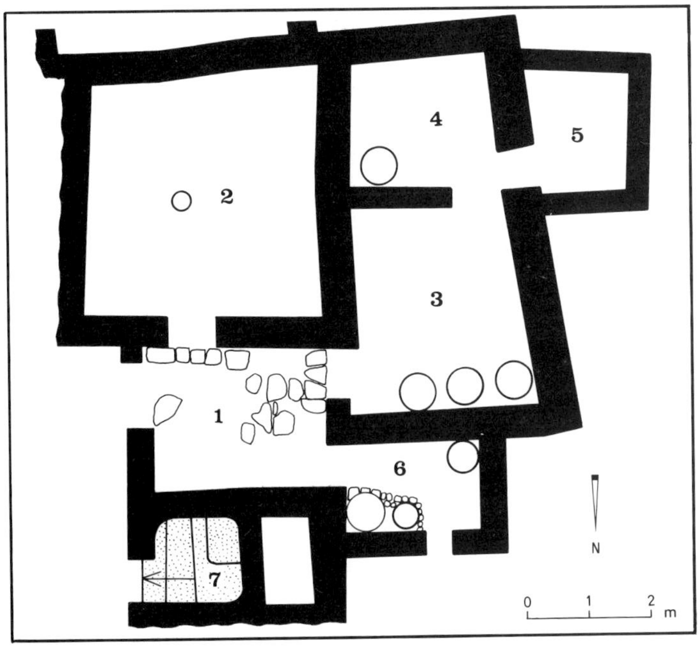

General view of the Burnt House.

First Jewish Revolt against Rome were found on the floors of the rooms. The house clearly burned down at the time of Jerusalem's destruction in 70, when the Romans occupied the Upper City, on the 8th of Elul, one month after the burning of the Temple, as reported by Josephus. Further evidence of the consequences of the war on the household was provided by an iron spear found leaning in the corner of one room and by the bones of a young woman's hand and arm found against one of the kitchen walls.

NAHMAN AVIGAD

Mount Zion: plan of the Herodian buildings.

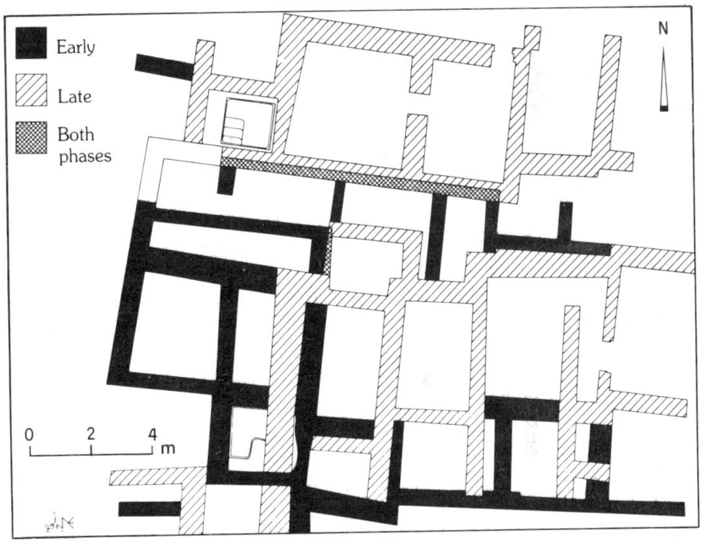

Remains of a magnificent residential building were discovered by M. Broshi (1971–1972), in the present area of the Armenian monastery (the House of Caiaphas) on Mount Zion. A piece of painted plaster was discovered that bears a drawing of a bird—an unusual motif in the Jewish artistic repertoire of the Second Temple period.

Remains of masonry, quarrying, and various water installations, such as the characteristic stepped ritual pools (mikvehs) of Second Temple times, have come to light in excavations conducted since the end of the nineteenth century in all parts of Mount Zion and on the slopes of the hill: the extensive excavations by Bliss and Dickie (1894–1897) in the southern part of Mount Zion and on its southern and eastern slopes; excavations by J. Margovski (1969) and by M. Ben-Dov (early 1970s) south of the Old City, along the wall from the Zion Gate to the Dung Gate; an excavation by E. Eisenberg (1983) in front of the Dormition Church on Mount Zion; and the excavation by S. Margalit and B. Pixner (early 1980s) on the southern slope of Mount Zion. Most probably, too, some of the water installations, quarrying, and fragmentary masonry exposed since 1890 by J. Germer-Durand in the precincts of the Church of Saint Peter in Gallicantu on the eastern slope of Mount Zion, as well as some remains discovered when foundations were laid for the Dormition Abbey in 1899, date to the Second Temple period. Kenyon's excavations on the eastern slope of Mount Zion also revealed what she considered evidence for settlement in the Second Temple period—but not before the reign of Agrippa I (see above, First Wall). Y. Gat's excavations in 1975 at the foot of the southeastern slope of Mount Zion, near the Siloam Pool, revealed remains of Second Temple period masonry. Y. Shiloh's area H, at the foot of the eastern slope of Mount Zion, revealed remains from Hasmonean times (stratum 7).

Mount Zion: general view of the Herodian buildings.

Herod's Palace. One of the most prominent buildings in the Upper City in Second Temple times was Herod's palace, which was built, as Josephus reported (*War* V, 176), at the northwestern corner of the hill. The excavations carried out there have provided some idea of the enormous size of the podium Herod built for it. Excavations by Amiran and Eitan in the courtyard of the Citadel (1968–1969); by Tushingham (as part of Kenyon's 1962–1967 excavations) in site L in the southern part of the Armenian Garden south of the Citadel; and by Bahat and Broshi (1970–1971) in the northern part of the Armenian Garden—all revealed the remains of the podium. It was impressive both for its size and the quality of its construction; its estimated dimensions were 330 by 130 m. It was built of a series of retaining walls, built crosswise, with earth fills in between, to elevate the ground level artificially by some 4 to 5 m. According to Tushingham, the podium collapsed some time after Herod's death and was repaired by Agrippa I. The Amiran–Eitan excavations in the Citadel courtyard also exposed a few sections of the superstructure of the palace complex itself, which bore patches of painted plaster (stratum IV). The remains discovered in the Citadel courtyard may belong to a military barrack associated with Herod's palace; the palace proper extended mainly over the area of the Armenian Garden farther to the south. When Herod's palace was built, various Hasmonean buildings were buried beneath the podium. Prominent among these is a wall with a gateway, complete with the original lintel (stratum VI in the Amiran–Eitan excavations). The monumental column base found by Solar and Sivan (1984–1988) in the southern fosse of the Citadel may also be associated with Herod's palace. In addition, a staircase 17 m wide, mostly cut in the bedrock, was exposed in the Citadel's eastern fosse. The beginnings of this structure date to the Hasmonean period, but its nature is as yet unclear. South of the Citadel, S. Gibson (1983) investigated a rock-cut drain, covered with stone slabs, running beneath the walls of the Old City. It is associated, in Gibson's view, with Herod's palace. During that period, the foundations of the outer face of the First Wall to the west of the palace were strengthened (see above, the First Wall).

THE SECOND WALL

The line of the Second Wall and the date of its construction constitute one of the most complex unsolved problems in the study of Jerusalem in the Second Temple period. Josephus describes it briefly (*War* V, 146) as beginning at the Gennath Gate in the First Wall and ending at the Antonia fortress, at the northwestern corner of the Temple Mount. Fourteen towers stood along the Second Wall (*War* V, 158). It was the northern line of Jerusalem's fortifications at the time of the Crucifixion, so that the location of its remains and determination of its course are critical clues to the location of the site of that event—that is, the Hill of Golgotha and the nearby sepulcher, both traditionally placed in the Church of the Holy Sepulcher in the Christian Quarter.

It is generally agreed that the Second Wall ran along a line north of the First Wall, in the area presently occupied by the Christian and Muslim quarters in the northern part of the Old City. Since the mid-nineteenth century, scholars have associated various segments of masonry—discovered by chance in that general area—with the Second Wall. The widely dispersed positions of these remains and their relationship to the location of the sacred sites within the Church of the Holy Sepulcher has inspired various scholars to suggest several alternative, winding lines for the course of the Second Wall, none of which can be confirmed by archaeology. In view of the crowded construction in the Christian and Muslim quarters, it is impossible today, as in the past, to expose the remains of the Second Wall. Moreover, the surface in this area reveals no prominent topographical features that might indicate its course. Thus, today no remains of ancient fortifications can be attributed with any confidence to the Second Wall. Nevertheless, the evidence from recent excavations may contribute to the formulation of an accepted solution, at least regarding the course of the Second Wall from the Gennath Gate to the north.

Any conclusions about the line described by the northernmost section of the Second Wall will depend directly on the location of the Third Wall (see below, Third Wall): the maximalists, who extend Jerusalem at the end of the Second Temple period as far as the wall exposed by E. L. Sukenik and L. A. Mayer (some 400 m north of the Damascus Gate), reconstruct the Second Wall along a line running north from the First Wall to the Damascus Gate; here, they argue, the Second Wall turned southeast and continued on toward the Antonia fortress. On the other hand, the minimalists, who limit the part of Jerusalem encompassed by the Third Wall to an area within the present-day northern wall of the Old City, along the line of the Damascus Gate, trace the line of the Second Wall from a point just north of the Gennath Gate, veering east toward the Antonia fortress at a certain point south of the Damascus Gate.

A large structure considered by several scholars to be part of the Second Wall was discovered underneath the Damascus Gate, in the middle of the present-day northern wall of the Old City. R. W. Hamilton (1937–1938), excavating beneath the present Ottoman gate, found the remains of the gate of the Roman city of Aelia Capitolina. It consisted of three openings between two projecting towers. The gate was built of typical Herodian ashlars with drafted margins, evidently in secondary use. In the foundations of the western tower, the excavators exposed the remains of an earlier wall; only one course of stones survives. It was built of large ashlar blocks, dressed in similar fashion to the stones in the later Roman gate above it; the short section exposed was a corner at an obtuse angle. Hamilton dated the wall to the Herodian period; Avi-Yonah and others believed it to be the remains of a gate tower at the northern end of the Second Wall. New excavations by M. Magen (1979–1984) at the Damascus Gate proved beyond a doubt that the ancient gate was contemporary with Aelia Capitolina. The earlier stretch of wall should probably be ascribed to a gate from the Second Temple period. The new finds reject the view of Kenyon and J. B. Hennessy, who dated the first stage of the Aelia Capitolina Damascus Gate to the Second Temple period (at which time, they believed, it constituted part of the Third Wall; see below, Roman Period).

In the 1870s, a corner of an ancient structure with openings was unearthed on the grounds of the Russian Hospice east of the Church of the Holy Sepulcher. It was built of large ashlar blocks with characteristic Herodian drafted margins. Vincent and others identified it as a gate in the Second Wall from the Second Temple period; it is today generally dated to the time of Aelia Capitolina (see below, Roman Period).

As already stated, both the ancient Damascus Gate and the masonry corner discovered in the Russian Hospice are built of large, typically Herodian ashlars; a careful examination of the details of the construction shows that in both the stones are in secondary use. The stones probably originated in luxurious buildings or in the walls of the Temple Mount in Second Temple times. They would have been dismantled to provide masonry for the important buildings in Aelia Capitolina.

In 1962, Kenyon discovered remains of ancient quarries in bedrock in her site C in the Muristan, southeast of the Church of the Holy Sepulcher. They were buried some 13 m beneath earth fills and the remains of buildings from later periods. Excavations by U. Lux and H. J. H. Vriezen (1970–1971) beneath the foundations of the Lutheran Church of the Redeemer, slightly north of Kenyon's site C, revealed identical stratigraphy: remains of ancient quarries in bedrock, at a considerable depth, under enormous spills of earth which the excavator attributed to the northern shift of Jerusalem's walls in the reign of Agrippa I. The finds at the site made it clear that the massive wall, discovered when the Lutheran church was built in 1893, was not part of the Second Wall.

An examination of the finds from Kenyon's and Lux's excavations and from excavations beneath the foundations of the Church of the Holy Sepulcher indicates that the slope of the hill now occupied by the Muristan in the Christian Quarter was the site of quarries, from which masonry was taken for Jerusalem's buildings, beginning in the First Temple period. Kenyon believed that the Second Wall had been built along a rock-cut scarp that rose some 3 m on the eastern side of the quarry; the quarry itself served as a fosse defending the Second Wall. This view accords well with Avigad's findings, which led him to locate the Gennath Gate—located by Josephus in the First Wall, with the Second Wall running north from it—in the northern part of the Jewish Quarter, a short distance south of the Muristan (see above, First Wall).

Lacking either confidently identifiable remains of the Second Wall or precise historical data, scholars are also divided over the date of its construction. On the evidence provided by Josephus (*Antiq.* XIV, 476), Jerusalem may have had two city walls as early as 37 BCE, when Herod occupied the city. It is probable, therefore, that the Second Wall was built as far back as the Late Hasmonean period, in order to protect the marketplaces in the upper part of the Tyropoeon Valley. Although some scholars put the date farther back, to the end of the First Temple period, still others prefer a later date, under Herod.

The sparse remains from the Second Temple period found in the area estimated to have been encircled by the Second Wall are described below (see the Temple Mount and Its Environs, the Third Wall, the New City).

THE TEMPLE MOUNT AND ITS ENVIRONS

The Herodian Temple Mount enclosure, supported by its massive retaining walls, was the most prominent and impressive architectural complex of Jerusalem in the Second Temple period. The magnificence of the entire complex—which was larger than other sacred enclosures of the time—and the Temple itself aroused the awe of the ancient world. Something of this magnificence is still conveyed by the outer walls of the Temple Mount, which are preserved to a considerable height and are visible today. The beauty and majesty of the enclosure and the Temple were repeatedly mentioned by Josephus and other historians, and the Rabbis said, "whosoever has not seen Herod's building [= the Temple] has never seen a beautiful building" (*B.B.* 3b). The Temple was destroyed when the Roman legions overran Jerusalem in 70 CE. There are no visible remains of it. It rose above the enclosure on Mount Moriah; its position (according to the commonly accepted view) is now marked by the Dome of the Rock.

Most of what is known about the remains of the Herodian Temple Mount

Reconstruction of the Temple Mount and the buildings surrounding it, as built by Herod.

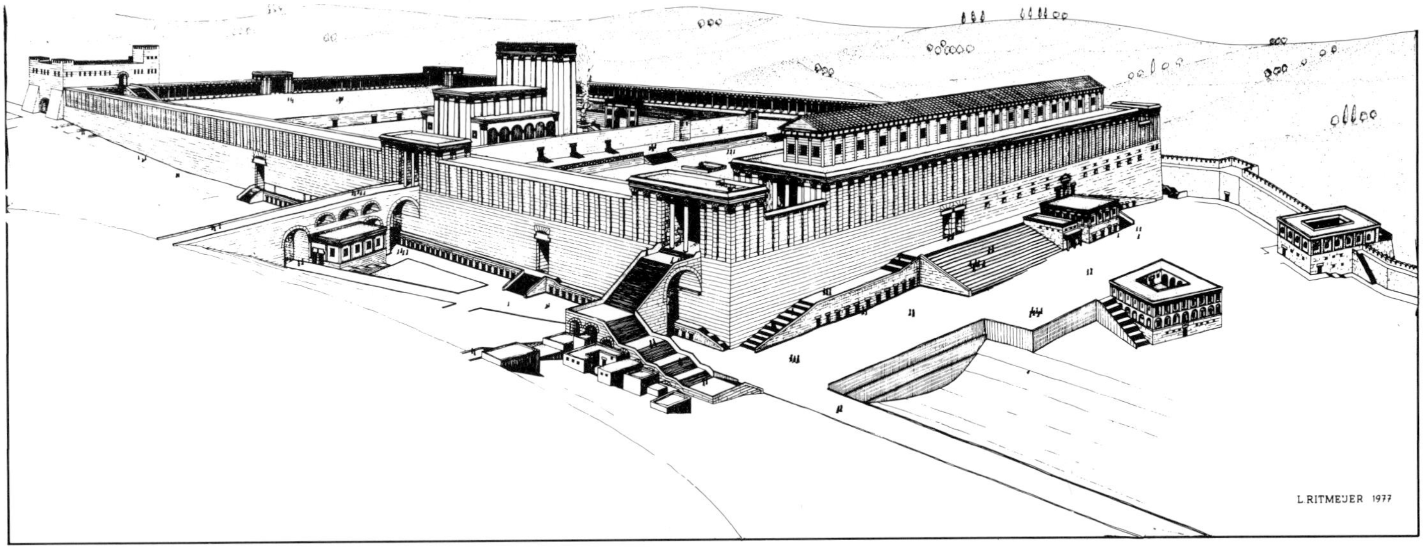

comes from C. Warren's indefatigable explorations between 1867 and 1869. His excavations added significantly to the information furnished by the survey and measurements made by C. Wilson in 1864. Warren sank numerous deep shafts just outside the walls of the Temple Mount; when he could go no farther, he sank more shafts at a distance from the walls and then ran horizontal tunnels right up to and along their foundations. As he documented his finds so precisely, publishing them in detail in his books, they are still used by researchers to study the construction of the walls around the Temple Mount as they were built by Herod.

Between 1968 and 1978, B. Mazar conducted extensive excavations along the southern wall of the Temple Mount and a small section of the southern end of the western wall, up to the Gate of the Mughrabis. His excavations added to what was known about the construction of the outer walls of the Temple Mount enclosure and furnished a comprehensive picture of Herod's monumental public construction along the southern and western walls.

Herod expanded the area of the Temple Mount beyond the natural dimensions of Mount Moriah, bridging the valleys surrounding it. The northeastern corner of the enclosure was built over the course of the Bezetha Valley, extending the Temple Mount area to its northern bank. The southwestern corner was built approximately 35 m west of the bed of the Tyropoeon Valley, at the foot of the eastern slope of the city's southwestern hill. In the northwestern corner of the Temple Mount, the masons cut into the rock, which originally rose above the summit of Mount Moriah; on the rest of this hill, Herod built the Antonia fortress. Simultaneously, the riverbed that once created a natural moat between Mount Moriah and the southwestern hill was dammed.

The Herodian Temple Mount enclosure was shaped like a rectangle with sides of unequal length. The length of the western (and longest) wall is 485 m; the eastern wall is 470 m long; the northern wall is 315 m long; and the southern (and shortest) wall is only 280 m long (there are slight differences between measurements made by different researchers). The area of the enclosure is 144,000 sq m—which is exceptionally large, compared with other well-known sacred enclosures in the classical world, such as that of Bel at Palmyra and Jupiter at Damascus. It is evident from the plan that the enclosure was designed as a symmetric complex, incorporating ancient remains in the east (see below), on the pattern of a gigantic temenos with the Temple at its center. The construction of such a large artificial area in a hilly region, where building conditions were far from favorable, is remarkable.

The walls around the Temple Mount, whose lower parts functioned as retaining walls, were founded for their entire length on bedrock, following the local topography. In the southern corners and in the vicinity of the northeastern corner, where the rock level is particularly low, the foundations

The Temple Mount and the excavated remains on the Ophel, looking north.

Plan of the Temple Mount as built by Herod.

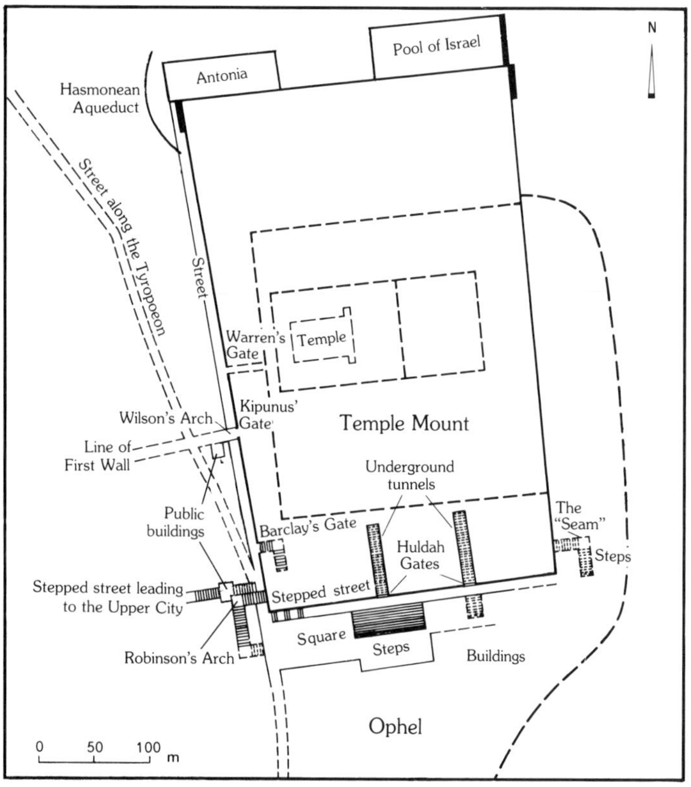

were laid at a greater depth below ground than in the northwest and in the center of the southern wall, where the rock surface is higher. In some places, the foundations of the walls lay deep below the contemporary street level, and the walls themselves sometimes rose to a height about 30 m above the street. There were presumably towers at the corners of the Temple Mount, accounting for an additional height of some 5 m. Thus, the maximum height of the original wall in the south reached some 50 to 55 m above bedrock. The present state of preservation of the walls depends on the local topography. They are particularly well preserved below the level of the Temple Mount's inner esplanade. In the north of the eastern wall, where it crosses the bed of the Bezetha Valley, the original masonry survives to a maximum height of some 40 m. The northeastern corner itself has survived to a height of about 7 m above the present paved level of the Temple Mount. The height of preservation is also considerable at the southern corners. The original masonry is particularly impressive at the southeastern corner, built on the steep eastern proclivity of the hill, where it dips down to the Kidron Valley. This corner stands today to a height of thirty-five original courses, for a total height of some 42 m above bedrock. In the southwestern corner, fifteen courses of original masonry survive above the street at the foot of the wall, in addition to eight courses buried underground, going down to bedrock. In the vicinity of the so-called Western Wall (or Wailing Wall), up to seven original courses rise above the level of the present pavement; a larger number of courses reaches bedrock under it. In all, the wall survives here to a total height of more than 20 m. The northwestern corner survives to the height of a few original courses above the level of the Temple Mount esplanade.

The walls around the Temple Mount were built of large ashlars. Their outer faces are dressed with a margin 10 to 20 cm wide, leaving a smoothed boss in the center that projects only very slightly from the surface. In some stones in the foundation courses—below ground level outside the Temple enclosure as it was in Second Temple times—the projecting bosses are somewhat coarser. In the northern part of the western wall, the natural rock was also tooled in imitation of the drafted masonry of the overlying wall. The play of light and shade created by the dressed margins contributed to the beauty and dramatic appearance of the massive walls. Above the level of the Temple Mount's inner esplanade, the outer face of the walls was decorated with engaged pilasters, which were observed by C. R. Conder in a short section of the northern part of the western wall. A fine example of this style of construction is furnished by the walls of the Ḥaram el-Khalil (Cave of Machpelah) at Hebron, which are also believed to be of Herodian construction. There are no signs of such pilasters in the tower at the northeastern corner of the Temple Mount, which, as stated, has survived above the level of the inner esplanade. This may be because the Temple enclosure on this side did not face the city, or the intention may have been to adapt the style of construction to that of the eastern wall of the Temple Mount, whose foundations in some sections are pre-Herodian.

The stones of which the Temple Mount walls were built are approximately 1–1.1 m high, but their length is uniform. Most of them weigh from 2 to 5 tons. The stones in the southern corners of the enclosure are particularly large; some of them are as much as 10 m long and about 2.5 m wide. These exceptional stones, which reach 50 tons or more, were laid as headers and stretchers in the corners in order to bond the walls together. At the height of the threshold of the Huldah Gates in the southern wall, the so-called *nidbakh rabba* ("master course" in Aramaic) is visible—the twenty-eighth course in the southeastern corner. Its stones are almost twice as high as the average stones, and it may be found along certain sections of the southern and western walls of the enclosure. The "master course" was apparently a kind of girdle around the complex structure of the Temple Mount walls, to stabilize and bind them, especially on the sides where the masonry rose to a particularly great height. The weight of one stone in this course, in the southeastern corner, is estimated at some 100 tons. An exceptionally large stone was also discovered in the western wall, north of the Wailing Wall. It is 12.1 m long and 3.5 m wide, and a careful estimate of its weight puts it approximately at 300 tons. The stones were laid in rows, in courses athwart the wall, with particularly long stones performing a bonding function. Each course in the wall is recessed 2 to 3 cm, compared with the one below it, so that the outer face of the walls is recessed a few dozen centimeters for its full height. This gradual recess presumably reinforced the strength of the retaining walls of the enclosure and, moreover, compensated for possible optical distortion.

The technique employed to construct these retaining walls is still unclear. The stones presumably were quarried north of Jerusalem's boundaries at that period, where the terrain rises above that of the city, and then were transported to Mount Moriah, thus obviating the need to expend great effort in raising the stones to great heights.

Various examinations and a geoelectric survey put the thickness of the western and southern walls at about 4.6 m. A similar conclusion follows from

Construction from Herod's time in the southern wall of the Temple Mount.

an examination in a tunnel dug at the eastern end of the Mount's southern wall. The wall was probably particularly thick where the eastern wall crosses the deep bed of the Bezetha Valley.

This mode of construction—using particularly large ashlar blocks laid side by side without any bonding material—guaranteed the stability of the walls, which served mainly as immense retaining walls for the Temple Mount enclosure. The construction of such a solid platform as a means of artificially elevating the surface level is characteristic of Herod's construction and was also used in building Herod's palace in the Upper City, as well as other buildings outside Jerusalem, such as at Herodium.

The inner space of the Temple Mount, as delineated by the walls, was probably filled with earth for the most part; in some places, where the height of the walls permitted, the overlying esplanade was supported on systems of vaults, as attested by the (Crusader) so-called Solomon's Stables at the southeastern corner, believed by some scholars to have been built in the Second Temple period. This inner vaulted area presumably relieved some of the enormous outward pressure exerted on the walls, mainly at the southern corners of the enclosure. It also provided a solution to the halachic problem of construction over graves. As mentioned in the Mishnah: "The ground beneath the Temple Mount and the courts was hollow, because of deep-lying graves" (*Par.* 3:3).

THE SOUTHERN WALL OF THE TEMPLE MOUNT AND REMAINS IN THE OPHEL. Two walled-up gates are visible today in the southern wall of the Temple Mount: the Double Gate to the west and the Triple Gate to the east. They are the remains of two gates from Herod's time that probably continued the Huldah Gates built in the Hasmonean period, and referred to in the Mishnah: "The two Gates of Huldah in the south serve for entry and exit" (*Mid.* 1:3). The Double Gate is in the west and the Triple Gate, in the east. The distance between them is 65 m. Both originally led to broad, stepped tunnels, built of large ashlars, that climbed to the level of the Temple Mount esplanade 14 m above. The tunnels were built in the vaulted space beneath the esplanade and ran beneath the royal stoa that Herod built at the southern end of the enclosure. The more familiar structure today is that of the western Huldah Gate, which was incorporated in the structure known as el-Aqsa el-Qadima, under the el-Aqsa Mosque at the southern end of the Temple Mount. The width of each opening in the Double Gate is 5.5 m and its estimated height is more than 10 m. The lintel above the eastern opening of the western Huldah Gate today consists of a large stone topped by a shallow relieving arch. Preserved inside the gate is a system of four stone domes supported by arches resting on central columns. Still visible on two of the domes are magnificent carved geometric and floral motifs. The Herodian eastern Huldah Gate is not extant; the Triple Gate seen today was built in a later period. One theory holds that this gate was also originally a double gate; others believe, however, that the present tripartite plan reflects a continuation of the original Herodian structure.

Near the Triple Gate Warren discovered a system of winding tunnels reaching deep into the precincts of the Temple Mount. The tunnels are cut in the rock and roofed with stone slabs. He conjectured that they drained water from the great cisterns in the southern part of the Mount. Another stone-built tunnel was discovered in B. Mazar's excavations here. It runs north for about 20 m until it is blocked by fallen debris. Mazar suggested that the tunnels were the *mesibbot* mentioned in the Mishnah (*Tam.* 1:1), although the sources can also be interpreted as referring to structures built somewhat farther to the north, within the area of the Temple Mount.

The complex of public buildings just outside the southern and western walls of the Temple Mount, like the Temple Mount enclosure itself, was planned on a monumental scale and impressively well constructed. From the north–south main street along the Tyropoeon Valley, a paved street branched off to the east near the southwestern corner of the Temple Mount and ran along the southern wall. From the western end of this street to the threshold of the Huldah Gates there was a climb of approximately 6 m; the street was 6.6 m wide and demarcated on the south by a wall. The street climbed eastward on a gentle gradient, in groups of three steps each. Beneath the street was a series of double rooms of the same size (3.4 by 2.8 m). Warren discovered in his excavations that the walls of the rooms were founded on bedrock. This series of rooms probably continued to the east, as far as the western Huldah Gate. They were roofed by vaults and were apparently used as shops that opened onto a paved square to the south. This square in turn was bordered on the south by a massive wall, of which only the foundation survives, some 11 m from the front of the vault. Between the two Huldah Gates the street was level. East of the eastern Huldah Gate, as reconstructed by the excavators, the street descended by steps supported on vaults whose piers were found in situ. Here, too, the vaulted spaces were probably used as shops open to the south. The stones of the walls at the rear of the vaults were found cracked and blackened with soot, hinting at the strong conflagration that had raged here during the destruction of Jerusalem in 70 CE.

South of the street, alongside the southern wall, the remains of two flights of steps were found. The width of the western flight, whose remains were exposed opposite the Double Gate, was 65 m; the other, opposite the Triple Gate, was apparently only 15 m wide, judging from a vault left standing opposite the gate. Between the two flights of steps were remains of masonry, including a few rooms and ritual baths. To their south were the remains of a spacious public square.

Along the southern wall the excavators found piles of stone debris, in which a few fragmentary inscriptions and parts of columns, capitals, friezes, and

The Ophel: decorated architectural fragment from the Temple Mount.

The Ophel: stairway in front of the southern wall of the Temple Mount, Herodian period.

Herodian paved street and stairway along the southern wall of the Temple Mount.

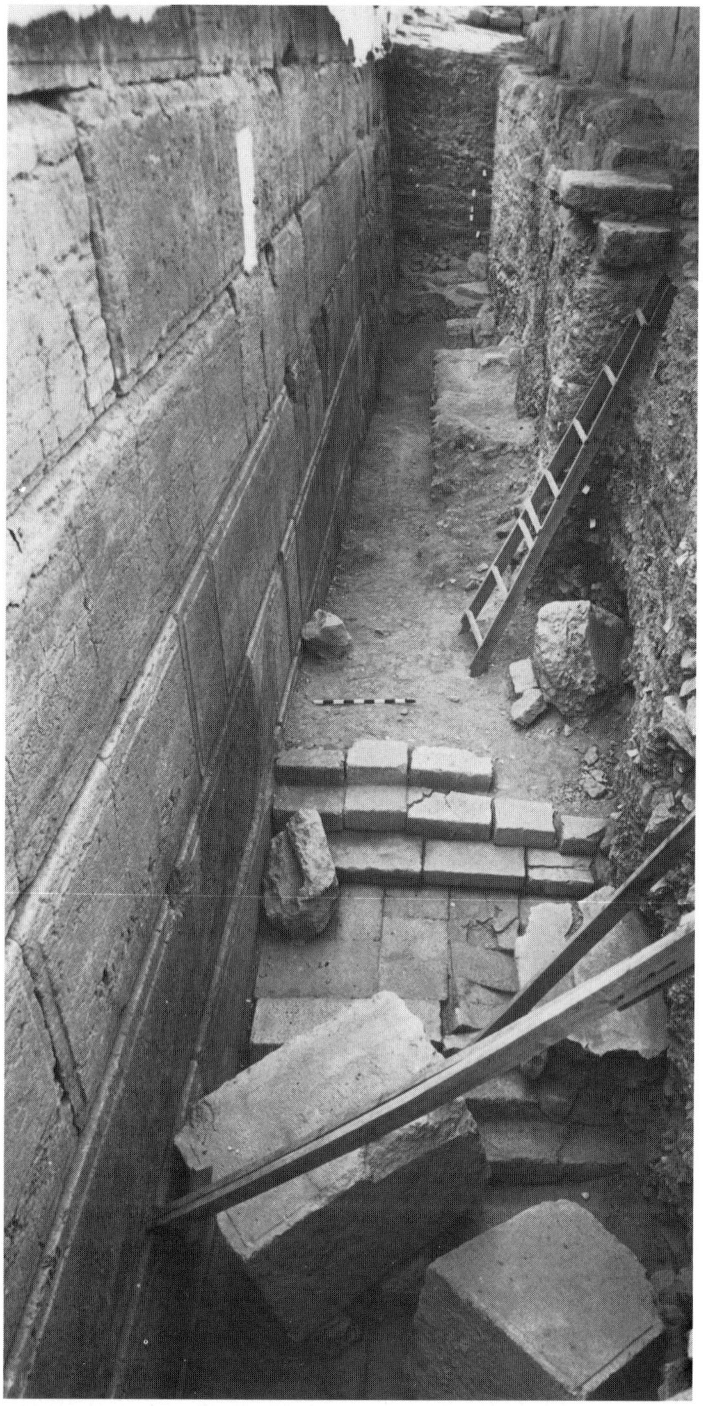

cornices were also found. These silent witnesses to the destruction in 70 CE were sometimes piled to a considerable height above the remains of Second Temple period buildings. Many of the stones are decorated with motifs characteristic of the artistic repertoire of Second Temple times: geometrical patterns in complex combinations, floral patterns such as rosettes inscribed in octagons, trailing branches of acanthus and ivy leaves, bunches of grapes, and palmettes. Identical motifs appear in the decoration of the domes in the Double Gate and on some of the most magnificent tomb facades and sarcophagi from the Second Temple period discovered in Jerusalem. Some fragments still bear the remains of gilt decoration, recalling descriptions in the Mishnah and in Josephus' works (*War* V, 190–227). These stones came from the Huldah Gates, the magnificent Royal Stoa that Herod built in the southern part of the Temple enclosure and also, perhaps, from other buildings that graced the enclosure in the Second Temple period. Found in the street at the foot of the southwestern corner were some ashlar blocks tooled and decorated in a style that enables a reconstruction of how the top of this corner of the Temple Mount looked. Engraved on the top corner stone was a fragmentary inscription: לבית התקיעה לה[. . . (to the Trumpeting Place to [. . .). Of the many proposed reconstructions of the missing last word, the most likely seems to be לה[כריז], "to declare" or לה[בדיל] "to distinguish," based on a passage in Josephus (*War* IV, 582) and on the Mishnah (*Suk.* 5:5).

In addition to the impressive public buildings just outside the southern wall of the Temple Mount, Mazar's excavations uncovered additional remains from the end of the Second Temple period, mainly in the area of the Ophel. A building in the southeastern part of the Ophel is unique in size and construction: its walls incorporated those of an earlier, massively built structure from the late First Temple period (see above). The new building, probably erected during Herod's reign, consisted of perhaps ten rooms, a few cisterns, and stepped mikvehs. Another imposing residential building—with cisterns, remains of vaults, and a mosaic floor—was discovered in the western Ophel, outside the walls of the Old City. In the remains of another building pieces of stucco fashioned in the likeness of various animals were found. There were remains everywhere in the excavated area of stepped mikvehs, including a particularly interesting one in the eastern Ophel. Probably intended for public use, it had flights of steps on all four sides. A small part of the masonry unearthed on the Ophel and dated to the Second Temple period constitutes remains of buildings cleared before Herod's massive construction projects were begun. Prominent among these remains are those of a pool and a few walls considered by Ben-Dov to have belonged to the Seleucid Acra (see above, the Acra). Among Mazar's finds dating to the Second Temple period were a Greek inscription from the Herodian period, marking the contribution of a person from Rhodes to some paving project (*SEG* 35, no. 1546); numerous fragments of stone vessels, some with incised decorations, one of them bearing the inscription *qrbn* (sacrifice); stone weights, some with incised inscriptions; bone artifacts; and a large quantity of coins.

THE WESTERN WALL OF THE TEMPLE MOUNT AND REMAINS IN THE TYROPOEON VALLEY. B. Mazar also excavated a stretch 75 m long along the western wall of the Temple Mount, from the southwestern corner up to the Gate of the Mughrabis. His finds testify to the exceptional planning of Herod's construction in this area.

Twelve m north of the southwestern corner of the Temple Mount, projecting from the western wall, are the remains of the so-called Robinson's Arch. The arch is named for the researcher who identified it in 1838 as the remains of the eastern end of the bridge he believed linked the Temple Mount to the Upper City to the west in the Second Temple period. Wilson and Warren discovered the remains of the pier on which the other side of the arch had rested. Warren, in fact, dug a series of seven shafts running westward at regular intervals up the southwestern hill from the arch, but found no evidence of additional piers. Nevertheless, the existence of such a bridge, supported on a row of arches, was taken almost for granted, until disproved by Mazar's excavations.

The pier that supported the western arm of Robinson's Arch stood 13 m distant from the western wall and was built of large ashlars, similar in tooling to the stones in the walls of the Temple Mount. The length of the pier was 15.2 m and its width 3.6 m; it was preserved to a height of some 5 m. In it were four small hollow spaces, possibly used as shops open onto the street that ran beneath Robinson's Arch. Shallow arches above the lintels of these spaces relieved the pressure from the superstructure; the remains of these arches are carved with convex upper sides, and are still in position on the lintels. The surviving remains of Robinson's Arch itself are three courses where the arch was attached to the wall of the Temple Mount. The arch was supported on this side by a course of projecting stones; there was probably a similar course in the opposite spring of the arch (in the pier), as such stones have been found in secondary use in a later building. The diameter of the span of Robinson's Arch was 13 m and its width was equal to the pier's. It hung 17.5 m above the street. The collapsed remains of the arch, including pieces of the steps built on top of it, were found on the street pavement. Found southwest of Robinson's Arch were the remnants of a series of vaults running at right angles to the arch. The length of the vaults was a little less than that of Robinson's Arch, and the diameter was 5 m. Six vaults were found, for a total length of 35 m, gradually increasing in height from south to north. The vaults, together with Robinson's Arch, supported a monumental flight of stairs. They were built during Herod's reign to link the street in the Tyropoeon Valley, at the foot of the Temple Mount, with the Royal Stoa in the southern part of the Temple Mount enclosure, as described by Josephus (*Antiq.* XV, 410–411).

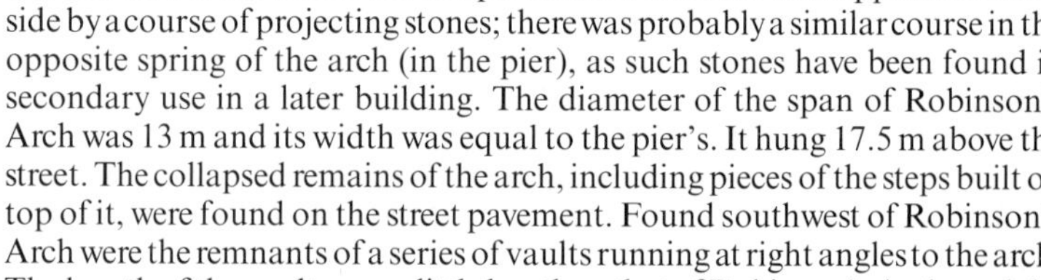

Hebrew inscription found near the southwest corner of the Temple Mount: "to the Trumpeting Place to [. . ." (probably "to declare" or "to distinguish").

Temple Mount: southwest corner and the remains of Robinson's Arch.

Robinson's Arch was an integral part of an extensive structure, the remains of whose rooms were exposed attached to the northern side of the arch. In view of the size and position of the building and the quality of its construction, Mazar conjectured that it might be the Jerusalem archives mentioned by Josephus (*War* VI, 354).

At the foot of the southwestern corner of the Temple Mount the remains of a street were discovered—a major traffic artery in the Second Temple period that ran along the bed of the Tyropoeon Valley. It was 10 m wide, paved with large stone slabs, most of them 2 to 4 sq m in area, and bordered on both sides by raised curbstones. It was buried under the rubble of ashlars from the walls of the Temple Mount. Beneath the street was a drain, sometimes as much as 4 m deep, mostly roofed by a vault. The drain's winding, irregular course is evidence that the workmen had tried to take advantage of the hollows created by First Temple tombs encountered along the way. Part of the street's southern continuation, farther down the Tyropoeon, and the drain beneath it were discovered by Bliss and Dickie at the end of the nineteenth century, north of the Siloam Pool. Kenyon reexposed a section of this street in her site N, and near it the remains of what was probably a public building built of ashlars. After some deliberation, she dated the street and the building to the Herodian period. This conclusion obviously ran counter to her hypothesis (see above) that this part of the Tyropoeon Valley was not part of the walled city of Jerusalem until the reign of Agrippa I. Near the Siloam Pool, Bliss and Dickie found an additional section of paving from the same street. The drain beneath the street left the city limits through gate C2 in the First Wall.

Drainage channel under the street running along the western wall of the Temple Mount.

Herodian street opposite the western wall of the Temple Mount. The street pavement is covered with fallen stones from the wall of the Temple Mount.

At the southwestern corner of the Temple Mount, the main street split into a side street that ran north on a higher level, alongside the western wall of the Temple Mount. Its width was 3 m and it was supported by a series of vaults. The vaults, in turn, were probably shops that opened onto the main street to the west (similar to the street and underlying vaults running alongside the southern wall). The remnants of the northern extension of this upper street along the western wall were probably those exposed by Warren in his shafts near Barclay's Gate and Wilson's Arch. A paved section of the continuation of that street was recently exposed near the northwestern corner of the Temple Mount (see below). At the southwestern corner of the Temple Mount another street split off the main street, climbing up eastward to the Huldah Gates (see above). Yet another street ran west, north of Robinson's Arch, and ascended to the Upper City by way of a flight of stairs, some of which were supported by underground vaults.

Some 80 m north of the southwestern corner of the Temple Mount, at the southern end of the present-day Western Wall, the lintel of the so-called Barclay's Gate is still visible. It was erroneously identified with Kipunus' Gate, mentioned in the Mishnah (*Mid.* 1:3). Warren exposed the threshold of the gate, which is now walled up, and examined its interior in a later cistern (no. 19) in the southwestern part of the Temple Mount esplanade. When the Second Temple was still standing, an underground stepped tunnel led up to the east from Barclay's Gate and turned south toward the Temple Mount esplanade. Barclay's Gate was 5.6 m wide and eight courses, or 10 m, high. The threshold was at the level of the upper street that ran along the western wall of the Temple Mount; it was approached from the main street in the Tyropoeon Valley by way of a (reconstructed) flight of stairs, supported by an arch, mentioned in this area by Warren. The lintel of the gate is a single large stone, more than 7 m long and about 2 m high.

Approximately 100 m north of Barclay's Gate, the so-called Wilson's Arch, explored by him in 1864, springs from the western wall of the Temple Mount. The arch, which is complete, is identical in length to Robinson's Arch, but is built at a level only slightly lower than the supposed level of the Temple Mount enclosure in the Second Temple period. Many scholars are of the opinion that the present arch was built in the Byzantine period or in the Early Arab period. However, Warren and Conder argued that it is possible that the three lower courses of the arch where it meets the Temple Mount wall, as well as the pier on its other side, originate in the Second Temple period. The remains of the original arch from that period were discovered, in their opinion, a few meters below the present level. Recent excavations at the eastern end of the Street of the Chain, above the level of Wilson's Arch, brought to light new evidence supporting its antiquity, dating it to the Second Temple period (see below, Roman Period). Wilson's Arch is considered to have been the easternmost of a series of arches that supported a bridge that, in Second Temple times, spanned the Tyropoeon Valley and linked the Upper City in the west with the Temple Mount esplanade in the east. This may be the location of the bridge referred to by Josephus (*Antiq.* XIV, 58; *War* II, 344).

Near Wilson's Arch are the remains of a magnificent hall from the Second Temple period; Warren discovered and named it the Freemasons' Hall. Today it is also called "the Hasmonean Hall." The walls are built of ashlars. Pilasters at the corners and along the walls originally bore Corinthian capitals, one of which is preserved in the northeastern corner. In the eastern wall was a double door with a lintel. Today the hall has a vaulted ceiling, of later construction, supported on a central pillar. The original hall was presumably part of a large Herodian public building that some scholars have identified with the Chamber of Hewn Stones (the Xystos) or with the Council Building, both referred to by Josephus as being in this area (*War* V, 144).

The outer face of the western wall of the Temple Mount enclosure, from Wilson's Arch to the northwestern corner, was first exposed in the 1970s in a tunnel dug under the supervision of M. Ben-Dov and later of D. Bahat beneath buildings in the present-day Old City.

The remains of the so-called Warren's Gate can be seen in the western wall about 40 m north of Wilson's Arch. The interior of this gate was examined by Warren in a cistern (no. 30) in the western part of the Temple Mount esplanade; it was originally an underground staircase providing access from the street level to the esplanade above (as in Barclay's Gate). The gate's exterior was as wide as Barclay's Gate. Most of the original elements of Warren's Gate have disappeared. Today it is roofed by an arch, of later construction than the Second Temple period, which was found walled up.

Temple Mount: the western wall north of Wilson's Arch.

North of Warren's Gate, the natural rock rises steeply. As a result, the foundations of the western wall not far from the northwestern corner of the Temple Mount were laid on a rock-cut scarp that stands even higher than the level of the street running alongside the wall. It is apparent that the street was never completed in this area. Work was interrupted in the Second Temple period itself, as the builders came up against the high, broad rock face, which they were unable to remove; long quarrying marks are still visible here in the rock. Thus, an uncut salient was left in the rock in the northwestern corner of the Temple Mount, more than 40 m long and some 3 m wide. Above it a tower, projecting 2.5 m from the line of the western wall, was discovered by Conder in the late nineteenth century; flat pilasters were built along its outer surface. Circling the rock projection is an aqueduct, running north–south, which was hewn in the rock and covered with large stone slabs. First investigated in 1867 by Conder and Warren and reexposed in 1987 by Bahat, it is broken off in the north by the Struthion Pool, which is associated with the Antonia fortress; its southern continuation, where it turns east, was severed in the Herodian period, when the western wall of the Temple Mount was constructed. In Bahat's opinion, the aqueduct was hewn by the Hasmoneans to drain rainwater from the upper reaches of the Tyropoeon into the newly built fortress (Baris), just outside the northwestern corner of the Temple Mount.

NORTHERN WALL OF THE TEMPLE MOUNT AND THE ANTONIA. The only known remains of original (Second Temple period) masonry from the northern wall of the Temple Mount are at the eastern end of the wall mainly where the Pool of Israel abuts it. Herod built the Antonia fortress north of the northwestern corner of the Temple Mount enclosure, on the site of a long series of citadels—generally known as the *Birah* in Hebrew or *Baris* in Greek—from the time of Nehemiah, through the Ptolemies and the Hasmoneans. It is possible that the Seleucid Acra was located here as well (see above). Herod's Antonia fortress and its formidable fortifications are described in great detail by Josephus (*War* V, 238–245). Thus, it is known that it was erected on a high rock, with towers at all four corners, and that the tower at the southeastern corner was higher than the other three. Christian tradition identifies the Antonia with the Praetorium, the seat of the Roman procurators in Jerusalem, where Jesus was tried and sentenced to be crucified (Mk. 15:1–20).

Some impressive remains of buildings exposed north of the northwestern corner of the Temple Mount were mistakenly associated by some scholars (and consequently by Christian tradition) with the Antonia fortress. Most of these remains were discovered in the 1860s during the construction of the Sisters of Zion Convent, in which they are now incorporated. They were described by Clermont-Ganneau. Additional excavations were conducted at the site in 1931–1932 by Sister Marie-Aline de Sion and L. H. Vincent. The site was reexamined in 1972 by P. Benoit and once again in the 1980s while conservation and reconstruction work was in progress.

The most salient and confidently identified vestige of the Antonia fortress is

Hasmonean aqueduct next to the northwest corner of the Temple Mount.

a rectangular, cut rock mass, some 120 by 45 m in area, that rises a few meters above the northwestern corner of the Temple Mount enclosure. Its southern scarp, clearly visible from the direction of the Temple Mount, is today the site of the 'Umariyyeh School. To the north, within the precincts of the Sisters of Zion Convent, is a pool from Second Temple times identified with the Struthion Pool, which is referred to in Josephus (*War* V, 467) as having been hewn in the northern fosse of the Antonia (see below, Water Supply).

Some impressive remains of masonry, believed to date to the Roman colony of Aelia Capitolina, were once incorrectly associated with the Antonia fortress. They are the stone pavement known as the Lithostrotos; the vaults over the Struthion Pool, which support the Lithostrotos; and the Ecce Homo Arch, which is actually part of an ornate tripartite gate (see below, Roman Period).

On the basis of these remains and the contours of some of the rock-cuttings, Vincent, together with Sister Marie-Aline, Avi-Yonah, and others, proposed reconstructing the Antonia as an enormous building (c. 150 by 90 m in area) protected by four towers and built around a central paved square (the Lithostrotos), beneath which was the Struthion Pool. The largest, southeastern tower stood on the great rectangular rocky mass abutting the Temple Mount. The northern towers of the fortress stood, according to this opinion, north of the present Sisters of Zion Convent. The plan of both is identifiable from the contours of the rock in the area. This extensive reconstruction, based mainly on remains now dated to the time of Aelia Capitolina and on rock cuttings of unknown origin, has been severely criticized by other scholars; presently it appears to lack sufficient substantiation.

Benoit and others envisaged a considerably smaller Antonia fortress, limited mainly to the rectangular rocky mass abutting the Temple Mount. This reconstruction leaves the Struthion Pool outside the fortress to the north, which is in agreement with Josephus (*War* V, 467). Benoit's proposal is probably more widely accepted today.

Farther to the east, in the present-day Street of the Lions' (St. Stephen's) Gate, north of the Temple Mount, M. Magen (1980–1981) excavated the remains of a paved street that in Second Temple times ran along the northern wall of the Temple Mount.

EASTERN WALL OF THE TEMPLE MOUNT. In the eastern wall of the Temple Mount, sections of original masonry are clearly visible for the entire length of the wall. Some sections are in fact earlier than Herod. Quite probably, because the original slopes of Mount Moriah were particularly steep on this side of the Temple Mount, measures were necessary even before the Second Temple period to level and fortify the natural terrain—Josephus ascribes these activities to the time of King Solomon (*Antiq.* XX, 221; *War* V, 184–185). The Mishnah also states that "All the walls that stood there were high, except for the eastern wall" (*Mid.* 2:4).

At the northern end of the eastern wall of the Temple Mount, where original masonry has survived above the level of the Temple Mount esplanade from Second Temple times, a salient in the wall forms a corner tower, like the tower at the northwestern corner. The length of the tower is 25 m; it projects 2.1 m from the wall.

About 275 m north of the southeast corner of the Temple Mount is the so-called Golden Gate (also known as the Gate of Mercy). The present structure is later than the Second Temple period. Some scholars believe that it was erected over an earlier, Second Temple period gate. The remains of an ancient arch, also undoubtedly later than the Second Temple period, were discovered by chance buried beneath the present gate. This find may reinforce the above hypothesis, as it indicates the continuity of a tradition of locating gates at this point.

Thirty-two meters north of the southeastern corner there is a vertical "seam" in the masonry of the eastern wall of the Temple Mount. North of this "seam," the wall is built of ashlars with drafted margins and a projecting boss laid in alternating courses of headers and stretchers. Similarly tooled stones are found farther north, particularly near the Lions' (St. Stephen's) Gate. This agrees with the above-mentioned evidence from the Mishnah and Josephus that the eastern wall of the Temple Mount was older than the other walls. It is clear from the present state of the remains that the masonry north of the "seam" is older than the 32-m-long addition south of the "seam," which is built of characteristically Herodian masonry. High up in the added section south of the "seam" are the remains of arch springers; above them are the vestiges of a double gate. This may indicate the existence of an eastern flight of stairs, perhaps communicating with the structure known as Solomon's Stables and built in the same style as Robinson's Arch in the western wall. Scholars are divided over the date of the earlier masonry north of the "seam," commonly considered a remnant of the pre-Herodian Temple Mount enclosure that Herod incorporated in his much-expanded structure. Some researchers present the style of the masonry as proof of construction in the First Temple or Persian period; others date it to the early Hellenistic (pre-Hasmonean) period, identifying it as the remains of the Seleucid Acra, or to the Hasmonean period. It is also possible to ascribe it to the Herodian period, on the assumption that Herod built a smaller enclosure before building on the 32-m extension to the south, where he erected the Royal Stoa.

REMAINS WITHIN THE TEMPLE ENCLOSURE. Within the Temple enclosure (the present-day Ḥaram esh-Sharif) there are only a few definite remains from the Second Temple period. Surveys and measurements carried out at the end of the nineteenth century by Wilson, Warren, Conder, and Schick mainly indicate the existence of thirty-seven cisterns beneath the Temple Mount esplanade—some rock-hewn, some stone-built, mostly irregular in shape. Some of them may date to the Second Temple. Other known subterranean features are the tunnels leading to the Huldah Gates, Barclay's Gate, and Warren's Gate and the structure known as Solomon's Stables (see above). The present-day level of the esplanade is estimated to be only slightly higher than it was in Second Temple times.

In 1970, Z. Yeivin examined a fragment of ancient masonry accidentally exposed when the ground in the eastern part of the Temple Mount esplanade was dug up. A 5-m-long stretch of this wall was exposed between two vertical rock-cut scarps; its width was 2 m and it was built of two rows of large ashlars, among which were stones with characteristically Herodian dressing. For lack of additional data it is difficult to propose an exact date for this wall, but it may be a remnant of Herodian masonry.

An attempt was made by B. Mazar and L. Ritmeyer to trace the early, smaller phase of the Temple Mount enclosure. Its traditional measurements are stated in the book of Ezekiel (42:15–20) and in the Mishnah (*Mid.* 2:1) to have been 500 by 500 cubits (262.5 by 262.5 m). This attempt is based on mutually complementary pieces of archeological evidence: the remains of masonry and rock cutting still visible in the northern part of the enclosure and the tunnels through which access was gained to the esplanade when the Second Temple was still in existence.

Of the Temple itself, which stood in its splendor above the elevated enclosure of the Temple Mount, there is today not a single definite remnant above the level of the present-day esplanade. Its reconstruction is based on the description of Josephus and the Talmudic sources. Even its precise location relative to the *even ha-shetiyyah* ("foundation stone")—the rock now enshrined in the Dome of the Rock—is a matter of pure conjecture. The common traditional view is that the Temple stood more or less where the Dome of the Rock now stands. An attempt by A. Kaufman to "shift" the location of the Temple slightly to the north of this traditional site, relying on unclear archeological remains he ascribes to the Second Temple period and on other evidence, lacks concrete proof.

Greek inscription from the Second Temple period forbidding entry to foreigners to the inner court of the Temple Mount.

Outside the limits of the Temple Mount the remains of two Greek inscriptions were discovered. Originally the inscriptions were fixed on the parapet wall that fenced off the inner court of the sacred enclosure. One complete inscription was discovered in 1870 by Clermont-Ganneau, north of the Temple Mount (*CIJ*, no. 1400). A fragment of an identical inscription was discovered in 1935 outside the Lions' (St. Stephen's) Gate. Both inscriptions forbid gentiles from entering the inner court of the Temple Mount. The existence of such inscriptions is known both from the Mishnah (*Kel.* 1:8) and from Josephus (*Antiq.* XV, 417, 5; *War* V, 193; VI, 125). A translation of the text follows: "No foreigner shall enter within the balustrade of the Temple, or within the precinct, and whosoever shall be caught shall be responsible for (his) death that will follow in consequence (of his trespassing)."

THE THIRD WALL

The Third Wall was the northernmost of the three walls of Jerusalem's defenses in the Second Temple period. The identification of the course of this wall and its remains—long a major subject of scholarly contention—has a direct bearing on the attempt to determine the line of the Second Wall south of it (see above). According to Josephus (*War* V, 147), the Third Wall began at the Hippicus Tower, at the northwestern corner of the First Wall—today in the Citadel area—and continued northward to the Tower of Psephinus. At this point, it turned east and ran on toward the Kidron Valley, passing such sites as Helene's Monument, the burial caves identified as the Tombs of the Kings, the Corner Tower, and the Fuller's Monument. Subsequently, the Third Wall turned south and ran parallel to and above the Kidron Valley to meet the walls of the Temple Mount. Along this line stood ninety towers (*War* V, 158). Josephus reports that the Third Wall was begun by Agrippa I (between 41 and 44 CE) but was not completed until the Great Revolt (66–70 CE) (*Antiq.* XIX, 326–327; *War* II, 219).

The remains of the Third Wall were first identified in 1838 by Robinson, about 450 m north of the Old City wall. Wilson, Schick, and others carried out limited trial excavations of these fortifications at the end of the nineteenth century. The major exposure of the remains of the Third Wall was made by E. L. Sukenik and L. A. Mayer between 1925 and 1927 and in 1940. They revealed eight segments of a wall, running west–east, for a total length of some 800 m, from the eastern slope of the hill now occupied by the Russian Compound to the American School of Oriental Research (the Albright Institute) in the east.

These segments of wall are described here from east to west.

1. A wall 30 m long.
2. A wall 56 m long, including a tower, 12 m long, whose western side projected 9 m from the wall.
3. A wall 81.7 m long, in which it is possible to reconstruct a tower projecting 12.4 m from the wall line (its remains are now in front of the U.S. Consulate on Nablus Street).
4. A short wall, 8.8 m long.
5. A wall and tower whose overall length is 16.1 m.
6. A wall 15 m long, including a tower projecting 7.5 m from the wall. East of this were the remains of a gate, some 6 m wide on the inside, found walled up; beyond the gate the wall continued for an additional 5 m.
7. A wall 23 m long, including a tower 12 m long, projecting 9 m from the wall.
8. The remains of a tower, at least 20 m wide, projecting approximately 7.5 m from the wall; in this section, the wall alters its course and turns southeast.

Together with the segments that were already known in the nineteenth century, 1,000 m of the length of the Third Wall have now been recognized. It is 4 to 4.5 m wide, but it is not preserved to a substantial height. It was built on a solid foundation layer consisting of a mixture of stones and bonding material. Most of the foundation was laid in accordance with the (natural or artificially cut) rock surface, in order to create a level surface. On this surface the builders placed large ashlar blocks, tooled with the characteristic Herodian dressed margins and smoothed bosses projecting only slightly. The length of these stones in the various stretches of the wall varies from 1.7 to 5.5 m; their maximum height is 1.75 m. In most cases, only the foundation of the fortification has survived, sometimes topped by one course of the wall's superstructure. Sukenik and Mayer believed that the wall segments they uncovered were the remains of the Third Wall. Their construction indicates that the wall was erected in considerable haste. This led the excavators to suggest that the remains were mainly the sections of the Third Wall built by the Zealots when they seized control of Jerusalem at the outbreak of the Jewish Revolt. The Third Wall along the Sukenik–Mayer line was built along this winding course in order to enhance the defenses of the shallow valleys to the north and mainly the upper branch of the Kidron Valley (Wadi el-Joz). Worthy of note is the uniform size (12 by 9 m) of most of the towers in the wall, which were built at regular intervals of 30 to 32 m.

The Sukenik–Mayer theory has been accepted by most scholars, including Albright and Avi-Yonah. However, an alternative theory—advanced by Vincent, J. Simons, Kenyon, G. J. Wightman, and others—argues that the line of the Third Wall should be traced along the present northern wall of the Old City, in line with the Damascus Gate. To substantiate this view—which considerably curtails the area enclosed by the Third Wall—Kenyon's expedition to Jerusalem reexamined the two proposed lines of the Third Wall.

Between 1964 and 1966, J. B. Hennessy exposed the outer face of the eastern tower of the ancient Damascus Gate, which Hamilton had begun to excavate in 1937–1938. This side of the gate, which was well preserved, included an arched side entrance and, on the east, a projecting tower. The finds exposed opposite the front of the gate proved, in Hennessy and Kenyon's view, that the gate had its origins in the late Second Temple period and should therefore be considered part of Jerusalem's Third Wall. Hennessy's conclusion was at odds with Hamilton's dating of the gate to the time of Aelia Capitolina, as well as with the view expressed by Wightman, who published the results of Kenyon and Hennessy's excavations at the site. Wightman's views have now been definitively confirmed by Magen's recent excavations.

In 1965, E. W. Hamrick conducted a series of soundings in area T, along the remains of the Sukenik–Mayer Third Wall between Nablus and Saladin streets. The earth layer contemporary with the fortification was found to contain sherds dating to the first century CE and coins of the Roman procurators of Judea of 54 and 58–59 CE. Hamrick concluded that the fortifications in question had indeed been built toward the end of the Second Temple period and suggested that they were the remains of yet another wall—a fourth wall—erected as a kind of barrier wall by the Zealots during the revolt. He could not explain why Josephus does not mention this wall. Thus, despite his convincing finds, Hamrick, too, traced the line of the Third Wall along the Old City wall in line with the Damascus Gate.

Foundations of the Third Wall.

Hamrick's interpretation was one of many attempts by supporters of the minimalist view to explain the presence of the Sukenik–Mayer fortifications. Vincent explained them as the remains of a city wall put up by the rebels to protect Jerusalem during the Bar-Kokhba Revolt (132–135 CE)—contrary to the findings of recent excavations along the line of the wall and archeological evidence from Jerusalem as a whole for this period. Kenyon first suggested that the Sukenik–Mayer city wall might be part of the wall of the camp built by the Tenth Legion during the siege of Jerusalem, before it was permanently stationed on the southwestern hill (after the occupation of the city). Later, she was inclined to identify it as the circumvallation erected by the Roman army around Jerusalem during the siege. Benoit's compromise proposal was that Agrippa I had indeed begun to build the Third Wall along the line of the Damascus Gate, but that, with the subsequent expansion of urban Jerusalem, the northern defenses were relocated, by necessity, to the Sukenik–Mayer line.

Between 1972 and 1974, S. Ben-Arieh and E. Netzer reexcavated a section of the Sukenik–Mayer line west of the U.S. Consulate. They, too, uncovered mainly the foundations of the wall, for a length of some 75 m, including a tower 12 m long projecting 9 m north of the wall. This segment of wall was identical in width and construction to the already known segments. On the inside of the wall the remains of a building were discovered, with first-century CE finds. Following Sukenik and Mayer, Ben-Arieh and Netzer also identified their discoveries as pertaining to the Third Wall, which was built in this area, as they believed, by Agrippa I. In excavations begun in 1990 and conducted by V. Tzaferis, A. Onn, and N. Feig, additional remains of the Third Wall's foundations were found between sections 2 and 3 of the Sukenik–Mayer wall.

The results of the latest excavations along the line of the Sukenik–Mayer wall fix the time of its construction to the first century CE. It is also significant that there are practically no burials dating to the Second Temple period between the northern wall of the Old City and the line of the Third Wall. These finds lend further credence to the hypothesis that the remains excavated by Sukenik and Mayer are indeed those of Josephus' Third Wall. This view is also reinforced by the lack of any clear-cut remains of fortifications from the Second Temple period in any excavation along the northern Old City wall, on either side of the Damascus Gate.

Remains of the Sukenik–Mayer Third Wall have come to light only along its northern line; various trial soundings carried out in recent years, on either side of the known segments of the wall, have not revealed any traces of the eastern and western continuations of the wall. Judging from Josephus' description, and taking the local topography into consideration, it would appear that the Third Wall continued to the east along the steep bank of the Kidron Valley, east of the Rockefeller Museum, running on southward along the line of the present-day eastern wall of the Old City, until its juncture with the Temple Mount enclosure.

Remains of the Third Wall as excavated in the early 1970s.

At the end of the nineteenth century, Schick described the remains of a large tower, with dimensions similar to "David's Tower," unearthed slightly north of the Lions' (Saint Stephen's) Gate, along the line of the wall of the Old City. He suggested that the tower had been built in the Second Temple period; there is, however, no concrete evidence to that effect and it is possible that it was built in medieval times.

West of the Sukenik–Mayer wall, the Third Wall climbed up the moderate slope of the hill (the present site of the Russian Compound), reaching a point at which it turned south. It is commonly held that the Third Wall ran south along the present-day western wall of the Old City, up to the area of the Jaffa Gate and the Citadel ("David's Tower") to its south. The remains of an ancient tower exposed under the northwestern corner of the wall of the Old City were considered by Vincent and others to be the remains of the Tower of Psephinus, which stood at the northwestern corner of the Third Wall (*War* V, 133, 147). Renewed excavations at the site in 1971–1972, by D. Bahat and M. Ben-Ari, proved that the remains are those of the Crusader Goliath's Tower (see below, Early Arab to Ayyubid Periods). In addition, several soundings carried out by H. Geva in 1980 beneath the foundations of the Old City wall, in the segment of the wall running north from the Jaffa Gate, revealed no traces of earlier fortifications.

In 1989, A. Maeir began to excavate the remains of a large fortified structure from the first century BCE outside the Old City walls, north of the Jaffa Gate. The nature of this building and its relationship to the city's defenses in Second Temple times are not yet clear.

North of the traditional "David's Tower," a massive wall was discovered at the end of the nineteenth century; according to the account published at the time, this wall, which ran north, was built of large ashlar blocks with dressed margins. This wall has sometimes been described in reconstructions of Jerusalem's defenses in antiquity as part of the Second Wall of the city in the Second Temple period, or of the city wall in the Roman-Byzantine period. However, the location—just north of "David's Tower," which should be identified with the Herodian tower of Hippicus (see above, the First Wall)—and the style of construction, which is clearly characteristic of monumental masonry in Jerusalem under Herod and his descendants, suggest that this might actually be a remnant of the Third Wall. If so, its western point of issue must be placed slightly farther east than the conventional view, which traces the wall north from the Jaffa Gate along the present Old City wall.

THE "NEW CITY"

There are few clear-cut remains of construction from the Second Temple period in the northern part of Jerusalem, in the area of what was then the quarter called the New City, enclosed in the first century CE by the Third Wall. There are fragmentary and unreliable reports of past discoveries of remains of ancient masonry, some certainly from Second Temple times, when foundations were being dug for various new buildings in the area (now the Christian and Muslim quarters) and even farther north outside the Old City. The major remains in this category are the public water pools of the city from that period and the adjacent remains, such as those uncovered near the Pool of Bethesda (see below, Water Supply).

Additional remains and finds from the Second Temple period have been unearthed in limited excavations recently carried out on Christians' Street, in the Muristan and the Church of the Holy Sepulcher, in the Antonia, in the area north of the Temple Mount, on the Via Dolorosa, in the Damascus Gate, along the northern wall of the Old City, and along the Sukenik–Mayer Third Wall.

In 1879, C. Schick published the remains of an ancient structure built in the Roman opus reticulatum technique, that was accidentally exposed some 250 m north of the Damascus Gate. He reexamined the site in 1893, but the remains were subsequently covered over and almost forgotten. In 1977, S. Ben-Arieh and E. Netzer excavated the site. The structure, built on a low rock salient, consisted of two concentric circles cut into the subsurface rock to a depth of some 2 m. The circles were 33 m and 8.8 m in diameter, respectively. The inner circle was surrounded by a wall that enlarged the diameter to 12.4 m. Only the inner face of the rock wall in the outer circle was found covered with opus reticulatum, which was also used in the Herodian palaces at Jericho and Banias. The building in question was an imposing structure whose superstructure was built of ashlar blocks (some decorated), a few of which were found scattered around the site. Schick identified this unique structure as the remains of a sumptuous public building, perhaps an amphitheater or the like. Ben-Arieh and Netzer believe, however, that it may represent the remains of "Herod's monument," mentioned by Josephus as standing in the northern part of Jerusalem (*War* V, 108, 507).

The nature of the finds unearthed within the Third Wall in the northern

Building constructed in the opus reticulatum technique, north of the Damascus Gate.

part of Jerusalem from the Second Temple period is indicative of a sparsely populated residential area, which developed toward the end of the period, mainly in the first century CE.

WATER SUPPLY

Jerusalem's expansion in the Second Temple period, taking in areas quite distant from the city's traditional source of water—the Gihon Spring and Siloam Pool—required a continuous effort to develop alternative sources to ensure a regular supply of water for the residents and the thousands of pilgrims visiting the city. Apart from the complex water-storage systems found both on the Temple Mount and in private homes (see above), numerous cisterns, public pools, and reservoirs were built in Second Temple times, as well as an aqueduct that brought water from distant springs to the heart of the city.

The entrance to the ancient water-supply system of biblical Jerusalem, Warren's Shaft, was repaired in the Second Temple period by the addition of a vault to support the earth spills that threatened to block it as well as an upper entrance tunnel with a gabled stone ceiling. The Siloam Pool functioned at this time as the main site for drawing water coming from the Gihon Spring, as is clear from Josephus (*War* V, 140) and the New Testament (Jn. 9:7). The appearance of the pool, probably as far back as the Second Temple period, can be reconstructed based on the remains discovered there by Bliss and Dickie. The system of walls that dammed the issue of the Tyropoeon Valley was apparently reinforced as early as the Hasmonean period by the so-called buttressed wall (see above, First Wall). The large water reservoir thus created, known today as Birket el-Ḥamra, was filled with overflow from the Siloam Pool and the winter flood waters gushing down the Tyropoeon.

In 1977, D. Adan discovered a few remains of a large pool from the Second Temple period, in the Kidron Valley southeast of the City of David. He believed that this might be the Pool of Solomon referred to by Josephus in his description of the First Wall (*War* V, 145).

Most of Jerusalem's large public pools were built in valleys in northern sections of the ancient city that, judging from the archeological evidence, had been occupied only since the Hasmonean period. The construction of these pools can be dated to the Second Temple period, but in some cases conclusive archeological proof to that effect is lacking.

On the grounds of the Church of Saint Anne, near the Lions' (Saint Stephen's) Gate, a pair of large pools was originally hewn in the bed of the Bezetha Valley. These pools are now identified with the New Testament pool of Bethesda (Probatica) (Jn. 5:2–4). It is highly probable that they coincide with the Sheep's Pool of Second Temple times. A small portion of the pools was cleared by the architect C. Mauss and the White Fathers (who own the site) in partial excavations in 1863–1876, 1888–1900 and since 1914. Additional excavations were carried out at the site in 1956, directed by J. M. Rousée. They exposed part of the corners of the two pools, the partition between the pools, and other evidence, all of which permit estimating their dimensions at 95 by 50–60 m. Most of the pools and the partition between them were hewn out of the rock; the rest consists of ashlar masonry. They are nearly 15 m deep and show the traces of several coats of plaster over their long period of use. No traces were found in the excavations of the five porticoes that, according to the New Testament and numerous Christian descriptions from the Byzantine period, adorned the pools (four around them and a fifth in between); these porticoes were reconstructed by Vincent on the basis of the written sources. The excavators dated the first construction of the pools to the Hasmonean period. At that time this area was north of the city walls (it was included in the walled area of the city when the Third Wall was built, under Agrippa I). Besides the pools, the site produced additional remains from the Second Temple period, prominent among which are a few rock-cut stepped ritual-immersion pools, of a type typical of the period, and probably also rock-cut vertical scarps bearing a few traces of colored plaster. A few shallow natural caves and drainage systems found on the slope of the hill east of the double pool indicate, in the excavators' opinion, that this was the site of a pagan healing center, established as early as the Hellenistic period, that continued in use after the destruction of the Second Temple (see below, Roman Period).

Adjoining the eastern end of the northern wall of the Temple Mount enclosure is a pool known as Birket Isra'il (Pool of Israel), which was built in the Second Temple period, at the same time as Herod's Temple Mount. Its structure was investigated in 1869 by Warren; some time later it was sealed and fell into disuse. It is aligned east–west and measures 110 by 38 m. The bottom was cut in the rock; all sides but the one on the west were built of large ashlars. Particularly noteworthy is the eastern wall (14 m thick), which also dammed the flow of the Bezetha stream, in which the pool had been built.

The Struthion Pool lies north of the northwestern corner of the Temple Mount. Although it is mentioned by Josephus (*War* V, 467) in connection with the Antonia fortress, its precise location in relation to the fortress is still a matter of debate. The pool was discovered at the end of the nineteenth century, when the Sisters of Zion Convent was being built. It is now incorporated in the convent's crypt. Today the Struthion consists of a pair of parallel pools aligned northwest–southeast and separated by a late wall in which there are openings. The bottom is hewn in the rock, while the sides are ashlar-built walls; two vaults span the pool that may be attributed, together with the separating wall and the Lithostrotos pavement, to the time of Aelia Capitolina. The size of the original pool, which lay in the open in Second Temple times, was 52 by 14 m. The depth of the pools is not uniform, varying from 12 m in the north to 17 in the south. They were probably dug in the northern moat of the Antonia during Herod's reign, thus severing the Hasmonean aqueduct that continued south (see above, the Temple Mount).

At the end of the nineteenth century, just inside the Jaffa Gate, Schick investigated the Pool of the Towers mentioned by Josephus (*War* V, 468), known today as Hezekiah's Pool. This pool was cut in the rock, here sloping down to the southeast; the construction of its eastern wall was particularly massive, as it also functioned as a dam. The pool is 44 m wide and (today) 73 m long. Another massive wall (3.5 m thick), built of ashlars with drafted margins, was discovered slightly north of the pool, indicating that the pool may once have been about 95 m long. Its depth varies from 6 to 7.5 m.

Birket es-Sultan, sometimes identified with the Second Temple period Serpents' Pool (*War* V, 108), is located southwest of the Jaffa Gate. The pool was examined in 1973 by Kloner, who found that the hewn rock served as the sides of a reservoir created by a wall that once dammed the upper Valley of Hinnom in the position of the present-day wall, which is of Ottoman construction.

AQUEDUCTS. The expansion and population growth of Jerusalem at the end of the Second Temple period demanded a regular supply of large quantities of water, in addition to that provided by the local reservoirs, whose capacity was limited. The problem of Jerusalem's water supply was partly solved by constructing an aqueduct that brought water by gravitation from distant springs south of the city.

As far back as the mid-nineteenth century, Wilson identified and surveyed the aqueducts that had supplied the city's water. At the end of the nineteenth century, Schick discovered a system of aqueducts that had brought water from a group of springs in Wadi 'Arub and Wadi Biyar, in the Judean Hills, to the reservoirs known today as Solomon's Pools. In 1969, A. Mazar carried out a comprehensive survey and measurement of the aqueducts that brought water to Jerusalem. Summarizing the data produced by these various studies leads to the conclusion that there were two aqueducts: a "low-level aqueduct," dating to the Second Temple period, and a "high-level aqueduct," which is commonly dated to Aelia Capitolina, following the destruction of the Second Temple (see below).

The low-level aqueduct set out from the lowest of the three Solomon's Pools, some 10 km from Jerusalem; it followed a winding topographical course more than 24 km long. Combined with the Wadi 'Arub aqueduct, its length reached 61 km. The aqueduct was built on a very moderate gradient, in order to help the water overcome the height differential of some 30 m between its issue at Solomon's Pools and its final destination—the Temple Mount. The cross section of the channel was rectangular or square and its depth varied. Some parts were cut in the rock and others were built with stones cemented together and waterproofed with a hard plaster. On its way, the aqueduct traversed several ridges by tunneling in the rock, crossing low-lying areas on dams and stone walls. It traveled through the Bethlehem region in a tunnel some 400 m long, skirted on the east the hill now occupied by Kibbutz Ramat Raḥel, and cut across Jebel Mukaber (Government House) through another tunnel 370 m long. The aqueduct subsequently ran along the western bank of the Hinnom Valley, beneath the present-day neighborhood of Yemin Moshe. South of the Jaffa Gate it crossed the Hinnom Valley and continued south, along the east bank of the valley, beneath the southwestern corner of the Old City wall. Its remains in this area, exposed in 1978, were found to be partly cut in the rock, with a retaining stone wall in the west. The aqueduct then skirted Mount Zion on the south, entering the city (in the Second Temple period) under a stretch of the First Wall discovered by Bliss and Dickie in the southern part of Mount Zion. Its continuation to the northeast was exposed a few years earlier by Warren. Another segment of the low-level aqueduct was cleared in 1968 by J. Margovski and in the early 1970s by M. Ben-Dov south of Burj Kibrit (the Sulfur Tower) in the southern wall of the Old City; north of this point the remains of the aqueduct are within the walled area of the Old City today. A rock-cut stretch of the aqueduct was investigated by Avigad beneath the new building of the Porat Yosef Yeshivah in the southeastern part of the Jewish Quarter. Farther to the north, the aqueduct cut into the rock scarp marking the eastern border of the present-day Jewish Quarter, opposite the Western Wall. It then probably crossed the Tyropoeon Valley on Wilson's Arch and delivered its water to the system of cisterns in the southern part of the Temple Mount.

Map of the aqueducts to Jerusalem, Second Temple period.

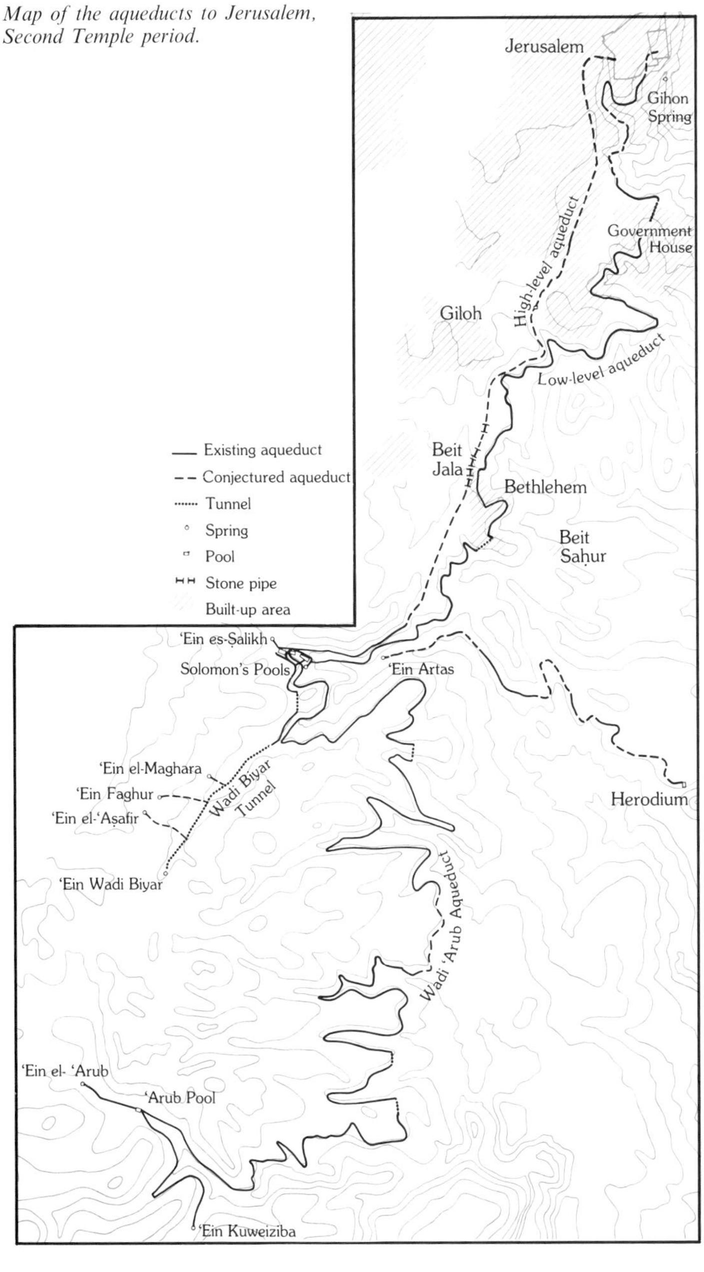

The aqueduct that supplied Jerusalem's water is referred to in the Talmudic literature (J.T., *Yoma* 41a; *Lam. Rab.* 4:7). We also know that the Roman procurator Pontius Pilate (early first century CE) confiscated temple funds to construct or repair the Jerusalem aqueduct (*Antiq.* XVIII, 60). The available data are still inadequate to determine whether the low-level aqueduct was built by Herod or, as some scholars believe, earlier—perhaps at the end of the Hasmonean period. It remained in use, with numerous repairs and alterations, until the Ottoman period.

It is generally agreed that the second aqueduct to Jerusalem, the so-called high-level aqueduct, which brought water over a shorter route from Solomon's Pools and entered the city from the west, in the region of the present-day Jaffa Gate, was built at the time of Aelia Capitolina (first half of the second century CE; see below, Roman Period). Nevertheless, it is possible, as was the opinion of Wilson and others, that the high level aqueduct had already been built by Herod, to supply water to his palace and the Upper City, on the southwestern hill.

TOMBS

The necropolises that surrounded Jerusalem in the Second Temple period have been investigated by various scholars. Partial summaries of the early studies were written by Clermont-Ganneau, Schick, K. Galling, and Macalister. In the 1930s and 1940s, the tombs in and around Jerusalem were studied by Sukenik and Avigad, and in the 1950s and 1960s by L. Y. Rahmani and others. The building boom in Jerusalem following the unification of the city in the wake of the 1967 Six-Day War led to the exposure of many additional tombs, in areas that had been part of the city's necropolis in the Second Temple period. The main discoveries pertain to the northern part of the city: the region of Mount Scopus and the new residential neighborhoods of Giv'at ha-Mivtar, French Hill, and Ramot Eshkol. A recent, comprehensive review of the finds by A. Kloner presents a complete and detailed picture of the architecture of tombs from Second Temple period Jerusalem, as well as their dates and distribution around the city.

About eight hundred tombs are now known from surveys and excavations in a radius of 5 km around the city limits of Jerusalem in the Second Temple period. Some seven hundred of them are concentrated in a narrow ring up to 3 km around the city. Within the present limits of the Old City, including regions that were undoubtedly included in the walled city at the end of the Second Temple period, there are only a few known tombs (such as those in the precincts of the Church of the Holy Sepulcher and north of the Damascus Gate). They probably were cleared when the urban area of Jerusalem was enlarged. This confirms the strict observance of the prohibition on burying the dead within the city limits.

Burials around Jerusalem in the Second Temple period betray no traces of a central plan. The tombs are seemingly distributed at random. The relative density of burials and the alignment of the tombs seem to have depended mainly on the type of rock and local topography. It also appears that burials were deliberately kept distant from the main roads out of the city. The tombs were hewn in the rocky banks of valleys and slopes of hills around the city, mostly in the soft *nari* stone, which is characteristic of Mount Scopus and the Mount of Olives, east of Jerusalem. A small proportion was cut in the harder *melekeh* or *qa'qulah* rock, common in the hilly areas surrounding the city on its north, west, and south.

Most of the tombs from this period around Jerusalem are small and simple. However, in some burial caves, the continuous use and reuse of the tombs over several generations created a complex system of burials, with several burial chambers communicating by doors. Sometimes, the builders, while digging a tomb, inadvertently breached the wall of an earlier one, thus creating an unintended communication between two tombs. Many Second Temple period tombs were broken into and plundered in antiquity, and most of their portable artifacts were looted. Some tombs were destroyed by late quarrying; others were reused for burial or other purposes in later periods, mainly in the Byzantine period.

A few architectural motifs are characteristic of most tombs in Jerusalem in this period—some, in fact, are typical of contemporary tombs throughout Judea. Approximately one half of the tombs have an open, rock-cut forecourt whose area depended on the richness or splendor of the tomb: large and particularly ornate tombs boasted a large, spacious court. In some cases benches were built along the sides of the court and a mikveh was cut for the mourners' use. The entrance to the tomb itself was generally cut in the rock to form a smooth wall with a doorway that was, on average, less than one meter high. In a considerable number of tombs, the open forecourt communicates with the burial chamber itself through a low entrance corridor. The opening was thoroughly sealed with a square stone, set in a depressed frame

Map of cemeteries and tombs in Jerusalem, Second Temple period.

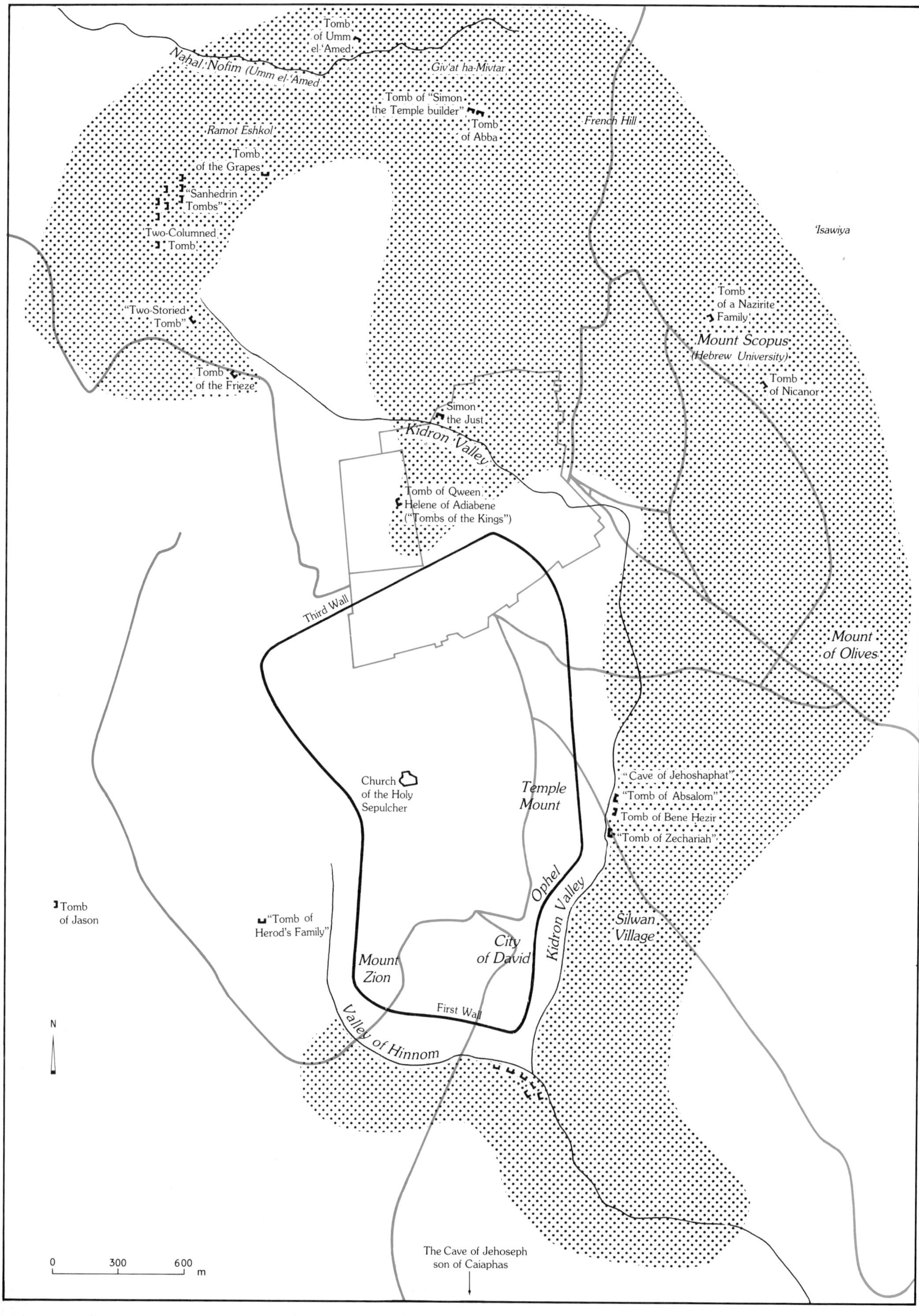

that was cut to fit. In only a few caves was there a circular rolling stone, weighing a few hundred kilograms, that could be moved in a fixed track between two rock-cut or artificially built walls.

The burial chamber, with its ceiling, was hewn into the rock. Sometimes, where the local rock was crumbly, or if a particularly rich tomb was desired, the chamber walls were faced, partially or entirely, with ashlars. The most characteristic feature of the Second Temple period tombs in Jerusalem is the loculi, or burial niches (*kokhim*), in which the bodies of the deceased were laid

Decorated ossuaries from the Second Temple period.

in primary burial. Such loculi were cut in approximately 450 of the tombs known from this period. The number of loculi in each tomb varies—from a few to a few dozen. Cut at right angles to the walls of the burial chamber, they were generally about 2 m long, 0.5 m wide, and slightly more than 0.5 m high. Sometimes a depression for a sealing stone was hewn around the aperture of the niche. Double sized loculi, or loculi arranged in two levels, perpendicular to the walls of the burial chamber, are found in some tombs. Approximately one quarter of the tombs found in Jerusalem also include repositories for bones that are usually smaller than the average loculus. These were used to collect the bones of the deceased after the flesh had decayed; sometimes they accommodated the ossuaries in which the bones were placed for secondary burial. Approximately one hundred tombs have been found containing arcosolia or burial benches cut in the shape of shelves along the burial chamber walls. The length of a typical arcosolium is about 2 m, and its height from the floor is about 1 m. Sometimes the ceiling above an arcosolium was hewn to form a shallow arch. In a very few tombs, arcosolia are carved into the shape of a trough. They form a kind of fixed sarcophagus that was covered with a stone slab. In approximately two hundred tombs a "standing pit" was cut in the floor in the center of the burial chamber, generally from 1.3 to 1.6 m long and one meter wide and one meter deep. Only seldom are these pits lined with stones; in a few cases their sides also contain loculi.

THE DECORATED TOMBS. A few dozen particularly large, elaborate tombs were found in the vicinity of Jerusalem, mainly to the east and north. They are hewn in hard rock, and some are very well preserved. Their magnificent facades were adorned with rock-carved architectural decorations, and each tomb has its own special character. The prevalent architectural styles—Doric and Ionic—were used mainly in capitals and friezes. Sometimes they were used in combination. Egyptian architecture is represented by pyramids and concave cornices. The architecture of tombs in Jerusalem in Second Temple times was influenced by East Greek architecture, but adapted to the artistic concepts of the Jews of the time. Sometimes the entrance to the burial tomb was decorated with a finely shaped frame, topped by a gable on which a plethora of floral motifs was carved: interlocking foliage, acanthus leaves, and fruit (as in the "Cave of Jehoshaphat" and the "Tombs of the Sanhedrin"). A unique feature in the facade of some tombs is a wide opening adorned with distyle in antis—two freestanding columns between pilasters, sometimes bearing a decorated frieze (Tomb of Queen Helene). The Cave of Umm el-ʿAmed is unique for the walls of its facade and entrance corridor, which were hewn in the rock in imitation of Herodian-style drafted masonry. Of particular significance are the monumental tombs in the Kidron Valley—the so-called Tomb (or Pillar) of Absalom and Tomb of Zechariah. Both were hewn in the rock but detached from the surrounding rock scarp. The "Tomb of Zechariah" is undoubtedly a *nefesh*—a monument to the memory of the deceased buried in a nearby grave. The "Tomb of Absalom" is a combination tomb and *nefesh* that also commemorates those buried in the adjoining "Cave of Jehoshaphat." Striking parallels to the architecture of these tombs can be found in the rock-cut Nabatean tombs at Petra.

DATING OF THE TOMBS. The earliest known use of tombs in Jerusalem of the type just described was in the second century BCE. However, most of them were cut and used in the first century BCE and continued in use until the destruction of the city in 70 CE. The finds indicate that the first use of arcosolia came later than the use of loculi. Not all the tombs discovered to date in Jerusalem were actually used through the destruction of the Second Temple; some fell into disuse long before. However, the number of known tombs is large, in contrast to the very scant information available about burial in the Persian and the Early (pre-Hasmonean) Hellenistic periods.

BURIAL IN OSSUARIES. The number of the stone chests known as ossuaries found to date in tombs from the late Second Temple period in Jerusalem is estimated at several thousand. The ossuaries are invariably shaped like an elongated chest with rectangular sides, sometimes standing on short legs. They were probably designed in imitation of chests used at the time to hold various household objects, as indicated by the name *gelusqema* (see Mishnah *Semaḥot* 12:9), a Greek loanword in Hebrew that originally denoted any kind of chest or box. Ossuaries were made of the soft, easily carved Jerusalem limestone. They were approximately 45 to 70 cm long; 25 to 30 cm wide; and 25 to 40 cm high. The lids were gabled, rounded or flat, sometimes fitting into grooves carved in the sides of the ossuary.

Many of the ossuaries were decorated on their long sides—some were painted red or yellow before the decorations were carved. The decoration was executed in a technique known as *Kerbschnitt* (chip-carving), once thought to have originated in wood carving; however, the technique may well be associated with the highly developed Jerusalem stone industry in the late Second Temple period, as suggested by Rahmani. The most frequently used ornamental motif in ossuaries from Jerusalem in the late Second Temple period is a stylized rosette, executed with a compass, with six or more petals in a circular border that also is drawn with a compass. Other floral motifs are acanthus leaves, palms and palm fronds, palmettes, ivy leaves, and fruit. Geometric and architectural motifs are also common, such as facades of tombs, ornamental entrances, columns, and even courses of ashlars with drafted margins. Exact parallels to these patterns can be seen in the most magnificent tombs in Jerusalem from the same period. Sometimes the names of the deceased and other identifying details or inscriptions—in Aramaic and/or Greek—were written in charcoal or incised on the ossuaries. Ossuaries began to be used in Jerusalem in the first century BCE, persisting mainly in the period ending in 70 CE. Wooden ossuaries, which have not survived, may have been used before that.

The great number of ossuaries found in Jerusalem attests to the custom, clearly prevalent in the late Second Temple period, of deliberately collecting the bones of the deceased and reinterring them in specially prepared receptacles (ossuaries). It is commonly believed that the source of the custom was the belief in the corporeal, individual resurrection of the dead, which emerged in Judaism at that time. Numerous passages in the Mishnah and the Talmud prescribe the shape of tomb and modes of burial. The custom of reinterring the bones of the dead is described in the Jerusalem Talmud (*Mo'ed Q.* 1:5, 80c): "First they buried them in arcosolia; when the flesh had decayed they collected the bones and buried them in cedar-wood." The custom of primary burial (with no subsequent collection of bones) was also practiced at the time, but only about twenty stone sarcophagi from the late Second Temple period, some of which were decorated, have been discovered in Jerusalem.

HILLEL GEVA

Burial cave in the German Colony: the inscription on the lid of the ossuary reads "Dositheus our father, and do not open."

Kidron Valley: interior of the Tomb of Bene Ḥezir.

Kidron Valley: "Tomb of Absalom."

DESCRIPTION OF THE TOMBS. Following is a description of the most prominent Second Temple period tombs found in Jerusalem:

Tomb of Bene Ḥezir. The Tomb of Bene Ḥezir is characterized by a pure Doric facade: two Doric columns between pilasters support a Doric frieze. On the architrave a Hebrew inscription states that it is the tomb and *nefesh* of several individuals referred to by name, who were priests of the Bene Ḥezir family. The *nefesh* probably stood beside the facade. The burial cave consists of a porch, chambers with loculi, a flight of stairs leading up to ground level, and a passage connecting the cave with the area to the south, where the so-called Tomb of Zechariah stands. The Tomb of Bene Ḥezir is dated to the end of the Hasmonean period; the inscription is dated to the beginning of Herod's reign.

"Tomb of Zechariah." The monumental so-called Tomb of Zechariah in the Kidron Valley is freestanding, but carved out of the surrounding rock in the form of a cube (length of each side 5 m) crowned by a pyramid. All four sides of the monument are decorated with Ionic columns and an Egyptian cavetto cornice. The monument was the *nefesh* for a tomb. A small chamber was discovered in its lower part, but it is not clear when it was cut.

"Cave of Jehoshaphat." The so-called Cave of Jehoshaphat is a tomb with eight chambers. Its large entrance is surmounted by a pediment adorned with a relief of vine leaves and fruit.

"Tomb of Absalom." In front of the "Cave of Jehoshaphat" stands the so-called Tomb (or Pillar) of Absalom, the highest (20 m) and probably the most complete tomb monument in Israel. It is in two main parts. A lower, square structure, most of which is rock-cut, contains a small burial chamber with arcosolia. The four walls of the square structure are ornamented with Ionic columns, a Doric frieze, and an Egyptian cornice—an unusual combination of styles. The upper part of the tomb is a round structure built of stones in the form of a pedestal (tholos) topped by a concave conical roof. This round structure is the monument, or *nefesh*, for the tomb below and perhaps also for the so-called Cave of Jehoshaphat. The "Tomb of Absalom" is dated to the first century CE.

Kidron Valley: "Tomb of Zechariah" and Tomb of Bene Ḥezir.

Tomb of Jason: drawing of a warship.

Tomb of Queen Helene of Adiabene ("Tombs of the Kings"): the facade.

Tomb of Jason. The Tomb of Jason was discovered in 1956 in the Reḥavia neighborhood and was excavated in the same year by L. Y. Rahmani. It consists of two courts, a porch, a burial chamber with loculi, and an ossuary chamber. The overall length of the structure is 22 m, and the length of the facade is 4.5 m. In the wide entrance to the porch, a single Doric column stood between two pilasters. The column is built of stone drums. This is the only tomb in Israel with a single column instead of the usual two, in the classical style. Above the porch rose a pyramid, some of whose stones were found in the surrounding rubble.

On the walls of the porch are charcoal drawings of ships, a Greek inscription, and several Aramaic inscriptions, the longest of which is in three lines, lamenting Jason, the deceased. In the tomb a considerable amount of pottery and coins were found, mostly Hasmonean, but some from the reign of Herod. The tomb is therefore dated to the beginning of the first century BCE. It continued in use until the beginning of the first century CE.

Tomb of Queen Helene of Adiabene. This is the largest and most magnificent tomb in Jerusalem. It is mentioned in ancient sources and in reports of travelers from the sixteenth century onward. In 1863, F. de Saulcy excavated the tomb, mistakenly attributed it to the kings of Judah, and named it the Tombs of the Kings. It has a 30-m-long forecourt with a 9-m-wide staircase, leading down to the main courtyard. This courtyard (26 by 27 m) was hewn into the rock to a depth of 8.5 m. The design of the tomb's facade, which was 27.5 m long and partially destroyed, is distyle in antis. A decorative band of carved leaves adorns the architrave, which supports a Doric frieze. Instead of continuing the triglyphs and metopes in the center of the frieze, a bunch of grapes, wreaths, and acanthus leaves are carved there. Josephus reported that originally there were three pyramids above the facade.

The burial cave consists of a porch, a main chamber, and eight burial chambers with loculi or arcosolia. The entrance was closed by a rolling stone and was accessible through a depression in the floor of the porch. The stone was apparently moved by some secret mechanism. The cave contained several decorated sarcophagi, one of which bore the inscription צדן מלכתה (Queen Ṣaddan.) The tomb is ascribed to Helene, Queen of Adiabene (in northern Mesopotamia), a convert to Judaism who—as related by Josephus—was brought to Jerusalem for burial together with two members of her family, at some time after 50 CE.

Tomb of Queen Helene of Adiabene ("Tombs of the Kings"): stairway descending to the courtyard.

Tomb of Queen Helene of Adiabene ("Tombs of the Kings"): reconstruction of the facade, after Vincent.

Tomb of Nicanor. The Tomb of Nicanor was discovered in 1902 on Mount Scopus, on land now occupied by the Hebrew University. The plan of the burial cave, which is one of the largest in Jerusalem, consists of a court, a porch, and four branches of burial chambers with loculi radiating from the center and descending to form several "stories." Two stone pillars stood at the entrance to the porch. The length of the facade is 17 m. The cave contained several decorated ossuaries, one of which bears an inscription in Greek. The inscription relates that the ossuary contained the bones of the sons of Nicanor of Alexandria, who had donated one of the gates (of the Temple). Below the inscription, the names of his two sons (Nicanor and Alexa) are written in Hebrew. The tomb is to be dated to the first century CE.

Cave of Umm el-'Amed. The Cave of Umm el-'Amed is at the northern extremity of the necropolis of Jerusalem in Wadi Umm el-'Amed. This cave

Cave of Umm el-'Amed: reconstruction, after Avigad.

Mount Scopus: Tomb of Nicanor.

has been visible for many decades. It consists of a court, a porch, and two chambers with loculi. Although the facade is mostly destroyed, its remains indicate that it had a distyle in antis facade (7.5 m long). Above the Doric frieze, extending along the entire length of the facade, is a row of dentils and a cornice with Doric guttae. It seems that it is one of the few places in Israel where guttae have been found underneath a cornice. The tomb had a most impressive facade. The walls of the facade and the porch are hewn in the rock in courses of ashlars with drafted margins in imitation of Herodian style masonry.

Two-Columned Tomb. The Two-Columned Tomb in the Sanhedria neighborhood is a burial cave with loculi. It had two columns in the entrance to the porch (one is missing). The architrave is undecorated. Benches were found in the court.

"Two-Storied Tomb." A two-storied burial cave on Shmuel ha-Navi Street has two columns between pilasters (distyle in antis) and a Doric frieze. The tomb's facade was hewn out of the rock in the form of two stories—that is, a second row of flat pilasters was carved in the rock wall above the usual facade. The tomb has been completely destroyed.

Tomb of the Grapes. The Tomb of the Grapes lies northeast of the "Sanhedrin Tombs." Above the entrance a pediment is ornamented with vine tendrils and bunches of grapes. Decorative reliefs in floral and geometric patterns are also found inside the porch. The tomb consists of a porch, a central chamber, three rooms with loculi, and one chamber with arcosolia.

"Sanhedrin Tombs." A burial cave situated near the Sanhedria neighborhood is popularly known as the Sanhedrin Tombs because of the great number of burials it contains, which approximate the number of members of the Sanhedrin. It was excavated by E. H. Palmer in 1898. In front of the cave is a spacious court. The entrance to the porch is crowned by a pediment with acroteria. Stylized acanthus leaves fill the entire area of the pediment, with pomegranates and other fruit scattered among them. The style and workmanship are characteristic of Jewish decorative art at the end of the Second Temple period. Another, smaller pediment, decorated with acanthus leaves, surmounts the entrance to the cave itself. The large central hall (6 by 5.5 m) is unique in having two rows of loculi, one above the other. Openings lead to two other rooms with loculi. Stairs in two corners of the floor lead down to other burial rooms. One of these rooms was not completely hewn, so that the method of cutting such tombs is illustrated clearly here.

Tomb of the Frieze. The Tomb of the Frieze is located on Shmuel ha-Navi Street. The entrance is ornamented with a Doric frieze and an elaborate Corinthian cornice. The tomb consists of a porch and a burial chamber with loculi.

"Tomb of Herod's Family." The so-called Tomb of Herod's Family was discovered in 1892 near the King David Hotel. The entrance is sealed by an unusually large rolling stone. The burial cave differs in plan from the other tombs: it has four chambers arranged around a small central hall. The walls of the chambers are faced with ashlars whose workmanship is very fine. Several stone sarcophagi decorated with floral patterns were found in the tomb. This was apparently the tomb monument of Herod referred to by Josephus. Near the cave the foundations of a structure were found that was probably the tomb's *nefesh*.

Burial Cave in the Schneller Compound. The burial cave in the Schneller Compound was discovered in 1906. The bilingual Greek and Hebrew inscriptions incised on ossuaries found in the cave attest that it belonged to a Jewish family from Beth-Shean (Scythopolis):

ΑΜΜΙΑ ΣΚΥΘΟΠΟΛΙΤΙΣΣΑ	(Ammia from Beth-Shean)	*'myh hbšnyt*	אמיה הבשנית
ΑΝΙΝ ΣΚΥΘΟΠΟΛΕΙΤΗΣ	(Ḥanin from Beth-Shean)	*ḥnyn hbšny*	חנין הבשני
ΠΑΠΙΑΣ ΚΑΙ ΣΑΛΩΜΗ ΣΚΥΘΟΠΟΛΕΙΤΑΙ	(Papias and Salome from Beth-Shean)	*ppys hbšny*	פפיס הבשני

Burial Cave in the Qaṭamon Neighborhood. A burial cave was discovered in 1912 in the Qaṭamon neighborhood. It contained six ossuaries with inscriptions indicating that all the burials belonged to the Qallon family. This family was very likely related to the priestly family of Bene Jeshebab from the time of the Second Temple. The names on the inscriptions included יהועזר בר שמעון בר קלון (Jeho'ezer, son of Simeon, son of Qallon); שלמציון אתת יהועזר בר קלון ברת גמלא (Shelomẓion, wife of Jeho'ezer, son of Qallon, daughter of Gamala [Gamaliel]); מרים יועזר שמעון בני יחזק בר קלון מן בני ישבאב (Miriam and Jo'ezer and Simeon, children of Jeḥezaq, son of Qallon of the Bene Jeshebab family); and ΙΩΣΗΠΟC ΚΑΛΛΩΝ (Iosephos Kallon).

Tomb in the Kidron Valley. A small burial cave was discovered in 1924 in the Kidron Valley. The ossuaries in it bear numerous inscriptions: יהוסף בר שמעון (Jehoseph, son of Simeon); שלון בת ליעזר (Shallon, daughter of Li'ezer); שלום

"Sanhedrin Tombs": gable of the facade.

אשת אלעזר (Salome, wife of Eleazar); אבונה שמעון סבא יהוסף ברה (our father Simeon the Elder, Jehoseph his son); and others.

Burial Cave in the German Colony. A one-room burial cave was discovered in 1926 in the German Colony. A pit in the floor led down to another room containing twelve ossuaries. Most of the ossuaries bear incised inscriptions, such as שלם ומתיה ברה (Shalom and Mattiah her son); אתת מתיה וברה (the wife of Mattiah and her son); שלמצין אמנה (Shelomẓion, our mother); בני אלעזר (the children of Eleazar); and others. One of the ossuaries, belonging to the head of the family, bears the inscription אבא דוסתס (Father Dositheus.) On its lid is a warning against opening it: דוסתס אבונה ולא למפתח (Dositheus our father, and do not open).

Cave on the Mount of Olives. A single-room burial cave was discovered in 1928 on the Mount of Olives. In it thirteen ossuaries were found. Some of them are ornamented and some bear Hebrew and Greek inscriptions, as, for example, בת תדטיון (daughter of Theodotion), ΘΕΟΔΟΤΙΩΝΟΣ (Theodotionos), and ΣΑΠΙΡΑ (Sapira). One of the ossuaries has the inscription תדטיון—"Theodotion"—on one side and ΔΙΔΑΣΚΑΛΟΥ—"of the teacher"—on the other.

Tomb near Giv'at Ram (Sheikh Badr). A small burial cave was discovered in 1929 on Giv'at Ram. It consists of one chamber, a loculus, and a niche. The objects found in the cave are of special interest: a pottery ossuary was found here together with a stone one, as well as iron nails, indicating that there also had been a wooden ossuary. Also found were glass vessels, a bronze mirror, and round pottery lamps. The finds attest that the cave was used for burial in the second century CE after the destruction of the Second Temple.

Burial Cave on the Western Slopes of Mount Scopus. The burial cave discovered in 1932 on the western slopes of Mount Scopus consists of a court, a chamber with loculi, and another room. Twenty-three decorated ossuaries and pottery vessels were found in the cave. The pottery included a group of lamps of the three most common types found in pre-Herodian and Herodian cave tombs. The ossuaries are inscribed with names such as גרידה (Gerida), מתתיה (Mattathiah), שמעון (Simeon), בוטון (Boton), and ΜΑΡΘΑ (Martha). The excavator believed this cave to be the tomb of the Baithos family, a priestly family from the end of the Second Temple period.

Burial Cave in Wadi Ṣal'ah. The burial cave discovered in 1934 in Wadi Ṣal'ah in the Kidron Valley has a spacious porch and a chamber with nine loculi. Five ossuaries were found here, one of them bearing the inscription יהודה בר יהוחנן בר יתרא (Judah, son of Jehoḥanan, son of Jethra.) One of the loculi was found blocked with plastered stones; a warning written above it in Aramaic reads: כוכה דנה עביד לגרמי אבהתנה ארך אמין תרתין ולא למפתח עליהן (This loculus has been made for the bones of our fathers; it is two cubits long, and do not open it).

Tomb South of the Village of Silwan. A tomb was discovered in 1941 south of the village of Silwan. It consists of a single chamber with a large pit sunk in the floor. Ossuaries with Greek and Hebrew inscriptions were found, as well as a group of complete pottery vessels from the Herodian period. Among the numerous inscriptions is one mentioning Alexandros *Qrnyt*. It can be assumed that this tomb belonged to a Jewish family from Cyrene.

Cave South of Karm esh-Sheikh in the Kidron Valley. The burial cave discovered in 1941 south of Karm esh-Sheikh consists of two chambers and two loculi. Eighteen ossuaries were found. One of them is of special interest because of its unusual motif of four Ionic columns, with three Greek inscriptions set between them in *tabulae ansatae*:

ΣΑΛΩ ΙΩΣΗΦ	(Salo[=Shalom] Joseph)
ΜΑΡΙΑ ΚΟΡΑΣΙΟΝ	(Maria the maiden)
ΙΩΣΗΦ ΚΑΙ ΕΛΙΕΖΕΡ ΔΙΔΥΜΟΙ	(Joseph and Eliezer the twins)

Burial Cave in the Talpiot Neighborhood. The burial cave discovered in 1945 in Talpiot is a one-chamber tomb cave with five loculi, in which eleven ossuaries were found, most of them decorated with rosettes. Pottery typical of the Herodian period was found with them, as well as a coin of Agrippa I. The tomb is dated to the beginning of the first century CE. On the walls of one of the ossuaries were charcoal drawings of large crosses; two other ossuaries had Greek inscriptions reading Ἰησοῦς ἰός, (Jesus woe!) and Ἰησοῦς ἀλώθ (Jesus and Aloth). The excavator interpreted the crosses and the inscriptions as expressions of sorrow at the crucifixion of Jesus, an interpretation not accepted by other scholars.

Tomb on Jebel Khalet et-Turi. A burial cave was discovered in 1955 on Jebel Khalet et-Turi south of Silwan village. The cave contains two chambers with loculi. In one of the rooms thirty ossuaries were found along with a group of pottery vessels that included lamps of the three common types (pre-Herodian and Herodian). The decoration on the ossuaries varies: some bear short inscriptions, and on the lid of one of them a warning is written in Aramaic: כל די אנש מתהנה בחלתה דה קרבן אלה מן דבגוה (Whatever a man may find for his benefit in this ossuary is an offering to God from him who is within it). This warning is unique for tombs from the Second Temple period, which have, as a rule, only the short phrase: "Do not open."

Tombs at Dominus Flevit. A huge necropolis from the Roman period, stretching over an area of about 1.5 a., was discovered in the early 1950s at the site known as Dominus Flevit on the Mount of Olives. This was the largest discovery of its kind in Jerusalem. Some twenty arcosolium burial caves were cleared, as well as about thirty-eight pit tombs. These date to the third and fourth centuries CE and continued in use in the Byzantine period. The Second Temple tombs with loculi are all the usual type, with one or two chambers and loculi cut into the walls. The floors of the main hall have a pit in the center. The entrances are small. Some of the small rooms were used for storing ossuaries. A rich collection of ossuaries, sarcophagi, and pottery was found here.

Seven hard limestone sarcophagi were found, some adorned with elaborate reliefs of rosettes, wreaths, leaves, and vine tendrils. The tombs contained 122 ossuaries, most adorned with rosettes, with slight variations; in some, the variations were more pronounced.

Altogether there were forty-three inscriptions on the ossuaries—in Aramaic, Hebrew, and Greek—some of which are of considerable interest for onomastics and paleography. The names that commonly appear are Zechariah, Jeshua, Maria, 'Azariah, Shelomẓion, Simeon, and Shapira. The inscriptions include Martha, our mother; Salome and her son; Salome, the wife of Shapir (the masculine form of Shapira); Jehoni, the artisan; Menaḥem of the family of Jakhin, the priest; Φίλων Κυρηναῖος (Philon the Cyrenean); Διογένης Προσήλυτος Ζηνᾶ (Diogenes, the proselyte, the son of Zenas). On one of the ossuaries the monogram XP appears. The excavators attribute it to the burial of a Judeo-Christian, a claim that is doubtful.

The Uzziah inscription.

Uzziah Inscription. An inscription incised on a stone tablet (35 by 34 cm) was discovered by Sukenik in 1931 in the antiquities collection of the Russian Convent on the Mount of Olives. The inscription, in Aramaic, commemorates the reburial of the remains of Uzziah, king of Judah:

Hither were brought	לכה התות
the bones of Uzziah	טמי עוזיה
King of Judah	מלך יהודה
and do not open	ולא למפתח

NAHMAN AVIGAD

Since 1967, many important Second Temple period burial caves have been discovered in Jerusalem. Following is a description of the most important of them:

Tomb of a Nazirite Family. Discovered on the grounds of the Hebrew University on Mount Scopus, the tomb of a Nazirite family was excavated by Avigad in 1967. (When the new university campus was built, the tomb was dismantled and reconstructed on the southeast side of the Mount Scopus botanical gardens.) The tomb consists of a central chamber from which three side chambers branch off. Both the tomb's facade and interior are faced with fine ashlar masonry, most of it displaying the characteristic drafted margins of Second Temple period Jerusalem. The central part of the facade ends in an arch; the central burial chamber is roofed with a barrel vault. There are no burial installations in the tomb. Two sarcophagi and fourteen ossuaries were found in the tomb. One of the sarcophagi is particularly elaborate, with rich, carved reliefs in floral motifs, mainly vine tendrils with bunches of grapes. Of

Mount Scopus: decorated sarcophagus from the Nazirite family tomb.

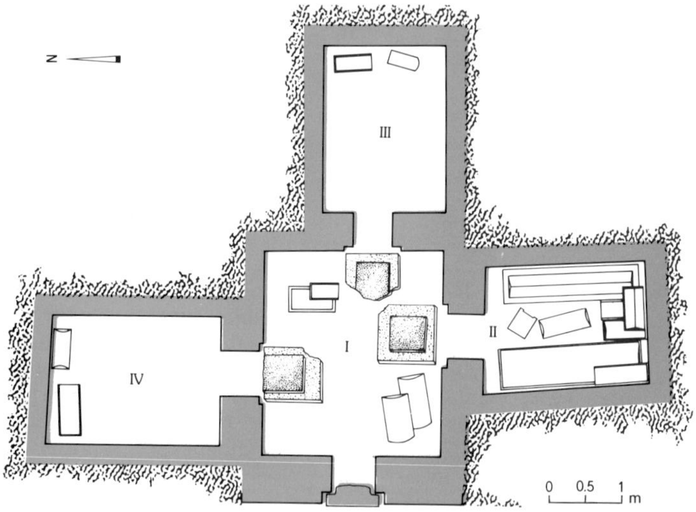

Plan of the Nazirite family tomb.

Mount Scopus: chamber II in the Nazirite family tomb.

special interest are two of the inscriptions on the ossuaries, which were written in Hebrew cursive script of the end of the Second Temple period: חנניה בר יהונתן הנזר (Hananiah son of Jehonathan the Nazirite) and שלום אנתת חנניה בר הנזיר (Salome wife of Hananiah son of the Nazirite). The tomb was in use in the first half of the first century CE. Its building style and the decoration on the elaborate sarcophagus recall parallels in Herod's family tomb in west Jerusalem (see above).

Tomb of Simon the Temple Builder. The Tomb of Simon the Temple Builder is one of a group of four burial caves excavated by V. Tzaferis in 1968, on Giv'at ha-Mivtar in northern Jerusalem. It consists of an upper burial chamber with a standing pit and four loculi, and a second burial chamber on a lower level, with eight loculi. It was in use at the end of the first century BCE and in the first century CE. The tomb contained eight ossuaries, one bearing two inscriptions in Aramaic, both reading (with a few orthographic variations): סמונ בנה הכלה, סמונ בנא הכלה (Simon the Temple Builder). The ossuary was presumably that of a man who had taken part in the building of the Temple in Jerusalem and wished to record the fact for posterity. Among the bones in one of the ossuaries were two heel bones transfixed by a large iron nail, probably indicating that the person in question had been crucified. This find received considerable publicity, in view of the parallel to the crucifixion of Jesus and the information to be gained about the method of crucifixion.

Tomb of Abba. The Tomb of Abba was discovered in 1970 on Giv'at ha-Mivtar and was excavated by Tzaferis. It consists of a forecourt, south of which is a rectangular chamber with a rock-cut bench. At the foot of the bench is a vertical pit with a loculus at its end, in which a decorated ossuary was interred. From this chamber, a passageway leads to another chamber in the east, with benches in its walls; a second long, narrow passageway leads back to the forecourt. South of the eastern chamber a repository was found empty. Above it was a seven-line Aramaic inscription in Paleo-Hebrew characters that is unique in the context of tombs in Jerusalem from the Second Temple period. It reads:

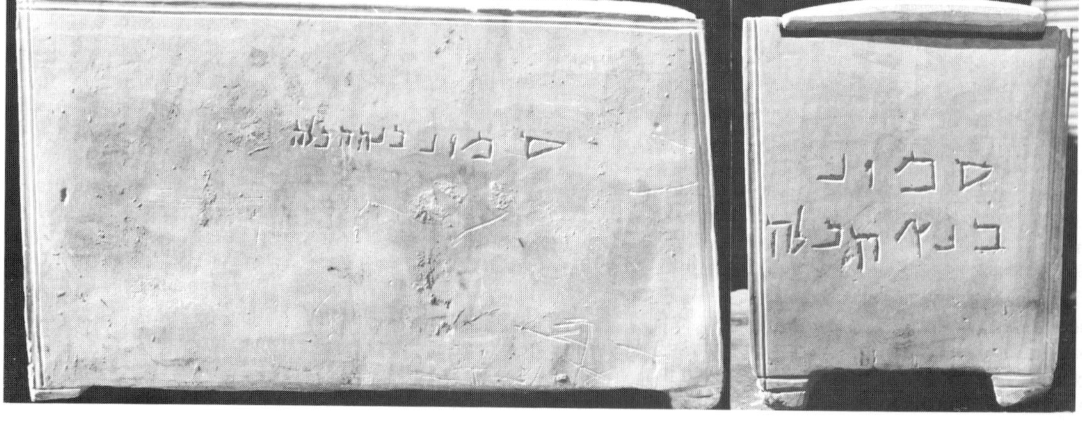

Giv'at ha-Mivtar: ossuary of "Simon the Temple Builder."

Giv'at ha-Mivtar: the "Abba" inscription.

I, Abba, son of the priest	אנה אבה בר כהנה א
Eleaz(ar), son of Aaron the high (priest),	לעז‹ר› בר אהרן רבה אנ
I, Abba, the oppressed	ה אבה מעניה מרד
and the persecuted(?), who was born in Jerusalem,	פה די יליד בירושלם
and went into exile into Babylonia	וגלא לבבל ואסק למתת
and brought (back to Jerusalem) Mattathi(ah),	
son of Jud(ah), and buried him in a	י בר יהוד וקברתה במ
cave which I bought by deed.	ערתה דזבנת בגטה

The inscription's content aroused considerable interest in the scholarly world. Some proposed identifying the remains in the decorated ossuary found in the cave as those of Mattathias Antigonus, the last monarch of the Hasmonean dynasty. This identification cannot be substantiated, however, and was not upheld by the examination of the bones.

Burial Cave on Giv'at ha-Mivtar. A burial cave on Giv'at ha-Mivtar was excavated by Kloner in 1971. It consists of a square central chamber with a standing pit and a large number of loculi cut in the walls. Sixteen ossuaries, some of them decorated, were found in the cave, as well as a few vessels of the Herodian period. Some of the ossuaries bear such names as אבשלום (Absalom), קריה (Kyria), and שמעון (Simeon.) Incised on the edge of one of the ossuaries is the inscription שלבידוד *šlbydwd*, possibly reading "of the House of David." This interpretation, referring to the Davidic dynasty in Second Temple times, arouses interesting historical questions.

Burial Cave on French Hill. A burial cave on the southern slope of French Hill was excavated by Kloner in 1975. It includes a rectangular court that led to two chambers: a northern chamber, containing a standing pit with benches and six loculi around it; and a southern chamber, with a standing pit and benches. In addition, a single loculus was cut in the western wall of the court. No ossuaries were found, but the tomb contained the remains of a great number of corpses. The pottery testifies to the tomb's use from the mid-second century BCE to the mid-first century CE.

Tombs on the Western Slope of Mount Zion. In 1975, Kloner examined several tombs on the western slope of Mount Zion, just below the southwestern corner of the Old City wall. These tombs differed from the familiar pattern in the Second Temple period: they are shallow, rock-cut depressions that were used for secondary burial. The finds, which included an ossuary found in situ and a few juglets, attest to the use of the area—which was outside the walled city—as a burial ground in the first century CE.

Tomb West of the Old City. An elaborate burial cave, west of the Old City, beyond the Hinnom Valley, near "Herod's family tomb," was discovered and partly surveyed by Schick at the end of the nineteenth century. It was re-examined in 1976 by Kloner. Owing to quarrying activities, it was found in a very ruined state. It was hewn in the first century CE, on the eastern side of a large, rectangular rocky mass that projects some 4 m above the surrounding terrain. The entrance was from the east, through a stone-built chamber that led into the cave itself through a doorway originally sealed by a rolling stone. In the center of the cave there was presumably a chamber that led to other chambers on the north, west, and south. Rectangular depressions were cut in the walls of the chambers at floor level, probably to hold sarcophagi; of the latter, only a few isolated fragments were preserved. The sparse remains are sufficient to indicate that the original burial cave must have been quite large and luxuriously appointed, perhaps similar to "Herod's family tomb" nearby.

Giv'at ha-Mivtar: inscription šlbydwd *(of the House of David) on an ossuary.*

Tomb on Mount Scopus. In 1976, Y. Gat excavated a burial cave on the east slope of Mount Scopus, below the Augusta Victoria Hospital. It consists of two sets of chambers that branch off a central entrance chamber: a western chamber contains seven loculi and a small room with benches around a central standing pit that originally contained two or three sarcophagi and an ossuary; and a southern chamber with benches around a central standing pit and a broad loculus that had contained three ossuaries. The pottery attests to continued burial in this tomb until the mid-second century CE.

Tombs on Ketef Hinnom. From 1975 to 1989 G. Barkay conducted five seasons of excavations in a late Second Temple period necropolis on Ketef Hinnom, on the southwest bank of the Valley of Hinnom. The unusual feature

Kidron Valley: decorated wall in a burial cave, Second Temple period.

Mount Scopus: decorated ossuary bearing the inscription "Jehoseph son of Ḥananiah the scribe."

of the graves was that they were dug in the ground, sometimes faced with field stones and covered with undressed stone slabs. All the graves had apparently been used for primary interment; some of them were found empty of bones, indicating that the remains had been collected and taken elsewhere for secondary burial.

Burial Caves in the Kidron Valley. Three burial caves were excavated in 1989 by G. Avni and Z. Greenhut, on the western bank of the Kidron Valley, near the monastery of Haceldama. The caves contain several chambers. Loculi and arcosolia are cut in the walls. The chambers were sealed with stone doors, some of which were found in situ. One door still had an iron bar and a key hole above it. The walls in one chamber were decorated with carved and painted geometric patterns. The entrance to another chamber was decorated with a frame of architectural patterns in the Doric style. Many ossuaries were discovered in the caves. Some of them bear decorations and inscriptions.

Burial Cave on Mount Scopus. A burial cave from the Second Temple period was excavated in 1989 by V. Sussman, on the southwestern slope of Mount Scopus. The cave consists of one chamber with loculi cut in its walls. In it many ossuaries were discovered, decorated in various patterns. On a stone that sealed one of the loculi, an Aramaic inscription was written in five lines, but it is too faded to be deciphered.

The Cave of Jehoseph Son of Caiaphas. A burial cave with loculi was excavated by Greenhut in 1990 in the Peace Forest in northern Talpiot. In it a few ossuaries were discovered. The most elaborate of these bears the inscriptions יהוסף בר קיפא and יהוסף בר קפא (Jehoseph son of Caiaphas). It is very likely that the person is to be identified with the person by that name known from the New Testament as the high priest at the time of Jesus' crucifixion. One of the skulls exposed in the tomb contained a coin. In the excavator's opinion, this testifies to the adoption of a pagan custom not attested in the other cemeteries of Second Temple Jerusalem.

Ossuary of Jehoḥanna, Granddaughter of the High Priest Theophilus. The inscription incised on the decorated facade of an ossuary reportedly found north of Jerusalem was published by D. Barag and D. Flusser. The three-line inscription is in Aramaic. It refers to Theophilus, known to have officiated as high priest in the first century CE, on the eve of the destruction of Jerusalem in 70 CE:

Jehoḥanna	יהוחנה
Jehoḥanna daughter of Jehoḥanan	יהוחנה ברת יהוחנן
son of Theophilus the high priest.	בר תפלוס הכהן הגדל

HILLEL GEVA

Government House: ossuary bearing the inscription "Jehoseph son of Caiaphas."

General: For excavations in Jerusalem and remains discovered up until the 1930s, see L. A. Mayer and M. Avi-Yonah, *QDAP* 1 (1932), 163–193, with supplementary information in *QDAP* 2–14.
See also C. Wilson and C. Warren, *Recovery of Jerusalem*, London 1871; C. Warren, *Underground Jerusalem*, London 1876; id.–Conder, *SWP—Jerusalem*; Clermont-Ganneau, *ARP* 1; L. H. Vincent, *Jérusalem Antique*, Paris 1912; id.–Abel, *Jérusalem Nouvelle* 2–3; id.–Stève, *Jérusalem* 1–3; J. Simons, *Jerusalem in the Old Testament*, Leiden 1952; K. M. Kenyon, *Jerusalem: Excavating 3000 Years of History*, London 1967; id., *Digging up Jerusalem*, London 1974; J. Wilkinson, *PEQ* 106 (1974), 32–51; id., *Levant* 7 (1975), 118–136; *Jerusalem Revealed* (ed. Y. Yadin), Jerusalem 1976; *Student Map Manual: Historical Geography of the Bible Land*, Jerusalem 1979, sect. 14; E. W. Cohn, *New Ideas about Jerusalem's*

Topography (Studium Biblicum Franciscanum Guide Books), Jerusalem 1987; W. H. Mare, *The Archaeology of the Jerusalem Area*, Grand Rapids 1987, 119–215; N. Avigad, *Archéologie, art et histoire de la Palestine: Colloque du centenaire de la section des sciences religieuses, École Pratique des Hautes Études, Sept. 1986*, 3 (ed. E.-M. Laperrousaz), Paris 1988, 133–142; M. Broshi, *Israel Museum Journal* 7 (1988), 13–23; J. D. Purvis, *Jerusalem, The Holy City: A Bibliography* (American Theological Library Association Bibliography Series 20), Metuchen, N.J. 1988; G. Barouch, *'Atiqot* 18 (1989), Supplement, 48–57; E.-M. Laperrousaz, *Transeuphratène* 1 (1989), 55–65; *MdB* 60 (1989), 3–49; N. H. Bailey, *PEQ* 122 (1990), 34–40; *Jerusalem: 5000 Ans d'histoire* (Les Dossiers d'Archéologie 165–166), Paris 1991.

Unusual finds: N. Avigad, *IEJ* 24 (1974), 52–58; D.T. Ariel, *LA* 32 (1982), 273–326; S. Gibson, *IEJ* 33 (1983), 176–188.

City of David: H. Guthe, *ZDPV* 5 (1882), 7–204, 217–277; Clermont-Ganneau, *ARP* 1, 295–297; L. H. Vincent, *Jérusalem sous terre*, London 1911; R. Weill, *La Cité de David* 1913–1914, Paris 1920; ibid. 1923–1924, Paris 1947; R. A. S. Macalister and J. G. Duncan, *Excavations on the Hill of Ophel* (PEFA 4), London 1926; J. W. Crowfoot and G. M. Fitzgerald, *Excavations in the Tyropoeon Valley 1927* (PEFA 5), London 1929; J. W. Crowfoot, *PEQ* 61 (1929), 9–16, 75–77, 150–166; M. Avi-Yonah, *IEJ* 4 (1954), 239–248; Y. Shiloh, *Excavations at the City of David 1, 1978–1982: Interim Report of the First Five Seasons* (Qedem 19), Jerusalem 1984; D. T. Ariel, *Imported Stamped Amphora Handles, Coins, Worked Bone and Ivory and Glass: Excavations at the City of David 1978–1985*, 2 (Qedem 30), Jerusalem 1990.

Acra: M. Avi-Yonah, *IEJ* 21 (1971), 168–169; E.-M. Laperrousaz, *VT* 38 (1988), 399–406; K. Decoster, *ZDPV* 105 (1989), 70–84; B. Pixner et al., ibid., 85–89; G. J. Wightman, *BAIAS* 9 (1989–1990), 29–40.

Southwestern Hill and First Wall: C. R. Conder, *PEQ* 7 (1875), 7–10, 81–89; F. J. Bliss and A. C. Dickie, *Excavations at Jerusalem 1894–1897*, London 1898; J. Germer-Durand, *Maison de Caiphe*, Paris 1914; R. W. Hamilton, *PEQ* 67 (1935), 141–143; C. N. Johns, *QDAP* 14 (1950), 121–190; A. D. Tushingham, *ZDPV* 95 (1979), 39–55; id., *Excavations in Jerusalem 1961–1967* 1, Toronto 1985; ibid. (Reviews), *Biblica* 68/3 (1987), 443–446. — *IEJ* 40 (1990), 229–230; id., *Levant* 19 (1987), 137–143; id., *PEQ* 120 (1988), 142–145; H. Geva, *IEJ* 31 (1981), 57–65; 33 (1983), 55–71; S. Gibson, *PEQ* 119 (1987), 81–96; N. Avigad, *The Herodian Quarter in Jerusalem: Wohl Archaeological Museum*, Jerusalem 1989; D. Chen and S. Margalit, *ZDPV* 105 (1989), 85–95; B. Pixner (et al.), ibid., 86–95; id., ibid., 96–104; R. Riesner, ibid., 105–109.

Second Wall: R. W. Hamilton, *QDAP* 10 (1944), 1–54; K. M. Kenyon, *PEQ* 96 (1964), 14–16; R. Amiran, *IEJ* 21 (1971), 166–167; U. Lux, *ZDPV* 88 (1972), 185–201; J. D. Purvis, *Jerusalem, The Holy City: A Bibliography* (op. cit.), 52–66; B. E. Schein, *BA* 44 (1981), 21–26.

Temple Mount and its environs: R. Hestrin, *Israel Museum News* 3/3 (1968), 51–52; R. Grafman, *IEJ* 20 (1970), 60–66; E.-M. Laperrousaz, *Syria* 50 (1973), 355–392; V. R. L. Fry, "The Warning Inscriptions from the Herodian Temple" (Ph.D. diss., Southern Baptist Theological Seminary 1974; Ann Arbor 1986); B. Mazar, *The Mountain of the Lord*, Garden City, N.Y. 1975; id., *Biblical Archaeology Today*, Jerusalem 1985, 463–468; B. Isaac, *IEJ* 33 (1983), 86–92; A. S. Kaufman, *BAR* 9/2 (1983), 40–59; R. Hachlili, *Ancient Jewish Art and Archaeology in the Land of Israel* (Handbuch der Orientalistik VII/I/2/4), Leiden 1988; J. D. Purvis, *Jerusalem, The Holy City: A Bibliography* (op. cit.), 178–192; R. Reich, *IEJ* 39 (1989), 63–65; K. Ritmeyer and L. Ritmeyer, *BAR* 15/6 (1989), 23–53; P. Segal, *IEJ* 39 (1989) 79–84; D. Chen, *10th World Congress of Jewish Studies* B/2, Jerusalem 1990, 9–14; K. Koenen, *ZDPV* 106 (1990), 180–182; L. D. Sporty, *BA* 53 (1990), 194–204; 54 (1991), 28–35; D. M. Jacobson, *BAIAS* 10 (1990–1991), 36–66.

Antonia: L. H. Vincent, *RB* 42 (1933), 83–113; 61 (1954), 87–107; S. Marie-Aline de Sion, *La Fortresse Antonia à Jérusalem et la question du pretoire*, Paris 1955; P. Benoit, *Harvard Theological Review* 64 (1971), 135–167; E. W. Cohn, *PEQ* 111 (1979), 41–52; G. J. Wightman, *BAIAS* 10 (1990–1991), 7–35.

Streets: R. W. Hamilton, *QDAP* 1 (1932), 105–110; 2 (1933), 34–40.

Opus reticulatum structure: E. Netzer and S. Ben-Arieh, *IEJ* 33 (1983), 163–175.

Third Wall: C. Schick, *PEQ* 20 (1888), 115–124; L. H. Vincent, *RB* 36 (1927), 516–548; 37 (1928), 80–100, 321–339; 54 (1947), 90–126; E. W. Hamrick, *BASOR* 183 (1966), 19–26; id., *BA* 40 (1977), 18–23; id., *Levant* 13 (1981), 262–266; K. M. Kenyon, *PEQ* 98 (1966), 87–88; M. Avi-Yonah, *IEJ* 18 (1968), 98–125; J. B. Hennessy, *Levant* 2 (1970), 22–27; S. Ben-Arieh and E. Netzer, *IEJ* 24 (1974), 97–107; P. Benoit, *Studia Hierosolymitana* 1 (1976), 111–126; J. Blomme, *RB* 86 (1979), 244–271; G. Schmitt, *ZDPV* 97 (1981), 153–170; A. D. Tushingham, *Excavations in Jerusalem 1961–1967* 1: *Excavations in the Armenian Garden on the Western Hill*, Toronto 1985; H. Shanks, *BAR* 13/3 (1987), 46–57; G. J. Wightman, *The Damascus Gate*, Jerusalem (*BAR*/IS 519), Oxford 1989.

Water supply: C. Mauss, *La Piscine de Béthesda à Jérusalem*, Paris 1888; C. Schick et al., *PEQ* 20 (1888), 115–124; C. R. Conder, ibid. 22 (1890), 122–123; L. Cre, ibid. 33 (1901), 163–165; R. de Vaux and J. M. Rousée, *RB* 64 (1957), 226–228; J. M. Rousée, ibid. 69 (1962), 107–108; L. Vetrali, *LA* 17 (1967), 149–161; D. Adan, *IEJ* 29 (1979), 92–100; F. W. Cohn, *New Ideas about Jerusalem's Topography* (op. cit.), Jerusalem 1987; J. D. Purvis (op. cit.), 43–51.

Tombs

General: N. Avigad, *IEJ* 1 (1950–1951), 96–106; P. Kahane, ibid. 2 (1952), 125–139, 176–182; 3 (1953), 48–54; L. Y. Rahmani, *BA* 44 (1981), 171–177, 229–235; 45 (1982), 43–53, 109–119; J. D. Purvis, *Jerusalem, The Holy City: A Bibliography* (op. cit.), 67–87; *'Atiqot* 21 (in prep.).

"Tomb of Zechariah": H. E. Stutchbury, *PEQ* 93 (1961), 101–113.

Jason's Tomb: A. Ben-Eli, *Sefunim* 1 (1966), 40–42.

Two-Columned Tomb: N. Avigad, *PEQ* 79 (1947), 119–122; L. Y. Rahmani, *'Atiqot* 3 (1961), 96.

"Two-Storied Tomb": K. Galling, *ZDPV* 59 (1936), 111–123.

Tomb of the Grapes: L. H. Vincent, *RB* 8 (1899), 297ff.; R. A. S. Macalister, *PEQ* 32 (1900), 54ff.

"Sanhedrin Tombs": J. J. Rothschild, *PEQ* 84 (1952), 23–28; 86 (1954), 16–22 (tomb 14); L. Y. Rahmani, *'Atiqot* 3 (1961), 93ff.

Tomb of the Frieze: L. H. Vincent, *RB* 10 (1901), 448; R. A. S. Macalister, *PEQ* 34 (1902), 118.

"Tomb of Herod's Family": C. Schick, *PEQ* 24 (1892), 115–120; R. A. S. Macalister, ibid. 33 (1901), 397–402; Vincent–Stève, *Jérusalem*, 342–346.

Burial cave in the Schneller Compound: Lutybarski, *Ephemeris* 2 (1906), 191–199; Frey, *Corpus* 2, 314f.

Burial cave in the Qaṭamon quarter: H. Haensler, *Das Heilige Land* 57 (1913), 85–95, 124–144; Frey, *Corpus* 2, 303f.

Tomb in the Kidron Valley: L. A. Mayer, *BBSAJ* 1 (1924), 56–60.

Burial cave in the German Colony: E. L. Sukenik, *JPOS* 8 (1928), 113–121; 9 (1929), 45–49; G. Avni, *ESI* 9 (1989–1990), 147.

Tomb south of Silwan: N. Avigad, *IEJ* 12 (1962), 1–12.

Burial cave in the Talpiot quarter: E. L. Sukenik, *AJA* 51 (1947), 351–365.

Tomb on Jebel Khalet et-Turi: J. T. Milik, *LA* 7 (1956–1957), 232–262.

Tombs at Dominus Flevit: B. Bagatti and J. T. Milik, *Gli Scavi del Dominus Flevit*, Jerusalem 1958; M. Avi-Yonah, *IEJ* 11 (1961), 91–94.

Tombs on Giv'at ha-Mivtar: N. Haas, *IEJ* 20 (1970), 38–59; J. Naveh, ibid., 33–37; V. Tzaferis, ibid., 18–32; id., *BAR* 11 (1985), 44–53; Y. Yadin, *IEJ* 23 (1973), 18–22; V. Moller-Christensen, ibid. 26 (1976), 35–38; J. Zias and E. Sekelef, ibid. 35 (1985), 22–27.

Burial cave with the "Abba" inscription: J. Naveh, *IEJ* 23 (1973), 82–91; E.-S. Rosenthal, ibid., 72–81; P. Smith, ibid. 27 (1977), 121–124.

Burial cave on French Hill: A. Kloner, *IEJ* 30 (1980), 99–108.

Tombs on Ketef Hinnom: H. M. Rösel, *Biblische Notizen* 35 (1986), 30–36; A. Lemaire, *VT* 38 (1988), 220–230, n. 15.

Tombs on Giv'at Ram (the Botanical Gardens): R. Ruchman, *ESI* 6 (1987–1988), 60–61.

Ossuary of Jehoḥanna: D. Barag and D. Flusser, *IEJ* 36 (1986), 39–44.

THE ROMAN PERIOD

HISTORY

The information available about Jerusalem's history in the Roman period—from the destruction of the Second Temple in 70 CE to the Byzantine period at the beginning of the fourth century CE—is extremely fragmentary, owing to the dearth of contemporary historical accounts.

Josephus (*War* VII, 2–5) states that the Tenth Roman Legion Fretensis was stationed in the ruins of Jerusalem after its destruction. The legion's camp was built near the three towers—Phasael, Hippicus, and Mariamme—and near the part of the western city wall that had not been destroyed.

During Hadrian's visit to Judea in 130 CE, it was decided to establish a Roman colony on the ruins of the city that had been destroyed in 70 CE. There are two conflicting opinions about the exact date on which the colony of Aelia Capitolina was founded. According to Dio Cassius (*Hist.* LXIX; 12, 1–2), the decision to establish a Roman colony in Jerusalem was the immediate cause of the outbreak of the Bar-Kokhba Revolt in 132 CE. The account of Eusebius, the church historian, dates the foundation of Aelia Capitolina to 136 CE, after the revolt was suppressed (*HE* IV, 6, 4). The discovery of hoards of coins from the time of the Bar-Kokhba Revolt, including coins of the colony of Aelia Capitolina itself, suggests the existence of the Roman colony during the revolt (132–135 CE).

The full name of the colony Hadrian founded in 130 CE was Colonia Aelia Capitolina. In the third century CE, the name was expanded to include the elements Commodiana, Pia Felix, and Antoniniana. The abbreviated name Aelia continued to be used throughout most of the Byzantine period, and even into the Early Arab period.

The Medeba map preserves the basic features of the town plan of Hadrianic

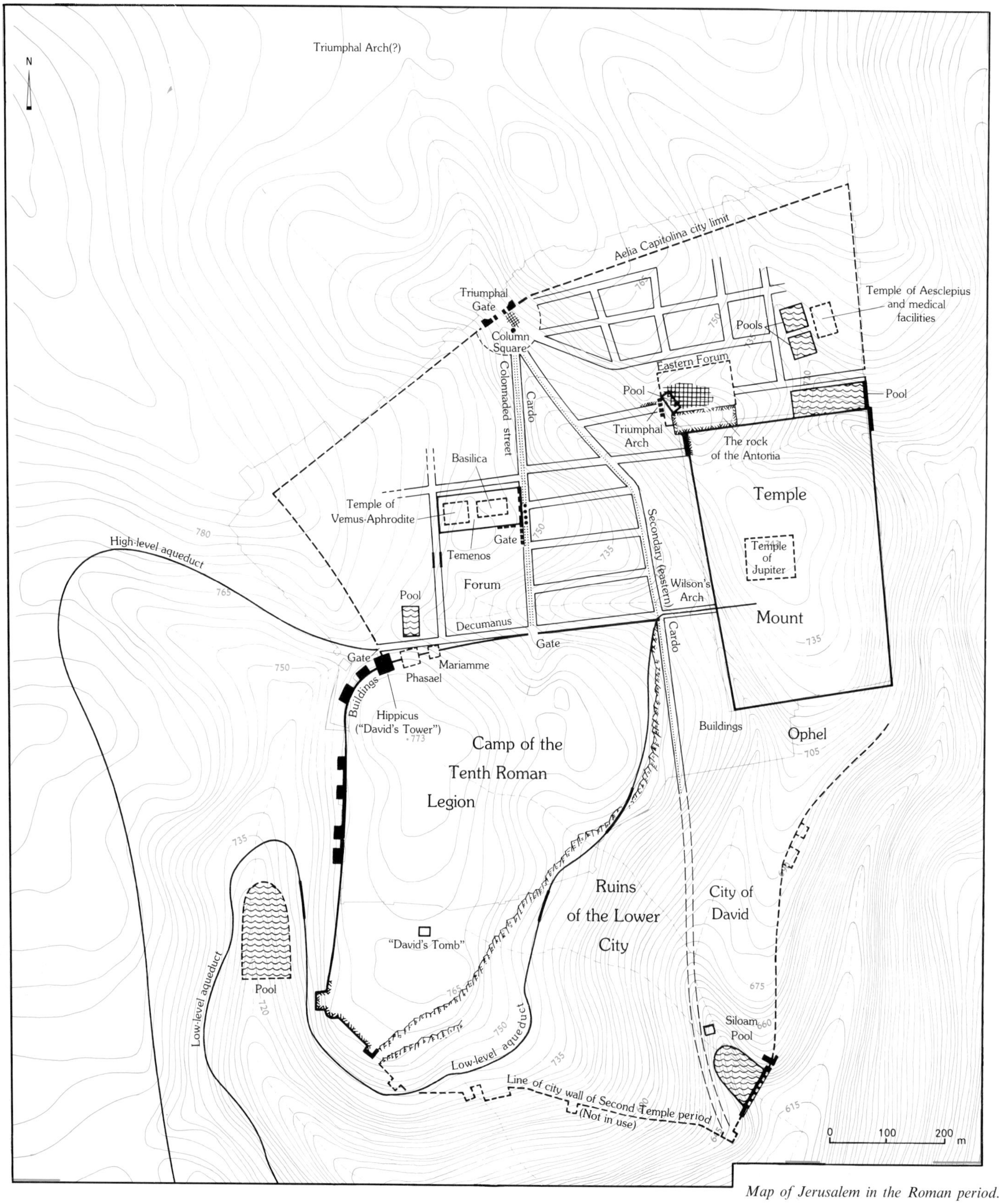

Map of Jerusalem in the Roman period.

Coin of Aelia Capitolina from the time of Lucius Verus with a depiction of a she-wolf suckling Romulus and Remus.

Aelia Capitolina (see Medeba). A later source, the *Chronicon Paschale*, describes the city's appearance at the time of its foundation: it was divided into seven definite quarters and included a few prominent central buildings. These buildings cannot be identified with certainty in the archaeological remains of the Roman period unearthed in Jerusalem; nevertheless, the description given in this source is testimony to the magnificence of Aelia Capitolina.

Many coins minted in Aelia Capitolina, from its foundation to the middle of the third century CE, attest to the pagan rituals practiced in the city in the Roman period and to the importance of the Tenth Legion in the pattern of city life. Dio Cassius (*Hist.* LXIX, 12, 1) writes that when the colony was founded a temple of Jupiter was built on the Temple Mount; its existence and that of others can also be inferred from their depiction on coins and references in inscriptions discovered in Jerusalem.

The decision to forbid Jews to settle in Jerusalem and to establish a pagan Roman colony there was responsible in part for the outbreak of the Bar-Kokhba Revolt. There is no archaeological evidence for a Jewish presence in Jerusalem in the Roman period, including during the Bar-Kokhba Revolt itself. Only a few of the coins issued by the Jews during the revolt have been discovered up until now in excavations in the area of ancient Jerusalem. It is probable that even if Jerusalem was occupied by Jewish forces then—and it is by no means certain that it was—they did not hold the city long enough to leave their mark in the archaeological record. At the end of the second century CE, the emperor Septimius Severus apparently visited Aelia, confirming the status of the city and its residents. The emperor's visit was commemorated by the minting of a special coin.

In the mid-third century, Aelia Capitolina began to lose its standing as a major city of Roman Palestine. The Tenth Legion gradually began leaving its camp in the city and its various outposts; the process was completed by the end of the third century, probably under Diocletian. Jerusalem only regained its former status at the beginning of the Byzantine period, in the reign of Constantine the Great, when it became the most important religious center in the Byzantine Christian Empire.

Archaeological finds from the Roman period unearthed at Jerusalem in the past, as well as many additional finds from the excavations since 1967, have contributed much to what is known of the topography of the city in that period. The cumulative evidence now enables a more precise reconstruction of the map of Aelia Capitolina and its internal division as well as the tracing of its urban development. The city is now known to have been divided into two parts that differed from one another in their nature and in the buildings they housed. The southern part of the city—the present-day Armenian and Jewish quarters and Mount Zion—was occupied by the Tenth Legion's camp, built in 70 CE. In the northern part of the city—the Muslim and Christian quarters—Hadrian's builders erected the city's civil and municipal complex. How Aelia Capitolina was defended in the Roman period has not yet been settled; however, the new evidence corroborates the theory that the city was unwalled for most of the period—at least until the end of the Roman period.

THE FINDS FROM 70 CE TO THE FOUNDING OF AELIA CAPITOLINA

Only a few finds can be confidently associated with the time that elapsed between the destruction of the city in 70 and Hadrian's founding of Aelia Capitolina in 129/130. B. Mazar, in his excavations south of the Temple Mount, found fragments of stone columns bearing dedicatory inscriptions in Latin referring to Vespasian and Titus, erected in Jerusalem by the Roman army to mark the city's defeat and occupation. R. Amiran and A. Eitan, excavating in the Citadel ("David's Tower") in 1968–1969, identified two occupation levels from the early stage of the legion's presence. The earlier level (IIIB) was a transitional stratum from the end of the first century, consisting of part of a floor overlying the remains of masonry from the end of the Second Temple period. Above this floor, a later stratum (IIIA) also from the end of the first century, included part of a building and a drain, built of stone sections, running between the building and the city wall. It was at that time, in the excavators' view, that a short stretch of the inner face of the First Wall from the Second Temple period was rebuilt with additional masonry (see below, Aelia Capitolina, the Camp of the Tenth Legion).

A few tombs from the Second Temple period in Jerusalem show signs of having continued in use between 70 and the foundation of Aelia Capitolina, but this does not imply a permanent Jewish presence in the city at the time; nor is there any evidence to that effect within the city itself. The available finds indicate that Jerusalem, in the interim period from 70 to the establishment of Aelia Capitolina, was populated mostly by the Tenth Legion's military camp on the southwestern hill.

AELIA CAPITOLINA

The bulk of the archaeological finds from the Roman period in Jerusalem dates to the period after Hadrian founded Aelia Capitolina on the ruins of the Second Temple period city. It was previously thought that the Roman colony of Aelia Capitolina was built according to the traditional Roman town plan—which resembles the plan of a square, fortified Roman military camp—with a network of streets crossing one another at right angles. As proof, scholars cited the depiction of Jerusalem on the Medeba map, as well as the present plan of the Old City, whose walls and some of whose streets, it was claimed, reflect the original plan of Aelia Capitolina. However, the new archaeological finds seem to clash at least partly with this view. They indicate that the plan of the Old City and the present course of its walls have a long and much more complex history.

THE CAMP OF THE TENTH LEGION. The camp of the Tenth Legion continued to occupy the southwestern hill after the foundation of Aelia Capitolina, retaining the features it had when it was built, just after the Roman conquest in 70. The Roman period occupation level excavated on the southwestern hill is generally extremely fragmentary, and in most places it is difficult to identify. The most common find indicating the presence of the Tenth Legion, including the period of Aelia Capitolina, are thousands of broken ceramic roof tiles, and to a lesser extent, bricks and pipes, many of them bearing a rectangular stamp featuring various combinations of the legion's abbreviated name LEG(IO) X FRE(TENSIS). The presence of the legionary camp in Jerusalem at the beginning of the Roman period is also attested to by fragments of roof tiles bearing a circular stamp with the abbreviation, L·X·F, of the legion's name, together with its insignia—a galley and a wild boar. Hundreds of stamped tiles of all kinds were found in excavations on the southwestern hill but they were also found elsewhere in Jerusalem; some have been found in several sites in the city's environs. In N. Avigad's excavations of the Jewish Quarter (1969–1982), the roof tiles were found in a well-defined stratigraphic layer, containing no masonry, from the Roman period. Most of them were found out of context, in later strata, mainly from the Byzantine period. The abundance of roof tiles is in striking contrast to the paucity of contemporary pottery, coins, and other finds anywhere on the southwestern hill.

C. N. Johns, excavating in the Citadel ("David's Tower") south of the Jaffa Gate in 1934–1947, exposed the corner of a massive structure from the time of Aelia Capitolina. Between it and the city wall was a portion of a water-pipe made of ceramic sections, some stamped L·X·F in a rectangular frame. As already mentioned, Amiran and Eitan, digging in the same site in 1968–1969, discovered occupation levels from the Roman period in their stratum III,

Jewish Quarter: fragments of roof tiles stamped with the seal of the Tenth Legion.

The Citadel: clay pipes stamped with the seal of the Tenth Legion.

Tombstone of Tiberius Claudius Fatalis, a Roman soldier in the Tenth Legion, discovered between the Damascus Gate and Herod's Gate.

dating to the period just before the foundation of Aelia Capitolina. They dated Johns's finds to stratum II, from the period of Aelia Capitolina, while not discounting the possibility that some of these elements had been added in the Byzantine period.

In H. Geva's excavations at the southern part of the Citadel's courtyard (1979–1980), only a few meager buildings' sections dating to the Roman period were exposed. The main find from that period was a segment of a pipe made of clay sections, some stamped L·X·F in a circular frame. Many roof tiles stamped with the Legion's stamp were found in 1962–1967 south of the Citadel, in the southern part of the Armenian Garden (area L). In A. D. Tushingham's view (published in his final report), that area was unoccupied before the Byzantine period. However, in the report published by K. Kenyon following the excavation season of 1963, a few meager remains of walls from the time of Aelia Capitolina were reported.

Some scholars date the ancient walls that are now part of the so-called David's Tomb structure on Mount Zion to the end of the Roman period (see below, Byzantine period).

The Tenth Legion is mentioned in a few inscriptions from the Roman period discovered in Jerusalem. Among the best known is the one discovered north of the Citadel at the end of the nineteenth century, when the Imperial Hotel was being built (the pillar bearing the inscription now stands in the center of a building at the site). It is a dedicatory inscription in honor of Marcus Junius Maximus, a legate of the Tenth Legion, that probably dates to the beginning of the third century. Other inscriptions referring to the Tenth Legion were discovered in the northern part of the Old City. One fragmentary inscription was found on a stone in secondary use in the Old City wall north of the Jaffa Gate. Between the Damascus Gate and Herod's Gate in the northern wall of the Old City, a tombstone was discovered in the 1930s referring to one Tiberius Claudius Fatalis, a soldier in the Tenth Legion at the end of the first century. Another fragmentary inscription was discovered by J. B. Hennessy (1964–1966) in front of the Damascus Gate. Only one inscription from the Roman period is known from the supposed location of the legion's camp on the southwestern hill. It was discovered at the end of the nineteenth century, in secondary use in the Zion Gate, in the southern wall of the Old City. The inscription mentions the Third Legion Cyrenaica and probably dates to 116/117. East of the Damascus Gate an inscription was discovered that refers to the Eleventh Legion.

A summary of the finds from the many excavations carried out in various parts of the southwestern hill indicates that a small military unit of the Tenth Legion was stationed there. Although the legion's camp extended over the entire hill, its headquarters were apparently located at the northwestern corner, near the three towers of Phasael, Hippicus, and Mariamme. The towers, built by Herod, were left standing by Titus's command when the rest of the city was destroyed (Josephus, *War* VII, 1–2). The Tenth Legion was stationed there for a long time, probably in buildings scattered over the hill on the ruins of what had been the Upper City in the Second Temple period. Additional units of the Tenth Legion were stationed elsewhere around Jerusalem—at Ramat Raḥel, south of the city, and at Giv'at Ram, to the west, where Avi-Yonah excavated what he interpreted as the remains of the legion's brickworks. In nearby Moẓa (the Arab village of Qalunya, whose name preserves the Latin word "colonia") a colony for retired Roman veterans was established in this period. Roof tiles of the legion have also been found at other sites, of a civilian nature, in the vicinity of Jerusalem—at el-'Azariya and 'En Ya'el. The wide distribution of the roof tiles indicates that the produce of the legionary brickworks was extensively used in civilian construction.

Archaeological finds on the southwestern hill do not confirm the presence there of a well-defended military camp, meeting the usual Roman standards: no evidence has surfaced of fortifications erected in the Roman period in the camp's estimated location. This negative evidence is particularly striking along the line of the present-day south wall of the Old City, which, scholars believed, followed the same line as far back as the Roman period. Excavations along the south wall, on both sides, have uncovered no evidence of fortifications prior to the tenth century CE. Hence, it appears that the defenses of the legion's camp on the southwestern hill were based in this area on the First Wall of the Second Temple period; its eastern defenses probably exploited the rock scarp facing the Temple Mount.

The Tenth Legion maintained its camp in Jerusalem until it was transferred to Elath at the end of the third century (apparently in the reign of Diocletian). By the beginning of the Byzantine period, the southwestern hill was again inhabited, but the remains do not attest to any uniform plan. This can be seen in the present-day layout of the southern part of the Old City, which shows no signs of planning; in the northern part, on the other hand, vestiges are still preserved of Aelia Capitolina's town plan (see below).

CITY PLANNING. Remains of magnificent construction dating to the early

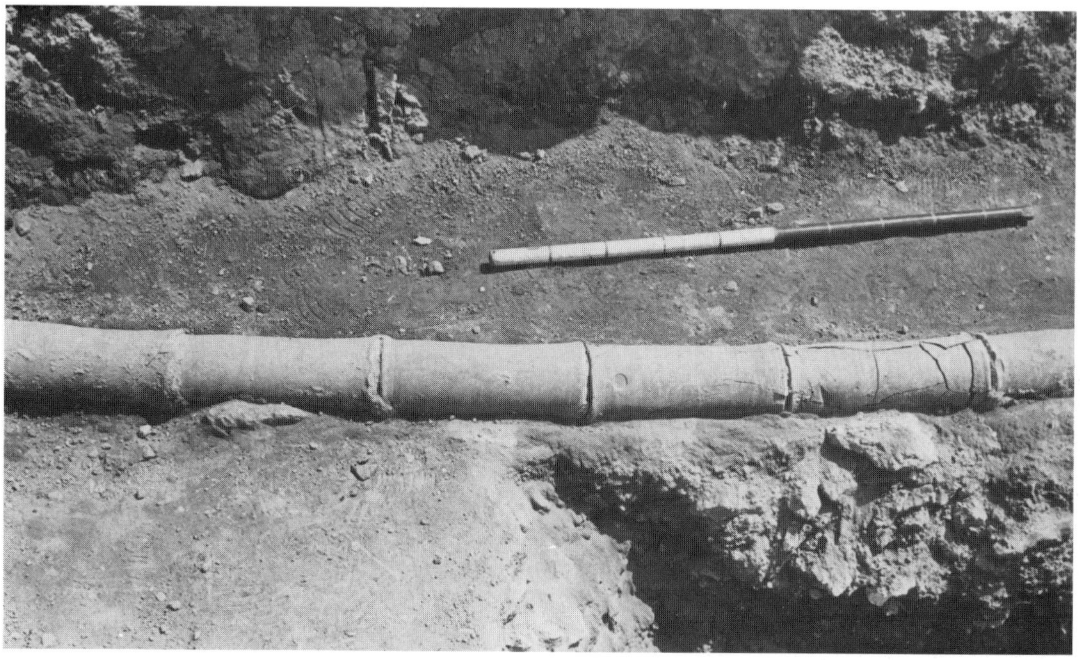

The Citadel: clay pipe in situ, Roman period.

Damascus Gate: plan of the elaborate gate built by Hadrian in the early 2nd century on the northern side of the colony of Aelia Capitolina.

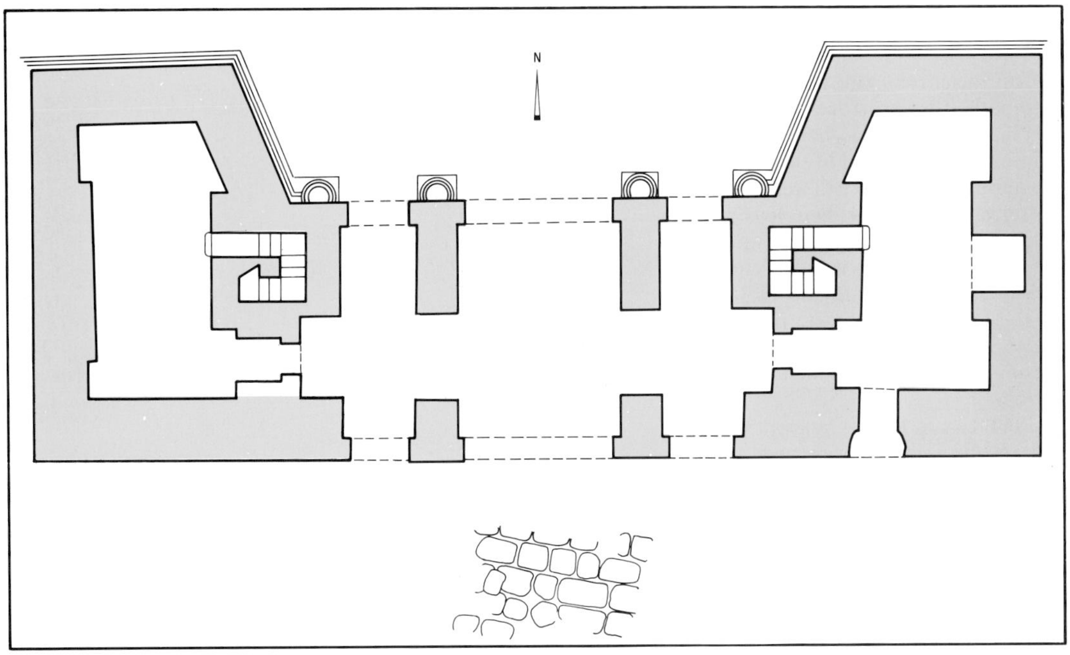

years of Aelia Capitolina in the Roman period have been located hitherto only in the present-day Christian and Muslim quarters, in the northern part of the Old City. This reinforces the view that Hadrian located the new colony's civilian municipal part of the city to the north of the Tenth Legion's camp on the southwestern hill. Analysis of the finds indicates that this part of the city was based on a precise geometric plan: a network of streets that crossed each other at right angles and along which the city's public buildings were erected. The deliberate rectangular layout of Aelia Capitolina's street network is still readily visible under the maze of modern streets in the northern part of the Old City.

THE NORTHERN GATE OF AELIA CAPITOLINA (DAMASCUS GATE) AND THE CITY'S FORTIFICATIONS. The most impressive surviving remains of Aelia Capitolina are those of the Roman Damascus Gate. They have been exposed in several seasons of excavations beneath the foundations of the Ottoman Damascus Gate in the northern wall of the Old City. Some upper parts of the gate's facade, a section of the wall near it, and part of its inner side were uncovered by R. W. Hamilton in 1937–1938; most of the facade at the eastern entrance was exposed by Hennessy (1964–1966), under the auspices of the Kenyon expedition. Beneath the foundations of the Roman gate a section of a wall dating to Second Temple times was also discovered (see above, Second Temple Period—Second Wall). Between 1979 and 1984, M. Magen continued to clear the remains of the gate: primarily the interiors of the two towers flanking it, the rear of the western tower, and a section of the paved square just inside it. Essentially, all the remains of the gate structure have been exposed. It was an impressive gate, with three entrances, of which the central one was wider and higher than the two side entrances; it was defended on either side by massive towers, the bases of whose northern facades had a fine profile. Only the eastern entrance has survived in its entirety, indicating that all three entrances were spanned by arches with a stepped, recessed profile. Of the engaged columns that originally flanked the entrances, all that remains are bases on raised pedestals on either side of the eastern entrance. Fixed above the arch of today's eastern entrance is a fragmentary inscription in Latin, probably in secondary use, which ends "by decree of the decurions of Aelia Capitolina." The surviving elements of the eastern entrance are its vaulted ceiling, threshold, and floor, the latter made of large stone slabs. The entrance was 2.36 m wide and 4.85 m high; a narrow corridor led eastward to the interior of the eastern tower. The walls of this tower, like those of the entire gate, were built of large ashlars dressed in typical Herodian style—mostly in secondary use, as indicated by their disposition. The eastern tower's interior was 11.5 m long and 6 m wide. It survives to its original height of 11.8 m, although the present ceiling is a late addition. In the southern wall of the eastern tower, a door provided access to the city. In the eastern wall was a square chamber (2 by 2 m). In the western wall, a door leading to a flight of steps is preserved in its entirety; the steps led to the upper part of the eastern tower. The western tower of the Roman Damascus Gate is preserved to a height of 11 m; it is identical in plan to the parallel, eastern tower, but the southern wall has disappeared.

Hamilton's view, since accepted by most scholars, was that the gate was built when Aelia Capitolina was founded. Hennessy and Kenyon, however, dated its beginnings to the Second Temple period, arguing that it continued to serve Aelia Capitolina, with some renovations and the addition of the upper part. Recent excavations have proved beyond doubt that the construction of the gate was indeed contemporary with the colony's founding. This was also the conclusion of G. J. Wightman, who in 1989 published the report on Hennessy's excavations. The gate's builders clearly made use of many ashlar blocks with typically Herodian dressed margins, undoubtedly taken from the ruins of the fine buildings and fortifications of Second Temple period Jerusalem. Hadrian's masons built the Damascus Gate as a triumphal arch to mark the northern city limits of the colony of Aelia Capitolina. Its structure shows several architectural features characteristic of Roman triumphal arches built in the second and third centuries in various cities in the Eastern empire, such as Gerasa in Transjordan. Other gates with three entrances were built in this period elsewhere in Jerusalem: north of the Temple Mount (the Ecce Homo Arch), and perhaps also east of the Church of the Holy Sepulcher and north of the Damascus Gate (see below).

The recent excavations in and around the Damascus Gate have revived the old question of whether Roman Aelia Capitolina was walled. The most commonly held view is that the city was unwalled at least until the end of the third or beginning of the fourth century. Repeated excavations along the line of the present Old City wall—which follows the supposed course of the Roman city wall—have failed to reveal definite evidence of fortifications dating to that time. Hamilton's excavations along the outer side of the Old City wall, west of the Damascus Gate, exposed a short segment of the outer

Damascus Gate: (below) eastern opening of the Hadrianic Roman gate; (above) the Damascus Gate, from the reign of Suleiman the Magnificent, mid-16th century.

Damascus Gate: interior of the east tower of the gatehouse, Roman period.

face of an ancient city wall, built mostly of smoothed, square stones and preserved to a considerable height. He dated this wall to the end of the third or beginning of the fourth century, and suggested that the two lowest courses in the foundation of this wall might be the remains of a wall contemporary with the Hadrianic gate. However, these remains, too, are inadequate to provide a definite solution to the puzzle of Aelia Capitolina's fortifications.

In 1864, C. Clermont-Ganneau reported the discovery of the remains of a triumphal arch, with three entrances, north of the Old City, alongside the present-day Nablus Road. The best-known element in these remains are fragments of a Latin inscription referring to Hadrian and the head of a marble statue found nearby; it is not clear whether the sculpture had anything to do with the gate or whether it should be identified as a representation of Hadrian. The gate was built outside the city limits, astride the main road to Aelia Capitolina from the north (see below, Byzantine Period, Saint Stephen's Church).

THE CARDO. Inside the Roman Damascus Gate, at the level of its entrance, Magen uncovered a section of a paved square (30 by 6–10 m) dating to the time of Aelia Capitolina; it was made of large, thick stone slabs up to 2 m long and, on the average, 1.2 m wide. Some of these stones were striated to prevent slipping and were worn with use. This paving was probably part of the inner square, with a pillar in the center, depicted on the Medeba map just inside the northern gate of Jerusalem.

In the 1970s, S. Margalit reexcavated massive paving stones along the present-day Beth ha-Bad Street, which cuts down the northern part of the Old City, southward from the Damascus Gate. The characteristic paving stones are probably remnants of the Cardo, the main street that ran the length of the Roman-Byzantine city. The Cardo is pictured in detail on the Byzantine Medeba map: a row of columns runs down either side of the street that bisects Jerusalem lengthwise from the inner square of the northern gate to Mount Zion in the south.

Some limestone columns, now in secondary use in the walls of the roofed bazaars in the middle of the Old City—which follow the line of the Cardo—have been identified as columns from the Roman Cardo. Among them, a column in the wall of a building on Beth ha-Bad Street marks the "Seventh Station" of the traditional Via Dolorosa. Additional fragments of dark granite columns, standing on high, finely carved pedestals, have been known since the mid-nineteenth century. They are on the grounds of the Russian Alexander Hospice, east of the Church of the Holy Sepulcher. In Aelia Capitolina these columns were part of the facade of a basilica and temple erected by Hadrian. These remains of pavements and columns belong to the northern, Roman part of the Cardo, built when Aelia Capitolina was established. At that time the Cardo ran south from the Damascus Gate, but only as far as the northern edge of the legion's camp on the southwestern hill (up to the present-day Jewish Quarter). This was confirmed by Avigad's excavations in the Jewish Quarter: all the evidence of the finds indicates that the southern section of the Cardo, exposed by Avigad, was built only toward the end of the Byzantine period by Justinian. There was no previous Roman street along the same line, as might have been expected according to the traditional view—that the entire length of the Cardo as shown on the Medeba map was already in existence in the Roman period (see below, Byzantine Period).

THE DECUMANUS. The main street crossing ancient Jerusalem at right angles to the Cardo—the Decumanus—is generally reconstructed along the line of David Street and the Street of the Chain, from the Jaffa Gate in the west to the Temple Mount in the east. The remains of part of the Roman Decumanus were exposed in 1990 by L. Gershuny and R. Abu Ria in the easternmost part of the Street of the Chain, near the Temple Mount. The remains consist of two sections of large, thick slabs. This is the first evidence discovered to date of the Decumanus in Roman Jerusalem; it is doubtful that it, like the Cardo, had flanking rows of columns.

The location of the tetrapylon, which marked the intersection of the Cardo and the Decumanus in many cities in the Roman period, is still unknown. Its identification with the building that houses the modern el-Bashura Cafe, at

Damascus Gate: pavement of the inner square, Roman period.

Christians' Street: street from the Early Byzantine period with Roman paving stones in secondary use.

the northern end of the Street of the Jews, is untenable. It is quite possible that there was no tetrapylon in the usual sense in Roman Aelia Capitolina. **THE FORUM AND SURROUNDING BUILDINGS.** Aelia Capitolina's central forum adjoined the Cardo. The city's basilica and the Temple of Venus-Aphrodite were to the north. Scholars locate the Roman forum in the area of the present-day Muristan, bounded by the Church of the Holy Sepulcher to the north, the Street of the Christians to the west, David Street to the south, and the three vaulted bazaars south of Beth ha-Bad Street (along the line of the Cardo) to the east. Remains of Hadrianic buildings on the northern side of the forum were discovered in the nineteenth century on the grounds of the Russian Hospice, east of the Church of the Holy Sepulcher. Extensive excavations in the Church of the Holy Sepulcher, carried out in 1960–1969 and in the 1970s by V. Corbo, C. Coüasnon, and others as part of the restoration work at the site, have revealed additional remains, some of which have been dated by the excavators to the establishment of Aelia Capitolina. The Roman remains discovered in the church itself are extremely fragmentary. Only the foundations of walls were discovered; the upper courses were presumably removed, as described by Eusebius, when the Constantinian basilica was built here at the beginning of the fourth century. However, the Roman date of these remains suggested by Corbo is not conclusively proven by the finds as reported in the excavation's final publication. Coüasnon has suggested another view of the date and nature of some of these remains and the building on the site in the Roman period that departs in many essential details from Corbo's theory.

Among the remains of Roman masonry identified in the church were stretches of walls that form two parallel corners. The walls were discovered in the church's Armenian section, south of the rotunda, and in the Latin section to the north. Corbo, citing Eusebius' assertion that Hadrian built his temple on the site of Jesus' tomb, identified these walls as remains of the temple at the forum's northwestern corner. Beneath the paved floor of the rotunda, north of the edicule built over the sepulcher, is a vaulted space that may have been used as a *favissa* under the Roman temple.

The largest vestige of Hadrianic masonry discovered in the Church of the Holy Sepulcher was a massive wall, preserved to a great height as the northern wall of a late cistern, now situated under the northern edge of the church's forecourt (parvis). The wall is exceptionally well built, of large, ashlar blocks with drafted margins. Corbo identified this wall as the western continuation of the southern retaining wall of the temenos that, he believed, surrounded the Roman temple. The southeastern corner of the temenos wall can be seen today in the Russian Hospice east of the Church of the Holy Sepulcher. This corner and the nearby segments of masonry were already familiar to many scholars in the mid-nineteenth century; among those who refer to them are M. de Vogüé, E. Pierotti, C. Wilson, and C. Clermont-Ganneau. The corner consists of two walls of unequal thickness, both running for a considerable distance and meeting not exactly at a right angle. The walls are built of large ashlars with typical Herodian dressed margins, probably taken from the ruins of Second Temple period buildings. The facade of the southern wall is built with engaged pilasters, while the eastern wall is founded on a rock-cut ledge. There were originally three openings in this wall, of which only two are extant—the southern opening in the Russian Hospice and the central, largest gate, now incorporated in a shop north of the hospice. Most scholars believe that the gates were hewn at the beginning of the fourth century—when the Constantinian basilica in the Holy Sepulcher was being built—into an older wall that dates to the establishment of Aelia Capitolina under Hadrian. Corbo was inclined to the view that the openings should also be dated to the original, Hadrianic phase. Previous theories identified these remains as part of the Second Wall of Jerusalem in the Second Temple period (see above, Second Temple Period). In Corbo's view, they formed the southeastern corner of the elevated temenos, built here by Hadrian. As against that view, Vincent and Coüasnon argue that these are the remains of the basilica. As already mentioned, a few of the original granite columns from the Roman Cardo were found opposite this structure's eastern facade. Incorporated in the corner, on the east and south, are additional segments of masonry that have been reconstructed as parts of a magnificent tripartite gate similar to the Roman Damascus Gate. This gate stood at the northeastern corner of the forum and provided access to the forum square.

Corbo suggested that Hadrian had built a Temple for Jupiter on the elevated temenos—the Capitolinum. He estimated the size of the temple at 41.5 by 37 m and reconstructed a broad flight of stairs ascending to it from the Cardo on the east. Although admitting that the actual remains of the temple were extremely sparse, Corbo considered them sufficient evidence of the temple's existence. Other scholars hold that Hadrian dedicated the temple to Venus-Aphrodite. Some scholars in fact believe that the temple was circular, this feature being preserved in the shape of the rotunda in the Church of the Holy Sepulcher (the earliest stages of which are known, from recent excavations and studies, to have originated in the Constantinian structure; see below, Byzantine Period).

In Coüasnon's view, the northern wall of the Chapel of Saint Helena, in the eastern part of the Church of the Holy Sepulcher, was built in the time of Hadrian as a stylobate supporting one of the colonnades of the Roman basilica. On this basis, he suggested that the fourth-century Constantinian basilica was essentially modeled on the Roman basilica that had stood at the northeastern corner of the forum.

In 1975–1976, M. Broshi, excavating in the rock-cut hollow now known as the Chapel of Saint Vartan, near the Chapel of Saint Helena, discovered three well-built walls. He suggested that they had originally supported the elevated floor of the temenos (one of these walls is the eastern continuation of the northern wall in the Chapel of Saint Helena).

Kenyon, excavating in 1960 in her site C in the Muristan, southeast of the Church of the Holy Sepulcher, found an earth fill that, she suggested, had been deposited to a considerable height in the extensive leveling operations that preceded the construction of the forum of Aelia Capitolina. In the fill she found a section of a drain that was part of the original construction of Aelia Capitolina.

In 1893, during the construction of the Lutheran Church of the Redeemer, north of Kenyon's site C, the builders discovered a wall that was once thought to be part of the Second Wall of Jerusalem in Second Temple times (see above, Second Temple Period, The Second Wall). Excavations by U. Lux in 1970–1971 ascertained that the wall in fact dated to the construction of Aelia Capitolina.

In 1977, Margalit, Chen, and Solar, working in Christians' Street, west of the Church of the Holy Sepulcher, exposed a section of a paved street laid at the beginning of the Byzantine period (see below, Byzantine Period). The style of the paving stones indicates that they may be of Roman workmanship, originally part of some pavement, of unknown origin, that was dismantled and whose stones were taken for secondary use in this Byzantine street. **THE SECONDARY (EASTERN) CARDO.** This eastern Cardo is shown on the Medeba map with a colonnade running along one side only. Its northern part ran southward, down the Tyropoeon Valley, and continued, according to the archaeological evidence, along the rock-cut scarp visible today along the eastern edge of the Jewish Quarter, overlooking the Western Wall. Some of this street's original paving was exposed on ha-Gai Street, which follows the old course of the Secondary Cardo (see below, Byzantine Period). In the early 1930s, Hamilton, excavating north of Wilson's Arch, discovered sections of two superimposed paved streets, with underlying drains; he suggested that the lower of these streets might date to the Roman period. In 1980, Magen, working at the junction of the Via Dolorosa and ha-Gai Street (opposite the "Third Station"), exposed a section of a street paved with large stones, some striated and worn with use. In the 1970s, outside the Dung Gate, M. Ben-Dov discovered a broad section of a paved street from the beginning of the Byzantine period; this was a continuation of part of the same street previously discovered inside the Old City wall. The street had a row of columns along its western side and was paved with large stones. The paving stones in the sections exposed along ha-Gai Street are very similar to the large, well-worn paving stones in the square just inside the Damascus Gate. They may therefore date to the Roman period, although some of them were undoubtedly reused here when the street was repaired in the Byzantine period. Despite the fragmentary evidence, it is reasonable to assume that the general line and detailed layout of the Secondary (eastern) Cardo date to the establishment of Aelia Capitolina. It continued in use for a considerable period, during which various sections along it were repaired.

THE EASTERN FORUM. The eastern forum was built north of the Temple Mount in the Roman period. The principal remains known today include the pavement known as the Lithostrotos and part of a triple-arched triumphal gate, the central arch of which is known as the Ecce Homo Arch. Christian tradition presents these as the remains of the Antonia fortress of the Second Temple period, identified with the Praetorium, the prison where Jesus' trial took place (Mk. 15:16).

The Ecce Homo Arch is referred to as a relic of antiquity in the nineteenth-century accounts of the earliest explorers of Jerusalem, such as Pierotti, Wilson, and Warren. Its remains, and the Lithostrotos pavement in which it is incorporated, were first discovered in the early 1860s, when the Sisters of Zion Convent was being built, and they were first described by Clermont-Ganneau. The remains were reexamined in 1931–1932 by Vincent and Marie-Aline de Sion. Further examinations were conducted at the site by Benoit in 1972 and again in the 1980s in the course of conservation work. Archaeologists have been able to prove fairly conclusively that these magnificent remains date to the time of Aelia Capitolina. Part of the gateway and most of the pavement are today in the Sisters of Zion Convent, while another part of the pavement is in the Chapel of the Condemnation, farther to the east.

The Lithostrotos pavement is impressively constructed. It consists of large paving stones, well dressed and laid close together in rows. The stones are considerably worn, owing to long use. A section of the pavement was actually

The Ecce Homo Arch: central arch in the gate of the eastern forum, Roman period.

Sisters of Zion Convent: the northern side entrance in the gate of the eastern forum, Roman period.

Sisters of Zion Convent: the Roman Lithostrotos pavement.

part of a main east–west passageway and its stones were striated to prevent slipping. Shallow grooves were cut in the paving stones to drain rainwater. Preserved on the eastern side of the exposed paving is part of a stylobate that originally supported a row of columns. Designs identified as board games were found incised on some of the paving stones. Part of the pavement was laid on vaults (also built at this time) spanning the Struthion Pool, which during the Second Temple period lay in the open. A narrow flight of steps, its lower part hewn in the rock, led up from the pool to the forum courtyard.

Incorporated in the pavement was, as already mentioned, a triple-arched gate, similar in structure to Aelia Capitolina's northern (Damascus) gate. The central and northern arches of this gateway have been exposed. The width of the central opening is 5.2 m, and the height of the Ecce Homo arch above it is 6.25 m (part of the arch is visible today spanning the Via Dolorosa). The smaller, northern entrance is 2.36 m wide and 5.2 m high (similar in size to the entrance in the Damascus Gate). The gate is built of finely hewn stones. Niches are cut in the wall of its western facade, between the openings.

The pavement discovered in the Sisters of Zion Convent was laid during Hadrian's reign, when it formed part of a public square—the eastern forum of Aelia Capitolina. The square was probably decorated with a row of columns, and some of the buildings and rooms whose remains were exposed to the north were used as shops. The triumphal arch in the forum square provided access to the city from the east.

Remains of masonry and other finds from the Roman period were discovered on the grounds of the Church of Saint Anne near the Lion's (Saint Stephen's) Gate. The site was excavated for many years, beginning with C. Mauss and the White Fathers at the end of the nineteenth century, and, after 1956, by M. J. Pierre and J. M. Rousée. The finds included walls and a subterranean vault bearing patches of painted plaster, small fragments of decorated mosaic floors, a sophisticated system of water channels, and a central pool. All these remains have been dated to the end of the Roman period. The excavators believed these finds to be associated with a temple and a system of water and bathing installations, for medicinal purposes, connected with the worship of Aesclepius-Serapis in the first centuries CE. The practice of some such ritual in this temple was confirmed by characteristic finds, some of which were brought as votive offerings, such as a fragment of a marble leg dedicated by one Pompeia Lucilia, votive stone models of ships, and fragments of reliefs. One of the most striking reliefs features the facade of a building with a snake and a figure bringing an offering of ears of wheat.

The Ophel: bronze statuette of a horseman, Roman period.

THE OPHEL AND THE SOUTHWESTERN CORNER OF THE TEMPLE MOUNT. Masonry remains and many finds from the Roman period, dating mainly to after the founding of Aelia Capitolina, were recovered by B. Mazar from 1968 to 1978 on the Ophel, south of the Herodian Temple precinct, near its southwestern corner. The Temple Mount itself, which remained largely in ruins in the Roman period, was occupied—as emerges from the sources—by Hadrian's Temple of Jupiter, near which stood statues of two emperors. Some scholars identify the temple enclosure at this time with the "codra" referred to in the *Chronicon Paschale*.

Found on the Ophel, inside the Old City wall, were the remains of a well-built structure, originally built in the Roman period, that continued in use, with some changes, in the Byzantine period. Two Latin inscriptions were found in secondary use in the remains of the Umayyad palace built on its ruins: a fragment of a column with a dedicatory inscription to Vespasian and Titus, and a fragment of a stone plaque bearing the end of a dedicatory inscription to Septimius Severus, Caracalla, and members of their families. The plaque had probably been affixed in some prominent position in Aelia Capitolina, at some time between 202 and 205, to mark the completion of a municipal construction project. As far back as the nineteenth century, another inscription, probably referring to Antoninus Pius, was identified in secondary use in the southern wall of the Temple Mount, east of the lintel of the Double Gate.

Two rooms of a large Roman structure were discovered near the southwestern corner of the Temple Mount. Not far from Robinson's Arch the remains of another, four-room building were found. When originally constructed in the Roman period, its floor was covered with a thick layer of plaster, into which several round baking ovens were sunk. Also found in this building was a rectangular seal with the Latin inscription PRIM, perhaps used to mark loaves of bread baked here.

B. Mazar's excavations produced a wealth of finds from the Roman period, mostly scattered and not found in situ: fragments of fine marble statues, bronze statuettes, many fragments of figurines of the Beit Natif type, and a large quantity of contemporary coins, some even minted in Aelia Capitolina. Particularly prominent among the finds were large quantities of broken ceramic roof tiles, pipes, and bricks stamped with the name of the Tenth Legion (L·X·F), in many variations. An interesting discovery was a bathhouse from the Umayyad period, found north of Robinson's Arch, whose installations contained a large number of reused round bricks stamped with the name of the Tenth Legion. Some fragments of roof tiles found in the area bore the stamp C(olonia) AEL(ia) C(apitolina), similar to roof tiles previously found in the northern part of the City of David. The abundant remains and finds from the Roman period uncovered on the Ophel and near the southwestern corner of the Temple Mount attest to the vigorous building activities in this area at the time, part of which may be associated, as B. Mazar suggested, with the activities of the Tenth Legion, which was then stationed in the city.

CITY OF DAVID AND THE SOUTHERN TYROPOEON VALLEY. The extensive excavations carried out in the City of David produced only scant remains dating to the Roman period. In 1965, Kenyon unearthed what she considered evidence, in her site V (adjoining the ancient quarries that Weill had excavated in the early twentieth century in the southern part of the City of David), that the area had been quarried for stone in the second century CE. (Shiloh, however, believed that the first exploitation of these quarries was earlier; see above, Second Temple Period.) Kenyon found remains of quarries from the Roman period elsewhere as well—in her site M, in the northwestern part of the City of David, and in her site S on the Ophel. In the northern part of the City of David, Macalister and Duncan (1923–1925) and Crowfoot and Fitzgerald (1925–1927) found mainly broken roof tiles with the stamps of the Tenth Legion. Shiloh's extensive excavations in the City of David (1978–1985) produced only sparse finds from the Roman period (stratum 4). A summary of the finds indicates that for most of the Roman period the City of David remained largely outside the built-up municipal area of Aelia Capitolina, serving mainly as a source for building stones.

The ancient remains of the Siloam Pool at the southern issue of the Tyropoeon Valley were first examined by Güthe and partly excavated by Bliss and Dickie toward the end of the nineteenth century. The pool (c. 25 by 24 m) was hewn in the rock and surrounded by a wall built of large stones. Covered stoas, supported by an arcade, presumably stood around the four walls. The pool received water from the Gihon Spring through Hezekiah's Tunnel. West of the pool, part of a stepped street descending to the south was found; it was limited on its west by the rock-cut scarp and on its east by the wall of the pool. Approximately 9 m wide at its northern end, the street narrowed to about 7.5 m at the southern end. Thirty-four steps were exposed, some of them stone slabs, others cut in the rock; they formed a regular, alternating sequence of one narrow and one wide step (similar to the flight of stairs that led up to the Huldah Gates in the southern wall of the Temple Mount in the Second Temple period).

Following Bliss and Dickie, most scholars date the masonry of the Siloam Pool to the Roman period. Bliss and Dickie identified the masonry as the quadriporticum mentioned by the Traveler of Bordeaux at the beginning of the fourth century (*Itin. Burdig*. 592, 1). Vincent identified this stage of the pool with the tetranympheon mentioned in the *Chronicon Paschale* as one of the main buildings in Aelia Capitolina. Bliss and Dickie, in their report, provide no convincing arguments for a Roman date. Various details of the construction indicate that this plan of the Siloam Pool and the street may be earlier, perhaps originating in the Second Temple period.

WATER SUPPLY

The "high-level aqueduct," so called to distinguish it from the "low-level aqueduct" from the end of the Second Temple period, was built in the Roman period. Its course and the details of its construction were resurveyed in 1969 by A. Mazar, with due attention given to the details reported by Wilson and Schick in the nineteenth century.

The "high-level aqueduct" ran for a distance of some 10 km (6 mi.), generally following the line of the watershed and today's main Bethlehem–Jerusalem road. Its source lay at Solomon's Pools, at an altitude of 790 m above sea level, and it ended at the Jaffa Gate, at 765 m above sea level. Some sections were hewn in the rock and others were built of field stones and mortar. The shallow depression west of Bethlehem was bridged in a closed stone pipe that operated on the principle of connected vessels (siphon). This sec-tion was about 2.5 km long, but only a few of its parts are preserved; the most familiar of these can be seen east of the Hebron–Bethlehem road, south of Rachel's Tomb. The pipe was composed of a large number of interlocking stone sections, firmly connected with a bonding material. The pipe's inner diameter is 38 cm. Some of the siphon's stone sections bear brief incised inscriptions in Latin, with the names of centurions in the Tenth Legion. Farther on, the aqueduct ran through a tunnel, built west of the modern neighborhood of Yemin Moshe, and reached the Mamilla Pool. In 1989, A. Maeir uncovered a Byzantine period section of this aqueduct outside the Old City, north of the Jaffa Gate. The "high-level aqueduct" entered the city through the Jaffa Gate, probably terminating nearby in Hezekiah's Pool.

It is commonly believed that the "high-level aqueduct" was built and maintained in working order by Tenth Legion personnel, in order to supply the large quantities of water Aelia Capitolina required. However, its beginnings may lie as far back as the Second Temple period (see above, Second Temple Period).

HILLEL GEVA

TOMBS

Outside the walls of Aelia Capitolina several late shaft tombs ascribed to the Roman city were discovered. A shaft—at the bottom of which was a stone that sealed the burial chamber—led down to a vaulted room with a narrow passage in the center, on both sides of which stone parapets enclosed burial places. A tomb of this type was found from the third century. In the fourth century, the form of the tomb underwent a change. The shaft was replaced by an entrance with steps built on one of the narrow sides of the burial chamber. Such tombs were found near Birket es-Sulṭan (also called the Serpent's Pool) in the Valley of Hinnom; on the Mount of Olives, especially on the road leading to the village of eṭ-Ṭur; north of the wall of the Old City, between the Damascus Gate and the "Tombs of the Kings"; near the Church of Saint Stephen outside the Damascus Gate; and along the Jaffa Road and Mount Zion.

Because the transition from the Roman to the Byzantine period is not marked by any destruction, the tombs from the fourth century are distinguished only by their finds. Finds of a clear pagan nature attest to non-Christian tombs. In 1934, graves of this type were discovered by Hamilton

The "high-level aqueduct" to Jerusalem in the Bethlehem area. This part was a pipe composed of interlocking stone segments.

Ketef Hinnom: cremation burial in a cooking pot, Roman period.

and Husseini near the intersection of Saladin Street and Nablus Road, south of the so-called Tombs of the Kings. Four types of tombs were discovered there: shaft tombs with a shelf in the lower part supporting stone slabs that covered the burial; a similar type, but with two superimposed burials, in which the cover of one burial forms the bottom of the other; tombs in which the shaft widens into a bell-shaped room, at the bottom of which the tombs are cut into the rock (the burial chamber is closed from above by a stone slab on which more stones are heaped); tombs with an open shaft, with individual graves covered with stone slabs—each grave compartment contained either one or two superimposed burials. Finds included lamps—by which the burials were dated—various kinds of jewelry, amulets, and ivory pins.

Another type of tomb from the third century was excavated in 1932, west of the YMCA building. Built of ashlars, the tomb consists of a narrow passage, near which the burials are dug into the rock. The first tombs on this site date to the third and second centuries BCE. Finds in the built tomb include three lead coffins, on one of which bulls and two cupids with bunches of grapes are depicted. A similar coffin, with a Nike and cupids, was found in a tomb excavated in 1879 near the Schneller Compound. In a shaft tomb excavated by Bliss between 1894 and 1897, the remains of colored frescoes of masks, wreaths, and depictions of Nikes with wreaths were found.

In 1935–1936, a Roman tomb was discovered during the widening of the street in front of the Lions' (Saint Stephen's) Gate. It was in two parts: the burial cave, with a remnant of a vault above it, and a structure with several rooms, the largest of which was also vaulted and perhaps had formed the foundation of the structure prior to its destruction.

MICHAEL AVI-YONAH

Between 1972 and 1974, Ben-Arieh and Netzer discovered five shaft graves dug into the foundation of a section of the Third Wall from the Second Temple period they had exposed north of the Damascus Gate. The graves contained some pottery from the end of the third and the beginning of the fourth centuries.

Barkay conducted five seasons of excavations (1975–1989) along Ketef Hinnom, on the southwest bank of the Valley of Hinnom. Here he discovered a burial ground in which the deceased were cremated and their ashes buried in cooking pots in the ground. It would appear that this area was a burial ground for the soldiers of the Tenth Legion, whose camp lay nearby, on the southwestern hill of Jerusalem, just across the Valley of Hinnom. Remains of cremated burials from the Roman period were also found in front of the Damascus Gate and along the Third Wall from the Second Temple period. Also found on Ketef Hinnom were deep pit graves, hewn in the rock and covered with stone slabs, used for burial in the third century.

HILLEL GEVA

General: For excavations in Jerusalem and remains discovered up until the 1930s, see L. A. Mayer and M. Avi-Yonah, *QDAP* 1 (1932), 163–193, with supplementary information in *QDAP* 2–14.
See also Warren–Conder, *SWP—Jerusalem*; Clermont-Ganneau, *ARP* 1; Vincent–Abel, *Jérusalem Nouvelle*; R.W. Hamilton, *PEQ* 84 (1952), 83–90; L. Kadman, *The Coins of Aelia Capitolina* (Corpus Nummorum Palaestinensium 1), Jerusalem 1956; J. Wilkinson, *Levant* 7 (1975), 118–136; *Jerusalem Revealed* (ed. Y. Yadin), Jerusalem 1976; D. T. Ariel, *LA* 32 (1982), 273–326; J. Briend, *MdB* 29 (1983), 35–37; W. H. Mare, *The Archaeology of the Jerusalem Area*, Grand Rapids 1987; M. Broshi, *Israel Museum Journal* 7 (1988), 13–23; J. D. Purvis, *Jerusalem, The Holy City: A Bibliography* (American Theological Library Association Bibliography Series 20), Metuchen, N.J. 1988, 200–218; R. Jacoby, *IEJ* 39 (1989), 284–286; S. Margalit, *Judaica* 45 (1989), 45–56; Y. Meshorer, *The Coinage of Aelia Capitolina* (Israel Museum Cat. 301), Jerusalem 1989.
The sites: S. Merrill, *PEQ* 18 (1886), 72–73; C. Mauss, *La Piscine de Béthesda à Jérusalem*, Paris 1888; F. J. Bliss, *PEQ* 27 (1895), 25; J. Germer-Durand, *Maison de Caiphe*, Paris 1914; R. A. S. Macalister and J. G. Duncan, *PEFA* 4 (1926); J. W. Crowfoot and G. M. Fitzgerald, ibid. 5 (1929); R. W. Hamilton, *QDAP* 1 (1932), 105–110; 2 (1933), 34–40; 10 (1944), 1–54; M. Avi-Yonah, ibid. 8 (1939), 54–57; id., *IEJ* 18 (1968), 196–197; C. N. Johns, *QDAP* 14 (1950), 121–190; Marie-Aline de Sion, *La Fortress Antonia à Jérusalem et la question du pretoire*, Jerusalem 1955; K. M. Kenyon, *PEQ* 96 (1964), 16–18; 98 (1966), 88; id., *Digging up Jerusalem*, London 1974, 256–264; J. B. Hennessy, *Levant* 2 (1970), 22–27; P. Benoit, *Harvard Theological Review* 64 (1971), 135–167; U. Lux, *ZDPV* 88 (1972), 185–201; P. J. Briand, *Sion* (Studium Biblicum Franciscanum Guide Books), Jerusalem 1973; S. Ben-Arieh and E. Netzer, *IEJ* 24 (1974), 97–107; M. Gichon and B. H. Isaac, ibid., 117–123; C. Coüasnon, *The Church of the Holy Sepulchre in Jerusalem*, London 1974; G. B. Sarfati, *IEJ* 25 (1975), 151; Y. Blomme, *RB* 86 (1979), 244–271; V. C. Corbo, *Il Santo Sepolcro di Gerusalemme* 1–3, Jerusalem 1981–1982; A. D. Tushingham, *Excavations in Jerusalem 1961–1967* 1: *Excavations in the Armenian Garden on the Western Hill*, Toronto 1985; ibid. (Reviews), *Biblica* 68/3 (1987), 443–446. — *IEJ* 40 (1990), 229–230; id., *PEQ* 120 (1988), 142–145; F. W. Cohn, *New Ideas about Jerusalem Topography* (Studium Biblicum Franciscanum Guide Books), Jerusalem 1987; S. Gibson, *PEQ* 119 (1987), 81–96; P. T. Crocker, *Buried History* 24 (1988), 54–59; E.-M. Laperrousaz, *Archéologie, art et histoire de la Palestine: Colloque du centenaire de la section des sciences religieuses, Ecole Pratique des Hautes Etudes, Sept. 1986*, Paris 1988, 143–148; M. Magen, *BAR* 14/3 (1988), 48–56; Weippert 1988 (Ortsregister); H. Stark et al., *ESI* 7–8 (1988–1989), 90–91; W. B. Sweeney and P. Visona, *Revue Numismatique* 33 (1991), 263–268; G. J. Wightman, *The Damascus Gate, Jerusalem* (*BAR*/IS 519), Oxford 1989; Z. Greenhut, *ESI* 9 (1989–1990), 147; id. (et al.), *Jerusalem Perspective* 4/4–5 (1991); A. Kloner and H. Stark, *ESI* 9 (1989–1990), 145; V. Sussman and H. Stark, ibid., 54–55.

THE BYZANTINE PERIOD

HISTORY

In the Byzantine period, from Constantine's reign (324 CE) onward, Jerusalem gained importance as a major religious center of the Byzantine Christian empire. The city's official name was Aelia, with the pagan adjective Capitolina omitted. Numerous historical sources describe Jerusalem in the Byzantine period, concentrating, naturally, on its churches and other sacred buildings. This voluminous literature includes various chronicles, such as that of Eusebius, relating the history of the Christian Church (*Historia Ecclesiastica*) and that of Jerome; liturgical works that describe rites and attest to the existence of many churches and holy shrines; biographies of monks such as Peter the Iberian, Euthymius, and Sabas that refer to the buildings associated with their activities in Jerusalem; and Procopius' account of the construction activities in Jerusalem in the reign of Justinian. Of particular importance are the many itineraries written by pilgrims who visited the city in that period, searching for the holy places mentioned in the Gospels—the Pilgrim of Bordeaux, Egeria, Antoninus of Placentia, and Arculf (the latter visited Jerusalem at the beginning of the Arab period).

From the historical sources it emerges that the preference of Jerusalem as a religous center led to an intensive construction of churches and other religious institutions in the city, some financed by the imperial coffers and others by private donors. That activity contributed to the Christian character of Byzantine Jerusalem as reflected by its buildings and its population. Church-building activities began in Jerusalem in the reign of the emperor Constantine, with the construction of the Church of the Holy Sepulcher inside the city and the Eleona Church on the summit of the Mount of Olives. In the Early Byzantine period, perhaps while Constantine was still reigning, a wall was built around Jerusalem.

Between 361 and 363 the emperor Julian the Apostate planned the rebuilding of the Jewish Temple on the Temple Mount. The failure of that attempt, due to a sudden outbreak of fire and the death of the emperor, was to determine the character of Jerusalem as a Christian city from that time until the beginning of the Arab period. It sealed the fate of the Temple Mount which remained desolate for the duration.

The building activity in Jerusalem increased in the fifth century, in the second half of which the city bishop was granted the status of patriarch. Among the more important churches erected at this time were the Church of Holy Zion on Mount Zion and the Church of the Ascension on the summit of the Mount of Olives. A major figure in Jerusalem in the mid-fifth century was Empress Eudocia, who invested considerable funds in the city's development and construction. A new wall was built on Mount Zion, a church was erected at the Siloam Pool, and another church, dedicated to Saint Stephen, was built north of the city.

In the fifth century, the influx of Christian pilgrims to Jerusalem gradually increased; some of them, in fact, made their home in the city. The population thus included, in addition to the permanent, native-born residents, many foreigners—Syrians, Armenians, Anatolian Greeks (Greeks from Asia Minor), and others. It was at this time that important centers of monasticism were founded in the Jerusalem vicinity, headed by monks from the Judean Desert, such as Euthymius, Theodosius, and Sabas, whose activities were a major factor in determining the city's character and religious leadership. It seems that in the Early Byzantine period Jews still were prohibited from settling in Jerusalem.

Byzantine Jerusalem reached the zenith of its splendor and greatness in the sixth century. Under the emperor Justinian, numerous building projects were undertaken, of which the best known are the "Nea" Church and the southern continuation of the Cardo. By the end of the Byzantine period, the municipal territory of Jerusalem extended beyond the city walls, taking in the suburbs to the north and west. These residential areas, which were only sparsely built up and populated, also contained churches, monasteries and convents, and burial chapels, as well as commercial and industrial buildings. The areas north of Jerusalem and on the Mount of Olives were the scene of considerable religious construction by the Armenian community. There is also evidence of a small Jewish community in Jerusalem at this time, apparently concentrated near the Temple Mount.

In 614, the Persians occupied Jerusalem, burning many churches and monasteries and slaughtering thousands of Christian laymen and leaders. The event is reported by the monk Strategius who describes thirty-five central sites and buildings in the city where the bodies were collected. Shortly thereafter, the patriarch Modestus embarked on repairs to some of the ruined churches, in particular the Church of the Holy Sepulcher.

In 628, Jerusalem was returned to Byzantine hands during the emperor Heraclius' reign, and some efforts were made to restore the city to its previous splendor. However, the attempt was doomed to failure; in 638, the city surrendered to the Muslim army—a surrender that saved it from destruction.

Christian Jerusalem slowly declined in the seventh and eighth centuries, gradually becoming a Muslim city.

JERUSALEM AS DEPICTED IN MOSAICS

How Byzantine Jerusalem looked during its Golden Age, at the end of the sixth century, is depicted in the celebrated Medeba mosaic map (see Medeba), which features a rather large (54 by 93 cm), detailed, bird's-eye view of the city as seen from west to east. In the mosaic, the shape of the city is oval and it is surrounded by a wall with some twenty towers and several gates. Jerusalem's main gate in the Byzantine period was Saint Stephen's Gate in the north (gate A). This was undoubtedly the magnificent gateway built when Hadrian founded Aelia Capitolina in the second century, the remains of which have been located beneath the foundations of the present-day Damascus Gate (see above, Roman Period). Inside the gateway was a spacious square, in the center of which stood the pillar (1) erected by Hadrian. From this square two main streets ran south, down the length of the city. The first of these, the Cardo (I), bisected the city from north to south, finally reaching a gate (B), beyond which, to the south, was the area known today as Mount Zion. The Cardo is shown in full detail on the Medeba map, its scale enlarged: it was flanked by colonnades whose roofs rest on two rows of columns. Based on the archaeological evidence, the northern half of the Cardo dates to the time of Aelia Capitolina, while the southern half was built only at the end of the Byzantine period (see below). The course of the Roman-Byzantine Cardo can still be

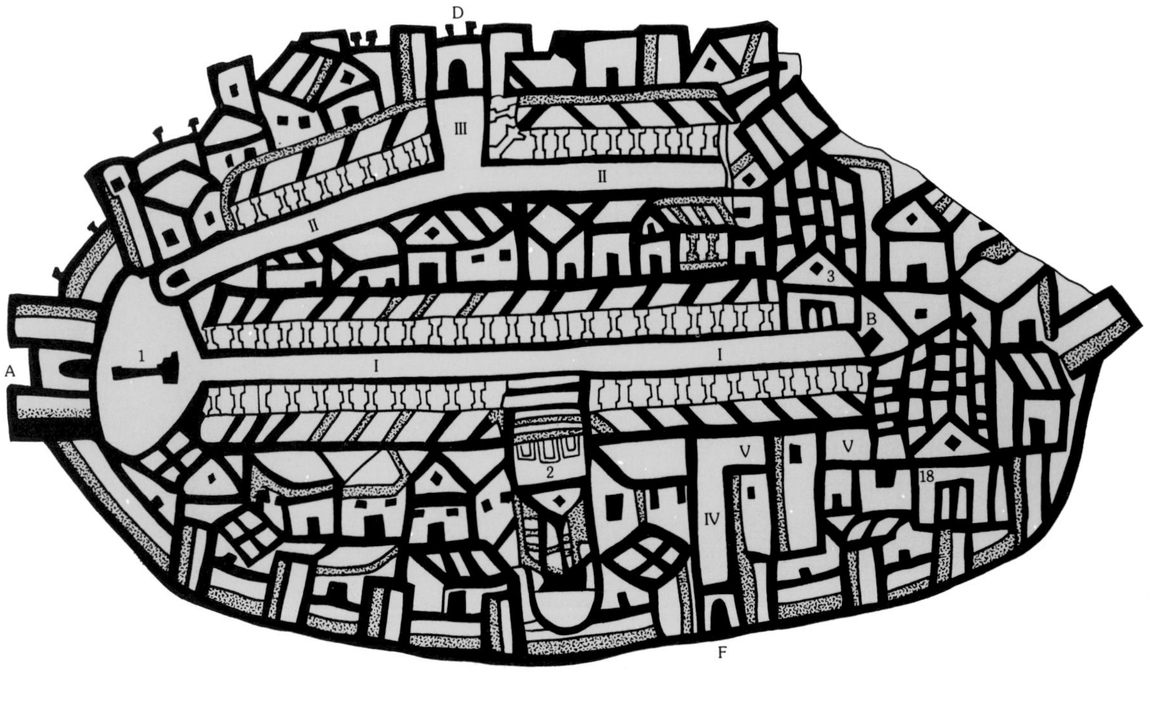

Schematic drawing of the map of Jerusalem in the mosaic floor at Medeba.

Map of Jerusalem in the Byzantine period.

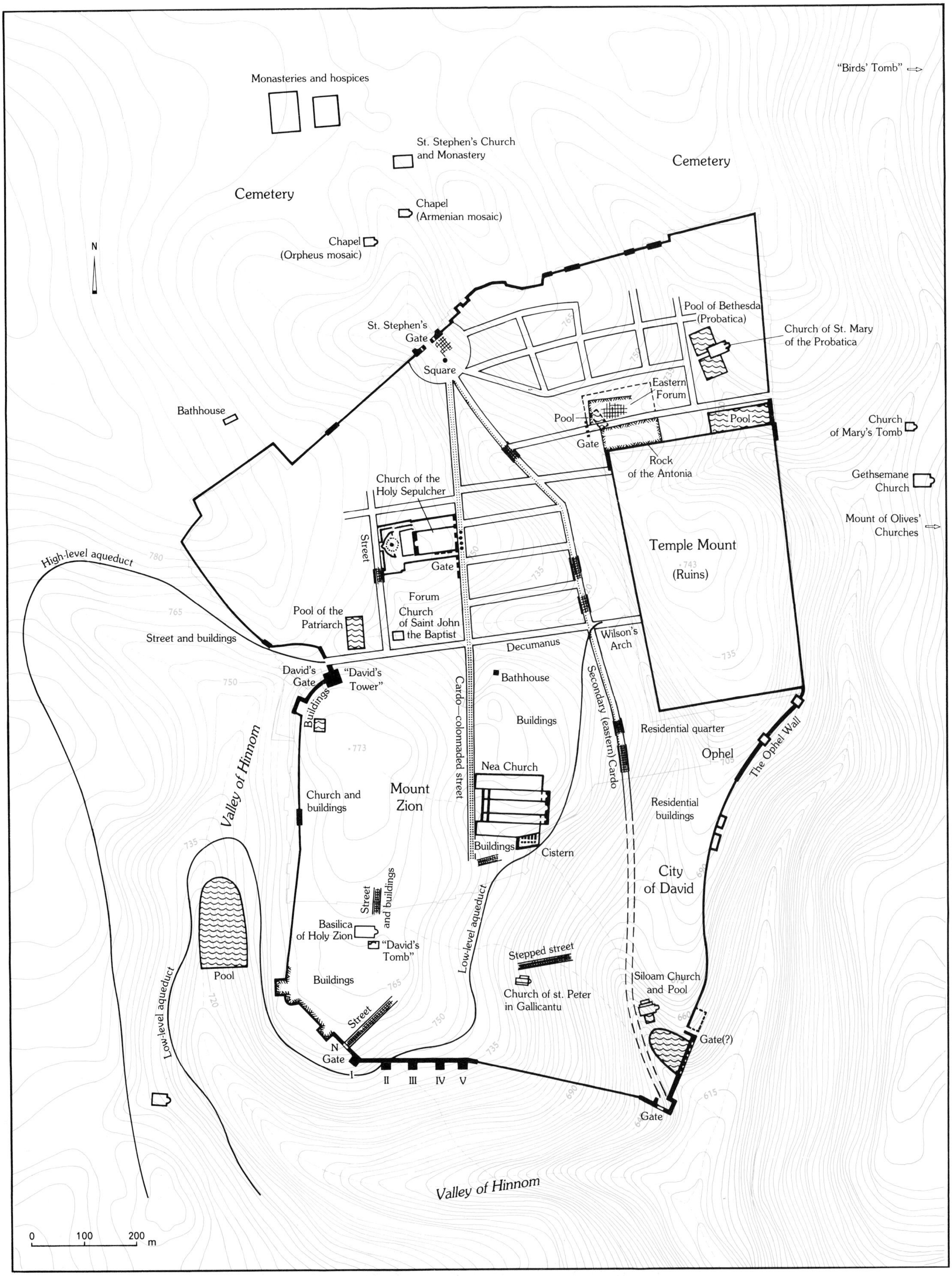

traced, along the main street that cuts down the Old City from north to south: it begins at the Damascus Gate and continues southward along Beth ha-Bad Street (Khan ez-Zeit), through the three parallel, roofed bazaars in the center of the Old City, and farther southward along the Street of the Jews and Ḥabad Street, ending in the vicinity of the present-day Zion Gate.

The Secondary (eastern) Cardo (II), which also runs south from the square just inside Damascus Gate, is shown on the Medeba map with only one colonnade. Its course runs mainly along the Tyropoeon Valley—that is, tracing the present-day course of ha-Gai Street, from the Damascus Gate in the north to the Dung Gate in the south. Another street (III) branches off street II to the east, running along the present line of the Via Dolorosa to the Gate of Benjamin (D), now known as Saint Stephen's Gate (or Lions' Gate), in the eastern city wall of the Old City. On the other side of the city, in the western city wall, the map shows David's Gate (F) at the present site of the Jaffa Gate. A street (IV) runs east from David's Gate, skirts "David's Tower," turns south as street V and continues on down the present-day Armenian Patriarchate Street, or slightly to its east, until it reaches Mount Zion. The central and most prominent buildings in the city shown alongside the Cardo are the Church of the Holy Sepulcher on the north (2) and the "Nea" Church (3), whose remains were recently identified in the southern part of the Jewish Quarter; shown on the summit of Mount Zion is the Church of Holy Zion (18), whose remains were exposed on the site of the present-day Dormition Abbey. Houses and buildings are also shown on the map, crowded within the city walls; scholars have tried to identify some of these with various churches and other buildings of Byzantine Jerusalem, in conformity with the information from the literary sources and the excavations.

According to the Medeba map, Byzantine Jerusalem's town plan and layout preserved the main municipal framework of the Roman city of Aelia Capitolina, but the many buildings added, particularly those of a religious nature, transformed the city into a Christian-Byzantine metropolis. The plan of Roman-Byzantine Jerusalem is still discernible in the map of the Old City of Jerusalem.

A record of Jerusalem in the Late Byzantine period, with an emphasis on the major Christian buildings as they were at that time, is the mosaic floor of the eighth-century Church of Saint Stephen, discovered in the 1980s at Umm er-Rasas in Jordan. In the mosaic, Jerusalem is shown from a north-to-south perspective, with the Damascus Gate in the foreground, flanked by its two towers; behind the gateway is a circular structure, its conical roof resting on three high pillars. The excavators identify this structure as the edicule over Jesus' tomb in the rotunda of the Church of the Holy Sepulcher—a familiar motif in Byzantine iconography. The building shown in the mosaic may actually be the rotunda, which towered proudly above Jerusalem's roofs. Another exceptionally high building visible behind this structure is "David's Tower"; two of Jerusalem's important churches are also visible.

EXCAVATIONS

The study of Byzantine Jerusalem was first concentrated on ancient churches, whose remains were discovered from time to time when new churches were built on the sites of earlier ones. Since the end of the nineteenth century, however, attention has also been devoted to the remains of the city's walls and to the residential areas south and north of the Old City. The extensive excavations conducted in Jerusalem since its reunification in 1967 have produced an abundance of new finds, giving scholars a more accurate picture of the city and of the general pattern of city life in the Byzantine period, including its street plan, its residential areas, and the location of its many churches and other religious buildings.

THE CITY WALL

The nature of the construction and line of Jerusalem's city wall in the Byzantine period are known from the many fortification remains excavated along its course. On the eastern side of the Ophel, south of the Temple Mount, C. Warren (1867–1870) examined a portion of a Byzantine wall (240 m long) that became known in the scholarly literature as the Ophel Wall. To the north, it adjoined the southeastern corner of the Herodian Temple Mount enclosure. From there it ran along the crest of the eastern slope of the Ophel, overlooking the Kidron Valley, in a southwesterly direction. K. Kenyon's 1967 excavations at her site SII exposed a short stretch of the inner face of the Ophel Wall, confirming its Byzantine date. Most of this inner face was exposed in the 1970s by B. Mazar in his excavations on the Ophel. The new finds indicated that the wall was built at the beginning of the Byzantine period. It was approximately 3 m wide; the two faces were built of smooth, square stones, with a core of field stones. The wall rested on a broad foundation consisting of several recessed courses. Along the wall several towers projected on both sides. Toward the end of the Byzantine period, or immediately afterward, a new wall was erected along the same line, built of coarsely hewn stones. This wall survives for some 30 m from the corner of the Temple Mount; it was built on top of or alongside the earlier wall.

South of the Ophel, the Byzantine wall apparently ran along the crest of the eastern slope of the City of David hill, overlooking the Kidron Valley, following the line of the First Wall from the Second Temple period. Part of a defensive complex consisting of a wall and two towers—excavated by R. A. S. Macalister and J. G. Duncan (Shiloh's area G)—and an additional stretch of fortification to the south—uncovered and examined by R. Weill and later by Y. Shiloh (area D)—were originally built in the Second Temple period as part of the First Wall. It is quite possible, however, that parts of this wall were still in use, in some form or another, as the eastern wall of Byzantine Jerusalem.

In area A2, on a rock scarp above the Siloam Pool, Shiloh discovered a few broad retaining walls that, he suggested, may have been part of the City of David's southern defenses in the Byzantine period (stratum 3).

The issue of the Tyropoeon Valley was closed by a wall, probably built along the ancient dam sealing Birket el-Ḥamra on the south. On the western side of the Tyropoeon, southwest of the Siloam Pool, Bliss and Dickie un-

Outer face of the Ophel Wall, Byzantine period.

The Ophel, looking east: (right) inner face of the Ophel Wall, Byzantine period; (foreground) Byzantine structure, (upper left) corner of Umayyad palace.

covered a gateway in the First Wall from the Second Temple period in which they identified two later, Byzantine phases of use. Kenyon, who reexcavated the gateway (1961–1963) in her site F, proposed that it had been used primarily in the Byzantine period. In front of the gateway, Bliss and Dickie investigated a massive structure, perhaps the remains of an outer tower protecting the gate; in Kenyon's opinion this tower was probably built in the Byzantine period.

Along the southern slope of Mount Zion, Bliss and Dickie (1894–1897) examined a few sections of a Byzantine wall, for a length of a few hundred meters, that included five towers and a gateway. The Byzantine city wall here ran along the line of the Second Temple period First Wall, sometimes actually founded directly upon it and sometimes separated from it by a layer of earth. It was built mainly of smoothed, square stones, as well as stones in secondary use.

At the eastern end of the Byzantine wall examined by Bliss and Dickie, stood tower V, a 10-m-long tower projecting 4.8 m from the wall. From this point, the wall ran west for 21 m to tower IV, 7.8 m long and projecting 3 m from the wall. From tower IV, the wall traversed a distance of 36 m to tower III, 9 m long and projecting 3 m from the wall. The wall then continued to the west for another 36 m to tower II, whose size was the same as tower III, and then for another 36 m to the corner tower (I). Tower I showed two phases of construction; the upper phase was a Byzantine addition to an earlier, Second Temple period phase. From tower I the wall ran 45 m, in a northwesterly direction, to reach the Second Temple period tower ABC. In this part of the wall was gate N, which was 2.4 m wide on the outside and 2.9 m wide on the inside. Bliss and Dickie reported that they could discern four stone thresholds in the gate, that had been superimposed one on another in the Byzantine period, at the end of which the gateway was blocked with masonry. Beneath the gate ran a drain, which continued beneath the paved street ascending northeastward from the gate. Between 1979 and 1986, the gate complex and the nearby remains were reexamined by B. Pixner, D. Chen, and S. Margalit; they dated the gate's original construction to the Second Temple period, above which were two phases of use in the Byzantine period.

A short segment of the inner face of Jerusalem's western city wall at the end of the Byzantine period was exposed by A. D. Tushingham (1962–1967) under the auspices of the Kenyon expedition, in site L, in the southern part of the Armenian Garden, south of the Citadel ("David's Tower"). A parallel segment, built of smoothly dressed square stones, of the outer face of the Byzantine wall was found by M. Broshi (1973–1976) beneath the foundations of the Old City wall. This wall is a local repair of the Second Temple period First Wall, dating to the Byzantine period.

R. Sivan and G. Solar (1981–1984) exposed a 13-m length of wall in the southern fosse of the Citadel and underneath the Kishleh building to its south. It was built of coarsely hewn stones and dated to the end of the Byzantine period.

In the Citadel courtyard, H. Geva (1976–1980) continued the excavation, begun by C. N. Johns, of the southern tower in the First Wall. The new finds indicate that the tower was reused at the beginning of the Byzantine period, when a new wall was being built along its western side and bonded to the surviving walls of the Second Temple tower.

Johns (1934–1947) uncovered the western side of a length of wall that ran north from the Herodian tower (the traditional "David's Tower") in the northeastern part of the Citadel. This wall was built of smoothly dressed square stones on a broad, stepped base; in Johns's opinion it was built at the end of the third and the beginning of the fourth centuries. Geva, who reexamined the stratigraphy here, proposed a later date: the beginning of the Byzantine period. The clearing of the wall was completed by Sivan and Solar, who were able to identify its inner, eastern face beneath the foundations of the Citadel's late (medieval) walls. The continuation of the city wall north of the Citadel has been identified in a wall discovered at the end of the nineteenth century (see above, Second Temple Period). In 1983, H. Goldfuss excavated a stretch of the city's medieval western wall in front of the Jaffa Gate. He suggested that some of the lower courses might be dated to the Byzantine period.

Several sections of Byzantine Jerusalem's northern city wall were discovered in the 1920s by Sukenik and Mayer and later, in 1937–1938, by Hamilton, beneath the foundations of the Old City's northern wall. Adjoining the Damascus Gate to the west, Hamilton exposed a short section of the outer face of the ancient wall, preserved to a considerable height—more than ten courses—and built of smoothly dressed square stones, like the other known sections of the Byzantine city wall. The wall courses postdate the construction of the Roman gate (except for the two lowest courses, which Hamilton dated to the time of the gate's construction in Hadrian's reign; see above, Roman Period). The finds in the earth fills cleared in front of the wall implied, to Hamilton, that it had been erected at the end of the third century or the beginning of the fourth. In area B, east of the Damascus Gate, Hamilton uncovered ten courses of an ancient wall under the present-day Old City wall. The lowest courses date to the third and fourth centuries; the overlying ones had been built during late repairs to the wall in the sixth and seventh centuries. In area C, west of Herod's Gate, Hamilton uncovered a stretch of fortification wall similar in construction and date to the others.

In 1976, A. Kloner reexamined the line of the ancient wall east of Herod's Gate. In 1979, west of the Damascus Gate, D. Tarler, A. De Groot, and Solar examined a section of an earlier city wall. Here, again, the foundations of the Old City wall were found to include portions of the Byzantine city wall, preserved to a height of several courses.

Construction and Date of the Wall. The finds point to certain characteristic architectural features common to all, or most, parts of the Byzantine city wall that have been excavated to date. The wall was built for the most part of smoothly dressed, square stones; more elongated stones, with two projecting bosses and margins around and between them, are also found occasionally. There was considerable secondary use of stones with dressed margins, taken from Second Temple period ruined buildings and fortifications. The stones were laid along both faces of the wall, with the space in between filled with stones and mortar. The joints between the stones in the walls' face were sometimes filled with plaster. The wall is only about 3 m thick—less than the thickness of Jerusalem's earlier walls. In some locations the wall rested on a broader foundation, consisting of several stepped courses. Foundations of this sort were intended to create a solid base for the wall where it was not built on bedrock or on the remains of earlier masonry. Towers of similar sizes were found in the southern part of Mount Zion, some spaced at regular intervals along the wall. It is interesting that, in the Byzantine period, the southern gates in the First Wall, from Second Temple times, and in the northern (Damascus) gate, originally built at the time of Aelia Capitolina, continued in use, with renovations—although the side entrances of the latter were probably sealed.

The wall of Byzantine Jerusalem on the eastern Ophel was apparently built slightly west of the Second Temple period First Wall. Just how it continued to the south along the eastern slope of the City of David hill is not clear. South and west of Mount Zion, the Byzantine wall adhered to the line of the First Wall, sometimes being built on the latter's ruins and sometimes incorporating its remains. Along the northern part of the city, the new wall encircled the built-up area of Jerusalem as it had been when Aelia Capitolina was established in the second century (the line of the present-day Damascus Gate).

Judging from the archaeological evidence, the Byzantine wall of Jerusalem can be dated as a whole to the late third or early fourth century (end of the Roman period to the beginning of the Byzantine). The refortification of Jerusalem at this time may be related to the evacuation of the Tenth Legion from its camp in the southern part of the city, at the end of the third century (probably in Diocletian's reign), which left the city largely undefended. It was, however, mainly motivated by Jerusalem's growing religious significance since the time of Constantine, in the early fourth century. It would seem, therefore, that Jerusalem, the unwalled Roman colony of Aelia Capitolina, was surrounded by a wall at the very beginning of the Byzantine period, perhaps already under Constantine the Great.

Bliss and Dickie, relying on the historical sources, identified the wall they discovered on the southern part of Mount Zion as the wall built by Empress Eudocia in the mid-fifth century to enclose Mount Zion. However, the archaeological evidence offers no definite proof either of this identification or of its implications for the previous line of the city wall in the south. The detailed construction of the Mount Zion wall exactly resembles that of the other known sections of the Byzantine wall—such as the Ophel Wall and the sections discovered in the Citadel and near the Damascus Gate—which have been confidently dated to the end of the Roman and beginning of the Byzantine periods. It is therefore a reasonable assumption that the city wall south of Mount Zion should also be associated with the fortification of Jerusalem at the beginning of the Byzantine period. This conclusion is reinforced by the lack of any fortified remains predating the tenth century in the present-day southern wall of the Old City.

At the end of the Byzantine period, some sections of the city wall were repaired. Large, coarsely hewn stones were characteristically used, such as those found on the eastern Ophel, in the fosse of the Citadel, and perhaps also in the northern part of the city. Some scholars, however, prefer a later date for these repair operations—the Early Arab period.

CITY OF DAVID AND THE SOUTHERN TYROPOEON VALLEY

Between 1923 and 1925, Macalister and Duncan exposed the remains of private houses from the Byzantine period in the central, northern part of the City of David. The main find in the earliest stratum from this period is a building, alongside a street, consisting of a central courtyard surrounded by four rooms. The excavators called it the House of Eusebius, as this name was found stamped on a fragment of a convex tile used as part of a drainage pipe beneath the building. The rooms were paved with mosaics laid in geometrical patterns, and the walls were coated with light-colored plaster. Beneath one of the rooms was a cistern with fish painted on its wall plaster. The excavators mistakenly ascribed the house to the Roman period, but Avi-Yonah, on the basis of the style of construction and the mosaics, assigned it to the Byzantine period.

In the stratum overlying the House of Eusebius, the excavators found fragmentary remains of private houses with mosaics and cisterns they ascribed to the Byzantine period. Particularly noteworthy was part of a relatively complete house with three rooms—one paved with mosaic, the other two with stone. Also found in this stratum were sections of two streets. These remains should probably be assigned to the end of the Byzantine period.

Crowfoot and Fitzgerald (1925–1927), excavating at the northwestern end of the City of David spur, found numerous remains of buildings in the two Byzantine strata. Most were found west of the ancient gate of the City of David—the Valley Gate. To the early Byzantine stratum here (up to the mid-sixth century) the excavators attributed a few sections of masonry, representing several different building phases. Among them were a particularly large cistern, partly rock-cut and partly built with stone, and the remains of a building with a long room and two adjoining smaller rooms in which the walls were coated with light-colored plaster. The ceilings of these rooms rested on central arches that sprang from engaged pillars in the walls.

The private houses in the later stratum presented excellent workmanship and were well preserved. They stood on either side of a street (c. 5 m wide) that descended gradually from north to south. The street, paved with large stones, was preserved for 20 m; its continuation could be traced for an additional 40 m, thanks to the main drainage channel running beneath it. Drains from the buildings flanking the street flowed into the main channel. Fifteen rooms were cleared in these buildings, some of whose walls were preserved to a height of about 3 m. The rooms opened onto the street; some were paved with mosaics and were found to contain various plastered stone installations, indicating that they had been roadside shops. A room in a house on the eastern side of the street contained a collection of bronze and glass vessels. As the name Anastasius was incised on one of the bowls, the excavators named the building the House of Anastasius. They dated the buildings in this stratum to the second half of the sixth century. The buildings were damaged in the Persian invasion of 614 but later reoccupied. According to J. Magness, analysis of the finds from the buildings proves that they continued to be used without interruption well into the Early Arab period.

In 1928, Crowfoot dug to the south of the main excavation area, whose finds have just been described. He exposed another section of the paved street and fragmentary remains of buildings that had stood along it at the end of the Byzantine period. Some of the rooms were hewn in the rock and had mosaic floors, fragments of which were preserved. Found in the center of one mosaic floor was a seven-line Greek inscription in a circular frame.

Remains of Byzantine buildings were also exposed by Kenyon (1961–1967) in the City of David—in her sites M, N, and R. In 1983, Shiloh, working in his area K in the southern part of the City of David, uncovered a building constructed in the fourth century (stratum 3), in which four consecutive building phases from the Byzantine period were discernible. The facade of the building, which included a doorway and a window, and the forecourt were hewn in the rock.

The various finds in the area provide evidence of vigorous and intense construction activities in the Byzantine period, mainly in the northern part of the City of David and in the Tyropoeon Valley, farther to the west. The buildings unearthed in these areas are the remains of Jerusalem's crowded residential neighborhoods at the end of the period and resemble those discovered in B. Mazar's excavations on the Ophel.

THE CHURCH OF SILOAM. Bliss and Dickie (1894–1897) exposed the remains of the Church of Siloam, which was probably built in the mid-fifth century by Empress Eudocia. It was built north of the Siloam Pool and was well preserved—some of its parts to a height of more than 2.5 m. Because of the difficult topographical conditions and the need to accommodate the pool, the plan of the church was unique: the entrance was in the north, leading down to the church proper through an atrium, a stepped narthex, and vaults sup-

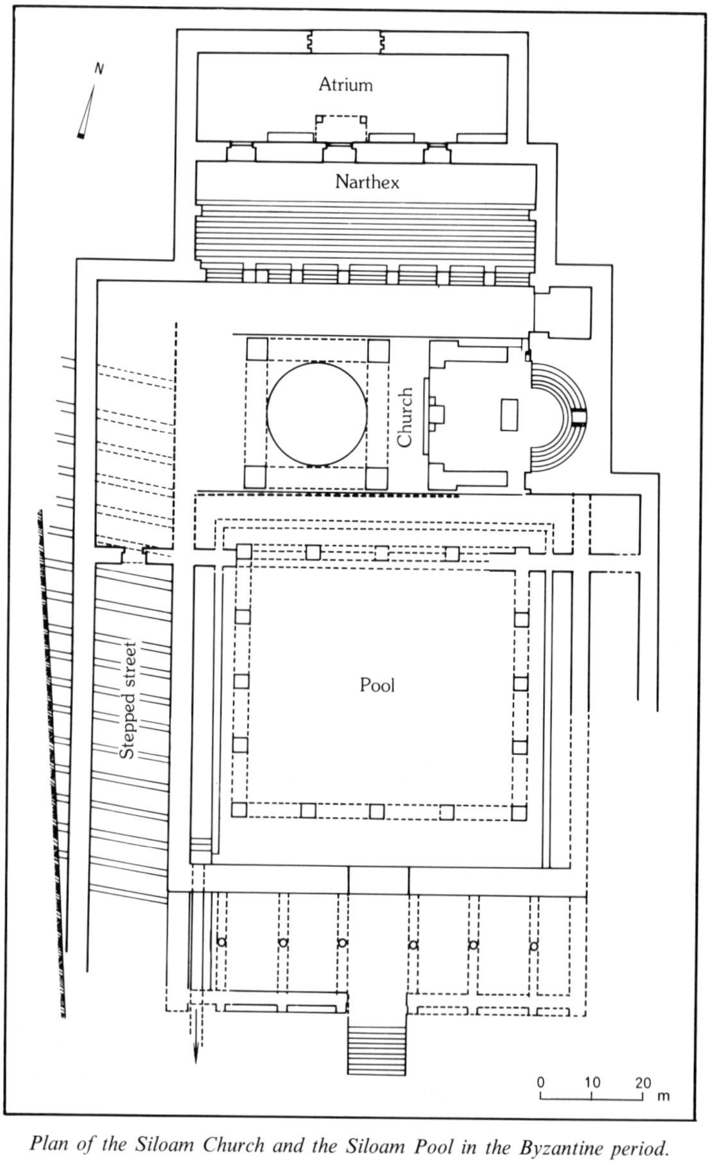

Plan of the Siloam Church and the Siloam Pool in the Byzantine period.

ported by a row of square piers. The church (16 by 28 m) had two building phases. It was divided into a nave and two aisles by four square piers. The aisles were paved with mosaics featuring patterns typical in the Byzantine period. The southern aisle opened onto the Siloam Pool through a kind of open portico. As reconstructed, the center of the nave was roofed by a dome and paved with mosaics. It ended in the east in an apse lined with benches paved with marble tiles in geometric patterns; the position of the altar was still visible. At the northern end of the apse, near the opening in the wall separating it from the northern aisle, a rectangular depression in the floor was lined with well-dressed stone slabs; the excavators interpreted it as a reliquary.

THE OPHEL AND THE REMAINS NEAR THE SOUTHWESTERN CORNER OF THE TEMPLE MOUNT

B. Mazar's excavations (1968–1978) on the Ophel and around the southwestern corner of the Temple Mount uncovered an impressive level of occupation from the Byzantine period, comprising several building phases. At the beginning of the period, in the fourth and fifth centuries, a residential neighborhood—including a few buildings scattered around the area without a master plan—was built on the Ophel. The buildings were of the peristyle type, the typical plan being an open courtyard with rooms arranged around it in two stories. The walls were built of smoothed stones, sometimes plastered and decorated with frescoes and stuccowork. The roofs were presumably made of wooden beams resting on stone arches set in the middle of the rooms. The floors were either beaten earth or paved with stone slabs. Beneath the buildings were cisterns for storing water. Building 7066, originally constructed in the Roman period near the southwestern corner of the Temple Mount, continued in use into the Early Byzantine period, with some additions and alterations. The building was partly destroyed by fire; judging from the numismatic finds, the fire probably occurred when Jews came to live in Jerusalem, near the Temple Mount, under Julian the Apostate, in 361–363. A similar date may be assigned to an inscription incised on one of the stones of the western wall on the Temple Mount, under Robinson's Arch, featuring the biblical verse: "You shall see, and your heart shall rejoice; your bones [shall flourish] like the grass . . ." (Is. 66:14).

A denser occupational level, from the end of the Byzantine period (sixth century), was found in the excavations on the Ophel, mainly where the remains had been damaged less seriously by construction in the Umayyad period. In fact, the municipal planning of the area at the end of the Byzantine period can be traced. Remains of numerous private houses, some completely preserved, were found here. Their plan is more or less uniform: several rooms arranged around a central courtyard, into which the doors and windows of the rooms open. Similar buildings were found in early excavations in the northern part of the City of David (see above). The buildings were two stories high, with rock-cut cellars that were used for storage and as workshops. Preserved on the walls of one cellar with one or two niches on its eastern side were the remains of colorful paintings. The central courtyard of the ground floor communicated via a broad flight of stone-built stairs with the building's upper story. Both faces of the walls were coated with a thick layer of waterproof plaster. The floors were paved with stone and mosaics; almost every house contained some rooms with coarse mosaic floors, some laid in simple geometric and floral patterns, some with Greek inscriptions quoting from the Bible. The ceilings were made of wooden beams supported on a central stone arch—one of the most typical features of houses on the Ophel and in the northern part of the City of David in the Byzantine period. Some of the roofs were tiled; some tiles

The Ophel: Byzantine dwelling.

*Hebrew inscription of verse from Isaiah (66:14) on a stone in the western wall of the Temple Mount, next to Robinson's Arch: **(below)** facsimile; **(above)** photograph.*

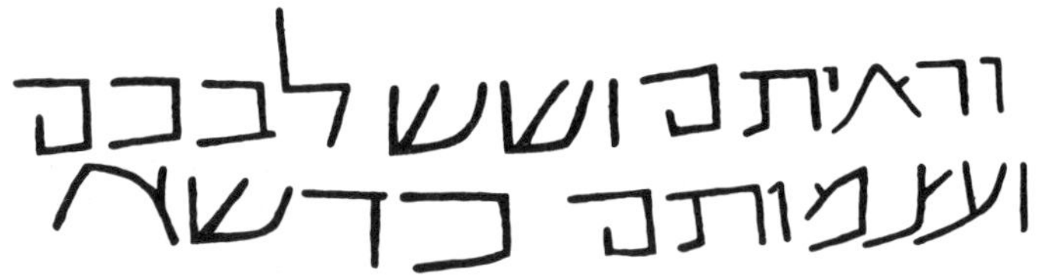

were inscribed with the names of about ten different manufacturers, most of them probably from outside Palestine. Marble was a commonly used material, as indicated by the numerous fragments found. A complicated system of clay pipes collected rainwater from the roofs and courtyards, feeding it into central cisterns hewn underneath the buildings. The remains of various industrial installations were found both in the courtyards and in the surrounding rooms: dyeing and tanning installations, as well as smelting furnaces. Some houses contained the remains of cooking stoves and other kitchen installations. The remains of a lavatory were found in the concealed back courtyard of one house. Some of the buildings showed signs of alterations carried out at various times in the Byzantine period. Various objects typical of the period were found: a variety of pottery, small artifacts, and thousands of coins, mainly from the end of the Byzantine period. A most impressive and finely constructed building from the period was found south of the Triple Gate in the southern wall of the Temple Mount. Both stories above the basement were well preserved, consisting of several rooms. The central courtyard on the ground floor was partly covered by a roof resting on stone pillars, each on a carved, elevated base. The excavators assigned this building to the time of Empress Eudocia, in the mid-fifth century, and interpreted it as a hospice or monastery. The structure showed signs of three phases of occupation; in the latest phase the southern wing was split off when the communicating doors were blocked with masonry.

The remains of part of a bathhouse, probably originating in the Byzantine period (or at the beginning of the Early Arab period), were discovered northwest of Robinson's Arch. Of the original spacious building, the excavators exposed some of the brick-built hypocaust columns that had supported the floor, a small pool in the south of the building, a small room with part of its original ceiling intact, and a pool to the north. An interesting discovery was the secondary use of bricks with the stamp of the Tenth Roman Legion.

Some of the buildings on the Ophel were apparently destroyed during the Persian invasion of 614 and never rebuilt.

On the floor of a building near the southwestern corner of the Temple Mount, a stone lintel, covered with white plaster was found. Painted on the lintel were a seven-branched candelabrum (menorah), an incense shovel, a lulab, and, perhaps, a shofar and an ethrog—the characteristic symbols in Jewish iconography in the Byzantine period. The plaster obscured a cross previously engraved on the lintel. Other drawings of menorahs were found on walls in this building. A notch to hold a mezuzah was found on a doorjamb. Engraved menorahs were found in the large building south of the Triple Gate as well. These finds suggest that Jews settled temporarily in the Byzantine Christian houses near the Temple Mount, after the Persian invasion in 614 or perhaps after the Arab occupation in 638.

Toward the end of the Byzantine period, an intricate irrigation system—a central pool and channels—was constructed south of the southwestern corner of the Temple Mount. This agricultural area was bounded on the south by a thick wall, running parallel to the southern wall of the Temple Mount at a distance of approximately 70 m.

Some of the Byzantine structures on the Ophel continued to be used alongside the Umayyad palaces built there in the seventh and eighth centuries (see below, The Early Arab and Crusader Periods). All of them were ruined in the earthquake that destroyed Jerusalem in 747 (or 749, according to a different view). In the large building south of the Triple Gate, which was probably also destroyed then, a group of vessels was found that include a bronze cross (35 by 60 cm), bronze suspension lamps, the remains of metal hoops for wooden chests, and a knocker in the shape of a ring with a flat, cross-shaped clasp to attach it to the door. These objects were presumably the property of a Jerusalem church and had been brought to this building for safekeeping.

A great number of architectural elements was found incorporated in the masonry of the Umayyad palaces: columns—some inscribed with crosses, engraved, or in relief—and fragments of a decorated stone lintel. These elements undoubtedly came from the city's ruined Byzantine churches.

THE SOUTHWESTERN HILL

The numerous excavations since the mid-nineteenth century, and in particular the recent ones, have uncovered the remains of a dense and multifaceted Byzantine level of occupation on Jerusalem's southwestern hill. Particularly noteworthy are the remains of churches—chief among them the Nea—and sections of streets, including the Cardo, the main thoroughfare of Byzantine Jerusalem. As a result of the quantity and quality of the remains, an accurate picture of the "Mount Zion Quarter" of Byzantine Jerusalem can be reconstructed.

Judging from the finds, civilian settlement and building on the southwestern hill in the Byzantine period began after the Tenth Roman Legion vacated its camp there at the close of the third century. The main development of the area, however, came later, particularly in the sixth century. The unplanned, haphazard development of the Mount Zion Quarter in the Byzantine period is faithfully reflected on the modern map of the southern section of the Old City, which shows no signs of a master plan.

The most important finds from the Byzantine period on the southwestern hill emerged from Avigad's excavations in the Jewish Quarter (1969–1982). The many excavated areas, scattered all over the quarter, produced the remains of a level of occupation from this period, sometimes comprising more than one building phase. Most of the remains were fragmented, owing to intensive construction in the area in later periods. Among the more complete remains, in addition to the Cardo and the Nea Church, was a long wall running north–south, built of ashlar blocks, with a gateway, found on Ararat Street, on the border of the Jewish and Armenian quarters (area R). A public bathhouse from the end of the Byzantine period, heated by a brick-built hypocaust and containing a bathtub lined with marble slabs, was discovered in the northern part of the Jewish Quarter (area C). Among the finds in other areas were sections of massive walls, as well as mosaic floors typical of the period. All these provide evidence of a densely populated residential neighborhood in this part of Byzantine Jerusalem. The construction reached its

The Ophel: inscription in a mosaic floor, "Happy are those who dwell in this house," Byzantine period.

Jewish Quarter: reconstruction of the southern part of the Byzantine Cardo.

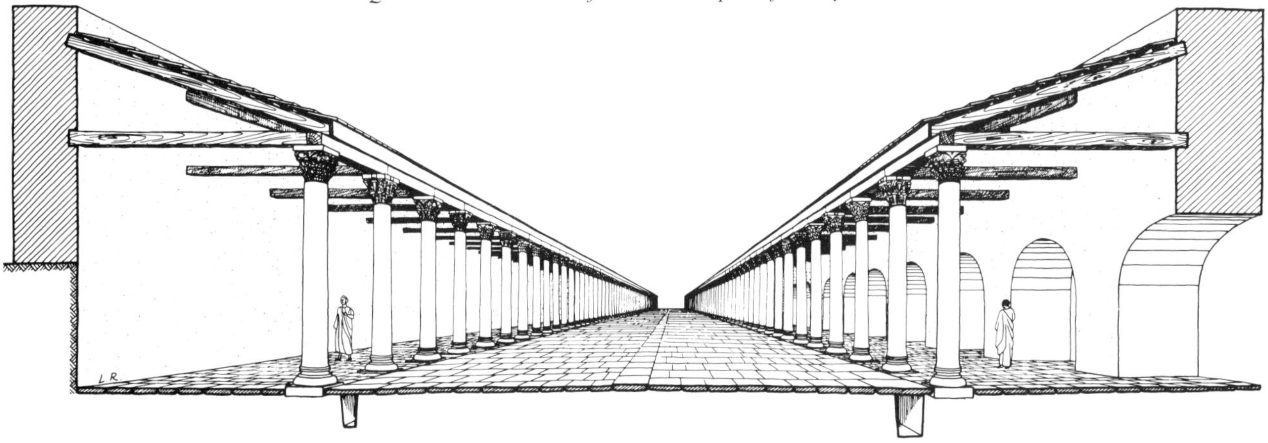

zenith with the monumental projects of the Cardo and the Nea Church during the sixth century.

THE CARDO. Between 1976 and 1981, Avigad exposed the remains of the Byzantine Cardo in area X. The remains lay along the course of the present-day Street of the Jews and Ḥabad Street, which bisect the Jewish Quarter from north to south. This plan and the location of the street confirm the Medeba map's representation of the Cardo. The Cardo's exposed sections total a length of some 200 m. The southern part of the Cardo was made by quarrying the bedrock, which left a scarp some 6 m high west of the street; the paving stones were then laid directly on the leveled rock. The northern part of the Cardo, however, was laid on earth fills, heaped to several meters. This covered the remains of the First Wall from the First and Second Temple periods (area X-2). The excavators unearthed broad sections of the street, which consisted of large, well-hewn paving stones, laid in parallel rows at right angles to the direction of the street. The stones laid along the middle of the street formed a raised ridge, from which the street sloped down on either side. The paving stones were well worn and in fact were split and cracked with age. The street's western border was a stone wall that survived in one place almost to its original height. It was built of large ashlars, with piers projecting into the street. Along the eastern side of the street ran an arcade of arches, built of large stones, supported on ashlar-built piers. Some of the original arches survived and were incorporated into later construction; the main survivals from this arcade, however, were the piers that supported the arches. The street (22.5 m wide) was divided by two rows of columns into a broad, unroofed central street with a covered passageway (stoa) on either side. The roofs of the stoas, which have not survived, were probably made of wooden beams covered with tiles: the roofs probably sloped toward the center of the street. The niches that originally accommodated the horizontal roof beams were found high up in the wall along the western side of the street.

The stylobates supporting the two rows of columns were built of large, smoothly dressed stones, in which square, cut depressions held the column bases. In the south, where the street was quarried out of the rock, the bases rested on a rock-cut ledge. Alongside the stylobates, on the side facing the street's center, deep drains, covered with paving stones, drained rainwater to the north. Except for two bases, the other column parts (bases, fragments of monolithic columns, and capitals) were not found in situ but in secondary use in later buildings or scattered about. The bases, which were carved in a degenerate Attic profile, were not uniform in size; some bore Greek letters—masons' marks. The shafts and bases were made of hard limestone; the capitals were carved from softer limestone, in the Corinthian style typical of the Byzantine period. The columns rose to a total height of some 5 m. Along the western side of the Cardo's southern part, several roadside shops were cut in the rock scarp. The thresholds and doorposts of these shops were rock-cut or stone-built. Some of the shops had wooden roofs, as attested by the niches visible in the rock face; others were covered by high vaults, one of which is preserved intact. Some large, profiled stones found scattered along the main axis of the Cardo testify to the style of the other architectural elements that once adorned the street.

The part of the Cardo exposed in the Jewish Quarter was built in the reign of Justinian (527–565). The evidence for this dating is stratigraphic and ceramic, in addition to points of architectural style and the design of the architectural elements, and the postulated connection between its construction and that of the Nea Church. It was built as a continuation of the northern part of the Cardo, which had been built in the Roman period but traversed only the northern part of Aelia Capitolina, from the Damascus Gate in the north to the Tenth Legion's camp on the southwestern hill in the south (up to the line of the present-day David Street and the Street of the Chain). Justinian's intention in extending the Cardo was to create a single, central thoroughfare linking Jerusalem's two principal churches—the Church of the Holy Sepulcher in the north and the Nea, which he himself built, in the city's southern sector. It was a magnificent street: its southern section adhered to the plan of the northern, Roman section but in the Byzantine style (clumsily executed architectural details). Topographical conditions forced the course of the southern Cardo to deviate slightly to the west, relative to the line of the northern, Roman Cardo.

Toward the end of the Byzantine period, or at the beginning of the Early Arab period, some sections of the Cardo's western colonnade (and probably also of the eastern colonnade) were replaced by square piers that supported vaults in place of the covered colonnades. Square capitals with receding, stepped profiles topped the piers. The arch visible in the stone wall at the

Restored southern part of the Byzantine Cardo.

Jewish Quarter: remains of the Byzantine Cardo at the time of excavation, looking west.

Plan of the Byzantine, Crusader, and Arab remains in the southern part of the Jewish Quarter.

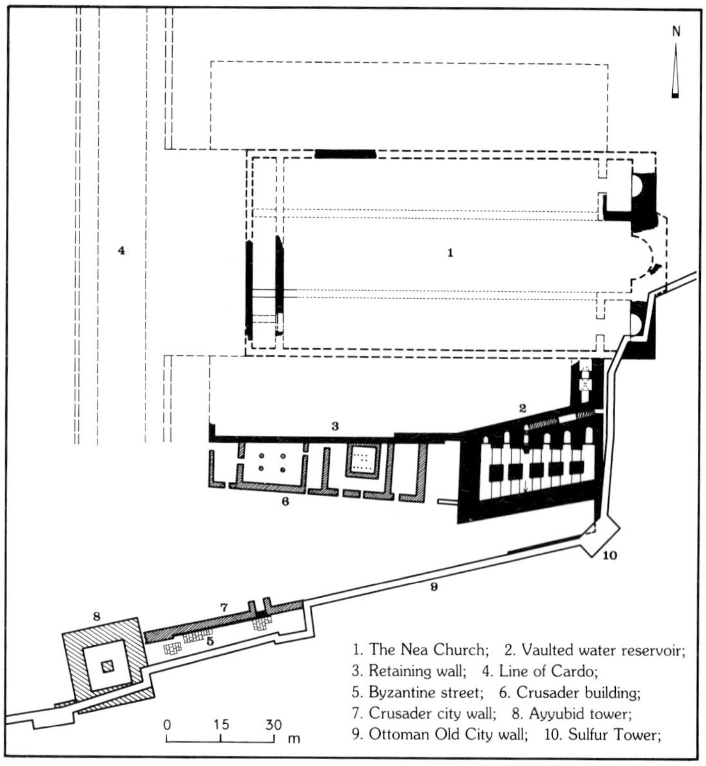

northern end of Ḥabad Street, where it meets Saint Mark's Street, once identified as the Second Temple period Gennath Gate, should be attributed to this period.

Following Avigad's excavations, the remains of the Cardo were restored and reconstructed. They now form an integral part of the new passage cut between the Street of the Jews and Ḥabad Street in the Jewish Quarter.

THE NEA CHURCH. The remains of the "Nea" Church complex were uncovered by Avigad (area T) in several seasons of excavations from 1970 to 1982. They were found in the southern part of the Jewish Quarter, exactly where the Medeba map shows a structure that scholars had long identified as the Nea. The Nea Church was built by Justinian and dedicated in 543. Damaged either in the Persian invasion of Palestine in 614 or the Arab invasion in 638, it was finally destroyed in the ninth century. The church, whose full name was New Church of Mary, Mother of God, was described in detail by the contemporary historian Procopius.

A section of a wall identified as belonging to the Nea Church (although no proof was available at the time) was exposed in 1862, when foundations were being dug for the Batei Maḥasseh complex at the southern edge of the Jewish Quarter.

The entrance to the Nea lay in the west, off the Cardo (area T-1). Part of the monolithic threshold of one of the main entrances is extant; it is founded on a solid wall that was part of the podium on which the building stood. To the east of this wall was a section of a marble-paved floor. A few sections of the eastern wall of the church were exposed in Avigad's excavations. The northernmost of these sections (13 m long and 6.5 m thick), in area D, was founded on bedrock 8 m below the surface; it was built of large stones with mortar. An inscribed apse in this wall (diameter, 5 m) was identified as the northern of the three apses presumably built in the church's eastern wall. The southeastern corner of the church was exposed in 1975 by Ben-Dov beneath the southern wall of the Old City. Its outer face was built of large stones, resembling those in the northern section (containing the apse), 35 m away. Near the corner, but inside the Old City wall, the church's southern apse was discovered in 1982; it was identical in size and construction to the northern apse. The church's southern retaining wall was exposed on the slope below the Batei Maḥasseh

Jewish Quarter: eastern wall of the Nea Church and its northern apse.

Jewish Quarter: Justinian inscription in the vaulted reservoir.

complex, some 40 m north of the Old City wall (area T-2). A 66-m-long section of the wall was exposed; it was found to consist of a row of vaulted openings, spanned by arches to relieve the pressure. The wall was preserved to a height of 7.5 m, primarily because it had been incorporated in a Crusader building built against it to the south.

The massive walls of the Nea Church were intended to support the earth fills deposited between them in order to raise and enlarge the area of the church and the complex of ancillary buildings, some of which were built on the steep southern slope of the hill. The remains that have come to light indicate that the Nea Church occupied an area east of the southern end of the Cardo. Avigad conjectured that the church was built on the plan of a basilica with a narthex in the west, toward the Cardo, and three inscribed apses in the eastern wall (although the central, as yet undiscovered, apse may have projected to the east). The estimated measurements of the church were 115 by 57 m, and the roof was probably supported on four rows of columns.

On the slope to the south of the church, Avigad unearthed a huge, impressively well-preserved underground vaulted structure (area T-7). The interior had been explored in the mid-nineteenth century by T. Lewin and J. T. Barclay, and Warren in fact published its plan. Judging from their report, the building was still intact. Its interior (9.5–17 by 33 m) was divided into six parts, roofed by a series of vaults supported by arches resting on rectangular piers (5 by 3.5 m and c. 10 high). Only the two easternmost vaults have completely survived; in the western part of the structure, they were in ruins, and the building's interior was found filled with earth. The walls, piers, and some of the vaults were built mostly of field stones with mortar. The floor was cut into the rock. The building's interior was coated with a thick layer of hard plaster. Two rows of deep niches were built in the northern wall. Beyond it, to the north, a stepped corridor descends to the west, parallel to the structure, and then turns south and enters the interior of the structure, opposite the third vault from the west. High on the southern wall, opposite the entrance from the corridor, a Greek inscription was found in a molded, red-painted plaster relief inside a *tabula ansata* above a large cross, also in relief. The inscription commemorates the building of the structure and explicitly mentions the builder—Emperor Justinian—and the year of its dedication—probably 549/550, according to the excavator's translation. It reads: "And this is the work which our most pious emperor Flavius Justinianus carried out with magnificence, under the care and devotion of the most holy Constantinus, priest and hegumen, in the thirteenth [year of the] indiction."

Jewish Quarter: interior of the vaulted reservoir adjacent to the Nea Church.

The huge structure, which was used as a water reservoir, was also meant to act as a raised podium for the southern wing of the Nea complex. Overlying the vaults, part of a courtyard was paved with well-dressed stones. Found standing to a considerable height, in situ, in the northeastern corner, were a few white-plastered walls of the building that adjoined the church to the south. A long wall, aligned east–west, was found in the center of the structure, with other walls built at right angles and spaces open to a courtyard in the south. The walls and the northern, upper part of the vaulted structure were built of alternating courses of stones and flat bricks, a technique that is not common in Byzantine construction in this part of the Byzantine Empire.

The method of construction of the Nea Church, its size, and the complex of vaults to its south conform well with Procopius' detailed account of Justinian's construction of this church (*Building* V, 6).

South of the Nea complex, parallel to the inner face of the Old City wall, Avigad uncovered the remains of a stepped road descending eastward from the southern end of the Cardo toward the Tyropoeon Valley and the City of David.

THE CITADEL AND THE ARMENIAN GARDEN. The many years of excavation in the southwestern part of the Old City, the area now occupied by the Citadel ("David's Tower") and the Armenian Garden to its south, have produced important evidence of settlement in the Byzantine period. Johns (1934–1947), excavating in the Citadel courtyard, cleared parts of buildings and white mosaic floors from the end of the Byzantine period. The remains were found along the inner face of the Second Temple period wall that traverses the middle of the courtyard. A noteworthy find was a fragment of a lintel bearing the remains of a Greek inscription flanking a cross.

Amiran and Eitan continued to excavate buildings from the Roman-Byzantine stratum in the Citadel in 1968–1969. To stratum I (Byzantine period) were assigned some segments of walls and water installations cleared by Johns's expedition; the excavators suggested that they may belong to different building phases.

Geva, excavating the southern part of the Citadel courtyard in 1979–1980, exposed remains of various buildings, mainly from the end of the Byzantine period. Among them were small rooms, paved with white mosaics, built up against the inner side of the southern tower in the part of the city wall that was renovated at the time. In the southeastern part of the courtyard, the excavator found a large room, also paved with mosaics; its ceiling was supported on a central arch, and beneath its floor was a large cistern. Johns associated the remains of the Byzantine stratum with the monastic activities in the vicinity of the Citadel during the fifth century known from the descriptions Cyril of Scythopolis. The buildings were destroyed in the Early Arab period, when the large circular corner tower was built in the southern part of the courtyard. Working in the southern fosse of the Citadel Sivan and Solar (1984–1988) uncovered a large, plastered Byzantine pool hewn in the rock.

Kenyon and Tushingham's excavations (1962–1967) in the Armenian Garden south of the Citadel (site L) unearthed various finds from the Byzantine period. The earliest stratum (I), from the second half of the sixth century, included the remains of a church—the foundations, part of the apse, and a small portion of a colored mosaic. The lower part of the mosaic featured a fanlike pattern and its upper part, a hare; between the two parts was a Greek inscription, whose ending is missing. The excavators first associated the construction of this church with a woman named Bassa, who is mentioned by Cyril of Scythopolis (*Life of Euthymius*, 30). In the final report, however, Tushingham retracted this identification. Strata II and III, from the end of the Byzantine period, included a building with a central courtyard and rooms that had been used either as a pilgrim hospice or commercially.

MOUNT ZION

MONASTERY AND CHURCH ON THE GROUNDS OF THE CHURCH OF SAINT PETER IN GALLICANTU. The remains of a Byzantine monastery and church were discovered in 1889 by the Assumptionist Fathers on the grounds of the Church of Saint Peter in Gallicantu, on the southeastern slope of Mount Zion. They were built on the ruins of a Second Temple period structure identified by Christian tradition as the House of Caiaphas, the high priest at the time of the Crucifixion. The results and finds of the excavations, published by J. Germer-Durand, imply the following reconstruction of the Byzantine church. In order to level the slope in preparation for construction, the rock was cut in the west and high retaining walls were erected in the east. The church's estimated measurements are 20 by 14 m. It included a rock-cut crypt, known traditionally as the prison where Jesus was kept on the night he spent in Caiaphas' house. The church has a typical basilical plan, with a central apse on the east (diameter, 5 m), flanked by rooms (4 by 3.5 m). On the west was the atrium, estimated at 16 by 9 m. The entrance to the church was on the north, from the stone-paved stepped street running east down the slope of the hill (see below). On either side of the church remains of rooms were found, some with mosaic floors; one contained a Greek inscription quoting from Psalms 121:8: "The Lord will keep your going out and your coming in . . ."; another had the inscription, "For the Salvation of Mary." These were probably from the monastery next to the church. West of the church, the remains of a bathhouse—walls, brick hypocaust columns, and a furnace—probably dating to the Byzantine period were found.

CHURCH OF HOLY ZION. In the Byzantine period the Church of Holy Zion was founded on the summit of Mount Zion. Built in 340 by Maximus, bishop of Jerusalem (or somewhat later, in the time of Bishop John II, 386–417), on the traditional site of the Last Supper (Mt. 26:17–29), it was one of the most important churches in Byzantine Jerusalem. Also known as the Mother of all Churches, it traditionally marked the place where the Apostles of Jesus had gathered (Acts 2:1–4). The Medeba map shows this church in the southern part of Jerusalem, south of the Cardo. When the Persians invaded Palestine in 614, they mainly damaged its interior. It was later repaired by Modestus and was still in use at the beginning of the Early Arab period.

Some scant remains of the church were discovered in 1898–1899, during the construction of the Dormition Church on Mount Zion, south of the Zion Gate in the Old City wall. At an early stage of the excavations, F. Palmer exposed a few portions of walls, on one of which two crosses were incised. The bulk of the excavations were carried out by M. Renard, who unearthed a network of walls belonging to the western wing of the church.

Reconstructions of the Church of Holy Zion were proposed, on the basis of the sparse remains, by Renard and later by L. H. Vincent. In view of the dearth of concrete remains, these reconstructions are purely theoretical, particularly for the eastern wing. Renard's view, especially his location of the church's site, is more widely accepted by modern scholars. He reconstructed the Byzantine church as a basilica with four rows of columns (52 by 37 m, including the narthex), ending in the east in three external apses. He suggested that the remains uncovered were actually the foundations of the narthex and part of the stylobates supporting the columns; of the latter, a few pillar fragments and two bases were found. Fragments of mosaic floors and small tesserae, some of gilt glass, attest to the splendor of the church, which was decorated with wall mosaics. According to Renard, "David's Tomb" was a southern annex to the Church's main building (see below).

Vincent's reconstruction differed in several details. He, too, reconstructed the church as a basilica (55 by 34 m) with four rows of columns, but with one central external apse. He rejected Renard's suggestion of a narthex at the western end, and included "David's Tomb" in the building's southeastern corner. Vincent thus placed the church slightly farther to the south than Renard.

In 1983, E. Eisenberg, digging west of the Dormition Church, discovered a stretch of wall, including a doorway and two fallen columns, that apparently are also associated with the Byzantine Church of Holy Zion.

"DAVID'S TOMB." The present walls of the so-called David's Tomb on Mount Zion incorporate sections of ancient masonry, consisting of large, well-dressed, square stones. In 1949, J. Pinkerfeld examined the building and found that the northern wall—behind the traditional tombstone—was also ancient, and contemporary with the southern and eastern walls. The thickness of the northern wall was 2.8 m, as against only 1.3 m for the southern and eastern walls. The southern face of the northern wall contains a niche oriented north (to be precise, northeast). The length of the building could thus be estimated at 10.5 m from north to south; the width could not be determined, as the building is now delimited on the west by a wall of later construction. In its first, original stage, the building had a stone-paved floor and the niche was about 1.92 m above it. In the second stage, the floor was paved with a mosaic featuring geometric patterns. Pinkerfeld discovered a few barely legible Greek graffiti on the wall plaster. These inscriptions were published by E. Testa and B. Bagatti, who read them as prayers to God and to Jesus.

Pinkerfeld dated the ancient masonry in the walls of the present-day "David's Tomb" to the Roman period. He interpreted them as the remains of a synagogue oriented toward the Temple Mount—the niche in the northern wall having housed the Torah Scrolls. He based this theory on architectural points of similarity between this building and the ancient synagogues at Eshtemoa in the southern Judean Hills and at Naveh in the Hauran. Another possibility is that this was the synagogue (of the Judeo-Christian community) described by the Bordeaux Pilgrim, who visited Jerusalem at the beginning of the fourth century (*Itin. Burdig.* 592). However, Y. Tsafrir considered the structure to be the remains of an elaborate pagan building from the Roman period, incorporated in the greater complex of the Church of Holy Zion in the Byzantine period.

OTHER STREETS AND STRUCTURES. Nineteenth-century excavations on Mount Zion, particularly the extensive explorations by Bliss and Dickie, revealed the remains of various buildings and water installations dating to the Byzantine period. It is difficult to determine the nature of these remains because they were inadequately published. One of them, the corner of a building with a white mosaic floor, was discovered on the grounds of the Bishop Gobat School. South of "David's Tomb" a small cistern with a cross and a Greek monogram inscribed on its wall was discovered. A room with massive walls, paved with a colored mosaic (7.5 by 5.7 m), was found in the Latin cemetery on Mount Zion; this room was probably part of a Byzantine public building or monastery. The mosaic's central carpet was divided into ten squares arranged in two rows, with guilloche patterns around and between them.

A few fragments of mosaic floors were found in the precincts of the Greek monastery west of the Dormition Church. Remains of mosaic floors and a small apse, possibly part of a Byzantine church, were also found in the area of the Armenian monastery (the House of Caiaphas).

K. Kenyon found only sparse remains from the Byzantine period (her sites B, D, and E) on the eastern slope of Mount Zion. Worthy of note was a cave, originally hewn in Second Temple times and later incorporated in a Byzantine building erected over it. Byzantine remains were exposed in 1970–1971 by J. Margovski near and west of Burj Kibrit (the Sulfur Tower) in the southern wall of the Old City. The finds included the remains of private houses with mosaic-paved rooms, a section of a street, and part of an aqueduct. Particularly striking was a building (c. 30 by 20 m) containing approximately twenty rooms paved with stone slabs or mosaics. The building was originally constructed in the Second Temple period; according to the excavator, it continued in use, with some modifications, as a public building or convent, in the Byzantine period (sixth and seventh centuries). Another structure from the same period was also found to contain a central courtyard with rooms around it. In 1975–1977, M. Ben-Dov discovered various remains of private houses from the end of the Byzantine period, between the Sulfur Tower and the Dung Gate, in the southern wall of the Old City. At the foot of the eastern slope of Mount Zion, in his area H, Y. Shiloh uncovered the corner of an impressive building from the Byzantine period. Adjoining it were a few poor remains of masonry presenting evidence of two building phases (stratum 3).

Northwest of the Church of Saint Peter in Gallicantu, J. Germer-Durand discovered the remains of a large, magnificent atrium building constructed around a stone-paved central courtyard. M. Avi-Yonah dated the building to the time of Aelia Capitolina, but the proximity of copious Byzantine remains makes a Byzantine date more probable. Not far from this building was a room with a mosaic floor featuring a depiction of sandals and the inscription, "Good luck, Stephanos."

Various ancient streets discovered in the past cut across Mount Zion and its environs in different directions. Bliss and Dickie found a street ascending from gate N in the southern wall of Byzantine Jerusalem, in a northeasterly direction. They were able to trace the course of the street for about 140 m, mainly by following the drain that ran beneath it. The street was 5.4 m wide and paved with stone slabs interspersed with leveled sections of rock. Some parts of this street were reexamined by B. Pixner, D. Chen, and S. Margalit (1979–1986). Other sections of streets, published by Germer-Durand and C. Schick, were also 5.4 m wide. Of particular note is the stepped street descending the slope toward the east, north of the Church of Saint Peter in Gallicantu. A section of this street (100 m long) was cleared and was found to be the standard width for streets of the period.

Additional excavations have been carried out in recent years, mainly near the summit of Mount Zion and on its eastern slopes. M. Broshi, in 1971–1972, excavated 24 m of a long, narrow building and a few mosaic floors of a public (religious) building from the Byzantine period, in the courtyard of the Armenian monastery (the House of Caiaphas), just south of the Zion Gate. These remains may be associated with the Church of Holy Zion. The most prominent find in this area from the Byzantine period was part of a street (44 m long) running north–south; its width was 5.4 m (6.4 m with the curbstones), like that of most other Byzantine streets discovered on Mount Zion. It was paved with large, well-dressed stone slabs. The street showed two building phases, one overlying the other, with a drainage system underneath each phase. The excavator suggested that this might be one of the main streets of Byzantine Jerusalem, visible on the Medeba map running west of and parallel to the Cardo.

SECONDARY (EASTERN) CARDO

As already mentioned (see above), the Medeba map depicts a secondary, eastern Cardo in Byzantine Jerusalem, with a covered colonnade running along one side. Sections of a paved street identified as remains of this Cardo were exposed along the present-day ha-Gai (Valley) Street, which runs roughly north–south from the Damascus Gate along the Tyropoeon Valley, toward the Dung Gate.

In the early 1930s, C. N. Johns, followed by R. W. Hamilton, uncovered two levels of a paved street, with underlying drainage systems, at various points along the part of ha-Gai Street between Suq el-Qattanin (the Cotton Merchants' Market) and Wilson's Arch. The upper level, probably dating to the Byzantine period, consists of well-dressed stone slabs laid diagonally with respect to the direction of the street. In 1977, O. Hess and E. Eisenberg exposed another section of the ancient paved street a few dozen meters farther north, along the modern street; it is identical in construction to the previously known remains. In 1980, M. Magen discovered yet another section of the street at the junction of ha-Gai Street and the Via Dolorosa (opposite the Third Station).

In the 1970s, Ben-Dov, working outside the Old City walls west of the Dung Gate, located the southernmost section of the Secondary (eastern) Cardo discovered so far, which he dated to the beginning of the Byzantine period. Another section had been discovered as early as the 1930s inside the Dung Gate. The width of the Secondary Cardo in this section was approximately 12 m. It was paved with large, thick stone slabs, well worn with use, with a drain running beneath them. Of the columns that originally stood along the western side of the street, a few bases were found in situ in specially hewn, rock-cut depressions. West of the row of columns a paved sidewalk extended for some 3 m, beyond which was a row of spaces, probably used as shops. At the southern end of the exposed section, another street branched off, climbing westward up Mount Zion; the main street continued southward, down the Tyropoeon Valley, as a stepped passageway.

The remains of the Secondary (eastern) Cardo exposed in ha-Gai Street were built in the Byzantine period. However, it can be assumed that the line of the street and its details date to the town plan of Roman Aelia Capitolina. In the north, the Secondary Cardo followed the upper course of the Tyropoeon Valley. It continued southward along the rock-cut scarp visible today at the eastern edge of the Jewish Quarter, facing the Temple Mount Western Wall. It is of interest that this southern section of the Cardo does not follow the line of Jerusalem's main thoroughfare in the Second Temple period, which ran along the western wall of the Temple Mount.

CHURCH OF THE HOLY SEPULCHER

The Church of the Holy Sepulcher was built in Jerusalem between 326 and 335, on the traditional site of the crucifixion and burial of Jesus (Mt. 27). It became the most important church in Jerusalem and in fact in the whole country. Eusebius, in his *Vita Constantini*, renders a detailed account of the building, describing its various parts. From him it was learned that the church had been built on the site of a Roman temple. Other details in this and other literary sources from the Byzantine period, as well as from the detailed representation on the Medeba map, indicate that the Byzantine complex of the Church of the Holy Sepulcher comprised several buildings. The four main elements, listed in order from east to west, were the (eastern) atrium of the basilica; the basilica itself (martyrium); the atrium of the rotunda (known as the Holy Garden); and the rotunda (Anastasis). Around these buildings were a variety of chapels and rooms, adding up to a unique architectural complex of impressive size and magnificence. It probably occupied an area of some 130 by 60 m between the Cardo (Beth ha-Bad Street) in the east and Christians' Street in the west. The complex is an example of a central commemorative structure, combined with a basilica, in which the daily prayer ritual could be practiced.

The first thorough, modern study of the ancient remains in the Church of the Holy Sepulcher was published in 1914 by L. H. Vincent and F. M. Abel. In 1933–1934, W. Harvey conducted an architectural survey of the present building. In 1960 to 1969 and in the 1970s, a comprehensive survey, including a series of trial soundings beneath the foundations, was undertaken in the church, under the supervision of V. Corbo, C. Coüasnon, and others, as part of reconstruction and restoration operations on behalf of the Christian communities. Among the discoveries were remains of ancient masonry, which provided important information about the church's original plan. Byzantine remains were preserved to a considerable height above the original floor level, mainly in the west, in the area of the rotunda; in the eastern part of the complex most of the remains did not rise higher than the wall foundations. Corbo's dating of some of the masonry to the Byzantine period was not conclusively confirmed by his final report of the excavations. Coüasnon, in a comprehensive historical-architectural study of the Church of the Holy Sepulcher, covering the entire history of the edifice, rejected some of Corbo's conclusions, with corresponding implications for the reconstruction of the ancient church's original plan. Corbo's and Coüasnon's conclusions occasionally contradict those of Vincent and Abel.

At the eastern end of the Byzantine complex stood the atrium of the basilica, which Eusebius describes as surrounded by colonnades. The surviving remains indicate that the atrium was trapezoidal and measured some 36 by 28–22 m. Its shape was dictated by the need to incorporate earlier (Roman) walls in the new structure. Coüasnon reconstructs a kind of narthex at the western side of the atrium, between it and the basilica. The Medeba map shows steps leading up from the Cardo to three entrances in the atrium's eastern wall. The southern wall of the atrium and part of its eastern wall, including the southern and central entrances, were discovered in the nineteenth century and are now visible in the Russian Hospice and in a shop north of the latter, both east of the present-day Church of the Holy Sepulcher. It is commonly believed that these walls were originally part of the podium of the Roman temple, and that the three entrances were breached in the eastern wall only when it was incorporated in the eastern wing of the church. Corbo, however, suggested that the entrances themselves might already have existed in the Roman period (see above, Roman Period). In the Byzantine period, the wall was covered with marble slabs; this is indicated by small depressions in its stones. In front of the building four pillars on a high base from the Roman period were preserved.

Three entrances led from the atrium into the basilica (martyrium), which was the principal ritual element of the church complex in the Byzantine period. Eusebius describes the basilica as being impressive in size; four rows

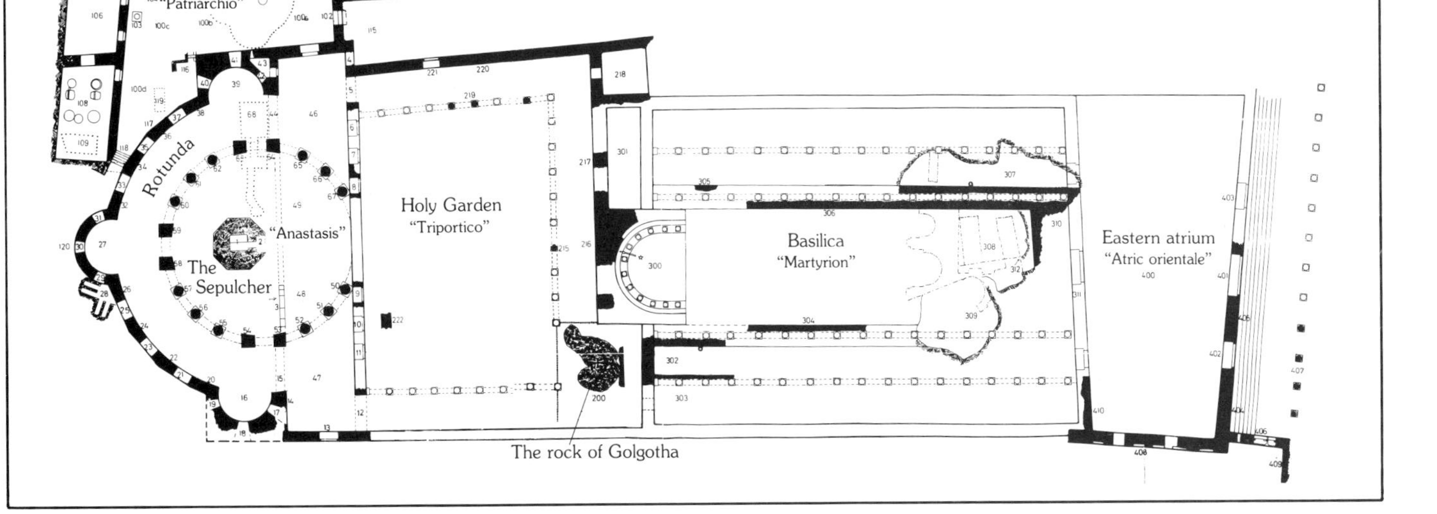

Plan of the Church of the Holy Sepulcher in the time of Constantine, after Corbo.

Facade of the Church of the Holy Sepulcher, Crusader period.

of columns stood in it, and its apse was surrounded by twelve columns, symbolizing the twelve Apostles.

Masonry remains exposed east of the Catholicon in the present church (the former location of the atrium of the rotunda in the ancient church) enable a reconstruction of the basilica's original design. The lines of the basilica's walls are preserved in the parallel walls of the later buildings. These also indicate the basilica's estimated dimensions: 58 by 40–38.5 m according to Corbo, 46 by 36 m according to Coüasnon.

Beneath the apse of the present-day Catholicon, excavators exposed part of the apse of the Constantinian church. It was an inscribed apse (diameter, 8.2 m), pointing west, toward the Sepulcher, rather than east, as was customary in Byzantine churches.

The position of the apse indicates that the axis of Constantine's basilica was a continuation of a line extending farther east, defined by the central entrance of the eastern atrium from the Cardo; it was thus identical with the axis of the present-day Chapel of Saint Helena. Toward the west, this axis ran slightly to the south of the axis of the rotunda's atrium and of the rotunda itself. The reason for this discrepancy between the alignments of the two main constituents of the Holy Sepulcher complex was that the builders of the basilica and the eastern atrium made partial use of earlier, Roman walls still standing on the site.

The positions of the rows of columns in the basilica can be determined by the remains of their foundations, which have been located in excavations. The northern and southern walls of the Chapel of Saint Helena incorporated earlier walls, some of which were actually hewn in the rock. Coüasnon suggested that the northern wall might be dated to the Roman period. In his reconstruction, these two parallel walls in the Chapel of Saint Helena supported the two central rows of columns in the Constantinian basilica, implying that the width of the central nave was 15 m. On the basis of these data, Coüasnon conjectured that Constantine's basilica was in fact identical with the Roman basilica from the time of Aelia Capitolina, though of course modified and adapted to its new purpose. In 1975–1976, Broshi exposed two walls at right angles to one another in a rock-cut cave east of the Chapel of Saint Helena (the so-called Chapel of Saint Vartan). These two walls were also ascribed to the foundations of Constantine's basilica. The main wall, which ran east–west, was yet another part of the stylobate supporting the northern row of columns in the basilica's nave. A considerable length of this wall was exposed, preserved to a height of 12 m. One of the walls contained a stone with a drawing of a boat and the Latin inscription, DOMINE IVIMUS ("O Lord, we shall go") beneath it.

Corbo and Broshi were each of the opinion that the presently accessible subterranean parts of the Church of the Holy Sepulcher, comprising the Chapel of Saint Helena, the Grotto of the Finding of the Cross, and the cave excavated by Broshi (Chapel of Saint Vartan), were sealed in the Byzantine period and access to them was blocked by walls. This hypothesis was contrary to the view of Coüasnon and Vincent, who contended that in the Byzantine period the Grotto of the Finding of the Cross was accessible through a partly hewn passage.

West of the basilica stood the central and most important element in the whole complex—the Sepulcher itself. Eusebius describes the Sepulcher in Constantine's church as surrounded by columns and elaborately ornamented. Adjoining it was an open courtyard, with colonnades along three of the walls. From the description rendered by Egeria (*Itinerarium*, 24–25), the fourth-century traveler, it appears that the Sepulcher was already enclosed in a covered structure—the rotunda (Anastasis).

Numerous masonry remains from the Byzantine period were found in the precincts of the present-day Catholicon and the rotunda to its west, some only as foundations under the current floor, others standing to a considerable height and built into the existing structure. Wherever bedrock was exposed there were clearly visible hewing marks, indicating that the slope of the hill, which had been a quarry in early periods, was systematically cut in Constantine's time to prepare the ground for the church. These operations created

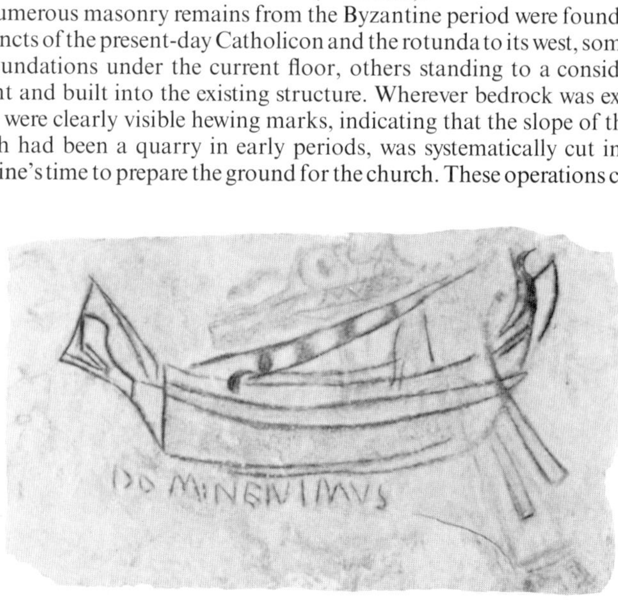

Church of the Holy Sepulcher: boat drawing and inscription ("O Lord, we shall go"), from the Chapel of St. Vartan.

a level area, lower than the Sepulcher; the Sepulcher thus rose above the surroundings as a commanding monument.

A circular wall (diameter, 35 m) around the Sepulcher contained three apses. The northern and southern ones were inscribed in a massively built wall; the western one was partly hewn in the rock, which was detached at its rear from the rest of the hill. Vincent held that this apse, and indeed the other two apses as well, were not integral parts of the circular wall but had been inserted at a later phase of the Byzantine period. The circular wall and the apses are preserved in some parts to a considerable height. The western apse is some 11 m high; the lowest 4 m consist of the rock-cut surface. Each apse is about 6 m in diameter and ends in a vault containing arched windows. Also visible are the holes in which the marble slabs covering the circular wall were fitted.

There are essential differences between Corbo's and Coüasnon's reconstructions of the western part of the Church of the Holy Sepulcher—namely, the immediate surroundings of the Sepulcher itself, when constructed under Constantine the Great. Corbo was of the opinion that the entire rotunda, including the circular wall and its apses, was completed in Constantine's reign and that the Sepulcher was, consequently, enclosed in a covered structure. Between it and the basilica to the east an open courtyard, surrounded on three sides by porticoes, functioned as a kind of atrium to the rotunda (Corbo called this courtyard the Triportico). A vestige of the northern wall of this courtyard is incorporated in the present structure. On the east, according to Corbo, the courtyard was sealed by the rear of the basilica's western wall (the apse wall). On the west—where there was no portico—the courtyard was sealed by a wall, in which a central entrance with four additional entrances on each side afforded access to the rotunda. Parts of this wall, including some of the doorways, still survive to a considerable height, incorporated in the facade of the Catholicon. Coüasnon, however, proposed a different plan for the Constantinian building: Excavations in the Armenian section of the church, south of the rotunda, and in the Latin section to the north, revealed two parallel stone-built corners. Coüasnon suggested that these were the stylobates supporting the porticoes that surrounded the open courtyard on three sides. In his reconstruction, the Sepulcher adjoined the courtyard on the west, surrounded by columns, as a kind of niche inscribed in the courtyard's western wall. The construction of the circular wall and the three apses—which also involved rock-cutting operations—began, Coüasnon believed, under Constantine, at the same time as the construction of the open mausoleum containing the Sepulcher. The rotunda, however, was not completed then, for lack of time; the work was finished only at the end of the fourth century, as implied by Egeria's report. Only then did the circular wall and the three apses become an integral part of the structure. When the rotunda was completed, the new wall with its nine openings was erected to the west, to separate the rotunda from the courtyard, which remained open, on the east.

Around the Sepulcher itself, a circle (diameter, 20 m) of twelve columns, in groups of three each, alternated with four pairs of square piers; the latter survive to a considerable height in the north. Two of the original columns are preserved in the northern part of the rotunda; they are actually two halves of a monolithic column, whose original height was 7.15 m. Corbo suggested that during the Constantinian construction operations the columns were removed from their original location in front of the Roman temple (the Capitolinum) for use in the rotunda. He concluded, therefore, that in the Byzantine period the rotunda had an upper gallery. Coüasnon, on the other hand, believed that the columns stood to their original height when Constantine's construction was in progress, having been removed only in the eleventh century, under the emperor Monomachus, as part of the repair operations. The space between the circle of columns and piers and the circular wall with the apses became an ambulatory. In the Byzantine period the rotunda had a roof, probably of wood.

Scholars have advanced various hypotheses as to the source of the rotunda structure in the Church of the Holy Sepulcher. The most popular explanation is that it was built as a concentric structure, a kind of mausoleum, enclosing the Sepulcher of Jesus. The Sepulcher itself was not in the exact center of the rotunda but displaced slightly west of the center, to leave room for a transept Corbo believed was built in the eastern foreground. The transept (8 by 43.5 m) and parts of the walls of its northern wing have survived to the impressive height of 11 m. The Sepulcher itself is marked by a hewn rock, on which an edicule was built, apparently in the time of Constantine. The form of this structure in the Byzantine period is known mainly from its depiction on special lead pilgrim's flasks from Monza and Bobbio in Italy cast in Jerusalem at the end of the Byzantine period.

The rock of Golgotha, the traditional site of the Crucifixion, was specially shaped by cutting during the construction of the Constantinian basilica; it rose to a height of some 5 m in the southeastern corner of the open courtyard (Holy Garden) between the rotunda and the basilica. A small structure, supported by four piers, was built around the rock at the end of the Byzantine period, under the patriarch Modestus.

North of the rotunda the remains of various rooms and courtyards, originally part of the Byzantine church complex, were found. Some survive to a considerable height, and in one case the original paved floor is extant. There was probably a baptistery south of the rotunda in the Byzantine period. As it is impossible to excavate the area, conclusions have been drawn based on the plans of walls in the present buildings. On this side of the church a large cistern, its ceiling supported by a row of piers, was built in the Byzantine period. Today this cistern is underneath the church's southern forecourt (parvis), utilizing, on its north, a fine Hadrianic wall. Coüasnon reconstructed courtyards and rooms north and south of the basilica. Particularly worthy of note is a long wall containing niches that open toward the south; Coüasnon suggested that this wall was built in the Byzantine period, south of and parallel to the basilica.

Various architectural fragments, probably originating in the Byzantine Church of the Holy Sepulcher, were found in secondary use in later buildings in the vicinity. Among these were bases of columns, some featuring crosses in relief; basket capitals; and capitals with monograms in relief.

The Byzantine Church of the Holy Sepulcher was apparently damaged in the Persian invasion of Jerusalem in 614. Shortly thereafter the building was partly restored by Modestus between 616 and 626, but it fell short of its original splendor. The appearance of the church at the end of the seventh century, after its restoration, was described by the traveler Arculf (Adamnanus, *De Locis Sanctis* I, 2–8). The Byzantine church was razed to the ground by the Fatimid caliph el-Hakim in 1009, to be rebuilt on a limited scale by the Byzantine emperor Monomachus in 1042–1048. Some walls from this church and its Byzantine predecessor are incorporated in the walls of the present structure, built by the Crusaders.

THE MURISTAN AND NORTHERN PART OF THE OLD CITY

Several remains of masonry from the Byzantine period were found in the Muristan, south of the Church of the Holy Sepulcher. In the southern part of the Muristan (site C) Kenyon uncovered a wall, containing a doorway, of a mosaic-paved room from the Byzantine period.

In 1977, excavations by Margalit, Chen, and Solar on Christians' Street, west of the Church of the Holy Sepulcher, revealed at a relatively shallow depth a portion of a paved street laid at the beginning of the Byzantine period. The street ran north–south and was paved with large stones, some striated and well worn with use. The shape of the stones suggested that they had been dismantled from some Roman pavement and reused here.

CHURCH OF SAINT JOHN THE BAPTIST. The Church of Saint John the Baptist is south of the Muristan. Its trefoil-shaped ground floor is preserved in its entirety. It has an external (eastern) apse and, north and south of it, two additional inscribed apses. A second floor was built on an identical plan in the Crusader period. However, some scholars hold that there is no conclusive proof for the Byzantine origin of this church.

CHURCH OF SAINT MARY OF THE PROBATICA. Northwest of the Temple Mount, on the grounds of Saint Anne's Church, near the Lions' (Saint Stephen's) gate, the remains were found of a Byzantine church, probably dedicated in memory of the healing of the paralytic (Jn. 5:1–9).The Virgin Mary is held by tradition to have been born nearby. The first, partial excavations were conducted at the site by C. Mauss and the White Fathers, who own the land, at the end of the nineteenth century, and again beginning in 1914. On the basis of the finds, Vincent reconstructed a church (c. 20 by 28 m), oriented west—unlike most churches from the Byzantine period. Extensive excavations were carried out at the site beginning in 1956, under the direction of M. J. Pierre and J. M. Rousée. They unearthed many additional finds, from which the exact plan of the church and the details of its construction could be reconstructed. Built at the beginning of the fifth century on a basilical plan (c. 20 by 50 m), the church was oriented, as usual, to the east. Its western part was founded on the two ancient Bethesda pools; its nave rested on the wall between the two pools (see above, Second Temple Period). Its southern aisle was partly supported on a row of high piers, from which sprang arches (one of which is preserved). The piers stood on the bottom of the southern pool, some 13 m beneath the church floor. The church's northern aisle rested partly on the remains of a building from the Roman period constructed in the northern pool. The eastern wall of the church was to the east of the pools; when it was built, most of the earlier remains on the site were destroyed and buried. Still extant on the site's eastern side are the remains of the wall that contained three apses, the central one external and polygonal. The church had a mosaic floor, featuring geometric designs, part of which survived on the northeastern side of the excavated area. A higher mosaic floor was assigned by the excavators to repairs made following the severe damage caused to the church in 614. Beneath Saint Anne's Crusader Church, remains of a room, cut partly in the rock and containing a Byzantine mosaic floor, were exposed. According to Vincent, the room was a chapel marking the Virgin Mary's birthplace; however, there is no evidence to support this.

HILLEL GEVA

REMAINS OUTSIDE THE BYZANTINE CITY

The remains of several churches and monasteries from the Byzantine period have been found outside what was then the walled area of Jerusalem. In addition to churches, the contemporary residents of Jerusalem also built chapels over tombs or near them; these are usually identifiable by their surviving mosaic floors or by dedicatory inscriptions in the mosaic. Such structures are, however, difficult to date.

NORTH OF THE CITY. Church of Saint Stephen. North of the city, outside the Damascus Gate, Empress Eudocia founded a church dedicated to Saint Stephen. This church, consecrated on June 15, 460, was cleared by the Dominican Fathers between 1885 and 1893. They erected their church and monastery on the site, which also houses the Dominican École Biblique. In the excavations, a basilical church (20 by 33 m) with a projecting apse was discovered whose outer wall is polygonal. The church's northern aisle is largely preserved. To construct the colonnades around the atrium, the builders of the ancient church seem to have reused columns, capitals, and the epistyle of the triumphal arch, which stood nearby (see above, Roman Period).

Church Near the Third Wall. In 1937, D. C. Baramki, on behalf of the Mandatory Department of Antiquities, excavated a mosaic-paved chapel near the Third Wall. The chapel (3.05 by 6.1 m) had been part of a hall twice its length that was afterward divided in two by the wall of the apse. West of the chapel was a narthex, and beyond it were two other rooms. A long narrow corridor passes south of all the rooms. The excavator considered these the remains of a fifth-century Byzantine monastery, but judging from the style of the mosaics, a date in the seventh century seems more justified.

Tombs and Chapels. North of the Damascus Gate, a large burial site extended to the banks of the Kidron Valley. Some of the chapels adjoining the tombs are noteworthy: 1. On the land of the Swedish School, a Byzantine chapel, of which remains of two walls and a mosaic floor with geometric patterns survive, was discovered during excavations of the Third Wall. The mosaic has an inscription naming the tomb as that of Anatolia of Arabissus, perhaps the sister of Emperor Mauricius (582–602). 2. Twenty meters south of the Church of Saint Stephen, two chapels were discovered above Jewish tombs reused in the Byzantine period. 3. Two tomb chapels found near the Damascus Gate contained mosaics of outstanding workmanship. One of them (3.9 by 6.3 m), with a small apse on its east side, was found in 1894 on ha-Nevi'im (Prophets') Street. In its mosaic floor ("the Armenian mosaic") animals and various objects are depicted, probably offerings, such as baskets of fruit. An inscription accompanying these designs contains a dedication: "To the memory and for the salvation of all the Armenians the names of whom the Lord alone knoweth." Its similarities to the Shellal and Ma'on mosaic pavements date it to the sixth century. Another chapel (3.2 by 5.7 m) with a mosaic floor was cleared in 1901 at the entrance to the Damascus Gate. In the center of the mosaic Orpheus is represented surrounded by animals, with Pan and a centaur at his feet. Below this scene are two female figures, labeled Theodosia and Georgia, and below them the figure of a hunter. This mosaic is to be dated to the second half of the sixth century. A similar tomb was found in 1932 on the grounds of the American School of Oriental Research. Judging from the more than one hundred bodies buried there, this was a common grave dug either during a war or an epidemic.

MICHAEL AVI-YONAH

Other Remains. The recent excavations (1972–1974) along the Third Wall by Netzer and Ben-Arieh exposed the remains of a large Byzantine monastery, some of whose rooms had been uncovered in the 1920s by Sukenik and Mayer. The building's several rooms, some paved with mosaics, were arranged around a spacious courtyard (or around several courtyards). Cisterns adjoined the building; a large cross was found molded in the plaster on the wall of one of them.

Excavations since 1990 along the line of the Third Wall, by V. Tzaferis, A. Onn, N. Feig, and E. Sukron, revealed the remains of a few complexes that served as monasteries and hospices in the Byzantine period. The spacious buildings include many rooms and chapels paved with mosaics, water installations, and tombs. The nearby chapel and rooms excavated by Baramki

"Armenian mosaic" in a Byzantine chapel north of the Damascus Gate.

in 1937 were part of one of these complexes. Excavations in 1990–1992 north of the Damascus Gate, by D. Amit and S. Wolff, revealed the remains of a monastery, including a mosaic floor with an Armenian inscription.

In 1987, A. Chambon discovered the remains of a Byzantine bathhouse on the grounds of the Notre Dame monastery, northwest of the Damascus Gate. The finds imply that a religious, Christian quarter existed north of the city in that period. It included monasteries and churches that still existed in the early Arab period.

In 1970, in the area of French Hill in northern Jerusalem, E. D. Oren discovered the remains of a fortified Byzantine building. It included a rectangular hall (7 by 20 m) adjoined by a cistern and a wing used in the manufacture of oil and wine. The remains probably belong to a monastic farm built in the fifth or sixth centuries.

HILLEL GEVA

Orpheus mosaic in a Byzantine chapel north of the Old City.

THE MOUNT OF OLIVES AND THE KIDRON VALLEY. Church of Eleona. No remains of the Church of Eleona, originally erected on the Mount of Olives, are visible on the surface. The White Fathers discovered it in 1910, and the Dominicans continued clearing it in 1918. Of the original church, primarily rock cuttings and remains of the foundations have survived. The church consisted of a courtyard surrounded by colonnades and a basilica (c. 30 m long). The basilica terminated with an internal apse. The crypt in front of its apse may be an ancient burial cave. Whether the apse was polygonal or rectangular was the subject of a controversy between L. H. Vincent and T. Wiegand. South of the church was a pit. On the site several mosaic fragments (mainly with geometric patterns), parts of the chancel screen, and a Corinthian, basketlike capital were found.

Church of the Ascension. In 378, the matron Poemenia founded the Church of the Ascension (*Ascensio*) on the summit of the Mount of Olives. It was named for the ascension of Jesus to heaven after his resurrection (*Lk*. 24:51). Excavations carried out in 1960 by the Franciscan Fathers, under V. Corbo's direction, revealed evidence of a circular church (rotunda). A row of columns stood along its round wall; another circle of columns in front of this wall supported the dome. Arculf, a pilgrim from the end of the seventh century, described the plan of the church, which was fully confirmed by Corbo's excavations. The diameter of the church was about 25 m. In the excavations, a dedicatory inscription was found mentioning Modestus, the patriarch who restored the church after its destruction by the Persians in 614. The restoration seems to have followed the original plan. Corbo's excavations showed that there is no evidence for the previous assumption that the Byzantine structure was octagonal. The octagonal form of churches is to be ascribed to the Crusader period.

Church South of the Russian Tower. The remains of another church were found south of the Russian Tower on the Mount of Olives. In a room to the west of the church proper, a mosaic floor was found with a dedicatory inscription and a prayer for the salvation of Eusebius the priest, the deacon Theodosius, and three monks.

Churches in Beit Ḥanina. The Franciscans, under the direction of S. J. Saller, cleared two churches, situated one above the other, in Beit Ḥanina, on the eastern slope of the Mount of Olives. Of the first church, only the apse, the prothesis and the diaconicon, and some fragments of a mosaic floor with geometric decorations are preserved. The excavators ascribe this church to the fourth or fifth century. The later date seems correct. The second church is built on top of the first one, except for the apse and the adjoining rooms, which were shifted 13 m to the east. This church probably dates to the sixth century.

Church of Dominus Flevit. At the site called Dominus Flevit, on the slopes of the Mount of Olives, the remains of a small church (7 by 14 m) were discovered in 1955 with a mosaic floor in geometric patterns and a dedicatory inscription mentioning the priest of the Anastasis. The church had one apse; the foundations of an altar and of a chancel screen in front of it were also found. J. T. Milik ascribed the building of the church to approximately 675, on the basis of the literary sources. Notwithstanding its clearly Byzantine style, it belongs to the Early Arab period.

Church of Gethsemane. In 385, Emperor Theodosius I erected a church at Gethsemane, where, according to Christian tradition, Jesus and his disciples spent the night before his arrest. From 1909 to 1920, the Franciscan Fathers,

Remains of a chapel in the Byzantine monastery north of the Damascus Gate.

under the direction of the architect A. Barluzzi and G. Orfali, excavated the remains of the Byzantine church and of the Crusader church here, at the foot of the Mount of Olives. The Byzantine church is a basilica (16.5 by 22.5 m) with a large external apse and two internal, lateral apses. Remains of a mosaic pavement with a wave-and-wreath pattern and geometric patterns in the intercolumnar spaces were found in the nave. A Corinthian capital belonging to the lower row of columns was also found. In the excavations conducted by Corbo in 1958 near the Church of Gethsemane, several rooms with mosaic floors, as well as architectural remains from the Byzantine church, were found.

Tombs and Chapels. In addition to churches, chapels and tombs were found on the Mount of Olives: 1. A chapel above a tomb (4.8 by 5.3 m) near the Greek Orthodox church Viri Galilaei has an inscription in the floor in memory of a woman named Susanna. 2. A small chapel with an apse and a mosaic floor was found beneath the Pater Noster Church. The mosaic was decorated with crosses but lacked an inscription. 3. Tomb chapels found north of the Russian Church on the Mount of Olives contain several mosaic floors with Armenian inscriptions. One is decorated with birds, fish, fruit, and the figure of a lamb in its center. A dedicatory inscription mentions Susanna, mother of Artaban. 4. Another, similar mosaic floor was uncovered, also displaying the figure of a lamb in its center and an inscription mentioning the (Armenian) bishop Jacob. In a subterranean chapel in the same vicinity, there is an Armenian dedicatory inscription to "Saint Isaiah." 5. Of the numerous Christian tombs on the slopes of the Mount of Olives, the most famous is the so-called Tomb of the Prophets (in Arabic, Qubur el-Anbia). It is entered from a flight of stairs that lead to a circular hall (diameter, 8.5 m), from which three rooms (9–12 m long) branch out. They lead to a semicircular burial corridor; there are twenty-six loculi in its outer wall. Another corridor, also rounded, connects the spokelike rooms but does not contain tombs. This tomb, which was explored by C. Clermont-Ganneau between 1870 and 1874, contains numerous Christian inscriptions in Greek.

MICHAEL AVI-YONAH

Church of the Tomb of the Virgin Mary. In 1937, C. N. Johns examined the the Tomb of the Virgin Mary in the Kidron Valley. Further excavations and examinations of the site were carried out in 1972 by B. Bagatti and in 1973 by Cyprianos. According to Arculf's account (Adamnanus, *De Locis Sanctis* I, 12), there were two churches here, a lower and an upper one, in the Byzantine period; the remains of the lower one, consisting mainly of a crypt, are an integral part of the present structure. These remains are rock-cut; the church seems to originally have been cruciform, with two apses, one toward the east and the other toward the west. The vaulted church was reached by a flight of steps on its south. The tomb, considered in Christian tradition to be that of the Virgin Mary, was cut from the surrounding rock. The church was probably built in the reign of Theodosius I, at the end of the fourth century. Lacking archaeological data, any reconstruction of the upper church, which was built in the fifth century, would be purely hypothetical.

Burial Cave. In 1974, A. Kloner excavated a Byzantine tomb on the western slopes of the Mount of Olives that contains a square burial chamber (1.8 by 1.8 m) whose ceiling is 1.65 m high. Arcosolia were cut in the walls. The tomb and its ceiling were plastered and decorated with multicolored drawings: vines drawn in the corners appear to be climbing to the ceiling, which is covered with spreading branches. A bird stands on either side of the vine's main trunk; other birds are depicted on the ceiling, one of them a large peacock (painted tombs featuring similar motifs are known from the environs of Jerusalem). Because the paintings do not feature crosses or pagan-mythological symbols, the excavator suggested that the cave might be a Jewish tomb from the third or fourth century.

HILLEL GEVA

REMAINS WEST AND SOUTH OF THE CITY. Church on Giv'at Ram. According to literary sources, Eudocia founded a home for the aged dedicated to Saint George (*gerontocomium Sancti Georgii*) "before" (πρό) the Holy City. In 1949, a group of buildings was discovered on Giv'at Ram (Sheikh Badr) that was excavated by M. Avi-Yonah on behalf of the Israel Department of Antiquities. A basilical church (14 by 17.5 m) and several rooms were cleared south of it, including a chapel with an apse and a mosaic pavement in which the inscription "O Lord, God of Saint George, remember the donor!" was set. West of the church were remains of monastic cells, with an underground burial chamber among them. The mosaics all show geometric and floral patterns. According to the excavator, it can be assumed that these are the remains of the monastery and of the home for the aged founded by Eudocia. (See the identification of Saint George's Church below, under Church on Ketef Hinnom.)

Tombs in the Valley of Hinnom and near the YMCA. Of the numerous tombs found in the Valley of Hinnom from the Byzantine period, most were reused

Ketef Hinnom: section of a decorated mosaic floor, Byzantine period.

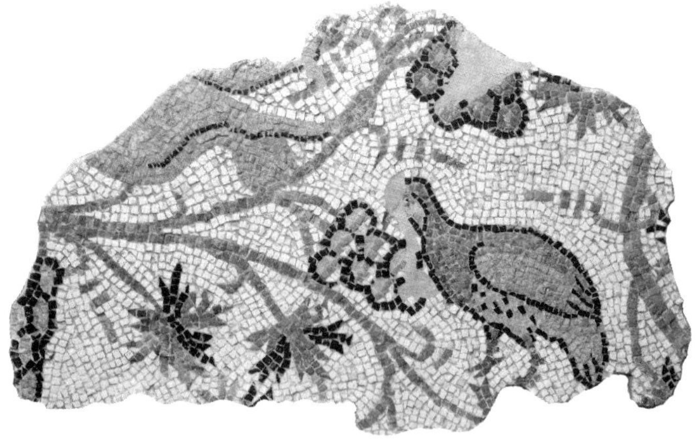

Jewish tombs. It is stated on the tombs that the deceased are from "Holy Zion" across the valley.

In 1932, a cemetery from the fifth to seventh centuries was discovered near the YMCA building on King David Street. It comprised very simple tombs dug into the rock and covered with stone slabs. Wherever the rock slopes, the tomb is completed with masonry. All the tombs are oriented east–west. Not far from them are the remains of walls, perhaps of a monastery. An inscription in a building near the monastery states that this is the private tomb of "Sa[muel] bishop of the Georgians and of his monastery which they purchased in the tower of David" (q.v. Monasteries: Jerusalem).

Tomb in Beit Ṣafafa. In the village of Beit Ṣafafa, on the outskirts of Jerusalem, J. Landau discovered a stone-built Byzantine tomb that he cleared in 1953, on behalf of the Israel Department of Antiquities. It consists of an underground chamber divided into eight cubicles—some containing lead coffins—and a chapel (7 by 8 m) with a mosaic floor and a square apse in its western wall. Near the apse an inscription mentions the founder, Samuel. It also gives a date of the year 6200 (of the creation era).

MICHAEL AVI-YONAH

Church on Ketef Hinnom. On a ridge on the west bank of the Valley of Hinnom, southwest of the Old City, G. Barkay excavated the remains of a Byzantine church for five seasons (1975–1989). Only fragmentary masonry remains were discovered, dating to the early fifth to early seventh centuries. The church (25 by 45 m) was paved with a mosaic, of which a small fragment, depicting a bird pecking at a bunch of grapes, was discovered intact. Three tombs, plastered and decorated with frescoes, were found beneath the floor level of the church, and a vaulted crypt was found underneath the narthex. Earlier excavations had recovered remains of buildings and cisterns in the vicinity that probably belonged to a monastery in the Byzantine period. The excavator identified the church as the Church of Saint George, which figures in the list of places in Jerusalem where Christian residents were massacred in the Persian invasion of Palestine in 614. Avi-Yonah, however, identified the remains of the Church of Saint George on Giv'at Ram (see above).

Remains of Structures and a Tomb West of the Jaffa Gate. In 1989, A. Maeir excavated the remains of Byzantine buildings outside the western wall of the Old City, opposite the Jaffa Gate. They are characterized by an identical layout—a street flanked by shops. The finds testify to the existence of a planned commercial and industrial center west of the city in the Byzantine period. It still existed in the Early Arab period. Part of an aqueduct leading toward the Jaffa Gate was also exposed at the site. The excavations were continued in 1990 by R. Reich. A rock-cut tomb with a mosaic-paved Byzantine chapel in front of it was found farther to the west.

HILLEL GEVA

General: For excavations in Jerusalem and remains discovered up until the 1930s, see L. A. Mayer and M. Avi-Yonah, *QDAP* 1 (1932), 163–193, with supplementary information in *QDAP* 2–14.
See also C. Wilson and C. Warren, *The Recovery of Jerusalem*, London 1871; Warren–Conder, *SWP—Jerusalem*; F. J. Bliss and A. C. Dickie, *Excavations at Jerusalem 1894–1897*, London 1898; Clermont-Ganneau, *ARP* 1; M. Renard, *Das Heilige Land* 44 (1900), 3–23; Vincent–Abel, *Jerusalem Nouvelle*; C. N. Johns, *QDAP* 14 (1950), 121–190; R. W. Hamilton, *PEQ* 84 (1952), 83–90; J. T. Milik, *MUSJ* 27 (1960–1961), 127–189; A. Ovadiah, *Corpus of the Byzantine Churches in the Holy Land* (Theophaneia 22), Bonn 1970, 75–98; id. and C. Gomez de Silva, *Levant* 14 (1982), 134–170; B. Bagatti, *The Church from the Circumcision* (Publications of the Studium Biblicum Franciscanum: Smaller Series 2), Jerusalem 1971; id., *The Church from the Gentiles in Palestine*, Jerusalem 1971; K. M. Kenyon, *Digging up Jerusalem*, London 1974, 265–280; Y. Tsafrir, *Reallexikon zur byzantinischen Kunst*, Stuttgart 1975, 525–615; J. Wilkinson, *Jerusalem Pilgrims before the Crusades*, Jerusalem 1977; *Student Map Manual: Historical Geography of the Bible Lands*, Jerusalem 1979, sect. 14–3; D. T. Ariel, *LA* 32 (1982), 273–326; D. Chen, *PEQ* 114 (1982), 43–45; A. D. Tushingham, *Excavations in Jerusalem 1961–1967* 1, Toronto 1985; H. Busse and G. Kretschmar, *Jerusalemer Heiligtumstraditionen in altkirchlicher und frühislamischer Zeit*, Wiesbaden

Remains of Byzantine structures west of the Jaffa Gate.

1987; W. H. Mare, *The Archaeology of the Jerusalem Area*, Grand Rapids 1987, 217–261; M. Broshi, *Israel Museum Journal* 7 (1988), 13–23; J. D. Purvis, *Jerusalem, The Holy City: A Bibliography* (American Theological Library Association Bibliography Series 20), Metuchen, N.J. 1988, 219–281, 303–367.
City of David: R. A. S. Macalister and J. G. Duncan, *PEFA* 4 (1926); J. W. Crowfoot and G. M. Fitzgerald, ibid. 5 (1929); J. W. Crowfoot, *PEQ* 61 (1929), 9–16; 75–77; Y. Shiloh, *Excavations at the City of David I 1978–1982: Interim Report of the First Five Seasons* (Qedem 19), Jerusalem 1984; J. Magness, "A Typology of the Late Roman and Byzantine Pottery of Jerusalem" (Ph.D. diss., Univ. of Pennsylvania 1989; Ann Arbor 1990).
Southwestern Hill: F. J. Bliss and A. C. Dickie, *Excavations at Jerusalem 1894–1897*, London 1898; J. Germer-Durand, *Maison de Caiphe*, Paris 1914; C. N. Johns, *QDAP* 14 (1950), 121–190; A. D. Tushingham, *PEQ* 100 (1968), 109–111; id., *ZDPV* 95 (1979), 39–55; N. Avigad, *IEJ* 27 (1977), 145–151; M. Broshi, ibid., 232–235; D. Chen, *ZDPV* 95 (1979), 178–181; J. Magness, "A Typology of the Late Roman and Byzantine Pottery of Jerusalem" (Ph.D. diss., Univ. of Pennsylvania 1989; Ann Arbor 1990).
Streets: R. W. Hamilton, *QDAP* 1 (1932), 105–110; 2 (1933), 34–40; C. N. Johns, ibid. 1 (1932), 97–100.
The Cardo: *BAR* 2/4 (1976), 19–21; 3/2 (1977), 4–5; 3/4 (1977), 10–12, 58; 8/4 (1982), 7; N. Avigad, *ESI* 1 (1982), 55–56; id., *IEJ* 32 (1982), 158–159; id., *Discovering Jerusalem*, Nashville 1983, 213–229; D. Chen, *PEQ* 114 (1982), 43–45; J. Feldman, *CNI Special Issue* (June 1985), 26–27; E. Niv Krendel, *BAIAS* 1985–1986, 48–52; R. Reich, *17th International Byzantine Congress: Abstracts of Short Papers*, Washington, D.C. 1986, 287–288; id., *IEJ* 37 (1987), 158–167.
Finds outside the Old City (including the tombs): R. W. Hamilton, *QDAP* 10 (1944), 1–54; V. C. Corbo, *Ricerche Archeologiche al Monte degli Ulivi*, Jerusalem 1965; J. B. Hennessy, *Levant* 2 (1970), 22–27; B. Bagatti, *The Church from the Circumcision*, Jerusalem 1971; id. et al., *New Discoveries at the Tomb of Virgin Mary in Gethsemane*, Jerusalem 1975; S. Ben-Arieh and E. Netzer, *IEJ* 24 (1974), 97–107; V. Tzaferis, ibid., 84–96.
Churches
General: Vincent–Abel, *Jérusalem Nouvelle*; M. Avi-Yonah, *QDAP* 2 (1933), 162–178; J. T. Milik, *RB* 67 (1960), 354–367, 550–586; id., *MUSJ* 37 (1960–1961), 127–189; A. Ovadiah, *Corpus of the Byzantine Churches in the Holy Land* (Theophaneia 22), Bonn 1970, 75–98; id. and C. Gomez de Silva, *Supplementum* to id. 1–3 ibid. (Levant 13 [1981], 221–225; 14 [1982], 134–143; 16 [1984], 136–138); Y. Tsafrir, *Reallexikon zur byzantinischen Kunst* 3, Stuttgart 1975, 587–615; J. D. Purvis, *Jerusalem, The Holy City: A Bibliography* (op. cit.), 303–367; G. R. Stone, *Buried History* 24 (1988), 84–97; P. Walker, *Holy City, Holy Places?: Christian Attitudes to Jerusalem and the Holy Land in the Fourth Century* (Oxford Christian Studies), Oxford 1990; *MdB* 68 (1991).
Church of the Holy Sepulcher: Vincent–Abel, *Jérusalem Nouvelle*, 40–300; W. Harvey, *Church of the Holy Sepulchre, Jerusalem*, London 1935; E. B. Smith, *The Dome: A Study in the History of Ideas* (Princeton Monographs in Art and Archaeology 25), Princeton 1950, 16–29; V. Corbo, *LA* 12 (1962), 221–304; 14 (1964), 293–338; 15 (1965), 316–318; 19 (1969), 65–144; 38 (1988), 391–422; id., *Il Santo Sepolcro di Gerusalemme* 1–3, Jerusalem 1981–1982; A. Ovadiah, *Corpus of the Byzantine Churches in the Holy Land* (op. cit.), 75–77; *Supplementum* 2, 134–138; M. T. Petrozzi, *Dal Calvario al S. Sepolcro* (Quaderni de La Terra Santa), Jerusalem 1972; D. Barag and J. Wilkinson, *Levant* 6 (1974), 179–187; C. Coüasnon, *The Church of the Holy Sepulchre in Jerusalem*, London 1974; id., *Atti del IX Congresso Internazionale di Archeologia Cristiana II 1975*, Vatican City 1978, 163–166; Y. Tsafrir (op. cit.), 587–600; M. Broshi, *IJNA* 6 (1977), 349; S. de Sandoli, *Calvary and the Holy Sepulchre: Historical Outline* (The Holy Places of Palestine), Jerusalem 1984; S. Eisenstadt, *BAR* 13/2 (1987), 46–49; G. S. P. Freeman-Grenville, *Journal of the Royal Asiatic Society* 2 (1987), 187–207; G.-W. Nebe, *Zeitschrift für die Neutestamentliche Wissenschaft* 78 (1987), 153–161; J. D. Purvis, *Jerusalem, The Holy City: A Bibliography* (op. cit.), 320–334; G. R. Stone, *Buried History* 24 (1988), 84–97; Y. Boiret, *MdB* 61 (1989), 41–43; N. Kenaan Kedar, ibid., 37–40; M. Biddle and B. Kjolbye-Biddle, *PEQ* 122 (1990), 152; A. Recio Veganzones, *Christian Archaeology in the Holy Land: New Discoveries* (V. C. Corbo Fest.), Jerusalem 1990, 571–589; Walker (op. cit.), 235–281; D. Pringle, *BAIAS* 10 (1990–1991), 108–110; J. M. O'Connor, *Les Dossiers d'Archéologie*, 165–166 (1991), 78–87; J. Patrich, *Ancient Churches Revealed*, Jerusalem (in prep.).
Nea Church: N. Avigad, *IEJ* 20 (1970), 137–138; 27 (1977), 145–151; 32 (1982), 158–159; id., *Antike Welt* 10/3 (1979), 31–35; id., *Discovering Jerusalem*, Nashville 1983, 229–246; A. Ovadiah (op. cit.), *Supplementum* 1, 221–222; Y. Tsafrir (op. cit.), 602; M. Ben-Dov, *BAR* 3/4 (1977), 32–37; 4/1 (1978), 48–49; id., *CNI* 26 (1977), 86–89; *Buried History* 14/3 (1978), 8–14; R. Reich, *17th International Byzantine Congress: Abstracts of Short Papers*, Washington, D.C. 1986, 287–288; K. Bieberstein, *ZDPV* 105 (1989), 110–122.
Church of Holy Zion: M. Renard, *Das Heilige Land* 44 (1900), 3–23; Vincent–Abel, *Jérusalem Nouvelle*, 421–490; A. Ovadiah (op. cit.), 89–90; id. *Supplementum* 2, 142; J. Briand, *Sion* (Cahiers de *La Terre Sainte*), Jerusalem 1973; Y. Tsafrir (op. cit.), 602; A. Le Borgne, *MdB* 55 (1988), 57; J. D. Purvis (op. cit.), 340–344; B. Pixner, *BAR* 16/3 (1990), 16–35, 60; Walker (op. cit.), 282–308.
Church of St. Peter in Gallicantu: J. Germer-Durand, *Maison de Caiphe*, Paris 1914; id., *RB* 11 (1914), 222–246; Vincent–Abel, *Jérusalem Nouvelle*, 506–515; A. Ovadiah (op. cit.), *Supplementum* 1, 225–226; M. B. Schlink, *The Holy Land Today*, rev. ed., Darmstadt 1975.
Church in the Armenian Garden: K. M. Kenyon, *Digging up Jerusalem*, London 1974, 273–274; A. D. Tushingham, *Excavations in Jerusalem, 1961–1967*, loc. cit.
Mount of Olives
General: A. Ovadiah (op. cit.), 87–89; A. Storme, *Le Mont des Oliviers*, 2nd ed. (Lieux Saints de Palestine), Jerusalem 1984; M. Küchler and C. Ühlinger, *Jerusalem: Texte, Bilder, Steine* (Novum Testamentum et Orbis Antiquus 6), Freiburg 1988; *MdB* 55 (1988); J. D. Purvis (op. cit.), 345–353; Walker (op. cit.), 199–234.
Church of Eleona: Vincent–Abel, *Jérusalem Nouvelle*, 337–360, 374–419; L. H. Vincent, *RB* 64 (1957), 48–71; A. Ovadiah (op. cit.), 82–83; *Supplementum* 2, 139; Y. Tsafrir (op. cit.), 606; M. Berder, *MdB* 55 (1988), 19–20.
Church of Dominus Flevit: B. Bagatti, *LA* 6 (1956), 240–270; J. T. Milik, *RB* 67 (1960), 552–554; A. Ovadiah (op. cit.), 83–84; *Supplementum* 2, 224–225; Y. Tsafrir (op. cit.), 607–610; A. Storme, *Le Mont des Oliviers*, 2nd ed. (Lieux Saints de Palestine), Jerusalem 1984, 127–148.
Church of the Ascension: Vincent–Abel, *Jérusalem Nouvelle*, 360–419; V. Corbo, *LA* 10 (1960), 205–248; A. Ovadiah (op. cit.), 85–87; *Supplementum* 2, 140–141; Y. Tsafrir (op. cit.), 606–607; A. Storme (op. cit.), 72–101; M. Berder, *MdB* 55 (1988), 17–19, 36–37; Walker (op. cit.), 202–217.
Church of Gethsemane: Vincent–Abel, *Jérusalem Nouvelle*, 301–327; P. G. Orfali, *Gethsémani*, Paris 1924; A. Ovadiah (op. cit.), 84–85; ibid., *Supplementum* 2, 139–140; B. Bagatti, *LA* 22 (1972), 236–290; 23 (1973), 318–321; id., *New Discoveries at the Tomb of the Virgin Mary in Gethsemane* (Studium Biblicum Franciscanum, Collectio Minor 17), Jerusalem 1975; A. Storme, *Gethsemane*, 2nd. ed. (The Holy Places of Palestine), Jerusalem 1972; Y. Tsafrir (op. cit.), 611; C. Katsimbinis, *LA* 26 (1976), 77–280; M. Breder, *MdB* 55 (1988), 22–31; J. D. Purvis, (op. cit.), 345–348; Walker (op. cit.), 229–234.
Greek Church (Gethsemane): A. Ovadiah (op. cit.), *Supplementum* 1, 221.
Church of the Tomb of the Virgin Mary: Vincent–Abel, *Jérusalem Nouvelle*, 808–810; 825–831; C. N. Johns, *QDAP* 8 (1938), 117–136; C. Katsimbinis, *LA* 26 (1976), 277–280; A. Ovadiah (op. cit.), 96–97; *Supplementum* 2, 142–143.
Church opposite the Bene Hezir Tomb: A. Ovadiah (op. cit.), *Supplementum* 3, 136.
Siloam Church: F. J. Bliss and A. C. Dickie, *Excavations at Jerusalem 1894–1897*, London 1898, 178–210; A. Ovadiah (op. cit.), 90–94; Y. Tsafrir (op. cit.), 602.
Qaṣr 'Ali: Y. Hirschfeld, *LA* 40 (1990), 287–294.
Church on Ketef Hinnom: A. Ovadiah (op cit.), *Supplementum* 1, 222–223.
Church of St. Mary (of the Probatica): C. Mauss, *La Piscine de Béthesda à Jérusalem*, Paris 1888; Vincent–Abel, *Jérusalem Nouvelle*, 669–742; J. M. Rousée, *Atti del VI Congresso Internazionale di Archeologia Cristiana*, Vatican City 1965, 169–176; A. Ovadiah (op. cit.), *Supplementum* 1, 223–224; Y. Tsafrir (op. cit.), 611; J. D. Purvis (op. cit.), 355–358.
St. Stephen's Church: Vincent–Abel, *Jérusalem Nouvelle*, 743–804; A. Ovadiah (op. cit.), 77–78; Y. Tsafrir (op. cit.), 611–613; J. D. Purvis (op. cit.), 365–367.
Church of St. John the Baptist: Vincent–Abel, *Jérusalem Nouvelle*, 642–668; A. Ovadiah (op. cit.), 78–79.
Church outside the Third Wall: D. C. Baramki, *QDAP* 6 (1938), 56–58; A. Ovadiah (op. cit.), 79–80; id. *Supplementum* 2, 138.
Ḥanania Hill: Deir Abu Tor: A. Ovadiah (op. cit.), 80–81.
Church on Giv'at Ram: A. Ovadiah (op. cit.), 81–82; id., *Supplementum* 2, 139.
Monastery of the Cross: A. Ovadiah (op. cit.), *Supplementum* 3, 137; A. Economopoulos, *Actes du Xe Congrès International d'Archéologie Chretienne* 2, Thessalonica 1984, 377–390; V. Tzaferis, *The Monastery of the Holy Cross in Jerusalem*, Jerusalem 1987; id., *Ancient Churches Revealed*, Jerusalem (in prep.); I. H. Dalmais, *MdB* 66 (1990), 45–47.
Mosaics: C. Schick and F. J. Bliss, *PEQ* 26 (1894), 257–261; M. Avi-Yonah, *QDAP* 2 (1933), 171–172; Y. Tsafrir (op. cit.), 613–614.
Orpheus mosaic: L. H. Vincent, *RB* 10 (1901), 436–448; M. Avi-Yonah, *QDAP* 2 (1933), 172–173; Y. Tsafrir (op. cit.), 613–614.
Via Dolorosa: A. Ovadiah (op. cit.), *Supplementum* 3, 138.
Mount of Olives mosaic: A. Ovadiah (loc. cit.).

EARLY ARAB TO AYYUBID PERIODS

HISTORY

EARLY ARAB PERIOD. Tumultuous events shook Jerusalem in the early seventh century. Within the span of a few years, the city changed hands several times. Each conquest brought with it destruction, followed by attempted reconstruction. The first occasion was the fall of Jerusalem to the Persian army under Chosroes II in 614. The Persian invaders, supported by a Jewish auxiliary force from the Galilee, broke into the city and slaughtered the Christian inhabitants. Christian religious institutions were systematically destroyed, including such important edifices as the Church of the Holy Sepulcher, the Church of the Ascension and many others.

After only fourteen years, a large Byzantine army headed by the emperor Heraclius—whose army the Persians had routed in 614—invaded the Persian Empire and Persian-occupied territories, including Syria and Palestine. In February 628 Heraclius marched into Jerusalem in a military-religious procession. Once again the city was to suffer acts of extreme violence. When the killing and destruction had abated, the Byzantine authorities set about repairing the ruins, particularly those of the holy places in and around Jerusalem. The excavations at the foot of the Temple Mount (see below) have revealed, besides the renovation work, evidence that the Temple Mount in particular had been the scene of large-scale, deliberate destruction. Perhaps Jewish involvement in the Persian occupation of Jerusalem and the ensuing destruction of churches inspired the Byzantine forces to wreak revenge by razing the already ruinous shrines on the Temple Mount. Lengthy sections of the walls of the enclosure were dismantled, their stones scattered in all directions. The excavators discovered many of the original, Herodian stones from the Temple Mount wall where they fell, on the ruins of private houses dated to the sixth century CE. The southern wall was particularly affected.

Only ten years later, Jerusalem changed hands again, falling to the Muslim Arabs. In 638, Jerusalem was conquered by the caliph Omar I, a newcomer from the Arabian deserts, who managed within a few years to defeat the two exhausted superpowers, Persia and the Byzantine Empire. Tradition has it that Omar himself, accompanied by his right-hand man Ka'b el-Akhbar, a converted Jew, visited the newly occupied city. It is told that he did not enter the precincts of the Church of the Holy Sepulcher to pray, but offered his devotions outside the building, in order to avoid offending Christian sensibilities and causing needless confrontations. On the other hand, he did ascend the ruined Temple Mount. There are no contemporary sources for events in Jerusalem in the first years of Islamic rule, nor is there anything in the archaeological record. Jerusalem became particularly important after the Umayyad caliphs came to power in 660. Realizing that physical force alone could not assure them of success in their struggle to supersede the Byzantine Christians as rulers of their newly captured possessions, they set about investing the city with religious significance for Muslims. It was the caliph Mu'awiyya who began to develop Jerusalem as a Muslim city. The development of Muslim Jerusalem reached its peak under his successors, and there was even an attempt to build a seat of political government in the heart of the city.

MEIR BEN-DOV

The reshaping of Jerusalem as a Muslim city, called Iliya or Ilya Bayt el-Maqdas by the Arabs, did not begin immediately after the Arab conquest of 638; most of the Christian population did not leave, and most of the Christian churches were left standing (although some had been damaged in the siege), as were the administration buildings. However, with the comimg of Muslim immigrants and the conversions that followed the Arab conquest, the proportion of Christians in the population fell steadily. The main changes in Jerusalem in this first stage took place on the Temple Mount and in its environs. The Dome of the Rock and el-Aqsa Mosque were built, the retaining walls of the mount were repaired, and a magnificent complex of government buildings was erected south and southwest of the mount. Historians believe that these activities expressed the conquerors' desire to demonstrate Islam's superiority over Christianity. Many scholars point to the similarity in plan and appearance between the Holy Sepulcher and the Muslim edifices on the Temple Mount as evidence of the competition between the two religions.

In the early years of the Early Arab period the authorities permitted Jews to settle in Jerusalem, for the first time in several centuries, and to establish their own quarter. The quarter may have been situated on the City of David spur (the exact location is still a matter of controversy), but later, in the eleventh century, it moved to the northeastern part of the city. The Early Arab period was also the formative period for the "ethnic" pattern of Jerusalem still apparent: the Muslim Quarter in the center of the city, the Christian Quarter in the northwest, and the Armenian Quarter in the southwest. There is almost no archaeological evidence for these processes, and our understanding is based exclusively on literary sources, the most important of which are the works of Muqaddasi (985) and Naṣir-i-Khosrau (1047) and letters found in the Cairo Genizah that describe Jerusalem as Jews saw it at the time.

Several violent earthquakes in the Early Arab period contributed to the lack of material remains for the period. The first occurred in 658. Even before the great construction projects of the Umayyads were completed, another strong earthquake (the so-called "quake of the seventh [Sabbatical] year") shook the country in 747 or 749, damaging the el-Aqsa Mosque; the mosque was damaged again in 765. The sources report another earthquake in 808 that affected the entire city, possibly also the Temple Mount shrines. In 1016, another earthquake toppled the dome of the Dome of the Rock. The worst quake occurred in 1033, toward the end of the Early Arab period, changing the entire appearance of Jerusalem. The city walls, which that quake destroyed, were repaired over the next three decades (1034–1064) and built along the lines they now occupy. It was then that Mount Zion and the City of David were left outside the walled area. Mount Zion was again enclosed by a wall only during Saladin's reign. Another cause of widespread destruction was the frequent changes of government: the Umayyads (660–750) gave way to the Abbasids (750–878); subsequently, Aḥmad Ibn Tulun seized power, purportedly in the name of the Abbasid caliphs, thus paving the way for the Ikhshid dynasty (935–969), which in turn was replaced by the Fatimids (969–1071 and 1098). The persecution of nonbelievers, which reached its peak in 1009 with the destruction of Christian religious institutions—above all, the Church of the Holy Sepulcher—obscured the character of the city and changed its appearance. Only the Temple Mount remained the same, although even the el-Aqsa Mosque underwent certain alterations to repair earthquake damage.

CRUSADER PERIOD. The Crusader conquest of Jerusalem, on July 15, 1099, ushered in a period of relative calm after decades of unrest. After the last vestiges of Muslim resistance (in the Citadel) had been suppressed, Jews and Muslims, considered unreliable elements by the new rulers, were expelled from the city, a "King of Jerusalem" was crowned, and a patriarch was elected. The sight of a fortified city was a novelty for most of its new Christian residents, for European cities were still in a primitive stage of development. At first, although they took over the property abandoned by the Muslims, the Crusaders, therefore, made no changes in the city's appearance. Only later did they initiate large-scale construction in Jerusalem—mainly of churches. The various markets, previously concentrated in the area of the Roman-Byzantine forum (see above, Roman and Byzantine periods), were now transferred to the main streets and shops were built along them; this feature of Crusader Jerusalem is still visible. When the Crusaders took Jerusalem, the city walls were only a few decades old, and so the conquerors changed nothing. Only after the Crusader period, under the Ayyubids, were the walls renovated; the Crusaders, for their part, refortified the Citadel, and the Templars built a new wall south of the Temple Mount. Here and there the Crusaders dismantled older buildings, as on the Temple Mount, where they destroyed any Muslim buildings they deemed useless—or detrimental—for their own needs. Thus, they converted the Dome of the Rock and el-Aqsa Mosque into churches, and the Temple Mount became a Christian site, invested with a variety of religious traditions. These Christian traditions were probably brought to Jerusalem not by the Crusaders, but by the city's indigenous Christian inhabitants, generally known as the "oriental Christians," who returned to Jerusalem and became a kind of link between the Early Arab and Crusader periods. In fact, they were the sole element that could teach the Crusader colonizers of Jerusalem, most of them of peasant backgrounds, how to run a city.

A distinctive feature of Crusader Jerusalem was its cosmopolitanism: the population was made up, on the one hand, of the oriental Christian com-

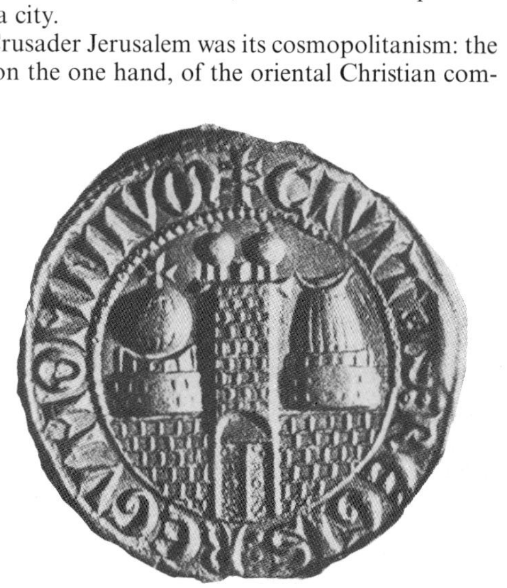

Royal Crusader seal with inscription: "the city of the king of all kings," and depictions (left to right) Church of the Holy Sepulcher, "David's Tower," and Dome of the Rock.

Map of Jerusalem in the Early Arab period.

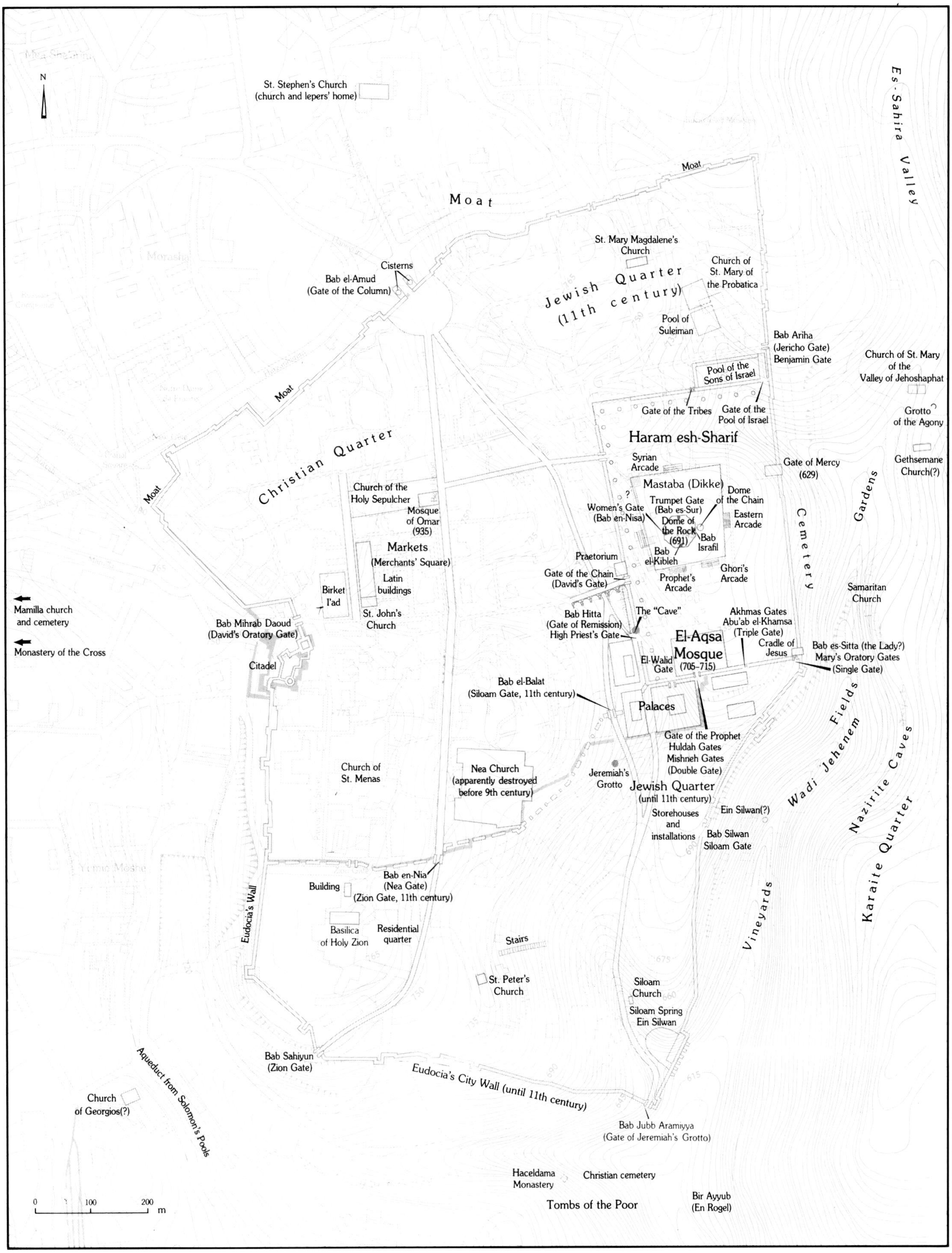

munities (Armenians, Georgians, Greeks, etc.) and, on the other, of the Franks, the newcomers from Europe. Among the latter were Frenchmen, Germans, Englishmen, Spaniards, Portuguese, and Hungarians. The large number of demographic elements in Jerusalem and the new settlement of Europeans required large-scale construction. Moreover, the Christian traditions relating to Jerusalem, both the older traditions that had long been current and those created in the Crusader period, prompted the construction of new churches and other religious institutions.

There exist a great variety and quantity of sources for the Crusader period, mainly documents of the religious-military orders and the major churches recording real estate transactions. As such documents concerning land and property generally included precise locations, they provide an important aid

Map of Jerusalem in the Crusader period.

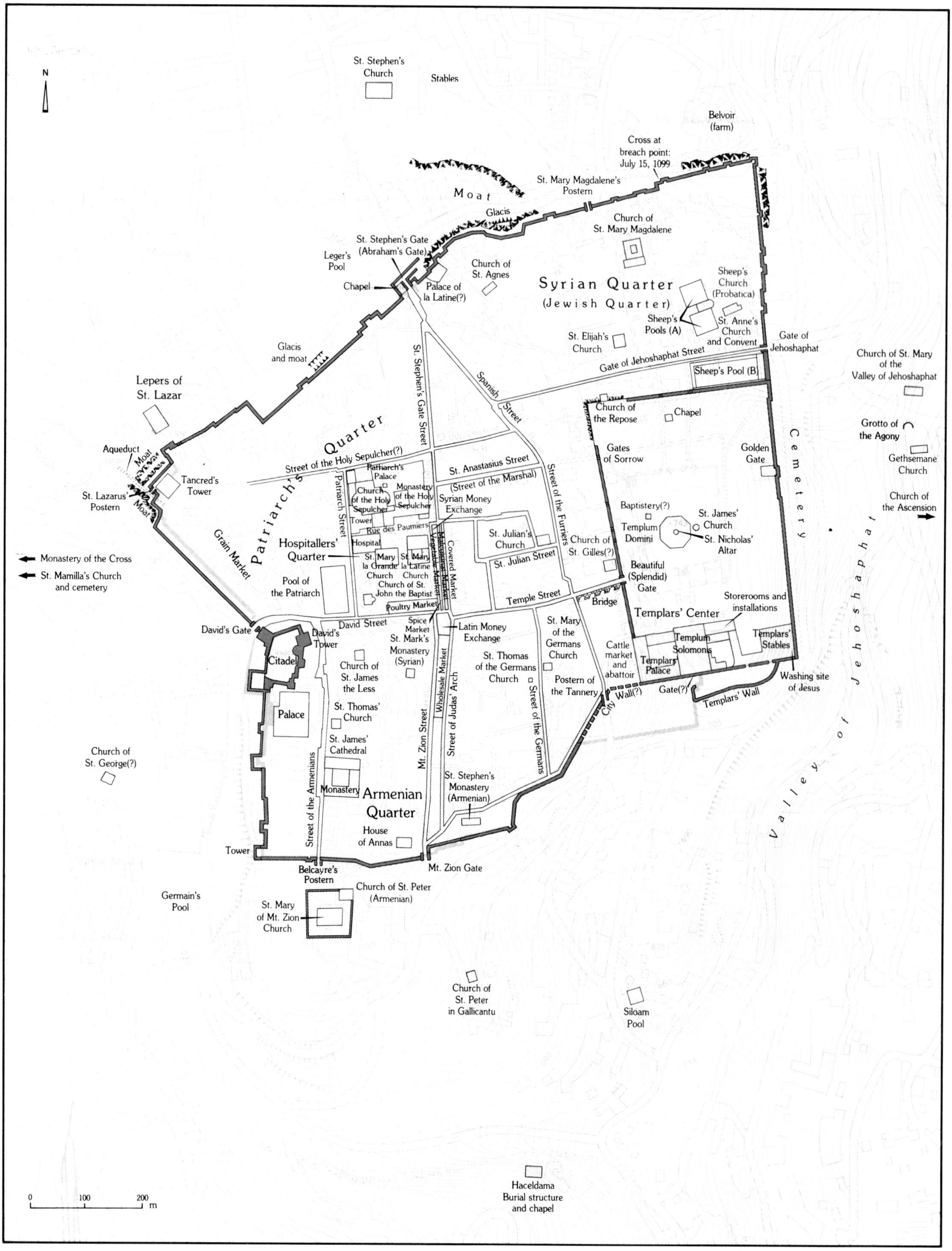

in identifying archaeological remains. The pilgrims who visited Jerusalem have also contributed to what is known of the Holy City, as do the descriptions written for Christians in Europe.

Because of Jerusalem's distance from the Mediterranean coast, the marine powers of the time (the Italian cities) had little interest in it and did not establish quarters here as they did, for example, at Acre. The privileges enjoyed by Christian settlers in Jerusalem, aimed at enlarging the city's Christian population, inspired a spate of economic activities and construction, all the more so as Jerusalem enjoyed considerable political calm for the whole of the twelfth century.

Architecture and architectural ornamentation in Jerusalem in the Crusader period were influenced both by the local—mainly Byzantine—and imported Romanesque art, then at its zenith in Europe. It was this commingling of the two styles that created the characteristic Christian art of Jerusalem. Most of the buildings of Crusader Jerusalem are still standing, although generally they are integrated in secondary use, in Muslim structures built in the Ayyubid and Mamluk period or later.

AYYUBID PERIOD. The Ayyubid period begins with Saladin's conquest of Jerusalem on October 2, 1187. The Crusader kingdom of Jerusalem enhanced the city's importance in the Muslim world. The new rulers began by effacing every possible sign of Crusader rule. The cross marking the point where the Crusaders had breached the city wall was removed, as was the cross crowning the Dome of the Rock. Churches were converted to mosques, and the most celebrated of these, Saint Anne's, became a Muslim *madrasa*, or religious school, and a residence for dervishes. A *minbar* (preacher's pulpit) fashioned by Nur ed-Din in Aleppo was now brought to Jerusalem and installed in the el-Aqsa Mosque. Christian artwork in the Dome of the Rock and el-Aqsa Mosque was dismantled or plastered over. Saladin also added an inscription of his own in the Dome of the Rock.

The Hospitaller hospital south of the Church of the Holy Sepulcher now became a hospital for Saladin's men. The Crusader patriarch's palace became a *khanqa*, a dervishes' residence. The Church of the Holy Sepulcher was returned to the Greek Orthodox, who had been its proprietors prior to the Crusaders' arrival, but only a few Latin monks were permitted to serve there.

The city walls, built about 120 years earlier by the Fatimids, were renovated. This project is widely described in the sources. Saladin himself took part in the work, setting an example for his nobles and commanders. His main concern was to fortify the line from the Damascus to the Jaffa gates; but he also fortified Mount Zion and built a wall around it. Archaeological evidence for this fortification project was discovered by Bliss and Dickie in their 1894–1897 excavations on Mount Zion and by the 1972 excavations in Ẓahal Square. These excavations exposed part of Saladin's system of walls and moats. After Saladin left Jerusalem, his brother el-Malik el-'Adil continued to fortify the city; part of an inscription dedicated by this ruler was discovered in the Citadel. El-'Adil's son, el-Malik el-Mu'azzem 'Isa, did more than any other member of the dynasty to build and fortify Jerusalem, as attested by his numerous inscriptions discovered in the city.

Saladin's reason for fortifying Jerusalem was the Third Crusade, one of whose leaders, Richard the Lion Heart, king of England, spent some time in Palestine and came so close to Jerusalem as to present a threat to the Ayyubid ruler. However, the Crusaders made no attempt to reoccupy the city, for fear that lack of manpower would make it impossible for them to hold it. Saladin permitted Christians to visit Jerusalem in order to mollify Christian anger over their loss of the Holy City.

In 1219, el-Malik el-Mu'azzem 'Isa decided to demolish Jerusalem's walls and fortifications, fearing that a Crusader army might launch a surprise attack and take advantage of its strongholds. This decision had an adverse effect on the city's residents, many of whom left, refusing to live in an unfortified city (only the "Tower of David" was spared). Drawings made by travelers in subsequent centuries show that the destruction consisted mainly of large breaches in the walls. El-Malik el-Mu'azzem 'Isa continued the demolition in 1220 and 1227. Meanwhile, another crusade reached Palestine, led by the king of Sicily and Holy Roman Emperor Frederick II Hohenstaufen of Germany. In 1229, the latter concluded an agreement with el-Malik el-Kamil, according to which Jerusalem—except for the Temple Mount—was handed over to the Christians. Christians ruled the city for the next fifteen years, but the Muslim inhabitants enjoyed considerable autonomy. Although a clause in the agreement between el-Malik el-Kamil and Frederick II prohibited any further fortification of Jerusalem, the emperor apparently received personal permission to fortify the city. It is not clear whether he made use of this permission, for he was in Jerusalem for three days (March 17–19, 1229), after which he returned to Europe. Before leaving, he bestowed gifts of property on the members of the Teutonic Order, which had assisted him—the Crusaders' royal palace (on the site of the present-day Kishleh, near the Jaffa Gate Citadel) and the nearby Church of Saint Thomas.

A peasants' revolt against the restoration of Jerusalem to the Christians was suppressed by a Crusader army from the north of the country (1230). Shortly thereafter, the Ayyubid el-Malik Naṣir Daoud attacked Jerusalem and besieged the Citadel. After a siege that lasted three weeks, he took the Citadel and decided to destroy it. (As the Citadel had been destroyed by el-Malik el-Mu'azzem 'Isa, it was probably rebuilt by Frederick II, and this new citadel was the one destroyed by el-Malik Naṣir Daoud.) In 1240, another agreement was concluded between the Egyptian sultan el-Malik Salaḥ Ayyub and Richard of Cornwall, who headed a new Crusader army. This agreement not only did not undermine Crusader control of Jerusalem, it in fact linked the city by a corridor to the Crusader kingdom in the coastal region. Further quarrels among the Ayyubid princes enabled the Crusaders to reach an agreement with the princes of Damascus (the Pact of Jaffa, 1244), which granted them the Temple Mount, which had been in Muslim hands since the agreement of 1229. Christian rites were then renewed in the Dome of the Rock. When the Egyptian Ayyubid prince realized that the Crusaders had collaborated with the princes of Damascus, he enlisted the aid of the Khwarizmians, who had been forced out of their homeland in Central Asia by the invading Mongols. The Khawarizmians stormed Jerusalem, routing the Crusaders and their Damascene allies. In July 1244, the almost unfortified city fell easily to the new invaders, who massacred the Christian inhabitants and put an end to Christian rule in Jerusalem.

DAN BAHAT

EL-ḤARAM ESH-SHARIF (THE TEMPLE MOUNT)

In the Arab period, the Temple Mount was called el-Ḥaram esh-Sharif, "the Noble Sanctuary" (often only the term "Ḥaram" is used). Physically the site corresponds to the Herodian compound.

According to various sources, after the Arabs conquered Jerusalem large amounts of rubble were carried away to clear the area for construction. Building activity on the Temple Mount can then be traced for some twelve centuries. All the monuments and architecture visible today postdate the Arab conquest.

In the Arab period the Temple Mount consisted of two levels: the one

Dome of the Rock: general view.

Dome of the Rock: section of the wall mosaic of the inner circular arcade, late 7th century CE.

Dome of the Rock: the "foundation stone" as viewed from the gallery of the dome's drum, late 7th century CE.

El-Aqsa Mosque: carved wooden panels used to strengthen the arches above the columns, 8th century CE.

encountered when entering from any of the various gates in the western and the northern walls (see below), which does not differ much from the Herodian level, and the irregularly shaped raised platform, essentially at the center of the compound. Eight flights of stairs on all four sides lead to the upper platform; they are crowned by arcades, four of which face the four openings in the Dome of the Rock. The stairs have apparently been there since the Umayyad period; by the tenth century two more are mentioned in the sources.

Shortly after the Arab conquest, a mosque was built somewhere along the southern wall of the Ḥaram esh-Sharif. A brief report by the European pilgrim Arculf, who visited the site in about 680, describes this first mosque as a rudimentary building. Little else is known about it, and nothing is left of it.

The turning point for all building activity on the Temple Mount took place in the Umayyad period (661–749). During that decisive period, the caliph ʿAbd el-Malik (685–705) developed the Ḥaram into a major Islamic center with two main poles: the Dome of the Rock and el-Aqsa Mosque.

THE DOME OF THE ROCK. Foremost is the Dome of the Rock in the center of the platform. This stone octagonal building, an architectural masterpiece, is also the most ancient Muslim monument in this country (it is sometimes erroneously referred to as the Mosque of Omar). It preserves its original inscription in Kufic, Early Arabic script, with the date 72 AH (691–692). Its inner space is divided into three areas by two arcades (*mawazin*, in Arabic): an intermediate octagon, parallel to the outer walls, and a circular arcade, around the rock in the very center, traditionally known as the site of the *akedah*, "the binding of Isaac" and of Muhammad's ascent to Heaven. This circular arcade supports the drum that is crowned by the dome. The dome is composed of two shells of wood ribs, inscribing one dome within the other, and an isolating space between the two. The length of each of the eight walls of the octagon averages 20.4 m, equaling the height of the dome and its diameter. Whereas much of the exterior decoration was redone through the centuries, most of the interior decoration is original, going back to the seventh century. The walls are paneled on both faces with slabs of marble. The coating on the polychrome glazed tiles on its exterior is a twentieth-century restoration that replaced seventh-century glass mosaics. The beauty and superior craftsmanship of the glass mosaics can be appreciated inside the monument, where they are preserved on both faces of the intermediate octagon, on the circular arcade, and on the drum.

The themes of the mosaics are based essentially on floral motifs; however, each one of the various sets of mosaics generates a distinct inner iconography. On the outer face of the intermediate octagon various trees with fruits and hybrid floral motifs are depicted. Its inner face is decorated with a rich collection of jewelry set into the floral motifs. The Kufic inscription (see above) runs on both sides of the intermediate octagon, above the decorative motifs. The circular arcade is decorated with scrolls emerging from jeweled amphorae; the mosaics around the drum are decorated in a similar fashion, but ending with pairs of winged motifs.

EL-AQSA MOSQUE. The second major building on the Ḥaram is the el-Aqsa Mosque, built along the southern wall of the Temple Mount. While the Dome of the Rock has preserved its original plan and much of its original decoration, the mosque has a different history. The area beneath it consists of hollow spaces (see below), which have contributed to the building's repeated destruction. Indeed, today the el-Aqsa Mosque is entirely different from what it was in the eighth century, when it was more than twice the size. It preserves nothing of its original plan and decoration. At least five stages can be traced in the building; the mosque in its second stage was apparently begun by ʿAbd el-Malik and completed by his son, Walid I. In a restoration in the 1940s, most of the interior was completely renovated. On display at the Rockefeller Museum and the Museum of the Temple Mount are examples of carved wooden panels that were the ends of the tie beams that supported the main roof in the eighth century. The extraordinary decoration of the wooden panels is in accordance with the style of the contemporary mosaic decoration of the Dome of the Rock. There is an abundance of floral motifs, such as pomegranates and vines, several arch frames, and some geometric patterns. The wood is apparently cypress.

THE DOME OF THE CHAIN. The small monument to the east of the Dome of the Rock, known as the Dome of the Chain, is another Umayyad memorial. On a smaller scale, it experienced many of the restorations the Dome of the Rock underwent. It, too, was originally decorated with glass mosaics; after having been restored twice in the Middle Ages, the glass mosaics were replaced with glazed tiles in the sixteenth century, under Sultan Suleiman the Magnificent. Unlike the Dome of the Rock, they were not replaced in the twentieth century. Its miḥrab, or prayer niche, which can be seen on its southern side, is post-Umayyad but is already mentioned in tenth-century sources.

OTHER BUILDINGS AND MONUMENTS. A systematic survey of the Ḥaram esh-Sharif numbered more than two hundred architectural units. They illustrate, to different degrees, the styles of the Ayyubid, Mameluke, and Ottoman periods. Only a few of the most significant examples of each one of these contributions to Islamic history and archaeology in this country are mentioned here.

The monumental gate in the middle of the enclosure's western wall leads to the Cotton Merchants' Market. The gate dates to the first part of the Mameluke period, in the first half of the fourteenth century, under the emir Tankiz. It preserves most of the features typical of Mameluke style.

Near the monumental gate is a small, exquisite fountain dating to the second half of the fifteenth century—the *sabil* (fountain of) Qaʾitbay—with a uniquely carved dome. The *madrasa* of that same Mameluke sultan, el-

"Solomon's Stables," probably 11th century.

Malik el-Ashraf Qa'itbay, is situated near the Gate of the Chain, farther to the south. An example of Ottoman architecture on the Ḥaram esh-Sharif, near the northern entrances, is a *sabil* from the time of Sultan Suleiman, in the first half of the sixteenth century.

Examples of various paleographic styles can be seen in their numerous inscriptions. The most important Ayyubid inscription is probably the four lines written above the main miḥrab in the el-Aqsa Mosque, commemorating Saladin's victory over the Crusaders.

MYRIAM ROSEN-AYALON

"SOLOMON'S STABLES." In order to build the Dome of the Rock and the el-Aqsa Mosque and convert the area into a sacred precinct, the Umayyad caliphs had to repair the Temple Mount enclosure. It was probably they who constructed the extensive subterranean vaulted space at the southeastern corner of the Temple Mount, popularly known today as "Solomon's Stables." Until the end of the 1960s, it was widely believed that the present structure dates to the Crusader period; it is now apparent that the Crusaders took over the Temple Mount as it was, merely converting the already existing mosques to churches. They may have added a few small structures of their own, but most of the precinct and its buildings were the work of their predecessors. The Templars used it as stables for their horses, as they did with various other existing buildings.

SOUTHERN GATES OF THE TEMPLE MOUNT. The Temple Mount, renovated by the Muslims, became a much frequented shrine, creating the necessity for several gates. In the south, the gates surviving from the Second Temple period were repaired: the Eastern Huldah Gate was rebuilt as a triple-arched gate and the Western Huldah Gate as a double-arched gate. In time, four columns with capitals were built in the western Double Gate, two to each arch, as well as a stone-carved arched decoration with floral and geometric patterns, in the best tradition of Muslim ornamental art. It was then named the Prophet's Gate, and the Triple Gate became the Gate of the Sufi Vaults (the vaults of Solomon's Stables were occupied by dervishes of the Sufi sect). These gates, situated as they were in the heart of the Umayyad government seat, were used by members of the royal court. Only after the palace and government buildings had been destroyed and abandoned did they become accessible to the general public. Inside the Double Gate, beneath the el-Aqsa Mosque, a tunnel was built, through which one could climb up to the Temple Mount plaza. The southern part of this tunnel, together with its domes and decoration, is actually of Second Temple period origin (see above, Second Temple Period), but its northern continuation was built by the Muslims when they renovated the Temple Mount precinct.

WESTERN GATES OF THE TEMPLE MOUNT. The earliest descriptions in Arab literature of the Temple Mount precinct and its gates are from the early tenth century; nevertheless, they describe the entire history of the area, from the Umayyad period on. The sources name seven gates on the western side of the Temple Mount, three of which can be identified. The southernmost gate on the west was that known as Barclay's Gate. It is the only gate to have survived from Second Temple times together with its posts, threshold, and lintel—although in the Umayyad period the threshhold was 3 m higher than the original level (see above, Second Temple Period). Visitors entering through this gate would ascend from the street running the length of the western wall of the Temple Mount, reaching the level of the Temple Mount proper through a stone-built tunnel. When the Umayyad government seat was located here, the gate was probably used exclusively by the caliph's party (see above). At the time it was known as the Gate of Forgiveness; its present name in Arabic is Bab el-Buraq, after Muhammad's legendary steed.

Some 150 m north of Barclay's Gate was another gate, discovered in 1867 by

Umayyad decoration above the Double Gate, 8th century CE.

Gate of Mercy: interior of the 7th-century structure.

the British explorers of the Palestine Exploration Fund expedition, who were engaged in a survey of cisterns on the Temple Mount. They named it Warren's Gate, after its discoverer, C. Warren. Excavations carried out on behalf of the Ministry of Religions beginning in 1968, under the supervision of M. Ben-Dov, exposed the outer face of this gate. Its lower part turned out to be of Second Temple period origin, while its upper part, including an arched lintel, had been renovated in the Roman or Umayyad period. Warren's Gate leads from street level—through an arched built tunnel—toward the Temple Mount plaza. During the Crusader period, the level of the city had been raised and this gate went out of use. It was blocked up and its tunnel was plastered and used as an enormous cistern.

South of Warren's Gate is a gigantic complete arch, known as Wilson's Arch, after its discoverer, C. Wilson. Above this arch is the Gate of the Chain, which was built by the Crusaders but includes repairs done by the Mamelukes. Warren and C. R. Conder, who first studied Wilson's Arch, dated it to the later part of the Byzantine period; Conder, in fact, believed it to be Muslim work, from the eighth century. Some later scholars (M. Avi-Yonah and others) claimed that it was originally built in Second Temple times. A re-examination of the structure during the Ministry of Religions' excavations corroborated Conder's date. The arch is part of the Umayyad construction projects in and around the Temple Mount precinct, although it is built on the remains of an ancient arch from the Second Temple period.

GATE OF MERCY. One of the most impressive monuments in the Temple Mount precinct is the Gate of Mercy in the enclosure's eastern wall. Some scholars identified it with the Shushan Gate or Priest's Gate from Second Temple times, but this is improbable in view of its architectural style, engravings, and construction technique. Most scholars date the gate to the Byzantine period. New studies of the gate have revealed, however, that it was one of the structures erected by the Umayyad caliphs on the Temple Mount. It was, in fact, built over the remains of earlier gates. In the Byzantine period, the Temple Mount was desolate and in ruins; there was no need then for gates, certainly not a monumental structure like the Gate of Mercy. The early remains may be vestiges of unfinished construction begun under the emperor Heraclius (628).

JERUSALEM'S FORTIFICATION AND CITADEL: EIGHTH TO ELEVENTH CENTURIES

The Arabs, after their conquest of Jerusalem in 638, continued to use the Byzantine fortifications. The tenth-century Arab historian el-Muqaddasi, a native of Jerusalem, described the city's gates and fortifications, counting eight gates. Vincent and others believed that the present course of the city walls, built by Suleiman the Magnificent in the sixteenth century, corresponds to "Muqaddasi's wall." They in fact tried to identify the present gates with those described by the Arab historian. They were faced, however, with explaining the discrepancy in the number of gates: there are only six in Suleiman's wall. Tsafrir's modified version of this theory identified the course of Suleiman's and el-Muqaddasi's walls, except for the area of the Umayyad government seat; however, this meant that there would have been five gates in the southern wall and only one in each of the other three sides of the city, for a total of eight. It is unlikely, however, that there were so many gates in the southern wall. Yet another suggestion is that the very reference to eight gates, some opening to the east and some to the south, implies that the course of the wall in el-Muqaddasi's generation still followed that of the Byzantine city wall. This would have meant including Mount Zion and the City of David, toward the Siloam Pool. In fact, the archaeological research outside the present Old City wall and west of the Dung Gate indicates that the area was then within the walls. This is in agreement with the large number (eight) of gates, particularly in the south, and the initial correspondence between the first stages of the Muslim city and the Byzantine city.

Excavations in the courtyard of the Citadel ("Tower of David"), near the Jaffa Gate, exposed the remains of a round tower and lengths of wall. This is part of the southeast corner tower of a citadel its excavators defined as an Umayyad structure. Ben-Dov believed this to be a citadel, or fortress, with round towers at the corners—a design typical of palaces, public buildings, and forts under the Umayyad and Abbasid caliphs. The remains uncovered to date are not sufficient to indicate whether this plan of the citadel was actually realized or the construction was interrupted, as was the case at the Umayyad government seat at the foot of the Temple Mount.

UMAYYAD SEAT OF GOVERNMENT

The most important archaeological discovery relating to Umayyad Jerusalem was made in the excavations at the foot of the southern wall and southwestern corner of the Temple Mount—a complex of Umayyad administrative buildings whose existence had not been reported in the written sources. The complex consisted of six buildings, two of them palaces with almost the same plan. Each palace (c. 95 by 85 m) was built around an open court, partly paved with stone, and probably partly planted with trees. Covered porticoes surrounded the court, which was reached through arched colonnades with pillars at the corners. Beyond the porticoes were long spaces, subdivided into small rooms. The solid foundations of both palaces reached bedrock or previous masonry, sometimes as much as 9 m deep. The foundations of the eastern palace in the southern wing were set on piers; this was probably the case for the first story, as well. One street (4.3 m wide) ran between the buildings and the southern wall of the Temple Mount; another one linked the two palaces. A well-designed sewage system constructed of clay pipes was discovered in the western palace. The pipes were installed vertically in grooves carved in the palace walls—a sure indication that the building had a second story. It is not known whether the construction of these buildings was ever completed. They were badly damaged in the Abbasid period, when the population of Jerusalem used them as a source of masonry and used the stones for lime. More than fifteen small lime kilns were found in the ruins of the western palace; around one of them scattered building stones from the Umayyad palaces, bearing vestiges of fine frescoes, were still visible in the excavation. The fresco fragments are an indication of the stage of construction that had been reached in the Umayyad palaces. The building blocks from these buildings were reused stones, partly from the walls of the Temple Mount (dismantled by the Byzantines in 628) and partly from Byzantine churches (including the Nea) destroyed in the Persian invasion of 614. That some of the stones came from churches is evident from the crosses on them.

Besides the two palaces, the Umayyad government seat included four other buildings. The easternmost of these stood on the Ophel, outside the southern wall, between the Triple Gate and the Single Gate. This building was only in the first stages of construction when the Umayyad complex was abandoned in 750. The other buildings were located to the west of the Temple Mount. Beyond the palace wall, a street ran the length of the western wall of the Temple Mount, continuing southward toward the Siloam Pool. West of this street was a court, without porticoes, surrounded by rooms with white or gray mosaic floors; the raw material for the mosaics, which were plain and unpatterned, was limestone or marble fragments. Because of the sloping terrain, these floors were laid on a higher level than those in the palace to the east. West of this building were signs of another building with a similar plan. Parts of its southern walls and rooms were unearthed in excavations outside and inside the Dung Gate (in 1975 and 1980, respectively), directed by Ben-Dov.

West of the Western Wall, beyond the street that ran along it, was a sixth building (c. 85 by 60 m). Its floors were partly stone-paved and partly mosaics. All that remained of this building were sections of its outer walls and foundations, from which its inner layout could be discerned. In its center was a small court, whose western part was open to the elements; piers were found within the building that probably supported the ceiling's domes and vaults.

The building's northwestern wing contained a bathhouse with its furnaces in situ. Although the bathhouse has only been partially cleared, it is evident

*Umayyad administrative complex: **(left)** plan; **(right)** aerial view, looking west.*

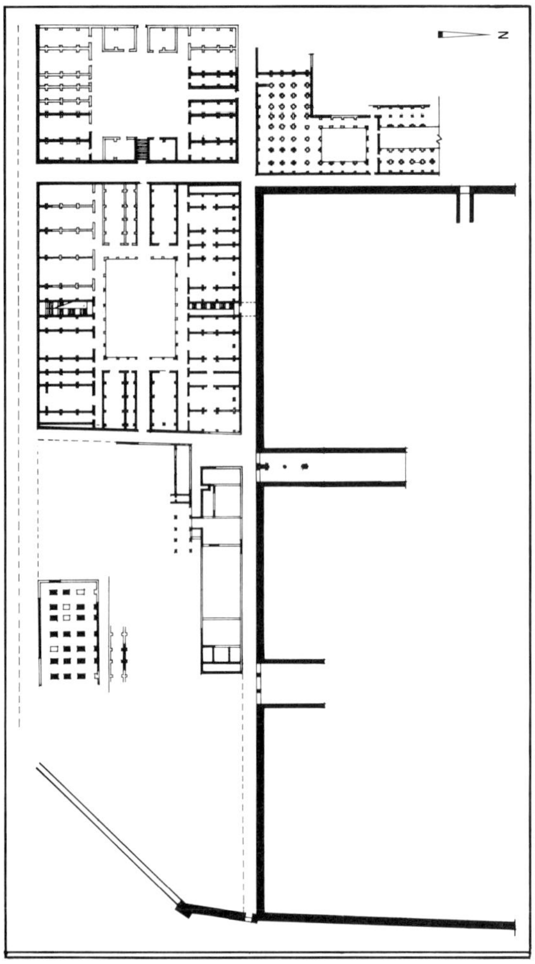

that the caldarium alone had an area of more than 1,000 sq m. Square flues ran up its walls from the furnaces, and the remains of benches, sheathed in marble tiles, were found in it. North of this room was a waiting room with a magnificent ceiling, from which bathers could enter the surrounding rooms. The latter have not yet been excavated; they may have been guest rooms, perhaps for the caliphs or their courtiers. They may also have been the scene of banquets, as at Khirbet el-Mafjar near Jericho. A hypocaust was found beneath the floor on the west; entrances were supported by pointed arches, the first discovered to date in an Umayyad bathhouse.

Large quantities of potsherds of Khirbet el-Mafjar ware were found in the drains and debris of the Umayyad government buildings. Of particular interest was the painted pottery, mainly small bowls and wine goblets adorned with representations of animals and geometric and floral motifs, as well as Arabic inscriptions. The ware is painted in white, black, and red, sometimes on a white background. This pottery should undoubtedly be considered palace ware. Other finds from the seat of government were various pottery and metal vessels, coins, bone and glass utensils, and remains of glass windows from the bathhouse ceiling. Found reused in the furnace floors were a few circular bricks stamped with the insignia of the Tenth Roman Legion Fretensis. The furnace pillars, vaults, and flues were all square, an Umayyad building tradition.

At the time this exceptionally ornate and large-scale government seat was being constructed in this part of Jerusalem, few architectural modifications were being made in the residential neighborhoods of the former Byzantine city.

FATIMID BARRACKS NEAR THE TEMPLE MOUNT. To the west of and above Wilson's Arch the Palestine Exploration Fund expedition discovered a building with many rooms, whose plan it published. Following the reunification of the city in 1967, in the context of maintenance work at and around the Western Wall, it was discovered that this structure was used then as part of

Large Umayyad palace south of the Temple Mount, 8th century CE.

Jerusalem's sewage system: the level of the city had risen since the Crusader period, making the structure subterranean. The entire system was cleared and exposed (under the supervision of Ben-Dov), revealing two clear-cut stages of construction. The structure consisted mainly of a vaulted corridor (c. 100 m long and more than 2 m wide). North of this corridor were several rooms, halls, and narrow corridors, all entered from the wider corridor. To the south of the corridor a series of rooms was entered from the south, but not from the corridor. On the eastern side of the structure, adjoining Wilson's Arch, several ground-floor rooms were discovered. On the west, along the course of the present-day ha-Gai Street, were several vaults, aligned north-south; there was access through some of them to the vaulted corridor. The vaults in the west functioned as a bridge-tunnel supporting ha-Gai Street on its course from the Damascus to the Dung gates; they also supported private houses and the Street of the Chain, which leads to the Temple Mount.

Remains of the structure were primarily found on its first floor (toward the east, part of its ground floor was also found). However, it originally consisted of two or three stories that fell into ruin and were built over in the Crusader and Mameluke periods, ignoring the substructure. Beneath the structure itself were remains of buildings from the Second Temple period, some of which had been repaired by the builders of the new structure, such as the hall known as the Hall of the Freemasons (see above, Second Temple period) and the one known as the Magnificent Hall. The vaulted corridor was built over the renovated Wilson's Arch, making it later than or at least contemporaneous with the Umayyad period.

In Ben-Dov's opinion, the structure with the long vaulted corridor was a military barrack adjoining the Temple Mount. It was probably erected in the second half of the tenth century, when the Fatimids ruled Jerusalem; as the city was then under pressure from the Abbasids and the Byzantine Empire, it presumably was necessary to strengthen its defenses and provide it with a permanent garrison. From the barrack, the governors of Jerusalem could keep activities on the Temple Mount under surveillance—fearing revolts breaking out when large crowds of worshipers were assembled. It also provided living quarters for the soldiers. The surviving ground floor incorporated storage, stables, and other service wings.

JERUSALEM'S FORTIFICATIONS: ELEVENTH TO THIRTEENTH CENTURIES

The present Old City walls, built by Suleiman the Magnificent in the sixteenth century, overlie the remains of earlier fortifications. Numerous excavations, carried out after the Six-Day War in 1967, both outside and inside the wall, have shown that Suleiman indeed kept to the course followed by the previous fortifications—sometimes incorporating surviving lengths of the earlier wall, suitably repaired. The excavations, directed by N. Avigad, M. Ben-Dov, and M. Broshi, concentrated mainly on the southern and western walls, exposing sections of walls, towers, and gates. At the northwestern corner of the Old City wall D. Bahat and M. Ben-Ari uncovered the medieval Goliath's Tower (see below). Several excavations focused on the area of the Damascus Gate, under the direction of R. W. Hamilton, J. B. Hennessy, and M. Magen (see below), and trial explorations were conducted west and east of the Damascus Gate by G. Solar and others (see below). Remains of the medieval fortifications were exposed in all of them. It is difficult to date these remains with any degree of certainty; nevertheless, they were clearly part of Jerusalem's fortifications in the eleventh to thirteenth centuries. The first rulers to renovate this line of fortifications were the Fatimids, in the eleventh century.

SOUTHERN WALL. One of the most impressive sections of these fortifications was discovered in the area of the Dung Gate. Several towers were erected along this course, including two gate towers: the Jews' Gate and the Tanners' Postern, the predecessors of the Zion and Dung gates, respectively. The masonry was generally large stones, not always well dressed, except at the corners and in embrasures. The stones were held together by good cementing materials containing a high proportion of lime.

In the Middle Ages, Jerusalem's southern defenses, which originally enclosed the City of David and the slopes of Mount Zion, were relocated toward the north, to the line of Suleiman's wall, exposing the southern part of the Temple Mount. The city wall no longer linked up with the southeastern corner of the Mount, to contain the entire southern wall of the enclosure in the walled area of the city. It thus became necessary to seal the southern gates of the Temple Mount. The Triple Gate was blocked by massive masonry, and the Double Gate was incorporated in a powerful tower built in front of it. The new city wall then ran from this tower, burying the remains of the Umayyad government seat beneath it. Deep underground, beneath Solomon's Stables, an escape tunnel was dug, breaching the southern wall.

Periodically, on the eve of important battles for Jerusalem, secondary fortifications have been added on the south to protect the Temple Mount and its blocked-up gates. Under the Fatimids, a defensive wall of this kind was built some 100 m from the southern wall; another such wall went up in the Ayyubid period, about 30 m south of the Temple Mount. Parts of these walls were discovered in the excavations on the Ophel.

THE CITADEL. Excavations in the Citadel ("Tower of David"), first by Johns and later by Geva, Solar and Sivan, unearthed remains going back as far as the First Temple period. It turned out that the now dominant structure of the Ottoman Citadel concealed remains from the eleventh to thirteenth centuries. However, it is not known when the earlier structure was built or who built it. In some places the medieval remains consist of two stories; sometimes the walls and towers were found completely breached. The construction of the earlier citadel resembles that of the medieval walls of Jerusalem in terms of building techniques, types and dressing of stone, and cementing materials.

MEIR BEN-DOV

EXCAVATIONS IN ẒAHAL SQUARE. An area just outside the northwestern corner of the Old City was excavated by D. Bahat and M. Ben-Ari in 1972 while landscaping work was in progress around the Old City walls. These excavations revealed that the Ottoman builders of the wall had left approximately 3 m of the tower known as Tancred's Tower, or Goliath's Tower (Qal'at Jalud), outside the city. The bulk of this great tower (35 sq m) was inside the walls. It was built at the northwest extremity of Jerusalem in the Middle Ages and was defended by the previous city wall, which then ran some 3 m to its north and west; a street separated the tower from the wall. The wall itself (3 m thick) was protected by a deep moat (c. 19 m wide), in which the excavators went down some 7 m without reaching bedrock. The city wall contemporary with the tower continues to the east and south beneath the Ottoman wall. Both the wall and tower were built of large, roughly hewn stones with a coarse central boss and margins made with a many-pointed hammer. In two places Crusader capitals, reworked in the manner just described, were found built into the masonry. In the nineteenth century, the remains of another tower had been found abutting the tower excavated in 1972. Both the archaeological evidence and the literary sources indicate that the tower and the wall were built in the time of Saladin and his successors (1192–1219) and were demolished later, along with Jerusalem's other fortifications. The structure was described as being in ruins as early as the late thirteenth century. The name Goliath's Tower appears in European sources only in the nineteenth century. The Tancred's Tower that figures in maps and descriptions of Crusader Jerusalem is probably the section of the eleventh-century tower now beneath the courtyard of the Collège des Frères in the Old City; it received its name in Crusader times because it was here that Tancred besieged Jerusalem in 1099. The tower continued in use throughout the Crusader period. An aqueduct that began in the Street of the Prophets and brought water to the cisterns in the Old City was discovered above a specially prepared passage in the medieval moat. The Ottoman builders leveled the ruins of the tower and the wall and built their wall over the ruins of the tower.

A small postern in the wall just west of the tower, noted in the nineteenth century by the Palestine Exploration Fund expedition, may be the ancient Lazarus' Postern referred to in contemporary sources.

NORTHERN WALL. In 1979, A. De Groot cut two trenches perpendicular to the northern wall. In the part of the western trench opposite Saint Savior's Convent, the excavators discovered fortifications, including a wall (4.5 m thick) 8 m from the Ottoman wall. This wall was preserved to a height of 3.5 m; to its north was a moat 14 m wide. The excavation showed that the Ottoman wall was clearly built over an earlier (probably Byzantine) wall. This may have been the course of the wall in the Middle Ages, as well. The remains are therefore probably those of the main wall, with a shallow, lower wall and a moat in front of it. These details agree with accounts of the Crusaders' successful siege of the city in 1099.

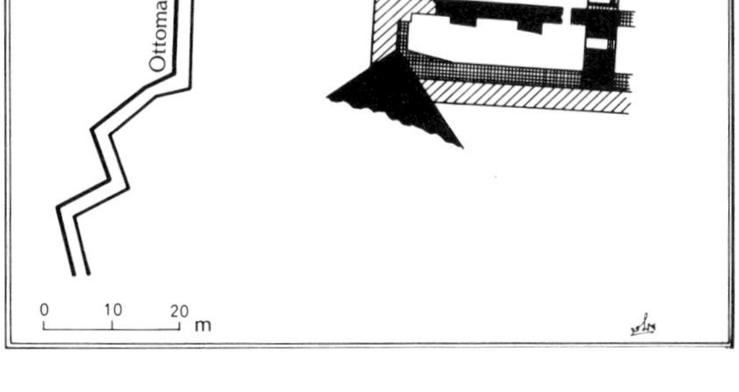

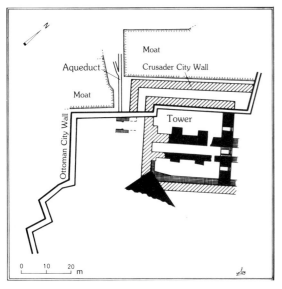

Plan of the excavations in Ẓahal Square.

Present-day butchers' market, originally of the Crusader period.

The eastern trench, 50 m from the other, also revealed remains of a sloping wall, probably the side of a moat. A similar wall was found east of the Damascus Gate. These two lengths of wall indicate the presence of fortifications with a moat to the north of the present-day Old City. Possibly, they were part of the fortifications of the Crusader city, but there is no written record of their construction in the Crusader period. There is, however, information about fortifications constructed some thirty years earlier, so it is possible that this system was constructed toward the end of the Fatimid period.

DAMASCUS GATE. The Damascus Gate was excavated by Hamilton in 1937–1938, on behalf of the Mandatory Department of Antiquities, and again by Hennessy as part of the Kenyon expedition between 1964 and 1968. From 1979 to 1983, additional excavations were carried out by Magen, as part of construction work to develop the area for tourism.

Most of the excavation, which revealed remains from the Middle Ages, was conducted outside the gate. In the present gate (1537–1538), which was built directly over the Roman gate, there are no traces of medieval masonry, except for the easternmost arch, which was blocked up by the Crusaders. Among the remains dated to the Crusader period was a barbican and passages linking it with the main gate. Three stages of construction were attributed to that period, in all of which entry to the city was indirect, through a narrow passage leading from the barbican to the main gate. There were various structures on both sides of the passage, including a chapel adorned with wall paintings depicting the Annunciation. Another structure collapsed during the excavations into an underlying Umayyad cistern. It may have been a customs house or some other administrative building connected with the gate. Both it and the chapel were added on to the gate in its second stage. In the third stage an additional story was added to the barbican and its piers were narrowed. Hennessy dated the gate to the twelfth century, although it is not mentioned in historical sources of that time. There are, on the contrary, thirteenth-century sources that describe a gate built in the brief span of Crusader rule in Jerusalem between 1229 and 1244. Confirmation of this date has come from a few coins discovered in the excavation, in particular a thirteenth-century coin found on the floor of the second stage. In the Crusader period, the gate was known as Saint Stephen's Gate, and the chapel found there was probably dedicated to the Virgin Mary, in her capacity as guardian of the city gates. The gate is believed to have been destroyed when the Khwarizmians sacked Je-rusalem in 1244.

CRUSADER(?) BUILDING IN CITY HALL SQUARE. In 1988–1989 Bahat and A. Maier excavated in the City Hall Square and exposed the northern and western outer walls of a large building. Along the wall were four supporting buttresses, but no floors were found in situ. The structure was dated on the basis of the debris, which consisted of stones dressed in typical Crusader style. One of the stones in fact bore a stonemason's mark—the letter A—which has been identified at other sites from the same period. The remains in question may be those of a hospital belonging to the Order of Saint Lazarus, or of a Mameluke caravanserai known from the sources.

EXCAVATIONS ON CHRISTIANS' STREET. In 1977, S. Margalit excavated on Christians' Street. At approximately 60 cm below the present street level, he discovered the original street, from the latter part of the Roman period and the beginning of the Byzantine period. This finely paved street survived until the Ottoman period. It was thus used in the Crusader period, when it was known as the Patriarch's Street. Evidence to that effect is the fact that the western entrance to the Crusader Church of the Holy Sepulcher was built at a level permitting easy access from it.

THE OLD CITY BAZAARS. The three bazaars in the heart of the Old City have been dated since the nineteenth century to the Crusader period, on the basis of inscriptions identifying them as property of Saint Anne's Church (only one of these inscriptions survives in situ). Various architectural elements in the bazaars can also be dated to the twelfth century, a date confirmed by the sources. In 1988, the owners of a stall in one of the bazaars, in clearing the plaster from the walls, revealed that all three bazaars were built up against the large bazaar along what is now David Street (also mentioned in the sources). The original eastern facade of the large bazaar was now exposed.

According to the historical sources, the junction of the Byzantine Cardo and Decumanus in the heart of the Old City was once marked by a plaza surrounded by Crusader remains; the area has, however, disappeared under more recent construction. South of this plaza the excavations in the Jewish Quarter revealed two bazaars from the Crusader period. One of these was a long, vaulted bazaar, built over the sixth-century Cardo. Here, too, an inscription referring to Saint Anne's Church was discovered. The street running the length of the bazaar was covered, with stalls on either side. The western stalls had almost no illumination, as they did not open onto the street, while the eastern stalls opened into today's Street of the Jews (called Street of Judas' Arch in the Crusader period) and were thus illuminated. The bazaar's narrow facade then pointed north, toward the above-mentioned plaza; it consisted of an ornamental arch resting on two capitals, one of which has remained in situ. The remains of the bazaar toward the south have disappeared, as they were destroyed when the later structures were built. Adjoining the northern ornamental arch was the second bazaar, a system of four stalls with a finely fashioned facade. It is clear from its relationship to the large bazaar that this group of stalls intruded into the central plaza and reduced its area. These stalls may be the street of shops built by Queen Melisande in 1152. Numerous stonemasons' marks were found in the four northern stalls.

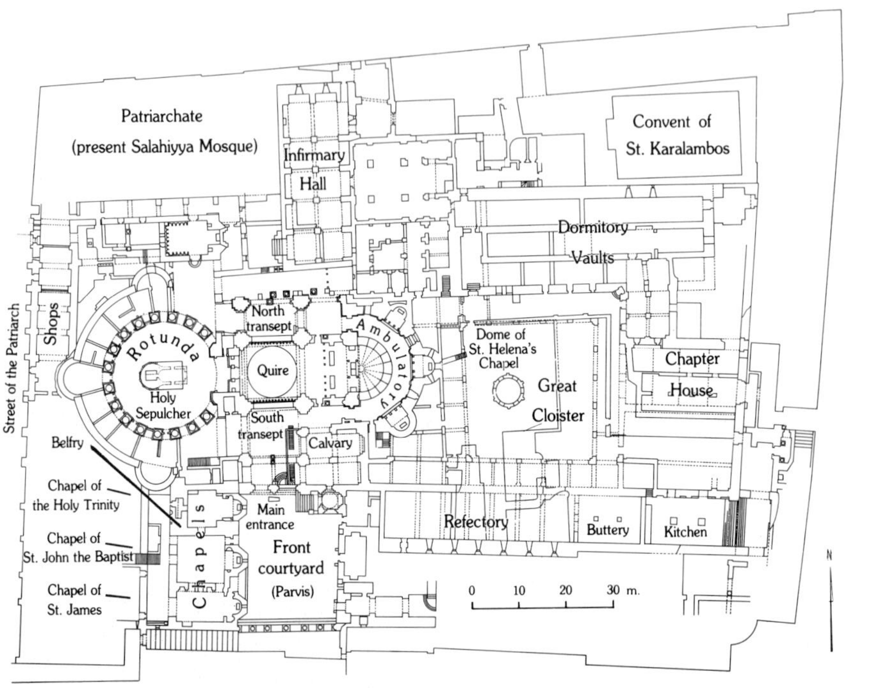

Plan of the Church of the Holy Sepulcher in the Crusader period.

INTERIOR OF THE DUNG GATE. Until the early 1980s, it was believed that there was no construction in the area just inside the Dung Gate in the Crusader period. In 1984, however, the area was excavated by Bahat, who discovered remains of an unknown nature from the Crusader period beneath a large public building from the Ottoman period.

CRUSADER ROYAL PALACE. In 1988–1989, during development work in the courtyard of the Kishleh near the Jaffa Gate, Bahat discovered a large public building, only part of which has been cleared (two rooms with cross vaults). The building blocks were all dressed in Crusader style. The building's facade was decorated with engaged pillars. This was probably the Crusaders' royal palace, which is known from the sources to have stood here. According to the documentary evidence, the building continued in use into the thirteenth century, when it became the Jerusalem headquarters of the Order of Teutonic Knights. It was probably destroyed in the mid-thirteenth century, by the Khwarizmians.

The southern walls of the palace, founded on bedrock, were discovered in the excavations in the Armenian Garden in 1971. One of its halls (17 m long) was discovered by Broshi and Bahat, above a cistern. A cross of Lorraine (a cross with two crossbars) was molded in the plaster of one of the cistern's walls. Various installations were discovered in the hall, perhaps pools for storing liquids (wine?).

CHURCHES

CHURCH OF THE HOLY SEPULCHER. Since the report of L. H. Vincent and F. M. Abel in 1922, excavations have been carried out in the church in 1960 to 1963, on behalf of various Christian communities (in the course of renovation work). The present Church of the Holy Sepulcher is basically the church built by the Crusaders. Upon arriving in Jerusalem, they found the eleventh-century church—an inadequate attempt made in 1042–1048 to renovate the Byzantine Church of the Holy Sepulcher. The Crusaders rebuilt it, here and there incorporating the foundations of the previous building. The Crusader structure is essentially modeled on European churches of the twelfth century: a basilical church with a transept and an apse containing an altar and surrounded by chapels. Excavations have ascertained that the crypt beneath the Chapel of Saint Helena, as well as the chapel itself, were also built in the Crusader period (and not earlier). However, unlike European churches, the Church of the Holy Sepulcher does not have a nave—instead of it, it incorporates the Byzantine rotunda, which was renovated in the eleventh century. The height of the rotunda dictated the height of the church (25.5 m), and the use of a pointed arch, which became increasingly common in this period. The bulk of the Crusaders' building activities took place in the so-called Holy Garden, which was the open part of the church as far back as the Byzantine period. The Crusader sculpture and molded items, some imported from Europe, the style of the capitals and the local decorative elements, such as the wall mosaics, ceiling mosaics and ornamentation of the arches, constitute the sole example in this country of this type of Crusader art. On the site of the Byzantine basilica (which was never rebuilt) the Crusaders built a monastery for the Augustinian canons who served in the church. The mon-

Interior of the Church of the Holy Sepulcher.

*Church of the Holy Sepulcher: **(above)** the western lintel depicting five events in the life of Jesus; **(below)** the eastern lintel.*

Church of Mary Magdalene: remains of the Crusader cloister.

astery was built around a square courtyard; some of the surrounding buildings are preserved, notably the refectory and parts of the basement of the monastery.

CHURCH OF MARY MAGDALENE. Development work near Herod's Gate, in 1978, revealed the remains of the cloister of a twelfth-century convent. The site, now occupied by the Mamuniyya School, was known before World War I to contain remains of the Church of Mary Magdalene. The identification of the church is confirmed by many sources. The cloister was apparently built in 1125. Its western wing was repaired later; according to the written evidence, the building became a *madrasa* in the Mameluke period. Only the southern and western sides are preserved. Three cross vaults were found on the western side, bordering the cloister court and supported by well-built piers. As was usual at the time, the arches were slightly pointed. Fragments of a Crusader-style cornice discovered here testify to the date of construction.

CHURCH OF SAINT JULIAN. Archaeological investigations in the Muslim Quarter of the Old City following the Six-Day War revealed a Crusader church on ʻAqabat Khaladiyya Street. The church was examined in 1978 by Bahat and Solar, who identified it as the Church of Saint Julian, mentioned in a contemporary document. Despite modifications to the building in its many years of use as a workshop, the church retained its original plan.

Of the three eastern apses, the northernmost ones survived. The characteristic cornice of Crusader churches was still evident in both apses, as is a window on the east. There were two small cells in the wall of the central apse, which was originally external, with a square projection into the neighboring courtyard. Because the courtyard has been built up since the survey, the projection is no longer visible. Two rows of three piers divided the building into three aisles. The piers were also decorated with cornices, which run along the northern wall. The western sections of the church have not retained their original shape, owing to numerous repairs, but it is nevertheless obvious that the three western bays were narrower than those on the east. The church's

Church of St. Julian.

Mount Zion: room of the Last Supper (the Cenacle).

dimensions are typical of a medium-sized Crusader church in Jerusalem (inner measurements 12.8 by 8.15 m; outer measurements 14.8 by 10.5 m).

CHURCH OF SAINT MARY OF THE GERMANS. The remains of the church of Saint Mary of the Germans are situated on Misgav Ladakh Street in the Jewish Quarter. It was known to the scholars working for the Palestine Exploration Fund in 1867. In 1968, A. Ovadiah carried out trial excavations at the site. The church (20 by 12 m) was built on a basilical plan: two rows of three piers each divided the building into a nave and two aisles. The ceiling was originally cross-vaulted. At the eastern end were three inscribed apses and a window that tapered outward. The altar was higher than the floor of the hall. Three doors were pierced in the western wall of the hall; a fourth door, in the southern wall, led into the adjoining complex of buildings on the south. The church was probably entered through an atrium (no longer extant) on the west.

South of the church was a two-storied building. The first floor was a hall, aligned east–west, divided into two parts by three piers. The upper floor, which was more or less on the level of the church floor, was similar in plan. Buildings may have adjoined the church on the north as well, presumably also used as a hospice (like the south wing).

The church was probably built along the standard lines of churches established by the German Knights of the Order of Hospitallers (from which the Order of Teutonic Knights developed in the late twelfth and the thirteenth centuries). The date of construction was probably not long after 1128, when the German knights were awarded special status within the Order of Hospitallers.

In the Mameluke period, walls were added to the building on the south and west, and the church seems to have become a residence for dervishes (on the evidence of the sources). The Mameluke accretions were removed when the church was reconstructed and prepared for public visits.

CHURCH OF SAINT THOMAS OF THE GERMANS. The Church of Saint Thomas of the Germans was discovered in the Jewish Quarter in the Palestine Exploration Fund's survey in the nineteenth century and rediscovered when debris was cleared from the ruined Jewish Quarter in 1969. It was found in the second story of a building on Ḥayyei 'Olam Street, the southernmost of the east–west streets in the Jewish Quarter. The hall (12.5 by 8.5 m—the length is only estimated because the western wall was not preserved) was divided into three aisles by two rows of three columns each; the apse at the eastern end was originally decorated with a "running cornice," and the capitals, which survive, were coarsely fashioned.

CHURCH OF SAINT PETER. At the southern end of the Jewish Quarter, Avigad discovered a large Crusader structure (62 m long) with several large rooms. The finest of them (16.3 by 11.4 m) was adorned with typical twelfth-century capitals resting on elbow-shaped consoles. The height of the hall was 7.4 m, and there were indications that the building had a second story. On the east were the remains of a contemporary bathhouse. In the Mameluke period, the building had an industrial use. The structure, built on a declivity adjoining the southern wall of the Byzantine Nea Church, fits descriptions of the Church of Saint Peter given by twelfth-century travelers. All accounts indeed describe the church as being located on the way to Mount Zion and stress that it was approached by descending a large number of steps. A later account reports that the building was converted into a bakery; this information, too, is borne out by the discernible changes in the Mameluke period.

CHURCH OF SAINT MARY OF MOUNT ZION. The Crusader Church of Saint Mary of Mount Zion, like the Byzantine church on which it was built, was discovered at the beginning of this century, during the construction of the Dormition Abbey. In 1983, its western part was excavated under the direction of O. Hess and E. Eisenberg, on behalf of the Israel Department of Antiquities and Museums; they exposed the northwestern corner of the Church of Saint Mary and additional sections of its walls (the northern wall was 2.2 m thick). Some sections of the church floor, which was paved in marble and probably also in mosaic, were also exposed. The remains suggest that the church was longer and wider than originally believed: instead of measuring 54 by 34 m, it was approximately 72 by 36 m. All but a few of its building stones were plundered to construct Saladin's walls, as reported in the historical sources.

CONVENT AND CHURCH OF THE TOMB OF THE VIRGIN MARY. (See above, Byzantine Period.) Two excavations were carried out in the Church of the Tomb of the Virgin Mary in 1973, one in the crypt, by Father Cyprianos, on behalf of the Greek Orthodox Patriarchate, and another farther north. In the crypt, the excavator discovered the burial place of Queen Melisande, wife of Fulk of Anjou and mother of Baldwin III. The excavation north of the crypt exposed a floor, consisting of a coarsely made mosaic and stones, and an inscribed tombstone bearing the date 985.

Church of the Ascension, 12th century.

CHURCH OF THE ASCENSION. In 1959, V. Corbo excavated the Church of the Ascension on the Mount of Olives. He worked in its southeastern corner, which had been surveyed toward the end of the nineteenth century and where magnificent Crusader capitals were preserved. The excavations revealed that the church had been protected by a nearby fortress. Incorporated in the fortifications were stables, in which mangers were discovered, and another building, basilical in plan, whose nature has yet to be determined.

AYYUBID REMAINS

BUILDINGS ON MOUNT ZION. Kenyon's excavations in the Armenian Garden on Mount Zion revealed evidence of Ayyubid construction in the area, mainly a large public building which the excavators interpreted as a khan, although its form suggests an administrative use. The "khan" was erected in a built-up residential area but was separated from the private houses by a street. The builders made use of the main walls of a Byzantine structure, still visible above ground.

The entrance to the khan was in the south (the building was not cleared all the way to the north). The rooms were roofed by barrel vaults. A second building stage, also Ayyubid, was characterized by the creation of raised platforms with well-made stone edges in the rooms. Such platforms continued in use into the Mameluke period, so that it was not always possible to tell the two periods apart in this building. In this same area, buildings were erected along the city wall, which was also repaired. They, too, were separated from the "khan" by a street. A historical source from the Mameluke period refers to Mount Zion (in the extended sense of the term) as an important center of Ayyubid activity.

The excavators dated the construction of the "khan" to the time of Saladin. The nearby private houses were demolished together with the city walls by el-Malik el-Mu'azzem 'Isa in 1219. However, the "khan" seems to have survived beyond that date, to 1227, when the same ruler demolished whatever fortifications had survived the destruction of 1219.

The many inscriptions of Ayyubid rulers on the Temple Mount suggest that they were particularly active there. There is a large Ayyubid inscription in the interior of the Dome of the Rock, and a *madrasa*, or religious school, north of the Temple Mount should be ascribed to el-Malik el-Mu'azzem 'Isa. The dome on the Temple Mount known as Qubbat en-Nahawiyya is still standing; although it has undergone changes over the centuries, its original form, also from the time of el-Malik el-Mu'azzem 'Isa, can still be reconstructed.

BUILDING WEST OF THE TEMPLE MOUNT. North of the Western ("Wailing") Wall plaza, excavation in the underground passages adjoining the western wall have revealed a large structure, consisting of four wings in the shape of a cross. Between the cross-vaults were four large piers, whose upper parts (as far as the vaults) were built of large stones, dressed in the style described above and attributed to the Ayyubids. Thus, these piers may have supported an Ayyubid building; this is also indicated by an inscription from 1198/99 that describes a building "beneath the vault, opposite one of the gates of the Temple Mount."

SUQ EL-QATTANIN. According to M. H. Burgoyne, Suq el-Qattanin (the Cotton Merchants' Market) that abuts the western wall of the Temple Mount, was built in two stages. The earliest comprised its western half; the eastern half was built merely to fill the space between the market and the walls of the Temple Mount. Burgoyne ascribed the facade of the market to the first stage, assigning the stones dressed in the "Ayyubid" style to a building dated to the time of Frederick II—that is, the thirteenth century. In this writer's opinion, the construction is specifically Ayyubid.

INSCRIPTION NEAR THE THIRD WALL. Excavations in the area of the Third Wall also unearthed an Ayyubid building inscription, mentioning a ruler (probably Saladin's son, 'Uthman).

DAN BAHAT

For excavations in Jerusalem, see L. A. Mayer and M. Avi-Yonah, *QDAP* 1, with supplementary information in *QDAP* 2–14 and later in *'Atiqot*, *ADAJ*, and the annual archaeological reports in *RB*. Roman, Byzantine, and Crusader remains discovered up until 1926 were primarily published in Vincent–Abel, *Jérusalem Nouvelle*.

See also C. M. de Vogüé, *Les Églises de la Terre Sainte*, Paris 1860; G. Le Strange, *Palestine under the Moslems*, London 1890 (index); Clermont-Ganneau, *ARP*, 116–126; R. Hartmann, *Palästina unter den Arabern 632–1516*, Leipzig 1915; M. van Berchem, *Materiaux pour un Corpus Inscriptionum Arabicum* 1–3, Cairo 1922–1923; E. Enlart, *Les Monuments des Croisés dans le royaume de Jérusalem* 1–2 (Bibliothèque Archéologique et Historique 7–8), Paris 1925–1928; L. A. Mayer, *ZDPV* 53 (1930), 222–229; K. A. C. Creswell, *Early Muslim Architecture* 1, Oxford 1932; id., *A Short Account of Early Muslim Architecture* (Revised and supplemented by J. W. Allan, Aldershot 1989); W. Harvey, *Church of the Holy Sepulchre*, Jerusalem, London 1935; S. D. Goitein, *JAOS* 70 (1950), 104–108; id., *Studies in Islamic History and Institutions*, Leiden 1966, 135–148; id., *Jerusalem Cathedra* 2 (1982), 168–196; D. Chitty, *The Christian East* n.s. 2/1 (1952), 22–32; V. C. Corbo, *Ricerche Archeologiche al Monte degli Ulivi*, Jerusalem 1965; id., *Il Santo Sepolcro di Gerusalemme* (Studium Biblicum Franciscanum, Collectio Maior 29), Jerusalem 1981; E. Kühnel, *Islamic Art and Architecture*, London 1966, 15–16, 185–186; T. S. R. Boase, *Castles and Churches of the Crusading Kingdom*, Oxford 1967, 1–24; J. Prawer, *Ariel* 19 (1967), 60–66; id., *The Latin Kingdom of Jerusalem*, London 1972, 416–468; id., *Recent Archaeology in the Land of Israel* (eds. H. Shanks and B. Mazar), Washington, D.C. 1981, 115–126; A. L. Tibawi, *The Islamic Quarterly* 12 (1968), 185–218; N. Avigad, *IEJ* 20 (1970), 137–138; id., *Discovering Jerusalem*, Nashville 1983, 247–257; M. Benvenisti, *The Crusaders in the Holy Land*, Jerusalem 1970, 35–73; J. B. Hennessy, *Levant* 2 (1970), 22–27; O. Grabar, *The Encyclopaedia of Islam* 3, Leiden 1971, 173–175; D. Bahat (with G. Solar), *RB* 78 (1971), 598–599; 85 (1978), 72–84; (with R. Reich), 93 (1986), 111–114; id., *IEJ* 22 (1972), 171; id., *Carta's Historical Atlas of Jerusalem*, Jerusalem 1973, 26–36; id., *BAR* 6/2 (1980), 46–49; id., *Archéologie, art et histoire de la Palestine: Colloque du centenaire de la section des sciences religieuses, Ecole Pratique des Hautes Etudes, Sept. 1986* (ed. E.-M. Laperrousaz), Paris 1988, 197–203; id. (and A. Maier), *ESI* 9 (1989–1990), 55–56; id., *Les Dossiers d'Archéologie* 165–166 (1991), 88–99; H. E. Mayer, *The Crusades*, Oxford 1972; M. Piccirillo, *LA* 22 (1972), 291–314; N. Kenaan, *IEJ* 23 (1973), 167–175, 221–229; C. Coüasnon, *The Church of the Holy Sepulchre, Jerusalem* (Schweich Lectures 1972), London 1974; H. Lazarus-Yafeh, *Jerusalem* (eds. M. Österreicher and A. Sinai), New York 1974, 211–225; A. Prodromo, *LA* 24 (1974), 202–226; B. Bagatti et al., *New Discoveries at the Tomb of the Virgin Mary in Gethsemane*, Jerusalem 1975; *Jerusalem Revealed* (ed. Y. Yadin), Jerusalem 1975; L. Y. Rahmani, *IEJ* 26 (1976), 120–129; M. Broshi and Y. Tsafrir, *IEJ* 27 (1977), 28–37; J. Folda, *A History of the Crusades* 4 (ed. K. Setton), Madison 1977, 251–280; id., *Levant* 10 (1978), 139–155; id., *Crusader Art in the Twelfth Century* (*BAR*/IS 152), Oxford 1982; B. Kühnel, *Gesta* 16/2 (1977), 41–50; Y. Tsafrir, *IEJ* 27 (1977), 152–161; 40 (1990), 280–286; J. Wilkinson, *Jerusalem Pilgrims before the Crusades*, Warminster 1977; J. D. Brady, *The American Numismatic Society Museum Notes* 23 (1978), 133–147; H. Buschhausen, *Die süditalieneische Bauplastik im Königreich Jerusalem von König Wilhelm II bis Kaiser Friedrich II* (Österreichischen Akademie der Wissenschaften, Philosophisch-historische Klasse, Denkschriften 108), Vienna 1978; D. Barag, *IEJ* 29 (1979), 197–217; id., *Israel Numismatic Journal* 10 (1988–1989), 40–48; Z. Jacoby, *Gesta* 18/2 (1979), 3–14; id., *IEJ* 30 (1980), 202–204; id., *Zeitschrift für Kunstgeschichte* 45 (1982), 325–394; 48 (1985), 441–450; E. Otto, *Jerusalem: Die Geschichte der Heiligen Stadt von den Anfängen bis zu Kreuzfahrerzeit* (Urban Taschenbücher 308), Stuttgart 1980, 198–226; A. Ovadiah, *Actes du 15e Congres International d'Etudes Byzantines* II, Athens 1981, 585–596; M. Rosen-Ayalon, *Recent Archaeology in the Land of Israel* (eds. H. Shanks and B. Mazar), Washington, D.C. 1981, 111–113; id., *Jerusalem: City of the Ages* (ed. A. L. Eckardt), Lenham 1987, 81–91; id., *Archéologie, art et histoire de la Palestine* (op. cit.), 205–215; id., *The Early Islamic Monuments of al-Haram al-Sharif: An Iconographic Study* (Qedem 28), Jerusalem 1989; ibid. (Reviews), *BAIAS* 9 (1989–1990), 56–58. — *RB* 97 (1990) 619–620. — *AJA* 95 (1991), 188–189. — *PEQ* 123 (1991), 133–135; id., *IEJ* 40 (1990), 305–314; id., *Les Dossiers d'Archéologie* 165–166 (1991), 100–111; M. Ben-Dov, *The Dig at the Temple Mount*, Jerusalem 1982, 343–354; M. Gil, *JNES* 41 (1982), 261–278; B. Z. Kedar, *Jerusalem Cathedra* 2 (1982), 318–327; D. Pringle, *The Ecclesiastical Architecture of the Latin Kingdom of Jerusalem*, Jerusalem 1982; id., *RB* 89 (1982), 92–98; id., *World Archaeology* 18 (1987), 341–362; id., *Levant* 21 (1989), 197–201; id., *BAIAS* 10 (1990–1991), 105–113; H. Geva, *IEJ* 33 (1983), 55–71; D. M. Jacobson, *PEQ* 115 (1983), 145–147; 119 (1987), 39–43; *Outremer: Studies in the History of the Crusading Kingdom of Jerusalem* (eds. B. Z. Kedar et al.), Jerusalem 1983; ibid. (Review), *ZDPV* 104 (1988), 188–189; E. Eisenberg, *ESI* 3 (1984), 47; A. Engle, *1000 Years of Glassmaking in Ancient Jerusalem* (Readings in Glass History 18), Jerusalem 1984, 88–95; A. D. Tushingham, *Excavations in Jerusalem 1961–1967* 1: *Excavations in the Armenian Garden on the Western Hill*, Toronto 1985, 105–107; K. Bieberstein, *ZDPV* 103 (1987), 178–184; 104 (1988), 152–161; M. H. Burgoyne, *Mamluk Jerusalem: An Architectural Study*, Buckhurst Hill 1987; ibid. (Review), *ADAJ* 31 (1987), 541–542; W. H. Mare, *The Archaeology of the Jerusalem Area*, Grand Rapids 1987, 263–292; G. Kühnel, *Wall Painting in the Latin Kingdom of Jerusalem* (Frankfurter Forschungen zur Kunst 14), Berlin 1988; E.-M. Laperrousaz, *Archéologie, art et histoire de la Palestine* (op. cit.), 143–148; J. D. Purvis, *Jerusalem, The Holy City: A Bibliography* (American Theological Library Association Bibliography Series 20), Metuchen, N.J. 1988, 282–292, 368–387; G. W. Wightman, *The Damascus Gate* (*BAR*/IS 519), Oxford 1989; ibid. (Review), *BAIAS* 9 (1989–1990), 61–62; Y. Boiret, *MdB* 61 (1989), 41–43; E. Grabiner, ibid., 27–30; N. Kenaan Kedar, ibid., 37–40; J. Richard, ibid., 13–17; A. Chambon, *ESI* 9 (1989–1990), 144–147; G. Fehérvári, *BAIAS* 9 (1989–1990), 66–67; A. M. Maeir, *IEJ* 40 (1990), 68–70; B. Pixner, *BAR* 16/3 (1990), 16–35, 60; J. Magness, *BA* 54 (1991), 208–217; *The Horns of Hattin* (ed. B. Z. Kedar), Jerusalem (in prep.).

HISTORY OF ARCHAEOLOGICAL RESEARCH IN JERUSALEM

The list below summarizes the major archaeological activities in the area of ancient Jerusalem and its environs, from the mid-nineteenth century to 1992. The list is arranged chronologically, according to the years in which the investigations and excavations took place. A brief summary of the main finds is provided in each case, in order of archaeological-historical periods—from the fourth millennium BCE to the Ottoman period. The dating of the finds and their identifications are those proposed by the excavators. Revisions were made only when new excavations and research proved such data to be wrong.

The locations of the excavated sites are shown on the following map of the Old City and its environs and on the maps assigned to the various periods.

1. F. de Saulcy, 1853–1865: Old City and environs
Documentation and exploration of ancient construction remains: Temple Mount and "Solomon's Stables."
Tombs: "Tomb of Pharaoh's Daughter" and "Tombs of the Kings"—the Tomb of Queen Helene of Adiabene.
(partial list)

2. M. de Vogüé, 1853–1862: Old City
Documentation and exploration of ancient construction remains: Temple Mount and Russian Hospice.
(partial list)

3. E. Pierotti, 1854–1869: Old City
Documentation and exploration of ancient construction remains: Temple Mount, "Solomon's Stables," Russian Hospice, marketplaces in the center of the Old City, Latin Patriarchate, Kishleh area, and Christ Church.
(partial list)

4. C. Mauss and the White Fathers, 1863–1876, 1888–1900: St. Anne's Church, Old City
Bethesda Pool (Probatica) and adjoining construction remains, Second Temple period; water installations and construction remains, Roman period; Church of St. Mary (of the Probatica), Byzantine period; chapel, Crusader period (for later excavations, see no. 41).

5. C. Wilson, 1863–1868: Old City and environs
Documentation and exploration of ancient construction remains: discovery of Wilson's Arch; exploration of roofed underground passages west of Wilson's Arch, Second Temple to medieval periods; survey of Jerusalem's water-supply systems, Second Temple to Ottoman periods and survey (with C. Warren) of cisterns on Temple Mount; examination of Third Wall and Church of the Holy Sepulcher.
Tombs: Garden Tomb.
(partial list)

6. C. Warren, 1867–1870: Old City and environs
Excavations, documentation, and exploration of ancient construction remains: discovery of Warren's Shaft and investigation of Gihon Spring, Siloam Tunnel, and Siloam Pool in City of David; exploration (with C. R. Conder) of Temple Mount walls; discovery of western pier of Robinson's Arch, sections of a street and underlying drainage channel; exploration (with C. Wilson) of Wilson's Arch and structures to its west, including the Freemasons' Hall, Second Temple to medieval periods; survey of cisterns and "Solomon's Stables" on the Temple Mount; Pool of Israel, Struthion Pool, Hasmonean aqueduct northwest of the Temple Mount, and the "low-level aqueduct" on Mount Zion; discovery of the Ophel Wall, Byzantine period, and of Damascus Gate, Gennath Gate, and Goliath's Tower, Roman to medieval periods.
(partial list)

7. C. Clermont-Ganneau, 1870–1874, 1881–1883: Old City and environs
Documentation and exploration of ancient construction remains: part of the fortifications in the City of David, Dome of the Rock, Golden Gate, Russian Hospice, and area of the Antonia fortress; discovery of the inscription forbidding gentiles entry to the Temple precinct, Second Temple period; remains of Byzantine period church at the Fourth Station on Via Dolorosa; Mount Zion.
Tombs: survey of First Temple period tombs in Silwan village, including "Tomb of the Royal Steward"; clearing of "Tombs of the Kings" and "Absalom's Tomb," Second Temple period.
(partial list)

8. H. Maudslay, 1871–1875: Mount Zion
City wall and tower at southwestern corner of the line of the First Wall, Second Temple period.

9. C. Schick, 1872–1901: Old City and environs
Documentation and exploration of ancient construction remains: Temple Mount, "Solomon's Stables" and Golden Gate, Bethesda Pool, Convent of the Flagellation, Muristan, Russian Hospice, Citadel ("Tower of David") and vicinity, Siloam Pool, Siloam Inscription.
Tombs: Garden Tomb, "Herod's Family Tomb."
(partial list)

10. H. Guthe, 1881–1885: Old City and environs
Investigation of the Siloam Tunnel and discovery of part of the fortifications in the City of David, Second Temple period(?); documentation of ancient construction remains, north of "Tower of David."
(partial list)

11. M. J. Lagrange and the White Fathers, 1881–1894: St. Etienne's Monastery north of Old City
Tombs, end of First Temple period; remains of monastery and church of St. Stephen, Byzantine period; chapel and adjoining buildings, Crusader period.

12. J. Germer-Durand and the Assumptionist Fathers, 1882–1912: St. Peter in Gallicantu, Mount Zion
Rock-cuttings and water installations, Second Temple period; monastery, church, and street, Byzantine period.

13. Franciscan Fathers, 1884–1889, 1901–1903: Convent of the Flagellation, Old City
Rock-cuttings and pavement, Roman period.

14. S. Merrill, 1885–1902: Old City and environs
Documentation and exploration of ancient construction remains: north and east of the Citadel ("Tower of David"), Third Wall, aqueduct to Jaffa Gate, Byzantine and medieval periods.
(partial list)

15. J. E. Hanauer, 1891–1907: Old City
Documentation and exploration of ancient construction remains: "Solomon's Stables," area of Antonia fortress, Russian Hospice.
(partial list)

16. F. J. Bliss, 1894: "Armenian mosaic" north of Old City
Remains of chapel, Byzantine period.

17. F. J. Bliss and A. C. Dickie, 1894–1897: Mount Zion and southern Tyropoeon Valley
Fortifications, including sections of city wall, towers, gates—"Essenes' Gate" and dam of the First Wall, Second Temple period; Siloam Pool and paved street, Second Temple period; fortifications, including sections of city wall, towers, and gate, Byzantine period (for later excavations, see no. 101); Siloam Church, buildings and streets, Byzantine period; buildings and enclosure wall, medieval period.

18. L. H. Vincent, 1900–1932: Old City and environs
Systematic detailed research and publication (with F. M. Abel and A. M. Stève) of ancient construction remains, Bronze Age to medieval periods; exploration (with M. Parker) of water-supply systems in Gihon Spring and Siloam Tunnel and discovery of part of the fortifications in City of David; investigation (with Marie-Aline de Sion) of ancient construction remains in Sisters of Zion Convent: Struthion Pool, Lithostrotos pavement and Ecce Homo Arch, Second Temple and Roman periods; excavations and investigation of Eleona Church, Church of the Ascension, and Dominus Flevit Church on Mount of Olives, Byzantine and Crusader periods; publication of the Orpheus mosaic.
(partial list)

19. R. A. S. Macalister, 1900–1908: around Old City
Survey and investigation of the city's necropolises, Second Temple period: Tomb of the Grapes, Tomb of the Frieze, "Herod's Family Tomb."
(partial list)

20. G. Orfali, 1909, 1919–1920: Church of Gethsemane, Kidron Valley
Remains of church, Byzantine and Crusader periods.

21. M. Parker and L. H. Vincent, 1909–1911: City of David
Discovery of part of the fortifications and exploration of water-supply systems: Warren's Shaft, Gihon Spring, and Siloam Tunnel.

22. R. Weill, 1913–1914, 1923–1924: City of David
Rock-cut caves erroneously identified as "Tombs of the House of David," First Temple period; part of the fortifications, system of retaining walls, Second Temple period (for later excavations, see no. 98); discovery of Theodotos inscription, Second Temple period.

23. R. A. S. Macalister and J. G. Duncan, 1923–1925: City of David
Fortification system, including city wall, two towers, and a stepped stone structure erroneously interpreted as part of Jebusite fortifications (for later excavations dating these remains to the Second Temple period, see nos. 45 and 98); buildings and streets, Byzantine period.

24. N. Slouschz, 1924: Kidron Valley
Clearing and exploration of "Absalom's Tomb" and "Tomb of Zechariah."

25. E. L. Sukenik, 1924–1946: around Old City
Exploration and publication of burial caves, including Nicanor's Tomb, Second Temple period; discovery of "Uzziah king of Judah" inscription.
(partial list)

26. E. L. Sukenik and L. A. Mayer, 1925–1927, 1940: north of Old City
Sections of city wall and towers along line of Third Wall, end of Second Temple period; section of city wall along northern line of Old City wall, Byzantine period; remains of buildings, Byzantine period.

27. J. W. Crowfoot and G. M. Fitzgerald, 1925–1927: City of David and Tyropoeon Valley
"Valley Gate," First Temple period(?) and mainly Second Temple period; buildings and streets, Byzantine period.

28. R. W. Hamilton, 1931: Ha-Gai (Valley) Street, Old City
Pavement of Secondary (eastern) Cardo, Roman and Byzantine periods.

29. D. C. Baramki, 1932: Karm esh-Sheikh (Rockefeller Museum), north of Old City
Dozens of tombs, Late Roman and Byzantine periods.

30. W. Harvey, 1933–1934: Church of the Holy Sepulcher, Old City
Examination and exploration of ancient remains, Byzantine and Crusader periods to modern times.

31. C. N. Johns, 1934–1947: Citadel ("Tower of David"), Old City
Sections of city walls and towers at the northwestern corner of the line of the First Wall, Second Temple period (Hasmonean and Herodian periods); remains of buildings from Tenth Legion camp, Roman period; sections of city walls, tower, and buildings, Byzantine period; round corner tower and buildings, Early Arab period; survey of remains of present-day Citadel, medieval to Ottoman periods (for later excavations, see nos. 53, 88, and 105).

32. K. Galling, 1936–1937, around Old City
Survey and publication of Second Temple period burial caves, including "Two-Storied Tomb."
(partial list)

33. C. N. Johns, 1937: Church of St. Mary's Tomb, Kidron Valley
Exploration of remains of church, Byzantine and Crusader periods.

34. R. W. Hamilton, 1937–1938: Damascus Gate and northern wall of Old City
Structure of the Roman Damascus Gate; sections of city wall, Late Roman and Byzantine periods (for later excavations, see nos. 45 and 100).

35. N. Avigad, 1945–1947: Kidron Valley, Silwan village, and north of Old City
Exploration of burial caves and monuments: "Tomb of Pharaoh's Daughter" and "Tomb of the Royal Steward," First Temple period; "Absalom's Tomb" and "Cave of Jehoshaphat," Tomb of Bene Ḥezir, "Tomb of Zechariah," Nicanor's Tomb, Cave of Umm el-'Amed, and Two-Columned Tomb, Second Temple period.
(partial list)

36. Y. Pinkerfeld, 1949: "David's Tomb," Mount Zion
Survey and exploration of remains, Roman and Byzantine periods.

37. M. Avi-Yonah, 1949, 1968: Sheikh Badr (Giv'at Ram), West Jerusalem
Pottery workshop, Second Temple period; pottery workshop of the Tenth Legion, Roman period; monastery and church of St. George, Byzantine period.

38. B. Bagatti and J. T. Milik, 1953–1955: Dominus Flevit Church, Mount of Olives
Remains of church and adjoining buildings, Byzantine period.
Tombs: burial caves, Second Temple and Byzantine periods.

39. R. Amiran, 1953–1960: West Jerusalem
Publication of Late Bronze Age burial caves in Naḥalat Aḥim neighborhood and late First Temple period tombs in Mamilla area; survey and excavation of tumuli in Qiryat Menaḥem neighborhood, end of First Temple period.

Map of the Old City and its environs.

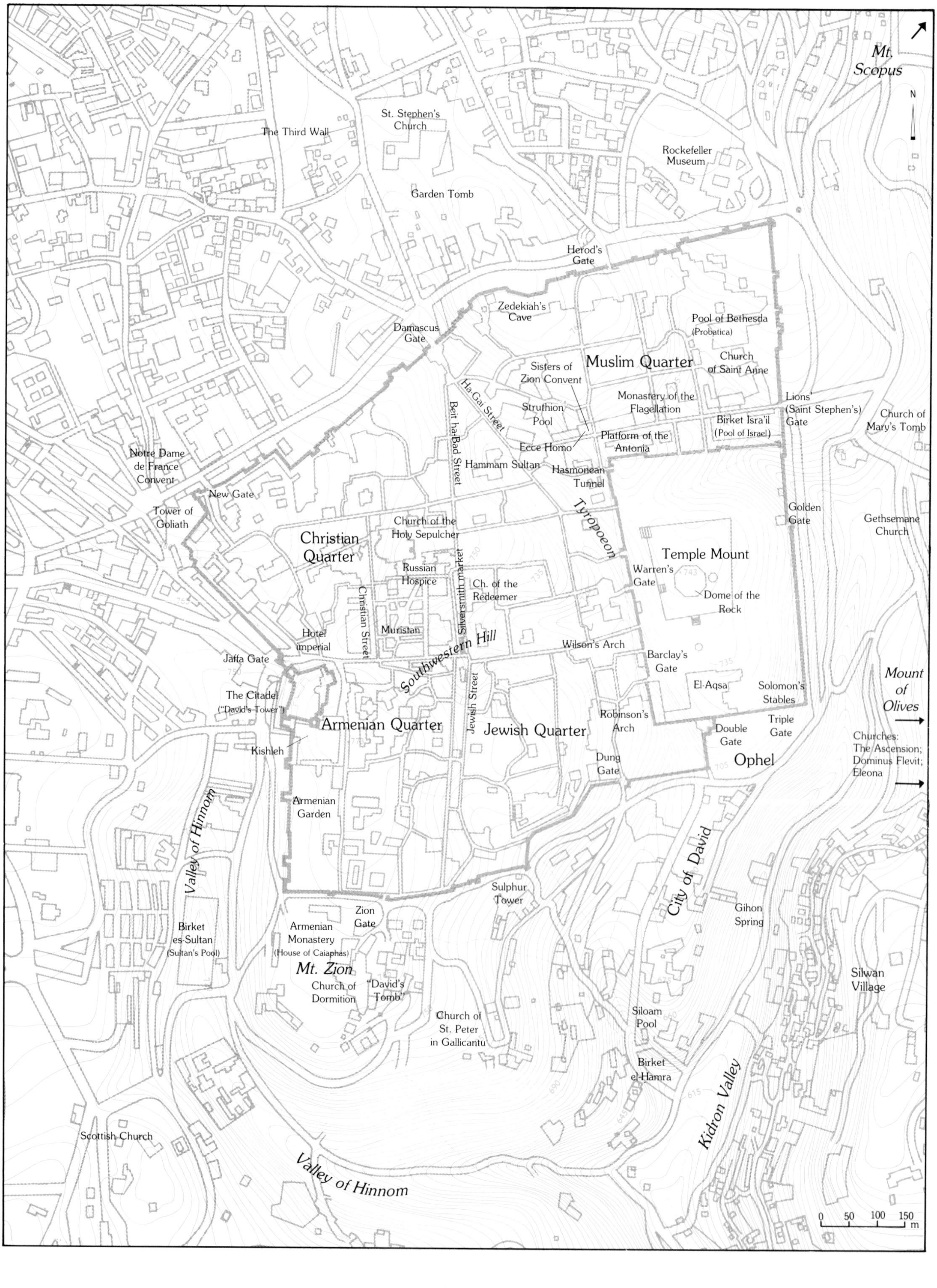
Mt. Scopus
N
The Third Wall
St. Stephen's Church
Rockefeller Museum
Garden Tomb
Herod's Gate
Zedekiah's Cave
Damascus Gate
Pool of Bethesda (Probatica)
Sisters of Zion Convent
Muslim Quarter
Church of Saint Anne
Ha-Gai Street
Beit ha-Bad Street
Struthion Pool
Monastery of the Flagellation
Lions' (Saint Stephen's) Gate
Church of Mary's Tomb
Birket Isra'il (Pool of Israel)
Platform of the Antonia
Ecce Homo
Hammam Sultan
Hasmonean Tunnel
Notre Dame de France Convent
New Gate
Tower of Goliath
Tyropoeon
Golden Gate
Gethsemane Church
Church of the Holy Sepulcher
Christian Quarter
Temple Mount
Russian Hospice
Silversmith market
Ch. of the Redeemer
Warren's Gate
Christian Street
Dome of the Rock
Muristan
Hotel imperial
Southwestern Hill
Wilson's Arch
Jaffa Gate
Barclay's Gate
Mount of Olives
The Citadel ("David's Tower")
Jewish Street
El-Aqsa
Solomon's Stables
Armenian Quarter
Jewish Quarter
Robinson's Arch
Triple Gate
Double Gate
Churches: The Ascension; Dominus Flevit; Eleona
Kishleh
Dung Gate
Ophel
Armenian Garden
Valley of Hinnom
City of David
Sulphur Tower
Zion Gate
Gihon Spring
Birket es-Sultan (Sultan's Pool)
Armenian Monastery (House of Caiaphas)
Mt. Zion
Church of Dormition
"David's Tomb"
Silwan Village
Church of St. Peter in Gallicantu
Siloam Pool
Birket el-Hamra
Kidron Valley
Scottish Church
Valley of Hinnom
0 50 100 150 m

40. S. J. Saller and A. Lemaire, 1954: Mount of Olives
Cemetery, Middle and Late Bronze ages.

41. M. J. Pierre and J. M. Rousée, 1956– : St. Anne's Church, Old City
Continued excavations of remains of Bethesda Pool (Probatica), Second Temple period; buildings, Roman period, and remains of Church of St. Mary (of the Probatica), Byzantine period (for earlier excavations, see no. 4).

42. L. Y. Rahmani, 1956: Northwest Jerusalem
Exploration and publication of burial caves in area of Sanhedria neighborhood, Second Temple period; excavation of Tomb of Jason in Reḥavia neighborhood, Hasmonean period.

43. V. Corbo, 1959: Church of the Ascension, Mount of Olives
Exploration of remains of church, Byzantine and Crusader periods.

44. V. Corbo, C. Coüasnon, A. Economopoulos, et al., 1960–1969: Church of the Holy Sepulcher, Old City
Survey and exploration of church complex; discovery of remains of quarries, end of First Temple period; temenos, Roman period; Constantinian church, medieval, mainly Crusader church.

45. K. M. Kenyon, 1961–1967: City of David, Old City, north of Old City, and Mount Zion
Excavations in several areas:

Bronze Age and First Temple period: Corner of tower, Middle Bronze Age (18th century BCE); system of retaining walls, "Millo" and remains of buildings, Late Bronze Age and First Temple period; city wall and buildings inside and outside the wall, end of First Temple period (site A-I–III and trench I, eastern slope of City of David); tower on line of Ophel Wall (site S), end of First Temple period; city wall at issue of Tyropoeon Valley (site F), end of First Temple period(?); remains in Armenian Garden (site L, with A. D. Tushingham) and in Muristan (site C), end of First Temple period (8th–6th centuries BCE).
Tombs: Mount of Olives, Middle Bronze Age I.

Second Temple period: Line of First Wall built in Persian period, addition of two towers, Hasmonean period (site A-I–III at top of eastern slope of City of David—for earlier excavations, see no. 23; for later excavations, see no. 98); investigation of system of dams and gate along line of First Wall at issue of Tyropoeon Valley (site F), Hasmonean period; street and buildings in Tyropoeon Valley (site N); fortifications along line of First Wall and podium of Herod's palace in Armenian Garden (site L); investigations (with E. W. Hamrick) along line of Third Wall (site T)—excavators mistakenly believed this was not the Second Temple period Third Wall (for earlier excavations, see no. 26; for later excavations, see nos. 71 and 123).

Roman period: Excavation (with J. B. Hennessy) of facade of Damascus Gate—excavators erroneously dated its beginnings to the Second Temple period (for earlier excavations, see no. 34; for later excavations, see no. 100); remains of quarries in southern Ophel and City of David.

Byzantine period: Several building phases and remains of church in Armenian Garden (site L; for later excavations, see no. 62).

Early Arab and medieval periods: Excavations (with R. de Vaux) of remains of monumental structure on the Ophel, erroneously dated to Byzantine period (for later excavations, see no. 51); outer gate complex of the Damascus Gate, Crusader period.

46. N. Avigad, 1967: Mount Scopus
Nazirite family tomb, Second Temple period.

47. V. Tzaferis, 1967: Giv'at Sha'ul, West Jerusalem
Fort, Hasmonean and Byzantine periods.

48. D. Ussishkin, 1968–1971: Silwan Village
Survey and publication of dozens of burial caves, 9th–7th centuries BCE.

49. M. H. Burgoyne, 1968–1975, Temple Mount and Muslim Quarter, Old City
Survey and publication of buildings, Mameluke period.

50. M. Ben-Dov, 1968–1985: Old City
Exposure of western wall of Temple Mount enclosure, Herodian period; exploration of networks of vaulted tunnels near Wilson's Arch, Second Temple to medieval periods (for later excavations, see no. 114).

51. B. Mazar, 1968–1978: Ophel and near southwestern corner of Temple Mount

First Temple period: Royal building—"house of Millo" (9th–8th centuries BCE; for later excavations, see no. 115) and tombs, First Temple period.

Second Temple period: Buildings and water installations, Hellenistic and Hasmonean periods; exposure of southern wall and southwestern corner of Temple Mount enclosure, with networks of streets, public squares, stairways to Huldah Gates, system of piers supporting stairway of Robinson's Arch, and various buildings, Herodian period.

Roman period: Buildings.

Byzantine period: Ophel Wall and its towers, various buildings, public building (hospice), bathhouse.

Early Arab period: Four Umayyad palaces (7th–8th centuries CE) and buildings from Fatimid period (10th–11th centuries).

52. A. Ovadiah and E. Netzer, 1968: Jewish Quarter, Old City
Exploration and survey of complex of Church of St. Mary of the Germans, Crusader period.

53. R. Amiran and A. Eitan, 1968–1969: Citadel ("Tower of David"), Old City
Exposure of inner face of northwestern corner on line of First Wall, with inner tower, Hasmonean period, thickened in Herodian period; buildings, Hasmonean period; and podium of Herod's palace; thickening of city wall and buildings, Byzantine period (for earlier excavations, see no. 31; for later excavations, see nos. 88 and 105).

54. V. Tzaferis, 1968: Giv'at ha-Mivtar, North Jerusalem
Burial caves with ossuary inscribed "Simon the Temple Builder" and remains of crucified man, Second Temple period.

55. N. Avigad, 1969–1982: Jewish Quarter, Old City
Excavations in several areas:

First Temple period: Fortifications along line of First Wall: "Broad Wall" (area A), gate or tower (area W), city wall and tower (area X-2), and buildings in various areas, end of First Temple period (8th–6th centuries BCE).

Second Temple period: Fortifications along line of First Wall: tower (area W), complex of fortifications—gate(?) identified with Gennath Gate (area X-2); buildings, Hasmonean period (areas E, J); street (areas E, J) and buildings, Herodian period: the PalatialMansion (area P), other buildings (areas F, M), and the Burnt House with evidence of the city's destruction in 70 CE (area B).

Roman period: Few finds and mainly Tenth Legion roof tiles.

Byzantine period: Cardo (area X), church, complex of buildings and cistern of Nea Church (areas D, T), bathhouse (area C), buildings in most excavated areas.

Early Arab period: City wall and gate (area T; 10th–11th centuries CE).

Crusader period: Public building (area T), vaulted marketplace (area X).

Ayyubid period: Gate or tower (area T; for later excavations, see no. 79).

56. A. Mazar, 1969: South of Jerusalem
Survey of aqueducts from Solomon's Pools to Jerusalem, Second Temple period and Roman to Ottoman periods.

57. J. Margovski, 1969: Jewish Quarter, Old City
Trial excavations: remains from Second Temple to medieval periods.

58. J. Margovski, 1969–1971: Mount Zion
Buildings and street, Second Temple period (Hasmonean and Herodian periods); public and other buildings, Byzantine period; Sulfur Tower (Burj Kibrit), medieval period; "low-level aqueduct," Second Temple to Ottoman periods.

59. O. Negbi, 1969: French Hill, North Jerusalem
Fort, end of First Temple and Persian periods.

60. E. D. Oren, 1970: French Hill, North Jerusalem
Fortified farmhouse, Byzantine period.

61. E. D. Oren, 1970: Valley of the Cross and Keren ha-Yesod Street, West Jerusalem
Watchtowers, Crusader and Mameluke periods.

62. D. Bahat and M. Broshi, 1970–1971: Armenian Garden, Old City
Fortifications along line of First Wall and podium of Herod's palace, Second Temple period; palace complex, Crusader period (for earlier excavations, see no. 45).

63. Z. Yeivin, 1970: Temple Mount, Old City
Wall, Second Temple period?

64. U. Lux, 1970–1971: Church of the Redeemer, Old City
Construction remains, Byzantine and medieval periods.

65. V. Tzaferis, 1970: Giv'at ha-Mivtar, North Jerusalem
Burial cave with inscription "I am Abba son of the priest," Second Temple period.

66. D. Bahat and M. Ben-Ari, 1971–1972: northwestern corner of Old City wall
City wall, Goliath's Tower, and moat, Crusader period.

67. M. Broshi, 1971–1972: Armenian monastery (House of Caiaphas), Mount Zion
Buildings, end of First Temple period (8th–6th centuries BCE); buildings, Second Temple period (Hasmonean and Herodian periods); remains of complex of Church of Holy Zion and street, Byzantine period; buildings, Early Arab period; enclosure wall of complex of Church of St. Mary of Mount Zion, Crusader period.

68. G. Barkay, A. Mazar, and A. Kloner, 1971–1972: north of Old City
Survey and publication of burial caves, end of First Temple period (8th–6th centuries BCE).

69. A. Kloner, 1971: Giv'at ha-Mivtar, North Jerusalem
Burial cave with ossuary inscribed "of the house of David," Second Temple period.

70. B. Bagatti, 1972: Church of St. Mary's Tomb, Kidron Valley
Exploration of remains of church, Byzantine and Crusader periods.

71. S. Ben-Arieh and E. Netzer, 1972–1974: north of Old City
Section of city wall and towers along line of Third Wall, end of Second Temple period; monastery complex, Byzantine period (for later excavations, see no. 123).

72. P. Benoit, 1972: Convent of the Sisters of Zion, Old City
Exploration of ancient construction remains, Roman period.

73. H. J. H. Vriezen, 1972–1974: Church of the Redeemer, Old City
Construction remains, Byzantine and Crusader periods.

74. M. Ben-Dov, 1975–1977, 1981: Mount Zion
Buildings and water installations, Second Temple period; Secondary (eastern) Cardo, corner of Nea Church and adjoining buildings, Byzantine period; wall, towers, and gate along line of southern wall of Old City, medieval period.

75. M. Broshi, 1973–1978: west of Old City
Structure and burial caves, end of First Temple period (8th–6th centuries BCE); fortifications along line of First Wall: tower from 2nd century BCE; city wall and four towers, Hasmonean period; thickening of towers, outer city wall, and gate entrance, Herodian period; section of city wall, Byzantine period; city wall and towers, Ayyubid period.

76. C. Katsimbinis, 1973–1974: Church of St. Mary's Tomb, Kidron Valley
Exploration of remains of monastery and church, Crusader period.

77. Cyprianos, 1973: Church of Gethsemane, Kidron Valley
Exploration of remains of church, Byzantine and Crusader periods.

78. A. Kloner, 1973: Sultan's Pool, Valley of Hinnom
Remains of the pool, Crusader and Ottoman periods.

79. M. Broshi, 1974: Mount Zion
Buildings, Second Temple period; buildings, Byzantine period; gate or tower, Ayyubid period (for earlier excavations, see no. 55).

80. M. Broshi and Y. Tsafrir, 1974: Zion Gate, southern wall of Old City
Gate or tower, Ayyubid period (for later excavations, see no. 116).

81. S. Margalit, 1974: Beth ha-Bad Street, Old City
Pavement of Cardo, Roman and Byzantine periods.

82. A. Kloner, 1974: Mount of Olives
Tomb with paintings, Byzantine period.

83. M. Broshi, 1975–1976: Church of the Holy Sepulcher, Old City
Remains of quarries, end of First Temple period; walls of Hadrianic temenos platform, Roman period; foundations of Constantinian basilica, Byzantine period.

84. G. Barkay, 1975–1989: Ketef Hinnom, southwest of Old City
Burial caves, end of First Temple period (8th–6th centuries BCE); cremation burials, Roman period; monastery and church of St. George, tombs, Byzantine period.

85. Y. Gat, 1975: southern Tyropoeon Valley
Construction remains, Second Temple period.

86. A. Kloner, 1975: French Hill, North Jerusalem
Burial cave, Early Hasmonean period.

87. A. Kloner and D. Davis, 1975–1978: west of Old City
Burial caves, end of First Temple period (8th–6th centuries BCE); tombs, Second Temple period; "low-level aqueduct," Second Temple to Ottoman periods.

88. H. Geva, 1976–1980: Citadel ("Tower of David"), Old City
Southern tower at northwestern corner of line of First Wall, including building phases from Second Temple period (Hasmonean and Herodian periods); construction remains of Tenth Legion camp, Roman period; sections of city wall, tower, and buildings, Byzantine period; round corner tower and buildings, Early Arab period; fortifications and buildings, medieval and Ottoman periods (for earlier excavations, see nos. 31 and 53; for later excavations, see no. 105).

89. Y. Gat, 1976: Mount Scopus
Tomb with sarcophagi, Second Temple period.

90. A. Kloner, 1976: northern wall of Old City
City wall, Byzantine period.
91. A. Kloner, 1976: West Jerusalem
Elaborate tomb complex, Second Temple period.
92. A. Kloner, 1976–1977: Ha-Gai Street, Old City
Wall–city wall(?), end of First Temple or Second Temple period.
93. D. Adan, 1977: Kidron Valley
Pool—"Solomon's Pool," Second Temple period.
94. O. Hess and E. Eisenberg, 1977: Ha-Gai Street, Old City
Pavement of Secondary (eastern) Cardo, Byzantine period.
95. S. Margalit, D. Chen, and G. Solar, 1977: Christians' Street, Old City
Pavement of street, Byzantine period.
96. E. Netzer and S. Ben-Arieh, 1977: north of Old City
Round opus reticulatum structure—"Herod's monument," Second Temple period.
97. A. Mazar, 1978–1979: Giloh neighborhood, South Jerusalem
Building surrounded by wall and tower, Iron Age I; watchtower, Iron Age II (see Giloh).
98. Y. Shiloh, 1978–1984: City of David
Excavation in several areas:

Chalcolithic period: Finds.

Bronze Age: Buildings, Early Bronze Age; city wall, Middle Bronze Age (18th century BCE), continuous layers of building on eastern slope of City of David (area E), Middle and Late Bronze ages.

First Temple period: Stepped stone structure on eastern slope of City of David (area G; 10th century BCE); city wall, end of First Temple period (area E; 8th–6th centuries BCE); dwellings: House of Ahiel, House of the Bullae, Burnt Room, end of First Temple period (area G; 8th–6th centuries BCE); clearing of Warren's Shaft, exploration of Siloam channel, First Temple period (area B); system of dams at issue of Tyropoeon Valley, First Temple period (area A).

Second Temple period: Sections of city wall and tower on line of First Wall, Persian and Hasmonean periods; earth glacis, Hasmonean period (area G; for earlier excavations, see nos. 23 and 45); section of city wall and blocked gateway along line of First Wall (area D), Hasmonean period; construction remains in dam of Tyropoeon Valley (area A); system of terraces on eastern slope of City of David, outside line of city wall (areas D and E), Hellenistic and Hasmonean periods (for earlier excavations, see no. 22); construction remains in Tyropoeon Valley (area H), Hasmonean period.

Byzantine period: Construction remains (area H) and partially rock-cut structure (area K).

99. D. Tarler, A. De Groot, and G. Solar, 1979: northern wall of Old City
City wall, Byzantine period; city wall and moat, Crusader period.
100. M. Magen, 1979–1984: Damascus Gate, northern wall of Old City
Complex of Damascus Gate and pavement of square inside it—Roman-Hadrianic periods (for earlier excavations, see nos. 34 and 45).
101. B. Pixner, D. Chen, and S. Margalit, 1979–1986: Mount Zion
Exploration of city wall, gate, and tower at southwestern corner of line of First Wall, Second Temple and Byzantine periods (for earlier excavations, see no. 17).
102. M. Magen, 1980: Ha-Gai Street, Old City
Pavement of Secondary (eastern) Cardo, Roman and Byzantine periods.
103. M. Magen, 1980–1981: Lions' (St. Stephen's) Gate Street, Old City
Pavement of street, Second Temple and Roman periods.
104. G. Edelstein, 1980, 1987 (with Z. Greenhut): Manaḥat hill, West Jerusalem
Settlement, Middle Bronze Age II and end of First Temple period (see Naḥal Rephaim).
105. G. Solar and R. Sivan, 1980–1988: Citadel ("Tower of David"), Old City
Fortifications and construction remains, end of First Temple period (8th–6th centuries BCE); exposure of outer face of northwestern corner on line of First Wall, with early "middle tower," "southern tower," and sections of city wall between them, Second Temple period (Hasmonean and Herodian periods); stepped installation—pool?, Hasmonean period; city wall, Byzantine period (for earlier excavations, see nos. 31, 53, and 88).
106. G. Edelstein, 1982–1987: 'En Ya'el, West Jerusalem
Farmhouse, Roman period (see Naḥal Rephaim).
107. E. Eisenberg, 1982–1990 (1985 season with G. Edelstein): Naḥal Rephaim, West Jerusalem
Settlement, Middle Bronze Age I and II (see Naḥal Rephaim).
108. S. Margalit and B. Pixner, 1982–1985: Mount Zion
Water installations, Second Temple period; street, Byzantine period.
109. E. Eisenberg, 1983: Mount Zion
Sections of walls associated with Church of Holy Zion, Byzantine period; Church of St. Mary of Mount Zion, Crusader period.
110. H. Goldfuss, 1983: western wall of Old City
Section of city wall, Byzantine(?) and medieval periods.
111. S. Gibson, 1983: western wall of Old City
Drainage channel, Herodian period.
112. G. Mazor, 1983: northern wall of Old City
Section of city wall, Crusader period.
113. D. Bahat, 1985: Dung Gate, Old City
Buildings and street, Mameluke and Ottoman periods.
114. D. Bahat, 1985–1990: west of Temple Mount, Old City
Renewed exploration of tunnel northwest of Temple Mount, Hasmonean period; exposure of city wall and tower at north end of western Temple Mount wall and nearby quarries and street, Herodian period (for earlier excavations, see no. 50).
115. E. Mazar and B. Mazar, 1986–1987: Ophel
Complex of royal buildings, including gate—Water Gate(?), fortifications, and storehouses, First Temple period (9th–6th centuries BCE; for earlier excavations, see no. 51).
116. A. Maeir, 1987: Zion Gate, southern wall of Old City
Gate or tower, Ayyubid period (for earlier excavations, see no. 80).
117. A. Chambon, 1987: Notre Dame, north of Old City
Bathhouse, Byzantine period.
118. G. Avni and Z. Greenhut, 1989: Kidron Valley
Elaborate burial caves, Second Temple period.
119. D. Bahat and A. Maeir, 1989: Russian Compound, north of Old City
Building—Hospital of the Order of St. Lazarus, Crusader period.
120. V. Sussman, 1989: Mount Scopus
Burial cave, Second Temple period.
121. A. Maeir, 1989: Valley of Hinnom, west of Old City
Corner of building, Second Temple period; complex of buildings, street, and aqueduct, Byzantine and Early Arab periods.
122. R. Abu Ria and L. Gershuny, 1990: Street of the Chain, Old City
Pavement of Decumanus, Roman and Byzantine periods.
123. V. Tzaferis, A. Onn, N. Feig, and E. Sukron, 1990: north of Old City
Section of Third Wall, end of Second Temple period; monasteries with systems of rooms, chapels, and tombs, Byzantine and Early Arab periods.
124. R. Reich, 1990: Valley of Hinnom, west of Old City
Burial caves, end of First Temple (8th–6th centuries BCE) and Second Temple periods; burial chapel, Byzantine period.
125. Z. Greenhut, 1990: south of Old City
Burial cave, with ossuary inscribed "Jehoseph son of Caiaphas," Second Temple period.
126. D. Amit and S. Wolff, 1990–1992: north of Old City
Armenian monastery with system of rooms and tombs, Byzantine and Early Arab periods.

HILLEL GEVA

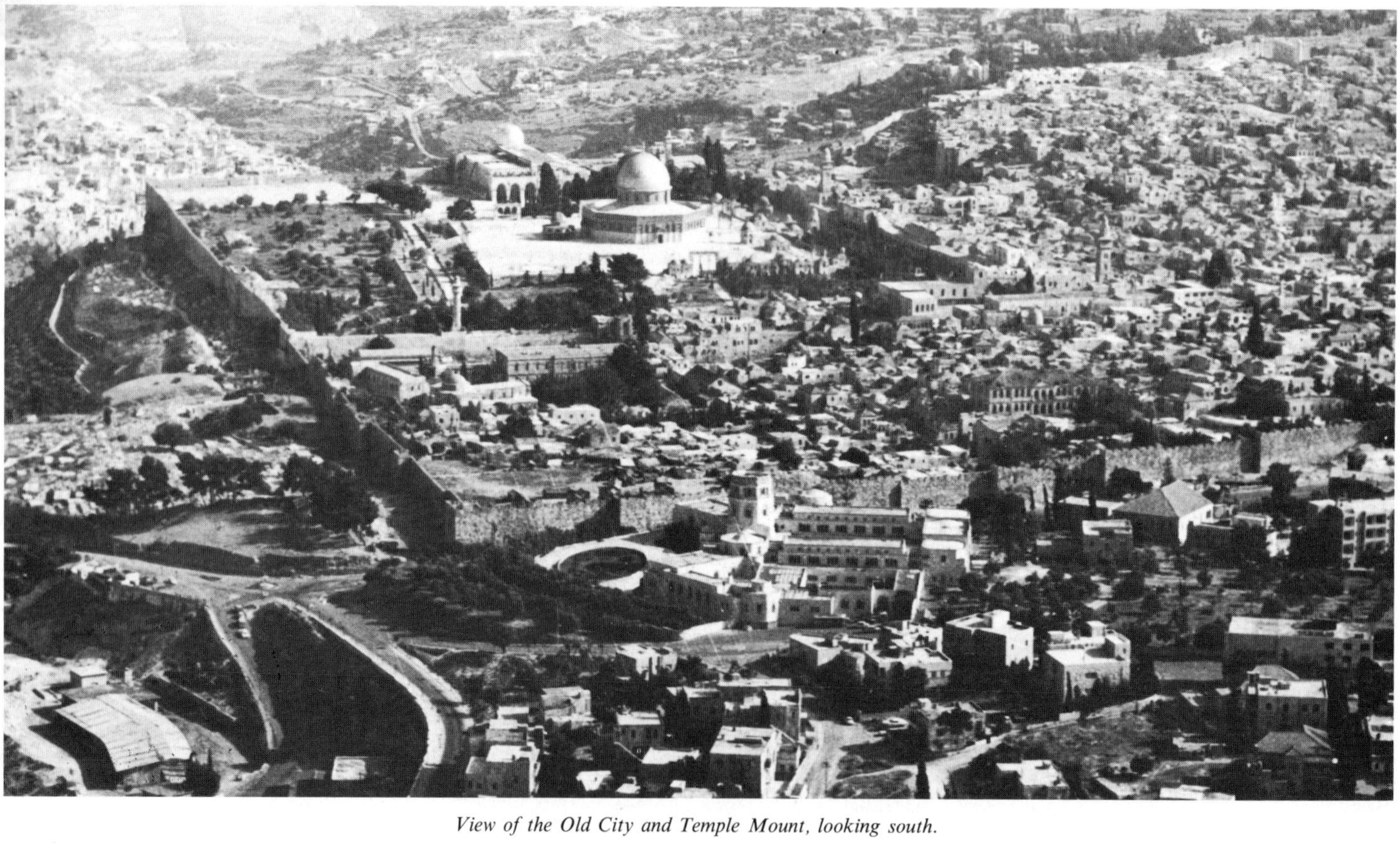

View of the Old City and Temple Mount, looking south.

MAIN EXCAVATIONS IN THE HOLY LAND

Additional sites appear on regional and subject maps

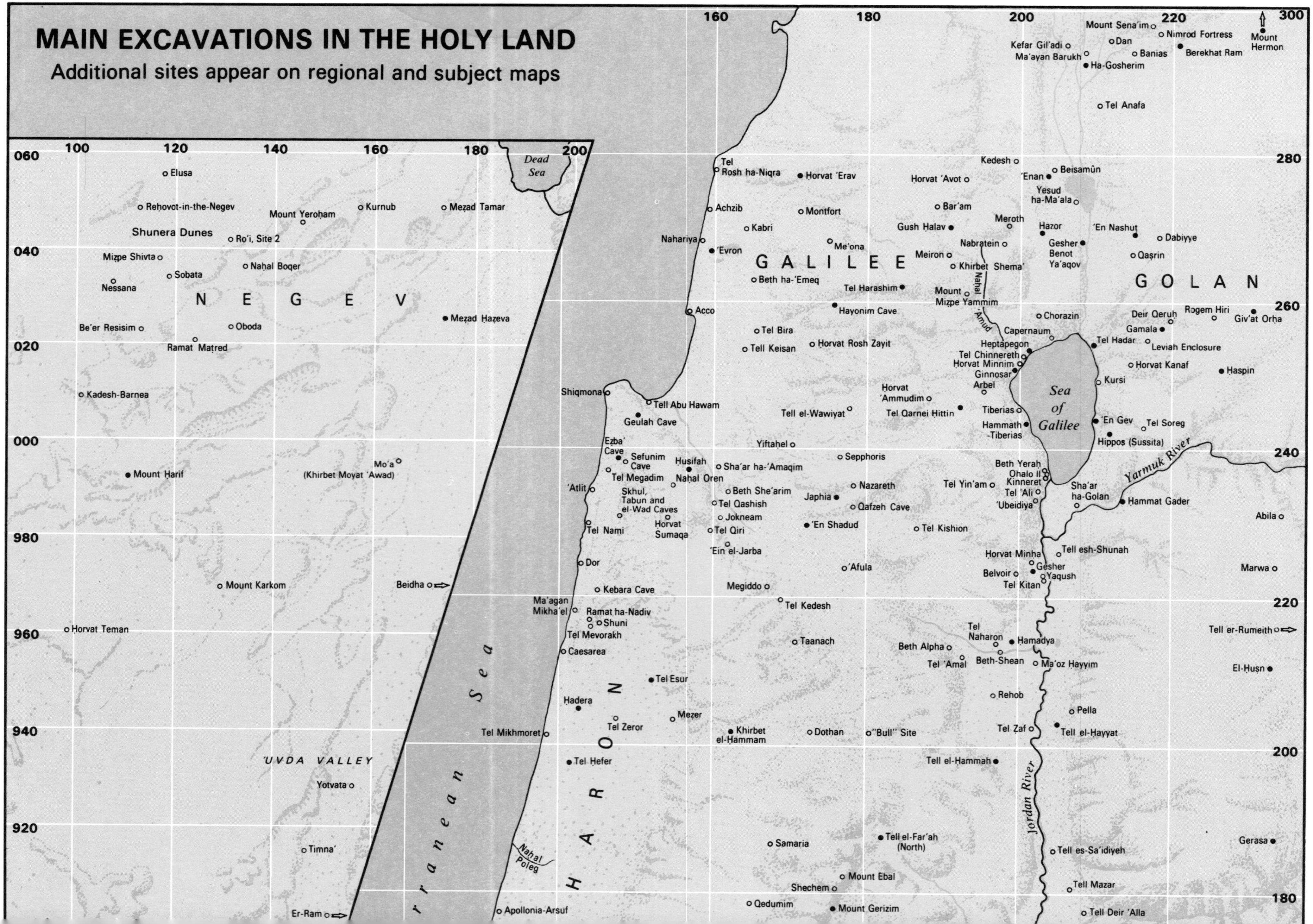